Disability and Rehabilitation Handbook

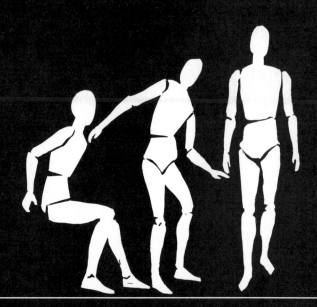

McGraw-Hill Book Company

New York   St. Louis   San Francisco

Auckland   London   New Delhi   Singapore
Bogotá   Madrid   Panama   Sydney
Düsseldorf   Mexico   Paris   Tokyo
Johannesburg   Montreal   São Paulo   Toronto

Disability and Rehabilitation Handbook

Robert M. Goldenson
Editor in Chief

Jerome R. Dunham
Charlis S. Dunham
Associate Editors

Library of Congress Cataloging in Publication Data:

Disability and rehabilitation handbook.

   1. Rehabilitation – United States – Addresses, essays,
lectures. 2. Handicapped – United States – Addresses, essays,
lectures. I. Goldenson, Robert M. II. Dunham, Jerome R.
III. Dunham, Charlis S. [DNLM: 1. Rehabilitation – Handbooks.
2. Handicapped – Handbooks. WB320 D611]

HD7256.U5D55   362.1   78-1441
ISBN 0-07-023658-5

Contents

Contributors and Reviewers

American Occupational Therapy Association, Rockville, Maryland.

American Social Health Association, Palo Alto, California.

Anderson, Ruth W., M.S.W., Consultant, Regional Cystic Fibrosis Center, and Clinical Social Worker, Department of Behavioral Sciences, Children's Orthopedic Hospital and Medical Center, Seattle.

Arthritis Foundation, Atlanta.

Barkaloo, Herbert, Ph.D., Special Education, Seattle Public School System.

Baum, Zelda, Executive Director, Cooley's Anemia Blood and Research Foundation for Children.

Bettmann, Ernest H., M.D., F.A.O.S., Orthopedic Consultant, Professor Emeritus of Orthopedic Surgery, University of Leipzig.

Bisaga, Jeffrey S., Ph.D., Staff Psychologist, Marianne Frostig Center of Educational Therapy, Los Angeles.

Bledsoe, Warren, Consultant, U.S. Department of Health, Education and Welfare, Office of the Blind.

Bowe, Frank, Ph.D., Director, American Coalition of Citizens with Disabilities, Washington, D.C.

Bowen, Angela, M.D.

Bruck, Lilly, Ph.D., Director of Education, New York City Department of Consumer Affairs.

Carlson, C. B., M.D., Director, Child Neurology, Children's Orthopedic Hospital and Medical Center, Seattle.

Carter, Ann, M.D., Seattle King County Health Department, and formerly Director of Cancer and Stroke Programs, Washington and Alaska Regional Medical Program.

Carty, Lee A., Director of Development, Mental Health Law Project, Washington, D.C.

Chaiklin, Sharon, D.T.R., American Dance Therapy Association, Columbia, Indiana.

Cystic Fibrosis Foundation, Atlanta.

Demmick, Martha.

Diggs, L. W., M.D., Consultant, Sickle Cell Center, University of Tennessee, Center for the Health Sciences.

Dudley, Jan, Northwest Project Director, Neurologic Disease Epidemiologic Study, School of Public Health, Seattle.

Dunham, Charlis S., M.A., Rehabilitation Psychologist and Supervisor, Seattle Mental Health Institute.

Dunham, Jerome R., Ph.D., Assistant Professor, Department of Rehabilitation, Seattle University, and formerly Administrator of Washington State Services for the Blind.

Dussault, William, J.D., Seattle.

Dysautonomia Foundation, New York City.

Edgar, Eugene B., Ph.D., Assistant Professor of Education, University of Washington, Seattle.

Ehrle, Raymond A., Ed.D., Secretary, Division 22 (Rehabilitation Psychology), American Psychological Association.

Ellenberg, Max, M.D., Clinical Professor of Medicine, Mount Sinai School of Medicine, and Attending Physician for Diabetes, Mount Sinai Hospital, New York.

Fahn, Stanley, M.D., Neurological Institute, New York City.

Farmer, Rae H., M.Ed.Psych., Supervisor, Chemical Dependency Program, Seattle Mental Health Institute.

Frostig, Marianne, Ph.D., Marianne Frostig Center of Educational Therapy, Los Angeles.

Gaynor, Harry J., Founder and President, National Burn Victim Foundation.

Gives, Virginia M., M.S.W., A.C.S.W., Chief Social Worker, United Cerebral Palsy Association of Westchester County, New York State.

Goldenson, Janet Codley, O.D.

Goldenson, Robert M., Ph.D., Psychologist for United Cerebral Palsy Association of Westchester County, New York State, and Professor at the International Graduate University, Switzerland.

Gregory, Mildred, Western Washington State Epilepsy Society.

Hall, Judith G., Associate Professor, Pediatrics and Medicine, University of Washington School of Medicine, Seattle.

Harrison, Hazel, Ostomy Mutual Aiders of Washington.

Hasselblad, Oliver W., M.D., Medical Consultant, American Leprosy Missions, Inc.

Hicks, John S., Ed.D., Coordinator of Special Education, Fordham University.

Holm, Vanja, M.D., Assistant Professor of Pediatrics, University of Washington School of Medicine, Seattle.

Houd, Helen.

Howell, Linda, M.A., Group Health Cooperative of Puget Sound, Seattle.

Institute of Rehabilitation Medicine, New York City.

International Association of Laryngectomees, New York City.

Iyer, Kamla, M.D., Institute of Rehabilitation Medicine, New York City.

Kliment, Stephen A., American Institute of Architects.

Kraft, George H., M.D., Associate Professor of Rehabilitation Medicine, University of Washington School of Medicine, Seattle.

Kriegman, Lois, M.A., Cofounder, Kriegman Clinic, Richmond, Virginia.

Laurie, Gini, Editor-Publisher and Founder, "Rehabilitation Gazette."

Leukemia Society of America, Inc., New York City.

Levenson, Robert M., M.D., Clinical Professor of Medicine, University of Washington, and Chief of Cardiology, Swedish Hospital, Seattle.

Lockhart, Jo, M.S., Recreation Specialist, Seattle.

Luppino, Anthony V., Ph.D., Vice-President of the National Burn Victim Foundation.

Macgregor, Frances Cooke, Clinical Associate Professor of Surgery (in Sociology), and Research Scientist, New York University Medical Center, Institute of Reconstructive Plastic Surgery.

McGwinn, Donna, book reviewer for "Rehabilitation Gazette."

McQuillen, Michael P., M.D., Chairman, Professional Education Committee, Myasthenia Gravis Foundation, Inc.

Metcalfe, Virginia M., Department of Health Services, University of Washington, Seattle.

Moser, Marvin, M.D., Senior Medical Consultant to the National High Blood Pressure Education Program, National Heart, Lung and Blood Institute.

Mosher, John, M.A., Blue Sky Consultants, Seattle.

Mund, Seymour, M.A., Research Utilization Specialist, Division of Vocational Rehabilitation, State of Connecticut.

Muscular Dystrophy Association, New York City.

National Amputation Foundation, Kenneth G. Robinson, C.P., Director.

National Council for Homemaker–Health Aide Services, New York City.

National Foundation – March of Dimes, White Plains, New York.

National Hemophilia Foundation, New York City.

National Tuberous Sclerosis Association, Laguna Beach, California.

Newcombe, Margaret H.

Northrop, Cedric, M.D., formerly Tuberculosis Control Officer, King County Health Department, Seattle.

Omenn, Gilbert S., M.D., Ph.D., Associate Professor of Medicine, Division of Medical Genetics, University of Washington.

Ostrow, Jonathan H., M.D., Clinical Associate Professor of Medicine, University of Washington School of Medicine, Seattle.

Pantell, Phyllis Ross.

Plaisted, Lena M., R.N., P.T., M.S., Professor Emeritus, Boston University, and formerly Chairperson of the Graduate Program in Rehabilitation Nursing.

Policoff, Leonard D., M.D., Chairman, Department of Rehabilitation Medicine, Rutgers Medical School.

Roman, Leo A., O.D., formerly Clinical Program Coordinator, American Optometric Association.

Rosenthal, Aaron, M.D., Physical Medicine and Rehabilitation, Fox River Hospital, Chicago.

Ruegg, Patricia, Director of Rehabilitation Workshop Administration, Seattle University.

Schut, Lawrence J., M.D., Medical Director, National Ataxia Foundation.

Scott, Roland B., M.D., Director, Howard University Center for Sickle Cell Disease.

Simkin, Peter, M.D., Assistant Professor of Medicine, University of Washington.

Simmler, Lynne, Ed.D., Rehabilitation Department, Seattle University.

Smallwood, Joan, D.T.R., American Dance Therapy Association, Columbia, Indiana.

Spina Bifida Association of America, Chicago.

Sternfeld, Leon, M.D., Medical Director, United Cerebral Palsy Research and Educational Foundation.

Strothers, Charles, M.D., Professor Emeritus, Department of Psychology, Psychiatry and Behavioral Sciences, University of Washington School of Medicine, Seattle.

Swanson, Philip, M.D., Board of Trustees, National Multiple Sclerosis Society, Seattle, and Head of Department of Neurology, University of Washington.

Thompson, John K., Coordinator of Region X Rehabilitation Education Program.

Ulman, Elinor, "American Journal of Art Therapy," Washington, D.C.

Wight, Penny Bigelow.

Winkle, Ronald S., M.D., Department of Physical Medicine and Rehabilitation, University of Washington.

A Word to the Reader

This volume is based on a dual approach, presenting detailed information on disabilities of every major type and on all phases of the rehabilitation process. These two aspects should be intertwined, for in all cases efforts should be made not only to understand each disability but to enable the affected person to utilize every available resource to overcome limitations as far as possible.

A disability may be defined as any chronic physical or mental incapacity resulting from injury, disease, or congenital defect. The range of disabilities is broad indeed, comprising such disparate conditions as cerebral palsy, mental retardation, diabetes, and orthopedic disorders, or sometimes a combination of several conditions. This broad range has determined the scope of the *Disability and Rehabilitation Handbook*. Rehabilitation comprises any process, procedure, or program designed to enable the affected individual to function at a more adequate and personally satisfying level. In its fully developed form this functioning includes all aspects of the individual's life—physical, psychological, social, vocational—and in the view of the editors of this book, only a total approach is deserving of the name "rehabilitation."

In this volume "rehabilitation" is used broadly, encompassing "habilitation"—the term sometimes applied to the special efforts designed to aid those disabled at birth or early in life. Rehabilitation is not something specialists do *to* disabled persons or *for* them, but something done *with* them. If the disabled are to avail themselves fully of the guidance and assistance of others, efforts must be made to enlist their cooperation, mobilize their energies, and overcome tendencies toward defeatism and dependency. A good part of rehabilitation must therefore be self-rehabilitation. Motivation is as important as technique.

In many instances the disabled (and their families as well) are unaware of the manifold resources available not only for treatment but for self-development and the chance to live a useful life. Only a team of professionals with various specialties, working together, can provide these opportunities; but the question in the mind of the disabled person and family members is where to go for help, what to expect, and what to demand of society. One of the prime purposes of this volume is to provide a practical guide in this pursuit.

It is with these considerations in mind that the authors offer a description of each disability from the standpoint of origin, incidence, treatment, prevention, and research; and a comprehensive account of the rehabilitation process, including its psychological aspects, the multidisciplinary approach, available facilities of all types, aids to independent living, and the contributions of education, vocational guidance, recreation, employment and self-employment, government benefits, and appropriate health agencies to the well-being of individuals with each type of disability.

These are the general outlines of the *Disability and Rehabilitation Handbook*. The volume is based on the urgent need for a single comprehensive source of information on an area of life that comprises no fewer than 25 million people in the United States alone, and one that directly or indirectly affects every member of the population. It has been conceived as a handbook written and reviewed by specialists in each field, and has been constructed in such a way that it can be readily consulted by professionals and paraprofessionals, the disabled and their families, social and health agencies, and the concerned public.

We take this opportunity to express our gratitude to the many associations, rehabilitation centers, and government departments which have cooperated with us in this undertaking. We are especially indebted to the specialists in each field who have contributed articles to the book or have given us the benefit of their critical reviews of its contents.

THE EDITORS

On the opposite page: Recreation therapy is an important part of the rehabilitation process. Here, a cerebral palsied girl is able to enjoy bowling by using a specially designed ramp. (United Cerebral Palsy Associations, Inc.)

1

Foundations of Rehabilitation

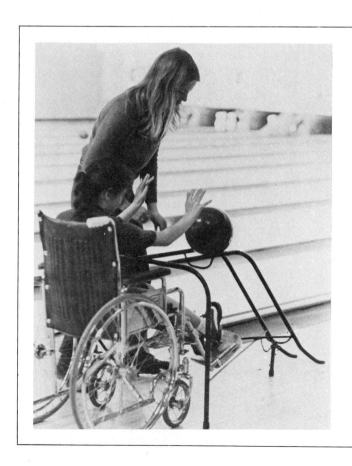

1

Dimensions of the Field

ROBERT M. GOLDENSON, Ph.D.

Disabilities are as old as humanity. Archeological research has demonstrated that skeletal disorders have been common since time immemorial; Egyptian mummies dating back 5,000 years show clear evidence of osteoarthritis and tubercular spine; and remains from the Neolithic Period indicate that illness, probably mental as well as physical, was combated by the heroic measure of trepanning, in which a hole was bored in the skull to permit evil spirits to escape.

It was not until the fifth century B.C., when Hippocrates appeared on the scene, that medicine began to separate from superstition and attempts were made to diagnose and treat physical and mental disease. In spite of this forward step, the Greeks were so enamored of physical perfection that the Athenians flung defective children from a precipice and the Spartans abandoned them on a mountainside. The only anticipation of modern methods was the Greek and Roman bath, which combined hydrotherapy with exercises and social interchange – but the baths were limited to the few who could afford this luxury.

The slow advance toward enlightenment came to a halt during the Middle Ages, when the primitive belief in spirits and demons again prevailed, and it was not until centuries later that the groundwork for an attack on disabilities and defects was laid.

HISTORICAL HIGHLIGHTS: EIGHTEENTH AND NINETEENTH CENTURIES

Orthopedics was probably the first medical specialty to develop: during the eighteenth century an institute for the crippled and deformed was opened in Switzerland by Jean André Venel. Bacteriology and pathology, so important in dealing with diseases causing disability, had to await the experiments of Louis Pasteur in the 1860s, the gradual development of high-powered microscopes, and the discovery of x-rays by W. K. Roentgen in 1895. Neurology did not become a separate medical field until the turn of the century, when J. M. Charcot successfully identified causes of cerebral hemorrhage, described the effects of spinal injury, and gave the first accurate descriptions of multiple sclerosis, poliomyelitis, paralysis agitans, and tabes dorsalis. Although the scientific study of mental disorders and their treatment started with Philippe Pinel in about 1800, psychiatry did not become a fully recognized discipline until a century later when Emil Kraepelin constructed the first classification of mental diseases and Sigmund Freud introduced the psychotherapeutic approach.

While the medical approach to disabilities was being developed during the nineteenth century, the concept of rehabilitation was also beginning to take shape. The emphasis on training and restoration which prevails today was foreshadowed by humanitarian attitudes toward the physically and mentally defective and the moral treatment era in psychiatry. Early in the nineteenth century a few homes for crippled children were established in Europe, but the emphasis with few exceptions was on custodial care rather than on medical treatment, education, and job training. In 1906, however, Conrad Biesalski conducted the first census of crippled children, in Berlin, and this led to the establishment of the Oscar-Helene Heim, often credited with being the first comprehensive rehabilitation center in the world. That distinction, however, can be disputed, for in the United States the Hospital for the Ruptured and Crippled, in New York City, opened its doors in 1863, followed by the Cleveland Rehabilitation Center in 1889 and the Boston Industrial School for the Crippled and Deformed in 1893, all of which offered vocational training as well as medical care. Meanwhile, the moral treatment movement in psychiatry introduced a compassionate, constructive approach to mental disorder, which emphasized, in the words of Charles Dickens (*American Notes for General Circulation*, 1842), "Trust of patient, interaction between patients and staff without paralyzing fear, little or no use of restraint, a diversity of occupations and recreations, and the expectation that behavior could become well modulated even in the severely deranged, and that the future held out promise for these unfortunates if they were cared for properly." Unfortunately this enlightened approach was put aside when mental patients were crowded into the cold, impersonal institutions of the late nineteenth and early twentieth centuries.

PROGRESS IN THE TWENTIETH CENTURY

The development of the rehabilitation movement was slow and halting before World War I. The first state to make direct provision for medical care of crippled children was Minnesota, starting in 1897; and the first organizations to study the overall problems of the disabled were the Russell Sage Foundation and the Bureau of the Handicapped of the New York City Charity Organization Society, dating from 1908. Before the turn of the century, Horace Mann and Samuel Gridley Howe recognized the needs of mentally retarded children, and the Rev. Thomas Gallaudet developed an educational program for these children as well as the deaf and blind. By 1914 special classes for slow learners had been established in Baltimore, Chicago, Cleveland, Detroit, New York, and Philadelphia schools. However, most of today's voluntary agencies for the physically and mentally disabled were not organized until decades later. The first was the National Society for Crippled Children and Adults (Easter Seal Society), founded in 1919.

From World War I to World War II the emphasis was on physical restoration and vocational rehabilitation of men injured in military service or in industries serving the war effort. This was the prime function of the Red Cross Institute for Crippled and Disabled Men (later the Institute for the Crippled and Disabled, and now the ICD Rehabilitation and Research Center), founded in 1917 in New York City. Another step was taken when the Soldiers Rehabilitation Act was passed and the Federal Board for Vocational Education was established in 1918. Other steps were taken in 1920 when President Woodrow Wilson signed the Smith-Fess Act, which extended the training program to disabled civilians, and in 1936 when the Randolph-Sheppard Act authorized the states to license blind persons to operate vending machines in federal buildings.

The longest strides toward a full rehabilitation program were taken during and after World War II. In 1943 the Vocational Rehabilitation Act, which originally (1920) covered only the physically disabled, was extended to include the mentally ill and mentally handicapped and to provide for medical and surgical treatment and prosthetic devices. Amendments adopted in 1954 further enlarged the program to include research and demonstration projects and the training of professional personnel. Additional amendments adopted in 1965 provided for increased services for the severely disabled, a National Commission on Architectural Barriers, and the construction of sheltered workshops, rehabilitation centers, and residential accommodations for the mentally retarded, in cooperation with state and voluntary agencies. Federal legislation since that time has provided for additional mental retardation facilities; community health services for patients with diabetes, arthritis, and other chronic disabling conditions; construction of hospitals and public health centers; the Social Security Medicare program for people sixty-five and over; the organization of community mental health centers in response to President John F. Kennedy's demand

5

for a "bold new approach" to mental illness; the Rehabilitation Act of 1973, which provides for individualized rehabilitation programs for the severely disabled; and, in 1974, the extension of monthly Social Security payments (Supplemental Security Income) to the disabled.

From World War II to the present the concept of rehabilitation has greatly expanded, and the need for a national program covering all types of disabilities has been more and more clearly recognized. A number of pioneers contributed immeasurably to this burgeoning field. Dr. Howard A. Rusk developed a total rehabilitation program for the Army Air Force with the aid of Dr. George G. Deaver, Medical Director of the Institute for the Crippled and Disabled. The program, designed to hasten convalescence and return to duty, was later extended to the Veterans Administration and, shortly after the war, to civilian patients under treatment at Bellevue Hospital, in New York, the first municipal hospital to have a department of rehabilitation. The moving force behind the government vocational rehabilitation programs was Mary E. Switzer; as commissioner, she conducted the first survey of the nation's rehabilitation needs, in 1952. Dr. Henry Kessler organized a rehabilitation program for the Navy during the war, established a leading institute in New Jersey, and disseminated the message of rehabilitation to countries around the world as president of the International Society of Cripples (now Rehabilitation International). Another pioneer, Dr. Henry Viscardi, Jr., established the first work center exclusively for the disabled, Abilities, Inc. From its founding in 1952, it has competed with industry on the open market and has enabled hundreds of presumably unemployable individuals to earn a livelihood.

RECENT PROGRESS

During the past two decades there has been an increasing recognition that the disabling effects of disease, accidental injury, and congenital defect constitute one of the greatest responsibilities not only of medicine but of society itself. This has led to seven important developments, summarized below.

1. National health surveys have made society more aware of the extent of the problem of disability. Its dimensions can be indicated by citing a few recent facts and figures. More than one out of ten individuals in the United States population are seriously enough disabled to need partial or total rehabilitation. The number of potential vocational rehabilitation cases has been estimated at 10,300,000. Approximately 5,000,000 persons suffer from rheumatoid arthritis, the most crippling form of the disease. According to figures published by the Children's Bureau of the Department of Health, Education and Welfare (HEW), 2,425,000 persons under twenty-one were afflicted with orthopedic handicaps in 1970. Over 475,000 Americans are legally blind, and 330,000 totally deaf. The 2,800,000 retarded young people (up to twenty-one) all require special education or training, and many need everyday care as well.

Approximately 1,750,000 mental patients require hospital care and treatment in the course of a year. (For details and further figures, see PART 4, SECTION 1: STATISTICS.)

2. The concept of disability has been refined. As used today, it denotes any relatively severe chronic impairment of function resulting from disease, accident, or congenital defect. The impairment, or limitation, may be in one or more of the following spheres: (a) physical, affecting ambulation, coordination, speech production, vision, etc.; (b) mental, affecting ability to think, remember, and comprehend, or general learning ability; (c) social, affecting ability to communicate and establish relationships with other people; (d) emotional, affecting self-image, self-acceptance, mental health; (e) occupational, affecting vocational or homemaking ability. In general, a condition is considered disabling when it interferes with activity or adjustment in a substantial, material way, not when it produces only mild discomfort or transient limitation. Ordinary farsightedness, flat feet, or occasional mild depression would not be described as disabilities, but all the conditions mentioned above, such as crippling arthritis and mental retardation, would certainly qualify.

3. The burden which disability places on society and the individual is more fully appreciated than ever before. The economic cost of disability is staggering. Alcoholism is estimated to cost the American economy $15 billion a year in treatment, rehabilitation, and loss of earning power. The annual cost of all forms of arthritis has been estimated at over $9 billion. According to HEW, mental illness costs the economy $21 billion each year. Rehabilitation itself is immensely expensive: for example, a cerebral palsy day program serving 100 clients operates on a budget of over $500,000 per year, or about $5,000 per client, exclusive of capital costs (the building and equipment) and medical and surgical expenditures. And it should be borne in mind that disabilities are, by definition, chronic disorders that usually require many years of care, treatment, and rehabilitation.

If the economic cost of disability is staggering, the human cost can only be described as incalculable. How can one measure the loss of self-worth in an individual who has lost not only his earning power but his ability to take care of himself? How can one calculate the burden of frustration, anxiety, dependency, and physical distress that is the daily lot of so many disabled persons? And how can one fully appreciate the effect of the social rejection and job discrimination that are still so prevalent? The fact that many are able to bear these burdens with dignity does not alleviate the problem of disability. That can be done only through an enlightened social policy, a wide-scale research effort, and an ever expanding rehabilitation program.

4. During the past twenty years the goals of rehabilitation have been broadened, and the process has been extended to every type of disability, mental as well as physical. Rehabilitation is no longer focused almost exclusively on vocational retraining, but is directed

toward adequate functioning in all areas of life. Nor is it limited to restoration after accidental injury, emotional breakdown, or acute disease, but includes developing the capacities of individuals affected by mental retardation, learning disability, and congenital defect, a process which some call habilitation rather than rehabilitation. This inclusive approach is expressed in the statement by Frank H. Krusen (*Handbook of Physical Medicine and Rehabilitation*, W. B. Saunders, Philadelphia, 1971) that "rehabilitation involves treatment and training of the patient to the end that he may attain his maximum potential for normal living physically, psychologically, socially and vocationally."

In accordance with this broader concept, rehabilitation is now conceived as a dynamic, holistic process based on a comprehensive, ongoing evaluation of each disabled person's specific limitations, abilities, and needs. It is also a flexible process focused on different facets at different times — but in general, it falls into four interlocking phases. (a) Physical rehabilitation includes prescription of medications, corrective surgery, application of special treatments such as hydrotherapy and range-of-motion exercises, adapted sports, and use of such equipment as respirators or kidney machines, orthotic and prosthetic devices, and functional aids. (b) Vocational rehabilitation involves counseling, testing, occupational and work adjustment training, and, if possible, job placement. (c) Social rehabilitation is carried out through participation in discussion groups, sociotherapy, sex and marital education, self-government and advocacy activities, day or resident camps, and a wide range of club and recreational activities. (d) Psychological rehabilitation consists of personal counseling, psychotherapy where needed, and supportive and motivational measures directed toward increased self-acceptance and full cooperation in the entire rehabilitative effort.

In addition to these general phases, the rehabilitation process involves many activities designed to meet special needs. Among them are mobility instruction for the blind, lip reading and sign language for the deaf, educational therapy for the learning disabled, special classes for the mentally retarded, services for the homebound, and intensive treatment and readjustment training for the mentally ill. Nor should one lose sight of the fact that the effectiveness of the entire program is dependent on many practical factors: government assistance programs (Medicaid, Medicare, etc.), the fund-raising efforts of voluntary agencies, federal and state approval of construction projects, the solution of transportation problems, and the elimination of environmental barriers. If rehabilitation is to be viewed in its totality, as this book will attempt to do, all these factors must be given due consideration.

5. It is now recognized that total rehabilitation requires a multidisciplinary effort involving a wide range of professionals, paraprofessionals, and aides. Any account of the process must therefore do full justice to the specific contributions of the physiatrist, who plans and directs the individualized program; the various medical spe-

cialists responsible for treatment; the physical therapist, who develops or restores basic functions through exercise and training; the occupational therapist, who provides training in self-care, the use of assistive devices, homemaking, arts and crafts, and functional skills; the social worker, who helps the family and the patient utilize community resources and cope with practical problems such as medical bills and housing; the psychologist, who assesses the patient's emotional and intellectual status and provides supportive therapy; the vocational rehabilitation counselor, who evaluates the patient's skills and capacities and plans a placement, self-employment, or workshop program with the individual. In addition, many other specialists must be available to perform needed services: special educators, who provide remedial or developmental programs; recreation specialists, who organize a program of games, sports, dramatics, etc.; the speech pathologist, who analyzes and corrects faulty speech and communication patterns; the rehabilitation nurse, who provides physical care and emotional support in the hospital or other treatment center; and many others who may be involved on a full-time or part-time basis: orthotists and prosthetists; music, art, and dance therapists; industrial and manual arts therapists; mobility and driving instructors; corrective therapists; homemakers; and a corps of volunteer workers.

6. The number of agencies and facilities devoted to disabilities and rehabilitation has grown. No fewer than 27 federal bureaus, commissions, and departments are wrestling with this problem, not only in the Department of Health, Education and Welfare but in a wide scattering of agencies. Over 250 national voluntary agencies are actively engaged in service and research activities. According to the Association of Rehabilitation Facilities, the number of rehabilitation facilities now exceeds 3,000. Although physical medicine and rehabilitation was not approved by the American Medical Association as a specialty until 1947, about one-third of the 114 medical schools in the United States now offer training in this field. In the field of mental retardation, there are 38 university-affiliated service and research facilities. The number of special schools and community colleges offering training in physical therapy, occupational therapy, nursing, and other allied health fields exceeds 1,400, and over 1,000 colleges and universities offer courses in special education. In the field of mental disabilities, the number of patients is greater than ever before, but fewer are confined to large-scale institutions and more are being actively treated and rehabilitated in community mental health centers, general hospitals, clinics, and halfway houses. Another indication of growth is the increase in the number of professional journals in the field; there are now approximately 130 periodicals devoted to disabilities and rehabilitation. (See PART 4, SECTION 2: VOLUNTARY ORGANIZATIONS; SECTION 3: FEDERAL ORGANIZATIONS; SECTION 4: PERIODICALS.)

7. Rehabilitation has proved its effectiveness. There is ample evidence, as the individual chapters of this volume will show, that rehabilitation *can* work *if* the process is carried out with tireless

effort, *if* it calls upon the skill and understanding of a team of specialists, and *if* it involves the total life of the disabled person — physical, psychological, occupational, and social. And it works in a number of specific ways. Studies have shown that, as Howard A. Rusk (*Rehabilitation Medicine,* C. V. Mosby, St. Louis, p. 21, 1964) has put it, "The neglect of disability is far more costly than an early aggressive program of rehabilitation which restores the individual to the highest possible level of physical, economic, social and emotional self-sufficiency." The reason is that rehabilitation, in general, shortens the hospital stay, decreases the readmission rate, results in earlier return to employment, and reduces the need for costly maintenance services. Moreover, rehabilitation "pays" in economic terms: for every dollar spent on vocational rehabilitation alone, an estimated $5 will be returned to society in the form of federal income taxes during the first five years of employment, and $35 will be earned in the individual's lifetime.

But the question as to whether rehabilitation works can be better answered in human terms — in terms of stemming deterioration, avoiding complications, overcoming limitations, and increasing the patient's independence, feeling of usefulness, and ability to face the future with hope. A paraplegic may never be able to walk, but she can be trained to do a job at home or in the community. A retarded child may not be able to achieve normality, but she can learn to take care of herself and get some enjoyment out of life. A laryngeal cancer victim cannot be given a new larynx, but he can be taught to speak again. A mentally disturbed person may never be restored to perfect health, but the rehabilitation process can help him meet the demands of life with some degree of adequacy. A cerebral palsied child cannot be cured, but her condition can be improved and she can learn to surmount many of her limitations. In all these cases the disabilities remain, but the handicaps are diminished.

A review of progress, such as the one just given, may give the impression that the situation is well in hand. This is by no means the case. Many types of facilities, professions, and techniques have been developed in recent years, but the attack on disability is still in the first stages. One reason is that opportunities for rehabilitation are unevenly distributed throughout the country, and in some areas they are almost entirely lacking. A second is that the development of the research effort, which has made a good start toward effective treatment and prevention, is seriously hampered by insufficient funds, both public and private. A third is that vocational rehabilitation, the first area to be developed and enacted into law, cannot keep up with the need: a 1975 study showed that less then one-third of potential cases are actually getting this crucial form of assistance — and those who do receive it are still likely to be faced with prejudicial attitudes when they apply for a job. Fourth, many obvious needs of the disabled are not being met, such as access to public transportation, barrier-free residences and schools, and the opportunity to avail themselves of advanced functional aids already developed by bioengineers. And fifth, study after study has shown that chronic disorders and disabilities of practically every type are most prevalent among low-income families, and the problem of poverty is still widespread. In short, there is no reason for complacency.

The substance of this introductory chapter can be briefly stated. The major disabilities that beset humankind have been identified, and their prevalence can be estimated with some degree of precision. People are more aware than ever before of the scope of the problems, physical, personal, and social, posed by disabling conditions. These problems are being actively attacked by a large number of voluntary and government agencies. Many new professions have been developed to deal with them, and many rehabilitation techniques have been devised. Society has therefore made a start toward solving the gigantic, many-sided problem of disability, and a new chapter is being written in the relief of human distress and the freeing of the body and spirit from the shackles of disorder. That account is recorded in the following pages.

2

Psychosocial Aspects of Disability

JEROME R. DUNHAM, Ph.D., and CHARLIS S. DUNHAM, M.A.

Most people, including the disabled, do not usually differentiate between "disability" and "handicap." Indeed, many of those who do make a distinction between the "disabled" and the "handicapped" still use these terms, as well as terms like "affliction" or "impairment," interchangeably in their discourse. In special education, children are not referred to as "disabled" but as "handicapped." Government programs and legislation, as well as popular literature, rely on the term "handicapped." The early working title of this book was *Handbook on the Handicapped,* but later the editors felt strongly that such a title would deny the major philosophy and intent of the work.

"DISABILITY" VERSUS "HANDICAP"

Those who prefer to show a difference between "disability" and "handicap" are trying to demonstrate that there is more involved than can be contained in a single category. The "disabled" person is one who is structurally, physiologically or psychologically, different from the normal person because of accident, disease, or development problems. A person who is "handicapped" feels less adequate than others, either in general or in a specific situation.

A disabled person may feel handicapped in some situations and not in others. A blind individual coming into an out-of-town hotel for the first time is handicapped in discerning the pattern of the elevator buttons; but when he returns to his job as an x-ray technician, his blindness is an asset in the darkroom. A young woman with one functional arm was handicapped in her attempt to move patients and carry trays as a nurses' aide, but found no difficulty in being helpful in the field of child care.

A normal person may feel that he is handicapped for reasons not apparent to others. A young man who experienced early success as a promoter and administrator found himself out of work in depressed times. He talked about himself as being more "handicapped" than any disabled person he knew, and was full of self-doubt and feelings of inadequacy and failure.

When the naïve bystander, observing a disabled person doing a task with considerable confidence and success, remarks that the disabled person did that as well or better than he could have, he is beginning to understand the difference between "handicapped" and "disabled." For the person who is "different," the incessant struggle toward such insights in other people is a continual reminder of the one-down position in which he is held. Bob Barnett, past administrator of the American Foundation for the Blind, was heard to say with exasperation, "There's not one sighted person I want to be 'just like.'"

Many who do differentiate between the two terms think of "disability" with a positive connotation and give "handicap" a negative connotation. A worker who differentiates in this way might look upon a newly disabled person who has not yet learned to cope with the disability as a "handicapped" person. The newly disabled person may not wish to join the population of the "disabled" because he (or she) thinks of "those people" as being less adequate than people in general. The newly disabled person, in this case, would *not* be differentiating between "disability" and "handicap," which is to be expected. Everyone is a product of the environment, and a person who becomes disabled or is brought into a family imbued with the prevailing negative attitudes is likely to view himself and his potential in the light of those attitudes.

Differentiating between "disability" and "handicap" becomes more controversial with the mentally ill. Some writers feel that mental illness does not exist as a medical entity (T. S. Szasz, *The Myth of Mental Illness*, rev. ed., Harper & Row, New York, 1974). They hold that society puts down the person with a deviant life-style because of its discomfort and tries to force conformity in the guise of "treatment for mental illness." The concept gets even more blurred when applied to the criminal, the obese, the drug addict, or the alcoholic. This is partly because many people believe that a person's willpower alone decides whether he or she will commit the crime, eat that much food, smoke, drink, or shoot that particular drug. In conversation with one ex-drug addict who counseled other addicts, the author was told, "We don't want to be included with the disabled, no matter how 'unhandicapped' they are." She wanted to be free of the stigma she felt toward the disabled, that of being impotent to affect or control her own fate.

The ability to manage oneself in accordance with one's own goals and in harmony with surrounding pressures is not entirely predicated on physical strength, sensory acuity, or cognitive achievement. Therefore, a disability need not be a handicap.

ATTITUDES TOWARD THE "HANDICAPPED"

People with disabilities have a wide variety of experiences regarding prejudice. Some individuals may encounter few evidences of prejudice in their lifetimes; others feel that their entire existence is marred by their being trapped in a stereotypical box. The most common experience of persons with a disability is to encounter a range of subtle and not so subtle prejudices almost every day of their lives.

To some extent, the variety of experiences is due to the existence of a wide range of attitudes toward disability. There are those who believe that if the disabled are allowed to exist at all they should be contained in some out-of-the-way place where they need not be observed in everyday life. There are also religious beliefs that illness or disability is a punishment from God, and families influenced by these beliefs are tormented with the idea that the disability is the direct result of someone's sinning. Many a disabled individual has had a complete stranger stop to "lay hands on him" and fervently pray for God's forgiveness—an embarrassing experience for most and sometimes extremely disturbing to a young child with a disability.

The assumption is often made that disablement is a continuing tragedy, and since the disabled still continue to pursue practically all life activities, perhaps with considerable confidence, some people feel that the disabled must have unusual courage to carry on through their travail or at least with a bit more divinity than most people grasp. Some who assume that living with disablement must be an almost unbearable cross reason that the disabled should be cared for and have a chance to be as happy as possible, but should not attempt to compete or participate in the mainstream of life.

In the article "Handicapism in America" (in the journal *WIN*, 1976) Douglas Biklen and Robert Bogdan compare some of the similarities of racism, sexism, and handicapism. They define handicapism as

> . . . a theory and set of practices that promote unequal and unjust treatment of people because of apparent or assumed physical or mental disability. It manifests itself in relations between individuals, in social policy and cultural norms, and in the helping professions as well. Handicapism pervades our lives, but the concept of handicapism can also serve as a vital tool by which anyone can scrupulously examine personal and societal behaviors toward disabilities.

Since disablement is a state with which most people are not intimately acquainted, it takes on the characteristic of ambiguity along with its unfamiliarity. The general public are often not sure how to relate to the disabled person. Biklen and Bogdan enumerate the following common reactions:

> First, there is a tendency to presume sadness on the part of the person with a disability. For example, one woman who has a physical disability and who, incidentally, smiles a lot, told us of an encounter with a man who said, "It's so good that you can still smile. Lord knows, you don't have much to be happy for."
>
> Second, there is the penchant to pity. You might have heard, "It is a tragedy that it had to happen to her; she had so much going for her." Or people sometimes tell us, "It is so good of you to give up your lives to help the poor souls." Or "My, you must be so patient to work with them. I could never do it."
>
> Third, people without disabilities sometimes focus so intensely on the disability as to make it impossible to recognize that the person with the disability is also simply another person with many of the same emotions, needs, and interests as other people. This attitude is reflected in the perennial questions, "What is it like to be deaf?" "It must be hard to get around in a wheelchair," and "You must really wish you could see sometimes."
>
> Fourth, people with disabilities are often treated as children. Notice for example, that feature films about people with mental retardation and physical handicaps are so frequently titled with first names: "Joey," "Charley," "Larry," and "Walter." We communicate this same message by calling disabled adults by first names when full names and titles would be more appropriate and by talking in a tone reserved for children.
>
> Fifth is avoidance. Having a disability often means being avoided, given the cold shoulder, and stared at from a distance. The phrases "Sorry, I have to go now," "Let's get together sometime (but not now and not any specific time)," and "I'd like to talk but I have to run" are repeated too consistently for mere coincidence.
>
> Sixth, we all grow up amidst a rampage of handicapist humor. It must take a psychological toll. "Did you hear the one about the moron who threw the clock out the window?" "There was a dwarf with a sawed-off cane . . ." "Two deaf brothers went into business with each other . . . a blind man entered their store."
>
> Seventh, people with disabilities frequently find themselves spoken for, as if they were not present or were unable to speak for themselves. In a similar vein, people without disabilities sometimes speak about people with disabilities in front of them, again as if they were objects and not people.
>
> In terms of personal relations, then, if you are labelled "handicapped," handicapism is your biggest burden. It is a no-win situation. You are not simply an ordinary person.

Disability is often confused with illness. The person with curtailed mobility due to a stroke may describe herself as being sick. Parents may think of their cerebral palsied child as ill. The "sick" person is in a dependent state, requiring attention and service to meet her vital needs. A newly disabled individual, handicapped by her condition, is in a similar position and may have a preference for viewing her condition as a "temporary" illness. Growth is taking place when the individual moves from the concept of being temporarily sick to that of acceptance of a permanent, unalterable condition.

A new version of an old theme comes from the psychosomatic approach and may be the most subtle form of prejudice. In this theory an individual subconsciously directs his particular style of life and is therefore responsible for his state of mind or body. Because of frustration, anxiety, neurotic distortion (or lack of faith in mind-over-matter religions), the individual may experience asthma, hypertension, ulcers, or accident proneness. There is growing evidence that even diseases such as cancer, arthritis, or the common cold correlate to some degree with states of tension, and such studies may point to important aspects of life. It is vital, however, to get rid of judgmental attitudes about the handling of stress. The bystander overinfluenced by psychosomatic thinking may wonder, when observing a person in a wheelchair or a blind person with a white cane, what kind of self-directed rage caused the person to be in this situation, and why he was so extremely stressed as to "suffer" so grave a disability. Many disabilities could not possibly have been influenced by the individual, but more than that, it would seem more realistic to view the world as exerting "universal pressure" with which all must deal. One or another problem along the way is part of living, not a fault or cause for guilt.

For years experimenters in many fields have attempted to find the different psychological makeup of the disabled; that is, they believed there might well be a "coronary personality," a "diabetic personality," a "deaf personality," or an "epileptic personality." The latest disability-personality type to have been investigated is the "alcoholic personality." It seemed also logical to believe that the disabled would experience more frustration and that they would in turn be more maladjusted than the ordinary population. On the basis of several careful investigations, it can be said with confidence that there is no evidence to support claims that the personality of disability groups is different from that of the normal population. In fact, as a whole they do not appear to be more maladjusted or more frustrated, or to be living a prolonged tragedy.

Many disabled persons have been known to join the general population in accepting prejudicial attitudes toward other disability groups. A person confined to a wheelchair marvels to learn that a blind colleague is traveling alone to a distant city although she has traveled the world in her wheelchair. The age-old discussion of "Which is worse, blindness or deafness?" is not only carried on in the population at large, but within the two disability groups as well. Quite understandably, individuals in each prefer what they know, and regard the other as having the greater difficulty. This argument may have undertones of prejudice and pity which the one group has for the other.

Most people respond to the adequacy they perceive in a disabled person, regardless of the prejudices they may hold. A newly blinded individual just beginning travel training will use the cane awkwardly, bumping into posts, and a shopkeeper in the neighborhood will look at her with an expression of pity, saying, "That's the saddest thing in the world." Several months later, as the same blind person strides down the street confidently, using the cane gracefully to give her information, the shopkeeper will take notice with admiration and say, "That is the most wonderful thing in the world." The shopkeeper then is reacting to the adequacy he sees before him. Employers may continue to feel that being in a wheelchair is an impossible state, but if the young woman applying for the job has a top background and presents herself with vigor and assurance, handling the wheelchair independently in the interview, she may well get the job.

Along with the general response to the adequate functioning of the individual, many people have a picture in their heads of what the disabled person is like. When the person does not fit that picture, they are confused and uncomfortable. The rehabilitation process involves making the disabled aware of these attitudes and capable of expressing individuality in ways that communicate his or her real capacities and feelings to other people.

SELF-CONCEPT

An individual's self-concept is the way he appears to himself. Personality theorists, behavioral scientists, and persons rehabilitating the disabled are concerned with the development of this concept; how the body image influences it; the discrepancies between its ideal and actual versions; and how social forces modify the picture that the person has of himself. Everyone has a constantly changing sense of his or her own worth and adequacy. Certain experiences build confidence and self-esteem; others arouse anxiety and feelings of self-doubt.

Those concerned with the physically disabled have been interested in the effects of body image on the person's sense of worth, confidence and belief in capabilities—particularly in a society where physical perfection is stressed in the media. Most disabled people become aware early on that they are looked upon as less than adequate, stigmatized by their fellows. They incorporate these attitudes, or a reaction to them, in their own self-concept.

There are many situational factors which can affect the disabled individual's sense of worth. The person in a wheelchair is at a lower level than the throngs of walking or standing adults. The blind person is not sure that the person she talks to is giving full attention. The deaf person wonders what others are saying and if they might be talking about him. The spastic individual may be regarded as limited in intelligence and ignored by impatient conversationalists. Many who are different in some way long for the physical closeness and warmth, the handshake, the arm-around-the-shoulder which seem to be easily shared by others.

Part of the richness of life is playing a variety of roles. A person can be a leader in one situation, a devoted follower in another, an angry rebel in a third, and perhaps a wise counselor or a sexually assertive individual on other occasions. It appears that with many disabled people role exploration is limited. The transactional analysis theories of Eric Berne and others describe three major ego-states of Parent (the should-be's and judgments), Child (the I-want's and creative expansiveness), and Adult (the rational fact-exploration). The self-actualized adult employs the proper ego-state for the situation at hand and is able to flow easily from one ego-state to another as he lives his life. A retarded teen-ager may always play the "child" role with his peers, although capable of the full range of behaviors. Other disabled persons may take the role of passive dependency or of an object of pity, or be placed by others in such roles.

One of the problems is to discern how a particular disabled individual pictures himself and his relation to the world around him. One example is a thirty-year-old cerebral palsied man who told his counselor that he could not be around children, that as a child he was told to keep away from other children. He was surprised and delighted to discover that he did not have to be entirely cut off from relationships with children. When asked if he thought he would hurt the children or if they would hurt him, he realized that he had never thought it through, but had just accepted this as part of the cerebral palsy limitations.

The struggle to find out who one is, is complicated in the case of disability by limitations imposed on the variety of experiences needed to develop a full concept of oneself. Therefore, one of the goals of rehabilitation is to remove physical and attitudinal barriers that stand in the way of exploring various roles and various aspects of the disabled's personality. If this process of self-exploration were available for the development of humankind in general, the self-actualization of the disabled would be a more easily attainable goal.

An important strategy of rehabilitation work should be to provide artificial (role-playing) and real recreational, social, and vocational experiences. Giving the disabled the opportunity to be teacher, leader, or vital team member may be the key to building his or her sense of ego strength. The "positive thinking" approach aimed at helping people believe in themselves; the use of religion to imbue greater faith in self, the surrounding world, and particularly, one's Maker; and the self-acceptance gained through psychotherapy have all been explored and make a contribution to the rehabilitation process. Psychiatrists, psychologists, social workers, and counselors seem to operate on the assumption that the more a person knows himself, his motivations, fears, and real interests, and the better he understands why other people behave as they do, the greater his sense of worth. On the other hand, occupational therapists, physical therapists, home economists, mobility instructors, educators, coaches, etc., emphasize that the more a person learns how to accomplish tasks, the more independent he can become and the more skills he has, the better he will feel about himself. Behavior modification enthusiasts hold that shaping the person's behavior is the primary endeavor. Most rehabilitation programs provide an array of approaches. Some, however, offer individually prescribed programs, and others insist that clients conform to the philosophical bias of the program.

Many rehabilitation facilities arrange for disabled people to engage in group discussions on the assumption that as they share information, problems, solutions, and particularly, how they feel about their disability and the way they are treated, they will realize that they are not alone. There is comfort in sharing as one goes through the adjustment process — a lessening of pain and anxiety — and perhaps even an increased confidence generated by greater awareness of where one is similar to and different from others.

A group of similarly disabled individuals who have shared their frustrations and difficulties over a prolonged period of time, however, may become embittered and locked into a minority subgroup. They may see themselves primarily in relation to discrimination if that is overemphasized.

As is true of people in general, disabled persons have changing needs, accomplishments, capacities, and limitations. As they go through adolescence, face advanced training, get jobs, lose jobs, get married or divorced, raise children, age, lose loved ones — as they face life, their adjustment is variously affected. An individual whose disability is not handicapping at one period of life may be quite differently affected at another. The person in a wheelchair who gets around quite adequately in college may at forty have gained weight and find the capacity for mobility more restricted. The blind person whose auditory acuity lessens with age may find that while she has been expert with cane travel, she must now think of using a guide dog. The retarded person who has functioned well in the community, at work, and even socially, may be less able to cope after the loss of devoted parents.

Combinations of disability seem to have an effect of "geometric progression"; two disabilities are more than twice as handicapping as one. A young woman said with poignant anguish, "I don't mind being Indian, and I don't mind being blind, and I don't mind being a girl, but to be a blind Indian girl is more than I can bear."

To quote Biklen and Bogdan again:

> However, while much has already been accomplished in the fight against handicapism, much remains to be done. The time has come to abolish handicapism, and it will require a concerted effort. The following ten points are a possible platform of action:
> 1. Learn to identify and correct handicapist statements in yourself and others.
> 2. Demand equal access for all people, regardless of disability, to all services and facilities.

3. Agencies should be funded only if they operate non-handicapist programs.

4. Start a national publicity campaign to fight handicapism.

5. Support a moratorium on the construction and funding of segregating facilities and programs.

6. Identify handicapism in the media and mount boycott campaigns if necessary to eliminate it.

7. Hold professionals accountable for the elimination of handicapism in their own practice.

8. Demand that human services be considered a right, not a privilege.

9. Support and develop national, state and local groups with enforcement power to monitor the abolition of handicapism in human services.

10. Organize an international committee to identify and eradicate handicapism.

3

The Role of the Family

CHARLIS S. DUNHAM, M.A.

In recent years changes have been occurring in the makeup of the family, with predictions of greater modifications in the future. Nevertheless, the role that family members play or fail to play in the adjustment of a disabled member has not been significantly altered. Love and acceptance as well as freedom to work through antagonisms and rivalries continue to have an important impact on the development and adjustment not only of the disabled but of all other family members. Whether the disabled person is an infant with a congenital disorder, a youngster at the time of onset of the disability, or an older person who is trying to adjust to conditions which force life changes, the family's support and understanding or lack of it can make the difference between his being part of the world or set apart from the society in which he lives.

Therapists skilled in facilitating communication between family members have a great deal to offer when the family is feeling strained in coping with the needs of its members. Families of disabled persons may benefit greatly from family therapy experience. Families also benefit from sharing experience and information with other families of similarly disabled persons; and the many parent groups which have evolved from the needs of blind, retarded, cerebral palsied, or deaf children become potent forces for family self-help.

Attitudes of Parents

In raising a child, parents harbor a complicated set of expectations and dreams which usually represent the way they themselves have experienced or hoped to experience life. When their infant comes into the world with a significant difference in physical or mental makeup, these hopes are badly shaken. A crisis takes place and is bound to produce some degree of individual and family disorganization. How this crisis is resolved is of crucial importance to the future.

There is evidence that conditions which are not detected early, such as profound deafness, interfere less with interpersonal development than those detected at birth. It has been postulated that when anxiety of parents is not aroused immediately, and significant early relationships are established with naturalness and spontaneity, the child will gain a foothold on life and will have a better chance for normal development. Likewise, if the disability occurs later on, after parents have been able to establish a close bond with the child, basic family relationships can be called upon to assist all members in coping with the crisis. But when there is early recognition that the child is defective in some way which may interfere with mobility or social interaction, the fears of what the future holds for the child and the parents themselves can affect all relationships within the family.

The immediate reaction of one or both parents may be to withdraw from the child and reject him or her. In some cases rejection takes the form of denying the disability; in other words, rejecting the part of the child that causes so much anxiety and concern. Frequently parents have difficulty in expressing anger toward the disabled child, making it impossible to set limits and provide discipline. Overprotection and indulgent permissiveness may themselves be forms of parental rejection, and the consequent behavior difficulties add to an already stressful family situation. If these reactions are brought to the surface, they can usually be dealt with. It is when anger, resentment, and disappointment are not acknowledged that they cause damage.

Frequently the disappointment experienced by the parents, along with the usually unrealistic but nonetheless commonly experienced guilt, seems to push the partners away from each other. Nagging thoughts of blame, fear of showing one's own "weak" or "dark" thoughts, and inability to give or accept comfort all serve to isolate the parents from each other and may build barriers which become more painful as the years go by, and may never be overcome.

The complicated development of parental feelings of identification with the child and rejection of the disability often results in hypersensitivity to the attitudes of others. Many families of disabled individuals report varying degrees of isolation from the larger family, neighbors, and friends. These families believe they are being rejected, when actually they are attributing to others the rejecting feelings they have toward the disabled child. One mother bitterly related slight after slight at church, in the neighborhood, and in the family because her son had a learning and behavioral disorder which had been a diagnostic and treatment puzzle for years.

During family counseling, in which she was able to express angry feelings and unburden herself of the accumulated pain and hurt, she began to relax in communicating with her husband and other children. She also began to perceive others differently. In an early session she described an experience in which she was in a store and was thinking how rudely people were staring at her and her son John, then she had suddenly realized that he was not even with her. In a later session she demonstrated an increasing ability to accept John and allow others to do so when she joyously related how workmen had let him explore their tractor and had been patient and kind to the boy. Soon she began to find acceptance for herself and her family in other situations as well.

With communication and the deep sharing of experiences and feelings, people become truly close, and many families are able to uncover newfound strengths and bonds in the process of nurturing a child with unusual difficulties. A mother of a disabled child expressed the closeness when she said, "I get more 'tenderation' from him." Countless families courageously and uncomplainingly provide an endless measure of devotion and ingenuity in helping their disabled child obtain opportunities which make a vast difference in his or her life—for example, in learning special means of communication with the child (signing, Braille, etc.), massaging and patiently exercising malformed limbs, carrying heavy braces, chauffeuring

At a cerebral palsy center the therapist teaches the mother how to work with her disabled child so that training can continue in the home. (United Cerebral Palsy Associations, Inc.)

long distances to get to assistance services, and, most importantly, in caring and believing in the worth and capabilities of the disabled child.

All over the United States in all kinds of specialized fields, parents have written an incredible record of innovating, spearheading, and demanding programs to meet the needs of their children. In many instances independent-thinking parents have led the way against professionals who did not believe in the abilities of the disabled individual and who, although meaning well, moved in what sometimes proved to be unenlightened directions. Prior to the 1950s, for example, parents of severely handicapped children were told en masse to institutionalize their children, even in some cases to forget them. Many parents, however, had the strength to insist on developing programs to serve their children while they lived at home, in the face of what was practically unanimous "expert" opinion to the contrary. (See CHAPTER 56: REHABILITATION FACILITIES AND SERVICES.)

Possible Negative Attitudes by Professionals

In other instances parents have not had negative advice, but have encountered confusion and a lack of meaningful help. Specialists can become calloused to the effect of their pronouncements, and parents sometimes report that they were told such things as, "Your child has epilepsy. Give her this medicine as directed and come back for a checkup in a year." "Your child is brain damaged. Nothing can be done for him. Keep him at home as long as you can, but you will probably have to send him to an institution eventually." In the case of persons who are deaf, some educators, reinforced by the medical profession, have for years insistently opposed training in sign language. Even today, when workers attempt to help deaf persons develop total communication, and consequently once again teach standardized sign language, they often have trouble convincing parents who have been told by prestigious physicians that sign language is old-fashioned and will keep their child from adjusting optimally. Not only has this position tended to prevent several generations of deaf persons from developing essential concepts, but it has also made them feel that who they are does not matter and what comes naturally to them is not desirable. The notion that the use of vocal speech and reading lips will be the only way in which a deaf person might find acceptance in the larger community reflects an institutionalized sense of inferiority which often hampers rehabilitation efforts.

In this example and many others, physicians have played a significant role. Since doctors devote their energies and talents to treating the problems (orthopedic, visual, auditory), there is a natural feeling that a person who cannot benefit from corrective measures is hopeless and that nothing significant can be done. In recent years, however, the medical profession has come far in recognizing the psychological dynamics working against their acceptance of the disabled person and his or her potential for adjustment. This has resulted in a change of attitude, and today in medical schools and ongoing education increasing numbers of doctors are collaborating closely with educators and rehabilitation specialists and are becoming aware of new vistas of adaptation for the individual for whom medical correction or restoration is not possible. But despite these enlightened efforts, there are still so many persons in treatment roles who are unaware of their emotional bias that it seems necessary to assess the knowledge and experience in rehabilitation which the treating physician does or does not possess. Rehabilitation specialists themselves are not immune to some negative bias regarding the potential of the disabled, and constant vigilance is necessary to check against subtle and insidious limits which can prevail when insight and perspective are blocked.

Sometimes the helping persons seem to "take over" and come between the parents and their children instead of facilitating family interaction. Frequently parents have been made to feel inadequate in comparison with the "expert's" ability to meet the child's needs. Moreover, it is still hard to find services for special children which are truly family-centered, that is, services which focus on the goals and values of the individual family and assist them in cohesive development of the family unit with the "special" child functioning as a well-integrated member. On the other hand, practically all programs serving disabled children express a philosophy which stresses the significance of the family, and in most cases service is provided to parents in the form of counseling, group discussion, or some sort of group organization.

Parental Overprotection

Much has been written about the problem of parental overprotection of the disabled child, with frequent emphasis on domination as an expression of covert rejection. Other aspects, however, are equally significant. When children are hospitalized for long periods of time, are affected by disturbing symptoms such as seizures and high temperature, or must go through repeated surgical intervention, the parents are bound to react. When one painstakingly helps a frail infant to survive or has experienced the wear and tear which a prolonged childhood illness can entail, the tendency to hover over the child is understandable. Special-education teachers are often aware of the tendency for parents to keep the child at home at the slightest sign of a sniffle as they fearfully remember past fragility — in spite of the fact that the child coping with a disabling condition needs all the school hours possibly available. Difficulty in setting limits and providing discipline for the disabled child is also common but not insurmountable.

Another manifestation of parental anxiety is perhaps at the opposite extreme. This is the approach which seeks to compensate: Johnnie must be the most capable cerebral palsied child that ever lived, or little Suzy must become a second Helen Keller. Well-intentioned parents at times overstimulate and overchallenge their child, and in extreme cases such demands can cause the child to withdraw as the only response to the unbearable pressure.

Helpful Organizations Founded by Parents

Some parents have extended their concern and knowledge from their own child to a larger group of similarly disabled children. Many of the organizations described in this book were founded by groups of parents. Society has benefited immeasurably from such efforts and, for the most part, so have the families involved in leadership roles. There are times, however, that these families have great difficulty in accepting the very benefits they have worked to make available to others. Workers find themselves in the untenable position of being "employee" and counselor simultaneously. Board members, parent group workers, and professionals need to be alert to these situations which come about gradually. Families should not be cheated out of objective assistance because of their leadership role, and arrangements can often be sensitively made to find the help they need elsewhere in the community.

Siblings of the "Exceptional" Child

Brothers and sisters sometimes have it roughest of all. The Smothers Brothers comedy team had an entire nation laughing in identification with the soulful line, "Mom always liked you best." Feelings of rivalry are practically universal and are usually resolved without much conscious attention, but when the person you are feeling jealous of is in a wheelchair, or cannot be allowed to cry very much because it interferes with her breathing, or for some reason arouses special emotional reactions from Mother and Dad, it makes it almost impossible to work through a competitive relationship. In some cases the brother or sister is hampered throughout life by guilt-laden feelings of resentment or unresolved problems of competition. When attention is paid to the development of all the children in the family, siblings are capable of inspiring acceptance of and devotion to their disabled brother or sister. There was, for example, the treasured moment when eight-year-old Ann was overheard answering a playmate who had made a negative remark about her hyperactive brother: "He was very sick when he was a baby. We almost lost him and we're lucky we didn't. Besides, he's learning better."

A Desirable Outlook

Parents of disabled children need to strike a balance the best they can, just as in any family — balancing each member's needs, balancing encouragement and expectations of achievement against acceptance of each child as "a good thing to be" without needing to prove his or her worth to the world. Perhaps most important is adopting a philosophy which recognizes that no one experiences everything there is in life. No one tastes every taste, sees every sight, develops physical powers to the ultimate. When someone significant to us experiences the world differently, we tend to lament what he is missing. It takes time and effort to appreciate that he may be experiencing his own unique set of phenomena, and it takes a good deal of experimentation to see how much we can share with each other. How much we miss what we do not experience has a great deal to do with the attitudes around us. Animals adapt to disability with greater ease than humans, possibly because no one stands around solemnly telling them they cannot. A blind and a sighted youngster were overheard talking in this vein: Joe: "Say, Billy, what's it like to be blind?" Billy: "What's it like to be sighted?" Joe: "I dunno." Pause. Billy: "I guess we both know what we know and don't know what we don't know."

This is not to minimize the discomforts, the frustrations, and the endless patience required of the person who is different. In our society there does, however, seem to be a growing capacity for people to accept individual differences more and more comfortably. All parents have hopes of seeing their children become independent adults with a sense of purpose and fulfillment. All parents have moments of concern and doubt about what the future holds for their children. Emphasis on abilities rather than disabilities, and acceptance of unique ways of developing one's potential—this is the challenge which faces families of disabled persons. It can be an enriching experience for all.

SELECTED REFERENCES

Becvar, R. J., *Skills for Effective Communication: A Guide for Building Relationships*, John Wiley, New York, 1974.

Glick, Ira D., and David R. Kessler, *Marital and Family Therapy*, Grune & Stratton, New York, 1974.

Goldstein, Joseph, Anna Freud, and Albert J. Solnit, *Beyond the Best Interests of the Child*, Free Press, Riverside, New Jersey, 1973.

Gordon, Thomas, *Parent Effectiveness Training*, David McKay, New York, 1970.

Jackson, Donald, and William J. Lederer, *The Mirages of Marriage*, W. W. Norton, New York, 1968.

Patterson, G. R., *Families: Applications of Social Learning to Family Life*, Research Press, Champaign, Illinois, 1971.

Patterson, G. R., *Living with Children*, Research Press, Champaign, Illinois, 1968.

Satir, Virginia, *Peoplemaking*, Science and Behavior Books, Palo Alto, California, 1972.

Weiss, Robert S., *Marital Separation*, Basic Books, New York, 1975.

4

Social-Sexual Relationships

CHARLIS S. DUNHAM, M. A.

Sexuality is integrally entwined with every individual's self-concept, and certainly with marriage and family life. Its expression is also surrounded with problems of many kinds, not the least of which is the conflict between repressive and permissive attitudes in American society. Yet despite the social and emotional difficulties attendant on sexual development, most of the world's populations, including our own, somehow grope toward a solution and gradually find ways of achieving fulfilling intimacy and satisfying sexual identification and gratification.

Society's Negative Attitudes

This situation does not apply to the majority of the disabled among us. Prejudicial thinking and active suppression have combined to deprive them of a successful sexual existence, one that meets their need not only for physical stimulation and satisfaction, but for a feeling of self-worth and acceptance, expressions of tenderness, and a sharing of both the joys and sorrows of life with a loved one. One of the greatest obstacles to achievement of these enriching relationships is the idea that the disabled are not sexual beings, that they are of neuter gender. Myths of nonsexuality surround spastic, blind, deaf, paraplegic, and retarded individuals, just as they are imposed upon children and the elderly. Too often these myths have the effect of denying the disabled the very foundations on which social-sexual life is built—early experiences with the opposite sex, masturbation without guilt, basic information on the "facts of life," and the privacy that is necessary if romantic attachment is to develop.

Experiences in our society repeatedly deny the handicapped person equality. In the 1960s, for instance, a landlady rented a room to a thoroughly virile blind adult male in a boarding house for ladies only. This example might suggest that prejudice is not always disadvantageous, but most experiences of discrimination are not humorous or in any way positive.

Sexual development is so emotionally charged that there are often complications in parental acceptance of the experimental sexual experiences of their adolescent offspring. When the child is disabled, these concerns are usually intensified. Raising a child who experiences the world differently in major areas such as sensory intake or independent mobility makes for increased fears about the hurts and rejections he may experience in life. Parents may have painful doubts about their disabled child's capability for future independence and general coping, let alone his capacity to manage in the complex social-sexual world.

An Enlightened Approach

In Sweden, Bengt Nirje referred to a Normalization Principle in a 1969 paper on the mentally retarded. This principle established the goal of "making available to the mentally retarded patterns and conditions of everyday life which are as close as possible to the norms and patterns of the mainstream of society." That principle is now being applied to all disabled individuals, not just the retarded. Jean Edwards, Director of Habilitation Programs at Portland State University in Oregon, stresses the need to recognize not only physical gratification but human relationships and social-sexual needs:

> Those needs are the same for all of us. What the handicapped want, you and I want: *a friend* — someone to talk to, to share important things with; *some warmth* — someone to touch, put their hands on my shoulder in a way that says, "I like you"; *approval* — a message from others that tells me, "I'm O.K."; *affection* — demonstrated love, feeling and knowing you are loved, not necessarily in a sexual way; *dignity* — some communication from others that you are of worth; *social outlets* — avoiding loneliness and experiencing the above; *identity as a sexual being* — feeling a sense of what one is as a man or woman; *sexual satisfaction* — lustful, biological need for sex and sexual stimulation.

Ms. Edwards concludes that the last mentioned need, although genuine and strong, is often of lesser significance than the other real human needs.

As of the 1970s, the topic of human sexuality is just beginning to appear on rehabilitation conference programs. Films and books on sex and disability are proliferating. Little by little, rehabilitation counselors and medical personnel are discussing sexual problems with their clients. Nevertheless, many persons who face life with permanent disabling conditions have no one to talk with or help them adjust to one of the most pivotal and absorbing concerns of their lives: their personhood as sexual beings.

Enlightened specialists in each disabling field are familiar with particular needs and the adjustments which can be made to satisfy them. Frank discussion of these matters is not so important for the specific "how to" information as it is for the individual's attitude of acceptance and belief in his or her sexual vitality, which is so necessary if one is to be free to explore the unique depths of sexual experience openly and curiously. In this connection it might be helpful to encourage parents of a congenitally blind child to be comfortable enough to allow him to touch their genitals in some natural way—bathing together, for example—or to feel the body of an infant being diapered. Special lifelike dolls have also been developed to provide blind youths with sexual information. In these ways the congenitally blind can begin to develop concepts of sexual differences, information which sighted people gain through illustrated books or merely by looking around.

Persons with dysfunctional limbs (paralysis, paraplegia) have often been misinformed and "raped" of their sexuality. In some cases it has been emphatically predicted that these individuals would never be able to experience sexual gratification, and they have discovered that they could; or that they could not conceive a child, and they have indeed been able to do so; or that they would not be able to bear a child successfully, and they have. Paraplegic males who do not have erections have learned that they can derive great satisfaction from bringing ecstasy to their loved one, and that they can do so with their hands or mouth or by using devices such as dildoes or vibrators. This is not to suggest disregard of medical opinion in matters of sexuality and procreation, but to urge against docile acceptance of prevailing ideas and to encourage the disabled to consult specialists who are open to individual possibilities in an unfettered, unprejudicial way.

As Milton Diamond states in an article entitled "Sexuality and the Handicapped" (*Rehabilitation Literature*, February 1974):

> The client should realize that guilt is an inappropriate feeling, not because the individual is less able, but because no standards for anyone, able-bodied or not, are legitimately imposed. One needn't worry about being different sexually because anything goes that is functional and mutually acceptable. Oral-genital stimulation, manual stimulation, anything that the couple or the individual can find satisfaction in doing is okay and we as professionals and agencies have to make our permission and sanction (because we have the power to grant such) very clear. We must not put a negative value on any practice found acceptable, whether it involves masturbation, oral-genital relations, a female superior position, or anything else that satisfies the couple.
>
> For this we have to train ourselves against being judgmental and considering some practices preferable to others. This doesn't mean that we have to force on any client any practice he or she may find objectionable. We also shouldn't force our own

or society's guilt-laden values on the person or couple. We may encourage experimentation into previously personal or socially taboo areas. We should do all we can to help remove whatever inappropriate guilt feelings may exist in the achievement of sexual satisfaction.

Sterilization

Many doctors and counselors have advised disabled individuals to be sterilized because they were convinced that they could not raise or support children—thus revealing a lack of belief in their capacity to cope with life. On the other hand, some disabled persons themselves decide on permanent sterilization, and most would agree that there can be sound and constructive reasons for making such a decision. It should, however, be very well thought through, and every attempt should be made to understand all factors and explore all feelings surrounding the issues. Modern methods of contraception are varied and have a high degree of reliability, so that permanent, irreversible changes can sometimes be avoided. On the other hand, surgical sterilization can sometimes benefit individuals by freeing them from anxiety and worry which may be inhibiting sexual growth and fulfillment. The essential point is that such decisions are important and may profoundly affect the entire life of the individual and therefore should be made with extreme care.

The Mentally Retarded

Perhaps no disability group is less understood sexually than the mentally retarded, who have been stereotyped either as having uncontrollable sexual appetites or as being sexless, infertile "children." With few exceptions, the sexual development and expression of feelings and desires of the retarded correspond to the patterns found in the "normal" population. However, if appropriate behavior is not reinforced throughout development, they may not manifest normal social-sexual behavior. It is not unusual to meet a twenty-five-year-old in an institutional setting who will kiss a stranger and say "I love you." Unfortunately this young adult (male or female) is living in an environment that does not reinforce appropriate behavior, and as a consequence the action will be viewed as inappropriate and childlike. The reason is simply that he or she has never been taught to shake hands and develop other social skills that are taken for granted in our society.

Masturbation is also a question of learning appropriate behavior. When done privately, it is considered normal and acceptable, but retarded persons are frequently not taught where private places are located, or may have lived under conditions where there is no privacy. One should accept this behavior calmly if it occurs inappropriately, and assure him or her that it is "O.K." but should be done in privacy. With consistent, firm, positive reinforcement retarded persons can learn to deal with a whole set of social-sexual behaviors just as they learn to dress themselves, wash, and talk. Reinforcement of appropriate behavior in grooming, cleanliness, and sexual expression is an important key to normal social development.

Parents, counselors, educators, and society as a whole are also fearful that the retarded person will be exploited sexually. Some advocate early sterilization to prevent this, overlooking the fact that sterilization does not destroy sexuality. While there is no easy answer to this problem, sex education which employs role playing, videotape, and patient, clear, behavior-shaping reinforcement seems to be proving effective in some settings. Verbal admonitions, attempts to instill fear, and prohibition of normal outlets such as dancing, movies, and sports are not effective controls and, in fact, are bound to interfere with the development of nonexploitive relationships.

Relating to Others

In many instances it appears that more widespread and serious consequences of prejudicial thinking regarding the sexuality of the disabled occur in social behavior preliminary to intimacy than in activities related to sexual intercourse and procreation. If a person cannot relate easily to others, cannot touch or be alone with someone attractive, or cannot find ways to give sexual pleasure to another person, then questions of having children are quite remote. A young man reacting to a lifetime of unrealistic, withdrawn, and painfully shy behavior poignantly asked his counselor, "Do you think I will ever be able to get married?" He was told that he needed first of all to become involved with people, to overcome his difficulty in relating to others. His longing for closeness was understood and provided the strong motivation he needed to risk new and often uncomfortable situations.

An individual with a disability often has to help other people to relate to him or her. A person in a wheelchair with a hand impairment may need to tell a standing friend that she likes to shake hands; a blind person will usually be the first to thrust out her hand even though unsure of the reaction of the other person; a deaf individual may need to write a note telling her friend how to get her attention and give warm personal contact. It is interesting to observe how attractive and sought-after some disabled individuals can be when they have a sense of their own worth and a chance to experiment in getting their personalities across to others. One may deduce that certain dynamic, attractive persons actually turn their disability into a source of admiration and interest, particularly to persons of the opposite sex.

All manner of ingenious accommodations and adaptations have been discovered by human beings when they are sufficiently motivated. Social closeness and sex are powerful motivators. It probably takes a good deal of effort to interfere with the normal gravitation people have toward one another.

Many parents and rehabilitation workers fail to recognize that severely handicapped persons have a normal need for intimate relationships. To quote an article by Giovanna Nigro in the *Journal of Rehabilitation*, February 1976:

> Many long-term alliances or engagements that I have witnessed have given the couples involved, who feel that they could not manage marital life, a semblance of normalcy and many years of satisfaction and emotional fulfillment. Also, of course, not all handicapped people want to marry or find suitable mates, just as is true for able-bodied people . . . And the right to establish a meaningful intimate relationship with another human being can be the difference between a solitary empty life and a rich sharing partnership between two people, which can make the lives of both of them so much more rewarding.

Marriage to an Able-bodied Person

Parents usually wish their disabled child could marry an able-bodied person—first, because they believe an able-bodied person would make life easier for the partially dependent person; second, they may still be affected by the notion that disabled people are inadequate and that a marriage between two disabled persons could not possibly succeed; and third, they are concerned about the children of such a union. In this last case it would be more helpful to encourage the parties to seek genetic counseling than to make prejudgments about the transmission of congenital defects to the couple's offspring.

Views of the Disabled Themselves

Finally, many of the ideas presented in this chapter were expressed in personal terms by a group of disabled young people at a regional conference of the National Rehabilitation Association held in Hawaii in 1973 and moderated by Dr. Milton Diamond of the School of Medicine, University of Hawaii. There could be no more appropriate way to end this chapter than to listen to their views:

> JERRY: Well, I don't really think that I had any idea that things were going to be so different after the operation on my back. I thought my sexual life was going to be the same as it always was and it turned out to be completely different.
>
> MICKIE: I think at first I felt a sense of desolation that the emotional side of my life was all over with and that I've been condemned to the life of a robot or a zombie . . .
>
> BILL: I've been paralyzed for over 20 years and it's been so long ago that I've forgotten what "normal" sex was. But as I recall, it had to do with sex being pretty much equated with an orgasm. But since I've been paralyzed and had a few chances for sex, I've realized that orgasm is not so important in sex; in fact, it actually hinders the enjoyment of it because when you don't worry about the orgasm and don't think about the orgasm, sex just continues on and on and it's never over . . .
>
> MICKIE: Well, since being paralyzed and getting out of the more severe part of it, I find that I am perfectly normal except that the mechanics of the thing are different. My legs and back are

totally paralyzed. As far as feelings are concerned, if anything, they're heightened because the type of polio I had made me hypersensitive. I find that it's just mostly the mechanics that interfere. And, of course, the preconceived idea that, because you're in a wheelchair, "Don't bother with her — she can't do anything anyway."

DR. DIAMOND: Well, we find that even able-bodied persons begin to find that there is more than one way to skin a cat and probably the handicapped find this out a lot quicker . . .

JERRY: With me, it was a problem, I believe, of creating a new self-image. I thought that I had to be the virile male and live up to my wife's expectations (which she didn't have) of me. She was perfectly satisfied with what I was able to give her after the accident but I was always trying to do more, and finally I just sat back and enjoyed it, and it was great!

DR. DIAMOND: Why couldn't it have been this way before?

JERRY: Yeah, why did I have to go through all this misery of thinking that I wasn't performing and that I had lost my capabilities.

DR. DIAMOND: Isn't that a problem with all of us — we become spectators, rather than participants. We ask, "What am I supposed to be doing?" rather than, "What can I do?" Shouldn't we concentrate on what we have, rather than on what we don't have? . . .

JERRY: I really believe that the biggest problem was living up to an expectation that wasn't expected at all.

DR. DIAMOND: But now you don't worry about it at all?

JERRY: No, I don't worry about it. That's just the way it is. My wife is a wonderful woman. She's very loving and we've established a new relationship on a different level.

DR. DIAMOND: You just don't have the movements.

JERRY: Right.

DR. DIAMOND: Bill, how about yourself?

BILL: I agree with that. That the most important thing is to get your own self-confidence and just do what comes naturally when you're with your girl.

DR. DIAMOND: How do you do that?

MICKIE: Well, you throw your inhibitions out the window and let it all hang loose . . .

DR. DIAMOND: Mickie, you said something I think is crucial about getting rid of your inhibitions. How about those feelings with guilt? That you may be doing something that somebody else says is not normal?

MICKIE: That is a very hard thing to overcome, but you've got to make up your mind; either you're going to take happiness now while it's there waiting for you or forget it because you're not going to come back and do it again. You know — it's that simple. It isn't like having a piece of cheese in the "refrig" and a week later going and getting it out. There's no way that you're going to be able to do that. So you've just got to say — maybe we'll try something else.

DR. DIAMOND: Sex, in terms of genitals, is important but, in terms of personal worth, getting along with somebody and self-worth are perhaps more important.

MICKIE: Oh, I think so!

SELECTED REFERENCES

Brenton, Myron, "Sex and the Physically Handicapped," *Physician's World,* September 1974.

Cook, Rose, "Sex Education Service Model for the Multi-Handicapped Adult," *Rehabilitation Literature,* September 1974.

De la Cruz, F., and G. D. La Veck, eds., *Human Sexuality and the Mentally Retarded,* Brunner/Mazel, New York, 1971.

Diamond, Milton, "Sexuality and the Handicapped," *Rehabilitation Literature,* February 1974.

Eisenberg, M., et al., *Sex and the Cord-Injured Person* (pamphlet), Veterans Administration Hospital, 10701 East Boulevard, Cleveland, OH 44106.

Hohmann, G. W., "Considerations in Management of Psychosexual Readjustment in the Cord-Injured Male," *Rehabilitation Psychology,* vol. 19, no. 2, 1972.

Johnson, Warren, *Sex Education and the Mentally Retarded* (pamphlet), American Association of Sex Educators and Counselors.

Multimedia Bibliography for Sex Educators and Counselors, American Association of Sex Educators and Counselors.

Romano, Mary D., and Robert E. Lassiter, "Sexual Counseling with the Spinal-Cord Injured," *Archives of Physical Medicine and Rehabilitation,* December 1972.

Selective Bibliography on Sex and the Handicapped: Selected Professional References, Sex Information and Education Council of the United States.

5

Independent Living: Ways and Means

ROBERT M. GOLDENSON, Ph.D.

The most basic rehabilitation is self-rehabilitation, for what disabled persons learn to do for themselves is more important than what others do for them. The reasons are clear. Self-dependence, even in small measure, helps individuals preserve their sense of dignity and personal worth, while dependence tends to deprive them of initiative, self-esteem, and hope for the future. Moreover, people who do not learn to do as much as possible for themselves are bound to compound their frustrations, and their disability will inevitably become a handicap instead of a limitation. And if they go further and come to expect or demand care from others when it is not necessary, they deprive the others as well as themselves of freedom. But if, on the other hand, they use every possible means of becoming self-dependent, they will feel that they are to a large extent the master of their fate and will be able to resist the debilitating effects of oversolicitude and overprotection.

This is not to say that the ideal is total independence and self-sufficiency. As Gil S. Joel (*So Your Child Has Cerebral Palsy*, University of New Mexico Press, Albuquerque, 1975), severely disabled himself, has pointed out:

> We CPs hear these terms constantly. We grow up with them. But their meaning is lost to us because they no longer have meaning. Handicapped or not, the "self-made man" is as extinct as the brontosaurus . . . The strength of our society comes, oddly enough, from man's dependence on his fellow man . . . If a person with no physical limitations needs help

from those around him, how can the handicapped be expected to achieve total independence?

All people, then, have limitations and need help, and there is no contradiction in saying that disabled persons cannot help themselves unless they are helped by others.

The goal, therefore, is not the impossible dream of doing everything for themselves, but of preserving a balance between what others do for them and what they do for themselves. This balance can be achieved if the entire rehabilitation process—medical treatment, physical therapy, occupational therapy, social and recreational therapy—is directed toward overcoming limitations, and if the disabled person is encouraged to use every available device and technique that will contribute to comfort and independence. Since other phases of rehabilitation are described elsewhere, this chapter will be devoted to the functions of everyday life, such as dressing, eating, mobility, and homemaking.

Even though our focus will be on daily living, it is important to recognize at the outset that self-help actually starts in the hospital or rehabilitation center. The treatment and restoration process is so complex and so highly professionalized that it is easy to lose sight of the vast amount contributed by the patients themselves. They must cooperate with the physician by taking their medication, and with the physical therapist by performing their exercises, even though tedious or even painful—and the more they cooperate, the more rapidly they progress. The same applies to cooperating with the occupational therapist, nurses, and other allied health personnel, such as orthotists and prosthetists, who may be involved. By now it is almost universally recognized that rehabilitation is not something that is done *to* the patient, but something done *with* the patient.

It must also be recognized, however, that some patients are unable to cooperate fully, and ordinary encouragement and reassurance may be insufficient. They may have gone through a life-threatening experience that has deprived them of their will to cooperate or even their will to live. They may be consumed by resentment ("Why did it have to happen to me?"), or they may be preoccupied with finding other people to blame for their plight. Others may be discouraged by the slow rate of improvement and the enormous effort that must be expended to achieve what appear to be very slight results. In such cases the temptation to adopt a "take it or leave it" approach, or even to write them off, may be strong. But instead, every effort should be made to understand their reactions and help them overcome these inner obstacles. One way is to involve family members by making them aware of the patient's feelings as well as potential for improvement. Another is to find a staff member, such as a nurse, who can establish a personal relationship with the patient and give the needed support. Still another is to bring a psychologist or psychiatrist into the picture to help the patient explore and, hopefully, overcome negative feelings. And in some cases the key may lie in demonstrating the possibilities of improvement through films, or by having the patient watch others who are actively participating in the rehabilitative process, or by arranging for the patient to talk with a volunteer or member of the staff who has been able to cope successfully with the same condition. In most instances one of these approaches, or a combination of several, will induce patients to cooperate and thereby help themselves.

The achievement of the highest possible degree of independence in such basic activities of daily living as feeding, dressing, toileting, and ambulation is one of the major goals of the rehabilitation process. This objective applies equally to children with developmental disabilities and to older people with acquired limitations resulting from injury or disease. All these patients require special training and practice under the direction of nurses, occupational therapists, and physical therapists, as well as carefully selected assistive devices adapted to the specific disability. Often, too, medical or surgical treatment may be needed to help the patient achieve greater manual control for feeding and dressing, or the sphincter control required for successful toilet training.

Feeding and Personal Cleanliness

Helping an infant or young child with feeding depends on many factors: the strength of sucking, swallowing, and chewing responses; parental awareness of precautions that must be taken; the availability of special aids; and infinite patience. In her helpful book, *Handling the Young Cerebral Palsied Child at Home* (Dutton, New York, 1975), Nancie R. Finnie outlines the steps involved and the problems encountered not only in feeding severely disabled children but in helping them learn to eat and drink self-sufficiently. Some of the common problems are a constantly open mouth; tongue thrust, which prevents food from being taken into the mouth; and an excessively strong bite reflex. Techniques have been developed for solving such problems — for example, swallowing with the mouth shut as a means of overcoming tongue thrust. In another excellent book, *Functional Aids for the Multiply Handicapped* (Harper and Row, New York, 1973), Isabel P. Robinault describes and illustrates a wide variety of feeding and eating equipment, from special bottles and nipples to utensils with built-up handles and plates with suction bottoms. She also gives directions and precautions for their use — for instance, positioning the child to prevent aspiration of food; the use of straws to encourage sucking; and various slings and supports for both children and adults afflicted with involuntary movements, arm paralysis, or other disorders that interfere with self-feeding. For an inventory of aids and devices, see the list of eating and drinking aids at the end of this chapter, based primarily on the Robinault book and the encyclopedic *Aids to Independent Living: Self-help for the Handicapped,* by Edward W. Lowman and Judith L. Klinger (McGraw-Hill, New York, 1969).

An equally broad range of devices is available for all other phases of self-care — toileting, washing, bathing, brushing the teeth, grooming, and dressing. But here, too, training must precede or go hand in hand with their use. Such training, given in developmental and rehabilitation centers as well as at home, is directed to improving basic physical functions such as manual coordination, sensitivity to bodily needs, and perception of temperature differences. The three books just mentioned, as well as pamphlets obtainable from individual organizations such as the Muscular Dystrophy Association, United Cerebral Palsy, and the Easter Seal Society, give specific instructions in this area. To cite a few examples, the mother must learn how to hold a flaccid baby as she bathes it, what kind of bath toys are most helpful, and the special supports and devices needed to develop skill and maintain a sense of security as the child learns to bathe itself. Older children and adults will need assistance and instruction in the use of special bathing aids, such as a nonslip surface, a shoulder shower, a bathtub lifter, grab bars, and transfer devices.

Patients who have difficulty with grasping can often learn to use a toothbrush with a special handle or a strap that goes around the hand, and in cases where the hands are nonfunctional a spongelike tooth cleaner can be chewed. Toileting often poses especially difficult and lasting problems. As with other children, the mother must become aware of signs of need, but even before that, Nancie Finnie recommends "potting" the child every hour in order to establish a regular routine, always letting the child know what is expected. In cases where head and trunk muscles are not strong enough to maintain a sitting position, it will be necessary to lend support with the hands or place the child on a potty chair with back and arm rests. For later use there are special seats with handgrips, chair commodes, and different types of urinals. If control cannot be fully developed, sanitary pants can be used, and if the hands are nonfunctional, there is an efficient but expensive device called the Clos-O-Mat which automatically cleanses the patient after elimination with a warm water douche followed by a jet of warm air.

Dressing

Independence in dressing requires a combination of ingenuity, careful choice of clothes, repeated practice, and special functional aids. (See the list of clothes and aids at the end of this chapter.) To begin with, there are a few tricks and techniques that make dressing oneself easier. For those who cannot stand well, it is usually possible to put on clothes while sitting or lying on a bed. It may be necessary to roll from side to side and pull up pants with a pair of tongs or a stick attached to the waistband with a clamp. Pull-on devices are also available for hose and socks. Gloves are easier to get on if they are somewhat oversize and made of stretch material, and the teeth can be used to grip them. Children should be encouraged to dress and undress themselves at the earliest possible age, even if it takes extra time. Various positions should be tried, but in most cases they can succeed if they lie down, sit in a large chair, or prop themselves against a corner wall.

Good grooming is an essential aspect of self-care not only because it is an integral part of personal hygiene but because it contributes to morale, a positive self-image, and acceptance by others. A slovenly, dilapidated appearance is an almost sure sign that the mentally or physically disabled person has given up on self-sufficiency. For these reasons most rehabilitation centers provide basic training in grooming, including makeup, manicuring, hair and skin care, and if facilities allow, practice in shampooing, bathing, and showering. For boys and young men, training may include practice in shaving, polishing shoes, brushing the hair, and choosing simple but neat clothing. (See the end of this chapter for a list of grooming aids.)

In recent years rehabilitation specialists, home economists, and manufacturers have developed many practical articles of clothing for the disabled. In general, they recommend wrinkle-resistant, easily cleaned fabrics fashioned into garments that are attractive and varied but also sturdy enough to withstand the wear and tear of crutches, wheelchairs, and braces. But there are other considerations as well: the clothing must be designed with particular types of disabilities in mind, so that it will be easy to put on and take off and comfortable to wear, and will allow ease of movement. For individuals with poor manual control, pullover shirts and sweaters are usually easier to manage than garments with buttons. Where closure is necessary and the hands are weak, oversize buttons and buttonholes are recommended, as well as zippers with large, easily grasped pulls. Sleeve buttons can be eliminated by wearing short sleeves or by replacing them with Velcro fabric-strip fasteners or elasticized thread. For women, skirts with front or side zippers or an elastic waistband and front-opening or stretch bras are recommended; and for men, clip-on ties or, better yet, a polo shirt or turtleneck.

For women who are wheelchair-bound or in braces, pants suits, stretch-knit slacks, and pleated skirts are suggested. Long, loose sleeves with large, open cuffs should be avoided because they are a safety hazard and easily become soiled from contact with chair wheels. Shoulder seams often need to be reinforced when a wheelchair or pair of crutches is used. Some of the many attractive accessories for disabled women are stretch watchbands, ornamental zipper pulls, and bracelets that cannot be caught in equipment. Men in wheelchairs find that short suit coats and jackets get less crumpled than the longer length and that shirts should always have pockets because pants pockets are hard to reach. Wide, double-knit trousers are easiest to get into and should be lined for extra wear if a brace or prosthesis is worn. A vinyl poncho is easier to get on and off than a raincoat, and a wheelchair cape is easier to manage than a topcoat or overcoat.

The most practical shoes for men, and sometimes for women and children as well, are slip-ons; but if shoes with closures are used, simple buckles, a shoe-lock fastener, or pretied elastic laces are best. In many cases shoes have to be specially made at considerable expense to conform to deformed feet or provide extra support. There are trade-in centers for those who require only one shoe or a different size for each foot: the National Odd-Shoe Exchange, 1415 Ocean Front, Santa Monica, CA 90401; the Shoe and Glove Exchange, 1115 Langford Drive, College Station, TX 77040; and Handicappers of America, R. R. 2, Box 58, Canby, Indiana.

The prime considerations in selecting children's clothes are not only comfort and attractiveness but freedom of movement and independence in putting them on and taking them off. Chubby-size clothing for girls and huskies for boys are often chosen if braces are worn, and reinforced seams, iron-on patches, and raglan sleeves are recommended if crutches are used. If children are in a wheelchair, pants, jeans, and dresses with pockets in front provide extra storage space for the trinkets they like to carry. Soft knits and jerseys, as well as minimum-care and soil-resistant finishes are especially practical for both boys and girls.

Mobility

For severely disabled infants and children, the first step toward mobility, and the independence it brings with it, is often the development of postural control. Spastic and athetoid children, for example, have far greater difficulty than able-bodied children with the various stages through which postural control is developed: turning over, lifting the head, creeping, crawling. Parents must help the child learn to turn, help support the head, and use sandbags or other objects to prop the child up. As Berta and Karl Bobath, Gosaku Naruse, and others have demonstrated, exercises and manipulations are needed as early in life as possible to help the child overcome tonic neck reflex, muscular imbalance, uncontrolled movements or other defects that interfere with mobility. The training process can also be advanced through the use of various kinds of equipment during the first years of life, such as sitting aids and creeping aids. As the child grows older, standing, walking, and jumping aids may be utilized, as well as physical training and playground equipment designed to increase strength, coordination, and balance.

For both young people and adults, preambulation training is usually carried out in the hospital during the recovery period. As Lowman and Klinger point out, proper "bed mechanics" are needed to assure adequate rest and the prevention of decubiti, contractures, or deformity. Many bed posture aids are available for patients with such conditions as spondylitis or spinal injury: a bedboard under the mattress, leg or head elevator, backrest, special neck pillows, footboard, heel protectors; as well as manually or electrically adjustable beds. The next step toward independence involves transferring from the bed to a standing or sitting position. Here, too, many aids are available: an adjustable-height bed, wooden blocks to raise bed legs, metal supports and rails for hands, portable parallel bars for ambulation training at bedside, wheelchair with removable arms, sliding board for placement between wheelchair and bed, rope ladder to enable the patient to pull up, overhead trapeze, mechanical or electric patient lifter.

An almost unlimited variety of mobility equipment, ranging from canes and crutches to wheelchairs and vans, is on the market today, and new variations are constantly appearing. But there are many problems as well: finding devices that are best suited to the particular disability instead of limiting oneself to the nearest pharmacy or hospital supply house; obtaining professional advice in making the selection, and professional training in learning to use the aid; obtaining financial assistance for the purchase of expensive equipment; finding an experienced mechanic who will make necessary adaptations or repairs.

Since major types of mobility equipment are listed at the end of this chapter, only general recommendations and precautions are covered here. Durability is a prime consideration, since uncontrolled movements, weak muscles, and other symptoms put extra strain on equipment. Adjustability is also essential—for example, it may be necessary to lengthen or shorten a cane or alter the height of a walker. Two other considerations are particularly important in choosing a wheelchair: ease of cleaning and maintenance, and availability of accessories or special features that enhance the comfort of the patient—for example, heel and toe straps, removable headrest, or a safety harness.

The ability to drive a car certainly offers advantages for the disabled person. It not only opens the road, quite literally, to greater opportunities for social and recreational life, travel, and sightseeing but to opportunities for education, vocational training, and actual employment. It also increases the feeling of independence, lightens the burden on the family, and helps one picture oneself as a more normal, capable person. For all these reasons, plus the fact that public transportation makes little or no provision for the physically handicapped, a growing number of rehabilitation centers and health agencies are making driver education available to their clients either as part of their own program or in conjunction with an Office of Vocational Rehabilitation.

The first step in driver training is a careful assessment of the individual's previous driving experience, if any, and the exact nature of the physical limitations. Personality makeup and emotional status must also be taken into account. If training is recommended on the basis of this evaluation, it should be carried out by a driver educator who has had experience in teaching the disabled. It is interesting that at the Institute of Rehabilitation Medicine, where a professional driver program is offered, there have been no student failures in over ten years.

A thorough evaluation is needed to determine the individual's potential as a driver and the type of car and special equipment needed. Wheelchair patients are now driving vans equipped with automatic or semiautomatic lifts, placed either at the side or the back, to raise the chair to the level of the interior. Special straps, lock-down devices, and wheel wells are available to keep the wheelchair in place, and where extra headroom is required, a bubble-top roof is also available. The bulk of disabled drivers, however, use ordinary passenger cars equipped with special hand or foot controls in addition to automatic transmission, power steering, power brakes, and adjustable seat. The available self-help devices are so varied that they can be chosen with the particular disability in mind. Among them are a gear shift extension for the left hand; hand-operated brakes, accelerator, and dimmer switch; a right-hand signal lever; a steering wheel spinner; heel stabilizer; grab bars; safety harness; and sliding board for transfer from a wheelchair. Studies have shown that properly trained disabled individuals who drive well-equipped cars have at least an average safety record. Nevertheless, it is advisable to take certain precautions, such as carrying a disabled-driver distress signal, patronizing service stations and motels that do not present architectural barriers, and traveling as much as possible on interstate highways, which usually have accessible rest areas. For long trips, special equipment will make travel easier, such as a soup or coffee heater that plugs into the cigarette lighter or an electric skillet for preparing packaged meals in a motel room.

Homemaking

Another important phase of independent living is homemaking. Today many rehabilitation centers provide basic training in cooking, cleaning, laundering, and other household activities. There is also an almost limitless array of aids and devices which make these chores more manageable. Some have been created especially for the rehabilitation market, but most have been developed for the average homemaker who wants to lighten and speed up the daily work. The fact that so many of these labor-saving devices have been developed for the open, competitive market not only ensures variety and availability but helps to keep the price down.

So many appliances, small and large, are manufactured today that the disabled individual can, theoretically at least, choose products that are best adapted to the particular limitations. A wheelchair patient will usually find it easier to use a front-opening washing machine and dishwasher and an ordinary oven, while an arthritic who cannot bend easily will manage better with a wall oven and machines that open from the top. Many appliances that ordinarily fall into the luxury category are veritable boons for the disabled person who can afford them: a trash compactor, sink garbage disposer, microwave oven, smooth-surface range that can double as a counter top, self-cleaning oven, automatic icemaker in the refrigerator. Easy-to-use electrical appliances are available for every type of operation: frying, baking, grating, blending, grinding, juicing, slicing, can opening — and an all-in-one unit has recently come on the market, though it is too costly for most homemakers. There is a similar wide range of smaller kitchen aids, such as jar openers, one-handed eggbeater, peeler, and an electric knife which can be used by persons with a paralyzed hand. A mixing bowl with a suction base, a pair of long tongs (perhaps from a barbecue set), mitten-type potholders, lightweight pots and pans—all these make cooking and cleaning up easier. For other items, see the list of kitchen aids at the end of this chapter.

Food preparation can be simplified by using convenience foods wherever possible, since they eliminate such operations as peeling, chopping, and mixing. Among these are innumerable frozen items such as vegetables, rolls, waffles, cakes, pies, juices, and entire dinners; prepared meats, packaged soups and gravies, cake mixes, powdered potatoes; and canned fruits and vegetables of all kinds. Casseroles and one-pot meals are also first-rate work savers, and two meals can be prepared almost as easily as one. Cleaning up can be facilitated by using paper napkins, throwaway pans, nonstick cookware, paper plates, and plastic cups. For a complete guide to all types of kitchen equipment, simple but nutritious meals, and techniques for cooking and cleaning up, see *Mealtime Manual for the*

Though arthritis restricts her movements, this woman can still manage certain household tasks by using special devices such as this "extended arm." (Arthritis Foundation)

Aged and the Handicapped, by Judith L. Klinger et al., Institute of Rehabilitation Medicine (Simon & Schuster, New York, 1970). See also *Homemaking Aids for the Disabled,* Elizabeth Kenny Institute, 1959.

Many methods and materials have also been developed for lightening the burden of housecleaning and laundry work. Much energy can be saved by keeping supplies within easy reach and sitting down while doing such jobs as dishwashing, bedmaking, ironing, and folding clothes. A secretary's chair or stool on casters will make it possible to move about while in a sitting position. Examples of labor-saving equipment are a canvas laundry cart on wheels, a basket for cleaning supplies attached to the wheelchair, a long-handled dustpan, a lightweight carpet sweeper or vacuum cleaner on rollers, a sponge mop with squeeze attachment, and an ironing board hinged on a wall. When such equipment is used in combination with carefully chosen cleaning materials, easy-care carpeting and vinyl floors, and minimum-care clothes, household cleaning and laundry chores will be far more manageable than they were a generation ago.

Finally, the home as a whole should be planned and designed with the disabled person in mind. There are two general approaches to this problem. One is to build the residence to order, an approach which is now limited to a few individual homes and a small but growing number of apartment houses which provide special suites for the handicapped. The model homes are all on one floor, with steps and thresholds eliminated, and have an open plan which reduces hall space and groups the kitchen and living and dining areas at one end. Such homes closely resemble standard ranch-style dwellings found in many areas.

The second approach is to adapt an existing home or apartment to special needs, in some cases with financial assistance from the state office of the Rehabilitation Services Administration. A number of rehabilitation agencies arrange to have an occupational therapist or home service specialist visit the home to suggest special equipment or modifications. Many severely disabled persons, even quadriplegics, can now live in apartments or in houses with minimal help instead of being placed in institutions.

Even though the model homes and apartments are few in number, they incorporate many features that can be used in existing residences. Among them are elimination of unnecessary doors or replacement with folding doors, widened doorways, substitution of ramps for steps, easy-access storage walls, front-operated faucets and range controls, raised electrical outlets and lower light switches and elevator buttons, casement or awning windows, sliding windows, doorknobs with levers added, shallow shelves, rotating book and kitchen shelves, low-pile carpet, nonslip tile floors, and telephone jacks in every room. The bathroom may be remodeled to provide a built-in sink-vanity combination with ample room underneath for a wheelchair, and such special aids as grab bars for tub and shower, a nonslip mat in the tub, a wall-hung toilet placed at the most comfortable height (or a toilet on a platform), and a bath lift or shower chair where needed. Kitchens can be redesigned by repositioning appliances, cabinets, and counter space and by installing such devices as a single-lever faucet in the sink, roll-out drawer-shelves or rotating shelves in the cabinets, and a pegboard to keep utensils within easy reach.

A number of guides to designing or adapting homes and apartments are available, notably *No Place Like Home*, by Irving R. Dickman, United Cerebral Palsy Associations, 66 East 34th Street, New York, New York; *Wheelchair Houses*, Paralyzed Veterans of America, 7315 Wisconsin Avenue, Washington, DC 20014; *Model Housing Units for Paraplegics*, Veterans Benefit Office, 2023 M Street N.W., Washington, DC 20421; and *Aids to Independent Living*, cited earlier, which contains an illustrated description of the model Horizon House developed in collaboration with the Institute of Rehabilitation Medicine.

Infant Care by the Disabled Mother

In her excellent book, *What You Can Do for Yourself* (Drake, New York, 1974), Patricia Galbreaith comments that not nearly enough has been written on the care of an infant by a disabled mother. Her own suggestions, however, are so practical and helpful that they go a long way toward filling this gap, as the following résumé indicates. Breast versus bottle feeding is still a moot question, but breast feeding has special advantages for a mother who finds it difficult to prepare the formula, sterilize the bottle, and get up in the middle of the night to heat it. On the other hand, if the decision is to bottle-feed, this can be accomplished with minimum wear and tear by using already-prepared liquid rather than powdered ingredients. Some mothers prefer throwaway nurser kits, others would rather sterilize a regular bottle, but in either case steps can be saved by keeping an electric bottle warmer on the night table. Energy can also be conserved by keeping the baby's crib beside the mother's bed instead of in another room. After the first few weeks, the easiest way to feed the baby may be to sit on the bed and put it in an infant seat propped against pillows. The process can be further simplified if all necessary items (food utensils, food and liquids, vitamins, damp cloth, etc.) are placed on a tray near the baby. When the child is older, spills can be avoided by using a covered cup with a drinking spout.

The disabled mother will also find bathing easier if she puts the baby on her bed or in a Bathinette placed at a comfortable height. A sponge bath is simplest to manage, but the child can also be bathed in a plastic dishpan or tub—again with necessary supplies placed within reach. After six months or so, the baby can be strapped into an infant seat and bathed in the bathtub or sink, whichever is easier. A sink spray or shampoo hose will lighten the work, and in any case the baby will be less slippery if dried before being lifted out.

The problem of dressing the baby and caring for its clothes can be simplified by using throwaway, no-pin or prefolded diapers;

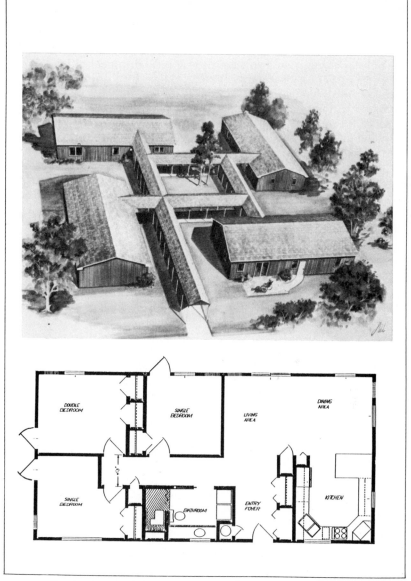

Barrier-free housing is important for independent living by the disabled using wheelchairs. In this design, four modular homes are connected by sheltered outside passageways. The floor plan for each house (overall dimensions 23 feet 8 inches by 50 feet, or 7.2 meters by 15 meters) includes wheelchair turning space, oversize bathroom with enlarged shower area, and 3-foot-wide (92 centimeter) doorways. The design also includes safety doors with ramps, and convenience kitchens with adjustable-height counters, appropriate knee and toe space, and front-opening appliances. (Independent Living Systems, Inc., Princeton, NJ 08540)

waterproof pants; dresses or other articles of clothing with snaps or Velcro closures; soft knits and permanent press outerwear that need little or no ironing; and shoes with elastic shoelaces that do not need tying.

A wheelchair-bound mother can transport her baby from room to room by placing it on a soft lap pillow held in place with a strap or by putting it in a "kangaroo pouch" made by folding a receiving blanket into a V-shape. Various supplies can be kept in a large bag attached to the chair. If she is on crutches, the baby can be easily pushed around if it is placed in a small portable crib on wheels, which can double as a playpen. A stroller can also be used by the mother who cannot carry her child. A car bed or even a large laundry basket will make a good portable crib not only for the car but in the backyard. A list of child care aids is given below. (See CHAPTER 55: ILLUSTRATIVE CASES, O. A Bridge between Hospital and Home; PART 4, SECTION 8: SOURCES OF INFORMATION AND SUPPLY).

SELECTED REFERENCES

American Heart Association: *Heart of the Home; Take It Easy.*

Copeland, Keith, ed., *Aids for the Severely Handicapped,* Grune and Stratton, New York, 1975.

Functionally Designed Clothing and Aids for the Chronically Ill and Disabled: A Seminar, Vocational Guidance and Rehabilitation Services, 2239 E. 55th Street, Cleveland, OH 44103.

Gilbert, Arlene, *You Can Do It from a Wheelchair,* Arlington House, New Rochelle, New York, 1974.

Goldenson, Daniel R., and Robert M. Goldenson, *A New Barrier-Free Modular Home for the Handicapped Designed for Individual and Congregate Use by Public and Private Groups,* Independent Living Systems, Inc., Princeton, New Jersey, 1977.

Hallenbeck, Phyllis N., "Special Clothing for the Handicapped: Review of Research and Resources," *Rehabilitation Literature,* February 1966.

Hofkosh, J. M., Jiri Sipajlo, and Leon Brody, "Driver Education for the Physically Disabled: Evaluation, Selection and Training Methods," *Medical Clinics of North America,* vol. 53, no. 3, May 1969.

Homemaking Aids for the Disabled, Sister Kenny Institute, Occupational Therapy Department, 1800 Chicago Avenue, Minneapolis, MN 55404.

Homemaking Hints, National Lung Association, 1740 Broadway, New York, NY 10019.

Institute of Rehabilitation Medicine, New York: *A Functional Home for Easier Living; A Manual for Training the Disabled Homemaker; Planning Kitchens for Handicapped Homemakers.*

Klinger, Judith L., *Self-help Manual for Arthritic Patients,* Arthritis Foundation.

Klinger, Judith L., et al., *Mealtime Manual for the Aged and Handicapped,* Institute of Rehabilitation Medicine, Simon & Schuster, New York, 1970.

Lowman, Edward, and Judith L. Klinger, *Aids to Independent Living: Self-help for the Handicapped,* McGraw-Hill, New York, 1969.

May, Elizabeth E., Neva R. Waggoner, and Eleanor B. Hotte, *Independent Living for the Handicapped and Elderly,* Houghton Mifflin, Boston, 1974.

Manual on Motion Economy Techniques, City of Hope Medical Center Rehabilitation Department, Duarte, California.

Olson, Sharon C., and Diane K. Meredith, *Wheelchair Interiors,* National Easter Seal Society, 1973.

Paralyzed Veterans of America, 7315 Wisconsin Avenue, Washington, DC 20014: *Wheelchair Houses; The Wheelchair in the Bathroom; The Wheelchair in the Kitchen.*

Robinault, Isabel, ed., *Functional Aids for the Multiply Handicapped,* Harper & Row, New York, 1973.

Rusk, Howard A., and Eugene J. Taylor, *Living with a Disability,* Blakiston, New York, 1953.

Vehicle Controls for Disabled Persons, American Automobile Association, Engineering and Safety Department, 1712 G Street N. W., Washington, DC 20006.

Washam, Veronica, *The One-Hander's Book: A Basic Guide,* John Day, New York, 1973.

Wheelchair Prescription, U.S. Public Health Service Publication no. 1666.

Independent Living Aids

DAILY LIVING AIDS

Eating

Hot plate; plastic bowls and dishes with suction cups; foam or suction pad for plate (Little Octopus); nonslip place mat; detachable rim guards; metal tongs or plastic holder for sandwich; utensils with built-up handles (bamboo, plastic, wood, foam); utensils with extended handles, angled handles, swiveling handles, or handles curving around the hand; other special utensils (rocker knife, scissors spoon, knife-fork combination, spoon-fork or "spork"; one-arm knife; nonspilling stay-level spoon); cock-up or rocker splints and overhead slings for hand support.

Drinking

Infant's wide-neck nursing bottle with special nipple; plastic squeeze bottle; cup with straw holder or built-in straw (Sippit); baby training mug; vacuum cup; ridged plastic tumbler; thermal tumbler or cup with double wall insulation, or with built-in straw (Thermo-Sip); flexible straw; nonslip terrycloth glass jacket; wooden or metal glass holder; tip-proof suction coaster; nonspilling cup for supine drinking (Wonderflo).

Personal Hygiene

Long-handled toothbrush; round-handle toothbrush; toothbrush with hand strap; electric toothbrush; toothpaste squeeze key; automatic toothpaste dispenser; Masti-Clean chewable tooth cleaner; glass-holder with handle; bathtub seat; bathtub lifter; bathtub hammock; bath pillow; bath rails; shower chair; shower and bathtub safety treads and mats; shower extension; shoulder shower; back scrubber; soap mitt; children's potty chair; elevated toilet seat; elevated or lowered wall-hung toilet bowl; cushioned toilet seat; manual or hydraulic elevating toilet seat with handgrips; toilet safety rails; incontinence pants and bloomers; over-toilet commode glider; stationary and wheeled commodes with receptacle; easy chair – commode combination; toilet aids for the bedbound (bedpan, inflatable bedpan, urinal); bidet – toilet seat combination.

Dressing

Aids: Zippers with ring instead of tab; zip-up chain; long-handle shoehorn; permanently tied elastic shoelaces; zipper or buckle shoe closure; stocking pull-on; sock, shorts, and pants pull-on (long dowel with cup hook at end); bootjack for removing shoes; Velcro closure for shoes; buttoner.

Women's Clothes: Wraparound skirt, dress, blouse with simple closure (Velcro, large-button, hook); pants with side zipper or Velcro; wheelchair cape and all-weather coat; front-opening bra; stretch bra; bra-slip combination; half-slip; zippered girdle; Velcro-fastened wraparound garter belt; garterless hose; Bermuda shorts.

Men's Clothes: Loose-fitting T-shirts and shorts; slacks with side or front zipper as needed; short wheelchair coat; wheelchair cape; turtleneck shirt; pretied neckwear; shoes with wipe-shine finish; loafers.

Children's Clothes: Overalls with large buttons or shoulder straps; loose-fitting coat dress; pullover jumper; loafers.

Grooming

Electric shoe polisher; spray shoe polish; plastic-roller lint pickup; rechargeable vacuum clothes brush; pressurized shaving cream; safety razor with hand strap; wooden extender for safety razor; lightweight battery shaver; electric shaver with hand strap or metal extension arm attached to table; lipstick with built-up handle or extension arm; long-handled comb and brush; comb and brush with handcuffs;

electric hairbrush; extension mirror for wheelchair patient; around-the-neck mirror; shampoo sprays and rinsers designed for wheelchair or bed; portable hair dryer; dress shields and antiperspirants.

SITTING, STANDING, AND MOBILITY AIDS

Sitting Aids

Propping devices (sandbags, pillows, rubber tire, wooden support, carton open at top); modified rocking horse; captain's chair with footrest; all-adjustable kitchen chair; adjustable potty chair; relaxation chair with wheels, tray or cut-out table, and footrest; seat belts for chair, wheelchair, car; vest for trunk support; child's car seat; adult swivel chair on wheels; foot and leg rests; slatted seat rest; chair with seat cushion lift (electric or spring-driven); reclining chair; commode chair.

Creeping and Crawling Aids

Barrel or beach ball; creeper on wheels; crawler on wheels; Scoot-A-Bout propelled by arms.

Standing Aids

Prone-stander; sit-in table (for one or two children); adult stand-in table; vertically positioned tiltboard or Stryker frame with body belts; raised workbench with or without arm rests; stand-up desk; wheeled stand-alone unit.

Canes

General Types: Hardwood; aluminum (adjustable, nonadjustable).
Variations: Special handles (curved, T-grip, spade, offset); cane-seat combination; quad cane (four legs, adjustable, with or without two wheels); tripod (crab cane); cane glider (two wheels, two tips); special tips (for ice, etc.); special handgrips (molded plastic; padded); long white canes for the blind.

Crutches

General Types: Hardwood or aluminum, double-upright, axillary (underarm), in various sizes, and usually adjustable; single-upright, adjustable; forearm, with arm cuff or trough forearm; underarm offset.
Accessories: Safety tips; rubber underarm pads; knob grips; contoured handgrips; forearm supports; utility bag; briefcase support.

Walkers

Types: Aluminum, with four legs (adjustable, nonadjustable); folding, nonfolding; with two or four wheels; stair walker; walker-chair combination; infant and child models; training walker with body support; one-sided walkerette; child walker with brakes.
Accessories: Basket; carryall; arm rests; axillary supports, tray.

Wheelchairs

Types and Variations: Standard chair with fixed armrests, stationary or swinging footrests, with or without elevating leg rests, upholstered or nonupholstered seat and back, folding; amputee chair; semi- and full-reclining chair; economy model; lightweight model; tiny tot and "growing" chair; junior chair; institutional model; light- and heavy-duty clinical models; chair with hydraulic elevating seat; one-arm drive chair; chair with tilt seat; motorized chairs (folding, nonfolding; guided by adapted hand control, chin, head, or breath); stair-climbing chair.
Accessories: Tray; lapboard; worktable; arm slings; heel and toe loops; heel strap; storage pocket; crutch and cane holder; removable headrest and head wings; seat belt; adjustable footrest with or without toe block; wrist cuffs; ventilated seat insert; slotted seat; removable solid seat; foam or inflatable rubber seat cushion; safety straps and vest; pneumatic tires; knobs attached to wheel rims for propelling; lever-type brakes; width reducer for narrow spaces; neck pillow; detachable armrests that can be raised or lowered; skirt guard; elevating leg rests.
Glider Chairs: With and without arms; large or small casters; with or without footrest; with bedpan; commode chair; shower chair; mobile lounge chair; chair-table combination; walker-chair combination; electric (Sleyride-Selectra, Lectro-Lift).

Road Vehicles

Small Vans: For group transportation, with wide door on right side and emergency rear door, equipped with safety belts, floor fasteners for wheelchairs, grab bars, back or side door ramp or ramp-stairs, hydraulic wheelchair lift.
Cars: Transfer and safety equipment includes grab bars and grips attached to car; retractable running board; car

door opener; folding wheelchair ramp; wheelchair loader; lifting devices for transfer of patient to and from car; safety belts and supports; adjustable back and seat rest; child's safety seat; back and headrest pillows.

Driving Equipment: Emergency devices (first-aid lights, citizen's band two-way radio, distress signs); motor-driven garage door opener, operated by transistor radio or pushbutton; hand controls adapted to individual limitations: accelerator, brake, dimmer switch, steering wheel spinner, extension for operating turn signal with right hand, hand control for parking brake, extension for operating shift lever with left hand, adjustable steering wheel; foot controls for drivers with inadequate use of hands; leg rests; heel stabilizers.

Adapted Vehicles: Electric car–wheelchair combination; invalid car; golf cart; small car adapted for stand-up or wheelchair driving.

HOMEMAKING, HOME FURNISHING, AND CHILD CARE AIDS

Furniture, Furnishings

Chair with seat lifter (spring-driven or electric); swivel stool (with or without casters and back); folding recliner; pole with hand grasp for rising from chair; foot and leg rest; swivel desk chair; bedside commode chair; bedboard; adjustable bed for head or leg elevation or body slant; bed backrest; bed footboard; blanket support; tilt-table standing device; bed rails; bed trapeze; rope ladder for rising in bed; lifting hammock; stair ramp (built-in or portable); stair lift; stairwell elevator; porch elevator; electrically operated window; curtains in place of closet doors; bifold or accordion closet doors; sliding closet doors; low closet rods; pole hangers; hangers on nylon rollers; closet rods with nylon hanger glides; closet organizers (for shoes, handbags, etc.); roll-out racks for shoes, etc.; kitchen storage devices (pull-out shelves, turntables, wire frames for vertically stacked dishes, sliding pan rack, wall rack, pegboard); countertop burner, electric skillet, oven; wall oven; range with front controls; refrigerator with swing-out shelves; sink with side faucets; beds mounted on casters; fitted sheets; electric blanket; drop-leaf desk mounted on wall;

worktable mounted on wheels; folding utility table.

Kitchen Aids

Easy-to-use peeler, grater, chopper; electric blender; electric meat grinder; electric juicer; electric mixer; safety devices (long matches, pushbutton extinguisher, stove guards); disposable metal pans; metal tongs and other long-handled utensils for reaching foodstuffs, serving, etc.; metal serving cart; hot tray; foldable wire shopping cart; shoulder shopping bag; one-hand electric can opener; wall-hung jar opener; long-handled bottle and can openers; lid flipper; vise-type jar opener; clamps and holders for one-hand kitchen work.

Cleaning

Long-handled duster and dust pan; hardwood pickup scissors; wet mop with high control; lightweight vacuum cleaner; metal all-purpose tongs; long-handled bathtub cleaning sponge; dish and glass brushes with detergent in handle; sink mat to reduce breakage; suction-based brushes for kitchen counter; hooped apron; front-opening dishwasher and washer-dryer; roll-around laundry cart and sorter; retractable clothesline; sit-down ironing board; traveling ironing board for use on wheelchair arms; travel and lightweight irons; folding ironing valet on casters; extended faucet opener.

Child Care Aids

Adjustable-height crib; crib with swing-side; crib-top changer; Bathinette; padded adjustable baby seat; infant chair on wheels; portable toilet with armrests; bathtub seat with suction cups; prefolded diapers; prepared formula in ready-to-use bottle; bottle thermal unit for night feeding; bottle holder attachment for crib; suction-based dish; child carrier for mother's back.

READING, WRITING, AND COMMUNICATION AIDS

Reading Aids

Book rack (wood or wire); overhead book holder; prismatic glasses for prone reading; clip-on book light; nonautomatic page turners (rubber-tipped stick or thimble; stick with magnet; mouth stick with suction cup); automatic page turners (Lakeland;

Turn-A-Page); microfilmed books with ceiling or wall projector; experimental Visotoner and Visotactor (for the blind and deaf); talking books; large-type books. (See Chapter 20: Blindness and Visual Impairment.)

Writing Aids

Felt-tip pen; ballpoint pen with angled tip; magnetized writing board for holding paper; clipboard; rubber, wood, and Velcro pencil holders; thumb and finger pencil holders (elastic, aluminum, wire); molded fiberglass writing cuff; mouth and head stick pencil holders; special armrests and overhead slings for weak arms.

Typing Aids

Light, compact manual typewriter; electric typewriter (with or without key guard and armrest); breath-controlled Possum typewriter; head and chin sticks for operating keys; Vista instant scanning typewriter adapter, activated by one key when the correct letter lights up; typing aids (copyholder, paper roll device, extended carriage return lever).

Telephone Aids

Extension bracket with tray for phone; Trimline handset for easy dialing; shoulder rest for receiver; pillow phone; Speakerphone (with mike and loudspeaker); Rehabaphone, for minimal muscle control; Touch-Tone pushbutton phone; dialing and pushbutton mouth stick; dialing tool; automatic pushbutton dialer for 500–1000 numbers; Card Dialer phone; handset with amplifier; portable amplifier; Tele-Muff (foam ring to attach to earpiece, for mild hearing loss); Sensicall (converts signals into Morse code, either as light flashes for the deaf or as vertical motion for the blind).

Communication Boards

For the nonverbal (aphonic): alphabet board (letters, numbers, Yes, No); word board (selected words according to age and need); magnetic board with movable letters and numbers; Illuminaid (buttons pushed with the finger, elbow, etc., to illuminate numbers, words, or pictures).

Electronic Aids

Tape recorder for correspondence (portable, battery-powered, or 110-volt, with reels or cassettes; pushbutton or voice command); intercom system (portable, built-in, or Home Interphone from phone company; pocket Bell Boy; walkie-talkie).

6

Educational Programs

JOHN S. HICKS, Ed.D., Coordinator of Special
Education, Fordham University

During the past seventy-five years, the field of educating children with handicaps has developed a wide spectrum of both services and approaches which are used in teaching. Historically, the trend has been toward providing more and more complex and varied types of services. At the beginning of this century, the major facilities and educational programs available for handicapped children were residential institutions or special private schools. In many cases, these were state-supported institutions which dealt with the very severely disabled child, with either a severely handicapping physical condition, such as total deafness or blindness, or severe mental retardation or mental illness.

HISTORICAL BACKGROUND

At the beginning of the twentieth century, public school facilities began to appear which attempted to deal with certain kinds of handicapping conditions. The public school programs were instituted in larger cities and were, for the most part, designed to deal with the mentally retarded. The growth of public school programs for mentally retarded children during this period parallels the growth of the field of mental testing in the United States during the early part of the twentieth century. The development of individual and group intelligence tests gave an impetus for the development of educational programs which could be adjusted to the level of intellectual functioning of the child.

A side effect of this movement of intellectual testing as it was applied to the field of handicapped children was the passage of many state laws in the 1910s and 1920s which allowed for the sterilization of retarded adults in the hope that such mental incapacity could be prevented. By 1930, an overwhelming majority of states had legislation allowing for this sterilization. Later developments in the field were quick to indicate that mental retardation could not be controlled through this kind of approach. During the 1930s and early 1940s, the major changes in programming for handicapped children seemed to focus on the development of more expertise in the medical professions concerning the etiology of handicapping conditions. Great progress took place in understanding that certain forms of retardation, blindness, and deafness could be caused by severe illness in childhood, brain damage during birth, or a host of prenatal conditions during pregnancy.

One of the major forces for social change and modified attitudes toward the handicapped child appeared to be directly attributed to World War II. As a number of authors have cited in their historical reviews of the field, the impact of the war was very positive in terms of handicapped children. The change resulted as a very large number of physically disabled soldiers returned home and had to be assimilated back into both the work force and their communities. During the last half of the 1940s, the public was forced to reconsider the stigma which had been attached to severe physical disabilities. It eventually became apparent that children with similar kinds of disabilities needed to be thought of in a different way, and certain forms of stigma seemed to abate.

At the same time, another major impetus for change which appeared in the field of educational programs for exceptional children was the development of a large number of parent groups during the late 1940s and early 1950s. These parent groups were traditionally attached to a particular kind of disability. Parent groups for retarded children, such as the National Association for Retarded Children, trace back to this era. (Such parent groups are considered advocate groups in the 1970s.) These groups began to look at legislation, educational programs, and the responsibilities of boards of education, and began to work through state and national legislatures to initiate or improve services for a variety of exceptional children. These services were no longer confined to institutional programs and became very widespread in public school programs.

The late 1950s and early 1960s are known in the field as periods of federal intervention. The federal government, through the U.S. Office of Education, began to stimulate a variety of new programs. There was an expansion of programs on the institutional, private, and public school fronts. Disabled children were being educated in many new ways. Various federal programs to train teachers of handicapped children were implemented, since it became obvious that the country lacked sufficient specialized teachers. The period saw a rapid proliferation of new, separate programs for handicapped children.

During the middle and late 1960s, the major change in the field of educational programs for exceptional children occurred. There appeared a number of legal challenges to traditional programming for handicapped children. Almost every state had legislative regulations or educational policies which allowed for the exclusion of children either for severe forms of disability or for severe forms of behavioral variation. These children were classified as uneducable and legally categorized as ineligible for services in public educational programs. Court challenges were made in a number of states, notably Pennsylvania and Mississippi, and in Washington, D.C., where the parents of handicapped children brought civil actions against the state or local educational boards, saying that no programs or inappropriate educational programs were being provided for their children. In most of these court cases, the persons bringing the suit won the case. These court rulings forced public educational programs to be responsible for a wide range of disabled children who previously would have been placed in institutional programs and outside the realm of public educational responsibility.

The changes seen in the first half of the 1970s in educational programs for exceptional children have reversed several of these trends. For the first seventy years of this century, the struggle has been to establish separate educational programs for exceptional children and to establish the right of the exceptional child to a specialized type of education. The major focus of the 1970s has been one of mainstreaming, which, in its simplest form, is the reintegration of the handicapped child into the general educational life of young children and adolescents in American public education.

TYPES OF SERVICES

The field of educational programs for exceptional children has developed, as was mentioned earlier, to the point where a wide range of services in a variety of settings are presently available to different kinds of handicapped children. In general, the historical precedent has been that the degree of severity of the handicap and the type of disability has in some way been related to the kind of service provided to the child. The policies are beginning to change, and this direct correspondence between degree of severity and type of service is no longer an iron-clad rule.

For example, it has long been the role of the state institutions to deal with and to care for the most severely and most complexly disabled children. State departments of mental hygiene, of institutions and agencies, or of education are responsible for severely handicapped or multihandicapped children placed in institutions. In a good number of cases, where a family, school, community, or court makes a decision that the child is so disabled that he or she cannot profit from public education or private school education, the child is remanded to the state for institutional placement. These institutions have been very large, usually overcrowded, and have generally provided both health care services and educational programs.

It must be remembered that there are a large number of severely handicapped children who cannot be served in public school programs and who cannot be placed in educational programs as they exist now in public or private schools. Consequently, mental institutions, institutions for retarded children, schools for the blind, and schools for the deaf continue to serve a purpose in cases of very severely or multihandicapped children. Until very recently, there was a differentiation between the legal responsibilities of the state education department and those of state institutions that dealt with retarded or emotionally disturbed children. In the case of New York State, the Department of Mental Hygiene has been responsible for services to children in state institutions, while the State Department of Education has been responsible for the other forms of public education.

The degree to which a state and its public school programs have been responsive to the needs of disabled children varies very greatly. In some cases the state still maintains and directly controls institutions or schools for handicapped children. However, the majority of programs in terms of exceptional children outside of state institutions and agencies are attached to local school districts or county-wide school districts, or cooperative district arrangements where the tax funds are used to provide educational programs for state residents.

One of the major developments of the 1960s and 1970s has been cooperative arrangements, usually known as BOCES (Boards of Cooperative Educational Service), where local districts combine and share their programs. For children with different types of disability of low incidence, very specialized services can be provided across geographic boundaries. While one district cannot provide such an expensive service, if two or more districts combine, they share the costs. This form of cooperative educational programming has become widespread in both suburban and rural communities where the incidence or rates of populations suggest that a cooperative effort be considered.

In addition to state public programs for educating handicapped children, there is another segment of services which have traditionally been offered to disabled children through the private sector. These private schools developed years ago when the public and state institutional programs did not provide services for specific kinds of disabled children. In many cases, parent groups, foundations, or religious groups developed programs to help meet the needs of these disabled children. Probably the best example of this form of service in a good number of states has been the case of the crippled child. In a large number of instances, a nonprofit organization, such as a cerebral palsy association, instituted educational programs and classes for severely physically handicapped and severely retarded children when the state or the local public school system simply refused and classified these children as ineligible for education.

The private schools and facilities have continued, and today represent a large segment of educational programs for exceptional children. Private facilities for emotionally disturbed children, founded to provide specific kinds of therapeutic treatment centers, have also provided educational programs. In many cases, private programs have also provided for preschool children where educational systems have not been legally responsible for the establishment of preschool programs. Many private facilities have been leaders in providing early intervention programs so that severely handicapped children can be given the kinds of stimulation which will help them develop their potential.

Several comments should be made concerning the range of services in terms of ages which have been provided for disabled children. Historically, the majority of services have always been channeled into the elementary school age range. The reason is that the elementary school is the initial point of public responsibility; educators have felt that the formative years of childhood are most critical in terms of lifelong adjustment; the elementary curriculum has traditionally dealt with the skills of basic educational literacy. The educational programs for handicapped children have been geared toward these ages so that exceptional children would acquire the literate skills of reading and writing and certain social skills, and get a good foundation in terms of adult life.

The emphasis on the adolescent child has been much less pronounced. Programs for the mentally retarded have been the most widespread in adolescent programs, because there is a very strong need for vocational education and vocational training if retarded adolescents are going to complete school and compete for jobs on the adult market. Junior and senior high school programs that dealt with other types of disabled adolescents have been much less extensive. If the child is intellectually capable, the child has been channeled through the public educational system on the junior and senior high school level. The majority of programs for emotionally disturbed adolescents have been exclusionary and have been related to programs which dealt with both emotionally disturbed and socially aggressive behavior. The current trend in educational policy appears to be moving toward an extension of special education services into the adolescent years.

As mentioned earlier, the legal responsibility for programs on a preschool level has never been fundamental to the public school systems. The impetus for the extension of programs for disabled children onto the preschool level has only recently developed as the U.S. Office of Education and the Bureau of Education for the Handicapped have begun to allot money to special projects, hopefully to stimulate preschool programs. The new federal law, Public Law 94-142, has a section which deals with preschool programs for exceptional children and provides federal money as a stimulant for educational programs to move down into the early ages.

EDUCATIONAL APPROACHES

Several trends have developed in the field of classroom programming for disabled children: (a) the diagnostic-prescriptive approach; (b) a cross-categorical approach; and (c) the individually prescribed curriculum. These three major trends in special education are seen in the different kinds of public and private programs and in the different age levels on which services are provided to exceptional children.

The oldest and most fundamental of the trends is the diagnostic-prescriptive approach. Responsibility for this development has been attached to the "medical model." The medical model suggests that if a teacher understands the "nature" of the disability and the nature of the learning problem, the teacher can prescribe educational remediation, just as medicine is prescribed. This has probably been the major curriculum model in special education for the past forty years. The diagnostic-prescriptive approach indicates that the more one knows about the handicaps that are present, the more one can diagnose and prescribe in terms of educational needs. This approach historically has led to a splintering in the field. As the diagnostic instruments have become better and better, the kinds of disabilities have become more and more discrete. While several years ago all children with severe emotional disorders might have been classified as schizophrenic, at this point in time the diagnostic categories are becoming smaller, and children are being classified as childhood autistic, symbiotic, or childhood psychotic as well as schizophrenic. The diagnostic-prescriptive process has led to an overextension of categories to the point where sometimes the teacher who is certified to teach brain-injured children is not certified to teach retarded children or emotionally disturbed children. There have been some situations in which the establishment of categories and the understanding of the nature of the disability are very important to the transformation of the curriculum into appropriate educational programming. However, the past tendency has been to seriously overemphasize the categorical approach.

The second major trend is a response to this, that is, a cross-categorical approach. During the last fifteen years in the field, it has become obvious that two major problems exist. The first problem is that a variety of categories are sometimes seen in any individual handicapped child. A child may be brain-injured, mildly retarded, and have an emotional overlay. It is very difficult to classify children into discrete categories in practice, while it may be possible in the textbooks. This has led to a broader approach so that professionals working in the field must know the rudiments of a variety of disabilities, because in reality the classroom is not that pure in terms of the kinds of disabilities that are the instructional responsibility of the teacher. In addition, the cross-categorical approach has become important because it has been found, in the last fifteen years, that while the specific disabilities grow to be more and more differentiated, they still retain many of the common curriculum modifications which are shared with a host of other disabling conditions. Consequently, teachers who are working with brain-injured children very often modify their instructional curriculum in much the same manner as do teachers who work with mildly retarded or mildly emotionally disturbed children. The cross-categorical approach has been practiced because the curriculum modifications are basically very similar across the disability categories.

A third major trend is the individualization of the curriculum. One of the evaluative criteria of special education programs appears to be the degree to which an individual child is given an individually prescribed program. The large difference between public education and special education appears to be the degree to which instruction is individualized. A disabled child may, in many ways, learn in the same manner as the normal child in either individual or group instruction. What makes the special child different is the degree to which that particular child needs special instruction to implement the learning that should be accomplished in the regular classroom. Consequently, the modification and individualization of curriculum allows the handicapped child to approach the same or similar content in terms of curriculum, but from different points of view and with different techniques and different modalities of learning. The individualization of a curriculum and the individualization of teaching, then, on a very small group basis or on a one-to-one basis, is a central theme in special education.

Within this area of individualizing to meet the learning needs of exceptional children, there have been a series of curriculum modifications which must be discussed. Basically, these modifications fall into four areas and are typically present in most programs that deal with disabled children. These areas are perceptual abilities, intellectual variations, social or adjustment behavior, and language development.

The field of the physically handicapped child, approximately twenty years ago, had a splinter group break off from it. This group of brain-injured children were only mildly physically handicapped but appeared to have perceptual difficulties. While they retained the characteristic of a physical involvement because a central nervous system disorder was hypothesized to be involved, the major behavioral characteristic was not severe retardation or severe losses in locomotion or lack of coordination, but rather the inability of the child to deal with the information which was being processed by the sensory fields. The perceptual disabilities were defined in terms of discriminating auditory and visual stimuli, and included the ability to coordinate movement with the messages in the sensory environment, to discriminate within a set of messages, or among the messages that the perceptual environment offers the disabled child.

These perceptual factors were the major reasons for modifying a major part of the special education curriculum. Consequently, perceptual training, auditory discrimination, visual discrimination, multisensory modalities, cross-modality learning and teaching, reinforcements in a variety of tactile-kinesthetic-visual modes have all been assimilated into the teaching strategies of handicapped children. Most classrooms that include handicapped children have in their curriculum activities a variety of multimodality activities.

The field of the mentally retarded child has developed a large body of knowledge concerning the intellectual variations of children. There are some qualitative differences in the way that retarded children learn when the intellectual level of performance is on a severely retarded level as compared with a normal child. While the area of gifted children has remained peripheral in the field of special children, the gifted child has revealed many things about the way the mind works and the way children learn. The psychological studies of cognitive learning in mentally retarded children have provided an abundance of information concerning patterns of cognitive processing which tend to suggest that there is a need for more concrete experiences, for more reinforcement of learning, for cross-modality learning experiences, for stronger reinforcement schedules of learning, for more transfer of learning, for a vast variety of concrete and also abstract forms of activities if the learning is to approach that of the normal child.

The area of the socially maladjusted or emotionally disturbed child has suggested a large series of modifications in the curriculum. In this area of disability, the assertion is that the teacher and the educational program are fundamentally involved in the emotional adjustment of the child, that is, the world of affective functioning, of relationships with people, of a sense of self, and of understanding the feelings of both positive and negative events in life. The major curriculum approach in the area of children with emotional problems has been therapeutic, attempting to provide a milieu in which the child can explore and learn about his or her own feelings and can learn to understand and control the various relationships with peers and adults. There have been a variety of curriculum materials produced in this area, such as Goldstein's Social Learning Curriculum; the Duso program, which comes out of American Guidance Services; and Dupont's Toward Affective Development, also from American Guidance Services, which helps the child explore the world of appropriate feelings.

In addition to the therapeutic approaches, a major input into the field of educational programs for emotionally handicapped children has been the growth of behavior modification. This has been a substantial phenomenon in the last fifteen years. The modification of inappropriate learning, the reduction of aggressive behavior through reinforcement schedules, through token economies, through aversive conditioning, through paired-associate learning, are major forces within most of the curriculum strategies for a variety of exceptional children. The work with behavior modification of severely withdrawn, schizophrenic children has been generalized to the extent that most of the programs which deal with disabled children have reinforcement or behavioral components. Both learning and behavior are dealt with through behavior modification in day-to-day activities. Examples are the Santa Monica Project or the engineered classroom of Frank Hewett.

There still remains a wide segment of curriculum modification dealing with certain forms of disability. This typically relates to the use or learning of language in severely visually impaired or deaf children where the physical disability has a tremendous impact on the way they comprehend and use language as both a communicative and a learning tool. The classes and programs which deal with deaf children, for example, have long been in combat over two theoretical positions. One position indicates that deaf children should learn to speak orally and develop a language consistent with the oral language of hearing children; the second position allows the child to develop a language through the use of gestures and signing, in which the child basically learns to communicate through the use of a series of hand movements. The language developed in programs for deaf children is typically a combination of the two, and except in a few instances the deaf child is taught to use both oral and sign language as an aid to understanding and learning.

The educational programs for blind children, however, have consistently been programs which have pushed the blind child into the regular classroom. The child listens and learns through auditory channels and can, for the major part, adjust to and succeed in regular classroom instruction, as long as some modifications are made to offset the visual instruction in reading and blackboard work. The overwhelming majority of blind children are found in the normal classroom, because they can hear and can participate through the use of oral language. Their language is not as impaired, other than in certain aspects of cognitive structures which deal with visual messages and basically visual discriminations.

The area of the physically handicapped child has been one where certain modifications such as braces and posture support apparatus and the use of wheelchairs and special chairs provide means through which the child can adjust to the disability. The range of physical impairments is the least of the problems in dealing with physically handicapped children. The major problems are typically social—lack of social interaction with other children and the issues of either self-concept or social adjustment. In some cases there is a problem of severe intellectual retardation related to the damage to the brain which has caused the physical disability. In a variety of cases, for the severely physically handicapped, homebound instruction is provided so that the child can pursue an academic program in spite of limitations.

Elementary and secondary school programs have been adapted to the needs of severely injured, hospitalized, or permanently physically disabled students. Home instruction, itinerant teachers, and the media of this technological age can bring the classroom to the home of the disabled student. Telephone and video systems allow the homebound student to actually participate in the classroom activities of the regular community school when systems are willing to provide the equipment required.

Instruction through educational television channels and programming, videotape cassettes, and other forms of communication systems will allow a wide variety of electronic teaching in the future. Currently, high school equivalency tests do not require a student to attend school, and a number of disabled high school students are able to complete course sequences without actually entering the school building. A recent program in California allows for a certificate of proficiency which is equal to a high school diploma and is given upon passing a written exam. What is novel about this development is that a student may sit for the exam if the tenth grade has been completed, allowing the student to move on to college immediately.

The speech-impaired child is often dealt with in educational programs for handicapped children. The program adjustments are usually in the form of supportive services, such as speech therapy, or classroom reinforcement of clinical training so that the speech development can increase to the appropriate level. For the major part, the curriculum adjustments in special education are geared to the cognitive disabilities, the perceptual disabilities, or the necessary social adjustments, and the lesser of the problems is always the physical adjustment which must be made in order to allow the child to become a successful learner.

FUTURE TRENDS

One of the most recent federal laws could have a tremendous impact on the educational programs for disabled children: the Education for All Handicapped Children Act (Public Law 94-142, passed November 1975). It is the culmination of a series of pieces of state and national legislation which have spoken to the educational needs of handicapped children. The congressional authors have attempted to incorporate a variety of educational policies and trends into this major legislation, which assures, from the point of view of federal law, all handicapped children of the right to an adequate education. Several important aspects of this law will probably be instrumental in spelling out the progression of the field for the next fifteen to twenty years. The major aspects are as follows.

By definition, the handicapped or disabled child in American society is described primarily as one who needs special educational programming to meet the potential of an education for adult life in our society. The federal law provides a 12 percent limitation on children who may be designated as handicapped or who may receive services under this federal legislation; that is, 12 percent of all children in school ages can now be classified as handicapped and can thus receive special services. Because of the emergence of Learning Disabilities as a category within the field of special education, the legislation has limited the range of services to the learning disabled at 2 percent of the school age population. There are no other regulations concerning the rates of incidence of disabilities among the categories.

Classification or diagnosis of a handicapped child is both positive and negative. It causes a certain stigma, but it also allows for certain services, and the payment for services, which the normal child does not receive in school. Because of the negative aspects attached to classifying a child as handicapped, there are certain restrictions in the diagnostic method and the classification procedure built into Public Law 94-142. In brief, the parents have the legal right to be a part of the diagnostic process; they have the legal right to be represented by attorneys in protecting their child; the school system is obligated to apprise the parents of all the information which would lead to a diagnosis; and the parents have the right to appeal both through higher educational agencies and also directly to the courts if the parents feel the diagnosis is improper.

Another major feature of the law is that the diagnostic process must be carried out in the native language of the child and must include more than one diagnostic instrument which is used for classification purposes. This is an outgrowth of a series of legal actions which have occurred in California concerning the classification of Mexican-American children as retarded through the use of intelligence tests which do not have adequate standardization in Mexican-American communities. The diagnostic process outlined in the new federal law requires an adequate instrument for diagnosis by a licensed diagnostician and is designed to protect the rights of both the school and the child being evaluated for services.

The diagnosis must lead to a categorization for state or federal aid as well as a prescriptive program to meet the educational needs of the disabled child, that is, an individually prescribed remedial program must be the end result of the diagnostic process. Along with a diagnostic classification of the child as mentally retarded, emotionally disturbed, etc., the individual prescriptive program which is not a part of the diagnostic process is a responsibility of the school unit. If the child is classified as handicapped and placed in an educational program for handicapped children, a review of this educational prescriptive program is mandated legally at least every year. The parent must have access to information concerning the degree to which the prescribed program is implemented and the degree to which the child is responding to the prescribed program.

Public Law 94-142 also established several agents which are intended to be advocates for the child as well as for the family unit. School districts are mandated to establish Committees of the Handicapped, which will, in essence, represent the handicapped child, whether the school is private or public. The public law also mandates "child find" services, where the states and local community schools are obligated to find handicapped children who are not presently being served or who are not being served to the maximum from which they could benefit. This is a result of studies which indicate that 3–4 percent of most school populations are being served as handicapped, while the evidence from the literature suggests that 10–12 percent of children in the school ages need services. Obviously, the need is not being met.

Another aspect of the federal law provides money for preschool programs. The intention is to stimulate activity both in finding exceptional children at a very early age and in providing remedial services for them. Hopefully, if appropriate remediation is started at an early age, the services can have a greater impact on the total life of the child. Direct grants to districts which initiate early childhood programs are available under the legislation.

It must also be noted that since this is a federal law, it is not a program which is temporary or which will expire at a particular date. The federal law was designed to be an ongoing part of the legislative rights of the citizens of the country, and is intended to be a permanent aspect of federal programs for our children. In this regard, it should be noted that federal support for this new legislation goes from a total of $387 million in fiscal year 1978 to a total of $3.16 billion in fiscal year 1982.

Another major component of Public Law 94-142 focuses on the obligation of local and state educational agencies to develop plans for the implementation of educational programs for handicapped children. Specifically, local agencies must submit plans providing for the educational programming for these handicapped children to state agencies. States in turn must submit to the U.S. Commissioner of Education plans for providing services to the handicapped children on a yearly basis.

Several other trends should be mentioned in terms of educational programs for handicapped children. There are a variety of developments in the field of technology which indicate a tremendous potential for use by handicapped children. Some of these have worked their way into programs for deaf and blind children; others may have a more general impact on educational programs in the years to come.

For example, there are a variety of computer-assisted instructional systems available which will help the teacher implement the strategy of individually prescribed instruction for handicapped children. A number of school districts have done research on the individualization of instruction through the utilization of computer programs, computer libraries, and computer banks which have developed the capability of adjusting programs to the needs of handicapped children. While the field of computer-assisted instruction is well known in regular education at this point, the majority of commercial organizations have not found it profitable to modify their systems to suit the needs of small numbers of handicapped children. One can hope that in the future this will occur, so that the resources of computer-assisted instruction will be available to teachers who wish to program for specific deficits in learning among classes of handicapped children.

Moreover, there is a wide range of technological instrumentation which can help the physically handicapped adjust to learning situations. Sensory probes known as Optacons have been developed and allow blind children to read from the printed page. By passing a scanning probe over a regular book, a printed page can be felt through a device much in the way that Braille uses raised dots. If the blind or visually impaired are taught to use this device, the total library resources can be open to them. The deaf child is being taught through a series of instrumentations where the child is bombarded through auditory systems in the total room. Amplification of sound in deaf children is a common occurrence in special educational programs. The physically handicapped are being helped to adjust to the limitations of buildings through the modification of the architectural designs, which allows these children to become mobile. Severely disturbed schizophrenic children are being taught with the aid of computerized "talking typewriters."

The educational programs which used to stop at the high school level for academically talented handicapped children have become available on the college level for the youth who is capable of profiting from these experiences. A number of colleges in the public and private sector are modifying their physical structures so that the handicapped students can utilize television or physical facilities in their daily learning experiences. It should also be remembered that a variety of nontraditional college programs are now available to both the handicapped and the nonhandicapped student. These range from home instruction by television or telephone, credit for life experiences, written home study courses, the College Level Examination Program offered by universities and state education departments, and specially tailored community college programs. Colleges without walls are presently open to a number of students, and the handicapped student finds it easier to participate in such programs as long as the necessary support services are provided. These may include tutors, readers, tape recorders, and books on records, and in most cases the Office of Vocational Rehabilitation will make these adjustments possible.

In addition, a good number of elementary and high school programs are developing both recreation and physical education programs for the handicapped. The institution of physical education activities in the lives of adolescent handicapped students seems to indicate that the handicapped child is being allowed to become more competitive and to understand the pleasure of being involved in physical competition. Clubs, community agencies, and professional groups which sponsor physical recreation for the handicapped are beginning to appear in communities throughout the country. One of the most outstanding appears to be the summer programs for recreation and physical education for handicapped children, where communities plan for the full range of handicapped children during the summer months.

SUMMARY AND CONCLUSIONS

This chapter has attempted to review various educational programs which are currently available to disabled children. The Selected References will provide the reader with further information concerning programs which have been mentioned. It seems necessary to reiterate that the focus on handicapped children at this point in history appears to be on the reintegration of the handicapped as members of the American educational system. The degree to which this can be accomplished is something which must be experienced in the future. The degree to which the handicapped child can find a place in American society and the degree to which our pluralistic society can realize the goal of accepting a disabled child into it remain something which the professionals in the field can hope for, and which seemingly only time can measure. (See CHAPTER 12: LEGISLATION AND CONSUMER RIGHTS; CHAPTER 14: RECREATION FOR THE DISABLED; CHAPTER 37: LEARNING DISABILITIES; PART 4, SECTION 8: SOURCES OF INFORMATION AND SUPPLY, Educational Materials.)

SELECTED REFERENCES

Barbe, Walter B., and Joseph Renzulli, eds., *Psychology and Education of the Gifted*, Halsted Press, New York, 1975.

Birch, Jack W., *Mainstreaming: Educable Mentally Retarded Children in Regular Classes*, Council for Exceptional Children, Reston, Virginia, 1974.

Cruickshank, William M., and G. O. Johnson, eds., *Education of Exceptional Children and Youth*, 3d ed., Prentice-Hall, Englewood Cliffs, New Jersey, 1975.

Dunn, Lloyd M., ed., *Exceptional Children in the Schools*, 2d ed., Holt, Rinehart & Winston, New York, 1973.

The Education of All Handicapped Children Act, Public Law 94-142.

Goodman, Leroy V., "A Bill of Rights for the Handicapped," *American Education*, June 1976.

Hammill, Donald D., and Nettie R. Bartel, *Teaching Children with Learning and Behavior Problems*, Allyn & Bacon, Boston, 1975.

Hewett, Frank, and Steven Forness, *Education of Exceptional Learners*, Allyn & Bacon, Boston, 1974.

Irwin, J., and M. Marge, *Principles of Childhood Language Disabilities*, Prentice-Hall, Englewood Cliffs, New Jersey, 1972.

Jones, Reginald L., *Problems and Issues in the Education of Exceptional Children*, Houghton Mifflin, Boston, 1974.

Lerner, Janet W., *Children with Learning Disabilities*, 2d ed., Houghton Mifflin, Boston, 1976.

McCarthy, James J., and Jean R. McCarthy, *Learning Disabilities*, Allyn & Bacon, Boston, 1973.

Reynolds, M. C., and M. D. Davis, *Exceptional Children in Regular Classrooms*, University of Minnesota Press, Minneapolis, 1971.

Robinson, Holbert, and Nancy Robinson, *The Mentally Retarded Child: A Psychological Approach*, McGraw-Hill, New York, 1965.

Smith, R. M. *An Introduction to Mental Retardation*, McGraw-Hill, New York, 1971.

The Unfinished Revolution: Education for the Handicapped, annual report of the National Advisory Committee on the Handicapped, Department of Health, Education and Welfare.

VanWitsen, Betty, *Perceptual Training Activities Handbook*, Teachers College Press, New York, 1967.

7

Vocational Rehabilitation; Employment; Self-employment: A. Vocational Rehabilitation Process

SEYMOUR MUND, M.A., Research Utilization Specialist, Division of Vocational Rehabilitation, State of Connecticut

In most cases rehabilitation is not considered complete until the individual is able to work and become self-sufficient. To assist in this goal a system of federal-state programs has been organized in all the fifty states and almost all United States territories to help develop and restore the working usefulness of physically and mentally handicapped individuals. Since 1920 this system of vocational rehabilitation has made it possible for many thousands of disabled people to enter or reenter the world of work. Any handicapped individual who can be reasonably expected to profit from rehabilitation services may apply. The following is a summary of the process a client would go through to attain independence.

Initial Referral

The first step for most people needing vocational rehabilitation is to be referred. This referral process may be as simple as a client walking into a Division of Vocational Rehabilitation (DVR) office and asking for service or as complex as passing through a maze of social agencies before someone calls the local DVR office on the individual's behalf. There are over seventy-five different potential referring sources listed on the Federal Statistical Reporting Form. Some of these are hospitals, doctors, welfare agencies, employment services, individuals, other health agencies, etc.

No matter how the referral is made to the DVR agency, the first and most important person the client comes into contact with is the rehabilitation counselor. The counselor is the key to the client's rehabilitation (see CHAPTER 57: REHABILITATION PROFESSIONS).

The initial contact with the counselor is usually a very important time for the client. At this point the counselor reassures the client and attempts to relieve any anxieties, clear up any misconceptions, and increase the individual's readiness for counseling. Through the counselor's friendly, unhurried, and pleasant manner, a good rapport and trust can be developed that will expedite the cooperation needed between client and counselor. Also at this time intake paper work is done and facts are collected to enable the counselor to begin to determine whether the individual can qualify as a client of the agency.

Qualification for Acceptance

Eligibility for acceptance as a client for vocational rehabilitation is based on the following criteria: (1) presence of a physical or mental disability which, for the individual, constitutes or results in a substantial handicap to employment; and (2) a reasonable expectation that vocational rehabilitation service may benefit the individual in terms of employability. The facts to document the decision for acceptability are collected from many sources, including hospitals where the client was treated, schools which the client attended, and places where the client worked.

Each individual being evaluated must have a general medical examination. This physical is arranged with the client's physician, if there is one, or with another doctor in the community. There is no cost to the individual for the evaluation. The individual may be sent for other tests, as needed, including psychological or psychiatric evaluation.

After the reports are in, in most cases a determination can be made in a very short time. However, for very severely disabled individuals a longer period of evaluation may be needed. This extended evaluation period may mean that the client will be given many services normally provided only to accepted clients, to see if the services are likely to enable a return to gainful employment. This extended evaluation period can last no longer than eighteen months, but most determinations of acceptance are made before then.

Vocational Rehabilitation Services

A person accepted as a client of the vocational rehabilitation agency is eligible for any or all of the following services needed for rehabilitation:

1. Counseling and guidance as an ongoing process during the whole rehabilitation program.

2. Physical and mental restoration services, purchased for the client as needed.

3. Vocational and other training services, including remedial education.

4. Maintenance and transportation when needed to help the client receive the benefits of other rehabilitation services.

5. Services to members of the client's family which are neces-

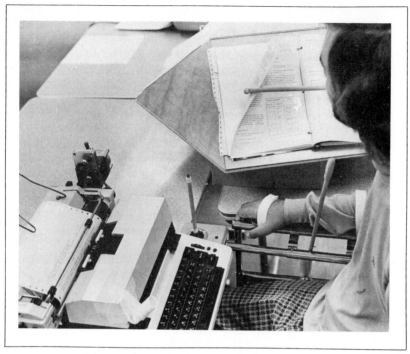

This patient with a spinal cord injury has acquired a work skill by learning to operate an electric typewriter with the aid of a mouth-held stick. (Woodrow Wilson Rehabilitaton Center, Fishersville, Virginia)

sary to the adjustment or rehabilitation of the handicapped individual.

6. Interpreter services for the deaf.

7. Reader services, rehabilitation teaching services, and orientation and mobility services for the blind, provided through special services for the blind in some states and directly through DVR in others.

8. Telecommunications and sensory and other technological aids and devices.

9. Placement in suitable employment after completion of rehabilitation.

10. Postemployment services when necessary to assist handicapped individuals maintain suitable employment.

11. Occupational licenses, tools, equipment, and initial stocks (including livestock) and supplies for a small business or job where warranted.

12. Other goods and services which can reasonably be expected to benefit a handicapped individual in terms of employability.

Starting the Process

An interview with the client is held at the time of acceptance. The vocational rehabilitation counselor and client (or, as appropriate, the parent, guardian, or other representative), working together, develop an individualized written rehabilitation program which will be initiated and continuously updated with the handicapped client. This plan or program emphasizes primarily the determination and achievement of a vocational goal. A copy of the written plan is given to the client.

The plan includes the specific vocational rehabilitation services to be provided in order to achieve established employment goals, and the terms and conditions for the provision of such services. Also included are tentative dates for completion of services and other important details needed in setting the course for the individual's rehabilitation.

Duration and Scope of Services

The length and kind of services a client will receive are, of course, dependent on individual needs and goals. For example, one client may need extensive medical restoration or even hospital or surgical care. Another may only need training, tutoring, or remedial education. Some may need four years of college to attain a vocational goal in line with their abilities and physical limitations, while others may only need counseling and guidance to return to gainful employment. For some, especially the severely retarded, a sheltered workshop type of employment may be the ultimate goal.

A unique facet of the Federal-State Program of Vocational Rehabilitation is that each client of an agency is considered to be an individual having very specific needs and wants. The individual is never put into a large group and made to fit. All the services a client may need are tailored to that person as an individual.

Job Placement and Follow-up

Each service and program has as its goal the placement of the individual into gainful work. As the relationship between client and counselor develops and each service is completed, both are taking steps leading to placement into employment. The counselor contacts employers, and the client registers with the employment service. Other community agencies are contacted; some of these may have worked with the client in other phases of the rehabilitation process. On-the-job training leading to employment in a local company may be tried. Work readiness activities may be needed at a rehabilitation center or sheltered workshop. Finally, the client is actually placed on a job which relates to training and utilizes individual skills and personality characteristics.

Even after the client has been working, the counselor follows up to see that all is going well and that the client has adjusted to the work situation. This follow-up may continue for an extended period of time, but by law cannot be less than sixty days.

Closure and Postemployment Services

When a client has been working successfully and both the counselor and the individual agree that all is going well, the case is closed. However, sometimes it may be indicated from the type of disability or work situation that future help will be needed to keep the person employed. If this is the case, arrangements can be made for postemployment services. These services are actually written into the individual's rehabilitation plan. But even if no problem is foreseen before closure, services can still be offered to some extent after the case is closed.

Conclusion

The Federal-State Program of Vocational Rehabilitation has proven that it is not the individual's disabilities but the abilities he or she possesses or can develop that are important. Evidence lies in the fact that in 1975 alone more than 392,000 individuals were rehabilitated and over 1,326,000 were serviced. Moreover, for every dollar the agency spends to rehabilitate a client, $5 is returned to society in the form of taxes alone when the individual goes back to work. (See PART 4, SECTION 1: STATISTICS. For a description of some personal cases, see CHAPTER 55: ILLUSTRA-TIVE CASES, J. Three Vocational Rehabilitation Cases. For a more detailed discussion of a comprehensive vocational rehabilitation center, see CHAPTER 56: REHABILITATION FACILITIES AND SERVICES.)

SELECTED REFERENCES

In House State Plan, Connecticut State Department of Education, Division of Vocational Rehabilitation, Hartford, September 30, 1977.

Soares, Louise M., et al., *The Rehabilitation Counselor*, Monograph no. 4, SRS Project Grant no. RD 1818G, U.S. Department of Health, Education and Welfare, Bridgeport, Connecticut, 1969.

Vocational Rehabilitation Programs: Implementation Provisions, U.S. Department of Health, Education and Welfare, November 25, 1975.

B. Employment and Job Placement

JOHN MOSHER, M.A., Blue Sky Consultants, Seattle

Reviewed by JOHN K. THOMPSON, Coordinator Region X Rehabilitation Education Program

Figures obtained from the United States 1970 Census indicate that 85 percent of the employable disabled are not working (Lawrence D. Haber, "Social Planning for Disability," *Journal of Human Resources*, vol. 7, supplement). Yet disabled workers are performing nearly every job imaginable. There are chemical engineers and diesel mechanics who are blind, counselors and welders who are deaf, clerk-typists who are retarded, and four recent United States presidents (Franklin Roosevelt, Dwight Eisenhower, John Kennedy, and Lyndon Johnson) who could have met the disability criteria for eligibility as clients of the federally funded Vocational Rehabilitation Programs. Clearly, a disabling condition is not totally incapacitating.

Since the federal government set up the first Vocational Rehabilitation Program in 1920, the rate of successful rehabilitations has remained approximately the same, regardless of the economy, hire-the-handicapped programs, and the steady growth of rehabilitation programs. Hiring the handicapped receives much lip service. However, the hope-crushing reality is different: a random sample of 120 employers in one state developed over 200 job openings in thirty-two firms; follow-up to all thirty-two resulted in only one actual job placement. What is the problem?

Discrimination

Efforts in the last ten years by minority groups and women to acquire the right to equal opportunity have uncovered widespread social stereotyping and personal prejudices. The disabled are similarly discriminated against, not only in employment but in every other area of social functioning — education, sexual expression, recreation, travel, and even in the physical space that nondisabled persons take for granted. Much of this discrimination is due to the lack of information or the preponderance of misinformation prevalent in the nondisabled population.

Attitudes

Research into attitudes of nondisabled persons toward the disabled reveals an uneasiness in the presence of a disabled person due to a lack of social contact. Many nondisabled persons reject close relationships with the disabled: "I wouldn't want my daughter to marry one." The disabled are thought to be better off with their own kind, perhaps even deserving of their affliction. Disabled persons are thought to be bad-tempered, self-conscious, hypersensitive (even if they seem outwardly adjusted), sexually disturbed, and manipulative, using their handicaps to get what they want.

Further research indicates that many nondisabled persons reject the disabled but feel guilty about it. There may be an identification with the disability and an anxiety about one's own vulnerability, leading to a compensatory overprotective attitude advocating tolerance and special treatment (rather than acceptance and an equal chance). There is often a mystification about the disability. The disabled person is seen as helpless mentally, physically, morally, yet also as possessing special supernormal gifts, such as extrasensory perception, extraordinary patience and humility, or a mystical closeness to the essentials of life.

Employer Prejudices

Employers can be expected to participate in these cultural stereotypes in their limited contact with disabled individuals. In addition, there are special employer prejudices. They may feel, for example, that the disabled employee will somehow cost them more money; that insurance rates for workmen's compensation will go up (generally false, especially in states where second-injury clauses are in effect); that productivity will go down (false); or that training costs will go up (which may not be the case, and for which on-the-job training funds are usually available through the state Vocational Rehabilitation Program). Records of companies employing disabled workers show, moreover, that disabled workers perform as well or better than nondisabled workers, with the most severely disabled often the top performers. Further, employers may feel that the disabled employee will not fit in socially, or may foresee special problems in firing, promoting, or transferring a disabled person. Again employment records show this to be untrue. And again, the disabled applicant remains just an applicant.

Self-fulfilling Prophecies

The potency of expectations has been proved. Self-fulfilling prophecies have been studied in schools, on the job, on the psychiatrist's couch, in vocational rehabilitation agencies, and in the home — with similar findings: those expected to succeed, do; those expected to fail, fail. For the few who shake loose from the seduction of a negative stereotype there is little reward or recognition. They are seen as maladjusted exceptions; their success is redefined as failure to fit expectations; and they are faced with hostility rather than praised for their achievements. In every community there are likely to be disabled persons who have transcended the stereotypes limiting their growth. Yet, for the most part, the disabled have remained invisible, the prejudices unexamined. Those who break the mold are seen as exceptions to the rule. The expectations of life-long dependency and helplessness, emotional instability, and social rejection set up self-fulfilling prophecies that are difficult to overcome. A disability is not a handicap. A disability is a loss of some physical, mental, or sensorial function; attitudes of the nondisabled toward a person with a disability are handicapping.

Vocational Choice and Expectations

When the genetic makeup of an individual is being established, thousands of vocational possibilities dim while other thousands brighten as the sex is determined, various aptitudes are inherited or, for a few, congenital disabilities are passed on. Vocational choice is a process, part accidental, part deliberate, which starts at the beginning of life and continues until the end.

Some vocational choices we are born to, some we seek out and work for, and some we have thrust upon us. The most difficult battle for a disabled person is in overcoming the erroneous belief that the disabled have few, if any, vocational choices. The disabled person first encounters and internalizes cultural expectations in the home. Eventually he or she can decide to fulfill, reject, or transcend them, and to a large extent this decision is influenced by the degree to which family members fall into the stereotypes.

Stereotyping in the Home

In addition to fitting our perceptions into our belief system, we also structure social, physical, and psychological environments to fit our expectations. Little Jimmy gets a tricycle for Christmas; Mary gets a luscious doll that dances and flirts; and blind Blake gets a talking book machine. As these children begin expanding their action territories, thus developing skills that will later affect vocational choices, each is encouraged (more or less subtly) in those areas which their parents and significant others approve. The parents of Blake may never know what he is capable of doing; at age ten he still cannot use a fork — mostly because his parents fear he may poke himself in the mouth. The point is that the unexamined expectation that the disabled are helpless leads parents to make the world "safe" for their disabled child by restricting the environment and thus affecting vocational choices.

Definition of Work and Skills

Any task, be it throwing a party, balancing a checkbook, scoring a touchdown, mowing a lawn, or preparing a meal, that involves a series of activities directed to a purposeful goal is work, even if we think of it as play or are not paid for it. The same criteria used to analyze the skills necessary for jobs in the employment marketplace can be used to analyze any task (see the *Dictionary of Occupational Titles*, 1965, or *A Handbook for Job Restructuring*, 1970, both from the U.S. Department of Labor). The more activities a disabled child engages in, the more skills he or she tests and develops. There are three types of skills: adaptive, functional, and work skills. Adaptive skills involve self-management, such as the ability to control impulses, to be patient, to stick to a task, to take directions or criticism, to ask for information, to relate to authority figures, to adjust to change, to conform, or to learn new things.

Functional skills develop out of aptitudes like artistic talent, problem solving, salesmanship, writing, musical talent, sociability, entertaining, using tools, and mechanical ability. Thus one's functional skills are likely to be particularly good in certain areas and less good in others. For the learning individual, the more tasks tried, the more functional skills tested.

Work skills are acquired through actual job experience and are job-specific. Thus a person might take functional mechanical ability and adapt it to mechanical engineering or repairing domestic automobiles. Later the adaptive skills of learning new things and adjusting to change may be needed to switch to foreign car repair. Except for the most profoundly disabled, every child has more functional skills than he or she will ever be consciously aware of, can learn adaptive skills, and can choose a career or life-style that will put to use the skills that are most valued.

Suggestions to Parents

Here are five important steps that parents of disabled children can take.

1. *Examine for prejudices.* Parents can carefully examine any "limiting factor" in their child to see if it is merely a prejudice. Doctors and counselors can be as subject to prejudice as nonprofessionals, so trial and error should be applied to advice from any source. The object is to leave all doors open; parents cannot know in advance what their disabled child can do. As for what the disability prevents the child from doing, no one can predict the aids that medicine or technology will develop. So, never say never.

2. *Permit mistakes.* Parents can allow their disabled child to make mistakes, including the right to get hurt. This is, in effect, a permission to learn through the experience of success and failure. Parents can reinforce experimentation and exploration by resisting the impulse to red-pencil their child's efforts and by making more of successes than failures. (In truth, this is a permission they could well extend to themselves and all the family.) There are books on what disabled children cannot do; what they can do, however, is uncharted territory. Fear of making a mistake can paralyze parents as well as their disabled children.

3. *Enrich the environment.* Parents can offer more choices to their child by enriching the environment rather than restricting it. The more tasks attempted, the more skills discovered.

4. *Identify skills.* Parents can help their child with skills identification. Very simply, this means telling the child what skills are being used for different tasks. Robert, a cerebral palsied child, has put a 300-piece puzzle together by himself. Mom or Dad could say:

> "You really showed a lot of determination in finishing that puzzle." (adaptive skill)

> "You were really patient." (adaptive skill)

> "You showed a lot of independence doing that by yourself." (adaptive skill)

> "You really have a knack for recognizing abstract shapes." (functional skill)

> "You used a lot of finger dexterity." (functional skill)

> "I was proud of the way you arranged your pieces ahead of time. You really got organized and planned well." (functional skill)

> "Putting all the pieces shiny side up and finding all the edge pieces first so you could set up your boundaries was terrific problem solving." (functional skill)

> "Tomorrow I'll get you one of those round puzzles to try." (reinforcement)

If the parent just said, "Gee! That's really great!" the comments focus on the process and the skills required to perform it, and are thus open-ended.

If Robert were to do something away from home, his parents could explore with him what he did, how he did it, and his feelings about it, noting the skills used and naming and describing them. There is a kind of "name magic" to skills, and knowing what to call what he has done goes a long way toward helping him internalize and own the skills. The exercise has the added advantage of helping Robert develop the adaptive skill of using his memory and the functional skill of verbal communication, among others.

Most important in the skill process is allowing the child to self-evaluate skills. Experiences of success and failure can do the job as well or better than criticism from parents, and the side effects of the latter can be quite handicapping.

5. *Provide contact with work.* The world of work in the last hundred years has increasingly become a separate area of social functioning which requires special skills to enter, and to perform, stay and advance in. Special behaviors and ways of relating are defined. Taboos (not coming in late or leaving early) and rituals (punching a time clock) are imposed. Work occurs at special times and in special places. Any child whose knowledge of the world of work is limited to seeing a parent leave home dressed for the job and return home later all tired out, or to watching television or movies is not equipped to make vocational choices. The disabled child needs access to the world of work through whatever means available: books, field trips, educational films, responsibility for chores at home, paper routes, summer jobs. The more contact, the better.

In one community, parents of disabled children banded together to make sure that their children received the best services available. Twenty years later they were dismayed to find their college-educated children moping around at home unemployed. Not one of them, parent or child, had the slightest idea of where to apply all those refined adaptive and functional skills. Yet the collective job opportunities represented by the parents (two owned companies hiring over fifty employees) were a rich and unthought-of resource. As the children were growing up, their parents had a combined access to hundreds of real jobs and a wide variety of vocational experiences. In a meeting called to discuss this unemployment problem, the parents reacted to the suggestion of hiring their own college-educated children with astonishment, rejected it, and then became aware of their own underlying and unexamined prejudices — that is, hiring the handicapped is good for somebody else's business.

Assisting the Newly Disabled

The newly disabled child or adult can also be assisted through the above five steps, with appropriate modifications. Of special importance for the newly disabled adult is the skills identification process. The so-called spread effect, the extrapolation of the loss of some skills to the loss of all skills, can affect disabled adults as much as those around them. A bank executive suffered a stroke from which she recovered with her speech and gait permanently impaired.

When she attempted to resign, her superiors refused, giving her a vacation instead. She later returned to resume her former duties. The bank was able to recognize what she could not: that her years of experience and special skills had not been affected by her stroke.

The experiences of the newly disabled are not always so favorable. An insurance executive who lost his eyesight agreed with his company's opinion that he should resign. He was relatively happy with that decision until he entered a vocational exploration group. There he identified hundreds of skills used before his blindness through skills identification processes. To his growing disbelief, one by one the skills were fully examined to see if he, indeed, could no longer perform them. Of the 247 skills identified, only 6 were eliminated by his blindness. About 40 were impaired, but procedures and aids were available that he could learn to use. Unfortunately, when he tried to get his old job back, he found his ex-employer to be as disbelieving as he himself had once been.

Vocational Training

The vocational terrain is changing in the United States, and these changes are being reflected in the schools. In the past, vocational training, beginning in elementary school and finishing in technical school or college education, was designed to fit an industrial model. Future workers were conditioned to be perfect (for quality control), to follow orders (for efficiency), and to respect authority (for effectiveness). Those who failed to conform were weeded out of the system. Toward the end of the educational process, greater emphasis was placed on learning work skills, for the benefit of employers, and on fitting students into predesigned slots on the industrial assembly line.

The greatest changes in education are occurring on the preschool and elementary school levels. These changes are largely due to the impact of civil rights legislation as it relates to discrimination against disabled students, and to the development of new teaching techniques based on discoveries about brain functioning and the learning process. Open classrooms allowing for individualized teaching, programmed instruction to meet individual needs, enriched classroom environments, and behavioral modification programs are the chief areas of development.

The civil rights legislation, both on the federal level and in some states, requires school districts to provide equal opportunity to disabled students in neighborhood schools. Thus some disabled students are leaving special schools and entering neighborhood schools. Since young children seem to be the most rejecting of their disabled peers, this development is likely to be a mixed blessing. To alleviate this problem, parents can advocate programs designed to open communications between disabled and nondisabled children.

The new teaching techniques provide a foundation for discovering and developing the adaptive and functional skills so important to the vocational choice process. In California, for example, students thought to be incorrigibly behaviorally disordered were taught the principles of behavioral modification. They were also taught specific social skills such as smiling, making "I" statements about feelings or wants, giving compliments, and offering behavioral descriptions of the offensive actions taken against them by peers or teachers. These skills were to be used as reinforcements in a behavior modification program of their choice, a program to modify their teachers' behaviors. The results were in some cases astonishing (Farnum Gray, Paul S. Graubard, and Harry Rosenberg, "Little Brother Is Changing You," *Psychology Today*, March 1974).

Other areas where specific training techniques are available for adaptation in those schools attempting to integrate disabled students are value clarification processes, assertiveness training, and creative aggression training. The latter two are especially threatening but are particularly important. Many disabled persons develop highly passive behaviors in response to the stereotyping they encounter. Resentments build with few outlets. Normal anger and frustration are internalized because there is guilt associated with expressing them toward "helpful" people. Creative aggression can teach students how to express these feelings constructively. Assertiveness training can show students how to ask for what they want, and eventually can be applied to performing the hardest "job" of all, finding a job.

Training for the older student is still traditional for the most part. Because of the limiting stereotypes, many disabled students are expected to enter skilled, semiskilled, or unskilled vocational areas, which are the easiest to train for. Job descriptions are identified and students are trained to perform the tasks, or work skills, necessary to do the job. There are various vocational training programs for the disabled, but many who graduate from them fail to find work because their functional and adaptive skills have been neglected. More people are rejected for job openings or terminated from employment for lacking adequate adaptive skills than for lacking work skills. An ace mechanic who is hostile to the supervisor will not last long. However, most of the disabled become more competitive as they move up the skills levels to positions which depend on their functional and adaptive skills, providing they have developed self-confidence. The work techniques of skilled, semiskilled, and unskilled jobs rely to a much greater degree on physical and sensorial capabilities. Also, these jobs are much more likely to be replaced by machines or technology.

The individual whose only work skills have been taken over by a machine has an uphill battle against a tremendous blow to self-esteem. Pigeon-holing, the process of slotting workers into predesigned jobs, is damaging for disabled and nondisabled alike. Some studies suggest that up to 80 percent of the work force feel unchallenged and unmotivated by their work. Pigeon-holing is also a very uncreative use of personnel, and is unresponsive to reality if no two clerk-typists (or what have you) perform exactly the same job. It is doubly damaging for the disabled person, who may not be able to perform every one of the work skills in a rigid job description, thus being less competitive with nondisabled workers even though skilled in many required areas. Another reality is that the occupational emphasis is shifting from industrial areas to service and technological areas where work skills may be highly specialized and subject to rapid change, thus requiring high adaptive and functional skills. In short, the emphasis on work skills should be carefully examined and demands for the development of adaptive and functional skills should be made by parents and students.

Job-Seeking Skills

Finding a job is a task that itself involves adaptive skills such as the ability to persist and follow through in the face of failures, the ability to maintain interest over a long period of time, and the ability to adjust to change. It also involves functional skills such as planning, organizing, coordinating, persuading, following directions and, for the job-seeking disabled person, educating the employer. In addition, job seeking involves work skills such as filling out an application, preparing a résumé, doing research (using resources such as the employment office, a vocational counselor, newspapers, the library), and using tools, especially a filing system, the telephone, and a pen or typewriter.

Many people are dreadful job seekers. We approach the process with few job-seeking skills, lowered self-esteem, and many destructive myths about how to find work. As a result, we are likely to suffer weeks of needless rejection shock and accept underemployment out of desperation. This does not take into account the influence of discrimination upon job seekers who are not white, male, middle-class, experienced, over twenty-one and under forty years old, and able-bodied.

The Old Model. The common notion of job seeking is that employers discover a need for a new employee, make the opening public, accept applications or résumés, and then select the most qualified job seeker. Thus, job seekers play a numbers game, and the odds are with the house. They check want ads and job listings, apply or send a résumé, and accept the implication of their deficiencies if they are, most probably, rejected. Only one person is selected for the job; all the others are rejected. The applicant may drop in on employers or send unsolicited résumés; however, the result will probably be the same. Experts estimate, for example, that one can expect five answers and maybe three interviews in response to a hundred résumés.

The New Model. The reality is quite different. Employers do not always know of job openings. A well-informed, assertive job seeker can often persuade an employer that hiring him or her will help the business. Only a small minority of job openings are actually publicized—at most 15 percent. With most inexperienced job seekers going to the same small source of jobs, the competition is merciless, especially for disabled applicants. The idea that the application form contributes to the selection process is also faulty; applications and résumés, especially historical, work-experience résumés, often screen seekers out rather than letting them in.

The most qualified job seekers do not always get the job. Sometimes it goes to the prettiest, the best talker, or to a friend of a friend. A survey of employers conducted by the Minneapolis Rehabilitation Center shows that work skills (that is, experience) are not even the prime focus of the selection process. According to the survey, employers are looking for self-confidence in the seeker's ability to do the job; ability to get along with fellow employees; knowledge of the job and company; dependability; ability to fit the company image on and off the job; and few personal or environmental problems. As this survey shows, the hiring process is dominated by adaptive skills.

Using the New Model. Work is a social environment and jobs are rewards given or withheld for social purposes. A job is a social reinforcement, and may be as close as next door. Job seekers must learn to tap the social network of the people who know them, picking up leads and information leading to the job market, including specific employers who need their skills. They need to know who to talk to, what jobs are available or what need they can fill in proposing their own job, and how hiring them will benefit the employer. All of this information is available through personal contacts, city directories, the chamber of commerce, trade journals, interviews with company employees, federal agencies, and the employment office. Job seekers also need to know how to get and engage in an interview.

During the interview they must know what their skills are and how to explain them in terms of what they can do, how they do it, where they have done it before, and why it is important to the employer. They must anticipate problem questions and objections and answer them on their own. Thus, if their disability requires a special way of performing a task, they are responsible for letting the employer know how they have resolved that problem. They must anticipate the stereotypes and voluntarily counter them at appropriate opportunities. Some employers in interviewing disabled applicants do not want to hurt their feelings, so they silently object—and reject. Job seekers must be appropriately prepared for the interview, and conduct themselves in a confident, assertive manner, showing interest and enthusiasm for the company and the job. As author Richard K. Irish has put it, you have to *Go Hire Yourself an Employer* (Doubleday, New York, 1973). Other books highly recommended are Richard Bolles's *What Color Is Your Parachute?* (Ten Speed Press, Berkeley, California, 1976) and Bolles and John Crystal's *Where Do I Go from Here with My Life?* (Seabury Press, New York, 1974)

Assertive Job Seeking. Here are three examples of what we have been talking about:

J., a young man with a congenitally deformed arm, was a teacher in a street school set up for high school drop-outs. Among his duties were setting up a curriculum, finding part-time work for the students, and generally running the school. When funding ran out, J.

was out of a job in the rural town he wanted to stay in. He looked for work in the usual way with no luck. Months passed until one afternoon he met B., a mildly retarded man living in a nearby group home. What started out to be another commiseration conversation suddenly turned into a brainstorming session in which the two planners hatched an idea for a business that would change both their lives. The result was a new company consisting of members of the group home who pooled their meager resources and hired J. to find them jobs, using his old contacts. Soon offers were spilling in — to mend fences, paint barns, butcher beef, clear fields, plant forests. All the home residents took responsibilities in the business. J. got a volunteer from the Small Business Administration's SCORE program to help set up the paperwork. J., his copartners, and the Group Home Company are still flourishing after three years of operation.

After her release from the state mental hospital, M. was directed to the Department of Vocational Rehabilitation, where she was referred to secretarial school despite the fact that she was afraid of being around a lot of people. M., instead, proposed janitorial work, which was considered inappropriate by her counselor. M. finally refused the Department's services, enrolled herself in a janitorial training program which she paid for out of her Social Security income, graduated, and found her own job. "You know," she later said, "it was really funny. My counselor kept telling me I had to become independent. But he wouldn't give me any help unless I did what he said. It makes me wonder who is crazy."

D. is a visually impaired, mildly retarded, club-footed dwarf. He peers proudly through his thick glasses at the goings and comings in the hotel where he works as a bell captain. Three years ago he wanted to be a television sportscaster, and he blew every interview for lesser jobs set up for him. His desire for work kept him coming in for counseling, and after lengthy sessions D. was asked where *he* thought his desire to be in the limelight and to be of service to people could be fulfilled. "How about being a bell hop?" was his suggestion. D. went back to the downtown hotel he lived in, asked to see the manager, and arranged for a two-week tryout for room and board. The arrangement led, ultimately, to his present position.

Professional Placement

There is a vocational place (not necessarily a job) for everyone who asks for it — providing that he knows: who he is and likes himself, what he can do and is proud of it, where he wants to do it and for whom, and how to get there and stay there. Those who cannot ask for their place in the scheme of things will have to be satisfied with where others place them.

The best placement is self-placement. Barring that, the next best is professional placement, and for the disabled this is hard to come by, although efforts are now being made to provide better placement services. The placement counselor is, quite simply, a job seeker on behalf of someone else. Thus counselors have a dual responsibility — to the client and to the employer. If they work for an agency, they must represent its interests as well. The typical placement person will be 50 percent salesman, 30 percent counselor, and 20 percent bureaucrat. What the best placement counselors will have to offer is a network of contacts among employers — people whom they can contact to discover those unpublished job openings and to whom they can personally recommend, in return, qualified job applicants.

Approaches to Employers. Placement counselors can choose from three common approaches to employers. The first is the "tin-cup" approach. Here the job developers go to an employer they know little about and beg him to "hire the handicapped." Such job developers have little faith in the disabled person they are trying to place and believe employers feel the same way. They are subject to current placement fads (darkroom work for the blind, key-punching for the deaf), since they do not consider the disabled to be capable individuals.

The second is the "missionary" approach. The job developers contact employers known to be "soft" on the handicapped. A few standard pats on the back are exchanged and another routine job is filled by the placement persons, who are likely to view their function with cynicism and the employer as a do-gooder, an exploiter of cheap labor, or a recipient of government welfare in the form of on-the-job training funds.

The third is the "professional" approach. Here job developers do their homework. They know the employer and his needs and the client and his skills, they educate the employer on the benefits of hiring the clients they refer, and follow up on placements on behalf of the client and the employer.

Placement and the Rehabilitation Process. Professional placement persons are on hand at the very start of the rehabilitation process. Their focus is always on placement: "What does this client need in order to be placeable among employers I know?" They keep a watchful eye on indicators of the client's self-esteem, the way he handles his problems, the degree of family support and stability, the kinds of skills he possesses, and his awareness of the work world and job-seeking skills. They are wary of standardized tests as the only source of information on clients' interests and aptitudes. They know that when the client is ignorant of work the validity of the tests suffers. They will be especially interested in the degree of participation offered by the client in drawing up his rehabilitation plan, knowing that the more the client is involved in the process the better the placement prospects. They will make sure they can believe in the client.

Vocational Exploration Groups. They will offer to the most inexperienced or fearful clients a vocational exploration group for training in job-seeking skills and for work on those factors limiting placeability. This small-group process will provide information, experiences, straight feedback from peers, and professional and job-seeking skills. The placement counselor recognizes that job seeking is not a step-by-step procedure but, like the rehabilitation that supports it, a complex process, with many interrelated skills on demand at the same time. The best way to learn a process is to experience it; this is the role of the vocational exploration group.

Serving Business Contacts. In the meantime, professional placement persons are out in the field maintaining contacts among employers. Effective job developers can always generate more jobs than the number of clients ready for work; to keep their contacts rewarded for job openings, they share leads with other counselors. They realize that for every employer who says yes there have been three to say no. Experience tells them that they have to contact interested employers four or five times before employers finally agree. In contacts with employers they have answers to objections and they directly address the employers' fears. They assist employers in any way they can, by providing information, referring employers to other professionals, or developing on-the-job training funds. They respect the social nature of their network of contacts as well as the professional demands of the job.

They know how to develop new contacts out of this ongoing network as well as general market-survey techniques. Before approaching a new contact, professional placement persons know what resources to look at for information about employers. They probably have a contact among the industrial relations representatives of the local employment office. They know from published lists who the federal contractors with contracts of over $2,500 are. (The 1973 Rehabilitation Act requires employers with federal contracts to develop a plan to hire disabled persons.) They also find out if the company they are researching has any affirmative action complaints filed against it, as they can offer such a company a very important service. Before ever talking to an employer they also find out what services or products are offered, number of employees, and types of jobs. They know the safety record of the company and the turnover rates for each job category. When placement professionals make contact with an employer, they come across as professionals from the start.

Follow-up. To protect their contacts, professionals see that only qualified applicants are referred to job openings. Satisfied employers therefore want to keep in touch. When a placement is made, placement counselors remember that the hiring employer is part of their job-market network. They follow up on both the client and the employer to see what is happening, and maintain contact with the employer even after the client's case is closed and recorded as rehabilitated. They are prepared to help the employer resolve supervisory problems that may arise, although they probably have talked with the client's supervisor beforehand. They also follow up on failures to determine what went awry and what can be done in the future to ensure success.

The Fight against Discrimination

The efforts of the placement professional and the independently job-seeking disabled have been enhanced by federal and state legislation developed to ensure the rights of the disabled. There is no national law protecting the civil rights of the disabled except Section 503 of the Vocational Rehabilitation Act of 1973 which, as stated above, requires all federal contractors with contracts of over $2,500 to take affirmative action in employing and advancing qualified disabled individuals. Employers must submit affirmative action plans for review to the contracting agency. This act covers about one-third of the United States employers.

According to the act, employers are responsible for removing architectural barriers and revising non-job-related demands that would interfere with hiring a disabled person. Any generalized statement of policy such as "All jobs in the company requiring eyesight" would be evidence of discrimination. Concerning the realism of such demands, the burden of proof is on the employer.

Enforcement. The Employment Standards Administration of the Department of Labor is enforcing the law. Penalties for noncompliance include court action by the government for breach of contract, withholding of payments due under the contract, cancellation of the contract, and disbarment of the contractor from future government contracts.

To file a discrimination complaint, the disabled person must be "certified" as disabled on a special form by the Department of Vocational Rehabilitation. Complaints are filed with the Employment Standards Administration.

State Efforts. In addition to the Vocational Rehabilitation Act of 1973, a few states have passed laws providing some (usually not much) protection from discrimination to disabled persons. These states include Alaska, California, Connecticut, Illinois, Iowa, Kansas, Maine, Massachusetts, Minnesota, Montana, Nebraska, Nevada, New Jersey, New Mexico, North Carolina, Oregon, Rhode Island, and Washington. Some cities have passed ordinances protecting the rights of the disabled.

Conclusion

It has been only in the last few years that attitudes toward the capacities of the disabled have progressed, and this change is especially reflected in the trend toward viewing the disabled as a minority group to be protected by law. No minority group experiences greater discrimination in employment than the severely disabled. In 1970 the nationwide unemployment rate among severely disabled noninstitutionalized men was 75 percent; for women, it was virtually 100 percent. Most of those who were working did so on a part-time basis only. And the unfortunate reality is that to obtain an income providing even a modest standard of living there are few realistic alternatives to paid employment. These alternatives need to be explored. We do not have a full employment economy and are not likely to in the foreseeable future. With this in mind, how can the right of everyone to actualize his or her full potential be ensured? (See CHAPTER 55: ILLUSTRATIVE CASES, F. Employing the Handicapped.)

SELECTED REFERENCES

Bolles, Richard N., *What Color Is Your Parachute?: A Practical Manual for Job-Hunters & Career-Changers*, Ten Speed Press, Box 4310, Berkely, CA 94704, 1972.

Dictionary of Occupational Titles, vols. 1, 2, and supplement, 3d ed., U.S. Department of Labor, Employment Service, 1965.

Haber, Lawrence D., *The Physically Disabled Worker: Myth and Reality*, U.S. Department of Health, Education and Welfare, Division of Survey Operations, National Center for Educational Statistics.

Irish, Richard K., *Go Hire Yourself an Employer*, Doubleday/Anchor, Garden City, New York, 1973.

Occupational Outlook Handbook, U.S. Department of Labor, Employment Service, 1974–1975.

Sears, James H., "The Able Disabled," *Journal of Rehabilitation*, pp. 19–22, 1975.

C. Self-employment by the Disabled

ROBERT M. GOLDENSON, Ph.D

A wide variety of successful enterprises have been undertaken by individuals confined to their homes by physical or psychiatric disabilities. Self-employment may also be the only recourse for partially disabled individuals who have the skill, competence, and even stamina for outside jobs but who are excluded from the labor market by reason of prejudicial attitudes, transportation problems, or preference for the able-bodied when work is scarce.

A home business offers many benefits. It can provide extra income, a feeling of usefulness, an antidote to boredom, and it may also help to satisfy the homebound individual's need to maintain contact with the world. Moreover, these goals can be achieved through either part- or full-time work, without the expense and effort of travel. It is also important to recognize that home businesses offer special benefits to the community as well; since the overhead is likely to be low, products and services can often be offered at a savings. Moreover, the homebound can offer services, such as telephone answering or teaching, after the usual business hours, and can provide services such as clerical work to businesses that are temporarily overloaded or shorthanded. The fact that they are meeting genuine needs should be borne in mind by disabled individuals whose self-image may have been damaged, and who may be tempted to offer their services in an apologetic manner.

The problem of finding suitable home employment is not easy to solve. It requires imagination, determination, a candid look at both abilities and disabilities, and the capacity to learn from failure instead of being defeated by setbacks. In addition, it is important for the budding entrepreneur to find and accept guidance and assistance from others. The ideal of the totally "self-made" person is as unrealistic within the home as it is outside. The following guidelines to self-employment have been gathered from a variety of sources.

1. *Making a choice.* Before deciding on a business, homebound individuals should talk with a vocational or government rehabilitation counselor and take any available aptitude tests in order to objectively evaluate abilities.

2. *Advice.* They should discuss possible businesses with experienced advisers such as friends familiar with the community's needs, retired business persons, a Small Business Administration (SBA) representative, and well-trained individuals in the field.

3. *Finances.* If funds are needed to start the enterprise, as is usually the case, a loan might be arranged at a bank or through the SBA, especially if it is backed by a friend or family member. The regional or local Office of Vocational Rehabilitation may also supply information on financial aid. It is important to recognize that most businesses are started on borrowed capital.

4. *Getting started.* A home business, like any other enterprise, must be organized in a businesslike manner. If it is a store, sales slips should be used, the books should be kept properly, and every available source for salable merchandise should be explored. If it is a service, such as bookkeeping or telephone answering, the necessary equipment must be purchased. If it is a repair shop, a workbench and a full set of tools and supplies will be needed. If the home business person is physically disabled, special assistive devices such as a lapboard, bed table, or telephone aids may be required. A business card and a descriptive leaflet should be printed.

5. *Publicity.* All possible means of reaching potential clients and customers should be explored: posting notices on bulletin boards in schools, colleges, plants, and offices; asking friends to distribute leaflets and business cards at religious gatherings, lodges, community centers, etc.; placing paid or unpaid announcements in newspapers; and making direct telephone calls—for example, calling schools to obtain pupils for tutoring or calling hardware stores for appliances in need of repair.

6. *Learning the ropes.* Most homebound workers need to brush up on old skills or learn new ones before starting their enterprise. A correspondence course may be taken, or a tutor may be engaged to provide the necessary training in typing or other clerical skills. Here again it would be advisable to obtain guidance from an Office of Vocational Rehabilitation counselor or from a school vocational counselor.

7. *Making contacts.* If the business is to be maintained and expanded, new contacts will have to be made. Three useful techniques are: enlisting the aid of a local club or lodge; purchasing mail-order lists; and obtaining specialized directories (such as doctors) from the local library.

The following is a representative list of actual businesses successfully run from the home:

Office services: Mailings, bookkeeping, accounting, typing, telephone answering service, mimeographing, extra secretarial help for small businesses or professionals.

Selling: Magazine subscriptions, insurance, ads for newspapers or radio stations, cosmetics, gift items, hobby materials, jewelry, souvenirs, mail-order items.

Contract work: Nearby manufacturing concerns can be contacted for piecework performed under contract, such as light assembly or packaging small articles such as pens, tools, and cosmetics. If the company will not deliver or pick up the items, family members or friends may help out.

Writing and writing services: Magazine articles, book reviews, short stories, poetry, proofreading, translating, research service for authors or editors, condensing books, clipping service.

Teaching: Tutoring children in school subjects; teaching arts and crafts or music to children or adults; teaching the retarded or physically disabled.

Arts and crafts products: Leatherwork, candlemaking, paper folding, clay modeling, découpage, artificial flowers, wood carving, photography, driftwood arrangements, bottle cutting, placemats, greeting cards, shell collages.

Pets: Boarding dogs or cats; raising canaries or parakeets, rabbits, hamsters, or tropical fish; grooming and clipping dogs.

Plants: Raising indoor plants for sale; greenhouse gardening; specialties such as African violets, cacti, or terrariums.

Repair work: Small appliances, cameras, guns, fishing tackle, clocks, collector's items, knife and scissors sharpening, musical instruments, small electrical items (lamps, radios, recorders), typewriters and other business machines.

Service work: Providing after-school supervision for children of working mothers; companion for the elderly; baby-sitting; providing room and board for college students or other guests.

Needlework: Alterations, mending, slipcovers, knitting, needlepoint, quilts, embroidery, doll clothes, fancy pillows, stuffed toy animals, rya rugs, rag rugs, crocheting, weaving.

Cooking: Cakes and cake decoration, jellies and jams, bread, pies, candies.

Other home services: Telephone surveys for various businesses, collections for doctors or others, political campaign calls, conducting an office skills employment service.

SELECTED REFERENCES

The Blind Person Can Do the Job (pamphlet), New York State Federation of Workers for the Blind, September 1972.

Cull, John G., and Richard E. Hardy, *Vocational Rehabilitation: Profession and Process,* Charles C. Thomas, Springfield, Illinois, 1972.

Gerald, Poldi, "Career Development for the Severely Disabled," *American Rehabilitation,* September–October 1975.

President's Committee on Employment of the Handicapped, Washington, DC 20210: *Affirmative Action to Employ Handicapped People* (Rehabilitation Act, 1973); *Careers for the Homebound: Home Study Opportunities; Guidelines for Hiring Handicapped Workers; Myths about Hiring the Handicapped.*

8

The Sheltered Workshop

ROBERT M. GOLDENSON, Ph.D.

Reviewed by PATRICIA RUEGG, Director of Rehabilitation Workshop
Administration, Seattle University

T he sheltered workshop is a strong and unique link in the chain of rehabilitation services available to the severely handicapped. Its uniqueness lies in its ability to provide them with an opportunity to make a useful contribution to society and to their own well-being through productive work. Its strength lies in its adaptability to practically every type of chronically disabled individual: the orthopedically handicapped, the visually impaired, the mentally retarded, the emotionally ill, and the chronically diseased.

Definition

The sheltered workshop has been defined by the key organization in the field, the Association of Rehabilitation Facilities, as "a work-oriented rehabilitation facility with a controlled working environment and individual vocational goals, which utilizes work experience and related services for assisting the handicapped person to progress toward normal living and a productive vocational status." As this definition indicates, the workshop experience constitutes, for many individuals, the vocational phase of the rehabilitation process. The term "controlled working environment" refers to the fact that the work is done under the supervision of a trained staff, and that the setting is adapted to the special needs and limitations of the workers. The "related services" are directed toward the goal of total rehabilitation, and include medical, psychological, and social services designed to protect the client and to assist with personal problems.

Objectives

The character of the sheltered workshop has undergone considerable change in the past few years. The first facilities, established during the 1920s and 1930s, were conceived on a custodial care model, and were aimed primarily at keeping the chronically disabled occupied in a more or less constructive manner. There was little or no conception that they might advance to a point where they could develop marketable skills and take their place in competitive industry. In contrast, the objective today is to help the vocationally handicapped achieve the highest level of functioning of which they are capable. The emphasis is upon development and progress toward the goals of economic self-sufficiency and a job in the outside world. At the same time, it is recognized that many trainees will not be able to attain these goals. For this reason most workshops are designed to serve two types of clients: (1) the severely disabled person who can profit from intensive training, adjust to the work situation, and develop a high enough level of skill and productivity to enter the labor market; and (2) the severely disabled person who accepts the work situation and develops some skill and productivity, but is unable to meet the requirements of the open labor market.

The term "transitional employment workshop" is applied to a workshop that is geared to moving the client to the open labor market, extended employment in the sheltered situation, additional education, or further supportive services. The terms "extended employment" or "long-term workshop" are applied to settings that offer continuing, remunerative employment to clients who have adjusted to the transitional work experience but cannot sustain competitive employment. The two services are usually offered by the same workshop. Efforts should be made to keep clients from feeling that a change from transitional to extended status is a sign of failure. They should also be evaluated periodically, since some may eventually be capable of outside employment.

Growth of Workshops

During the past two decades the concept of rehabilitation has expanded to include vocational development, and according to a study conducted for the Rehabilitation Services Administration the number of certified workshops in the United States increased from 855 at the end of 1966 to 2,766 in 1975. The number of handicapped workers participating in these workshops is now over 410,000, with an estimated 180,000 completing the programs annually.

Advantages

The benefits offered by the sheltered workshop are many and varied. The experience increases the disabled person's self-respect and self-esteem by offering an opportunity to make a useful social contribution. It provides the personal satisfaction of restoring old skills or developing new ones that help to compensate for an impairment. It encourages the disabled person to keep active and alert instead of lapsing into a state of inertia and despair. It provides a work setting that is especially adapted to individual needs and limitations, under the watchful eye of specialists not only in vocational training but in total rehabilitation. It gives an opportunity to work with others facing similar problems, and to communicate and build social relationships instead of living an isolated life. It exposes the disabled to many of the demands and disciplines found in a real work situation, and gives an opportunity to test personal ability and adaptability in a benign atmosphere before venturing into competitive employment. And finally, the individual not only works under the supervision of vocational experts, but has the added benefit of receiving care from physicians, social workers, psychologists, and other professionals.

Planning a Workshop

The impetus for establishing a workshop may come from a variety of sources: a professional person interested in rehabilitation, a hospital or clinic, a single social agency, the local Council of Social Agencies, a handicapped individual, or families of the disabled. In any case, the first concrete steps must be undertaken by a planning committee which conducts a fact-finding survey and, on the basis of its findings, formulates definite plans and recommendations.

The planning committee should be headed by an outstanding community leader and should represent organizations that will take responsibility for different phases of the operation, as well as groups and individuals who will provide moral and financial support. It should include representatives of medical and health agencies (medical society, hospital, public health department, mental health clinic, and chapters of national health organizations); educational agencies (Department of Education, State Vocational Education Division, and educational facilities for the handicapped); vocational rehabilitation agencies (state, Veterans Administration, private employment and vocational services); social agencies (public assistance department, Community Chest, Council of Social Agencies, and family casework agency); churches, civic clubs, and service organizations; business, trade, and labor organizations; government officials (mayor, county, court, and police officials); influential and philanthropic individuals; and representatives of the press, radio, and television. The committee should be familiarized with the objectives of sheltered workshops, their place in the rehabilitation picture, and the distinction between transitional and extended employment facilities.

Community Survey. The first major function of the planning committee is to initiate a community-wide survey to be carried out by a social agency or qualified professional on a fee basis. Its object is to collect data on: (1) the severely disabled in the community (number of each type, number of vocationally handicapped, number who might be interested in a workshop, and such characteristics as age, sex, and rehabilitative needs); (2) other workshops in the community; and (3) a number of specifics, such as availability of professional and technical staff, resources for technical advice on management and marketing, possible plant facilities, availability of suitable work to be performed for business or industry, possible employment opportunities for graduates, and evidence for sustained community support.

Type of Work. The committee's second function is to make a number of basic decisions and recommendations on the type of work to be performed, type of work training, supportive services, financing, and housing for the facility. The type of work must be based on the capacities of the disabled personnel, the availability of plant and equipment, the markets for manufactured products, and the labor market available to graduates.

Four workshop patterns have been developed: (1) *Industrial subcontract work* has the advantages of training to industrial standards, a variety of materials supplied by customers, and an objective basis for evaluating cost; however, the work may be seasonal or sporadic, and production pressures may conflict with training needs. (2) *Service contracts,* a newer approach which is becoming more popular, permits contracting for janitorial service, gardening, motel maid service, food services, etc. (3) *Renovating and process-*

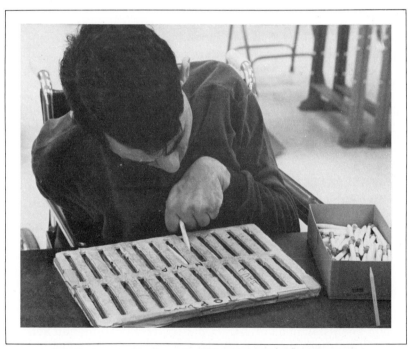

In a sheltered workshop a cerebral palsied worker packs ball-point pens by using a jig. (Photograph by Elinor Stecker; United Cerebral Palsy Association of Westchester County, New York State)

ing of used materials enlists broad community support, provides a relatively high cash return, and permits a continuous work load and flexible production schedule, but has the disadvantages of requiring extensive advertising promotion and more capital equipment. (4) *Manufacture of new goods* permits easier control of work load, provides training to industrial standards and objective evaluation, and may offer higher wage possibilities, but involves risks of product development, purchase of raw materials, and sales and inventory costs.

The Wagner-O'Day Act (P.L. 92-98) has been extended to bring government contracts within the reach of all handicapped as it once did for the blind.

Type of Training. The pattern of operation as well as employment opportunities provided for graduates will determine the type of training to be offered. In most cases, workshop training is primarily at the unskilled or semiskilled level, although industrial subcontracts may involve more skilled operations. If the workshop operates a retail outlet, training in selling, accounting, and other white-collar functions may be included in the overall plan.

Supportive Services. Supportive services are an integral part of the responsibility of a sheltered workshop and must therefore be included in the initial plan. Continuing medical supervision must be provided in order to determine physical tolerance for work activities, prevent exacerbation of disorders, and ensure collaboration with treatment or rehabilitation programs in progress. Psychiatric er psychological services are also required, ranging from treatment for mental or emotional disorders to counseling aimed at adjustment to vocational limitations and work stresses. Employment counseling and job placement activities are likewise essential, and recreational programs may also be undertaken. One of the responsibilities of the planning committee is to find community resources that will supply these services, since the workshop cannot be expected to provide them all.

Financial Program. In outlining its financial plan, the committee must be prepared to submit a realistic estimate of operating costs as well as estimated subsidy requirements, since workshops are inevitably conducted on a deficit basis. Possible sources of income include: production revenue (from sale of products, contract work, or repair work); fund raising and donations; value of goods donated for resale; Community Chest support; government or private grants; contributed staff; fees for services to clients of referring agencies, such as the Vocational Rehabilitation Division or the Veterans Administration; and free consultative services from other agencies.

Government Support. The committee should acquaint itself with the Federal Vocational Rehabilitation Act of 1973 and subsequent amendments, which are carried out by the Rehabilitation Services Administration. The act authorizes state vocational rehabilitation agencies to make federal matching funds available for meeting the costs of construction and equipping rehabilitation facilities, including the expansion and remodeling of existing buildings and the purchase of workshops and facilities for work evaluation and personal and work adjustment. The federal government is authorized to insure up to 100 percent of any mortgage covering construction of a public or nonprofit rehabilitation facility, including equipment to be used in its operation. The act also provides grants for programs and construction planning, initial staffing (for four years three months), residential accommodations for mentally retarded workers and those with severe mobility problems, and training services directed toward career advancement (occupational training, work testing and evaluation, tools and equipment used in training, job tryouts, plus a weekly allowance for the trainee and any dependents). Grants are also available for workshop improvement (analyzing and expanding professional and technical services). A provision of this act is that a study be carried out on the role of technical problems. Applicants for grants should secure the advice and assistance of the State Vocational Rehabilitation Agency and submit the final application to this agency for review.

The Small Business Administration in 1973 established Handicapped Assistance Loans, in which the SBA will loan a private or public nonprofit sheltered workshop up to $350,000 for up to fifteen years, or guarantee up to 90 percent of a loan to this amount which is made by a private lending institution. The money must be used to "enable them to produce and provide marketable goods and services."

Physical Plant. Plans for a workshop facility should be based on the following considerations: (1) accessibility to all clients, with public transportation in an urban center and adequate roads in a rural area; (2) service by commercial carriers for delivery of materials and supplies and pick-up of finished work; (3) adequate parking space for clients in wheelchairs, in braces, or on crutches; (4) eating facilities in the immediate vicinity unless provided by the workshop; (5) selection of building in terms of architectural suitability, ease of remodeling, neighborhood, possible expansion, and public image; (6) zoning ordinances; (7) adequate plant layout; (8) safety; (9) space for supportive services, such as medical examination, interviews, testing, counseling, physical therapy, staff conferences; and (10) compliance with requirements of the Federal Vocational Rehabilitation Act for government financing.

Organizing the Workshop

The first step in the actual organization of a workshop is a legal one: incorporation. This is essential for a number of reasons: to qualify for state and federal tax exemption privileges as a nonprofit organization, to conform to regulations of the Internal Revenue Service, to attain added prestige as well as legal status, to establish the right to sue and be sued, and to absolve the members of the governing group from personal liability. Incorporation requires a carefully drawn statement of purpose based on the findings of the planning committee, and should be carried out with legal advice.

The second step is the selection and organization of a board of directors to be responsible for formulating the overall policy, determining the program, evaluating community needs and resources, setting standards, interpreting workshop activities to the public, obtaining financial support, selecting and giving general direction to the executive director, outlining accounting standards, evaluating the operation, and initiating new services. Since the project is dependent on the board of directors for prestige, continuity, and stability, the members should represent all major community groups with an interest in rehabilitation — business, organized labor, social agencies, etc. — and should be chosen not only on grounds of competence and interest, but on their ability to elicit community support. In most cases the board selects a small steering or executive committee which will take responsibility for blueprinting the program (number and type of clients, type of work, equipment, and supportive services), organizing community resources (establishing relations with agencies for referrals and negotiation of fee arrangements), selecting a site or building, developing a staff plan, and preparing a budget and financing plan.

The third step is establishing criteria for the clientele in terms of age, type and severity of disability, location of residence, etc. A decision must be made as to whether the workshop will serve clientele with a single disability or those with different disabilities. Eligibility criteria for each type of workshop must be established: Individuals who have never worked, who need to be retrained or to learn a new skill, or who need to develop work tolerance should be eligible for the transitional workshop. Eligibility for the extended workshop is determined by the inability to produce at a competitive rate even after a training period or to be placed due to a tight labor market, advanced age, or enforced retirement.

The fourth step is application for a certificate from the Wage and Hour and Public Contracts Division of the U.S. Department of Labor, if the workers are engaged in producing goods for interstate commerce and are unable to earn at least the current minimum wage. Application forms may be obtained from the regional director of the Division.

The fifth step is finding a suitable location for the physical plant, as outlined above.

The sixth is staffing the workshop. This entails the preliminary responsibility of establishing sound personnel practices, formulating policy with respect to salaries for staff and wages for clients, and selecting an executive director who will administer the organization, develop job descriptions for all specialized positions, and select all other personnel. Although many workshops will have to start with limited personnel, a full staff will be of two types: (1) professional personnel, who will provide medical, social, psychological, and counseling services; and (2) technical personnel, who will provide management, training, supervision, and sales services.

The seventh step is drawing up an estimated budget to be presented to the community to gain its financial support, since the workshop cannot be self-supporting and will need to be subsidized.

This entails setting up four separate funds: (1) adequate capital funds for acquiring, building, or leasing a plant, and for machinery, tools, office equipment, etc.; (2) a revolving fund for purchase of raw materials and payment of wages to clients; (3) operating funds for salaries of technical staff, repairs, telephone, light, heat, and maintenance; and (4) a fund for the services of the professional staff or services provided by cooperating agencies under contract to the workshop.

The eighth step is establishing record-keeping and accounting practices, including payroll records that conform to federal government requirements under the Fair Labor Standards and Walsh-Healey acts, and cost accounting procedures, with periodic review and annual auditing by a certified public accountant.

The final step is a public relations plan designed to build community confidence in the workshop. The activities and reputations of board members will contribute materially to its success, but many special facets must be developed with or without the aid of professional consultants: regular public accounting of expenditures, publicity for the program's accomplishments, dramatic examples of successful graduates, and facts to demonstrate that the workshop is meeting the needs of the community.

Workshop Program

The workshop program is a five-stage affair. The *intake* process is the responsibility of a trained interviewer, such as a vocational counselor or social caseworker who is fully acquainted with the agency's objectives and approach. This interviewer obtains data for the case record (name, age, disability, physician, family, etc.), clears the case through a central social service exchange if there is one in the community, and reviews or assembles the following types of evaluation: medical (examination, diagnosis, prognosis, capacities, and limitations); psychological (intelligence level, learning ability, occupational aptitudes and preferences, social maturity, results of tests given by the State Employment Service, etc.); social (social history, role in family, financial situation); educational and vocational (academic and vocational schooling, specialized training, work history, and attitudes). On the basis of this information, a complete case record is constructed, for the double purpose of planning the rehabilitation program and charting the client's progress.

Before the client embarks on the *work tryout*, or evaluation, period, the job counselor devises a work program designed to evaluate physical capacities, learning ability, special aptitudes and skills, and ability to maintain social relationships and meet the demands imposed by the work situation. The tryout may include one or more of the following situations: office work (duplicating, addressing, etc.); quality inspection; service activities (cafeteria, messenger, maintenance, etc.); bench work (packaging, assembling); production machine operation; and tending, as in greenhouse work. During this period the client is observed and assessed for ability to follow directions, sensory capacities, efficiency, strength and fatigue level, as well as work pace, tolerance for routine or monotonous work, aspiration level, punctuality, dependability, frustration level, and attitudes toward coworkers and supervision. On the basis of this comprehensive appraisal, the counselor and client together determine vocational objectives and, if the client has been previously employed, whether training should be focused on a modified version of the former occupation or on a new occupation.

The next stage, *work conditioning and training,* must be long enough for the client to learn a specific job and, if necessary, develop skills that will compensate for personal limitations. During this period the client is instructed in the use of tools and equipment, and receives training in the economical use of raw materials, manipulative skills and coordination, industrial safety, and concepts of time, spatial relationships, and money value, as needed.

The *job placement* stage is reached when the client is ready to take a job in competitive industry or extended employment. Extended employment is remunerative work carried out in a different area of the workshop. Placement in industry requires extensive job search and promotion activities on the part of the workshop itself, the state rehabilitation agency, or the department of the state employment service devoted to the handicapped. The workshop job counselor should visit nearby firms and observe actual jobs in action in order to assess the fitness of his clients for the work. When a suitable opening is found, the counselor informs the client about the company and the nature of the work, helps one fill out an application, and arranges and prepares one for the employment interview.

The final stage is the *follow-up* period, in which the counselor keeps in touch with the client in order to evaluate progress, to make sure that a satisfactory adjustment is taking place, to help obtain medical or casework assistance as needed, and to see that the client is not exploited. Periodic case reviews are scheduled for all workers, whether they are placed in extended employment or on an outside job.

During this entire process the workshop experience is reinforced by supportive services, particularly those of a medical and psychological service nature. Although few workshops have a full-time physician on staff, and few offer extensive restoration services, all should have a medical consultant who performs initial medical examinations and reexaminations during the program and before placement on a job, and gives medical attention if new symptoms or disabilities develop. Medical guidance will also be valuable in planning the physical setup of the workshop and in developing vocational objectives for individual clients. Psychological service includes work and personal adjustment counseling by individuals with psychiatric, psychological, vocational, and social work experience. The objective is to help the client build a positive self-image, overcome tendencies toward overdependency and oversensitivity, and adapt more fully to the world of work by improving work habits, personal appearance, and social skills, as well as the ability to work with others and adjust to special demands, such as time pressure, noise, and the discipline of training.

Operational Considerations

A sheltered workshop must be organized on sound business lines if it is to be fully effective in serving clients and in attracting community support. This means that it must model itself after competitive industry in such essential areas as management practices, marketing activities, plant layout, industrial engineering, safety measures, wages and hours, government regulations, accounting, and personnel practices. Each of these areas will be briefly outlined. Consultation on all these aspects is available through the Rehabilitation Services Administration and State Divisions of Vocational Rehabilitation.

Management Practices. The principles of sound management — planning, organization, and control — apply to workshops as fully as to other business and social institutions: "It is not possible to control what is not organized, nor is it possible to organize what has not been planned." Personnel, production, processing controls, sources of supply, equipment, and analysis of price trends and market conditions must be subjected to intensive and continuous study. It is also necessary to isolate and attack special problems that arise in serving the disabled, such as maintaining a balance between production requirements, special training, and supportive services that take up the workers' time; or releasing a trainee from placement when the work flow is dependent on the trainee's operation and another person has to be trained as replacement. Professional management consultants may have to be called upon to solve especially complex problems.

Marketing Activities. Advice from consultants (business persons, State Department of Commerce, university professors) may also be needed in developing a market for manufactured goods. Again, the same principles apply as to other business enterprises: (1) salability, which depends on good design, good workmanship, and responsiveness to current market demands; (2) competitive pricing; and (3) effective merchandising, which requires ingenuity and skill in presenting the products either to the consuming public directly, as in a store, or to businesses that use the products or services provided by the workshop. In making bids to industry, it is important to take into account all costs involved, including raw materials, handling, and storage; and labor, shipping, and overhead (supervision, accounting, administration, rent or amortization payments, heat and maintenance, and selling).

Plant Layout. The following are major considerations in planning and preparing the physical plant: space for work stations (100 to 150 square feet, or 9 to 14 square meters, for each), ample storage space, convenient loading docks, a wide-open interior with high ceilings if possible, sturdy floors for storage and heavy equipment, wide doors (at least 32 inches, or 82 centimeters) for wheelchairs, broad aisles, grab bars or railings on ramps and stairs and in washrooms, separate dining room where possible, rest rooms with a stall for wheelchair clients, ample lighting and ventilation, and modern production tools and equipment.

Industrial Engineering. To ensure maximum productivity and earning power for the workers, every effort should be made to simplify the work and maintain efficiency. Stools, workbenches, and tools should be arranged with the workers' physical limitations in mind, and jigs and fixtures should be used wherever possible. Time-motion studies should be carried out where possible; the services of an engineering consultant may be obtained through a chapter of the American Society for Training and Development. The consultant can also assist in designing a flow chart that will expedite the work process and eliminate backtracking and excessive handling of materials.

Safety Measures. Since the workers are disabled, every possible safeguard against accidents must be used: well-marked aisle space, clean and uncluttered floors, orderly arrangement of all materials and equipment, safe stacking of materials, safety training for all workers, safety devices on all machines, adequate first-aid service, and thorough training of staff in handling emergencies.

Wages and Hours. The basic work week should be determined by individual capacities and physician's recommendations, but should not exceed the standard forty hours. Premium pay, usually $1\frac{1}{2}$ times the regular rate, should be given for work in excess of forty hours. Holidays, paid vacations, and sick leave should follow accepted practices in the area. Compensation should be calculated on a piecework basis wherever possible, in order to provide maximum incentive and make rewards commensurate with measurable achievement. If contract work is performed, the rates should be determined by time studies based on the job method or, in some cases, by union or trade association officials. Clients not engaged in direct production (packers, shippers) must be paid hourly wages based on prevailing rates in the area but related to individual performance — that is, if the prevailing wage is $4 per hour and the client produces half the standard amount, he or she will receive $2. To stimulate improvement, the performance of every worker should be periodically reviewed and adjustments should be made for individual progress. In some instances, wages will have to be supplemented in order to bring them up to the minimum fixed by the certificate for the workshop. Some workshops also provide additional supplements to less productive clients as a subsidy.

Government Regulations. Since some states have laws or regulations that govern employment in sheltered workshops, the executive director should write to the State Department of Labor for this information. On a federal basis, the Fair Labor Standards Act establishes a minimum wage for employees engaged in producing goods for interstate commerce. It also establishes overtime pay of at least $1\frac{1}{2}$ times the regular rate above forty hours, sets a basic minimum age of sixteen for general employment, and requires equal pay for equal work without discrimination as to sex. This law does not apply to state-operated sheltered workshops. The Walsh-Healey Public Contracts Act sets standards for federal government supply contracts in excess of $10,000 (and smaller contracts in certain circumstances), and applies to state-operated as well as other workshops. The minimum wage under this law is the prevailing wage in the particular industry, and the child labor provision establishes sixteen years as the minimum age for boys and eighteen for girls.

An application should be filed for a sheltered workshop certificate with the appropriate regional office of the Wage and Hour and Public Contracts Division of the U.S. Department of Labor. This certificate sets a minimum wage for the entire workshop, which may be less than the statutory minimum. It may also set a different minimum for different departments and different clients, and may establish a special training rate. In addition, it sets hourly and piecework rates based on rates for nonhandicapped workers for the same type and amount of work; and requires the workshop to keep accurate payroll and productivity records for all workers covered by the law. The certificate must be renewed yearly.

Accounting. A sound cost-accounting system is imperative, not only to evaluate the efficiency of the operation, but to provide a basis for requesting a subsidy from the community. A detailed cost determination system and a break-even point analysis can be found in the appendix to *Sheltered Workshops: A Handbook,* published by the Association of Rehabilitation Facilities.

Personnel Practices. The Commission on Accreditation of Rehabilitation Facilities (CARF) establishes guidelines on personnel for workshops wishing to be accredited in this area. The overall staffing plan is determined by the board of directors on the basis of services offered, number of clients, and available funds. The executive director develops (1) job descriptions for each position, detailing responsibilities, skills to be practiced, and physical requirements; and (2) qualifying requirements, including professional training or education, experience, personality, and physical capacities, if significant. Since there is a shortage of trained personnel at present, every recruitment resource should be utilized: state employment services, the registry and employment service of the National Society for Crippled Children and Adults (2023 West Ogden Avenue, Chicago), professional schools and universities, want ads in rehabilitation journals, employment exchanges of professional associations (American Psychological Association, American Personnel and Guidance Association, etc.), private employment agencies, experienced retirees, publicity and word-of-mouth, and the consultation service of the Association of Rehabilitation Facilities. In addition, professional internships, usually on an on-the-job basis, may be offered through a local college or university.

Other details of the personnel program are standard for social agencies. They include a written statement of policies and procedures, employment applications and interviews, a preemployment medical examination, a probationary period, a basic forty-hour five-day week, compensation for overtime, legal holidays, annual vacation with pay, specified sick leave, health insurance paid jointly by agency and staff, and benefits under state and federal legislation, including Federal Old Age and Survivors Insurance, State Disability Insurance, and State Workmen's Compensation Insurance. Salaries should be adequate and consistent with the prevailing scale for comparable positions in the community, with a range based on years of service and periodic raises until the maximum for the grade is reached. Staff development should be a continuing process, including in-service orientation sessions, on-the-job training, special training for supervisory staff, professional conferences and meetings and, where possible, graduate study partially underwritten by the agency.

9

Housing and Home Services

GINI LAURIE, Editor-Publisher and Founder,
Rehabilitation Gazette

$\mathbf{H}$ousing for the disabled does not simply mean a place of residence. "Housing" has become a blanket term referring to the problems of education, training, employment, transportation, architectural barriers, recreation, and home services.

Housing for the disabled is not a problem that can be separated from the problems facing the rest of the community, or that can be dissected, analyzed, and solved by designing special features into a building. The entire United States is in the midst of a severe housing crisis. One out of every five families suffers from housing deprivation. Four out of five persons with incomes under $5,000 experience serious housing problems. Millions of moderate- and middle-income persons in urban, suburban, and rural areas find it increasingly difficult to provide adequate housing for themselves and their families. A lasting solution to the housing problems of all people requires a comprehensive attack on a variety of social injustices. An essential dimension of a comprehensive housing strategy is action on unemployment and inadequate income.

No Wholesale Solution

There is no wholesale solution to the housing problems of any person. As do all people, disabled individuals need individual solutions. Their primary emotional needs are the same — to be fulfilled as persons, to love and be loved, to be needed, to have friends and a useful niche in life, and to be a part of a community. They must have opportunities to make mistakes and to take risks. They must be able to progress, as do their nondisabled peers, from family life to dormitory life, to student apartments, to shared apartments, to young-marrieds' apartments, to larger apartments, and to their own homes or farms. They must be able to develop their particular capabilities to the maximum and to choose life-styles to match each stage of development.

To accomplish independent life-styles, all persons need motivation, sources of information, training in life skills, employment or other source of income, and transportation from home to work, school, or recreation. Besides these essentials, the severely disabled also require human assistance with the basics of living, mechanical equipment to equalize the loss of movement of limbs, and adaptations for mobility.

Evolvement from Institutionalization

At the time of World War II, domestic help all but disappeared and big families split up into apartments and small homes. Many elderly, disabled, and mentally retarded persons who could no longer be cared for at home were shunted into nursing homes or other institutions. Coincidentally, improved medical management drastically increased the numbers of the elderly and disabled. Consequently, the nursing home industry boomed and state institutions filled up. Among the first to rebel against this institutionalization were the parents of mentally retarded and cerebral palsied children. From their concern grew two very effective organizations, the National Association for Retarded Citizens and the United Cerebral Palsy Associations. Eventually, the two organizations were the catalysts for legislation which has resulted in the nationwide system of Councils on Developmental Disabilities.

These organizations have discovered many innovative approaches to deinstitutionalization. Their projects and literature should be carefully studied by all who are interested in housing. A particularly helpful publication of the National Association for Retarded Citizens (P.O. Box 6109, 2709 Avenue E East, Arlington, TX 76011) is *The Right to Choose*. Another useful publication by the United Cerebral Palsy Associations, Inc. (66 East 34th Street, New York, NY 10016), is *No Place like Home*. An excellent source of information is the President's Committee on Mental Retardation (Washington, DC 20201). The monograph *Home Is a Good Place*, which provides an overview of group homes for retarded citizens, is available from the American Association on Mental Deficiency (5201 Connecticut Avenue N.W., Washington, DC 20015), another good source of information.

These organizations have accomplished deinstitutionalization through group homes, hostels, halfway houses, foster homes, sheltered living homes, mobile homes, and apartment living. They have been particularly attuned to the need for a system of protective and supportive services, for training to live independently, for growth through learning and experience, and for progression from dependency to varying degrees of independence.

All of these basic essentials of independent living are typified by the Tanya Towers Hostel Apartments, which United Cerebral Palsy of New York City sponsors. For some of the residents this is a transition stage toward their own apartments, for others it is a permanent home. For all, this program of assisted living and going to work at the UCP Center is an important step to normal living. (Details of this and related programs are available from UCP of NYC, 122 East 23d Street, New York, NY 10010.)

Veterans Administration Projects

One of the first specialized housing projects to be planned was a circular building designed specifically for paraplegics and quadriplegics toward which the Eastern Paralyzed Veterans Association worked for many years. By the time the plan was abandoned due to a lack of funds, the EPVA's philosophy of housing for the disabled had changed. It was felt that the original plan would have been too isolated from the community and that a realistic housing program must integrate disabled individuals within the mainstream of society. To accomplish this, the EPVA created an excellent model of a transitional housing system that is the final step in the rehabilitation of the disabled back into the community.

Called Rogosin House, the project is named in memory of its benefactor, the late Israel Rogosin. The project provides wheelchair-accessible furnished apartments to spinal-cord-injured veterans on a transitional basis. The average length of stay is between six and nine months. During this time the resident is assisted in finding employment and permanent housing and in making the adjustment back to normal living. Each resident is responsible for a share of the rent, telephone, utilities, food, and housekeeping. Apartments are available both to hospitalized veterans and to those who are living outside the hospital in inadequate housing. (More information may be obtained from Eastern Paralyzed Veterans Association, 432 Park Avenue South, New York, NY 10016.)

In a further effort to bring veterans back into normal living, the Veterans Administration has expanded its hospital-based home care program to include "house calls" to facilitate the transfer from hospital to home. The service involves a physician, social worker, nurse, and administrative person as a core group, with other professional persons added as needed. Patients receive the same specialized services in their homes that they would receive in the hospital. (Details are available from Mrs. Essie Davis Morgan, Chief, Socio-Economic Rehabilitation, Spinal Cord Injury Service, Veterans Administration Central Office, 810 Vermont Avenue N.W., Washington, DC 20420.)

Long-term Residential Facilities

One of the few successful long-term residential facilities in the United States is the Occupational Home of the Christian League for the Handicapped in Wisconsin. It was started in 1948 by the Rev. Charles E. Pederson, the present director, and a small group of disabled individuals. The project has been funded entirely through local groups and foundations. It has grown gradually to meet the needs of the community. It offers employment, transportation, recreation, therapy, and attendant services. With meals, the thirty-four single and double rooms rent for $305 for a private room and $210 for a shared room. State nursing home regulations, which are unnecessarily stringent for young disabled residents, have resulted in the development of apartments rather than rooms with board. The apartments are leased on a lifetime basis, with attendant care available as needed. (Additional information is available from Christian League for the Handicapped, Box 98, Walworth, WI 53185. Any group contemplating a long-term residential facility would be well advised to contact Reverend Pederson and discuss the problems of a residential facility as opposed to apartments with services.)

Existing Apartments with Services

Though some choose the shelter of collective living in a long-term residential facility, for many it is too confining and too isolated from the community. For the majority, using existing apartments and adding adaptations and services through umbrella organizations have great potential for truly independent living. In addition to the obvious benefits of freedom of choice of location and integration within the community, these programs have the advantage of being able to expand or contract to fit demand.

Many variations of this combination of apartments and services are being tried by groups of disabled individuals and by voluntary organizations representing the developmentally disabled. Examples of these, and the many other types of housing around the world are detailed in Gini Laurie's *Housing and Home Services for the Disabled.*

The best known of this type of program is the Fokus System, originated in 1964 by Dr. Sven-Olof Brattgard, a paraplegic, in Sweden. One of the first of similar programs in the United States is Independent Living for the Handicapped, which was started in 1970 by the Richard S. Weinberger Fund, Inc. (9 Winthrop Street, Brooklyn, NY 11225). Acting as an ombudsman, the program assists disabled individuals to live as they wish to live. The organization offers assistance in locating apartments and personal assistants, subsidized transportation, counseling, and interpretation of social and welfare programs.

The most exciting program and the one that is being most frequently copied in the United States is the Center for Independent Living (2539 Telegraph Road, Berkeley, CA 94704). Staffed entirely by blind, deaf, and wheelchaired individuals and funded by the Department of Health, Education and Welfare, the State of California, and private foundations, the services of the center cover every facet of independent living. It is a very potent source of psychological strength and information. The center has effected curb ramps throughout the area; furnishes transportation by van to the public transit system; operates a wheelchair repair shop; maintains a registry of attendants and assists in their training; keeps files of accessible apartments and adapts them with ramps or makes bathroom and kitchen alterations; maintains a peer counseling service; offers welfare rights counseling on Supplemental Security Income (SSI) and welfare programs; instructs the newly blind in mobility; acts as a referral agency to service agencies; and trains rehabilitation counselors to deal with the problems of the severely disabled.

HUD-Assisted Housing

Between 1967 and 1974, the Department of Housing and Urban Development (HUD) supported eight projects with a total of 1,085 units specially designed wholly or partly for occupancy by disabled persons. Though infinitesimal compared to the need or to the 500,000 units for the elderly (some of which had 10 percent made accessible to wheelchairs) which HUD supported between 1958 and 1974, the construction and operation of the eight projects contributed to the knowledge of housing for the disabled. Specifically, the following lessons were learned:

1. Housing without attendant services is useless to the severely disabled.

2. Housing is fully liberating to the less severely disabled only if other essential services are also available.

3. Information and referral services are essential.

4. The problems of housing, rehabilitation, and transportation are intertwined.

5. Small units, scattered throughout a city, are preferable to large, segregated housing projects.

6. Young disabled and elderly do not mix well.

7. Some disabled individuals like to live with other disabled; others do not.

8. The disabled cannot be classified as a unit; they are individuals with the same infinite variety of human tastes, needs, and values of all people.

9. Equipment must be adapted to individual needs.

10. The surrounding environment must be accessible.

11. Housing should be near shops and activity.

Details of the eight HUD-assisted projects are outlined below. The analyses of the Toledo project and the Highland Heights project will be of special interest to all who are planning a housing project, whatever the type or size.

1. Vistula Manor, 400 Nebraska Avenue, Toledo, OH 43602. Sponsor: Toledo Metropolitan Housing Authority; 164 units for elderly and disabled; low-rent public housing.

2. Pilgrim Tower, 1233 South Vermont Avenue, Los Angeles, CA 90006. Sponsor: Pilgrim Lutheran Church of the Deaf; 112 units for deaf and elderly; Section 202 Direct Loan.

3. Center Park Apartments, 825 Yesler Way, Seattle, WA 98104. Sponsor: Seattle Housing Authority; 150 units for elderly and disabled; low-rent public housing.

4. Walter B. Roberts Manor, 1024 South 32d Street, Omaha, NE

86105. Sponsor: Omaha Association for the Blind; 42 units for blind and elderly; Federal Housing Authority (FHA) Section 221(d)(3).

5. Highland Heights, 1197 Robeson Street, Fall River, MA 02722. Sponsor: Fall River Housing Authority; 208 units for elderly and disabled; low-rent public housing.

6. New Horizons Manor, 2525 North Broadway, Fargo, ND 58102. Sponsor: Fargo Housing Authority; 100 units for all disabilities; low-rent public housing.

7. Independence Hall, Airline Drive at Burress Street, Houston, TX 77022. Sponsor: Goodwill Industries; 202 units for elderly and disabled; FHA Section 236.

8. Creative Living, 444 West Eighth Avenue, Columbus, OH 43210. Sponsor: Creative Living, Inc.; 18 units for severely disabled; FHA Section 236.

Housing and Community Development Act

Under Section 231 of the Housing and Community Development Act of 1974, HUD may provide construction loans to nonprofit organizations, profit-motivated groups, and public agencies sponsoring the construction or rehabilitation of specially designed rental housing for the elderly or handicapped. Under Section 202, construction loans may be made available to nonprofit and corporate sponsors of housing specially designed for the handicapped that participate in the Section 8 Housing Assistance Payments Program. There is concern, however, that this special housing may be too segregating. Sponsors should plan to use it principally for transitional learning experiences and should ensure that there are sufficient alternatives so that segregation is a matter of choice, not necessity.

The new Section 8 rental assistance program, on the other hand, is a real gold mine for disabled who are unemployed or earning less than the area's median income. In this program, an individual pays only 25 percent of income for rent. The program takes into consideration the expenses of disability and has an extended cutoff period for those whose income increases past the median. (Details of the program are available from local housing authorities.)

Attendant Care

Attendant care is the keystone of independent living for severely disabled individuals who are unable to perform the basic activities of daily living. Many severely disabled individuals can be dressed and fed in the morning and then left alone to work independently until the noon and evening meals and the undressing routine of evening. Consequently, they can get along with part-time help or help that is on call.

With limitless ingenuity many severely disabled individuals live independently. They adapt their apartments or homes to their individual needs, and find their attendants from newspaper ads, religious and school bulletins, and word-of-mouth. These attendants include high school and college students, housewives, mildly retarded persons, religious missionaries, persons recently released from mental hospitals, aliens, and persons who are mildly disabled. For most, several attendants are better than one—particularly a combination of family, neighbors, volunteers, and paid staff. Severely disabled individuals usually want to hire, train, and if necessary fire their own attendants.

Funding and payments for attendant care vary widely from state to state. In California, a severely disabled individual may receive a maximum of $505 a month for attendant care. In addition, SSI and supplemental payments amount to about $280 a month. Most states do not participate in Medicaid home health. In 1974 Missouri spent only $4,637 on 36 people for home health expenditures. In the same year New York State spent $15.5 million on 33,000 persons. The maximum allowed in New York is $206 per month plus up to $20 a day for an attendant. The average payments to nursing homes in New York amount to $900–1,500 per month.

Oklahoma uses Medicaid for an effective and economical system of personal care service. To comply with Medicaid regulations, the care must be recommended by a personal physician, and 50 registered nurses supervise 2,383 providers. Some work short hours, others live in. The daily rate of vendor payment is $5.31. The average monthly cost is $140, while the average nursing home is $410 per month.

Another approach to funding attendant care is being proposed by the Massachusetts Council of Organizations of the Handicapped, which is endeavoring to have personal care attendants included under Title XX.

Self-determination

The disabled are becoming increasingly determined to attain their rights and to make the decisions that affect their lives. The American Coalition of Citizens with Disabilities (1346 Connecticut Avenue N.W., Room 308, Washington, DC 20036) has united organizations that represent many disabilities and whose membership totals about 5 million disabled individuals. A social action group of disabled in Minnesota, the United Handicapped Federation (1951 University Avenue, St. Paul, MN 55104), worked for three years with private and governmental agencies to construct a ninety-unit apartment building. The three-story complex, known as 2100 Bloomington, was opened in 1976. Every detail is designed to be usable by the disabled. The complex was planned for persons with limited incomes, and rental assistance is provided for all ninety units.

A young quadriplegic summarized these feelings of self-determination: "Persons with long-term disabilities are not asking to be taken care of. They are asking for their rights to be a part of the mainstream of society. This is not a medical question or a psychological question but rather a question of effective enforcement of civil rights."

Complexity of Solutions

The solutions to the complex comprehensive problems of housing for the disabled are themselves complex. The following are some of the more frequently suggested solutions:

1. Disabled Americans Act, similar to the Older Americans Act.
2. Centers for Independent Living, staffed by disabled, that provide information and referral services on a nationwide basis.
3. National health insurance that includes attendant care.
4. A proportion of accessible housing at all income levels.
5. Building codes that contain adequate provisions for accessibility.
6. More widely used rental assistance plans.
7. Seed monies for experimental living arrangements.
8. More realistic public housing income levels that allow for the expenses of disability.
9. Accessible public transportation.
10. A national housing policy actually related to disabled persons, including long-range service support, long-range financing, training for independent living, and zoning.

In short, the problems of housing for the disabled will be solved when living in the community is as feasible as subsistence in a nursing home, when vocational rehabilitation assumes its rightful responsibility for ongoing rehabilitation and adjustment to independent living, when the disabled themselves are involved in the solutions, and when people who are disabled can move as freely as the rest of the population and can choose where and how they wish to live.

SELECTED REFERENCES

Dickman, Irving R., *Help at the Door: A Manual on Home Services for Individuals with Cerebral Palsy and Other Developmental Disabilities*, United Cerebral Palsy Associations, New York, 1975.

Dickman, Irving R., *Independent Living: New Goal for Disabled Persons*, Public Affairs Pamphlets, New York, 1975.

Dickman, Irving R., *No Place like Home: Alternate Living Arrangements for Teenagers and Adults with Cerebral Palsy*, United Cerebral Palsy Associations, New York, 1975.

Fay, Frederick A., *Housing Alternatives for Individuals with Spinal Cord Injury*, Reprinted from *Selected Research Topics in Spinal Cord Injury Rehabilitation*, Tufts University, Boston, 1975.

Freedom of Choice: Report to the President and to the Congress on Housing Needs of Handicapped Individuals, Architectural and Transportation Barriers Compliance Board, Washington D.C., 1976.

Goodwill Industries of America, *Proceedings of National Conference on Housing and the Handicapped, September 10–12, 1974, Houston, Texas*, Health and Education Resources, Inc., Bethesda, Maryland.

Heaton, Edythe L., *Skills in Living . . . Toward a Richer Tomorrow: For Adults and Teenagers with Cerebral Palsy*, United Cerebral Palsy Associations, New York, 1976.

Helsel, Elsie D., "Residential Services," *Mental Retardation*, vol. 3, pp. 76–102, 1971.

Hofstra University, Department of Special Education and Rehabilitation, *Housing for Disabled Persons: Annotated Bibliography*, United Cerebral Palsy Associations, New York, 1975.

HUD Challenge, Special Issue on the Handicapped, U.S. Department of Housing and Urban Development, March 1975.

Jeffrey, Dorothy A., "A Living Environment for the Physically Disabled," *Rehabilitation Literature*, vol. 34, no. 4, pp. 98–103, April 1973.

Laurie, Gini, *Housing and Home Services for the Disabled: Guidelines and Experiences of Independent Living*, Harper & Row, Hagerstown, Maryland, 1977.

O'Connor, Gail, *Home Is a Good Place: A National Perspective of Community Residential Facilities for Developmentally Disabled Persons*, American Association of Mental Deficiency, Washington, D.C., 1976.

People Live in Houses: Profiles of Community Residences for Retarded Children and Adults, President's Committee on Mental Retardation.

Rehabilitation Record, Special Issue on Housing, vol. 13, no. 6, November-December 1972.

The Right to Choose: Achieving Residential Alternatives in the Community, National Association of Retarded Citizens, Arlington, Texas, 1973.

10

Removing Environmental Barriers

STEPHEN A. KLIMENT, American Institute of Architects

As a result of improved rehabilitation methods, healthier diets, better sanitary conditions, and improved medical care, far greater numbers of disabled individuals now have the potential to live useful and relatively independent lives.

Not everyone who is disabled can be classed as handicapped. Conversely, not everyone who is handicapped in necessarily disabled. For example, a person who is deaf, epileptic, or blind may be defined medically as having a disabling condition, but the condition is not one which will deter those affected from overcoming most common architectural barriers. On the other hand, a person pushing a loaded shopping cart home from the supermarket is not medically disabled, but is certainly handicapped. Hence, a handicapped person, in this context of buildings and adjacent spaces, is anyone who is hampered in mobility or functioning (as compared with an able-bodied person) as a result of obstacles caused by the design of a building, the choice of hardware and equipment, and the arrangement of outside spaces. The following list provides a general overview of three broad categories of individuals who, at one time or another, come under this definition: (1) *Temporary condition:* fracture; pregnancy; movement of large or heavy loads; and convalescence from an operation or illness. (2) *Characteristic condition:* childhood; dwarfism; frailty due to old age; frailty due to physical size or build; gigantism; and obesity. (3) *Long-established condition:* sight disabilities; hearing disabilities; nonambulatory disabilities due to which an individual walks, climbs, bends or stoops, reaches, waits, or carries modest loads with difficulty; and coordination disabilities due to brain, spinal, or peripheral nerve injury. Where barriers have been removed, an individual, however disabled, may no longer be handicapped in entering and using a building.

ANSI Standard on the Physically Handicapped

Federal, state, and local laws and regulations which specify barrier conditions to be corrected began to be enacted in the early 1960s, and can by and large be traced back to the development of the key document guiding barrier-free legislation. This document, Standard 117.1, was published in 1961 by the American National Standards Institute, Inc. (ANSI). "Specifications for making buildings and facilities accessible to, and usable by, the physically handicapped" (to give the standard its full name) has been the underlying basis of most legislation and regulations now on the books. It identifies certain *requirements* (sizes and functioning of a wheelchair and crutches) and *handicapping conditions* (blindness, deafness, semi- and nonambulatory disabilities, and disabilities that stem from incoordination and old age). It responds to these requirements and conditions by establishing minimum provisions of parking, site grading, building design, dimensioning of washroom and other facilities, and design and disposition of signals and controls. The formulators hoped that these provisions would, if observed, make a building accessible.

The standard has lost some of its usefulness over the years. As the first model document of its kind, it was geared to the social climate of fifteen years ago. Today citizens are more aware, more concerned, and will agree to tougher standards. ANSI 117.1 did not include residential buildings and left equivocal such public or semipublic accommodations as hotels, motels, and college dormitories with their heavy content of living, cooking, and washing activity.

Revising the Standard

To compensate for these shortcomings, the University of Syracuse began an intensive two-year project to revise ANSI 117.1. Under a $256,000 grant from the Department of Housing and Urban Development, the project is centered in the School of Architecture and the All-University Gerontology Center. Project director is Edward Steinfeld. The project will expand the scope of ANSI 117.1 to include dwelling units and related exterior spaces, single-family as well as multifamily housing, and mobile homes.

TYPICAL BARRIER PROBLEMS OF THE HANDICAPPED

The goal of barrier-free design is "autonomous functioning" of the handicapped individual. In other words, any person with a handicap should be able to participate without help in such everyday activities as acquisition of goods and services, living and em-

This demonstration against environmental barriers, staged
at the City Hall in Cleveland, Ohio, had successful results.
The members of the National Paraplegia Foundation are led
by Councilman William Franklin. (Photograph by the Cleveland
Plain Dealer; National Paraplegia Foundation)

ployment, leisure, entertainment, and schooling. The following are
the kinds of barriers which hamper autonomous functioning.
(Underlying all barrier-free planning is the principle that *all
prosthetic devices*—a broad term that includes artificial limbs,
ramps, accessible toilets, raised numbers on elevator buttons, etc.—
be linked in a continuous sequence. In other words, it does no good
to have a barrier-free toilet stall on the second floor if the only way
to reach it is up a flight of steps.)

1. *Parking and approaches to building entrance.*
   a. Parking: Space too narrow to permit transfer to wheelchair or
   crutches. Space not level. A curb or step from space to paved
   walk. Parking meter out of reach.
   b. Approaches: Street between parking space and building entrance. No curb cut or traffic light at crossing. Curb cut
   blocked by a car. No snow removal. Step between sidewalk
   and entrance level. Ramp, if provided, too steep for wheelchair or crutches.
   c. Entrances: Doors too narrow to admit wheelchair. Revolving
   doors which operate while flush side doors are locked. Distance between outer and inner door too short. Excessive pressure needed to operate doors.

2. *Travel within building.*

   a. Stairs: Steps open or have projecting nosing under which toes may be caught. Risers exceeding 7 inches, or 18 centimeters. Handrail too high or low, or hard to grasp due to its size or shape, or not extending beyond steps.

   b. Elevators: Entrance too narrow to admit wheelchair. Cab's floor level out of alignment with building floor. Control for upper floors out of reach. Buttons flush, precluding unaided use by blind. Audible arrival signal which does not indicate to the blind whether cab is on the way up or down. Cab size too small for wheelchair.

   c. Floors: Floors between different parts of the building not level, and connected by steps. Floors slippery or carpeted with deep pile carpeting.

3. *Services.*

   a. Rest rooms: Closest accessible rest room three floors away, or for the other sex only. "Modesty barriers" (two doors in sequence) situated so wheelchair user must have both doors open at same time to pass through. Toilet with door that scrapes the sides of a wheelchair passing through. No free space for a wheelchair to turn.

   b. Toilets: Toilet stall door too narrow to admit wheelchair. No grab bars either at the side or rear of the stall. Toilet seat too low for transfer.

   c. Lavatories: Clearance below bowl too small to permit wheelchair to slide under. Uninsulated hot water line. Towel bar, soap, and paper towel dispensers and disposal out of reach.

   d. Water fountains: Spout and controls out of reach. Fountain in alcove too narrow for wheelchair.

   e. Coin-operated telephones: Nearest phone two floors away or in an enclosed booth. Free-standing, but lacking space beneath for wheelchair. Coin slot, dial, and handset out of reach.

   f. Miscellaneous: Windows, curtains, heat controls, light switches, and fire alarms out of reach of persons in wheelchairs, or so constructed as to be inoperable by those with physical or coordination disabilities.

4. *Hazards.*

   a. General: Doors leading to boiler rooms and other hazardous spaces not identifiable by the blind. Floor access panels or holes left unprotected. Gratings and joints in paving which snag wheelchair wheels.

   b. Alarms: Signs, fixtures, or cantilevered building elements hung so low as to be a danger to the blind. Changes in level and other hazards in and out of the building unlit at night. Fire alarms solely audible, neglecting the hard of hearing. Corridor exit signs not distinct enough to be distinguished by partially blind persons.

5. *Housing* (includes single-family homes, apartments, hotels and motels, and dormitories).

   a. Kitchens: Cabinets and cooking areas reachable only by parking wheelchair parallel to counter. Storage areas too high or too low. Door swings which obstruct free wheelchair movement.

   b. Motels, hotels, guest rooms: Arrangement of bed and other furniture which obstructs movement of wheelchair or prevents transfers.

   c. Bathrooms: Shower without grab bar, seat, safety controls, water overflow controls, nonslip surface.

   d. Dining rooms: Table undersides too low to permit wheelchair to slide under.

   e. Bedrooms: Mattress too low or too high for transfer.

6. *Schools and universities.*

   a. Lecture halls and auditoriums: No special-level station for wheelchair. No existing seats removable to accommodate wheelchair. Aisles to stage or dais stepped, not ramped. Access by turnstile only.

   b. Laboratories: Work stations permitting only "parallel" parking of wheelchair. No low workbench provided. Aisles too narrow for wheelchair.

   c. Physical education: Lockers inaccessible. No special toilet and shower facilities.

   d. Campuses: Travel between campus buildings involving steps, steep ramps, delayed winter snow removal.

7. *Places of worship, restaurants, stadiums, and stores.* The handicapped person also usually encounters barriers in most places of worship, shopping, and public entertainment. In church or temple, pews are laid out so the aisle is the only place for the wheelchair, and transfer to a pew is not feasible. In a restaurant, seating is in booths, tables lack sufficient clearance beneath, and toilets are inaccessible. Seats in football stadiums can often be reached only via stairs. A handicapped person's selection of shops and department stores is limited by the aforementioned common barriers in parking, approach, clearances, and facilities.

8. *Transportation terminals.* The terminal building or station poses special barrier problems, over and above those a handicapped individual finds elsewhere. Travel-oriented facilities, more so than others, require sharp and sudden changes of level, long walking distances, and such focused checkpoints as baggage inspection points and turnstiles. Moreover, the handicapped person tends to be encumbered with luggage and, because of typical crowds, emotional anxiety is added to purely physical obstacles. Finally, because of the many choices of direction, gates, tracks, etc., open to the traveler, the person handicapped by a visual or hearing impairment requires (but does not always find) the big, clear signs and audible signals or announcements needed to locate and reach the proper spot.

9. *Product design.* Most products, for example, door handles, water fountains, television and appliance controls, and even packaging, are based on criteria derived from so-called normal groups. Pushing for development of design criteria and standards that

accommodate most classes of handicapped persons will result in the creation of far more universal products. For example, a door handle requiring downward pressure instead of a twisting motion will help not only those with loss of hand function but all able-bodied people, especially those carrying loads.

Of course, the question arises of what to do about existing buildings. Nearly all existing buildings, since they were erected before the barrier-free movement began to emerge, have barriers. Legislation, as well as court decisions, at first focused on new construction but is now concentrating more on making existing buildings barrier-free. State codes such as that of Massachusetts and municipal codes such as Chicago's stipulate, with certain provisos, that any remodeling on buildings to which the public has access must be made barrier-free. North Carolina has made a $2 million fund available for remodeling state facilities to make them accessible.

In general, such regulations recognize three classes of projects: (1) Those projects in which alterations affect a very small area or in which the extent of alterations over a large area is very superficial, such as painting. (2) Those projects in which alterations are substantive, such as rewiring and air-conditioning, or entail a major added new structure. In those cases, the entire complex of buildings must be raised to barrier-free standards. (3) Those intermediate situations in which the work is substantial enough to justify barrier removal but not extensive enough to require a total adaptation. A typical measure is to stipulate a percentage range — usually between 25 and 50 percent of the cost of the original structure. If the cost of modernization or addition falls in this range, only the area of the work must meet barrier-free criteria. Sometimes key areas, such as entrances and toilet access, *must* be accommodated.

INTRODUCTION TO MINIMUM STANDARDS

Barrier-free standards seek to: (1) determine the size, shape, and location of spaces within or adjacent to a building, such as parking and stairs; (2) control the size, shape, and location of objects, such as door handles, rest rooms, toilets, water fountains, and control knobs; (3) indirectly place a limit on both personal energy output by the handicapped person — by limiting, say, the angle of ramps — and on the degree of hazard to be encountered — for example, by modifying door hardware design to alert blind people when doors lead to hazardous spaces; (4) specify the size and nature of signs and signals that guide a handicapped person in entering and using a building.

The following are highlights of current standards. (The section is divided into logical parts related to the way a handicapped person typically approaches and uses a building. The data are drawn from the checklists of John C. Worsley, AIA, California State Architect, and of the New York State University Construction Fund.)

1. *Parking and approaches to building entrance.*
   a. Parking: Locate near building. Identify parking spaces for use by handicapped only. Make level. Minimum width: 12 feet, or 3.6 meters. Clear step-free route from reserved space to building entrance.
   b. Approaches: Minimum width: 5 feet, or 1.5 meters; 1 in 20 maximum gradient. Nonslip surface. Curb cuts if road crossing required. No downspouts discharging onto walkway. Change in paving texture to alert visually impaired, especially when there are ramps or curb cuts.
   c. Ramps: Avoid. If inevitable, 1 in 12 maximum slope. Handrail on at least one side 32 inches, or 82 centimeters, above ramp surface, extending 12 inches, or 31 centimeters, beyond top and bottom of ramp. Nonslip surface. Snow-melting apparatus if outdoors. Six feet, or 1.8 meters, of straight clearance at top and bottom. Level rest platform at 30-foot, or 9-meter, intervals and at turns.
   d. Entrances: One primary entrance barrier-free, with access to elevators. *Clear* door opening 32 inches, or 82 centimeters, wide. View panel at 3-foot, or 92-centimeter, height if two-way door. Less than 8 pounds, or 36 newtons, of pressure needed to operate. Doorsill flush with floor. If vestibule, 6½ feet, or 2 meters, between doors. Adequate night illumination.
   e. Stairs (exterior): No protruding nosings. Nonskid surface. Lit for nighttime use by ambulatory handicapped. Riser: 5¾ inches, or 15 centimeters (maximum); tread: 14 inches, or 36 centimeters (minimum). Handrails 32 inches, or 82 centimeters, high, extending 30 inches, or 76 centimeters, horizontally at top and bottom.
2. *Movement within building.*
   a. Stairs: No protruding nosings. Maximum riser height: 7 inches, or 18 centimeters. Handrails 32 inches, or 82 centimeters, above tread at face of riser, extending 12 inches, or 31 centimeters, beyond top and bottom parallel to floor. Handrails circular or oval, 1¾ to 2 inches, or 4.5 to 5 centimeters, thick.
   b. Elevators: Install in all buildings of two or more stories. Cab dimensions and cab doors to conform to wheelchair dimensions and movement constraints. Minimum cab size: 5 feet deep by 5½ feet wide, or 1.5 by 1.7 meters. Doors to have safety edge with sensing device. No control higher than 4 feet, or 1.2 meters, from floor. Control buttons to have raised or notched information adjacent to buttons.
   c. Corridors: Minimum: 5 feet, or 1.5 meters, wide.
   d. Floors: Nonslip surface. Differences in level connected by ramps.
   e. Doors: See "Entrances," above.
3. *Services.*
   a. Toilets: Stall size 3 feet wide by 5 feet deep, or 1 by 1.5 me-

ters (minimum), with an outswinging door providing 32 inches, or 82 centimeters, of clearance (4 feet 10 inches by 5 feet for lateral transfer, or 1.4 by 1.5 meters). Wall-mounted toilet with seat 17 inches, or 43 centimeters, from floor. Grab bars (1½ inches, or 4 centimeters, in diameter and 1½ inches from walls) on both walls, 33 inches, or 84 centimeters, from floor. Add rail at rear if stall over 40 inches, or 102 centimeters, wide.

b. Lavatories: Clearance to bottom of apron: 2½ feet, or 76 centimeters (minimum). Faucet handles easy to operate. Shield hot water line and trap. Mirror bottom, soap and towel dispenser, and other accessories not over 40 inches, or 102 centimeters, above floor. Do not slope mirror.

c. Urinals: At least one fixture 15 inches, or 38 centimeters, above floor.

d. Water fountains: Upper edge of basin not over 3 feet, or 92 centimeters, above floor. Controls and spouts at front. Recess, if present, not less than 3 feet wide.

e. Coin-operated phones: Do not place phone in booths. Dial, coin slot, and handset 3–4 feet, or 92–122 centimeters, from floor. Hearing disabilities compensated for.

f. Controls: Light and other switches 3–3½ feet, or 92–107 centimeters, from floor, with unobstructed access. Lever handles (versus rotating). Foot operation included where possible.

4. *Hazards.*

a. Obstructions: Low-hanging door closers, signs, ceiling fixtures: 7 feet, or 2.1 meters (minimum), clearance above floor.

b. Lighting on ramps: 1 footcandle, or 10.8 lumens/square meter (minimum).

c. Alarms: Visual signal to alert hearing-impaired. Audible signal to alert visually impaired.

The preceding standards are geared to three relatively fixed design conditions: the individual in a wheelchair, the person on crutches, and the blind.

The Blind Individual

When properly trained, blind persons have a somewhat greater freedom of mobility than those confined to wheelchairs. Widely held is the view that by including certain kinds of barrier-free design provisions, architects make access to and use of buildings easier not only for the blind but for other categories of handicapped too, especially the wheelchair-bound. Typical of these provisions are grade-level entry and the elimination of steps.

Other design provisions to expand access to the blind should include: (1) *Floor texture changes.* (2) *Color contrast.* Since many individuals who are classified as blind in fact have some usable vision, color contrast is a valid way to warn against hazards. Even those with 3 percent vision can react to color change, especially when of high contrast, such as dark blue versus beige. (3) *Elevator indicators.* Some kind of acoustic indicator would help the blind know whether the elevator they have called is heading up or down. (A two-tone signal has been suggested — high-pitched for "up" and lower-pitched for "down.")

In any case, many authorities on the problems of the blind feel that mobility training for the blind should focus not only on touch and the cane but also on developing greater sensitivity to such stimuli as sound and air currents.

Number of Facilities for Disabled

Most codes and guidelines suggest minimum quantities or percentages of barrier-free facilities. Typical requirements or recommendations are as follows:

> Parking places: 5 percent
> Coin-operated phones: one per bank of phones
> Toilets: one per sex per floor
> College dormitory rooms: 2 percent
> Motel or hotel rooms: 5 percent (Massachusetts)
> Laboratory work stations: one station or 1 percent
> Spaces in auditorium: 1 percent

Adaptable Design

A second kind of approach is emerging, however. Known as adaptable design, it allows an entire building to be designed so any or all spaces and facilities can be made accessible by adding or subtracting design elements. For example, a toilet is so sized and laid out that it can be adapted for side access and transfer. Attachments are incorporated into the initial structure so that prosthetic aids such as grab bars can be simply attached as needed. Toilets can be designed so the seat can be raised or lowered to any reasonable height. Auditorium seats are removable to make room for varying numbers of wheelchairs.

Conclusion

A frequent argument deals with the economic value to the United States of raising the employment opportunities of handicapped persons by reducing barriers at places of work. No one really knows how many of the unemployed handicapped are willing and able to work. Taking even the lower estimates as to the numbers of noninstitutionalized handicapped in this country, however, the net increase in gross national product and tax revenues would be considerable. But does this in itself make the case for reduced barriers? Any handicapped person may quite justifiably resent having the argument for eliminating barriers based purely on financial grounds. Economic benefits should more correctly be seen as the *results* of a totally accessible environment, and should not be used to argue the case for it.

(This article is based in part on material developed for the American Institute of Architects under a grant from the Rehabilitation Services Administration of the Department of Health, Education and Welfare.)

SELECTED REFERENCES

Architectural Facilities for the Handicapped, ICTA Information Centre, Fack S-16103, Bromma, Sweden.

Architectural Planning for the Physically Handicapped: A Checklist of Recent Publications, National Easter Seal Society, May 1975.

Barrier-Free Site Design, American Society of Landscape Architects Foundation and HUD, Superintendent of Documents, Government Printing Office, Washington, DC 20402.

Goldsmith, Selwyn, *Design for the Disabled*, McGraw-Hill, New York, 1967.

Jorgensen, Jay, *Landscape Design for the Disabled*, American Society of Landscape Architects Foundation, 1750 Old Meadow Road, McLean, VA 22101, 1975.

Kirk, Larry, *Accent on Access*, American Society of Landscape Architects Foundation, 1974.

Kliment, Stephen A., *Into the Mainstream: A Syllabus for a Barrier-Free Environment*, American Institute of Architects, 1975.

Lassen, Peter, *Barrier Free Design: A Selected Bibliography*, Paralyzed Veterans of America, 1974.

Mace, Ronald, and Betsy Laslett, eds., *An Illustrated Handbook of the Handicapped Section of the North Carolina State Building Code*, North Carolina Department of Insurance, P.O. Box 26387, Raleigh, NC 27611, 1974.

Reports of the Architectural and Transportation Barriers Compliance Board, Room 1004, 330 C Street S.W., Washington, DC 20201.

Reports of the National Center for a Barrier-Free Environment, 8401 Connecticut Avenue, Chevy Chase, MD 20015.

11

Transportation

JEROME R. DUNHAM, Ph.D.

$\mathbf{A}$lthough housing and clothing may show the greatest contrasts among different types of people in a community, it is transportation which is most consequential when it is limited by the inequalities imposed by poverty, disability, and lack of knowledge. Having no means to transport oneself restricts chances for employment, recreation, medical help, and sometimes obtaining food and clothing.

The situation as it exists today for the average disabled person is accurately described in the following excerpt from *Amicus* (National Center for Law and the Handicapped, January 1976):

> If President-elect Franklin D. Roosevelt, traveling in 1933 from Hyde Park, New York, to Washington, D.C., for his inauguration, had been forced to rely solely on ordinary transportation services, he would not have arrived. He could not have walked up the steps of a bus or train. If he had chosen to fly, he probably would have been denied passage unless he had an able-bodied companion with him. Once in Washington, he would have found not only more inaccessible buses, but also a fleet of taxi drivers reluctant to pick up a wheelchair passenger.
>
> Today a similarly disabled person would encounter the same obstacles on a journey to almost any city in the United States. It is a paradox that in the 40 years since Roosevelt reached a pinnacle of American political power and exercised that authority vigorously to reshape so much of our national life, the status of millions of his fellow disabled citizens has changed very little.
>
> Few issues are as important to disabled people as accessible

transportation services. Transportation can make the difference between meaningful work and mere subsistence, between sharing the community of one's friends or being isolated, between enjoyment of the world of art, sports, and public affairs or being deprived of those dimensions of existence. The availability of accessible transportation affects directly the quality of life.

There is an additional importance to the transportation issue. Nothing symbolizes more vividly this nation's ostracism of disabled people than the inaccessibility of buses, subways, trains, and airplanes. While the non-handicapped can whiz away to the mainstream of life, the disabled are excluded from that society as if signs had been posted on the outskirts of civilization proclaiming, "Handicapped may not enter." The disabled are thus effectively banished from sight, and the non-handicapped are relieved from dealing with the discomforting aspects of physical and mental disability — its slowness, its labored moving about, its fundamental unattractiveness. Accessible transit systems would mean that our society has taken a step toward integrating the disabled into one phase of our collective life and thereby overcome at least some of its fear.

For those to whom driving is a commonplace event, the world can seem to have an infinite number of cars, traffic frustrations, and delays. One worries about rising fuel and maintenance costs, as well as paralyzing fuel shortages. It seems as if almost everyone drives a car, and it may be startling to realize that, in most statistical estimates, the number of people not able to get around independently ranges from a third to more than half of the United States population. The very young, old, poor, and the severely disabled may not be able to drive or even to utilize transit systems, if they exist.

There are two aspects to the problem of transportation for the disabled. One is technological and the other is attitudinal. Design barriers are built into the vehicles, street curbs, stairs and turnstiles, preventing wheelchair travel. Highways and downtown streets are frightening, dangerous places filled with obstacles, noise, and vehicle exhaust pollution that can trouble persons with chronic lung disease, the timid, or the blind who must try to hear their way among the throngs. An elderly couple reluctantly gives up its car because of expense or fear of accidents, although they know this will isolate them even more from their dwindling social contacts. An impoverished mother with a sick or handicapped infant knows only too well the frustration of living beyond the end of a bus line, with no money for a cab, and is hesitant to rely on uninterested neighbors to take her and the baby to the clinic.

It is probably not yet technologically possible to manufacture a six-legged mechanical donkey that will kneel low for transfer from a wheelchair and then, at a slight signal from the paraplegic driver, run effortlessly up stairs, down hills, over mountain streams, and through the woods, always providing a smooth ride by lengthening or shortening its remarkable chromium legs. However, it is likely that technology could provide a blind person with a wrist speaker that could be used to receive recorded information from the corner traffic light. We do not have a pocket screen to translate spoken words into a visual presentation for a deaf person, but we could design a bus that pulls up to a curb and extends a hydraulic lift for an entering wheelchair. Few individuals can afford specially equipped vans or minibuses of their own, but many rehabilitation centers provide them.

Most technological problems are the result of history and habit. The old horsedrawn tram had a row of wooden benches along its length. The seats in a bus or streetcar are often just cushioned counterparts of those old benches without a thought given to what might be safer or more feasible at the much greater speeds of modern equipment. Catherine Stewart, writing for the Mitre Corporation, points out the need for research on the kinds of safeguards a frail elderly person should have during the fast deceleration of a braking bus. She outlines a series of kits that could adapt city buses for a variety of disability groups. These kits concern route identification, public address, handles/handrails, stanchions, raised seat, extended step, interior surfaces finish policy, interior ambient lighting, reading lights, and display/control panel lighting. A large sign with the bus's number or route number, just to the left of the door, would help everyone, and if it were in raised print a blind person could reach up and read it with the fingers; however, a loudspeaker at the door would be more helpful, and a good public address system on all buses could identify stops for passengers able-bodied and disabled alike. Wide ramps with thick handrails could help those with weak hips or hands, as well as many other passengers with less severe handicaps.

Most designers and architects have not been concerned about deviant populations, as they were attempting to serve crowds in the cheapest and most efficient manner possible. It has taken legislation to change priorities. It has also taken the time of many dedicated people to argue that design features which are good for the disabled will be safer and more comfortable for everyone. The designers of Bay Area Rapid Transport (BART) went out of their way to include disabled persons in its advisory committees, but the Washington, D.C., subway had to be closed even before service began, because of a suit that directed officials to modify architectural barriers to comply with the Urban Mass Transportation Act Amendments of 1974, Section 16, which states:

> (a) It is hereby declared to be the national policy that elderly and handicapped persons have the same right as other persons to utilize mass transportation facilities and services; that special efforts shall be made in the planning and design of mass transportation facilities and services so that the availability to elderly and handicapped persons of mass transportation which they can effectively utilize will be assured; and that all Federal programs offering assistance in the field of mass transportation (including the programs under this Act) should contain provisions implementing this policy.

(b) In addition to the grants and loans otherwise provided for under this Act, the Secretary is authorized to make grants and loans —

(1) to States and local public bodies and agencies thereof for the specific purpose of assisting them in providing mass transportation services which are planned, designed, and carried out so as to meet the special needs of elderly and handicapped persons, with such grants and loans being subject to all of the terms, conditions, requirements, and provisions applicable to grants and loans made under section 3(a) and being considered for the purposes of all other laws to have been made under such section; and

(2) to private nonprofit corporations and associations for the specific purpose of assisting them in providing transportation services meeting the special needs of elderly and handicapped persons for whom mass transportation services planned, designed, and carried out under paragraph (1) are unavailable, insufficient, or inappropriate, with such grants and loans being subject to such terms, conditions, requirements, and provisions similar insofar as may be appropriate to those applicable to grants and loans under paragraph (1), as the Secretary may determine to be necessary or appropriate for purposes of this paragraph.

Of the total amount of the obligations which the Secretary is authorized to incur on behalf of the United States under the first sentence of section 4(c), 2 per centum may be set aside and used exclusively to finance the programs and activities authorized by this subsection (including administrative costs).

Attitudes are revealed in the kind of priorities established by the transportation system; for instance: how many specially modified railroad cars were purchased for the disabled, or does an airline make allowance for wheelchairs at its security checkpoints? Attitudinal problems are often most clearly revealed in the face-to-face interchanges between disabled persons and transportation employees. Since it is usually assumed that indignities to people arise largely out of ignorance, many agencies, organizations, and individuals have attempted to "educate the public." These attempts have not usually been formalized or prolonged, and have primarily dealt with only that disability group of concern to the "teachers." The etiquette of how to lead a blind person, how to communicate with a deaf person, and how to properly assist a quadriplegic is demonstrated and explained, and the audience is assured that persons in this particular disability group are "just like them" and want to be regarded as normal people who happen not to be able to see or hear or walk. But there is usually no systematic follow-up, and as personnel changes along with policies and leadership, disabled persons usually discover they are being handled by a concerned but naive individual who may be somewhat embarrassed or may believe that the disabled should not travel on the transportation system at all.

Training on a more comprehensive scale has been undertaken by the American Rehabilitation Foundation in Minneapolis, through a Demonstration Grant from the Division of Research and Demonstration Grants, Social and Rehabilitation Service, Department of Health, Education and Welfare. Under the title of the Wheelchairmanship Project, the Foundation developed audio-visual packages that can be sent to industry for in-service training. They suggest that local agencies of organizations be responsible for the training and follow-up contacts. Their report states, in summary:

> Nationally, Wheelchairmanship training materials were incorporated into the training programs of 23 U.S. airlines out of a total of 32 contacted, or 71%. In terms of percentages of industry personnel trained, however, the figure, if available, would be considerably higher since eight of the nine that did *not* establish Wheelchairmanship as a regular part of their employee training were small local carriers and the ninth does not operate domestically in the U.S. . . . Although airline management groups were highly accepting of the training program and cooperative in incorporating it into their in-service programs, the other industries studied were much more reluctant to recognize the need and desirability of such training. However, airlines training programs were also the only industrial training programs where all new employees are taught a structured, organized curriculum. It would appear from project experience with management groups that lack of formal training programs, rapid turnover in service employees, difficulty in job scheduling and release of employees for in-service training as well as refusal to admit the need for service improvement all contribute to negate the urgency to train employees in Wheelchairmanship.

By the time most of us become adults, we have had many experiences in negotiating transportation. We can recall getting on the wrong bus or experiencing confusion in a strange part of town, and learning how to get help and thereby reach our destination. A person who, for some reason, is prevented from the usual development of travel confidence operates at a great disadvantage. Having a doctoral degree is of little consequence if one cannot get from home to a job.

There seems to be an optimum time for reaching out beyond our accustomed area, when motivation is high enough to offset risks. If the individual has been disabled throughout childhood, the freedom to explore and try new behaviors, as well as the anticipation of future independence, is very important throughout the developmental period. One may need to develop special skills in learning how to handle a mechanical wheelchair, manipulate special hand controls on an automobile, compensate in traffic for muffled sound cues, or use a cane to obtain information about the terrain and surrounding buildings. If prior experience has been lacking, remedial intervention is necessary to overcome resistance and fears and to experience the satisfaction of independent travel. For a newly blinded person urban traffic is often a source of terror. Scientifically developed methods of using a long cane or, for a small percentage of vigorous walkers, a guide dog have been developed to facilitate independent movement. The efficiently mobile also become proficient at helping sighted people give them helpful information and assistance.

Piecemeal methods are not adequate in designing equipment or educating personnel. It is taking a long period of time for disabled people and their friends and advocates to succeed in getting passage of legislation for the removal of architectural barriers. It will take a longer time for the educational system to teach all of us how to relate and empathize with all deviant groups. A disabled person traveling in public conveyances is exposed to many hazards, most of them attitudinal. For example, a woman in a wheelchair may feel the need to stop drinking liquids some time before leaving on a plane trip because she cannot get into the washroom. She may also be refused entry to a plane because it is believed that she will make escape difficult for other passengers if the plane has to be abandoned. One of the authors, who is blind, once asked another passenger if he might walk along with him to the embarcation lounge so that a busy employee would not have to be inconvenienced. The employee told the passenger not to take the responsibility because he could be sued if the blind person were to fall on the escalator.

Despite rising fares, public transportation systems have been in trouble throughout the United States due to staggering deficits; a 1973 estimate ran to $400,000,000. The dilemma which baffles planners is that the very people for whom public transportation is the most essential, the disabled, are not able to use public conveyances as they are now designed. Therefore the Department of Transportation, through the 1974 amendments to the Urban Mass Transportation Act (UMTA), has become involved in much experimentation to attempt to make public transportation available to disabled persons. The Summer 1975 issue of *Accent on Living,* a publication disseminating information to disabled persons, surveyed the transportation scene and described what the government is doing to explore the problem and to fund demonstration projects offering solutions. For example, small buses outfitted with hydraulic lifts and handrails are available in a few communities for trips to medical, social, or employment destinations. Demonstration projects are testing vehicles of different sizes; various operating techniques such as subscription services, dial-a-ride, and two-way radios; and new types of marketing methods, fare structures, and cost-sharing plans. In 1975, $1 billion was available under UMTA on an 80:20 match ratio, and it is hoped that local governments will assume responsibility for furthering this work.

Because of a long history of passively accepting isolation and second-class citizenship, most disabled people are not demanding transportation. Until there are places to go and reasons to go to them, transportation systems, although specially equipped, may be underutilized. On the other hand, participation in the community is not possible if there is no way to get around. There is a necessity for the concurrent development of both a broader scope of living for the disabled person and an adaptation of transportation methods.

In the meantime controversy clouds the issues and frustrates everyone. One group of disabled persons appears to implore the city governments to invest in specialized transportation equipment, while another group states that it would not use such a system. A transit system attempting to aid blind passengers by designating a special area for seating blind persons with guide dogs is attacked as discriminating. Some wheelchair-bound persons resent having the wheelchair strapped into a vehicle, while others want to be very sure such precautions are taken.

There is overwhelming evidence that the entire public will need to reexamine attitudes about transportation in the light of operational costs, fuel shortages, and problems of pollution. The additional problem of meeting the transportation needs of the poor, young, elderly, and disabled is a challenge whose solution will depend upon the efforts of the disabled and their friends as well as leaders in human services fields.

(For a discussion of driver training and special controls, see CHAPTER 5: INDEPENDENT LIVING: WAYS AND MEANS.)

SELECTED REFERENCES

Accent on Living, Transportation for the Disabled Issue, P.O. Box 700, Bloomington, IL 61701, Summer 1975.

Bray, Peter, and Don M. Cunningham, "Vehicles for the Severely Disabled," *Rehabilitation Literature,* April 1967.

De Benedictis, J. A., *A Directory of Vehicles and Related Systems Components for the Elderly and Handicapped,* Department of Transportation, Urban Mass Transportation Administration, Washington, DC 20590.

Michaels, R. M., and N. S. Weiler, *Transportation Needs of the Mobility Limited,* Northeastern Illinois Planning Commission, 10 S. Riverside Plaza, Chicago, IL 60606.

Performance, Transportation Issue, President's Committee on Employment of the Handicapped, August 1974.

Transportation for the Handicapped: A Bibliography, Department of Transportation, Library Services Division, Washington, DC 20590.

Urban Mass Transportation Act of 1964 and Related Laws Amended through November 26, 1974, Department of Transportation, Washington, DC 20590.

12

Legislation and Consumer Rights:
A. Federal and State Laws

WILLIAM DUSSAULT, J.D., Seattle, and LEE A. CARTY,
Director of Development, Mental Health Law Project,
Washington, D.C.

For the past hundred years, indifference and neglect have characterized attitudes toward handicapped persons in the United States,
and those who have tried to function in the mainstream of society
have met with outright discrimination. The presence of disability—
especially mental disability or obvious physical deformity—has
historically generated anxiety among "normal" persons ("There,
but for the grace of God, go I"). Modern society has tended to deal
with this anxiety by segregating the disabled in the name of benign
paternalism. State institutions were built to provide ostensibly
helpful (often custodial) services, usually as far as possible from
population centers. But little attention was paid to developing alternatives in housing, education, public transportation, employment, or any other aspects of community living that most nondisabled citizens take for granted.

Before the 1970s, most social policy changes of benefit to handicapped persons came about through efforts by organizations of parents or friends of persons with similar types of disabilities. The
National Association for Retarded Children (now Citizens), the
National Association for Mental Health (now the Mental Health
Association), and the National Federation for the Blind, for example, lobbied vigorously in the 1960s for piecemeal legislation.
Federal laws began to reflect their emphasis, authorizing funds for
the construction of community-based facilities for care, treatment,
and rehabilitation—for example, the 1963 Community Mental
Health Centers Act (P.L. 88-164)—and expanding entitlements for

handicapped persons in amendments to the Social Security Act (notably Medicaid), Elementary and Secondary Education Act, and Vocational Rehabilitation Act.

During the 1970s, a new focus developed, based on the recognition that citizens who are handicapped—whether as a result of mental retardation, physical disability, or sensory impairment—have the same legal rights as all other citizens. The recent assault on societal attitudes and policies has employed two principal weapons: test-case litigation and legislation.

Landmark lawsuits have established a number of basic rights which pertain specifically to disabled persons: the right to education, the right to be free from discrimination in employment and public accommodations, the right to fair and impartial classification, the right to suitable treatment (and to receive it in the least restrictive setting consistent with individual need), the right to vote, the right to live in the community, and other basic tenets of citizenship, all of which nonhandicapped persons usually fail to consider because their rights in these areas are rarely threatened. (For some of the significant cases and their effects, see CHAPTER 13: ADVOCACY.)

Recent legislation not only provides for services to handicapped persons, but it also recognizes their rights as citizens and sets forth concrete methods for vindication of these rights through entitlements, service programs, and individual enforcement actions. These statutes thereby provide a base for overall change.

Education

Perhaps the most important early victories were obtained in the area of education. In 1971 only sixteen states had enacted mandatory education for handicapped children. Mandatory education requires local school districts to provide educational programming for all school-age children residing within district boundaries, regardless of handicap. In the space of five years, thirty-two additional states adopted mandatory education as a result of judicial rulings that all handicapped children must receive appropriate education at public expense.

Most of the legal underpinning for the right to education can be found in the United States Supreme Court decision, *Brown v. Board of Education* (347 U.S. 483 [1954]). Of course, the *Brown* case had nothing to do with handicapped students per se; the issue was, rather, the education of racial minorities in segregated as opposed to integrated schools. However, the doctrines and dictums set down in that historic ruling are as true for handicapped students today as they were (and still are) for students within a racial minority. As Chief Justice Earl Warren stated: "Education is perhaps the most important function of state and local governments. It is the very foundation of good citizenship . . . the principal instrument in . . . helping [the child] to adjust normally to his environment. In these days, it is doubtful that any child may reasonably be expected to succeed in life if he is denied the opportunity of an education."

On November 28, 1975, President Gerald Ford signed into law the Education for All Handicapped Children Act (P.L. 94-142), calling for a sharply increased federal commitment to assist states in educating handicapped youngsters. The bill was four years in development in Congress, where testimony revealed that fewer than half of an estimated 8 million school-age children with disabilities were receiving appropriate educational services. The act finally won overwhelming endorsement, with the House of Representatives approving the Conference Report by a vote of 404 to 7 and the Senate by 87 to 7. It sets out a formula of entitlements to states to provide education appropriate to the handicapping condition of each child. Past history showed Congress that school districts tended to ignore the most severely handicapped children. Therefore, priorities were set, directing implementation of the new act first to those children currently unserved, and next to those whose educational needs are inadequately met by existing programs. In order to qualify for federal assistance under the act by September 1, 1978, states must provide education for all handicapped children between ages three and eighteen and, by September 1, 1980, for all between three and twenty-one. The law also sets out due-process provisions to allow a means for appealing placement in programs thought to be inappropriate for a child's particular handicap. Sanctions include withholding of federal funds to the state or to local education agencies when compliance is deficient.

These legislative advancements at the state and federal levels were won against a backdrop of test-case litigation which established not a constitutional right to education, but a right to due-process protections in relation to educational classification or exclusion from publicly supported educational systems. The key suits have been *Pennsylvania Association for Retarded Children v. Pennsylvania* (334 F. Supp. 1257 [E.D. Pa. 1971]), known as the "PARC case," and *Mills v. Board of Education* (348 F. Supp. 866 [D.D.C. 1972]).

The PARC case established for the first time that mentally retarded children, regardless of the severity of handicap, had the right to an appropriate educational opportunity at public expense and, further, that they had the right to appeal the placement provided by a school if it was believed inappropriate or inadequate. Though settled by a consent decree, the PARC case sent shock waves across the country in the area of special education. The *Mills* case, brought by the Mental Health Law Project a year later, made solid legal precedent when the federal court ruled that not only mentally retarded children but all handicapped children — whether the disability was due to alleged mental, behavioral, physical, or emotional disability or deficiency — had a right to education. The court found that "due process of law requires a hearing prior to exclusion, termination [or] classification into a special program," and ordered the local government to plan for and develop constitutionally adequate educational placements. Since the PARC and *Mills* cases, there have been right-to-education suits brought in more than half of the states, and in each instance the court has upheld the right of the handicapped child to appropriate education at public expense. (See CHAPTER 6: EDUCATIONAL PROGRAMS.)

Discrimination

Another federal legislative recognition of the rights of handicapped persons, the Rehabilitation Act of 1973 (P.L. 93-112 as amended by P.L. 93-516), may ultimately be even more important in giving stronger sanctions to enforce the right to education (such as the threat of withholding *all* federal assistance to a state's educational system), as well as to improving the condition of handicapped persons in a variety of daily living situations. Sections 503 and 504, respectively, call for affirmative-action programs in hiring and prohibit discrimination on the basis of mental or physical handicap by all programs and facilities receiving federal assistance, including schools, universities, libraries, community health and mental health centers.

Originally, Section 504 was proposed as an amendment to the Civil Rights Act of 1964, and it gives handicapped persons similar protections. While by circumstance appended to the "Voc-Rehab" Act, Section 504 broadens the definition of the term "handicapped individual" to include a person "mislabeled" as handicapped as well as anyone with a substantial limitation to functioning in one or more major life activities; the definition is thus not limited to any specific handicap in relation to employment, vocational objectives, or potential benefits from vocational rehabilitation services.

However, there has been an inordinate delay in administrative enforcement of Section 504. As a result of pressure brought by groups representing handicapped individuals (including a lawsuit, *Cherry v. Mathews;* see CHAPTER 13: ADVOCACY), the Secretary of Health, Education and Welfare published proposed regulations (41 F.R. 29548 [July 16, 1976]), which elicited extensive public comment and congressional and administrative legislative revision. Given the concern that compliance could be costly, especially in terms of special programs and architectural refinements to make facilities accessible, detailed inflationary-impact studies were required. They demonstrated that the benefit in increased taxable earning power of handicapped persons would outweigh the expense of bringing federally assisted facilities into compliance. Nevertheless, by early fall of 1977 neither the outgoing nor the incoming administration had promulgated final regulations for implementation of Section 504.

Several states have also taken an aggressive stance in providing discrimination protection for handicapped citizens. For instance, in the Revised Code of Washington (Chap. 49.60, Sect. 49.60.010):

The legislature hereby finds and declares that practices of discrimination against any of its inhabitants because of race, creed, color, national origin, sex, marital status, age or *the presence of any sensory, mental, or physical handicap* are a matter of concern, that such discrimination threatens not only the rights and proper privileges of its inhabitants but menaces the institutions and foundations of the free democratic state [emphasis added].

This section goes on to state that the right to be free from discrimination is recognized and declared to be a civil right, including but not limited to the right to obtain employment without discrimination; the right to full enjoyment of any accommodations, advantages, facilities, or privileges of any place of public resort, accommodation, assemblage, or amusement; and the right to engage in real-estate, credit, or insurance transactions without discrimination.

New Jersey has also passed legislation proscribing discrimination against the physically handicapped (1972 amendment to New Jersey P.L. 1945, C. 169, [C. 10:5-5]). This state is unusually aggressive in protecting the rights of handicapped persons through its unique independent Department of the Public Advocate. A conciliation of more than $4,000, made through the state's Department of Law and Public Safety Division on Civil Rights, between the American Smelting and Refinery Company of Cranford and an epileptic employee terminated as a result of his epilepsy was most likely the first instance of a monetary victory by a handicapped person against private industry.

Enforcement

Such broad federal and state declarations of civil rights offer great encouragement to handicapped consumers. But few states have taken such diligent enforcement action as New Jersey, and there is too little public awareness of protections under either state or federal law. While intrinsically an inefficient mechanism for long-range social change, individual litigation on a case-by-case basis remains the primary tool for enforcement.

A major legislative reform passed by Congress in late 1976 may increase the incidence and effectiveness of legal advocacy on behalf of handicapped persons. The Civil Rights Attorney Fees Act (P.L. 94-559) authorizes federal courts to award reasonable attorneys' fees to a prevailing party in cases arising under certain civil rights statutes [specifically, 42 U.S.C. §§1981, 1982, 1983, 1985, 1986, and 2000 (d), generally prohibiting denial of civil and constitutional rights in such areas as employment, housing, and contractual relationships] and the Internal Revenue Code. Most private attorneys have been understandably reluctant to undertake complicated and potentially lengthy lawsuits seeking to vindicate the civil rights of handicapped persons, and legal-service lawyers have been overburdened with a huge load of poverty-law cases. With the carrot of attorneys' fees added to the stick of stronger statutory causes of action, it seems likely that increased individual litigation (or its threat) will hasten compliance with new federal antidiscrimination legislation on all levels.

Other provisions in new federal legislation may help in a similar fashion. Independent state advocacy systems are an important requirement of the 1975 Developmental Disabilities Assistance and Bill of Rights Act (see CHAPTER 13: ADVOCACY). They are expected to ensure implementation of the act's requirements of minimum standards for least restrictive facilities and appropriate services for developmentally disabled persons. As with the Education for All Handicapped Children Act, lack of compliance can bring about cutoff of federal assistance to state and local programs. While for many large states this sanction may be of negligible impact in a single programmatic area, if applied across various programs and in umbrella legislation such as Section 504, and if enforced through increasingly sophisticated litigation, the potential aggregate loss of federal monies to state and local budgets could wield significant clout.

Guardianship

Some other areas of individual civil rights pertain to particular subgroups of handicapped persons rather than to the general population. With regard to mentally handicapped adults, seldom recognized is the right to be treated as competent and emancipated unless proved to be incompetent. Far too often state law presumes absolute incompetence on the part of a person under civil commitment to an institution. Inmates are thereby deprived of a spectrum of rights, from the right to vote to the capacity for assisting in their own treatment or rehabilitation decisions. The wholesale presumption of incompetency that follows the labeling of an individual as mentally retarded is even more distressing. While some device is often needed to assist mentally disabled persons who are substantially incapacitated, this device must relate to the specific area of handicap — in financial matters, for instance — and should take into account the pride and dignity of a mentally handicapped person who has some ability in other areas.

A traditional judicial tool for dealing with persons who are in some degree incompetent to handle their "persons or estates" is guardianship or conservatorship. Historically, guardianship has been utilized paternalistically by someone desiring to provide legal protection and assistance for another, less able individual. In most states, the area of guardianship has no due-process protections, few burden-of-proof requirements, and substantial procedural and substantive abuses. An article by Robert J. Hodgson in *Albany Law Review* (vol. 37, no. 3, 1973), "Guardianship of Mentally Retarded Persons: Three Approaches to a Long Neglected Problem," sets forth the main obstacles. Too often, in order to provide any of the protections associated with guardianship, the proposed ward is determined to be totally legally incompetent. Thereupon, the ward loses the majority of his or her legal rights and becomes for most purposes a "nonperson." Only the declarations of the guardian have any legal bearing.

Some states, notably New York, Colorado, West Virginia, Washington and, recently, California, have taken steps to remedy the problem. Washington law (Revised Code of Washington, Chaps. 11: 88 and 11:92 as amended by Chap. 95, Laws of 1975) is perhaps the most progressive in the country. While recognizing the due-process rights of the allegedly incompetent or disabled ward and providing substantial protection for those rights, the law allows for protection of the individual in the specific area of incompetency. In *The Rights of Mentally Retarded Persons* (Avon Books, New York, 1976), Paul Friedman describes application of the least-restrictive-alternative principle to guardianship, which "has led to creation both of specialized forms of guardianship," such as "guardians of the estate" (dealing with the management of property and income), "guardians of the person" (dealing with the right to determine where and how the ward shall live), and guardians *ad litem* (that is, appointed for the specific purpose of conducting litigation on behalf of their wards). Friedman adds, "On a continuum, guardianship can be viewed as a less restrictive alternative to institutionalization." However, "Experts argue that neither institutionalization nor guardianship are necessary for most mentally retarded persons if there are adequate supportive social services to expand the range of choices in areas like housing, employment and education, along with adequate personal-support services in such areas as homemaking and money management." Therefore, an advocate may be a better choice than a guardian, "both to create pressure for better social-service programs for his client and to help his client to locate and secure access to existing services" without the control (and concurrent loss of dignity) inherent in guardianship.

Accessibility

For the physically handicapped, accessibility is a matter of vital importance. Virtually none of the rights mentioned earlier can be enjoyed by physically handicapped citizens if they have no practical access to the community. It is all very well to say that a handicapped person has a right to be free from discrimination in public accommodations, but there are no fully accessible public transportation facilities anywhere in the United States. Several communities have attempted to provide a few buses forming a demand-related transportation system, as in Denver. The one possible exception could be the Washington, D.C., subway system, now under construction. A lawsuit has resulted in an order calling for accessibility to all stations and trains for handicapped persons (*Urban League v. WMATA*, Civil No. 776-72 [D.D.C., plaintiffs' motion for summary judgment granted October 9, order issued October 24, 1973]). The Federal Urban Mass Transportation Act of 1972 provides that in order to acquire the 80 percent federal match monies available to a metropolitan transportation system, special provisions must be made for handicapped citizens in the purchase of new transportation equipment. Unfortunately, "special provisions" do not necessarily equal full accessibility. Lifts, ramps, or other devices to make buses accessible to persons with wheelchairs, walkers, crutches, or canes, or to persons with limited mobility, are simply not required. The life of the average metropolitan bus is about twenty years. Therefore, currently inadequate standards seem to be programming continued inaccessibility for another two decades.

Major metropolitan transit systems have been assailed in the last two years with suits to provide greater accessibility, both under the Urban Mass Transit Act and state antidiscrimination laws (see Seattle, *Martin v. Metro;* San Francisco, *Bohlke v. Golden Gate Bridge Highway and Transportation District;* Birmingham, *Snowden v. Birmingham–Jefferson County Transit Authority).* One of the standard rebuttals to considerations of transportation accessibility is that the cost is prohibitive in the context of such a small segment of the population as the disabled. But that population may not be so small. A 1972 Department of Transportation study of the needs of the handicapped and elderly indicates that as many as 20 percent of the total population may need special assistance in public transportation.

Even if transportation were made accessible today, physically handicapped citizens might still be unable to make use of it. They might be unable to leave houses or apartments built with stairs. Without help, they could not get past curbs or into most business buildings, and once inside they could not use rest rooms, telephones, escalators, water fountains, or other conveniences that "normal" people take for granted. "Movement, we are told, is a law of animal life; as to man in any event, nothing could be more essential to personality, social existence, economic opportunity – in short, to individual well-being and integration into the life of the community – than the physical capacity, the public approval and the legal right to be abroad in the land" (Jacobus tenBroek, "The Right to Live in the World: The Disabled and the Law of Torts," 54 *California Law Review* 841 [1966]).

While both the Federal Architectural Barriers Act of 1968, as revised (42 U.S.C. §§4151–4156 [1970]), and similar laws in every state require that architectural barriers be eliminated in most new construction and many types of renovation, enforcement is generally weak. Architects, planners, and developers continue to construct old "standard" door frames, stairways, and other barriers to mobility for the physically handicapped – defending their rigidity on grounds of economy (even though actual cost increments for accessibility at the new-construction stage are less than 1 percent). Therefore, the legal right to travel freely is routinely denied to many handicapped persons. (See also "Abroad in the Land: Legal Strategies to Effectuate the Rights of the Physically Disabled," *Georgetown Law Journal,* vol. 61:1501, and Jack Achtenberg, "'Crips' Unite to Enforce Symbolic Laws: Legal Aid for the Disabled—An Overview," *University of San Fernando Law Review*, vol 4, no. 2, Fall 1975.)

Entitlements and Social Services

The foregoing is merely an overview of some of the important recent federal legislation designed to help disabled persons attain maximum self-sufficiency. Unfortunately, for lack of enforcement, these laws are still in large measure merely statements of policy based on the newly perceived constitutional rights of handicapped persons. Also of recent vintage, through amendments of the 1970s, are a growing range of federal entitlement programs which offer financial assistance and social welfare benefits to mentally and physically disabled persons: Social Security disability insurance, Supplemental Security Income (SSI), Aid to Families with Dependent Children (AFDC), Medicare and Medicaid, and benefits for military personnel and their families under the Civilian Health and Medical Program of the Uniformed Services (CHAMPUS). However, the way to claiming benefits under these programs is often blocked with red tape; in some states, consumer groups have set up citizen advocacy systems to help disabled persons apply for and receive these personal entitlements. There are also a number of federally funded programs which support services for disabled persons. Two of the most important are the Vocational Rehabilitation Program, administered in each state by a Department of Vocational Rehabilitation, and the range of social services programs (such as work-activities and day-care centers) provided by each state with funds under Title XX of the Social Security Act.

Most of the new legislation is based on recognition of the rights of the disabled as consumers rather than "alms seekers." Now it will take the aggressive action of the consumers themselves, their advocates, and their attorneys to enforce these laws and expand the legal rights of disabled persons. This process has already begun. On January 21, 1977, a consortium of thirteen organizations representing handicapped consumers (signers of the letter are consumer and public-interest advocacy organizations: the American Coalition of Citizens with Disabilities, American Council of the Blind, American Foundation for the Blind, Association of Rehabilitation Facilities, Children's Defense Fund, Council for Exceptional Children, Education Law Center, Epilepsy Foundation of America, Mental Health Law Project, National Association of the Deaf, National Association of the Physically Handicapped, National Association for Retarded Citizens, and United Cerebral Palsy Associations) wrote to the incoming Secretary of Health, Education and Welfare to demand as a first order of business of the new administration the final promulgation of the long-delayed regulations to implement Section 504 of the Rehabilitation Act. In addition to the Action League for Physically Handicapped Adults, plaintiff in the case which placed the outgoing Secretary under a court order to release the regulations, the list of these groups illustrates a new activism among disabled persons themselves. Just as ethnic and racial minorities achieved meaningful success in vindicating their rights only when they joined fully in their own advocacy, so this next stage in the fight for full citizenship may add functional gains to theoretical victories for handicapped persons. As other minorities have learned, it is a long and difficult battle, never fully won. But dignity and self-determination are the prize, and they are worth the extraordinary effort.

SELECTED REFERENCES

Barrier Free Site Design, U.S. Department of Housing and Urban Development, Office of Policy Development and Research, 1975.

Federal Laws and Regulations Affecting the Handicapped, National Association of Coordinators of State Programs for the Mentally Retarded, annual.

Law Reform Project, Ohio State University, *Zoning for Community Change: A Handbook for Local Legislative Change; Zoning for Community Homes: A Handbook for Municipal Officials*, 1976.

The Legal Rights of Persons with Epilepsy, Epilepsy Foundation of America, 1976.

Mental Health Law Project, *Mental Health Legislative Guide*, produced under contract with the National Institute of Mental Health, 1977.

NARC's Government Report, Governmental Affairs Office, National Association for Retarded Citizens, monthly.

Programs for the Handicapped, Office for Handicapped Individuals, Department of Health, Education and Welfare, monthly.

A *Summary of Selected Legislation Relating to the Handicapped*, Office of Human Development, Department of Health, Education and Welfare, annual.

UCPA Legislative Priorities for Action: A Status Report on the 94th Congress 2nd Session, 1976, United Cerebral Palsy Associations Governmental Activities Office.

Weintraub, F., A. Abeson, and D. Braddock, *State Law & Education of Handicapped Children: Issues and Recommendations*, Council for Exceptional Children, 1972.

Word from Washington, a newsletter issued jointly by United Cerebral Palsy Associations, Epilepsy Foundation of America, and National Society for Autistic Children.

B. Consumer Rights for the Disabled

FRANK BOWE, Ph.D., Director, American Coalition of
Citizens with Disabilities, Washington, D.C.

As Frank Bowe points out below, the disabled have always depended on others to speak for them. This situation arose largely for two reasons: first, many disabled people accepted the prejudicial image which society foisted on them — that they did not have the capacity to think or act for themselves; and second, they lacked organizations through which their voices could be heard and their demands met. Both of these situations are now being rectified, and within a relatively short period of time an entirely new and highly promising development has gathered force: the disabled consumer rights movement.

This movement has provided much of the impetus for the legislation summarized in the first part of this chapter, and for the litigation reported in the following chapter on advocacy. As a bridge between these two chapters, it is appropriate — indeed, essential — to focus on the consumer rights movement itself by presenting an article by Frank Bowe on the new militancy of the disabled and a brief account by Lilly Bruck of one of the rights that has been almost totally neglected to date.

Although disabled individuals and groups are speaking for themselves with an ever stronger voice, they are rarely attempting to "go it alone," but are working with advocacy organizations, committees, and individuals who are genuinely concerned about their interests and rights. In an article published in *Amicus* for May 1976, Marie L. Moore, National Advocacy Coordinator of United Cerebral Palsy Associations, has identified the following types of workers and services: Case, or individual, advocacy is carried out by (1) the citizen advocate, who is a volunteer member of a Citizen Advocacy Board of a private association or agency; (2) the ombudsman, who is a member of an advocacy council of a private agency or a State Human Rights Commission; (3) the legal advocate, who may be connected with an agency; (4) the case manager advocate, who is a member of a public or private agency which ensures that adequate service is being provided; and (5) protective services such as guardianship and trusteeship which are mandated by legislation and carried out by a state board or council. Class, or group, advocacy consists of (1) legislative advocacy, in which representatives of consumer organizations use the legislative process to mandate changes and secure rights for the disabled; (2) community organization advocacy, in which community or statewide planning groups, consumer advocacy groups, and the disabled themselves work for increased communication and cooperation between agencies; (3) program brokerage, in which consumer representatives work with governmental and private agencies to seek expanded services and to remove barriers to program development; (4) protective services, in which a state board or council provides guardianship and other advocacy services; and (5) consumer action advocacy, in which independent organizations and consumer committees act as pressure groups to effect desired changes in such areas as treatment and care, education, transportation, trusteeship, removal of environmental barriers, and opportunities for housing.

[ROBERT M. GOLDENSON]

When the U.S. Department of Transportation made accessibility in public transit buses optional rather than mandatory, twelve groups of disabled people went to court contesting the decision. Five months later, in December 1976, a coalition of disabled leaders held a press conference at the entrance of a Washington, D.C. subway station to protest its reopening after having been closed as inaccessible by a federal judge. And on his last day in office as Secretary of the U.S. Department of Health, Education and Welfare (HEW), David Mathews was under court order to sign regulations affecting disabled people. The order was temporarily suspended just two hours before midnight. On Joseph Califano's first day after confirmation as Mathews's successor, disabled activists brought the regulations to his attention and requested his signature. These regulations were designed to carry out Section 504 of the Rehabilitation Act of 1973, which has been called the "Bill of Rights" for disabled people:

> No otherwise qualified handicapped individual in the United States, as defined in Section 7 (6), shall, solely by reason of his handicap be excluded from participation in, be denied the benefits of, or be subjected to discrimination under any program or activity receiving Federal financial assistance.

Action on these regulations had been held up for over three and a half years, and was again postponed to give the new administration a chance to review them. Finally, after another series of delays, organizations belonging to the American Coalition of Citizens with Disabilities held sit-in protests in the Washington office of HEW and in regional offices in ten other cities—and on April 28, 1977, HEW Secretary Califano signed the regulations, which in his words would "usher in a new era of equality for handicapped individuals."

Are disabled people becoming radical? What do they want? Why are they joining together now to plead for their own causes? Disabled people have been excluded from the mainstream of American life for more than 200 years. The reasons for their exclusion offer answers to the questions which their growing militancy raises.

Secluded Settings

The first programs serving disabled people in the United States were established in the early 1800s. As institutions providing custodial and educational services for mentally retarded and deaf children and youth, the programs were also instruments of a society that wanted to keep disabled people out of sight and out of mind. Together with often inferior education, this imposed isolation kept disabled people out of the community and rendered them politically powerless. Equally important, their isolation meant that community construction and program planning went forward with little or no consideration for their needs. Indeed, the more removed from the everyday lives of community residents disabilities became, the more frightening and threatening these conditions seemed. This led to discriminatory laws banning marriage, forbidding children, and denying the right to vote. Throughout the late 1800s and early 1900s, disabled people were becoming more, not less, removed from society.

It took a war to halt the backward slide and inaugurate the first tentative steps toward equality for disabled Americans. Veterans returning from World War I often came back with arms amputated, eyes blinded, or ears with seriously impaired function. A new program of vocational rehabilitation was designed to help these veterans train for new occupations. Gradually, concern spread to children and others with more long-standing disabilities, and special education came into its own as a field of human service. Then, during World War II, with tens of thousands of workers drafted into the armed forces, disabled individuals were given an opportunity to demonstrate that, as they had often contended, it was ability, not disability, that counted. They proved this by successfully taking over jobs on the home front. Yet after the war the jobs were returned to the able-bodied workers and the disabled individuals were again displaced. In part to compensate for this, but more to assist returning veterans who had become disabled, the Vocational Rehabilitation Program was expanded considerably and began to take on much of its present character as a nationwide federal-state program combining medical services, education, and job placement.

Between the two world wars, social clubs of disabled people had emerged in unprecedented numbers throughout the country. The gradual growth of special education and rehabilitation had helped prepare hundreds of thousands of disabled people for employment, and this in turn had increased their involvement in community activities and their awareness of injustices perpetrated upon them because of their disabilities. These social and recreational functions served to bring disabled people together and permitted them to discuss their mutual problems and concerns. Yet, because they were few in number and their members relatively inexperienced in social activism, they met with little success. The accelerated growth of rehabilitation and special education that followed World War II increased the awareness of many disabled adults and helped produce state and national organizations.

Throughout the 1950s and 1960s, however, these groups remained focused upon single disabilities and continued to be relatively ineffective. The civil rights struggle of ethnic minority groups, and later the consciousness-raising efforts of women, inspired disabled people to join together across disabilities in an attempt to finally end 200 years of exclusion and second-class citizenship.

A Coalition

The Rehabilitation Act of 1973 contained historic measures benefiting disabled people, including the first provisions of basic civil rights protection ever proposed on their behalf. President Richard Nixon vetoed the measure twice, and in an attempt to secure an override of his vetoes disabled people at last came together. Soon after the act became law, they convened in Washington to establish formally the coalition that had successfully lobbied for the override. In April 1974, 150 disabled adults formed the American Coalition of Citizens with Disabilities, Inc. (ACCD). The Coalition, as it was called, has since concentrated its efforts upon securing implementation and enforcement of the Rehabilitation Act and other vital legislation which promises to enhance the human and civil rights of disabled people. ACCD has continued to grow and now numbers among its organizational members such pivotal groups as the American Council of the Blind, National Association of the Deaf, National Association of the Physically Handicapped, National Paraplegia

139

Foundation, Paralyzed Veterans of America, and Teletypewriters for the Deaf, as well as several national organizations that serve disabled people, such as the Epilepsy Foundation of America, National Association for Retarded Citizens, and United Cerebral Palsy Associations. The Coalition has concentrated its work on areas of concern to all disabled Americans and has been successful in bringing different groups of disabled people together to protect and obtain basic human and civil rights. It joined the suit against the Department of Transportation over public transit accessibility, for example, and led the fight to get the regulations for Section 504 of the Rehabilitation Act of 1973 signed. Its press conference at Gallery Place in Washington over the inaccessible subway station, and its role in forging consumer involvement for disabled people in the Carter administration are other instances of its work.

No, disabled people are not yet becoming radical. To use the courts and the press as forums for civil rights advocacy after extensive efforts through channels have proved unsuccessful in securing basic protection for disabled people is far less radical than much of the strident demonstrating minority-group members and women have used to gain their rights. What disabled people seek today is monumentally simple: the right to an education, to access to public transportation and public buildings, to employment, to housing, and to health care. And they are achieving these basic rights gradually in a peaceful and dignified manner.

Their progress, recent as it is, reflects the basic appropriateness of their conviction that they must now speak for themselves. In the past women have spoken for women, Blacks for Blacks, and Indians for Indians. By contrast, children and disabled people have always relied on others to be their representatives. Disabled adults have begun to chart their own directions and forge their own places in modern American society. Their quiet legal approaches are working, and as long as this remains true, militancy will not be necessary. But there are already those who are impatient for progress. In Washington, New York City, and San Francisco, small groups of disabled adults are beginning to talk about mass demonstrations, picketing, and office takeovers. Whether they are right that only through militant protests will their rights be secured, or whether the more conservative segments of the disabled community are correct that working within the system is the appropriate way, only time will tell. The past two decades have witnessed free speech in Berkeley, busing in Selma, and bra-burning in Miami. Will the next decade see wheelchairs blocking doors and stairways in protest across the nation?

C. Disabled Consumer Bill of Rights

LILLY BRUCK, Ph.D., Director of Education, New York
City Department of Consumer Affairs

In 1962 President John Kennedy proclaimed a "Consumer Bill of Rights": the right to be informed, the right to safety, the right to choose, and the right to be heard. In 1975 President Gerald Ford added the right to consumer education. Needed now is a "Disabled Consumer Bill of Rights": the right to *access* for the mobility-impaired; the right to *information* for the vision-impaired; the right to *communication* for the hearing-impaired; and the right to *consideration* for the mentally impaired.

Increasing numbers of disabled persons, freed by medical technology and vocational rehabilitation from lives of dependence and isolation, make the disabled community a growing presence in today's society. This minority is pushing for housing, employment, quality education, and other rights of first-class citizenship. Recent and pending legislation extends to disabled persons many of the antidiscrimination protections accorded to other minorities.

As consumers, citizens with disabilities are entitled to equality in the marketplace. Whether limited in mobility or impaired in sight or hearing, consumers are deprived of their rights when environmental and attitudinal barriers deprive them of access, information, and communication.

There are two sides to the needs of consumers with disabilities: (1) equipment and services for disability-related needs; and (2) goods and services related to their nondisabled selves, that is, goods and services which everybody consumes, but which cost the disabled more because they are denied advantages available to other shoppers.

In the purchase of goods and services for special needs, comparison shopping, an elementary precaution preceding a purchase, is difficult or impossible for some disabled consumers. Availability of information on cost and delivery over the telephone should be required by local legislation, as well as some supervision, by registration or licensing, over suppliers of medical devices and their conditions for repair and service. Inflated prices, due to payment by third parties (such as Medicaid, the Office of Vocational Rehabilitation, or insurance) for unconscionably high charges without a dispute, make customers who are self-supporting and work for a living pay twice: once in excessive cost and again in their tax dollars that go to Medicaid and other government agencies. Some control over suppliers and increased accountability of third-party payers would alleviate the situation.

In the purchase of goods and services related to their nondisabled selves, mobility-impaired consumers suffer from lack of accessibility; the visually impaired are disadvantaged by lack of information; and the hearing-impaired not only are denied person-to-person communication, but are even deprived of all the messages advertisers and consumer educators send over the airways.

In doing research for *Consumer Rights for Disabled Citizens* (1976), the New York City Department of Consumer Affairs sent questionnaires to airlines, banks, department stores, and supermarkets. Questions were specific—relating to the width of doors and aisles and the accessibility of dressing rooms and rest rooms; how information was disseminated to the visually impaired; how communication was handled with the hearing-impaired; and what staff orientation toward disabled consumers was given and what accommodations were available to them. Responses were received from seven out of ten airlines, but from only two out of ten banks, five out of nineteen department stores, and eight out of twenty-six supermarket chains. This majority of "no-shows" seems to indicate the general lack of concern of business for the needs of the disabled.

The submitted questionnaires, summary of responses, and names of responders and no-shows are published in the book, preceded by an introduction:

> It will be up to the disabled community to effect changes, to demand accommodations and to vote with their shopping dollars for those merchants who cooperate, giving customers with disabilities equal access to their services.
>
> We'd like to make a suggestion: use the questionnaires on the following pages to evaluate your suppliers of goods and services from your own point of view: positive points—your banking, shopping, traveling will be made easier; negative points—remember that competition is the lifeblood of American business and the assurance of service for the consumer!

The extraordinarily enthusiastic reception of this book, locally and nationally, confirms the thesis that citizens with disabilities want to be recognized as consumers. They want to spend their shopping dollars where business accommodates and welcomes them as customers.

While federal, state, and local laws relating to access to public buildings may not yet apply to privately owned establishments, places used by the public, such as stores, markets, and any public business place, should be accessible to all the public, with no exceptions. And accessibility is not enough: where there are rest rooms, at least one for each sex should be suited to use by shoppers in wheelchairs; where there are water fountains, at least one should be low enough to reach from a wheelchair; and at least one public telephone should permit the use of a hearing aid via magnetic spillover.

Public pressure and the recognition of the profit potential from a new market segment may influence private enterprise, but a more effective means would be to make what is presently required in publicly funded buildings mandatory in privately owned but open-to-the-public buildings—or at least in those of a certain size or those doing a certain volume of business. What must be achieved, and quickly, is a marketplace where there are no second-class citizens. The disabled community will have to insist on their rights — in the public and in the private sector of society.

13

Advocacy

LEE A. CARTY, Director of Development, Mental Health
Law Project, Washington, D.C.

In 1971, of the 5,000 residents of Bryce Hospital, a state psychiatric facility in Alabama, about 1,000 were mentally retarded and 1,600 were geriatric patients. The hospital was built in the 1850s. Filth and vermin prevailed, residents were often straitjacketed, and were physically abused by the staff and each other. The food budget was fifty cents per day per resident. There were only three medical doctors with some psychiatric training—no board-certified psychiatrists—and one psychologist with a Ph.D. to evaluate and treat all 5,000; there were no specialists in retardation or geriatrics. Most of the residents were confined against their will; many would spend decades—even their lives—in these circumstances.

These facts and more came out in expert testimony during a landmark class-action lawsuit, *Wyatt v. Stickney*.[1] They led a federal judge to enunciate the "right to treatment," the first of a series of basic constitutional rights of disabled Americans which have been defined in recent public-interest litigation.

With variations in the gruesome details, that was the picture at the majority of state mental hospitals in the United States. Jammed together in purely custodial surroundings were the violent (sometimes committed for criminal offenses), the aging (often there only for lack of other recourse for personal-care services), mentally

---

[1]*Wyatt v. Stickney*, 325 F. Supp. 781 (M.D. Ala. 1971), 334 F. Supp. 1341 (M.D. Ala. 1971), 344 F. Supp. 373, 387 (M.D. Ala. 1972), *aff'd in part, modified in part sub nom., Wyatt v. Aderholt*, 503 F. 2d 1305 (5th Cir. 1974).

retarded or autistic children and adults, persons with epilepsy, and even others whose presence at home was merely inconvenient (such as a troublesome adolescent or a wife who refused to grant her husband a divorce). State retardation facilities were no better.

Even with some increases in funding and attention in the years since 1971, in most states improvements have been merely cosmetic. But there is a significant trend, a new emphasis on advocacy, which may pave the way for real improvement in the public services available to the mentally and physically disabled. In hearings on the 1975 Developmental Disabilities Assistance and Bill of Rights Act, Senator Harrison Williams of New Jersey summed up congressional intent in adding strong advocacy provisions to new service-delivery legislation:

> All indications point toward little change, unless substantial legal and advocacy pressure is forthcoming. While much can be said about the lack of funds to improve conditions at these [public] institutions, at some point this country must draw the lines. The abuses are too commonplace to point at a single institution or a single abuse and say that it is an anomaly.[2]

Advocacy is generally defined as pleading the cause of another as if it were one's own. The various forms are loosely grouped into "case" and "class" advocacy.[3] Case advocacy usually involves representation of one individual by another—a lawyer or ombudsman, for example. Class advocacy, such as lobbying, public-interest litigation, and public-relations campaigns, may be performed by individuals or by groups acting on behalf of constituencies with a similar problem. (See CHAPTER 12: LEGISLATION AND CONSUMER RIGHTS, B. Consumer Rights for the Disabled.)

The civil-rights movement of the 1960s exemplified class advocacy, where a variety of activist groups spoke out on moral grounds for the rights of previously powerless racial and ethnic minorities. Basic rights to equality of opportunity were defined and enforcement tools were established by legislation. In the 1970s, public-interest organizations have sought protections for consumers—a group powerless by virtue of its inclusiveness—by using technological data to convince courts, legislatures, and administrative agencies.

In the context of the emerging advocacy on their behalf, disabled persons are both a traditionally underrepresented minority and "consumers" of health and habilitation services. Their powerlessness as a class is compounded by the effects of their disabilities and, often, their segregation from society in institutions or other "special" surroundings.

In the 1970s, class advocacy on behalf of the disabled has led to a new public awareness of their legal rights and to a backdrop of law

---

[2]Congressional Record S9362, June 3, 1975.
[3]A chart listing component activities within these categories has been developed by Marie L. Moore, National Advocacy Coordinator, United Cerebral Palsy Associations, Inc., 66 East 34th Street, New York, NY 10016.

on which case advocacy may be based. Much of this new body of law has evolved around issues primarily affecting so-called mentally ill and mentally retarded persons. In a paper prepared for the White House Conference on the Handicapped, "Advocacy for the Mentally Disabled" (1976), Wilson, Beyer, and Yudowitz cite the particular need of mentally disabled persons for advocacy because "the law is involved in a much more intrusive sense in the treatment of the mentally ill and mentally retarded than it is in the provision of other kinds of health services." While most medical treatment for physical illness is voluntary, both adults and children who are found incompetent may be committed to institutions or may, like ex-convicts, "lose substantial rights which those not so afflicted take for granted, such as the right to enter contracts, to join certain professions, to hold a driver's license or to vote."

Persons with certain physical disabilities suffer similar deprivation. They often end up in mental hospitals or retardation facilities. Cerebral palsy, epilepsy, and autism, along with mental retardation, have been designated as "developmental disabilities" for the purpose of federal assistance. The Developmental Disabilities Act covers conditions originating before the age of eighteen which will probably continue indefinitely and which substantially handicap a person in functioning normally in society.

This legislation goes beyond other federal laws for the protection or advancement of disabled persons (see CHAPTER 12: LEGISLATION AND CONSUMER RIGHTS) in actually mandating an independent system in every state "to protect and advocate the rights of persons with developmental disabilities."[4] These rights include both general rights enjoyed by all citizens and special rights that accrue by virtue of the disabling condition, enumerated in Section 111 of the act.

Other disabled populations may also win federal advocacy programs. In 1976, Rep. James J. Florio introduced a bill (H.R. 10827) calling for mental health advocacy programs in states receiving federal assistance under the Community Mental Health Centers Act. In 1975 Congress created a Commission for the Control of Epilepsy and Its Consequences under the Department of Health, Education and Welfare (HEW) to survey legislation required to fill gaps in research, prevention, identification, treatment, and rehabilitation of persons with epilepsy. In a paper prepared for the commission, John Niemitz of the Epilepsy Foundation of America discussed the concern that while epilepsy is covered under the Developmental Disabilities Act, state programs with a primary focus on the mentally retarded might neglect some of the special problems and characteristics of persons with epilepsy—frequent employment discrimination, for example. Advocacy programs might be distinctive also, said Niemitz, in that "most people with epilepsy

---

[4]Section 113 of Title II. Emphasizing the nature of advocacy—pleading another's cause "as if it were one's own" rather than paternalistically, Section 113 also lays down an essential criterion: state advocacy systems must be "independent of any State agency which provides treatment, services or habilitation."

are clearly able to plead their own cause," unlike most mentally retarded persons, and would therefore be more active participants in their own advocacy.

Such a flurry of planning and legislation "follows an era of unprecedented expansion of the constitutional and statutory right to counsel [of disabled persons subject to state intervention] and extraordinary reliance on the courts as agencies of reform," wrote Fred Cohen in the chapter on advocacy in *The Mentally Retarded Citizen and the Law* (Free Press, New York, 1976). He outlined similarities in advocacy needs of "persons assigned to the categories of 'sick,' 'bad,' or 'dependent-deprived' [who are] officially labeled as deviant and eligible for incarceration . . . The language varies with the process, but the underlying concerns and objectives spill over."

Calling for the development of effective case-advocacy systems, Cohen lists some of "the rights either won or currently being litigated on behalf of the mentally retarded—the rights to treatment and habilitation, education, fair classification, custody of children, compensation for institutional labor, and damages for a failure to treat— . . . a tribute to a small and dedicated group of attorneys" who have combined qualities of the civil rights and the consumer movements into a new kind of class advocacy. By systematic cooperation between specialized public-interest lawyers and mental health and retardation professionals, the mental health law movement has established a base of legal precedent for case advocacy by client-service attorneys. Moreover, the publicity surrounding trials and landmark court orders has aroused public concern for the human rights of the disabled, giving political legitimacy to both state and federal legislative reform efforts.

A pioneer in this movement has been the Mental Health Law Project, a nonprofit public-interest organization based in Washington, D.C. While other public-interest attorneys have won major court victories and the number of specialized legal advocates for the mentally and developmentally disabled is growing accordingly, a description of the Project's comprehensive litigation record illustrates most of the relevant issues.

Right to Treatment

The Project grew out of *Wyatt*, the first federal case to establish that persons confined against their will to public mental institutions and retardation facilities have a constitutional right to receive appropriate, individualized treatment or habilitation.[5] The federal court heard evidence of the abhorrent conditions at Bryce Hospital and Alabama's other institutions and ruled that "to deprive any citizen of his or her liberty upon the altruistic theory that the confinement

---

[5]"Treatment" was defined by the *Wyatt* court as the provision of such adequate and appropriate care as is necessary to give each committed person "a realistic opportunity to lead a more useful and meaningful life and to return to society." In regard to developmentally disabled persons, the "right to treatment" becomes the "right to habilitation." The term "habilitation" is used by services appropriate for mentally retarded individuals to increase skill or level of adjustment.

is for humane therapeutic reasons and then fail to provide adequate treatment violates the very fundamentals of due process" specified in the Fourteenth Amendment. But who could determine the nature of minimally adequate treatment and how could its provision be enforced?

To find answers, the judge asked several national organizations to serve as *amici curiae* (friends of the court), evaluating existing programs and working with both plaintiffs and defendants to draw up minimum standards in the context of "three fundamental conditions for adequate and effective treatment: [a] humane physical and psychological environment, [qualified staff] in numbers sufficient to administer adequate treatment," and individualized treatment plans. These "friends of the court" were the American Civil Liberties Union, American Orthopsychiatric Association, American Psychological Association, and American Association on Mental Deficiency. (When the case was appealed, the National Association for Mental Health and the National Association for Retarded Children also joined as *amici.*) The lawyers representing these professional and consumer groups knew how to get at the pertinent facts and how to present them to the court; the mental health and retardation experts knew what to look for and what services were needed.

In April 1972 the court ordered standards which included minimum staffing ratios, a human rights committee at each institution, minimum nutritional and sanitary requirements, provisions for individualized evaluations and programs, and the right of every resident to the least restrictive setting necessary for treatment.[6] In response to the court requirements, the Alabama legislature increased funding to pay for these institutional services.[7]

To the attorneys representing the *amicus* organizations, the case offered a model technique to expose and halt the egregious abuses which occurred regularly behind the locked doors of remote, outdated institutions and, perhaps, to stimulate improvement in public services and living conditions for the disabled. In mid-1972, with some of the experts who had worked on the *Wyatt* standards, these attorneys formed the Mental Health Law Project (MHLP) to sustain the momentum of their cooperative class advocacy.

Other Mental Disability Issues

Other cases surfaced as vehicles for effecting lasting reform in additional areas of need: persons committed to institutions without a hearing or the right to counsel; experimentation on residents as well as arbitrary and sometimes excessive use of strong psychotrop-

---

[6]The standards served as a model for revision of mental health and mental retardation policies in other jurisdictions, and the precedent has supported a number of other decisions for the right to treatment and the right to habilitation, for example, *Welsch v. Likins*, 373 F. Supp. 487 (D. Minn. 1974), *enforced*, No. 4072-Civ. 451 (D. Minn. Oct. 1, 1974) and *Davis V. Watkins*, 384 F. Supp. 1196 (N.D. Ohio 1974).

[7]This is, of course, an oversimplification of the effects of the *Wyatt* order, which also resulted in some "dumping" of residents from the institutions to meet staff-resident ratios. While the state's mental health budget rose from $25,000,000 in 1971 to $84,000,000 in 1975, representing significant improvement in conditions and services at the institutions, in late 1976 compliance with the standards continued under *amici's* review and the standards themselves remain subject to revision.

ic drugs, electroshock, psychosurgery, and other dangerous or intrusive therapies (often apparently for institutional convenience rather than for a resident's benefit); residents forced to perform maintenance work without pay; and "dumping" of helpless people from overcrowded state hospitals and retardation facilities into substandard board-and-care homes, into welfare hotels, and onto city streets. Problems facing disabled people in the community also came under scrutiny: handicapped children being denied admission to public schools; zoning ordinances prohibiting residence by formerly hospitalized persons; undue dissemination of diagnostic and treatment records; discrimination in employment, housing, and licensing (to drive or for certain kinds of work) against persons perceived as mentally handicapped. All of these problems have been the focus of MHLP's research and litigation; for some, the door to resolution has now been opened by landmark court orders.

Right to Protection from Harm

Originally brought to seek the right to treatment for the 5,209 mentally retarded residents of Willowbrook Developmental Center in New York, *New York State Association for Retarded Children v. Carey*[8] led to a second constitutional principle which advocates for the disabled can use to press for institutional reform: the right to protection from harm, based upon the Eighth Amendment's prohibition against cruel and unusual punishment. Commonly called the Willowbrook case, the class action was resolved by an extensive and detailed consent decree specifying concrete "steps, standards and procedures" to protect residents from such abuses as seclusion, corporal punishment, degradation, medical experimentation, and the routine use of restraints. It sets as the primary goal of Willowbrook the preparation of each resident for development and life in the community at large. To that end, the decree mandates individual plans for education, therapy, care, and development for each resident, and calls for increased state funding for services at the institution and, within six years, for its replacement with a network of homelike facilities and positive programs for mentally retarded persons in their own communities.

Testimony presented during the three-year litigation described bruised and beaten children, maggot-infested wounds, assembly-line bathing, inadequate medical care, and gross insufficiency of habilitation programs at Willowbrook. It also cited studies which demonstrate that residents of large, crowded mental hospitals and retardation centers deteriorate in intellectual, social, and physical functioning as a result of institutional confinement, becoming apathetic and unable to relate meaningfully to others.[9] Therefore, the Willowbrook consent decree established standards for "a

---

[8]393 F. Supp. 715 (E.D.N.Y. 1975), 357 F. Supp. 752 (E.D.N.Y. 1973).

[9]This phenomenon, sometimes termed "institutionalization," is described by E. Goffman in *Asylums: Essays on the Social Situation of Mental Patients and Other Inmates* (1961). See also R. Barton, *Institutional Neurosis* (1966), and N. Hobbs, *The Futures of Children* (1975).

certain level of affirmative intervention and programming" which, Federal Judge Orrin B. Judd wrote in a memorandum opinion accompanying ratification of the decree, "is necessary if [the] capacity for growth is to be preserved and regression prevented."

While the outcome of the Willowbrook case was similar to the *Wyatt* decision and standards, the right to protection from harm "goes beyond the right to habilitation [treatment] in one important respect," states Paul Friedman in the American Civil Liberties Union handbook *The Rights of Mentally Retarded Persons* (1976): The right to habilitation may be limited to persons who have been "involuntarily" deprived of their liberty for the purpose of habilitation. By contrast, the Willowbrook "right to protection from harm" theory would apply to any mentally retarded resident for whom the state has accepted responsibility—whether on an involuntary or a voluntary basis.

Right to Refuse Treatment

With the definition of the right to receive treatment, concern has also arisen about the imposition of potentially hazardous or intrusive treatment upon objecting recipients. Activist ex-inmate groups have conducted a vigorous public-relations campaign against forced administration of psychotropic drugs and electroconvulsive therapy (commonly called electroshock or ECT), and have filed a class-action lawsuit seeking definition of a constitutional right to refuse such treatments. An MHLP survey of the social science research supporting the use of psychotropic drugs on institutionalized mentally retarded persons[10] demonstrated that "medical and institutional personnel who prescribe and administer these drugs are operating in a scientific vacuum concerning their effects on the mentally retarded."

The survey led to conjecture that major tranquilizers were most often used not for residents' benefit but for the convenience of institutional management.[11] The 1975 movie made from Ken Kesey's book, *One Flew Over the Cuckoo's Nest*, vividly dramatized the injustice of intrusive therapy—in this case, a lobotomy—used for institutional convenience.

Among judicial decisions supporting refusal of treatment on religious grounds, *Winters v. Miller*[12] obtained a federal appellate court ruling that a mental patient objecting on religious grounds cannot be forced to accept nonemergency medication or physical treatment.

Certain therapies which have traditionally been administered at the unquestioned discretion of treatment professionals now require informed consent by institutionalized persons in some states. These include surgery (especially sterilization and psychosurgery),

---

[10]A 1968 National Institute of Mental Health study showed that 51 percent of the residents in retardation facilities were on psychotropic drugs. It appears that the situation is no different today.

[11]"Institutional Drug Abuse?" (Editorial) *Mental Health Law Project Summary of Activities,* March 1975.

[12]*Winters v. Miller,* 446 F.2d 65 (2d Cir. 1971), *cert. denied,* 404 U.S. 985 (1971).

psychotropic drugs, ECT, certain forms of behavior modification (especially those involving aversive conditioning, that is, punishment and deprivation), and many experimental procedures. In 1974 Congress set up a National Commission for the Protection of Human Subjects of Biomedical and Behavioral Research to recommend guidelines for research which uses children, prisoners, and institutionalized mentally disabled persons. The report on psychosurgery has been released, lifting a moratorium on that procedure and recommending certain controls. Other reports are expected by the end of 1977.

It is especially important—albeit difficult—to formulate such controls. They should allow consumers to benefit from high-risk treatments and conscientious therapists to administer them confidently. At the same time they must provide protections against misuse of these procedures and against violations of individual rights to privacy and autonomy, to freedom from cruel and unusual punishment, and to due process.

One of the treatment standards ordered by the *Wyatt* court, Standard Nine, dealt with the right of patients at Alabama's psychiatric hospitals to refuse certain therapies: "Patients have a right not to be subjected to . . . unusual or hazardous treatment procedures without their express and informed consent after consultation with counsel or interested party of the patient's choice." Three years later the court accepted revisions prohibiting all psychosurgery and similar surgical procedures. The revised Standard Nine allows ECT only for persons of age eighteen or older, under specific standards governing the qualifications of those recommending and administering it. It similarly forbids aversive conditioning except in accordance with special procedures which, like those for ECT, include elaborate precautions to ensure that a patient's consent is truly "informed." Where informed consent to ECT is impossible—when a person is incompetent to give it due to age or disability—advance approval by a multidisciplinary outside Extraordinary Treatment Committee is required.

Friedman, who is MHLP's managing attorney, discusses the matter of substitute decision-making for incompetent persons in the context of those who are mentally retarded:

> Ordinarily, the vicarious decision-maker would be a relative or guardian. But because hazardous or intrusive procedures may infringe fundamental First, Eighth or Fourteenth Amendment rights, additional protections—such as review by an independent "human rights committee"—would seem to be required to insure that the procedures imposed are in the "best interest" of the retarded person and are no more intrusive than necessary to accomplish the legitimate therapeutic or behavioral goal.

Thus, human rights committees, such as those set up by court orders in *Wyatt* and the Willowbrook cases, have become another kind of advocacy group. Their role includes both case advocacy (making decisions in the best interests of a single incompetent resident of an institution) and class advocacy (supervising enforcement of standards for the protection of all institutional residents).

Right to Fair Compensation

"Institutional peonage" describes the widespread practice of employing residents in institutions—mental hospitals, Veterans Administration hospitals, and retardation facilities—to perform productive labor for the maintenance of the institution without adequate compensation. While personal housekeeping work is reasonable—making one's own bed and keeping one's own room clean, for example—too often state institutions have economized by exploiting residents, requiring them to perform cleaning, laundering, kitchen work, and other maintenance tasks with token or no compensation. Residents were thereby denied benefits such as workmen's compensation and retirement plans as well as the therapeutic value of an appropriate financial reward.

A major step in the abolition of institutional peonage was the federal court decision in *Souder v. Brennan*,[13] which extended the minimum-wage and overtime provisions of the 1966 Amendments to the Fair Labor Standards Act to employees, including resident-workers, at "hospitals, institutions and schools for the mentally handicapped." While it is difficult to distinguish between work and occupational therapy or vocational training, the court stated: "Economic reality is the test of employment and the reality is that many of the patient-workers perform work for which they are in no way handicapped and from which the institution derives full economic benefit."

However, in 1976 the United States Supreme Court issued a decision in *National League of Cities v. Usery*[14] which declared federal regulation of wages in state-operated facilities unconstitutional. Resident-workers in state facilities are therefore no longer guaranteed a federal minimum wage, although they are still entitled to the state minimum wage. However, the *Souder* decision still applies to residents of private facilities. And there remains the potential for successfully challenging refusal to pay residents under the Thirteenth Amendment's prohibition of involuntary servitude.

Due-Process Rights of Persons Facing Commitment

How do mentally disabled persons arrive in public institutions? Some enter of their own volition, seeking treatment; many are signed in by parents, spouses, or guardians; others are committed by courts under states' parental and police powers.[15]

Police power commitments serve to protect society from dangerous persons—and there is enormous controversy as to what consti-

---

[13]*Souder v. Brennan*, 367 F. Supp. 808 (D.D.C. 1973).
[14]*National League of Cities v. Usery*, 44 U.S.L.W. 4974 (June 24, 1976).
[15]In 1972, for example, of 403,924 admissions to state and county mental hospitals, 169,000 were admitted on an "involuntary" basis, 23,000 as "nonprotesting," and 193,000 on a "voluntary" basis. Others came through the criminal process (National Institute of Mental Health, Statistical Note #105).

tutes "dangerousness" and how it can be proved[16]—while the state's parental power *(parens patriae)* is used to protect minors, establish guardianships, and provide for the rehabilitation of the mentally disabled through involuntary commitment to a treatment or habilitation facility. In a late 1976 draft of a mental health legislative guide prepared under a contract with the National Institute of Mental Health, Project attorneys pointed out one of the difficulties of civil commitment:

> Civil commitment is often seen as necessary to provide beneficial care or treatment to the mentally impaired who cannot recognize their need for professional help. It is also advocated as more protective and humane than criminal prosecution. But questionably broad criteria for commitment have turned well-intentioned laws into vehicles to care for and house many old people who might be unable to survive on their own; to gain expedient social control over deviant behavior or feared violence; to relieve families of the burden of intolerable or untolerated individuals; and to impose treatment on competent persons who would otherwise refuse it.

Given the massive deprivation of liberty inherent in commitment, the gross deficiencies of institutional services, and the minimal likelihood of reintegration into society for those committed to state institutions,[17] procedural safeguards under the due-process clause of the Constitution are essential to ensure that committed persons are treated with dignity and have access to suitable treatment. Such safeguards include, at a minimum, the right to notice and a hearing and to counsel. Various states and federal courts have, in recent years, required other protections, such as the right to one's own examiner or witness, the right to a jury trial, durational limits on commitment, and requirements that commitment be to the least restrictive facility necessary for treatment of the individual's disability.

Legal advocacy for persons subject to the civil commitment process is obviously vital. Yet as recently as 1971, although forty-two of fifty-one jurisdictions had a statutory right to counsel for respondents in civil commitment actions, only twenty-four mandated appointment of counsel.[18] Furthermore, as Fred Cohen describes the inadequacy of most such legal representation, the "lawyer representing a prospective patient in a typical commitment proceeding is a stranger in a strange land without benefit of guidebook, map, or dictionary."[19] However, representation by attorneys with some ex-

---

[16]See B. Ennis and T. Litwack, "Psychiatry and the Presumption of Expertise: Flipping Coins in the Courtroom," 62 CALIF. L. REV. 693 (1974).

[17]According to the Joint Commission on the Mental Health of Children, one-fourth of the children admitted to one state's mental hospitals can anticipate being permanently hospitalized for the next fifty years of their lives. Mentally retarded institutional residents, 90 percent of whom were initially admitted as minors, have a current median stay of fifteen years.

[18]American Bar Foundation *The Mentally Disabled and the Law*, Brakel and Rock, eds. (1971).

[19]Cohen, "The Function of the Attorney and the Commitment of the Mentally Ill," 44 TEX. L. REV. 424 (1966).

pertise in the mental health area can, it appears, greatly reduce the rate of civil commitment. Eighty-one cases were studied by Wenger and Fletcher.[20] In sixty-six, the patients were not represented by counsel; sixty-one were institutionalized. Of fifteen patients represented by attorneys, only four were admitted.

Children are generally admitted to institutions "voluntarily" by their parents for treatment or habilitation. But they do not have the right of "voluntary" adult residents to leave the institutions when they choose; nor, in most states, have they the due-process rights available to involuntarily committed adults. In 1975 a landmark class-action lawsuit in Pennsylvania[21] ruled that minors placed in state mental facilities have due-process rights to a hearing shortly after admission and to consult with counsel. The United States Supreme Court heard argument in the case in December 1976; at this writing the decision has not been rendered.

In an *amicus curiae* brief filed with the Supreme Court on behalf of seven professional and consumer organizations,[22] MHLP cited numerous studies demonstrating the harmful "impact of institutionalization upon the intellectual and emotional development of children [which] can result in irreversible damage to their future potential as adults." Additionally, just as with civilly committed adults, a record of institutionalization "carries with it a stigma which may cause them to be denied admission to employment, licenses, higher education and access to health benefits" following release.

In the lower court, testimony for the plaintiffs showed that parental intentions in admitting children to institutions are not always altruistic. The *amicus* brief summarized the problems:

> Parents are generally driven to hospitalization as a result of inability to cope with the problems of the child when they are under conditions of great stress . . . they are often ignorant of or unable to find alternatives by themselves and their own best interests or the interests of other family members are likely to be in conflict with what is best for the child.

Therefore, *amici* argued for "the rational application of due process to the commitment of children," with provision for a limited exception up to two weeks for respite care or evaluation of children of age twelve and younger.

Right to Liberty

Another landmark decision by the Supreme Court prevents the civil commitment of nondangerous persons for purely custodial pur-

[20]Wenger and Fletcher, "The Effect of Legal Counsel on Admissions to a State Hospital: A Confrontation of Professions," *Journal of Health and Social Behavior* (1966).

[21]*Bartley v. Kremens*, 402 F. Supp. 1039 (E.D. Pa. 1975), *on appeal* (U.S. Sup. Ct., No. 75-1064).

[22]American Orthopsychiatric Association, American Psychological Association, Federation of Parents Organizations for the New York State Mental Institutions, National Association for Mental Health, National Association for Retarded Citizens, National Association of Social Workers, and National Center for Law and the Handicapped.

poses. In June 1975 the Court ruled in *O'Connor v. Donaldson*[23] that it was illegal to confine without suitable treatment "a nondangerous individual who is capable of surviving safely in freedom by himself or with the help of willing and responsible family members or friends." Kenneth Donaldson had been committed to a state hospital in Florida for almost fifteen years, receiving no treatment yet also denied his persistent requests for release. The Project took his suit for damages up through the courts, seeking to vindicate his right either to receive suitable treatment or to be released.

There was no determination as to whether the state can override a nondangerous person's right to liberty in order to provide treatment under its parental power. However, the Supreme Court noted that "the mere presence of mental illness does not disqualify a person from preferring his home to the comforts of an institution" and made it clear that "mere public intolerance or animosity cannot justify the deprivation of a person's physical liberty."

Least Restrictive Alternative

In the context of the *Donaldson* decision, another new right is of crucial importance: the right to receive suitable treatment in the least-restrictive-alternative setting consistent with individual need. The *Wyatt* standards include recognition of this right; the Willowbrook consent judgment orders development of less-restrictive community facilities for almost all of that institution's mentally retarded residents. As long ago as 1961, the Joint Commission on Mental Illness, Action for Mental Health, stated the goal of the mental health system: to "enable the patient to maintain himself in the community in a normal manner." The Developmental Disabilities Act of 1975 specifically states that "the treatment, services and habilitation for a person with developmental disabilities . . . should be provided in the setting that is least restrictive of the person's personal liberty."

Yet "warehousing" of residents in twenty-four-hour institutions continues, for lack of sufficient community-based alternatives. For example, a survey of public retardation facilities showed that lack of community services was the primary reason given for 50 percent of readmissions in 1974. The directors estimated that the total residential population could be decreased by 52 percent if community services were available.[24] An equivalent evil is "dumping"—a real possibility under the *Donaldson* ban on purely custodial confinement. Dumping, the wholesale release of helpless, disabled people into substandard board-and-care homes, welfare hotels, and onto city streets, has been documented in newspaper exposés and congressional testimony. Clearly there is a need to accelerate the development of a network of quality community residential facilities

[23]*O'Connor v. Donaldson,* 422 U.S. 563 (1975) (43 U.S.L.W. 4929, June 26, 1975), 493 F. 2d (5th Cir. 1974).
[24]National Association of Superintendents of Public Residential Facilities, *Current Trends and Status of Public Residential Services for the Mentally Retarded* (1975).

and services for disabled persons, such as halfway houses, foster homes, sheltered workshops, and nursing and personal-care homes.

In December 1975 a federal court rendered a landmark decision in a major class-action lawsuit, *Dixon v. Weinberger*.[25] Two years earlier, the Project had filed the case on behalf of over 1,000 patients inappropriately confined in St. Elizabeth's Hospital in the District of Columbia, seeking adequate local facilities so that vindication of the right to alternative treatment would benefit rather than harm the patients to be released. The court ordered the federal and District governments (jointly responsible for the patients) to create and fund suitable alternative facilities and to develop and monitor minimum standards for their operation to prevent the dumping syndrome.

Plans for such facilities are still in the developmental stage. Summarizing the decision in MHLP's newsletter, Patricia Wald stated:

> *Dixon v. Weinberger* is still only a beacon. It came fast on the heels of the Supreme Court's decision in *Donaldson* which proclaimed the right of the mentally ill to freedom and participation in community life if they are not dangerous and are capable of surviving by themselves or with friends and family. *Dixon* extends that right to community life for those who are mentally ill and not dangerous, but devoid of willing friends and family and so incapable of surviving without society's help in the community. Both groups deserve a meaningful chance to live, to work and to socialize in the real world outside the hospital. With determination, perseverance and advocacy, we hope to help them secure that right.[26]

Rights of the Disabled in the Community

With the "deinstitutionalization" process under way nationwide, based on decisions such as *Donaldson* and *Dixon* and on fiscally strapped states' reduction of institutional populations, the rights of disabled persons in the community have gained attention and urgency. As noted earlier, formerly institutionalized persons suffer stigma and discrimination; so also do those labeled as "handicapped" either by evident physical disabilities or by medical or classification records attesting to mental retardation, epilepsy, learning disabilities, or other conditions.

Intensive class advocacy by disabled-constituent organizations and public-interest groups probably deserves credit for recent federal legislation which offers new causes of action on behalf of disabled persons subject to discrimination in many areas. Legislative evolution of the 1975 Education for All Handicapped Children Act included extensive testimony by attorneys involved in landmark right-to-education cases. (See CHAPTER 12: LEGISLATION AND

---

[25]*Dixon v. Weinberger*, 405 F. Supp. 974 (D.D.C. 1975).
[26]*Mental Health Law Project Summary of Activities*, March 1976.

CONSUMER RIGHTS.) Law professor Jack Achtenberg writes[27] that increased "pressure on the establishment [by] the disabled themselves, and those familiar with their plight . . . resulted in the landmark 1973 Vocational Rehabilitation Act," also described in Chapter 12. But regulations for implementation of Section 504, which prohibits discrimination by federally assisted programs, had not yet been issued by February 1977, despite extensive comment and input from Congress, administrative agencies, and many advocacy organizations, as well as a lawsuit[28] brought by a physically handicapped individual and a consumer group, the Action League for Physically Handicapped Adults. However, while not setting a deadline, the federal court has ordered the Secretary of Health, Education and Welfare to promulgate final regulations and has retained jurisdiction—a move advocates hope will speed implementation of these broad antidiscrimination provisions.

In the interim, case law is slowly developing through suits filed on behalf of persons who had received psychiatric treatment and were subsequently denied readmission to universities or employment, or who were discriminated against in rehiring and promotion in jobs previously held.

Other Rights in the Community—Licensing and Voting

Licensing—to drive and to work in certain areas, such as barbering and realty—is often a problem, especially for persons with controlled epilepsy, mild mental retardation, or a history of psychiatric treatment. The Epilepsy Foundation of America seeks revision of 1971 Federal Motor Carrier Safety Regulations, which prohibit the licensing of persons with a history of epilepsy. As a result of thirty-seven states' issuance of similar regulations, many truck drivers with years of safe-driving records have suddenly found themselves jobless, the Foundation reports. The Foundation and MHLP are also surveying licensing regulations and procedures by all state motor-vehicle agencies to learn whether blanket permit refusals or casual review procedures violate citizens' rights to equal protection of the law and privacy of confidential medical records.

Other common types of discrimination against those labeled as disabled include denial of health and life insurance, and annulment of adoptions or refusal of custody of children to the "disabled" person in divorce proceedings. While not an issue of livelihood, barriers to voting by disabled citizens received considerable public attention in 1976, a presidential election year. Test cases on behalf of the physically handicapped have led to nearly all states' permitting absentee voting by disabled electors or requiring that polling places be located in buildings accessible to the handicapped. But in many states institutionalized persons are still dis-

---

[27]"'Crips' Unite To Enforce Symbolic Laws: Legal Aid for the Disabled," SAN FERNANDO L. REV. 161 (Fall 1975).
[28]*Cherry v. Mathews,* 419 F. Supp. 922 (D.D.C. 1976).

franchised by laws prohibiting voting by "idiots," "persons of unsound mind," or those under the implied guardianship of the state by virtue of institutionalization. While some states have revised such outdated statutes as a result of landmark litigation establishing the right to vote for residents of schools for mentally retarded persons,[29] few institutionalized persons are registered due to lack of awareness of their rights by both advocates and residents.

Housing — The Right to Live in the Community

Disabled persons also encounter discrimination in their efforts to live in residential neighborhoods. Any parent of a severely disabled child will attest to rejection by neighbors. Individuals released from institutions face reluctant landlords; personnel in after-care programs must often ghost-sign leases for former mental hospital patients. Zoning ordinances, too, have been used to prevent formerly institutionalized individuals from living in a community. Long Beach, New York, passed an ordinance which provided that "any person requiring continuous psychiatric or medical or nursing services shall not be registered" in Long Beach hotels. While this ordinance clearly reflected the nationwide phenomenon of community backlash against "dumping" from state institutions, it was nevertheless found unconstitutional by a federal court as violating the right to travel, the right to be treated in the least-restrictive-alternative setting, and the right to privacy.[30]

The prevailing problem, however, lies in the use of zoning ordinances to keep small, homelike group residences for the disabled (or for ex-inmates of mental hospitals or prisons) out of residential areas. Halfway houses and family-care homes are thus relegated to commercial districts and urban ghettos. As important as litigation in advocacy for the right of disabled persons to live in the community, says Friedman, is its coordination "with good community relations: efforts to communicate with neighbors about the program, practical steps to alleviate their concerns, meaningful guarantees that the residential facility is adequate for the purposes envisioned."

Right to Privacy

Closely tied to discrimination is the problem of confidentiality of health records, especially those relating to psychiatric treatment. Leading health writer Natalie Davis Spingarn has asserted that "the threat to confidentiality is of even greater concern to psychiatry than to the rest of medicine."[31] As described in the *Harvard Law Review:*

> A former mental patient may suffer from the social opprobrium which attaches to treatment for mental illness and which may have more serious consequences than do the formally imposed

[29]E.g., *Carroll v. Cobb*, Civil Action No. L-6585-74-P.W. (Burlington County, N.J. Super. Ct., Nov. 1974), *Boyd v. Board of Registrars of Voters*, 334 N.E. 2d 629 (Mass. 1975).
[30]*Stoner v. Miller*, 377 F. Supp. 177 (E.D. N.Y. 1974).
[31]*Confidentiality: A Report of the 1974 Conference on Confidentiality of Health Records*, 1975.

disabilities. Many people have an "irrational fear of the mentally ill." The former mental patient is likely to be treated with distrust and even loathing; he may be socially ostracized and victimized by employment and educational discrimination.[32]

With insurers—private insurance companies and governmental programs such as Medicaid—increasingly requesting and computerizing details of health services for which payment or reimbursement is asked (not to mention the prospect of national health insurance), both therapists and psychiatric patients are concerned for the protection of "confidential personal revelations" which are the "very essence of psychotherapy."[33] Yet clients of mental health services need to have their bills paid, and third-party payers assert legitimate claims to treatment information lest they pay unfounded or excessive claims.

The outcome of the 1974 conference reported by Spingarn is the recent formation of a National Commission on Confidentiality of and Access to Health Care Records, composed of health-care professional and consumer-representative organizations and insurers' groups. The Commission intends to develop guidelines and seek legislation to preserve the privacy of health records.

Test-case litigation has also attempted to clarify the right to privacy of treatment records. In one case, MHLP has filed suit against a county government on behalf of a social worker turned down for a job because she refused to answer highly intrusive questions on a health form—for example, had she ever suffered from "depression or excessive worry" or "terrifying nightmares"—and to divulge any treatment received in the previous five years from any "clinics, physicians, healers or other practitioners."[34] The Project was also part of a consortium of organizations which forced the United States Civil Service Commission to eliminate Question 29 from preliminary employment-application forms. The question asked if the applicant has or has had "heart disease, a nervous breakdown, epilepsy, tuberculosis or diabetes." The question was deleted, but it took further pressure and the threat of litigation two years later to halt continuing use of the old form—still in plentiful supply—without advice to applicants that they did not have to answer Question 29.

In other cases the Project has represented both patients and therapists seeking court orders to eliminate patient-identifying data from computerized records of treatment[35] and prescriptions.[36] Poor security of data files was cited among the threats to clients' privacy. Another area in which confidentiality is endangered is in publication of research, when the subject's identity is insufficiently disguised. Traditional civil rights advocates part ways here. An *amicus curiae* brief to the Supreme Court on behalf of three professional

[32]"Developments in the Law, Civil Commitment of the Mentally Ill," 87 HARV. L. REV. 1193, 1200 (1974).
[33]Slovenko, *Psychotherapy, Confidentiality, and Privileged Communication* (1966).
[34]*Womeldorf v. Gleason,* Civ. Act. No. B-75-1086 (D.C. Md., filed August 6, 1975).
[35]*Volkman v. Miller,* Index No. 01209 (Sup. Ct. N.Y. Co., filed January 23, 1974).
[36]*Whelan v. Roe,* 403 F. Supp. 931, *cert. granted,* 96 S. Ct. 1100 (1976).

organizations in such a case,[37] involving an injunction against distribution of a book published by a psychoanalyst, summarized the conflict:

> On the one hand, there is the doctor's interest in publication purportedly protected by the First Amendment as embodied in the prior restraint doctrine. On the other hand, there are the patient's interests in confidentiality, which is essential for effective mental health treatment, and in privacy, which is essential for a happy and productive life.

A third area of concern is access by patients to their own treatment records, often denied by hospital authorities on one of two grounds: The administrative burden of opening records for patient viewing with a mental health professional available to interpret them, and the fear that some of the information may be harmful to a patient who misunderstands it.

Patients seek access to their records for a variety of reasons: for example, to bring suit against the hospital or the therapist; to write about their experience at an institution; or to view and, if necessary, correct the contents of records before consenting to their release to employers, insurers, lawyers, or family members. Some state laws provide grounds for access, but the Project's attempt to obtain a constitutional ruling was not successful.[38]

A survey of forty-two hospitals in Maryland, Virginia, and the District of Columbia conducted by the Psychiatric Institute showed that a majority of the hospitals allowed patients access to their records, "yet only a fraction allow patients to add an amendment to those records if they feel the information in them is incorrect."[39]

The Future of Advocacy

In the ACLU handbook, Friedman refers to new legislation protecting disabled persons against discrimination. But, he adds:

> Having these laws on the books does not guarantee that they will be observed . . . Securing a declaration of legal rights is only the first step. Monitoring, muckraking, lobbying, political pressure and continuing judicial intervention must all be used by advocates in order to assure that the rights of the mentally retarded are actually enjoyed.

As clearly demonstrated in the enforcement of the Civil Rights Act since 1964, such advice applies to advocacy on behalf of all disadvantaged groups. However, it is particularly valid in the case of mentally and developmentally disabled persons. A discussion pa-

---

[37]*Roe v. Doe,* 42 A.D. 2d 559, 345 N.Y.S. 2d 560 *aff'd,* 33 N.Y. 2d 902, 352 N.Y.S. 2d 626, 307 N.E. 2d 823 (1973), *dismissed* (February 19, 1975), brief filed by the Mental Health Law Project for the American Psychiatric Association, the American Psychoanalytic Association, and the American Orthopsychiatric Association.

[38]*Gotkin v. Miller,* 379 F. Supp. 959, E.D.N.Y. (July 25, 1974), 514 F. 2d. 125 (2d Cir., 1975), in which a formerly hospitalized writer sought access to write a book. MHLP attorneys alleged that Janet Gotkin was denied her rights to liberty and property without due process, her right to autonomy, and her right to be free from unreasonable searches and seizures.

[39]"The Right to Know vs. the Right to Privacy," *Focus,* December 1976.

per prepared by Staney Herr for the Department of Health, Education and Welfare, "Advocacy under the Developmental Disabilities Act" (1976), points out:

> Rights of the developmentally disabled are no more self-enforcing than rights of others. There is, however, an obvious and special need for advocacy services for those so disabled in general, and the institutionalized in particular. Effective representation is currently provided to only a very small minority of developmentally disabled persons with socio-legal problems. The default of legal and human rights is occasioned in part by lawyers' lack of familiarity with mental retardation, autism and other disabilities which impair self-advocacy and the special problems arising from that condition or social status. And disabled people's use of the courts, lawyers and the law has tended to be episodic and unsystematic. No matter how aggrieved they feel or how well intentioned their advocates, without access to sustained socio-legal backup assistance, violations of their legal and human rights may neither be identified nor corrected. In the majority of states just such a socio-legal backup center is conspicuously lacking.

There are in a few states legal advocacy programs providing competent and specialized case advocacy for mentally handicapped persons. New York, Massachusetts, New Jersey, and Ohio have innovative legal advocacy programs which are independent of the mental health administrative departments.[40] Other state programs are offshoots of the national Legal Services Corporation (formerly the Office of Economic Opportunity, or OEO), funded through state health or social-services agencies.[41] As MHLP's legislative guide describes it, in a chapter recommending state advocacy legislation:

> Such programs, and establishment of an American Bar Association Commission on the Mentally Disabled, indicate that some elements in the legal profession are awakening to their responsibilities in this area. However, nationwide the mentally handicapped generally continue to receive grossly inadequate legal services.

In the area of class advocacy, public-interest legal organizations like MHLP and the National Center for Law and the Handicapped can play a leadership role, bringing test-case litigation (which often

---

[40]New York's Mental Health Information Service is responsible for informing institutionalized patients of their legal rights and representing them at hearings; it is a direct arm of the state's judicial system. Massachusetts' Mental Health Legal Advisors Committee is under the control of the state's Supreme Judicial Court; it trains and compensates private attorneys to represent mentally handicapped persons before the courts. In New Jersey a Division of Mental Health Advocacy is part of the state's unique independent Department of Public Advocacy; it has three neighborhood offices, staffed by lawyers and nonlawyers in equal numbers. The Ohio Legal Rights Service, a statutorily created body independent of other state agencies, was established in mid-1975 to protect the rights of mentally retarded persons in regard to present, past, or potential institutionalization.

[41]The Seattle–Kings County Legal Aid Services' representation of institutionalized mentally handicapped persons operates within the Legal Aid Bureau and is financed by the Washington State Department of Social and Health Services. The Minnesota Developmentally Disabled Advocacy Project is funded by the state's Council on Developmental Disabilities and is operated by the Legal Aid Society of Minneapolis, a Legal Services grantee.

calls for novel legal strategies), publishing research findings, providing backup to state advocacy programs, and serving as an information clearinghouse for case advocates and consumer groups. But their numbers are limited and their funding is insecure.

At this writing, the outcome of a case on appeal before the Fourth Circuit Court of Appeals is therefore worth watching. In *United States v. Solomon*,[42] the Department of Justice had filed a right-to-habilitation class action on behalf of mentally retarded residents of a Maryland institution, alleging "severe and widespread deprivation" of their rights in the overcrowded, understaffed facility. The lower court dismissed the case on the basis that the Justice Department lacked the power to bring such a suit, fearing that judicial recognition of such a power would "threaten the delicate balance of power. . . between the federal and state governments." On behalf of the Justice Department's appeal, the Project filed a brief for *amici curiae*—the American Association on Mental Deficiency, the National Association for Retarded Citizens, and the National Coalition for Children's Justice—arguing:

> [T]here is a documentable and universally acknowledged "national emergency" involving the widespread and pervasive deprivation of constitutional rights of institutionalized residents. Congress has found that constitutional abuses are endemic in state institutions and committed itself to helping these residents enforce their legal rights [through such legislation as Title II of the Developmental Disabilities Act] . . . The ranks of private advocates for these residents are entirely too thin and undernourished to begin to meet the need. The retention of the presence of the Attorney General, with his superior resources for maintaining complex and protracted litigation, is indispensable to the Congressional aim of protection of civil rights for the institutionalized.

Public-interest law programs, through their specialized class advocacy, "have virtually created new bodies of law to protect the rights of . . . the mentally ill and the mentally retarded," according to the report issued in late 1976 by the Council for Public Interest Law, *Balancing the Scales of Justice: Financing Public Interest Law in America*. The report recommends several methods of financing public-interest law centers, among them legislation which allows attorney's fee awards in public-interest litigation, passed by Congress in October 1976. But the report adds:

> The longer-term problem calls for a more fundamental look at the legal system. The problems of public interest law ultimately are not separable from the larger problems of the legal process, and the long-term solution . . . is tied to larger questions of law reform. The groups that most need legal advocacy to help them overcome inherent disadvantages in wealth, sophistication, and access to technical expertise are most likely to be

---

[42]*United States v. Solomon*, No. N-74-181 (D. Md., July 8, 1976), *appeal docketed*, September 3, 1976.

shortchanged. The procedures of our courts that tolerate expensive proceedings and delays disadvantage the groups least able to function effectively in such settings.

But in the interim, while progress of legislation to protect the rights of the disabled appears slow and problems of implementing new court orders loom large, there is a new public awareness of the human rights of disabled persons. As a result of intensive and specialized class advocacy, their "fate," wrote Judge Judd in his memorandum opinion on the Willowbrook case, "has passed from an arcane concern to a major issue both of constitutional rights and social policy." It is on this issue that new and effective advocacy programs can be built. (See PART 4, SECTION 2: VOLUNTARY ORGANIZATIONS for advocacy organizations.)

SELECTED REFERENCES

BOOKS

Basic Rights of the Mentally Handicapped, Mental Health Law Project.

Berlin, I., ed., *Advocacy for Child Mental Health*, Brunner/Mazel, New York, 1975.

Bradley, V., and G. Clarke, *Paper Victories and Hard Realities: The Implementation of the Legal and Constitutional Rights of the Mentally Disabled*, Health Policy Center, Georgetown University, 1976.

Brakel, J., and R. Rock, *The Mentally Disabled and the Law*, rev. ed., University of Chicago Press, 1971.

Brooks, L., *Law, Psychiatry and the Mental Health System*, Little, Brown, Boston, 1974.

Ennis, B., and P. Friedman, eds., *Legal Rights of the Mentally Handicapped*, 1974.

Ennis, B., and L. Siegel, *The Rights of Mental Patients: An American Civil Liberties Union Handbook*, Avon, New York, 1977.

Friedman, P., *The Rights of Mentally Retarded Persons: An American Civil Liberties Union Handbook*, Avon, New York, 1976.

Kindred, M., J. Cohen, D. Penrod, and T. Shaffer, eds., *The Mentally Retarded Citizen and the Law*, Free Press, Riverside, New Jersey, 1976.

Mental Retardation: Century of Decision, President's Committee on Mental Retardation, 1976.

Mental Retardation . . . The Known and the Unknown, President's Committee on Mental Retardation, 1975.

Sigelman, C., ed., *Protective Services and Citizen Advocacy*, §1401, Research and Training Center in Mental Retardation, Texas Tech University, 1974.

Silent Minority, President's Committee on Mental Retardation, 1973.

Stone, A., *Mental Health and Law: A System in Transition*, National Institute of Mental Health, DHEW Publication no. (ADM) 75-176, 1975.

Wolfensberger, W., *Citizen Advocacy for the Handicapped, Impaired and Disadvantaged: An Overview*, Government Printing Office, Washington, D.C., 1972.

Wolfensberger, W., *The Principle of Normalization in Human Services*, 1972.

ARTICLES

Achtenberg, J., "'Crips' Unite to Enforce Symbolic Laws: Legal Aid for the Disabled," *University of San Fernando Law Review* 161 (Fall 1975).

Andalman, E., and D. L. Chambers, "Effective Counsel for Persons Facing Civil Commitment: A Survey, a Polemic, and a Proposal," 45 *Mississippi Law Journal* 43 (1974).

"Developments in the Law: Civil Commitment of the Mentally Ill," 87 *Harvard Law Review* 1190 (1974).

Ferleger, D., "A Patient's Rights Organization: Advocacy and Collective Action by and for Inmates in Mental Institutions," 8 *Clearinghouse Review* 597 (1975).

Friedman, P., and R. Beck, *Mental Retardation and the Law: A Comprehensive Summary of the Status of Current Court Cases* (September 1975).

Halpern, C., "The Legal System Focuses on the Rights of the Mentally Handicapped," 41 *D.C. Bar Journal* 9 (January–June 1974).

Handel, R., "Role of the Advocate in Securing the Handicapped Child's Right to an Effective Minimal Education," 36 *Ohio State Law Journal* 349 (1975). (§905).

Herr, S., *Advocacy under the Developmental Disabilities Act*, U.S. Department of Health, Education and Welfare (1976).

Kannensohn, M., and N. Kessler, "Representing the Public Interest: A Report on New Jersey's Department of the Public Advocate," 48 *State Government* (4) 252 (1975).

Mahan, S., S. Maples, S. Murphy, and G. Tubb, "A Mechanism for Enforcing the Right to Treatment: The Human Rights Committee," *Law & Psychology Review* 131 (Spring 1975).

"Symposium: The Legal Rights of the Mentally Retarded," 23 *Syracuse Law Review* 991 (1972).

"Symposium: Mental Disability and the Law," 62 *California Law Review* 671 (1974).

Verkuil, P., "Ombudsman and the Limits of the Adversary System," 75 *Columbia Law Review* 845 (May 1975).

Wald, P., and L. Schwartz, "Trying a Right to Treatment Case: Pointers and Pitfalls for Plaintiffs," 12 *American Criminal Law Review* 125 (1974).

"The Wyatt Case: Implementation of a Judicial Decree Ordering Institutional Change," 84 *Yale Law Journal* 1338 (1975).

14

Recreation for the Disabled:
A. Activities for Specific Groups

JO LOCKHART, M.S., Recreation Specialist, Seattle

This section discusses the development of appropriate recreational activities for the hearing-impaired, the visually impaired, the intellectually handicapped, and the physically handicapped. A listing of suggested recreational and physical training equipment is given at the end of the section.

Hearing-Impaired

Several factors should be considered in planning recreational activities for the hearing-impaired. First, whatever form of communication is used must be clearly understood by everyone involved in an activity. Generally, confusion occurs when the form of communication to be used has not been defined. For example, if sign language is used it should be used consistently, always keeping in mind the vocabulary level of the people involved. Second, if possible, knowledge of the recreational background of the individuals involved in a program is helpful, to avoid starting at either too simple or too complicated a level.

Recreation can be important to the hearing-impaired for a number of reasons. Depending on the activity, it can allow them to be more actively involved in the community. For example, field trips to interesting places can be an invaluable experience in familiarizing them with the community and in showing them areas they can explore further in their leisure time. These trips can include visits to bakeries, factories, stores, etc. Visiting such places can involve learning new vocabulary as well as providing extensive insights into the environment in which they live.

Primarily because communication is much easier, deaf people tend to spend their leisure time together. Recreation, however, can provide opportunities for interaction with hearing people. Often deaf people are left out of activities because they do not understand rules or vocabulary necessary to take part effectively. However, by working with small groups of adults or children, vocabulary pertinent to the activity can be taught. This method is especially effective with small children.

Entire programs can operate for weeks by teaching one game such as kickball. Not only can children learn vocabulary and rules, but they can also be introduced to the concepts of strategy and team play as they grow older. These concepts can then be applied to other team sports such as baseball or football. Working in small groups helps to increase self-confidence and interest in recreational programs. These benefits, in turn, often provide the incentive necessary to facilitate the deaf person's involvement in more advanced activities with a greater variety of people.

By starting with deaf children at a very early age, a wide range of cultural, artistic, and sports-oriented activities can be offered. They can participate fully in all such forms of recreation, provided they are given the requisites of vocabulary and acquired skills to ensure total involvement.

Visually Impaired

Planning, organization, implementation, and evaluation of a recreational program for visually impaired individuals should be initiated with the thought that many blind persons will be interested in any form of normal recreational activity. In determining recreational programs, consideration should be given to whether the individual is newly or congenitally blind and to the age and ability of the individual. With integration into normal community recreational activity as the ideal goal, programs must be developed to meet the needs of three types of blind individuals: (1) those whose lack of sight, coupled with other handicapping conditions (that is, deafness, mental retardation, or cerebral palsy), will always necessitate some form of specialized recreational activity; (2) those who, with training, will at some time in the future integrate successfully into community recreational activities; and (3) those who, due to lack of knowledge of or exposure to current community recreational opportunities, are hindered from participation in otherwise accessible programs.

Recreation programs should be initiated at the earliest possible age, but no later than the grade school level. Interaction and socialization with both sighted and nonsighted persons fosters the integration process. Activities oriented around group encounters (field trips, camping) should be as extensive as individual activities (hobbies). Experience has proved that from a sound integrated rec-

Amateur radio is an ideal hobby for the disabled, keeping them in touch with the world. Dick Eichhorn, WB0CPC, blind for more than ten years, coordinates the activities of the Courage Handi-Ham System in Golden Valley, Minnesota. Gene Conop, WB9IBA, of Rice Lake, Wisconsin, keys with his right toe by using a specially designed "bug" since he lacks speech and arm control. (American Radio Relay League)

reation base, increased worthwhile use of leisure time by the visually impaired will ensue.

Integration is especially important for individuals who have been visually impaired from birth. The congenitally blind need more social skill development as they relate to recreational programming, whereas the newly blind already have the social skills but need to learn to adapt them to previous recreational activities. Total segregation of the visually impaired is a negative situation which should be avoided. However, in many cases a recreational program may begin by being segregated only until certain skill levels (social skills, game skills) are attained.

As an individual becomes older, at the junior and senior high school level, for example, activities should be largely oriented toward recreational opportunities in which the individual can take an active part with or without sighted friends and family (such as bowling, sporting events, and swimming).

Recreational leaders need to know only a few of the mobility (sighted guide techniques) and motivational techniques that may be needed in a given situation when conducting activities for the visually impaired. The main criterion for leadership is the ability to adapt the activity to the individual until a skill level is reached where it is possible to participate with sighted peers in a community recreational program. The leader should guard against the tendency to stereotype the visually impaired individual and thus impose personal restrictions when in fact he or she may be capable of successful accomplishment in a given skill.

Intellectually Handicapped

Recreation for the intellectually handicapped person is carried out on three levels of programming based on individual needs. The first level is concerned with the person who, with encouragement, can participate in regular community recreational programs. The second level is for the retarded person who needs extra assistance, instruction, and encouragement before becoming able to move into the normal recreational community. The third level meets the needs of the retarded who will always require special leisure time programs. Since recreation is usually readily available to the first group of individuals, this discussion will be concerned primarily with those who require special assistance in pursuit of their leisure time needs.

The recreational activities which can be adapted to the abilities and needs of the mentally retarded can be divided into social, physical, and self-help programs. Social recreation incorporates games, arts and crafts, special events, parties, and dances. These activities encourage the mentally retarded to participate with others in a fun-filled, relaxed atmosphere, which in turn leads to personal socialization and increased expertise. In establishing a social recreational program, one should first decide what the primary focus of the program is to be (that is, dancing, games, field trips, or music). After a basic design has been established and the handicapped group has been identified and notified, the participants should be asked how they want to spend their leisure time. The general public chooses its own recreation, and so should the mentally handicapped public.

Physical recreation for the mentally handicapped is well received by all who participate and, depending on the severity of the handicap, a great deal of success can be attained. These activities range from individual sports such as bowling, swimming, track and field, and gymnastics to team sports such as football, baseball, and floor hockey. All types of physical activity are feasible for the mentally retarded. The basic requirement is that each skill be broken down into workable units which, once learned, are reassembled into the complete activity. The Kennedy Foundation sponsors Special Olympics for mentally retarded youths and adults, giving these people a chance to compete for local, state, and national honors with athletes on their own level of ability. (Information on establishing a Special Olympics program can be obtained through the Joseph P. Kennedy, Jr. Foundation, 1701 K Street N.W., Washington, DC 20006.)

Self-help programs fit within the recreational framework in that they allow mentally retarded participants to learn skills which assist them in enjoying a full spectrum of leisure time activities. These skills include learning to ride public transportation to and from community recreation centers; money management in relation to paying for their recreational activities; and field trips through the community to learn what recreation activities it has to offer. Cooking, sewing, shopping, and grooming are also included as supplemental programs in schools and living units. The individual who is well rounded and confident in these basic living skills will be more likely to seek out and enjoy recreational activities within the community.

The basic premise of recreation for the intellectually handicapped is to move the participant from individual recreational activity through activity with an object (such as a ball, television set, or books) to recreation with other people in a comprehensive program within the community.

Physically Handicapped

Recreational opportunities for the physically handicapped vary greatly with the severity of the handicap. Generally speaking, those who are able to function in daily life with the help of a wheelchair or some sort of ambulatory device have a wide range of activities from which to choose. Almost any kind of sport or game (such as bowling, basketball, archery, and table tennis) can be adapted by means of special apparatus or rules. Many municipal recreation departments have information about state and national wheelchair games, and some metropolitan departments have a special recreation section that plans and supervises programs for handicapped populations. Many programs are now being implemented that involve physically handicapped and nonhandicapped individuals in the same activities. An example is bowling teams composed of an equal number of both groups. Basketball and baseball teams exist in which all players, handicapped or nonhandicapped, have to compete in wheelchairs. Camping, boating, and many other outdoor activities have been adapted to meet the needs of physically handicapped persons.

Transportation is one of the major problems in programs for the handicapped, but many agencies provide vans, and some individuals can use private or public transportation. When this problem is overcome, this group of physically handicapped are relatively easy to serve. Arts and crafts activities and quiet games should be available for this group, but they are often overemphasized and become unpopular. Social programs and dances are particularly appealing, and there are numerous groups of wheelchair square dancers in large metropolitan areas. Most recreation activities, including table games, can be adapted or adjusted to fit the needs of this group.

The second group of physically handicapped individuals includes those unable to use wheelchairs or walking devices. This group is more difficult to plan for because most sports and game activities range from very difficult to impossible for them to participate in. The most successful type of programs for this group involves mental rather than physical skills. All types of word games are popular. Examples of these are Twenty Questions, Who Am I, and many other question-and-answer games. Communication skill is sometimes a consideration for certain activities. Swimming is usually an appropriate physical activity for this group, but it demands a one-to-one instructor-pupil ratio. A bowling program can be implemented with the aid of special apparatus. Camping, socials, and arts and crafts are also popular activities. Trips and tours are well received, although special apparatus is often needed for transportation.

Because most of these individuals are unable to drive or use public transportation, it is often difficult to conduct programs that require the participants to meet at a central location or community recreation center. This problem can be eliminated by conducting recreational activities in sheltered workshops, nursing homes, schools, or any other agency that attracts groups of handicapped individuals. This is frequently the best method of reaching the greatest number of people.

Recreational and Physical Training Equipment

Indoor Equipment: Lightweight bowling set; candle pin bowling set; Tally Pins game; carpet bowling; bowling ball ramp; handle grip bowling ball; table tennis set (with or without side walls); suction dart set; rubber horseshoe set; bumper pool table; small or standard pool table; table games (baseball, marble board, basketball, knock-hockey); card-playing (card holder, Solitaire board, one-hand and electric shuffler); beanbag game; Kik-It hockey game; cloth crawling tunnel; Rocky Board (curved rocking board with ropes on sides); trampoline; putting game, with or without automatic ball return.

Indoor-Outdoor Equipment: Tetherball; shuffleboard; gym scooter; pitch back; stilts; pogo stick; rollerskates; swimming aids (belt with removable floats, inflatable swim vest, water wings, body float, hydraulic lifter); quoits.

Outdoor Equipment: Safety bat and baseball; volleyball; badminton; croquet; polyethylene softballs; safety and professional hockey sets; kickball; playground ball; cage ball; jump rope; paddle racket set (with wrist straps); Crosse Game (La Crosse); inflated car or airplane tire tubes (for sitting, swinging, floating); golf (motorized cart, rubber ball pickup, sitting cane, putting course); fishing (electric reel, rod holder attachment for boat rail or seat; pellet-propelled lures; spinning reel with extra-large lever); archery set; amputee baseball glove; shuttlecock.

Clay Modeling, Pottery, Ceramics:

Wedging cart; wedging table; mortar and pestle; sieve; scale; lifters; potter's wheels (kick type, electric type, portable and bench models); kilns (standard, high-fire, metal enameling, economy models); glaze sprayer.

Woodworking: Workbench with vise; adjustable-height workbench (crank and hydraulic types); hand tool set; tool cabinet; rehabilitation woodworking machine with bicycle exerciser; ankle-exerciser saw and sander; treadle therapeutic saw; band saw; arbor saw; drill press; hand power-tools (drill, scroll saw, grinder, jig saw, sander, sabre saw, sprayer, router, polisher, etc.).

Weaving: Rehabilitation loom (with graded weights for upper and lower extremities exercise; can be used by wheelchair patients); table and bed looms; folding loom; master loom; rug frame; Inkle loom (7 inches, or 18 centimeters, wide, for belts, braids, etc.); hooked rug loom; rya rug loom; tapestry loom.

Leathercraft: Shears; rawhide mallet; edge beveler; straightedge square; rotary punch; needle-nose pliers; skive knife; stamping tools.

Painting: Sponge rubber ball grip for brush; extended balsa mouthstick for brush; suction cups to keep paint containers upright; hand sling attached above, to support painter's arm.

Needlework, Sewing: Needle threader (wire threader, automatic threader); self-threading seeing-eye needle; Magic Stitcher; large-headed pins; thread clippers; pattern tracing wheel;

left-handed scissors; adjustable-tension scissors; electric scissors; knee clamp and table clamp holders for darning egg or embroidery frame; self-standing embroidery frame for one-handed use; floor stand for needlework frames; portable table-model sewing machine with elbow or knee control; crochet and knitting needles with built-up handles.

Gardening: One-handed cane basket; yard cart with tools and supplies; garden stool on wheels; wheelchair with gardening accessories attached; steel cart with large wheels; long-handled forks and trowels, and short-handled rake and hoe for wheelchair use; long-handled clippers for reaching flowers and shrubs without stretching.

Indoor gardening equipment includes free-standing, attached, and window greenhouses; window plant shelves; hanging pots; plant stands; plant grow-lights; trigger spray; automatic waterer.

Photography: Cartridge-loaded camera with electric eye exposure control, automatic film advance, and built-in flash holders (still or movie); small tripod for wheelchair use; cartridge film movie projector with automatic threading, projection, and rewind mechanism; remote-control slide projector.

Music: Harmonica with "no-hands" holder; special brackets for one-handed playing of wind instruments; handcuffs for holding drumsticks; recorder; Magic Zither (with song sheet under wires); Autoharp (with chord-bar keys); xylophone; vibraphone; armrest for playing piano; rhythm instruments for children (tom-tom, maracas, wrist bells, tambour set, sand blocks, jingle clogs, rhythm sticks, tone blocks, tambourine, cymbals, triangle, castanets).

Balance Control: Floor sitter; barrel roll; wheeled coaster; rocker board (large or small); large inflated exercise ball; push scooter; circular scooter; adapted tricycle (with body support and foot attachments); trainer bicycle; air-inflated cylinder; stilts; pogo stick; bouncing tube (rubber tube with canvas top, used like trampoline).

Crawling Skills: Crawler with body support; crawling training unit for homolateral and cross-pattern crawling; cloth crawling tunnel; rubber hands-and-feet crawling pattern set; barrel with incline; large crawl-through shapes and blocks; crawling

obstacle course (a combination of the preceding equipment).

Standing, Walking, Jumping: Colored disks for standing and walking; footprints; walk-on numbers and letters; foot placement ladder; balance square; balance beam; slanted walking board; bicycle tires or plastic hoops for walking and hopping; bouncing board; bouncing tube; trampoline (with or without handrail); high jump stand; jump rope; stretch rope; parallel bars (adjustable, with or without platform; folding type for the home; wall type); exercise and training stairs.

Climbing: Ramp with nested steps; staircase with handrails; climbing stools; climbing pyramid; climbing net; wooden and rope ladders; Lind climber (incline, ladder, etc.).

Throwing, Catching, Batting, Kicking: Balls (large cage ball, kickball, plastic football, 36-inch or 90-centimeter vinyl ball, beach ball, fleece ball for indoors); beanbag game; quoits; ring toss; horseshoes; plastic safety bat and base; pitchback net.

Playground Equipment: Fence climb; space platform; catwalk beams; net scrambler; parallel bars; tunnel crawl; wheelchair maze and tunnel; benches; sandbox; sand-and-water trough; slide; swing; metal rocking tub.

Other Indoor Equipment: Gym mats; protective helmets; incline mats; posture mirror; large and small foam-filled shapes for piling and exercise; adjustable basketball standard (to be used while sitting or standing); folding gym (with trapeze, chinning bar, climbing ropes, horizontal and vertical ladders, rings); exercise chair; wheelchair exercise unit; ankle and leg exerciser; safety walking belt; head strap; shoulder weight bag; quadriceps boot; foot drop boot; restorator (clinical and home models); knee exercise unit; suspension apparatus; shoulder wheel; leg exerciser; pulley system; dumbbell set; calf flexor; rotary wrist machine; shoulder ladder; circumductor table; exercise skate; heel stretcher; hip circumductor; hand exerciser; weight bags; exercise ankle cuffs; foot stirrup; exercise weight bars; rowing machine; health walker; medicine ball; side horse; punching bag set; doorway chinning bar; hand exercise putty; finger and wrist exercise boards; hydraulic resistive exercise table; wall pulleys; treadmill; weight and flexion units.   [ROBERT M. GOLDENSON]

171

B. Day Camps

Sections B through G by ROBERT M. GOLDENSON, Ph.D.

Day camps offer many benefits to the disabled: healthy out-of-doors activities, nature experiences, acquisition of new skills and interests, and opportunities to develop independence, initiative, and group relationships. If well planned and organized, they provide a varied program on a relatively inexpensive short-term basis (usually two weeks to one month per group) to children for whom long-term "sleep-away" camps are not feasible, or in cases where the child needs preparation for residential camping.

Day camps are generally organized and administered by social or health agencies in cooperation with parents, teachers, specialists in camping, community leaders, and a medical advisory committee. The sites vary considerably; most common are parks, recreation centers, churches, school grounds, and facilities provided by health agencies. Private estates, sport clubs, and wooded areas may also be used, especially if there is a swimming pool, pond, or beach nearby.

Referrals are usually made by individuals or by hospitals, clinics, schools, or agencies which serve the handicapped, and examination by a physician is generally required. Most of these camps are coeducational, and a mixture of ambulatory and nonambulatory campers is common. Counselors who have had training or experience with the handicapped are preferred, and an in-service training program for both staff and volunteers is usually held before the opening of the season. A ratio of one trained staff worker to four severely disabled campers is often maintained, but a ratio of one worker to eight or ten campers may be considered sufficient for the less severely handicapped.

Campers frequently share in planning the program with the professional staff. The activities may be limited by the camp location, but often include trips to zoos, aquariums, and farms; constructing terrariums; bird watching; tree, plant, animal, and insect identification; nature walks and hikes (even in wheelchairs); learning to use camp tools, such as knives and axes; making rustic shelters; trail blazing; signaling; knot tying; fire building; cooking one-pot meals; nature crafts (with pods, seeds, shells, feathers, etc.); music (action songs, folk songs, rounds, rhythm band); dramatics (pantomimes, skits, charades); storytelling; flag ceremonies; games and sports (archery, swimming, boating, fishing, horseshoes, etc.); instruction in health and safety; production of a camp newspaper and, in some camps, varied activities focused on a single theme, such as pirates, pioneers, beachcombers, gypsies, Indians, or cowboys. In addition, some day camps include overnight camp-outs for younger campers and camping trips to state parks for older campers.

For details, see Grace Mitchell, *Fundamentals of Day Camping*, Association Press, New York, 1961; Virginia Musselman, *Day*

Camping, National Recreation Association, 1963; and Janet Pomeroy, *Recreation for the Physically Handicapped,* Macmillan, New York, 1964.

C. Residential Camps

Ideally every child, able-bodied or disabled, should have an opportunity to attend a residential summer camp, or if that is not possible, a day camp. Many of the values inherent in the two kinds of camp experience are basically the same, and a number of them have been mentioned in Section B. However, residential camps offer special advantages to the handicapped because they give both younger and older children an opportunity to fend for themselves outside the protective, often overprotective, atmosphere of the home. Going away to camp is usually the child's first chance to be independent and to function in new surroundings with new people. Although handicapped children may experience some separation anxiety, they usually adapt themselves successfully and come home more mature, resourceful, and independent people.

In his article "Camping for the Physically Handicapped: A Rationale and Approach," in the May 1973 issue of *Rehabilitation Literature,* Gary M. Robb points out that the question is not so much whether handicapped children should attend a summer camp, but what type of camp they should attend. In fully integrated camps, handicapped children occupy the same cabins as able-bodied campers; in semi-integrated camps, handicapped children either live together in one cabin, or a few live in a cabin with non-handicapped children; and in the fully segregated camp, all campers are handicapped. In the last type, the camp may be made up of children with a variety of disabilities, or with a single disability such as diabetes, blindness, orthopedic disorders, emotional disturbances, or mental retardation.

At this point there appear to be strong arguments in favor of each of these alternatives, and no definitive studies are available on which an overall decision between integration and segregation can be based. Robb, however, states that "increasingly, sentiment is shifting toward integrating the physically handicapped into 'regular' camp programs . . . [but] for the present, at least, we must be realistic in assuming that the severely physically handicapped will primarily be involved in segregated programs." The camp which Robb himself directs is of the segregated variety and includes children with many types of handicap. This camp appears to be so representative of progressive concepts that permission has been obtained to quote a large portion of the camp brochure:

> Located in Bedford, New Hampshire, Camp Allen, Inc. has
> attempted to meet the tremendous challenge of providing en-

riching summer experiences for *all* physically handicapped children—those with mild, moderate, and severe disabilities, the blind, the cerebral palsied, the deaf, and those with spina bifida or muscular dystrophy; many other youngsters with congenital and traumatic physical involvements are included . . . The primary emphasis of the Camp is on providing a variety of therapeutic recreation activities designed and adapted to develop independence through *involved* participation. This involvement is specifically directed toward the camper's ability and his potential for development of social, psychological, and physical awareness. The camper is treated as an individual, a person, and *not* a handicap.

At Camp Allen the handicap becomes, for the first time in many of the children's lives, of secondary importance. We are certainly not entrenched in the naïveté that a two- or four-week stay at camp will relieve the ever-present anxieties, frustrations, and fears which are intrinsically woven into the personality of each camper. However, as a result of the camp structure, i.e., diversified program, opportunities for new experiences, opportunities for positive relationships with staff and other campers, and a conscious accelerated effort at integration into the community, a child will very often gain new hope, confidence, and self-esteem, which carries over into old and new routines after his leaving camp. With campers accepted who differ greatly in ability and in handicapping condition, attainment of the above goals has accelerated.

In reconciling a program that requires a huge staff (ratio $1:1\frac{1}{2}$), that demands long days of physical and emotional involvement, and that necessitates a tremendous budget, one must look at the structure and effectiveness of the program.

A well-oriented, trained staff is the key to successful camp programs. Counselors at Allen are involved in an intense pre-camp orientation and training session. Supervision and guidance are also received throughout the summer. Supervisory staff are employed and begin preparatory activities many weeks in advance. Included among the staff of almost 50 are 2 registered nurses, occupational therapists, adapted physical education and therapeutic recreation specialists and students, and water safety instructors with certificates in swimming for the handicapped. The Camp is also medically supported by a consulting physician, pediatric group, and local general hospital. The Camp also provides a counselor-in-training program of the highest quality.

The core program consists of almost every conceivable activity area, including aquatic activity; physical recreation and education; domestic, creative, and manual arts; nature and outdoor education; and special instruction in personal hygiene and management. These activities, which campers help choose and develop, may be found in many camps with top-quality programs and in themselves are not unique. Campers participate in groups of 7 to 10; the groups consist of campers of both sexes, similar ages, and diverse physical ability.

Creativity, expression, and communication are major objectives. Skill, although a concomitant objective, is developed through working with each camper individually and encouraging him to progress as rapidly as he is ready. Competition, unlike in many other camps, is not a major emphasis but is utilized occasionally to develop enthusiasm and a spirit of esprit de corps.

These structured activities are only one component of the total camp program. The program provides the camper with many other opportunities for choice in activity of special interest through the inclusion of special "club" activities. Daily programs also consist of evening programs, campwide and by dormitory, and include such activities as a coffeehouse, campfires, evening swimming, and movies and a gamut of others that the campers and staff might choose or create. Overnight campouts, held weekly, are eagerly anticipated by most campers.

A major part of the Camp Allen experience includes a community outreach program. This multidimensional program consists of a number of approaches. Semiweekly bus trips take each camper to points of interest, education, and entertainment. Previous trips have included deep-sea fishing; visits to amusement parks, science centers, and aquariums; major league baseball; fairs; horseback riding; and days at the beach. In addition small groups of campers often "invade" the local communities for the purpose of shopping, eating out, attending movies and plays, bowling, and participating in other community programs.

Campers not only have the chance to mingle in the community, but many efforts are made to bring the community to the Camp. On a weekly basis, arrangements are made for groups to come to the Camp and participate *with* and, at times, perform *with* the campers. Traveling theaters, rock and Irish singing groups, community organizations and groups, along with many individual citizens, have participated with the campers in the programs at camp. Annually, one day is set aside especially for a "community picnic." Twice during the summer Olympic Days and water carnivals are held. Parents, friends, and anyone interested are welcome to attend, observe, and participate in a variety of activities.

This outreach program has proved very helpful in bridging the gap between the handicapped and the community and has been a fruitful endeavor for campers as well as community citizens . . .

Through sleeping, eating, playing and working together, campers develop tremendous empathy for each other, and, regardless of handicap, they are in some measure able to look upon their own lives with hope and anticipation. Following this intense, if brief, experience away from the protected environment of home or institution, the handicapped youngster comes away with new and exciting experiences never before attained. When all of these opportunities and experiences are put together, the child is definitely a step closer to the community of which he is struggling to become a part.

The following publications can be obtained from the National Easter Seal Society: *Directory of Resident Camps for Persons with Special Health Needs, Easter Seal Guide to Special Camping Programs,* and *Maximum Utilization of Camp Facilities.*

D. Scouting

Scouting offers disabled youngsters an opportunity not only to lead as normal a life as possible, but to participate in enjoyable activities that help them overcome their limitations. The Scout and Campfire programs offer a number of basic benefits that are essentially the same as for able-bodied children: physical fitness, exposure to outdoor life, social relationships, the satisfactions inherent in identification with a national movement, a sense of personal worth derived from being of service to others, and the stimulation and challenge of tests involving knowledge and skill. Some of these values are especially applicable to the disabled: wider social contacts help to counteract tendencies toward isolation and withdrawal; the development of new skills and interests compensates for limitations that are often imposed on them; and the winning of merit badges or other forms of recognition helps them overcome feelings of inadequacy.

The question of organization inevitably presents itself: Should handicapped children be integrated into regular units or become members of a unit of their own? There is no ready formula for answering this question. In some cases mildly handicapped boys and girls, and even some in wheelchairs who do not require special facilities or a great deal of extra care, can function well in a regular unit. In fact, it is good training for other members to learn to accept them and adapt to their needs. However, where specially trained leaders, special activities, and much supervision are required, an all-handicapped unit appears to be the most practical solution.

The Boy Scouts of America has published several pamphlets for leaders of handicapped scouts. Among its recommendations for the physically disabled are the following: It is important for the parents to submit an application describing the child's disability, capabilities, and limitations, necessary appliances and equipment, and any special help needed. If the child joins a mixed unit, it is essential to guard against an overprotective and oversolicitous attitude on the part of both the leader and fellow scouts, since this would prevent the development of independence. For children with neuromuscular disorders, semiactive games (such as table football) should be planned, but they should also become involved in the usual competitive games even if they can only serve as umpire or scorekeeper. When the group is all-handicapped, it is important to slow down the pace of games and ceremonials, to experiment with activities especially suited to the disabled, and to make allowances for different degrees of participation due to such factors as fatigue and short attention span. With these considerations in mind, most disabled children, including those in wheelchairs, can engage in short hikes, overnight camp-outs, individual sports such as archery and swimming, and a variety of team sports such as adapted baseball played with plastic bats and balls. They can also earn many activity badges, since the Scout manual permits a helping hand and substitutions when merit badge requirements are beyond a child's physical capability.

In its pamphlet on scouting for the visually handicapped, the Scout organization cites two false notions that should be discarded—that blind children are helpless and incapable of fun and enjoyment, and that they lack other basic skills such as coordination and dexterity. The fact is that many skills are highly developed in blind children as a compensation for their visual disability, and in most cases they can pass such standard tests as knot tying, Morse code, fire building, cooking an outdoor meal, and pitching a tent. In learning manual skills, the blind scout simply places the hands on those of the leader, and then goes through the motions with the leader's hands as guides. In many dens and troops, visually handicapped leaders have proved to be the best teachers. Blind scouts can also participate in exciting group activities such as canoeing and hiking, and can learn to identify trees and shrubs by touch and birds by sound. Special training aids are available from Library of Congress branches and the American Printing House for the Blind, including Cub and Boy Scout manuals and merit badge pamphlets in Braille and talking-book editions, bird call records, topographic maps, and Braille compasses.

The mentally retarded usually derive the most benefit from scouting if they are in units of their own, since the entire pace of the program must be slow and the leader must devote much time to explanation and motivation. These units are usually sponsored by a group or association of parents, or a public institution such as a school or residential facility. Program guidance and leadership training are often provided by a Scout commissioner or a local chapter of the National Association for Retarded Citizens. Boys are permitted to register as Cub Scouts a year or two past the age of ten, and may remain in the Boy Scout program after age eighteen. Although rank itself is of minor consequence to the retarded, and they may not always be able to earn the usual insignia and merit badges, they usually respond well to recognition in the form of applause, special certificates, and awards. The Cub Scout program is particularly relevant because achievement is based on doing one's best, and substitute requirements are permitted. Even though the Boy Scout program is more rigid, many retarded scouts can earn merit badges in activities for which they have been trained in special education classes—for example, crafts, printing, and woodwork. With patient instruction and the use of special teaching aids, they may also be able to learn the Scout oath, tie a square knot, engage in simplified games, read a compass, give the basic rules for fire safety and first aid, and explain what to do if one becomes lost in the woods.

See *Scouting for the Physically Handicapped, Scouting for the Visually Handicapped,* and *Scouting for the Mentally Retarded,* Boy Scouts of America, New Brunswick, NJ 08902; *Leaders of Handicapped Girls,* Camp Fire Girls, Inc., 1740 Broadway, New York, NY 10019; and Marian Barnett, *Handicapped Girls in Girl*

Scouting, Girl Scouts of the USA, 830 Third Avenue, New York, NY 10017.

E. Wheelchair Sports

Wheelchair sports programs are playing an increasingly significant role in the rehabilitation of many types of handicapped individuals. Among the conditions which frequently require confinement to a wheelchair are paraplegia, polio, cerebral palsy, muscular dystrophy, multiple sclerosis, and amputation of the lower limbs. The choice of sports and extent of participation should be made on the basis of a thorough medical evaluation.

Many rehabilitation centers or agencies devoted to specific handicaps offer limited wheelchair sports such as bowling. Others offer a wide range of activities which may include several of the following: wheelchair basketball, archery, "dartchery," table tennis, lawn bowling, fencing, swimming, slalom, weight-lifting, shot put, discus, javelin, and such track events as dashes and relays. In a few places the wheelchair program includes not only standard sports, but square dancing in which both men and women execute practically all the standard patterns and movements.

Wheelchair sports began to develop spontaneously when disabled veterans of World War II organized basketball teams with rules adapted to their special characteristics. In 1946 a team known as the "Flying Wheels," of Van Nuys, California, toured the country and not only aroused an interest in wheelchair sports but demonstrated the potential resources of the disabled. By 1950 various sports were organized and introduced in the United States and at the Stoke Mandeville Hospital in England, and in 1957 the first National Wheelchair Games were held at Adelphi College on Long Island, New York. During the 1960s, international wheelchair competitions were held in England, Israel, Canada, and Japan, as well as in Rome in association with the Olympic Games. Currently over 10,000 athletes are participating in organized wheelchair competition throughout the United States, and over fifty other countries are engaged in similar programs.

In an article published in 1970 in the *International Rehabilitation Review,* Benjamin H. Lipton, Chairman of the United States International Wheelchair Athletic Association, ably summarized the manifold benefits of wheelchair sports as a form of rehabilitation: They supplement the prescribed exercise and physical therapy program; provide social and recreational experiences; restore self-esteem and self-confidence through participation in competitive activities; combat feelings of frustration and apathy; give the patient an outlet for energies which may have been allowed to lapse through disuse; help to overcome tendencies toward withdrawal, introversion, or depression; improve "body image" by demonstrating that the handicapped person is more physically capable than was realized; and motivate the individual to engage to the fullest degree in other phases of the rehabilitation process.

There are other benefits as well. News reports of teams and competitions stimulate public interest in the disabled and show that they are doing everything possible to overcome handicaps. In many cases increased public awareness prompts people in the community to work as volunteers for agencies dealing with the disabled, or to contribute to their financial support. Another important effect is to increase employer awareness of the capacities of disabled persons, and to demonstrate to them that "ability not disability counts." In addition, the sports program may help to encourage the participants themselves to seek employment or engage in vocational training.

The National Wheelchair Athletic Association (40-24 62d Street, Woodside, NY 11377) was founded by Benjamin H. Lipton to give permanently disabled persons an opportunity to compete vigorously in as many standard sports as possible under the regular rules except for adaptations allowing for the use of wheelchairs, safety of participants, and different degrees of disability. Membership is open to competitors, supporters, and organizers of wheelchair sports.

The major activities of the Association include: (1) organization of the United States Wheelchair Sports Fund, Inc., to encourage wheelchair sports within the United States and between the United States and other countries; (2) sponsorship of regional sports groups which organize competitions in their area; (3) planning, scheduling, and establishing regulations for the annual National Wheelchair Games; (4) organizing and selecting competitors for the Wheelchair "Paralympics" team representing the United States in international competition; (5) maintenance of the Wheelchair Sports Hall of Fame to honor distinguished wheelchair athletes and others who have contributed to the development and promotion of wheelchair sports; (6) establishment of official rules which define wheelchair sports participants, wheelchair specifications, and various disability categories in order to ensure fair competition between participants with similar degrees of disability; and (7) establishment of official rules governing wheelchair competition in target archery, bowling, various field events, table tennis, swimming, track events, and weight-lifting.

Other organizations active in the field are the Indoor Sports Club, 1145 Highland Street, Napoleon, OH 43545; National Association of the Physically Handicapped, 76 Elm Street, London, OH 43140; National Paraplegia Foundation, 333 North Michigan Avenue, Chicago, IL 60601; National Wheelchair Basketball Association, 110 Seaton Building, University of Kentucky, Lexington, KY 40506; Paralyzed Veterans of America, 7315 Wisconsin Avenue, Washington, DC 20014; and American Alliance for Health, Physical Education and Recreation, 1201 16th Street N.W., Washington, DC 20036.

F. Hobbies

A hobby, as distinguished from a pastime, is far more than a transient diversion or way of filling, or killing, time. It is an enduring avocation actively and often systematically pursued. Unlike a vocation, it is not imposed by necessity but is pursued for pleasure not profit, for life rather than livelihood. Moreover, it is not merely followed, but is *developed*, becoming an integral part of the hobbyist's personality, and is a source of constantly increasing satisfaction and self-expression.

The general rewards and values of hobbies apply equally to the able-bodied and disabled: a sense of achievement; self-development and self-realization through ever-growing knowledge, skill, and productivity; relaxation and refreshment of spirit through a change of pace; the awakening of unsuspected capacities, such as latent skill and creative ability; recognition from others; and the enhancement and enrichment of life through widened horizons, broader social contacts, and new dimensions of interest, stimulation, and self-discovery.

But while disabled people can share in all these general rewards, they may also experience a number of special benefits. Too often emphasis is placed upon their limitations and handicaps; hobbies shift the focus from disability to ability. Too often their lives fall into a dreary routine; hobbies, by their very nature, offer a constructive antidote to monotony and boredom, and do so by evoking the individual's own resources. Too often the disabled live vicarious lives, with the emphasis on passivity and spectatorship; a well-chosen hobby will keep them active and interested, and will provide an opportunity for them to contribute to the lives of others through the articles they make or the objects they collect. Too often the attitudes of others, much more than the disability itself, lead them to lose confidence in themselves and accept a meager lot with resignation; a hobby will almost inevitably improve their self-image, arouse enthusiasm, and give them a much-needed feeling of adequacy. What can be more exciting than decorating one's home with one's own creations, turning a hobby into a small business enterprise, or becoming a specialist or even an authority in a recognized field of activity?

More specifically, a suitable hobby can enable the homebound or wheelchair-bound not only to find a healthy outlet for emotions and energies, but to reach out to other people through the mails by joining a hobby association or by establishing a pen pal relationship with other enthusiasts. A retarded individual can experience a sense of accomplishment from a simple art or craft such as sponge painting or paper folding, and perhaps can be motivated to read instructions and care for materials used. Mentally ill individuals can often increase their feeling of well-being through avocational activities which help to combat apathy and despair, tension, and overexcitement, and at the same time to maintain contact with the real world.

But it is important to recognize that disabled people usually need special encouragement, guidance, and assistance in finding a satisfying hobby and deriving maximum benefit from it. The following suggestions apply both to families and to health agencies:

1. If the individual has already expressed an interest in a particular activity or general area (collecting objects, making things, nature study, etc.), build on this interest wherever possible; if not, help the individual explore and experiment until an interest is expressed.

2. Watch for clues to special abilities and talents, and provide materials — even simple kits — that will encourage their development. Plan outings, if possible, to museums and exhibits, craft and hobby stores, flea markets, and collectors' shops.

3. Suggest talking over budding interests with available arts and crafts teachers, recreation specialists, and hobbyists themselves. Explore the possibility of enrollment in a local adult school course.

4. Visit the local library, taking the individual with you if possible, to talk to the librarians and examine books, periodicals, and pamphlets on hobbies. Other possible activities include consulting the sections on leisure-time pursuits in the *Encyclopedia of Associations*, writing for information and possible membership in organizations of interest, or inquiring about local hobby clubs at the library or community center.

Finally, if disabled individuals are to find a stimulating hobby, they should be aware of a wide range of possibilities, so that they can choose the one that best matches interests and abilities. Since the disabled vary in both of these characteristics as much as other individuals, the following list of potential activities is as inclusive as possible:

Hobbies

CRAFTS

Carving, Modeling: ceramics; clay modeling; gem cutting; plaster casting; puppets and marionettes; scrimshaw; soap carving and stone carving; whittling and wood carving.

Cloth and Needlework Hobbies: appliqué; batik; burlapcraft; crewel; crochet; embroidery; feltcraft; knitting; needlepoint; quilting; tatting; tie dyeing; upholstery.

Drawing, Painting, Photography: art media; crayoncraft; fabric decoration; finger painting; glass decoration; photography; porcelain painting.

Metalcraft: coppercraft; damascening; jewelry making; nail sculpture; pewtercraft; repoussage; tin can – craft; wirecraft.

Paperwork: bookbinding; cardboard craft; carton craft; Découpage; origami; paper decoration; papercraft; paper making; paper sculpture; papier mâché.

Printing Crafts: calligraphy; etching; linoleum block printing; potato printing; printing; rubbings (frottage); screen painting; wood block printing and engraving.

Weaving and Knotting: basketry; caning; macramé; netmaking; plaiting; rug hooking; rya knotting; square knotting; weaving.

Other Arts and Crafts: beadcraft; bottle cutting; candlemaking; collage, montage, and assemblage; doll making; enameling; flower arranging; flower making; flower preserving; fly tying; foamcraft; glassblowing; home maintenance; kite making; leatherwork; mask making; mobiles; model building; mosaics; nature crafts; picture framing; plastic craft; scrapcraft; shellcraft; stained glass craft; string craft; woodworking; bread dough craft; chenille craft; craft sticks; dioramas; egg craft; Indian crafts; marble craft; quilling; ribbon straw craft; sock craft; stabiles; stone painting.

COLLECTIONS

Autographs; automotive accessories; barbed wire; beer cans; bells; bookplates; books; bottles; boxes; buttons; calendars; cartoons; carved wood; catalogs; checks; china and porcelain; Chinese snuff bottles; clippings; clocks and watches; coin banks; coins; comic books; dolls; fans; firearms; fireplace equipment; furniture; furniture specialties; games; glass; greeting cards; Indian artifacts; insulators; ivory; jewelry and accessories; keys and locks; kitchenwares; lace; lighting equipment; maps; matchbooks; menus; military insignia and medals; mirrors; music makers; nails and screws; needlework; newspapers; paperweights; paperwork items; pens and pencils; pewter; pipes; playing cards; political memorabilia; postcards; posters; postmarks; prints; recordings; scent bottles and vinaigrettes; scientific devices; sewing accessories; silhouettes; silver; souvenirs; spoons; stamps; stoves; swords and daggers; tapestry; tea and coffee articles; tin containers; tin and toleware; tokens; tools; toys; trade cards and merchandise labels; trays; valentines; viewers; weathervanes.

Other Collections: art deco; ashtrays; baskets; cigar and tobacco cutters; circus memorabilia; cuspidors; desk and office equipment; doorstops; fire marks; gambling and vending machines; hooks and brackets; horse brasses; knife rests; mortars and pestles; napkin rings; parasols; salt cellars; scales and measures; scrimshaw articles; stands; stevengraphs; string and twine holders; telephones; wood samples.

MISCELLANEOUS

Food and Drink: cheese tasting; cooking; home brewing; wine hobbies.
Nature: animal breeding; beekeeping; bird watching; cats; dogs; fish; fossils; gardening (indoor); gardening (outdoor); insects; leaves; pigeons; plants; reptiles and amphibians; rocks and minerals; shells; taxidermy.
Science and Communication: amateur (ham) radio; archeology; cave exploration (spelunking); research hobbies; stargazing; weathercasting.
Service: volunteer work; community committees, etc.
Transportation: antique airplanes; antique automobiles; balloons and airships; buses; classic cars; railroad trains; steamships.

Finally, it can be safely stated that any and every hobby listed above can be pursued by *some* disabled individuals. However, the approach may have to be modified in certain instances. A physically limited person may not be able to explore caves, restore antique cars, or participate in an archeological dig, but he may be able to gather photographs, articles, and books and become an expert in any of these fields. Similarly, the person who cannot attend auctions or visit exhibits or shops may specialize in paperweights, greeting cards, bottles, or almost any other collector's item by corresponding with other collectors and by watching the ads and notices in association newsletters or such magazines as *Hobbies* and *Early American Life.*

G. Travel

A few years ago, travel opportunities for the physically disabled were severely limited, and only a fortunate few could take extended trips in the United States or abroad. Practically all were defeated by such obstacles as vehicle design, architectural barriers, airline regulations, and lack of personnel trained to deal with the handicapped. Today that situation is gradually changing for the better, and more blind, deaf, neurologically impaired, and wheelchair-bound individuals are widening their horizons and enriching their lives through travel.

One factor which has brought about this change is improved equipment—for example, a narrow, two-wheeled boarding chair for airplanes and a touring bus with a mechanical elevator that lifts wheelchairs and their occupants to the door. Some hotels have built ramps, and a few have widened doorways or will remove bathroom doors in order to accommodate wheelchair guests, and a growing number of cities are providing ramped curbs. Many of the newer airports are designed with wide doors, accessible toilets, and elevators in addition to stairs; and in some cases personnel are trained to handle disabled passengers. A few airports also operate intra-airport buses with wheelchair hoists. Such facilities made it possible for the author to take two cerebral palsied patients, one in a wheelchair and the other ataxic, to Switzerland to participate in a summer course in brain damage and cerebral palsy, and to undergo a month's intensive treatment at the International Graduate University in Leysin (now in Lugano). A minimum of difficulty was encountered during air passage and on various side trips, including the ascent of Mont Blanc and the Diablerets via cable car.

In some instances religious groups and other organizations arrange vacations for the disabled, but one of the most promising developments is the commercial travel agency specializing in tours for the handicapped. The growing number of such tours has encouraged hotels, city governments, and certain airlines to facilitate travel and sightseeing by the disabled. The Federal Aviation Administration is now working on a set of regulations designed to ensure comfortable and safe flights. However, it must be recognized that tours for the handicapped require extra preparation and effort, briefing of the handicapped group, and investigation of travel facilities, hotels, and entertainment and sightseeing opportunities that offer a minimum of obstacles. Among the special services provided by these agencies are a sign language expert for deaf groups; a portable hydraulic elevator to lift wheelchair patients into tour buses; and escorts experienced in helping disabled clients with special needs.

A list of agencies operating these tours will indicate the scope of travel opportunities already available for the disabled who can afford to take trips. Most agencies offer group travel, and some also provide companions or aides. Flying Wheel Tours (148 West Bridge Street, Owatonna, Michigan) runs trips for wheelchair travelers and for the blind and deaf to various points in the United States and Hawaii. Evergreen Travel Service (19429 44th Street, Lynnwood, Washington) offers a variety of tours to points as far away as Great Britain, Alaska, and the South Pacific, for retarded, blind, and other handicapped clients. Handy-Cap Horizons (3250 East Loretta Drive, Indianapolis, Indiana) operates on a nonprofit basis and specializes in people-to-people contacts in other countries. Rambling Tours (P.O. Box 1304, Hallandale, Florida) offers tours to Europe and North Africa. Hill Travel House (2628 Fair Oaks Boulevard, Sacramento, California) runs tours to Hawaii, Europe, and Israel. Kasheta Travel (139 Main Street, Far Rockaway, New York) takes disabled people to Europe, the Orient, and Hawaii. Grand Travel Consultants (427 Broad Street, Shrewsbury, New Jersey) specializes in Caribbean cruises for the deaf.

Other sources of information are three books by Ernest M. Gutman, all from Erncar Publications, Fort Lauderdale, FL 33308 *(Cape to Cape by Wheelchair, Middle Europe by Wheelchair, and A Travel Guide for the Disabled); Where Training Wheels Stop,* published by the Paralyzed Veterans of America; *The Wheelchair Traveler,* published by Douglas Annand, Ball Hill Road, Milford, NH 03055; *List of Guidebooks for Handicapped Travelers* and *A Guide to the National Parks and Monuments for Handicapped Tourists,* both available from the Superintendent of Documents, Government Printing Office, Washington, DC 20402; and the Travel Information Center, Moss Rehabilitation Hospital, 12th Street and Tabor Road, Philadelphia, PA 19141.

(See CHAPTER 56: REHABILITATION FACILITIES AND SERVICES, E. Recreation Center; CHAPTER 57: REHABILITATION PROFESSIONS, Recreation Specialist, Occupational Therapist, Art Therapist, Dance Therapist, Music Therapist.)

SELECTED REFERENCES

Access Travel: A Guide to the Accessibility of Airport Terminals, Architectural and Transportation Barriers Compliance Board, 330 C Street S.W., Washington, DC 20201.

Adams, R. C., A. Daniel, and L. Rullman, *Games, Sports and Exercises for the Physically Handicapped,* Lea and Febiger, Philadelphia, 1972.

Alkema, C. J., *Art for the Exceptional,* Pruett, Boulder, Colorado, 1971.

American Association for Health, Physical Education and Recreation: *Activity Programs for the Mentally Retarded; Aquatic Therapy: A Real First Step to Rehabilitation; Competitive Sports for the Handicapped; A Guide for Programs in Recreation and Physical Education of the Mentally Retarded; Special Fitness Test Manual for the Mentally Retarded; Special Olympics Instruction Manual . . . From Beginners to Champions; A Year-Round Camping and Outdoor Education Center for the Mentally Retarded in the Northern Locality of the U.S.;* these pamphlets and reprints are available from NEA Publications – Sales, 1201 16th Street N.W., Washington, DC 20036.

Brooks, H. D., and C. J. Oppenheim, *Horticulture as a Therapeutic Aid,* Institute of Rehabilitation Medicine, 1973.

Carlson, Bernice W., and D. R. Ginglend, *Play Activities for the Retarded Child,* Abingdon, Nashville, 1961: *Recreation for Retarded Teenagers and Young Adults,* Abingdon, 1968.

Case, Maurice, *Recreation for Blind Adults,* Charles C. Thomas, Springfield, Illinois, 1966.

Chapman, F. M., *Recreation Activities for the Handicapped,* Ronald Press, New York, 1960.

Frye, Virginia, and Martha Peters, *Therapeutic Recreation,* Stackpole, Harrisburg, Pennsylvania, 1972.

Ginglend, D. R., and Winifred E. Stiles, *Music Activities for Retarded Children,* Abingdon, Nashville, 1965.

Gordon, Ronnie, *The Design of a Pre-School Therapeutic Playground,* Institute of Rehabilitation Medicine, 1972.

Hunt, Valerie V., *Recreation for the Handicapped*, Prentice-Hall, Englewood Cliffs, New Jersey, 1955.

Klappholz, L., ed., *Physical Education for the Physically Handicapped and Mentally Retarded*, Croft Educational Services, New London, Connecticut, 1969.

Kramer, Jack, *Gardening without Stress and Strain*, Scribner, New York, 1973.

Lindsay, Zaidee, *Art and the Handicapped Child*, Van Nostrand, New York, 1972.

A List of Guide Books for Handicapped Travelers, President's Committee on Employment of the Handicapped, Washington, DC 20210.

Moore, Robert A., *Sports and Mental Health*, Charles C. Thomas, Springfield, Illinois, 1966.

National Easter Seal Society: *Directory of Camps for the Handicapped; Recreation for the Handicapped: A Selection of Recent Books and Pamphlets.*

Nelson, John G., *Wheelchair Vagabond*, Project Press, Santa Monica, California.

Outdoor Recreation Planning for the Handicapped, U.S. Bureau of Outdoor Recreation and National Recreation and Park Association.

Pomeroy, Janet, *Recreation for the Physically Handicapped*, Macmillan, New York, 1964; *State of the Art in Community Recreation for the Handicapped*, Recreation Center for the Handicapped, San Francisco, 1975.

Rathbone, Josephine L., *Corrective Physical Education*, W. B. Saunders, Philadelphia, 1965.

Robinson, F. M., *Therapeutic Re-creation: Ideas and Experience*, Charles C. Thomas, Springfield, Illinois, 1974.

Schattner, Regina, *Creative Dramatics for Handicapped Children*, John Day, New York, 1967.

Schmidt, Alfred, *Craft Projects for Slow Learners*, John Day, New York, 1968.

Swimming for the Handicapped: A Manual for the Aide, American National Red Cross, Washington, DC 20006.

United Cerebral Palsy Associations: *Day Camping for the Cerebral Palsied; More than Fun: A Handbook of Recreational Programming for Children and Adults with Cerebral Palsy.*

Yanowitch, R. E., and J. P. Sirkis, "Air Travel and the Handicapped," *Aerospace Medicine*, August 1974.

15

Financial Aid and Special Services

VIRGINIA M. GIVES, M.S.W., A.C.S.W., Chief Social
Worker, United Cerebral Palsy Association of
Westchester County

Contemporary America offers an increasingly impressive array of
health care agencies and services for the handicapped. Unfortunately, to disabled individuals the myriad of potential resources
may be mind-boggling. How do they know which agencies will be
of real value to them and which ones provide only nominal services? How can they keep from becoming hopelessly enmeshed in
the intricacies of eligibility requirements and bureaucratic procedures? Where do disabled persons go if they need to supplement
the monthly food budget? How can they obtain help to finance that
badly needed wheelchair? Is there any way to take that special
drivers' education course that will put them on the road to economic self-sufficiency?

GOVERNMENT GRANTS FOR THE DISABLED

The best place to start is at the local Social Security Administration office. When the Social Security Act was enacted in 1935, it
covered only the insured worker upon retirement. In 1939 the law
was changed to pay survivors if the worker died, as well as certain
dependents when the worker retired.

Disability insurance was added in 1954 to give workers protection against loss of earnings due to total disability. There are three
basic situations which permit the payment of monthly disability
benefits:

1. Insured workers can collect disability benefits for themselves

(and their family) if they suddenly become disabled. The term "disabled" means that they have a physical or mental impairment which (a) prevents them from doing any substantial gainful work and (b) is expected to last (or has lasted) for at least twelve months or is expected to result in death. Blindness, for purposes of simplification, is here considered within the category of "disabled." It is specifically defined as vision no better than 20/200 in the better eye with corrective lenses, or visual field restriction to 20 degrees or less. In the case of blind or disabled workers, their own earnings record is the basis for computation of their benefits.

2. "Childhood disability benefits" are payable to unmarried individuals disabled before age twenty-two who are likely to continue to be severely impaired. The definition of "disability" is the same as for a disabled worker, but the calculation of benefits in this case is based on the earnings of the deceased, disabled, or retired parent.

3. Disabled widows or widowers (and, under certain circumstances, disabled divorced spouses) are eligible for disability benefits upon the death of an insured worker. The amount of benefits is based on the earnings of the deceased spouse. In this case, a widow or widower may be considered disabled only if she or he has a condition which is so severe that it would ordinarily prevent a person from working and which is expected to last at least twelve months. An important difference in this situation from that of the disabled worker or child is that vocational factors such as age, education, and work experience are not considered in making the disability determination.

Supplemental Security Income

What happens to a person who is disabled but is unable to qualify for regular Social Security benefits based on either one's own or someone else's earning record? Since January 1974, such an individual has been eligible for cash benefits under the Supplemental Security Income (SSI) program.

SSI is designed to assist the aged, blind, and disabled who have limited income and little or no other resources. It has essentially replaced the previous programs for these people that were administered by state public assistance agencies. A person does not need to have worked to qualify for SSI, nor are there any age restrictions if one is blind or disabled.

The criteria for assessment of disability, as well as the definition of blindness, are the same under SSI as for regular Social Security benefits. The applicant must be a United States citizen or lawfully admitted alien. Since economic need is a basis for determining SSI eligibility, monthly income and assets must be below the maximums stipulated by the federal government. Figures for income, assets, and monthly benefits vary from time to time.

Income. The following were in effect on January 1, 1977: An individual qualifies for SSI if income is less than $157.70 a month; a couple may apply if their income is less than $236.60. In assessing financial eligibility, the first $20 a month of any kind of income is disregarded. In addition, the first $65 per month of all *earned* income is not counted. One half of all monthly earnings over $65 is also disregarded. There are other types of income, such as scholarships and certain payments for foster care of children, which are also excluded. A full listing may be found in the pamphlet "A Guide to Supplemental Security Income," available at any Social Security office.

Assets. A person may apply for SSI and still retain ownership of a house regardless of market value, a car worth $1,200 or less, and life insurance with a total face value of up to $1,500. An individual may have additional resources, such as savings, of up to $1,500; a couple may have resources totaling up to $2,250.

Disabled children who live with their parents may file for SSI as independent adults when they become eighteen years old, or at age twenty-two if still students. At that time, only their own income and resources will be considered. Prior to age eighteen (or twenty-two if attending school), the parents' income and assets are calculated in making the SSI determination.

Amount of Monthly Benefits. The federal Supplemental Security Income payment is $157.70 per month for an individual and $236.60 for a couple, both of whom are disabled. However, most states supplement this amount with additional funds. For example, as of July 1, 1977, the monthly living allowances in New York State were as follows: (1) $342.64 per month for a couple, each of whom qualifies separately for SSI; (2) $238.65 per month for an individual living alone; (3) $185.98 per month for an individual sharing an apartment ("sharing" is determined by the amount of contribution made by each individual); (4) $126.72 per month for an individual living in another person's household, such as a disabled child living with parents.

Special payment rates have also been established for aged, blind, and disabled individuals living in family care or residential facilities in New York State. These "congregate living allowances" are allocated as follows: (1) $636.70 per month for a Residential Treatment Center (Level III), which provides a full program for the resident. Psychological, recreational, and other ancillary services are usually included. (2) $396.70 per month for a Proprietary Home for Adults (Level II), which provides some minimal personal care and supervision. The program is generally provided elsewhere. An example would be a hostel for mentally retarded individuals who attend a sheltered workshop at another location. (3) $246.70 per month for a Residential Facility for the Aged. Residents here are generally capable of self-care and receive meals but few additional services.

How to Apply

A disabled individual who is able to go to the local Social Security office in person should do so. Otherwise, a claims representative will come to one's home to take the application, but the waiting period may be a lengthy one. A parent may apply for a disabled child, who need not be present when the application is filed.

The following supporting documentation is needed: (1) birth or baptismal certificate for the applicant; (2) proof of naturalization or permanent residence if not a native-born United States citizen; (3) marriage certificate in the case of a disabled widow or widower; (4) Social Security number for the applicant and the person on whose earnings record the claim is being filed (in the case of a disabled child, request for a Social Security number may be made at the time the application is filed); (5) W-2 form and savings account books, if applicable; (6) list of all doctors and relevant treatment sources, with addresses, phone numbers, and dates of treatment.

MEDICAL ASSISTANCE

Often the medical expenses incurred by a disabled individual can be as financially devastating as the illness is physically crippling. To offset these tremendous costs, medical assistance programs have been instituted at both the federal and the state level.

Medicare

Medicare is essentially an insurance program, financed by monthly premiums, paid jointly by the insured person and the federal government. Practically everyone sixty-five or older is eligible for Medicare. Disabled individuals qualify for Medicare regardless of age if: (1) they have been receiving Social Security disability benefits for two consecutive years or more, or (2) they need dialysis treatment or a kidney transplant. (Family members of insured individuals are also eligible if they require this type of treatment).

Specifics of Medicare Coverage

Hospital Insurance (Part A of Medicare). Briefly summarized, this section of Medicare coverage helps pay for services received while the disabled person is in the hospital. The benefits include:

1. Up to 90 days of inpatient care in any participating hospital in each benefit period. (A "benefit period" starts the first time the individual enters the hospital once the Medicare coverage has begun. After one has been out of the hospital for 60 consecutive days, a new benefit period starts the next time one is hospitalized.) There is no limit to the number of benefit periods a person can have.

2. A "reserve" of 60 additional inpatient hospital days, which can be used if the individual needs more than 90 days in any given benefit period. Each "reserve" day used reduces permanently the total number of reserve days left.

3. Up to 100 days of care in each benefit period in a skilled nursing or rehabilitation facility, provided certain conditions are met.

4. Up to 100 "home health care" visits by a visiting nurse, physi-

cal therapist, or selected health care professionals. These visits must take place within twelve months after discharge from a hospital or skilled nursing facility.

The specific criteria for provision of these services, as well as the deductibles which must be met for each aspect of this plan, are outlined in the pamphlet "A Brief Explanation of Medicare," distributed by the Social Security Administration.

Medicare does not pay for inpatient care that is considered purely custodial in nature, that is, if the individual is admitted primarily because help is required in dressing, eating, or other activities of daily living.

Medical Insurance (Part B of Medicare). This section of Medicare coverage generally pays for outpatient as opposed to inpatient treatment. The basic services it covers are:

1. Physicians' services, whether rendered in the hospital, the doctor's office, or the disabled individual's home. However, payment for psychiatric treatment outside a hospital is limited to $250 a year.

2. Outpatient hospital services in an emergency room or clinic.

3. Up to 100 "home health care" visits as authorized by a physician. (Part B of Medicare, unlike Part A, pays for these services even if the disabled individual has not been hospitalized. If one has been discharged from a hospital, one can receive these visits in addition to those provided under Part A.)

4. Outpatient physical therapy and speech pathology services provided under a doctor's supervision. However, payment for an independent physical therapist's services is limited to $80 a year.

5. Various other medical and health services, such as x-rays, braces, splints, casts, artificial limbs, wheelchairs, and oxygen equipment are covered when specifically ordered by a physician. (It is best to call the local Social Security office to verify coverage on individual items.)

6. Certain ambulance services.

7. Limited services by chiropractors.

The disabled individual must pay the first $60 of medical expenses incurred each year. Once this $60 deductible is met, Medicare will pay 80 percent of the "reasonable charges" (set by local fee schedule) for all covered services for the rest of the year.

Medicare does not pay for any services that are considered elective on the part of the disabled person and that are not needed for diagnosis or treatment. It also will not cover:

1. Routine physical checkups.

2. Prescription drugs and patent medicines.

3. Glasses and eye examinations to fit glasses.

4. Hearing aids and examinations for them.

5. Immunizations.

6. Dentures and routine dental care.

7. Orthopedic shoes.

8. Personal comfort items.

9. The first three pints of blood received in each calendar year.

Medicaid

Suppose an individual still needs help in paying for some of these other medical items, such as eyeglasses or a hearing aid. What can a person do if one is disabled but does not meet any of the criteria for Medicare as outlined above? Fortunately, almost all states have some type of assistance program (usually termed Medicaid) for those residents who cannot meet the cost of the medical care they need. In New York State, as an example, the following provisions apply.

Medicaid Eligibility

Individuals receiving Supplemental Security Income (SSI) are automatically entitled to Medicaid, since they have already proved disability and economic need. Financial eligibility for other individuals is determined according to the accompanying table, which lists the amounts of earnings and allowable reserves, or assets, an applicant may have.

In determining a family's eligibility for Medicaid, the first $500 of savings, including cash value of life insurance, is exempt as a burial fund. This $500 exemption applies to each member of a family, with a maximum of $2,000 per family. Additional savings equal to one-half of the annual net income exemption are also allowed.

For families larger than seven, the exemption is increased by $600 for each additional person; for allowable reserves, the exemption is increased by $300 for each additional person. In addition, the first $20 per month of any income for each person in the family household who has income and is blind, disabled, or sixty-five years of age or over will be disregarded.

Some individuals are fearful that they will have to surrender their home or car in order to apply for Medicaid. These fears are groundless, as both of these items are exempt from consideration in determining Medicaid eligibility. So, too, are personal effects, such as furniture, clothing, appliances, and business equipment.

Medicaid also makes provision for assisting individuals who need chronic care and families who must cope with catastrophic illness. In cases of catastrophic illness, Medicaid will pay for inpatient care when it exceeds 25 percent of annual net income, or the

Medicaid Eligibility Table (as of September 1976)

Number in family	Annual income	Allowable reserves
1	$2,800	$1,900
2	$4,000	$3,000
3	$4,200	$3,600
4	$5,000	$4,500
5	$5,800	$4,900
6	$6,500	$5,250
7	$7,400	$5,700

amount of such income in excess of public assistance levels, which-ever sum is smaller.

For example, a person earning $5,000 annual net income who incurs a bill of $2,000 must pay $1,250 (25 percent of $5,000) and Medicaid will pay the remaining $750.

For an individual who needs chronic care, such as in a nursing home or hospital, Medicaid will meet the medical costs remaining after the disabled person exhausts income. The individual can keep $28.50 a month for personal expenses, and apply whatever is need-ed for the support of dependents, but the rest of the income must be applied to medical care.

Other large medical bills may be covered by Medicaid if the monthly cost of care exceeds the income exemption determined on a monthly basis. For example, suppose the services of a physician or dentist cost $300 in a month and the family's income exceeds the exemption by only $50. The family would pay $50 and the re-maining $250 would be paid by Medicaid.

Services Covered by Medicaid

Once financial eligibility is established, Medicaid pays for:

1. Necessary services provided by physicians, optometrists, po-diatrists, chiropractors, and other professional personnel.

2. Dental services, such as extraction of teeth, fillings of cavities, routine preventive dental care, and other essential treatment.

3. Care, treatment, maintenance, and nursing services in hospi-tals or nursing homes, including the infirmary sections of public institutions for the mentally retarded.

4. Home health care services, including home nursing services and services of home health aides.

5. Drugs, sickroom supplies, eyeglasses, and prosthetic appli-ances.

Medicaid Application Procedures

Application for Medicaid is made by completing an application form, available at the local Department of Social Services. The ap-plication will be accepted or rejected within thirty days. If accept-ed, the applicant receives a Medicaid identification card to be used in obtaining services.

SERVICES FOR DISABLED CHILDREN

Every state has a Crippled Children's Agency, or similarly titled organization, whose function is to locate children with disabling conditions and assist them in obtaining services needed for diagno-sis and treatment. No cash grants are paid directly to the children or their parents, but these agencies do help pay the cost of whatever health care is indicated. Financial support for crippled children's services comes from tax revenues, usually from the state with matching funds from the federal government.

Each agency operates under a law passed by the state legislature which gives some guidelines for the type of handicaps to be covered by the state agency. All states include individuals under twenty-one years of age who have some kind of handicap that needs orthopedic treatment or plastic surgery, such as congenital malformations or cerebral palsy. Nearly all states service children with heart disease, epilepsy, cystic fibrosis, and visual or hearing problems. Many states are now also beginning to include the mentally retarded under their programs for crippled children.

The state agency may staff local field clinics, or it may refer children to university medical centers or local specialists. The range of services and procedures for application vary from state to state. In some instances, services for special children are administered at the county level, as with the Bureau of Medical Rehabilitation in Westchester County, New York. Others may require direct application to the state agency.

However, since all states provide at least some services, the individual with a disabled child can always obtain basic information regarding this program by contacting the state's Department of Health.

PRIVATE INSURANCE

A disabled individual who has Medicare or Medicaid may still wish to retain private insurance coverage. Of course, individual insurance carriers will vary greatly in the amount of coverage they provide, and the available plans differ throughout the country.

In the New York City area, many employers participate in the insurance program provided by Blue Cross/Blue Shield of Greater New York. Depending upon which plan is selected, the insured individual may be eligible for up to 120 days of hospital care covered in full by Blue Cross. It will usually cover up to 30 days in any twelve-month period for care of mental or nervous disorders. In addition, most Blue Cross policies provide benefits for x-ray and radium treatments, physiotherapy and rehabilitation, and up to 100 home care visits by a registered nurse, physical therapist, or other health care professional.

Blue Shield, the part of this plan which covers out-of-hospital treatment, pays for doctors' visits, x-rays, laboratory tests, and other services performed on an outpatient basis. Payment is based on a fee schedule of "reasonable charges," which are usually applicable once a deductible is met.

Insurance carriers such as Blue Cross/Blue Shield generally also offer various "major medical" plans, which provide extended coverage for an increased premium. In addition, these plans often pay for surgery maternity services, shock therapy, and other medical needs ordinarily not met under the basic hospitalization insurance contract.

The insurance underwriter may face quite a quandary when confronting an individual who is already disabled and wishes to apply for hospitalization or disability income insurance. The options are:

(1) issuing a policy at standard rates; (2) issuing a policy with a restriction, that is, excluding the preexisting impairment from coverage, particularly if it is a condition such as back injury which may have a psychosomatic component; (3) charging a higher premium; (4) limiting the extent of benefits provided; or (5) declining coverage completely.

Typically, disability insurance premiums are higher for individuals with preexisting impairments. The arguments advanced by insurance carriers for this seeming inequity are twofold: (1) with added injury, the handicapped person will be even more incapacitated than a nondisabled individual with the same injury, and (2) the disabled are more likely to have accidents.

All insurance decisions are based on individual circumstances. Social factors, the length of time for which the handicap has existed, and the individual's adjustment to it are all important considerations. Purchasers of insurance should be aware that in most states there is a "two-year contestable clause," which permits a company to rescind a policy or deny benefits if any facts were misrepresented at the time of application.

One possible recourse for a disabled individual seeking insurance is to obtain group coverage, such as the Blue Cross/Blue Shield plan cited above. In general, underwriting standards are not as strict for group coverage as for individual policies. If the disabled person is not employed by a firm which offers a group plan, group coverage can sometimes be obtained through an organization like the National Rehabilitation Association. In some cases one may be able to join a "true group," a relatively new option in which a number of individuals draw up a plan based on factors such as their age, sex, occupation, and income. This plan is then submitted to a specified insurance company which derives appropriate premium rates for the group and readjusts them at the end of a year, based on claims actually submitted. The "true group" option is unique because no medical information is required.

Finally, although the purchase of hospitalization and disability insurance presents the greatest problem for the handicapped, obtaining life insurance is not without its problems. Static disabilities such as deafness and amputation are usually accepted at standard coverage rates. Difficulties may arise due to the etiology of the disability, however. For example, amputation due to trauma represents less of an insurance risk than amputation due to diabetes, when the disease may be progressive and eventually life-threatening. In these instances reinsurance companies provide insurance companies with statistics which guide them in making individual decisions.

Auto insurance is usually granted on the basis of a physician's statement indicating what effect the impairment is expected to have on the applicant's driving ability. Coverage may be denied, provided at standard rates, or provided at higher rates. Frequently, the disabled person is given a trial period as a "substandard risk," after which one may be elevated to "preferred (normal) risk" status.

MISCELLANEOUS SOCIAL SERVICES AND AID PROGRAMS

This discussion has summarized some of the financial assistance programs and medical benefits available to the disabled person. These programs are basically designed to provide the individual with bare subsistence, that is, food, lodging, and health care essentials.

The handicapped individual often has a variety of other unmet needs, however. For example, although one's monthly SSI check provides some ready cash, one may be physically unable to get to the store to shop. Some sort of recreation program may be needed to avoid becoming a social isolate. Unless totally disabled, the individual will probably be interested in some type of retraining program directed toward eventually meeting the demands of life as independently as possible.

To cope with these problems, there are both public and private agencies, as well as some special programs for people who have suffered particular types of traumatic injury.

Public Agencies

Department of Social Services (DSS). Because this state agency is often associated with "welfare" recipients, many people do not realize that it provides a whole range of services for individuals and families with limited income:

1. Food stamps—Eligibility for these coupons, which are used like money to buy food at grocery stores, is based upon household size and gross annual income. Ownership of a home, a car, or life insurance does not render a person ineligible for food stamps. See the accompanying table.

An individual may be eligible for food stamps even if gross income is higher than figures in this table. Other factors affecting eligibility are high medical costs, child care payments, high rent or mortgage costs, educational expenses, and court-ordered child support payments. When an application for food stamps is approved, the applicant then receives a card once or twice a month that entitles one to purchase food stamps at a bank or other licensed outlet. The card states the dollar value of the stamps (such as $160), and the discount price to be paid for them (such as $100).

2. Homemaker services and home health aides — The Department

Guideline Used in Applications for Food Stamps

Household size	Gross annual income
1	$3,900
2	5,400
3	6,800
4	8,800
5	10,600

Note: "Gross annual income" is income considered before any deductions.

of Social Services contracts with licensed agencies to provide these health care personnel to assist needy individuals in their own homes. Usually a "homemaker" or "home manager" will do light housekeeping, shopping, cooking, laundry, and similar household chores. Frequently, this type of service is provided to families when the person who would ordinarily perform this work becomes disabled. If some type of personal care is needed, for example, bathing or lifting a disabled individual, then a "home health aide" or "personal attendant" is utilized. Ordinarily, a physician's recommendation is needed for these services, and in some cases a small fee may be charged to the client.

3. Family planning services — The Department of Social Services offers counseling and referral for medical services, including provision of contraceptive devices and supplies.

4. Housing services — The Department of Social Services will assist an individual in locating a suitable apartment and in applying for gas, electricity, and telephone service.

5. Protective services — The Department of Social Services helps eliminate dangerous living conditions and attempts to safeguard the rights of dependent individuals. In particular, it is one of the main community resources available to prevent child abuse.

6. Hot meals for the elderly — Individuals sixty years old or over who cannot afford adequate food or who are unable to shop and prepare meals are eligible for the nutrition program funded by the Department of Social Services. In some areas a "meals on wheels" service is available.

7. Counseling services — The Department of Social Services maintains a service unit to help with all types of family problems. It also provides information and referral services to assist in cases of alcoholism and drug addiction.

Office of Vocational Rehabilitation (OVR). This state agency is designed to help physically or mentally handicapped individuals obtain the education, training, equipment, and other services required to enable them to perform gainful work activity. Services provided include:

1. Diagnosis and comprehensive evaluation, to help the disabled person decide where interests and abilities lie.

2. Ongoing counseling by a trained rehabilitation counselor, to help overcome frustration, discouragement, and other obstacles.

3. Education and training in a new skill, if needed.

4. Assistance in payment for prostheses, tools, equipment, and supplies needed to ensure employability.

5. Transportation and maintenance during rehabilitation.

6. Employment placement services.

Commission for the Blind and Visually Handicapped. Services provided by this state agency are aimed at making individuals with a visual loss become self-sufficient. In general, it offers the same services as the Office of Vocational Rehabilitation; in fact, some states do not have a separate Commission for the Visually Handicapped and service these individuals under the OVR umbrella.

In most states, some attempt is made to meet the special needs of the blind for mobility training. Instructors also call at the homes of the blind to teach homemaking and self-care in addition to Braille, typing, and simple handcrafts.

"Talking Books," recorded on discs or magnetic tapes, are available for the blind (and also for those physically handicapped individuals who experience difficulty in handling printed matter). The Commission for the Visually Handicapped will provide assistance in obtaining this service, or application can be made directly to Division for the Blind and Physically Handicapped, Library of Congress, Washington, DC 20542.

Private Agencies

In addition to the public agencies described above, countless private agencies provide services for individuals with specific disabling conditions. For example, there are many local chapters of the National Association for Retarded Citizens, which provides help for retarded persons. Other major organizations which provide services are the American Heart Association, American Cancer Society, Epilepsy Foundation of America, National Multiple Sclerosis Society, American Lung Association, United Cerebral Palsy Associations, National Foundation – March of Dimes (formerly National Foundation for Infantile Paralysis), and National Society for Crippled Children and Adults (Easter Seal). Their services range from financial assistance, in some cases, to education, sheltered workshops, home health care, and special equipment.

The Goodwill Industries and the Salvation Army are two other agencies that help handicapped people. They provide a number of social services and, in some instances, on-the-job training. Many communities also provide special recreational facilities for the handicapped, which enable the disabled to participate in swimming, camping, and other activities. (See PART 4, SECTION 2: VOLUNTARY ORGANIZATIONS; SECTION 3: FEDERAL ORGANIZATIONS.)

Special Situations

There are some individuals whose disabilities entitle them to special benefits because of the manner in which their injuries were incurred.

Veterans are probably the most widely known category of disabled people who receive special benefits. In addition to a cash allowance for service-connected disabilities, they are eligible for extensive vocational rehabilitation services and counseling through the Veterans Administration. The government pays all costs for training, tuition, books, supplies, and subsistence. Subsistence allowance is in addition to veterans' compensation payment. Placement services are also available.

Individuals disabled as a result of on-the-job injuries are eligible for Workmen's Compensation benefits. These programs are generally administered at the state level. Cash awards are made, but vocational rehabilitation services are provided through the appropriate state agency as outlined above.

Sixteen of the fifty states have special compensation laws to aid victims of violent crimes. To administer these laws, the states usually set up a crime victim compensation board. In some cases the disabled victim may receive compensation for lost wages and medical expenses not covered by insurance. Since this program is relatively new in most states, there is still a lag in offering the additional services needed to minimize the disabled person's adjustment problems following traumatic injury.

Internal Revenue Service Deductions

Most disabled individuals, or their responsible relatives, are aware of the obvious income tax deductions allowed under medical and dental expenses for physicians and hospital fees, medicine, etc. Following is a list of some of the lesser-known deductions permitted under "medical expenses":

1. Tuition costs, room and board for a special school or institution for the handicapped (Revenue Ruling 58-280).

2. Charges for special instruction or training to alleviate a handicap, such as lipreading, Braille, speech therapy (Revenue Ruling 68-212).

3. Cost of sheltered workshop training (Ruling 58-280).

4. Transportation expenses (train, bus, taxi fare) incurred by a handicapped person traveling to and from special schools or institutions and doctors' offices (R. T. Olson 23 TCM-2008); if a private car is used, parking fees and tolls, as well as a 6-cents-per-mile fuel allowance, may be deducted.

5. Parents may deduct their transportation costs when visiting a child at a special school but only if their visit is deemed a necessary part of treatment.

6. In some instances the cost of parents' attendance at group meetings for parents of disabled children may be interpreted as a deductible expense if it is essential for the child's welfare.

Final Word

This chapter has attempted to provide an overview of the financial aid programs and special services available to the disabled person, primarily on the federal and state levels. Most geographic areas have some type of Community Service Council, usually operational on a citywide or countywide basis, which can be an additional and valuable resource in finding specific programs on a local level.

SELECTED REFERENCES

Davis, Speed, "Guide to Supplemental Security Income," *Rehabilitation Gazette*, vol. 18, 1975.

Employment Assistance for the Handicapped: A Directory of Federal and State Programs To Help the Handicapped to Employment, President's Committee on Employment of the Handicapped, Washington, DC 20210.

State Department of Social Services, 1450 Western Avenue, Albany, NY 12243:

Food Stamps Can Give You Extra Buying Power; Publication no. 1201 C, revised August 1976; *Medicaid: How New York State Helps When Illness Strikes,* Publication no. 1006, revised September 1976; *Social Services for the Aged, Blind, and Disabled,* Publication no. 1173, August 1974.

U.S. Department of Health, Education and Welfare, Public Health Service, *Services for Crippled Children,* Health Services Administration, Bureau of Community Health Services, Rockville, MD 20852.

U.S. Department of Health, Education and Welfare, Social Security Administration, *A Brief Explanation of Medicare,* DHEW Publication no. 75-10043, 1975; *Disabled? Find Out about Social Security Benefits,* DHEW Publication no. 74-10068, February 1974; *Guide to Supplemental Security Income,* DHEW Publication no. 75-11015, July 1975; *Social Security Benefits for People Disabled before Age 22,* DHEW Publication no. 74-10012, February 1974.

On the opposite page: At a
rehabilitation center a physical therapy aide helps a patient
use a leg exerciser. (Woodrow
Wilson Rehabilitation Center,
Fishersville, Virginia)

2

Disabling Disorders

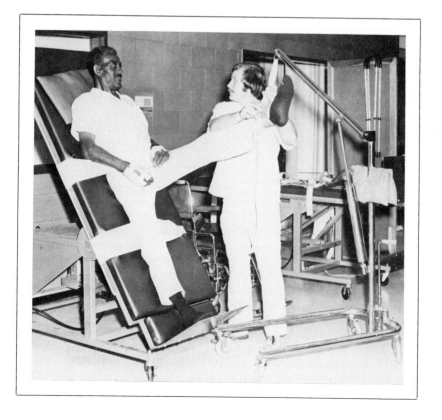

16

Alcoholism

RAE H. FARMER, M.Ed.Psych., Supervisor, Chemical Dependency Program, Seattle Mental Health Institute

Alcoholism is a complex, progressive addictive disease typically characterized by varying degrees of psychological and physiological dependence on alcohol. Although the use of alcohol as a mood-changing drug, with pleasurable effects, has been a part of human existence since the beginning of recorded history, little attention was paid to the social and medical aspects of the excessive use of alcoholic beverages until the beginning of this century.

Probably no disabling condition of our times remains so stigmatized as alcoholism, and it is difficult to exaggerate the extent to which ingrained attitudes, misconceptions, and archaic thinking have delayed and limited the development of effective treatment programs. Social drinking is greatly encouraged and tolerated in our society, and a conservative estimate suggests that at least two-thirds of the adult population of the United States use alcohol regularly in social and family situations. Yet when alcoholism is the result, as in a considerable number of instances, the drinker is ostracized, rejected, and despised. Even when a more enlightened attitude is held — for instance, by physicians, counselors, and others of the helping professions — there tends to be a greater degree of negative expectations for outcome of counseling, with emphasis on "reform" rather than treatment, than is the case with any other condition. Alcoholism, along with other forms of drug abuse, obesity, and various kinds of neurotic behavior, is too frequently related to willful misconduct, and a relapse usually evokes moralistic disapproval.

In recent years, since the addictive nature of alcohol has become better understood (that is, its ability to induce an acquired increased biochemical tolerance leading to increased physical dependence), it has become generally recognized that in most cases alcoholism is a disease entity and not necessarily a symptom of underlying psychopathology. When a society approves drinking and tolerates drunkenness, whether all of the time or on special occasions, many people will drink to excess. Some of these people will become alcoholic for various reasons — constitutional, biochemical, physiological, or psychological. Unfortunately, societal ambivalence and judgmental attitudes contribute to the problem. We must all recognize that the alcoholic is a sick person, and it is certain that if that person continues to drink, progress toward a chronic, deteriorated condition is inevitable.

With the growing understanding of alcoholism as a complex disease which deserves and can respond to treatment, the federal government is responsive to urgent public demands for the widespread availability of treatment and rehabilitation services. Legislation in the early 1970s and the recently established National Institute of Alcohol Abuse and Alcoholism (NIAAA, 1971) are now providing a broad impetus for urgent comprehensive services to treat the medical, emotional, and social problems of alcoholic men and women. Effective treatment of alcohol dependency is not an impossible goal. Encouraging results are being obtained in certain areas of critical concern, such as ASAP (Alcohol Safety Action Project) and specialized industrial alcoholism programs. Countermeasures instituted by ASAP have shown a 9 percent decrease in traffic accident fatalities for the first year's operation in ASAP areas, in contrast to a 2 percent increase in non-ASAP areas in the same states (NIAAA, *Alcohol and Health Notes*, December 1973). In a statement recently released by NIAAA, M. E. Chafetz reports that some industrial alcoholism programs are producing an 80 percent recovery rate (1973), while K. Rouse notes that several business and industrial programs show a rate of abstinence as high as 50 percent ("Employees with a Drinking Problem," Kemper Insurance Group, 1975).

Many workers in the field of alcoholism with specialized knowledge and understanding of the complexities of this illness are finding it one of the more gratifying areas of helping experiences. The optimistic and persevering counselor who demonstrates a nonjudgmental attitude and comfortable acceptance of alcoholic individuals can accomplish a great deal in helping them to achieve sobriety and then to learn better ways of developing a more satisfying emotional life through rewarding relationships with others.

Incidence

According to a major study of American drinking practices, about 95 million adults drink alcoholic beverages at least occasionally, and approximately 17 million young people between fourteen and eighteen experiment with alcohol. Although the overwhelming majority drink responsibly and estimates vary considerably, it is now thought that three out of every ten persons who use alcohol regularly will probably develop some form of drinking problem. Contrary to popular belief, at least 95 percent of these will consist of employed or employable, family-centered individuals. They reside in respectable neighborhoods, live with husband or wife, may send their children to college, attend church, and pay taxes. Many continue to function with varying degrees of effectiveness as bank presidents, housewives, farmers, salesmen, stenographers, teachers, clergymen, and physicians. Contrary to popular belief, many people on Skid Row are not alcoholics, and those who are probably make up less than 5 percent of the total alcoholism problem population.

Although men and women who have drinking problems constitute a relatively small portion of the total American population, the misery they cause themselves and others is enormous. According to the National Council on Alcoholism, there are an estimated 9 million alcoholics in the United States. Their life expectancy is usually shorter by ten to twelve years than that of nonalcoholics. Forty percent of all male admissions to state mental hospitals suffer from alcoholism, and the number of beds for alcoholic patients has increased by as much as 50 percent in some areas during the past few years. Fifty percent of all fatal automobile accidents involve alcohol, and at least 50 percent of these fatal accidents involve an alcoholic individual. Alcoholics account for at least 40 percent of all cases brought to family court, and many cases of child abuse suggest alcoholism as a causative factor. Thirty-one percent of those who take their own lives are alcoholics. Their suicide rate is fifty-eight times that of nonalcoholic individuals.

If one considers only the personal cost of problem drinking, the price is exorbitant. The effects of alcoholism, however, are not limited to the drinker alone. Family, employer, and society at large are all harmed by the drinker's behavior, and all have a stake in helping to prevent this disease from becoming more severe. Statistical data related to the ill effects of problem drinking on families of the drinkers suggest that some 36 million Americans can be regarded as caught in alcohol's web. Unhappy marriages, broken homes, desertion, divorce, impoverished families, and deprived or displaced children are all part of the toll. The cost to public and private agencies for support of families ravished by alcohol problems has been estimated at many millions of dollars a year. It is clear that the cost in human suffering is incalculable. (See PART 4, SECTION 1: STATISTICS.)

Types and Degree of Severity

Alcoholism is not easy to define, and no single definition is suitable for all purposes. At present, there is no formal definition for alcoholism which is universally accepted. Perhaps the best functional definition of alcoholism is one used by Harry Milt (Public Affairs Pamphlet no. 426, "Alcoholics and Alcoholism"), in which he describes alcoholism as "a chronic disorder in which an individual is unable, for physical or psychological reasons, to refrain from frequent consumption of alcohol in quantities sufficient to produce intoxication, and ultimately, injury to health and functioning." Milt describes the essential element as compulsive, uncontrollable drinking. "While others can decide whether to drink or not and whether to keep on drinking after the second or third drink, the alcoholic cannot. He has lost choice or decision in respect to this act and this is alcohol addiction."

It is important to recognize that there is no single "alcoholism" but several different "alcoholisms." The above description specifies the characteristic loss of control of gamma alcoholism, which is predominant in the United States, Canada, and other Anglo-Saxon countries. The progression of gamma alcoholism is as follows: (1) acquired increased tissue tolerance to alcohol; (2) adaptive cell metabolism; (3) withdrawal symptoms and "craving," that is, physical dependence; and (4) loss of control. Another species, delta alcoholism, is becoming more prevalent in these countries. This shows a similar progression with the exception of "loss of control" and instead there is an "inability to abstain" as a characteristic factor. In distinct contrast to the gamma type, the ability to control the amount of alcohol intake on any given occasion remains virtually intact, but there is no ability to abstain for even a day or two without the manifestation of withdrawal symptoms. This form is more frequently found where there is general acceptance of high alcohol intake by the society to which the drinker belongs.

Although there is no simple diagnostic procedure for detecting alcoholism, particularly in the borderline, or early, stages of the illness, there are symptoms that can be recognized. Dr. E. M. Jellinek, pioneer researcher in alcoholism, identified a typical sequence of symptoms in its development. Not all symptoms occur necessarily in all alcoholics, nor do they occur in the same sequence. Nevertheless, in the majority they seem to appear gradually and with increasing frequency and intensity over a period of years until most of them are invariably present. Jellinek clustered symptoms together into three identifiable progressive stages or phases of alcoholism (the second and third stages constituting addiction):

Early alcoholism — With increasing frequency, individuals drink too much. "Blackouts," or temporary amnesia, occur during or following drinking episodes. They drink more rapidly than others. They sneak drinks and in other ways conceal the quantity that they drink. They resent any reference to their drinking habits. Increased preoccupation with drinking occurs.

Acute or middle-stage alcoholism — Individuals begin to lose control as to time, place, and amount of drinking. They get drunk when they do not intend to. They hide and protect their liquor supply. They drink to overcome the hangover effects of prior drinking. They try new patterns of drinking as to time and place. They attempt cures by moving to new locations or by changing drinking companions. They get into morning drinking, alibis, remorse, and loss of interests.

Chronic or advanced alcoholism—Individuals become loners in their drinking. They make excuses and rationalizations to explain their drinking. There are personality and behavioral changes, even when not drinking, that adversely affect all relationships—family, employment, community. Extended binges result in physical tremors, hallucinations, and delirium. The outcome is complete rejection of social reality, malnutrition with accompanying illness and disease, and early death.

In 1952 the Alcoholism Subcommittee of the World Health Committee distinguished between two categories of alcoholism—"alcohol addicts" and "habitual symptomatic excessive drinkers" (frequently described as nonaddictive alcoholics). The "loss of control" factor appears to be the basis for this differentiation. Jellinek's phases of alcohol addiction were developed from the drinking histories of alcohol addicts, that is, gamma species, where loss of control is typically experienced. It has less relevance for delta alcoholism, where loss of control is not a factor, yet where there is undeniable evidence of both psychological and physiological addiction. Strict adherence to Jellinek's stages is not always helpful when attempting to assess an individual's problem with alcohol, particularly in the early stage or in borderline cases, and it is essential to recognize that continued alcohol excess will undoubtedly speed up the entire deterioration process.

Despite difficulties in accurate assessment, there are three important behavioral criteria by which one can usually form a descriptive basis for defining an individual's alcohol problem, and these are: (a) the victims find themselves drinking when they intend not to drink, or drinking more than they had planned; (b) there is evidence of functional or structural damage—physiological, psychological, economic, or social; and (c) the frequent use of alcohol is pursued as a kind of universal therapy by which the individuals try to keep their life from disintegrating, and they exhibit an intense need for alcohol-induced mood modification for coping with life in general.

Etiology

It is now generally accepted that the development of alcoholism involves complex psychological, social, and physiological factors related to the individual and the total environment. Earlier explanations labeled alcoholics as maladjusted people with serious psychoneuroses or personality disorders and usually described them as belonging to one of two groups: antisocial persons who seek to rebel against society, and those whose inner tensions are so great that they must attain relief from alcohol regardless of society's disapproval. This simplistic approach fails to account for the behavior of many alcohol-addictive individuals. There are persons who by tradition and culture use alcohol freely to socialize and for business reasons. Many of these individuals have no basic personality problem, and yet, of this group, some who drink excessively will progress from heavy drinking to a marked dependence on alcohol. There are others who are by nature shy and inhibited and, upon finding the magical qualities of alcohol, may unwittingly begin to use alcoholic beverages to overcome such feelings. A considerable number of such people who drink excessively may soon experience both psychological and physiological dependence. As tolerance to alcohol develops, increased amount and frequency of consumption are required to reach either the limit of socially acceptable behavior or the desired level of effect.

Others present a more complicated picture which indicates that alcoholism is probably secondary to serious personality problems, neurosis, or even psychosis. Since the prolonged, excessive use of alcohol can have devastating effects on psychological and physiological functioning, it is usually impossible to determine if these manifestations are the cause or result of destructive drinking, particularly when the individual is still drinking or is in the early post-withdrawal period of abstaining. The assumption that alcoholism is the result of unconsciously motivated factors is highly controversial, since this theory is based on inference and ignores basic research into the mechanisms of alcohol tolerance. Hard evidence simply confirms that there are many kinds of drinking problems, many types of people who have them, and many reasons why they begin and continue to drink to a harmful degree.

High-Risk Individuals

Although the search for the cause of alcoholism has not yet been successful, it is possible to identify people in the community who are clearly more susceptible and have a higher risk, according to statistics, for developing alcoholism should they, in fact, drink: children of alcoholic parents; children from broken homes with absent or rejecting fathers, or from families where there is a history of recurrent depression in one or more generations; people from families where a history of teetotalism is found; and Irish, French, and Scandinavian people. Certain occupations also seem to involve a higher risk, such as the catering trades, businesses, or sales jobs where alcohol is used to facilitate transactions. Those with executive responsibilities run a high degree of risk since they frequently use alcohol while negotiating, then later as a means of obtaining relief from the stress and tension produced by executive life.

Other situational circumstances increase the risk factor, such as being in the military, seagoing occupations, and the "country club set." In such situations, the acceptable code of relatively heavy drinking can gradually reduce the body's ability to handle alcohol and all too frequently "they become—biochemically speaking—alcoholic" (J. Smith, "Orientation to Alcoholism," Shadel Hospital, Seattle). There is ample evidence that situational dependence is a significant factor in moving social drinkers into problem drinking and alcoholism.

Treatment

The alcoholic person usually seeks treatment in one of the following ways: at a doctor's office (or hospital), when suffering from alcohol-related injuries or illness, where gentle probing or sensitively phrased questioning can soon produce a frank discussion of the patient's drinking history and current problems; at an alcoholism center, clinic, or counselor's office, with the patient either in a state of temporary sobriety and seeking help under duress from a relation, employer, courts, etc., or in a confused, disorganized state resulting from acute intoxication.

Acute Intoxication. The first move is to have the individuals withdrawn from alcohol, that is, detoxification. This is designed to overcome the immediate toxic effects of excess alcohol, and patients may need immediate physical measures to treat or prevent serious withdrawal symptoms. The severity of withdrawal is determined by the degree of physical dependence on alcohol, and patients even in the early stage of alcoholism frequently experience symptoms of acute anxiety, sleeplessness, nausea, and general discomfort when they stop drinking. In more advanced cases, the symptoms consist of an acute brain syndrome identifiable by severe psychomotor agitation, that is, severe shakes, auditory hallucinations and, in some cases, delirium tremens, which generally begins two to five days after abrupt cessation of very heavy drinking. Delirium tremens, known colloquially as the "the DT's," is a serious and sometimes fatal condition in which the patient is confused, has little awareness of surroundings, and is sometimes convulsive. The patient may have terrifying hallucinations or seizures, and recent studies indicate that a rapid and dramatic drop in blood sugar could produce a hypoglycemic coma and perhaps result in death. It is estimated that about 5 percent of alcoholics in hospitals, and perhaps 25 percent who suffer DT's alone and unattended, die from this condition.

Treatment usually consists of sedative drugs, polyvitamin therapy (especially the vitamin B group), administration of minerals to provide maintenance of proper electrolyte balance (sodium, potassium, magnesium), and a high protein-carbohydrate diet. Recent evidence indicates that massive intramuscular doses of vitamins and the presence of a highly concerned person providing personal supportive care throughout this critical period can reduce both the severity and duration of symptoms as effectively as the more frequently used tranquilizing or sedative compounds. This suggests that patients with close friends or family relationships can probably survive withdrawal at home more comfortably and safely than in the past. Another recent finding indicates that patients are not dehydrated during withdrawal as previously thought. For many years patients were routinely treated with large doses of intravenous fluids, but it has now been determined that a declining blood-alcohol concentration actually leads to overhydration, and if fluids are given at all, they should be given orally in many small drinks simply to quench the patient's sensation of thirst.

Detoxification is best carried out in a general hospital ward if severe symptoms are expected; however, many general hospitals are still unwilling to accept alcoholics, primarily because they often appear dirty, disheveled, and in a state of acute intoxication. For this reason, special facilities have been developed throughout the country to help alcoholic patients in the early withdrawal drying-out period. These have not been entirely successful, since they tend to perpetuate the "revolving door" syndrome, by repeatedly drying out the same population and turning persons out into the street who are still sick, confused, and without any future treatment plans. Detoxification units are now making a more concerned effort to direct alcoholic persons into appropriate treatment programs prior to discharge from the facility, recognizing that drying-out is just the first step along the long road to successful recovery from alcoholism.

Physical Consequences of Alcoholism. When over the acute stages of withdrawal, the patient must start a long-range treatment plan which may involve various forms of expert care. Medical assessment may be necessary to determine what physical and mental deterioration has already occurred. The excessive use of alcohol can measurably impair every system of the body, and although some systems are not involved to a fatal degree, there are three systems where fatal or permanently crippling damage is encountered: (1) the cardiovascular system, comprising the heart and blood vessels; (2) the nervous system, comprising the brain, spinal cord, and nerves running to all parts of the body; and (3) the liver.

A large number of alcoholics die of heart disease as a result of hardening of the arteries, or atherosclerosis. Excessive quantities of alcohol will inevitably produce a raised blood level of fats, which may progress to the point where a crippling or even fatal heart attack can occur. Heart disease secondary to malnutrition (thiamine deficiency) frequently occurs, as well as the characteristic alcoholic cardiomyopathy found in even comparatively young persons—a condition due to the direct toxic effect of alcohol on the heart muscle itself. As in other alcohol-related illnesses, absolute abstinence from alcohol is a prerequisite for successful treatment, and many patients with bed rest, improved nutrition, and abstinence will fully recover. Some, however, have irreversible heart disease by the time they are seen by a physician.

The entire nervous system is susceptible to the effects of alcohol, and specific neurological disorders constitute the most direct relationship between nutritional deficiencies and medical complications of alcoholism. A deficiency of one or more B vitamins is responsible for a condition known as peripheral neuropathy, in which degenerative changes occur in the nerve cells, initially affecting the toes and feet—hence the term "peripheral." The symptoms of tingling, gradual loss of sensation, weakness, and motor loss can gradually spread toward the trunk if early medical treatment is not undertaken. With the correction of thiamine and other vitamin deficiencies, this condition is reversible, although irreversible neurological damage may occur in more deteriorated patients who are unable to adequately utilize essential vitamins and protein. (See CHAPTER 43: NEUROLOGICAL DISORDERS.)

The effect of prolonged, excessive drinking on the brain results in diffuse cerebral atrophy, cerebellar deterioration, and the Wernicke-Korsakoff syndrome. These conditions are identified by a selective memory loss, confabulation, difficulties in concentration, and frequently a disturbance of gait and balance. There is also a gradual decline in intellectual ability with the progressive brain cell destruction. It has been noted in all of these conditions that significant improvement can be expected with prolonged abstinence and a high intake of thiamine, vitamin B_1. Recent studies have shown that even abnormal electroencephalogram (EEG) tracings can frequently revert to normal with long-term abstinence in some subjects, suggesting temporary damage rather than irreversible cell destruction (A. E. Bennett). The major point is that it is essential the patient discontinue any alcohol intake as soon as a diagnosis of alcoholism is made for neurological reasons alone. If one continues drinking, mental functioning will inevitably deteriorate, and one may be forced to live in a highly supportive or protected environment such as a nursing home or mental hospital.

The role of alcohol toxicity and nutritional deficiency in the development of liver disease is well established. The chronic use of alcohol causes tiny droplets of fat to accumulate in the liver, pancreas, blood vessels, and other parts of the body. Fatty infiltration of the liver impairs its ability to metabolize nutrients essential for its own healthy functioning and for other vital organs, and a vicious cycle is set up. Malnutrition resulting from impaired liver functioning contributes to further liver cell destruction, and yet further malnutrition. The damage is reversible if the injuring process from alcohol is stopped and an adequate diet containing essential vitamins and nutrient supplements is provided. However, if alcohol intake is continued, the fatty infiltration progresses to further cell destruction, with resulting scar tissue constricting blood vessels and reducing blood supply, thus causing further liver cell damage and, finally, cirrhosis, or hardening.

It was assumed for many years that cirrhosis was primarily due to the poor diet habits of alcoholics; however, this damaging sequence of events can occur in spite of a nutritionally adequate diet, and cirrhosis of the liver occurs in apparently well-nourished individuals who continue to use excessive amounts of alcohol. Liver failure leads to failure in other vital processes, with increased ammonia and other poisons accumulating in the bloodstream, producing mental confusion, lethargy, a comatose state, or death. It is unfortunate that the progression of symptoms in liver damage usually occurs without significant pain or warning. In all cases, it is essential to determine what degree of liver damage exists and then urge the patient to preserve whatever liver function is left.

Other medical conditions frequently associated with alcoholism are acute or chronic pancreatitis, gastritis and peptic ulcer, alcohol-induced hypoglycemia, and adrenal insufficiency. Individuals can frequently suffer from one or more of these conditions, and medical attention at all times must be directed not only to the presenting illness, but also to the underlying disease of alcoholism if the patient is to avoid inevitable progression to irreversible physical and mental deterioration.

Personal and Social Rehabilitation

Once clearly addicted, the alcoholic person suffers from loss of respect of family and friends and a sense of growing isolation and loneliness. The gradual awareness of personal self-destruction turns life into a nightmare such as only the alcoholic knows. A process of simple separation from alcohol (sometimes in a *detoxification unit* at a medical facility) will enable the individual to become sober, but the task of helping the person to remain sober sufficiently long enough to cope with the tangled morass of problems that drinking has imposed is much more difficult. No one single treatment method has been found to be more effective than others, and a combination of treatment approaches may be necessary not only to help different patients but often to help the same individual in different stages of the illness.

There is reason to believe that the best result is obtained if treatment begins on an inpatient basis and is followed up by planned regular outpatient treatment. *Residential treatment programs* are often indicated and, indeed, preferable for individuals with an unstable home life, the more socially isolated, and those who cannot stay sober for more than one or two weeks at a time. The major advantage of residential treatment lies in providing a stress-free environment totally conducive to sobriety where the patient is kept sober long enough to initiate more appropriate and effective ways of coping with the personal life situation. Treatment usually varies from thirty to ninety days, and a wide range of group, individual, socialization, and educational activities is provided. The highly trained staff themselves frequently are recovered alcoholics, who are therefore able to approach other alcoholics without hostility or contempt. Patients also obtain considerable benefit from the mutual support of other members in group therapy sessions, which enable them to express shared feelings of rejection and loneliness. Most residential programs have their own Alcoholics Anonymous (AA) groups, and arrangements are usually made for follow-up services and continued contact with AA groups in the community prior to leaving the treatment facility.

It is estimated that 10 percent of total recovery in alcoholism takes place during intensive residential treatment, and 90 percent occurs in the community. For this reason, community helping agencies are making a determined and coordinated effort to provide a multidisciplinary approach in treating the varying psychological and physical needs of alcoholic individuals and their families on an outpatient basis. *Alcoholism information and referral centers* are located in many communities and specialize in assessing the extent of a person's involvement with alcohol. They provide clients and others in the community with information and sponsor educational classes concerning problem drinking and the nature of alcoholism. They also make direct referrals, and on occasion staff members accompany clients to appropriate treatment facilities or social service agencies to ensure early management of the problem.

Specialized alcoholism outpatient clinics have the single purpose of treating alcoholics and helping their families by individual counseling, group therapy, or family counseling. Many of these clinics are selective, and some general criteria for accepting clients are as follows: (1) the person is not seriously brain damaged, and (2) not in acute withdrawal; (3) the person accepts that alcohol has interfered with his or her functioning and has motivation to accept help, and (4) accepts the clinic philosophy that emotional conflicts are related to drinking or family problems; and (5) the individual has personal resources which permit psychotherapy, that is, normal intelligence, fairly good physical health, history of stabilization in his or her life, and potential for change (Alcoholism Treatment Clinic, Seattle). Specialized outpatient facilities sharing this basic philosophy prefer working with relatively stable, employed, family-oriented persons, with whom they are most successful. Many alcoholics do not meet these criteria, and *community mental health centers* are now attempting to respond to the problems of all alcoholic persons in the community, including the indigent, mentally ill, "street people," and other disadvantaged groups. Mental health centers have the advantage of being able to utilize the numerous services which are already available to the community at large for this purpose. Walk-in emergency care, crisis intervention, and advocacy for housing or legal problems are frequently provided in addition to longer-term group, individual, and vocational counseling services. Mental health workers are now receiving intensive advanced training and orientation in the treatment of alcoholism, and it is expected that they will be even more responsive in the future to early identification, treatment, and prevention of alcoholism problems within the community.

Special adaptive services are sometimes necessary to ensure continuity of care for some individuals. *Partial hospitalization* can provide daily treatment, supervision, and suitable daytime activities for those who need intensive treatment, yet are able to return to their own living arrangements at night. Another form of partial hospitalization allows the client to continue work or participate in a community day-care program and then return to the protected environment of a residential facility at night. The *halfway house* is frequently used for this purpose and can be particularly helpful for the transition from hospital residence back into community living. Alternatively, placement in *foster homes* or small group homes may be needed to provide support, constructive use of leisure time, and a gradual return to effective social functioning.

A more rarely used form of treatment is the conditioned reflex or *aversion therapy,* in which the essential procedure is to induce an extremely unpleasant sensation in response to the taste, smell, and sight of alcohol. The patient is given an injection of a drug which will produce vomiting, and very shortly afterwards given alcohol; the patient vomits and subsequently establishes an alcohol reaction. This procedure is repeated several times in the course of a treatment session, and about half a dozen sessions take place over the course of several days. Finally, a distasteful association with alcohol has been made, and the individual develops nausea when handling a drink. The aversive reaction is reinforced by further treatment courses at intervals later on, and although the treatment is drastic, it has been consistently reported to produce good results. Possibly it is less frequently used because it can be administered only under strict medical supervision and because it has been primarily successful for patients from a higher socioeconomic group who are very well motivated to overcome their addiction.

Some patients remain abstinent through the use of a chemical deterrent drug, disulfuram, commonly known as *Antabuse.* Again, the principle of this method is to introduce a drug into the system of the drinker which, when combined with alcohol, will produce an extremely unpleasant reaction. The patient is instructed that such a reaction will be experienced if alcohol is ingested within the next three to five days after taking the dose of Antabuse. Although this drug has proved effective for some highly motivated persons, its use has declined due to severe side effects and contraindications.

From a learning theory viewpoint it is clear that the alcoholic person will probably remain sober when not drinking is found to be more rewarding than drinking. *Alcoholics Anonymous* recognizes this, and the AA program has become widely acknowledged as probably the most effective and successful way to help alcoholic individuals and their families recognize the seriousness of excessive drinking and the realistic implications of continued drinking. Its members are dedicated to helping themselves and others stay sober by a plan based on open self-scrutiny, admission of defects, and reparation for harm done to others in the past. Increased self-esteem, group approval, and renewal of social contacts in AA undoubtedly reward nondrinking behavior. AA is a worldwide organization with scheduled meetings in most cities in many different countries, and it has been estimated that "50 percent of those who accept the program achieve sobriety. Another 25 percent, after slips occasioned by over-confidence and/or neglect of some part of the program, permanently abstain from alcohol. The other 25% never get back." (S. Hartley, "Alcoholism: Facets of Recovery in AA," 1973). Al-Anon is the family or spouses' organization designed to help family members work together with the alcoholic in a program of maintaining sobriety, self-growth, and renewed responsibility. AA participation is strongly emphasized in all treatment programs as an important part of an overall long-range therapeutic plan, and membership in Al-Anon and Ala-Teen (for children of alcoholic persons) undoubtedly helps family members gain better understanding and effectiveness in dealing with whatever social and emotional difficulties they are experiencing. AA has the least success with alcoholics who are not gregarious and cannot tolerate the pressure of intimate relationships with others, but it can be a life-changing experience for those who are sociable and derive satisfaction from helping others.

Vocational rehabilitation is very important. Most alcoholic individuals are already in the work force, and the fear of job loss due to impairment in performance and poor on-the-job relationships frequently motivates them to seek treatment. In many instances the alcoholic worker is highly experienced and has no difficulty returning to the previous job or finding new employment after successful response to treatment. This is not the case for the indigent alcoholic, or others with marginal job skills, limited education, and poor previous work experience. Vocational rehabilitation services are an essential part of the total rehabilitation effort for these persons. Upgrading education through appropriate vocational training and placement services which can lead to satisfying, adequately paid employment has now become the major goal of state rehabilitation and public welfare agencies in attempting to rehabilitate this complex disability group.

Although sobriety is a prerequisite for vocational rehabilitation services, sobriety alone cannot solve the problems of survival for vocationally disadvantaged alcoholics. The opportunity to become a constructive, independent, and productive worker in our society will clearly go a long way to meet the needs of the alcoholic and family members.

The entire network of treatment services must be available in order to meet the various needs of individuals at different stages in the rehabilitation process, and the services may be particularly crucial for the more disadvantaged alcoholic persons whose lives have usually lacked opportunity for economic and social stability. Until comparatively recently, most treatment plans were determined more by limitation in available services than by careful assessment of individual need. More humanistic treatment efforts now recognize that services must be specifically tailored to individual need if they are to yield greater benefit for many more persons than in the past. The pessimistic and negative attitudes of some workers in this field have resulted from the fact that most treated alcoholics have come from the more severely disabled portion of the total alcoholic population and seem to have the least potential for successful recovery. If attitudes and outcome of treatment are to change, more personalized service must be directed at the whole individual within the context of the total environment rather than dealing exclusively with the alcoholism problem itself. At the same time, increased efforts to identify and motivate individuals in the early stage of the illness will clearly be less costly and more effective than when the problem is far advanced.

Although sobriety (an alcohol-free life) is the primary goal of treatment, long-term supportive care is often needed to sustain the sober alcoholic through the many problem areas the patient encounters while attempting to reconstruct life without alcohol. Counseling strategy should aim at helping the alcoholic accept himself or herself as a worthwhile person and then help to develop realistic objectives based on the positive reinforcement of abstinence. Honest, direct communication between the worker and the client can neutralize tendencies to minimize the severity of the drinking problem and can lead to a gradual willingness to accept responsibility for dealing with the drinking and other major life problems. Workers can offer reasonable hope of recovery and thereby reduce the need for denial, rationalization, and compromises which have long supported the continued use of alcohol despite its obvious harmful effects. Patient, understanding workers provide the alcoholic person with hope for the future and help toward achieving a more fully satisfying life through continued personal growth and self-understanding.

Prevention

Preventing alcoholism is a major public health goal in our country and must rest ultimately with the private decisions and behavior of individuals. We must also accept a personal responsibility to educate those who drink with regard to the effects of excessive use of alcohol. Experts agree that if the incidence of alcoholism is to be lowered, two types of social change will have to come about. "Certain characteristic American drinking practices will need modification, and conditions leading to improved mental health of individuals will have to be encouraged" (R. Straus, "Alcohol and Society," *Psychiatric Annals*, vol. 3, no. 10, 1973). Drinking is repeatedly depicted by the mass media as appropriate to many work and leisure situations and is invariably associated with status, prestige, wealth, and success. Repetitive drinking in young persons is usually labeled as "sowing wild oats" and rarely thought of as problem drinking since we seem unable to accept the fact that alcoholism can occur at relatively early periods of life. Our social climate also supports the use of chemicals for all types of coping purposes, and this influences the way many people rationalize their drinking and routinely combine alcohol with various other chemical substances despite the potential danger of a synergistic effect and increased probability of addiction.

The traditional public health approach has been applied to the prevention of alcoholism by M. E. Chafetz and H. W. Demone, Jr., who describe prevention as follows: primary prevention is the use of various procedures to prevent the onset of alcoholism; secondary prevention consists of early intervention in excessive drinking to prevent major consequences of alcoholism: and tertiary prevention involves rehabilitation of the chronic alcoholic to avoid further complications of the illness and prevent the spread of its influence to other members of society (*International Psychiatric Clinics*, vol. 3, no. 2, 1966). Primary prevention involves an increased knowledge about alcoholism at every level of the community, which should also include education about alcohol and a greater understanding of how alcohol and the individual interact. Social change requires a change in attitudes of the general public, and a healthier national attitude toward drinking will be achieved when we can all agree on the following considerations: It is not essential for people to drink at all, and those who do can learn how to do so with maximum safety to themselves and others. Those who decide not to drink should not be subjected to pressure by others. Excessive drinking does not indicate status, virility, or social competence, but instead can lead to frequent occasions of intoxication. Tolerance to alcohol is individually determined by physiological as well as psychosocial factors, and an increased tolerance, rather than being viewed as an accomplishment, might instead suggest the acquired increased tissue tolerance characteristic of physical addiction.

Young people are the drinkers and abstainers of tomorrow and should be the prime audience for education in the responsible use of alcohol. Schools usually present objective facts about drinking in a neutral manner, recognizing that parents are the most influential teachers by establishing responsible drinking patterns in the home. It is unfortunate that families often disagree among themselves on drinking and agree only when it comes to judging the drinking practices of other families. Alcoholism will be prevented if alcohol is consumed infrequently, in small amounts, adequately diluted, and preferably with meals. Efforts to encourage more desirable drinking habits must also aim at reducing the overall level of alcohol consumption if the prevalence and severity of alcoholism is to diminish in future years.

Secondary prevention relies on earlier identification of problems related to excessive drinking so as to prevent progression into more severe manifestations of alcoholism. More young people and even teen-agers are becoming increasingly involved in excessive drinking due to changing drinking practices in our affluent society. A key problem in imposing controls on individuals who are already having difficulties with alcohol is that controls must be self-imposed as well as instituted by formal social measures. Unfortunately, formal controls often seem to produce the very opposite of what they intend, and many problem drinkers will not accept the need for self-imposed control until distinct symptoms of alcoholism are being experienced.

Despite the difficulties of effecting change in social custom and in the early detection of problem drinking, the National Council on Alcoholism and other organizations are mounting a massive attempt to make their message reach everywhere: "Alcoholism is a disease and the alcoholic is a sick person. An alcoholic can be helped, and is worth helping. It is a major public health problem and a public problem and a public responsibility." Continued nationwide research is necessary to further describe and measure the extent of the problem and to document changes which may occur as a result of disseminating factual information and other control efforts. New methods to influence or modify attitudes must be sought and then tested to determine their effectiveness in changing drinking behavior. Alcoholism is now being confronted as one of our gravest social problems, but we are at least beginning to find a way to face this problem more openly, rationally, and humanely than at any time in the past.

Sources of Information

Al-Anon Family Groups and Ala-Teen, P.O. Box 182, Madison Square Station, New York, NY 10010.

Alcoholics Anonymous, General Office, 468 Park Avenue South, New York, NY 10016.

National Council on Alcoholism, 2 Park Avenue, New York, NY 10016.

National Institute of Alcohol Abuse and Alcoholism, National Institute of Mental Health, 5600 Fishers Lane, Rockville, MD 20852.

North American Association of Alcohol Programs, 1130 17th Street N.W., Washington, DC 20036.

Rutgers Center for Alcohol Studies, Rutgers University, New Brunswick, NJ 08901.

Each state has alcoholism agencies; consult State Government listings in the telephone directory, etc.

SELECTED REFERENCES

Bennett, A. E., A. L. Mowery, and J. T. Fort, "Brain Damage from Chronic Alcoholism: The Diagnosis of Intermediate Stage of Alcoholic Brain Disease, *American Journal of Psychiatry*, vol. 116, pp. 705–711, 1960.

Chafetz, M. E., and H. W. Demone, Jr., *Alcoholism and Society*, Oxford University Press, New York, 1962.

Edwards, G., "The Status of Alcoholism as a Disease," in R. V. Phillipson, ed., *Modern Trends in Drug Dependence and Alcoholism*, Appleton-Century-Crofts, New York, 1970.

Mardones, Jorge, and Israel Yady, *Biological Basis of Alcohol*, Wiley-Interscience, New York, 1971.

Mell, N. K., "Behavior Studies of Alcoholism," in B. Kissin and H. Begleiter, eds., *The Biology of Alcoholism*, Plenum Press, New York, 1972.

Milt, Harry, *Alcoholism*, Scribners, New York, 1976.

National Institute of Alcohol Abuse and Alcoholism, *Alcoholism Problems, Progress and Programs*, DHEW Publication no. (HSM) 72-9123, revised 1972.

Rubington, Earl, *Alcohol Problems and Social Control*, Charles E. Merrill, Columbus, Ohio, 1973.

17

Amputations

CHARLIS S. DUNHAM, M.A.

Reviewed by RONALD S. WINKLE, M.D., Department of Physical Medicine and Rehabilitation, University of Washington, and the National Amputation Foundation, Kenneth G. Robinson, C.P., Director

While the term "amputation" applies to the removal of any projecting portion of the body, it is here discussed with reference to the arms and legs, or extremities. The surgical removal of a limb or portion of a limb is usually a lifesaving treatment procedure, and the first step in a complex rehabilitative process.

There is evidence of amputation in skeletal remains dating back to prehistoric times. Throughout the world there are records of limbs severed for religious sacrifice, punishment, or proof of stamina and courage. In 484 B.C. the Greek historian Herodotus wrote of a soldier who escaped from captive chains by cutting off his foot, replacing it later with a wooden substitute. An artificial leg was found in a Capua tomb which is thought to date back to about 300 B.C. Many amputations were performed during the great wars of the Middle Ages, but today about 12½ times as many amputations result from civilian accidents and diseases as from combat injuries. As society becomes more mechanized, there are more accidents, and as people survive to greater longevity, there is more need for restorative measures.

Incidence and Causes

The 1971 Department of Health, Education and Welfare Health Interview Survey reported approximately 274,000 persons with absence of major extremities (leg, foot, arm, hand) in the civilian noninstitutionalized population. In addition, the Veterans Administration has recently reported about 86,000 amputees among war veterans (1977). A two-year study ending June 1967 reported that of 8,698 persons obtaining artificial limbs (prostheses) in thirty states, 60 percent of the amputations were caused by disease, 29 percent by trauma (accidental injury), 6 percent by tumor, and 5 percent were of congenital origin. Most amputations from disease occur when persons are in their seventies; those caused by accidents reach their highest frequency in the third decade of life; and those due to tumors tend to be performed when people are in their twenties. Males incur more amputations from all causes, at the rate of 2 to 1 from diseases, 10 to 1 from trauma, and 1.2 to 1 for both congenital causes and tumor.

Among the specific factors that render amputation necessary are the following: *trauma,* involving crushing injuries or lacerations which are so extensive that reconstruction is not possible, or in which the destroyed tissue and loss of blood threaten the life of the victim; *vascular disease,* involving cutting off the blood supply so that gangrene cannot be prevented, which may be a complication of diabetes, peripheral arteriosclerosis, blocking of blood vessels, or a consequence of thermal injury such as frostbite or excessive burning; *chronic infection* of the bones or joints such as tuberculosis or chronic osteomyelitis; *soft tissue injury* of a long-standing nature such as ulcerated tissue or contracture; *tumor,* involving a malignancy, such as osteogenic sarcoma; *congenital deformity or paralysis,* where the limb is not capable of functioning and there is extensive loss of nerve supply or muscle power.

Automobile, industrial, and combat injuries together account for more than 50 percent of the approximately 4,000 accident-caused amputations each year. Farm, train, and gunshot accidents occur in significant numbers, and thermal and lawn mower injuries result in a small number of amputations. Fourteen percent of cases studied are unique accidents which do not fit into the above categories.

Individuals with congenital underdevelopment or malformation of limbs have been helped by amputation of the nonfunctional limb and fitting of a prosthesis.

Types

When an amputation occurs at the limb joint, it is designated as a disarticulation—for example, shoulder, knee, wrist, or hip. An amputation above the pelvic ring is called a hemipelvectomy. An amputation performed on the mid-foot is termed trans-metatarsal, and one performed between the wrist and fingers is termed trans-metacarpal. Amputations are also described by the area of loss, such as below or above the knee or elbow.

Great care is taken to preserve as much of the limb as possible. A special technique is sometimes used, called cineplasty, in which a portion of a muscle is connected with an apparatus to be attached to the prosthesis. The apparatus enables the patient to move the prosthesis through the voluntarily controlled power of the muscle.

Treatment and Rehabilitation

The orthopedic surgeon begins the rehabilitation process by preparing the stump of the amputated limb for greatest possible use of the prosthesis. Skilled repair of the involved muscles, blood vessels, nerves, bone, subcutaneous tissue and skin, including placement of the scar, are all important for maximizing postoperative functioning.

A "phantom limb" phenomenon (persistent awareness of the amputated limb) may occur immediately after surgery or later. It may be experienced as a feeling of pressure, burning, or throbbing, or a sense that the limb is in the posture held at the time of amputation. These sensations are usually temporary, becoming infrequent or disappearing entirely, particularly when the prosthesis is applied early, as in the "immediate fit." The exact cause is not yet known, though in some instances it may be related to the individual's body concept and, significantly, people who are born with a limb missing or who undergo amputation very early in life do not experience phantom reactions: In a small percentage of cases, severe phantom pain persists to the point where psychiatric treatment is necessary.

Exercise. The need to strengthen recovering and newly important muscles and to develop stamina requires concentrated collaboration between the amputee and the physical therapist in an individualized regime of exercise. The musculature, neural, and skeletal structures of the body are delicately balanced, and the person with an amputation must gradually become accustomed to new ways of functioning with a minimum of strain and fatigue.

Hygiene. Whenever there is intervention in normal bodily functions, special attention must be paid to hygiene. The amputee needs to become extremely particular about daily washing and drying the stump of the amputated limb, the sock or bandage, and the socket of the prosthesis. Detailed procedures will be explained, such as cleansing the stump at bedtime to minimize dampness or slight swelling when the prosthesis is attached for the day's use, or not using hot water on socket or socks. Elastic bandaging is often necessary, and competence in the proper application of the bandage must be developed. Most important is the necessity of medical attention for even minor abrasions, blisters, or infection, so that serious difficulties do not arise.

Education. Despite the fact that growing children require frequent refitting of expensive equipment, prostheses are increasingly advised for young amputees so that they will become proficient in their use. Individuals who are close to children with congenital lack of limbs are in particular need of a positive attitude toward the prosthesis, since the device may seem more troublesome than helpful at first. A great deal of encouragement is needed, and the child should be given interesting toys and rewarding tasks which require the use of the artificial limbs. It has been shown that child amputees are best prepared for a full life in society if they attend regular school. Classmates soon accept them after the initial reaction, particularly when the teacher and other adults are comfortable with the disabled children. There seems to be little basis for concern that children might use their prosthesis as a weapon; however, common sense dictates than an arm prosthesis should be removed when the child is involved in body contact activities, to avoid inadvertent injury to self or others.

Training to Use the Prosthesis. Whenever a person is fitted with a prosthesis, there is need for well-planned training. Even a person being refitted with a new device benefits from expert instruction. The program is usually carried out by a physical or occupational therapist with special experience, and includes knowledge of how the device works and how to take care of it. Instruction time varies—a matter of days, weeks, or months, depending on the complexity of the device, limb or limbs amputated, and extent of amputation, past experience, and attitude of the amputee. Appearance and gracefulness are considered. In the lower extremity amputee, it is important to master techniques of falling and rising from a fall. In some cases the prosthesis is fitted immediately after surgery, and the training process is begun within a day or so. From then on, it progresses in a systematic way, each step laying the groundwork for the next. For example, in the case of lower extremities, balance is achieved first, then walking in a straight line until the gait is smooth and rhythmic, then pivoting, turning, negotiating stairs, and finally sitting and rising from the floor.

In some cases of lower extremity amputation, a cane or crutches may be used along with the prosthesis. There are also persons who for lack of balance or other reasons are unable to use any prosthesis. In these cases, a wheelchair may be needed for mobility. A striking example of the degree of adaptation of which the human being is capable is Dr. Harold Wilke, who without arms has been able to develop the use of his legs and feet to write on a blackboard, turn pages at a podium, shave while standing on one leg, and feed himself gracefully at any banquet table. There are others who manage household tasks, dressing, and even typing without arms. (See CHAPTER 55: ILLUSTRATIVE CASES, Introduction.)

Vocational Rehabilitation. Single extremity amputees under fifty years of age who learn to use a prosthesis have a 75 percent chance for full restoration—that is, functioning is restored to normal, and they can return to their former occupation and social life. In some cases, when the former job relied on use of limbs, such as typing or climbing ladders or poles, preparation for a different occupation must be arranged. Amputees are currently functioning in virtually all vocational fields, and with the physical demands of jobs decreasing, there seems to be an increase in suitable work opportunities for the trained amputee.

Aids and Devices

Any rehabilitation conference exhibit brings forth an astonishing array of artificial limbs and accompanying gadgetry, such as adaptations for operating an automobile and household appliances, or motorized wheelchairs operated by movement of the eyes, or capable of climbing stairs or functioning as a motorized street vehicle. (See CHAPTER 5: INDEPENDENT LIVING: WAYS AND MEANS.)

The Veterans Administration Prosthetic and Sensory Aids Service publishes a *Bulletin of Prosthetic Research.* The American Orthotic and Prosthetic Association (1440 N Street N.W., Washington, DC 20005) publishes an annual listing of firms and suppliers around the world, and pledges itself to promoting high levels of orthotic/prosthetic services to the handicapped. In collaboration with the American Academy of Orthopaedic Surgeons, it identifies practitioners and certifies facilities engaged in the manufacturing and fitting of prostheses. There is an ever-growing body of literature reporting study and research on these devices, and the collaboration of physicians, bioengineers, and prosthetists has brought a high level of professional service to all parts of the United States.

Organizations

The federal government, through the Veterans Administration and U.S. Public Health Service, provides treatment and rehabilitation for military personnel and members of the U.S. Maritime Service. In recent years federal and state programs have also provided these services to civilian amputees. Children are assisted through the Children's Bureau of the Department of Health, Education and Welfare, and adults through the Vocational Rehabilitation Departments in each state. Nonprofit private rehabilitation centers, almost universally sponsored by voluntary organizations, supplement government programs in many areas. The National Amputation Foundation Prosthetic Center (12-45 150th Street, Whitestone, NY 11357) is devoted to the fabrication of prosthetic devices and research projects in the field.

SELECTED REFERENCES

Bender, Leonard F., *Prostheses and Rehabilitation after Arm Amputation,* Charles C. Thomas, Springfield, Illinois, 1974.

Committee on Prosthetic-Orthotic Education, *Geriatric Amputee: Principles of Management,* National Academy of Sciences, 1971.

Committee on Prosthetics Research and Development, *The Child with an Acquired Amputation,* National Academy of Sciences, 1972.

Humm, W., *Rehabilitation of the Lower Limb Amputee,* Williams & Wilkins, Baltimore, 1969.

Mital, Mohinder A., and Donald S. Pierce, *Amputees and Their Prostheses,* Little Brown, New York, 1971.

18

Arthritis

ROBERT M. GOLDENSON, Ph.D.

Reviewed by PETER SIMKIN, M.D., Assistant Professor of Medicine,
University of Washington, and by the Arthritis Foundation

The literal meaning of "arthritis" is inflammation of a joint, but the term is now broadly applied to nearly 100 different conditions which cause aching and pain in joints and connective tissues throughout the body, not all of which involve inflammation. The word "arthritis" is synonymous with "rheumatism," a term preferred in Great Britain and also used in America. A physician specializing in the care of arthritis patients is a rheumatologist, and physicians speak of rheumatology departments and of rheumatic diseases.

The key factor in the most serious forms of arthritis is inflammation, evidenced by heat, swelling, redness, stiffness, and pain. Inflammatory reactions occur when body tissue is damaged, but the inflammation itself may produce damage. In many cases a vicious circle develops which leads to irreversible changes in the bones and joints, making them stiff and in some cases so distorted that movement becomes difficult or even impossible.

Types of Condition

The major forms of arthritis are chronic diseases, that is, they are persistent and may last for life. Unlike illnesses such as colds and measles, arthritis generally produces tissue changes which do not simply heal "as good as new" but tend to be permanent, and may become progressive unless early treatment, proper precautions, and different types of treatment are continuously applied. The five most widespread kinds of arthritis are the following:

Rheumatoid arthritis is the most serious, painful, and crippling type. The inflammation attacks primarily the joints but can also affect the skin, blood vessels, muscles, spleen, heart, and even the eyes. In addition to painfully tender, swollen, and stiff joints, many patients feel "sick all over" and develop such symptoms as fever, fatigability, poor appetite, loss of weight, anemia, enlarged lymph glands and spleen, excessive sweating, and cold, tingling hands and feet. About one in five develops small lumps under the skin of the joints known as rheumatoid nodules. Rheumatoid arthritis tends to subside and flare up unpredictably, causing progressive, irreversible changes in tissue. Three times as many women as men are affected. Among children the disease is known as juvenile rheumatoid arthritis (Still's disease). Distinct forms of juvenile rheumatoid arthritis have been recognized. One starts violently, with a rash and a fever. Another has a very insidious onset, often affecting only one or a few joints. For some reason not yet understood, the latter may be associated with a serious but treatable eye condition.

Osteoarthritis, or degenerative joint disease, used to be regarded primarily as a wear-and-tear disease that affects the weight-bearing joints (knees, hips, spine) in older people, but today the medical profession recognizes that it may affect younger people as well. Unlike rheumatoid arthritis, it does not cause general illness, and is usually mild and noninflammatory. Sometimes, however, there is considerable pain, and mild to severe disability may gradually develop. The pain results from fraying of the normally smooth cartilage between bones, and the disability is caused by muscle weakness and inability to move the joint easily. In advanced cases changes occur in the bone ends, which become thicker and develop knobby spurs. Evidence of joint damage can usually be found in x-rays.

Ankylosing spondylitis (Marie-Strümpell disease) is a chronic, rather rare inflammatory arthritis of the spine which usually begins in the teens or early twenties, and affects ten times as many men as women. A common early symptom is pain in the lower back and legs; the hips and shoulders may be involved later. Stiffness of the spine may develop, and the patient may take on an increasingly stooped position. In 1974 it was discovered that 90 percent of patients suffering from ankylosing spondylitis have a genetic marker called B-27 (this marker occurs in only 7 percent of the general population). Eventually this marker may enable doctors to identify patients at risk of developing ankylosing spondylitis and institute preventive therapy.

Rheumatic fever is an acute systemic disease which follows streptococcus infection and frequently damages the heart. It also involves arthritis in the joints, but this condition subsides quickly if treated with suitable antibiotics. In such cases it is not crippling and does not damage the joints permanently.

Gout, also called gouty arthritis, is an intensely painful disease which most often attacks the joints, particularly the big toe. It is sometimes, but not usually, inherited, and most victims are men. Gout is a prime example of crystal-induced arthritis. In this group of diseases, small crystals form, become lodged in the joints, and cause an acute inflammation. In gout these crystals are sodium urate. They are formed either because the patient does not break down uric acid rapidly enough, or because his body manufactures an excess of uric acid. The understanding and successful treatment of gout is one of the great success stories of twentieth-century medicine. Several medications (allopurinol, Benemid) can keep the uric acid levels of a patient within normal levels.

Other Forms of Arthritis

Psoriatic arthritis is similar to rheumatoid arthritis in its effects and occurs in about one out of ten cases of psoriasis, a common skin disease of unknown cause whose major symptom is an irritating rash occurring in different parts of the body. Psoriasis affects more then 4 million Americans, of whom about 400,000 are afflicted with arthritic complications. *Systemic lupus erythematosus* (SLE) is a disease of unknown cause which inflames and damages connective tissue throughout the body, affecting the skin, joints, and internal organs. Painful arthritis is part of the problem in nine out of ten cases. About 80 percent of victims are women, most frequently between the ages of twenty and forty. The disease follows an irregular, chronic course, with unpredictable periods of exacerbation and improvement. Among the common symptoms are fever, skin rash, weight loss, weakness, fatigue, joint pains, anemia, kidney problems, and emotional disturbance. *Bursitis* is an inflammation in one or more bursae, the small sacs containing slippery fluid which serve as a cushion at points of friction around the joint structure. The inflammation is triggered by irritation from pressure or injury, and the bursa becomes extremely tender and painful and often red and swollen. The shoulders are most often affected, but the inflammation may also occur in the hips or elbows (tennis elbow). *Fibrositis,* sometimes called muscular rheumatism, is not a specific disease but a combination of unexplained symptoms comprising aches, pains, and stiffness in various parts of the body. It is not a serious or crippling condition and does not seem to be related to joints or body movements. Victims tend to be nervous, tense, and weak, and the condition may be aggravated by excitement, overfatigue, or emotional upset. *Scleroderma* is a serious connective tissue disease of unknown cause with accompanying symptoms of arthritis in the joints. Its most prominent features are a thickening and hardening of the skin, sometimes with inflammation and scarring of muscles and internal organs. More women than men are afflicted, and though onset may occur at any age, it usually starts in the forties and fifties. Some cases progress rapidly, while others show ups and downs over the years. *Infectious arthritis* is caused by common infectious organisms which invade joints and produce acute or chronic disease. Joint destruction is often extremely rapid, and the condition should be diagnosed as quickly as possible. Infectious arthritis often accompanies tuberculosis (one case out of twenty-five), meningitis, and gonorrhea. The current upsurge in venereal disease has resulted in a great number of acute cases. The condition is frequently overlooked because many physicians are unfamiliar with its manifestations. Correct diagnosis is based on the identification of the infectious agent in joint fluid. The condition responds to suitable antibiotics.

Warning Signs and Symptoms

Since aches and pains in and around the joints may be due to a wide variety of conditions, an accurate medical diagnosis is absolutely essential. This should be done as soon as possible, since treatment measures are most effective when started early. Moreover, arthritis rarely clears up by itself, tends to progress insidiously, and usually becomes greatly aggravated if neglected. Unfortunately, sufferers wait an average of four years before seeking proper medical diagnosis and care and in many instances become afflicted with irreparable crippling symptoms which could have been avoided. Accurate diagnosis is not easy and may require many types of tests: blood tests, urine tests, joint fluid tests, tissue biopsies, and x-ray examinations.

The following warning signs should be taken seriously, and the individual should see a qualified physician: (1) persistent pain and stiffness on getting up in the morning; (2) pain or tenderness in one or more joints; (3) swelling in one or more joints; (4) recurrence of these symptoms, especially when more than one joint is involved; (5) pain and stiffness in the neck, lower back, and knees and other joints; (6) tingling sensations in the fingertips, hands, and feet; (7) unexplained weight loss, fever, and weakness.

Prevalence

Arthritis is often called the country's number one crippling disease. Approximately 22 million Americans are severely enough affected to require medical care. There are 250,000 new victims each year. The disease occurs in mild, moderate, or devastating form at all ages from infancy on, but is more likely to strike older than younger people. In 97 percent of all individuals over sixty, the joint symptoms are sufficiently advanced to be visible on x-ray films. Approximately 5 million people, usually in the prime-of-life years between twenty and forty-five, suffer from rheumatoid arthritis, the most crippling form of the disease. Ten million develop osteoarthritic symptoms serious enough to cause painful problems. Gouty arthritis is more prevalent than is generally recognized; there are at least 1 million cases in the United States. All told, approximately three times as many women as men suffer from arthritis.

Arthritis is one of the most incapacitating of all diseases. An estimated 3,500,000 people in the American population are disabled at any one time. They account for 240 million days of restricted activity and 14,898,000 days lost from work annually. In monetary terms, the annual cost to the national economy of all forms of arthritis is estimated as $9,226,000,000.

Causes

Although the precise cause of rheumatoid arthritis is still unknown, there is some evidence that the inflammation may be triggered by the sudden activity of a latent or dormant viruslike organism. Many scientists think that it represents an autoimmune reaction against the body's own joints and tissues. The disease is not directly inherited, but some persons may be born with a predisposition or susceptibility to the disease, and therefore several members of one family may be affected. Emotional disturbances may also be contributing factors, since symptoms sometimes appear after a period of tension or a traumatic event. In patients who already suffer from the disease, the symptoms may be exacerbated during periods of upset and subside when the stress is relieved.

A variety of causal factors may contribute to the development of osteoarthritis. Though precise knowledge is still lacking, these may include degeneration of tissue attendant on the normal aging process due to wrong joint alignment, since moving parts of the body are affected; abuse of special joints, including the knees or hips of overweight people; joints overused in sports or injured by accidents; or joints with hidden birth defects. Small, often painful, bony enlargements over the end joints of the fingers (called Heberden's nodes) which can develop in patients suffering from osteoarthritis are often hereditary.

Gouty arthritis is usually due to a defect in body chemistry, sometimes hereditary, resulting in overproduction of uric acid. It may also be due to a failure to break down this substance quickly enough. The excess acid is retained by the kidneys and leads to the formation of needlelike crystals in the joints, which in turn produce severe inflammation. The affected joints may be in almost any part of the body, but in three out of four cases the large joint of the big toe becomes hot, swollen, and painfully tender. Contrary to public opinion, the basic cause of gout is not "high living," although overeating and overindulgence in alcohol and coffee may trigger attacks in some patients who are already afflicted.

The cause of ankylosing spondylitis is unknown, but predisposition plays a part. Although the basic cause of psoriatic arthritis has not yet been discovered, it is a well-known fact that the psoriasis itself may be aggravated by emotional tension. No significant progress has been made toward discovering causal factors in scleroderma and fibrositis. Bursitis, as noted above, seems to be associated with injury or repeated pressure over the joints in the elbow, shoulder, or hips, as in excessive tennis playing. Rheumatic fever, which usually involves joint inflammation, is believed to be caused by a streptococcus infection.

Treatment

Rheumatoid arthritis can now be effectively controlled in most cases if a full, individualized program is faithfully carried out over a long period. Since the disease is complex, the objectives are many: to relieve pain, reduce inflammation, prevent damage to the joints, forestall the development of deformities, and keep joints movable and functioning. In some cases spontaneous remission occurs for varying periods, and in one out of five of these cases the symptoms do not return. However, some patients experience severe flare-ups which may require temporary hospitalization.

Prime elements in the overall treatment program are: (1) medication, including one or more of the following: carefully regulated doses of aspirin or aspirinlike drugs, gold salts, phenylbutazone, indomethacin, or cortisone or related steroids; (2) rest as needed, sometimes with individual joints held in removable plaster cast splints; (3) gentle exercises designed to keep joints mobile, to strengthen muscles, and to correct deformities; (4) prescribed heat, such as hot baths, hydrotherapy, hot packs, heat lamps, or paraffin

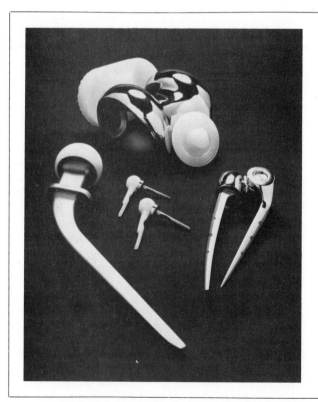

These prostheses are utilized in joint replacement surgery to help arthritic patients regain mobility. At top is a knee joint replacement, and below (left to right) are hip, finger, and elbow replacements. (Arthritis Foundation)

229

wax applications; (5) surgery directed toward preventing damage by removing diseased tissue to allow normal tissue to grow back, as well as techniques designed to undo crippling effects, as in releasing frozen joints, stabilizing useless joints by fusion, or inserting artificial joints to restore lost functions.

Although osteoarthritis cannot be completely cured, it is often possible to retard the disease process, ease the pain, and prevent disabling effects. Treatment, however, must continue throughout life, and consists of drugs, rest, special exercises, and heat, as well as orthopedic surgery and rehabilitation procedures where indicated. In special situations cortisonelike drugs bring temporary relief when injected directly into affected joints. It is also essential to protect these joints from stresses and strains, and for this reason reducing diets are prescribed for overweight patients. Today total replacement of a joint with a metal-plastic implant has restored mobility to many patients.

Gouty arthritis can now be treated effectively by reducing the level of uric acid in the system. Colchicine, phenylbutazone, and indomethacin are widely used in controlling acute attacks. Other drugs, such as probenecid, are prescribed to stimulate the discharge of uric acid, and still others, such as allopurinol, are aimed at reducing its production. Medication of one type or another must be continued for life. Although there is no special diet for gout, doctors warn against overeating, excessive use of alcohol, and such foods as kidney, liver, and sweetbreads.

The discomfort and deformities resulting from ankylosing spondylitis can usually be controlled by prompt use of medication and exercise. The disease often subsides of its own accord after several years, and even though stiffness persists there is relatively little pain, and most patients can lead a productive life. Treatment of psoriatic arthritis is essentially the same as for rheumatoid arthritis.

There is no complete cure for systemic lupus erythematosus, but pain-relieving medications and anti-inflammatory drugs are frequently administered with good effect. Patients should be under close medical supervision. Rheumatic fever may require treatment with antibiotics to prevent streptococcal infections, and the treatment is usually continued indefinitely since the disease tends to recur. A variety of treatments may be necessary in cases of bursitis: pain-relieving drugs, injections of cortisone, rest, physical therapy, and sometimes surgery. Fibrositis is difficult to treat, but some cases respond to heat and injection of an anesthetic or special massage. Scleroderma is even more stubborn and baffling, but in rare cases the inflammation can be controlled with steroid drugs such as prednisone. In cases of arthritis due to infection, the specific bacteria involved must be identified before prescribing the appropriate antibiotic.

It is important to recognize that arthritis is a happy hunting ground for unscrupulous promoters who offer sure cures and miraculous remedies. Special diets, health spas, across-the-border clinics, uranium cures, alfalfa tablets, "immunized" milk, magnetic rings and copper bracelets, books full of high-sounding nonsense—all these forms of quackery not only rob innocent sufferers of a total of $400 million a year, but waste valuable time during which the disease may do irreversible damage that could have been avoided by proper medical treatment. Some of these remedies, especially the diets, are relatively harmless, but totally ineffective; others are downright dangerous; still others merely consist of specially named drugs whose chief ingredient is aspirin, which can be purchased in ordinary form at a fraction of the cost. In some cases the most outlandish treatments seem to work for a time, but this is only a trap based on the fact that spontaneous, transient remissions frequently occur in arthritic diseases. All medications and devices offered over the counter or through the mails should be checked with the family physician or local chapter of the Arthritis Foundation before purchase. Some of the more obvious clues to quackery are "secret" devices and formulas, advertising backed by testimonials, the promise of a quick and easy cure that cleanses the body of "poisons" and makes medical treatment unnecessary, accusations against the "medical establishment" for persecuting the maker or thwarting progress, and refusal to submit the medication or device to proper authorities for scientific testing and evaluation.

Posture. Correct posture is essential since the tendency of arthritics is to keep painful joints bent for long periods. This leads to greater stiffness, loss of motion, and eventual deformity due to increased cartilage damage. Good posture includes standing straight with head high, stomach in, and hips and knees straight; a normal walking gait with arms swinging; not carrying heavy packages or pocketbooks that put a strain on affected muscles; sitting erect with feet on the floor in a straightback chair with back support and preferably with armrests; lying on a firm mattress with a board underneath, flat on the back with arms at the sides and knees and hips straight, and with only a small pillow under the head and none under the knees.

Rest. The amount and kind of rest depend on the severity of the condition. Too much rest may lead to stiffness in joints and muscles; too little may result in damaged joints and increased pain. As much rest as possible is recommended if joints are acutely inflamed, especially if accompanied by fever and general weakness. In general, the patient is advised to assume the correct posture while resting, to sit rather than stand whenever possible, and to rest for short periods during the day rather than for one long period. Splints, braces, canes, and crutches may be prescribed for partial rest of involved joints.

Exercises. Again, the program must be prescribed and supervised by the physician and, in special cases, should be planned by a physiatrist and carried out by a physical therapist, occupational therapist, or public health nurse.

Rehabilitation

The many variations of arthritic disease symptomatology have varying vocational significance ranging from virtually none at all to very significant handicap to any remunerative employment. Each individual must understand the nature of his or her own condition and relate future developments to the particular vocational situation. Unlike an acute illness with a finite course, arthritis is a chronic condition which, while it may not progress rapidly or may even be arrested, has the potential of becoming more debilitating in the future. It is well to make vocational preparations with this in mind. For example, if one is an insurance salesman, heavily dependent on active mobility for successful interaction with customers, it might be well to explore other roles in the insurance business which are less apt to require the mobility, if one faces the possibility of decreased capacity to maneuver. Greater haste in vocational retraining might be indicated if one were a lumberjack and one's condition was of the rheumatoid variety. Just as in daily living, where the goal is to remain as optimally functional as possible, this is the goal vocationally. Aids and devices are applicable to office and business as well as home. Emotional stresses are apt to be more critically significant than physical requirements, and the extent of tension and anxiety in a given work situation should be considered in relation to management of the disease. The natural tendency to deny the disability is unfortunate if there is interference with realistic planning and adaptation so that the person can have the best possible chance to minimize the toll of the arthritic condition.

Research

There are three basic areas of research in arthritis: (1) a search for the causal agent, which is thought to be a virus that remains dormant in the body for a long period until somehow activated; (2) a study of the body's response to the causal agent, that is, the immune or antibody response which evidently goes wrong and begins to produce cells which attack tissues in joint areas; and (3) study of the actual process of inflammation of the joints.

One area of activity is the development of drugs to suppress inflammation or to suppress the specific antibody-producing cells. Another is the perfecting of surgical techniques for removal of the synovial lining of joints and total joint replacement. Fortunately, research in arthritis ties in with other areas of research into the body's immunological responses, such as the work on organ transplants. Findings in these other areas may have direct application for solving the problem of arthritis.

The Arthritis Foundation

Located at 3400 Peachtree Road N.E., Atlanta, GA 30326, the Arthritis Foundation is the national voluntary health agency devoted to "seeking the total answer—cause, prevention, cure—to the nation's number one crippling disease . . . through programs of research, patient services, public health information and education, professional education and training." The core of the program is direct service provided by the local chapters of the Foundation. These chapters serve two basic purposes. They are, first, information centers which distribute factual literature and sponsor forums and lectures for both patients and physicians; and second, they are referral centers which direct patients to available community services. Many chapters also support arthritis clinics and home care services that provide complete patient care from diagnosis to back-to-work programs. Others provide mobile clinics, staffed by teams of specialists, which travel to smaller communities and work with local physicians in the treatment of patients.

All chapters play a vital role in the search for the answer to arthritis and related rheumatic diseases by supporting medical investigators and clinical research centers. These centers study individual patients to discover clues to the disease, provide comprehensive team care, conduct trials of new drugs and treatments, and train young physicians, scientists, surgeons, and allied health workers in the arthritis specialty. As the central office states, "the goal of the Foundation is to extend the benefits of such center programs to all Americans who suffer from crippling arthritis."

The scientific program is the key to final victory over arthritis. To spur research, the Foundation annually awards research fellowships to promising young physicians and scientists for specific studies to be carried out both in the laboratory and at the bedside. In addition, two professional associations work with the Foundation on critical problems: the American Rheumatic Section, representing the world's largest professional society of rheumatologists, governs the Foundation's medical and scientific programs; and the Allied Health Professions Section, representing physical and occupational therapists, medical social workers, nurses, and others, devotes itself to overcoming the shortage of specialized health workers in the arthritis field.

(See CHAPTER 55: ILLUSTRATIVE CASES, N. Danny and Donny Share a Room, and Much More.)

SELECTED REFERENCES

PROFESSIONAL

Ehrlich, George E., ed., *Total Management of the Arthritis Patient*, Lippincott, Philadelphia, 1973.

Hollander, Joseph Lee, and Daniel J. McCarthy, Jr., eds., *Arthritis and Allied Conditions*, 8th ed., Lea & Febiger, Philadelphia, 1972.

Primer on the Rheumatic Diseases, 7th ed., Arthritis Foundation, 1976.

PATIENT GUIDANCE AND INFORMATION

Aladjem, Henrietta, *The Sun Is My Enemy* (concerning SLE), Prentice-Hall, Englewood Cliffs, New Jersey, 1972.

Blau, Sheldon P., and Dodi Schultz, *Arthritis: Complete, Up-to-date Facts for Patients and Their Families*, Doubleday, Garden City, New York, 1974.

Corrigan, A. B., *Living with Arthritis*, Grosset & Dunlap, New York, 1971.

Crain, Darrell C., *The Arthritis Handbook: A Patient's Manual on Arthritis and Rheumatism and Gout*, Arco, New York, 1971.

Jayson, I. V., and Allan St. J. Dixon, *Understanding Arthritis and Rheumatism*, Random House, New York, 1974.

Self-help Manual for Arthritis Patients, Arthritis Foundation.

19

Birth Defects; Genetic Counseling
A. Disabling Birth Defects

LINDA HOWELL, M.A., Group Health Cooperative of
Puget Sound, Seattle

Reviewed by the National Foundation

A problem or disability is referred to as a birth defect if it is present at birth and is a disorder of body chemistry or other body function (including mental function), a malformation, or a defect of structure. At one extreme the defect can be inconsequential, with no disabling aspects. At the other it can be severely disabling, affecting multiple body systems and functions. Birth defects often have profound effects not only on the infant or child but on the lives of others involved.

Incidence and Prevalence

Of the more than 3 million babies born every year in the United States, approximately 250,000 are born with defects. At any one time, an estimated 15 million United States residents have one or more birth defects. These defects take a great toll of human life, especially if one considers the number of defective babies who die before or during birth each year. Understandably, this entire area is now attracting great concern, study, and therapeutic effort.

Types and Causal Factors

Specific birth defects of fairly high incidence are dealt with in detail in other chapters in Part 2 of this book. A general description of the types of defects and how they occur will be presented here.

In simplest terms a birth defect is either inherited or has an environmental causation or is a combination of these two factors. Approximately 20 percent of all birth defects are inherited, 20 percent are due to environmental factors during pregnancy, and 60 percent are a combination of the two.

An inherited disorder is one which is passed on through the genes (contributed by egg and sperm) to the offspring by the parent or parents, who may have the defect themselves or may be hidden carriers of the defective gene. Some examples of inherited diseases are sickle cell anemia, Huntington's disease, cystic fibrosis, Tay-Sachs disease, muscular dystrophy, phenylketonuria (PKU), hemophilia, thalassemia, albinism, and Niemann-Pick disease.

An example of a well-known birth defect which is genetically determined but not necessarily inherited in this same sense is Down's syndrome (mongolism or trisomy 21), in which there is an excess chromosome, number 21. This results in a condition of mild to severe mental retardation and structural defects. This extra chromosome appears spontaneously in the sperm, maturing egg cell, or fertilized egg during the process of cell division.(In about 3 percent of cases the extra chromosome is inherited from parents who are hidden carriers.) Since the frequency of Down's syndrome is believed to be related to certain aspects of the mother's condition (advanced age and health factors), this birth defect might be attributed to environmental causation of genetic change (the environment in this case being the mother's ovaries in which the egg matures). Radiation in sufficient doses is known to produce genetic

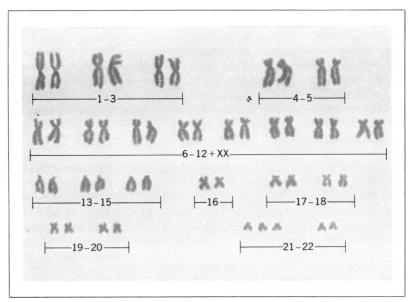

The chromosome complement of a girl with Down's syndrome. Note that chromosome number 21 is present in triplicate. (With the permission of P. E. Ferrier, M.D., from the McGraw-Hill Encyclopedia of Science and Technology, 4th ed., vol. 14, p. 116, 1977)

changes sometimes detrimental to a developing organism, and may be one of the rarer causes of mongolism.

Familiar examples of environmental causation of birth defects are cases of maternal disease — notably rubella (German measles) during the first three months of pregnancy. This viral infectious disease interferes with the normal development of the fetus and can have a range of negative consequences, including eye, heart, and hearing defects and mental retardation. Some drugs may seriously alter development. This is most dramatically seen in the anomalies of the thalidomide era. (See CHAPTER 32: FACIAL DISFIGUREMENT.)

Congenital syphilis is an illness of the pregnant mother which, if left untreated, may result in underdevelopment and other problems for the child, including death. (See CHAPTER 53: VENEREAL DISEASE.)

Examples of familiar structural-developmental birth defects brought about by interference of some kind with "normal" prenatal development include certain cases of blindness and deafness, additional or missing fingers or toes, clubfoot, hip dislocation, cleft lip and cleft palate, defects of the internal organs (especially heart, kidneys, and liver), incomplete closure of the spine (spina bifida), and hydrocephalus. There are many other bone, muscle, joint, circulatory, and nervous system defects.

A number of conditions reflect metabolic birth defects. There are defects involving carbohydrate metabolism (diabetes mellitus), protein metabolism (phenylketonuria, or PKU), metal (copper) metabolism (Wilson's disease), amino acids (maple sugar urine disease), and lipid metabolism (gargoylism, Tay-Sachs disease); thyroid deficiency (cretinism); and pituitary defect (dwarfism). These diseases tend to be directly inherited or represent the results of a genetic-environment interaction.

Another source of birth defects is blood type incompatibility. If a pregnant mother has Rh-negative blood type while the father has Rh-positive, the fetus may inherit the father's blood type. The mother's body may develop antibodies to resist the "foreign" substance. This battle of chemistries can produce birth defects such as mental retardation, congenital anemia, heart defects, and cerebral palsy.

Clearly, mental retardation is by far the most commonly occurring birth defect. This is because it occurs in conjunction with many other physical problems — PKU, hydrocephalus, Down's syndrome, and Tay-Sachs disease. Blindness, deafness, and lesser visual and auditory impairments are the next most frequently occurring results of adverse preconceptional and prenatal factors.

There are certain factors which, if found to characterize a woman, cause her to be rated "at risk" during pregnancy. Some of these risk factors include extremes of age, low socioeconomic status, inadequate diet, presence of disease (especially metabolic disease such as diabetes or toxemia), addiction, a history of difficult prior preg-

Newborn intensive care units (NICU) are not only increasing the survival rate of babies with low birth weight, but are reducing the number of abnormalities among them. (National Foundation/March of Dimes)

nancies, previous children with birth defects, family history of congenital defects, and Rh incompatibility.

Treatment and Prevention

There are as many treatment modalities as there are birth defects. Some structural defects lend themselves to surgical repair with varying degrees of success. Examples are cleft lip, cleft palate, congenital heart defects, spina bifida, and hydrocephalus. Some defects of metabolism or body chemistry can be treated with substantial success by diet or medication, such as diabetes mellitus and phenylketonuria. In many instances treatment of a birth defect may be primarily educational in its thrust to allow the child or adult to maximize potential and to compensate for deficiencies where possible.

There are many special birth defect clinics in medical centers all over the country which provide diagnostic aid, treatment, counseling, and educational services. Some specialize in particular problems such as central nervous system defects, metabolic disorders, orthopedic problems, genetic-chromosomal abnormalities, or urologic defects.

Many birth defects are preventable and for this reason the emphasis is clearly on prevention. One approach to prevention is improved prenatal medical care with regular visits to a physician, attention to diet, avoidance and treatment of disease, and, in general, concentration on making the fetal environment a favorable one for development. It is strongly recommended that unprescribed drugs be avoided by pregnant mothers, and there is increasing evidence that maternal alcoholism may be a factor in some cases.

A vaccine against rubella has been developed, and is responsible for a sizable reduction in the incidence of cerebral palsy and other congenital brain disorders. An Rh vaccine is also available which, if injected in the mother within seventy-two hours following the birth, miscarriage, or abortion of an Rh-positive child, will protect the next Rh-positive child from assault by her immunity system. (See CHAPTER 26: CEREBRAL PALSY.)

Genetic or inheritable disorders are not preventable in the same manner as environmentally caused problems. Genetic counseling is available in many centers for "at risk" parents or any others who would like to avail themselves of this service. Screening is done in many places for sickle cell and Tay-Sachs carriers. Individual genetic testing can be carried out to identify carriers of the defective gene of nearly 100 diseases. If the inheritance pattern is known, parents can be informed of the statistical risks of having a child with a birth defect. (See B. Prevention through Genetic Counseling.)

Diagnosis is possible during pregnancy through a procedure called amniocentesis, which is performed in the second trimester. A thin, hollow needle is inserted through the abdomen to the uterus in order to obtain a sample of the amniotic fluid surrounding the fetus. The cells of the fluid are prepared in a laboratory for culture and study. All chromosomal defects and about seventy biochemical abnormalities can be detected, such as Down's syndrome (chromosomal) and Tay-Sachs disease (biochemical), but it should be noted that not all genetic disorders are detectable by this method.

In its booklet, "What Are the Facts about Genetic Disease?", the National Institute of General Medical Sciences states, "Studies to date reveal that the economic gain from screening and prevention can exceed by ten- to twenty-fold the cost of caring medically for genetic disease victims. This calculation does not, of course, take into account the alleviation of anxiety and suffering by patients and their families." Two examples are given. The cost of fifty untreated cases of PKU would be $19,250,000 for lifetime institutional care, as contrasted with $800,000 that would have been spent for screening these children as newborns, and $50,000 for dietary treatment. The cost of fifty Tay-Sachs cases given palliative treatment to death would be $1,750,000, as compared to $250,000 that would have been spent on screening married couples at high risk, and $17,500 for prenatal diagnosis and abortion.

Research

Research in the area of birth defects is taking many directions, but the three basic areas of focus are (1) the study of causal factors, (2) the study of preventive techniques, and (3) the study of treatment modalities. Detailed basic research into embryonic development will eventually yield information relevant to many forms of birth defects. Much work is being done in immunology, the study of the nature of immunity (such as the mechanism of antibodies) in living organisms. This work will have implications for many disorders other than those termed birth defects. Enzyme activity is a major field of scientific interest. Other work involving the role of nutrition, hormones, and drugs in fetal development will have important implications for prevention. In the field of genetics, the amniocentesis technique is being constantly refined with increased effectiveness. Ways of identifying carriers of hereditary diseases are continually expanding. Environmental sources or causes of chromosomal birth defects are being investigated. At a very basic level, chromosomes are studied to determine their genetic pattern and how they bring about certain effects, such as Down's syndrome. In the area of treatment, drugs are being developed to treat hereditary blood diseases, and unusual surgical techniques, including organ transplants, are being refined to help the individuals with birth defects that affect organ systems.

Organizations

Founded in 1938 by President Franklin D. Roosevelt, as the National Foundation for Infantile Paralysis, the National Foundation/March of Dimes (Box 2000, White Plains, NY 10602) is now the major voluntary health organization devoted to the prevention and treatment of birth defects. According to recent annual reports, the Foundation is currently allocating over $7 million per year for research support, another $7 million for public health education, over $2 million for professional health education, over $5 million for community services, over $6 million for medical services, and $1 million for the Salk Institute for Biological Studies. These funds support a wide-ranging basic and clinical research program, patient care through a network of over 275 medical service program centers and clinics, and preparation and distribution of films, film strips, exhibits, and other educational materials to both professional and lay groups. Publications of the Foundation include the *National Directory of Genetic Services* (biennial) and a series of monographs on birth defects. (See CHAPTER 39: MENTAL RETARDATION.)

A large number of birth defects are under investigation by the National Institutes of Health — for example, phenylketonuria, Tay-Sachs, cleft lip/palate, cystic fibrosis, thalassemia, sickle cell anemia, Down's syndrome, galactosemia, and hemophilia. The NIH allocates approximately $100 million a year to research related to genetic disorders, of which a high proportion is administered by the National Institute of General Medical Sciences, which has designated ten national centers for such research.

B. Prevention through Genetic Counseling

GILBERT S. OMENN, M.D., Ph.D., Associate Professor of Medicine, Division of Medical Genetics, University of Washington

Reviewed by the National Foundation

Genetic counseling has become an important facet in the care and education of patients with handicapping diseases. Patients and their families typically seek answers to the following questions: Is this disorder hereditary? Is there any way to prevent passing it on? Can other members of the family get it through contact? What is the precise diagnosis and what will be the course of the disease? What can be done to treat or minimize the effects of this disorder?

There has been tremendous progress in the past fifteen years in medical genetics. The federal government (National Institutes of Health) and the National Foundation – March of Dimes now support birth defect clinics and genetic clinics at many major medical centers, with out-reach or satellite clinics throughout many regions of the country.

Table 1. Therapy of Genetic Diseases by Conventional Means

Treatment approach	Examples
1. Add missing substance (product)	Thyroid hormone, cortisol, insulin, anti-hemophilic globulin, gamma globulin, blood cells, vitamin B_{12}
2. Prevent accumulation of toxic precursor (substrate)	Phenylalanine in phenylketonuria; galactose-1-phosphate in galactosemia
3. Replace the defective enzyme	Plasma pseudocholinesterase deficiency; Fabry's disease (glycolipid lipidosis); metachromatic leukodystrophy
4. Use drug therapy (inhibit enzymes)	Allopurinol to prevent gout
5. Induce enzyme by drug	Phenobarbital for jaundice in newborn
6. Remove toxic substance	Metal-removing drugs for copper (Wilson's disease) or iron (hemochromatosis)
7. Surgically remove organ	Colon in congenital polyposis; spleen in spherocytosis; lens with cataracts
8. Transplant	Kidney (polycystic kidneys, cystinosis); bone marrow (thalassemia); cornea
9. Use artificial aids	Eyeglasses; hearing aids; kidney machine
10. Block physiological (immune) response	Rh-immune globulin treatment of Rh-negative mothers who deliver Rh-positive babies

Source: G. S. Omenn, "Genetic Engineering: Present and Future," in R. H. Williams, ed., *To Live and to Die: When, Why, and How,* Springer-Verlag, New York, 1973.

For a long time people thought of hereditary conditions as diseases "you couldn't do anything about." That is no longer the case. Now a great variety of treatments can be applied specifically to certain diseases, treatments which utilize present-day approaches — giving special diets, using certain drugs, performing surgery or transplantation, immunizing against Rh incompatibility. These approaches are summarized in Table 1, with examples of diseases in each category. Nowadays the popular conceptions of genetics include such ambitious ideas as true "genetic engineering," in which a faulty gene would actually be replaced. The complicated process which would be required is diagramed in the figure in

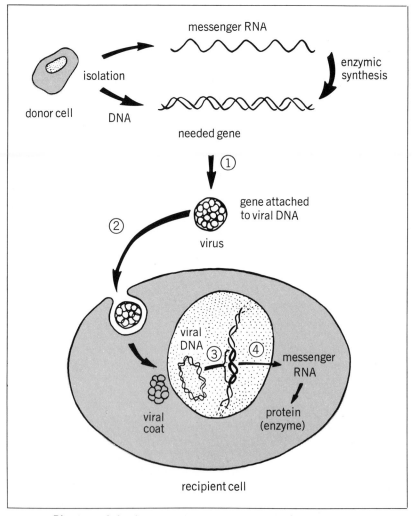

Diagram of the four steps (see text) involved in genetic engineering to replace a disease-causing gene. (Courtesy of Gilbert S. Omenn)

four steps: (1) preparation of the gene (deoxyribonucleic acid, or DNA) involved in that disease, from among the millions of genes in every human cell; (2) delivery of the gene into the organ needing it, such as the liver for phenylketonuria, a cause of mental retardation, utilizing a hepatitislike virus which "homes" in on the liver; (3) insertion of the gene into the proper chromosome among the twenty-three pairs of human chromosomes in each cell; and (4) regulation of the function of the gene according to the needs of the body.

When a patient and the family come for genetic counseling, they are usually seen by a team of physicians and other health professionals who specialize in these disorders and who are highly sensitive to the emotional impact of birth defects and other handicapping conditions. For families who are upset or bitter because of the occurrence of a serious disorder in a child, it is often helpful to point out that about 5 percent of all live-born children either have major congenital malformations or develop severe mental retardation or both. The problems the parents face are shared by many, many others.

Careful diagnosis is the cornerstone of proper medical care. Often there are many different disorders which produce similar-appearing handicaps; for example, there are more than two dozen different causes of cleft lip or cleft palate. There are several dozen different causes of severe mental retardation, yet these all together account for only about 30 percent of cases. The rest of the causes have not yet been pinned down. In disorders of the brain causing ataxia, some are inherited as autosomal dominants, occurring in parents and children; others, appearing clinically the same, may be transmitted as autosomal recessives, occurring only in siblings, not in the parents, and rarely passed on to grandchildren.

Kinds of Genetic Disorders

At this point, the kinds of genetic disorders should be differentiated according to the pattern of transmission in the family. Certain disorders are due to abnormality of just one gene, while others (common birth defects) involve the combined action of many genes. The first category is characterized further in Table 2 into autosomal dominant, autosomal recessive, and X-linked recessive patterns of genetic transmission. Genes occur in pairs, one carried on the chromosome from the mother's egg and the other carried on the homologous chromosome from the father's sperm. The exception occurs in males, who have an X chromosome from the mother and a Y chromosome from the father, the so-called sex chromosomes. Girls have two X chromosomes.

The *family pedigree*, identifying affected and normal members of the family, often reveals the most likely pattern of inheritance. Thus, *dominant* conditions occur in more than one generation of the family; a single dose of the abnormal gene, from either parent, can produce the disease. The risk for children or siblings of an affected person is 50 percent to get the abnormal gene and up to 50

Table 2. Features of Mendelian Patterns of Inheritance

	Autosomal dominant	Autosomal recessive	X-linked recessive
Pedigree features	Vertical trans-mission	Only siblings affected	Vertical trans-mission
Sex affected	Both	Both	Maternally related males
Clinical features	Variable expres-sivity Incomplete penetrance Late age of onset	More severe and more uniform	May be mild manifestations in female carriers
Risk to relatives of index case:			
Children	50%	Nearly zero	50% for boys; nearly zero for girls
Siblings	50%	25%	50% for boys; nearly zero for girls
Parents	50%	Nearly zero	Nearly zero, ex-cept mild signs in carrier mother
Significance of "negative family history"	Common problem: a. new mutation b. different father c. nonpenetrant in parent d. later onset in parent	Expected, unless multiple siblings	Common problem: a. Search for male relatives through successive females b. New mutation
Consanguinity	Irrelevant	Greatly increases risk over general population	Irrelevant
Biochemical mechanism	Multichain pro-teins or cell sur-face mosaics with normal + abnor-mal components	Deficiency of enzymes or other functional molecules	Deficiencies

percent to get the disease. However, it is a feature of dominant diseases that the clinical manifestations of the disease can vary quite a lot, sometimes not even being recognized. Sometimes the genetics of the disorder must be recognized by knowledge of the clinical disease, since no other members of the family appear to be affected. There are many good reasons for such a "negative family history" (Table 2), but children of the affected person will still have a 50 percent risk of getting the abnormal dominant gene, even though he or she is the first affected person in the family. Examples of dominant disorders are Marfan's syndrome and other disorders of the bones, neurological syndromes such as many ataxias, polycystic kidney disease, and some cases of cleft lip or palate and of blindness and deafness. The precise biochemical lesion is not known for any of these diseases.

Autosomal *recessive* conditions require a double dose of the abnormal gene, meaning that the child must get an abnormal gene from each parent. The parents also have a normal copy of that gene and appear to be normal; that is why the abnormal copy of the gene is termed "recessive." If the disease is quite rare, like primary microcephaly as a cause of mental retardation, the abnormal gene is infrequent in the population; the chance that one person who is a carrier for this recessive gene will marry another person who carries the same abnormal gene is greatly enhanced if they are related, as first cousins, for example. Such first-cousin matings are called consanguineous and are illegal in many states. Many recessive disorders are now known to be due to deficiency of a particular enzyme or protein, for which biochemical tests are quite feasible. The carriers (both parents and two-thirds of clinically normal siblings) have one-half the normal level of that specific enzyme and can be identified by appropriate tests as well. Screening programs for sickle-cell anemia carriers and for carriers of the gene for Tay-Sachs disease, a cause of mental retardation and blindness, utilize blood tests for such biochemical abnormalities in the carriers.

Finally, *X-linked recessive* disorders, including Duchenne's pseudohypertrophic muscular dystrophy and hemophilia, occur almost exclusively in boys and are transmitted through the generations on the mother's side of the family. Affected family members may include brothers, uncles, male cousins, and sons of the mother. Often there are no affected family members except for the affected patient. The reason may be that there were few male relatives on the mother's side or that they were all lucky (each son of a carrier mother has a 50-50 chance of not getting the abnormal gene and the disease) or the abnormal gene may have arisen by mutation (change in the gene) only in them or their mother. Biochemical tests to detect carriers of these diseases have been developed and are very important in counseling the families. In a common counseling situation, the normal sister of a boy with Duchenne's dystrophy or hemophilia comes to the clinic for advice about her risks of "having a child like my brother." Often they have helped their parents care for the brother for years, only to see him crippled or helpless as a teen-ager. If the sister is a carrier (tests can prove that), her risk is 50 percent to have an affected boy among the boys, but essentially zero among the girls, half of whom would be carriers like her; thus, the overall risk is 25 percent. Some couples in this situation would prefer unaffected girls over the risk of having an affected boy (see below). If she is not a carrier, her risk of having such an affected child is zero.

Polygenic inheritance is the cause of many common birth defects, including many cases of cleft lip and palate, congenital dislocation of the hip, and clubfeet. It is best to think of these disorders as involving complex embryological formations of the middle part of the face, the pelvis and hip, and the feet. Obviously, a great many structures and enzymes are involved, each determined by one or more genes; the whole process then depends upon many genes. A different term, "multifactorial," is used to describe the interaction of genes and presumed environmental factors, as might be the case for spina bifida and meningomyelocele (neural-tube closure defects).

In contrast to specific disorders of the genes, the medical profession recognizes syndromes due to *gross chromosome abnormalities*. The most important by far is Down's syndrome (formerly called mongolism), which is due to trisomy of chromosome 21 (Figure 2). There are no abnormal genes, but there is a gross imbalance in genes, because of the third set of the genes carried on the twenty-first chromosome. Usually this trisomy results from fertilization of an egg containing both of the number 21 chromosomes from the mother, instead of the usual single chromosome; however, the extra chromosome can come from the father. One in every 700 to 800 births is a child with Down's syndrome. Other syndromes with an extra autosomal chromosome cause even more severe physical and mental handicaps than Down's syndrome. Disorders due to an extra sex chromosome (XXX, XXY, XYY) are less severe, but include some physical and mental abnormalities in many cases. Modern techniques of examining the chromosome structures are revealing more subtle abnormalities in additional patients with various handicaps. (See CHAPTER 39: MENTAL RETARDATION.)

Amniocentesis and Prenatal Genetic Diagnosis

The most dramatic clinical development in medical genetics is the procedure of amniocentesis for genetic diagnosis in the first part of pregnancy. This test drastically changes the situation for the parents who must decide about having further children. In the absence of such a test, they must decide on the basis of the statistical risk, 50 percent for dominant diseases, 25 percent for recessive disorders, usually 3 to 5 percent for common birth defects (polygenic), and about 1 percent for recurrence of trisomy 21. For testable diseases, they can now find out whether that particular fetus has or does not have the disease about which they are worried. The procedure involves the insertion of a long needle, like that used for lumbar punctures, through the abdominal and uterine walls into the amniotic fluid sac around the fetus. A small amount of fluid (5–10 milliliters or 1–2 teaspoons) is removed for analysis. The fluid contains some cells from the fetal skin, respiratory tract, and urinary tract. The chromosomes can be counted and examined, and certain biochemical tests can be performed on these cells once they have multiplied by growth under laboratory conditions. The amniocentesis is done in the thirteenth or fourteenth week of pregnancy (counting from the last menstrual period), when there is sufficient fluid, and the tests usually take about three weeks to complete in the laboratory. Only those conditions for which specific chromosomal or biochemical abnormalities are known can be tested for, leaving a great many genetic disorders for which no tests are presently available.

For example, among autosomal recessive conditions, certain specific enzyme deficiencies can be tested for, like Tay-Sachs disease or Hurler's disease. But the enzyme deficiency in phenylketonuria involves a liver enzyme not normally expressed in amniotic fluid cells. Similarly, sickle-cell anemia involves blood cells, which are not routinely obtained during amniocentesis. For cystic fibrosis, the most common severe autosomal recessive disease among Caucasians, doctors do not yet have any clue to the biochemical lesion, so there is no test.

It cannot be overemphasized that these tests do *not* assure a "normal" baby; these tests only rule out the presence of specific disorders for which that baby appears to be at high risk, warranting the test procedure. The current indications for amniocentesis are given in Table 3. A few other means of diagnosis in early pregnancy have been utilized in special cases. These cases include radiography of the fetus in a family with the autosomal recessive disorder of absent radius bones and bleeding disorder due to low platelets; ultrasound for head size in a family with previous children mentally retarded because of primary microcephaly; and analysis of the linked genetic marker system determining secretion of ABH blood group substances in the amniotic fluid in families with myotonic muscular dystrophy.

With progress in elucidating the biochemical mechanisms of

Table 3. Indications for Amniocentesis

	Test	Risk of recurrence
1. Chromosome disorder		
a. Previous child with Down's syndrome	Chromosomes	1%
b. Mother over age thirty-five (risk of Down's syndrome rises with mother's age)	Chromosomes	0.2–2%
2. Neural-tube closure defect (anencephaly, meningomyelocele, spina bifida), previous child affected	Biochemical for alpha-fetoprotein	4%
3. Autosomal recessive disorder with known and testable enzyme deficiency (such as Tay-Sachs disease)	Enzyme assay	25%
4. X-linked recessive disorder with no known enzyme deficiency (such as hemophilia, Duchenne's muscular dystrophy)	Chromosomes for sex	50% males
X-linked recessive disorder with known enzyme deficiency (such as Hunter's syndrome, Lesch-Nyhan syndrome)	Enzyme assay	25%

human diseases and devising tests, it is hoped that many more diseases will be diagnosable early in pregnancy. At present all that can be offered in these cases is the test result, providing great reassurance that the baby will be unaffected with a particular dread disease or, in the minority of instances, demonstrating that the fetus is already affected. The couple may then decide to terminate that pregnancy and try again. In the future, it may be possible to initiate early intrauterine treatment or be ready at birth for children with specific handicapping conditions.

SELECTED REFERENCES

Apgar, Virginia, and Joan Beck, *Is My Baby Alright: A Guide to Birth Defects*, Pocket Books, New York, 1974.

Bergsma, Daniel, ed., *Contemporary Genetic Counseling*, National Foundation – March of Dimes, 1973.

Howell, R. Rodney, "Genetic Disease: The Present Status of Treatment," *Hospital Practice*, October 1972.

Lynch, H. T., D. Bergsma, and R. J. Thomas, eds., *International Directory of Genetic Services*, 5th ed., National Foundation – March of Dimes, 1977.

McKusick, V. A., *Mendelian Inheritance in Man: Catalogs of Autosomal Dominant, Autosomal Recessive, and X-linked Phenotypes*, 4th ed., Johns Hopkins University Press, Baltimore, 1975.

Milunsky, A. *The Prenatal Diagnosis of Hereditary Disorders*, Charles C. Thomas, Springfield, Illinois, 1973.

Omenn, G. S., "Genetic Engineering: Present and Future," in R. H. Williams, ed., *To Live and to Die: When, Why, and How*, Springer-Verlag, New York, 1973.

Robinson, N. M., and H. B. Robinson, *The Mentally Retarded Child: A Psychological Approach*, 2d ed., McGraw-Hill, New York, 1976.

Smith, D. W., *Recognizable Patterns of Human Malformation: Genetic, Embryologic, and Clinical Aspects*, W. B. Saunders, Philadelphia, 1970.

What Are the Facts about Genetic Disease?, National Institute of General Medical Sciences, National Institutes of Health.

20

Blindness and Visual Impairment

JEROME R. DUNHAM, Ph.D.

Reviewed by WARREN BLEDSOE, Consultant, U.S. Department of Health, Education and Welfare, Office of the Blind, and JANET CODLEY GOLDENSON, O.D.

A person with normal eyesight is said to have twenty over twenty (20/20) vision. This means that what this individual can see at twenty feet (6 meters), other normal persons can also see at twenty feet. If one can see at twenty feet what the ordinary person can see at fifteen feet (4.5 meters), then one's vision would be 20/15, better than normal. If a person has 20/70 vision, visual ability is noticeably lessened, and the individual may not drive a car. If the vision is 20/200 in the better eye with correction, then the person can be considered legally blind. A person with no perception of visual stimuli is totally blind.

Visual impairment takes many forms. Some may see a tiny spot of the visual field, and if the diameter is twenty degrees or less, even though that spot of vision is 20/20 in itself, they may also be considered legally blind. Fuzzy vision, vision out of one corner of the eye, vision that is poor in dim light or poor in well-lighted environments, trouble with color—all make the description of visual impairment difficult for people to completely understand. This is particularly true when a sighted person is in contact with a visually handicapped person who has fluctuating vision or whose vision seems to fluctuate because of changes of light and familiarity of environment.

History

Although the majority of blind people down through the ages have lived in humble circumstances, or even in sordid poverty without encouragement or opportunity, there have been in each land and culture a handful of blind people who were considered to be outstanding. Sometimes these were famous personages who, like John Milton, became blind later in life but still carried on in behalf of themselves and others. Less frequently, blind persons through their own courage and creativity became famous while blind.

Homer is usually considered one of the first historical blind persons who made a lasting contribution to his culture. In the Middle Ages blind persons were either beggars or confined to asylums. King Louis IX of France created the "Three Hundred" (Quinze-Vingts)—a combination asylum and commercial establishment for the blind. It was established in 1260 and is the oldest institution for the blind continued into this century. Also in France, in 1785 Valentin Haüy organized classes for blind persons, and the system that gradually developed was copied in other parts of Europe. In 1832 three schools in the United States were opened in Boston, Philadelphia, and New York. Schools then spread throughout the country, frequently in combination with facilities for orphans and delinquents. Although there were a few schools that combined the blind and deaf, these usually were not particularly successful and showed a considerable lack of understanding about the two disability groups. At the same time that schools for the blind were being constructed, workshops were being established where blind persons could make certain items such as brooms, brushes, and mops. These workshops fabricated only a few items, differing in various countries. For instance, in the United States blind persons were not believed to be capable of constructing barrels, whereas in one country in Europe barrels were the only things the blind were believed to be able to make.

In the 1920s and 1930s several blind persons in the United States and Canada innovated placement techniques in industry. They went to employers and demonstrated that blind persons could operate punch presses, drill presses, lathes, etc. This paid off during World War II, when many blind people got their first opportunity for competitive employment in the defense plants. The Social Security Act of 1935 provided the basis by which some state agencies for the blind were formed, and the Rehabilitation Acts of 1943 and 1954 strengthened the capacities of state agencies to rehabilitate blind persons.

The American Foundation for the Blind began to provide research and development leadership in 1921. The American Printing House for the Blind, which had been funded by Congress in 1879, provided educational resource materials. Many other services developed to encourage workers for the blind to be more knowledgeable about blindness and the opportunities that might be held out to them. Throughout the 1950s and 1960s rehabilitation centers for the blind formed teams that were trained in helping blind people gain skills in communication (Braille, typing, tape recorders, talking book machines); use of tools; daily living problems such as dialing the phone rapidly and accurately; identification and separation of coins and the proper separation of folding money so that the denominations could be ascertained by the position in the wallet or by clips; taking care of personal possessions by marking them in Braille; teaching people to use various devices such as Braille watches, Braille rulers, and Braille playing cards. The rehabilitation center clients were also taught how to get around with a cane, and how to be more discriminating with use of auditory perception and the senses of touch and smell in maintaining contact with their environment. The rehabilitation centers themselves did not teach dog guide mobility but frequently referred clients to one of the dog guide foundations. Long before the rehabilitation center movement, home teachers (now called rehabilitation teachers) taught these same skills in the blind person's home or in workshops, social centers, or other special facilities. (See CHAPTER 57: REHABILITATION PROFESSIONS, Orientation and Mobility Instructor.)

Today some federally funded state rehabilitation agencies work only with the blind, but in most cases they are generalized rehabilitation agencies or programs which work with all disabilities.

Incidence

The exact number of blind persons in the United States is unknown, and it certainly is not known how many partially sighted people there are. In the late 1960s the National Institute of Neurological Diseases and Blindness set up model reporting areas in various states, where it was hoped an accurate register could be maintained to provide definitive statistics. These states, employing careful sampling techniques, have provided a basis by which all states have estimated their blind populations.

Estimates vary, but it is usually agreed that there are approximately 500,000 legally blind persons and 1 million more with significant visual impairment in the United States. In retirement villages there are apt to be more blind people since visual impairment is often associated with aging. Also, in certain areas of the world, because of the prevalence of unsanitary conditions and epidemic diseases that attack the eye, there are much larger percentages of blind people in the population. For instance, it is estimated that India has one-fourth to one-fifth of the world's estimated 14 million blind persons.

Types and Causes

As mentioned, poor vision takes many forms and there are many degrees of impairment. When light enters the eye the rays are bent by its curved surface, and bent again slightly by the lens in order to focus on the retina at the back. When the curved surface or the lens is irregular, the person is said to have astigmatism, and a lens ground in a prescribed manner is required to eliminate the distortions caused by the irregularity. If the eyeball is elongated so that the focusing point is in front of the retina, the person is said to be nearsighted (myopic). If the eyeball is too short, the image effectively focuses behind the retina, and the person is said to be farsighted (hyperopic). When the two eyes do not track together because of varying muscular strength, the resulting imbalance produces a condition termed strabismus, in which misalignment of one eye may be inward (cross-eyed), outward, up, or down.

In the center of the retina (macula) thousands of tiny cone-shaped cells are packed together. The cones enable one to see clearest in strong light and also to perceive color. Toward the edge of the retina, serving the periphery of the visual field, are rod-shaped sensory cells which function best in dim light. They are not stimulated by color, and after being in strong light there is a time lag before they can adapt and enable one to see under dimmer conditions. Individuals with color problems vary from those who have difficulty with slight hue changes in the red end of the spectrum, through those who have difficulty telling blue and green apart, to those extreme cases who apparently see only different shades of gray or brightness. About sixteen times as many men as women have color difficulty, and it is a hereditary trait.

Blindness can be caused by physiological conditions, diseases, or accidents. These usually affect the eye itself; however, hemorrhage or insufficient blood supply in the brain can also reduce vision. The visual cortex is in the back of the brain (the occipital lobe), and occasionally blindness is caused by severe trauma to that area. The optic nerves come together behind the bridge of the nose (optic chiasma), and some of the fibers cross over to the opposite hemisphere of the brain. If a pituitary tumor develops, these crossed fibers may be blocked from functioning, and half of each eye can see toward the nose but cannot see toward the temple (bitemporal hemianopsia). Also, after a cerebral vascular accident or trauma to one side of the brain, the patient may be able to see only from one side of each eye (hemianopsia).

Perhaps the primary cause of blindness is cataract, a condition in which the normally clear lens in the pupil of the eye becomes milky or clouded. As the opacity increases, more and more light fails to reach the rear chamber of the eye, and vision gradually diminishes. Cataracts, however, are usually easily removed, and the percentage of good vision after the operation is high. However, it takes several weeks to get used to the necessary artificial lens. When a contact lens is used for the correction, nearly normal vision can usually be obtained.

In the past most permanent blindness was caused by glaucoma—a condition in which more fluid enters or is formed in the eyeball than can escape through the canal that ordinarily removes it. The obstruction or narrowing of this area causes pressure to increase inside the eyeball. As this pressure intensifies, the outside fibers of the optic nerve are kept from functioning, and side vision is reduced. If glaucoma is uncontrolled, the individual may have only a tiny spot of vision in the immediate center of the visual field, and eventually total blindness sets in. Another disorder that usually results in a small central area of vision ("tunnel vision"), and sometimes total blindness, is the hereditary condition termed retinitis pigmentosa, in which there is dystrophy of the rod-shaped cells in the retina. There are various types with different genetic characteristics, and anyone with retinitis pigmentosa in the family should receive genetic counseling.

Another cause of visual impairment, although not usually of total blindness, is macular degeneration. The macula is in the central part of the retina where vision is clearest, and when it becomes affected the person may still have good peripheral vision but cannot see well enough to read or drive a car. The individual is able to get around adequately and may be able to ride a bicycle on quiet streets.

As the number of diabetics has increased, diabetic retinopathy has increased and is now one of the more common causes of visual impairment and total blindness. The person who has been a diabetic for a number of years may undergo vascular changes which cause hemorrhaging in the retina, and as a result may experience a flood of spots in his visual field, first red but darkening later. Quite often the blood reabsorbs and fairly good vision returns for a long period of time. Occasionally, depending on the condition of the retina and the vascular problems, blindness may come on quite suddenly and be permanent.

Eye banks are not always understood by the general public. The whole eye cannot be transplanted, but many times a burn or acid victim suffers damage to the outside membrane of the eye (cornea). Scar tissue begins to grow over the affected part, and this makes for unclear vision. The eye bank provides clear corneas from donors who have willed their eyes for that purpose. A clear cornea is surgically placed in the damaged eye, and if successful the transplant results in a clear field of vision.

The ophthalmologist, or eye physician, may feel defeated once the patient's eyes no longer respond to treatment. The doctor may therefore fail to refer the patient to rehabilitation services. The ophthalmologist may fail to give the patient brochures, or to report the cause of blindness to the state rehabilitation facilities, probably feeling that this is an infringement of the person's rights, or that the client is ashamed of the new condition. Whatever the type or degree of poor vision the person may have, it is essential that information about services to visually handicapped people be made available as soon as possible.

Prevention and Treatment

It is customary to say that half of blindness is preventable. As the pattern of the diseases and conditions that cause blindness gradually change, this may not be as true as it once was. At one time there was much more blindness as a result of syphilis, gonorrhea, and trachoma, which are largely preventable. With diabetic retinopathy and poor vision as a result of the aging process, prevention still offers difficulties. In most states, however, there have for many years been programs that provide information and funding to help people conserve vision or prevent blindness. The National Society for the Prevention of Blindness has in many states strong programs to

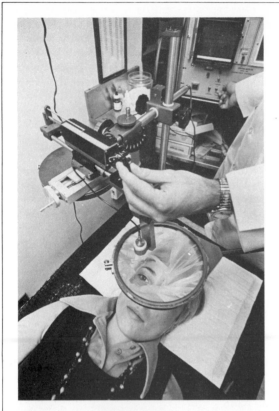

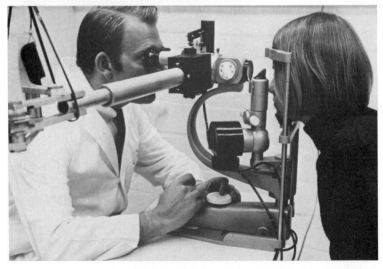

Two examples of modern technology applied to visual disorders: (top) ultrasound diagnosis and (bottom) laser beam treatment. (Research to Prevent Blindness, Inc.)

promote screening, to help with legislation to provide safety glasses, and to assist people in recognizing the danger signs for glaucoma. Occasionally an eye is blinded when children play with sharp sticks or firecrackers. In some industrial plants workers who are lax about wearing safety helmets may suffer eye injuries. However, in most states safety rules and plastic glasses have cut down industrial accidents to a considerable degree.

Poor people may still not get the eye care they need. But Prevention of Blindness programs, Medicare, Title XIX of the Social Security Act, and accident and health insurance have all helped in a variety of ways to provide good eye care to more and more people. At this writing the prospect of national health insurance is gaining and, if it comes to pass, will probably further prevention programs.

When some adults notice that they cannot see the fine print in the phone book as well as they once did, they may well go to a store and sort through spectacles until they find a pair that works. It is a better choice to go to an optometrist and have a pair of glasses prescribed. However, there are certain situations in which individuals should go to an eye physician — an ophthalmologist — because their condition does not require lenses or vision training as much as it requires medical treatment. When a child is found to have crossed eyes, the child should be taken to the eye doctor right away. Since in this condition the two eyes look at slightly different pictures, the brain cannot integrate the images and one eye will soon stop seeing (amblyopia). (See CHAPTER 57: REHABILITATION PROFESSIONS, Ophthalmologist; Optometrist.)

A person who finds that the field of vision is shrinking may be noticing the first signs of glaucoma. This disorder can usually be controlled through use of eyedrops. Occasionally this does not work, and some other measures have to be taken. But one of the problems is that after a few months of taking the eyedrops some people decide that it is not really helping them to see better, so they discontinue the drops. This mistake comes about because they do not realize that the eyedrops are used to improve the function of the canals in the eye so that fluid can get out — in other words, to maintain a lower pressure in the eye. This does nothing to help the person see better within the restricted visual field, but once the pressure again elevates and more vision is lost, the damage is irreversible.

An eye that is cut or bruised should be kept cool and clean, and the individual should get to the doctor as soon as possible. An eye so damaged that it can no longer function may sometimes have to be removed so that it does not cause blindness in the good eye (sympathetic ophthalmia).

Syphilitic blindness has seldom been encountered in the last fifty years; however, this may increase as the venereal disease itself is increasing (see CHAPTER 53: VENEREAL DISEASE). In gonorrhea a baby does not automatically become infected when the mother has the disease; however, its eyes may become infected during its birth passage. This possibility is usually taken care of by the medication put into a newborn infant's eyes (silver nitrate). During the 1940s and 1950s a large number of premature babies were blinded as a result of excess oxygen in the incubators (retrolental fibroplasia, or RLF). Occasionally a baby is still seen with RLF because it is very difficult to achieve exactly the right balance of oxygen: too little oxygen may cause brain damage, and a slight increase in the oxygen may cause RLF.

In the middle 1960s a rubella (German measles) epidemic caught a number of mothers in their first trimester, and as a result a number of children were born with rubella syndrome. This syndrome can have a number of complications, one of which may be very poor vision. Immunization has reduced the number of rubella cases in recent years.

Occasionally an eye that has a tumor or is extremely nearsighted will have its retina detached from the nutritive layer right behind it. There are a variety of techniques to reattach the retina, which then may remain in place for an indefinite period. Still another source of visual impairment is occupational hazard, such as in welding or overexposure to bright light. Although all kinds of exposure cannot be prevented, the more knowledgeable a person is, the better the chances to make enlightened choices such as wearing safety glasses or dark glasses in specific situations.

Education

During the 1940s and 1950s an increasing number of children did not attend the School for the Blind in their state. Instead parent groups gradually convinced school systems to include blind and partially sighted children in neighborhood schools. Itinerant teachers visited from school to school, resource room teachers established a study hall for blind children, and sightsaving classes for partially sighted youngsters were introduced into the public school system. The resource room often provided special equipment such as talking book machines, tape recorders, Braille writers, typewriters, arithmetic devices, and Braille dictionaries and encyclopedias. Volunteers were recruited in many communities to prepare Braille and recorded textbooks for the students. Many of these volunteers were housewives, but a large amount of work was also done in prisons.

Braille is still used in school systems and schools for the blind up through the twelfth grade. Usually college students use Braille for language and mathematics, and many blind lawyers have a large library of Braille reference books. However, an increasing amount of literature for college and high school students is available on tape reel or cassette recordings. This is partly because the aural form is so much faster, but primarily because of storage. Braille is light but very bulky. For instance, the *World Book Encyclopedia* comprises 145 large volumes in Braille, and a dictionary may cover most of the bookshelving in a student's room. Although volunteers do a great deal, most of the textbooks and other educational material come from the American Printing House for the Blind in Louisville, Kentucky. Journals and books about education of the visually handicapped can be obtained from the American Foundation for the Blind or from the Association for the Education of the Visually Handicapped. The Association publishes *Fountainhead* and other newsletters; the Foundation publishes the *Journal of Blindness and Visual Impairment.*

In the United States there are no colleges and universities for blind students such as there are in some countries. It was decided to have blind students attend regular colleges and universities, where by and large they have been well received. In some colleges with a larger number of blind students rooms have been set aside equipped with the Braille reference books and special equipment, much like the resource rooms in elementary and secondary schools. Philanthropic organizations sometimes fund these facilities.

Because of parental pressure and legislative changes, common schools are taking more responsibility for the education of all children, including those who deviate from the norm. The population of blind children also is shifting to a greater incidence of the multiply handicapped. In the past the parents of a blind child needed considerable assurance and counseling to help them realize how to stimulate and help the child learn to explore its environment. Parents who have a multiply handicapped child need even more assurance, and more time and energy have to be given to assisting the child to attain self-sufficiency or whatever measure of independence is possible. New programs have been developed to help with these children, such as group homes where parents can be relieved of some of the responsibility for a severely handicapped child, and workshops and activity programs where severely handicapped young people can learn to do various kinds of work and experience recreational and socializing activities.

Rehabilitation

The newly blinded adult may not know what assistance is available to blind persons. In some cases it may take months to discover that a broad array of services may be obtainable (800 agencies in the United States offer assistance). The rehabilitation program for blind persons is a part of a general agency in many states, but in some states a separate agency or commission for the blind will make contact with a newly blinded person, explain services that are available, and start to plan what steps the blind person can take in order to get back to making a living and fulfilling family and community responsibilities. Usually the first step is to get a general physical and an eye report. Often the first contact is made by a rehabilitation teacher who comes to the blind person's home and begins to teach how to handle some of the daily problems in dealing with the environment and compensating for the loss of vision.

If the first step is to go through a rehabilitation center, then the blind person is transported to a facility that has had some experience in systematically teaching the blind to perform a great number of activities. The program usually includes work in a shop and a

An editor of this book, Dr. Jerome R. Dunham, who has been blind since adolescence, at an exhibit of the Tactile Arts Program, Henry Gallery, Seattle. (Photograph by John A. Moore, Office of Information Services, University of Washington, Seattle)

home economics area, development of communication skills, learning to get around with a cane, retraining of senses, and exploring attitudes toward blindness. Many rehabilitation centers focus on the blind person's self-image as well as concepts of sighted people and other blind persons. One also has to learn how to cope with people who grossly over- or underestimate the blind person's capabilities. Many people stereotype the blind, usually in the form of providing too much help.

Family members have to learn when to assist the blind person and when to allow independent exploration and accomplishment of tasks. The disabled person has to decide how dependent or independent to be. This comes from experience, but it is also determined by background, age at the onset of blindness, how good hearing might be, health, and the nature and personality of family and friends. The blind person will invariably need some kinds of help — for instance, in reading mail or being transported in a car. Usually the counselors or rehabilitation center personnel attempt to help the blind person gracefully accept realistic dependency but maintain some control over the situation, so that the disabled individual still feels a whole, adequate person.

Unfortunately the family of a blind person is not always given adequate training or counseling. As a result, it sometimes happens that family members do not appreciate the new skills or the white cane, and because of their feelings of shame discourage the blind person from appearing in public. Also, the spouse or parents may enjoy the new role of having the blind person dependent on them and resist attempts at independence.

It is said that there are more than 7,000 different occupations in which blind persons are successfully competing. In general it is harder for a blind person to handle a common laboring job and easier to do well in a job that requires verbal skills and a good memory. But there are many blind persons who prefer to do heavy or mechanical work or agricultural tasks, and many exhibit unusual manual dexterity. A newly blinded person is likely to ask what kinds of jobs blind people can do. Instead of simply listing them, an experienced rehabilitation counselor will usually help blind persons explore patterns of interests, abilities, and past experience in order to identify a particular job category that suits them, and then will find out how close they can come to that type of job in a position that does not require vision.

The newly blinded person and many sighted people find it difficult to understand how people can do many tasks without vision. They are so familiar with using vision in most activities that it takes time and a good deal of experience to learn how to do things in a different way. The rehabilitation process includes counseling, training, diagnosis, physical restoration, and placement with follow-up services when required. Placement of a blind person on a job is usually done by the rehabilitation counselor or a placement specialist. After the blind person has been on the job for sixty days, the individual is usually asked if everything is going all right, and if the employer is satisfied the case is closed. Services can be resumed if the blind person wishes to change fields for a legitimate reason, loses a position, suffers a radical change in health, or encounters a family situation which necessitates retraining for another occupation.

Special considerations have been given to blind persons — for instance, an extra exemption on income tax and a slightly different set of rules on Supplemental Security Income. There is certain legislation that has helped the blind person secure employment — for example, the Randolph-Sheppard Act, which provides for a program set up by a state agency which will give the blind person rent-free use of a snack bar, cafeteria, or cigar counter business enterprise in a public building. In most states the state program trains the blind person in salesmanship, business practices, facility sanitation and upkeep, and inventory control. When the blind person wishes to give up the stand, the licensed authority, usually the state program, requires that the inventory be restored to its original level, and will place another blind person in that location to continue the business. The contractual relationship is between the licensing authority and the building management. Furnishing vending machine service is often included in the contractual arrangement. The blind person maintains, repairs, and gets the profit from the machines. The licensing authority usually purchases or rents them for the use of the blind vendor and the people in the building.

The Wagner-O'Day Act provides that blind and other disabled persons have first priority in supplying services and products for governmental contracts. Usually it has been goods required by the government, such as ashtrays, military ties, navy signal flags, and mattresses. (See CHAPTER 8: THE SHELTERED WORKSHOP for further information about the Wagner-O'Day Act.)

Aids and Devices

Many public and private agencies for the blind maintain a supply of canes, Braille equipment, tools, and other devices that have been modified or selected because they can be easily used without vision. One category of special devices is supplied by a low-vision clinic or optical aids program in which a variety of light filters and magnification systems are maintained. The usual fitter of lenses attempts to improve vision in general for the person, sometimes more specifically for near or distant viewing. In the optical aids programs, however, an attempt is made to help the visually impaired person do one particular job; for instance, a college student may be able to take care of all studies except mathematics, but with a closed-circuit TV and zoom lens one may actually be able to watch one's own writing and read the formula on the page made with a felt pen. This may increase one's speed and accuracy in mathematics severalfold. Or perhaps a light-sensitive albino person may utilize glare-reducing polarized lenses to move about freely on a bright sunny day. Or through a system of contact lenses, spectacles, and a lens on the end of a jeweler's loop, a very severely impaired person might be able to read the meters on equipment at work.

In exploring the use of an optical aid program, a visually impaired person should, wherever possible, attempt to obtain a referral to the clinic from his or her own eye doctor. However, many eye physicians do not see the importance of a particular optical aid. They realize that the magnification will not generally improve the vision, but do not always appreciate the fact that for this individual being able to do one task more easily is very important. There should be a caution, however. Many people will purchase a particular lens and then not make use of it. Most optical aid programs offer an opportunity to practice with the preferred magnification system until certain whether it will be more helpful than troublesome, before actually purchasing the item or requesting it from a rehabilitation agency.

There is a large range of tools and devices constructed for the blind, such as circuit analyzers, light detectors, bread slicers, Braille dials on electric fry pans, and needle threaders. These devices are sold by several concerns. The American Foundation for the Blind publishes the largest catalog for general usage, and Science for the Blind offers more technical equipment. Howe Press and the American Printing House for the Blind direct their efforts more toward communication and educational materials.

Many blind persons get about regularly and freely with the assistance of a travel aid. For some elderly people, for those who have never learned to get around by themselves, and for some deaf-blind persons, this travel aid should be another person. For the deaf-blind, the guide may also act as interpreter in communication with others. For a relatively small percentage of people, the travel aid may be a dog guide. There are eleven dog guide facilities in the country; the oldest and best known is Seeing Eye, Inc., in Morristown, New Jersey. (See the list of dog guide facilities at the end of the chapter.)

A common occurrence in a community where people discover that one of their fellow citizens is newly blinded is to offer to chip in and purchase a dog guide. This is a good neighborly spirit but is not always well directed. Without cost, most dog guide facilities will fly the blind person to their training facility, provide a month's training and the dog, and take care of the return trip. It is usually better, however, for the newly blinded person to find out how to get about with a cane. One needs to retrain the senses and to learn how to handle oneself as a blind person. And then, if after experience and deliberation, it is decided to use a dog guide, the decision will be made out of greater knowledge.

There are a variety of canes. The ones currently used have evolved from the short, sturdy orthopedic cane. The long, light canes of today are measured according to the person's height, length of stride, speed of walk, length of arm, and other factors determined by the orientation and mobility instructor. The instructor teaches the blind person how to best use the cane in a graceful and safe manner, and to get the most information from its tip. Today's canes can be rigid or can fold up and fit into a coat pocket or purse. These are particularly useful for those blind persons who do a lot of traveling on bus, train, or plane. At this writing electronic canes are still in experimental form. A laser cane is being distributed to a few agencies for further field testing. It provides beams to alert the blind person to overhead obstructions, to detect an object or person several feet ahead, and to detect a hole or stepdown. These obstacles are communicated to the blind person by a vibrating button under the forefinger or by two different tones. The sounds are usually so low in volume that they do not disturb others or bring unwelcome attention to the blind person. There is also an ultrasonic device that fits into a pair of spectacles, with small tubes leading to the ears, enabling the blind traveler to tell a great deal about the environment several feet away. The device takes training and usually does not entirely eliminate the use of a cane.

For more than fifty years inventors have turned their attention to helping blind persons read print. A variety of devices have been developed, including a movable sensing device that can be pushed along the line of print, and a box that gives out a variety of tones indicating the pattern of the various letters. This approach is probably best exemplified by the Visatoner, which is provided to blind veterans by the Veterans Administration. Another device that has recently been widely sold is the Optacon, which has the same movable sensing device, but in this case the pattern of the letters is presented tactually rather than aurally. The blind individual's finger is placed on a slightly concave area of 144 pins that vibrate, so that a wave of vibration is felt that can be detected as a particular letter coming halfway around the extended finger. Most people with training and adequate motivation can learn to read by this method, but rather slowly and laboriously. However, several people have reported speeds from 60 to 100 words a minute, which shows promise since most people do not read Braille any faster than this. However, exceptional Braille readers can sometimes read as fast as 250 words a minute. The ordinary reading speed by sound, that is, listening to a tape recorder or a person reading, is approximately 125 words a minute. With the new devices that compress speech and register it on tape recorders and record players, speeds of considerably higher rate can be reached while still maintaining adequate comprehension.

Since many blind people became disabled in adulthood, and do not read Braille particularly well, there has been great emphasis on tape recorders for note-taking and communication. Although there are blind persons who have Ph.D.'s in mathematics, computations are clumsy in Braille. The recently developed audio calculator is a breakthrough that should open new jobs and make mathematical tasks much simpler. As each button is pushed down for a number or function, the name of that number or function is read aloud through chip circuitry.

Braille continues to be the basic form of communication for many blind persons, and there have been many advances in producing it quickly. The "slate and stylus" is the original means of writing Braille: with a little awl, holes are punched into paper placed on a framework that has precise rows of dents formed for that purpose. The Braille writer looks somewhat like a typewriter except that it has only nine keys. With this equipment Braille can be produced much faster, since several dots can be formed at once by pushing down more than one key at a time. The IBM Braille Typewriter is a large electric machine: the untrained sighted secretary or volunteer can push down a letter on a keyboard and produce the Braille equivalent. In Braille a number of contractions are ordinarily utilized, and the IBM typewriter is arranged so that some of these contractions can be produced. For the last fifteen years the Thermoform machine has been the primary duplicating device for Braille; that is, a piece of plastic is placed over the Braille page and is heated and vacuumed down. The same method is used for duplicating maps and charts; a raised line drawing is made on aluminum foil or a wheel makes raised punches on Braille paper, then this is placed into the machine and the plastic duplicates the form.

Research

There continues to be extensive medical research into the causes of the various kinds of blindness. At this writing this applies particularly to research in diabetic retinopathy. Laser coagulation of retinal hemorrhages and of diabetic diseased tissue holds out hope of preventing much blindness. Other research projects are being conducted on the causes of diseases like macular degeneration and retinitis. These include the use of fluorescent photography; a plastic intraocular lens implanted after cataract surgery; a new drug, Ara-AMP, which combats herpes infection of the eye, the major cause of corneal blindness; and further investigation of vitrectomy, a surgical technique in which cloudy vitreous fluid, which fills the center of the eye, is removed and replaced by a clear solution.

There continues to be research in improving Braille and sound recording for the education of blind persons. A good deal of attention is being given to some exotic television camera devices hooked up to electrodes implanted in the blind person's visual cortex, or optic nerve, or retina, to discover whether, through this means, the blind can be made to see. A number of studies are being conducted on occupational information and the means of disseminating and retrieving information about work for the blind and the kinds of jobs they are doing around the country. And the research in travel devices still intrigues many blind persons and many inventors who are challenged by the problems of the blind moving about in a changing environment. As an example of current research, the June 1975 issue of *Research Bulletin*, published semiannually by the American Foundation for the Blind, includes the following reports: "On the Possibility of an Entirely Extracranial Visual Prosthesis," "A Method for the Comparative Evaluation of Visual and Auditory Displays," and "Spelled Speech as an Output for the Lexiphone Reading Machine and the Spellex Talking Typewriter."

Organizations and Foundations

In almost every city there is at least a small society of blind persons who meet together to socialize, to exchange information, or to work on a project. Most of these societies are affiliates of statewide organizations, and most of the state organizations are affiliates of one of the two national organizations of blind people. The oldest and largest is the National Federation of the Blind, headquartered in Des Moines, Iowa. The other is the American Council of the Blind, with national headquarters in Washington, D.C. These two organizations are concerned with broadening the opportunities for blind persons to participate in the mainstream of life, to increase the number of training and employment opportunities, and whenever discrimination toward a blind person is found, to attempt to educate the parties involved about the capacities of blind persons. Sometimes the National Federation, particularly, will bring suit to right what it feels has been an injustice toward blind persons.

The national organizations of the blind, besides holding yearly conventions and publishing monthly newsletters, have a variety of informational sources they can tap to help blind persons. They play a client watchdog role with agencies for the blind. They introduce legislation, inspect bills that may have an effect on work for the blind, and maintain a lobby in Washington, D.C., and in many state legislatures. Organizations of the blind have traditionally been the strongest and best organized of any of the disability groups.

The American Association of Workers for the Blind (AAWB) and the Association for Education of the Visually Handicapped (AEVH) are parallel organizations that have influenced work for the blind throughout the century. They hold national conventions and publish journals and yearbooks; they have state and regional chapters and organize special committees or launch projects to research particular problems or fill a special need. Although the two organizations have many interests in common, they have seldom met together nationally. AAWB has a membership primarily composed of those concerned with rehabilitation of adults; AEVH is primarily concerned with education of children.

A number of organizations are engaged in research programs, including Research to Prevent Blindness, Association for Research in Vision and Ophthalmology, Fight for Sight, National Eye Research Foundation, National Foundation for Eye Research, National Retinitis Pigmentosa Foundation, and National Society for the Prevention of Blindness. Research to Prevent Blindness has been particularly active not only through its extensive research grants but through its leadership role in the creation of the National Eye Institute of the National Institutes of Health. The total operating budget of the Institute for 1976 was $50,212,000, practically all of which was allotted to research-oriented projects. (See PART 4, SECTION 2: VOLUNTARY ORGANIZATIONS for all addresses.)

Dog Guide Schools

Eye Dog Foundation for the Blind, 408 South Spring Street, Los Angeles, CA 90013.

Eye of the Pacific Guide Dogs, 3008 Kalei Road, Honolulu, HI 96814.

Guide Dog Foundation for the Blind, 109-19 72d Avenue, Forest Hills, NY 11375.

Guide Dogs for the Blind, P.O. Box 1200, San Rafael, CA 94902.

Guiding Eyes for the Blind, 106 East 41st Street, New York, NY 10017.

International Guiding Eyes, 5431-35 Denny Avenue, North Hollywood, CA 91603.

Leader Dogs for the Blind, 1039 Rochester Road, Rochester, MI 48063.

Pilot Dogs, 625 West Town Street, Columbus, OH 43215.

The Seeing Eye, P.O. Box 375, Morristown, NJ 07960.

SELECTED REFERENCES

Apple, Loyal E., and Marianne May, *Distant Vision and Perceptual Training: A Concept for Use in Mobility Training for Low Vision Clients*, American Foundation for the Blind, 1971.

Dickey, Thomas W., and Louis Vieceli, "A Survey of the Vocational Placement of Visually Handicapped Persons and Their Degree of Vision," *New Outlook for the Blind*, February 1972.

Gilpin, Joy, *Teaching Housekeeping to Blind Homemakers*, Brooklyn Bureau of Social Service, 285 Schermerhorn Street, Brooklyn, NY 11217.

Hardy, Richard E., and John G. Cull, *Social and Rehabilitation Services for the Blind*, Charles C. Thomas, Springfield, Illinois, 1972.

Lowenfeld, Berthold, *The Changing Status of the Blind: From Separation to Integration*, Charles C. Thomas, Springfield, Illinois, 1975.

Rehabilitation Centers for the Blind and Visually Impaired: The State of the Art, 1975—Final Report of the National Workshop on Rehabilitation Centers, American Foundation for the Blind.

Rusalem, Herbert, *Coping with the Unseen Environment: An Introduction to the Vocational Rehabilitation of Blind Persons*, Teachers College Press, New York, 1972.

Sullivan, Tom, *If You Could See What I Hear*, Harper & Row, New York, 1975.

21

Blood Disorders:
A. Cooley's Anemia

ZELDA BAUM, Executive Director, Cooley's Anemia
Blood and Research Foundation for Children

Named after Dr. Thomas A. Cooley, a Detroit physician who first diagnosed it, in 1925, Cooley's anemia derives its alternative name, thalassemia major, from the Greek *thalassa*, meaning "sea." The reason for the latter term is that the disease is believed to have originated more than 50,000 years ago in the Mediterranean basin, possibly because of a protective value against malaria. Today Cooley's anemia is particularly prevalent in Italy, Sicily, Sardinia, Greece, Crete, Cyprus, Syria, and Turkey, but it is also found farther east, in Asia, including southern China, and in central Africa. In the United States the "melting pot" has distributed the disorder through intermarriage to approximately 200,000 individuals.

Cooley's anemia is the result of a genetic defect due to recessive inheritance. When only one defective gene is transmitted, the result is thalassemia minor, and the inheritor, although carrying the trait, is not sick and may lead a normal life. But when both parents carry the gene, each of their children has a 25 percent chance of developing thalassemia major.

The adverse effects of the two faulty genes are centered in the hemoglobin, the pigment that endows red blood cells with their color and carries out the essential job of transporting oxygen to body tissues. As molecules go, hemoglobin is large, containing 10,000 atoms. Even so, each red cell normally contains more than 250 million hemoglobin molecules, each capable of transporting eight atoms of oxygen.

Hemoglobin is a chromoprotein—a combination of a protein,

globin, and a colored, iron-containing compound, heme. In Cooley's anemia, both the amount of hemoglobin and the number of red cells are strikingly reduced, and as a consequence the blood cells are pale and cannot perform their oxygen-carrying function fully. Moreover, normal red cells have a life-span of three to four months, and as they die are continuously replaced by new cells. In Cooley's anemia the red cells cannot survive for more than a few weeks.

Most children born with the disease appear healthy at birth. Gradually symptoms begin to appear, often at one or two years of age, sometimes as early as three months. The child becomes pale, listless, irritable. A mother may notice that the baby does not have the strength to finish a meal. Growth is retarded.

Meantime, a devastating chain of events is occurring. The spleen is working excessively. Charged with normal removal of old worn-out red cells, it is inundated with young destroyed cells. Over a period of time it will hypertrophy, or enlarge, much like an overworked muscle. The liver enlarges too, and after a time the abdomen swells because of the two overgrown organs.

The bone marrow works hard trying to compensate for the rapid destruction of red cells by producing more—but its desperate efforts, even though almost continuous, are abortive. Because of the hyperactivity of the marrow, changes occur in the bones: they become brittle, break easily, take ten times longer to heal. And often there is a thickening of the cranial bones, producing facial traits like those of mongolism, and a vast overgrowth of the maxilla (upper jawbone) with protruberant teeth.

Meanwhile, because of the severe chronic anemia, the heart, working harder to pump more blood to oxygen-starved tissues, enlarges. Finally, as the overexerting heart loses its pumping vigor, the patient may succumb to congestive heart failure.

Hypertransfusion Treatment

The outlook for Cooley's anemia victims was invariably bleak before the 1960s. Iron compound medications (hematinics) failed to increase the amount of hemoglobin. Treatment was largely symptomatic, consisting of periodic blood transfusions in an attempt to keep hemoglobin concentrations from falling to dangerous levels. Transfusions were, however, used only sparingly because of the risks of transfusional hemosiderosis, the deposition of large amounts of iron in all tissues of the body. Iron deposition was recognized to be a serious hazard in Cooley's anemia not only because of the quantities introduced by transfusion but also because anemic patients absorb much greater amounts than normal from dietary sources under the stimulus of the anemia and ineffective red cell formation. And if iron stores are excessive, the iron spills over from its normal storage sites in the blood, spleen, liver, bone marrow, and lymph nodes into functioning tissue cells in the liver, pancreas, and other glands. It even gets into the heart, where it acts as a poison, causing fibrosis, necrosis, and eventual organ failure, leading to cirrhosis, diabetes, hypogonadism, and heart failure.

Then, in 1964, the unexpected happened. An investigator, Dr. I. J. Wolman, discovered the benefits of intensive, as contrasted with sporadic, transfusion in bringing hemoglobin levels up higher, approaching normal, and keeping them there. Survival was not influenced, but up to about age thirteen his young patients were not afflicted with chronic illness and listlessness and were almost indistinguishable from normal children on the surface. Bone fractures and dental problems associated with facial malformations were virtually eliminated, and liver and spleen enlargement was reduced. Iron overloading was still going on, but it appeared that hypertransfusion made it no greater than restricted transfusions. If the increased transfusions added more iron, at the same time they removed the stimulus of chronic anemia to increase intestinal absorption of iron.

At least to puberty the lives of patients were vastly improved. At puberty, however, the normal growth spurt and secondary sexual development failed to occur because of endocrine gland damage from iron overload. Heart enlargement and congestive heart failure associated with severe anemia could be postponed by hypertransfusion, but they occurred at a later age and were related to huge iron overload of the heart. Moreover, the diabetes and other endocrine disturbances and the cirrhosis of the liver that tended to occur in older thalassemia patients could not be significantly changed by hypertransfusion; they seemed more related to iron overload than to tissue oxygen shortage from anemia. But hypertransfusion had succeeded in raising life expectancy from well under ten years to between fifteen and twenty-five years for most patients.

Treatment for Iron Poisoning

Efforts to get rid of excess iron go back many years. Some compounds, called chelators, have the ability to sequester and bind metallic ions into their molecular rings. Chelators of many types have been studied for their usefulness in iron removal. Most have been discarded because of lack of potency or selectivity for iron or because of toxicity. But, at last, one chelator with very high affinity for iron and without serious toxicity has become available for use in Cooley's anemia and in other serious disorders requiring multitransfusional therapy. This drug is desferrioxamine, now officially called desferoxamine (Desferal, Ciba).

Desferal is not a new drug, and its value in combating iron overload has been recognized for some time. It was originally introduced as a treatment for acute iron poisoning, in which the death rate was about 50 percent, mainly in children. It was remarkably effective, as indicated by a 1966 study of 172 patients and a 1971 study of 474, in which mortality was reduced to close to 1 percent. Clearly, Desferal was a potent iron chelator, with the specific ability of forming a water-soluble complex, ferrioxamine, which prevents the iron from entering into further chemical reactions and carries it out of the body in the urine.

New Treatment for Cooley's Anemia

In view of these results, it seemed that Desferal might be useful in thalassemia cases. Early investigations appeared to indicate that, in the short term, intramuscular injection of the compound on a daily basis did not bring all patients into iron balance. But a few investigators – in Greece, Australia, and Britain particularly – persisted, and by 1974 it had been reported that long-term treatment without serious toxicity was feasible. The reports from abroad led to a reawakening of interest in the United States – to no small extent helped by the efforts of the Cooley's Anemia Blood and Research Foundation to promote research through grants and seminars.

In April 1976 a report was submitted by an Ad Hoc Working Group that had been appointed by the National Heart, Lung and Blood Institute's Division of Blood Diseases and Resources to develop a policy position on the chronic use of Desferal in the treatment of iron overload. After examining all major studies conducted to date, the Working Group observed that treatment with the drug has not been carried on long enough to determine definitively whether survival is prolonged. Nevertheless, they found several studies that indicated a prolongation of life, and concluded: "Desferrioxamine is safe as well as potent and specific in removing iron from patients with excessive iron overload. The drug may be effective in reducing the morbidity associated with iron overload, preventing or delaying the tissue damage from excessive iron stores, and prolonging life in patients with transfusional iron overload." The report therefore went on to say: "With the present state of our knowledge we recommend that desferrioxamine be made available to promote iron excretion from patients with thalassemia and other chronic anemias associated with iron overload."

As of 1977, research is continuing on the administration of Desferal as well as on techniques for increasing the supply in the United States. Dr. Richard D. Propper and his associates at the Harvard Medical School and the Children's Hospital Medical Center in Boston have treated the thalassemic patients with sixteen-hour intravenous infusions and have suggested the use of a lightweight portable intermittent-infusion pump. Tests are now under way in which a pump with a drug-filled syringe is worn strapped to the body. Production of Desferal is a complex process, presently carried out in Italy. In view of the increased interest in the drug and its possible use not only with thalassemia patients but with other conditions which require repeated transfusions, such as sickle cell anemia and chronic leukemia, efforts are being made to estimate the amount required by American physicians, and to make adequate supplies available.

Organization

Founded by parents of thalassemia children in 1954, the Cooley's Anemia Blood and Research Foundation for Children is headquartered at 647 Franklin Avenue, Garden City, NY 11530. Its overall objective is to provide a full program of patient services, education, and research. The Foundation helps patients obtain blood products, offers wheelchair and transportation services when needed, and arranges for screening tests and insurance counseling. The educational program includes a comprehensive reference library, a speakers' bureau, and distribution of an informative film. Some of the locations where research projects are currently funded by the Foundation are the College of Physicians and Surgeons, Columbia University; Institute of Child Health, in Athens, Greece; Osborn Laboratories of Marine Sciences; Nassau County Medical Center; Boston Children's Hospital Medical Center; Albert Einstein College of Medicine; and the Catania Clinic, in Italy.

B. Hemophilia

ROBERT M. GOLDENSON, Ph.D.

Reviewed by the National Hemophilia Foundation

Hemophilia is an inherited disorder of the blood characterized by a deficiency of the specific factor in blood plasma which produces clotting. Due to lack of this factor, coagulation is abnormally delayed in both internal and external bleeding. Hemorrhaging may occur throughout life, and may arise spontaneously or result from a bruising bump or blow. Usually these painful episodes cannot be controlled or arrested without medical treatment, and if they occur repeatedly or are inadequately treated they may lead to serious disability and even deformity due to the effect on muscles, joints, and vital organs.

Hemophilia patients are technically termed hemophiliacs and popularly known as "bleeders." The disorder has also been called the "disease of kings," since it was transmitted through Queen Victoria to her male descendants among the royal families of England, Russia, and Spain. Today it often affects average families who lack the means of coping with the continuous, crushing financial and emotional toll it exacts.

Types and Diagnosis

There are a number of hemophilias or hemophilialike diseases, each characterized by a blood factor deficiency which can be determined by standard tests that measure clotting time. The two most prevalent types are hemophilia A, or classic hemophilia, and hemophilia B, also known as Christmas disease. In both types the plasma component responsible for blood coagulation is absent or not functionally available. In hemophilia A this component is termed Factor VIII, and in hemophilia B, Factor IX. In both types the severity of the disorder varies considerably. Patients who are mildly affected (25 to 50 percent of the factor present) or moderately affected (5 to 25 percent present) often go undiagnosed until they undergo a surgical procedure during which bleeding cannot be readily controlled. Individuals with 1 to 5 percent of Factor VIII or IX have a moderately severe deficiency and may also go undiagnosed for long periods. These patients rarely hemorrhage spontaneously but bleed profusely after a minor injury. Children at this level are allowed to live a normal existence, but the patients are cautioned to consult a physician if there is any question of bleeding.

The plight of the severely affected (those with less than 1 percent of the factor) is far more serious. In these cases the diagnosis is often made at birth on the basis of hemorrhage or family history, but if not, it may be made at the time of circumcision. The affected experience spontaneous hemorrhage all their lives, for reasons unknown, though there are data suggesting that the bleeding may be provoked by emotional stress in some instances. Special precautions must be taken with these patients — for instance, deep intramuscular injections should be avoided since they may induce internal bleeding, and even inoculation and vaccination must be performed with extreme care. If spontaneous bleeding into the joints occurs, it commonly affects the knees, elbows, ankles, and wrists and must be treated immediately, since the major cause of infirmity and chronic disability in these patients is secondary joint deformity. It is also imperative to attend to hemorrhage into the bones and muscles, since this may also result in disability.

Incidence and Prevalence

About 1 out of 4,000 American boys in every racial and socioeconomic group is affected with hemophilia, and the total number of cases is estimated at 100,000. The incidence of Factor VIII hemophilia is estimated at $1/2$ to 1 per 10,000 newborn males. The incidence of Factor IX cases is less certain since it is rarer. According to a study published by the National Heart and Lung Institute in 1972, about 25,500 cases under treatment fell into the severe or moderate categories. Factor VIII deficiency accounted for approximately 80 percent of all these cases, factor IX approximately 20 percent, and there were considerably more severe cases among the former than among the latter type. Hemophilia has also been found in females, but is extremely rare.

Etiology

Hemophilia has been recognized as an inherited disorder as far back as the Old Testament. It is a sex-linked recessive condition transmitted through the mother to male children almost exclusively. Though the female is always the carrier, she herself does not show signs of the disease; and when a hemophiliac himself has children, his sons are all normal but his daughters are carriers. The transmitting mechanism is one of the mother's two X (sex) chromosomes; each of her sons will have a 50 percent chance of being a hemophiliac, and each daughter a 50 percent chance to be a carrier.

Despite this general genetic pattern, only about 70 percent of known cases show a family history of bleeders. A few of the remaining 30 percent may be due to hidden inheritance through generations of female carriers, but by far the larger number are "new" cases which have arisen through genetic mutation. The rate of these spontaneous mutations, which create new carriers of hemophilia, is believed to be the highest among all known sex-linked genetic disorders. A number of experimental laboratory tests have been devised for detecting these and other carriers, but as yet no standard, reliable test is available.

Prevention

Since hemophilia is an inherited disorder, genetic counseling is recommended whenever it is found in a family. This usually consists of carefully explaining the nature of the disorder, the inheritance pattern, and the risk of having a hemophiliac son. The parents, or potential parents, are given informative literature to read, but the final decision as to whether to bear a child is left entirely to them. Known carriers who are already pregnant may be advised to undergo amniocentesis (study of the amniotic fluid) in order to detect the sex of the child. If the test results indicate that the fetus is a boy, the mother may decide to have an abortion. Amniocentesis is an expensive technique and is not always undertaken. At present there are no statistics on how often abortion is used as a means of preventing hemophilia. (See CHAPTER 19: BIRTH DEFECTS; GENETIC COUNSELING.)

When a hemophiliac son has already been born, two other forms of prevention are in order, one of a psychological and the other of a physical nature. Counseling is often made available to the mother to prevent her from feeling guilty about transmitting the disease to her son and to help her avoid overprotection and oversolicitude. The father, too, may need counseling to discourage him from withdrawing emotionally from his wife and son, leaving the mother to cope with the boy's problems by herself. The other preventive approach focuses on the physical aspects of the disorder. Its aim is to reduce the likelihood of crippling effects by providing preventive medical and hospital care when needed, and by prophylactic treatment in the form of regular infusions of the clotting factor, as outlined below.

Treatment and Management

Until recently transfusions of whole blood or plasma were used to replace the deficient factors in hemophilia. In either case relatively large amounts were required, and even then an adequate supply of the clotting factor could not always be achieved. Moreover, there was always a danger of overloading the vascular system, a condition known as hypervolemia. Today this danger is avoided by the infusion of blood-clotting concentrates, which the National Hemophilia Foundation has called "the single most significant advance to date in the history of the treatment of hemophilia . . . Concentrates have the power to cut down or even head off bleeding episodes, which means a drastic reduction in the pain, crippling, hospitalization and mortality of most victims." The concentrates offer the additional advantage of permitting patients to undergo elective major surgery and regular dental work never before possible.

The mainstay of therapy for Factor VIII hemophilia is intravenous infusion of this factor extracted from plasma. Recently, too, concentrates of Factor IX have also become available. Several methods of extraction are used, but the most common is precipitation from fresh frozen plasma. These cryoprecipitates are easily prepared and stored and, even more important, can be given in small amounts that will not overload the intravascular space. The physician, however, must be aware of possible side effects, such as hives (urticaria), fever, anemia and, very occasionally, hepatitis.

Another aspect of the treatment program is management of bleeding episodes, which are often called to the physician's attention by the patient himself when he is in pain. Bleeding may occur at any time and without warning, and the pain is often a clue to its nature and location even before there are any objective findings. If there is evidence of gastrointestinal, intra-abdominal, pharyngeal, or intracranial bleeding, or bleeding into other internal organs, immediate hospitalization is indicated. In addition, alleviation of the pain is usually required, although analgesics must be carefully chosen, since some anti-inflammatory agents, including aspirin, may prolong the bleeding time.

This is by no means the whole story regarding treatment and management. Today the emphasis is on a total care approach, and when it is followed almost all hemophiliacs can live relatively normal lives, even though there is no cure for the condition. As Dr. Louis M. Aledort, Medical Director of the National Hemophilia Foundation, points out:

> One of the major developments in hemophilia management has been the emergence of the team approach to the long-range care of the hemophiliac patient now increasingly practiced in various medical centers throughout the country. Ideally, every hemophiliac child or adult should be regularly evaluated by his physician as well as by an interdisciplinary hospital team. The team consists of a pediatrician, internist, hematologist, orthopedist, dentist (for the difficult problems related to repair of caries and to extractions), physiatrist, social service personnel, and psychologist or psychiatrist (to help the patient and his family cope with the anxiety, guilt, and other emotional stresses that often are a part of the picture). Educational and vocational counselors may also be needed, because the hemophiliac often has serious problems in maintaining his education and his earning potential. Working together, the practitioner and the specialty team have been able to make today's hemophiliac a more active and productive member of society.

Life Effects

Many hemophiliac patients still lack the assistance provided by a comprehensive team of specialists—and even with that assistance they will be faced with problems. Although there is no evidence of an intrinsic relationship between hemophilia and intelligence level or academic achievement, the school performance of some children may be affected by absenteeism resulting from the disorder. Some parents enroll their son in a school for the handicapped, but both the National Heart, Lung and Blood Institute and the National Hemophilia Foundation are opposed to this practice and strongly recommend enrollment in a regular school. They also suggest that wherever possible the parents and even the child learn home treatment techniques as described and illustrated in the *American Journal of Nursing* article listed below. By learning to infuse the clotting factor, they will avoid many trips to the physician or clinic and many absences from school.

These organizations also recommend that the teacher and school nurse be provided with a full record of the diagnosis and severity of the disorder, and be prepared to cope with emergency bleeding episodes and to contact the physician if they occur. It may also be necessary to provide a hemophiliac boy with a splint, crutches, or cane to rest a body part for a time. These children can take any course, even shop, but safety measures appropriate for all children should be given special emphasis. Contrary to popular opinion, exercise is not to be avoided—in fact, it is vital for the hemophiliac child since good physical condition reduces the frequency and severity of bleeding episodes and helps muscles and joints resist permanent damage. However, such sports as swimming, bicycling, and tennis are recommended over body contact sports, such as basketball and football, in which bumps and bruises are likely to occur. Another precaution, for adults and children alike, is to wear a Hemophilia ID Disc supplied by the National Hemophilia Foundation, bearing their diagnosis and blood type.

Vocational guidance geared to individual needs, interests, and abilities is highly advisable, as it is with other children. It should be recognized that some hemophiliacs can cope with a vocation involving more physical stress than others, and for this reason the severity of their condition should be borne in mind. Many hemophiliacs attempt to conceal their disorder from employers for fear that they will be turned down or lose their job, but a study by Alfred Katz has shown that those who reveal their condition tend to remain on the job for longer periods of time and experience better relationships with their employers. It is also important to recognize that hemophiliacs who conceal their disorder run the double risk of being assigned to hazardous jobs and of being unable to obtain plasma therapy or other medical care during working hours. The Katz study also showed that although absenteeism is a common problem, hemophiliac workers who had received adequate education and training tended to retain their jobs regardless of frequent absences. To correct current inequities, it has been recommended that (a) the state pay for their injuries under Workmen's Compensation; (b) vocational counseling should be started during the junior high school years and be included in state rehabilitation programs; (c) social service workers in hemophilia clinics and state Crippled Children's Services should work with school systems to develop resources that will enable these young people to stay in school; and (d) severe hemophiliacs should be trained for job opportunities which stress social contact or social service.

Another problem faced by hemophiliacs and their families is the heavy financial burden of treatment. Today the cost of concentrate medication alone can amount to as much as $22,000 a year. In its role as consumer advocate, the National Hemophilia Foundation has repeatedly testified in Washington on the urgent need for designating hemophilia a chronic condition in proposed legislation to assist those who suffer from catastrophic illness. It has also supported coverage for blood and blood products in any national health insurance program that is finally enacted. Meanwhile Congress has approved Public Law 94-63, which includes a provision for establishment of "Comprehensive Hemophilia Diagnostic and Treatment Centers" as well as "Blood Separation Centers," and has appropriated $1 million for the first type of center and $2 million for the second for fiscal 1976. Administration of both programs has been assigned to the Bureau of Maternal and Child Health Services of the Department of Health, Education and Welfare.

Research

Most hemophilia research is funded by the National Heart, Lung and Blood Institute. A portion of the National Hemophilia Foundation's budget is also spent on research projects and fellowships. Among the most active research areas are data on circulating anticoagulants; better means of carrier identification; basic genetic information; better definition of the Factor VIII molecule and how it works to form a clot; attempts to duplicate the factor synthetically, and to produce it in a tissue culture; use of animal organ transplants to discover how the defect can be limited or corrected; improved screening techniques for hemophilia; increasing the yield of Factor VIII in various plasma preparations; and finding ways of eliminating hepatitis from Factor IX concentrates.

National Hemophilia Foundation

Located at 25 West 39th Street, New York, NY 10018, this organization is the basic voluntary agency in the field. It was founded in 1948 to provide a voice for individual patients and their families and to ensure availability of necessary facilities and services. Its goal is to develop a national program focused on research and clinical studies, early diagnosis, effective treatment, and training of professional personnel. The board of trustees includes presidents of the more than fifty chapters across the nation, and a National Medical Advisory Council advises on therapy and publications, both lay and professional.

The Foundation supports research activities, seeks to interest federal agencies in sponsoring hemophilia projects, promotes legislation on behalf of hemophiliacs, and conducts symposia and institutes. A wide range of specific services is also provided. The Foundation promotes the establishment of comprehensive care clinics to meet the need not only for effective medical treatment but also for supportive psychological and social services. It has identified more than 200 specialized treatment programs in the United States, and publishes a *Directory of Hemophilia Treatment Centers* as well as a *State Resources Guide for Hemophiliacs*. It offers scholarships to hemophiliac students and encourages the organization of summer camp programs for affected children. Through the United Airlines Pilots' Association, airlift services are provided for children needing treatment that is unavailable where they live. It has successfully advocated federal legislation to support demonstration treatment centers, and works with federal and social agencies to provide financial aid for hemophiliacs and their families. And thanks to efforts of the Foundation and its chapters, sixteen states have enacted hemophilia assistance programs which generally provide payment for blood products not covered by insurance.

SELECTED REFERENCES

Aledort, Louis M., "The Management of Hemophilia," *Drug Therapy*, March 1971.

Katz, Alfred, *Hemophilia: A Study in Hope and Reality*, Charles C. Thomas, Springfield, Illinois, 1970.

National Hemophilia Foundation: *The Hemophilic Child in School; New Perspectives on Hemophilia; What You Should Know about Hemophilia; Your Child and Hemophilia: A Manual for Parents.*

Petit, Caroline R., and Harvey G. Klein, *Hemophilia, Hemophiliacs and the Health Care Delivery System*, U.S. Department of Health, Education and Welfare, National Heart and Lung Institute, 1976.

Sergis, Elaine, and Margaret W. Hilgartner, "Hemophilia: Teaching Transfusion for Home Care," *American Journal of Nursing*, November 1972.

C. Leukemia

The Leukemia Society of America, Inc.

Leukemia is commonly considered a disease of the blood, yet in fact it is a disease of the tissues and organs where the body's blood supply is made: bone marrow, lymph nodes, and spleen. In the leukemia patient, overproduction of abnormal white blood cells disrupts the production of red blood cells and interferes with oxygen transport and clotting.

In lymphoblastic (also known as lymphocytic) leukemia these white cells are lymphocytes, produced in the lymph nodes and other lymphoid organs. Myelocytic leukemia (also known as granu-locytic or myelogenous leukemia) affects the granulocytes, the white blood cells produced in the bone marrow. Both lymphocytic and myelocytic leukemia occur as acute and chronic diseases.

In the acute forms of leukemia the predominant abnormal cell is one that is very immature and does not achieve normal maturation. Early in the acute form, one usually notes abnormalities of other cells produced in the bone marrow as well, so that the clinical pic-ture, initially, may be more abnormal. In chronic leukemia the pre-dominant cells are mature in appearance although their function may be deranged.

The age group most often affected is over forty years, with men afflicted more frequently than women. At the same time leukemia claims the lives of more children from four to fourteen than any other disease.

Leukemia and related disorders (lymphomas, including Hodg-kin's disease) will strike an estimated 50,800 during the coming year, and 33,000 will die because of the disorders in the same peri-od (estimate by the National Institutes of Health).

To date, there is no known way of preventing leukemia; how-ever, early detection and proper treatment have now been shown to prolong life for increasingly longer periods of time. Therefore any suspicious signs, such as easy bruising, bleeding without clotting, fever, continual weakness, pain in the joints and bones, and chro-nic fatigue, should bring a person promptly to a physician for a checkup.

It is obvious that early diagnosis of the disease — when fewer numbers of leukemic cells are circulating — will produce quicker response to treatment. Leukemia is not treated surgically. In both acute and chronic leukemia certain powerful drugs are used to pro-long life. At present there are more than twenty drugs which can be administered one at a time or in combination and appear to be capa-ble of controlling some forms of the disease, specifically acute lymphoblastic leukemia. Radiotherapy (x-ray or cobalt treatment) is used in conjunction with chemotherapy in some forms of the dis-ease.

A number of studies have shown that the most encouraging treat-ment takes place in a medical center or hospital where doctors, nurses, and paramedical personnel specializing in leukemia work together as a team. Once the diagnosis has been made, the patient should be transferred, if possible, to such a center. When the pa-tient is in remission, and the course of future treatment planned, the patient can be returned home to the care of the family physician or pediatrician. When a patient is in remission, there is a return to a state of normal health with no apparent sign of disease.

If children with acute lymphoblastic leukemia are treated at a center with the trained personnel and facilities needed for optimal treatment, five out of ten will be alive after five years, in contrast to twenty-five years ago, when these five children would have died two months after diagnosis. Today 15 to 20 percent of children with the disease live for more than five years after diagnosis. It will take time to see if these children are indeed cured.

The encouraging results with acute lymphoblastic leukemia in children are not yet being achieved in adults with this form of leukemia. Although increasing numbers of grownups with this disease go into remission, physicians still do not know how to maintain these remissions for prolonged periods.

Acute myelocytic leukemia makes up 90 percent of cases of acute leukemia occurring in adults, and 10 percent of those in children. Although remission can now be achieved in at least two-thirds of those with this form of leukemia, the median survival time is approximately one year for patients who achieve remission and only a few months for those who do not. Fewer than 5 percent of patients with acute myelocytic leukemia survive more than five years. The recent improvement in remission rate in this disease suggests that the point has been reached where physicians can concentrate more on prolongation of such remissions. That point was reached in childhood acute lymphoblastic leukemia about fifteen years ago.

The median survival time in chronic myelocytic leukemia has not changed in the last fifty years and is still three or three and one-half years despite numerous trials of radiotherapy, chemotherapy, surgery, and combinations of these. In the last four or five years physicians have realized that more research into more aggressive treatment is needed in chronic myelocytic leukemia.

Chronic lymphocytic leukemia has a median survival of four years; some patients may die from the disease in the first year, while others may live for fifteen or twenty years with few or no symptoms.

Hodgkin's Disease

Hodgkin's disease is a disorder of the lymphatic system where the body manufactures plasma cells and white blood cells (lymphocytes)—major links in its chain of defense against infection. The most frequent first symptom of Hodgkin's disease is a swollen lymph gland, usually in the neck, but also in the armpits or groin. Sometimes pain may occur in the abdomen, back, or legs along with persistent fever, sweating, itching, appetite loss, nausea, and vomiting. The commonness and obscurity of these symptoms make the disease difficult to diagnose. Definite diagnosis can be reached through clinical examinations and laboratory tests.

The most effective treatment during the early localized stages of Hodgkin's disease is intensive irradiation of the lymph regions over a period of several weeks. Distressing disease symptoms usually subside under effective x-ray treatment. It is possible to save an estimated 80 to 90 percent of those afflicted with Hodgkin's disease in its beginning stages.

Drug therapy is most beneficial for patients in the later stages of the disease and has produced encouraging results. The carefully orchestrated combinations of drugs are somewhat similar to those used against leukemia. Under such treatment 60 to 80 percent of the patients achieve remission, and some of these with disseminated Hodgkin's disease may lead normal, productive lives for many years, perhaps indefinitely.

Research

An important aspect of leukemia research and treatment has been the realization that these procedures have provided a "window" to the treatment of solid tumors. The effectiveness of chemotherapy in treating leukemia can be readily observed. Day by day, or week by week, the patient's response to treatment can be measured by examination of the blood or bone marrow. Such close observation is not possible with most other human tissue.

Great progress has been seen in some forms of leukemia, with remission coming quickly and lasting for months or years. Following the success of combination drug therapy with many leukemic patients, the chemotherapists are now encouraging the surgeons and radiologists who treat malignant solid tumors to follow up surgical or radiation procedures with a regimen of drug treatment. The results have been very promising in some forms of tumors with high risk of recurrence, especially some types of cancer of the breast.

The Leukemia Society of America has as its goal the control and prevention of leukemia and closely related diseases. This goal is being achieved through continuing research—research that is aimed at developing better therapeutic measures to cure all forms of leukemia; research to understand what goes wrong with normal cells that make them become leukemic cells; and finally, research that seeks the cause of leukemia.

The cause or causes of the different types of leukemia are still unknown. In acute leukemia the participation of a virus in the causation is widely suspected, since in many species of animals in which similar leukemias are seen, viruses have been found to play a causative role. In chronic myelogenous as well as acute leukemia, ionizing radiation has proved to be an important causative factor. Thus the incidence of leukemia of these types increased sharply in the Japanese population exposed to the atom bomb in 1945. Radiation does not seem to be a factor in chronic lymphatic leukemia.

Organization

The Leukemia Society of America, Inc., at 211 East 43d Street, New York, NY 10017, a national voluntary health agency, conducts a three-pronged attack against leukemia. Through its research program the Society is supporting more than 100 scientists throughout the world seeking the cause, cure, or control of leukemia. Besides supporting researchers and clinicians who look specifically for new chemical, immunologic, and other treatments to cure human leukemia, the Society also strongly supports the view that leukemia will probably not be eliminated as a deadly disease until much more is understood about the normal cell and how it becomes transformed into a malignant cell. Therefore scientists are studying cell membranes, viruses, and hormones, and conducting many other basic biologic research projects, all of which are potentially related to the cause, behavior, or treatment of leukemia.

In addition, the Leukemia Society provides financial aid to outpatients being treated for leukemia, the lymphomas, and Hodgkin's disease. The program covers payment for: (1) drugs used in the care, treatment, or control of leukemia and allied diseases; (2) transfusing of blood, processing, typing, and cross-matching only; (3) transportation to and from a doctor's office, hospital, or treatment center; (4) x-ray therapy in amounts up to $300 for patients in the early stages of Hodgkin's disease (stages I and II), in which the disease is considered to be potentially curable; (5) x-ray therapy in amounts up to $300 for cranial (not spinal) radiation for children with acute lymphoblastic leukemia.

In addition to financial assistance to meet the expenses involved in the management of the disease, the chapters offer referrals to other means of help within a community and work closely to coordinate such services in the best interests of the patients.

Through the professional education program, the Society brings to physicians, nurses, and paramedical personnel the latest advances in treatment and research. Each year in conjunction with its annual meeting the Society conducts a medical symposium highlighting the research being conducted under the Society's sponsorship. In addition, the Society cosponsors with the National Cancer Institute of the National Institutes of Health a biennial international meeting on leukemia and related diseases, as well as specific programs at the meetings of the American Hematology Society and the International Hematology Society. Chapters conduct symposia each year for their medical community.

The public education program alerts members of the community to the dangers of leukemia and what they can do if leukemia strikes.

SELECTED REFERENCES

Clemmesen, J., and D. Yohn, eds., *Comparative Leukemia Research 1975*, S. Karger, White Plains, New York.

Leukemia Society of America: *Hodgkin's Disease; Leukemia: A Guide to the Management of the Disease; Leukemia: Nature of the Disease; What Is Leukemia?*

National Cancer Institute, National Institutes of Health: *The Leukemic Child; Progress against Leukemia.*

D. Sickle Cell Anemia

MARGARET H. NEWCOMBE

Reviewed by ROLAND B. SCOTT, M.D., Director, Howard University Center for Sickle Cell Disease, and L. W. DIGGS, M.D., Consultant, Sickle Cell Center, University of Tennessee, Center for the Health Sciences

Anemia means that there is less than the normal amount of the red component of blood, hemoglobin, which serves to carry the oxygen required by the body's organs and tissues. In sickle cell anemia the hemoglobin is highly sensitive to decreases in oxygen, so that the usually round, red blood cells become distorted. These distorted cells, often sickle-shaped, do not flow easily through the blood vessles, particularly the tiny capillaries. If they pile up and form a "logjam" in the circulatory system, the oxygen-deprived tissues and organs become intensely painful — a condition termed a sickle cell "crisis." In sickle cell anemia (HbS) a large number of sickle cells are present in the circulating blood under normal living conditions. This contrasts with other hemoglobinopathies such as HbC, D, and G.

Incidence and Etiology

Sickle cell anemia is most prevalent among the groups of people whose ancestors came from certain parts of Africa, the Mediterranean rim, and India. In these areas individuals whose blood cells contained some sickle hemoglobin were more apt to survive the widespread, often fatal disease of malaria, so that it became a genetic advantage to possess this trait. In the United States it is estimated that 1 in 500 blacks is afflicted with sickle cell anemia. This incidence among blacks is higher than that of other disorders which receive far more public attention.

Sickle cell disease is inherited. One out of twelve black Americans inherits a genetic trait known as the sickle cell trait, which in itself is harmless except under certain unusual circumstances. While carriers of the trait are not affected themselves, they can pass it on to their children. When two carriers mate and produce children, the chances are 1 in 4 that a child may inherit sickle cell anemia, 1 in 4 that the child will not inherit either the trait or the anemia, and 2 in 4 that the child will inherit the sickle cell trait. If a sickle cell trait carrier marries someone who does not carry the trait, the chances are 2 in 4 that each child will also carry the trait but will not inherit the disease.

Prevention and Symptoms

Sickle cell anemia is still incurable, but as a disease with a clear-cut pattern of inheritance it is preventable. Detection programs usually include genetic counseling. Carriers are told of the risk they run of having children with sickle cell anemia if they marry another sickle cell carrier. At present these detection programs are generally aimed at the age group at highest risk, i.e., at puberty or childbearing age, continuing up to thirty or so.

The disease rarely manifests itself before a child is four months of age. Early symptoms are general signs of pallor, anemia, and enlargement of organs such as heart, liver, and spleen. Young children with the disease may experience painful swelling of the hands and feet (hand-foot syndrome). Later these symptoms tend to shift to other parts of the body — to the head, including the eyes, back, abdomen, chest, central nervous system, sex organs, etc. Pregnancy in women with sickle cell anemia is characterized by relatively high morbidity and mortality rates for the child and for the mother. In adults chronic ulcers may develop on the lower part of the legs and ankles.

It has been estimated that a person with the disease has on the average two to four crises per year. These painful attacks tend to be less frequent as the individual grows older. The attacks may have no apparent immediate cause or may be brought on by physical stress (cold, infection, intoxication, etc.).

Diagnosis and Treatment

A screening laboratory procedure for detecting sickle cell anemia involves a solubility test and electrophoresis. Additional confirmatory laboratory procedures may be necessary for a definitive diagnosis, including tests on other members of the family.

Crises of swelling, pain, and fever may require direct medical treatment, depending on the duration of the symptoms and the particular parts of the body involved. Typically, medical treatment is directed toward easing pain and relieving dehydration and increased viscosity. Blood transfusion may be recommended in some cases.

Management and Rehabilitation

Frequently the number of specific crises can be reduced if the patient takes care to avoid significant physical stress. Children, however, should not be overly restricted, because of the psychological harm this could cause. It is also important for every person with the disease to be knowledgeable about it. Patients themselves can treat uncomplicated crises at home if they are aware of the nature of the trouble, and should alert physicians about their condition before asking for medication or before undergoing surgery. Adults should select an occupation which will be appropriate to their physical capacities and limitations.

Research

Although the deformed sickle cell was discovered by Dr. James B. Herrick in 1910, research on the prevention and treatment of the anemia has received significant government support only in the 1970s. Recently some promising experiments which show potential for reversing the sickling of the blood cells have been conducted.

The sudden surge of interest in sickle cell anemia and the resultant publicity have had some adverse effects — for example, there is widespread misunderstanding among physicians, employers, and the public about the difference between having the disease and carrying the trait. Hope for prevention and cure of this painful, crippling, and sometimes fatal disease lies in increased support for research and in an informed and enlightened public.

Organizational Help

The national sickle cell program, supported by the National Institutes of Health (Bethesda, Maryland), has authorized the setting up of a number of Comprehensive Sickle Cell Centers, which sponsor research, education, and patient care. One of these centers is located at Howard University in Washington, D.C. Another is in operation at the University of Tennessee in Memphis.

Mass screening for identification of sickle cell trait carriers is being conducted in many areas. To date, more than thirty states are operating or planning to operate detection programs, and forty-one federally funded clinics in addition to the centers have been organized throughout the country. Numerous private foundations, community groups, and city and county governments also support sickle cell detection programs. Many cases of sickle cell anemia as well as other blood abnormalities have been discovered through these screening programs.

SELECTED REFERENCES

Abramson, H., J. F. Bertles, and D. L. Wethers, *Sickle Cell Disease: Diagnosis, Management, Education, and Research*, C. V. Mosby, St. Louis, 1973.

Diggs, L. W., "Sickle Cell Crises," *American Journal of Clinical Pathology*, vol. 44, no. 1, July 1965.

Olafson, F., and A. W. Parker, eds., *Sickle Cell Anemia: The Neglected Disease*, Health Center Seminar Program Monograph Series no. 5, University Extension, University of California, Berkeley, 1973.

22

Brain Damage

LINDA HOWELL, M.A., Group Health Cooperative
of Puget Sound, Seattle

Reviewed by VANJA HOLM, M.D., Assistant Professor of Pediatrics,
University of Washington School of Medicine, Seattle

The brain is the body's master organ. Damage to the brain is revealed in a multitude of disorders and disabilities. Disorders which may involve the brain in their pathology include: (1) those where the primary lesion is known to be in the brain—cerebral palsy, epilepsy, Parkinson's disease, stroke; (2) those which involve the whole central nervous system, including brain and spinal cord—amyotrophic lateral sclerosis, multiple sclerosis, poliomyelitis; (3) those in which brain dysfunction is apparent but there is no readily documented cause—learning disabilities, some forms of mental retardation; (4) those conditions which may have as their cause cerebral pathology—speech disorders, blindness, hearing disorders, mental illness; and (5) those which at some point may bring about pathological changes in the brain—alcoholism, venereal disease, cancer, spina bifida, diabetes, sickle cell anemia, hypertension. (See the chapters in Part 2 on each of these disorders.)

Some of these disorders present neurological symptoms which are peculiar to the particular condition. Others present signs which require careful diagnostic differentiation. Conditions in which damage to the brain is due to infection, tumor, toxicity, and trauma will be discussed here as a unit, since there is considerable overlap in the ways in which the damage is manifested. This discussion also has application in many of the disorders mentioned above.

Causes and Physical Effects

Infection of the brain may be generalized or localized. One type of generalized infection is encephalitis, which is an inflammation of the brain due to viruses, syphilis, tuberculosis, or other types of invading organisms. There are changes in nerve tissue and swelling (edema), with increases in pressure and sometimes hemorrhage from brain blood vessels. In meningitis there is inflammation of the meninges, the membranes enveloping the spinal cord and brain. The meninges most often become infected through the bloodstream and (seldom nowadays) by direct extension of infection from the ear, face, nose, sinuses, or abscesses in the brain. The inflammation may cause increased intracranial pressure and abnormal nervous system function. A localized infection is termed a brain abscess. Bacteria may invade the brain through the bloodstream or directly, as in meningitis. There will be an area of pus and dead neural tissue accumulation which can eventually become encapsulated by fibrous tissue. This also leads to increased intracranial pressure and dysfunction of the nervous system.

Brain tumors may be primary, developing out of the cells of the structures surrounding the brain or within the brain tissue, or they may be secondary metastases from other parts of the body. Nearly 10 percent of all tumors originate in the central nervous system, and most of these are in the brain. Tumor growth destroys, displaces, and compresses brain tissue and may block the flow of cerebral spinal fluid, which will lead to further displacement and compression.

Toxic agents damaging the brain include carbon monoxide, lead, and other obvious poisons, as well as alcohol and anoxia (lack of oxygen). Toxins destroy tissue or cause impaired functioning which may in turn lead to permanent injury.

Trauma can be defined here as direct closed or penetrating head injury — concussion, skull fracture, contusions. (Note that this would include brain surgery.) Head injuries may cause direct tissue destruction, or brain cells may be affected indirectly, as through pressure being exerted or by interruption of blood flow through the brain.

Early Signs and Diagnosis

Signs of infection in the brain usually include high fever, severe headache with vomiting, and decreased alertness. Delirium, and even coma, may set in. In very young children these symptoms are frequently not as obvious. Diagnosis is made by lumbar puncture. Cerebrospinal fluid in meningitis is cloudy, contains bacteria and pus cells, and is under relatively high pressure. In viral encephalitis the cerebrospinal fluid yields a cellular (lymphocyte) reaction in the acute phase, and there are behavioral signs of involvement of the central nervous system.

The same early signs may be evident in the initial stages of brain abscess, but as the abscess becomes encapsulated the symptoms change to reflect intracranial pressure. Specific symptoms depend on the area and size of the abscess. Brain tumors cause symptoms similar to those of encapsulated abscesses. The first significant sign of trouble may be a seizure. Depending upon the cause of the convulsions, this may be a temporary symptom or may become a permanent condition which requires regular medical treatment for control. (See CHAPTER 31: EPILEPSY.) Tumors and abscesses can be diagnosed by using a range of techniques and instruments. X-ray of the skull may give evidence of distortion. Air can be introduced into the ventricular, or cerebrospinal fluid—circulating, system in the skull, and then x-rays are taken (producing a pneumoencephalogram). The electroencephalograph (EEG) technique involves measurement of the electrical activity of the brain as transmitted through the skull. Alterations of normal activity are seen with seizures, coma, tumors, etc. Angiography is another technique in which a radiopaque dye is injected into a carotid or vertebral artery. Its progress through the cerebral vessels is followed by a rapid sequence of x-rays in order to detect evidence of stoppage or distortion. The most recent and most revolutionary radiographic technique is computerized axial tomography (CAT), in which an x-ray beam scans the brain at six to eight levels in about ten minutes, producing cross-sectional images which can reveal such conditions as aneurysm, hemorrhage and hematoma, hydrocephalus, abscess, tumor, meningioma, atrophy, and infarction.

The diagnosis of the presence of a toxic substance in the body is seldom based mainly on neurological symptoms. History of exposure is important, and many laboratory tests are available for diagnosis. A history is also very important for establishing the existence of a closed head injury, but the patient is not always able to give a history because the memory may be involved. The laboratory techniques mentioned above may be used to clarify the situation.

Significant Symptoms and Effects

As a rule, brain damage in a child has more widespread or general effect on later functioning and behavior than the same amount of damage to the same part of the brain in an adult. As the brain becomes more differentiated and patterned over time, brain damage in an adult typically results in more specific deficits with many areas of functioning left largely unaffected.

In the youthful and relatively undifferentiated brain there is a greater capacity for compensation than in the adult brain. The best-documented example is with the speech-language centers, which are usually located in the brain's left hemisphere. If the left hemisphere is damaged in a young child, the right hemisphere may take over its function and the speech-language centers will develop in the right hemisphere. In adults with damage to these centers the deficit is more permanent—there is apparently no shift of function to the opposite hemisphere. However, the adult has the advantage of already having learned skills and information, and much of what has been learned will be available for relearning.

Normally the two hemispheres of the brain show a division of function which, when one side or the other is damaged, yields a somewhat characteristic result. Because the speech-language centers are in the left hemisphere, damage on that side may produce a range of disorders of language expression and comprehension— from slight changes in fluency and rhythm to a situation where the patient is completely cut off from language and written symbols and is unable to communicate meaningfully with others. (See CHAPTER 49: SPEECH AND LANGUAGE DISORDERS.) When the right hemisphere is damaged, verbal functioning may remain intact, but different kinds of perceptual impairments — especially visual — may be apparent.

In order to put into context the following information on changes caused by brain injury, it should be emphasized that the configuration of symptoms varies greatly from case to case, just as the causes, locations, and periods of time for development of symptoms are diverse. At this stage in understanding the brain, there are relatively few clear correlations between these latter factors and specific significant symptoms. For any form of handicap, illness, or disability, the tendency of the observer and of the patient as well is to focus on what is wrong and what is different. In the following discussion an attempt will be made to relate diagnostic signs to the experience of the individual involved.

Specific Symptoms

Fundamental areas of functioning which may undergo temporary to long-term changes when the brain is attacked in some manner include: (1) consciousness; (2) motor ability; (3) sensation; (4) intelligence (including perception and memory); and (5) emotion.

Consciousness is usually weakened or even lost (coma, semi-coma, stupor, lethargy) in the acute phase of generalized infection, toxicity, or head injury, and a long period of unconsciousness is a negative sign in the prognostic picture. As consciousness gradually returns, the individual may go through a period of reduced alertness or "clouding" of consciousness in which confusion is expressed as to what has been and is now happening. One's personal experience may not match one's objective context. This can lead to misunderstandings, bizarre behavior, confusion of dreams with reality, and perhaps even to the development of a state of fear or anxiety as one is unable to grasp or master the situation.

Motor ability, involving control and coordination, is often disturbed by brain injury. The nature, extent, and duration of impairments depend on the areas of the brain which are involved, the source of dysfunction, and the permanence of the injury to nerve tissue. (Central nervous system nerve cells do not regenerate after destruction, but those cells and fibers not actually destroyed will recover functioning.) One form of impairment is paralysis (hemiplegia) or weakness (hemiparesis) on one side of the body. This happens, for example, when there is damage to the motor areas of the hemisphere of the brain opposite to the side on which the paralysis occurs. This reversal is due to the crossing-over of most motor and senosry nerve fibers from one side to the other within the pathways to and from the brain. Hemiplegia is typically of sudden onset in a vascular accident (see CHAPTER 52: STROKE) and head injury, but may come on gradually in cases of tumor and other brain disease. If there is damage to both hemispheres, motor function of both sides of the body may be involved (such as in cerebral anoxia). A fairly discrete lesion may produce weakness or paraylsis of a single limb or other limited area of the body. If there is involvement of the cranial nerves at the base of the brain, this produces characteristic defects.

Muscles paralyzed due to brain damage usually exhibit spasticity or increased muscle tone and exaggerated reflex action which in turn produces involuntary movement. There is a tendency for some joints to stay in flexion or in extension positions. These tendencies may in time produce contractures (joint rigidity) if left untreated. Another type of impairment of the motor system is evidenced by incoordination of movements. This may be grossly apparent, as in an ataxic or staggering gait where equilibrium is disturbed, or in dysarthria where, due to incoordination of the oral musculature, there is loss of proper articulation in speech. Impairments may be observed only in the execution of very fine or skilled movements. The automaticity of motions may be broken up. One serious sequel of encephalitis is parkinsonism, the symptoms of which may develop several years after the initial illness (see CHAPTER 47: PARKINSON'S DISEASE). In many cases there is considerable recovery of motor function, but the more skilled and complex the movement, the less likely it is to recover fully. The time period in which there may be recovery of muscle power and coordination is generally limited to two years, with most of the recovery taking place in the first few months. Some of this recovery is due to the natural, spontaneous reduction and absorption of the edema in the traumatized areas and to the return of more normal circulation.

Lack of voluntary muscle power, especially when it comes on suddenly, leaves an individual feeling very helpless. Activities which were long taken for granted seem overwhelmingly difficult, even impossible. Paralyzed individuals often liken their situation to that of helpless, dependent infants with the whole world asking for their attention, daring them to try things, laughing at their mistakes.

Sensation involvement in brain injury may entail loss, decrease, or even an increase in sensation of one or more kinds — touch, pain, temperature, position sense, taste, smell, vision, or hearing. Motor impairment and sensory impairment most often manifest themselves in the same parts of the body, but they can exist independently of one another, based upon the location of injury in the brain. Some early sensory signs of something going wrong in the brain, such as a tumor or abscess, are a decrease in awareness of external stimulation (such as touch) to some part of the body, blurring of vision, double vision, and visual field defects. Careful notation and measurement of sensory deficits can be of great assistance in localizing a lesion in the brain.

Loss of sensation in any part of the body makes that part particularly susceptible to injuries such as burns, cuts, and pressure sores (decubiti). People who develop any gross impairment of sensation must function without information previously taken for granted.

Their behavior at times may appear to be odd, confused, or to reflect poor judgment. Odd behavior may mean that brain-injured persons are not fully aware of their deficits and have not yet developed effective means of compensation. The more automatic or routine the activity, the less they may recognize that their information is faulty until, of course, they find their course of action unproductive or counterproductive.

Sensation may also return to normal levels, but the return differs somewhat from the motor situation in that it tends to occur early after injury and the chances for improvement later on are very limited.

Intelligence is another area of functioning which may undergo change. When we think of the brain we normally think of the mind, of the intellect, and, in general, we associate brain damage primarily with mental changes and only secondarily with physical problems.

Intelligence is not a directly measurable entity in the same sense as motor power or sensation. Most people who have not previously experienced serious injury have normal muscle power, sensation, and range of motion against which the brain-injured person can be compared to determine deficits, if any. Intelligence is so variable in its manifestations that changes are sometimes hard to pinpoint unless the diagnostician has detailed information about the person prior to this problem—which one rarely does. Nevertheless there are some kinds of intellectual changes which are well known and well documented by students of brain damage. These changes can be divided somewhat arbitrarily into the following areas: (1) perception; (2) memory; (3) learning, thinking, and reasoning.

Perception refers to deriving meaning from incoming sensory information. The perceptions of some who sustain brain damage may not correspond to the "reality" of the stimulus. Therefore the person is misled as to this input and may respond "inappropriately," as one might when sensory input itself is faulty. One common perceptual deficit is loss of ability to distinguish fine details—for example, inability to distinguish between similar-sounding words. This perceptual change is a kind of regression to an earlier, simpler perception of the world. A more serious perceptual change is more frequently found in persons with damage to the right or nondominant hemisphere of the brain, especially to the parietal lobe. In these cases there is gross distortion of perception—for example, mistaking an unfamiliar person for a familiar one; being unable to make out familiar symbols, shapes, and objects; confusing body image and position; neglecting body parts; and even ignoring direct sensory (notably visual) input. Such misperceptions create many problems and mishaps, making relearning in other areas especially difficult.

Memory is a second aspect of intelligence which can be impaired by brain injury. In cases of relatively acute onset, there is typically some discontinuity in the recall of events which occur around the onset period. There may be loss of memory for events which occurred prior to injury. This is called retrograde amnesia. Usually only the most recent memories are lost and, in time, there may be some return of these. Anterograde amnesia is the inability to recall events at the point of and following the trauma. Anterograde amnesia occurs in disease of slow onset as well as rapid onset. The person's attention span and short-term memory span may be shortened by a loss of control functions. This person may seem distractible, confused, and appear to have poor concentration ability. Attention span and short-term memory may be relatively normal, but the brain's ability to process the information in such a way that it is retained and available later from long-term memory is somehow deficient. In these cases the person appears to be alert and retaining information, but later is found to have little or no recall. Memory for events of the remote past is seldom disturbed by brain injury as far as can be determined through retrospective study. The particular type of memory loss, or change in memory functioning, is related to the nature and location of the injury, although this has not been so clearly delineated as it has been for motor and sensory function. Except in extreme cases (such as bilateral destruction of temporal-hippocampal areas of the brain) memory will improve over time, although in some instances it may never be as efficient as it was previously. An older adult tends to experience comparably more change in memory functioning than a younger person, given the same degree of brain injury.

Human beings are very sensitive to and threatened by changes in their memory capacities. Some may respond to such changes with depression and withdrawal or they may respond in a denying or defensive manner—"I have so much on my mind, I just can't concentrate on that," or "It's been so long since I was in school." A more extreme defensive response is confabulation, which simply means the person fills in the memory gaps with imagined or familiar information. This happens in cases of fairly severe memory loss. It is most commonly noted in cases of chronic alcoholism. It also seems to be related to the person's premorbid character, that is, to a pattern in which the person is typically inclined to deny personal fault, weakness, or conflict.

A third area of intellect which draws directly on the other two can be described as involving learning, thinking, and reasoning. Brain damage may cause a deterioration in these basic cognitive functions. In general terms, there can be a slowing down of functioning and some reduction of thinking capabilities. Characteristically, after brain damage a person may be less adaptable and less able to shift from one thing to another. One tends to be repetitive, and ability to monitor or check one's own behavior is less reliable, especially in the early stages of illness and recovery. One way to describe many of the changes is to say that the capacity for abstraction is reduced: the individual approaches the world with a more concrete attitude; there is a narrowing of interests; one becomes more tied to the immediate environment and tends not to look beyond; flexibility and insight in organization and problem solving are poorer. With these changes the person obviously has a lessened ability to learn new things.

Just how significant changes in learning capacity may be depends on the preinjury level of functioning and also on a person's life situation. If a person has a job in which complex decision making and solving new problems are required, a change to one of the many work roles which require little new learning, decision making, or problem solving may be necessary.

Emotion is the final area which may be affected by brain damage. The emotional adjustment of a person who has had brain damage can change in significant ways. A few of the changes may reflect underlying changes in the nervous system—a decrease in inhibitory controls, for example. Other reactions — irritability, euphoria, or emotional lability (rapid mood shifts) — are frequently observed but vary considerably from one person to another. These characteristics also are most apparent soon after injury, largely diminishing over time. They tend to be accentuated if the person is under stress in addition to the illness. Some flattening or dulling of affect may be a more permanent consequence of injury, especially if the more anterior parts of the brain are involved.

Most observable changes in emotionality reflect patients' reaction to their new status and their efforts to cope with it. Usually the greatest determinant of how they cope is the individual's personality, character structure, or habit patterns. Depression is probably the prevailing emotional reaction to disability in general in its early stages, and it is characteristic of the brain-injured as well. At some level persons are aware of loss. Some are acutely aware of changes; others are aware at a level less than consciousness. There is fear that these losses will be permanent and that their usefulness is gone. One way to handle the anxiety aroused by this awareness, often seen in the newly brain-injured, is denial that there is anything wrong—problems are not dealt with because there are no problems. This defense is usually temporary, except in cases of extensive damage.

Some of the people who are likely to experience difficulty in adjusting to a disability and in learning how best to compensate for loss are those with undeveloped problem-solving abilities, rigid attitudes and rigid behavior patterns, or a particular horror of sickness or disability; or those who have never envisioned another lifestyle, line of work, or role for themselves.

The source of injury may have an effect on the attitude of the individual. That is, one may become overloaded with guilt and self-reproach in a case where one was somehow at fault in bringing about the disability, or may become relatively emotionally incapacitated by bitterness and resentment at having been the victim of some kind of attack. Fatalistic attitudes which are common in our society—"My number was up"—sometimes help the person to avoid these extreme reactions.

Treatment

Specific medical treatment depends upon the source or cause of the brain damage and upon the part or parts of the brain affected. Meningitis is treated with antibiotics (penicillin, ampicillin, sulfonamides, streptomycin, tetracycline, etc.) chosen according to the known affecting organism. Disabling late complications are sometimes unavoidable, and sometimes they result from delayed or inadequate treatment. They may require rehabilitative treatment. This may also be true for complications from encephalitis, which is not susceptible to antibiotic treatment. However, symptoms such as headache and convulsions may be amenable to symptomatic treatment. Brain abscesses are usually handled surgically. The skull and brain are perforated and the abscess is punctured; antimicrobial agents such as penicillin or sulfa are administered, and the pus of the infection is aspirated or drained. When an abscess is firmly encapsulated, it can be excised if this surgical procedure does not inflict great damage to surrounding tissue or endanger vital centers.

Brain tumors are best diagnosed early, and completely or partly removed (resectioned). Some tumors are located deep within the brain and are not subject to removal because of the extensive damage that might be done in surgery. X-ray or radiation therapy is used in some cases to slow the growth of the tumor. If increased pressure of the cerebrospinal fluid develops, leading to dilation of the ventricles and compression of brain tissue, a condition known as hydrocephalus develops. A surgical procedure can be performed to shunt this excess fluid into the bloodstream.

Head injuries are treated according to the symptoms. Intracerebral hemorrhage is common. Excess blood, blood clots, or bone fragments may have to be removed by the cutting of the skull (craniotomy) to reveal the area of damage. Toxic conditions require the removal of the toxic agent and supportive therapy (for example, artificial respiration). More specific forms of treatment depend on the particular toxic agent involved.

Rehabilitation and Management

Impairment of muscle power and coordination as a result of brain injury should receive immediate treatment involving proper positioning of the patient to prevent contractures and other complications, and maintenance of the range of motion by exercising the affected limbs. The unaffected parts of the body should also be actively exercised. Usually the patient learns how to propel a wheelchair if initially unable to ambulate. The patient progresses to muscle strengthening, gait training, learning of new motor patterns, building endurance and coordination, and use of various assistive devices, especially in the relearning of self-care techniques. Motivation may suddenly increase if efforts are made to help the person look more attractive, healthy, and less disabled. Attention to hair, clothing, and makeup is very important.

If there are sensory and perceptual changes, the person may be trained to compensate for inadequate sensation (such as for a visual field loss or lack of position sense in a weakened lower extremity), and be trained in basic eye-hand coordination and visual discrimination skills, etc. When speech is involved — usually this would be in the form of aphasia or dysarthria — speech therapy is instituted in retraining or for very basic language stimulation in severe cases of aphasia. A person with brain damage may profit from supportive counseling, which would ideally continue when the patient returns to the community. More traditional forms of insight therapy are typically rather unproductive, however. Supportive therapy from a group of fellow patients can be beneficial in reducing the isolation of the newly disabled, giving them some perspective on their condition and allowing them to discover areas of intactness by being able to fall back on old and trusted social conventions.

Vocational guidance is necessary for men and women who have been in the labor market or wish to reenter it. This is best done when there is some stabilization of the disability or condition in order to make a realistic appraisal of potential. The interests of the person, motivation for achievement and, most importantly, past experience must be carefully studied. An evaluation of potential is made in the light of the current level of endurance, frustration tolerance, physical capacities, perceptual status, speech-language levels, rate of working, general adjustment, and degree of compensation for losses. From such an evaluation a reasonable plan of action can be set.

A key factor in the rehabilitation of any person is the supportive help available from the professional rehabilitation staff and, more significantly, from family and friends. The necessary support can make rehabilitation a reality, while lack of support or the wrong kind may diminish the person's chances for adjustment. Educating the family about the disability or condition and enlisting their participation in a program of rehabilitation is a major responsibility of rehabilitation personnel.

Because of a decrease in adaptability which occurs with many kinds of brain damage, persons will function best in familiar situations and surroundings, doing overlearned tasks. They will be more successful if responsibility is lessened and sources of distraction (especially noises) are eliminated or controlled. This will tend to alleviate anxiety. In time they may be able to test for themselves what they can and cannot do, to find their own limits, and to accept them. One reaction to anxiety generally, and a common reaction of the person with brain injury, is compulsivity — controlling the situation by repetition and thoroughness in one's activities. This kind of behavior tends to minimize mistakes, but it may also diminish creativity, spontaneity, and variety.

Research

Brain research involves scientists of different disciplines (neurologists, surgeons, pathologists, bioengineers, etc.) and is one of the promising frontiers of scientific endeavor. In basic research the scientist asks such questions as: How does the brain work? How does it interpret, process, and retain information? More specifically, which part of the brain does what? How does one part interact with another for a certain result? What is the function of a particular fiber type or chemical process or neural pathway? The most difficult and also most intriguing question concerns the learning-storage-retention capacity of the brain. Chemical explanations for the permanence of learning have had the widest acceptance and interest, as in the protein-synthesis and neurotransmitter hypotheses of how information is coded and recalled.

The basic thrust of this research is with the normally functioning brain. Currently most brain research or "neuroscience" research is done with animal species. Yet there are implications for understanding the results of pathological processes, for preventing damage, and for treating or retraining human deficits, although these last are probably the most neglected aspects of brain studies. A good deal of the understanding of the normal brain has derived from studies of human beings who have experienced brain injury of various kinds (stroke, tumor, hematoma, trauma, etc.). Type, locus, extent, and duration of injury are correlated with behavior measures — motor function, memory, sensation, intelligence, etc. — to yield a pattern of integration and functioning of the brain.

The National Institute of Neurological Diseases, Communication Disorders and Stroke of the National Institutes of Health, U.S. Department of Health, Education and Welfare, sponsors much of this research, and private foundations are also contributing. Research takes place in most universities and in private and industrial laboratories.

Organizations and Assistance

Because the causes and results of brain injury are so diverse, those who experience brain injury do not tend to find help from any particular organization. The National Easter Seal Society for Crippled Children and Adults, 2023 West Ogden Avenue, Chicago, IL 60612, serves persons of all ages with neurological disabilities, and many other disorders as well. This organization provides direct rehabilitation services — diagnosis, therapy, education, counseling, recreation, and vocational assistance — and indirect services such as public education, research, and support for legislation.

Stroke victims and persons with other forms of brain injury share many experiences and problems. Stroke clubs should be, and in many cases have been, broadened to include those with other sources of injury such as have been discussed in this chapter. These clubs can provide socializing opportunities and other services. The Easter Seal Society promotes these clubs in many areas.

If brain-injured individuals develop epilepsy as a result of their illness, the Epilepsy Foundation of America should be approached for help (see CHAPTER 31: EPILEPSY).

(For other organizations and Selected References on individual brain disorders, see the chapters on the relevant disorders, referred to in the first paragraph of this article.)

SELECTED REFERENCES

Bender, Lauretta, *A Visual-Motor Gestalt Test and Its Clinical Use*, American Orthopsychiatric Association, New York, 1938.

Halstead, Ward C., *Brain and Intelligence*, University of Chicago Press, 1947.

Hebb, Donald O., *The Organization of Behavior*, Wiley, New York, 1949.

Hodgkins, Eric, *Episode: Report on the Accident inside My Skull*, Atheneum, New York, 1968.

Mountcastle, Vernon B., ed., *Interhemispheric Relations and Cerebral Damage*, Johns Hopkins Press, Baltimore, 1962.

Geschwind, Norman, "Language and the Brain," *Scientific American*, 226:76, 1972.

Strauss, A. A., and L. E. Lehtinen, *Psychopathology and Education of the Brain-Injured Child*, Grune & Stratton, New York, 1947.

Talland, G. A., and N. C. Waugh, eds., *The Pathology of Memory*, Academic Press, New York, 1969.

Weinstein, E. A., and R. L. Kahn, *Denial of Illness*, Charles C. Thomas, Springfield, Illinois, 1955.

23

Burn Injuries:
A. Causes, Types, and Treatment

HARRY J. GAYNOR, Founder and President, National
Burn Victim Foundation

According to the National Institutes of Health and other reporting organizations, 2 million Americans experience a burn injury each year. Of these, 300,000 are seriously burned and 50,000 to 70,000 are hospitalized for a period ranging from six weeks to two years. Moreover, the National Commission on Fire Prevention reports that of those who suffer serious burns 12,000 die every year; and there is evidence that 50 percent of these fatalities occur before arrival at the hospital emergency room.

A second measure of the burn problem is the cost of treatment. In 1972 the daily cost during intensive care in highly specialized facilities was between $250 and $400. By 1974 these figures had jumped to between $350 and $800, and by the end of 1976 patient charges for the same services were running between $500 and $1,100 per day. It is estimated by some experts in the National Institutes of Health that burn patients will be paying as high as $2,000 per day in 1980.

But the most important measure of this problem is the effect of burn injuries on the victims and their families. There are few if any injuries requiring long hospitalization that are more traumatic than severe burns. The frightening circumstances of the injury, the long isolation from the family, the continuous pain during recovery, the stigma of disfigurement—all these contribute to a deep despondency and frequently loss of the will to live. Moreover, the toll taken by this tragedy must be measured in terms of those who grieve the loss of loved ones, and those who are left jobless or impoverished be-

cause of permanent disability, as well as those left with the staggering cost of hospital bills.

Causes of Burn Injuries

Although the estimates cited above give some concept of the
general scope of the burn problem, there is an appalling gap in
knowledge of the number of different types of burn injuries, the
types of burns most frequently admitted to hospitals, and the incidence of burns in different segments of the population. One reason
for the lack of scientific data is that, generally speaking, hospitals in
the United States are not required to report or maintain records on
burn injuries. Another is that state departments of health have
been reluctant to allocate funds to obtain burn data. Still another
reason is that different organizations are concerned with different
aspects of the problem, and none of them sees the situation as a
whole. For example, the National Commission on Fire Prevention
and Control has published a report, "America Burning," which
deals solely with fire problems and flame injuries. This report
leaves many questions unanswered, such as: Are all the 300,000
seriously burned victims cited in the report fire-related injuries?
Are all the 12,000 burn deaths due to fire and flame? If these data
are based upon fire injuries only, as representatives of the National
Fire Prevention and Control Administration in Washington assert,
the nation's toll in burns would be more than double the estimates,
since injuries caused by scalding, electric current, chemicals, sun-
burn, and even frostbite are considered burn injuries.

Data provided by all national sources, including the National Institute for Burn Medicine and the National Smoke, Fire and Burn
Institute, as well as the organizations cited above, also indicate that
one-half of the 300,000 seriously burned are children, with senior
citizens representing 25 percent and the remaining 25 percent
spread among the sixteen to sixty-five age groups. These estimates,
too, may be open to question. In an effort to obtain accurate data in
one highly industrialized state, New Jersey, the National Burn Victim Foundation distributed a reporting form to hospitals, first-aid
squads, and fire departments for one year (1976). The resulting data
indicate that the greatest concentration of injuries occurred in the
age range from sixteen to fifty-nine instead of among children and
the elderly. The study also revealed that the number of burns due
to scalding exceeded those due to flames. While the Foundation
recognizes that the sources of ignition and combustion which cause
flame burns may vary from state to state, it also points out that the
potential of burn injuries from scalding is a constant, if often unrecognized, hazard in homes, restaurants, such trades as plumbing and
steamfitting, public buildings, and industries utilizing steam and
boiling liquids in their operations.

Until the federal government or state health agencies make burns
a reportable injury and fund the cost accordingly, full data on the
specific causes of burns and the population most frequently involved will be lacking — and without adequate data researchers will

continue to depend upon assumptions. Intelligent planning for a solution to the huge problem of burns must be based on facts, not guesswork.

Types of Burns

One area on which there is general agreement is the classification of burns. *Superficial* (first-degree) burns are confined to the epidermis, or outer layer of the skin, which does not contain blood vessels. Circulation is not affected, and the local symptoms are warmth, tingling sensation, and pain. The general appearance is red or pink (erythema), and some swelling and peeling may develop.

Partial thickness (second-degree) burns involve the dermis, the interior, thick layer of the skin which contains blood vessels and nerve endings. Penetration beyond the skin is possible in deep second-degree burns involving the subcutaneous fat tissue, but circulation is not affected. Local symptoms are soreness or pain, tingling, and warmth. The general appearance is red and swollen, with areas of superficially mottled pink or red. If a deep second-degree burn occurs, the skin will be dull white, tan, or cherry red, with dark streaks of coagulated capillaries and blisters containing clear fluid. (If blisters contain milky or grayish fluid, infection is probably taking place.)

Full thickness (third-degree) burns penetrate through the epidermis and dermis into subcutaneous tissue or beyond. Congestion occurs beneath coagulated areas, circulation is not intact, nerve endings have been destroyed, and there are no viable epithelial cells. The general appearance is leathery, dusky, or blackened (char burns). Since the nerve endings have been destroyed, there will usually be no immediate pain. A distinct burn odor is present, and if the area is char (fourth-degree), the burn has penetrated the fascia (fibrous tissue) and muscle and may have damaged the bone.

Treatment

While the details of treatment are beyond the scope of this book, it is important to point out that emergency efforts are absolutely essential and that different types of burns (flame, electrical, chemical, scalding, etc.) require different first-aid procedures. While first-degree burns are readily handled by commonly known measures, second- and third-degree burns require specialized knowledge and specially trained personnel. Treatment in the emergency department of a hospital is recommended for all major burns, and includes such steps as plotting the burn wound and calculating the percentage of total body surface burned, as well as such procedures as cleaning the wound, application of antibacterial salve, fluid therapy, catheterization, immunization against tetanus, and intravenous sedation. (For an outline of emergency procedures, see John A. Flood, Jr., *Burn Therapy in the Emergency Department*, National Burn Victim Foundation.) Hospitalization is indicated for all patients with above 20 percent of total body surface involved in partial or full thickness burns (10 percent for small children and adults over sixty-five). There are several reasons for hospitalization: the necessity for frequent administration of antibiotics and for monitoring vital signs; use of special equipment and nursing techniques to prevent pressure sores; and in some cases the necessity of isolating the patient from infection by others. Another important reason is to guard against complications such as septicemia, renal shutdown, and pneumonia, which might result in death if not detected early. Moreover, to stop loss of skin functions it is necessary to remove destroyed skin (debridement) and replace it with autografts (from another part of the patient's body) or homografts (from another person). Pigskin heterografts are also used to help retain body fluids and protect the wound from external infection. Reconstructive surgery may be required at a later date.

Treatment Facilities

Since release of the National Commission on Fire Prevention and Control report "America Burning," in 1973, legislation has been introduced by United States senators and congressmen seeking appropriations exceeding $200 million to develop and build highly specialized burn centers throughout the country. It is important, however, to distinguish between burn centers, burn units, and burn programs. The designation "burn center" is generally applied by the medical community to a facility isolated from the mainstream of major hospital activity, yet an integral part of the hospital's service capability. It is an area set aside solely for the treatment of burn patients. Research and medical education programs are emphasized, and the center is usually associated with a medical school or has other sources providing heavy financial support.

Burn units are hospital facilities set aside for the specific treatment of burns, but generally do not emphasize research or medical education. Burn programs are conducted in hospitals which have developed consistent management of burn patients under the direction of physicians with specialized skills in burn treatment.

Burn centers and burn units which set aside beds solely for treatment of burn patients generally experience high financial losses annually since these beds are not fully utilized. The combination of hospital losses and overwhelming patient charges has led to the development of other approaches. A study of seventy-three general hospitals in Florida has presented strong evidence that there is little difference in the outcome for patients treated in general hospitals having physician expertise in burn treatment and those treated in specialized burn units. The study also pointed out the need for more burn education programs, particularly aimed at physicians serving in emergency rooms, and noted that a large proportion of patients with minor burns admitted to hospitals could have been treated on an outpatient basis or hospitalized for shorter periods. Physicians at Yale University Medical School have also demonstrated that physicians skilled in burn treatment can effectively treat burns without a specialized burn unit, but using regular hospital facilities, such as the intensive care unit where needed, and trained nurses and physical therapists. A community hospital in Dayton, Ohio, provides a flexible system based on the burn team concept involving physicians and hospital support personnel who have attained skills in the treatment of seriously burned patients. A major advantage of this concept is that the burn team can function in other areas when not needed to treat burn patients. In addition, hospital beds may be utilized for other patients when not needed for burn patients.

A unique system for handling and treating seriously burned patients has been developed by the National Burn Victim Foundation in New Jersey. Prior to this system, no coordinated approach existed, and many patients had to be needlessly transported out of state to expensive hospitals specializing in burn treatment. The Foundation therefore identified physicians in the state who had developed special skills in treating burn injuries, and established a twenty-four-hour emergency telephone system enabling hospital emergency room physicians to contact the burn specialists and obtain consultation at no charge to the patients. If it is decided that the patient cannot be treated at the initial hospital, arrangements are made to transfer the patient to a hospital as close to home as possible that provides physician expertise, facilities, and personnel to carry out the treatment. This system has been characterized by burn experts as efficient and effective, and received national attention for its role in handling the twenty-eight seriously and severely burned survivors of the American Chicle Company disaster in Queens, New York, on November 21, 1976. Ten of these patients were treated by burn surgeons in New Jersey hospitals. The system has also significantly reduced the number of burn victims sent to out-of-state burn centers and units, and in some instances New Jersey residents burned in out-of-state accidents have been brought home for treatment.

Organization

The National Burn Victim Foundation, with headquarters at 439 Main Street, Orange, NJ 07050, is a nonprofit public foundation dedicated to finding solutions to a wide range of burn-related problems. Organized in 1974, it has had an impact on several major burn problems: treatment facilities, medical educational programs for emergency-level personnel, and innovative burn prevention programs for the general public.

B. **Psychological Rehabilitation**

ANTHONY V. LUPPINO, Ph.D., Vice-President of the
National Burn Victim Foundation

We are all cognizant of the awesome physical consequences of serious burns: suffering, scarring, facial disfigurement, and loss of function. These consequences alone would certainly constitute a substantial trauma. However, this trauma is exacerbated by the fact that the seriously burned patient will spend more time in acute hospital care than is required on the average by any other major illness. Despite such lengthy and highly expensive care, the chances are that the burn victim will have to adjust to living with significant scarring and functional losses. In all, then, to incur a major burn is to incur a major crisis. The crisis is of such proportion that it can be truly said that burns happen to families, not individuals.

Under the impact of a crisis of such magnitude, the individual's emotional resources are placed under strain severe enough that seriously debilitating psychological reactions can be expected. The patient's vulnerability is increased by the fact that those who normally constitute the major support system to assist in withstanding crises, members of the victim's family, are facing the debilitating effects of their crisis. While comparatively little research has been directed to investigating the psychological consequences of burns, the problem is well known to those who treat burns, and several studies report that emotional problems are indeed a prevalent concomitant of serious burns.

Caplan's important contribution to the field of mental health is instructive here (see Selected References, 3). As in any crisis, individuals suffering major burns require immediate psychological intervention to avoid the empty victory of saving a life, restoring as much physical function as possible only to see that individual totally disabled by the more potent secondary effect of psychiatric illness. One of the few studies which have taken the pains to follow patients after discharge (ref. 1) reports that fully 30 percent of those patients were suffering emotional consequences up to five years postburn. Unfortunately no study was found which compared premorbid functioning in terms of employment, income, social involvement, etc., with postburn involvement in such activities. It is not unreasonable to expect decrements in all of these areas, decrements which would not meet the requirements for a psychiatric diagnosis, but decrements which timely, effective intervention could have prevented.

It may be predicted, however, that few of these victims are afforded professional help. Considering the fact that of the estimated 300,000 serious burns per year only 8 percent are treated in burn centers and burn units, 92 percent of the victims are left to be treated in general hospitals. While burn centers normally have professional mental health support, it is unusual for burn units to have

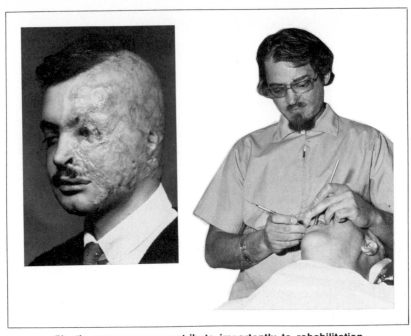

Plastic surgery may contribute importantly to rehabilitation in burn cases. In an automobile crash flaming gasoline destroyed the left side of this young dentist's face. Through fourteen operations over a three-year period his face was reconstructed, and he was able to resume his practice. (Institute of Reconstructive Plastic Surgery, New York University Medical Center)

such support available and unlikely that general hospitals have such services. Thus the conditions for long-term debilitating secondary psychiatric disability are present for the vast majority facing the burn crisis.

Recognition of these facts led the National Burn Victim Foundation to include among its major goals that of providing for the psychological well-being and rehabilitation needs of burn victims. A part of that goal is satisfied by education, training, and research efforts of the Foundation. It is not possible, however, to meet the needs of individual burn victims by tapping the already overextended pool of available mental health professionals. Happily there is no need to do so. Recent developments in the field of mental health, best exemplified in the work of Caplan and his associates at Harvard Medical School's Laboratory of Community Psychiatry (refs. 3, 4), offer a framework for interventive action which promises more effective help than professionals can offer on a one-to-one basis. In short, the National Burn Victim Foundation decided to utilize former burn victims and their families in a person-to-person dual role of crisis intervention and continuing mutual support system.

This group of former burn victims and their families is known as Burns Recovered. It is essentially a mutual help support system of the type discussed by Marie Killilea (ref. 4). The activities of the group are based on an appreciation of the fact (a) that serious burns constitute a severe crisis in the life of an individual, and how that individual deals with this crisis will dictate the eventual level of recovery, including the social, economic, and interpersonal spheres; (b) that the most important and powerful support system available to the individual, the family, is undergoing a crisis which threatens to render it ineffective; (c) that the visual evidence of the likelihood of recovery is important in the early stages; and (d) that certain social institutions need to understand the burn victim's needs in order to foster reintegration of the victim into society at the most productive level possible.

The initial focus of the Burns Recovered group is the burn victim's family. Speed is important. As soon as the Foundation is advised of a serious burn, a Burns Recovered family which has expressed interest in contacting new victims is informed. The major goal is to offer support to the family to ensure that it, in turn, can continue to function in its vital role as primary support system for the patient. The family needs to see that another family can come through the experience intact and still be as vitally involved in the normal activities of life as before the burn. The contact can provide a mechanism for the ventilation and reconstruction of thoughts and feelings concerning the new situation being faced, and appropriate models through members of Burns Recovered who have already faced and negotiated similar situations. The contact also provides the family with general information about what to expect, thus providing a framework for understanding which helps the family deal with the overwhelming anxiety which is part of dealing with unknowns. Further, the Burns Recovered family is ready to extend itself to provide concrete person-to-person forms of help (baby-sitting, helping with meals, rides, etc.). And finally, the contact provides an opportunity to assess special needs of the family or victim. The special needs can be communicated (with the family's permission) to the National Burn Victim Foundation for intervention or proper referral. In some cases it is advisable to bring together families who are currently undergoing the crisis.

The timing of the initial visit with the burn victim must await the physician's judgment that the patient is past the critical initial medical emergency and ready to have visitors. The emotional reactions of burn patients are not different from those encountered in any patient facing major trauma. The behavioral manifestation of these reactions, both in terms of severity and character, is more a function of the individual's premorbid adjustment than of the fact that the injury is due to burns.

The newly burned patient is facing a number of problems: fear of imminent death; sudden forced dependency; unrelenting painful procedures; threats to identity, competence, and autonomy owing to disfigurement and loss of function; and the need to handle strong emotions of guilt, anger, and hostility. Likely reactions are depression, regression, management problems, denial, and withdrawal.

At some point virtually all seriously burned patients can be expected to display these reactions. For those who demonstrate marked reactions, professional intervention is, of course, required. For many, however, one must assume that with supportive intervention offered by volunteers from Burns Recovered many who might otherwise develop severe reactions would be able to mobilize their strengths to cope with crisis, thereby avoiding long-term disability.

Burns Recovered volunteers are prepared. They are encouraged to use the sensitivity they have earned in dealing with the patient. They do not undercut the patient's defenses but follow the patient. They are an example that burn patients can and do resume normal lives and acquire acceptable appearance. The patient is allowed to ventilate, and Burns Recovered volunteers can tolerate this because they know from their own experience its meaning and have no need to cut the patient off.

Several studies (refs. 5, 7) discuss the recovery mechanisms utilized by the patient. These include the mobilization of hope, the restoration of interpersonal relations, and development of group relationships. The mobilizing effect of seeing concrete evidence of the likelihood of a level of recovery that allows full enjoyment of life and family, especially during the early phase of treatment, has been noted informally by investigators (ref. 2). It is this role that Burns Recovered volunteers can fill more effectively than anyone else.

SELECTED REFERENCES

1. Andreasen, N. J., A. S. Norris, and C. E. Hartford, "Incidence of Long-Term Psychiatric Complications in Severely Burned Adults," *Annals of Surgery,* no. 174, 1971.

2. Andreasen, N. J., R. Noyes, Jr., and C. E. Hartford et al., "Management of Emotional Reactions in Seriously Burned Adults," *New England Journal of Medicine,* vol. 286, 1972.

3. Caplan, G., *Principles of Preventive Psychiatry,* Basic Books, New York, 1964.

4. Caplan, G., and M. Killilea, eds., *Support Systems and Mutual Help,* Grune & Stratton, New York, 1976.

5. Hamburg, D. A., B. Hamburg, and B. A. deGoza, "Adaptive Problems and Mechanisms in Severely Burned Patients," *Psychiatry,* vol. 16, 1953.

6. National Burn Victim Foundation: *Burn Therapy in the Emergency Department,* by John A. Flood, Jr.; *Burn Therapy Team: An Approach to Burn Care in a Community Hospital; Burn Units: Is There Another Way?*

7. Visotsky, H. M., D. A. Hamburg, M. E. Gross et al., "Coping Behavior under Extreme Stress," *Archives of General Psychiatry,* vol. 5, 1961.

24

Cancer

CHARLIS S. DUNHAM, M.A.

Reviewed by ANN CARTER, M.D., Seattle King County Health Department, formerly Director of Cancer and Stroke Programs, Washington and Alaska Regional Medical Program

Cancer is characterized by unrestrained proliferation of cells which, if continuing uncontrolled, will cause death. A neoplasm is a new, abnormal, nonfunctional growth within the body; thus cancer is also known as "neoplastic disease." Cancer is also frequently called a "malignancy." Malignancy refers to a very dangerous or virulent condition, likely to cause death, by dictionary definition, and has come to be synonymous with cancer because of the high degree of fatality in the past. In recent years, however, advances in early diagnosis and treatment methods have resulted in the survival of one in three persons who develop cancer. The American Cancer Society estimates that in the United States alone there are 1.5 million men, women, and children who have survived cancer and are restored to an active, often their preillness, mode of life. The data are further interpreted to mean that of every six persons who get cancer today, two will be saved, a third person will die but probably would have been saved had proper treatment been received, and the other three cannot be saved with current knowledge.

The increase in the incidence of cancer is related to the fact that modern technology has allowed humans to escape death from other causes and live longer. In an excellent Public Affairs pamphlet, "Facts about Cancer" (no. 38A, p. 4), Dallas Johnson states: "In 1900, when the average person could expect to live to be 49, tuberculosis was the first cause of death. Heart disease was No. 3 on the list, and cancer No. 7. Now that the average infant at birth can expect to live to the ripe old age of 70, heart disease has moved up to first place and cancer is second."

There appears to be no single cause of cancer, and the conditions responsible for the disease in one organ may be completely different from conditions responsible for it in another. Therefore it is probably more accurate to think of cancer as a group of diseases depending on the primary location of the pathological process (skin, lung, breast, intestine, blood, etc.). The degree of localizaton of the disease, the age at onset, and many other factors greatly affect the estimate of chances for recovery (the prognosis).

Some common characteristics of the disease that usually hold true, whatever the specific form, are as follows: (1) there is higher rate of cell growth than that of normal tissues and cells, with the proliferating cells tending to spread and destroy other cells or (2) failing to maintain the boundaries of normal tissue and organs; (3) the proliferating cells have a microscopic appearace suggesting resemblance to immature tissue; (4) if not checked, in late stages of the disease, these cells tend to spread to parts of the body distant from the original site, a condition termed metastasis.

We think of cancer as a human disease, but it precedes humans on earth and goes back to the earliest cellular organisms. There is evidence in the bones of animals that lived millions of years ago, and in every kind of living thing today, both plants and animals. Cancer is mentioned by the Egyptians in the Ebers Papyrus, written about 1550 B.C., and also in medical writings of the Hindus, dating back to about 2000 B.C. The ancient Greeks likened the disease to the spreading claws of a crab and called the disease *karkinos* (hence the medical term "carcinoma"). The Latin translation of the word is *cancer*. There have been many false beliefs about cancer, encouraged by the high incidence of the disease and, until the 1930s, the very high degree of fatalities. It was popularly held for many years that cancer was contagious and therefore abundant in certain districts or villages, and that it was derived from animal disease or from plants. It was also thought that cancer was produced by a blow. As more sophisticated research and data collection took place, these notions were ruled out. It is important to recognize that it is only recently that detection and treatment techniques have made survival possible, in comparison with the many years when a diagnosis of cancer was a death sentence. Ignorance of the chances for survival may cause an individual to deny symptoms and avoid medical examination which, in turn, heightens the probability of doom — a self-fulfilling prophecy.

Warning Signs and Detection

There are early symptomatic signs which everyone should know: (1) unusual bleeding or discharge; (2) a lump or thickening in the breast or elsewhere; (3) change in size or color of a wart or mole; (4) sores that do not heal; (5) change in bowel or bladder habits; (6) chronic hoarseness or coughing; and (7) chronic indigestion or difficulty in swallowing.

Since there are instances when symptoms are not experienced but the disease can be detected by physician's examination, annual physical examinations are important, particularly for adults over forty, when the greatest number of persons contract the disease. The Pap test for females and proctoscopy for both men and women are particularly urged. Dr. George N. Papanicolaou developed a technique for microscopic study of small amounts of tissue scraped from the uterine wall, to predict the presence or absence of the disease in that area of the body with a great degree of accuracy (cytologic test). The proctoscope is a lighted tube which, when passed into the rectum and lower colon, permits the physician to inspect the walls of these organs visually. Because of the high incidence of cancer of the colon and rectum (75,000 cases in 1971), and because 60 percent of these cases result in fatalities although three out of four could be saved with early diagnosis, the temporary discomfort of this examination seems highly worth enduring.

There has been considerable effort to inform women about self-examination for lumps in the breast, since this simple technique leading to early detection can significantly affect the degree of survival. Breast self-examination (BSE) may be a monthly routine, or women may examine themselves regularly while bathing or dressing. If a lump is noted, a more thorough check can be made. The individual should lie down with one arm raised, hand behind the head. The breast should be felt in a concentric pattern so that the entire area is examined. Then the process should be repeated with the opposite breast. Eighty percent of breast lumps prove to be noncancerous. If a growth is suspected, an x-ray of breast tissue (mammography) can detect breast cancer at very early stages. Measurement of the heat patterns of the breast (thermography) detects cancer by temperature of the affected area.

When cancer is suspected, often a biopsy is done in which a small amount of tissue of the suspected organ is studied under the microscope for detection of atypical cell growth.

Incidence and Prevention

According to present rates, it is predicted that one in four persons, or 55 million Americans now living, will eventually have cancer, affecting two out of three families. In the 1970s it has been estimated that there would be 3.5 million cancer deaths, 6.5 million new cancer cases, and 10 million under medical care for cancer at any given time. In a 1977 American Cancer Society report, there were 700,000 new cases, not including skin cancer. More than one-half the cancer fatalities are persons over sixty-five, with a ratio of fifty-five men to forty-five women. More old men than old women die of cancer, but between thirty and fifty-five years of age there are more cancer deaths among women than men.

While researchers are continuing their fight to prevent the disease as a whole, prevention of fatality has been extremely successful. In 1937 one in five cancer patients was alive five years after treatment, in 1971 one in three. In 1937 uterine cancer was the chief cause of fatality in women; in 1977 the death rate was reduced by 66 percent, and could be even more dramatically reduced if early diagnosis were achieved in more cases. In 1937 there were no prospects of controlling the ever-mounting incidence of lung cancer; today, 80 percent of the cases could be prevented. The goal for 1977, with early detection and current treatment techniques, was to save 350,000 lives, or half of those who develop cancer each year.

Skin cancer occurs most frequently, with about 300,000 new cases reported in the United States each year. It also has the highest rate of cure. Avoidance of overexposure to sun would help to prevent much skin cancer, and immediate reporting of skin sores which do not heal would make it possible to cure approximately 95 percent of cases.

Breast cancer, with 91,000 new cases in 1977, is the leading type in women, with a high degree of survival, 85 percent, when treated before the cancer spreads to the lymphatic system. Current apathy about early detection has much to do with the fact that breast cancer leads as the cause of female deaths (34,000 estimated in 1978).

It is known that tobacco smoking is the leading cause of lung cancer, which is difficult to detect in time for successful treatment. About 71,000 men and 22,000 women were predicted to die of lung cancer in 1977. It is the leading cause of male cancer deaths, and the rate is rising. A U.S. Public Health Service 1975 survey showed 30 million persons as exsmokers—two-thirds of the adult population are now nonsmokers versus 50 percent ten years ago. Since the correlation between smoking and lung cancer has been identified, teen-age smoking dipped for a time, but seemingly has risen again in the fourteen- to eighteen-year range. There has been some effort on the part of the cigarette industry to reduce the hazards of smoking by lowering amounts of tars and nicotine and by manufacturing more filtered cigarettes—at the same time avoiding admission that cigarette smoking is dangerous to life. Research to the contrary is convincing. Lung cancer has been experimentally induced in dogs from smoking. Currently the death rate for lung cancer was ten times as high among regular smokers, and twenty times as high among those who smoke two packs a day, compared with those who have never smoked tobacco.

In a small percentage of cases, irritations of occupational origin are found to be associated with cancer—for example, bladder cancer has been high in the dye industry, and the asbestos industry has recently been implicated. Prevention is accomplished by removing the irritating agent from contact with humans, as in avoiding certain types of red dye and having asbestos workers wear masks in better-ventilated factories.

Although frequently thought of as a childhood disease, leukemia is actually found more often in adults. The age group most often affected is over forty. Incidence in men is twice that of women. It is estimated that leukemia and related lymphoma disease will affect approximately 41,000 persons per year in the United States, and 32,000 will die of these diseases during the same period (source: National Institutes of Health). (See CHAPTER 21: BLOOD DISORDERS, C. Leukemia.)

Despite the appalling loss of life due to cancer, there are growing numbers of persons alive today who have been cured of cancer – in 1977 nearly 2 million persons. One is considered to be cured or free of the disease when the physician concludes that special follow-up watchfulness is no longer necessary. This may be after five years free from recurrence, but in some cases one or three years, and in some cases a close watch is maintained for even longer than five years. There are also instances where benign conditions such as cysts and warts become malignant, and such conditions should be examined routinely for some time.

Types of Cancer

Cancer that begins in the skin is called epithelioma; in the glands, carcinoma; in muscle, fibrous tissue, tendon, or bone, sarcoma; in lymph tissues, lymphoma; and leukemia is a disease of the white blood cells. There are malignancies of the gastrointestinal tract, the genitourinary system, the neurological system, and of various other organs such as the lungs and eyes. As an entity, cancer has been identified in about 200 different forms.

Significant Factors

Heredity. Cancer is a common disease, and some familial "clustering" would be expected on the basis of chance. The result of research with animals on strain differences in the risk of cancer suggests that future human research should study familial risk patterns for specific forms of cancer rather than all forms together. Limited current data suggest some greater-than-chance family clustering of cancer of the stomach, breast, large intestine, and some other sites, but many other temperamental and environmental factors may be involved. Research into hereditary factors is inconclusive; however, family members of cancer patients should be particularly alert to regular preventive physical examination.

Retinoblastoma, a rare malignancy in the retina of the eye, is known to occur due to a mutation transmitted through the chromosomal makeup of the parents. Retinoblastoma is also the only disease entity significantly associated with higher-than-average intelligence, but the reason for this correlation is unknown.

If localized cancer goes untreated or is undiscovered for too long a time, diseased cells may break off and metastasize to other parts of the body. If the disease involves systems which spread throughout the body, such as the lymphatic or blood system, it is not possible to destroy all of the diseased cells; however, drugs and hormones can give temporary relief and improvement to many.

Socioeconomic Factors. Low socioeconomic groups have above-average incidence and mortality rates related to cancer. This is not fully understood, but differences in medical care and degree of exposure to the carcinogenic materials in the environment might be among the reasons. Certain customs and habits, such as smoking tobacco, chewing betelnut, placing tobacco and lime in the mouth, holding hot vessels against the abdomen, and wearing loincloths are also associated with higher incidence of cancer. Alcohol consumption and diet (especially excessive use of condiments) may involve repeated irritations or may otherwise play a role in raising tissue susceptibility to cancer-producing materials (cocarcinogenesis). Some synthetic substances used in foods, cosmetics, and toilet articles have been found to produce cancer in animals; however, the research into their effect on humans is generally inconclusive. There have been many notions held about diet and cancer, but scientific investigation on human populations has not provided evidence of the connection. Obesity has also not been proved to be of significance.

Psychological Factors. Many researchers have investigated lifestyles and personality complexities which appear to have some bearing on the incidence of cancer. Claus Bahnson, Ph.D., characterizes the current approaches as follows:

> 1. Loss-depression theories, which relate the clinical onset of malignancies to life events bringing object loss, depression, and hopelessness.
> 2. Repression of affect theories, suggesting that repressive ego defenses predispose an individual to cancer.
> 3. Central nervous system, autonomic nervous system, and endocrinological theories which specify by which channels psychological events may influence the malignant process.
> 4. Theories relating immune responses both to cancer and to different types of life events with psychological implications.

The loss-depression phenomenon seems to be related to unresolved relationships with parents which resurface in attempting to establish close emotional relationships with the spouse or through making substitute investments in creativity or work. When these precariously established relationships in adulthood break down, the original despair reemerges. Ego-defense hypotheses turn the focus on coping patterns and structure of personality, also related to early developmental experiences. Such defense mechanisms as loss of affect and dependency needs, and suppression of emotional problems and conflicts seem to correlate with incidence of cancer. Hormonal activity, which is related to personality and emotionality, has been shown, in combination with virus, to be highly carcinogenic. Rats raised with closeness and petting had significantly greater resistance to cancer than rats raised in isolation, without handling. One study suggested that the habit of smoking at night hastened the onset of lung cancer in middle-aged men who have impaired capacity for emotional gratification.

Psychophysiological cancer research is a reminder of the complexity and interrrelatedness of physiological and psychological phenomena in human existence.

Treatment

Treatment is usually through surgery, radiation with x-ray or radioactive materials, administration of chemicals, medications, and hormones, or a combination of these methods. Surgery can remove the area of cancerous growth; x-ray can destroy cancer cells without damaging essential normal tissue in the area, and chemicals and hormones control or stop growth of cells.

Continuous refinement of surgical techniques makes it possible to accomplish safe removal of areas heretofore inaccessible. Improved anesthesia and infection control have greatly increased surgical success. Methods of radiation have also been greatly improved in recent years. New equipment is capable of greater precision. Radioactive isotopes of cobalt are used for diagnosis and therapy, and the older method of implanting radium capsules in patients at the site of the cancer is still employed.

Treatment with chemicals (chemotherapy) has had limited success but is stimulating important research into the nature of cancer cells. Nitrogen mustard has been found helpful in treating Hodgkin's disease, and other chemicals are found to be valuable in controlling the disease process in acute leukemia.

Quackery has long been a problem in the field of treating cancer patients because of the extreme anguish and desperation experienced by patients and their families who deny the symptoms of the disease or, once cancer has been diagnosed, seek to avoid the difficult realities they must face. It is tragic when pretended remedies delay essential treatment which might be life-saving. It is almost as unfortunate when unrealistic treatments drain already-depleted material and emotional resources of persons facing terminal disease. In contrast, an enlightened approach focuses on making the patient as comfortable as possible, and wise counsel can assist the patient and family to cope with the course of the illness in a united and realistic way (Public Affairs Pamphlet no. 286, "When a Family Faces Cancer"). The dignity and comfort derived by the cancer patient and the family from knowing that together they have done the best they can in providing care and support can be a significant comfort even when fatality is inevitable.

Treatment of cancer sometimes brings about extreme body changes, as compared with that of nonmalignant diseases, and creates extensive associated disability. In many cases the treatment-associated disability presented by the cancer patient does not differ greatly from that associated with other diagnostic causes. For example, amputations resulting from cancer involve the same treatment and rehabilitation considerations as other amputations. In a study on rehabilitation of cancer patients (HEW no. RD 2311-M, 1971), it is pointed out that persons experiencing amputations due to cancer, being aware of the diagnosis, may be more able to accept the loss as more obviously life-saving than persons experiencing amputation due to other causes. (See CHAPTER 17: AMPUTATIONS.) Surgery of neck or face results in disfigurement which involves the same kinds of adjustments and rehabilitation experienced by persons dealing with such disfigurement from other causes. Cosmetic restoration, even of limited potential, may be of great significance in increasing interpersonal relating and adequate sense of self—to actually face the world. (See CHAPTER 32: FACIAL DISFIGUREMENT.) Cancer involving the nervous system is sometimes amenable to retraining processes to minimize debilitating effects and restore the individual to optimum functioning, just as other neurological impairments might be accommodated.

Rehabilitation

General Rehabilitation Guidelines. These include: (1) careful consideration of the treatment and rehabilitation goals as early as possible; (2) preoperative preparation which includes knowledge of possibilities; (3) feeling understood by the physician and having trust in the physician as well as others of the rehabilitation staff with whom the patient will be working after the surgery; (4) supportive relationships and knowledge throughout the necessary dependency period of hospitalization, with assistance to face realities during the convalescent and rehabilitation periods after surgery; (5) family counseling and vocational guidance as vital components of the rehabilitation process.

The physical impairments which sometimes result from cancer are often not as disabling as the emotional and attitudinal problems which the cancer patient must face. In some cases physical and self-image changes are great; there is fear of recurrence of the disease with anticipation of unbearable pain or death. These fears must be dealt with and overcome so that one can continue to live and fulfill oneself.

The following treatment techniques commonly employed to stop the disease process present certain management and rehabilitation problems which seem best discussed in connection with each technique: mastectomy, colostomy, and laryngectomy.

Mastectomy. The surgical procedure itself is usually extensive, involving removal of the surrounding muscles and lymph nodes in addition to the breast itself. This is to more nearly ensure that the disease will not recur. After surgery there is usually limitation of arm movement for some time. A regime of physiotherapy and exercise usually overcomes difficulty with arm mobility and also helps to avoid or relieve postoperative complications such as the swelling of tissue due to fluid (edema). Some researchers report as many as half of the mastectomy patients in their group experience some postoperative edema. The swelling is usually slight and subsides without intervention. If, however, the condition persists, it is important that it be brought to the attention of the physician, who can employ various treatment measures such as instituting a salt-free diet, massage, compression, or administration of medications which reduce water content in tissue (diuretics). Some persons report difficulty with balance just after surgery, but usually readjustment of carriage and posture is soon achieved.

Changes to our bodies, even slight ones such as the loss of a tooth, affect us. We have a sense of comfort in remaining the way we are accustomed to being. There is also a widespread myth in our culture about physical perfection, which is actually attained by no one but desired by all. Additionally, considerable sexual significance is placed on the breasts of females, and pleasure is experienced by both males and females in caressing the breasts. In most cases of mastectomy, psychological adjustment is further complicated by the fact that the patient enters surgery not knowing whether she will have a small biopsy or, if the biopsy yields positive results of the presence of cancer, radical surgery. It is therefore very important that individuals have an opportunity to understand facts and express their feelings before surgery in order to make the best adjustment. Counseling with both the woman and her mate might be indicated. It is the fears and loss which are not frankly discussed that cause the most problems. Sharing experiences, difficult ones as well as joyous ones, builds bonds between people and can deepen the loving relationship. Human beings are capable of expressing closeness in a great variety of ways, so that with genuine communication there need not be sexual problems resulting from the mastectomy.

When clothed, the prosthetic breasts are natural-looking. Bathing suits require ingenuity but can be worn in many cases. The prosthesis should be fitted while the person is still in the hospital.

Group support regarding rehabilitation needs of mastectomy patients and individual counsel and support from other mastectomy patients who are accommodating to the surgery have proved helpful. The American Cancer Society sponsors Reach to Recovery, which organizes the rehabilitation effort to include all details which might be helpful regarding the breast forms, clothing adjustments, exercises, factual information, cosmetic devices for camouflaging scars, and individual and group support to work through feelings and problems.

Colostomy. Another life-saving procedure which is performed on approximately 45,000 persons a year is colostomy, in which the diseased intestine is removed, the end of the bowel is brought through the abdominal wall, and the feces are expelled through the artificial opening. The person must master an entirely new technique of emptying the bowels—a task that has been effectively learned by thousands and can be performed for many years without interfering with the vocational, social, recreational, or intimate life of the colostomee. (See CHAPTER 46: OSTOMIES.)

Laryngectomy. The surgical removal of the diseased larynx, or voice box, may involve just the vocal cords or also the surrounding structure. There are approximately 7,000 new cases of laryngeal cancer each year, and it is estimated that there are approximately 25,000 persons with laryngectomies in the United States. When the disease is discovered early enough, and has not spread beyond the larynx, the prognosis is good. When the surgeon removes the diseased organ, an opening called a stoma is created in the front part of the neck and joins the trachea, or windpipe, to it. The laryngectomee continues to eat and drink through the mouth, but a new method of speaking must be learned. Group support from Lost Chord Clubs has proved of great value in the rehabilitation process, and there are devices and aids which assist in adjustment. (See CHAPTER 36: LARYNGEAL CANCER.)

Vocational Rehabilitation

It is unique to the condition of cancer that there is frequently a short period of time between identification of the condition and treatment. In many cases the cancer patient does not become eligible for vocational rehabilitation services as soon as such services are required for optimum effectiveness. The physician who is aware of these problems can refer the client for rehabilitation services with explanation and recommendation for services early in the course of care.

Many individuals surviving cancer and adjusting to the procedures of treatment resulting in altered physical capability or appearance are able to return to their previous careers. Cosmetic problems may interfere with employment for some or cause withdrawal from accustomed occupational interaction. If the changes caused by the disease or treatment of the disease necessitate occupational change, realistic preparation for a new career will play an important part in the person's recovery and subsequent adjustment. In the HEW research project conducted by J. Dietz and G. Robbins (January 1971), "Rehabilitation of Cancer Patients," no. RD 2311-M, it is stated: "Rehabilitation therapy early in the period of disability will eliminate development of periods of hopelessness, frustration and despair. Preoperative training and counsel for the patient about to undergo surgery will add both psychological and physiological benefits."

The development of an adequate self-concept and of hope for the future significantly influences recovery. Today a great many persons who have had cancer look forward to a full life-span with productivity and independence. If, however, one is not informed about the realistic chances for survival, is operating out of a depressed mood with morbid fantasies of future suffering, and is isolated from rewarding relationships, then that person is experiencing a thousand deaths daily. All that any of us can strive for is a productive, relatively harmonious, valuable life for as long as possible. There are individuals who, with or without realistic cause, live in fear of the future. The individual recovering from cancer will usually experience a period of depression and shock; however, the opportunity to discuss the facts of one's condition and to make use of rehabilitative support should encourage the development of a more hopeful outlook and the ability to direct energy into new coping techniques. When medical, volunteer, institutional, or agency resources are called upon in the readjustment period, the person will usually profit from a cooperative effort. If after a reasonable period of time the person cannot begin to make adjustments, accept assistance, and assimilate available information, professional counseling should be obtained to help the individual work through the personal grief and anger.

Family Support of the Child with Cancer

One child in 7,000 will be likely to develop cancer. This is not a frequent childhood occurrence, but it is not exactly rare either. More schoolchildren die of cancer than any other disease. There are adults living today who were cured of cancer in childhood. Wilm's tumor of the kidney has a good rate of cure when detected and removed early enough. Retinoblastoma (eye tumor) has a low incidence of recurrence with proper treatment.

Because of the more rapid growth and development of cells in the young, the present rate of survival in some types of childhood cancer is low. The pain of facing the terminal illness of one's child is compounded by lack of preparation and lack of recognition on the part of society of what is involved in losing a child to disease. Without good help, many families break under the blow, causing suffering to all the members. The child with cancer also has a right to as good a quality of life as possible. Peter G. Koltnow of the Candlelighters in an article, "The Child with Cancer—The Family" (June 23, 1972, Atlanta, American Cancer Society), states: "One of the chief hopes that guides parents in the care of the sick child and the family is that their youngster will live a normal, healthy life as long as possible. To parents a normal, healthy child means a child that fits happily into the family; a child comfortable with himself; able to cope with the ordinary pressures of childhood as well as the abnormal conditions that attend periodic treatment and relapse."

Parents need to stay in communication with each other, to understand and support each other through the loss. Often parents feel guilt, although it is unrealistic; and they lack knowledge of their child's condition, of available services, of how they can collaborate with the medical personnel in watching the symptomatology and in treating their child. Help from professional counselors and parent groups as well as hospital staff can make a tremendous difference in the kinds of experiences the child and the family have.

Research

Over half of the individuals developing cancer today could be cured if treated early enough. Only further research will make it possible to save the many for whom there is not currently a cure. The National Cancer Institute research projects listing cites the following areas of investigation: (1) the biological and chemical processes that underlie cancer to try to learn how cancer starts; (2) improvement of the two established methods of treatment, surgery and radiation; (3) new, improved detection methods; (4) investigation of chemical treatment, particularly for leukemia; (5) investigation of virus as a possible cause of cancer; (6) the study of immunology; that is, how the body fights against cancer, and a search for a preventive vaccine; (7) study of hereditary factors including the body's enzyme system, hormones, glandular secretions, reproduction of cells, and cell growth psychogenic components.

All of these problems are being actively investigated, since they have a bearing on the development of cancer and therefore may one day shed light on how to cure its various types. Research allocations by the National Cancer Institute amounted to $815 million in 1977 alone.

Organizations

The American Cancer Society (ACS) has been providing service to cancer patients and funding research and public education since 1913. The national headquarters address is 377 Third Avenue, New York, NY 10017. There are fifty-eight incorporated chartered divisions of the Society, one in each state, one in the District of Columbia, and seven in metropolitan areas. It is a voluntary organization, and programs are planned by a national board of 107 voting volunteer directors representing all the divisions of the Society. At least half of the board must be physicians, dentists, or other scientists, according to the bylaws. The long-range objective of the Society is to eliminate cancer; the immediate goal is to save more lives and diminish suffering from cancer as much as possible. ACS has developed effective techniques of public education using all communication media, and particularly calling the attention of the country to the seven warning signs through the annual door-to-door, citizen-operated April Crusade. Professional education, both in preparation of specialists and keeping practitioners informed about new advances, is funded by the Society.

The following direct services are provided by ACS Chapters: (1) counseling for the patient or the family; (2) loan closets of sickroom necessities; (3) surgical dressings prepared by volunteers; (4) patient transportation to and from doctors' offices, hospitals, and clinics for diagnosis and treatment; (5) home care programs. Sometimes local chapters also support detection programs, tissue examination services, approved tissue registers, social work services, medications, and approved rehabilitation services. The Society has fostered self-help organizations of persons with ostomy, mastectomy, and laryngectomy. A wide range of research is funded by ACS ($24 million in fiscal 1976–1977), and the vast, detailed statistical information compiled by the Society has been instrumental in the battle against cancer. Contact with the national headquarters or a local chapter can provide clear, up-to-date information on all aspects of cancer as well as direction and services.

SELECTED REFERENCES

American Cancer Society: *The Clergy and the Cancer Patient; Post-Mastectomy Lymphedema; Rehabilitation of the Patient with Colostomy; What Is Reach to Recovery?*

Bahnson, Claus, ed., "Second Conference on Psychophysiological Aspects of Cancer," *Annals of New York Academy of Sciences*, vol. 164, October 14, 1969.

Dietz, J. Herbert, Jr., *Rehabilitation of the Patient with Disability Resulting from Cancer or Its Treatment*, Institute of Rehabilitation Medicine, New York.

Georgetown University Medical Center Cancer Symposium, *The Successfully Treated Cancer Patient: New Problems and Challenges,* January 1974.

Krusen, Frank H., Frederic J. Kottke, and Paul M. Ellwood, Jr., *Handbook of Physical Medicine and Rehabilitation,* W. B. Saunders, Philadelphia, 1965.

Mozden, Peter J., "Neoplasms," in Julian S. Myers, ed., *An Orientation to Chronic Disease and Disability,* Macmillan, New York, 1965.

Wilhelm, Morton C., Saul Batten, and Judith Morgan, "Cancer Trends," *Virginia Medical Monthly,* vol. 101, June 1974.

25

Cardiac Disorders

HELEN HOUD

Reviewed by ROBERT M. LEVENSON, M.D., Clinical Professor of Medicine, University of Washington, and Chief of Cardiology, Swedish Hospital, Seattle

B y 1980 it is projected that in the United States there will be 90 million persons over forty-five years of age, the age group in which cardiac disease is most prevalent. At present the monetary cost of heart disease to the nation exceeds $26 billion annually. In addition to lost income and expenditures for medical care, 52 million workdays are lost each year. Other hidden costs – losses in management skills, production know-how, and personnel training – are difficult to determine. And this does not include the intangible losses in happiness, comfort, and equanimity of the individual and family.

Cardiovascular disease (CVD) is the leading cause of death in this country. A total of 31,290,000 Americans have some form of heart and blood vessel disease: 23,660,000, hypertension; 4,050,000, coronary heart disease; 1,770,000, rheumatic heart disease; and 1,810,000, stroke. In 1974, the latest year for which statistics are available, cardiovascular disease claimed more lives than all other causes of death combined – that is, 1,035,273, or 54 percent of the total mortality. This figure compares with 360,472 deaths due to cancer, 104,622 from accidents, and 434,021 for all other causes. In view of wide publication of these facts, cardiovascular disease is disabling both intrinsically and by implication. Because the fear associated with heart disease is so widespread, many persons who have made a good medical recovery consign themselves to an unnecessary invalidism. Some cardiologists contend that fear creates more cardiac invalids than does injury to the heart chambers or primary vessels. Patients have images of themselves as fragile persons in need of protection.

Heart and Circulatory System

The heart is a four-chambered double pump that beats 100,000 times a day while moving 4,300 gallons (16,300 liters) of oxygen-rich blood through the circulatory system. The system functions to provide a continuous circulation of blood to and from the cells of the body, and through the lungs for the purpose of oxygenating the blood and releasing carbon dioxide.

The heart, located a little to the left of the midline and behind the sternum, is slightly larger than a closed fist and weighs just under a pound (450 grams). Contractions of the thick muscle wall (myocardium) pump blood from the heart through 60,000 miles (96,000 kilometers) of blood vessels. The heart rests only a fraction of a second between beats. The normal adult circulatory system contains about eight pints (3.8 liters) of blood, which is recirculated continuously.

There are two pumping stations, each made up of two chambers: the right atrium and right ventricle, the left atrium and left ventricle. The right heart receives the blue, or deoxygenated, blood after it has delivered nutrients and oxygen to the body tissues. The lungs cleanse the blood of waste gas (carbon dioxide) and provide a fresh supply of oxygen. The left heart receives this recycled, bright red blood from the lungs and pumps it through the circulatory system. The heartbeat is activated by a small node in the right atrium — actually an "electrical" impulse center — that normally regulates the heart beat at sixty to eighty times a minute. The sinoatrial node sends out electrical impulses which travel through the heart's own intricate conduction system.

The circulatory system is a complex arrangement of vessels — arteries and arterioles (small arteries), capillaries, veins, and venules (small veins). They branch out from one to another to distribute oxygenated blood to every cell of the body and carry off wastes. The entire body depends on this interdependent system.

Diseases affecting this system can be inherited, can result from living habits, or can be caused by injuries from embryonic life on. Some diseases primarily affect the blood vessels, others only the heart itself.

Major Cardiovascular Diseases

These diseases include high blood pressure, atherosclerosis, heart attack, stroke, congestive heart failure, rheumatic heart disease, and congenital defects.

High blood pressure is a silent killer. It has no characteristic symptoms, and in more than 90 percent of the cases the cause is unknown. If hypertension is not controlled, serious cardiovascular complications may result. One in every six adults has some elevation of blood pressure. If severe and persistent, this condition can result in stroke or congestive heart and kidney failure, and is a major risk factor in coronary artery disease. It is a major cause of death of black Americans.

The causes of primary hypertension are complex. In the majority of individuals the small arteries constrict and thus more force is required to pump the blood. The maintenance of this additional pressure increases the work load of the heart, and hypertensive heart disease may develop. Treatment is aimed primarily at correcting the hypertension. Chemotherapy is effective in most cases. (See CHAPTER 34: HYPERTENSION.)

Congestive heart failure is not a disease but a complication of either a cardiovascular or lung disease. It is a circulatory failure which occurs when the heart is unable to pump sufficient blood to meet the requirements of the body. Failure may develop as an immediate complication of the acute stages of arteriosclerotic heart disease, or it may appear as the end result of a disease which over a period of years has made inordinate demands on the heart.

The disease may manifest itself by enlargement of the heart (cardiac hypertrophy) to compensate for the extra load which has been placed upon it. The kidneys fail to excrete sodium and water adequately. The patient's most pronounced symptoms are usually related to congestion in the lungs. There may be shortness of breath (dyspnea) with exertion or the inability to breathe lying flat (orthopnea). Gastrointestinal symptoms, such as loss of appetite, nausea, and vomiting, may occur with congestive heart failure as a result of congestion of the liver and other organs.

Treatment of congestive heart failure is directed to the underlying disease. The work load on the heart is reduced, and usually sodium intake regulated. Diuretics are administered to rid the body of excess fluid, and medication, such as digitalis, is prescribed to increase cardiac output.

Arteriosclerotic heart disease, or atherosclerosis, is the most common cause of heart disease. It is slow and progressive, and is characterized by heart attack and stroke. The disease, which has its beginning early in life, deposits fibrin (a clotting material), cellular debris, and calcium in the arteries. As this buildup on the inner walls increases, the arteries lose their ability to expand and contract, and the blood moves with difficulty through the narrowed channels. This makes it easier for a clot to block the channel and deprive the heart, brain, or other organs of blood. When the blockage occurs in a coronary artery, the result is a coronary thrombosis, or heart attack; when it occurs in the brain, the result is a cerebral thrombosis, or stroke.

It is presumed that the high consumption of fatty foods increases the deposits of fat molecules of the blood in the innermost coat (intima) of the artery. Hereditary factors seem to predispose some people to the disease. It is higher among men than women. Though it characteristically appears in middle or later years, atherosclerosis can develop in persons in their mid-teens or early twenties. Autopsies of children killed in accidents, or who have died from other causes, reveal the beginnings of the atherosclerotic process. And autopsies of servicemen killed in the Korean War revealed that in some cases the atherosclerotic process had already reached advanced stages by the early twenties and thirties.

Physicians are emphasizing early identification and modification of the risk factors, particularly high blood pressure and elevated blood cholesterol, to help retard or prevent the development of atherosclerosis and the heart attack and stroke that may result.

Heart attack, or myocardial infarction, occurs when the coronary artery is completely blocked (occluded) and a portion of the heart muscle is suddenly deprived of blood. The occlusion may occur as the result of either a progressive or sudden closure of the artery, as the end product of the atherosclerotic process. More often, the blood flowing over a plaque will form a clot (thrombus) which blocks the blood vessel. The tissue in that portion of the heart muscle which has been deprived of oxygen becomes dead or necrotic and the patient has a myocardial infarction.

The symptoms are characterized by prolonged chest pains, and may be accompanied by profuse sweating, overwhelming weakness, and sometimes shock. Some individuals may develop chest distress with exertion. This is termed angina pectoris.

When a myocardial infarction occurs, physical demands on the heart must be reduced. The essence of treatment is complete bed rest, usually in a hospital, so that minimal demands are made on the damaged heart until the healing process has taken place, and also to prevent the complication of acute muscle injury. To enable the heart muscle to heal, small blood vessels open up to detour more blood through the damaged area. This is called collateral circulation, and is the heart's own life-saving method in which other blood vessels take over the functions of the blocked artery. As healing progresses, part of the injured area may be replaced by scar tissue. A period of about six weeks is usually required for the healing process to be complete. Anticoagulants and other medications are sometimes used as additional therapy for infarctions.

Coronary occlusions may be immediately fatal, and the patient who survives may develop complications such as congestive failure, shock, or various forms of arrhythmia. Most patients who sustain a myocardial infarction recover and are able to resume their normal level of activity.

Extensive studies of family history, physical conditions, and lifestyles have identified several factors as contributing to an increased risk of heart attack and stroke. These factors include heredity, sex, age, race, cigarette smoking, high blood pressure, elevated blood cholesterol, diabetes, electrocardiographic abnormalities, stress, and lack of exercise. An epidemiological study by the U.S. Public Health Service, based on long-term observations of health of the inhabitants of Framingham, Massachusetts, has documented the significance of the major risk factors in heart attack and stroke. It also shows that the more risk factors present, or the greater degree of abnormality of any factor, the greater the risk.

Rheumatic heart disease is usually a childhood disease, and most frequently strikes between the ages of five and fifteen. The disease develops as the result of rheumatic fever, preceded by a streptococcal infection, usually a sore throat. During the acute stage of rheumatic fever there may be involvement of the joints and damage to the heart muscle, as well as the valves. The joint symptoms subside shortly, and the heart muscle recovers, but the damaged valves indefinitely impair the health of the patient.

The mitral valve, located between the atrium and the ventricle on the left side of the heart, is most frequently involved. If the margins of the valve thicken, or the edges become so scarred that they do not meet in the closing process, blood regurgitates back into the chamber instead of flowing along its normal course. In either instance the work of the heart is enormously increased, and if the valvular damage is severe, congestive heart failure can ultimately be expected. If the valve edges become fused, less blood may flow between the atrium and ventricle (mitral stenosis).

Streptococcal infections can now be effectively treated by antibiotics so that the incidence of rheumatic fever has dropped. However, persons who have rheumatic heart disease are susceptible to repeated streptococcal infections and must be given antibiotics or sulfonamides prophylactically.

In the case of rheumatic fever, if treatment is early and adequate, the patient can make a full recovery without permanent damage to the heart. However, rheumatic heart disease affects an estimated 100,000 children and 1,670,000 adults, and was responsible for 13,302 deaths in 1974.

Congenital heart disease describes defects which are present at birth and usually are detectable almost immediately. The infant may evidence difficulty in breathing (dyspnea) and may be cyanotic, or "blue," in appearance, if blood is being shunted into the arterial system without being oxygenated.

Among the common congenital defects are openings in the septum, or dividing wall, of either of the atria or the ventricles; the persistence of openings between structures which are normal during fetal life but should close soon after birth (patent ductus arteriosis or patent foramen ovale); extreme constriction of the main arterial channel (coarctation of aorta); and closing of the pulmonary valves (pulmonic stenosis). The tetralogy of Fallot is a combination of defects in which the infant has malpositioning of the aorta, which is the large vessel rising from the left ventricle and the main stem of the arterial tree; right ventricle enlargement (hypertrophy); constricted pulmonary artery (pulmonic stenosis); and a hole in the wall between chambers of the heart (ventricle septal defect). Tetralogy of Fallot heart repair surgery is usually performed at age six to eight and makes possible a normal life.

The outlook for children with congenital heart disease has immeasurably improved in recent years through advancement in cardiac surgery. The heart can now be virtually reconstructed, with abnormal openings closed and valves repaired, as the result of a combination of innovations: improved techniques in anesthesiology, electronic monitoring, induction of hypothermia, and the use of the heart-lung machine, permitting the oxygenation of blood outside the body during prolonged reparative procedures.

Each year more than 25,000 infants are born with heart defects, many of which can be repaired surgically. As diagnostic and surgical techniques improved, deaths due to heart defects were reduced from about 8,000 a year to 6,698 in 1974.

Both rheumatic fever and congenital malformations are responsible for subacute bacterial endocarditis, which is a severe infection of the heart lining, and the mortality rate is about 90 percent. The infection becomes implanted upon a valve that has been damaged by rheumatic fever, or at the site of a congenital malformation. Antibiotics have greatly reduced the mortality rate and the disease has become quite uncommon as a result of antibiotics. However, in recent years the disorder is again on the increase, particularly among drug addicts.

Congenital cardiac defects can be greatly reduced if all women, prior to pregnancy and during the early months of pregnancy, would take the following precautions:

1. Avoid excessive use of tobacco and alcohol.
2. Avoid use of drugs, particularly in early pregnancy.
3. Avoid exposure to x-ray.
4. Avoid exposure to virus disease, particularly in the early months.
5. It would be desirable for every female child before age twelve to be immunized to German measles (rubella).

Relevant Factors in Cardiovascular Disease

Sex. Young women are less likely to have heart attacks than men. After menopause, the mortality rate for heart attack in women increases sharply.

Race. Black Americans are twice as likely to have high blood pressure as whites. High blood pressure is one condition that contributes to heart attack and stroke, and blacks suffer more strokes at an earlier age and with more severe results.

Cigarette Smoking. The risk of heart attack increases in direct relation to the number of cigarettes smoked. A man who smokes more than a pack of cigarettes a day has nearly twice the risk of heart attack and nearly five times the risk of stroke as a nonsmoker. However, the death rate of people who stop smoking is nearly as low as that of people who have never smoked.

Diet. A diet low in saturated fat and cholesterol, which contains the number of calories needed to maintain optimal body weight, may help reduce the risk of heart attack and stroke, and prevent overweight as well. Cholesterol is a fatty substance found normally in all living tissue. The body gets it in two ways—through diet and by manufacturing it. However, in some circumstances it can build up on the walls of the arteries, narrow the passageway (lumen), and set the stage for heart attack and stroke. A physician can measure the amount of cholesterol in the blood and prescribe drugs and diet regimens to maintain it within a normal level. (See CHAPTER 44: OBESITY.)

Stress. This is a common environmental factor which may contribute to cardiovascular disease. Only the individual can alter stressful life-style and control emotional reactions to daily events. There is not always a need to restrict one's life, but rather to change one's reaction to life problems.

Exercise. Many studies have shown that people who lead sedentary lives run a higher risk of heart attack than those who get regular exercise. The doctor should test the individual carefully to determine the reserve and capability of the cardiovascular system, and then prescribe the appropriate kind and amount of exercise.

Diabetes. Diabetes, or a familial tendency toward diabetes, is associated with an increased risk of heart attack and stroke. A physician can detect diabetes and prescribe drugs, diet regimens, and weight control programs to keep it in check. (See CHAPTER 29: DIABETES MELLITUS.)

High Blood Pressure. Modern medicine has not yet identified the basic cause of most high blood pressure, but has a wide variety of drugs with which to control it.

Electrocardiogram Abnormalities. The presence of such abnormalities increases the risk of heart attack.

Surgical Advances

During recent decades dramatic advances have been made in repairing both congenital and acquired cardiovascular abnormalities. Surgery has progressed to the point where it is used as a method to repair and replace damaged portions of the heart and blood vessels.

One of the most significant advances has been the development of the heart-lung machine, which enables surgeons to operate inside the heart while it takes over the functions of heart and lungs. As the machine pumps and oxygenates the blood, the heart can be exposed and can be opened to correct defects. Heart valves, deformed by birth defects or rheumatic heart disease, can be repaired surgically or, when necessary, replaced with artificial valves.

A recent development is coronary artery bypass surgery, which is currently undergoing evaluation to determine whether it can significantly prolong and improve the quality of life of coronary patients. Strides have been made in treating blood vessel diseases, contributing factors to heart attack and stroke. Damaged arteries are replaced by transplanted healthy vessels or flexible synthetic tubing, restoring circulation to major arteries which supply the brain, kidneys, and legs.

Electronic pacemakers can maintain regular heart beat for patients suffering from irregular heart rhythms. This is a small power pack which is implanted under the skin and wired to the heart, and provides electric impulses to control rhythm and rate of heart beat.

Cardiac Rehabilitation

Cardiac rehabilitation is a process whereby a patient is restored to and maintained at optimum physiological, psychological, vocational, and social states. Implicit in this process is the institution of those measures which will prevent progression of the underlying disease process and the development of additional impairment. The rehabilitative process may be instituted at any of several points in the history of coronary heart disease, the most obvious starting point being at the onset of myocardial infarction. The extent, form, intensity, and duration of care vary from patient to patient.

During immediate crisis the patient and family must be reassured and comforted. For example, oxygen should be explained as a helpful aid in allowing the heart to function with less demand, and should not be interpreted by the family as a harbinger of doom. The entire course of illness should be projected to the family, the patient should be reassured in general terms, and the specifics left to be discussed as the occasion arises. Therefore the quality of communication with the patient and the family during the initial period of treatment, usually in a specialized coronary care unit, is the first step in rehabilitation.

Frequently individuals are sent to a cardiac rehabilitation unit after the first three to seven days of treatment, when the patient's condition is uncomplicated and stable. In this unit the patient and family can receive appropriate counseling regarding dietary regulations, physical activity, sexual activity, life-style, and whatever questions come to mind. In those instances in which family attitudes are overprotective, guilt-ridden, unsympathetic, or otherwise antitherapeutic, there is great need for education and counseling. Ideally rehabilitation is a team effort involving the medical staff, the patient, and the family. Many individuals do not have family resources, and may need encouragement to develop a structure of supportive relationships in their lives.

Convalescence begins with discharge from the hospital and lasts until the patient returns to work. During this stage the patient recuperates at home, and the immediate care is transferred to family members. Convalescent facilities may be required for single patients. The patient can take care of personal needs, eat meals with the family, perform routine tasks, and take short walks in the house and about the neighborhood. A companion can play a significant role by assisting in modifying dietary requirements and monitoring the patient's response to various stimuli, such as physical exercise.

Family relations are usually complex, particularly when a major shock threatens the stability of the roles that have been built up over the years. Guilt, anger, or frustration can be unspoken, but still very much a force in relationships.

The patient may return to work from six to fourteen weeks after hospitalization. Initially the patient may return to part-time employment, gradually increasing the working day over a period of about two weeks. The level to which the patient progresses depends on the presence or absence of symptoms, and can be monitored physiologically by an occasional measurement of the heart rate.

Prior to a return to normal activities, each patient is reevaluated by the physician. In addition to the physical examination, electrocardiogram, and chest x-ray, an exercise stress test may be performed. The results provide the patient with appropriate guidelines for the performance of physical exercise. The introduction of exercise stress testing has had as important an impact on cardiac rehabilitation as has the introduction of the cardiac care unit to the acute care of the myocardial infarction patient. Its value in adding to the diagnostic yield of latent or overt ischemic heart disease has been well established. The indications for an exercise stress test now include: (a) evaluation of unexplained chest pain; (b) evaluation of an individual's fitness for either work or sport; (c) evaluation of a specific therapeutic intervention or of a particular rehabilitation regimen.

Sexual Adjustment. The attitudes toward sexual life of the post-myocardial infarction patient have changed as dramatically during the past twenty years as have the positions taken toward early ambulation, exercise stress testing, and active rehabilitation programs. Although the return to sexual adequacy is related to the seriousness of the illness and to the presence or absence of symptoms, there is every reason to reassure cardiac patients that they can expect to return to a normal sexual adjustment when they recover.

Some patients withdraw from sexual activity because of fear of dying. However, in a study of 5,559 cases of sudden death, only 34 were reported to be coital deaths. Of the 34 coital deaths, 24 were extramarital, and were associated with an excess of alcohol consumption as well. The implication is obvious. The patient who desires sexual activity in a compatible sustained relationship runs little risk, while the patients who place themselves in a potentially stressful environment increase the risk of fatal cardiac event.

Other Behavioral Patterns. Cardiac impairment of any type in an individual who was previously healthy and unlimited leads to a series of emotional reactions which, in themselves, can produce limitations and disability. A valuable concept on the role of behavior in coronary heart disease was reported in 1959 by M. Friedman and R. H. Rosenman, who classified personality patterns as Type A and B. Type A persons are characterized as possessing: (1) a tense, sustained drive to achieve self-selected but usually poorly defined goals; (2) a profound eagerness to compete; (3) a persistent drive for recognition and advancement; (4) a continuous involvement in multiple and diverse functions constantly subject to deadlines; (5) a habitual propensity to accelerate the rate of execution of many physical and mental functions; and (6) an extraordinary mental and physical alertness. Type B individuals lack these qualities.

In further studies of the same personality concepts the Type A patient has an incidence of coronary heart disease six times that of Type B, and autopsies on Type A show six times as severe atherosclerosis.

The immediate emotional impact of myocardial infarction may manifest itself in deep depression and anxiety. These symptoms are often expressed as fear of impending death, concern over unmet obligations, and focusing on issues in the home situation. In most instances these emotional reactions are alleviated by strong reassurance on the part of the physician. However, in those patients whose precoronary personality profiles were characterized by significant depression and hypochondria, the cardiac event may aggravate these characteristics to the extent of producing prolonged psychological impairment. Such patients may require psychotherapy.

If the patient does possess the Type A personality pattern, it is imperative that he be made aware of its features so that the characteristics may be modified. Many actively rehabilitated patients have modified their total life-style, even though physical exercise was the only apparent therapeutic approach involved. Sedentary patients decrease only their level of cigarette smoking. In other words, even selection into an active rehabilitation program is related to the precardiac behavior pattern. Patients who volunteered and adhered to the program for three months or longer invariably had a history of participation in vigorous physical activity from high school years. Those patients who maintained or reduced their preinfarct activity levels following recovery were usually sedentary types in puberty.

Return to Work. The primary goal of comprehensive cardiac care is the restoration of the patient to previous life pursuits. The emotional impact of the disease is increased when the patient is unable to return to former employment. About 70 to 90 percent of cardiac patients return to their former employment within a period of three to six months, and of these patients 54 percent had unblemished attendance records for a year or longer, while their absence frequently was only 25 percent of the general absentee rate.

There are, of course, some job situations in which a myocardial infarction patient should not be employed, such as any occupation in which a population is placed at additional risk because of the unpredictability of sudden death. Aside from these limitations, the patient who has recovered from a myocardial infarction can return to work, and often can do exactly the same type of work performed before the onset of the illness. There are instances where well-intentioned employers reduce the responsibilities of the cardiac patient. The patient may be under far greater stress from anxiety over lowered status and thwarted opportunities than would have been the case if the former position had been resumed.

A cardiovascular disorder can impose permanent limitations on an individual's physical activity and may, in some instances, leave a person entirely disqualified vocationally. However, the disabilities imposed by these diseases have been greatly exaggerated. A person with severe congestive heart failure may be a dubious employment risk because tolerance for physical exertion is extremely limited, and the disorder can become acute under some situations. The person whose congenital heart disease has been corrected surgically should function normally. The outlook for the person with rheumatic heart disease varies with the severity of the valvular damage. If there is adequate cardiac compensation and no congestive failure, moderate or heavy physical activity may be permitted. The person with hypertensive heart disease can work, usually without restrictions.

In the past more cardiac patients were consigned to the role of the permanently disabled than the realities warranted. Potential employers felt that hiring a cardiac patient was costly and ill-advised. Some employers are fearful that insurance premiums will be increased.

Perhaps even more of an obstacle than the employer's reluctance is the patient's possible self-image as a fragile person in need of protection, an image which the counselor occasionally reinforces. Rest is admittedly important in the treatment of myocardial infarction and in the management of the acute phases of other cardiovascular disorders. But the need for rest is not interminable, and the cardiac patient can be done a disservice by a counselor who caters to existing anxieties.

The American Heart Association, along with its local chapters, has been instrumental in setting up work evaluation units to help assess the functional capacity of the heart and its relationship to work capacity. This was a milestone in the realistic consideration of the work outlook for cardiac patients. The objective of these units is a complete evaluation of the individual client to answer the following questions: What are the medical diagnosis and prognosis as determined by cardiac function studies? What physical demands are made in the course of a day's work, not only in performing the job but in getting to and from work and in necessary ambulation during the work day? How much exertion is involved in meeting the commitments of the social environment? To what extent is unwarranted fear a barrier to the rehabilitation of the client?

Through the American Heart Association a uniform system of classifying patients with diseases of the heart has been widely used. Patients are classified therapeutically and in terms of their functional capacity. This classification serves as a guide and provides an abbreviated system of communicating heart information. By means of this classification, information needed by the counselor or the employment interviewer can be transmitted via a uniform terminology, clarifying with exactitude the client's functional capacity.

Some significant conclusions reached as a result of extensive experience with work classification investigations are: (1) persons with cardiovascular disease who can walk comfortably outdoors are generally capable of working, regardless of the type of disease; (2) if they are well motivated for work, they probably will become employed; (3) the cardiac patient in a properly selected job usually produces as much as does the average worker and continues to work for a substantial period of time.

As research continues in the determination of those predictors which reflect progression of the atherosclerotic process or of additional impairment, more and more patients enter activity programs and are placed in positions of responsibility. Employers have increasingly recognized that the cardiac individual may continue to be a valuable worker. And it may well be remembered that Presidents Eisenhower and Johnson, chronically at risk from another cardiac event, guided the destiny of the United States.

Research

During recent years research in this vast field has been focused on such projects as development of two-dimensional echocardiography, in which ultrasound waves are used for diagnosis and evaluation; methods for reducing the extent and severity of heart muscle damage from acute heart attacks, such as use of nitroglycerine in combination with phenylephrine, "balloon pumping" in which a balloon-tipped catheter is introduced into the descending portion of the aorta, and use of various drugs such as propanolol, mannitol, and certain steroids; development of automated systems for large-scale measurement of lipid (cholesterol, triglyceride) levels as a step toward prevention of coronary heart disease; investigation of the possibility that the tendency to excessive cholesterol in the blood (hypercholesterolemia) may be inherited as a dominant trait; study of the underlying mechanism by which the liver and other organs control the production of blood fats; refinement of lifesaving techniques after cardiac arrest (medications such as lidocaine, D-C shock therapy, monitoring), which have already reduced in-hospital death from heart attack by 30 percent; further development of anticoagulant therapy to reduce thrombosis and embolic strokes; further development of cardiac surgery, including new types of valve replacements, coronary bypass procedures, and pacemakers; the development of antihypertensive drugs which reduce the risk of angina, coronary insufficiency, myocardial infarction, and death; and studies of the underlying mechanism which governs blood circulation within the brain.

Organizations

The American Heart Association, with headquarters at 7320 Greenville Avenue, Dallas, TX 75231, comprises 55 affiliates and 1,190 local subdivisions, of which 127 are chapters with a national membership of 40,000 physicians and more than 65,000 other members, who have joined together to help solve the problems posed by the cardiovascular diseases. The Association has played a major role in stimulating public support of cardiovascular research, and has channeled more than $268 million into this effort since its first Heart Fund campaign in 1949, including $19 million in 1976 alone. Another major role of the Association is professional education conducted through scientific meetings, teaching institutes, teaching scholarships, medical symposia, films, technical publications, and scientific journals. Its public education program is directed toward reduction of premature death and disability by providing information on early recognition, diagnosis, and effective treatment. Community programs are carried out through health professionals, community organizations, local Heart Associations, and the media, to help physicians, patients, and the general public prevent heart attack, stroke, hypertension, and rheumatic fever; to identify, through screening, children and adults at risk; to reduce risks through programs aimed at controlling diet, smoking, and hypertension; and to provide training in resuscitation and emergency care. Association periodicals include *Circulation, Circulation Research, Stroke,* and *Cardiovascular Nursing.*

The National Heart, Lung and Blood Institute of the National Institutes of Health was created as the National Heart Institute in 1948 to conduct research into the causes, prevention, diagnosis, and treatment of cardiovascular diseases; to foster, support, and coordinate cardiovascular research and related activities in public and private agencies; and to provide training related to such diseases. Its research appropriations for cardiovascular diseases have increased from about $10 million in 1950 to about $81 million in 1975.

SELECTED REFERENCES

American Heart Association: *After a Coronary; Children with Heart Disease: A Guide for Teachers; Heart Facts, 1977; How to Live with Heart Trouble* (Public Affairs Pamphlet); *How to Reduce Your Risk of Heart Attack; If Your Child Has a Congenital Heart Defect; Master Catalog of the American Heart Association; National Program Awards for CV Research.*

Benney, Celia, Leah Lawentman, and Harriet Vern, "Comprehensive Service to Cardiac Patients in a Work-Oriented Rehabilitation Center," *New York State Journal of Medicine,* August 1, 1964.

Friedman, Meyer, and Ray H. Rosenman, *Type A Behavior and Your Heart,* Knopf, New York, 1974; Fawcett World, New York, 1976.

Halberstein, Michael, and Stephen Lesher, *A Coronary Event,* Lippincott, Philadelphia, 1976.

The Heart and Heart Diseases, Division of Thoracic and Cardiovascular Surgery, University of Texas Medical Branch, Galveston.

Jezer, Abraham, "The Workshop in the Coronary Spectrum," *Journal of Rehabilitation,* March–April 1966.

Needs and Opportunities for Rehabilitating the Coronary Disease Patient, National Heart, Lung, and Blood Institute, 1974.

Research Conference: Rehabilitation in Cardiac Disease, 1966, Tufts University School of Medicine, Division of Physical Medicine and Rehabilitation, Boston, MA 02111.

Scheingold, Lee, and Nathaniel Wagner, *Sound Sex and the Aging Heart,* Behavioral Publications, New York, 1975.

Vocational Rehabilitation and Heart Surgery, University of Texas Medical Branch, Galveston, 1969.

26

Cerebral Palsy

ROBERT M. GOLDENSON, Ph.D.

Reviewed by LEON STERNFELD, M.D., Medical Director, United Cerebral Palsy Research and Educational Foundation

Cerebral palsy is a group of nonhereditary disorders resulting from brain damage, characterized primarily by inadequate control over the muscles and in some cases by sensory and intellectual impairment as well. The following definition has been adopted by United Cerebral Palsy Associations (UCPA): "Cerebral palsy is the general term applied to a group of permanently disabling symptoms resulting from damage to the developing brain that may occur before, during or after birth and that results in loss or impairment of control over voluntary muscles."

One form of this disorder, cerebral spastic diplegia, in which both sides of the body are affected, was described in 1862 by an English surgeon, William J. Little, who attributed the condition to "Abnormal Parturition, Difficult Labours, Premature Birth, and Asphyxia Neonatorum." It was not until the 1930s, however, that all forms were grouped under a common heading by Winthrop M. Phelps, of the Johns Hopkins Medical School. He selected the term "cerebral palsy" to indicate that the common denominator is a paralysis (palsy) due to central nervous system (cerebral) impairment. The most frequent symptoms of the disorder are muscle spasms, uncontrolled movements, staggering gait, guttural speech, and grimacing, although seizures, visual defects, hearing loss, and mental retardation may also be involved.

Incidence

Cerebral palsy is the most common of all nonprogressive disabilities. The total number of cases in the United States today is estimated at 750,000, or approximately 4 per 1,000 population. In 1950, 25,000–30,000 babies were born with the disorder, but since then the number has declined to 12,000–15,000 due to increasingly widespread application of the preventive measures described below.

Major Types

Cerebral palsy is an extremely varied condition, since different areas of the brain may be affected. The motor regions, however, are primarily involved, and for this reason the disorder is defined in terms of muscle control. The motor difficulty most commonly involves one side of the body (hemiparesis, hemiplegia), but parts of both sides may be involved (diplegia), or in some instances all four extremities (quadriparesis, quadriplegia). In other persons the symptoms are so mild that except for some clumsiness the defect may go unnoticed. Others may be extensively handicapped, and require crutches, a walker, braces, arm slings, or a wheelchair. The more severe cases may also require assistance with the basic activities of daily living, such as feeding, dressing, bathing, and toileting.

The basic disorder, defective motor control, may take any one or any combination of three major forms, each of which may be mild, moderate, or severe. *Spastic* individuals suffer from hypertonicity (excessive muscle tension), contractures (permanent fixation of ankle, elbow, wrist, or other joints in an abnormal position), and clonus (rapidly alternating contraction and relaxation of muscles). They usually hold their head on one side, and walk, if they are able, with a scissors gait (knees together, feet apart). Spasticity is due to a lesion in the motor cortex. The *athetoid* patient is characterized by involuntary, uncontrolled movements of hands or feet, often accompanied by slurred speech and defective hearing. Athetosis is due to a lesion found primarily in the basal ganglia. The *ataxic* individual has a disturbed sense of balance and faulty depth perception, walks with a staggering gait, frequently misjudges distances, and may have to be protected from falling or have to wear a plastic helmet. The ataxic form is due to a fixed cerebellar lesion.

In addition to the symptoms characterizing spastic, athetoid, and ataxic types, tremor is sometimes also considered a major symptom. It usually takes the form of a fine tremulousness, but may also be of the intention type—that is, it may appear only during purposive activity such as reaching or writing. Also, a small number of patients are afflicted with rigidity (the "lead pipe phenomenon"). Their movements are extremely slow, and they may require institutionalization due to microcephaly (small head and brain), with severe mental retardation. In some cases they may exhibit severe opisthotonos, or tetanus dorsalis, a rigid forward convexity of the entire spine and extremities.

Associated Symptoms

Many additional symptoms may be associated with cerebral palsy, and the majority of patients can therefore be described as multihandicapped. A large number have mild to severe speech problems due to defective articulation. A small but appreciable number are afflicted with some degree of hearing loss, and a larger number with strabismus or other visual difficulty. Perhaps one-third are subject to seizures, particularly in childhood, but rarely continuing for life. A large number have specific learning disabilities involving conceptual, perceptual, or language disorders. Dental abnormalities are also common, especially caries and irregular positioning of the teeth.

At least half of cerebral palsy patients are mentally retarded, though mostly in the mildly retarded range. These persons are generally educable, and practically all, even in severely retarded categories, are trainable. Unfortunately, many persons with cerebral palsy are mistakenly labeled as retarded due to such characteristics as an open mouth, drooling, dysarthric speech, or grimacing. These are purely physical symptoms and are not indicative of intellectual capability, which may be very high.

Finally, while many patients, including the severely involved, accept their disability with remarkable equanimity and realism, many others are in need of sociopsychological help. Their emotional disturbances range from mild to severe, and frequently involve a poor self-image, depression, feelings of inadequacy, frustration, and withdrawal. Many of these emotional problems are caused or aggravated by cold or overprotective family attitudes and inadequate efforts to help the patients achieve as normal and independent a life as possible.

Diagnosis

It is generally recognized that a complete and certain diagnosis of cerebral palsy cannot be made until several months after birth, since the central nervous system does not come into full operation until that time. As Alfred L. Scherzer ("Early Diagnosis, Management, and Treatment of Cerebral Palsy," *Rehabilitation Literature,* July 1974) points out, the motor patterns are not present at the time the precipitating cause occurs, but

> . . . emerge as the result of the maturation of an abnormal nervous system. The spastic type of cerebral palsy, for example, is not apparent usually before one year to 18 months of age. The athetoid form frequently is not seen before 18 months to two years, and the ataxic form may not be seen before even three years of age. The emergence of these major motor patterns is correlated with maturation of the brain from functioning on a brain-stem level at birth to gradually moving toward higher functions with age.

However, as he also points out, considerable progress is being made in identifying very early signs of brain dysfunction, and "accordingly it is no longer acceptable practice to await the obvious presence of major motor types of cerebral palsy before making a diagnosis."

How, then, is this tentative diagnosis made? First, as suggested by an article in *Patient Care* ("Cerebral Palsy: My Baby Is Slow . . . ," January 30, 1972), "The likelihood of brain damage would be foremost in your thinking if an infant were premature, if there were a history of rubella during the first trimester of gestation, a low Apgar score at one and five minutes after birth, hyperbilirubinemia [kernicterus, jaundice], or complications of delivery." (This etiological, case history approach will be summarized in more detail in the next part of this chapter.) Second, the physician would look for cerebral palsy if there were evidence of even one of these "cardinal signs": delayed motor development, unusual patterns of motor development, persistence of primitive reflexes, or abnormal muscular tone. The parents may give clues to one or more of these signs by reporting that the baby has trouble sucking or pushes the nipple and food away, that they cannot get the child's legs apart to change diapers, or that the child never moves spontaneously or crawls "like a bunny." They may also report other signs, such as inability to turn over by two months of age, listlessness and lack of interest in the environment, extreme irritability, or extreme right- or left-handedness before eighteen months of age.

These warning signs are not diagnostic in themselves, but they do indicate that a series of tests should be performed as soon as feasible — tests of reflex activity, muscle tone, motor coordination, balance, speech mechanisms, sight, and hearing. A full evaluation may eventually require consultation with many specialists, such as orthopedists, neurologists, ophthalmologists, otologists, and speech pathologists; but the pediatrician is usually responsible for the initial diagnosis and must therefore be equipped to identify some of the more specific signs of possible cerebral palsy. Among the indications in newborns are excessive "floppiness" of the body (hypotonia); unusual hypertonia, especially if deep tendon reflexes are exaggerated, an extensor (rigidly extended) posture when prone; lack of spontaneous movement; and tremor in the extremities after four days.

Some of the possible indications in older infants are a clenching of the thumb in the palm or keeping one hand fisted after four to five months, kicking the legs in unison rather than bicycle fashion, moving the tongue in and out continuously, hyperextension of the neck when the head is not supported, assumption of a fencing position when the head is turned after six months (obligatory tonic neck reflex), failure of the neck-righting reflex, nystagmus (oscillation of the eyeballs), dropping of the chin on the chest unless supported, persistent use of one hand, failure to lift the head and chest from the table after five months, inability to pull a cloth off the face after six months, collapsing forward in the sitting position after eight months, or wormlike involuntary movements after eighteen months. A combination of these overt signs may be sufficient to make a presumptive general diagnosis, but there are also some early signs of specific types of cerebral palsy. For example, a normal baby pulls the legs up or bicycles when picked up under the arms from behind, whereas a spastic infant will go into extensor thrust or scissors, and an ataxic baby will sit in the air with hips flexed and knees extended.

These are a few of the diagnostic signs. In any case, as the afore-mentioned article in *Patient Care* remarks, "When the clinical picture points to cerebral palsy, you'll want to refer the child and his family to a specialized clinic for specific diagnosis which will differentiate between the types of cerebral palsy such as spastic and tension athetosis. The ability to make this type of differential diagnosis requires varied experience, unusual for anyone without a special interest in cerebral palsy." It is also necessary to differentiate cerebral palsy from other disorders such as hypertonia due to hypocalcemia and immature motor patterns due to mental retardation.

Etiology

Extremely few cases of cerebral palsy can be attributed to hereditary defect. Approximately 85 percent are congenital, due to conditions occurring during the gestation period or the birth process, while about 15 percent occur in previously normal children during the early developmental period. At the present time, however, no specific cause can be found in about one-third of cases. But where the cause can be identified, it most often involves interruption of the oxygen and nutrient supply to the brain before, during, or just after birth—that is, in the perinatal period. This interruption may result from (1) premature separation of the placenta from the wall of the uterus, (2) an awkward birth position, (3) overextended or fore-shortened labor, (4) a twisted umbilical cord, or (5) prematurity. Other causal factors are (1) Rh or A-B-O blood type incompatibility between parents, resulting in abnormally high antibody levels in the baby; (2) infection of the mother by German measles (rubella) or other viral diseases (cytomegalic inclusion disease, diphtheria, typhoid fever, scarlet fever, etc.) in early pregnancy; (3) intracranial hemorrhage in the baby; (4) hyperbilirubinemia in the baby; and, in occasional cases, (5) induced labor; (6) postmaturity; (7) postnatal brain injury; (8) toxoplasmosis, (9) toxic disorder, such as lead poisoning, in the mother; (10) overexposure of the fetus to radiation; (11) forceps injury during delivery; (12) an enzyme defect inherited through the mother (Lesch-Nyhan syndrome); or (13) a number of conditions that may occur during the first few months of the child's life such as head injury; toxic disorder due to medications, heavy metals, or gases; and brain inflammation due to meningitis, epidemic encephalitis, or other severe infections.

Some of these causal factors require a word of explanation:

Studies have shown that the following factors are often associated with prematurity: infections in the mother's kidney or urinary tract, heavy smoking, a history of premature births, or a mother younger than sixteen or older than forty. Prematurity is involved more frequently than any other single factor, occurring in one-third of all cases.

Toxic disorders in the mother may be due to inhalation of metals used in industry (lead, manganese, mercury), inhalation of gases such as carbon monoxide, and excessive use of barbiturates or other drugs (psychotropic, stimulant, etc.).

Cytomegalic inclusion disease is characterized by the presence of inclusion bodies in oversized cells of various organs, resulting in enlargement of the liver and spleen, jaundice, erythroblastosis (yellow baby disease), and in some cases, brain damage.

Hyperbilirubinemia is a condition involving an excessive amount of bilirubin (a breakdown product of hemoglobin) in the circulating blood, which may result in kernicterus, an acute disease in the newborn child characterized by jaundice, anemia, a high-pitched cry, and in severe cases, brain damage, spasticity, and mental retardation. The disorder is often associated with blood incompatibility (Rh-positive children with Rh-negative mothers), prematurity, and severe neonatal sepsis (blood poisoning).

The significance of blood incompatibility lies in the fact that if a mother who lacks the Rh factor (Rh-negative) has a child by an Rh-positive man and the child is Rh-positive, she will produce antibodies which may affect subsequent pregnancies—that is, the antibodies may become attached to the unborn child's red blood cells, destroying them and causing anemia with mild to severe jaundice (erythroblastosis).

Toxoplasmosis is a parasitic disease contracted from animals; it may be transmitted from mother to fetus, but may also be acquired in infancy. In some instances the parasite attacks the brain and produces such symptoms as spasticity, convulsions, blindness, deafness, and occasionally hydrocephalus or microcephaly.

The Lesch-Nyhan syndrome is a rare type of cerebral palsy inherited through the mother and affecting males only. It is characterized by spasticity, a scissoring stance, involuntary movements of the extremities, aggressiveness, and self-mutilation. The condition has been traced to deficiency of a single enzyme (known as HGPRT for short), which leads to extreme overproduction of uric acid.

Recent studies have established a connection between prematurity and the inability of the undeveloped lung to synthesize and secrete a lining substance known as surfactant. If this substance is not produced in sufficient quantities, hyaline membrane disease develops, and unless special precautions are taken, two-thirds of the survivors will suffer brain damage due to oxygen deprivation.

Prevention

In recent years significant advances have been made in developing preventive measures, but much more remains to be done. Present measures include:

Improved gynecological and obstetrical care: (a) medical attention to slight kidney infections that may lead to prematurity; (b) surgical correction of anatomical defects that make it difficult to carry a child full term; (c) administration of medications that will delay the birth process until full term or adequate birth weight is reached; (d) administration of hormones to stimulate birth in cases of overdue babies; (e) administration of medications to prevent abrupt or prolonged labor; (f) wider use of obstetrical techniques that prevent birth injury.

Application of measures to prevent respiratory disorders in the newborn: (a) an amniotic fluid test for pulmonary surfactant; (b) delay in delivery until the lung matures; (c) experimental administration of corticosteroids to hasten lung development; and, where premature birth cannot be prevented, (d) identification and intensive care of the child at risk, including respiratory therapy, administering of intravenous fluids, adjustment of the thermal environment, continuous monitoring of respiratory and heart rates, and use of microchemical techniques to measure oxygen, hydrogen ion, and carbon dioxide content of the blood.

Administration of special tests to determine (a) Rh antibody level in the mother's blood; (b) bilirubin levels in the baby's blood before or after birth; (c) the presence of toxoplasmosis in the mother and newborn child.

Administration of Rh-immune globulin to Rh-negative mothers who have an Rh-positive baby or miscarriage, within seventy-two hours of delivery or abortion.

Intrauterine or postnatal blood exchange transfusion for the baby in cases of blood incompatibility and jaundice.

Administration of vaccine against German measles to children between one year and puberty. Though not universal as yet, rubella immunization has already reduced the incidence of cerebral palsy by at least 10 to 15 percent.

Routine immunization against other types of infection such as diphtheria, polio, mumps, and regular measles.

Detection and treatment of cytomegalovirus infection in the mother before or during pregnancy. A vaccine has not yet been developed for this infection, nor for toxoplasmosis.

Examination of a sample of amniotic fluid (amniocentesis) during pregnancy if the Lesch-Nyhan enzyme defect is suspected. Also, a simple screening test using prepared filter paper dipped into urine and analyzed for uric acid content is now available and being applied in the institutional population and in United Cerebral Palsy affiliates. Actual prevention, however, is not yet possible except by genetic counseling or abortion, but early dietary treatment (restriction of purines) is being tried.

Prevention of toxic disorders that may lead to brain damage — for example, through the use of nonlead paint and stricter regulation of the use of toxic substances in industrial processes.

Prevention of radiation overexposure through advanced radiologic techniques and avoidance of unnecessary x-ray examinations during pregnancy.

Therapy and Rehabilitation

Cerebral palsy is not generally a progressive disorder, since most patients do not deteriorate and some show improvement as they grow older. There is no overall cure, since brain damage cannot, as yet, be reversed. However, many of its effects can be remedied or corrected to some extent by medical, dental, and surgical procedures, and practically every patient can be taught or trained to develop capacities and learn to meet the demands of life — functional, social, emotional, and vocational — with increasing success and satisfaction.

Since cerebral palsy is a multifaceted disorder, the process of therapy and rehabilitation must be based on the total needs of each individual. The process is therefore highly complex, and can be carried out effectively only through the coordinated efforts of an interdisciplinary team working in a center that specializes in this condition. If it is to be successful, the program requires the active collaboration of both the client and the family. The major approaches are summarized below.

Medical-Surgical Therapy. Early treatment is based on a detailed evaluation of the child's reflex behavior (including sucking and swallowing), postural abnormalities, and muscle balance throughout the body. In attempting to correct or counteract abnormalities, the pediatrician pays particular attention to positioning, handling, and feeding the child. Early sensory and motor stimulation are especially important in aiding in the development of head, neck, and trunk control. Various devices are used to enable the child to progress through the stages of creeping, crawling, reaching and grasping, sitting, standing, and if possible ambulation: a bottle with a special nipple to encourage sucking, a splint to keep the thumb out of the palm, attractive toys that require the use of both hands, a special crawler to develop leg and trunk muscles, and carefully fitted braces, crutches, or walkers to promote ambulation. A full evaluation is made by an orthopedic surgeon before range-of-motion exercises are prescribed or surgical procedures are undertaken to correct muscle imbalance, to prevent deformity due to contractures and fixation of joints in distorted positions, or to correct congenital subluxation (incomplete dislocation) of the hips. Podiatrists may also be called upon to examine foot deformities, analyze gait patterns, and prescribe special shoes that will help to improve standing and walking balance.

As the child grows, many other medical procedures are used as needed: the prescription of muscle relaxants such as dantrolene sodium, Librium, and Valium to relieve spasticity, and anticonvulsants and sedatives (Dilantin, Mysoline, phenobarbital, etc.) to control seizures; eye surgery to correct strabismus and prevent amblyopia (dimness of vision) in one eye; exercises to improve eye muscle balance; ear surgery and hearing aids to improve hearing; tranquilizers to reduce hyperactivity and restlessness; medications such as L-dopa to relieve athetosis; and in extreme cases, brain surgery and, experimentally at least, implantation of a cerebellar stimulator to reduce seizures and hypertonicity. In addition, dentists experienced in treating disabled patients are frequently needed to treat tooth and gum disorders due to the limited diet of soft foods or to involuntary muscular activity that throw the teeth out of line. Orthodontia may also be required not only for health reasons but for improvement of speech and general appearance.

Rehabilitation Program. Since the many facets of the rehabilitation process, as well as the professions involved, are described in considerable detail elsewhere in this volume, this section will be limited to a brief summary. (See CHAPTER 8: THE SHELTERED WORKSHOP; CHAPTER 56: REHABILITATION FACILITIES AND SERVICES, B. Cerebral Palsy Centers.)

1. Physical therapy program: Evaluation of sitting, crawling, standing and walking; exercises for motor reeducation; gait training; instruction in use of special aids (canes, crutches, walker, wheelchair); practice in functional activities such as transfer from bed to chair, stair climbing, walking on different types of surfaces, and wheelchair management. Objectives: to develop strength, coordination, and balance, and to learn to use assistive devices.

2. Occupation therapy program: Focuses on the activities of daily living (ADL): self-feeding, bathing, toileting, dressing, and grooming. These activities require special training and the use of such aids as utensils with special handles, nonspill cups, and electric shaver with a hand strap. Other activities are writing, typing, arts and crafts, and basic cooking. Objective: to develop maximum independence in everyday life.

3. Recreational program: Indoor games (table games, darts, etc.); outdoor sports with adapted equipment; field trips; bowling league; wheelchair games; singing and other music groups; holiday parties; summer day camps; arrangements for "sleep-away" camp; Scout groups; social-recreational club for young adults; avocational program for the severely handicapped. Objectives: to provide opportunities for enjoyment, sociability, and new experiences.

4. Vocational program: Prevocational program in basic skills; vocational evaluation and counseling; personal adjustment and work training; sheltered workshop (transitional or long-term); selective placement in business or industry. Objective: to prepare for the performance of useful, paid work in sheltered setting or community.

5. Speech and hearing program: Evaluation of speech mechanism, speech patterns, and language ability; audiometer test and referral for hearing aid; speech therapy; training in nonverbal communication; development of verbal communication; auditory training. Objectives: to treat defective speech and hearing, and to develop communication skills.

6. Psychological program: Evaluation of intelligence level, personality development, and general aptitudes; assessment of trainability and educability; short-term counseling and therapy for emotional problems; identification of learning disabilities; participation in planning educational, social, and vocational program for individual clients; parent counseling. Objectives: to determine individual abilities and needs, and to provide counseling and psychotherapy.

7. Social service program: Application of a casework approach in

exploring the home environment, family attitudes, and the patient's interpersonal relationships; periodic interviews with parents to enlist their cooperation in meeting the client's needs; parent discussion groups; arranging for the use of community resources (other social agencies, camps, government assistance, homemaker service, residential placement). Objectives: to encourage family involvement, and to solve personal and practical problems.

8. Educational and training program: Developmental, or day care, program starting on an infant or nursery school level; school readiness program; special education classes in reading and other basic subjects for the mentally retarded and learning-disabled; instruction for older children in selected subjects such as social studies, music, art, and typing; instruction for teen-agers and adults in homemaking skills, sex education, current events, etc. Objectives: to develop intellectual, social, and self-care skills, and to remedy learning disorders.

9. Other activities and programs: Cerebral palsy centers frequently offer a variety of other services which contribute directly or indirectly to the rehabilitation process. These include a home service program for the homebound; training of students for special education and rehabilitation fields; client advocacy and consumer groups; and participation in research projects concerned with diagnostic and treatment techniques, new aids and devices, etc.

Research

An active research program is being carried out in all major areas: primary prevention such as prevention of prematurity; early detection through tests and other diagnostic techniques; medical treatments and rehabilitation procedures; and new biomechanical and bioengineering devices. Projects are funded by the United Cerebral Palsy (UCP) Research and Educational Foundation and other voluntary agencies (National Association for Retarded Citizens, National Foundation, National Easter Seal Society for Crippled Children and Adults, and others); and by government grants from the National Institute of Neurological and Communication Disorders and Stroke, and other agencies.

The UCP Research and Educational Foundation has expended over $14 million in grants since it was established in 1955. Its projects have helped in the development of a vaccine to immunize children against rubella; an electronic amplifier for the improvement of defective speech; nerve banks which make possible the regrowth of damaged nerves in the arm or leg; an electronic monitoring system that records heart rate in relation to uterine contractions and therefore permits the detection of fetal stress so that preventive measures may be undertaken; amelioration of brain damage due to anoxia, through infusion of carbohydrates in newborn babies who fail to breathe; the widely used Illinois Test of Psycholinguistic Ability; identification of the Lesch-Nyhan syndrome before birth; and tests of drugs for the alleviation of athetoid cerebral palsy.

Current research is being conducted in such areas as prevention of the Lesch-Nyhan syndrome; determination of the exact causes of onset of labor in order to develop agents which will prevent prematurity; studies of the effect of lead in the environment on the developing nervous system; investigation of cytomegaloviruses, which may account each year for over 3,000 cases of brain damage, including cerebral palsy; and many projects directed toward the prevention of cerebral palsy in newborn babies, such as a study of the causes, prevention, and treatment of jaundice, and the measurement of the effect of amino acid imbalance on the developing brain. A number of projects are also being devoted to improving the functioning of children and adults through the use of sensory feedback techniques, administration of L-dopa to athetoid patients, and the application of biomedical technology to the development of equipment that will improve the overall functioning of persons with cerebral palsy (in the areas of communication, learning, ambulation, working, and more independent living).

A recent United Cerebral Palsy film, *Something Different*, depicts a number of promising research projects. In one sequence a biofeedback device developed at the Krusen Center for Research and Engineering in Philadelphia is used in training a severely affected child to hold her head up. The device is contained in a helmet worn by the child, and each time she lifts her head even slight-

This cerebral palsied child is being trained to hold her head up; the biofeedback device attached to the helmet activates the toy train when her head is raised. (United Cerebral Palsy Associations, Inc.)

ly, a TV picture switches on or a toy train moves. In a second sequence a child at the Kennedy Memorial Hospital is shown using a "Magic Light Pen" devised by a Massachusetts Institute of Technology engineer. The object is to develop eye-hand coordination and motor control by following a maze: if the pen strays from the track, a light goes on and a sound is heard. Another sequence is based on a pilot project carried out by Robert M. Goldenson and Milton V. Kline, Director of the Institute for Research in Hypnosis, in which hypnotic relaxation was successfully used as a means of improving virtually unintelligible speech in cerebral palsied patients. (See CHAPTER 55: ILLUSTRATIVE CASES, C. Sensory Feedback Therapy.)

Organizations

The basic organization in this field is United Cerebral Palsy Associations, Inc. (66 East 34th Street, New York, NY 10016), a federation of more than 300 self-governing state and local groups devoted to treatment, care, educational and vocational services, and an overall, long-range attack on the entire problem. The UCP Research and Educational Foundation, which fosters and finances research and professional training, is part of the national organization. The Foundation publishes research reports, and UCPA publishes a monthly newsletter, *Word from Washington*, and a quarterly report, *UCP Crusader*. The American Academy for Cerebral Palsy and Developmental Medicine, in Washington, D.C., is the professional organization in the field, representing nineteen different specialties; it is devoted to evaluation of treatment methods, presentation of awards, and allotment of research grants. Other important groups concerned with cerebral palsy are the Easter Seal Society, the Association for the Aid of Crippled Children, and a number of government agencies, including the Office of Child Development, the National Institutes of Health, the Office of Vocational Rehabilitation, and the Bureau of Education for the Handicapped.

SELECTED REFERENCES

A Brief List of Publications in Print on Cerebral Palsy, National Easter Seal Society, January 1976.

Denhoff, Eric, *Cerebral Palsy: The Preschool Years—Diagnosis, Treatment, and Planning,* Charles C. Thomas, Springfield, Illinois, 1967.

Finnie, Nancie R., *Handling the Young Cerebral Palsied Child at Home,* E. P. Dutton, New York, 1970.

Gillette, Harriet E., *Systems of Therapy in Cerebral Palsy,* Charles C. Thomas, Springfield, Illinois, 1969.

Heaton, Edythe L., *Skills in Living . . . Toward a Richer Tomorrow for Teenagers and Adults with Cerebral Palsy,* United Cerebral Palsy Associations, 1975.

Helsel, Elsie D., and Earl C. Graham, *Tomorrow Is Today* (booklet on long-term care), United Cerebral Palsy Associations.

Hoffer, M. Mark, *Basic Considerations and Classifications of the Cerebral Palsied,* Rancho Los Amigos Hospital, Downey, California.

Hoffer, M. Mark, et al., "New Concepts of Orthotics for Cerebral Palsy," *Clinical Orthopaedics and Related Research,* July–August 1974.

Keats, Sidney, *Cerebral Palsy,* Charles C. Thomas, Springfield, Illinois, 1965.

Models of Service for the Multi-Handicapped Adult, United Cerebral Palsy of New York City, 12 E. 23d Street, New York, NY 10010, 1974.

Naruse, Gosaku, "Psychological Treatment of Motor Difficulty of the Cerebral Palsied Child," *Journal of Psychological Rehabilitation,* Kyushu University, Japan, 1974.

Nieburgs, Tamara, Robert Sigman, Robert M. Goldenson, Herbert Nieberg, and Milton V. Kline, *Hypnotic Approaches to Neuromuscular Impairment: Speech Rehabilitation of the Cerebral Palsied,* Institute for Research in Hypnosis, New York, NY 10023, 1977.

Phelps, Winthrop M., *The Cerebral Palsied Child,* Simon & Schuster, New York, 1958.

Research Report, United Cerebral Palsy Research and Education Foundation, 66 E. 34th Street, New York, NY 10016, March 1974.

Scherzer, Alfred L., "Early Diagnosis, Management, and Treatment of Cerebral Palsy," *Rehabilitation Literature,* July 1974.

The Second Milestone: A Conference on Life Enrichment Needs of Persons with Multiple Handicaps Who Are Socially and Culturally Deprived, United Cerebral Palsy Associations.

Wolf, James M., *The Results of Treatment in Cerebral Palsy,* Charles C. Thomas, Springfield, Illinois, 1969.

Wolf, James M., and R. M. Anderson, *The Multihandicapped Child,* Charles C. Thomas, Springfield, Illinois, 1969.

Wooldridge, C. P., et al., *Bioengineering in the Management of the Cerebral Palsied Child: Biofeedback Training,* Ontario Crippled Children's Centre, 350 Rumsey Road, Toronto, 1975.

27

Cystic Fibrosis

RUTH W. ANDERSON, M.S.W., Consultant, Regional
Cystic Fibrosis Center, and Clinical Social Worker,
Department of Behavioral Sciences, Children's
Orthopedic Hospital and Medical Center, Seattle

Reviewed by the Cystic Fibrosis Foundation

Cystic fibrosis (abbreviated CF; also known as mucoviscidosis
and pancreatic fibrosis) is a generalized disorder affecting the exocrine (outward-secreting) glands which produce mucus, saliva, and
sweat. These substances are abnormal in cystic fibrosis patients—
particularly the mucus, which is abnormally thick and sticky. This
viscid mucus disturbs primarily the respiratory and digestive systems. The unusual mucous secretions interfere with the flow of
digestive enzymes produced in the pancreas. As a result, food is not
completely digested. The viscid mucus also accumulates in and
plugs the small air passages in the lungs. This leads to pooling of
secretions, repeated bacterial infection, and progressive damage to
the lungs, resulting in impaired pulmonary functioning.

Incidence and Etiology

Cystic fibrosis occurs in approximately 1 in 1,600 live births,
which results in approximately 2,000 new cases annually in the
United States. CF is the most serious disease affecting the lungs of
American Caucasian children. In the United States, an estimated
30,000 children currently suffer from the disorder.

Cystic fibrosis is thought to be due to an inborn error of metabolism. The basic biochemical defect is caused by the inheritance of
two CF genes, and is not yet understood. The theory of genetic
transmission of CF derives from principles of simple Mendelian
recessive inheritance. When the CF gene is present in both parents, there is a 2 in 4 chance, with the birth of each baby, that the

child will not have cystic fibrosis, but will be a carrier; a 1 in 4 chance that the child will have cystic fibrosis; and a 1 in 4 chance that the child will not have the disease and will not be a carrier. It is estimated that 1 in 20 of the general population is a carrier of the CF gene. The probability of two carriers marrying is 1 in 400.

Preventive Measures

There is no test by which the carriers of one CF gene can be identified before they produce a child with cystic fibrosis. After the diagnosis has been made in a child, genetic counseling for the parents can provide them with statistical probabilities of recurrence of the disease in future offspring, and they can use this information to decide whether to attempt future pregnancies.

Current research is focused on determining the basic biochemical abnormality produced by the CF gene. An understanding of the nature of CF's inborn error of metabolism will help scientists develop a prenatal diagnostic procedure, as well as a screening tool and a carrier test for newborns.

Symptoms, Diagnosis, and Course

Early indicators of cystic fibrosis are sometimes confused with other conditions because of similar pulmonary symptoms or digestive manifestations. Diagnosis is currently made earlier and in milder cases because of increased awareness of the disease itself by pediatricians and other physicians who care for children. Gastrointestinal symptoms include persistent, bulky bowel movements and a failure to grow or gain weight despite a large appetite. The signs of pulmonary involvement include repeated episodes of wheezing, persistent cough with excessive amounts of mucus, and recurrent respiratory infections. Other signs are a salty taste to skin and nasal polyps. The diagnosis of cystic fibrosis is aided by a finding of elevated sodium and chloride levels in the sweat.

The effects of the disease vary—for instance, some individuals with CF do not have the digestive complications. The general condition of a cystic fibrosis patient is usually determined by the pulmonary involvement. The typical patient experiences increased disability in correlation with progressive lung impairment. In the severe cases, chronic respiratory insufficiency gradually results in a downward spiral, the extreme being cardiac failure and death.

Treatment

There is no cure for cystic fibrosis. However, treatments have been developed which, especially in the past decade, have lengthened and improved the lives of CF-affected individuals.

Medical Therapy. Intestinal problems are usually managed by vitamin supplementation and pancreatic enzyme replacement. A special diet is not usually recommended. However, foods with high fat content may not be well tolerated. The primary thrust of medical therapy concerns the lung complications. Treatment is directed toward removing the viscous mucus from airways by bronchial (postural) drainage and aerosol therapy. Antibiotics are used to combat the frequent pulmonary infections. Treatment is costly and time-consuming. Crippled Children's Services (CCS) vary from state to state, but help cover medical costs for those who are financially eligible. Except in eight states, CCS is limited to patients under age twenty-one. National health insurance appears to be the most viable solution for underwriting the cost of medical management of cystic fibrosis, particularly for the young adult.

The Cystic Fibrosis Foundation helps to support a national network of 120 Cystic Fibrosis Centers, which specialize in the diagnosis and comprehensive treatment of children, teen-agers, and young adults with CF. For information about locations of these CF Centers, contact local chapters of the CF Foundation or the organization's national headquarters (see below).

Psychosocial Problems. The CF Foundation is currently focusing more attention on the psychosocial issues of CF. The diagnosis of CF has a profound effect on the patient's sense of self, relationships within the family and the community, and expectations of others. These problem areas may vary according to age at the time of diagnosis, prediagnostic history, ordinal rank in the family, and the sex and status of siblings, that is, whether there are other CF children in the family, etc. Likewise, healthy siblings may be confronted with psychosocial problems and may develop coping processes which may be maladaptive to personality development.

The anxiety that parents experience may be increased by the possibility of the disorder occurring in subsequent offspring. They may be further strained by the unremitting medical costs (averaging $5,000 per year, excluding hospital admissions or catastrophic complications), the demands on their time for attending to aerosol therapy and postural drainage (which may be required two to three times a day), intermittent crises with acute illness, and the possible fear that they are losing the struggle. Patients or families may need the kind of comprehensive care that includes the services of a mental health professional. (Such comprehensive care is the hallmark of CF Centers.) If the needs of the total family are overlooked, members may experience emotional isolation, and the parents, as well as the patients, may be ill-prepared for the continuing challenge of psychosocial development through adolescence and adulthood.

Rehabilitative Considerations

The use of the term "rehabilitation" is imprecise for most individuals with CF, since their life experience requires a sequence of specialized adaptations rather than a reintegration during adulthood. The problems posed by their physical condition, which might be minimal or moderately to severely compromised, are compounded by the complexity of the disease, making it difficult to predict, hence plan, employment opportunities, vocational training, or pursuit of educational goals. The individual's receptiveness to vocational counseling will also vary to some degree according to the general level of maturity, apart from the consequences of CF.

As with all other individuals who have a handicap or disabling disease, CF patients vary in their realistic appraisal of the effect that the disease has on their capacity to function. Furthermore, it is difficult, at times impossible, for the physician to offer a reliable prognosis for use in long-range planning.

In response to the increased life expectancy for more CF patients, a Young Adult Committee has been formed by the Cystic Fibrosis Foundation. Collaboration of this committee with the Social and Rehabilitation Service of the U.S. Department of Health, Education and Welfare has produced a study of problems confronting young adults with cystic fibrosis. Its findings have revealed broad areas of need which have not been covered under state and federal programs for persons with disabling conditions.

The study confirmed the extreme difficulty that CF patients encounter in their effort to assume financial responsibility for their medical care. The patient who has been covered under the family's medical insurance plan is advised to try to convert this to a personal policy before the age of nineteen. It may be that application for medical insurance would be rejected at a later date due to a "preexisting condition" clause, though the family's policy provides coverage to age twenty-one or twenty-two. At the present time, the person with CF may be able to obtain coverage through a group medical plan, subsequent to employment. This possibility weighs heavily in the choice of a vocation, if such a decision involves further training or education. In some cases, when the individual is accepted for State Division of Vocational Rehabilitation programs, drugs and necessary equipment may be provided until the trainee or student attains competitive employment.

Research

Research continues to focus on isolating the basic biochemical abnormality of cystic fibrosis and on the development of more effective treatment. Thus far, the disease cannot be observed or induced in animals. The complexity of CF is such that significant therapeutic findings might be derived from research being conducted in the areas of respiratory and gastrointestinal diseases. Studies bearing on prevention are primarily being directed toward the development of a carrier test, prenatal detection, and newborn screening.

Recently, attention has begun to center on the psychosocial implications of CF, as evidenced by the following publications: *Psychosocial Aspects of Cystic Fibrosis: A Model for Chronic Lung Disease,* edited by Patterson, Denning, and Kutscher, Columbia University Press, New York, 1973; and "Psychosocial Aspects of Cystic Fibrosis: A Review of the Literature," *American Journal of Diseases of Children,* Gayton and Friedman, vol. 126, December 1973. Psychosocial aspects of CF were also explored at the 1976 international conference, "Cystic Fibrosis: Projections into the Future."

The Foundation and Other Organizations

The Cystic Fibrosis Foundation, incorporated in 1955, is a national voluntary health organization with 100 chapters throughout the United States. The funds raised by the Foundation and its chapters help to subsidize programs of clinical services, teaching, and research at Cystic Fibrosis and Pediatric Pulmonary Centers, as well as research projects at these and other institutions. Federal funds for research have been available since 1958 through the U.S. Public Health Service, National Institutes of Health. The Cystic Fibrosis Foundation also publishes and distributes informational materials prepared especially for parents of newly diagnosed patients and for young CF adults, as well as for scientists, physicians, and other members of the health care team. Pamphlets and current information are available by request from the offices of local chapters or from the national office (3379 Peachtree Road N.E., Atlanta, GA 30326).

SELECTED REFERENCES

Boyle, I. R., S. Sack, F. Millican, and P. A. di Sant'Agnese, "Emotional Adjustment in Adolescents and Young Adults with Cystic Fibrosis," in J. A. Mangos and R. C. Talamo, eds., *Fundamental Problems of Cystic Fibrosis and Related Diseases*, Symposia Specialists, Miami, 1973.

Cystic Fibrosis Foundation, *Educational and Vocational Counseling for Young Adults with Cystic Fibrosis; Fact Sheet on Vocational Rehabilitation Services; How Do I Get a Job?; Living with Cystic Fibrosis: A Guide for the Young Adult; Problems in Reproductive Physiology and Anatomy in Young Adults with Cystic Fibrosis; Problems in Sweat Testing; Psychosocial Aspects of Heterozygote Detection in Cystic Fibrosis; Research: Top Priority of the Cystic Fibrosis Foundation; Vocational Rehabilitation for Young Adults with Cystic Fibrosis.*

Matthews, L. W., B. C. Hilman, and P. Nathan, *Vocational and Life Adjustment Problems of Young Adults with Cystic Fibrosis*, Cystic Fibrosis Foundation, 1969.

28

The Deaf-Blind

JEROME R. DUNHAM, Ph.D.

When double disabilities occur, the compounding may bring unexpected consequences. For instance, the person who is both epileptic and arthritic may experience greatly exacerbated pains in joints after a grand mal seizure; or a double-hand-amputee blind veteran may have to undergo specialized surgery in order to use the two arm bones (radius and ulna) as a pincer to receive useful tactile sensations from his white cane. In the case of the double disability of deafness and blindness, the two primary sensory inputs are lacking. This leads to severe education and communication problems. The deaf child learns much through imitation. The blind child is educated primarily through verbal communication from others. The deaf-blind child lives in a world of vibrations, air currents, temperature changes, smells, and a great many tactile sensations and sensations from within the digestive system, muscles, joints, etc.

For the congenitally deaf it is difficult to understand language, and for the congenitally blind it is not simple to master the physical and social environment. The combination of the two defects leaves the child physically and socially isolated from the environment.

Deaf-blind adults probably have received the most sophisticated training available. They may be able to move about familiar environments with a cane or by means of other techniques; they may have a family and hold down a job in private employment. But they may still be confronted with a barrier when coming into contact with the general public. In fact, some people may be repelled by the deaf-blind person's "differentness." Because of the complex problems, universal, successful education of deaf-blind persons has been slow in coming. The phenomenon of Helen Keller seems a paradox since so many people know of her and, unlike their behavior toward other deaf-blind persons, people used to crowd around her in order to touch her sleeve, or stand quietly in her presence with almost religious awe.

Several factors are usually considered when discussing the deaf-blind. First, the deaf-blind are not usually entirely deaf or entirely blind; the usual definition of deaf-blindness is that the person has such auditory and visual impairment as to be unable to communicate or be educated in the usual fashion. Second, the person who is born blind and becomes deaf later in life has a different set of problems from one who is born deaf and becomes blind later. The age of onset of either disability and the severity of the losses modify the disabled person's experience—along with the usual factors of family understanding, neighborhood acceptance, educational opportunities, health, and cultural differences.

Since the number of deaf-blind persons is relatively few, usually only one in a given average community, they are ordinarily isolated from each other; only through governmental intervention are they brought together for a sharing of experiences.

The first deaf-blind person in the United States to come to general attention was Laura Bridgman (1829–1889), who was educated in the Perkins Institute for the Blind. Because of publicity about her through *American Notes* by Charles Dickens, Helen Keller's family discovered the Perkins School. Other schools for the blind, as well as sheltered workshops, occasionally worked with deaf-blind persons, and in the 1940s and 1950s several schools for the blind made a concerted attempt to offer an enriched program to several deaf-blind students. However, it was not until after the 1963–1965 rubella (German measles) epidemic that federal legislation concentrated on the problems of deaf-blind education. In 1968, Title VI of the Elementary and Secondary Education Act was amended by Public Law 90-247, Part C, to establish model centers for deaf-blind children through the Division of Educational Services in the Bureau of Education of the Handicapped of the U.S. Department of Health, Education and Welfare.

One year later, Congress appropriated funds, under P.L. 91-230, to establish ten regional centers for deaf-blind children. These centers, which cover the United States and its territories, surveyed the number of children with combined visual and auditory impairment, located facilities and teachers, organized parents, and began the difficult task of systematically trying to impinge on the awareness of these children. By the use of hearing aids, closed-circuit television, bright lights, loud sounds, behavior modification techniques, and much affection, dedicated teachers with a liberal number of assistants have worked daily to make small changes in the ability of these children to take care of themselves.

Another important step forward was taken when the Helen Keller National Center for Deaf-Blind Youths and Adults was established by an amendment to the Rehabilitation Act of 1973. The Center first operated by using the Industrial Home for the Blind in Brooklyn, and their facilities and staff. In 1974 ground was broken for the Center's own facility located at 111 Middle Neck Road, Sands Point, NY 11050.

Identification of deaf-blind persons in the United States is a major problem. The American Foundation for the Blind tried for years to set up an adequate registry but was frustrated in its attempts by the number of deaf-blind individuals who were hidden away by their families. The Helen Keller National Center for Deaf-Blind Youths and Adults estimates that the number of identified deaf-blind children is between 6,000 and 7,500; the number of identified deaf-blind adults is 5,000, with another 5,000 estimated but not identified. The numbers may not be large in this disability group, but the problems are great and the breakthroughs spectacular. Besides Helen Keller, Richard Kinney, Executive Director of the Hadley School for the Blind in Winnetka, Illinois, and Robert J. Smithdas, Litt.D., Director of Community Education for the Helen Keller Center, are individuals who dramatically demonstrate how much well-trained deaf-blind persons can accomplish.

Although many cases of deaf-blindness can be traced back to the mother having rubella during the first trimester of pregnancy, other conditions can result in this condition. Retinitis pigmentosa is a hereditary disorder that makes it particularly important for deaf children to have a retinal examination before they make vocational choices, since if they prepare for employment that requires vision and have the first signs of retinitis pigmentosa, they may have to change or repeat vocational training for other fields. It is, of course, mandatory for blind persons to have audiological examinations during the course of rehabilitation, whether they are known to have retinitis pigmentosa or not, because of the importance of hearing in the blind person's adjustment. In some cases accidents, systemic diseases, and infections can also result in both visual and auditory impairment.

It is important for trained counselors to work with the parents of deaf-blind children. The parents need not only reassurance but detailed information so that they can stimulate and guide their child's experiences. One phenomenon that occasionally occurs with rubella children is tactile defensiveness. For several months of pregnancy the mother may have been looking forward to holding and petting her newborn child, only to discover after birth that the slightest touch brings on automatic arching of the back and screaming. After weeks or months of prolonged screaming the mother may well feel rejected, and without patient counseling would not have the slightest idea of how to gradually habituate the child to being touched and held.

Communication is a primary problem with deaf-blind children and adults. In educational circles there has been some perplexity about the best method to use. It now appears that total communication is the preferred route. This includes sign language when the child has enough vision to see signs; the Tadoma method, in which the deaf-blind person places the fingers on the speaker's lips with the thumb on the speaker's throat in order to lip-read; finger spelling where the teacher spells each word and the child feels with both hands; tracing out a print letter by the teacher on the palm of the student's hand or some other part of the body; Braille, of course; or, if there is enough vision, using large print.

After communication the next greatest problem is mobility. The obvious problems of not seeing and hearing cues in the environment are made more difficult by problems of balance and difficulty in walking a straight line. Specially trained mobility instructors can teach the deaf-blind person how to explore the environment, and can provide instruction in the systematic use of a white cane to detect obstacles and drop-offs. Also helpful for mobility are preprinted cards that identify the individual as a deaf-blind person and indicate wishes or questions. The cards may indicate, for example, that the deaf-blind person wishes to board a particular bus or be directed to a specific destination. Students and travelers, however, may find it preferable to use an interpreter-companion both to guide them and to help them communicate with others.

It is too early to tell how far deaf-blind persons can go in their training and too soon to predict the percentage of deaf-blind persons who can strive for more than sheltered workshop employment, but it seems likely that concentrating deaf-blind persons in the National Center with its trained staff, plus the experience accrued from the teaching of many thousands of rubella children, will increase the likelihood of success in deaf-blind rehabilitation.

Deaf-blind persons use a number of devices that can be tactually identified, such as Braille watches, rulers, and thermometers, which are also used by the hearing blind. However, there are certain devices that are specifically designed for deaf-blind persons, such as a pocket vibrator box that is triggered by the doorbell; and the Tellatouch machine, which has an alphabetically arranged typewriter keyboard in front and a Braille cell with tiny pins in back, so that communication is accomplished by having the sighted person press down on a key which causes the appropriate Braille symbol to be pushed against the finger of the deaf-blind person.

There are a number of periodicals in Braille. However, the one Braille magazine specifically for this population, and free to all deaf-blind persons, is *The Hotline* (Twin Vision, 18440 Topham Street, Tarzana, CA 91356). This magazine helps the deaf-blind keep up with news events. The primary journal for those working in the field of deaf-blindness is *The Center News*, published by the Helen Keller National Center for Deaf-Blind Youths and Adults.

SELECTED REFERENCES

Kinney, Richard, *Independent Living without Sight and Hearing*, Hadley School for the Blind, Winnetka, IL 60093, 1972.

Smithdas, Robert, *Life in My Fingertips*, Doubleday, New York, 1969.

A complete bibliography of the literature on the deaf-blind can be obtained from the Helen Keller National Center for Deaf-Blind Youths and Adults, 111 Middle Neck Road, Sands Point, NY 11050.

29

Diabetes Mellitus

MAX ELLENBERG, M.D., Clinical Professor of Medicine,
Mount Sinai School of Medicine, and Attending
Physician for Diabetes, Mount Sinai Hospital, New York

Diabetes mellitus is a disease characterized by abnormalities of the endocrine secretion of the pancreas, resulting in disordered metabolism of carbohydrate, fat, and protein and, in time, structural abnormalities in a variety of tissues. The weight of current evidence indicates that a deficiency in insulin secretion by the pancreas is the primary pathogenic event, leading in mild cases to inadequate disposal of ingested glucose and in severe instances to overproduction of glucose, dissolution of body fat, and dissipation of protein reserves. In addition, abnormalities of glucagon secretion have been suggested as contributing to the metabolic disturbance.

Since the discovery of insulin by F. B. Banting and C. H. Best in 1921, the outlook for diabetics has much improved. Death from diabetic coma has become uncommon. Infections, including tuberculosis, have been sharply reduced. Pregnancy, formerly rare in diabetic females, is now so commonplace that most large hospitals find it necessary to maintain a diabetic pregnancy clinic. The lifespan of diabetics has been prolonged significantly, and most are now able to lead relatively normal existences as contributing members of the community. However, as diabetics live longer, it has become apparent that they are increasingly at risk for the development of severe complications.

Prevalence and Significance

Diabetes mellitus is a major health problem in the United States, annually draining the economy of over $5 billion in health care, disability costs, and lost wages. Some 10 million Americans have diabetes; 600,000 people are newly diagnosed each year; both the prevalence and diagnosis of diabetes have increased over 50 percent in the last ten years; as many as 300,000 deaths a year are now attributed to diabetes, making it the third-ranking cause of death, behind cardiovascular disease and cancer; and women are 50 percent more likely to have diabetes than men. Diabetes is the leading cause of new cases of blindness, and a major cause of heart attack, stroke, kidney disease, gangrene, and nerve damage. Diabetic nephropathy, a specific pathological involvement of the kidneys, has become the primary cause of death among juvenile diabetics; and neuropathic complications abound, including severe painful peripheral neuropathy, foot ulcerations, and a remarkably high incidence of impotence in the diabetic male. Pregnancy, although far more frequent and much more successful than in the preinsulin era, still carries with it a higher fatality rate for the offspring and a significantly higher incidence of congenital abnormalities.

Types

Although diabetes is characteristically divided into two types, juvenile and adult-maturity-onset, it would be more correct to characterize the two types as insulin-dependent and insulin-independent. The insulin-dependent type most frequently occurs in, but is not limited to, the juvenile; this group comprises between 5 and 10 percent of all diabetics. It is explosive in onset with sudden and dramatic manifestations of the classical symptoms of diabetes, namely polyuria, polydipsia, polyphagia, nocturia, rapid weight loss, and a ready tendency to develop diabetic ketoacidosis leading to coma. These patients are dependent upon insulin for survival. They are ketosis-prone, and the condition is often difficult to control. Shortly after onset and with proper therapy, they may go into the "honeymoon" phase, during which time their pancreas has apparently recovered the ability to secrete insulin and the patients may not require any insulin for three to six months. During this interval parents often doubt the original diagnosis and become very hopeful for complete recovery. Unfortunately, the diabetes always returns in force. In these patients the ability of the pancreas to secrete insulin progressively decreases, and eventually is completely lost. Another differentiating characteristic of this group is the lack of responsiveness to oral diabetic medications.

As indicated, most such patients are juveniles, but this type of diabetes does occur in the adult; actually some 10 percent of diabetic coma occurs in the adult. This group has a higher tendency to develop microangiopathy, specifically retinopathy, which may lead to blindness, and nephropathy, which may lead to kidney failure. These correlate best with the duration of diabetes. Early manifestations usually become evident after thirteen to fifteen years of diabetes and increase from then on both in frequency and severity.

The adult-maturity-onset type generally occurs in the older patients. They are insulin-independent from the point of view of the life-saving effects of insulin, but actually many do require insulin for better control. An outstanding characteristic is obesity, which applies to 80–85 percent of these patients. They are non-ketosis-prone, and the vast majority of cases can be controlled by dietary measures alone. Another feature is the tendency to develop complications. It has been estimated that one-third of all adult-maturity-onset diabetic patients are not diagnosed until a complication appears, such as acute coronary thrombosis, gangrene, or severe neuropathy.

Diagnosis

Diagnosis of diabetes is suggested by the symptoms of polyuria, polydipsia, polyphagia, and weight loss, and is made by finding abnormalities in carbohydrate metabolism. If the fasting blood sugar is clearly abnormal, then the diagnosis of diabetes is established. However, when there is doubt, a glucose tolerance test should be performed. The diagnosis of diabetes has a profound effect on the entire future of the patient from a medical and dietary point of view as well as an influence on applications for insurance and employment, and therefore if the glucose tolerance test is equivocal the diagnosis should not be made.

Hereditary and Acquired Factors

While heredity plays a major role in determining susceptibility to the development of diabetes, phenotypic expression is dependent on acquired factors as well, the most important of which is obesity. As stated above, a high percentage of adult-maturity-onset diabetics are obese, and the incidence of diabetes in these subjects is substantially greater than in the general population.

Some evidence suggests that acquired factors may result in diabetes by producing a diminution in insulin secretion. Several recent studies suggest that while certain viral infections do not produce clinical pancreatitis or insulinitis, they might nevertheless damage the islets of Langerhans, with subsequent impairment of insulin secretion.

Other environmental factors apparently influence the occurrence of diabetes as well. For example, the geographical transplantation of large groups of people from rural to urban areas is often attended by a sharp increase in the occurrence of diabetes. Factors of relative physical inactivity and changes in diet, including ingestion of more fats and sugar, have all been implicated.

Treatment

Treatment of diabetes includes a program of diet, exercise, and insulin or oral hypoglycemic agents as indicated. The fundamental approach in all of diabetes is diet, on which all other modalities are based. In general, the diabetic diet has increasingly approached the average daily diet in the United States with an ever-increasing amount of carbohydrates being permitted. However, the sharp restriction of sugar remains in effect.

In the juvenile type, insulin is essential to sustain life and must be taken daily. Often, to obtain greater stability and to avoid excesses in the range of blood sugar levels and thus prevent hypoglycemic episodes, the injections are taken twice daily. The insulin used is usually intermediate in activity, and to it may be added the short-acting form of insulin. In the adult, control of obesity is paramount. The majority of these overweight patients can often be completely controlled by achieving normal weight and maintaining an appropriate diet; in fact, in some instances the abnormal glucose tolerance test may even revert to normal. For those who cannot be controlled on diet alone, oral hypoglycemic agents are available, and these may help attain the desired result. The remainder require insulin. It should be emphasized that the juvenile, insulin-dependent type of diabetes does not respond to oral agents and hence these are contraindicated.

There is an ongoing controversy as to the effect of good control on the development, frequency, severity, and progression of complications. However, there is little argument as to the beneficial effects of control on the general state of the physical, mental, and emotional health of the diabetic.

Chronic Complications

It is important to appreciate the amazingly wide spectrum of clinical manifestations covered by the various complications of diabetes. There is virtually no organ or organ system in the body that cannot be involved. The chronic complications are classified as macrovascular disease, diabetic microangiopathy, and diabetic neuropathy.

Macrovascular Disease. Large-vessel disease in diabetes is characterized by: (1) increased frequency; (2) earlier onset; (3) accelerated progression; (4) more severe and extensive involvement; and (5) loss of sex protection, that is, the increased frequency of atherosclerotic involvement in the male as compared with the female does not obtain in diabetes, where both are at equal risk for these complications. Another very significant generalization concerns the relationship of the large-vessel disease to carbohydrate metabolism. Specifically, the carbohydrate metabolic abnormality may be minimal, and frequently the atherosclerotic complication is the initial clinical manifestation of the diabetes.

Approximately three-fourths of all cerebral vascular accidents are related to diabetes. Other than the increased frequency and the factors already alluded to that characterize the diabetic state, there is no special difference in the onset, course, or management of cerebrovascular involvement in diabetes. In view of the frequency, the numbers of patients who require rehabilitation in speech, physical activity, etc., are enormous.

About 50 percent of all heart attacks are related to abnormal carbohydrate metabolism. In all decades of life, regardless of sex, coronary occlusion is far more frequent in the diabetic than non-diabetic patient. The therapy in acute myocardial infarction is the same as in nondiabetics except that one must be especially careful to avoid hypoglycemia during treatment in the acute stage. The long-term prognosis in coronary artery occlusive disease is definitely worse in diabetics than nondiabetics.

The frequency, importance, and severity of peripheral vascular involvement in diabetes is underscored by the fact that out of every six amputations for gangrene, five are performed on diabetics. The frequency of gangrene in its various forms is conditioned by the following three factors.

1. Arteriosclerosis obliterans is a slow and insidious process usually accompanied by an attempt at the formation of collateral circulation. Intermittent claudication (painful lameness) is frequently an initial symptom.

2. Peripheral neuropathy is one of the most significant and characteristic features of "the diabetic foot," and accounts for the marked increase in gangrene. Because of impaired sensation, dry skin, and fissures, a minor trauma such as hot water, improper paring of corns, tight shoes, or a thread in a sock can result in major damage. Dry skin and fissures result from trophic changes secondary to autonomic nerve involvement.

3. Infection results from a combination of ischemia and neuropathy which makes the tissues more vulnerable and produces a poor response to therapy.

The recognition of the significance of peripheral neuropathy and infection on the course of gangrene has in great measure resulted in a diminution of the frequency of amputation. A concerted medical effort is frequently successful, especially since the introduction of antibiotics in those cases not resulting entirely from vascular insufficiency. When amputation is mandatory, the only decision is at what level, which is determined by the status of the circulation. This is then followed by the need for prosthesis and rehabilitation of the patient.

A major advance in therapy has been in the field of vascular surgery. Here, the newer knowledge of arteriography, the subsequent ability to pinpoint the site of the lesion or lesions, and the applications of vascular reconstruction, bypass, and thromboendarterectomy have proven of inestimable benefit. Nevertheless, these procedures in no way have any curative or decelerating effect on the basic problem of arteriosclerosis; and the indication for these procedures is considerably less in the diabetic by virtue of the fact that the runoff vessels are so frequently involved.

Microangiopathy. In the diabetic, retinopathy causes the greatest amount of permanent destruction as well as irreversible loss of vision. Proliferative retinopathy is associated with the greatest loss of vision in the diabetic patient since it leads to vitreous hemorrhage, retinal detachment, and secondary glaucoma.

The current phase of therapy for diabetic retinopathy is photocoagulation. This is accomplished through several different approaches involving various aspects of the laser beam. An on-going multicentered controlled study strongly suggests that photocoagulation may be of benefit in proliferative retinopathy.

For diabetic nephropathy no specific therapy is available at present, and symptomatic therapy is the mainstay of management. This includes control of hypertension, edema, and infection. Kidney transplant is a most satisfactory form of therapy, but in the absence of availability of a kidney, dialysis is beneficial.

Diabetic Neuropathy. Neuropathic involvement is significant in the diabetic due to its frequent occurrence, its involvement of virtually every system in the body, its appearance in so many different guises, and its mimicry of a multitude of disease states. The manifestations of diabetic neuropathy may be divided into two broad categories: somatic neuropathy and visceral neuropathy.

In somatic neuropathy, the most frequent presentation is peripheral neuropathy involving the nerves of the lower extremities, usually bilaterally symmetrical and predominantly sensory. There is no consistent relationship to the severity or duration of the diabetes. The outstanding symptoms are pain and paresthesias. A distinguishing characteristic of the pain is its nocturnal intensification, with relief by pacing the floor. The skin may be so sensitive that even the touch of pajamas or bedclothes cannot be tolerated. Paresthesias are usually described as coldness, numbness, tingling, or burning. Less common variants include foot-drop, amyotrophy, and mononeuropathies. Depression, irritability, and anorexia are often part of the clinical picture; lessening of these symptoms will often presage clearing of the neuritis.

Diabetic neuropathy is rarely thought of in terms of the upper extremities. It is important, therefore, to indicate that such involvement is common, has clinical significance, and is usually readily recognizable. The chief clinical manifestations may be categorized as atrophy, asthenia, sensory impairment, and radiculitis.

Although there is much variation in the objective findings, the most reliable and consistent sign of somatic neuropathy is the absence of knee or ankle jerks. Sensory findings, though commonly present, vary considerably and are unpredictable from patient to patient.

The symptoms and signs of visceral neuropathy have been referred to as "pseudotabes diabetica," since they mimic very closely the symptomatology of tabetic syphilis. This suggests that the site of the pathologic lesion is identical with tabes. The visceral involvement is of exceeding importance, since it results in the following syndromes that simulate many other disease entities.

1. The eyes. Extraocular muscle palsies are usually preceded by pain on the affected side, and are characterized by spontaneous resolution in six to twelve weeks. Pupillary reflex abnormalities, though common, rarely progress to the classical Argyll-Robertson pupil.

2. The gastrointestinal tract. Gastric neuropathy is characterized by delayed emptying of the stomach with marked retention. This may lead to poor diabetic control because of the unpredictable and irregular absorption of food. Diabetic enteropathy is customarily referred to as diabetic diarrhea; however, the former term empha-

sizes that the clinical symptomatology is attributable to dysfunction of the small intestine. The clinical picture is characterized by intermittent recurrent attacks of nocturnal fecal incontinence, a small-bowel deficiency pattern on x-ray, associated autonomic and peripheral neuropathy, and normal exocrine pancreatic function. Malabsorption has been described in diabetes with diarrhea. The necessity for proper diagnosis is underscored by the dramatic response of the malabsorption syndrome to gluten-free diet.

3. The genitourinary tract. Bladder involvement may progress to complete paralysis. Prompt recognition is urgent to avoid secondary infection which inevitably leads to ascending pyelonephritis and progressive renal impairment.

Impotence is remarkably frequent (50–60 percent) in the male diabetic patient. When the impotence is a neuropathic phenomenon, which is usually the case, the prognosis is poor. Frequently this is the presenting clinical symptom of diabetes. Prostheses may be surgically implanted in these cases. Retrograde ejaculation, which is a neuropathic feature, occurs more frequently than is realized, and is a cause of sterility and infertility.

4. Neuropathic arthropathy. The Charcot joint in diabetes is directly comparable to tabes in the extensive bone and joint destruction in the presence of an adequate blood supply, the remarkable freedom from pain, the absence of infection, and the presence of neuropathy. In diabetes, unlike tabes, the tarsal and ankle joints are most frequently involved. X-ray examination reveals extensive destruction and dissolution of the bones, unrelated to osteoporosis or osteomyelitis. This condition requires orthopedic treatment.

5. Neuropathic ulcer. This is usually painless, and occurs at a site of pressure, most often the head of a metatarsal bone. Since the lesion is neuropathic, there is usually an excellent blood supply. This lesion may attract the attention of the patient only because of the presence of a serous discharge on the sock.

6. The autonomic nervous system. The involvement of the autonomic nervous system in diabetes may be so extensive as to simulate the effects of a sympathectomy. Postural or orthostatic hypotension results from the presence of a dilated peripheral vascular bed which is unable to constrict, thus serving as a reservoir for a considerable proportion of the total blood volume. Further evidence of the lack of neural reflex is the absence of a compensatory tachycardia. Other evidences of autonomic nervous system involvement include anhidrosis, vasomotor instability, tachycardia, dependent edema, trophic skin disturbances, and reversal of the skin temperature gradient.

Some of the lesions of diabetic neuropathy recover spontaneously. Among these are the external ocular palsies, and the painful forms of peripheral neuropathy although recovery often takes six to eighteen months. Dilantin may be helpful in minimizing the need for addictive narcotic drugs. When conservative measures fail, the neurogenic bladder may be relieved dramatically by resection of the internal vesical sphincter. Diabetic gastropathy may be alleviated by bethanecol chloride. Diabetic diarrhea frequently responds to a broad-spectrum antibiotic. When the diarrhea is associated with malabsorption syndrome, there is a dramatic response to a gluten-free diet or corticosteroid administration. Charcot joints may be helped considerably by orthopedic devices that relieve weightbearing. Neuropathic ulcers may be treated by local surgery, including removal of the offending pressure-producing head of the underlying metatarsal bone. Postural hypotension is relieved by salt-retaining hormones and particularly by the application of an Air Force antigravity suit. General symptomatic measures, including warmth, good nutrition, relief of pain, and proper diabetic control, are indicated.

Psychological Aspects

The diagnosis of diabetes may be psychologically traumatic. Diagnosis is often followed by fear for the future and concern about the ability to hold a job, to perform routine domestic chores and child-rearing tasks, and to adjust to the normal demands of living. Tremendous apprehension occurs among parents of children with newly discovered diabetes. This is often a source of deep psychological upheaval during adolescence, and may be worsened by uncertainty of careers, marriage potential, and availability of basic opportunities. At this stage proper guidance and counseling is mandatory and often of great value. A simple yet thorough explanation of the facts as they exist will often allay the fear engendered by the unknown and the imagined.

Employment

The problem of employment in the diabetic centers chiefly on younger persons entering the labor market and on older diabetics seeking new jobs. In general, employed persons who become diabetic have no difficulty in retaining their positions. However, since diabetes is a chronic disease with potentially serious complications, there has been a great deal of reluctance to hire diabetics. Consequently diabetic applicants are placed at a disadvantage even though they may be fully capable of functioning in an appropriate job for many years. In fact, as a group, diabetics have work and absentee records comparing favorably with those of nondiabetics. The vast majority of jobs are suitable for diabetics; nevertheless, certain types are not. For example, diabetics should not fill positions where they will be risking their safety or that of others. They should not drive or fly for a living, nor should they work near heavy moving equipment or on ladders or scaffolding. Further, it is usually advisable that they not take situations which require frequent changes of shift or working hours that could interfere with diabetic management.

Insurance

Until fairly recently it was quite difficult and indeed at times impossible for diabetics to get insurance. This situation has significantly changed, so that now many companies are writing policies for diabetics. Today life insurance is increasingly available at reasonably satisfactory rates to most diabetics, especially those who are under good control, who have not had the disease for long, or who are not too advanced in years. Group insurance, of course, is the easiest way to get medical coverage, particularly for those who cannot obtain insurance otherwise. More recently individual health insurance has become available to diabetics, at least to some degree. As diabetes becomes better managed, advances in treatment continue, and the health and longevity of the diabetic becomes more assured, the outlook for ever-increasing insurance opportunities improves.

Recent Research Advances

The goal of diabetic therapy—normalization of the blood sugar—remains impossible at this time. An obvious solution would be to provide a source of insulin that simulates the normal pancreas, that is, a pancreatic transplant. This has been accomplished but remains a formidable surgical procedure, the availability of the organ is sharply limited, and above all there is the prospect of organ rejection. In the hope of avoiding rejection, the islets of the pancreas and the beta cells which manufacture the insulin have been isolated, grown in culture, and then injected into animals. However, tissue rejection is operative even for these microscopic elements. Thus, successful transplantation must await the ability to overcome tissue rejection. Efforts are now being made in the direction of an artificial pancreas, some of whose components have already reached the stage of completion.

An added incentive to mimic the sensitive homeostatic control of blood sugar is the increasing investigational evidence that suggests a link between control of the diabetes and the diabetic complications. Such information has been achieved through chemical, animal, and clinical studies.

A resurgence of the importance of the hormone glucagon—an anti-insulin factor—has followed the development of a method for measuring it. At present there is evidence to suggest that diabetes may even be a bihormonal disease. The recent discovery of another hormone, somatastatin, which affects insulin and glucagon, has opened new pathways of investigation.

In the area of heredity, the recent observation of differences in the types of histocompatibility antigens in juvenile and adult diabetes has indicated differences in transmission of these two types of diabetes. In addition, viral infections have been correlated with the occurrence of the juvenile type. This raises the exciting possibility of isolating the responsible viruses and developing a vaccine against them, immunizing susceptible youngsters, and thus preventing diabetes.

American Diabetes Association

It is important for diabetics, their family, doctors, and all others involved in their care to become fully familiar with the American Diabetes Association. This national association has headquarters in

New York City and 53 affiliates throughout the United States. Its interest in diabetes is manifested by a four-point program: patient education, professional education, public education, and research. To help attain these ends the Association sponsors many meetings and symposiums. Pamphlets are available and can be obtained by contacting the national organization headquarters at 1 West 48th Street in New York; those who live in other areas should contact their local affiliates. These pamphlets cover virtually every aspect of diabetes, including some of the latest trends in research. Most of them also include up-to-date information on various types of insurance availability and details of employment standards that are used by industry.

SELECTED REFERENCES

Barker, C. F., "Transplantation of the Islets of Langerhans and the Histocompatibility of Endocrine Tissue; Summary of the Twelfth Research Symposium," *Diabetes*, vol. 24, p. 766, 1975.

Ellenberg, M., "Diabetes: Current Status of an Evolving Disease," *New York State Journal of Medicine*, vol. 77, p. 62, January 1977.

Ellenberg, M., and H. Rifkin, *Diabetes Mellitus: Theory and Practice*, McGraw-Hill, New York, 1970.

Johnson, D. G., and P. W. Danan, "The Best Policy," *Diabetes Forecast*, vol. 30, p. 20, 1977.

Nerup, J., "HL-A Antigens and Diabetes Mellitus," *Lancet*, vol. 2, p. 864, 1974.

Tatersall, R. B., and S. S. Fajans, "A Difference between the Inheritance of Classical Juvenile-onset Diabetes and Maturity-onset Type Diabetes of Young People," *Diabetes*, vol. 24, p. 44, 1975.

30

Drug-Abuse Problems

RAE H. FARMER, M.Ed.Psych., Supervisor, Chemical
Dependency Program, Seattle Mental Health Institute

For many thousands of years, humans have used and abused a wide variety of mind-altering substances for a variety of reasons. Sometimes these reasons have social significance and their choice is culturally determined, as in the use of alcohol in Western society and hallucinogens in South America. More commonly, however, these substances are used for personal reasons, either to relieve feelings of anxiety imposed by internal or environmental pressures, or simply to induce a state of elevated mood or altered consciousness. Although use of opium, hashish, cocaine, alcohol, and some of the hallucinogens dates back into early historical times, it is only in quite recent years that the problem of drug misuse and abuse has aroused serious national and international concern. With the growing casual use of a wide range of drugs by an apparently increasingly youthful population, the whole area of drug abuse has become confused by myths, half-truths, and misinformation. Bewildered parents and other members of the public often feel frightened by the menace of drug abuse while, at the same time, prejudice and irrational attitudes toward the "addict" too often result in punitive measures that further alienate and isolate the drug abuser, instead of humane treatment efforts.

United States Statistics

While the prevalence of drug use and abuse in the United States is subject to considerable dispute, the following statistics (adapted from the Sixth Annual Eagleville Conference, 1973) are useful indications of the present situation with regard to overall drug use excluding alcohol, which is the most widely used drug of all.

Approximately 22,500,000 adults and 3,500,000 youths have used marijuana.

3,000,000 adults and 1,500,000 youths have experimented with inhaling volatile solvents.

5,500,000 adults and 750,000 youths have taken sedative drugs for nonmedical reasons.

8,500,000 adults and 750,000 youths have used tranquilizers for nonmedical reasons.

7,000,000 adults and 1,000,000 youths have used stimulant drugs and amphetamines for nonmedical reasons.

4,500,000 adults and 375,000 youths have tried cocaine at least once.

1,850,000 adults and 150,000 youths have used heroin at least once.

Current estimates of drug dependence are varied. The Drug Enforcement Agency sets the number of narcotic addicts at 560,000, while others place the figure as low as 225,000 or as high as 700,000. These figures do not take into account the speculations that another 500,000 to 1,500,000 persons in the general adult population may be addicted to narcotic drugs with medical sanction. Despite intensive federal efforts in 1972, there is a definite upward trend in the use of narcotics, a significant increase in chronic polydrug abuse—the aftermath of experimentation in the 1960s, and more frequent prescribing of tranquilizing, sedative, and stimulant drugs. The economic cost of drug abuse to the nation is staggering. According to President Gerald Ford's message to Congress in 1976, the cost from lost productivity, drug-related crime, and treatment and prevention programs may range anywhere from $10 billion to $17 billion each year. These statistics cannot reflect the tragic toll that drug dependence exacts on a personal level.

In order to help a person whose thinking, feeling, and behavior are affected by the use of some drug, workers in this field should be informed about the effects of different drugs and should also be familiar with terms commonly used in connection with drug abuse. There is a distinction among drug use, misuse, and abuse. Drug use applies when the effects of a drug are realized and there is minimal hazard, whether or not it is used therapeutically or legally. Drug misuse occurs when a drug is taken under circumstances and in doses that significantly increase the hazard to the individual or to others. Drug abuse is defined as persistent or sporadic excessive drug use, inconsistent with acceptable medical practice, where a drug is taken to such a degree as to impair the ability of the individual to adequately function, or cope. There is nothing intrinsically good or bad about drug taking and, in general, most illicit drugs, including alcohol, are at the "use" level. However, excessive misuse and abuse are problems for both the individual and society.

Drug Dependence Defined

The word "addiction" denotes a pattern of compulsive use rather than any specific pharmacological interaction, and it is a term that no longer has scientific or practical value. The World Health Organization Committee on Addiction-Producing Drugs has recommended that the term "drug dependence" be used for all conditions formerly described as drug habituation or addiction, and provides a good working definition (1969):

> *Drug dependence* is a state, psychic and sometimes also physical, resulting from the interaction between a living organism and a drug, characterized by behavioral and other responses that always include a compulsion to take the drug(s) on a continuous or periodic basis in order to experience its psychic effects, and sometimes to avoid the discomfort of its absence. Tolerance may or may not be present and a person may be dependent on more than one drug.

Psychological dependence is the condition that exists when the effects of a drug have become necessary to the individual in order to maintain an optimal state of well-being, and intensity may range from mild desire to strong craving for the drug's effects. *Physical dependence* refers to a state in which a definite biological change has taken place in the body following drug taking, and can therefore be measured with somewhat more precision than psychological dependence. This change initiates a physical need to continue taking the drug to avoid distressing withdrawal symptoms which are characteristic for specific groups of drugs. The particular set of symptoms is called a withdrawal syndrome, and the more abrupt the withdrawal, the more severe the syndrome. In the absence of a withdrawal syndrome there is no physical dependence. *Tolerance* can develop with chronic use of certain drugs and specifically relates to conditions where repeated equal doses of the drug have less and less effect, so that steadily increasing doses are required to achieve the same effect. Tolerance develops relatively quickly with certain drugs such as the opiates and the amphetamines, and is also often rapidly lost, leading to a fatal overdose if an individual then takes a formerly tolerable dose.

When describing the effects of various drugs, one must bear in mind that even the simplest of drugs has a wide range of effects. These vary with respect to the user's attitudes and expectations, the dosage, the route of administration, circumstances under which the drug is used, and countless other factors. The predominant effects of drugs, however, can be conveniently grouped into three basic categories: sedatives, stimulants, and hallucinogens.

SEDATIVES

Narcotic Analgesics

These drugs have a powerful pain-relieving action and possess the most intensive dependency-producing potential. Their place as pain-relieving drugs is beyond question; the widespread use of narcotics (namely, opium and later morphine) during the Civil, Prussian-Austrian, and Franco-Prussian wars created such a large opiate-dependent population that morphine dependence became known as the "soldier's disease." Following the isolation of morphine as a derivative of opium in 1805 and the invention of the hypodermic in 1854, the United States became what Edward M. Brecher describes as a "dope fiend's" paradise. Throughout this same period, countless nonprescribed opiate patent medicines were easily obtained by over-the-counter sales, and it is estimated that 1,250,000 (that is, 4 percent of the population) were regularly using opiate drugs. With the passage of the Harrison Narcotic Act in 1914, the unauthorized sale, possession, or purchase of narcotic drugs became a criminal offense, and the management of these drugs moved toward vigorous law enforcement controls and prosecution. Despite the good intentions behind the law, tens of thousands of addicts were driven underground, and a criminal hierarchy was created to enable addicts to pay for their habits. Currently, it is estimated that about 0.05 percent of the population is addicted to opiatelike drugs (A. Y. Cohen), which include opium, morphine, heroin, Demerol, codeine, Dilaudid, methadone, and a variety of other opiate derivatives and synthetic equivalents.

These drugs can be taken by mouth, sniffed, injected into the skin (skin-popping) or, for maximum effect, injected directly into a vein (mainlining). Narcotic analgesics are prescribed for the relief of pain, tranquilization, and sedation; unfortunately, physical dependence, tolerance of the drug, and habituation invariably occur if individuals are exposed sufficiently to these drugs. Regardless of the type of personality involved, anyone using opiates over a period of time will develop physiological changes characteristic of addiction. Narcotics have a generally depressant action on the central nervous system, resulting in almost immediate relief of physical tension when administered by hypodermic. The intense physical and emotional pleasure experienced, which induces a complete sense of well-being with the illusion of total mastery over life circumstances, tends to make narcotics particularly irresistible to individuals who find it difficult to cope with some of the unpleasant realities of life. Eventually the user tends to no longer experience the euphoric sense of well-being, but continues to use the drug to avoid distressing withdrawal symptoms. These symptoms can start four to forty-eight hours after the last use of the drug and may include a mild abstinence syndrome of a flulike or allergic reaction with sore throat, running eyes and nose, yawning, and a slightly elevated temperature. More severe withdrawal is characterized by increasing anxiety and restlessness, recurring waves of gooseflesh, and dilation of the pupils. Severe cramps in the legs and abdomen and twitching of muscles with vomiting and diarrhea are also common, and there is usually an increase in the metabolic rate, respiration, and blood pressure during the first three or four days of abstinence. In all cases, the symptoms vary with the individual, quantity of drugs used, and length of time of addiction. Although fear of withdrawal is one of the strong incentives in continued use of narcotics, most addicts have experienced withdrawal either "cold turkey," that is, with no medical assistance whatever, or by using other drugs, including alcohol or methadone, since most addicts cannot afford to support their large habits as their tolerance to ever-increasing doses develops. It is now recognized that narcotic-dependent individuals frequently request medical detoxification not to become totally drug-free, but to start over again and use smaller dosages.

In contrast to the deteriorating effect of excessive use of alcohol on all the major systems of the body, there are no direct harmful physical effects or physiological damage caused by narcotic analgesics, even with prolonged use. The hazards of narcotic addiction are essentially related to the use of dirty needles leading to abscesses, severe general infection, hepatitis, and chronic personal self-neglect of health. Loss of weight, malnutrition, and dental caries are other frequent consequences of addiction, while the total preoccupation with seeking and taking drugs, disruption of interpersonal relationships, and the fear of imprisonment for involvement with criminal activities to support the habit are other deleterious effects. There is also danger of death from heroin overdose, and it has been estimated that about $1\frac{1}{4}$ percent of the addict population in New York City dies each year from overdose. Many of these deaths have been attributed to substances used to adulterate the heroin, or have resulted from the use of alcohol or barbiturates in connection with heroin rather than from the overdose of heroin itself.

The nature of narcotic dependence is not yet fully understood and, meanwhile, controversy between the alternatives of mobilizing better law enforcement resources and providing better treatment and rehabilitation services continues. It is clear that abuse of these drugs is incompatible with the maintenance of a normal lifestyle and that our main attention needs to be focused more on problems of individuals who take these drugs and their environment rather than on stricter controls on availability of the drugs themselves, since controls tend merely to alter the existing patterns of distribution.

Sedative-Hypnotics

This is a large group of addicting nonopiate sedatives and depressant drugs, including alcohol, barbiturates, and barbituratelike drugs such as meprobamate and glutethimide. The minor tranquilizers Valium and Librium are also included in this group. All of these drugs can produce tolerance leading to increasing dosage, and have the potential for both psychological and physical dependence.

Barbiturates are probably the most important of this group and are widely used to promote sleep and as mild daytime sedation for tense or emotionally anxious people. They are also frequently used to control seizures in the treatment of epilepsy, and sometimes as preanesthetic sedatives or for complete general anesthesia, particularly for short operations where longer-acting anesthesia and total muscular relaxation are not important. With a few exceptions, barbiturates can be distinguished by the suffix "al," for example, Tuinal, Seconal, Nembutal, Luminal, etc., and are classified according to the duration of their chemical effects and the rate of onset. In general, the quicker the drug produces sedation, the shorter the duration of its effect. Slower-acting barbiturates, such as phenobarbital, have a delayed onset and a longer-acting duration with a moderate degree of hangover, whereas Seconal has a quick onset of action, a relatively short duration of effect, and less hangover. The short-acting barbiturates tend to be most popular with abusers of this drug because of their rapid intoxicating effect, which is very similar to that produced by alcohol. There is also cross tolerance, which means that increased tolerance for alcohol results in an increased tolerance for barbiturate drugs and also intensifies the effect of alcohol, so that they are often used interchangeably or in combination, and death from simultaneous use, either accidental or of suicidal intent, is common.

A person who has become physically dependent on barbiturates is by definition in a state of chronic intoxication. Anyone taking doses in excess of 600 milligrams per day for over twelve months is likely to show typical symptoms of physical addiction such as slurred speech, unsteady gait, and confused thinking. Early withdrawal symptoms can occur within twenty-four hours (for shorter-acting barbiturates), and include trembling, shaky hands, dizziness, and nausea. More severe withdrawal symptoms for longer-acting barbiturates do not occur before three to six days, and include the earlier signs with progression into seizures and delirium. Of all withdrawal states, barbiturates present the most serious physical problems, and both overdoses and acute withdrawal are serious medical emergencies and require immediate hospitalization. Self-medication with excessive amounts of barbiturates combined or alternating with stimulants such as the amphetamines and cocaine can produce a toxic psychosis and, again, the real danger of fatal overdose. Although the sale of barbiturates has been regulated in the United States by law since 1965 so that a prescription cannot be refilled more than five times, it is estimated that one-half of all barbiturates produced in the United States find their way into the illicit market. Meanwhile, acute intoxication with barbiturates accounts for 25 percent of all cases admitted to general hospitals for treatment of acute poisoning, and death from barbiturate overdoses is still increasing. In Cook County, Illinois, a 113-percent increase in barbiturate deaths was reported over an eight-year period (D. Mauer and V. Vogel).

Minor tranquilizer drugs, such as Miltown, Equanil, Librium, and Valium, are all capable of producing physical dependence and serious withdrawal symptoms when used in excessive amounts over a period of time.

It is fair to say that physical and psychological dependence on sedative and tranquilizing drugs is much wider in incidence than is generally realized, and this type of drug dependence has not received the attention it merits. Many in our society have the mistak-

Addictive Doses of Sedative-Hypnotics

Trade name	Generic name	Dependency-producing dose, milligrams per day	Number of days necessary to produce dependence
Librium	Chlordiazepoxide	300–600	60–180
Valium	Diazepam	80–120	42
Noctec	Chloral hydrate	2000–3000	
Equanil Miltown	Meprobamate	1600–2400	
Doriden	Glutethimide	200–3000	
Seconal	Sodium secobarbital	800–2200	35–37
Nembutal	Sodium pentobarbital	800–2200	35–37
Quaalude	Methaqualone	2100–3000	21–28

SOURCE: "Methaqualone: Dangerous New Drug Fad Sweeping West?", *Connection*, vol. 1, no. 1, 1972. Adapted from G. R. Gay, D. E. Smith, D. R. Wesson, and C. W. Sheppard, *Journal of Psychedelic Drugs*, vol. 3, no. 2, 1971.

en belief that pills can cure everything, and physicians have too often contributed to this belief by prescribing unnecessary and even inappropriate medication for their patients. Recognizing that recent reports of effectiveness for tranquilizers and antidepressants are less enthusiastic than earlier ones, and that dangers of dependence and idiosyncratic toxic reactions exist, more physicians are beginning to fulfill their professional responsibilities by referring troubled persons to agencies or other specialists. It must also be recognized that the use of alcohol greatly enhances the effect of tranquilizers and can be particularly hazardous for persons who are driving and operating heavy machinery. The ease with which alcohol and these drugs can be obtained makes them particularly tempting for vulnerable persons, and maintaining abstinence may be very difficult to achieve.

Marijuana is also classified as a nonopiate sedative and is the most widely used illicit drug, with an estimated 20 percent of Americans over the age of eleven having used it at least once. Although thousands of users do not consider themselves drug addicts since marijuana does not cause physical dependency, it can, however, produce psychological dependence and regular users do develop tolerance. Its effects vary with individual expectations, dosage, and the environment in which it is used, so that a lone user may become drowsy, and with others may become hyperactive and excitable. There are alterations in time and perception, a sense of euphoria, increased sociability, suggestibility, and disinhibition at the usual levels of social use. With higher doses, there are visual distortions, feelings of personal unreality, and sometimes psychoticlike effects, that is, hallucinations and paranoid thinking. In general, motor coordination and intellectual functioning are affected by marijuana intoxication, and there are consistent decrements in the performance of complex tasks, particularly for the inexperienced user.

While there is no evidence of harmful physical effects from occasional or infrequent use of marijuana, the effects of its long-term chronic use are less certain. Some studies have shown increased incidences of bronchitis, decreased respiratory function, and abnormal changes in bronchial tissue similar to those found in older heavy cigarette smokers. Other studies suggest that symptoms of mental sluggishness, apathy, loss of interest in appearance, memory problems, and confusion can be related to the toxic effects of chronic marijuana use on the brain. There are, however, no reliable objective ways of confirming that these symptoms are directly related to the level of marijuana use. The obvious seriousness, however, of this possibility would suggest that continued research on this question receive high priority. One of the major concerns regarding its frequent use is the possibility of involvement in a sociocultural group that approves of other, more dangerous forms of drug taking and experimentation. There is also increasing evidence that heavy use is correlated with social indifference and loss of motivation. On the other hand, youthful marijuana users see it as a harmless pleasurable substance and contrast it with the alcohol drinking of their elders with all its well-known dangers.

Marijuana, as in the case of other drugs, is neither inherently evil nor totally harmless, yet its users seem to invite extreme comments. Until the deleterious effects of long-term frequent usage are factually established, it must be considered simply as an intoxicant, frequently used by the young, possibly as a symbol of protest for some and by others for its pleasurable effects. As with other intoxicants, it has the relative potential for personal and social harm and, unfortunately, as is the case with other drugs, will tend to be used most frequently by those who probably run the greatest risk from its abuse. Sensationalizing the dire consequences of marijuana use might well have a reinforcing effect on potential abusers. Until more conclusive information is available, it would seem desirable to approach it with common-sense inquiry instead of the extreme positions it appears to invite.

Glue and volatile solvents are central nervous system depressants with effects that most closely resemble alcohol intoxication. They are readily available in many household products such as paint thinners, glues, enamels, varnishes, and lighter and dry-cleaning fluids. When the vapors of organic solvents are inhaled, there is an almost immediate exhilarating effect, disinhibition, and sometimes short hallucinogenic experiences which are apparently highly valued. With repeated inhalation more severe symptoms of incoordination, confusion, and disorientation occur; if used in high enough concentrations these solvents can cause quite severe brain damage, coma, and even death. In addition to these dangers, the common technique of placing a plastic bag over the head to retain the fumes can lead to the complication of asphyxiation. Glue sniffing, in particular, is much more common in relatively young children, and it has been suggested that publicizing its dangers by the mass media in the early 1960s may have encouraged experimentation by school children in epidemic proportions. The regular practice of glue sniffing, however, involves a much smaller number who tend to be more emotionally unstable and deprived youngsters who are predisposed by severely disorganized homes.

STIMULANTS

These drugs increase central nervous system activity, promote energy, alertness and, initially, a euphoric feeling of well-being. Drugs included in this group are cocaine, the amphetamines, and low-abuse-potential drugs such as caffeine and nicotine. Drugs such as lysergic acid diethylamide (LSD) and dimethyltryptamine (DMT) also stimulate the central nervous system, but are discussed according to their most vivid primary effect as hallucinogens.

Cocaine

This is a powerful stimulant derived from the coca bush found in some South American countries and used medically only as a local anesthetic. It is used by addiction-prone individuals primarily for its powerful stimulant effect and is usually sniffed, injected intravenously or, more rarely, chewed. Although cocaine is not considered a physically addicting drug, the intense excitement and elation experienced by its users make it so attractive that they can become extremely psychologically dependent on it in a very short period of time. With longer-term use and repeated administration of cocaine, its relatively short-term pleasurable effects are followed by strong feelings of anxiety, fear, and persecution. For this reason, cocaine is rarely used alone, but tends to lead toward excessive use of other drugs, namely heroin or alcohol, to counteract the unpleasant anxious reaction which follows the initial period of euphoria.

There has been a resurgence in the use of cocaine in the past few years, especially by the middle and upper class or others who consider themselves the "elite" of the drug culture. The euphoria, overalertness, and feelings of great power produced by cocaine are quite similar to reactions produced by a high dose of amphetamines, except that the effects of cocaine are much shorter-acting. This results in a need for rapid and repeated short-interval administration, which can cause the possibility of an intense toxic reaction characterized by frank paranoia and vivid hallucinations which sometimes precipitate unjustified acts of violence. Since there is no physical dependence, this drug is easy to withdraw, and discontinuing usually requires a fairly short time, attended by temporary depression and a strong craving for the drug. As in the case of other stimulant drugs, cocaine users will often deny their very real craving for it and cite its lack of physical addiction in its favor. Again, however, the preoccupation with illegal drug taking, disturbance in interpersonal relationships, and economic problems are clear evidence of its negative consequences.

Amphetamines

Common preparations of these drugs include amphetamine sulfate, Dexedrine, Benzedrine, Methedrine, Dexamyl (Dexedrine combined with a barbiturate), and the similar-acting Preludin. These drugs are closely related to ephedrine and adrenaline, producing an increased feeling of well-being, confidence, heightened alertness, and initiative. They have often been used to reduce fatigue and appetite; however, their long-term efficacy for these purposes is doubtful. Their current medical use is strictly limited to treatment for hyperactive children, narcolepsy (a condition characterized by an uncontrolled need for sleep), and short-term appetite control. The occasional user of amphetamines for a specific purpose is not to be compared with the vulnerable person who rapidly becomes psychologically addicted and finds abstinence most difficult. For these persons there is considerable satisfaction in the stimulating effect of these drugs when taken in larger amount than therapeutically prescribed.

Tolerance to amphetamines develops rapidly, and their abuse has become a major problem in the past few years, especially among young people. Commonly, they start with four or five tablets at a time, and gradually increase this dosage until all too often oral administration will change to intravenous injection, which has been described as among the most disastrous forms of drug use yet devised. Frequently, amphetamines are mixed with heroin and injected, a combination known as a "speed ball." Classical symptoms of intoxication with amphetamines include insomnia, restlessness, and agitation. Sometimes a toxic psychosis ensues in which there are paranoid ideas and vague hallucinations, and the person may become very anxious with delusions of danger and being attacked, often resulting in dangerous aggressiveness toward others. The "speed freak" typically injects the drug many times a day with each dose in the hundreds of milligrams, and may remain awake continuously for possibly up to six days, gradually becoming more tense and paranoid as the "run" progresses. These sprees are usually interrupted by bouts of very profound sleep which may last a day or two. Withdrawal from amphetamines on the whole is uncomplicated. The patient usually becomes very sleepy, gains weight rapidly over a period of days, and experiences states of irritable depression. There are indications that the individual may also subsequently reexperience these bouts of depression and lethargy, even long after drug use has been discontinued.

It is generally considered that amphetamine users are probably the most poorly adapted to the drug scene since they are usually middle class and quite inexperienced compared with the typical street drug addict. Their tendency to be highly agitated and suspicious frequently incapacitates them for legitimate employment, and relationships with family and friends who are not themselves drug abusers will invariably deteriorate. Total abstinence is difficult for many users primarily because of the feelings of fatigue and lethargy which frequently persist for a considerable period of time. The hazards of continued use, however, particularly when mainlining, are comparable to dangers when other substances are carelessly injected: subacute bacterial endocarditis and infections such as tetanus, syphilis, or viral hepatitis. It is also possible that enormous doses of amphetamines can over time injure brain cells. The warning poster "Speed Kills" has been validated by the serious physical and psychological deterioration, including psychotic breakdowns, which can undoubtedly follow from the prolonged excessive use of these drugs.

Hallucinogens

This diverse group of drugs produces radical changes in perception, thinking, mood, and self-awareness. They include LSD (the most potent), mescaline, psilocybin, DMT, and others. They are commonly taken orally, and produce strong psychological addiction and mild tolerance. They cause fundamental alterations in a person's perception of the outside world with vivid imagery, hallucinations, and distortions which often prove to be greatly valued by the user. Both subtle and striking changes are often described vaguely, yet are considered intense revelations by users who appear to derive some subjective benefits of a personal insightful nature. However, often the person may have an adverse, somewhat psychotic reaction with hallucinogens. There is no way of predicting who is more prone to such a reaction, or when it may occur. Similar "flashback" experiences may also occur up to eighteen months after using a drug such as LSD.

The most striking and primary effect of hallucinogens is on the autonomic nervous system—that is, on those parts of the nervous system that control respiratory rate, movements of the stomach, and heart rate—and occurs long before the hallucinogenic effect occurs. LSD has been described as probably the most powerful drug known since 25 micrograms will produce a mild effect in most people and doses of about 100 micrograms taken orally are considered average. The effects from such a dose are experienced within an hour and peak two or three hours after ingestion, with a waning of effect eight to twelve hours later. Tolerance develops rapidly to the same dose of LSD and is also lost rapidly, usually within forty-eight hours. There is cross-dependence between LSD, mescaline, and psilocybin, while sedatives and tranquilizers tend to counteract them. Serious side effects are considered minimal; however, the psychic aspects can sometimes result in a fantasy-laden experience where the ego may tend to fragment and where occasionally a complete loss of self-identity takes place. These feelings of estrangement and depersonalization are common and are particularly harmful to persons who have suffered from previous emotional disturbances. Although there is no clear-cut evidence that permanent signs of organic brain damage result from the use of hallucinogens, there tends to be a pattern of impaired memory and attention span, mental confusion, and difficulty with abstract thinking that persists for some time in heavy users.

Psychedelics (as hallucinogens are often termed) are considered by many to be mind-expanding and, most frequently, those who have used them were motivated by curiosity and had no particular interest in continuing their use. On the other hand, there are the "acid heads" who have taken LSD and other psychedelics in a variety of doses possibly hundreds of times in a religious and mystical search for meaning. There is a tendency for these users to make a virtue out of the habit and to be hung up on the illusory notion that these chemically induced transcendental experiences provide valid insights needed to stabilize their lives. Since the precise nature of the action of these drugs on the human body and mind are unknown at the present time, it seems obvious that they should be kept under control to prevent further spread of their abuse.

TREATMENT

Treatment of drug dependence presents many special and difficult problems. Studies related to the outcome of treatment show a high relapse rate, often on the order of 90 percent within the first six months after discharge from the hospital (U.S. Public Health Service Hospital, Lexington, Kentucky), and workers in drug treatment agencies are exposed to a continuing series of relapses and readmissions. It is therefore not surprising that treatment for drug abuse is apt to be approached with wary cynicism and pessimism, and it is not generally recognized that these negative expectations can have an important bearing on the outcome of treatment. In many cases, drug abusers are forced into treatment by parental concern, public agencies, or the criminal justice system, and are themselves unwilling to fully cooperate in the treatment process. Harsh and punitive attitudes held by many, including some workers in the field who should know better, only further alienate the drug-dependent individual and hinder rehabilitation efforts. Other difficulties arise from controversial viewpoints concerning differing theories of the nature of drug dependence itself, causation, and competing treatment methods. Unfortunately, factual knowledge of the nature of drug dependence and causation is still contentious, and it is oversimplistic to expect that one particular treatment method will be effective in all cases. It is a guiding principle that every client should be evaluated individually with regard to pattern of drug use, type of drug used, and frequency, quantity, and duration of use, within the total context of personality structure, personal history, and sociocultural milieu.

In recent years a number of federally funded agencies have been established throughout the country to provide several different types of treatment through affiliation with existing local treatment programs. These form a comprehensive cohesive network to care for drug-abuse clients with options that include detoxification (either methadone withdrawal or symptomatic), methadone maintenance, and various types of drug-free services in residential or outpatient treatment settings.

Methadone Detoxification

An initial intake assessment determines the need for withdrawal and, in the case of barbiturates, the necessity for immediate hospitalization. Withdrawal from narcotics is best accomplished in a methadone detoxification program, on either an in- or outpatient basis. This is usually a twenty-one-day detoxification program where clients are given gradually reducing doses of methadone to detox them from heroin, coupled with individual or group counseling. It is difficult to ascertain if outpatient withdrawal has been successful because of the tendency to substitute other drugs or to continue use of heroin to relieve withdrawal symptoms. Random surveillance of urine samples is routinely performed by most withdrawal programs, although positive findings are not used to penalize the client, but as an indication that other problems need to be explored with the client. A symptomatic detox is utilized when the client does not have extreme withdrawal symptoms, but does need some medication in order to become drug-free. This is usually accomplished by use of tranquilizing or sedating drugs to relieve the agitation and psychic discomfort most abusers experience during this period. They are also sometimes used to offset the panic reactions induced by a bad LSD trip, although other means to reassure and calm the patient are considered preferable. The obvious hazard of becoming dependent on tranquilizers can be avoided if their use is aimed at short-term alleviation of distress, and it is risky to assume that because they are medically prescribed they will not be abused, leading to tolerance, increasing dosage, and dependence. The primary goal during this period is to help the patient become drug-free as safely and speedily as possible. The withdrawal period is also used to help develop rapport and a trusting relationship with clients in order to sustain them in becoming drug-free and to help them explore longer-term viable alternatives to drug use which are essential to remaining drug-free.

Therapeutic Community

Postwithdrawal treatment plans must again take into account the individual's history, primary drug preference, and other factors. There are a variety of different treatment programs from which to select the one best suited to individual needs. Physical separation from drugs in a drug-free residential therapeutic community, frequently run by former addicts, is often the most effective treatment for the more serious drug abuser with no stable relationships or social supports in the community. Synanon, Daytop Village, Phoenix House, and others are well-known examples of this type of program and were initially used for hard-core heroin addicts whose entire life-style, attitudes, and values centered on procuring and using narcotics. In these facilities, clients experience a rigorous restructuring of their lives intended to help them adapt to a totally drug-free existence with a more responsible, active, and positive role. Although the philosophies of most therapeutic communities are based on the combined psychological and sociological theories of drug addiction and have important similarities, they do differ from one another. Daytop Village was consciously based on the Synanon model and originally began as a treatment center in 1963 for convicted male addicts on probation. It has greatly expanded since then and now accepts both men and women of all ages, irrespective of whether they are in difficulty with the law. Various kinds of encounter groups are used exclusively, focusing on present rather than past experiences, and all decisions are made by group process. New residents are asked to literally regress to an infantile level, becoming totally dependent on the group, and must strictly conform to all the rules. They are gradually allowed to progress through stages, assuming more responsibility as they become more self-confident about what they want to do. Residents who still remain in the program after twelve to eighteen months may enter the "reentry" phase of the program, which allows them to gradually become reintegrated into the community for a period of about six months while continuing to live at Daytop. Residents can then "graduate" from the program if they meet the following requirements: In addition to being drug-free, they must (1) have shown a consistently positive attitude toward self-development with increased self-confidence and self-sufficiency; (2) have demonstrated consistently positive responsibility and concern toward others with respect for authority; and (3) have developed a realistic workable plan by which they intend to live after leaving Daytop. Graduates are encouraged to maintain contact and to return for continued participation in therapy. Unfortunately, the traditional heavily confrontative groups and strict disciplinary methods are often too stressful for those with more serious emotional disorders, who frequently "split" even when sentenced there by the courts. In the first six years, about 110 individuals out of an unknown number that could well exceed 1,000 successfully completed the program, with two-thirds of these working either at Daytop or on the staff of other drug treatment programs.

Odyssey House, Inc., is another tough-minded, but more psychiatrically oriented, therapeutic community with pioneering (1969) concerns for child addicts and the special problems of addicted mothers. Odyssey now has thirty-three locations spread over six states, and while the phases of treatment are comparable with those at Daytop, aiming at total personality reconstruction through regression, earned privileges, increased authority, and reentry, there is more emphasis on vocational rehabilitation geared toward employment outside the field of drug addiction. Therapeutic communities have been criticized for their low success rate; yet, nevertheless, hundreds of former addicts who were sufficiently motivated to stay with these programs have learned to live successfully without drugs. Many of these programs are becoming more flexible in their approach, including the use of outside mental health services, increased emphasis on educational and vocational services, and shortened, varying lengths of residence. These changes are more likely to meet the individual needs of a more diverse drug-abuse population and undoubtedly will result in a higher rate of successful reentry into the community.

Methadone Maintenance

This is another form of long-term treatment for persons with a prolonged biochemical dependence on heroin, and has no role in the treatment of other kinds of drug abuse. It is intended to manage rather than cure addiction and involves oral administration of a fixed daily dose of methadone, a synthetic opiate with effects that develop more slowly and persist longer than heroin and are said to "block" the craving for drugs. A documented two-year history of addiction and repeated treatment failures to remain drug-free are the basic criteria for admission to a maintenance program. It was considered the first major breakthrough and was enthusiastically welcomed as the answer to the heroin problem following the initial Dole and Nyswander methadone research project in 1964. Over the years since then, however, it has been heavily criticized by opponents of maintenance for perpetuating addiction by merely substituting one addicting opiate drug for another and for accepting quite young people for maintenance with no verifiable substantial history of addiction. Furthermore, not all maintenance programs have achieved similar high success rates in terms of increased employment, improved social functioning, and decrease in drug-related crimes and arrests. There is also increasing evidence that more maintenance clients are seriously turning to excessive use of alcohol with the obvious danger of alcohol addiction, liver disease, and general apathy toward changing their drug-related life-style. No one is suggesting that methadone maintenance is the treatment of choice for all long-term heroin users. However, whatever the shortcomings of maintenance programs, it has been shown that more clients voluntarily stay in maintenance for far longer periods than in any other form of treatment; most totally abstain from using heroin; a high percentage lead a law-abiding life with a drastically reduced incidence of drug-related crime and arrests; and many receive training and obtain employment with improved functioning in the community. When high-quality supportive rehabilitation services such as counseling and vocational and education programs are provided in addition to methadone, treatment can be more effectively geared toward detoxification from methadone and continued social functioning in a drug-free state.

Outpatient Community Services

These mental health center drug treatment services are not effective for most narcotic addicts unless they have been drug-free for a considerable time and then find there are family, vocational, or psychological problems to be worked out. Therapy involving one or two hours a week can rarely meet the needs of these particularly difficult clients. Mental health programs are most helpful for drug abusers with other significant psychiatric problems, and particularly for the polydrug abuser who frequently finds traditional drug programs too stressful. David Smith has estimated that there are probably about 2,000,000 polydrug abusers with virtually no adequate programs for this ubiquitous population. These people tend to drift into using different drugs, depending upon availability or temporary mood state, and have no clear primary drug preference. There are indications of more severe psychopathology in multiple-drug dependence. and these individuals are more likely to respond to low-stress day-care and social and recreational activities with supportive counseling than to the heavy attack confrontation in therapeutic communities. A mental health treatment plan might include nonaddicting psychotropic medications combined with peer-support relationships and group activities. Psychotropics can probably be discontinued for most of these clients as emphasis shifts toward developing better coping mechanisms and other life-management skills.

Other Approaches

With the recognition that stricter law enforcement controls, mandatory treatment programs, and education stressing the undesirability of drugs have not made major inroads on drug abuse, other approaches are beginning to view this whole complex area from the perspective that many drug abusers are not necessarily criminal characters, immature, or mentally ill. C. Pinsky has suggested that for drug dependence to develop, the right drug must encounter the right individual, and that lack of some metabolic or neural function which a particular drug replaces will induce dependence. He bases this theory on the very recent discovery of an opiatelike substance "endorphin," found throughout the brain, and hypothesizes that addicts may be individuals with a deficit of this inborn narcotic substance. If this newly discovered brain neurotransmitter proves to be of importance, not only for the opiate drug mechanism but possibly in the craving for a variety of psychoactive chemicals, Pinsky sugfests that drug abusers would then best respond to a regimen of psychotherapy combined with individualized *pharmacotherapy* aimed at repairing deranged neurotransmitter functions.

Another treatment approach emphasizes that unfulfilled needs and aspirations are the basic motives for drug abuse. A. Y. Cohen's innovative programs are attempting to provide multivaried logical *alternatives* which correspond to the motives, needs, and aspirations that impel some persons toward drug abuse. He lists types of gratifications in categories such as physical, sensory, emotional, interpersonal, mental-intellectual, creative-esthetic, experiential, stylistic, social-political, philosophical, spiritual, and miscellaneous (such as a risk-taking need for adventure). These programs suggest that the choice of drugs and patterns of use vary, with individual kinds of gratifications being sought in each of these categories, and that a particular kind of drug effect will be the motive for its use. The alternatives approach attempts to systematically explore nonchemical alternatives that are realistic, attainable, and attractive, and satisfy the specific individual needs that have previously been sought in the use of drugs. The creative search for alternatives to drug use might include relaxation, yoga, recreation, sensory awareness training, biofeedback, transcendental meditation, artistic hobbies, and even personal political involvement. It is expected that the particular alternatives selected will be more effective in satisfying needs, as they require active assertion of will, effort, and commitment in contrast to the previous passive "taking in" of drugs and, indeed, the personalized search for alternatives might well be the most potent alternative of all.

Research

Research activities in drug abuse have greatly expanded in recent years, but for the most part are fragmented due to lack of coordination between specific research efforts and to poor dissemination of results. All federal research is basically aimed at determining what causes a person to turn to drugs, what treatment systems and methods are most effective for different types of client, and what characteristics of a client's profile can predict which particular treatment modality would be most effective. Research in this area produced the Pittell Drug Abuse Treatment Referral System (DATRS), which consists of a number of scales based on drug types and quality, frequency of drug use, and drug-related involvement (the drug index), and an overall assessment of personal and social resources (the prognostic index). Scores on these can maximize the probability of success for each kind of client by referral to the most appropriate of twenty-three different treatment alternatives ranging from "no treatment required" to "custodial care or incarceration." Other research efforts have led to advances in methods of detecting drugs, a measurement of the abuse potential of various drugs, and other chemotherapeutic alternatives for treating narcotic addiction. There is still a great need for follow-up studies on clients after leaving treatment to determine the relative effectiveness of prevention and treatment approaches, and a critical need for an integrated and coordinated overall federal research, demonstration, and evaluation effort.

Conclusion

Comprehensive treatment of drug dependence generally requires the strategic use of a variety of treatment modalities. It is effective only when adequate consideration of the needs of a particular client are integrated with timing of medical, psychological, and social interventions. It is an area of social concern where prejudice, oversimplification, and unjustifiable pessimism have hindered progress and logical inquiry.

Successful treatment must take into account chronicity of the problem and all the various perspectives regarding a client, including a pharmacological knowledge of the particular drugs being abused. Effective rehabilitation can be viewed as a long series of small progressive steps, each of which contributes to the reversal of previous treatment failure, and the challenge to participate in this can be a major source of gratification for enthusiastic and innovative individuals working in this field.

Relevant Organizations

Addiction Research and Treatment Corporation, 22 Chapel Street, Brooklyn, NY 11201.

Drug Abuse Council, 1828 L Street N.W., Washington, DC 20036.

Institute for the Study of Drug Misuse, 111 Fifth Avenue, New York, NY 10003.

National Association for the Prevention of Addiction to Narcotics, 175 Fifth Avenue, New York, NY 10010.

National Coordinating Council on Drug Education, 1526 18th Street N.W., Washington, DC 20036.

National Council on Drug Abuse, 8 South Michigan Avenue, Chicago, IL 60603.

National Family Council on Drug Addiction, 401 West End Avenue, New York, NY 10024.

Odyssey Institute, 1125 North Tonti, New Orleans, LA 70119.

Rubicon, Inc., 1208 West Franklin Street, Richmond, VA 23220.

SELECTED REFERENCES

Brecher, Edward M., *Licit and Illicit Drugs*, Little, Brown, Boston, 1972.

Cohen, Allen Y., *Alternatives to Drug Abuse, Steps towards Preventing*, National Clearinghouse for Drug Abuse, Rockville, Maryland, 1975.

Cohen, Sidney, *The Drug Dilemma*, McGraw-Hill, New York, 1969.

Densen-Gerber, Judianne, *We Mainline Dreams*, Doubleday, Garden City, New York, 1973.

Dole, Vincent T., and Marie Nyswander, "A Medical Treatment for Diacetylmorphine (Heroin) Addiction," *Journal of the American Medical Association*, vol. 193, no. 646, 1965.

Mauer, David, and Victor Vogel, *Narcotics and Narcotic Addiction*, Charles C. Thomas, Springfield, Illinois, 1973.

Pinsky, C., *Chemical Treatment of Alcohol and Other Drug Dependencies*, University of Manitoba, Winnipeg, 1976.

Smith, David E., "Polydrug Abuse and Comprehensive Treatment Intervention," presented at the National Drug Abuse Conference, New York, March 1976.

Smith, David E., "The Trip—There and Back," in L. Brill and L. Lieberman, eds., *Major Modalities in the Treatment of Drug Abuse*, Behavioral Publications, New York, 1972.

The Treatment of Drug Abuse, Joint Information Service, 1972.

Weil, Andrew, *The Natural Mind*, Houghton Mifflin, Boston, 1972.

Weismann, Thomas, *Drug Abuse and Drug Counseling*, Press of Case Western Reserve, Cleveland, 1972.

Willis, J. H., *Drug Dependence*, Faber and Faber, London, 1969.

31

Epilepsy

LINDA HOWELL, M.A.,. Group Health Cooperative of Puget Sound, Seattle

Reviewed by MILDRED GREGORY, Western Washington State Epilepsy Society, and C. B. CARLSON, M.D., Director, Child Neurology, Children's Orthopedic Hospital and Medical Center, Seattle

The word "epilepsy" is derived from the Greek *epilepsia,* meaning seizure. Since antiquity this disorder has been surrounded by mystery, superstition, fear, and wonder. The ancient Greeks thought that seizures were evidence of visitation by the gods. In Europe during the Middle Ages (and even today within certain religious groups) it was believed that those who had seizures were possessed by evil spirits. Exorcism by ritual and torture has been practiced in many societies.

Superstitious beliefs about the cause and meaning of epilepsy have tended to keep many victims of this disorder on the periphery of society. In spite of this fact, some of the great individuals in history—Alexander the Great, Julius Caesar, Handel, Socrates, and Tchaikovsky, for example—are known to have had epileptic seizures.

Prevalence

It is estimated that from 1 to 4 million people in the United States are subject to recurring convulsive seizures (0.5 to 2 percent of the population). Epilepsy occurs within all races and age groups and is found equally in both sexes.

Definition and Types

Epilepsy is not a disease, but a general type of brain disorder. Within the brain, nerve cells (neurons) work cooperatively with each other to regulate body functions. In the brains of certain people, this functional cooperation breaks down, resulting in occasional excessive discharge of electrical energy. The symptoms or manifestations depend upon where the discharge occurs, how extreme it is, and its extent or spread within the brain.

These symptoms of brain irritation and discharge can be categorized. The majority of epileptics have one type of seizure pattern; the rest have a combination of different seizure types. The most familiar form is the *grand mal*, or generalized convulsion, which accounts for 60 percent of cases. In the first, or tonic phase, there is loss of consciousness, stiffening of the body, heavy irregular breathing, drooling, skin pallor, and occasional bladder incontinence. After a few seconds the clonic phase sets in, characterized by acute spasms of the jaws and legs, usually followed by deep sleep. As part of the seizure, the person may first experience a kind of warning. This is called an *aura* (from the Latin meaning "breeze") and is simply one representation of neural activity change in the brain. Its form depends upon the location of the irritable tissue, and for this reason may be a peculiar numbness, noise, taste, smell, or other sensation. It may also consist of a premonition of impending doom or even a feeling of extreme well-being. Occasionally auras occur without subsequent seizures. Following the seizure, in what is called the "postictal" period, drowsiness, disorientation, or fatigue may be experienced.

Petit mal seizures are much more difficult to recognize. Usually the person undergoing such a seizure appears to be staring absentmindedly; a repetitive eyeblink may be observed. The lapse lasts from five to twenty-five seconds and may occur many times a day. After the seizure, the individual does not remember what has happened and is usually unaware of the loss of time but there is no postictal confusion. Seizures of this type occur most commonly in children and usually disappear as maturity is reached. The areas of the brain involved in both grand mal and petit mal seizures include those which control movement and consciousness.

Psychomotor convulsions may be described in terms of behavior that occurs involuntarily and that usually appears to be inappropriate or odd. Examples are chewing, lip smacking, or rubbing the hands or legs. The person may perceive noises and visual disturbances, and experience negative emotional changes (fear or anger) which may last for moments or minutes. Confusion and lack of recall after the attack are typical. These seizures are known to originate in the temporal lobes of the brain.

Other epileptic seizure types are relatively less common but deserve some mention. Infantile myoclonic and akinetic convulsions occur in infants and children. In infants the seizure takes the form of spasms or jerking of the extremities and may be quite frequent although brief. In older children these seizures appear as muscle spasms which may cause the child to fall to the ground. They are considered by some to be variations of petit mal. Difficult to control, this seizure condition is often accompanied by other kinds of neurological dysfunction.

Focal or Jacksonian seizures derive from the motor area of the frontal lobes of the brain — that area known to be a part of the brain which controls movement. When nerves discharge improperly, body parts corresponding to the areas of the strip involved will move or jerk in a regular pattern. In Jacksonian epilepsy the seizure starts on one side of the body and spreads to the other side, sometimes terminating in a generalized convulsion and loss of consciousness.

Etiology

Epileptic disorders are also grouped according to whether or not the cause of the problem is known. *Idiopathic* (primary) epilepsy implies that the cause is not apparent or has not been demonstrated. This type may represent some kind of genetic predisposition, sometimes described as a "low seizure threshold," or it could be that there has been an insult to the brain at some point which went undetected and only later produced the epileptic symptoms. About one-half of all epileptic disorders are of the idiopathic type, with the seizures usually appearing after age five. In cases where there appears to be a significant family history, genetic counseling is often recommended before having children.

Epilepsy of known causation is termed *symptomatic* (secondary). The cause and the symptom do not necessarily occur simultaneously. Symptomatic epilepsy may emerge in time as a result of direct injury to brain structures during fetal development, nutritional deficits which may bring about maldevelopment of tissues, or toxic chemical changes. It may also result from a head injury or lack of oxygen during the birth process. Later an individual may experience any number of traumas to the brain which could cause the irritation and electrical dysrhythmia which is termed epilepsy. Among them are head injury, infections which attack the nervous system directly (encephalitis and meningitis), cerebrovascular disease (especially in the elderly), oxygen and nutritional deficiencies, toxic conditions (such as drug overdose), other chemical or hormonal defects, tumors of neural or surrounding tissue in the brain, etc.

All of these different types of insults to the brain may result in various symptoms in addition to epilepsy. The brain is the body's master organ, and if it does not function properly many changes may become evident. Intellectual and perceptual functioning, motor abilities, or the emotional condition of the individual may be affected in some way. Epilepsy does not cause these other conditions; rather, epilepsy may be caused by the same insult which produces the other problems. With respect to intellectual functioning, studies of large numbers of epileptics show that normal intelligence is the rule, especially for the more common disorders, but a particular individual may develop a specific learning problem.

What causes a seizure to occur at any one point in time? A seizure may be triggered by different stimuli, or seemingly by nothing at all. Tension, emotional upset, boredom, overexertion, fatigue, and even fear of having a seizure may bring on an attack in some cases.

Occasionally, sudden sounds or lights flashing at certain frequencies may induce a seizure. Hyperventilation (rapid, deep breathing) during a period of excitement may also be a precipitating cause.

Symptoms and Diagnosis

Very young children may have convulsions which are not epileptic; these convulsions are transient and usually brought on by high fevers in their relatively undeveloped and vulnerable organisms. It is important to note, however, that any convulsion is sufficient reason to seek medical attention. Epilepsy may be indicated by any of the following signs, provided they have been repeatedly observed: staring spells or daydreaming, chewing and swallowing when not eating, tics, eye rolling, purposeless sounds and rhythmic head and body movements, lack of response, head dropping, or lack of recall of events.

The diagnosis of epilepsy is usually made in the following way: A careful history is taken of the events leading up to, characterizing, and following the "unusual" behavior. A complete physical and neurological examination is performed. In some cases x-rays of the skull may be required, as may a lumbar puncture. The electroencephalograph (EEG), an instrument which measures the frequency and strength of electrical (nerve) activity of the brain in different areas, is used almost routinely to determine the locus and degree of the problem. The dynamic nature of the condition, however, makes diagnosis sometimes difficult, and frequent testing may be required. A variety of other diagnostic techniques, such as a brain scan and computerized axial tomography (CAT), are available for more detailed study where warranted.

Prevention, Medical Treatment, and Management

The central nervous system defects which underlie the epilepsy syndrome are obviously not all preventable, especially those due to the accidents of living. The more hazardous one's environment, the greater the likelihood of insult to the brain and the greater the probability that an epileptic syndrome will develop. Seizures, however, are treatable and can even be completely eliminated in many cases. That is, they are "outgrown" by many people, especially children. Drug therapy is the primary treatment. Currently phenobarbital, Dilantin, and Mysoline are the three most commonly employed anticonvulsant agents. Numerous other agents are available, and more are being developed and tested all the time. Certain drugs are more effective in controlling specific types of seizures. The proper choice, combination, and dosage of these oral medications for each individual—proper in the sense of providing maximal control of seizures with minimal side effects—must be carefully evaluated over time. Gas-liquid chromatography (GLC), a scientific test of the levels of anticonvulsant medications in the blood, now makes it possible to study individual response to medication. Some persons have to take seizure medications indefinitely, and the dosage and drugs themselves may have to be changed periodically. Others may be able to reduce or discontinue use when the physician so advises—after a long period of good control, for example. Brain surgery is another form of treatment for epilepsy, but is seldom undertaken.

The life-style of the individual may require "treatment" to optimize the response to medication and control of seizures. Rest, relaxation, freedom from stress, good nutrition, and satisfaction with one's state in life—important for everyone—are particularly important for the epileptic's favorable response to medical treatment.

Rehabilitation

As most epileptics are indistinguishable from nonepileptics except for their seizure tendency, they should be living normally within the larger society. However, this is not always the case. Superstition and prejudice about this condition persist to this day, although there is a definite trend toward improved attitudes among the general public and among epileptics themselves. Next to medical control of seizures, education of the public is the single most important factor which would allow epileptics freedom of movement and opportunity.

The Epilepsy Foundation of America (EFA) estimates that about 50 percent of individuals with seizure disorders can, through good medical care and drug therapy, live completely free of convulsions, and that another 30 percent can have their seizures reduced to a minimum. Given adequate medical care, most members of these groups, totaling 80 percent of all persons with seizures, are capable of normal participation in the general educational, vocational, and social environment. The extent to which this potential is realized depends first of all upon the individual's own understanding and acceptance of the condition. A person with epilepsy may be inclined to deny the problem and resist its proper treatment. Or one may tend to isolate onself from normal social activity due to fear of seizures or the feeling that one is "different." An epileptic who has had particularly negative life experiences may need professional supportive help from social and mental health workers to develop a stronger self-image and make it possible to cope with situations more adequately. Families, too, may benefit from the services of professionals to learn how they can be truly supportive. They are often inclined to be too protective of the epileptic, especially a child, and may inadvertently prevent the individual from reaching a normal potential.

The goal of individual fulfillment depends upon the capacity of society's gatekeepers in education and the job world to deal openly and honestly with individuals rather than with the superstition which precedes them. Some schools, for example, bar all epileptics from entrance and education for the more severely disabled epileptic is extremely restricted. Also, the unemployment rate of medically controlled epileptics is nearly 25 percent according to the Epilepsy Foundation of America. Epileptics are exempt from military duty.

One cannot discount the reality that a seizure has an untoward effect on other people, let alone the discomfort and embarrassment it may cause the epileptic. Yet an attitude of understanding and acceptance among classroom teachers, camp counselors, and other adults will greatly lessen this effect and perhaps may render the experience educational for all involved. Children who have seen epilepsy in this light will grow into more understanding adults.

Independence and personal satisfaction in our society largely hinge upon employment and financial independence. In the world of work the kinds of jobs open to an individual with a seizure disorder vary according to the nature of the disorder. In general, since consciousness and motor control are almost always involved, work involving heights or around particularly dangerous machinery is not advised. Careful evaluation of the person's skills and abilities, as well as the extent of disability, is necessary to ensure the safety of the job situation and the greatest possible work satisfaction. Statistics show that epileptics have as good (or better) work records as any other group of employees.

Some epileptics feel they must hide their condition from an employer in order to get or keep a job. However, to the extent that the condition may affect work capability, and in order to ensure long-term employment, it is the epileptic's responsibility to discuss with the employer the epileptic condition and to outline procedures to be followed in case seizures occur. That is, the person undergoing a grand mal seizure may give the appearance of being in great pain, which may cause panic and overreaction by others. In fact, there is little pain involved, as the person is temporarily unconscious.

The Epilepsy Foundation has these suggestions when a seizure is encountered:

1. Keep calm. There is nothing you can do to stop a seizure.
2. Do not try to restrain the person.
3. Clear the area around the person to prevent self-injury.
4. Try not to interfere with movements in any way.
5. Do not force anything between the teeth. If the mouth is already open, you can place a soft object (rolled handkerchief) between the side teeth.
6. It is usually not necessary to call a doctor unless the attack is followed almost immediately by another major seizure, or unless the seizure lasts more than ten minutes.
7. Treat the incident in a calm, matter-of-fact way. After the seizure is over, let the person rest if so desired.

The American Medical Association provides a free "Emergency Medical Information" card to be carried by persons with health problems. Such identification may help to prevent unnecessary treatment or restraint in case of a seizure.

Some of the discrimination faced by epileptics has been legislated. Many local and state laws do not reflect the reality of the epileptic condition, but the prejudice and ignorance that have long existed in society. For example, some states still call for sterilization of epileptics under some conditions. The restrictions on getting drivers' licenses may in some cases be based on scientifically out-moded information about seizures and their control. In the past, workmen's compensation laws have tended to be written in such a way as to discourage employers from hiring persons with epilepsy. Epileptics may also be faced with high insurance rates, in spite of the fact that their accident rate is no higher than that for the general population, and the death rate is only slightly higher. Fortunately, any legal restrictions are subject to review and may be changed if enough information and effort are put forth.

Some epileptics are chronically disabled by uncontrolled sei-zures and by the effect of brain damage as well. In these cases, con-tinuous, specialized help is needed, and they may have to be placed in public or private chronic care institutions. Less severely disabled persons benefit from participation in special education classes in the public schools and elsewhere, and may gain some measure of productivity and independence through participation in sheltered workshops (see CHAPTER 8: THE SHELTERED WORK-SHOP). However, if medically supervised, the great majority of persons with a seizure tendency can live a normal life educationally, vocationally, and in every other respect.

Research Efforts

Basic research efforts are directed toward revealing the electro-chemical changes occurring in the brain leading up to and during seizures; the "trigger" phenomenon, or tendency of certain stimuli to provoke such a release of energy from the brain; and the nature of and reason for the "spread" of electrical activity. Applied re-search deals mainly with anticonvulsant medications—their side effects, efficacy in controlling seizures, and individual differences in response to medication. Cerebellar stimulation is also being in-vestigated as a means of treatment. There is neurosurgical research into improved techniques for isolating and removing or inactivating diseased brain tissue. One aspect of prevention research deals with pregnancy, prenatal care, the birth process, and the first few months of life—periods of relatively high susceptibility to damage.

National Agencies

The only major national agency dealing specifically with epilep-sy is the Epilepsy Foundation of America. It was founded in 1967 and has over 100 chapters in the United States. The Foundation's goals are to encourage research into the causes and treatment of epilepsy, to educate the public as to the nature of and treatments for this disorder, and to improve and promote services in all areas for epileptics. Its 1976 Research Training Institute grants totaled $121,598. The addresses of local chapters, which invite participa-tion of persons with epilepsy and other interested parties, can be obtained by writing to the Foundation headquarters at 1828 L Street N.W., Washington, DC 20036.

Among the federal agencies which are concerned with the prob-lem of epilepsy are the National Institute of Neurological and

Communication Disorders and Stroke, a research division of the National Institutes of Health; the Division of Developmental Disabilities, an educational agency, and the Rehabilitation Services Administration of the Social and Rehabilitation Service, concerned with vocational rehabilitation problems. Other vocationally oriented agencies concerned with epilepsy are the Veterans Administration, the Manpower Administration of the Department of Labor, and the President's Committee on Employment of the Handicapped. The National Institute of Neurological and Communication Disorders and Stroke spent $4,317,000 for research on the causes, treatment, and prevention of epilepsy in 1975, but other federal agencies such as the Rehabilitation Services Administration, the Veterans Administration, the National Science Foundation, and the Department of Defense also support research projects. The total research expenditure of over $4,000,000 per year contrasts with the estimated annual cost of epilepsy to the American economy of $4,000,000,000 for disability benefits, medical aid, loss of productivity, and vocational rehabilitation.

SELECTED REFERENCES

Cooper, I. S., and S. Gilman, "Chronic Stimulation of the Cerebellar Cortex in the Therapy of Epilepsy in the Human," *Neural Organization and Its Relevance to Prosthetics*, 1973.

Epilepsy Foundation of America, pamphlets and recommended readings.

Goldensohn, Eli S., and Howard S. Barrows, *Handbook for Patients*, Ayerst Laboratories, New York.

Livingston, Samuel, and Irving M. Pruce, *Living with Epileptic Seizures*, Charles C. Thomas, Springfield, Illinois, 1963.

32

Facial Disfigurement

FRANCES COOKE MACGREGOR, Clinical Associate
Professor of Surgery (in Sociology), and Research
Scientist, New York University Medical Center, Institute
of Reconstructive Plastic Surgery

F acial disfigurement is one of humanity's most intolerable handicaps. Wearing a defect where all may see, the facially disfigured suffer from the highest visibility. More than anything else it is the person's face that is the mediator between the individual and other people; and it is the face that defines one's identity because it defines the reactions of others. It is of singular interest, therefore, that in the broad context of physical disabilities and rehabilitation facial disfigurement has occupied so marginal a position. Because the disfigured do not necessarily suffer any functional impairment, as do those who are blind or crippled, their deprivations tend to be minimized when compared with those whose needs are better understood and better defined. Although it is true that a face that is marred or that deviates in some manner from the norm does not physically restrict one's ability to perform the basic tasks of daily life, research has shown that the social, psychological, and economic consequences may be far more serious than the loss of an arm or leg.

Types and Causes of Disfigurement

Facial abnormalities are incurred in a variety of ways. There are congenital anomalies, apparent at birth, and other malformations that manifest themselves as the child develops. For the most part, birth defects represent the interaction of genetic traits and environmental factors. Some result from disease such as maternal rubella

(German measles); others from being exposed to x-rays during pregnancy, or from the ingestion of such drugs as Thalidomide.

Of the wide variety of cranio-facial anomalies, most cases of cleft lip or palate are reparable in infancy. Hydrocephalus, a condition due to an increase in the volume of cerebrospinal fluid within the skull, will result in gross enlargement of the head and intellectual impairment unless surgery is performed to shunt the excess fluid into the bloodstream. Cretinism, a hypothyroid condition originating in fetal life or early infancy, is characterized by a large protruding tongue, large abdomen, low-grade mentality, and dwarfish stature. Acromegaly, a pituitary disorder in adulthood, involves an increase in size of the hands, feet, and face as well as the viscera and bones. Romberg's disease is characterized by atrophy of skin, bone, and muscle of the face, giving the affected side a "caved-in" appearance. There is no known effective treatment for Down's syndrome (mongolism), a congenital condition characterized by a broad face, flat or stubby nose, obliquely set eyes, open mouth, flaccid muscles, and mental retardation. Other congenital disorders involving facial disfigurement are:

Acrocephaly (oxycephaly): Deformity of the head in which the top is high and more or less pointed.

Apert's syndrome: Characterized by an abnormally high skull, usually with exophthalmic (bulging) eyes and wide separation of the eyes. Some of the toes or fingers are fused, or webbed (syndactyly).

Crouzon's disease: The face generally has a "froglike" appearance when viewed from the front. The nose is broad and hooked, resembling a parrot's beak. There is marked protrusion of the lower jaw (mandible), and the teeth in the upper jaw are irregular. The earlobes are often larger than normal, and divergent strabismus is frequent.

Gargoylism (Hurler's disease): Characterized by dwarfism, short fingers, depression of the bridge of the nose, heavy ugly facies, stiffness of joints, cloudy cornea.

Hypertelorism (Grieg's disease): A deformity of the frontal region of the cranium resulting in a low forehead, flattened bridge of nose, wide separation between the eyes, and divergent strabismus.

Macrocephaly: Gross enlargement of the head due to abnormal growth of the supportive tissue of the brain.

Microcephaly: A congenital hypoplasia (underdevelopment) of the cerebrum, with a thick skull and early closure of the fontanel, resulting in an abnormally small head.

Treacher-Collins syndrome: Characterized by pronounced underdevelopment of the malar (cheek) bone, which usually gives the cheeks a flattened appearance; also notching of the lower eyelids.

Acquired disfigurements come from many directions: traffic and industrial accidents, war, criminal assaults, and burns from explosions or faulty products such as flammable clothing. Others may result either from diseases such as cancer and Romberg's disease,

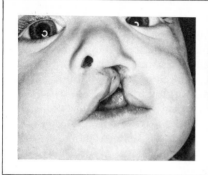

The child's cleft lip has been treated surgically so that the separated portions of the upper lip join in proper alignment. (Institute of Reconstructive Plastic Surgery, New York University Medical Center)

or from such treatments of these conditions as radical surgery or radiation.

Prevalence

Because the victims of conspicuously malformed or disfigured faces are reluctant to appear in public, the extent of this particular disability is not generally realized. While no specific figures are available, it is estimated that every year 52 million Americans suffer injury; and damage to the face, exposed and unprotected as it is, may be assumed to be very high. Unfortunately, the number of persons whose faces are grievously marred increases daily. Automobile accidents account for an appalling number of mutilated faces, while tissue-destroying burns alone, according to National Health Survey data, amount to approximately 2 million injuries per year, a high proportion of which are permanent and incapacitating. As for birth defects, it has been estimated that 1 out of 16 babies is born with some type of anomaly ranging from a minor cosmetic defect to heart deficiency, while 1 child in 700 is born with cleft lip or palate.

Social and Psychological Implications

As already stated, a facial disfigurement does not necessarily incapacitate a person physically, but (and herein lies its special irony) it becomes a handicap of major proportions because of our often arbitrary sociocultural standards and values, and the attitudes, prejudices, and reactions of the nonhandicapped toward those with unesthetic-looking or atypical facial features.

We live in a society that places high value on both a certain conformity and physical attractiveness. In our culture the way one looks makes a difference in the responses one gets. A person who is "ugly" is devalued and set apart. If one happens to look different, one is likely to receive differential treatment and in turn to begin to *feel* different. To be disfigured, therefore, as studies have shown, is to be an object of staring, curiosity, pity, rejection, ridicule, remarks, and discrimination. These reactions and attitudes are frequently more damaging to the individual's self-image than the reflection in the mirror. Such persons find it an ordeal to move about in public. Their anonymity is attacked, strangers question them, or they are shunned altogether. In addition to these humiliations, major obstacles confront them in their efforts to make friends, attract members of the opposite sex, marry, or find employment. As a consequence, such persons frequently develop personality problems or emotional and behavioral disorders that, in many instances, are more serious than the physical defect itself. These may range from feelings of inferiority, shame, self-consciousness, anger, hypersensitivity, anxiety, and paranoid complaints to complete withdrawal, antisocial behavior, and psychotic states.

The attitudes and reactions — mostly negative — of the nonhandicapped toward those who are facially disfigured depend on the type of disfigurement. Some may evoke feelings of revulsion and esthetic rejection — reactions that are spontaneous and visceral, even though the observer, moments later, may feel great pity and sympathy for the victim. Other reactions have their roots in myths, misconceptions, and prejudices that have been acquired and passed down from one generation to another and are perpetuated by unquestioning acceptance. For example, more often than one might suppose, congenital deformities are believed to be predestined, caused by some moral transgression, "God's punishment," or the result of impressions on the mother while carrying the child, such as being frightened by an animal or by the sight of an accident. In addition, it is frequently assumed that children born with malformed faces are mentally retarded. In this connection, some children have been known to be placed in institutions where, treated as if they are mentally deficient, they inevitably become socially retarded, thus validating the original but false assumption. For similar reasons adoption agencies find it all but impossible to place a child with facial stigmata.

Research has shown that there is no direct relationship between the severity of a disfigurement and the degree of psychic distress generated in the victim. The stereotyping of individuals based on their external appearance and on our tendency to assess personality, character, intelligence, and background accordingly, too often leads, in the case of those with facial deviations, to the imputation of socially unacceptable or discrediting traits. For example, a youngster with a receding chin is thought to be dull or weak of character; a youth with a facial scar or a paralyzed mouth a delinquent; or the child with Apert's syndrome mentally deficient. Equally humiliating are facial deviations that suggest caricature or tend to evoke laughter and ridicule. The person with protruding teeth, lop ears, a large nose, or crossed eyes is often the victim of nicknames, mimicking, and jokes that are no less damaging to self-image and self-esteem than the actual expression of horror at the sight of a more severe deformity. Indeed, research has shown that patients whose deformities provoked false character judgments or evoked ridicule exhibited more behavioral disorders and were more maladjusted in many instances than those whose gross disfigurements elicited strong emotional reactions such as pity or revulsion.

Prevention

A substantial number of persons could be spared the tragedy of a damaged face if more preventive measures were taken. In the case of birth defects, for example, parents or prospective parents concerned about transmitting a defect to a child or the recurrence of one in future children can obtain genetic counseling from their physician (usually a pediatrician) or from a genetic center (see CHAPTER 19: BIRTH DEFECTS; GENETIC COUNSELING). Medical supervision during pregnancy and the avoidance of certain drugs would also reduce the number of birth defects. Acquired disfigurements resulting from diseases such as cancer could often be avoided by obtaining immediate medical attention for any developing abnormality.

Only two areas of accident prevention will be mentioned here. (1) Auto accidents: There is incontrovertible evidence that the use of safety belts and, in 1974, the reduction of speed limits, has created a marked impact on the number of highway deaths and injuries. In this connection public cooperation is essential. (2) Burns: The incidence of burns, excluding those caused by auto accidents, could be reduced by more stringent legislation with respect to safety measures in buildings and in the manufacture and use of combustible and flammable products and of electrical devices (see CHAPTER 23: BURN INJURIES).

Management

The amelioration or correction of facial disfigurements requires specialists in the field of plastic surgery. Surgery for congenital defects should be undertaken as soon as possible to forestall possible lasting and adverse psychological effects. Immediate attention should be given to traumatic injuries to prevent what otherwise could become permanent and unsightly aftereffects. Unfortunately, however, no matter how skilled the surgeon, a severely disfigured face can seldom be restored to normal. Moreover, reconstruction and repair frequently involve multiple stages of surgical procedures undertaken over a period of months and even years. In such cases the major problems become the psychological management and support of the patient and family and require the cooperative efforts of all those involved—for example, doctors, nurses, social workers, psychiatrists, psychologists, teachers, and vocational counselors.

When a child is born with a facial anomaly, the parents generally react with shock, grief, anger, or guilt. This is a time when professional help is essential. Parents should be provided with as much information as possible concerning the causes and treatment of the

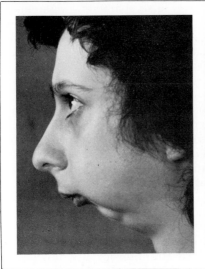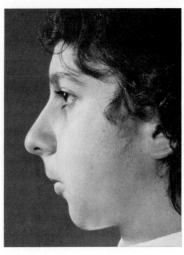

This case of micrognathia has been corrected by implant of an artificial chin. (Institute of Reconstructive Plastic Surgery, New York University Medical Center)

defect. If their feelings of grief or guilt persist, psychological help is indicated. Parental attitudes and behavior are of critical importance to the child's adaptation and adjustment. To prevent possible personality and behavioral disorders, the child should be neither over-protected nor rejected. Research studies have shown that if the child is treated within the family as if normal, and in the same way as siblings, he or she is less likely to develop emotional and psychological problems than if treated as someone different or special. The same is true of the particularly difficult time of entering school. Sometimes, by making an issue of the handicap overtly or covertly, well-intentioned teachers cause the child to feel conspicuous and set apart. The desire of most facially disfigured children is to be treated the same as everyone else.

Vocational Problems

Unlike those who incur functional impairment, the facially disfigured adult does not necessarily require a rehabilitation program to develop new skills to help compensate for those lost by the injury. The problem in this connection is not job training but job placement, and "cosmetic" damage when measured economically and vocationally may be extremely severe. Far too often such persons, although they may be able-bodied, intelligent, and educated, are, because of existing prejudices, forced to work in occupations where they will not be seen by the public. This economic and social reality is too often overlooked in situations involving insurance, compensation, and litigation.

Research and Recent Projects

Not until some twenty years ago was there any systematic and comprehensive scientific investigation of the social, psychological, and cultural implications of facial disfigurement (Frances C. Macgregor, "Some Psycho-social Problems Associated with Facial Deformities," *American Sociological Review*, vol. 16, no. 5, pp. 629–683, 1951; Frances Cooke Macgregor, Theodora M. Abel, Albert Bryt, Edith Lauer, and Serena Weissmann, *Facial Deformities and Plastic Surgery: A Psychosocial Study*, Charles C. Thomas, Springfield, Illinois, 1953). At present, further research is being conducted at the New York University Medical Center, Institute of Reconstructive Plastic Surgery. Studies concerned with specific deformities such as cleft lip and palate are being conducted at the University of Iowa and Duke University.

Organizations

The main agencies in this field are the Society for the Facially Disfigured, Institute of Reconstructive Plastic Surgery, New York University Medical Center, New York; the National Society of Crippled Children and Adults (Easter Seal Society); and state agencies for crippled children.

33

Hearing Disorders

JEROME R. DUNHAM, Ph.D., and CHARLIS S. DUNHAM, M.A.

Reviewed by HERBERT BARKALOO, Ph.D., Special Education, Seattle Public School System

Total deafness is rare. The term "deaf" signifies that human speech cannot be understood even with amplification. Hard-of-hearing persons can understand speech with the use of hearing aids. Since the sense of hearing is crucial to early intellectual development, and detection of a hearing disorder depends on information provided by the subject, deafness is often undetected until later in life, or at times not diagnosed at all. The "real" handicap of a hearing loss is the lack of language and consequently the communicative skills with which to express language and gain further knowledge. Due to the language deficit, the deaf person falls behind in many cultural fundamental skills unless there is intervention with special training.

From ancient times through the Middle Ages there is evidence that deaf people were misunderstood and ostracized, their condition being confused with the idiotic, the insane, and the possessed. In the 1500s Girolamo Cardano of Milan was the first to express the belief that deaf persons could be educated. During the 1500s and 1600s there were a handful of individuals teaching deaf students in western Europe, but the greatest breakthrough toward responsible preparation of deaf persons for a place in society is usually attributed to Abbé de l'Epée, who established a School for the Deaf in Paris in 1760, where he relied primarily on his newly developed silent hand-sign method for communication. Thomas Braidwood of Edinburgh developed schooling for deaf people about the same time, and from the educational efforts of the Braidwood family evolved the speech or oral method for teaching the deaf.

For over 100 years a battle known as "oralism" versus "total communication" has raged. Drs. Eugene Mindel and McCay Vernon, in their 1971 book, *They Grow in Silence,* have extensively explored this controversy which has been emotionally charged and deeply significant to the developmental experiences of deaf persons. There seems to be considerable evidence that well-meaning experts, out of zeal to bring about adjustment to the hearing world, have created an artificial emphasis on oral communication. They realized that deaf children communicated naturally by gesture or sign, and developmental psychology research indicated that learning had to commence early in life to be well ingrained. With the hearing person's bias, they imposed the oralist lip-reading methods with stringent vigor. Pediatricians and many other professionals were converted and mobilized to present the parents with overwhelming prestigious opinion that the deaf child's future would be limited unless speech and lip-reading were learned at an early age. As with other disabilities, normality was considered to be superior to a deviant, but natural, process, a bias with unfortunate consequences in terms of the self-concept of the disabled person. Research indicates that early manual communication, which facilitates development of concepts, does not retard the development of deaf students' speech.

New methods of standardized sign language which include more grammatical variances, combined with finger spelling, writing, speech, and lip-reading, provide the individual with greater language concept precision. Thus it seems that the total communication approach not only provides the deaf child with more opportunities for relating to others and for reinforcing a favorable self-concept, but may actually be better preparation for successful oral communication.

Prevalence

Hearing disorders are one of the most common chronic physical impairments in the United States; however, for many years no satisfactory tabulation of the number of hearing-impaired persons was available, because of difficulties in definition and classification, and such problems as case-finding among young children and the prevalence of multiple handicaps. This situation has been rectified by the definitive work of Jerome D. Schein and Marcus T. Delk, Jr., of the Deafness Research and Training Center at New York University. In their book, *The Deaf Population of the United States,* published by the National Association of the Deaf in 1974, based on a 1971 survey, they state that there are 13,362,842 Americans of all ages with hearing impairment sufficient to affect communication. Of these, 6,548,842 are affected by significant bilateral hearing loss, of whom 201,626 were afflicted prior to three years of age and 410,522 prior to 19 years of age.

Types

The *congenitally deaf* are those who have never heard, or were so young when hearing loss occurred that sound has little meaning for them. Others who become deaf later in life from disease or trauma are referred to as *adventitiously deaf*.

Conductive deafness occurs when sound waves cannot be transmitted in either the outer or middle ear. It may be due to a congenital blockage of the auditory canal or total absence of the passageway (congenital atresia). Frequently obstruction of the canal is caused by a condition which is temporary, such as a foreign object or an accumulation of wax, and can be successfully relieved. A more common cause of conductive deafness results from infection of the middle ear due to upper respiratory infection, diseased tonsils and adenoids, or other common childhood diseases. Middle ear infection (otitis media) has been estimated to cause about one-tenth of the severe cases of deafness in adults. Another common cause of conductive deafness is the development of a spongy growth of bone in the middle ear called otosclerosis.

Sensory neural or nerve deafness affects the inner ear or the auditory nerve leading to the brain. It can arise from a variety of causes, including German measles (rubella) in the mother during the first three months of pregnancy; complications of infectious diseases such as meningitis or diphtheria; or from some blow (trauma) or toxicity.

Degree of impairment varies considerably and is usually measured by audiometer tests, which indicate whether or not a person can hear pure tones at various frequency levels. Functional hearing is also measured by how well the person hears the human voice at different levels of loudness.

How well one utilizes what hearing one has is significantly affected by the age at onset, life experiences for conceptualization, comfort with self and others, the life-style of the individual, and the specific frequency loss (losses in the speech range are most limiting). The degree of functional hearing in relation to the development and education of the person is a highly individualized matter which requires the skillful evaluation and reevaluation by the medical specialist (otologist), the audiologist, the speech pathologist, and the teacher; sometimes a counselor, psychologist, or psychiatrist; and most certainly the deaf person and family. The extent of capacity to perceive communication from others and to respond to others determines the degree of handicap more than the extent of physiological loss.

Causes

Two major causes of congenital deafness are heredity and rubella. In modern times genetic factors have been the leading cause, except during epidemic periods of rubella. Genetic deafness often involves recessive genes, even when there is known deafness in the family. The unpredictability of genetics is such that many more persons carry these recessive genes than develop hereditary deafness. In cases where genetic deafness is suspected or definitely established, family members should obtain genetic counseling so that they are informed of all future possibilities. They should also obtain periodic ophthalmological examinations because there are cases of hearing loss where visual problems exist. (See CHAPTER 19: BIRTH DEFECTS; GENETIC COUNSELING and CHAPTER 28: THE DEAF-BLIND.)

Rubella in the mother during pregnancy may be so mild that she is not aware of the disease, and yet it can cause serious defects in the developing fetus. The period of greatest danger is the first three months of pregnancy, but damage can occur just prior to conception or as late as the eighth or ninth month. Preventive vaccines have been developed which give promise of eventually eliminating rubella as a major cause of deafness.

Premature births and complications of the Rh factor may also result in congenital deafness. Diseases in childhood which may result in deafness are meningitis (3 to 5 percent of children who contract it are affected) and encephalitis.

Treatment

In cases of otitis media, otosclerosis, and other types of conductive deafness, otological surgery offers restorative procedures. At the present time, nerve deafness is irreversible, and the major treatment emphasis is amplification of sound. Even when hearing aids do not bring human speech within the range of hearing, they sometimes help the deaf person to make volume judgments or hear warning sounds in the environment. When individuals have insufficient hearing to perform ordinary functions of life without special education (profound deafness), the major treatment thrust becomes a rehabilitative one to help the person acquire communication and other skills, develop individuality, and adjust to life.

Speech and hearing clinics (frequently called societies, centers, or leagues) are specialized centers for evaluation and rehabilitative treatment of deaf persons. More than half of the 350 speech and hearing clinics in the United States are connected with colleges, universities, and medical schools. Others are associated with schools for the deaf and hospitals, and are privately operated. Services of these clinics may include audiological and speech evaluation; medical (otological) examinations; hearing aid prescription; psychological assessment; personal counseling, group therapy, and social services; family counseling and training of preschool deaf children; auditory and speech training; speech and lip-reading; teaching sign language to deaf persons, families, and volunteers; social and recreational activities; vocational assessment, counseling, and job placement.

Education

When deafness occurs before language concepts have been formed, there is the need for a long period of specialized teaching

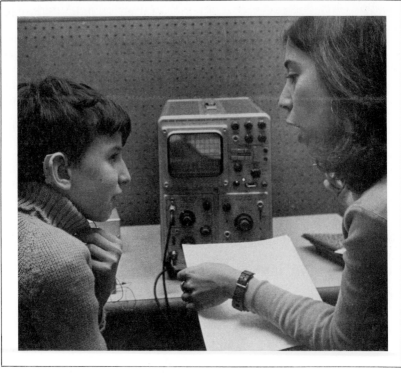

A deaf child receives speech training. (Lexington School for the Deaf, Jackson Heights, New York)

aimed at the development of the ability to put feelings, experiences, and facts into symbols which can be communicated. Early diagnosis and training are crucial for optimal development, and throughout the educational experience of the deaf individual there is the need for specialized aids and techniques.

There are a variety of settings in which education of the deaf can be achieved. Many schools start with children three or four years of age. Most states have public residential schools as well as day schools for deaf students integrated with hearing students. In addition there are a large number of private schools and classes, some of which are denominational. Most schools include speech training in the curriculum, and many have specialized programs for multiple-handicapped deaf children.

While there are exceptions, the majority of deaf students in the elementary grades are in self-contained classes and integrate with hearing students primarily for nonacademic classes, such as physical education and art. These children may also be in residential schools where little or no integration is possible.

Hard-of-hearing students may be in self-contained classes but tend to integrate more into the regular academic classes and are not usually placed in residential schools. In some systems, hard-of-hearing children are placed in regular classrooms and visited periodically by an itinerant speech therapist for tutoring or other assistance. Another arrangement for hard-of-hearing children is to be in the regular classroom with a resource room teacher available to them on a regular scheduled basis (usually one hour daily) for tutoring, language development, and other assistance.

Gallaudet College in Washington, D.C., founded in 1856, was the only liberal arts college for deaf students in the world for many years. California State University at Northridge is currently admitting deaf undergraduates and providing financial support, and other institutions will likely follow. The vocational-technical equivalent of Gallaudet is the National Technical Institute for the Deaf, within the administrative structure of the Rochester Institute of Technology. Other major federally funded programs are Seattle Community College, St. Paul Technical Vocational Institute, and Degado College in New Orleans.

State and federally funded vocational rehabilitation programs usually provide funding for tuition and room and board, as well as books and supplies on a quarterly basis for the deaf student approved to attend postsecondary programs. The success of the three junior college programs mentioned indicates that with counseling, interpreting, and tutorial services the deaf student can progress in the vocational-technical areas at about the same rate as hearing students. Some deaf and hard-of-hearing persons participate in vocational schools and colleges and universities with no special assistance, working out adaptations themselves.

Vocational Rehabilitation

Professionals and deaf adults are working to promote public and employer understanding of vocational capacities of deaf persons, individualized treatment, training in job and communication skills, and job performance standards equal to those of hearing employees. There is an emphasis on realistic career goals and personal life adjustment as well as the need for a wide variety of occupational training and better job opportunities without discrimination.

The bulk of rehabilitation costs are directly or indirectly paid for by state-federal rehabilitation programs. There are such programs in each state, and some of these have become effective in facilitating satisfactory vocational achievement of deaf persons by employing specialists who are experienced and intimately involved with the problems their clients face. The time needed for vocational training of deaf persons may seem long when compared with many other disability groups; however, as in the general education of deaf individuals, solidly acquired concepts take time to be achieved but can result in continued accomplishment and success.

Communications factors are significant in career choice and job placement of the deaf. It is necessary to determine the extent of communication needed on a particular job and the client's capability to meet the requirements as well as the degree of interaction with coworkers or the public, and the climate for accepting the deaf worker.

Job-sample and sheltered workshop experiences frequently help

401

prepare the deaf person to cope with the world of work. Follow-up support, after the job is obtained, can be crucial to success, because it is difficult to acquire the sophistication and social competence which the deaf must possess in order to maintain good work relationships with their hearing coworkers and supervisors. For example, changes on the job can result in misunderstandings, suspicion, and bafflement. Experienced rehabilitation workers recommend providing employers with easy access to vocational counselors as needed and periodic follow-up efforts with the deaf employee outside of work time so that supportive efforts do not inadvertently interfere with success on the job.

Employers are frequently reluctant to hire individuals who present differences with which they are unfamiliar; therefore, there is a need for interpretation of the ability, adaptability, and potential of the deaf employee, preferably by the deaf person. The federal government has provided many opportunities for deaf persons to demonstrate to private industry and business the remarkably fine work record they can maintain in a variety of clerical, mechanical, professional, and technical jobs. As more and more deaf persons function in a greater variety of jobs, employment doors are opening to careers commensurate with individual abilities and training.

Onset in Later Life

Many persons develop hearing loss in their mature years. Amplification is now available for most conditions, but there are some related problems. Sophisticated devices are very costly, and many persons on limited incomes cannot afford them unless subsidized by Medicaid or other insurance coverage. If all governmental programs fail, philanthropic organizations should be explored.

Perhaps a more frequent deterrent to using hearing aids than the high cost is a denial of the problem. Many individuals seem to feel that they will be treated with less respect or acceptance if they have a visible sign of disability. More often than not, the lack of communication and isolation resulting from impaired hearing causes far greater discomfort and rejection than one would experience due to the wearing of a hearing aid. Often the denial is partly a rejection of the aging process in general. These problems may make it very difficult to cope with the adjustment period required in some instances to the amplification of sound. Some people report considerable tension and must use their hearing aids gradually, but there are also cases of individuals who were immediately delighted with the ability to hear well again and who consistently wear their aids.

Aids and Devices

The hearing aid industry has attempted to ensure ethical and professional standards through voluntary self-regulation (National Hearing Aid Society, 2402 Grand River Avenue, Detroit, MI 48219). The doctor or evaluation clinic usually recommends several reputable dealers, and it is wise to select one conveniently located for subsequent service. If one has been told that a hearing aid will not improve a condition, it is advisable to check this out from time to time because technology in this electronic field advances at a relatively fast pace.

Ingenuity has been employed to produce visual cues in place of traditional sound cues — for example, light changes rather than the sound of a doorbell; adapting light so that it increases in intensity as the deaf person's voice becomes louder to aid in learning control; flashing-light Morse code for telephone communication.

One new device permits people with hearing disabilities to use the telephone. Called Phonetype, it connects an ordinary telephone to a teletypewriter. The impulses from the teletypewriter are converted to sound and transmitted through the telephone system to a receiver, where they are again converted for use by another teletypewriter. At present, there must be a teletypewriter and converter at both ends of the connection. The patented conversion device costs about $150.00, and several communications companies have donated surplus teletypewriters. Distribution of the unit is controlled by the National Association of the Deaf. This system frees those with hearing disabilities from depending on others to assist them in using the telephone. In some cities, police departments have Phonetype units so that deaf persons can request police or fire department assistance. Units in centers for deaf persons are in almost constant use, providing an opportunity for people who cannot afford their own units to take advantage of them.

Research

In fiscal 1975 the National Institute of Neurological and Communication Disorders and Stroke allocated $10,433,000 to research projects on disorders of hearing and related fields. In addition to government-sponsored research and the considerable amount of investigation done by individuals preparing to be teachers and counselors of the deaf, $1 million per year is being contributed from nongovernmental sources (private agencies, voluntary health agencies, and universities) for research in hearing. The Deafness Research Foundation alone made grants and awards totaling $303,772 in 1974, and has allocated over $5,000,000 to research since its founding in 1958. Normal and pathological functioning of the ear continues to be under investigation as well as many training and accommodation methods. Some of the benefits that have already accrued from research projects are microsurgery for conductive deafness, stapedectomy for otosclerosis, identification of viruses causing ear infections, and new surgical procedures for auditory nerve tumors.

Organizations

Many religious denominations conduct services, Sunday schools, Bible classes, and other religious instruction and devotions for deaf persons, and some parochial schools have outstanding special education programs.

The National Association of Hearing and Speech Agencies (814

Thayer Avenue, Silver Spring, MD 20910) and the American Speech and Hearing Association (9030 Old Georgetown Road, Bethesda, MD 20014) are composed of specialists in communication disorders. The National Association of the Deaf (814 Thayer Avenue, Silver Spring, MD 20910) has a number of cooperating state chapters, and there are also state associations not affiliated with the national one. The National Fraternal Society for the Deaf (6701 West North Avenue, Oak Park, IL 60302) lists groups in cities around the United States. The Alexander Graham Bell Association for the Deaf, Inc. (1537 35th Street N.W., Washington, DC 20007), established 1892, disseminates information and promotes speech and lip reading.

"A Directory of Services for the Deaf in the United States" is annually compiled and published by the *American Annals of the Deaf* (a journal published six times a year as an official organ of schools and instructors of the deaf; 5034 Wisconsin Avenue N.W., Washington, DC 20016), and is a comprehensive enumeration of educational, clinical, and organizational services.

SELECTED REFERENCES

Facts about Hearing and Hearing Aids, Superintendent of Documents, Government Printing Office, Washington, DC 20402.

Greenburg, Joanne, *In This Sign,* Holt, Rinehart & Winston, New York, 1970.

Hearing Loss: Hope through Research, National Institutes of Health, Office of Scientific and Health Reports, Bethesda, MD 20014.

Jacobs, Leo, *A Deaf Adult Speaks Out,* Gallaudet College Press, Washington, D.C., 1975.

Levine, Edna S., *Psychology of Deafness,* Columbia University Press, New York, 1960.

Mindel, Eugene D., and McCoy, Vernon, *They Grew in Silence: The Deaf Child and His Family,* National Association of the Deaf, Silver Spring, Maryland, 1971.

Opportunities for the Hard of Hearing and the Deaf, U.S. Department of Health, Education and Welfare, Office of Human Development, Rehabilitation Services Administration, Washington, DC 20201.

Schlesinger, H., and K. Meadow, *Sound and Sign,* University of California Press, Berkeley, 1973.

What Every Person Should Know about Heredity and Deafness, Public Service Programs, Gallaudet College, Washington, DC 20002.

34

Hypertension

ROBERT M. GOLDENSON, Ph.D.

Reviewed by MARVIN MOSER, M.D., Senior Medical Consultant to the
National High Blood Pressure Education Program, National Heart,
Lung and Blood Institute

Blood pressure is measured with a sphygmomanometer, which consists of an inflatable cuff wrapped around the arm, and a device for indicating the effect of the pressure on a column of mercury registering in millimeters. Levels vary considerably from individual to individual and tend to increase with age, body weight, and stress. In early childhood the average systolic pressure (registered at the moment of heart contraction) is about 80, and the normal diastolic pressure (registered when the heart is momentarily at rest) is 55. These values increase to 95–110 systolic and 65–80 diastolic during adolescence. The normal upper limit in adulthood has been arbitrarily established at 140/90.

Age, however, is still an important factor in adult life. As stated in the American Heart Association publication "How You Can Help Your Doctor Treat Your High Blood Pressure": "Usually in any person under the age of 40 a systolic pressure greater than 140–145 is elevated. However, in patients of 60 to 70 years of age a systolic pressure of 150–155 may be within normal limits. When the diastolic pressure is consistently greater than 90–95, the diagnosis of hypertension is justified."

Estimates based on the National Health Examination Survey indicate that 23 million Americans have a systolic blood pressure of 160 or more. Of these, 9.5 million show a diastolic pressure between 95 and 104, and 4.5 million show 105 or more. In the remaining 9 million the systolic is at least 160 but the diastolic is below 95.

The estimated number of hypertension cases by age is 1.4 million between ages eighteen and thirty-four; 2.8 million between thirty-five and forty-four; 4.6 million between forty-five and fifty-four; 5.5 million between fifty-five and sixty-four; and 8.7 million above sixty-five. The prevalence is about twice as high among blacks as among whites, and is slightly higher among white females than white males; but in general, women tolerate the condition better than men. Elevations are generally found to develop earlier and persist longer among relatives of hypertensive than among nonhypertensive individuals.

Diagnosis and Effects

Although the diagnosis of hypertension is primarily based on repeated blood pressure measurements, there are a number of other symptoms and signs. The most common and often most disabling symptom is a dull, pounding headache in the occipital region (back of the head). Long-term untreated cases may also develop such symptoms as lightheadedness, vertigo, flatulence, fatigability, heart palpitations, and excessive perspiration. These symptoms are not always present—in fact, many patients with elevated blood pressure have no symptoms or signs whatever. This is one of the major reasons why studies have shown that only 30 percent of affected individuals are aware of the disorder. It is also important to recognize that those who do become aware of the condition frequently develop emotional reactions of fear and anxiety (blood pressure consciousness or phobia), which not only cause distress but may actually aggravate the condition itself.

The physical effects of excessive blood pressure are serious and often critical. A Society of Actuaries study based upon life expectancy figures for males at age thirty-five indicates that even minimal elevations in blood pressure, if persistent, may shorten life. According to this study, the reduction in life expectancy for individuals with a blood pressure of 140/95 is 9 years, and for those with 150/100, 16½ years. Major elevations in blood pressure are one of the prime contributory factors to heart attacks and strokes, as well as kidney disease and visual disorders. Arteriosclerosis of the coronary and cerebral arteries tends to be more severe among individuals with high blood pressure than among normotensive individuals, resulting in a sharply increased incidence of heart attacks and strokes. Of the estimated 800,000 persons who suffer a first heart attack each year, 545,000, or 68 percent, have definite or borderline high blood pressure (42 percent definite, that is, at least 160/95; and 26 percent borderline, that is, 140–160/90–95). Of the estimated 400,000 who are afflicted with the first stroke, 300,000, or 75 percent, have hypertension (54 percent definite; 21 percent borderline). Hypertension is also frequently associated with arteriosclerotic heart disease.

A widely cited study conducted in Framingham, Massachusetts, concludes that the risk of every manifestation of coronary heart disease, including angina, coronary insufficiency, myocardial infarction, and sudden death, was distinctly and impressively related to the antecedent level of both systolic and diastolic blood pressure.

The risk of stroke is even greater than the risk of heart attack, and in both cases this risk increases as the pressure increases. (See CHAPTER 25: CARDIAC DISORDERS; CHAPTER 52: STROKE.)

The personal cost of these conditions in terms of anxiety and stress on the individual and the family is incalculable. The cost to the United States economy, however, has been estimated for the year 1972. According to the Social Security Administration Information Bureau, cardiovascular diseases as a whole cost this country $40 billion in direct and indirect medical care and loss of productivity. This figure represents 21 percent of the total economic cost for all diseases, which came to $189 billion for that year. A large percentage of the cardiovascular cost can be attributed to hypertension, which is often a major contributory factor to these illnesses, disabilities, and deaths.

Etiology

When blood pressure is high but fairly constant and there is no immediate danger, the hypertension is described as benign; but when it is rapidly progressive and dangerous, it is termed malignant. Over 90 percent of individuals with elevated blood pressure have essential hypertension—that is, the specific cause is unknown, though the condition may be of hereditary or constitutional origin. The small number of cases (some claim as few as 6 percent) in which the etiology can be definitely traced are due to such conditions as overactivity of the thyroid gland, arteriovenous fistula (narrowing of blood vessels due to disease or injury), oversecretion of the pituitary gland, adrenal cortical hyperfunction, or a rapidly expanding brain tumor.

In addition, psychogenic factors may be involved as contributory causes of hypertension, as described in the *Encyclopedia of Human Behavior* by Robert M. Goldenson:

> In many cases it appears to be due to a pre-existing tendency toward high blood pressure which is aggravated by emotional stress. The situations that contribute to hypertension often involve anger against people on whom the patient is extremely dependent. Some authorities believe this pattern originated early in life when the patient was unable to handle his ambivalent impulses toward his parents—that is, he was afraid of expressing his resentment fully and openly because at the same time he loved and depended on them. At any rate these patients get into the habit of repressing their hostility instead of releasing it through speech and action. Their pent-up anger then discharges itself through the vascular system, causing increased blood pressure. Not surprisingly, then, adult hypertensive patients tend to be outwardly calm, controlled and conforming—but these attitudes conceal inward urges of an aggressive character.

Treatment and Prognosis

The most pressing need in the hypertension picture today is for prompt, effective treatment even of moderate cases before they can lead to stroke, heart attack, or kidney failure. In a recent article,

"Long-Term Management of Hypertension," Marvin Moser, M.D., questions some of the common approaches to this problem and outlines a step-by-step procedure, the core of which is drug therapy. When repeated blood pressure measurements indicate a consistent elevation, the physician's first task is to take a thorough history and to perform a physical examination and certain diagnostic tests. Although some physicians hospitalize the patient for this work-up, a recent report by the Joint National Committee on Detection, Evaluation and Treatment of Hypertension indicates that hospitalization is rarely necessary and that time and expense can be saved if the basic tests are performed in the doctor's office. Among these tests are urinalysis, electrocardiogram, hematocrit, serum potassium, and in many cases, blood sugar, serum cholesterol, and chest x-ray.

Dr. Moser also suggests that too much emphasis is often placed on weight reduction, dietary restrictions, and a less active life, to the neglect of other forms of therapy.

> Many physicians suggest that hypertensive patients be placed on a low-salt diet, obesity be corrected, certain lifestyle changes such as "taking it easy" be implemented, and sedatives or tranquilizers be tried before specific drug therapy is begun. This approach may appear to be correct but is rarely effective in controlling elevated blood pressure other than the mildest forms.

He does not rule out these approaches but has found on the basis of twenty-three years' experience that it is usually enough to eliminate obviously salty foods such as pretzels, peanuts, and bacon; and he points out that control of blood pressure can be achieved without dramatic shifts of occupation or taking an hour a day off. It is also advisable to recommend moderation in smoking and avoidance of overexertion as well as excessive use of alcohol, and he states that "it is important for people to lose weight, but while weight is being lost, blood pressure should be treated more specifically with anti-hypertensive drugs," especially if the diastolic blood pressure is over 105, or is between 90 and 105 if the patient is a black male and shows other risk factors such as diabetes, obesity, and elevated blood cholesterol.

There are several steps in the basic drug therapy approach. First most cases of mild to moderate hypertension should be started on thiazide or thiazidelike diuretics, which have proven effective in 30 to 40 percent of cases because they eliminate excessive sodium from the body. If diuretics alone do not bring the blood pressure down to normal levels, a second-step drug such as alpha-methyldopa, rauwolfia, or propanolol is added to the diuretic.

If one of these combinations is not effective, as they usually are in 60 to 70 percent of cases, the addition of hydralazine or clonidine is suggested as a third step. And if this triple combination is inadequate, the addition or substitution of guanethidine for one of the other drugs, such as alpha-methyldopa, will frequently normalize the blood pressure.

A description of the specific nature and effect of each of these types of drugs will not be attempted here. In general, they reduce blood pressure by relaxing narrowed blood vessels through direct action on their muscular wall or by blocking the nerve supply that causes at least part of the narrowing. It is important, however, to recognize three other aspects of drug therapy. First, each of the drugs may have unpleasant or undesirable side effects on some individuals. These effects usually diminish or even disappear in time; if they do not, the physician will prescribe drugs that will counteract them, or switch to another medication. Second, the dosages must be carefully regulated for each individual, and this, too, takes time and patience. Third, once an effective formula is found, the medications must in most cases be continued indefinitely, since high blood pressure is a lifelong condition requiring ongoing treatment. This cannot be overemphasized, since patients frequently discontinue treatment when their symptoms subside. But studies show that if they continue to visit their physician three or four times a year even after their blood pressure has been normalized, they will maintain their improvement in at least 85 percent of cases, and the risk of disabling stroke, heart attack, or kidney failure will be sharply reduced. A close, supportive relationship of physician to patient is essential as a means of encouraging the patient to continue and periodically check the drug treatment, and in some cases psychotherapy is recommended as a means of alleviating anxiety and tension that may provoke flare-ups.

Research Expenditures and Needs

A recent volume, *The Killers and Cripplers*, compiled by the National Health Education Committee, clearly summarizes facts and figures on hypertension research provided by the National Heart, Lung and Blood Institute and other governmental and nongovernmental sources. In fiscal 1974 the Institute allocated $47,409,000 specifically to research in hypertension, including kidney disease. Large amounts were also devoted to research on other cardiovascular disorders which may have a bearing on the problem of hypertension. These include $60,487,000 allocated to arteriosclerosis, $3,482,000 to stroke, and $110,462,000 to other cardiovascular conditions. In addition, the National Institute of Neurological Diseases, Communication Disorders and Stroke spent $8,578,000 on stroke research in 1975; the U.S. Atomic Energy Commission, $2,667,000 on research in cardiovascular disorders in 1973; and the Veterans Administration, $10,164,000 on research dealing with stroke and other cardiovascular conditions in 1975. All these research expenditures add up to a grand total of $243,249,000 in federal funds. In the private sector, the American Heart Association and its affiliates spent $16,778,531 for research in 1973.

It is not easy to assess the results of these research programs, but the volume by the National Health Education Committee offers the following comments:

As a result of the medical research breakthrough in the development of many effective antihypertension drugs, (1) the death rate from hypertensive disease (as defined by the National Vital Statistics Division and not including its relationship to deaths from heart attacks and strokes) has declined more than 65% since 1950; (2) while the death rate from hypertensive disease has declined, the full impact of therapy now available for hypertension has not yet sufficiently affected the death rates from other types of heart disease and strokes in which hypertension is involved, since many victims of high blood pressure go undetected and untreated until the heart attack or stroke is actually experienced.

This again is a reminder of the urgent need for education of both the medical profession and the public that even moderate hypertension should be treated early in order to prevent the development of heart disease; and the need for the development and evaluation of new and more effective techniques for delivering long-term care to all hypertensive patients, since at present far too many of those who have been detected and treated leave therapy too early or receive inadequate treatment.

SELECTED REFERENCES

Goldenson, Robert M., *Encyclopedia of Human Behavior: Psychology, Psychiatry, and Mental Health*, Doubleday, Garden City, New York, 1970.

Kannel, W. B., Melvin J. Schwartz, and Patricia M. McNamara, "Blood Pressure and Risk of Coronary Heart Disease: The Framingham Study," *Diseases of the Chest*, vol. 56, no. 1, July 1969.

Moser, Marvin, *How You Can Help Your Doctor Treat Your High Blood Pressure*, American Heart Association, 1976.

Moser, Marvin, "Long-Term Management of Hypertension," in Albert Brest, ed., *The Cardiovascular Clinic*, Grune & Stratton, New York, 1977.

National Health Education Committee, *The Killers and Cripplers: Facts on Major Diseases in the United States Today*, David McKay, New York, 1976.

35

Kidney Disease

VIRGINIA M. METCALFE, Department of Health
Services, University of Washington, Seattle*

Normally functioning kidneys contribute to the maintenance of a
stable environment within the body by helping regulate the water,
electrolyte, and acid base content of the blood. The excretion of
urine, the watery solution of waste products of metabolism, is the
most obvious function of kidneys. Intact kidneys protect against the
extremes of dehydration and fluid overload by adjusting the volume
of fluid excreted according to a constantly changing amount of hy-
dration. By altering the acidity of urine, the kidney excretes excess
acid or retains acid to balance accumulating bases, thus assuring (in
conjunction with regulation of the amount of carbon dioxide ex-
haled) an extremely narrow range of pH (an indicator of acidity or
alkalinity) in blood and body fluids. Renal regulation of body stores
of several elements, notably sodium, permits large variation in the
amount ingested without the risks of intoxication or depletion. Ni-
trogen-containing end products of protein digestion, primarily
urea, are mainly excreted in the urine. Urine composition mirrors
closely the presence and quantity of normal and abnormal compounds in blood, and this is the reason that analysis of urine is so
important to assessment of health and diagnosis of disease.

*This chapter is condensed from material prepared for the *Renal Disease Services Criteria and Standards
Draft Monograph,* 1976, by Virginia M. Metcalfe, in cooperation with Christopher R. Blagg, M.D., Northwest
Kidney Center, Seattle, and Eli A. Friedman, M.D., Downstate Medical Center, Brooklyn. Graduate research
assistants Janet K. Edlefsen and Ursula Roosen-Runge assisted in developing portions of the monograph. The
monograph was prepared for the Bureau of Health Planning and Resources Development of the Department of
Health, Education and Welfare under contract no. HRA 106-74-56.

Every individual normally has two kidneys, each weighing about 4–6 ounces (113–170 grams), measuring approximately 4½ × 2–3 × 1 inch (11 × 5–7.5 × 2.5 cm), and located in the posterior abdomen at the junction of the thoracic and lumbar spine. Each kidney is composed of about 1 million separate functioning units termed nephrons. Within the nephron, blood is filtered at the initial portion (called the glomerulus), and the filtrate, free of blood cells and proteins, is modified in its subsequent course through the remaining nephron (called the renal tubule) until it passes into the ureter and then the bladder.

During its passage through the nephron, as the blood filtrate is modified to become urine, the kidney responds to body needs by either reclaiming substances (such as glucose) or adding wastes (organic acids). The importance of the filtration, addition, subtraction sequence can be judged from the fact that one-fifth of blood pumped from the heart flows through the kidneys. Approximately 180 liters of filtrate is produced at the glomerulus each day, and 1 to 2 liters of urine is excreted, an indication of the activity of the kidney in preserving needed body constituents. The additional endocrine functions of the kidney, notably in the control of blood pressure by secretion of the hormone renin, and in the stimulation of bone marrow synthesis of red blood cells, underscore the essentiality of renal functional integrity to life.

Disease

Kidney diseases are many and varied, ranging from minor, short-term ailments to serious, chronic disease. For each function of the kidney there is a disease or family of diseases relating to malfunction. For example, a patient unable to excrete acid through the kidney becomes acidotic even though other renal functions are intact. Similarly loss of the kidney's ability to conserve sodium may produce a disease in which depletion of the body sodium stores is the most prominent clinical feature.

Some diseases involve all functions of the kidney and eventually lead to renal failure, a condition in which the kidneys are unable to filter waste products from the blood adequately, characterized by life-threatening disturbances of the body's chemical balance. Renal failure may be acute and reversible or chronic and irreversible (end-stage renal disease, or ESRD). The exclusion of curable causes of renal failure, such as those due to urinary tract obstruction by an enlarged prostate or kidney stones, is essential before the patient is entered into a long-term program for management of chronic renal disease.

The major diseases causing ESRD are given below.

Glomerulonephritis. This is a general term which refers to inflammation of the glomeruli of the kidney, in most cases the result of an immune reaction in which the body produces antibodies that injure or destroy its own glomeruli. Acute glomerulonephritis is most common in young children, although it is found in individuals of all ages, and usually occurs as the delayed aftermath of a streptococcal infection. The risk of getting acute glomerulonephritis after a strep infection is extremely low. Chronic glomerulonephritis represents a heterogeneous group of disorders, each characterized by damage to the structure of the nephron, principally the glomerular portion. In most cases the glomerular damage is probably the result of an immune phenomenon, and it is only rarely associated with a streptococcal infection or with a prior case of acute glomerulonephritis. Chronic glomerulonephritis is the single most common cause of ESRD, accounting for 40 to 60 percent of all patients in dialysis and transplant programs.

Genetic Renal Diseases. Inherited renal diseases account for 10 to 20 percent of all cases of ESRD. The most common (8 to 14 percent of ESRD) inherited disease, polycystic disease, is a dominant disorder resulting in large cysts in both kidneys, and frequently cysts in the liver, pancreas, lungs, and other organs. Characteristically, adult patients of either sex are discovered to have polycystic kidneys in the third to fifth decade of life during the course of evaluation for a complaint of back pain, urinary tract bleeding, or infection. Loss of renal function progressing to ESRD occurs over five to ten years in about half of affected patients. Because it can be predicted that one-half of the siblings and one-half of the children of affected patients will also have the disease, genetic counseling is an important part of management. Other heritable renal diseases, each with different clinical expressions, include medullary cystic disease, interstitial nephritis with deafness (Alport's syndrome), cystinosis, oxalosis, Fabry's disease, renal tubular disorders, sickle cell disease, and infantile polycystic disease.

Pyelonephritis. This term implies a bacterial or viral inflammation of the renal tubules and the supporting structures between tubules—the interstitia. Development of ESRD in patients with pyelonephritis nearly always is associated with the presence of obstruction or other structural abnormalities in the urinary tract which predispose to the occurrence of repeated urinary tract infections. Confusing the elucidation of the cause of chronic pyelonephritis is the evidence that diseases of the kidney other than infection may also produce the microscopic findings associated with chronic pyelonephritis. These other diseases include excessive use of analgesics, gout, nephrotoxic drugs, renal irradiation, hereditary nephritis, heavy metal poisoning, renal vascular disease, and diabetes mellitus.

Obstructive Disease. Early recognition of urinary tract obstruction is important because of the potential for actual cure rather than palliative treatment. Surgical relief of obstruction due to an enlarged prostate is obviously preferable to effective dialysis or a successful transplant. In addition to prostatism, renal stones, tumors, and, rarely, blood clots may prevent free flow of urine and lead to "curable" renal failure, which, if undetected, may become ESRD.

Hypertensive Renal Disease. Systemic primary (essential) hypertension may induce secondary renal damage due to nephrosclerosis, and may lead to ESRD. Damaged kidneys, whether or not the initial injury was due to hypertension, may continue to cause hypertension through the secretion of renin, a hormone which activates angiotensin, a substance in plasma, which is a potent elevator of blood pressure.

Metabolic Diseases. Diabetes mellitus is an important cause of ESRD. In fact, 57 percent of all juvenile diabetics die in uremia, and renal failure is seventeen times more common in maturity-onset diabetics than in the population at large. Unfortunately the same degenerative vascular complications which destroy renal function in the diabetic also affect the eyes, heart, peripheral vasculature, and neurological system, thus lessening the chances for rehabilitation by dialysis and transplantation. Gouty nephropathy is a disease of the kidney in which uric acid deposits incite an inflammatory reaction in the tissues between the tubules. Obstruction of urine flow occasionally may result from blockage of tubules by urate deposits. Excessive mobilization of calcium from bone in hyperparathyroidism may produce obstruction of the urinary tract by calcium-containing stones, or may actually deposit large amounts of calcium throughout the kidney, thereby damaging the kidney.

Systemic Diseases. Included in this category are diffuse connective tissue disorders such as systemic lupus erythematosus and scleroderma, and diseases of unknown cause such as amyloidosis. The important point to be noted is that when a patient with systemic disease develops ESRD, the prognosis is tied to the multiple system involvement; treatment of ESRD may not affect rehabilitation when other organs have also failed.

Tumors. Tumors, malignant or otherwise, may cause ESRD, either by obstruction of urine flow or by infiltration and destruction of functioning renal tissue. Multiple myeloma is a malignant disease of certain white blood cells (plasma cells) in which renal failure is common.

Congenital Anomalies. Abnormalities of the kidneys, ureters, or bladder may be due to birth defects. X-ray of the urinary system usually reveals such anomaly.

Treatment

Establishment of a specific diagnosis assumes high priority in the treatment of each new patient with compromised renal function. Once a diagnosis has been made, it may be possible to forecast at what rate future deterioration of renal function will occur. For example, azotemia (the presence in the blood of excessive amounts of urea and other nitrogenous waste products normally removed by the kidney) in scleroderma or diabetic glomerulosclerosis heralds rapid deterioration, and usually indicates that uremia (the toxic condition associated with the retention of nitrogenous substances in the blood) will supervene in less than a year; a prolonged course, lasting five or more years, is probable in urate nephropathy and polycystic disease. Decisions relating to employment, marriage, and housing may depend on sound prognostication. Patients with inherited diseases such as cystinuria, medullary cystic disease, or the syndrome of hereditary nephritis and deafness frequently desire estimates of the risk that the disease will be transmitted to their children.

In mild and nonprogressive kidney diseases and in the early stages of progressive renal destruction, the kidneys usually continue to function adequately, and treatment consists of conservative management techniques. Conservative medical management refers to any treatment other than chronic dialysis or transplantation, and consists of attempts to reduce the excretory burden on the kidneys, delay their progressive destruction, and minimize symptoms in the patient. Conservative management may include drugs to control hypertension, low-protein, low-salt, or other modified diets, antibiotics to treat infection, iron supplementation to control anemia, and occasional dialysis to restore chemical balance.

For the patient whose kidney disease has progressed to the terminal or end stage, and for whom conservative management is no longer adequate, two types of treatment can extend life: dialysis and transplantation. Prior to the early 1960s, treatment that could sustain the end-stage renal disease patient was not available, and the fate for such patients was inevitable — death, usually within a few months. Now almost 90 percent of ESRD patients receiving maintenance dialysis or a renal transplant survive each year.

It is estimated that there are between 50,000 and 55,000 deaths related to some form of kidney disease each year in the United States. Though kidney transplantation and dialysis are accepted methods of treating end-stage renal disease, not all ESRD patients can benefit from treatment. An estimated 50-plus per million population, or about 10,000–11,000 new patients, are identified each year in this country who would benefit from dialysis or transplantation. During 1974 approximately 3,100 patients received kidney transplants and 5,000–6,000 new patients began maintenance dialysis. Since July 1973 all individuals with end-stage renal disease requiring dialysis or transplantation who are entitled to Social Security or Railroad Retirement benefits, or are spouses or dependents of such individuals, have been eligible for Medicare benefits. By mid-1975 over 25,000 renal disease patients had qualified for Medicare coverage of their treatment costs.

Transplantation and dialysis are not competitive, but are complementary, interdependent therapies. Should a transplant recipient reject the graft, the patient may be sustained on dialysis until the performance of a second or third transplant. Conversely a long-term dialysis patient may opt to have a transplant at any time during the course of treatment. In general, many of the younger patients may be better treated by transplantation, while patients in late middle age and beyond generally are better treated by long-term dialysis. Nevertheless even in younger patients dialysis is able to provide rehabilitation and a return to a useful productive life for many. This is important, because if a patient does not have a related donor to provide a kidney for transplantation, the patient may have to be maintained on dialysis for a considerable period of time until a cadaveric kidney becomes available.

The catastrophic nature of end-stage renal disease, the constancy and continuity of treatment needed to sustain life, and the resulting complications and emotional strains create certain special needs and requirements in treating ESRD patients. Returning the patient to a meaningful and satisfying position in society is an important goal of a comprehensive treatment approach. Treatment should be designed to restore the patient to as much normal function, and the life-style the patient desires, as is possible. This requires psychological, vocational, and rehabilitation counseling and the efforts of many types of support personnel, as well as the medical team. The most effective programs provide not only the medical treatment, but all of the supporting services required to enable the patient to remain a functioning member of society.

Transplantation

The first successful kidney transplant involved identical twins and was performed in Boston in 1954. Since 1963 the Human Renal Transplant Registry has kept centralized records of transplant data from throughout the world, and the recent Twelfth Report of the Human Renal Transplant Registry records data on a total of 16,444 kidney transplants. Of the 14,479 transplant recipients for whom follow-up data are available, 67.4 percent survive—46.8 percent with, and 20.6 percent without, a still-functioning graft.

Immunology and Graft Rejection. The central problem with transplanted organs is the immunological phenomenon, in which the body rejects and destroys tissue which comes from another individual. More than 60 percent of those kidney transplants which fail do so because of rejection or a complication associated with rejection.

The mechanism of rejection depends on substances called antigens and antibodies. Antigens from another individual are perceived as foreign and harmful proteins, and the body responds by producing antibodies to destroy them. Several antigen systems are involved in rejection of transplanted kidneys: the ABO system (the antigen system which determines an individual's blood group), the HL-A (human leukocyte-antigen) system, and other less well defined systems such as that represented by the MLC (mixed lymphocyte culture) test. Currently a variety of laboratory tests are used to type the tissues of recipients and donors in order to match them as closely as possible, and also to determine whether the recipient has already developed antibodies to any HL-A antigens of the proposed donor. Typing and matching ABO antigens is a simple and well-established process carried out by all blood banks. Tissue typing of the HL-A system and other tests such as MLC are more complex. At present, rejection remains the major obstacle to success of kidney transplantation, and will remain so until the immune phenomena involved are understood further so that appropriate countermeasures can be developed.

Rejection of a transplanted kidney is classified as hyperacute, acute, or chronic. Hyperacute rejection occurs on the operating table within minutes of connecting the kidney to the recipient's circulation; an acute rejection occurs within the first three months following transplantation; and a chronic rejection occurs at any time after three months posttransplantation. Rejections of the acute and chronic types may be difficult to diagnose, since the accompanying symptoms such as fever, malaise, and tenderness over the grafted kidney may be similar to those occurring with infection and other disorders.

Effects of Immunosuppressive Drugs. Currently the technique for minimizing rejection is the use of drugs to suppress the recipient's immune response to foreign tissue. The two major drugs used are azathioprine (brand name, Imuran) and prednisone or other corticosteroids. These drugs are effective in minimizing the rejection response but are associated with potentially serious side effects. The most important of these is an increased susceptibility to infection, as the patient's entire immune system, including those factors normally responsible for resisting bacterial, viral, and fungal infections, is suppressed. Infection, in consequence, is the single most frequent cause of death in transplant recipients, accounting for approximately 40 percent of deaths. Other possible side effects from these drugs include bleeding and ulceration of the gastrointestinal tract; bone disorders; cosmetic changes such as acne, puffy face, and weight gain; psychological changes; and an increased incidence of malignancies.

Antilymphocyte globulin (ALG) or antithymocyte globulin (ATG) is used by some transplant programs as an adjunct to the usual immunosuppressive drugs. Antilymphocyte globulin is antiserum produced in horses, goats, or rabbits following injection of human lymphocytes. Unfortunately techniques for standardization of antilymphocyte globulin are lacking, and some preparations may be relatively inactive. Consequently antilymphocyte globulin at present is under study, and is not used by all transplant programs.

Nephrectomy and Splenectomy. Kidney transplantation can be performed without removing the recipient's own kidneys. Nephrectomy (removal of the kidneys) constitutes an additional surgical risk and cost to the recipient and, furthermore, even badly damaged kidneys continue to produce erythropoietin (a hormone involved in the production of red blood cells) and other hormones, and may continue to put out an appreciable volume of urine, making management of the dialysis patient easier. Nevertheless bilateral nephrectomy prior to transplantation may still be required for recipients with infected or polycystic kidneys, and occasionally for patients with severe hypertension. Currently there is controversy as to the possible value of nephrectomy prior to transplantation in patients without hypertension or infection.

Removal of the spleen (splenectomy) may also be performed in association with bilateral nephrectomy prior to or at the time of transplantation. Splenectomy may be of value in those transplant patients who are to receive antilymphocyte globulin, but probably has no benefit in other circumstances, and may in fact present appreciable medical risks from infection later.

Donor Kidneys. There are three possible types of kidney donors: living related, living unrelated, and cadaver.

The ideal kidney donor is an identical twin, since immunological rejection then is zero. The next best donor is a sibling with identical HL-A antigens; kidney grafts from such a source have a two-year survival rate of 95 percent. Grafts from imperfectly matched siblings or from parents are somewhat less desirable, although recipient survival after such transplants still is appreciably better than with dialysis or with cadaveric transplantation.

Unrelated living donors have been used only rarely because their motivation for giving a kidney can be questioned, and because immunologic problems are as serious as with the use of unrelated cadaveric kidneys.

In the case of any living donor, whether related or unrelated, the benefits to the recipient must be carefully weighed against possible physical and psychological effects on the donor.

Cadavers are the most frequently used source of kidneys, and their use is increasing. The Twelfth Report of the Renal Transplant Registry notes that cadaveric kidneys have increased from 56 percent of grafts in 1967 to 70.4 percent of grafts performed in 1973. Use of cadaveric kidneys offers two major advantages: risks to living donors are avoided, and the potentially available pool of donor kidneys is increased greatly. This potential is not being realized at the present time, however, and a major factor limiting the number of transplants being performed in the United States is a continuing shortage of available kidneys. Efforts in several areas could help to alleviate this problem: public education to encourage donation of kidneys; resolution of ethical, medical and legal considerations in the definition of death; and establishment of improved networks for regional sharing of kidneys.

Use of cadaveric kidneys does, however, present some clinical problems also: (1) immunological problems exist; (2) the donor must be screened for complicating conditions such as infection, vascular disease which might involve the kidneys, malignancy, etc.; (3) graft failure is more frequent with cadaveric kidneys than with kidneys from related donors; and (4) appreciable renal damage interfering with function may occur at the time of death, or during the period between the removal of the kidneys from the donor and their transplantation into the recipients. Preservation techniques to maintain viable kidneys during this time include surface cooling and filling the kidney vasculature with a special electrolyte solution, or continuous pumping of specially prepared oxygenated blood plasma through the kidney in a special kidney perfusion machine. Current techniques allow for preservation of kidneys for as long as forty-eight to seventy-two hours before transplantation.

Graft Failure and Recipient Morbidity and Mortality. More than 60 percent of transplant graft failures reported by the Renal Transplant Registry are due to rejection; another 10 percent result from technical and surgical problems at the time of transplantation. In terms of patient death, infection or a combination of rejection and infection accounts for 40 percent of deaths. Other causes of patient death include gastrointestinal hemorrhage, 4.3 percent; myocardial infarction, 4.2 percent; stroke, 3.3 percent; and pulmonary embolism, 2 percent.

In addition, the incidence of morbidity is high, even in successful transplant recipients, and frequently is attributable to the immunosuppressive therapy used to prevent rejection. Reported disorders include such complications as infection, gastrointestinal bleeding, cardiovascular disease, malignancies, bone disease, iatrogenic Cushing's syndrome, recurrence of the original kidney disease in the grafted kidney, and other complications.

Because the results of transplantation vary from program to program, it is essential that individual patients be counseled as to the appropriateness of treatment by transplantation, with knowledge of the results of both patient and graft survival for both living related and cadaveric transplantation at the appropriate regional center, and that these be compared with the local results of dialysis.

Future of Kidney Transplantation. The greatest potential for improved success of kidney transplantation lies in the field of immunology. Techniques must be developed to block the immune response to grafted kidneys without reducing the response of the recipient to infectious agents. Further knowledge of the antigen systems involved in rejection may allow for improved matching techniques. Medical developments of this nature, coupled with greater availability of cadaveric kidneys and improved interregional sharing of kidneys, could result in transplantation becoming a more accessible and successful option for patients with end-stage renal disease.

Dialysis

At the present time the great majority of patients with end-stage renal disease in the United States must be treated by dialysis. Transplantation, although the treatment of choice for suitable patients, still is not sufficiently available, owing both to the scarcity of donated kidneys and to the yet unresolved immunologic problems.

Originally dialysis developed as an emergency procedure for the treatment of acute (short-term) kidney failure. In 1960, with development of the external (Scribner) shunt, dialysis treatment for the first time could be extended to patients who otherwise would have died from chronic renal failure. Since then, dialysis has become the predominant method of treatment for these patients, although as noted previously, if donor kidneys were available, transplantation would be preferable for at least some patients. The National Dialysis Registry, in existence since 1969, reported in

1975 that more than 14,000 persons in the United States were being treated with regular maintenance dialysis; it is estimated that the actual current number of dialysis patients in this country is closer to 20,000.

Theory and Procedures. Dialysis is a process during which water and diffusible solutes are removed from blood by bringing blood into contact with a membrane on the other side of which is a fluid that does not contain these solutes (or contains them in a different concentration). This specially formulated fluid is called dialysate. It is mixed in appropriate proportions with solutes similar to those present in normal blood so that these are not lost from the blood during dialysis. The membrane used in hemodialysis is contained in a device known as a dialyzer or an artificial kidney. (In the case of peritoneal dialysis, the peritoneal membrane lining of the patient's abdominal cavity is used as the membrane.) Dialysate is delivered to the dialyzer from a dialysate delivery system which either recirculates a large batch of dialyzing fluid through the dialyzer or repeatedly prepares and then discards the dialysate after it passes through the machine. The dialysate delivery system may include various devices to monitor both the patient and the dialysate.

Dialysis performs several essential functions normally performed by the kidneys: it maintains proper blood acidity, maintains salt and water balance, maintains other aspects of the body's chemical stability, and eliminates waste products of metabolism. Dialysis is, however, a relatively crude technique involving simple filtration, and it in no way replaces many of the complex and sensitively monitored processes of the normal kidney.

Dialysis treatment can be provided in a variety of settings and can be performed either by paid staff or by the patient and family members. Institutional dialysis refers to dialysis performed by trained professional staff, and can take place either in a hospital or in a nonhospital dialysis center. In-hospital dialysis is expensive and, as far as possible, should be reserved for patients requiring hospitalization rather than for regular maintenance dialysis. However, at the present time in the United States some 50 percent of patients on maintenance dialysis are being dialyzed in hospital units. Nonhospital institutional dialysis, often referred to as limited care dialysis, may take place in a dialysis center which provides no services other than in-center maintenance dialysis, or in a center which offers other services such as home dialysis training, supporting services for home dialysis patients, etc. Such out-of-hospital units may be nonprofit or may be proprietary for-profit institutions owned by a corporation or by individual physicians. Self-dialysis refers to dialysis performed by the patient (with or without the assistance of a helper), and can take place either in the home or in a self-care facility which provides space, equipment, and only minimal professional supervision. According to the most recent National Dialysis Registry data, approximately 25 percent of the dialysis patients in the United States are performing home dialysis, 50 percent are being dialyzed in hospitals, and 25 percent in out-of-hospital or limited care dialysis centers.

Hemodialysis. This is accomplished by connecting the patient's circulatory system to an artificial kidney (dialyzer), where blood and dialysate are brought into contact with a synthetic membrane. This procedure usually is carried out three times weekly for five to eight hours per session, although this is variable depending upon the patient, the dialyzer used, and other factors. Hemodialysis, efficient and less time-consuming than peritoneal dialysis (see below), is the technique used for 98 percent of dialysis patients.

One of the major problems with hemodialysis is the need for repeated access to the patient's circulation. Development of the external arteriovenous shunt by B. H. Scribner in Seattle in 1960 first made possible repeated dialysis and the use of dialysis as a maintenance (chronic) procedure. The shunt consists of two small silastic tubes (cannulas) surgically implanted into an artery and a vein in the arm or leg. These tubes, extending out through the skin, are connected to the dialyzer during dialysis, carrying blood to the machine and returning filtered blood to the body. The arteriovenous shunt has a number of disadvantages, including infection around the skin openings, blood clotting in the cannulas, and inconvenience to the patient associated with the presence of an external apparatus.

Another method of vascular access, the arteriovenous fistula, consists of the surgical joining of an artery or vein in the forearm or elsewhere. The higher pressure in the artery results in a high blood flow rate through the vein, causing the vein to enlarge and become readily visible and palpable. Such large veins with high blood flow can be punctured easily with large-diameter needles so as to withdraw and return blood from the vein to and from the artificial kidney. The use of an arteriovenous fistula gives the patient greater freedom of movement than with a shunt, since there is no external apparatus. The fistula also generally is free of problems of infection and clotting. However, dialysis using the fistula is more complex, and may be more difficult for some home dialysis patients. One or two large needles must be inserted into the vein with each dialysis, entailing some anxiety, discomfort, and the possibility of vessel injury. A blood pump must also be used, and this requires more complex monitoring and results in more frequent machine alarms during dialysis, so reducing the adaptability of this technique to overnight dialysis while sleeping.

The choice between use of external cannulas or a fistula must be made on an individual basis, taking into account both physical and psychosocial characteristics of the patient, and the situation in which the patient will dialyze.

Peritoneal Dialysis. This is accomplished by introducing sterile dialysate into the abdominal cavity through a small indwelling catheter. The dialysate spreads across the highly vascularized peritoneal membrane lining the abdominal cavity, and exchange across this membrane permits removal of water and solutes from the blood. The dialysate is left in the abdomen for twenty to forty minutes, then drained out, this process being repeated twenty or more times, until adequate dialysis has been achieved. Maintenance peritoneal dialysis is usually performed three times weekly for ten to twelve hours per session.

Thus a major disadvantage of peritoneal dialysis is that it is a time-consuming process. Although improved techniques and equipment together with strict emphasis on sterile procedures have greatly reduced the incidence of infection, the danger of inflammation of the peritoneal membrane, which may occur if bacteria enter the abdominal cavity through the catheter, remains a serious problem. Peritoneal dialysis does have a distinct advantage: it is relatively simple to perform and thus may be well suited for home dialysis, particularly for patients who have difficulty in mastering the more complex procedure of hemodialysis.

Currently, peritoneal dialysis is not used widely as a maintenance procedure; it is the treatment for only about 2 percent of all dialysis patients. However, with improved equipment becoming available, the advantages of peritoneal dialysis are becoming more apparent, and it is possible that this form of dialysis will be used more widely in the future.

Morbidity and Mortality of Dialysis Patients. The mortality rate among chronic dialysis patients currently is about 9 percent per year. Recent studies indicate that somewhere between 45 and 60 percent of these deaths are attributable to cardiovascular disease, and much current concern is focused on these alarming statistics. Other causes of death and disability common in dialysis patients include infections, anemia, hepatitis, neuropathy (nerve injury from accumulated toxins), bone disease, and psychosocial stress. Improved control of uremia through better and more frequent dialysis has reduced the incidence and severity of some of these complications, and further reductions in morbidity and mortality are to be hoped for. Nevertheless increasing use of dialysis for patients with serious complicating conditions such as diabetes mellitus and for older patients undoubtedly will result in an increased incidence of complications and poorer patient survival figures.

Future of Dialysis. Even if the problems with kidney transplantation are resolved, it is likely that dialysis will continue to be the treatment of choice for an appreciable number of patients. Future developments with dialysis may include improved techniques for and increased use of peritoneal dialysis; improved techniques of vascular access; smaller, portable, perhaps wearable dialyzers; short daily dialysis; and an improved understanding of the causes of morbidity and mortality in dialysis patients.

Research and Prevention: Future Possibilities

There is widespread recognition of the need for placing more emphasis on preventive care and research in the area of renal disease, though opinions differ as to the advisability of extensive application of currently available preventive and screening techniques. There is perhaps greatest optimism concerning the potential of management of hypertension in preventing or limiting renal failure. The relationship between hypertension and renal disease has been documented by a number of studies which have found that approximately one-half of hypertensive patients also have renal disease. Hypertension is a manageable condition in most individuals, and its control may prevent the subsequent development of renal disease. (See CHAPTER 34: HYPERTENSION.)

As stated by Dr. Arvin Weinstein, Chairman of the National Medical Advisory Board of the National Kidney Foundation, before the 1975 congressional hearings on Medicare's End-Stage Renal Disease Program:

> If you were to apply currently available knowledge, you could prevent end-stage renal disease . . . in a significant number of people.
>
> It is not because we have good curative drugs to treat all kinds of kidney disease, but because one of the major sources of end-stage renal disease . . . is untreated high blood pressure, particularly untreated high blood pressure in susceptible groups, more specifically the black population in this country . . .
>
> In all honesty, there are very few truly preventable end-stage kidney diseases. Hypertension is by all odds the most common. Some patients, a small percentage, with recurrent or persistent urinary tract infection would fall in this category . . . We know virtually nothing about how to prevent or cure most kinds of Bright's disease or glomerulonephritis which contribute at least 50 percent of all patients who enter this treatment modality [dialysis].
>
> That depends upon basic research . . .

Looking into the future, Dr. Weinstein provides the perspective of possible long-term developments in renal disease services:

> We are so hung up on improving dialysis machinery and doing better transplants that you might be led to believe that this is the ultimate possible. This represents the crudest stage of our capability! The fancy hardware and dramatic transplants will be looked back upon, hopefully within a decade or two, as that "crude, primitive period" we went through when we didn't know know how to prevent kidney disease.

Organizations

The basic voluntary organization in this field is the National Kidney Foundation, 116 East 27th Street, New York, NY 10016. In the fiscal year ending June 30, 1976, the Foundation spent $465,411 on public and professional education and patient and community services, and $249,906 on research. In the same year the National Institutes of Health allocated $46,576,219 to research in kidney and urinary tract disease.

SELECTED REFERENCES

Bailye, J. L., ed., *Hemodialysis Principles and Practice*, Academic Press, New York, 1971.

Becker, E. L., ed., *Kidney and Urinary Tract Infections*, Lilly Research Laboratories, Indianapolis, 1971.

Brown, T. M., et al., "Living with Long-Term Home Dialysis," *Annals of Internal Medicine*, vol. 81, pp. 165–170, August 1974.

Chojnacki, R., and K. Keady, "Hemodialysis in the Home," *American Family Physician*, vol. 11, pp. 149–153, February 1975.

Goldberg, R. T., "Vocational Rehabilitation of Patients on Long-Term Hemodialysis," *Archives of Physical Medicine and Rehabilitation*, vol. 55, pp. 60–65, 1974.

Harrington, J. D., and E. R. Brener, *Patient Care in Renal Failure*, W. B. Saunders, Philadelphia, 1973.

Mackenzie, J. C., "Advances in Renal Disease," *Practitioner*, vol. 211, pp. 499–509, 1973.

Merrill, J. P., "Present Status of Kidney Transplantation," *Disease-A-Month*, November 1974.

The Renal Disease Provision of Medicare, U.S. Department of Health, Education and Welfare, Social Security Administration, BHI Publication no. 013-75, May 1975.

36

Laryngeal Cancer

ROBERT M. GOLDENSON, PH.D.

Reviewed by the International Association of Laryngectomees

Cancer of the larynx is a malignant tumor involving either the vocal cords or the surrounding, supporting structure of the larynx, or voice box. If the malignancy is discovered in time, it is one of the most curable of all cancers, since treatment is effective in about 90 percent of cases. Although anticancer chemicals are prescribed in some cases, radiation is the treatment of choice for early, small, localized laryngeal cancer. In such cases the larynx is not removed. Aftereffects are minimal, and the only evidence that treatment has been administered may be a somewhat hoarse voice.

In more advanced cases, surgery or a combination of surgery with radiation is generally employed. The surgical treatment may require removal of only one vocal cord, which means that speech ability is altered but not lost. In some instances, however, a more radical procedure is required, and the patient is subjected to a total laryngectomy. This operation involves removal of both vocal cords and results in a permanent loss of normal speech. The patient can, however, be taught to use a substitute for normal speech.

Incidence

There are approximately 7,000 new cases of laryngeal cancer each year in the United States. About 3,000 of these are fatal, but a large proportion of these deaths could be prevented by early detection and prompt treatment. Fatalities are usually due to spread of the cancerous tumor directly into adjacent tissue, or to metastasis, a process by which cancer cells travel through the blood or lymph systems to other parts of the body, where they create new cancerous growths.

Cancer of the larynx affects about eight times more men than women, nearly always between the ages of forty and sixty-five. Among persons who undergo total laryngectomy, the ratio of men to women is about 10 to 1. The estimated number of laryngectomees, as these patients are called, is approximately 25,000 to 27,000 in the United States alone.

Diagnosis

The importance of early diagnosis cannot be overemphasized, since the danger of spreading is diminished and damage to the voice is usually slight if the tumor is treated while it is small and local. However, the symptoms that appear in the early stages of the disease are likely to be mild, and unfortunately many people brush them aside as due to smoking or a cold. The most frequent and significant of these early symptoms is persistent hoarseness; others are "a lump in the throat," soreness in the neck, and difficulty in swallowing. If any of these symptoms persist for two weeks, a doctor should be consulted.

Possible indications of cancer can be readily and painlessly detected by inspecting the larynx with a mirror that reveals visible abnormalities. In some cases the patient is found to have the disease known as keratosis, which may produce wartlike growths in the larynx. This is believed to be a precancerous condition, and should be considered a warning sign requiring frequent examinations. If the doctor suspects cancer, a sample of tissue is removed for a biopsy examination. Microscopic inspection of this sample will determine whether or not cancer is present. To locate a tumor or determine its extent, the doctor may also administer an x-ray or fluoroscopic examination.

Causal Factors

Although the precise causal mechanisms are not known, studies show a particularly high incidence of cancer of the larynx among heavy drinkers and heavy smokers. Regarding the latter, the United States Surgeon General's report on smoking and health states: "Cigarette smoking is a significant factor in the causation of laryngeal cancer in the male." For cigarette smokers the risk of developing this type of cancer is seven times as great as for nonsmokers. It is an interesting fact that the disease is almost never found among certain groups, such as Seventh Day Adventists, who do not smoke or drink. Studies also show that cancer of the larynx is more common in urban than rural areas, probably due to irritants contained in city air.

Prevention

Prevention of cancer of the larynx can be carried out on two levels. Primary prevention consists of avoidance of carcinogenic agents, which means cutting cigarette smoking down to a reasonable level (no more than half a pack a day) or, preferably, cutting it out altogether. It also means avoiding the excessive use of alcohol (no more than one or two drinks a day). Psychological help may be needed by those who cannot control drinking or smoking. The elimination of pollutants from the city atmosphere is a social problem, and everything possible should be done to solve it.

Secondary prevention consists of early detection and treatment. Men and women alike should have a thorough checkup every year, including careful examination of the larynx. Persistent hoarseness, coughing, or other signs of throat irritation should be taken seriously, and a full examination should be made. Early removal of the cancerous growth greatly increases the possibility of survival, and may make it possible to retain part of the speech mechanism so that the voice is not entirely lost.

The Laryngectomee

The laryngectomee is an individual who has lost the ability to speak normally as a result of surgical removal of the larynx. During the operation the surgeon creates an opening called a stoma in the front part of the neck and joins the trachea, or windpipe, to it. This eliminates any connection between the lungs and mouth or nose, and the patient breaths, coughs, sneezes, and "blows his nose" through the stoma. However, he continues to take food and liquid by mouth as usual.

Generally speaking, laryngectomees can engage in all activities that were possible before the operation except swimming, since the neck is open and water could enter the lungs. The greatest loss is the ability to speak. They also cannot laugh aloud or sing as before, although they may make a good try after learning a new speech technique. In addition, laryngectomees lose most of their taste and smell sensitivity, since they do not breathe through the nose. They also cannot lift heavy loads or put themselves under heavy strain, and are warned against trying, since they can no longer lock their breath in.

The acquisition of a new mode of speaking is the major concern of laryngectomees and the major step in rehabilitation. The lungs play no part in this process, since they can no longer expel air into the mouth. Instead the patient is gradually taught to take air into the mouth and swallow or force it into the esophagus by locking the tongue to the roof of the mouth. When the air is forced back up, it causes the walls of the esophagus and larynx to vibrate. These vibrations are transmitted to the column of air in the passages and produce a low-pitched sound. The entire process is actually a controlled belch or burp, but its effect is to give the laryngectomee the makings of a new voice, for one can gradually learn to articulate the sound into words with the tongue, lips, teeth, and palate, as normal speakers do.

Rehabilitation Program

The rehabilitation process is, in general, a three-step affair: a preoperative program, intensive postoperative speech therapy, and inspiration and instruction derived from attending meetings of a

427

Lost Chord Club. Ideally the preoperative services should include: (1) an explanation of the surgical procedures and aftereffects by the attending physician or surgeon, with as much assurance as possible that the prognosis for this type of condition is favorable; (2) an explanation of the development of esophageal speech by a speech clinician, supplemented by actual practice in speech production by this method, with cautions against the development of detrimental speech habits; (3) a visit by a laryngectomee who uses esophageal speech effectively and can give the patient encouragement; (4) an interview with a rehabilitation counselor to discuss postoperative employment and vocational training if needed. Experienced hospital nurses can also be an important factor both preoperatively and postoperatively. They can give reassuring answers to questions asked by the patient and family; help to relieve preoperative tension and apprehension; prepare the patient for surgery; give special postoperative care, including tube feeding and cleansing of the silver laryngectomy tube which is inserted in the stoma until it is healed, and teaching the patient to take care of it at home.

Speech Training. Speech training, the second stage of rehabilitation, is a complex, individual affair that can be described only in general outline in this book. It is important to assure the patient that even though the sound-making mechanism (the larynx) has been removed, the other components of speech production are left intact. Learning to speak is therefore a question of making sound once more available to the oral cavity so that the sound can be articulated into speech.

The actual training should start only when the physician considers the patient ready for it. The first goal is the production of esophageal sound by taking air into the upper section of the esophagus and expelling it at will. One technique is the swallow method referred to above, in which the patient is asked to imagine chewing and swallowing food, then bringing the air swallowed along with the food back up immediately, as in a simulated burp or belch. The swallow-belch method is one of the most effective procedures, but it has some disadvantages. The speech may have an undesirable belch quality, the time delay between the swallow and the belch may interfere with fluency and intelligibility, and excessive swallowing of air may produce gastrointestinal distress.

Two other methods may also be recommended. The aspirate or inhaling technique has the advantage of being more natural, since it does not dissociate the normal tendency to breathe out during speech from breathing out during the use of the pseudo voice. In other words, the patient exhales during voice production. In learning to use this method, the patient practices drawing air from the esophagus into the pharynx by opening the mouth slightly and, in the beginning, closes off the stoma for a moment with the hand. The third method, the injection technique, consists of trapping or locking air between the back of the tongue and the hard and soft palate, and suddenly forcing it backward and down far enough into the esophagus to be entrapped there before injection. Many esophageal speakers use this method without being able to explain how they do it.

Each patient is encouraged to use the method that works best for him or her. One is also urged to avoid unpleasant grimaces and to relax as much as possible, since tension makes esophageal speech almost impossible.

Once the esophageal sound is achieved, the patient is trained to prolong it and maintain volume by letting the air out a little at a time. Vowels are worked on first, then consonants and nonsense syllables, then finally one-, two-, and three-syllable words. Multi-syllable words may be broken up because for beginners only five to eight syllables can be produced during one expulsion of air. When the patient succeeds in producing words, the emphasis is on breaking them up into syllables and obtaining added volume and inflection. To avoid overfatigue, training sessions with the therapist and practice sessions at home must be kept short, especially during the first weeks after surgery. Encouragement and reassurance are important factors during the entire process.

Artificial Larynx. Some laryngectomees learn esophageal speech within a few weeks, while others may take as long as a year. About 35 percent, however, are unable to develop a satisfactory new voice for a variety of reasons. These include extensive surgery, advanced age, poor health, insufficient motivation, lack of practice, loss of confidence, embarrassment during the first attempts to speak, and early retirement with self-imposed isolation, which limits the opportunity to communicate. If a patient fails to make progress toward speech restoration in ninety days, an artificial larynx may be recommended. A few patients purchase artificial speech aids to enable them to return to work within a short time after surgery. In cases where extensive surgery prevents the development of esophageal speech, the patient may be given a speech aid while still in the hospital.

Two major types of artificial electronic larynx are available. One produces a sound (usually through a reed mechanism) and conveys it to the oral cavity by means of a rubber or plastic tube inserted in the mouth. The device may be activated either by natural breath pressure through a tube inserted in the stoma or by an electronic transducer held in the hand or inserted in the head of a smoking pipe, with controls available to modify the pitch or intensity of the voice. These devices are usually less noisy, bulky, and conspicuous than the second major type, which transmits the sound to the oral cavity through a battery-operated buzzer held against the soft tissue of the throat. In both instances the laryngectomee gradually learns to articulate the sounds into words in the same manner as with normal speech.

Both types of apparatus, however, have a number of inherent disadvantages. They are mechanical in nature and therefore subject to breakdown; usually require the use of one hand; call attention to the fact that the user is disabled; tend to produce a monotonous voice quality; make a continuous sound that interferes with intelli-

429

gibility; and are expensive both in initial cost and upkeep.

Lost Chord Clubs. Lost Chord or New Voice Clubs are the third major factor in rehabilitation. They have been formed throughout the country as an answer to the patient's need for support, understanding, and help, particularly during the trying period of readjustment. With the cooperation of the physician, members of the club call on the new laryngectomee in the hospital, often before as well as after surgery, to assure the patient that one will be able to live a normal life. They also assure that one will get all the help needed in learning to find a new voice. Above all, they demonstrate that speech is possible, for they are themselves laryngectomees who have been successfully taught to speak again.

The spouses of the members also play a vital role in the process. They frequently visit the wife or husband of the patient to assure that normal family life will still be possible, and to give tips on how to manage the patient, how to help overcome anxieties, and how to assist in speech retraining. It is important, too, to have the patient's wife or husband attend the club meetings with the patient.

The monthly meetings of the clubs are a key element in the rehabilitation of the new laryngectomee, and are actually group therapy of a very practical kind. They enable the patient to learn from the experiences of others who have faced and overcome the same problems. They keep the patient in contact with other people at a time when one may be tempted to withdraw from society. They give one an opportunity to view films on rehabilitation and speech training, or to observe speech therapists as they demonstrate their techniques in person. They bring to attention the devices and aids which will make life more comfortable, and show how to use them without sacrificing a neat and presentable appearance. Most important, the clubs offer the kind of motivation, instruction, and morale-boosting needed as one embarks on the long road toward total rehabilitation.

Psychological Factors. Loss of the larynx and the associated loss of voice are bound to have a severe psychological impact on patients. During the early days after surgery they suffer an emotional trauma which is in many cases magnified by the sense of shock experienced by the entire family. The reasons for these emotional reactions are understandable. Patients suffer from the dread of cancer and anxiety that it may spread. They are concerned that they will be unable to resume their former occupation or find a new means of livelihood. They are worried that they will be permanently deprived of a voice, and that not only their work life but their social life will be severely limited. They may be afraid their spouse will lose interest, and that their children will feel self-conscious about the handicap. They may picture themselves living in an isolated world, cut off from other people by inability to communicate in a normal way.

The particular psychological reactions to which these patients are prone include preoperative apprehension, self-pity, depression, withdrawal, and fear of embarrassment. The prevention of adverse reactions is not the province of a single person or specialist, and can only be minimized or alleviated if everyone involved gives the patient the support, encouragement, and information needed—including the general physician, the surgeon, the nurse, members of a Lost Chord Club, the family, the speech therapist, the rehabilitation counselor, and the employer. In some cases special psychological or psychiatric help may be required.

Rehabilitation Aids and Devices. Three general types of aids are recommended for use by all laryngectomees. First, the patient is urged to dress in a manner that covers the marks of surgery without interfering with the breathing process. Women use scarves, jeweled neckbands, or large costume jewelry to cover the stoma. Men are urged to wear a collar and tie or turtleneck rather than an open sport shirt. The second button of shirts should be snipped off and sewn on top of the buttonhole; this permits quick access to the stoma in case of coughing spells or mucous production.

Second, many types of shields are used to protect the stoma from foreign material or to prevent it from being sucked inward when breathing: an easily laundered cloth, bib, or a cover made of perforated plastic or aluminum and fastened around the neck with ties.

Third, to avoid the difficulties and dangers involved in showering and shampooing, there are rubber shields with a bell-shaped enlargement and holes beneath to admit air. These shields fit snugly around the neck, and are fastened by an adjustable snap buckle. In addition to these aids, special voice amplifiers are available, for even some good esophageal speakers are not heard well at a distance, in noisy places, or by persons with impaired hearing.

Where to Get Help

The treatment and rehabilitation of the laryngectomee requires a multifaceted approach. To assure full service, the patient and family or physician should contact one or more of the following local organizations: a speech and hearing center or clinic (usually connected with a hospital or university); an Office of Vocational Rehabilitation; a laryngectomee (Lost Chord, New Voice) club; a branch of the American Cancer Society; the Health Department; a rehabilitation center; the Department of Special Education under the local school board; a branch of the Society for Crippled Children and Adults. If these organizations are not available, assistance should be sought from the International Association of Laryngectomees, American Cancer Society, American Speech and Hearing Association, American Hearing Society, Office of Vocational Rehabilitation in the Department of Health, Education and Welfare, or National Society for Crippled Children and Adults.

The International Association of Laryngectomees, 777 Third Avenue, New York, NY 10017, is a voluntary organization sponsored by the American Cancer Society, currently comprising approximately 235 member clubs representing 45 states and 12 foreign countries. The organization was founded in Cleveland, Ohio, in 1952 as a means of coordinating the activities of individual Lost

Chord, Anamilo, or New Voice Clubs which had been spontaneously formed in many parts of the country. The purposes of the IAL are "to promote and support the rehabilitation of laryngectomized persons by the exchange and dissemination of ideas and information to the clubs and to the public; to facilitate the formation of new clubs; to foster improvement in laryngectomee programs; and to work towards the establishment of minimum standards for teachers of post-laryngectomy speech."

Special projects include publication of a bimonthly newsletter, "IAL News," mailed to approximately 23,000 persons in 55 countries; seminars or institutes for prospective teachers; a national program of special education in first aid and artificial respiration for laryngectomees; a registry of esophageal speech instructors; annual international conventions; and a program to inform employers about the reemployability of laryngectomees. Each member club sends delegates to an annual meeting to exchange ideas and elect the board of directors and officers. The national headquarters of the Association is located in the national office of the American Cancer Society.

Some helpful publications are available from the International Association of Laryngectomees: *First Aid for Laryngectomees (Neck Breathers); Helping Words for Laryngectomees; Laryngectomees at Work; Laryngectomized Speaker's Source Book; Rehabilitating Laryngectomees; Your New Voice*, by W. F. Waldrop and M. H. Gould (American Cancer Society reprint).

37

Learning Disabilities

EUGENE B. EDGAR, Ph.D., Assistant Professor of
Education, University of Washington, Seattle

Coined by Dr. Samuel Kirk in 1963, the term "learning disabilities" as a specific designation for individuals who have normal intelligence but are experiencing difficulties in learning is of fairly
recent origin. This type of individual, however, has been discussed
in medical, psychological, and educational literature for a least
100 years.

History and Significant Publications

The history of learning disabilities comprises varied theoretical
positions and suggested treatment procedures. To date, the professionals in education, psychology, optometry, and medicine have
been unable to agree on either a theory or set of procedures. The
crux of the problem is that no one can agree on a definition for the
learning disabled.

P. P. Broca, a French physican, reported in 1861 on patients who
suffered language disabilities due to specific brain damage. In the
1890s an English ophthalmologist, W. P. Morgan; an English
physician, James Kerr; and a Scottish ophthalmologist, James
Hinshelwood, reported on separate cases of "word blindness."
Kurt Goldstein was able to classify the typical behaviors of brain-
injured individuals based on his studies of World War I soldiers
who had suffered direct insult to the brain.

The first extensive work on children of normal intelligence who
were experiencing difficulties in language skills was published in
1937 by Dr. Samuel Orton. Entitled *Reading, Writing, and Speech*

Problems in Children, this book was the result of fifteen years of work with children who suffered from congenital word blindness, which Orton called strephosymbolia (twisted symbols). Based on Orton's theory of lack of hemispherical dominance in these children, Anna Gillingham and Bessie Stilman in their book, *Remedial Training for Children with Specific Disability in Reading, Spelling, and Penmanship,* developed a structured, phonic, multisensory reading program. The more recent work of Beth Slingerland, *A Multi-Sensory Approach to Language Arts for Specific Language Disability Children: A Guide for Primary Teachers,* is an adaptation of the Orton-Gillingham techniques. Concurrent with Orton's work was that of Grace Fernald. Working in the reading clinic of the University of California in the 1920s, Fernald developed a technique for teaching reading to nonreaders of normal intelligence which used visual, auditory, and kinesthetic modalities.

In the 1940s Alfred Strauss, Heinz Werner, and Laura Lehtinen-Rogan began their work with brain-injured mentally retarded children at the Wayne County Training School in Northville, Michigan. These researchers and their students have had the greatest impact of any single professional group in the area of learning disabilities. Strauss and Werner studied the behavioral differences of retarded individuals who had demonstrable brain damage and those whose retardation was due to other causes. From these studies came a list of behaviors associated with brain damage (such as distractibility, perseveration, catastrophic reactions). These scientists then made the assumption that individuals who exhibited these behaviors but did not have "hard neurological signs" of brain damage could also be considered neurologically impaired. This type of individual with "soft neurological signs" became known as the "Strauss syndrome child." Lehtinen-Rogan and Strauss developed the first educational strategies for this population in their book *Psychopathology and Education of the Brain Injured Child.*

One of the implicit assumptions of the Strauss group was that these individuals were suffering from impaired processing of information. Therefore, before these children could be taught academic skills, process training had to occur. Newell Kephart, a student of Strauss, expanded this concept in his classic book, *The Slow Learner in the Classroom,* published in 1960. According to Kephart, perceptual motor training is crucial to ameliorating these process difficulties. Gerald Getman, an optometrist who had collaborated with Arnold Gesell on the study of visual development in children, also collaborated with Kephart in 1956 in the development of visual-motor-perceptual activities for the Strauss syndrome child. Ray Barsch was influenced by both Kephart and Getman and developed a "movigenic" curriculum in 1965, a technique stressing the motor aspects of learning.

Working independently in Los Angeles in the 1950s but influenced by the work of Strauss and also that of Jean Piaget, Marianne Frostig did important work with disturbed children. She is best known for her Developmental Test of Visual Perception (DTVP) and the accompanying remedial worksheets. Like Kephart, Getman, and Barsch, Frostig feels that the process training deficit must be corrected before academic skill training can take place.

In 1961 William Cruickshank and his colleagues published *A Teaching Method for Brain Injured and Hyperactive Children.* Cruickshank also was profoundly influenced by the work of Strauss, Werner, and Lehtinen-Rogan, but rather than focus on the training of the mental processes he attempted to develop a controlled environment that would eliminate overstimulation and enable these children to learn.

An atmosphere conducive to the growth of new theories and techniques for the learning disabled was created in the early 1960s when federal funds were made available for children labeled as "learning disabled," and parent groups, especially the Association for Children with Learning Disabilities (ACLD), were formed.

In 1959 Carl Delacato, an educational psychologist, published *The Treatment and Prevention of Reading Problems: The Neurological Approach.* This book furnishes the basis of the Doman-Delacato approach to learning disabilities. Delacato and Glenn Doman, a physical therapist, have developed highly controversial motor techniques which, they claim, provide for neurological reorganization and thus a "cure" for neurological deficits.

In 1961 Samuel Kirk and James McCarthy developed the Illinois Test of Psycholinguistic Abilities (ITPA) in an attempt to provide an assessment device that would provide educationally relevant information for handicapped children. The ITPA is currently the most common assessment device used with learning disabled children.

Drawing on intensive work with deaf individuals, Helmar Myklebust and Doris Johnson published *Learning Disabilities: Educational Principles and Practices* in 1967. It advocates a clinical teaching approach for the learning disabled.

Various medical approaches have recently been advocated. Central nervous system stimulants such as Ritalin have been used for hyperactive children (children with minimal brain dysfunction). For some unknown reason these stimulants tend to act as depressants with some of these children. More recently Allan Cott has reported success with megavitamin therapy.

The most recent educational approach for children with learning disabilities has grown out of the work of B. F. Skinner and Ogden Lindsley. Norris Haring, a student of Cruickshank, has written extensively on the use of experimental analysis of behavior techniques for the learning disabled.

Definition

As with the educable mentally retarded, a classification which lumps together slow learners, the culturally deprived, acting-out students, as well as those students with below average intelligence scores, learning disability is an ambiguous term used to classify a diverse group of individuals. The National Advisory Committee to the Office of Education for the Handicapped in 1968 defined learning disabled children as:

> . . . children . . . [who] exhibit a disorder in one or more of the basic psychological processes involved in understanding or in using spoken or written language. These may be manifested in disorders of listening, thinking, talking, reading, writing, spelling or arithmetic. They include conditions which have been referred to as perceptual handicaps, brain injury, minimal brain dysfunction, dyslexia, developmental aphasia, etc. They do not include learning problems which are due primarily to visual, hearing, or motor handicaps, to mental retardation, emotional disturbance or to environmental disadvantage.

Hence, the learning disabled are defined by what they are *not*, as well as what they *are*.

The confusion that surrounds today's definition of learning disability can be traced to the historical events that have influenced present-day practitioners. The earliest roots of the field are closely tied to demonstrated brain damage. Orton was the first to write about children who did not have hard neurological signs. The work of Strauss and Werner extended this practice. However, each of the theorists used his own peculiar definition (such as word blindness, strephosymbolia, dyslexia, exogenous, brain injured, perceptually handicapped). When Kirk addressed the parent conference which was the forerunner of ACLD in 1963, he suggested the term "learning disabilities" in an attempt to provide a functional definition to the problem. Kirk warned the parents and professionals at the first meeting of the dangers inherent in a term used to classify a diverse group of individuals. Contrary to Kirk's wishes, a new category was begun. Although many attempts have been made since 1963 to clarify the terminology, especially the massive work of the National Institute of Neurological Diseases and Blindness task force headed by Clements in 1966, no operational definition of learning disabilities has yet evolved.

Some of the terms that are most often used synonymously with learning disabilities are *minimal brain dysfunction* (MBD), which is believed to be a result of an insult to the brain at or before birth affecting the functioning of the central nervous system; *brain injured,* which implies there is demonstrable evidence of brain tissue damage; *learning language disability* (LLD); and *specific language disability* (SLD).

There do exist individuals who appear to be capable (that is, have normal tested intelligence and no major sensory deficit) and yet do not learn to read or write. Other than this rather vague operational definition, the learning disabled child is essentially defined by whoever is working with him.

Incidence and Etiology

The incidence of learning disabilities is difficult to pinpoint because of the lack of an agreed-upon operational definition. The incidence figures usually range from 1 to 20 percent of the school age population. Three percent seems to be the figure most quoted in educational circles. A ratio of 5:1, males to females, is also often suggested.

Learning-disabled children are children who are thought to suffer a deficit in the psychological processing of information. Whether the cause of this problem is due to an inhibition of the development of the processes or to an interference with these processes has not been determined. Certainly basic physiological research as to the causes of these problems must continue. As of now, individuals charged with aiding the learning disabled must focus on the behaviors present and attempt to alter the inappropriate behaviors and increase the desired behaviors.

Behavioral Symptoms

While there is a wide range of behaviors associated with learning disabilities, only two must be present in all cases of learning disability: average tested intelligence and evidence of failure to learn to read (usually defined as two or more grade levels behind potential). Many other behaviors are often found in conjunction with these two, although they are not confined to the area of learning disabilities. (See CHAPTER 55: ILLUSTRATIVE CASES, E. Shali: Educational Therapy.) Some of these are:

Hyperactivity (Hyperkinetic). This refers to the "overly active" child. A firm definition of this term is difficult since the range of "normal" active behavior is tremendous.

Coordination. Often the learning-disabled child is uncoordinated or clumsy. Many tests and scales are available to measure motor behavior (such as the Purdue Perceptual Motor Survey). Included are both fine motor skills (writing) and gross motor skills (balance, skipping, etc.). It must be noted that many "clumsy" individuals are also outstanding readers.

Perseveration. Difficulty in switching from one topic to another or the continuation of a behavior for an unreasonable amount of time is often associated with learning disability. For example, when asked to print the letter "A," some children will fill a page with "A's."

Immaturity. Many children who have been labeled learning disabled lack social behaviors that are appropriate to their age level. These children are often termed "babyish" by their teachers. They giggle, express childish fears, and engage in play activities common to children much younger.

Attention. Poor attention or short attention span is associated with these children. Again this is difficult to document. These are children who do not stay with a task to completion and seem to move from one activity to another.

Following Directions. Often learning-disabled children do not follow multilevel directions. For example, if a parent directs the child to get a book, take it to the bedroom, and put it on the shelf, the child will get the book and then ask the parent, "What should I do next?"

Linguistic Disorders. Poor grammatical development is often associated with the learning disabled. Past tenses, pronouns, plurals, etc., are used inappropriately.

Memory. Learning-disabled children often exhibit memory deficits. They knew their "add" facts yesterday but have "forgotten" how to do them today.

There are numerous other behaviors which various people associate with the learning disabled according to the myriad theories that exist. It must be emphasized, however, that the only two behaviors which most professional people agree are present with the learning disabled are those of normal tested intelligence and a deficit in reading.

Treatment Strategies

As the brief overview of the historical developments indicates, there are no universally accepted treatment strategies for the learning disabled. Due to the lack of an operational definition of the disorder, comparative research analysis is impossible. As a result there are a great many diverse programs offered to the learning disabled, all with claims of success but without convincing substantiating data. An artificial, but useful, categorization of these strategies into those theories which purport to train basic psychological processes (the process group) and those theories which purport to directly train skills (the task group) helps clarify the different treatment strategies.

Process Group. This group of treatment procedures is focused on training the underlying psychological processes which enable the individual to better process information from the environment. Once these processes are functioning properly, academic training can begin.

1. Visual-motor theories: The works of Kephart, Getman, and Barsch recommend that vision training and motor training precede academic training. Emphasis is placed on seeing and doing simultaneously, such as walking on a balance beam, identifying body parts, drawing Harmon circles on a chalkboard, tracking with the eye, and copying shapes. These activities are prescribed for children who have demonstrated deficiencies in these areas.

2. Visual perception: Frostig stresses amelioration of the visual perceptual skills before the onset of academic instruction. The Developmental Test of Visual Perception (DTVP) tests the areas of (1) eye motor coordination, (2) figure ground, (3) form consistency, (4) position in space, and (5) spatial relations. The Frostig-Horne training program was developed to remediate these skills.

3. Neurological organization: There are neurological, psychological, and educational teams, some of which, like Doman-Delacato, purport to not only remediate the deficit process functioning but also bring about reorganization of the brain by evaluating the func-

tioning capacity of various areas of the brain using a checklist of behaviors.

Task Group. These theorists believe that the treatment of preference is to alter the teaching strategies used with the learning disabled and to teach, in fact, the desired academic behaviors.

1. Controlled environment: Cruickshank is probably the best-known current theorist of this persuasion. By eliminating distracting environmental stimuli and devising academic tasks that are at the level of the student, Cruickshank believes the learning-disabled child can make academic progress. Best known for his suggestions of a very bland environment, limited color, limited available materials, learning cubicles which further restrict stimulus input, and use of the multidiscipline team, Cruickshank methodologies intend to enhance the possibility for the learning disabled to make academic progress.

2. Visual, auditory, kinesthetic input modalities: The Gillingham and Slingerland techniques are based on the belief that the learning-disabled child learns to read by having a structured phonetic approach that uses auditory, visual, and kinesthetic input modalities. By matching these methods and ensuring that the child has learned each skill before moving on to the next skill, these children are capable of learning to be proficient readers.

3. Illinois Test of Psycholinguistic Abilities: Developed by Kirk and McCarthy, the ITPA claims to measure three types of psycholinguistic processes (receptive, organizational, and expressive) in two major communication channels (visual-motor and auditory-vocal) on two levels of organization (representational and automatic). Once the child has been tested and the strengths and weaknesses are noted in profile form, the teacher can determine discrepancies in the individual child and build an educational program that best fits the child's strengths.

4. Language approach: Myklebust is best known as an advocate of a language approach to learning disabilities. Basing his ideas on a rather complex theory of learning, Myklebust advocates a clinical teaching approach for these children which requires an intense diagnostic work-up to determine modality strengths, emotional factors, and academic level. From this information the teacher then builds an individualized remedial program for each child.

5. Experimental analysis of behavior: Dr. Norris Haring is perhaps the best-known proponent of the experimental analysis of behavior approach for the learning disabled. Haring has developed a set of procedures which can be used with all varieties of learning problems. These procedures consist of (1) the exact pinpointing of desired behavior; (2) careful selection of the methods and materials (antecedents); (3) reinforcement techniques (consequences) peculiar to each individual child; and (4) the precise and frequent measurement of the child's performance. The antecedents and consequences are manipulated until the child's performance is at the desired level.

Pharmacological Treatment

This approach attempts to alter the individual's capacity to handle stimuli through the effect of chemical agents on the central nervous system. The most popular chemotherapy is the use of central nervous system stimulants, especially dextroamphetamine (Dexedrine) and methylphenidate (Ritalin). Antianxiety agents such as thioridazine (Mellaril) and anticonvulsants such as diphenylhydantoin (Dilantin) have also been used with varying success. With some hyperactive children these drugs have tended to produce calming effects and increase attention spans. When this occurs, academic instruction becomes more feasible.

Research on Intervention Techniques

The relative effectiveness of any of the intervention techniques is difficult to evaluate for a number of reasons, primarily the lack of an operational definition. Each researcher has carefully selected a sampling of subjects fitting one definition which varies greatly from one research to another, the result being that the research findings are not comparable. Excellent reviews can be found in the works of Hallahan and Cruickshank; Chalfant and Scheffelin; DeLaCruz, Fox, and Roberts; and Myers and Hammill. The general conclusion of all the reviews of the research literature is that no one technique has proven successful for all children.

Future Considerations

Early Identification. Procedures for the early (preschool) identification of the learning disabled must be developed. No longer can professionals wait until children have experienced year after year of failure in school before attempting to provide help. High-risk children must be screened and helped before they lose confidence in themselves and the schools.

Several exciting techniques for early identification are currently being researched. Behavior checklists of various perceptual-motor skills have been developed that can be used with kindergarten children. Many pediatricians are becoming aware of the signs of hyperactivity and perceptual-motor problems and are referring high-risk children to diagnostic clinics for more complete work-ups. Some promising work has begun in the area of language delays in three- and four-year-old children. By carefully analyzing the linguistic characteristics of language-delayed children, researchers are attempting to identify critical language behaviors which may be the early warning signs of learning disability.

Care must be used, however, with any one-shot screening technique. All of the instruments used for early identification are of questionable validity and tend to provide information that is likely to be used for labeling children rather than providing relevant information for treatment. Some are urging diagnostic work by eclectic teams not devoted to one school of thought but conversant with the entire range. Careful observation of children in natural settings with multiple data points is the most efficient method of gathering assessment data. All of this information is meaningless if treatment programs are not available to the children identified as having developmental lags.

Needed Research. Research must continue on the various intervention strategies in an attempt to find the most efficient remedial techniques for these individuals. The luxury of using whatever technique "feels best" does not ensure adequate services for the learning disabled. Research into the possible etiological factors of learning disability must continue. Prevention would certainly be preferable to the remediation of learning disabilities.

Extended Programs. There is a movement to develop continuing education opportunities for the adolescent and young adult who are experiencing learning difficulties. Currently there are the beginnings of vocational education programs in high schools which can provide alternatives for the learning disabled. Additionally, some junior colleges are offering intensive remedial reading programs for adults, many of whom could be classified as learning disabled.

There have been some recent concerns expressed about the relationship between learning disabilities and juvenile antisocial conduct (juvenile delinquency). Judge Alfred O. Holte, of Snohomish County, Washington, has noted the high incidence of below-potential reading ability of many incarcerated youths. Although the relationship between learning disabilities and juvenile delinquency is tenuous at best, meaningful educational services need to be available to the learning disabled if these individuals are to live happy and productive lives.

Need for an Operational Definition. The need for a workable definition of learning disabilities is crucial to all future work in this area. Perhaps more than one definition is needed: an administrative definition for professionals engaged in providing service; a definition for research of the various intervention techniques; and a definition for physiological studies of the central nervous system. Until an operational definition is derived, systematic advances in the prevention and treatment of learning disabilities may be delayed.

Services and Organizations

Many public schools offer some type of special services for the learning disabled. Many private schools and private tutors are also available. At the local level, organizations for learning disabilities usually exist. The Council for Exceptional Children (CEC), Division for Children with Learning Disabilities (DCLD), 1920 Association Drive, Reston, VA 22091; The Association for Children with Learning Disabilities (ACLD), 2200 Brownsville Road, Pittsburgh, PA 15210; and the Orton Society, 8415 Bellona Lane, Towson, MD 21204, can provide information on local groups. (See CHAPTER 6: EDUCATIONAL PROGRAMS.)

SELECTED REFERENCES

Allen, K. E., J. Rieke, V. Dmitriev, and A. H. Hayden, "Early Warning! Observation as a Tool for Recognizing Potential Handicaps in Young Children," *Educational Horizons*, vol. 50, pp. 43–55, 1972.

Chalfant, J. C., and M. A. Scheffelin, *Central Processing Dysfunction in Children: A Review of Research*, U.S. Department of Health, Education and Welfare, NINDS Monograph no. 9, Bethesda, Maryland, 1969.

Clements, S. D., *Minimal Brain Dysfunction in Children*, U.S. Department of Health, Education and Welfare, NINDB Monograph no. 3, Public Health Service Bulletin no. 1415, 1966.

Cruickshank, W. M., F. A. Bentzen, F. H. Ratzeburg, and M. T. Tannhausser, *A Teaching Method for Brain-Injured and Hyperactive Children*, Syracuse University Press, Syracuse, New York, 1961.

Delacato, C. H., *The Treatment and Prevention of Reading Problems: The Neurological Approach*, Charles C. Thomas, Springfield, Illinois, 1959.

DeLaCruz, F. F., B. H. Fox, and R. H. Roberts, eds., "Minimal Brain Dysfunction," *Annals of the New York Academy of Sciences*, vol. 205, 1973.

Fernald, G. M., *Remedial Techniques in Basic School Subjects*, McGraw-Hill, New York, 1943.

Frostig, M., and D. Horne, *The Frostig Program for the Development of Visual Perception*, Follett, Chicago, 1964.

Frostig, M., D. W. Lefever, and J. R. B. Whittlesey, *The Marianne Frostig Developmental Test of Visual Perception*, Consulting Psychology Press, Palo Alto, California, 1964.

Gillingham, A., and B. Stillman, *Remedial Work for Reading, Spelling, and Penmanship*, Sackett and Wilhelms, New York, 1936.

Hallahan, D. P., and W. M. Cruickshank, *Psycho-Educational Foundations of Learning Disabilities*, Prentice-Hall, Englewood Cliffs, New Jersey, 1973.

Hedrick, D. L., and E. M. Prather, "A Behavioral System for Assessing Language Development," in R. L. Schiefelbush, ed., *Language of the Mentally Retarded*, University Press, Baltimore, 1972.

Holte, A. O., "Learning Disabilities and Juvenile Delinquency," presented to Shoreline Parents SLD Group, February 1, 1972.

Johnson, D., and H. R. Myklebust, *Learning Disabilities: Educational Principles and Practices*, Grune & Stratton, New York, 1967.

Kephart, N. C., *The Slow Learner in the Classroom*, Charles E. Merrill, Columbus, Ohio, 1960.

Kirk, S. A., J. J. McCarthy, and W. D. Kirk, *Illinois Test of Psycholinguistic Abilities*, experimental edition, University of Illinois Press, Urbana, 1961.

Lovitt, T. C., "Assessment of Children with Learning Disabilities," *Exceptional Children*, vol. 34, pp. 233–239, 1967.

Mardell, C. D., and D. S. Goldenberg, *Learning Disabilities/Early Childhood Research Project: Annual Report, 1972*. Illinois State Office of the Superintendent of Public Instruction.

Myers, P. I., and D. D. Hammill, *Methods for Learning Disorders*, Wiley, New York, 1969.

Orton, S., *Reading, Writing, and Speech Problems in Children*, Norton, New York, 1937.

Peters, J. E., J. S. Davis, C. M. Goolsby, S. D. Clements, and T. J. Hicks, *Physician's Handbook: Screening for MBD*, CIBA Pharmaceutical Company, Summit, New Jersey, 1973.

Slingerland, B., *A Multi-Sensory Approach to Language Arts for Specific Language Disability Children: A Guide for Primary Teachers*, Educators Publishing Service, Cambridge, Massachusetts, 1971.

Strauss, A. A., and L. E. Lehtinen, *Psychopathology and Education of the Brain-Injured Child*, vol. 1, Grune & Stratton, New York, 1947.

Sulzbacher, S. I., "Chemotherapy with Learning Disabled Children," in A. Talbot and H. Eichenwold, eds., *The Learning Disabled Child*, University of Texas Press, Dallas, 1974.

38

Mental Illness

CHARLIS S. DUNHAM, M.A.

While the term "mental illness" covers a vast range of disorders, including many neuroses, psychoses, and characterologic and organic conditions, there are common factors, both historical and cultural, which make it appropriate to discuss this broad area of human difficulty as a whole. All human beings attempt to function in their particular society in such a way that they are able to gain maximum satisfaction and minimize or cope with stress. There are a great variety of factors which interfere with each person's capacity for, and fulfillment of, potential for optimum adjustment and development. People who manage to get along "within normal limits" for their particular society or milieu inevitably encounter some significant problems; but in every cultural group there are those who manifest more extreme problems than the majority, and in Western society these manifestations are often designated as symptoms of mental illness.

Individuals sometimes develop ways of handling their feelings and needs that become problems in themselves. They may develop unrealistic compulsions (repeating certain behavior inappropriately); hysterical displacements (converting anxiety into physical symptoms); anxiety and panic; phobias (uncontrollable morbid fears); or some other type of neurotic defense. Others may act out their fears and angers against society by committing antisocial acts or by becoming dependent on alcohol or drugs — reactions characteristic of sociopathic or character disorders.

Some persons, on the other hand, withdraw into unrealistic, bizarre, overimaginative thinking dominated by suspicious or grandiose ideas, and may also experience hallucinations (imagined perceptions, not based on reality) or delusions (persistent false beliefs or opinions) as expressions of psychotic states or episodes. But it soon becomes apparent that many other and vastly different kinds of human experience are also termed psychotic: the strange autistic behavior of a baby almost from the beginning of life; the "break" experienced by a young college student just after a sad love affair or grueling competition; the acute depression that overwhelms a young mother just after the birth of her baby; the mounting eccentricity that characterizes the behavior of a man or woman over a period of years; the unfounded delusions of poverty or persecution that assail some individuals toward the end of their lives. In many instances modern treatment methods can enable such individuals to come to terms with their problems and function in a satisfactory manner; in some, however, treatment constitutes a long, slow struggle that yields only small increments of social competency.

Problems of Diagnosis

Descriptions of the different psychiatric syndromes are helpful in furthering understanding of complex symptoms, but they are often confusing when the attempt is made to apply them to actual human beings. Psychological makeup and personality are so multifaceted, dynamic, and everchanging that a single individual encompasses many strengths and problems, many defenses and strivings that are influenced by physical, environmental, and cultural forces—and a person may therefore present a more complicated set of behaviors than is usually included in any particular diagnostic category. Often as people's lives become more troubled, anxiety levels rise and the defenses which served before may not continue to provide comfort. People therefore give up on that level of adjustment (decompensate) and struggle to handle their stressful feelings in some other and usually less controlled or integrated fashion. Therefore an individual may appear "normal" at times, "neurotic" or "psychotic" at other times.

Interpersonal conflicts and needs, as well as mental and emotional processes, are in many ways similar for all. In mental illness they differ primarily in degree or timing, and psychiatric disorders do not, therefore, involve totally different kinds of experience or need. For example, almost everyone has felt for a fleeting moment that someone on the street looked oddly at him. A troubled person might be somewhat aware that she is supersensitive, but feel nevertheless that most of her acquaintances whisper about her or reject her. Sometimes people become enmeshed in an entire system of believing that messages have been planted all around them pertaining to their difficulties, that TV programs are about them, or that enemies are controlling or attempting to poison them. The fears and insecurities or feelings of self-importance are similar in all these instances, but can be understood as different in degree of intensity.

Some have thought of neurosis as a less severe form of emotional disability than psychosis. This is not always the case, because persons with neurotic tendencies can be severely crippled over a long period of time, and an acute psychotic episode may be treatable in a relatively short time and need not be a recurrent condition. In the light of modern treatment approaches, it is not accurate to think of psychotic states as necessarily more serious than severe forms of neurotic states. Usually neuroses interrupt life less than psychoses; however, it is possible that society's attitudes and the methods of treating psychosis have much to do with the severity and chronicity of this type of condition.

A Brief History

In practically every ancient culture there is evidence of attempts to understand behavioral deviations and to deal in some way with the individual manifesting the problem. "Insanity" was the term used by Roman lawyers to cover the diagnoses made by Hippocratically trained Greek doctors when they attempted to assess the responsibility of the deranged in the courts. During medieval times the mentally ill were believed to be possessed by demons, and were stoned and chained as a means of punishing them for vague and unfounded sins or of driving the demons out of their bodies. In England during the reign of Henry VIII the "insane" were incarcerated in an asylum, New Bethlehem, colloquially known as "Bedlam," a term that survives as an eloquent reminder of the conditions that prevailed in that institution. In the United States prior to the nineteenth century the psychotic were either ostracized and wandered about as beggars, or were confined to prisons along with paupers and criminals.

Virginia was the first state to provide a hospital exclusively for the psychotic, the Public Hospital for Persons of Insane and Disordered Minds, founded in 1768. Until 1800 Massachusetts committed "furiously mad lunatics" to a "house of correction," but established a mental hospital in 1818. During the mid-1800s a number of state hospitals were built, largely as a result of the untiring efforts of a humanitarian schoolteacher, Dorothea Dix. But state responsibility remained an uphill battle for some time since most of the care was under the direction of callous local committees and counties. Filthy, dark, impoverished conditions prevailed, and the "inmates" were under the control of ignorant, poorly paid, and often sadistic caretakers. Gradually, however, state hospitals began to develop into facilities where patients would be viewed as ill and efforts made to cure them. They also became centers for study and training with much more resourcefulness than was available at the local level. However, the mistake was made of creating enormous "warehouses" for so-called chronic patients, far away from community life and their families. The economics of the growing state hospital population also became a major concern, but unfortunately the states chose to deal with this problem at the expense of proper treatment, comfort, and adequate food. A rebellion against these conditions was led by Clifford W. Beers, who had himself been hospitalized in several institutions. He dedicated himself to organizing a citizenry independent of political considerations, and was instrumental in founding the National Committee for Mental Hygiene in 1909, whose prime objective was to bring about improvements in mental hospitals. Largely as a result of its efforts, impersonal care gradually evolved into intensive treatment, and the hospitals gradually changed from purely custodial institutions to therapeutic communities.

More recently a second basic change has taken place. The pessimistic attitude toward mental illness as a verdict of doom, which caused exile of "lost souls" to virtual prisons away from society, has been replaced by a more optimistic point of view based on new treatment techniques and on the role played by sociocultural factors, both in causing and in curing psychiatric disorders. Now the interaction between the individual and society is stressed, and abnormal behavior is viewed largely as a manifestation of extreme anxiety, frustration, and hopelessness arising out of that interaction. The approach, therefore, has become increasingly community-centered, with emphasis on reducing extreme anxiety with medication as quickly as possible and returning the person to the flow of life with the assistance of mental health centers, psychiatric departments of general hospitals, and various transitional facilities which enable the individual to become more socially competent and better able to cope with the problems of life. Treatment within the community offers many advantages: the patient's life is disrupted as little as possible, and studies show that the patient usually gets well quicker and at lower total cost. Moreover, treatment within the community enables the family to learn what behavior is abnormal and what is not, and to recognize their own special role in the recovery process.

In line with the new sociocultural emphasis, much attention is now given to the problems in society which produce abnormal behavior. There are many who believe the major approach to prevention must come from social advocacy and political action, with the objective of making society more responsive to human needs and more relevant to the human condition.

Incidence and Prevalence

Mental illness occurs in all races, ages, and economic and ethnic groups, although behavior manifestations differ from one condition to another. With some variations in predominant types, the symptoms understood as schizophrenia—the most prevalent and serious of all mental illnesses—appear at about the same rate in remote South Pacific isles, communist and capitalist societies.

In the United States a high correlation between severe mental illness and poverty has been documented, but there is evidence that the downward socioeconomic mobility experienced when a person becomes mentally ill is in part responsible for this correlation. Many of the people who become chronic public fund users, if not chronic psychiatric hospital and nursing home patients, were at one time productive middle and upper class persons with family and institutional resources, and capacities for independent functioning. Becoming isolated and unable to function socially is at the core of mental illness and frequently sets in motion the vicious cycle of illness-poverty-illness.

At the present time an estimated 21,500,000 people in the United States suffer from mental or emotional illness severe enough to require psychiatric or psychological treatment. This is one out of ten, a ratio that has been cited for many years. The total includes an estimated 500,000 children, many as young as two or three years of age, who suffer serious forms of mental illness.

The National Institute of Mental Health reported that 2,700,000 Americans were treated in mental hospitals, outpatient clinics, and other psychiatric facilities during 1971. At that time there were 601 psychiatric hospitals — 324 state and county, 158 private, and 119 under the Veterans Administration. The private hospitals accounted for only about 3 percent of beds devoted to mental patients, since these hospitals are not only fewer in number but usually much smaller than government institutions. The population of residential psychiatric hospitals has been declining, and the number of patients treated on an outpatient basis in community mental health centers, free-standing clinics, and general hospitals has been steadily increasing. Between 1955 and 1973 there was a more than 60 percent reduction in the resident population of state institutions, and that decline is continuing. This, however, does not mean that fewer patients are being treated — rather, the length of the hospital stay has been substantially reduced. Prior to 1955, when psychotropic drugs were introduced, the average length of stay in mental hospitals was 8 years; in 1968 it was 1.4 years; and in the more advanced hospitals the average length of stay for first-admission patients is now less than two months. Moreover, readmission rates for patients receiving continuing aftercare and rehabilitation are as low as 10 percent.

Many investigators associate other social and personality disturbances with mental illness, such as suicide, criminal behavior, delinquency, alcoholism, and drug abuse. Family breakdown and chronic unemployment are also correlated with mental and emotional problems. In 1973 approximately 24,440 people committed suicide in this country, and since it is estimated that there are eight suicide attempts for every suicide committed, perhaps as many as 400,000 people attempt suicide in a given year. There are an estimated 9,000,000 alcoholics in the United States, with 200,000 new cases expected to develop each year. The number of narcotic addicts, according to the Drug Enforcement Agency, is approximately 560,000. The economic cost of crime and delinquency, including law enforcement and justice administration as well as damage inflicted by offenders, has been estimated at more than $20 billion a year. (See CHAPTER 16: ALCOHOLISM; CHAPTER 30: DRUG ABUSE PROBLEMS.)

Types of Mental and Emotional Disorders

The disordered behavior of individuals suffering from *neurosis* is often attributed to an unsuccessful attempt to gain security and emotional balance when equilibrium has been disturbed by intense anxiety. Everyone seeks satisfaction of many emotional and physical needs. When a significant number of these needs are not met due to intervening human and nonhuman obstacles, and when at the same time the individual is lacking in emotional development, or develops misconceptions concerning personal experiences, the result is often a neurosis. Typically, one then exhibits anxieties and conflicts in relationships with others and with the world in general. The behavior probably would have been considered normal at an earlier stage of development—for example, extreme dependence on a parent or parent substitute; or it may be irrational in the circumstances, as in phobic fears or compulsive acts. One is intellectually aware that the behavior is not sound, and also experiences painful feelings of despair, inadequacy, self-disgust, helplessness, shame, and even hopelessness. Situations which make the person feel markedly inadequate are usually avoided, and one may as a consequence circumscribe one's life more and more in order to avoid the anxiety they produce. Since the individual has failed to develop adequate coping skills, the more one avoids what one fears, the more one experiences fear. Thus a destructive cycle evolves, and the neurotic patterns of behavior become so crippling that they prevent full involvement in life.

Psychosis includes the affective disorders of psychotic depression and manic-depressive reaction, and various manifestations of schizophrenia (simple, paranoid, catatonic, hebephrenic, schizo-affective, etc.) These are not sharply differentiated conditions, but rather a great complexity of reactions which are grouped together because of certain similarities. There is a continuing debate about the causes of psychosis and the part that may be played by social, hereditary, cultural, psychological, and metabolic and other physiological factors. Today many investigators emphasize the genetic, constitutional, biochemical, and neuropathological aspects of psychosis; but conclusive evidence of organic causation is still lacking. However, treatment advances are being made on the basis of the majority opinion that schizophrenia and manic-depressive psychosis are probably due to a complex, subtle interplay between all of these factors.

Depression and Its Treatment

Not long ago a news magazine cover story was based on the theme that depression is "the leading mental illness in the U.S., and is now virtually epidemic" (*Newsweek*, January 8, 1973). The article reported that 1 in 8 Americans will need psychiatric help for depression during his or her lifetime; that 125,000 of these are hospitalized each year, with another 200,000 treated in offices—and in addition, an estimated 4 to 8 million need help but are not aware of it. There is an ever-continuing debate on such questions as to whether events in the person's life are sufficiently stressful to produce the depression; why an individual reacts to certain conditions with depression at one time and not at another; and why similar situations produce depression in one person and not in another. Some investigators implicate perfectionism, rigid ritualistic makeup, or unresolved hostility toward the self. Others are working on the question of biochemistry, supported by the fact that medications are often effective in lifting depression.

The onset of depression may be sudden or gradual, and the degree may vary from chronic "blue" feelings to deeper feelings of dejection and discouragement accompanied by agitation or psychomotor retardation. Depressed individuals are usually preoccupied with worries and have difficulty with thinking, working, and sleeping. In extreme cases they may dwell on self-accusations and unrealistic, obsessional thoughts about the evil things they have done or experienced, or the mistakes they have made and the punishment they expect to suffer.

Several types of medication (particularly the tricyclics and MAO inhibitors) are often highly effective in elevating the patient's mood and preparing the way for psychotherapy. Realistic, supportive counseling may also be effective. When individuals are operating out of depression, they usually feel not only despondent but totally inadequate, and therefore treatment must be focused on situational factors and personality tendencies, as well as relationships and experiences that will build self-esteem and an appreciation of self-worth. In the more severe cases a short course of electroshock therapy has frequently proved remarkably effective.

When depression occurs, there is concern about suicide even though the patient may not bring up the subject. However, suicidal thoughts are common, and the opportunity to talk about them with a skilled counselor is helpful. Efforts should be made to see that an acutely depressed person is not left alone, and it has been found that such depressions are particularly dangerous when the patient begins to show some mild improvement.

The best way to be helpful to a person suffering depression is through a nonpitying recognition of problems without superficial optimism. The opportunity to air and discuss angry or guilty feelings is an important part of the therapeutic process, but it is also essential to help the person become active again in constructive pursuits that reinforce one's strengths. Reassurance that the therapist understands one's feelings and has faith in one's improvement is more helpful than insisting that things are not as bad as they seem. It is useful to recognize, and perhaps point out to the patient, that according to NIMH director Bertram S. Brown, with accurate diagnosis and insightful care the depressed individual has a 95 percent chance of returning to full functioning.

Manic-Depressive Psychosis and Its Treatment

People who experience swings from deep depression to euphoric highs, or sometimes just experience repeated high or manic states and then a leveling-off with an occasional depressive state, or vice versa, are diagnosed as having manic-depressive psychosis. Characteristically these individuals are relatively well adjusted and often high achievers when the disorder is in remission. A manic state may have a fairly gradual onset during which the patient seems amusing or jovial, but a little more talkative and witty than usual. The person may also engage in risky business enterprises, sometimes successful, or spend money extravagantly. As internal stresses increase, the mechanisms of the brain appear to be speeded up: the person jumps from one idea to another, becomes hyperactive, and talks "a blue streak" (pressure of speech). At this point one's business enterprises become sheer gambles and usually fail. As a consequence, one may become belligerent and easily upset for a time, but will usually regain the extreme euphoria and turn one's attention to a new and even more unrealistic scheme. Hyperactivity continues to increase until one can neither eat nor sleep and becomes physically exhausted. The person seems to be unable to recognize the social consequences of the behavior or to experience guilt, and therefore appears totally irresponsible. An experienced observer will sometimes sense deep depression underneath the fast-moving, excited behavior. The family and associates of a person afflicted with manic-depressive reaction may have to pay the debts incurred, or face embarrassment as a result of the behavior.

A physiological predisposition or an obscure biochemical error has long been suspected in these cases, but these factors have not been fully identified or verified. There is considerable evidence, however, that complex factors involving the patient's concept of self, and the patient's relationships with significant persons in the family, are close to the root of this cyclic illness. Therefore it is highly important for persons in intimate contact with the patient to learn to interact with the individual as constructively as possible.

The sooner this disorder is recognized and therapy obtained, the better the chances of recovery. A long-known medication, lithium carbonate, has been successful in stabilizing the mood swings of many of these patients. Management of life-style can also have a good effect. Motivated by a high level of aspiration, many individuals with manic tendencies acquire a great deal of the kind of knowledge and know-how that society recognizes and rewards. If they select a profession which will suffer relatively little from interruption, such as writing, or if they develop a specialized capability that is in increasing demand, they might be able to channel their abundant energy into constructive and satisfying directions. Recognition from society may help to prevent or at least moderate their periods of depression and thereby help to bring their mood swings within a manageable range.

Schizophrenia and Its Treatment

Some investigators maintain that close to 90 percent of hospitalized mental patients suffer from this disorder. The many labels, such as schizoid personality, chronic undifferentiated schizophrenia, and schizo-affective reaction, as well as the heated debates about possible causes, all seem to suggest that at the present time many different human problems may be called schizophrenia. It seems helpful to think in terms of a division into episodic and chronic types. The episodic, or reactive, type is one in which the individual has been functioning fairly well, but a traumatic experience or buildup of stress produces an emotional crisis that suddenly throws one into a psychotic state. The chronic, or process, type is observed in individuals who experience lifelong difficulty in meeting the demands of living and in developing stable interpersonal relationships. These patients have long appeared to be "different," and gradually become more and more withdrawn and unrealistic.

The symptoms collected under the general label of schizophrenia can be divided into five categories: (1) disturbances in testing the reality of phenomena, so that the patient thinks in bizarre or personalized ways; (2) feelings of estrangement or depersonalization—unreal feelings of being outside oneself looking on; (3) disturbances in emotional control such as total retardation of movement or sudden overwhelming excitement; (4) social isolation and longing for closeness, but at the same time fear of being close; (5) language and thought disturbances—initially vagueness, then more and more idiosyncratic or autistic expression, with neologisms, clang associations (relating words by sound rather than by meaning), and concrete thinking (with concomitant lack of abstract thought).

The diagnostic subcategories of simple, catatonic, paranoid, and hebephrenic which have been used for many years have recently been challenged because of the high degree of overlapping of symptoms and the changes in the way society views behavior. Paranoid, for example, has become a common word and is to some degree understood by a great many people who apply it to supersuspicious and self-important attitudes. The realization that human experience is a continuum of intensity, differing in degree rather than kind; and that people have a way of being so complex that their behavior does not conveniently conform to the diagnostic categories has prompted many workers from various disciplines and theoretical backgrounds to emphasize the dynamics of behavior rather than classification and differential diagnosis. It becomes important for treatment purposes to focus on such factors as the following: the capacity of the patient to relate to others; the onset of behavior changes; the nature of the patient's development prior to the current condition; the positive and negative aspects of the environment; and the degree to which one can respond to realistic expectations and mobilize one's healthy characteristics and capacities.

The phenothiazine medications offer significant assistance with acute phases of schizophrenia as well as long-term management of persistent anxiety and stress. These drugs are supplied in oral and injectable form; long-acting injections have been of great assistance to persons who have difficulty taking medication. Resistance to taking the drugs seems due in some cases to the desire to appear strong and not need a crutch. It is often a source of regret that persons who become "stabilized" (free of symptoms) on a prescribed dosage frequently stop taking the medication and "become ill again." Perhaps it is more helpful to recognize that the medication can artificially reduce extreme anxiety and prepare the way for a therapeutic relationship which will help the patient achieve closer touch with the environment. If the patient fails to develop greater hope and satisfaction in life, or if the therapist withdraws too soon, the individual may stop taking the medication and will once again express anguish in the form of symptoms. Without the medication it takes a long period of intense interpersonal effort to reach the patient who is unrealistic, and to help the patient gain the satisfactions needed—but the medication alone will not enable one to reach these goals. If the person ceases to take the medication and relapses, the setback will more likely be due to withdrawal of therapy and life support than to withdrawal of the drugs.

Some families and counselors exert pressure toward rejection of medication as a form of assistance. Others rely on it as a kind of magic or perhaps as a means of controlling the patient. Most helpful seems to be the attitude that the medication is a useful tool which the patient can come to understand and accept, even to the point of tolerating some unpleasant side effects such as dry mouth or impairment of visual acuity. Some of the side effects can be handled in commonsense ways—for example, increasing intake of water to relieve dry mouth, or protecting oneself from exposure to the sun where indicated. Medications may also be prescribed to minimize such side effects as restlessness and muscular tension.

Interpersonal management stresses appreciation of the extreme sensitivity to rejection experienced by individuals with schizophrenia. The therapist must be fully aware of the importance of his or her relationship with these patients, and be able to discriminate the subtle nuances of this relationship. The therapist must also be fully honest about what they understand and don't understand, and about the limits of their tolerance. The less manipulative, controlling, and judgmental, the better. An overassured, extroversive approach is apt to cause further withdrawal. Calm acceptance that is not over-friendly, and respect for distance (no touching) and for the patient's privacy are recommended. Too much probing can also do more harm than good. The therapist may have to offer 80 percent of the relationship at first in order to lend his own zest for living to the patient. It is also important for the family to have an opportunity to examine their own reactions honestly, since the sometimes strange psychotic behavior produces anxiety in others. A calm, understanding, tactful attitude on the family's part will tend to reduce their anxiety and at the same time allow the disturbed person to feel safe and accepted.

Organic and Toxic Conditions

Organic and toxic conditions can produce psychotic behavioral changes and must be carefully checked out by an experienced diagnostician. Endocrine imbalance, head trauma, encephalitis, cerebral arteriosclerosis, and a large number of neurological disorders such as Pick's, Alzheimer's, and Huntington's diseases often involve bizarre, withdrawn, or confused behavior quite similar to the mental illnesses attributed to disturbing experiences or other psychogenic factors. Toxic reactions from medications, drugs, or metallic poisons, as well as certain types of vitamin deficiency, may also result in psychoticlike behavior. Two types of conditions account for the great majority of cases of psychosis among the elderly—arteriosclerotic brain disorder and senile brain disease—and both are on the increase due to the lengthening of the life-span. Common mental symptoms in the first of these disorders are memory defect and inability to concentrate, progressing to clouding of consciousness, disorientation, and incoherence. The second type, which is also termed senile dementia, is due to degeneration of the brain and expresses itself in forgetfulness of recent events, preoccupation with bodily functions, confusion about temporal relationships, and intellectual impoverishment. Dementia may also crystallize into one of five fairly well-defined psychoses: the depressed and agitated type, in which the patient wrings the hands and exhibits hypochondriacal delusions; the delirious and confused type, characterized by bewilderment, disorientation, hallucinations, and extreme restlessness; the paranoid type, in which the patient first becomes quarrelsome and demanding and later develops delusions and hallucinations usually of a persecutory nature; the presbyophrenic type, in which the patient, usually a woman, becomes excessively jovial, frequently confabulates, and engages in rambling recollections and aimless behavior such as packing and unpacking clothing; and, most common of all, the simple deterioration type, characterized by apathy, memory defect, restricted interests, loss of judgment, and irritability, developing into loss of contact with the environment, personal neglect, confusion, and disorientation.

In all the conditions discussed in this chapter, degree of impairment varies, whatever the cluster of symptoms. Just as in most physical illnesses, the longer a person struggles alone with fear and hopelessness, the more intense the symptoms are likely to become. But fortunately most communities now have medical personnel, teachers, ministers, law enforcement officers, and businessmen who recognize early symptoms of mental illness, and for this reason therapeutic intervention is likely to be provided sooner than was the case even twenty years ago. It is for this reason that few people who experience mental illness today lapse into the deeply withdrawn, regressive symptomatology (catatonic stupor, hebephrenic personalized language, etc.) that was so prevalent in the past. Even the organic disorders just enumerated can frequently be relieved or moderated by the newer medications, and the senile conditions can be counteracted by tranquilizers, enriched diet, and a program of social and occupational therapy which will slow the process of deterioration even where it cannot be reversed.

It must be recognized, however, that at this stage in the development of psychiatry and psychology, there are still many patients who do not respond well either to available medications or to relationship therapies, although in some cases newer approaches such as behavior modification techniques can be applied to good effect. The patients who cannot be reached continue to present baffling problems to their families, their therapists, and, most of all, to themselves. (See CHAPTER 54: OTHER DISORDERS, E. Geriatric Rehabilitation; CHAPTER 55: ILLUSTRATIVE CASES, K. Huntington's Disease.)

Rehabilitation*

Rehabilitation has been defined as the process of helping individuals who have had a physical or mental disorder to participate in society to the fullest extent of their capacities. In the case of mental patients, this process is necessitated by two factors. First, during extended hospitalization they tend to lose touch with community and family life and may even develop a "disability syndrome" or "institutional neurosis" characterized by apathy, withdrawal, and resignation, and a period of readjustment is often required. Ideally the patient is carefully prepared for social and occupational participation in the community before leaving the hospital, but too often this preparation is neglected. Second, the term "rehabilitation" implies that residuals of psychiatric disorder may remain after treatment, and the rehabilitative process should be designed to cope with these residuals and keep them from interfering with social and occupational activities.

The goal of community rehabilitation, therefore, is to provide a bridge to normal life for the patient who has been released from residential treatment. Transitional facilities and aftercare programs have multiplied in recent years, but are still unavailable in many localities. They include day hospitals, providing all types of psychiatric treatment and all rehabilitative activities on an outpatient basis; halfway houses, where patients may live during the readjustment period, including not only group residential centers but subsidized apartments supervised by social workers, such as Horizon House in Philadelphia and Quarters House in San Jose; occupational rehabilitation under the federal-state rehabilitation system and private organizations, providing vocational counseling, job finding, and placement in industry or in sheltered workshops; expatient clubs for social and therapeutic purposes, run by either the patients themselves or the hospital as part of its aftercare program; foster family care in carefully selected families under the supervision of a social worker and visiting psychiatric nurse; care in the patient's own family, with the assistance of psychiatric or public health nurses and social workers who work with the family

---

*Based on Robert M. Goldenson, "Rehabilitation (Psychiatric)," *The Encyclopedia of Human Behavior: Psychology, Psychiatry, and Mental Health,* Doubleday, New York, 1970.

as well as the patient. (See CHAPTER 8: THE SHELTERED WORK-SHOP; CHAPTER 56: REHABILITATION FACILITIES AND SERVICES.)

Therapeutic Value of Employment

Although the community approach comprises many important facets—day treatment, sheltered housing, recreation, social life—one phase, employment, deserves special consideration. As Cecil Makota states in "Community Survival for Long-Term Patients" (H. Richard Lamb, ed., Jossey-Bass, San Francisco, 1976):

> Work therapy with long-term patients is an extremely effective activity that not only helps these patients remain in the community, but makes their lives more meaningful. It contributes to their mental health by increasing their feelings of self-esteem and mastery over their lives, and it often leads to their achieving independence through employment. It is viewed by many patients as the only means of extricating themselves from the mental health system and shedding their identity as mental patients. It is equally effective for those who will go into competitive employment and those who will remain in sheltered work situations.

The Seattle Mental Health Institute is an example of an organization that fully recognizes the therapeutic value of work. Its rehabilitation program includes fifty to seventy-five work stations throughout the community where clients can participate from one or two hours on one or several days a week to a full eight-hour, five-day-a-week schedule. The program starts with a close look at the individual client, after which the rehabilitation counselor arranges for work experience in virtually any type of appropriate endeavor—veterinary assistant, warehouse jobs, design, radio-TV, food services, health care, clerical activities, sales, landscaping—at an entry or advanced level, in small groups or large. Sheltered employment is also an important link in the program's continuum of work adjustment.

Enlightened policies regarding mental illness are growing among employers as stigma and fear are replaced by knowledge and understanding. Workers who have become seriously disturbed may be placed on sick leave, often for no longer than is the case with serious physical ailment, and they return to full work capacity after treatment of the acute stage has been completed. Employers are encouraged to keep their roles clear and make proper demands regarding the job, rather than giving sympathy and counsel. Acceptance of the recovered mental patient is an equally important matter. The employer who "walks on eggshells" or is fearful of making demands on the employee is bound to cause more problems. Generalizations are hazardous, but a good rule of thumb is to maintain candid and honest communication with the employee who has been ill. Employers often find that the emotional crisis and its treatment uncover hidden depths and strengths that were previously unrecognized.

Organizations and Associations

The Mental Health Act of 1963 created state mental health and mental retardation planning bodies and channeled authority for setting priorities and coordinating services in county governments. In the late 1960s there was a movement toward providing fees for services to those who could not pay for care themselves, and in the early 1970s there occurred a movement toward relying on state, city, and county governments to use shared federal revenue for providing some of the funding for human services. National health insurance legislation appears to be in the offing. This changing picture makes it very difficult to give helpful information about governmental structures which can be contacted for assistance with mental health problems. However, each state has some governmental agency designated as the Mental Health Authority, although the structure and titles differ from place to place.

Vocational rehabilitation agencies provide many guidance and training opportunities to psychiatric rehabilitants. Referral from physician, therapist, or agency is probably helpful, but individuals and families can make application directly.

Citizen organizations concerned with mental disorders date back to 1909 when Clifford Beers, as noted above, organized the National Committee for Mental Hygiene to combat abusive conditions in mental institutions. In 1950 that organization joined with the National Mental Health Foundation and the Psychiatric Foundation (part of the American Psychiatric Association and the American Neurological Society) to form the National Association for Mental Health, Inc., 1800 North Kent Street, Rosslyn, VA 22209. NAMH is a voluntary citizens' organization dedicated to combatting mental illness and advancing mental health. Its four major program categories are: (1) improved care and treatment for mental hospital patients; (2) provision of aftercare and rehabilitation services, posthospitalization; (3) treatment, education, and special services for mentally ill children; and (4) community mental health services. There are state organizations in almost all states and many metropolitan areas have local chapters. The more than 1,000 Mental Health Associations in the United States engage in a range of activities, including social action and providing of training and research opportunities; they also support a variety of direct services such as sheltered housing, socialization, family assistance, and sheltered employment projects. NAMH provides a large number of informative public information pamphlets at little or no cost, publishes a quarterly journal, *Mental Hygiene,* and works with mass media resources to disseminate educational information.

The National Committee Against Mental Illness, 1028 Connecticut Avenue N.W., Suite 1215, Washington, DC 20036, under the leadership of Mike Gorman, has played a significant role in the enactment of legislation supporting psychiatric hospital improvement and community and mental health development.

Since the Mental Health Act of 1946, the National Institute of

Mental Health, Bethesda, MD 20014, has been the federal government authority charged with the task of coordinated development of research, training, and services in the mental health area. NIMH has been a bureau in the Department of Health, Education and Welfare since HEW evolved, and has overseen grants throughout the country to support research, training, and mental health services as well as to conduct research and training in its own laboratories with NIMH staff. There are ten regional teams throughout the country and a Citizen's Participation Branch, Chevy Chase, MD 20203. In fiscal 1975 NIMH spent $225,041,000 for community mental health programs, including children's services; $242,010,000 for community narcotic addiction and alcoholism rehabilitation programs; and a total of $123,249,000 for research on general mental health, drug abuse, and alcoholism.

There have been significant groups working together for a specific period of time on particular tasks, such as the Joint Commission on Mental Illness and Health (1955 – 1962). The Commission's published report, *Action for Mental Health,* detailed recommendations for a national program, and it has had extensive impact on the direction which has been taken to improve care for the mentally ill.

Many other organizations have concerned themselves with mental health such as state social welfare organizations and professional groups of all disciplines. (For a list of associations, see PART 4, SECTION 2: VOLUNTARY ORGANIZATIONS.)

It is often extremely confusing to a family or individual faced with a mental health problem to know where to start to get help. Talking with a trusted helping person such as a physician, clergyman, or social agency worker might be of assistance in learning about the varied resources available in the community. In many places, public health nurses will come to the home and discuss the problem and various possible solutions. There seem to be a growing variety of options where there was little or no help in the recent past. (A number of these alternatives such as community mental health centers, family care, and clinics are described in CHAPTER 56: REHABILITATION FACILITIES AND SERVICES.)

SELECTED REFERENCES

Almond, Richard, *The Healing Community,* Jason Aronson, New York, 1974.

Bach, George, *Creative Aggression,* Doubleday, Garden City New York, 1975; Avon Books, New York, 1975.

Chu, Franklin, and Sharland Trotter, *The Madness Establishment,* Grossman, New York, 1974.

Deutsch, Albert, *The Mentally Ill in America,* Columbia University Press, New York, 1949.

Dreikurs, Rudolph, *Social Equality: The Challenge of Today,* Henry Regnery, Chicago, 1971.

Ellis, Albert, *Reason and Emotion in Psychotherapy,* Lyle Stuart, New York, 1962.

Erikson, Erik, *Identity, Youth and Crisis,* W. W. Norton, New York, 1968.

Fairweather, George, *Community Life for the Mentally Ill,* Aldine, Chicago, 1969.

Fromm, Eric, *The Art of Loving,* Harper & Row, New York, 1974.

Fromm-Reichman, Frieda, *Principles of Intensive Psychotherapy,* University of Chicago Press, 1971.

Frankl, Victor, *Man's Search for Meaning*, Simon & Schuster, 1970; New York Pocket Books, New York, 1975.

Goldenson, Robert M., *The Encyclopedia of Human Behavior: Psychology, Psychiatry and Mental Health*, vols. 1 and 2, Doubleday, New York, 1970; Dell, New York, 1975.

Green, Hanna, *I Never Promised You a Rose Garden*, Holt, Rinehart & Winston, New York, 1964.

Haley, Jay, *Problem Solving Therapy*, Jossey-Bass, San Francisco, 1976.

Hollingshead, A. B., and F. C. Redlich, *Social Class and Mental Illness*, Wiley, New York, 1958.

Knouth, Percy, *A Season in Hell*, Harper & Row, New York, 1975.

Kolb, Lawrence C., *Modern Clinical Psychiatry*, W. B. Saunders, Philadelphia, 1973.

Kriegman, George, and L. M. Harris, *Emotional and Mental Disorders*, Virginia Commonwealth University, Medical College of Virginia, Department of Psychiatry.

Lamb, H. Richard, and Associates, *Community Survival for Long-Term Patients*, Jossey-Bass, San Francisco, 1976.

Lazarus, Arnold, *Behavior Therapy and Beyond*, McGraw-Hill, New York, 1971.

Logan, Joshua, *Josh: My Up and Down and In and Out Life*, Delacorte, New York, 1976.

MacMurray, Val D., et al., *Citizen Evaluation of Mental Health Services*, Human Sciences Press, New York, 1976.

Parker, Beulah, *Mental Health In-Service Training*, International Universities Press, New York, 1968.

Rothwell, Naomi D., *The Psychiatric Half-Way House*, Charles C. Thomas, Springfield, Illinois, 1966.

Ryan, William, ed., *Distress in the City*, University Press Book Service, New York, 1969.

Srole, L., et al., *Mental Health in the Metropolis*, Harper Torchbooks, New York, 1975.

Steiner, Claude M., *Scripts People Live*, Bantam Psychology Books, New York, 1975.

Sullivan, Harry Stack, *The Interpersonal Theory of Psychiatry*, W. W. Norton, New York, 1953.

Sullivan, Harry Stack, *The Psychiatric Interview*, W. W. Norton, New York, 1954.

Yalom, Irvin D., *The Theory and Practice of Group Psychotherapy*, Basic Books, New York, 1975.

39

Mental Retardation

JEROME R. DUNHAM, Ph.D., and CHARLIS S. DUNHAM, M.A.

Reviewed by CHARLES STROTHERS, M.D., Professor Emeritus, Department of Psychology, Psychiatry and Behavioral Sciences, University of Washington School of Medicine, and LYNNE SIMMLER, Ed.D., Rehabilitation Department, Seattle University

The American Association on Mental Deficiency definition is as follows: "Mental retardation refers to significantly subaverage general intellectual functioning existing concurrently with deficits in adaptive behavior, and manifested during the developmental period." The upper limit of the developmental period is arbitrarily set at eighteen years of age. Adaptive behavior is defined in terms of the individual's ability to meet standards of personal independence and social responsibility expected of his or her age and cultural group. It covers a great many different functions, from the development of sensory and self-help skills and the beginnings of speech and socialization during the early years, to the complexities of reasoning and judgment, application of academic skills, communication and social interaction in the later developmental period.

Normal individuals differ greatly in the development of adaptive behavior, and retarded individuals also show a vast range of differences in adjusting to their environment. One retarded child may not be able to take solid foods until age four, or walk until age eight, while another may climb and drink from a cup at the usual ages, and function so well at an early age that the retardation goes unrecognized until the child begins to have problems in talking or responding to relationships like other children of that age.

Since intellectual and social abilities develop like building blocks in an interrelated way, and human beings mature in a sequence of capabilities, those who make a special study of young children can often identify retarded development in a specific case.

Sometimes the deficiency is identifiable in early infancy, and in rare cases it may be so severe that the child does not develop beyond this totally dependent stage. Most retarded individuals, however, are capable of learning and developing, but do so at a slow and limited rate. Early identification is important because of the help which can be provided by training efforts and stimulation, as well as by medical treatment and surgery in some cases. A retarded child may seem quietly content in the crib for long periods of time, but would profit from contact with the world of sights, sounds, smells, and touch to stimulate and encourage development.

The rejection and lack of understanding which are likely to surround retarded individuals, as well as their own frustrations in coping with the demands of life, often lead to emotional difficulties. Much mental retardation is also associated with complex physical problems and vulnerabilities, and in these cases the child is described as multihandicapped. Nevertheless, in spite of all these difficulties, increasing numbers of mentally retarded persons are finding a gratifying place in society. Many of them become self-supporting and gain great satisfaction from relationships with loved ones and the complex world around them.

In the United States specialized care for the mentally deficient dates back to 1848 with the establishment of the Perkins Institute in Boston. Many advances have been made since that beginning, but there remain to this day scandals of institutional neglect and deterioration which shock and sicken those who care. That society allows such inhumanities suggests a persistence of the ignorant myths and attitudes which prevailed up to the 1920s and 1930s. It was commonly believed that "feeblemindedness" was associated with increased sexual urges and uncontrolled, imprudent behavior; that most cases of retardation were hereditary, and since society was beginning to meet everyone's survival needs, more and more "defectives" were surviving, so that the primary emphasis was not on bringing fulfillment and dignity to retarded persons but on how to end their fearsome proliferation.

For many years sterilization and ostracism were practically the only answers offered. As late as the 1940s parents were advised by professionals that the best thing for the entire family was to send the retarded child to a state custodial institution as soon as possible. Retarded adults could often cope with rural life, but the economics and complexity of the cities resulted in the "warehousing" of human beings who apparently could not meet the demands of society.

It was only when some brave families with a high degree of determination were able to oppose professional advice and raise their children within the family, that it began to be apparent that many retarded persons could reach significant levels of independence, happiness, and fulfillment, given the proper stimulation, training, patient understanding, and love. In addition to these practical experiences and the growing concern over the institutional dilemma, research on learning pointed out that much retardation is related to nutritional, physical, and experiential deprivation during the significant formative years, and that these deprivations are in most instances associated with poverty.

Incidence and Degree of Retardation

It is estimated that about 3 percent of the population of the United States, or 6 million persons, are mentally retarded. This means that mental deficiency is the greatest single cause of disability among children, and probably among adults as well. According to the U.S. Department of Health, Education and Welfare ("The Problem of Mental Retardation," p. 2), approximately 2,454,000 are under twenty and 3,546,000 are over twenty years of age; 50 percent female and 50 percent male. The National Association for Retarded Children (now Citizens), in a 1963 investigation, estimated that 89 percent (5,340,000), were mildly retarded (I.Q. from 52 to 67), 6 percent (360,000) moderately retarded (I.Q. 36 to 51), 3.5 percent severely retarded (I.Q. 20 to 35), and 1.5 percent profoundly retarded (I.Q. 20 and untestable).

"Intelligence" is an abstract word that applies to a wide range of complex behavior, including reasoning, perception, comprehension, remembering, synthesizing, and other mental functions. Tests have been developed which indicate that in many cases the mentally retarded display a generalized intellectual deficiency of greater or lesser degree, although there may also be special weaknesses, as well as special strengths, in one or more areas. Specialized tests of individual abilities are often essential, since an adequate educational or training program must be planned with the child's special capacities and incapacities in mind. For example, retarded individuals are often unable to understand or use abstract concepts, but may be able to handle concrete ideas and materials quite adequately.

There is currently a good deal of justifiable concern about the abuses of intelligence testing. It is recognized that some children "test" retarded by school standards, but are extremely adaptive in their home and community environments. There are tragic instances where children have been incorrectly evaluated and placed in classes or institutions for the retarded. Serious problems arise from mass evaluation which emphasize the I.Q. level instead of a complexity of factors. Also, long-range predictions are often made on the basis of one evaluation at a given period in the individual's life. Skilled diagnosticians approach intelligence tests with a recognition of the interrelatedness of the aspects of intelligence and the continuum on which learning takes place; as well as the emotional, physical, and cultural factors which affect the normal, exaggerated, or neglected development of specific functions. Any assessment made at a given time provides an indication of developmental accomplishments and needs at that time. In order to provide meaningful information to teachers and families, assessment should continue throughout the developmental period of the individual's life, with greater frequency of readings as the time goes on, so that the person will have the benefit of all appropriate methods of teaching, training, or nurturing.

Not only are the interacting forces too complex for reliance on one evaluation to make vital educational decisions, but experiences and conditions affect the individual and produce changes throughout life. General intelligence levels do not always remain constant and, most certainly, if there is intervention in the adaptive pattern of the person, intertest patterns and specific intellectual capacities can often be altered. Sufficiently skilled analysis of behavior as measured by a battery of psychological tests can provide useful direction for the individual whether one learns at a very slow, average, or superior rate.

Special tools have been devised to evaluate potential abilities under special conditions such as sensory deprivation or communication difficulties. And in addition to standardized psychological tests, systematic observations are helpful in evaluating progress. This method is particularly useful with the severely retarded.

There are instances of functional retardation, sometimes termed pseudoretardation, in which the person performs and learns significantly below average, but gives evidence of being potentially capable of a more normal rate of learning. Education and treatment of the retarded varies subtly but significantly, depending upon whether the retardation is functional or organic, but essentially the approach is the same—starting where the individual is and patiently expecting and helping the individual to achieve the next step.

Early Indications

Early indications of mental retardation may show up in one or many of the areas of child growth and development. Most children follow a general sequence of learning activities leading to mobility, communication, and self-help. Many activities must be learned prior to achieving more complex behaviors. For example, before walking, children first learn to raise their head; roll over from back to stomach; support their own weight in a sitting position; bounce up and down; sit alone; creep and crawl; pull themselves up to standing position; walk holding on; and take their first faltering steps alone. All of this activity is motivated by curiosity to reach and get things and go to places and people. Other adaptive behavior also has its series of preliminary activities.

Individual children differ a great deal in the time they take to accomplish these skills. Many times concerned parents misinterpret individual variation in rate of growth as indicating a serious developmental lag. Nevertheless, marked delay in a number of areas may indicate to specialists in child growth and development, such as the pediatrician or child psychologist, that the youngster is retarded.

Examples of physical conditions in early infancy which should be carefully evaluated by a pediatrician are convulsions or spasticity, physical lethargy, such as sleeping long periods of time; and lack of emotional response to persons, sounds, or objects. Some-times organic brain damage associated with retardation is accom-panied by aimless movements, hyperactivity, lack of alertness, and difficulty in sucking, swallowing, and learning self-feeding skills. Conditions which involve physiological abnormalities, such as Down's syndrome and microcephaly, are readily identified by the physician.

Causes, Prevention, and Treatment

While some 200 specific causes of mental retardation have been identified, it is impossible to determine the precise etiology in 75 to 85 percent of actual cases. Usually the disease, trauma, or genetic determinant occurs and affects the brain at the time of conception, prenatal life, or just after birth. Full evaluation of brain functioning is usually not possible until several months later. Therefore the symptom is often discovered long after the causative agent has tak-en its toll. Additionally, aggravating environmental factors interact with organic factors in such a complex fashion that the developing overlay of problems blocks out forever the primary cause. Mathilde Krim ("Scientific Research and Mental Retardation," President's Committee on Mental Retardation Message, no. 16, January 1969) categorizes the causes of mental retardation into poverty, agents of organic defect, and genetic determinants.

Poverty. Poverty in rural and city slums means malnutrition, un-sanitary conditions, and poor housing, as well as physical, intellec-tual, and emotional deprivation. In areas of extreme poverty one finds more disease (for example, five to nine times more tuberculo-sis); three times more premature births; almost all cases of infant lead poisoning; more accidents—and there is often virtually no medical care or health education. These overwhelming burdens lead to hopelessness, apathy, and breakdown of family life, and a consequent lack of stimulation in early childhood. There is abun-dant evidence that a full-scale attack on poverty would significantly reduce the incidence of mental retardation. Nutritious food, decent housing, and health and educational services are absolute essen-tials, with early stimulation being of significant importance. Society remains plagued by blind spots which thus far have defeated efforts to meet the fundamental needs of poor people. Many workers in the mental retardation field hold that prevention in half of the cases (affecting approximately 3 million people) must start with social action.

In this connection, there are a growing number of young, anties-tablishment parents from middle and upper income backgrounds who, in their search for new freedoms and ethics, are turning away from the health and living standards of their families. Many of them live under poverty conditions of poor nutrition, inadequate hous-ing, no medical care, ignorance of the consequences of venereal disease, drug intake, and inadequate protection of their babies. There is an urgent need to direct preventive educational efforts and health services to this group of the "protesting poor."

463

Agents of Organic Defect. These "account for more cases of retardation than all those resulting from genetic defects" (Krim, p. 6). Pathological conditions in the mother during pregnancy are significant causes of retardation. Toxemia of pregnancy (excess of poisons or waste in the blood) is easily discovered and controlled; however, studies show that in many cities 30 percent of mothers do not receive prenatal care. A high percentage of these are young girls. Rubella, or German measles, during the first three months of pregnancy can cause severe damage to the unborn child. A recently developed vaccine can prevent this disease. Several other viral diseases are suspected of causing defects during prenatal development: hepatitis and chicken pox are among those under active investigation. It is strongly recommended that no live virus vaccine be given to women of childbearing age, in case they might be pregnant. Toxoplasma, a protozoan parasite transmitted by animals, may not harm the mother, but may attack the embryo brain, sometimes causing blindness, deafness, microcephaly, or hydrocephalus.

Metabolic and kidney disturbances during pregnancy can also cause fetal developmental problems. Congenital syphilis, after many years of declining incidence, is on the rise as a cause of brain damage and mental retardation. (See CHAPTER 53: VENEREAL DISEASE.)

Women exposed to excessive radiation during diagnostic or therapeutic x-rays, or while performing certain medical jobs, may give birth to mentally retarded offspring. There are advocates of a lifetime record of x-ray exposure, and much has been done to take special precautions and to reduce unnecessary use of this technique for routine testing.

At one time Rh incompatibility disease (erythroblastosis fetalis) placed 400,000 of the 4 million babies born in the United States each year in jeopardy, killed about 16,000 newborn, and left thousands of other babies mentally retarded and otherwise defective. This condition occurs in certain cases where the mother's blood lacks a factor known as Rh (from rhesus, a monkey in which it was first discovered) and the father's blood contains that factor, and the father's genes transmit it to the baby. The baby is then Rh positive and the mother is Rh negative. If the mother has had a previous pregnancy, she will have become sensitized to the Rh positive blood of the fetus and will have developed antibodies against it. In the course of the present pregnancy these antibodies will be acquired by the unborn child from maternal circulation, and will cause anemia with mild to severe jaundice (that is, erythroblastosis). One of the possible effects of this disease is cerebral palsy and another is mental retardation—and some children are afflicted with both conditions. For some years prior to 1960 the infant's blood was replaced by exchange transfusions in order to remove the hostile, sensitized blood before brain damage occurred. Today, however, it is customary to adopt the much less risk-ridden and costly solution of giving the mother Rh immune globulin within seventy-two hours of each delivery or miscarriage, as a preventive measure.

Other perinatal conditions can cause retardation, such as brain hemorrhage due to injury of the fetus during delivery; insufficient oxygen to the brain (cerebral anoxia); or premature separation of the placenta (see CHAPTER 26: CEREBRAL PALSY).

Postnatal causes of retardation take the form of either injury or disease. Head injuries result in brain damage in about 1 million children per year. Child abuse by disturbed and anguished adults may produce a condition known as battered child syndrome, which in some cases leads to mental retardation.

Deficient diet, lead or other metallic poisoning, and certain childhood diseases can leave permanent damage to intellectual and adaptive capacity. Complications of measles, whooping cough, encephalitis, meningitis, and tuberculosis can result in retardation. These diseases can often be prevented, or their complications controlled, by medical treatment and adequate child care and supervision.

Thus it would seem that better prenatal, infant, and child care in which well-known preventive measures are applied could do much to reduce organic brain damage resulting in retardation.

Genetic Determinants. Since the mid-1800s discoveries by the Austrian botanist Gregor Mendel, it has been recognized that many physical and mental characteristics are inherited and that knowledge of the combination of these traits carried by the genes of the parents can result in prediction of the characteristics of the offspring. Since 1957 the study of chromosomes and genes has made prediction of complex characteristics more precise. Genetic technology has developed to a point where the biochemical constitution of prospective parents can be investigated, and the chances of having children with serious limitations and disabilities assessed with some accuracy.

Some are troubled about the responsibility such knowledge places on society, but others look forward to routine genetic counseling for all, so that enlightened decisions can be made about mating, giving birth, artificial insemination, whether to have more children, adoption, or remaining childless. While large-scale population control programs do not exist, increasing numbers of concerned couples are seeking information from genetic counselors. This form of counseling includes investigation of a couple's genetic and physical history, a chromosomal count of both partners, and interpretation of the results of the investigation to the prospective parents. Physicians throughout the country can assist couples in locating genetic counseling resources, which are often associated with medical schools.

Since 1966 it has also been possible to safely analyze the chromosomal count of the fetus early in pregnancy in the event that damage is suspected. If the result is favorable, the parents will be reassured; if not, and if personal ethics and the law allow, they may elect abortion.

Chromosomal damage from certain drugs is under investigation. Although results are for the most part inconclusive, there is widespread concern that the use of drugs, such as LSD, may cause fetal damage. Women must be informed about the possible consequences of taking prescribed or nonprescribed drugs during pregnancy and discuss any use of drugs with their physician.

Today, due to increased opportunities for community living, many retarded adults are finding happiness and companionship in marriage. They may be capable of understanding the serious problems that would beset them and any children they might produce. With counseling, many retarded couples decide to forgo parenthood for their own and the potential children's sake.

There are instances in which parents who themselves show no abnormalities are carriers of abnormal traits or diseases. An example is Tay-Sachs disease, or cerebral lipoidosis: if both parents are carriers, there is a 25 percent chance with each pregnancy that the child will have the disease. A Tay-Sachs child appears to be normal at birth but begins to deteriorate at about six months of age and gradually develops loss of coordination, seizures, blindness, and severe mental retardation, rarely surviving beyond the fourth year. The disease is now known to be caused by the accumulation of a fatty substance (sphingolipid) chiefly in the brain, due to the absence of an enzyme (hexosaminidase A, or HEX A). A blood test has been developed to identify carriers and the condition can also be detected by amniocentesis during the third or fourth month of pregnancy, after which a therapeutic abortion is performed. Two other closely related diseases, Gaucher's and Niemann-Pick, also result in mental retardation. (See CHAPTER 19: BIRTH DEFECTS; GENETIC COUNSELING.)

Anomalies are deviations that occur in a random manner. While they may sometimes appear to be associated with certain factors, such as the age of the mother, the precise cause is not known. One of the more common of these conditions is mongolism, or Down's syndrome, which is now believed to be due to an accidental abnormality in the distribution of chromosomes in the cells of the developing embryo. Dr. John Langdon-Down, who first described this disorder, characterized it as "the largest group of single diagnostic clinical types of mental retardation." He called the syndrome mongolism because the victim's facial features roughly resemble those of the Mongolian race, but in recent years the disorder has come to be identified by his name instead, since this conforms to medical custom and avoids racial overtones. Certain foot- and hand-print abnormalities are characteristic of this condition, as well as lack of fold in the eyelids, broad nose, protruding lower lip, large thick tongue, stubby fingers, round face, and broad short skull. Down's syndrome children often have poor circulation and are susceptible to respiratory disease. In the past, these defects reduced life expectancy, but today they can often be corrected by careful medical attention. Other complications such as visual or dental disorder, congenital heart disorder, and speech defect may also be associated with Down's syndrome.

Chromosomal abnormalities result in Down's syndrome (about

fourteen different types have been identified), but it is not known exactly how the extra chromosome (trisomy 21) causes the disorder. Currently the condition is not thought to be inherited. Studies have shown some correlation with difficulty during previous deliveries; higher than usual incidence of breech births; and higher incidence when the mother is over forty years of age.

Many personality traits have been attributed to Down's syndrome children, such as an affectionate nature, love of music, and sense of mimicry, but these traits are often associated with family relationships and characteristics and are not realistic expectations of a clinical nature.

Structural anomalies of the head can also result in brain damage and retardation. Hydrocephalus, an enlargement of the head due to pressure of excess cerebrospinal fluid on brain tissue, can sometimes be arrested by an operation in which the fluid is shunted into the bloodstream. Craniostenosis, due to premature closure of the cranial opening, can also be partially relieved by surgery in some cases. Little if anything can be done for children born with microcephaly, characterized by a small, pointed head and miniature brain. Some cases are probably due to a single recessive gene, others to radiation treatment of the mother or infectious diseases such as toxoplasmosis. (See CHAPTER 50: SPINA BIFIDA.)

Cretinism is a severe thyroid deficiency disorder originating in fetal life or early infancy. It occurs with frequency where lack of iodine produces a high incidence of goiter, but it may also result from birth injury or infectious disease. If untreated, it can cause stunted growth, thick protruding tongue, large head, coarse hair, and intellectual retardation. When the child is treated with thyroid extract during the first few months of life, development can be close to normal.

Phenylketonuria (PKU) is a congenital metabolic disorder in which phenylpyruvic acid can be detected in the urine. The condition is often associated with severe mental retardation and affects 1 in 20,000 children. Since a urine test can identify the disorder soon after birth, it is possible in some cases to prevent or greatly limit brain damage by prescribing a diet low in phenylalanine.

It is becoming increasingly routine to check for body chemistry abnormalities at birth, and techniques are being developed to do so during pregnancy. Research is accomplishing more and more in the prevention of birth anomalies, but there is still a long way to go.

A number of other congenital disorders that frequently result in mental retardation (acrocephaly, Apert's syndrome, Crouzon's disease, gargoylism, hypertelorism, macrocephaly) are briefly described in CHAPTER 32: FACIAL DISFIGUREMENT.

Education

Although educational services for the retarded have greatly increased in the past twenty years, it is estimated that only half of the children in need of special education are currently receiving it (Philip Roos, "Trends and Issues in Special Education for the Mentally Retarded," National Association for Retarded Citizens). (See CHAPTER 12: LEGISLATION AND CONSUMER RIGHTS.)

The prevailing philosophy in mental retardation work emphasizes a "developmental model" which holds that all children, even the most profoundly retarded, have a capacity for growth and learning and that retarded persons experience the same needs, feelings, and sensitivities as everyone else. The retarded benefit from participating, as much as possible, in the mainstream of society, and there is evidence that society as a whole profits from integrating those with individual differences into the general group.

Education for every child begins long before the usual age for school, and the early experiences of mentally retarded children at home are just as crucial as for normal children, if not more so. There are excellent, clearly written books and pamphlets for parents providing practical suggestions to further the development of retarded children, and information which helps families achieve accepting attitudes toward them. One of these is "The Mentally Retarded Child at Home," by Laura Dittman (Children's Bureau publication no. 374, 1969, HEW), which deals with such areas of life as toilet training, dressing, mannerisms (head banging, rocking, drooling), speech development, discipline, play, group experiences, etc. Another is "The Retarded Child: Answers to Questions Parents Ask," by A. A. Attwell and D. A. Clabby, Western Psychological Services, Los Angeles, 1971.

At the present time family efforts to provide early experiences for retarded children are being supplemented in many areas by "developmental schools" established by local voluntary organizations, but there are plans to extend public education programs for the preschool retarded child. The 1975 Education for All Handicapped Children Act requires all states receiving federal aid to develop plans for educating all handicapped children in the mainstream to the fullest possible extent, but many people are concerned that in some cases exceptional children will be placed in regular schools without adequate preparation and resources, and that they will therefore be denied the best possible education.

Some children are so disabled that they may never walk, use language, achieve toilet training, or feed themselves. Although there is a trend toward expanding education programs to include the severely and profoundly retarded, too often the least skilled teachers are assigned to the most seriously impaired pupils. Moreover, many educators associate education only with teaching academic skills, which automatically eliminates the severely retarded. On the other hand, some severely retarded children and teen-agers are attending training schools and activity centers that provide appropriate stimulation and practice at a level consistent with their capacities.

The work of B. F. Skinner through the 1940s and 1950s has had a significant impact on education as a whole, but it has recently been recognized to be especially effective in the training of the mentally retarded. Operant conditioning, or behavior modification, is the systematic application of rewards and in some cases mild punishment for the purpose of shaping and reinforcing preferred behavior and eliminating unsatisfactory behavior. This approach is applicable to the profoundly retarded, and is used to develop feeding skills, control of elimination, and even social response. The technique can be taught to parents and paraprofessionals in a relatively short time, and is particularly effective because the goals and the minute steps leading to them are kept clearly in mind.

Retarded children who are given an opportunity to attend regular schools have the advantage of gradually learning to cope with their differences, and often become better equipped to participate in society during adult life. On the other hand, there are some who believe that segregation in special schools promotes the development of greater self-confidence, since the retarded children do not have to compete with those who learn at a normal rate. But the majority of specialists concerned with the welfare of mentally retarded persons adhere to a compromise position—that retarded children should attend special classes for academic subjects (those involving verbal and numerical concepts), and regular classes for such subjects as art, physical education, music, and shop.

There is a growing emphasis on practical education for the mentally retarded, focused on vocational preparation, daily living skills, and avocational and social skills. As adult education gains favor, it should be remembered that retarded adults also require continuing education to assist them in coping with a rapidly changing environment.

Educators make a distinction between children who are educable and those who are only trainable. The trainable children learn at a slower rate than the educable children and are not capable of handling abstractions, but may eventually become capable of taking care of themselves and of doing useful work under special direction. Some children are limited in their functioning because of hyperactive or restless, erratic behavior. Their limited attention span and "steamroller" activity interfere with learning and relating to others. (See CHAPTER 6: EDUCATIONAL PROGRAMS; CHAPTER 37: LEARNING DISABILITIES.)

As with all special education, the selection of the best setting for a particular child is a task requiring the careful consideration of the family and a team of specialists. The physical health and mental level of the child, as well as emotional factors and conditions in the home, play a part in the decision. There may be a need for reevaluation from time to time, and it may be beneficial to change from one mode or setting to another—that is, from residential school to day school, or vice versa. (See CHAPTER 55: ILLUSTRATIVE CASES, L. A Multihandicapped Child.)

Residential Care

Approximately 275,000 persons live in the nation's public and private residential facilities for the retarded. An essential problem with most residential facilities is that they tend to be custodial and to lack programs which promote growth and habilitation ("Policy Statement on Residential Care," National Association for Retarded Children, October 1968). Too often they are not based on individual needs, do not plan in terms of specific goals or span of time, and are not closely linked with the medical, educational, and welfare programs of the community. Many dehumanizing practices are followed in some overcrowded, understaffed institutions ("Dehumanization vs. Dignity," National Association for Retarded Citizens). Among them are: herding the "inmates" in groups; imposing uniform standards or rules geared to the least capable residents; specifying certain days for bathing or shaving; providing ill-fitting, inappropriate clothing; requiring the residents to ask for personal items; failing to provide privacy; having the police or sheriff bring them to school; locking them behind bars; discussing them as if they were not present; labeling and treating them as a "diagnosis"; failing to provide glasses, dentures, or hearing aids.

While there continue to be shocking instances in which essential health, safety, and humane standards are not met, some state residential schools for the retarded do provide positive programs and a therapeutic environment. Many state schools have also instituted large volunteer programs designed to provide more stimulation and human contact for their residents. A residential facility which strives to be treatment-oriented rather than merely custodial will have a specialized staff, offer opportunities for innovative programming, and provide long-range help for retarded individuals whose needs are not being met in the community.

Community foster homes and group homes have gained favor in recent years and are offering an opportunity for social and emotional satisfaction to retarded young people. Programs offering day facilities to retarded adults residing in their own homes, as well as temporary "respite care" of retarded children while their families regain strength for the task of meeting their needs, are also gaining in popularity.

Private schools and centers, both residential and day care, exist throughout the country. One of the best-known and most respected is the complex of Devereux schools ("Devereux Serves," Devereux Foundation Press, Devon, Pennsylvania, 1970) in several east, west, and southwest locations. Devereux serves children with a wide range of learning disorders, offering academic work from kindergarten to college for the potentially average or superior, along with highly individualized tutorial and vocational training programs for slow learners. A highly trained, multidisciplinary staff provides ongoing assessment and a broad scope of activities directed toward independence and personal fulfillment.

Vocational Rehabilitation

Mary Switzer ("This Isn't Kindness, This Is Business," NARC), the highly respected federal rehabilitation leader in the 1950s and

1960s, has pointed out that the number of mentally retarded persons moving into the competitive labor market is but a fraction of what it should be in view of their real potential for remunerative work. Employment of the mentally retarded in urban private business and industry is relatively new, and most employers do not realize that when properly placed they can do the job as well as and often better than others. Many industrial tasks are of such a repetitive, assembly-line nature that the jobs are disturbing or boring to workers capable of intellectual challenge, but can be accomplished with diligence, speed, and pride by mentally retarded workers. Service jobs in restaurants, laundries, and building maintenance are often suitable to persons of limited intelligence, and when given a chance they have usually achieved a positive record. Studies indicate low absenteeism, good safety records, no more than average time and cost for training, and high job satisfaction resulting in low turnover ("What a Mentally Retarded Worker Can Do," *Supervisory Management Magazine*, 1966). Labor unions are becoming increasingly supportive of the retarded worker in keeping with their commitment to opportunity and fulfillment for all.

Government has developed programs to reimburse the employer for one-half the salary for a month or so, in addition to offering placement and counseling support to the new employee. State employment services and the Division of Vocational Rehabilitation provide information about these programs. Sheltered workshops, such as Goodwill Industries, train the mentally retarded to develop work habits and skills, and also provide employment for those not capable of performing competitively. (See CHAPTER 8: THE SHELTERED WORKSHOP.)

Once having hurdled the employment barrier, the greatest problem for the retarded worker is usually not directly associated with the job but results from loneliness and leisure time impoverishment in an urban society. Community living for retarded adults is just beginning to receive widespread attention. Their prime needs are for companionship to meet their need for socialization and recreation, and for supportive assistance from time to time in coping with the complexities of modern life. When large numbers of people live in dormitory settings, they almost inevitably evolve into depersonalized institutions, but small hostels or cooperative apartments with shared recreational rooms have been gaining recognition as a solution to the retarded individual's living problem. There is also much interest in the potential of adult group homes, sheltered boarding homes (frequently called halfway houses), and adult foster homes.

Local community and national groups are providing citizen advocates and guardians for retarded adults who have lost touch with their families and find it difficult to develop new supportive ties. A volunteer "friend" who takes a personal interest and is available in time of difficulty can be of inestimable value in helping the mentally retarded individual adjust to the community.

(See Chapter 56: Rehabilitation Facilities and Services, J. Halfway Houses; K. Group Homes; L. Foster Families; O. Communities for the Retarded; P. A Training School for the Retarded.)

Research

The bulk of research in mental retardation is either carried out or supported by the federal government. In 1973 over $24 million was spent by the National Institutes of Health, including allocations by the National Institute of Child Health and Human Development to twelve Mental Retardation Research Centers located at the University of Chicago; Children's Hospital, Cincinnati; George Peabody College of Teachers, Nashville; University of Colorado Medical Center, Denver; University of Washington, Seattle; University of California, Los Angeles; Albert Einstein College of Medicine, New York; University of Kansas, Lawrence; Walter E. Fernald State School, Waltham, Massachusetts; Children's Hospital Medical Center, Boston; University of North Carolina, Chapel Hill; and University of Wisconsin, Madison. Other agencies of the Department of Health, Education and Welfare, such as the Office of Education, support research in their respective areas. A number of nongovernmental agencies, including the National Foundation, the Kennedy Foundation, the National Association for Retarded Citizens, the American Association on Mental Deficiency, and the Association for the Aid of Crippled Children, also support research related to mental retardation.

Current research areas include biochemical studies of inborn errors of metabolism, including methods of detection and treatment (enzyme replacement, for example) in Gaucher's and other diseases; studies of the way the rubella virus destroys immune response; investigation of the widespread infectious disease toxoplasmosis; a method of treating the estimated 30,000 Rh negative mothers who are already sensitized to Rh positive babies; further chromosomal studies of Down's syndrome; many projects in the field of genetics, designed to throw light on the transmission of hereditary defects; investigations of the legal and ethical problems relating to the mentally retarded.

Organizations

The two largest organizations in this field are the American Association on Mental Deficiency (AAMD), 5201 Connecticut Avenue N.W., Washington, DC 20015; and the National Association for Retarded Citizens (NARC), 2709 Avenue E East, Arlington, TX 76011. Other associations and foundations are listed in Part 4, Section 2: Voluntary Organizations. In addition to its headquarters in Washington, the AAMD comprises 11 regional groups and a total of about 10,000 members, including physicians, educators, administrators, social workers, psychologists, psychiatrists, students, and others interested in the general welfare of mentally subnormal persons and the study of the causes, treatment, and prevention of mental retardation. Its major publications are the *American*

Journal of Mental Deficiency and *Mental Retardation,* both bi-monthlies. The NARC consists of approximately 200,000 members, and 50 state and 1,500 local groups. The members are parents, professional workers, and other concerned persons who work on local, state, and national levels to promote treatment, research, public understanding, legislation, and parent counseling.

SELECTED REFERENCES

Accreditation Council for Services for Mentally Retarded and Other Developmentally Disabled Persons: *Standards for Residential Facilities for the Mentally Retarded; Standards for Community Agencies Serving Persons with Mental Retardation and Other Developmental Disabilities.*

Baroff, G. S., *Mental Retardation: Nature, Cause, and Management,* Wiley, New York, 1974.

Books for Mentally Retarded Children, American Library Association, 50 E. Huron Street, Chicago, IL 60611.

Grossman, M. S., ed., *Manual on Terminology and Classification in Mental Retardation,* American Association on Mental Deficiency, 1973.

President's Committee on Mental Retardation: *Century of Decision; Hello World; The Known and the Unknown; Past and Present; A Program Perspective; Trends in State Services;* Superintendent of Documents, Government Printing Office, Washington, DC 20402.

Stevens, H. A., and R. Heber, *Mental Retardation,* University of Chicago Press, 1964.

40

Multiple Sclerosis

JAN DUDLEY, Northwest Project Director, Neurologic Disease Epidemiologic Study, School of Public Health, Seattle

Reviewed by PHILIP SWANSON, M.D., Board of Trustees, National Multiple Sclerosis Society, Seattle

For more than 100 years multiple sclerosis (MS) has been identified as a chronic disabling disease of the central nervous system, yet it remains one of the most baffling diseases in existence. MS is called a demyelinating disease. That is, the myelin sheath, which is the fatty insulating material that spirals around the nerve fibers of the central nervous system (brain and spinal cord), is somehow destroyed and seems to cause a "short-circuiting" or blocking of the impulses that control the bodily functions. Of the various demyelinating diseases, MS is the most common.

In MS, demyelination occurs in patches called plaques. As the disease progresses, these plaques become more numerous and may combine to form even larger areas of demyelination, and thus cause dysfunction of the nerve impulses. The location of the plaques determines what symptoms manifest themselves. If the plaques occur in an area concerned with movement, there may be weakness. If an area involving sensation is affected, numbness or tingling may result. If the plaques are in "silent areas," there will be no sign of disease. This means that silent areas of the brain which are affected produce no visible effect on the system. Thus an individual may have MS and be unaware of it.

Incidence

MS is a disorder which usually appears during the prime of life. The peak age of onset is thirty years of age. Onset is characterized by the appearance of symptoms, although the agent that causes MS may have been existent in the body previous to any sign of symptoms. Onset of the disease before the age of fifteen or after the age of fifty-five is extremely rare. Responsible estimates place the number of Americans afflicted with the disorder at about 500,000 individuals. Men seem to show signs somewhat later than women, and the overall ratio is 1.5 women to 1 man. Most researchers believe that whatever the factors that cause MS, they occur before the age of fifteen and are external (exogenous) in nature, rather than of a congenital or genetic origin. While interest in the role of genetics has recently increased, it is suspected that this factor is minor in relation to the etiology of MS.

It is known that the prevalence of MS increases in proportion to the geographical distance from the Equator. The northern latitudes are considered to be high-risk areas (40 to 60 MS individuals per 100,000 around 46° latitude, as compared to 10 to 15 individuals per 100,000 at 34°). The exception to this is those populations in Asia. While little is known about research throughout most of Asia, studies in Japan reveal the incidence to be much lower than might be expected considering the latitude: 2 to 4 MS individuals per 100,000. At the opposite end of the spectrum, the Shetland and Orkney Islands of Scotland have a suspected rate of 150 to 200 MS individuals per 100,000. These islands are a particular focus for further research.

Symptoms

The onset of MS can be dramatic enough to encompass most of the symptoms listed below, or as subtle as a vague feeling of tingling or numbness in one area for less than twenty-four hours' duration.

One or more of the following signs or symptoms may appear during the first attack of the disease: slurred speech, blurred or double vision, vertigo, tingling sensations, muscle weakness, numbness or possible loss of coordination and balance, and in some cases an abrupt change of mood involving inappropriate euphoria or depression. A severe attack can include paralysis, muscle cramps, pain, and possibly total blindness. Usually an initial attack will recede within a few weeks and may leave the person with some perceptible change. Subsequent attacks may involve a recurrence of the initial symptoms and also introduce new conditions, such as tremor or loss of bladder or bowel control.

It should be noted that the usual case does not necessarily involve all these signs and symptoms. They are mentioned to illustrate the variety and variation of symptoms that each individual must deal with personally, since no case of MS is identical in its course to any other.

Diagnosis

The diagnosis of multiple sclerosis is exceedingly difficult. There is no definitive laboratory test that can specifically point to MS as the true diagnosis. Often years must elapse before the evolution of the symptoms rules out any other diagnosis. Some laboratory tests exist that can rule out other diseases or conditions, while certain tests such as examination of the cerebrospinal fluid can give indications that increase the probability of the diagnosis.

The difficulty of diagnosis and the natural caution of the examining physician can lead to resentment toward the medical profession and mounting frustration on the part of the patient who feels a strong need to know what disorder he or she may have.

Types and Degrees of Severity

Textbooks most often describe the "classic" case of MS as a series of attacks (exacerbations) and periods of stability (remissions). There is also a benign form which may show no perceptible symptoms and few attacks during the patient's lifetime, with little or no disability resulting from attacks when they do occur. There are a large number of benign cases. Occasionally the malignant form may appear, characterized by a steady downhill, debilitating course with death occurring in a few years. The majority of cases fall between these two extremes.

The usual course of the disease is that of exacerbations occurring every few years, each leaving some disability. Between attacks the patient often functions quite capably until the accumulation of changes becomes too disabling.

There is no way to predict the onset of the disease nor the onset of a new attack, but clinical impressions by physicians have led researchers to become interested in outside factors such as stress, injury, pregnancy, and infections. Further study needs to be done in this area.

The life expectancy of a person with MS is at least 75 percent of the normal span, and usually those whose lives are shortened by the disease die of complicating factors such as infections of the lung or urinary tract. Patients having this disease live for a long time with it, as do the members of their family, and special attention to this aspect warrants consideration of its emotional as well as financial impact.

Causes

Speculation as to the cause or causes of multiple sclerosis runs the gamut from external factors such as diet, temperature, sanitation, exposure to sunlight, and age of acquisition of childhood diseases to internal factors such as genetic predilection, immune response, and chemical deficiency. The possibility of viral causation is also under active consideration.

Presently there is no evidence that the disease is communicable or hereditary in nature. While there is an increased tendency for it to appear in families where there is already one case, the increase in risk is only 5 percent, which is not enough to convince investigators that heredity plays a significant role.

Treatment

As yet, treatment with medications has not shown consistent results. The response to drug therapy appears to be as individualized as the disorder itself. Adrenocorticotropic hormone (ACTH) has shown promise when used during an exacerbation, but this and other agents may produce adverse side effects. In many cases ACTH shows no beneficial results at all, and the use of this drug and other medications in treatment is cautiously evaluated.

Physical therapy in conjunction with medications has been useful in relieving some individuals of muscle spasms, contraction of muscles, and pain. In the event of more severe conditions, surgical procedures are sometimes feasible.

Most MS patients and neurologists will agree that emotional factors influence the course of the disorder. People with MS will sometimes experience an exacerbation when placed under emotional stress; therefore it is of prime importance that the psychological well-being of a patient be given attention. In a disease entity where there are many uncertainties, vague feelings, and fluctuating symptoms, it is understandable that many individuals will develop a personalized response to their situation. Counseling, which provides an opportunity to discuss the realistic fears that each patient can have relative to familial dependence, sexual activity, and financial concerns, may alleviate problems in dealing with the emotional stress associated with the long-term disabling disease. Evaluation by a specialist in emotional adjustment to disability such as a psychiatrist with rehabilitation experience may be invaluable to someone with MS.

Individuals with MS report a variety of treatment methods which relieve specific symptoms, such as diet control, vitamins, acupuncture, and exercise. Some researchers maintain that a low-fat diet is an effective means of controlling the disorder. The physician can also prescribe a regimen to maintain muscle tone and strength.

In the later stages of MS the individual is vulnerable to serious complications which may be prevented or alleviated through proper care. For the bedridden individual, pulmonary disease is often a threat. Other serious complications of the severely disabled person are bedsores and urinary tract infections. The prevention of such complications is accomplished by an awareness on the part of the individual of his or her condition and through quality nursing care which is sometimes difficult to obtain. The treatment of MS is not primarily a matter of medication, but rather the education of the individual in the management of the symptoms encountered in its course and the maintenance of personal capabilities at the highest level of functioning possible.

There are many appliances and devices (braces, wheelchairs, etc.) which can be used to reduce the effects of the loss of full utilization of the body. Instruction and counseling in their use should be part of the treatment of the disorder, not only for the individual's comfort and convenience but also for those who live with the person and assist in care.

Research

The National Advisory Commission on Multiple Sclerosis completed and published its findings in March 1974. This extensive report recommending specific areas of research and the requisite funding can be obtained through the Government Printing Office.

The report explains many reasons why MS has not been more widely researched. Since it appears to be a uniquely human disease, there is no animal model, and this severely limits experimentation. Often the enigmas and lack of significant breakthroughs discourage those interested in scientific inquiry, especially when the leads are scattered and the hope for fruitful results slim. Although other diseases with similar handicaps have been investigated, MS does not have the dramatic manifestations that characterize well-researched disorders such as polio or epilepsy. Diseases that affect children usually have an added emotional appeal for medical investigators. There is a growing conviction that society must support the appropriations by Congress that are needed for the development of measures to treat, prevent, and cure any disease.

> Few, if any, funds are being expended now on direct attempts to prevent MS, comparatively little on therapy directed to arresting the multiple sclerosis process, an unconscionably small amount on treatments directed to minimizing the complications of multiple sclerosis and the painful, disabling and crippling after-effects of the disease, and an exceedingly small amount for the development of sensitive diagnostic tests. (From vol. 1, *Report and Recommendations*, National Advisory Commission on Multiple Sclerosis.)

Two new technological developments show promise in the diagnosis and monitoring of the disease process: the EMI brain scanner developed in England which combines x-ray and computer techniques, and proton-beam (heavy particle) radiography which should be available for use shortly. The EMI scanner is now available, and many are on order for various clinics throughout the country.

The two areas receiving the most attention at present are virology and immunology. Viruses have long been suspected of playing a causative role in MS. As yet, the evidence is indirect and incomplete, but research in this field is quite varied. An exciting recent development was the recovery of an identical virus from the brain tissues of two MS patients through a new technique of fusing. Electron microscopy has aided in this new research. It remains to be seen if these viruses actually caused MS or were incidental invaders of brains damaged by MS. Several chronic degenerative diseases of the central nervous system have been shown to be caused by slow-acting viruses; that is, the disease develops only many months or years after infection takes place. MS is thought by some to be this type of disease, and researchers are focusing on this concept.

The immune process has captured the interest of many investigators, and funds have been allocated for research in this area. While the case for considering MS an autoimmune disease needs greater proof, investigations are being carried out at several medical institutions.

Presently the federal government, through its National Institute of Neurological and Communication Disorders and Stroke, is spending over $3 million a year for research that would be directly relevant to MS, and $31 million for basic biomedical research in neurological sciences. The National Commission has expressed the hope that both of these areas would be expanded by additional funding of $5 million allotted directly to MS research and an additional $4 million to basic research.

In addition to funds which are derived federally, the National Multiple Sclerosis Society spends about $3 million per year on research directed to the cause and cure of this baffling disease.

Sources of Information and Patient Services

The National Multiple Sclerosis Society, with headquarters at 205 East 42d Street, New York, NY 10017, has approximately 175 chapters in the United States. These chapters vary in their ability to provide for patient service. Some have medical facilities attached; others provide referral service to other organizations. The Society's clinical program includes 24 university-associated clinics, 25 community hospital neurological clinics, and 20 rehabilitation clinics. Most chapters have some equipment available to those in need, such as wheelchairs, braces, or canes. Another possible source of patient service is the nearest branch of the Easter Seal Society.

SELECTED REFERENCES

McAlpine, Douglas, C. E. Lumsden, and E. D. Acheson, *Multiple Sclerosis: A Reappraisal,* Churchill Livingstone, London, 1972.

Mackay, Roland P., and Asao Hirano, "Forms of Benign Multiple Sclerosis," *Archives of Neurology,* vol. 17, December 1967.

National Multiple Sclerosis Society: *Home Care Manual; Multiple Sclerosis Research.*

Schumacher, George A., "Multiple Sclerosis," in *Conn's Current Therapy,* W. B. Saunders, Philadelphia, 1970.

41

Muscular Dystrophy

ROBERT M. GOLDENSON, Ph.D.

Reviewed by GEORGE H. KRAFT, M.D., Associate Professor of
Rehabilitation Medicine, University of Washington School of Medicine;
and by the Muscular Dystrophy Association

M uscular dystrophy is not a single disorder but a group of chronic diseases whose most prominent characteristic is progressive degeneration, or wasting of the skeletal or voluntary musculature. The rate of progression varies in different types of dystrophy, but in general, the earlier clinical symptoms appear, the more rapid the progression. The disorder is generally painless. As the muscles deteriorate, the patient becomes weaker and more helpless. Eventually, as weakness progresses, the patient may become confined to a wheelchair or eventually to bed. In the more severe forms, the person may be unable to carry out the simplest activities of daily life and combat intercurrent infections. Premature death, where it occurs, usually results from respiratory failure or, in some cases, involvement of the heart muscle.

Prevalence

It has been estimated that 200,000 men, women, and children are afflicted with some form of muscular dystrophy in the United States. One-third are between the ages of three and thirteen, and 8 out of 10 are males. The incidence has been found to be approximately the same in all parts of the world.

Early Signs

The age of onset as well as the rate of progression vary according to the type of dystrophy involved. Among children the onset is so insidious that the disease may go unnoticed for months or even years. The hallmark of the disease is muscle weakness without sensory impairment. Early signs might be difficulty in climbing stairs and rising from a sitting or lying position, plus a tendency to fall frequently. Later the child's calf muscles may become enlarged and he may develop a waddling gait. Among adults, the early signs are a "flat" smile and inability to whistle or to drink through a straw.

Major Types

There are four major and three minor types of MD.

Pseudohypertrophic (Duchenne) is the most common and severe form of dystrophy. It occurs only in males. Initially involved are the proximal muscles of the pelvic girdle, producing postural defects (lordosis), a waddling gait, and difficulty in ascending stairs and rising from the floor. Muscles of the shoulder girdle are affected later. The distinctive characteristic is apparent enlargement (pseudo-hypertrophy) of the calf muscle caused by deposits of fat taking the place of wasted muscle tissue. Progression is rapid, with no remission, and death usually occurs within ten to fifteen years of clinical onset.

Facio-scapulo-humeral (Landouzy-Déjèrine) and all other types occur in both males and females. It usually has its onset in early adolescence, occasionally as late as the mid-twenties. Muscles of the face and shoulder girdle are the first to be affected, resulting in lack of facial mobility, difficulty in raising arms over the head, and a characteristic forward slope of the shoulders. The disease usually progresses very slowly, with long plateaus. It rarely shortens life and is probably the most benign type of dystrophy.

In the *limb-girdle* type, clinical onset occurs between the first and second decade of life, usually with involvement of the proximal muscles of the pelvic or shoulder girdle. The disorder progresses at a variable pace, but never as rapidly as the Duchenne type. Disability may be slight, and patients may reach an advanced age.

In *myotonic dystrophy* (Steinert's disease), the symptoms may appear in puberty, but more commonly in young adulthood. In contrast to most other types, the distal extremities are first affected. Common early symptoms are stiffness in limbs and difficulty in relaxing the handgrasp. The disability becomes severe in fifteen to twenty years, and patients rarely live to a normal age.

Less Common Types

Congenital dystrophy is a term which lumps together various myopathies characterized by small, weak, and markedly hypotonic muscles at birth. Occasionally there are multiple contractures, indicating that the disease was initiated at an early fetal stage. The span of life is short. *Ophthalmoplegic dystrophy* usually makes its appearance in adulthood and progresses insidiously. The extra-ocular muscles are the first involved, and the pharyngeal muscles also tend to be affected. The facial expression and especially ptosis (drooping) of the eyelids resemble symptoms of myasthenia gravis. An extremely rare form is *distal dystrophy*, which is chiefly characterized by initial and primary involvement of the distal muscula-ture (in the extremities), and is frequently confused with peroneal muscular atrophy, a disease of the nervous system.

There are many other disorders which are being more specifical-ly defined and delineated as research progresses. Some examples are central core disease, nemaline myopathy, mitochondrial dis-ease, myotubular myopathy, and idiopathic myopathy—all includ-ed among the dystrophies. These disorders run in families and are characterized by diffuse, mainly proximal, weakness on both sides, but in most cases are nonprogressive.

Another disease of the muscles is *myositis*, a localized or diffuse inflammation of skeletal muscle which is nonhereditary, and of unknown cause. It may be mild and chronic (with episodes of acute pain), severe and chronic (with fiber degeneration and weakness resembling muscular dystrophy), or acute with rapid progression leading to death within a few months. Corticoid therapy may be effective, especially among adults diagnosed early; spontaneous remission occurs in some children.

Causal Factors

Muscular dystrophy is for the most part a hereditary disorder, al-though some cases occur sporadically in which no hereditary fac-tor is evident. The genetic error gives rise to a metabolic defect, but it is not yet known whether the primary lesion is in the muscles themselves or in other parts of the body, such as the liver or hor-mone system. The genetic pattern varies in different types of dys-trophy, and will be briefly described only for the most common types. In pseudohypertrophic dystrophy the pattern is recessive and sex-linked, and transmitted through the female but affecting only male offspring (with 50 percent of females as possible carriers). In the facio-scapulo-humeral type the pattern is autosomal domi-nant, transmitted by either parent and affecting males and females equally, with 50 percent probability of incidence. The limb-girdle type is autosomal recessive, and therefore both parents must carry the defective gene, and the probability is that 25 percent of off-spring will be clinically affected (males and females equally), 50 percent will be normal but carry the gene, and 25 percent will be completely free of hereditary defect. In myotonic dystrophy the pattern is autosomal dominant, transmitted by either parent and affecting male and female equally, with 50 percent probability of incidence among offspring, although not always in the complete form.

Diagnosis

Muscular dystrophy is a disorder of muscle and must be distin-guished from primary nerve disorders causing weakness. It is also necessary to identify the specific type of muscle disease. Careful differential diagnosis must therefore be made, covering (a) family history (since the disease may be genetically determined); (b) not only a routine physical examination, but observation of gait, facial muscle patterns, ability to lift arms, rise from a supine position, lean over and pick up objects from the floor, etc.; (c) a biopsy in which a thin slice of muscle tissue is studied and examined under a microscope; (d) an electromyogram performed by inserting needle electrodes into suspected muscle groups to measure voltage (which is reduced in dystrophy); (e) serum enzyme tests to determine whether there is an increase in enzymes in the blood due to muscle breakdown (important for early diagnosis); the most sensitive of these is the test for CPK (creatine phosphokinase), which is also useful in detecting female carriers. Increased levels of other enzymes, such as aldolase, lactic dehydrogenase (LDH), and glutamic oxalacetic transaminase (GOT), are also diagnostically indicative.

Treatment

As yet there is no effective treatment for any of the dystrophies. Medical management is limited to relieving symptoms through physical therapy aimed at reducing side effects, such as contractures attendant on muscle weakness; and prescription of supportive devices at appropriate stages. These include walkers, crutches, braces, orthopedic shoes, night splints, surgical corsets, hospital beds and mattresses, hydraulic lifts, and wheelchairs with such accessories as ball-bearing feeders, commodes, specially padded cushions, and seatbelts.

Research

Wide-ranging research projects are being conducted under the sponsorship of the National Institute of Neurological and Communication Disorders and Stroke and the Muscular Dystrophy Association. In 1976 the Association allocated $10,580,835 to its worldwide research program, which supports ten major university-based research/clinical centers and over 300 individual scientific and medical grants and fellowships. In fiscal 1975 the National Institute spent an estimated $6,314,000 on muscular dystrophy and other neuromuscular disorders.

Among the current research projects are studies of nerve-muscle synapse formation; microscopic analysis of the contractile mechanism; acetylcholine metabolism in muscle; function and control of muscle membranes; tests for detecting female carriers of the recessive trait; biochemical abnormalities associated with the disease; clinical trials of D-penicillamine and other agents that might halt the progress or ameliorate the symptoms of muscular dystrophy; and the investigation of genetic mechanisms in animal models.

Muscular Dystrophy Association

The Muscular Dystrophy Association (MDA), with headquarters at 810 Seventh Avenue, New York NY 10019, was formed by a group of New York City parents in 1950, primarily to raise money for research in the almost neglected area of muscle disorders. Dr. Ade T. Milhorat, Professor of Clinical Medicine at Cornell University Medical College, a specialist in muscle disease, was appointed to chair the Medical Advisory Board. Chapter affiliates were created almost immediately, and now number 232, located in every state, the District of Columbia, Guam, and Puerto Rico. A national network of 164 clinics has been created, providing services at no charge to victims of muscular dystrophy and related diseases.

The programs of the Muscular Dystrophy Association encompass, in addition to the muscular dystrophies, the nondystrophic muscle disorder myositis, and other noninfectious disorders of the neuromuscular unit, including myasthenia gravis, progressive spinal muscular atrophy, amyotrophic lateral sclerosis (ALS), benign congenital hypotonia, infantile progressive spinal muscular atrophy (Werdnig-Hoffmann disease), juvenile progressive spinal muscular atrophy (Kugelberg-Welander disease), adult progressive spinal muscular atrophy (Aran-Duchenne type), peroneal muscular atrophy (Charcot-Marie-Tooth disease), Friedreich's ataxia, and such rare conditions as McArdle's, Pompe's, Thomsen's, and Tarui's diseases. (See CHAPTER 42: MYASTHENIA GRAVIS; CHAPTER 43: NEUROLOGICAL DISORDERS; CHAPTER 54: OTHER DISORDERS, B. Ataxia.)

MDA conducts a multifaceted service program applicable not only to muscular dystrophy itself but to related neuromuscular disorders. Authorized patient services offered by local chapters may include assistance in the purchase and repair of orthopedic appliances prescribed by a physician (walker, wheelchair, lift, etc.); physical therapy, consisting of stretching exercises and active and passive manipulation for a period of three months, renewable after medical examination; arrangements for inclusion of patients in existing elementary and secondary educational programs, plus promotion of legislation to eliminate architectural barriers in schools; recreational programs such as supervised excursions and summer camping; transportation, usually by volunteers, to and from clinics, schools, recreational events; flu shots, since influenza is particularly hazardous to patients. In urban areas, community clinic services are available, including complete examination for differential diagnosis with all necessary laboratory tests, on an outpatient basis and, if necessary, up to three days of hospitalization. The program also includes periodic reevaluation, medical advice, physical therapy under medical supervision, social work assistance with personal and family problems, cooperation with the personal physician, administration of carrier tests, and counsel on family planning.

SELECTED REFERENCES

Abrahamson, Arthur S., *An Approach to Rehabilitation of Children with Muscular Dystrophy*, Muscular Dystrophy Association, 1953.

Milhorat, A. T., "Progressive Muscular Dystrophy," *The Crippled Child*, August 1951.

Muscular Dystrophy: Hope through Research, National Institute of Neurological and Communication Disorders and Stroke, Bethesda, MD 20014.

Ogg, Elizabeth, *Milestones in Muscle Disease Research,* Muscular Dystrophy Association.

Patient and Community Services, Muscular Dystrophy Association.

Pearson, Carl M., "Muscular Dystrophy: Review and Recent Observations," *American Journal of Medicine,* vol. 35, no. 5.

42

Myasthenia Gravis

MICHAEL P. McQUILLEN, M.D., Chairman, Professional
Education Committee, Myasthenia Gravis Foundation, Inc.

Myasthenia gravis is a neuromuscular disease characterized by weakness and abnormal fatigue of the voluntary muscles. The weakness may affect any muscle, but most frequently involves muscles around the eyes, face, neck, and throat. The most severe problems develop in patients whose breathing and swallowing muscles are primarily involved.

Myasthenia gravis probably was described as long ago as 1672, but there was no effective treatment for the condition until 1934. Prior to 1934 the mortality rate was as high as 85 percent. Now the survival rate is at least 85 percent.

Incidence and Prevalence

The prevalence of myasthenia gravis in the population is not well documented. Estimates range from 1 in 10,000 to 1 in 7,000 (or 5,000–30,000 cases in the United States). More women are affected than men. Typically, the disease strikes women in their twenties, and men in their forties and fifties. However, it may be seen at any age, and occurs in all races.

Etiology

The cause of myasthenia gravis is unknown. Anatomically and physiologically, there are defects at the junction between nerve and muscle. In normal individuals, a nerve impulse arriving at this junction leads to the release of a chemical transmitter, acetylcholine, which attaches to receptors in a specialized area of the muscle membrane called the end-plate region. Acetylcholine so alters the receptors as to permit generation of a muscle impulse, or action potential. Ultimately, the muscle action potential is coupled to the contractile proteins inside the muscle fiber, and contraction of muscle ensues. Once this complex process occurs, it must be reversed in order to occur again. At the neuromuscular junction, reversal is governed by an enzyme, cholinesterase, which breaks down acetylcholine and terminates its action.

Myasthenia gravis may be viewed as an "acetylcholine-deficiency" disease. The standard form of medical therapy for myasthenia consists of drugs which inhibit cholinesterase, prevent the breakdown of acetylcholine, and permit the "deficiency" to be overcome. Some evidence suggests that the number of receptors is reduced in the end-plate regions of muscle in myasthenic patients. Recent work provides evidence that myasthenia gravis may be an immunologic disease: rabbits and other animals given an injection of end-plate receptor protein with other factors will develop an illness very similar to the human condition; and the physiology of mouse muscle can be altered to resemble the changes seen in myasthenia gravis by giving the mouse repeated injections of serum proteins derived from the blood of myasthenic patients. This work has pertinence to a long-standing concern over the role of the thymus gland in myasthenia gravis. This gland, located behind the breastbone in the chest, is very active early in life in "teaching" or regulating the body's immune systems. Tumors of the gland occur in myasthenic patients with much greater frequency (20 percent) than in the general population.

Except for rare instances, myasthenia gravis is not an inherited condition. There is a transient form of myasthenia seen in some children born to mothers with myasthenia gravis—one of the clinical observations which gave rise to the immunologic hypothesis described above.

Symptoms

Often the onset of myasthenia gravis is gradual, and because the symptoms are ubiquitous to the human condition (weakness, fatigue), the disorder may not be identified at first.

The most frequent first complaints have to do with the muscles of the eyes—double vision and drooping of the upper eyelid. The voice may become hoarse and chewing and swallowing may become difficult. There may be a change in facial expression, and weakness of the arms, hands, and legs. Difficulty in breathing, the most serious of the symptoms, usually appears later in the illness. Muscle weakness is greatly increased as activity is repeated. Rest will restore muscle strength, but only temporarily. Typically, the pattern of the disease is a long series of remissions and recurrences, but there are cases of total spontaneous remission.

Diagnosis

When symptoms suggest myasthenia gravis, diagnosis can be confirmed by the administration of drugs which inhibit cholinesterase. These include edrophonium (Tensilon), a short-acting drug given intravenously, and neostigmine (Prostigmin), given intra-muscularly or by mouth. The patient's strength and stamina are measured before and after the drug takes effect—and often after a placebo as well—since one of the main diagnoses with which myasthenia gravis may be confused is neurasthenia. Electromyographic studies, with repetitive stimulation of nerve and recording from muscle, show changes typical of myasthenia gravis in most patients. X-rays of the chest may show evidence of a thymic tumor, if present. Myasthenia gravis must especially be distinguished from other nerve and muscle disorders, such as the muscular dystrophies and neuropathies.

Medical Treatment

Without treatment patients with generalized myasthenia gravis often deteriorate. With proper care most can lead normal lives. The primary treatment is oral medication such as neostigmine, pyrido-stigmine (Mestinon), and ambenomium (Mytelase). As noted earlier, these are all anticholinesterase drugs, which prevent the breakdown of acetylcholine at the neuromuscular junction. Dosage is tailored to the needs of the individual patient (as with insulin for the diabetic); too much acetylcholine will lead to increased weakness (similar to that produced in the operating room by the muscle relaxant succinylcholine), and too little acetylcholine effect produces, in essence, the disease myasthenia gravis. Medication rarely allows the patient to recover full strength. Both the patient and physician must be sensitive to changing conditions, to ensure that the medication schedule is appropriate to the condition.

Together with the "wanted" effect on skeletal muscles, these drugs may produce "unwanted" effects on smooth muscles and mucous and sweat glands. Nausea, stomach cramps, diarrhea, and increased secretions in the mouth and chest may develop. Atropine may be used to counter these side effects.

Other forms of treatment include the administration of adreno-corticotropic hormone (ACTH) or corticosteroids and thymectomy (removal of the thymus gland). Generally these measures are reserved for patients with severe myasthenia gravis, although medical opinion varies on this question.

A patient may experience a myasthenic "crisis," often in relation to another condition (such as infection or emotional upset). During a crisis, breathing is difficult and artificial respiration may be required. Drug overdosage may produce serious weakness as well.

Management Treatment

The individual with myasthenia gravis must understand the medication and how it serves to alter complaints. It is important to have an adequate drug supply at hand, and to be alert to changes in the condition over time. The relation of complaints to emotional factors often is an important consideration.

The patient's vocational and educational aspirations must be adapted to the physical condition, especially to limited physical energy. If the patient is realistic about limitations, strengths or special abilities which do not require a great deal of physical exertion may be capitalized upon. Most people with myasthenia gravis lead productive lives.

Research

Most of the research in the United States into the cause, cure, and prevention of myasthenia gravis has been accomplished by investigators united through the Myasthenia Gravis Foundation and supported by grants from that and other private agencies, and from the National Institutes of Health (NIH). There are many research projects in progress investigating facets of the disease — immunologic mechanisms in patients and the animal model; the anatomy, physiology, and pharmacology of myasthenia and, indeed, of normal neuromuscular mechanisms; and the analysis of various treatment modalities (not only the standard anticholinesterase drugs but also other drugs, including corticosteroids, and thymectomy).

Organizations

The Myasthenia Gravis Foundation (230 Park Avenue, New York, NY 10017) was established in 1952 and has more than 50 local chapters in many parts of the country. Its purposes are to foster, coordinate, and support research into the causes of myasthenia gravis, its alleviation, cure, and prevention, and to disseminate information to interested persons. More than 45 percent of its annual budget is allocated to research. Local chapters often support drug banks through which myasthenic patients can buy prescribed medicines at reduced cost. The address of a nearby chapter or clinic which provides this service may be obtained from the national office.

The Muscular Dystrophy Association, with headquarters at 810 Seventh Avenue, New York, NY 10019, provides patient service through its local chapters, and also conducts a research program on the causes of myasthenia gravis as well as other neuromuscular disorders.

Literature

The scientific literature in regard to myasthenia gravis expands almost daily, especially in this era of developing animal models of the disease. The Myasthenia Gravis Foundation, through its Medical Advisory Board, has prepared manuals for the physician and nurse which contain annotated bibliographies, and pamphlets for patients as well. These are available from the Foundation in New York, and through its local chapters.

43

Neurological Disorders

LINDA HOWELL, M.A., Group Health Cooperative of
Puget Sound, Seattle

Reviewed by the Muscular Dystrophy Association

This article first discusses the neurological disorders involving the spinal cord, and then the peripheral neuropathies, involving myelin degeneration in peripheral nerve fibers.

DISEASES INVOLVING THE SPINAL CORD

Amyotrophic Lateral Sclerosis ("Lou Gehrig's Disease")

ALS is a gradually developing and then rapidly progressive neuromuscular disease which is most frequently observed in adults between forty and sixty years of age. However, cases have also been reported in the very young and very old. The disorder involves degeneration of the motor nerves in the spinal cord and brainstem, and is therefore described as a disease of both the upper and lower motor neurons. The cranial nerves may become involved in the degenerative process, but sensation is usually intact. Both increased tension (spasticity) and weakness or atrophy of the muscles develop, and there is much involuntary twitching (fasciculations). Which muscles are affected in which order is quite variable from case to case. One side may weaken before the other. The upper and lower extremities are involved, as are the tongue, palate, pharynx, and neck, causing difficulty in swallowing and speaking (hoarseness and dysarthria). Respiratory failure and quadriplegia may result. Physical debilitation and death usually occur within 5 years, but the course runs much longer in some cases.

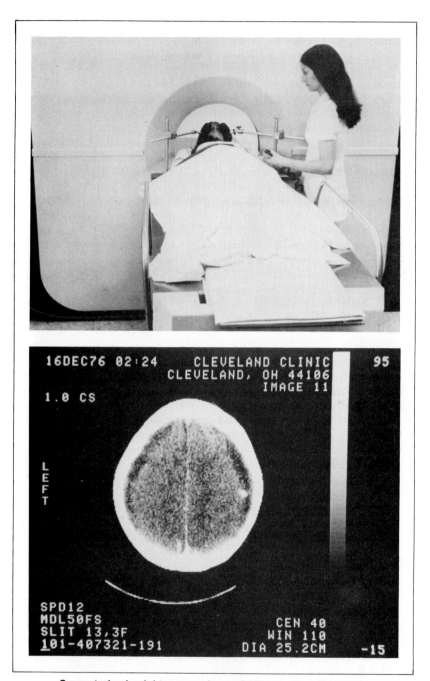

Computerized axial tomography, or CAT scan, is a diagnostic technique in which narrow x-ray beams are used to provide detailed pictures of the brain and the internal organs. Here, the reclining patient is positioned for a brain scan. The sample scan reveals a subdural hematoma. (Ohio-Nuclear, Inc., Solon, Ohio)

The incidence of amyotrophic lateral sclerosis is approximately 4 per 100,000 in the United States. It is more commonly found in men than in women. Its cause is not known. A family history of the disease is usually not in evidence, but the incidence of ALS is approximately 100 times the normal rate in Guam, and there may be many cases among related individuals there. The high incidence in Guam has provoked research into causal factors; a defective genetic inheritance and viral causation are alternative suggestions.

Treatment is symptomatic. At any stage some rehabilitation therapy — speech therapy, physical therapy, bracing, etc. — may have helpful, if short-lived, benefits. Also, medication may alleviate the spasticity and muscle fasciculations. (For other details, see CHAPTER 55: ILLUSTRATIVE CASES, D. Amyotrophic Lateral Sclerosis.)

The Muscular Dystrophy Association conducts a service and research program on ALS, and two other associations have recently been formed: the Amyotrophic Lateral Sclerosis Foundation (2840 Adams Avenue, San Diego, CA 92116) and the National ALS Foundation (185 Madison Avenue, New York, NY 10016). The National Institute of Neurological and Communication Disorders and Stroke of the National Institutes of Health is also involved in research on ALS.

Benign Congenital Hypotonia (Oppenheim's Disease)

This neuromuscular disease occurs at birth or soon after. The motor nerve (anterior horn) cells of the spinal cord or peripheral nerves deteriorate due to a genetic defect. The child is affected by symmetrical weakness of the muscles of the arms, legs, and neck. The condition levels off, leaving the patient much less crippled than in the more severe infantile spinal muscular atrophy (see below). The disease is autosomal recessive; that is, when both parents carry the defective gene, up to one-fourth of their offspring of either sex may inherit the condition and one-half may be carriers. There is no treatment other than supportive measures. However, spontaneous improvement occurs in some cases.

Infantile Spinal Muscular Atrophy (Werdnig-Hoffmann Disease)

This is a severe progressive hereditary disorder with onset prenatally, at birth, or shortly after, involving deterioration of the motor nerve cells of the spinal cord or peripheral nerves. The earlier the onset, the faster the disease progresses. Affected infants have symmetrically weak, flaccid muscles which make crawling difficult and walking impossible. The disease is autosomal recessive. There is no treatment other than through supportive devices, and survival is rarely beyond childhood.

Juvenile Spinal Muscular Atrophy (Kugelberg-Welander Disease)

This is a slowly progressive disorder with onset in late childhood or early adolescence, involving atrophy and weakness of the proximal leg muscles and later the neck and upper extremities. A degeneration of the motor nerve cells of the spinal cord takes place due to genetic defect. A normal or near-normal life-span can be expected. The disease is autosomal recessive. There is no specific treatment, but supportive devices may prove helpful in relieving symptoms.

Peroneal Muscular Atrophy
(Charcot-Marie-Tooth Disease)

This is a disease with onset any time from age five to age fifty or older. The earlier the onset, the more rapid the progression of atrophy in the muscles of both feet and legs as well as hands and forearms. A degeneration of the motor nerve cells of the spinal cord and of the peripheral nerves takes place due to a genetic defect. The inheritance of this disease is variable, either through dominant or recessive genes, and is transmitted to males and females. There is no specific treatment, but bracing and splinting may prove helpful. A normal life-span can be expected, with increasing disability. (For other details, see CHAPTER 55: ILLUSTRATIVE CASES, M. Charcot-Marie-Tooth Syndrome.)

Spinal Muscular Atrophy of Adults
(Aran-Duchenne Type)

This is a variably progressive disease with onset in the third to fifth decade of life. The distal muscles, especially of the hand, are weakened. The cause is unknown and the condition occurs in both men and women sporadically. No direct treatment is available.

The Muscular Dystrophy Association conducts service and research programs on all of the disorders outlined above. (See CHAPTER 41: MUSCULAR DYSTROPHY; CHAPTER 51: SPINAL CORD INJURY.)

PERIPHERAL NEUROPATHIES

In peripheral neuropathies of either slow or acute onset, there is degeneration of the fatty (myelin) sheath covering the peripheral nerve fibers. As a result, there is some deterioration of motor and sensory function of the innervated parts of the body. A paralysis of the limp or flaccid type may develop, with sensory changes ranging from loss of sensation, to numbness and tingling, to pain and extreme tenderness of muscles. Peripheral neuropathies occur primarily in adults.

Types and Causes

Peripheral neuropathies of acute or rapid onset are termed acute polyneuritis; there are many different descriptions and names of these syndromes. It has been suggested that they may all be variations of one basic disease. Guillain-Barré syndrome is perhaps the best known and came to national attention during the swine flu vaccination program of 1976. Usually there is progressive weakness beginning in the lower extremities, and even the cranial nerves. This progressive involvement takes place over a period of several days and may be accompanied by sensory changes. At the point of greatest involvement, the patient may be totally paralyzed and subject to respiratory crises. Death can occur at this point if respiratory and circulatory failure cannot be prevented. After a point of stabilization, a gradual return of function may take place if there is proper supportive treatment. This mysterious and overwhelming disease has no known cause. In some cases the symptoms develop after a period of mild illness with upper respiratory or gastrointestinal infection. A viral or bacterial cause has been suggested, as has some kind of allergic or autoimmune mechanism.

The first signs of *slowly progressive peripheral neuropathies* are usually fatigue and soreness of limbs, numbness of hands and feet, cramps in leg muscles, and sharp pains in legs. The progressive nature of these disorders may be due in part to nutritional deficiency of the peripheral nerves—especially vitamin B deficiency—or to toxins such as lead, arsenic, carbon monoxide, or mercury. The toxins are carried in the bloodstream to the terminal part of the nerves and then ascend along the nerve fibers. Examples of nutritional deficiencies are chronic alcoholism and pellagra. Diabetes and diphtheria may also cause this problem. The symptom patterns vary with the cause, and within any causal group there is a range of effects. In some cases the upper extremities—especially the hands—are most involved; in others, only the legs. In some patients the primary change may be sensory; in others, motor involvement is primary.

Alcoholic peripheral neuropathy is the most commonly occurring type. Early signs are pain and muscle tenderness in the legs, often progressing to great difficulty in walking or to complete inability to walk. Position sense in the lower extremities is also impaired, so that balance is difficult to maintain. If the condition is not treated early enough, a full flaccid paralysis with muscle atrophy may develop.

Diagnosis and Treatment

Diagnosis of peripheral neuropathy is based on x-rays, a myelogram, electromyographic conduction studies of the muscles, and in some cases a history of nutritional deficit or exposure to toxic substances.

Since only the peripheral nerves are involved, regeneration will occur and a natural recovery may take place quickly or within several months or a year or two. In acute and slow-developing cases, preventive treatment must be applied immediately in order to avoid permanent residuals such as foot drop, other contractures, and deformities which may develop when the limbs are flaccid and the patient is not positioned correctly. It is vitally important that the specific causal agent be determined in the slow-onset neuropathies, so that good nutrition can be maintained and any toxic agent removed from the system. Alcohol withdrawal can be a very difficult problem (see CHAPTER 16: ALCOHOLISM).

Regular range-of-motion exercise of the affected parts is needed.

Splints may be helpful to counteract deformities. Muscle strengthening must begin after the person is fully rested and the condition has stabilized. If the hands are particularly affected, coordination exercises are helpful, as is the use of assistive devices. The major focus of the rehabilitation program will probably be on strengthening the lower extremities and, if necessary, on ambulation training. (See CHAPTER 54: OTHER DISORDERS, B. Ataxia, and F. Hansen's Disease.)

44

Obesity

MARTHA DEMMICK

Reviewed by ANGELA BOWEN, M.D.

The storage of body fat in excess amounts is a normal, natural body function as well as a primitive protection against cold and famine. When the daily intake of food is inadequate, hormones slowly convert fat from storage to make it available for body energy.

Obesity, or the phenomenon of overweight resulting from excessive storage of fat, has become a major health problem in societies which have (1) sufficient technology to ensure preservation and storage of food, thereby creating an abundance; (2) a decreased need for exercise, or energy expenditure, in the business of survival; and (3) unbalanced dietary patterns which may result from eating overfattened meats, or other fatty foods, cultural food preferences, the need to follow social hospitality conventions, the desire for taste gratification, or simply a result of convenience. Psychological disturbances involving anxiety, frustration, and despair (due, for example, to personal-social problems or to disease or disability); lonelinesss; lovelessness; and boredom may also lead to overeating and the development of obesity. Socioeconomic factors are also involved, for obesity frequently occurs in low-income groups where people are unable to afford higher-priced protein sources and therefore eat primarily cheaper carbohydrate and fatty foods. There also appears to be a familial and possibly a genetic predisposition in some cases, and in a small percentage (perhaps 5 percent) an underactive thyroid or other glandular condition may be at the root of the problem.

Whatever the eating pattern, or however it is established, it becomes an integral part of the individual's personality. For example, an eating pattern established in childhood during the growing years on the mistaken assumption that "a fat child is a healthy child" may continue when growth has stopped and the body's demand for food has decreased, simply out of psychological and physiological habit. Similarly, a person may eat heavily during a period in life connected with heavy exercise, and continue that eating pattern even though the level of activity has changed (for example, in the case of disabled persons with activity limitations). Eating due to emotional stress may establish a pattern of association with food that is deep-rooted and difficult to identify and change.

Prevalence

Obesity is a matter of definition. Some define it as weight which is 20 percent above the average for a given height. Others regard an excess of 10 percent as an obese level. It is estimated that 25–35 percent of the adult population of the United States is 10 percent overweight. Also, about 15–20 percent of teen-agers are overweight. Weight (fat) tends to increase with age as activity level and the body's demand for food decrease. In the United States 30 percent of men and 40 percent of women over forty years of age are 20 percent above their optimal weight.

Effects of Obesity

Extreme obesity has a psychological effect on the individual in that it tends to increase feelings of loneliness, self-pity, frustration, anxiety, and self-hatred. Indeed, attitudes toward overweight in a society which fosters unhealthy attitudes toward food, and yet idolizes slimness, may be damaging to the self-image of even the slightly overweight. There is no question that the obese individual is likely to encounter discrimination in many areas of activity, including education and employment.

When food is habitually consumed in excess, there may also be drastic effects on physical health. To compensate for this excess food intake, the body produces more enzymes for converting the food into storage fat. It also produces more blood vessels to supply oxygen to the tissues, and additional products of digestion tend to be deposited within the vascular system, leading in some cases to coronary and arteriosclerotic disorders. Blood pressure may become elevated as a result of the additional area the blood must cover and the constriction of blood vessels due to fat deposits within them. Studies have also shown that diabetes is frequently associated with overweight. (See CHAPTER 25: CARDIAC DISORDERS; CHAPTER 29: DIABETES MELLITUS; CHAPTER 34: HYPERTENSION.)

Treatment

Once the individual has decided to do something about excess weight, treatment may be approached in a variety of ways. The most effective therapy for any case depends upon the individual; no hard and fast rules can be laid down. Available to the overweight are vast quantities of information — cookbooks, diet strategies, exercises, techniques for maintaining morale, charts of food values and caloric contents, elaborate programs designed to make basic changes in life-style. Nevertheless, it should be noted that with all these options and programs, the percentage of permanent "cures" for overweight is incredibly low. Perhaps the variety of techniques available has a tendency to keep the individual moving from one possibility to another, whereas systematic change appears to be the crucial factor in sustained weight loss.

It is estimated that overweight Americans, and Americans who neurotically believe themselves overweight or fear becoming overweight, waste $100,000,000 a year on phony reducing products and programs. Clinics, spas, belts, creams, baths, and machines offer the buyer individual attention, a hint of glamour, and the proposition that weight can be lost by a "scientific" program which need not involve much effort or any drastic restructuring of habits. This is the "wear-this-while-you-watch-TV-and-lose-weight" pitch.

The following survey of significant treatments is brief and mentions advantages and problems wherever possible. With a condition so controversial and complex as obesity, it is important to remember that no treatment will be easy or simple.

Diets

There are as many diets as there are food combinations — liquid diets, low-salt diets, low-calorie diets, low-fat/high-protein diets, crash diets, and even fasts.

1. A carefully balanced *low-calorie diet* (1,000 – 1,200 calories per day) is one of the most effective techniques for weight reduction. The advantage of this type of diet is that it allows one to eat a number of different foods and avoids the monotony of many other diets; it also tends to increase awareness of the calorie content of most common foods and accustoms the dieter to eating balanced, low-calorie meals. These factors are highly desirable, since the long-range goal of weight reduction is a permanently healthy eating pattern. In addition, the nutritional balance in a low-calorie diet which allows all foods, but in small quantity, ensures that prolonged adherence to the diet will be healthy in that it provides sufficient quantities of vitamins, minerals, proteins, etc. This factor is also important in encouraging the dieter to establish a consistently healthy eating pattern.

One difficulty with the low-calorie type of diet is that weight loss is small and gradual, not dramatic. For those needing dramatic results, the reinforcement may not be sufficient. In addition, since the diet restricts food (especially fats), hunger is barely satisfied; for those to whom a very full feeling is a symbol of security, a low-calorie diet may be more threatening than others. Nevertheless, its long-range results hit both targets: weight reduction and revised habit patterns.

2. The *ketogenic diet* (also called the drinking man's diet, the Mayo diet, the low-carbohydrate diet, the Wisconsin diet) is the other most effective type of diet program. This diet depends upon the incomplete combustion of food and body fat that occurs when carbohydrate intake is restricted. That is, in order to combust fat completely, carbohydrates must be burned in conjunction with it. With inadequate carbohydrate intake, fat is incompletely burned and the unused fuel is eliminated in the urine in the form of organic compounds called ketones — hence the diet is ketogenic, or ketone-producing. This diet is valueless unless the carbohydrate restriction is strictly observed. It supplies an intake of from 1,800 to 2,000 calories while offering the body only 1,000 calories of fuel for consumption. The advantages of the ketogenic diet are that the high fat and protein content eliminates hunger and can be selected from nearly any menu. It is also one of the easiest diets to follow and results tend to be more dramatic than with the low-calorie diet.

This kind of diet, however, may not be as useful as the low-calorie type in developing healthy eating habits which will be easy to maintain. One must be more careful about supplementing vitamins and minerals and especially careful about drinking lots of water, since the higher concentration of ketones in the system is likely to irritate the kidneys and could cause complications if not diluted with sufficient water. In addition, this diet is more expensive (high-protein), and may be more monotonous than the low-calorie type.

3. Periodic forty-eight-hour *fasting* in conjunction with a comprehensive habit-revision program can be beneficial both because the calorie deficit is greater and because fasting can disrupt old eating habits. It helps to change the pattern of secretion of enzymes which ordinarily determine hunger and appetite patterns. Obviously, prolonged fasting is inadvisable, because it deprives muscle of protein and produces general weakness. Also, the decision to fast must be tailored to the individual's psychological state. If the strain of food deprivation is too great for a person to whom food means security, the fast will likely be broken and no progress will be made toward habit revision. If used improperly, fasting may cause the person to despair of losing weight at all. Although for some cases the weight drop may be encouraging, in general it is best to build confidence through a comprehensive, reliable program which produces regular, realistic results.

4. Dieters have long been tempted by the idea of water reduction — and indeed, if one follows a *liquid diet*, one seems to lose weight quickly. This occurs because the dieter takes in more water than is necessary to digest solid food, and the excess is eliminated by the kidneys. Therefore the weight loss in this type of diet program is not due to a decrease in fatty tissue, but to a decrease in water. Also, it is important to recognize that the body retains more water depending on environmental temperatures. Moreover, experience has shown that even if weight is lost rapidly during a liquid diet regimen, it is also quickly regained afterward.

Medication

Appetite-dulling pills (such as amphetamine sulfate) are attractive to the potential reducer because they tend to check the impulse to eat and because control does not have to be developed through a change in attitudes and habits. However, even if short-term weight loss is enhanced by drugs, a relapse to former weight is likely for the individual who has not restructured eating habits and such a relapse can be more damaging than the original condition. In addition, these pills, due to their mood-elevating effect, have an addictive potential. However, in a carefully monitored, balanced reduction program, it may be beneficial for some persons to have their interest and faith in results encouraged by the short-term use of drug therapy.

Those who suspect they may have diabetes, thyroid, or other hormonal diseases should consult physicians with a special interest in these disorders before using these pills. Patients with a family history of these conditions are at especially high risk.

Surgery

Plastic surgery can be performed to remove the "roll" or "apron" over the abdomen in the very obese person. This can mean an immediate loss of considerable weight. Excessively large breasts can also be "reduced" in this manner. However, these procedures should be carried out only after lean body weight has been achieved.

As a last resort in extreme cases of obesity with concomitant medical conditions, such as severe diabetes or high blood pressure, some doctors agree to perform an operation which shortens the small-intestinal tract from twenty-three feet to about thirty inches. Since 5 out of 150 die in connection with this operation, it is not attempted unless the person's life is in danger due to the other complications. The effect is simply to allow less food to be digested.

Therapy Based on Psychological Theory

1. *Psychoanalysis or depth psychology.* Since obesity is a deeply rooted problem, often stemming from habits developed in early childhood, depth analysis seems to be a way of reaching the root causes. This approach may be appropriate for those who feel a need to solve comprehensive personality problems, one of the symptoms of which may be obesity. For most individuals the analytic process is too long, expensive, and discouraging during the early stages. There are, however, briefer forms of psychotherapy that can be highly effective.

2. *Behavior therapy.* This technique offers a relatively simple, fast, and (for many people) satisfying approach which can be used effectively in conjunction with dieting, exercise, and other methods. The basic objectives of behavior therapy are to unlearn old, negative behavior patterns (overeating), and to learn new, desirable patterns of behavior. Food is a primary form of reinforce-

ment. In order to effect behavior changes, other kinds of reinforcement (rewards, satisfactions) for behavior related to refraining from
eating must be introduced, and in some programs food itself may
gradually lose its reward value. The first step in a program of behavior therapy is usually for the patient to compile a very detailed record of eating and other behavior. This in itself promotes an awareness of eating problems and situations that prompt overeating. An
approach of this type can lead to a kind of prescription for change
reinforced by a system of rewards.

Another behavior modification technique is aversive therapy.
This is most suited to people who have a craving for certain kinds of
food. For example, a mild shock may be administered whenever
this food is presented until the patient no longer desires it, or the
patient may be required to count every bite of food in order to de-
tract from its appeal. The purpose of aversive conditioning is basically to suppress habits deemed undesirable. This method is limited
in application and generally somewhat less effective than a positive
conditioning program.

3. *Hypnosis.* Hypnosis or hypnotherapy is another psychological
approach to the problem of obesity. Essentially this is also a form of
behavior modification since the emphasis is on changing eating
habits. However, there is usually an attempt to change attitudes not
only toward eating but also toward the self. After eating habits and
attitudes are examined, the patient is trained to enter a trance during which the hypnotist gives positive suggestions to modify behavior. This technique brings about rapid improvement in habits,
but it is up to the patient to maintain that improvement.

4. *Group therapy and diet clubs.* Weight reduction in groups
combines behavior therapy with diet, moral support, peer pressure,
and competition with others. Take Off Pounds Sensibly (TOPS) is
an organization of this kind. Weight Watchers International, Inc.,
which has enjoyed great popularity with the overweight population, incorporates three phases: reducing, leveling, and maintenance. The effectiveness of this program depends on continued
involvement in order to avoid the backsliding so common in
obesity. The success rate in terms of permanent weight loss,
however, is quite low, as it is for many types of treatment for
obesity. Another organization, Overeaters Anonymous, with a
World Service Office at 3730 Motor Avenue, Los Angeles, CA
90034, looks upon compulsive eating as a "progressive illness,"
and bases its approach on the principles of Alcoholics Anonymous,
with an emphasis on spiritual motivation, group support, communication, and companionship.

5. *Family therapy approach.* This approach, including observation of mealtime behavior of family members, as well as the attitudes of the nonobese members toward the obese one, has been
gaining acceptance. Since overeating patterns have usually been
formed in the home, it is reasonable to attempt to re-form them in
the same setting. The family therapist can further this process by
increasing the family's understanding of the factors that brought

about these patterns, and by encouraging open discussion and exchange of ideas among all its members.

Vocational Implications

Extreme obesity can be a vocational handicap, and in some careers (such as a pilot) even a small degree of overweight is serious. Many judgmental attitudes prevail which unrealistically accuse the obese person of the faults of immature overindulgence, gluttony, or lack of concern about health and appearance. Supportive group programs, such as TOPS and Weight Watchers as well as group psychotherapy, have considerable value in developing feelings of self-worth among overweight persons. When one accepts oneself, there is greater likelihood of presenting oneself to an employer with confidence and poise, whatever the physical condition.

Specially designed clothes can be helpful in minimizing weight problems. Large stores frequently have fashion consultants who can be of great service, usually at no extra cost, in helping to find styles and colors that contribute to a better appearance, and thus enhance self-confidence.

In summary, effective treatment of obesity should be based on (1) desire for change; (2) gradual development of a positive body image and abandonment of tendencies to self-deprecation; (3) understanding of personal eating history and patterns and the psychological significance of these patterns; (4) knowledge of the physiology of obesity which will help to maintain discipline and understanding of the changes which take place in the body; (5) establishment of a new eating pattern; (6) medical support; and (7) a program of exercise.

SELECTED REFERENCES

Albrink, Margaret J., guest ed., "Obesity," in *Clinics in Endocrinology and Metabolism*, vol. 5, no. 2, July 1976.

Bray, George A., and John E. Bethune, eds., *Treatment and Management of Obesity*, Harper & Row, New York, 1974.

Hirsch, J., and J. L. Knittle, "Cellularity of Obese and Nonobese Human Adipose Tissue," *Federal Proceedings*, 29:1516–1521, 1970.

Mayer, J., *Overweight Causes, Cost and Control*, Prentice-Hall, Englewood Cliffs, New Jersey, 1968.

Obesity and Health, U.S. Public Health Service, Department of Health, Education and Welfare, 1966.

Stuart, R. B., and B. Davis, *Slim Chance in a Fat World: Behavioral Control of Obesity*, Research Press, Champaign, Illinois, 1971.

Stunkard, A. J., H. Levine, and S. Fox, "The Management of Obesity: Patient Self-help and Medical Treatment," *Archives of Internal Medicine*, 125:1067–1072, 1970.

Wade, G. N., "Gonadal Hormones and Behavioral Regulation of Body Weight," *Physiology and Behavior*, 8:523–534, 1972.

Wilmore, D. W., and B. A. Pruitt, "Fat Boys Get Burned," *Lancet*, 2:631–632, 1972.

Wollersheim, J. P., "The Effectiveness of Group Therapy Based upon Learning Principles in the Treatment of Overweight Women," *Journal of Abnormal Psychology*, 76:462–474, 1970.

45

Orthopedic Disorders

ERNEST H. BETTMANN, M.D., F.A.O.S., Orthopedic
Consultant, Professor Emeritus of Orthopedic Surgery,
University of Leipzig

Orthopedic disorders comprise all anatomical and functional abnormalities of the musculoskeletal system either manifest at birth or developing during the growth period (ages one to eighteen) or during the active vocational life (ages nineteen to seventy). These disorders are often the result of body neglect, environmental stress, and poor social habits which lead to "wear-and-tear damages" and "premature aging." The term "orthopedics" was derived from two Greek words, *ortho* meaning straight and *paidos* meaning child. The first definition of orthopedics was given by the French physician Nicholas André in 1742, who described it as "the art of preventing and correcting deformities in children."

Though some orthopedic problems are due to congenital conditions, birth injuries, or accidents, many others, especially those characterized by pain, declining joint function, and stiffness, are the result of neglect in childhood. Except for fractures and other injuries, the cause of these conditions may date back many years to a period when parents, teachers, and doctors did not pay sufficient attention to biological requirements—that is, to posture awareness, exercises, avoidance of gravity damage, and poor alignment. As a result, therapeutic efforts are usually confined to treatment of the effects only.

The treatment of congenital, acute, and chronic orthopedic conditions has undergone spectacular changes during the past fifty years, thanks to antibiotics and efficient bioengineered designs, such as internal fixation of fractures and joint replacements. A number of these approaches are reviewed in other chapters.

Historically speaking, humans emerged in the struggle for survival by adapting themselves to changing environmental demands and by assuming a harmonious posture as *Homo sapiens erectus.* However, during the industrial revolution increasing occupational and environmental stress together with unfavorable social habits have gradually resulted in a "postural decline," and many of us are having difficulty counteracting the deviating forces of gravity within our normal joint alignment and well-balanced muscle tone. In a society which depends more and more on automation and mechanization, we find ourselves increasingly alienated from "body culture" and "body analysis." In a word, we are in danger of becoming the slaves of our ingeniously constructed mechanical world. Moreover, there is the added danger that our musculoskeletal system, which has served us faithfully in the past, will go on strike. The signals are clear: pain and disturbed function constitute an "alarm reaction" when unnatural demands cannot be compensated for functionally or anatomically.

Prophylaxis and therapy for musculoskeletal disturbances is the concern not only of orthopedics, but also of specialists in the fields of metabolic, cardiovascular, gastrointestinal, respiratory, gynecological, and psychiatric disorders.

GENERAL THERAPEUTIC PRINCIPLES

Orthopedic treatment and rehabilitation involve the following general steps:

1. Exact diagnostic analysis with its implications shared with the patient and family.

2. Creation of rapport and an atmosphere of confidence between patient and physician, with the option of home, office, or hospital treatment.

3. Relief from physical pain and anxiety.

4. Physical and emotional rest, with comfortable positioning (support for painful joints and extremities) and avoidance of active or passive motion leading to malalignment, pain, or muscle spasm, especially in weight-bearing segments such as the spine, pelvis, and lower extremities.

5. For traumatic joint and bone conditions, including fractures, temporary and often prolonged immobilization through such devices and procedures as splints, casts, braces, skeletal traction, internal fixation (wires, screws, pins, plates, rods), air splints, and suspension.

6. After bone healing and subsidence of joint and tissue irritation, a regime of regular active, passive, and resistance exercises undertaken to prevent inactivity atrophy, contractures, joint stiffness, and bone demineralization (osteoporosis). The old saying, "If I rest I will rust," should serve as a motto. Early exercises adjusted

to the individual case hasten recovery except for inflammatory conditions and fractures. The amount of exercise depends on the patient's cooperation and motivation and on the ability to perform short, simple limbering-up exercises in bed, involving breathing, air bicycling, and sit-ups, as well as out-of-bed exercises such as walking, bicycling, and swimming, as prescribed by the physician.

7. Recovery or improvement can also be enhanced by selective use of the following procedures:

a. *Thermal applications.* These include ice, cold compresses, and ethyl chloride spray for acute painful swellings.

b. *Applied heat.* The old-fashioned hot water bottle should be replaced by moist heat compresses and poultices, which are more effective. As a compromise, a hot moist towel covered by a dry turkish towel with a hot water bottle on top may be used. The pain-relieving, spasm-diminishing effect of moist heat is due to active vasodilatation with enhanced tissue metabolism and tissue debris absorption.

c. *Radiant heat.* Any form of radiant heat (infrared, diathermy, microtherm), depending on the proper indications and the patient's response, will diminish pain and muscle-tissue tension while enhancing local cell metabolism and restoring vascular tissue harmony. This procedure is contraindicated in cases involving inflammatory changes and fractures.

d. *Iontophoresis.* The use of a low-voltage galvanic current combined with a vasodilating circulation-stimulating drug (histamine, acetylcholine, cortisone) or analgesic ointments will raise outer and deeper skin temperature for a longer time than other external heat stimuli, and has, in contrast to a faradic current, an analgesic-soothing effect.

e. *Ultrasound.* Ultrasound vibrations, with a frequency of several thousand impulses per second, are used to penetrate the cutaneous and subcutaneous layers by bombarding the cell membranes. This technique has an analgesic anti-irritant effect and can also be used for diagnostic purposes as a means of locating painful trigger-point areas. It has also been applied in conjunction with other modalities and medications, such as cortisone and analgesics.

f. *Sinusoidal stimulation (wave current).* Since the classical experiments of Galvani which demonstrated the contraction of leg muscles in the frog as a result of a current potential, as well as the discovery that a faradic current in a wire spool can produce an increment and decrement of electric discharges, it has been known that a wave current can stimulate muscle tone by contracting the fibers. This technique has the added advantage of increasing the patient's awareness of muscle contraction through a somatopsychic feedback experience.

g. *Massage.* Any skillful tender contact between a painful

505

body segment and the hand has a soothing effect. Manual massage based on palpating (feeling) anatomical and pathological changes (swelling, muscle spasm, tightening) is the oldest medical modality in existence, with modern variations that include vibrations, underwater massage, and whirlpool baths.

h. *Manipulation.* Like massage, manipulation requires skillful hands and thorough anatomical knowledge. Its object is to relax tight ligamentous and muscular structures in order to restore normal joint contact.

The inability of the orthopedic surgeon or physiatrist to "cure" every patient has driven a great number of disappointed individuals into the hands of chiropractors and osteopaths, who may be able to help them, often by combining physical therapy with secret medicines and by applying their own style of treatment for a great many sessions. It is well, however, to recall that Benjamin Franklin's saying, "God cures all diseases and the doctor sends the bill," is still valid for some practitioners.

Gently applied manipulations can cure an acute or subacute joint displacement, such as a dislocated shoulder, as well as displacements in other joints in the upper and lower extremities. The treatment requires clinical, neurological, and x-ray evaluation, followed by semirigid or rigid immobilization for several weeks. However, in the case of spinal disorders often misdiagnosed as "slipped disc" or "dislocated vertebra," manipulation can have harmful consequences. The "low-back syndrome" caused by many factors which have to be carefully analyzed requires an individualized therapeutic program with stretching, relaxing, and corrective and toning-up exercises.

i. *Traction.* It is important to recall that most of the quadrupeds and even birds stretch their torso or spread their wings as a prelude to daily muscle contraction and relaxation rhythms, and that these exercises enable them to gain power and speed and to traverse space more effectively. In humans, manual traction involving the cervical, pelvic, and lower leg regions, preferably with prolonged weight-pull exercises, releases muscle tension and enhances realignment of joint surfaces. Even more effective is motorized, intermittent traction such as cervical traction for whiplash injuries and the use of special traction tables for low-back derangements. It is interesting that woodcuts of the sixteenth century show patients suspended with their feet in a ladder incline and their own body weight exerting a therapeutic traction effect. This rather heroic method has been modified, particularly in Europe, by having the patient lie on a height-adjustable stretchboard with cervical and pelvic traction.

ORTHOPEDIC CONDITIONS

A great many acute and chronic musculoskeletal involvements, such as those due to poliomyelitis and tuberculosis, have been either prevented or cured thanks to the dramatic medical-surgical progress of the last fifty years. However, new orthopedic problems are emerging due to increasing traffic, sports, and industrial injuries, and to wear-and-tear reactions on weight-bearing joints and spine, together with postural decline and premature aging due to neglect of exercise needs and body culture. The following orthopedic disorders fall into these categories as well as into the category of congenital conditions.

Congenital Orthopedic Conditions and Treatment

1. *Congenital dislocation of hip.* This condition posed a serious orthopedic problem until fifty years ago due to delayed diagnosis of asymmetrical joint contact (hip dysplasia), but can be cured today before the child sits or walks. The classical so-called "unbloody" method of Lorenz (Vienna, 1910), in which the child is kept in a frog-leg plaster cast position up to twelve to sixteen months, has been replaced by x-ray confirmation shortly after birth, followed by early gentle manipulation during which both legs are kept at a 45-degree angle in abduction for several months. This method enhances proper centering of the growing femoral head into the socket through the use of a Dennis Brown or Fillauer splint. Many overlooked hip dislocations lead to joint degeneration, and the patients become candidates for hip replacement procedures many years later.

2. *Clubfoot.* This condition, sometimes hereditary, is also becoming a rarity today due to improved pre- and postnatal care. Treatment involves the use of corrective wedging casts with gentle corrective manipulation between them, followed by the use of overcorrecting shoe gear. This technique results in a less mobile but still useful foot. Clubfoot due to polio or special abnormalities still poses a complex surgical problem.

3. *Birth injuries.* The most common but fortunately harmless birth injury is the *collar bone fracture*, which will heal by itself due to the admirable regenerative power of the baby's bones. *Erb's palsy* and *epiphyseal separation* are usually the result of delivery complications, leading to a partially paralyzed shoulder with nerve damage. (Erb's palsy is a paralysis of the muscles of the upper arm; an epiphysis is a part of a bone separated from the shaft by cartilage but later united with it.)

4. *Scolioses.* Spinal curvatures are generally congenital and still pose an unsolved orthopedic problem. However, they can be partially corrected in some cases by long-maintained bracing with the Blount Milwaukee brace, "halotraction," or dynamic major surgery in which a metal strut is inserted to support the side which curves in. The life-span of these patients is often foreshortened because of

decreased vital capacity and inadequate respiratory and circulatory exchange.

5. *Other orthopedic deformities. Torticollis,* or wry neck, is due to abnormal pressure in utero, causing contractures of fetal lateral neck muscles. It is correctible by muscle dissection (myotenotomy) followed by active exercise and attention to posture. In rare cases the condition is due to vertebral or scapular (shoulder bone) anomalies (Klippel Feil syndrome). (For the use of biofeedback in treating torticollis, see CHAPTER 55: ILLUSTRATIVE CASES, C. Sensory Feedback Therapy.) *Congenital pes planus* (flatfoot) due to muscle weakness or bony anomalies may require surgical reconstruction procedures. However, in most instances symptomatic care in the form of exercises such as picking up marbles with the toes, corrective shoes, and arch supports are usually recommended. *Genu varum* (bowleg) and *genu valgum* (knock-knee) are in most cases the result of ligamentous knee weakness or due to asymmetry of the weight-bearing growing centers, particularly during the prepuberty growth spurt. These conditions can be partly compensated by systematic corrective exercises and corrective footgear. If the deformity is progressive, surgical correction in the form of osteotomies or epiphyseal stapling will be necessary. *Pes equinus* with shortened Achilles tendon (which joins the calf muscles to the heel) is often a manifestation of cerebral palsy. The condition requires surgical correction in the form of tenotomy followed by bracing — which is also necessary in case of *drop foot* due to peroneal (side of leg) nerve damage — to prevent overstretching of the foot extensors and progressive shortening of the Achilles tendon.

Orthopedic Growth Disturbances between the Ages of Four and Twelve

1. *Slipped epiphysis,* a not yet fully understood slipping off of the femoral (thigh bone) cartilaginous head, causing a sudden limp with pain, can be successfully treated (after x-ray examination) by gentle manipulation under anesthesia and internal fixation of the headcap reduced to its base by inserting several threaded pins (Knolls pins).

2. *Legg-Calve-Perthe disease,* first distinguished from tubercular bone disease about 1912, is due to inadequate circulation in the femoral head and upper neck portion of the femur, and results in bone cartilage necrosis (cell death) and deformity. Surgical procedures were found to be more harmful than beneficial, but fortunately a fully functioning though slightly deformed femoral head can be achieved spontaneously if weight-bearing is avoided for a long period, ranging from six to twenty-four months.

If slipped epiphysis and Legg-Calve-Perthe disease are neglected, joint disintegration is likely to set in. In such cases the only viable alternative is insertion of a painlessly functioning joint replacement unit which will, in most instances, enable the patient to participate in all normal activities, even sports. Charnley biomechanical joint replacement therapy is now applied to practically all joints,

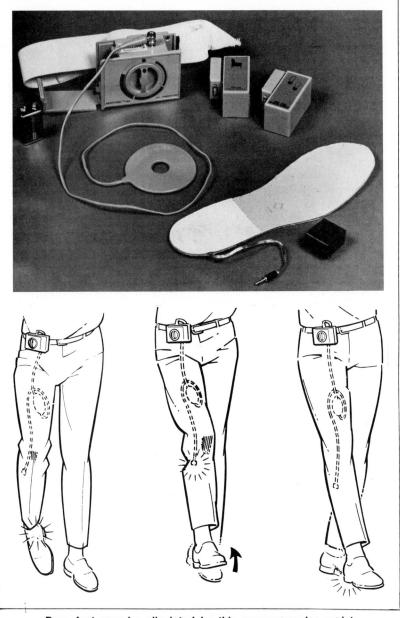

Drop foot may be alleviated by this neuromuscular assist device. In the diagrams, lifting the heel causes the heel switch system to activate the belt-suspended transmitter, which sends a radio-frequency signal along the antenna and through the skin to an implant, thus stimulating the peroneal nerve and dorsiflexing the boot; the heel strike against the ground terminates the sequence. (System developed at Rancho Los Amigos Hospital, Los Angeles, and Medtronics, Inc., Minneapolis)

with the reservation that it cannot be used as yet during the growth period.

Common Fractures and Injuries: Rehabilitation Principles

The following exclude compound fractures, infected fractures, and dislocations:

1. *Clavicle (collarbone) fractures, rib fractures,* and impacted (not displaced) *upper humeral (upper arm bone) fractures* require only semirigid fixation, such as the clavicle figure-eight sling, without correction or rigid fixation.

2. *Sport and daily activity injuries* include *wrist injury:* fracture of the distal end of the radius bone with "silver fork" deformity or Calles fractures; *ankle injury:* fracture of the distal fibula (calf bone), requiring immediate x-ray and reduction (usually under local anesthesia), followed by cast immobilization for five to eight weeks, then early active movement and gentle manipulation plus hydrotherapy and well-programmed exercises designed to forestall posttraumatic stiffness (traumatic arthritis). Internal (Rush) pin fixation of the long bones can usually obviate external fixation and lead to earlier use of the ankle. Fixation with an intramedullary nail also is used in femur and humeral fractures.

3. *Whiplash injury* is often the result of the most common car accident, the rear-end collision, and is characterized by later-appearing neck stiffness and pain. It sometimes involves disc and nerve root damage. The combination of muscle, ligamentous, and vertebral damage usually requires neck collar fixation, muscle relaxants, and moist heat applications. If the condition persists, intermittent traction, together with reassurance, may be indicated. Other traffic injuries may involve cerebral shock and compound fractures with internal complications such as infection and embolism. Such injuries may require surgery and many months of hospitalization.

4. *Common sport injuries involving torn or dislocated knee cartilages* require first-aid to relieve pain, as well as immobilization through the use of emergency splinting. Such injuries often require a long rehabilitation. *Fractured vertebrae or pelvic bones* heal in most cases, with remaining painless deformity, after several weeks of bed rest and bracing. These procedures should be followed by the most effective rehabilitation activity, swimming.

5. *Hip fractures and knee replacement* are most common after sixty and are increasing in number due to increased longevity. Fifty years ago they posed a serious therapeutic problem which required strict cast immobilization for three or more months, often leading to such complications as embolism, pneumonia, urinary disturbances, and bedsores, with a mortality rate of 35 percent. Today, thanks to the much modified technique of internal pin fixation, the patient will be out of bed the next day and ambulatory on crutches without weight-bearing on the involved leg. Moreover, by supporting the fractured area with a vitallium Austin Moore prosthesis or by replacing the entire joint and upper femoral portion with a total hip

replacement (Charnley), the patient will be able to ambulate with full weight-bearing after a few days. In the past few years, painful, stiffened arthritic knee joints have also been replaced with metal and acrylic components which allow full, painless weight-bearing with markedly increased motion range.

6. *Fractures of wrist, ankle, and upper and lower extremities* are properly aligned under general anesthesia, and then these body segments are immobilized with internal fixation devices such as the Rush pin compression-screw plate, Kventschner femoral rod, and Kirschner wires. Such devices allow for earlier joint mobilization and often replace prolonged rigid fixation. In addition, the plaster of Paris cast, which is still used for immobilization, is now available in lighter, waterproof material. As mentioned above, it is also used for therapeutic fixation of sport injuries involving severe spasms, tenderness, tears, knee derangements, and the like.

7. *Osteoporosis,* as the name implies, involves porous, brittle bones, and is due to prolonged immobilization, neurovascular changes after trauma, and physical changes associated with menopause or old age. The entire skeleton may become "rarefied" and demineralized, particularly the spine and hip. This frequently leads to spontaneous hip fractures and chronically painful collapse of the vertebrae. These patients require rehabilitation efforts directed toward developing their own "muscle corset" by exercising their back muscles. Back-bracing may be used to give the spine additional support. Among the available types of braces are the Camp-type corset, the McAusland brace which immobilizes the whole dorsolumbar spine, the light corrective Taylor brace, the Jewett brace, and the Williams brace for low-back derangements.

8. *Paget's disease (osteitis deformans)* received its classical description by James Paget over 100 years ago, but the etiology of this disease remains unknown. It manifests itself, in middle or late life, in the skull, spine, pelvis, and extremities, leading to enlargement of the skull and bowleg deformities with painful areas of local bone disintegration, rarely developing into malignant changes. Although new drugs (Calcitonin) have resulted in temporary relief, no definite cure has been reported. The disease is progressive in nature, and fracture may occur spontaneously or following trivial injury— nevertheless, Paget's does not cause total disability.

9. *The aching back* is a suitable ending for this condensed orthopedic-rehabilitation discussion. The most common American disorder, it affects 80 percent of the population. In the struggle for survival, humans have emerged from the evolutionary stages of fish, amphibians, reptiles, mammals, and primates as the only species with upright posture. This erect posture is based on the ability to support the body through the action of antigravity erector muscles suspended on a spinal base, with the pelvis as centerboard. However, humans pay for this posture by becoming afflicted with back pain due to constant gravity strain, environmental stress, and bad postural habits, all of which combine to put pressure on the lower spine. A condition known as spinal insufficiency results, and is of-

ten aggravated by overweight, muscular inactivity, poor feet, and nervous tension.

Education in good postural control with symmetrical joint alignment and strong muscle tone will combat sitting damage and wear-and-tear damage to delicate disc structures, and will often compensate for and correct potentially poor postural alignment and premature decline and aging of the central back structures, which so often occur among those who develop poor postural habits due to prolonged television viewing, sitting in bucket seats and easy chairs, or working and standing in awkward positions. The simplest and most basic recipe is to engage in walking and swimming plus breathing and abdominal muscle – strengthening exercises.

(For other conditions involving orthopedic treatment and rehabilitation, see CHAPTER 17: AMPUTATIONS; CHAPTER 18: ARTHRITIS; CHAPTER 26: CEREBRAL PALSY; CHAPTER 41: MUSCULAR DYSTROPHY; CHAPTER 54: OTHER DISORDERS, A. Arthrogryposis, C. Dwarfism, H. Osteogenesis Imperfecta, I. Poliomyelitis.)

46

Ostomies

HAZEL HARRISON, Ostomy Mutual Aiders of
Washington

Reviewed by ANN CARTER, M.D., Seattle King County Health
Department, and Former Director, Cancer and Stroke Programs,
Washington and Alaska Regional Medical Program

It is estimated that there are 1,000,000 ostomates in the United
States and Canada and that approximately 90,000 new ostomy sur-
geries are performed each year. Ileostomy, colostomy, and ureterostomy are surgical procedures in which an artificial opening, or
stoma, is made in the abdominal wall to excrete waste from the
body. With proper management and control techniques, the ostomy
presents a minimal handicap to the patient.

Ileostomy

When the entire colon or middle part of the large intestine is
diseased, the surgeon must remove it. A stoma is then formed from
the ileum, or lower part of the small intestine—hence, the name
ileostomy. This stoma is generally located on the right side of the
abdomen, about two inches below the waistline, and halfway between the right hipbone and the umbilicus or navel.

The first ileostomy surgery (in the early 1900s) was very simple;
antibiotics were unknown, and the danger of fatal peritonitis, or
inflammation of the abdominal walls, was very great. One procedure was to bring the appendix out as the stoma and use it as a tube
to wash the colon and to instill medication. Another method was to
bring the cecum, or first part of the large intestine, to the surface of
the abdomen and insert a tube for drainage and medication. Later a
technique was devised in which the terminal ileum was divided,
and a tube placed within for drainage. None of these methods was
very successful, and mortality was high. It was not until the 1940s

that Brian Brooke of England developed the present procedure of bringing the ileum through the abdominal wall, removing the affected colon. This surgery, thanks to antibiotics, steroids, and a better understanding of physiology, can now be completed in one operation. One other major advancement came in 1951 when Dr. Brooke devised a technique of eversion, or folding back the ileum on itself to prevent granulation and stenosis, or tightening, of the stoma.

The most recent development in ileostomy surgery has been the intra-abdominal reservoir operation, in which a loop of the ileum is formed into an inside pouch. Although ideally no outside pouch is necessary with this type of surgery after a period of training, there is need for frequent siphoning through the stoma. In spite of this, there may be leakage and, in addition, infection and stenosis are a danger. Presently this technique seems to possess too many disadvantages to be used extensively.

Ileostomy surgery is performed most often on patients with ulcerative colitis. This disease is found principally in adolescence or early adult life, but can occur at almost any age. In children it may lead to impairment of normal physical development. The danger of malignant tumors arising in cases of extensive ulcerative colitis is well established, particularly in those patients whose disease began in childhood.

The cause of ulcerative colitis is unknown. There are two forms: fulminating (acute) and chronic. The fulminating form must be treated surgically, often as a life-saving procedure. The chronic form, which gives rise to bleeding through the rectum and excessive diarrhea with excruciating pain, may be alleviated for years, but surgery is usually necessary eventually.

Ileostomy may be performed when there are many small growths on the colon. This condition, called familial polyposis, is a hereditary disease, transmitted as a Mendelian dominant, which may undergo malignant change. Also, ileostomy may be performed if amebic dysentery does not respond to medication, although this is infrequent.

Colostomy

The colostomy differs from the ileostomy in that the opening is to the colon, or large intestine. Sometimes the colon can be reconnected at a later date.

The first records of colostomy surgery date back to the eighteenth century. Prior to 1900, the operative mortality rate was over 20 percent. In the early 1900s, Ernest Miles developed the method of forming a permanent colostomy when the rectum was excised. At first the outlet was placed in the anal region, but this did not prove satisfactory because of difficulty in control. Gradually, surgeons turned their attention to the establishment of an abdominal outlet for the colostomy. This has proved much more satisfactory and is now the technique almost universally followed.

Permanent colostomy is most often performed because of malignant tumors, either in the rectal area or in some part of the colon. Temporary colostomy may be performed for conditions such as diverticulitis (an inflammation of pockets in the wall of the colon), blockages of the colon, fistulas in the anal area, and malformed or malfunctioning portions of the intestine in the newborn.

Ureterostomy

A ureterostomy is markedly different from either an ileostomy or a colostomy. Its purpose is to divert the urine from the bladder. One early method was to join the tubes which connect the kidneys with the bladder (ureters) to the colon, permitting discharge of both urine and feces through the rectum. A variation of this procedure was to form a colostomy through which the feces were diverted, and the tubes from the kidneys were connected to the lower part of the colon, thus creating separate outlets for feces and urine. A third method was to bring the ureters directly to the outside of the abdomen, one on each side, as stomas. All of these methods subjected a person to great danger of infection traveling to the kidneys. The ileal conduit operation is the one most generally performed today. A short segment, four to six inches, of the ileum is selected near where it joins the colon. This segment is severed, and the colon is reconnected so that continuity of the digestive system is not interrupted. The isolated section of ileum is placed so that one end is deep on the right side of the abdomen, and the other end is brought out through the abdominal wall and sewn in place as a stoma. The deep end is closed so no urine will escape inside the abdomen. The ureters are cut near the bladder and are connected to this segment of ileum. This arrangement then allows the kidneys to deliver the urine through the ureters into the ileal conduit, which propels the urine to the outside through the stoma.

Ureterostomy surgery is performed mainly for malignancy and dysfunction of kidneys or bladder in adults—for example, incontinence due to spinal cord injury; in children, it is performed usually for malformation or malfunction of the bladder.

Ostomy Appliances

Appliances consisting mainly of a rubber or hard plastic disc to which a rubber or plastic pouch is attached are needed for ileostomies and ureterostomies. They may or may not be needed for colostomies, depending on the consistency and control of the feces.

A simple, comfortable, nonirritating, inexpensive, inconspicuous, odor- and leak-proof appliance is essential to the well-being of the patient. The appliance may be attached to the body in various ways: with contact adhesive cement, double-faced adhesive discs, or karaya gum rings. Belts or waterproof tapes are often used to reinforce the adhesion.

The first ostomy appliances were large and boxlike. They were conspicuous, uncomfortable, and often leaked, causing severe burning and loss of skin (excoriation). Since the development of the adherent ostomy appliance in the early 1940s, through the combined efforts of Dr. Alfred Strauss, Henry Koenig (an ostomate who was also an artist, chemist, and mechanic), and Henry Rutzen, a businessman, no one need be aware of ostomy unless the patient wishes. There is a wide choice of appliances and aids to cover essentially all individual needs.

Ostomy Management

Ostomates must pay special attention to the following.

1. *Skin care* involves gentle cleansing without scrubbing in the ostomy area. If fecal matter comes in contact with the skin, excoriation will occur, so this must be attended to at once, using oil-free emollients so that the disc will still adhere to the surrounding skin.

2. *Granulation tissue* can cause difficulty in fitting the appliance. If profuse, it is usually controlled by cauterization with silver nitrate.

3. *Stenosis*, a tightening of the ostomy, is caused by natural scar formation at the junction between the skin and the mucous membrane. This can cause cramps, diarrhea, and excessive fluid loss. Surgery is usually necessary to correct stenosis.

4. *Prolapse* is essentially a herniation or protrusion of bowel through the stoma and must be reduced promptly. This should be done by a physician.

5. *Retraction* means a pulling in of the ostomy due to breaking of sutures, unexpected internal tension, or excessive weight gain. Retraction which occurs soon after the operation must be corrected promptly to prevent complete loss of the stoma and internal peritoneal soiling. Delayed retractions are a less immediate problem, but both require surgery.

6. *Drainage* from the wound can greatly inhibit normal activity. It can persist from six months to three years after surgery. Surgical refinements in the past ten years have reduced the frequency of this problem considerably.

7. *Blockage* must be overcome promptly by cleaning the walls of the small intestine by means of injections or by drawing off the fluids from the ureter (catheterization).

8. *Electrolyte imbalance* must be corrected. The colon normally helps to maintain the fluid and electrolyte balance of the body. Imbalance may be serious should diseases associated with loss of body fluids occur. Diarrhea must be treated, and saline drinks given as a first-aid measure.

9. *Perforation* of the colon as a result of irrigation is a risk. Perforation requires immediate surgical attention.

10. *Odor* is controlled by various deodorants manufactured especially for use by ostomates.

Rehabilitation

A comparatively new concept in rehabilitation is the training of entrostomal therapists, preferably those with a stoma, to assist surgeons during postoperative care.

Once the techniques of management have been mastered, the

average ostomate is not disabled. Continuance in a previous occupation is usually possible unless it is exceptionally heavy work, in which case changing to lighter work may be necessary. Naturally, the ostomate must ensure that supplies are always at hand. Patients with multiple ostomies may have considerably more difficulty adjusting. Prejudice against the ostomate has been encountered among employers and in medical insurance plans, but this is decreasing. Since 1972, provision of "colostomy bags and supplies directly related to colostomy care" has been included under the Social Security Act in cases of need.

Remaining Problems

Several problems remain to be solved. For example, there is still no sure method of preventing excoriation of the skin under the ostomy appliance. For some patients, handling waste disposal remains a problem. Better public awareness and understanding of ostomies would help the ostomy patient considerably. Finally, a breakthrough is needed in current knowledge of ulcerative colitis and cancer, the two main conditions necessitating ostomy surgery, if ostomies are to become a rarity rather than a not uncommon procedure.

Organizations

The United Ostomy Association, Inc., with international headquarters at 1111 Wilshire Boulevard, Los Angeles, CA 90017, is the most important comprehensive source of information for the ostomate. It publishes a paramedical quarterly which contains a complete listing of all local groups and a listing of distributors of ostomy products, and maintains a listing of current publications on ostomy care. The Association also has a hospital income plan for its members.

The National Foundation for Ileitis and Colitis, with headquarters at 295 Madison Avenue, New York, NY 10017, was established in 1965 to combat inflammatory bowel diseases which afflict an estimated 2 million Americans, including 200,000 children. The Foundation now comprises 7,500 members and twenty-five chapters, and since its founding has awarded $1.7 million in research grants to twenty-six major research centers. Among current projects are epidemiological studies to determine the background of individuals most vulnerable to these diseases, transmission studies to reveal specific agents which might cause them, and pharmacological studies designed to assess the effectiveness of various treatments. The Foundation also holds educational meetings and seminars for the public, and distributes informative literature to hospitals, physicians, and the public. In addition, it cooperates with the Digestive Disease Section of the National Institutes of Health.

Local *ostomy clubs* maintain contacts between persons having ostomies. There is at least one of these clubs in nearly every state and several in Canada. Contacts are made through referrals from doctors, the Visiting Nurse Service, the American Cancer Society, and bulletins published and exchanged by each club. Local ostomy clubs are funded primarily by dues and donations, often supplemented by grants from the American Cancer Society or a local corporation. The ostomate learns from the personal experiences of others, from medical articles, and through manufacturers' displays. Ostomy club representatives usually visit and encourage new ostomates.

SELECTED REFERENCES

Binder, D. P., *Sex, Courtship and the Single Ostomate*, United Ostomy Association (UOA), 1973.

Dericks, Virginia C., "Rehabilitation of Patients with Ileostomy," *American Journal of Nursing*, May 1961.

Gambrell, Ed, *Sex and the Male Ostomate*, UOA, 1973.

Gross, Linda, *Ileostomy: A Guide*, UOA, 1974.

Jeter, Katherine, *Urinary Ostomies: A Guidebook for Patients*, UOA, 1972.

Larson, Darlene, *Living Comfortably with Your Ileostomy*, Sister Kenny Institute, Minneapolis, 1973.

Lenneberg, Edith, *The Ileostomy Patient*, Charles C. Thomas, Springfield, Illinois, 1970.

Lenneberg, Edith, and Alan H. Mendelssohn, *Colostomies: A Guide*, UOA, 1969.

Lenneberg, Edith, and Miriam Weiner, *The Ostomy Handbook*, UOA, 1973.

Norris, Carol, and Ed Gambrell, *Sex, Pregnancy and the Female Ostomate*, UOA, 1972.

Ostomy Quarterly articles by E. D. Acheson, Spring 1964; J. H. Hertzler, Summer 1967; Albert L. Mendelhoff et al., Fall 1970; James J. Pollard, Summer 1964.

So You Have — or Will Have — an Ostomy, UOA.

Sparberg, Marshall, *Ileostomy Care*, Charles C. Thomas, Springfield, Illinois, 1971.

Parkinson's Disease

ROBERT M. GOLDENSON, Ph.D.

Reviewed by PHILIP SWANSON, M.D., Head of Department of
Neurology, University of Washington, Seattle, and STANLEY
FAHN, M.D., Neurological Institute, New York

Parkinson's disease, or parkinsonism, is a progressive neurological disorder primarily affecting certain regions of the brain that are important for motor control. Its history traces back to biblical times, and for generations it was known as "shaking palsy" (paralysis agitans). The first medical account of the disorder was given by the English physician James Parkinson in "An Essay on the Shaking Palsy," published in 1817, in which he noted the following characteristics: "An involuntary tremulous motion, with lessened muscular power in parts not in action . . . a propensity to bend the trunk forward and to pass from a walking to a running pace; the senses and intellect being uninjured." This description proved so accurate that the disease was named after him.

Prevalence

Parkinsonism is a leading cause of chronic disability in people over fifty years of age, but occasionally occurs earlier. Recent estimates indicate that 1 percent of the population aged fifty or over has or will develop the disease, and that it will strike 3 percent of people aged sixty-five or older. Estimates in terms of the total number affected vary between 500,000 and 1,500,000 for the United States alone. In view of the increasing proportion of older people in the population, it is likely that the incidence of the disease will increase.

Types

The majority of cases are classified as "idiopathic parkinsonism," or parkinsonism of unknown cause, since no specific causal factor or associated condition can be found. One type, however, is known as "postencephalitic parkinsonism," due to the fact that the symptoms appear during or after an infection of the brain by the virus causing encephalitis lethargica, or sleeping sickness, which swept the United States between 1917 and 1926. Sometimes the term "arteriosclerotic parkinsonism" is applied to older patients who develop both parkinsonism symptoms and cerebral arteriosclerosis, or hardening of the arteries which carry blood nourishment to the brain. Today, however, most investigators believe that these two conditions occur together only by coincidence.

Other Causes

Certain drugs, particularly the phenothiazines (Thorazine, Stelazine), can produce symptoms resembling parkinsonism. This is known as drug-induced parkinsonism, but the symptoms disappear when the offending drug is reduced or discontinued. Viruses and hereditary factors are under scrutiny for their passive role in the causation of idiopathic parkinsonism, although little if any positive evidence has thus far been discovered. Occasionally, more than one case occurs in a family, but this is generally considered to be coincidental. Since the factors responsible for the disease have not been determined, it is not yet possible to apply preventive measures. Pathological specimens usually show degenerative changes in a portion of the brainstem called the substantia nigra (black substance).

Symptoms and Diagnosis

In many cases the disease first manifests itself in a "proneness to trembling in some particular part," to use Parkinson's own words. The tremors most commonly appear in one of the hands, but in some cases the head and legs may be affected first. One major characteristic is that the limbs tend to shake when they are at rest; a second characteristic is the tendency to develop more pronounced tremors due to self-consciousness and the fear of being observed. Emotional tension of any type may also aggravate the symptoms. But since tremor may be due to other causes, an accurate diagnosis may sometimes be difficult to make.

Ordinarily the disorder develops gradually, and as months and years go by, the tremors may become more severe and spread to other limbs. Sooner or later another major symptom develops: muscular rigidity and slowness of movement (bradykinesia), frequently accompanied by loss of automatic movements such as those involved in blinking the eyes, facial expressions, and swinging the arms while walking. As a result, the face becomes masklike, the eyes appear to stare, and the head is held constantly in the same position.

The patient's posture and gait are also deeply affected. Not only are the arms held motionless at the sides, but the walk consists of short, rapid, shuffling steps, with head and neck bent stiffly forward. The patient may have trouble starting to walk, and once on the way usually manifests a hurried or "festinating" gait, with the feet moving faster and faster until stopping becomes difficult. The individual may even pitch forward and fall.

The major symptoms—tremors, rigidity, bradykinesia, and diminished automatic movements—vary in degree in different patients, and one symptom may be considerably more pronounced than another. In many cases the symptoms remain mild and increase only gradually over the years. In other cases they develop more rapidly, and the muscles may become so rigid that they cannot be relaxed. Such patients become afflicted with a permanent shortening of the muscles, frozen joints, and deformities of the hands and feet.

Parkinsonism frequently affects the patient's personality, increasing passivity and indecisiveness. There may also be some loss of intellectual capacity, but the patient's general health is not greatly affected. Only in rare cases is life-span shortened.

Medical Treatment

Two general types of procedure have been employed in treating parkinsonism: surgery and medications. At one time, brain surgery was used far more extensively than it is today. It is now rarely employed for treatment of parkinsonism in most hospitals. It is called upon only when drugs prove inadequate or produce severe side effects. The procedure is painless, and a local anesthetic is used in order to enable the patient to assist the neurosurgeon in locating the precise point to be excised. One of the newer surgical techniques is cryosurgery, in which an ice-cold fluid (liquid nitrogen) is carefully dripped through a fine tube, or cannula, inserted into the brain to deaden nerve fibers responsible for the symptoms. Operative procedures have provided relief from tremors and rigidity in many cases, but unfortunately do not alleviate other symptoms such as bradykinesia or the loss of automatic movements. Another drawback is that only one side of the brain can be operated on at a time, and a second operation performed on the other side involves considerable risk of serious complications.

Until recently the most common medications used in the treatment of parkinsonism were certain alkaloids, particularly atropine and hyoscine, which are derived from plants, and their synthetic analogs. These drugs were frequently effective in reducing tremor and rigidity, but produced uncomfortable side effects. Within the past few years, however, a breakthrough in chemotherapy has been made through the introduction of a compound known as L-dopa (levodihydroxyphenylalanine). This chemical is derived from the amino acid tyrosine and is the intermediate compound between tyrosine and dopamine, a brain chemical which has been demonstrated to be deficient in patients with parkinsonism. Tests con-

521

ducted by George C. Cotzias, Melvin D. Yahr, and others indicate that L-dopa dramatically relieves symptoms in about 80 percent of cases. High dosages are needed, however, and it must be administered with caution, due to the possibility of side effects. More recently, an enzyme inhibitor has been used in conjunction with L-dopa. This inhibitor reduces the metabolism of L-dopa in tissues outside the brain, allowing much less L-dopa to be administered and reducing some of the side effects, such as nausea and vomiting. In the United States the combination tablet containing L-dopa and the inhibitor is known as Sinemet.

Research Areas

One major center for research is located in the William Black Medical Research Building at the College of Physicians and Surgeons, Columbia University, where some thirty specialists representing all relevant scientific fields pool their efforts in an all-out attack on the disease. A broad range of projects is also being conducted in institutions in many countries. In addition to examination of the possible role of viruses, arteriosclerosis, and hereditary factors, as noted above, research includes experimentation on such brain structures as the basal ganglia and thalamus; investigation of the chemistry of nerve cells; and anatomical studies performed with the aid of the electron microscope and other instruments, directed toward revealing important structural changes in the brain of parkinsonism patients. Other important projects are directed toward the development of agents which will control the side effects of L-dopa, as well as new types of chemotherapy that may prove even more effective than this remarkable drug.

Rehabilitation Measures

The major approach is through physical therapy, except where contraindicated. A careful and exhaustive examination by a neurologist, preferably with the aid of a specialist in rehabilitation medicine (physiatrist), is mandatory in developing the most beneficial exercise program for the particular patient. The Parkinson's Disease Foundation makes available a free pamphlet entitled "Exercises for the Parkinson Patient," and it may be helpful to give a brief indication of the nature of this program. Its prime objective is to prevent rigidity or stiffness, which if untreated may lead to deformities and disabilities in later years.

The following general rules are recommended: lift the toes with every step; take small steps and keep the feet widely apart while turning; practice walking and turning at least fifteen minutes per day; swing the arms freely while walking; practice rising rapidly from a chair; carry a weight (shopping bag, for instance) with one hand to counteract the tendency to list to the other side; repeatedly practice tasks that are becoming difficult, such as buttoning a shirt or getting out of bed. Special exercises are suggested for improving standing and sitting posture, balance, walking, turning, getting in and out of a chair or bed, maintaining the use of the hands, observing safety in the bathtub and toilet, and overcoming difficulties with speech, facial expression, and chewing. In general, these exercises can all be performed at home, but to be of maximum benefit they must be repeated several times a day. In addition, an intensive course of therapy under a professional physical therapist is strongly recommended wherever possible.

Another key aspect of the rehabilitation program is to continue to engage in as many everyday activities as possible, including working, walking outdoors, shopping, doing household chores, gardening, traveling, going to the theater, and swimming and other sports. A full program of social activities should also be maintained, including frequent visits to friends and membership in senior clubs, church organizations, and Y's and other organizations devoted to health, recreation, and education.

Organizations

Established in 1957, the primary function of the Parkinson's Disease Foundation (640 West 168th Street, New York, NY 10032) is to stimulate research into the cause, prevention, and cure of the disease. Every dollar donated by the public is spent on research, since all administrative expenses are covered by an endowment provided by its founder and chairman, William Black. To date, the Foundation has awarded grants amounting to well over $1 million for support of studies conducted in over twenty-five institutions, including the Central Research Facility at Columbia University. The Foundation's Research Advisory Board, composed of leading neurologists in the United States, establishes research policies, makes recommendations for projects, and passes on applications for research support. To supply the necessary personnel, the Foundation provides financial support for periods of three to five years to experienced researchers working on Parkinson's disease at their own university or hospital.

Many research projects were stimulated by the national symposium conducted by the Foundation in 1960. Two other major programs were also recommended at this symposium and are now being carried out: maintenance of a registry of parkinsonism patients, and establishment of a "brain bank" at Columbia University Medical School to which victims of the disease could bequeath their brains for medical research on a scale hitherto impossible to achieve. Subsequent symposia have resulted in further substantial contributions reported in two books, *The Thalamus* (Columbia University Press, New York) and *Biochemistry and Pharmacology of the Basal Ganglia* (Raven Press, New York).

The National Parkinson Foundation, with headquarters at 1501 Ninth Avenue, Miami, FL 33136, maintains the National Parkinson Institute, which provides diagnosis, treatment, care, and rehabilitation; and conducts an educational program for physicians, patients, nurses' training schools, and health clinics. The United Parkinson Foundation (220 South State Street, Chicago, IL 60604) is a membership organization consisting of about 10,000 patients, family members, medical personnel, and other interested persons. It publishes informative material helpful to sufferers, fosters scientific research, and assists the patient and family through medical referrals and education. The objectives of the American Parkinson Disease Association (147 East 50th Street, New York, NY 10022) are to alleviate pain and suffering by subsidizing outpatient clinics and to provide funds for research to find a cure for the disease.

SELECTED REFERENCES

Bianchine, J., "Drug Therapy of Parkinsonism," *New England Journal of Medicine*, vol. 295, 1976.

Birkmayer, W., ed., *Proceedings of the Fifth International Symposium on Parkinson's Disease, Vienna* (clinical features, management, and basic mechanisms), 1976.

Pallis, C., "Parkinsonism: Natural History and Clinical Features" (neuropathology, physiology, and pharmacology), *British Medical Journal*, September 18, 1971.

48

Pulmonary Disease:
A. Tuberculosis

CEDRIC NORTHROP, M.D., Former Tuberculosis Control
Officer, King County Health Department, Seattle

Tuberculosis, formerly called consumption, has been known since medieval times in Europe. It was often thought to be an inherited affliction, and its communicability was suspected but never proved until 1882. In Europe the predominantly agrarian economy began to change with the Industrial Revolution, and cities with their slums and poverty caused a great increase in the tuberculosis rate. By 1700 it was estimated in Great Britain that one death in every three was due to tuberculosis. With improved socioeconomic status of the populations there began a slow decline in the frightful mortality, and this improvement first became discernible about 1850. In 1862 Louis Pasteur announced the germ theory of disease, followed by proof that tuberculosis was communicable — which J. A. Villemin demonstrated through animal inoculation in 1865 – 1868. On March 24, 1882, Robert Koch, a Prussian country doctor, read a paper describing the discovery of the tubercle bacillus. The stage was set for real progress to be made — but it took almost seventy years for significant results to be apparent.

Institutional Care

In the United States one landmark was the funding of the Adirondack Cottage Sanatorium at Saranac Lake, New York, in 1885 by Edward Livingston Trudeau. It emphasized the use of bed rest, open air, and superalimentation (in that order) as the therapeutic triad. By 1900 the use of pneumothorax (compression of the lung with air) as a treatment device was growing in acceptance. At that time the use of institutional treatment for active cases was undergoing a nationwide developmental phase, to attain its maximum extent about 1948–1960. Institutional care was advocated due to two factors: it provided the maximum opportunity for the patient to get well, based on scientific knowledge available at that time, and it protected the patient's family and the public from a communicable disease. An unfortunate by-product of the emphasis on open air treatment was the construction of many of the institutions in out-of-the-way places, far from the urban centers. Not until 1915–1920 was it proved that, other things being equal, tuberculosis patients in Massachusetts did as well as patients in Arizona or New Mexico.

Other Rehabilitation Approaches

Although there were occasional cases of tuberculosis which ran an acute course, the vast majority were chronic and characterized by exacerbations and remissions. The heartache and frustration to both the patient and those responsible for recuperation were readily apparent. It became a standard recommendation to patients to adopt a "new way of life," which meant to ease back into the "normal" routine very slowly over two to five years, and if they had been employed at heavy labor, a return to such work was seldom successful. Therefore, as a natural consequence of the institutional program, several offshoots were gradually developed: occupational therapy, work colonies, sheltered workshops, and true rehabilitation programs.

Occupational Therapy. Occupational therapy (OT) was the first and easiest program to institute, and involved minimum cost. It started simply with a library of newspapers, books, and magazines to make the stay of the patient more tolerable. Entertainment was therapeutically useful, progressing to listening to the radio in the 1920s, movies in the 1930s, and television beginning in the 1940–1950 era. For the patient of limited education, reading often had no appeal, so the development of activities utilizing crafts and skills gradually became essential. Starting with simple items, the program developed in variety and sophistication, from simple crafts to more complex activities such as printing. It almost seemed that some institutions derived more community support from their OT program than from statistical analysis of the results of medical care. Nevertheless, the OT department proved for more than sixty years to be one of the factors which could help to make the prolonged (one to three or more years) stay of the patient more tolerable.

Work Colonies. In order to try to help diminish the economic crises that tuberculosis imposed on many patients and families, a work colony was developed in many places in Europe, with the largest and best known located in England. Here workers could obtain preliminary rest treatment for tuberculosis, then enter a graduated program of decreasing rest and increasing work until they were able to return to society on a full-time basis. The most famous of this type was Papworth Village, Cambridgeshire, England, begun after World War I and continued until after World War II. However, the advent of modern chemotherapy for the treatment of tuberculosis diminished the need for this type of setup after 1960.

Sheltered Workshops. A moderate number were established in the period 1910–1930, possibly best exemplified by the Altro Workshops of New York. Started in 1915, the Altro Workshop provided opportunities for patients to be discharged from a sanatorium and undertake an initial work schedule of three hours daily. They would live at home but would work under supervision; this work schedule would gradually be increased to a maximum of eight hours. The results were medically good, but the difficulty in supplying an adequate work base provided an insurmountable obstacle to the majority of these projects. Another early sponsor of a sheltered workshop was Eastman Kodak, in Rochester, New York. An operation of a sheltered workshop of an "inpatient nature" has been carried on successfully at Finland Sanatorium at Seattle, in cooperation with the Boeing Aircraft Company. The manufacture of small airplane parts involving much handwork provided "pin money" for selected patients, and proved an excellent means to promote acceptance of hospitalization by tuberculosis patients. This sheltered workshop was started about 1950, enrolled at its peak nearly 100 patients, and continued on a diminishing scale until the closing of the institution in October 1973. (See CHAPTER 8: THE SHELTERED WORKSHOP.)

True Rehabilitation Programs. The first efforts to improve the status of crippled persons started about the time of the French Revolution, but development was slow and halting until the latter half of the nineteenth century. Some definite efforts at rehabilitation of the tuberculous began in France in 1896, but during the early part of the twentieth century the most important pioneer efforts were made by the British. In the United States the emphasis on rehabilitation received a significant boost with the passage by Congress of the Soldier Rehabilitation Act on June 27, 1918. It authorized the states to develop rehabilitation plans with federal financial aid. Massachusetts was the first state to adopt a plan, in 1918, and Minnesota was the second, in 1919, with many others soon to follow. In Minnesota the acceptance of the tuberculosis patient in need of rehabilitation was so rapid that by 1924 one-half of the total state load of patients under rehabilitation training were the tuberculous group. All tuberculosis sanatoriums in Minnesota participated, but at Glen Lake Sanatorium in Minneapolis the program was acclaimed as most outstanding and deserves special mention. During the first month after admission to the hospital, medical, social, and educational data were gathered and a summary prepared as to rehabilitation prospects of the patient. About six weeks after admission a conference was held, composed of the directors of education, occupational therapy, social service, and library; the physician in charge of the case; and the rehabilitation counselor (from the local office of the State Division of Rehabilitation). The potentialities of the patient were evaluated from all angles, and individual desires and hopes considered.

The excellent pioneer work in Minnesota was extensively copied elsewhere between 1945 and 1950, and became standard practice in all but the smaller institutions where it was not economically feasible.

Ever since the discovery of the tubercle bacillus, the hope had existed of a definitive treatment that would effectively reduce the period of time necessary and improve the results. For the next 60 years medications were introduced from time to time in the treatment of tuberculosis, only to turn out disappointing. In November 1944 S. A. Waksman and associates announced the discovery of the antibiotic streptomycin. In 1945 trials proved its protective value first in experimental animals, then in clinical treatment of patients. By 1946 it became widely available for treatment and though it was initially both expensive and toxic both shortcomings were rapidly reduced. In 1947–1948 a second medication, para-aminosalicylic acid (PAS), was introduced from Sweden, and its joint usage with streptomycin was widely accepted by 1950. Isoniazid (INAH), discovered in the United States and almost simultaneously in West Germany, was introduced in 1952. The list of available medications grew, but many were accompanied by serious toxic reactions which limited their usefulness. By 1973 there were four primary drugs (of first-rank value) available and seven secondary drugs (of lesser value for occasional use only), and the results of treatment were truly impressive. The mortality has dropped steadily since 1950. The first-rank drugs are isoniazid, ethambutol (EMB), rifampin (RMP), and streptomycin. These are usually used two or occasionally three at a time. There are ten other drugs with moderate to minimal value that can be used in exceptional circumstances.

The effectiveness of these medications has made it possible to shorten the hospital stay for many patients to as low as one to four months. In consequence, the prescription for many patients is a short-term stay in tuberculosis units located in general hospitals, rather than prolonged care in specialized tuberculosis institutions. Prolonged courses of medication have replaced the years of hospital care or bed rest. The elements of success in treatment are a knowledgeable physician familiar with tuberculosis management and other medical problems which the patient may have; availability of the necessary chemotherapy; and a patient who is willing to listen to the educational efforts of the physician and capable of following through on the recuperative program.

New Methods of Tuberculosis Case-Finding

Once the fact that tuberculosis is a communicable disease rather than an inherited illness was accepted, the value of contact examinations was increasingly appreciated. With the discovery of tuberculin in 1890 by Koch, a diagnostic tool for screening became available. The further discovery of x-rays by W. K. Roentgen in 1895 started a cycle of genuine progress in the case-finding effort. However, the x-ray film remained expensive and time-consuming until the introduction of the miniature chest film (photoroentgenography), which became a practical tool 1935–1940. It was destined to be used to screen 20 million persons in the United States armed forces between 1941 and 1944. By 1950 more than fifty mobile x-ray units were screening the civilian population, and surveys of the entire adult population of cities as large as Los Angeles were being undertaken.

The advent of steadily improving treatment of tuberculosis, with its reduction in the number of sanatorium patients, plus the wide coverage with chest surveys combined to create several results: (1) a slowdown in the establishing of new sanatorium beds, starting in 1950 and reaching a virtual standstill by 1960; (2) a reduction in the number of patients occupying sanatorium beds so that efforts were begun to discontinue the smaller sanatoriums with inadequate medical programs, or those with poor location far from urban centers; and (3) a steady diminishing of the need for rehabilitation programs. Patients could look forward to a return to former jobs in ever increasing numbers. By 1970 the need for rehabilitation service was only a small fraction of the experience of twenty years earlier— only the unusual patient was programmed for it at all.

Another change took place in the composition of the patient population in the sanitoriums. Earlier, when sanatorium beds were in short supply, no great effort was made in most states to try to manage the recalcitrant patient. The person who did not cooperate with institutional regulations (becoming intoxicated on the premises or leaving the institution without permission were the commonest problems) was often allowed to circulate in the community, possibly to spread the disease. The advent of the miniature chest film made it possible to do low-cost screening of persons being booked in jails and prisons. As the patient load began to fall in sanatoriums, together with x-ray surveys of jails and "skid row" populations, the ratio of alcoholic patients in the sanatoriums began to rise, From a pre–World War II level of an estimated 5 percent, the ratio rose to 35 percent, then to nearly 50 percent, and in a very few institutions as high as 65 percent. The problem of rehabilitation was proportionally a tremendous one, but slanted largely toward treatment of the alcoholism. It was observed that treatment of the patient's tuberculosis often became relatively routine, but treatment of the alcoholism often was very difficult, if not impossible. Obligatory quarantine was required by many health officers but remained legally controversial, although it was successfully employed in many urban centers. With the discontinuation of many tuberculosis sanatoriums in urban centers, procedures were developed for chemotherapy of alcoholic tuberculous patients while they remained in their own milieu. The long-range results may require another five to ten years for adequate evaluation.

This section has reviewed the highlights of the tuberculosis problem, with particular reference to the United States. The heyday of the tuberculosis sanatorium was in the period 1930–1960, and it was during those years that the maximum effort in rehabilitation training took place. As medical treatment improved during

1950–1965, the need for rehabilitation training declined markedly until it is now an unusual patient who requires it at all. The complete eradication of tuberculosis is still a hope for the distant future, but it is reasonable to conclude that further diminution of the problem will steadily take place. There may be a great deal to celebrate in 1982, the centennial of Robert Koch's discovery of the tubercle bacillus.

B. Chronic Obstructive Pulmonary Disease

JONATHAN H. OSTROW, M.D., Clinical Associate Professor of Medicine, University of Washington School of Medicine, Seattle

The term "chronic obstructive pulmonary disease" (COPD) encompasses several related disorders that share a common functional defect, the inability to expire air completely and rapidly from the lungs.

Types of Disease

The major types of chronic obstructive pulmonary disease include emphysema, chronic bronchitis, and chronic bronchial asthma.

Emphysema is defined as an anatomic alteration of the lung, characterized by an abnormal enlargement of the air spaces (alveoli) beyond the smallest conducting lung airways (terminal nonrespiratory bronchioles), accompanied by destructive changes of the air space (alveolar) walls. Matthew Baillie, an English anatomist, included a plate showing lung emphysema in his textbook in 1812, and the great French physician R. T. H. Laënnec, the inventor of the stethoscope, provided an accurate description of the clinical syndrome of emphysema in his text *A Treatise on the Diseases of the Chest and on Mediate Auscultation* as early as 1830. Thus, emphysema has been a medically recognized condition for about 150 years.

Chronic bronchitis is a clinical disorder characterized by excessive mucous secretion in the bronchial tree and manifested by chronic or recurrent productive cough, present on most days for a minimum of three months in each year for at least two successive years. Whereas emphysema is defined primarily by the anatomic appearance of the diseased lung, chronic bronchitis is defined in terms of the symptoms of chronic cough and sputum (phlegm) production. In emphysema, the visual abnormalities include overdistention of the small terminal air spaces in the lung (alveoli), accompanied by actual destruction of the terminal air space walls; in chronic bronchitis, the major abnormalities are located within the airways themselves rather than in the terminal air spaces, and consist of mucous gland enlargement, excessive secretion of mucus, scar tissue formation adjacent to the smaller airways, and a tendency for the smallest airways to collapse prematurely during the act of forcing air out of the lungs (expiration). Although the anatomic findings differ, these two conditions frequently share a common course, that is, steadily worsening breathlessness eventually leading to major disability.

A careful study of these two major types of chronic airway obstruction has led to descriptions of two types of sufferers. The person with emphysema has been called a Type A or Type PP (for "pink puffer") individual, characterized by an anxious expression, thin and barrel-chested rib cage, exaggerated use of neck, chest, and abdominal muscles while attempting to breathe, a tendency toward weight loss as the disease progresses, steadily progressive breathlessness (dyspnea) with scanty cough or sputum production, and a tendency for skin color or complexion to remain pink until the final stages of the illness. In contrast, the patient with chronic bronchitis may look deceptively healthy, except for a tendency to purplish or bluish discoloration of the lips and fingernails (cyanosis) and a daily hacking cough, resulting in constant spitting up of phlegm, most frequently upon arising in the morning. This individual, called Type B or Type BB (for "blue bloater"), may appear quite healthy until a cold or flulike illness develops, resulting in rapidly worsening breathlessness, blue lips and nailbeds, and a tendency to collect excessive amounts of fluid in the body (edema). Measurement of pulmonary function may show similar degrees of obstruction to outflow of air during respiration in Type A and Type B individuals, thus justifying the overlapping term "chronic obstructive pulmonary disease" for these two rather different clinical types.

Asthma, also known as asthmatic bronchitis, is another closely related obstructive airway disease. Asthma is a disease characterized by increased responsiveness of the major airways (trachea and bronchi) to various stimuli and is manifested by widespread narrowing of the airways that varies in severity, either spontaneously or as a result of treatment. The main differences between asthma and the other chronic obstructive pulmonary diseases is the potential for reversibility and, therefore, the tendency for the disease to wax and wane (exacerbations and remissions) in response to inhalation of specific substances (allergens), such as feathers, house dust, pollens, cat hair, or molds; to respiratory infection; or to other, unspecified stimuli, including psychological factors. Typical allergic (extrinsic) asthma begins in childhood or young adulthood, is characterized by wide fluctuations in symptoms (wheezing, breathlessness, and cough), and a potential for complete reversibility with removal of the noxious stimuli or vigorous medical treatment. Although less prevalent as a major cause of disability in adults than emphysema or chronic bronchitis, chronic bronchial asthma may sometimes result in severe pulmonary disability characterized by the need for constant daily medication, allergy shots (hyposensitization), inability to work in certain dusty or fume-ridden occupational environments and, rarely, the necessity for a geographic change in residence.

What emphysema, chronic bronchitis, and chronic bronchial asthma have in common is chronicity, the ability to render a suffering individual disabled as a result of severe breathlessness, cough, or wheezing and, unless detected early and treated vigorously, a tendency for gradual worsening (progression) of disability.

Incidence

Although emphysema has been described for 150 years and chronic bronchitis has been recognized in England as a clinical entity since before the turn of the century, only for the past few decades have the obstructive pulmonary syndromes been recognized as a major cause of disability. In part, this is due to the widespread popularity of cigarette smoking during the twentieth century, the health consequences of which were eventually revealed in the U.S. Surgeon General's reports. However, it is likely that the rising reported incidence of emphysema and chronic bronchitis is also due to increased recognition of the obstructive pulmonary disorders by physicians and the general public, as a result of major educational campaigns conducted by the U.S. Public Health Service and voluntary health associations.

It is estimated that 2 million Americans are known to have chronic obstructive pulmonary disease, whereas the actual prevalence may be as high as 6 to 9 percent of the population over age thirty, based upon screening pulmonary function testing done on recent samples of the United States adult population. Thus, it has been estimated that as many as 14 to 15 million Americans now have chronic obstructive airway disease, with clinical recognition in only about one person in seven. As of the late 1960s, the reported annual death rate from chronic obstructive pulmonary disease was increasing by about 20 percent yearly. Emphysema and chronic bronchitis make up the third largest specific cause of federal and state worker disability, ranking only behind musculoskeletal disorders and coronary (arteriosclerotic) heart disease. Thus, for example, in 1967, of 310,947 workers granted Social Security disability allowances, 19,227 were considered disabled with emphysema.

Degree of Severity

The stages of severity are based upon the usual progression of physiologic abnormalities that occur as lung destruction or airway obstruction progressively worsens. During the first, or asymptomatic, stage, anatomic changes of early emphysema may be present in the lung with no symptoms, no abnormalities upon physical examination, and no laboratory, x-ray, or pulmonary function abnormalities. In the second, or ventilatory, stage, patients have one or more of the following: cough; sputum; wheezing, especially upon exertion or with respiratory infection; breathlessness; and chronic fatigue. Usually, medical examination will reveal evidence of lung overinflation, resulting in a barrellike appearance of the chest, decreased breath sounds as heard through the stethoscope, a slowing of outward air movement (expiration), and the presence of abnormal lung wheezes and mucus rattling (rhonchi). Overdistended lungs may then also be recognized on the chest x-ray, and pulmonary function testing, by means of the forced expiratory spirograph, will reveal a diminished expiratory flow rate of air as the patient attempts to forcefully empty the lungs.

During the third, or hypoxemic, stage, the above symptoms may also be augmented by weight loss, loss of appetite, and weakness; and the medical examination, in addition to showing lung hyperinflation and wheezing, may also reveal bluish discoloration of the lips and finger nailbeds (cyanosis). The blood count may show abnormal overproduction of red blood cells (polycythemia), which is a compensatory response to low blood oxygen values. In the hypoxemic stage of severity, the ability of the lungs to extract oxygen from air has worsened so that the oxygen content of the arterial blood leaving the lungs begins to fall, which can be measured directly in the laboratory (arterial blood gas determination).

During the fourth, or hypercarbic, stage of severity, the carbon dioxide content of the blood begins to rise, due to further deterioration of gas exchange in the lungs, which now prevents full elimination of carbon dioxide gas by the lungs. As the dissolved carbon dioxide gradually increases in the blood and tissues, irritability, somnolence, and impairment of attention and mental concentration may occur which, when extreme, may progress to stupor and coma. The presence of hypercarbia is also confirmed by direct laboratory measurement of the arterial carbon dioxide tension.

The fifth, or final, stage of severity is reached when lung function has deteriorated to the point where "emphysema heart disease" (cor pulmonale) occurs. This is mainly manifested by weight gain and leg swelling; an enlarged, tender liver; and certain findings on physical examination, confirmed by electrocardiography, of strain to the right side of the heart, which may also be detected by enlargement of the heart shadow on the standard chest x-ray. By the time this fifth stage of pulmonary emphysema is reached, marked abnormalities of ventilatory function, as detected on the expiratory spirogram, and gas exchange in the lung, as detected by the arterial gas measurements of oxygen and carbon dioxide tension, have occurred.

Causes

The exact causes of chronic obstructive pulmonary disease are not known. Rarely, the disorder may be hereditary. Recently, a certain small percentage of all patients with chronic obstructive pulmonary disease have been found lacking in a specific enzyme (alpha-1 antitrypsin), which may allow certain other destructive (proteolytic) enzymes to cause premature disruption of walls of the smaller lung air sacs (alveoli). However, this specific abnormality is present in only a small minority of all patients with chronic obstructive pulmonary disease.

Most authorities agree that the main causal factor is heavy and prolonged cigarette smoking, which may result in either emphysema or chronic bronchitis, although the exact nature of the harmful ingredients in cigarette smoke remains to be determined. It has also been hypothesized that various air pollutants in urban industrial settings may be contributing to the gradual rise in morbidity and mortality from chronic pulmonary disease during the twentieth century; and certainly, excessive mortality has been observed among patients with known chronic obstructive pulmonary disease during periods of extreme smog or air pollution, particularly in highly urbanized areas, such as Los Angeles, Tokyo, and London. However, the exact relationship of chronic low-level air pollution to chronic obstructive pulmonary disease remains unknown.

Prevention

Prevention of chronic obstructive pulmonary disease is mainly directed at cessation of cigarette smoking. To be most effective, nonsmoking should begin long before the symptoms of obstructive lung disease occur, hence the great emphasis placed upon anti-smoking campaigns directed at children and young adults. Many people feel that the recent ecologic interest in environmental pollution and its control may also lead to a gradual reduction in chronic obstructive pulmonary disease in the future.

Symptoms, Diagnosis, and Effects (Warning Signs)

The main symptoms of chronic obstructive pulmonary disease are chronic cough; wheezing, particularly upon exertion or during periods of respiratory infection; and breathlessness, either constant or episodic. Those patients with chronic bronchitis (Type B) characteristically raise phlegm daily, in association with the chronic cough. The phlegm may be clear and mucoid in appearance most of the time, but becomes yellow or green during periods of respiratory infection, which characteristically causes the cough, wheezing, and breathlessness to worsen. Wheezing, particularly during exertion or with infection, is common in the chronic obstructive pulmonary syndrome, and is usually recognized by patients as the dry, high-pitched, rasping sounds made during attempts to empty the lungs. Observant patients can usually pinpoint the difficulty as inability to empty the lungs rather than to fill them.

Breathlessness is another major symptom. The degree of breathlessness may vary, particularly in those individuals with bronchial asthma, but also in those patients with emphysema and chronic bronchitis, where breathlessness may be markedly worsened during periods of respiratory infection. In the earlier stages of emphysema, it is frequently helpful to grade the degree of breathlessness

Standard Classification of Grading Breathlessness

Grade	Description
1	Can keep pace walking with person of same age and body build without breathlessness on level ground, but not on hills or stairs
2	Can walk a mile at own pace without dyspnea, but cannot keep pace with a normal person on level ground
3	Becomes breathless after walking about 100 yards (92 meters), or for a few minutes on level ground
4	Becomes breathless while dressing or talking

present to establish the degree of functional disability caused by the airway obstruction (see the table).

As a general rule, by the time that grade 3 or grade 4 breathlessness has appeared, individuals are unable to successfully perform physical activities that require moderate to vigorous physical exertion at a normal pace. Walking rapidly against a grade, climbing stairs, heavy or sustained lifting, or similar activities may result in extreme breathlessness accompanied by lightheadedness, weakness, sweating, and rapid pulse, requiring the affected individual to halt all physical activity for several minutes, until able to catch his or her breath. In addition to the primary symptoms of cough, sputum production, wheezing, and breathlessness, as the disease worsens, chronic fatigue, weakness, weight loss, loss of appetite, disturbance of normal sleep patterns, and mental irritability may occur; and the appearance of these symptoms is used to grade the advancing severity of the disease. Once emphysema reaches the fourth or fifth stage, the sufferer may experience so much disruption of powers of concentration, attention span, and memory as to seriously limit rehabilitation goals. In addition, many patients with advanced obstructive pulmonary disease become severely depressed as they realize the full impact of their disability.

Treatment

Treatment of chronic obstructive pulmonary disease utilizes a comprehensive approach aimed at educating the patient as to the nature of the disease, lessening the degree of airway obstruction, and ceasing cigarette smoking; treating intercurrent respiratory infections; improving general body conditioning, combating depression, and providing the severely affected individual with certain home devices such as supplemental oxygen and positive pressure breathing (IPPB) machines. For many patients, treatment and initial rehabilitation begin in the hospital where the sufferer arrives seriously ill as a result of a flare-up of the condition during a bout of respiratory infection. Other individuals first seek care in their own physicians' offices because of persistent cough end awareness of worsening breathlessness. Still others come to medical attention when they seek help in stopping cigarette smoking or when attending "breathing classes" conducted by local health departments or voluntary health organizations.

The usual comprehensive treatment program includes patient education in the relationship of cigarette smoking to emphysema and chronic bronchitis, the importance of seeking early treatment of respiratory infection, and the usefulness of certain controlled breathing techniques to move air in and out of the lungs more effectively. The patient is taught to avoid airway irritants such as tobacco smoke, air of low temperature and low humidity, air containing specific allergic substances, or air high in irritating dust, vapor, or fume content.

Next, patients are instructed to use various medications which help to reverse that portion of the airway obstruction due to spasm of the muscles surrounding the medium and smaller airways (bronchospasm) and to help thin and liquefy sputum. If phlegm production is voluminous, the patient is taught various postural positions to encourage the drainage of phlegm by gravity (postural drainage). Certain chest physiotherapy techniques, such as percussion (clapping, cupping, and vibration) of the chest wall during postural drainage will require the aid of another person, such as a visiting nurse or, ideally, a household member.

Patients are often given home supplies of "broad spectrum" antibiotics such as ampicillin or tetracycline and urged to take them whenever they have an upper respiratory infection or produce discolored (yellow or green) sputum. Sometimes patients are instructed to take antibiotics regularly, perhaps two weeks out of every four, or continuously during the winter months, when the hazard from respiratory infections seems greater in many communities.

For asthmatic individuals, and a minority of those with chronic bronchitis and emphysema, certain anti-inflammatory medications, notably the "corticosteroids" such as prednisone, may provide significant relief of wheezing (bronchospasm) and may also help to decrease sputum volume and improve a sense of well-being. However, the cortisonelike medicines have side effects in high doses and are not generally recommended for the average patient with emphysema or chronic bronchitis, unless asthma, uncontrolled by other means, is also present.

Frequently, sufferers in the more advanced stages of chronic obstructive pulmonary disease have regressed to a self-imposed life of invalidism, particularly if they have been misadvised by friends, relatives, or even their medical practitioners that they should avoid all physical activity and stay at home. For these unfortunate individuals, a major goal of treatment is the resumption of physical activity within their capability, such as daily walking on level surfaces or indoor exercises using a stationary bicycle, rowing machine, or treadmill.

If the disease has already progressed to low blood oxygen (hypoxemia), carbon dioxide retention (hypercarbia), and emphysema heart disease (cor pulmonale), then treatment is often augmented by giving supplemental oxygen therapy, either continuously or during periods of exercise, and by using IPPB machines. These may aid in providing more complete lung expansion, are effective methods of administering bronchodilator medications (aerosol therapy), and may help to decrease the actual work of breathing for the sufferer who now must devote a considerable proportion of energy expenditure to the act of breathing itself.

Ideally, when all possible treatment modalities are being used, arrangements have been made for follow-up care in the home by visiting nurses or respiratory therapists, family members have been educated in the nature of the disease, and the sufferer's other medical problems attended to, then the depression lifts and new methods of adjustment are learned that enhance self-image, increase independence, and allow the person to reachieve a level of improved financial security. Unfortunately, in spite of such comprehensive treatment programs, the chronic airway obstruction tends to slowly progress, as measured by deteriorating pulmonary function testing. However, in spite of inability to reverse the underlying disease process, the outlook for many patients in comprehensive treatment programs is markedly improved, due to increased exercise tolerance, improved self-care, reduced anxiety and depression, and treatment of medical complications, the most common of which is respiratory infection. The results of vigorous treatment can be measured in diminished need for hospitalization and may result in longer-term survival. Thus, although the disease itself may not be curable, many patients have less symptoms with therapy and are able to lead more independent and productive lives at home, while avoiding repeated and expensive hospitalizations.

A complete treatment program for the patient with chronic obstructive pulmonary disease implies utilization of services extending beyond the private physician's office. Patient education may be enhanced by antismoking campaigns and breathing classes provided at the community level under the sponsorship of state and local Lung Association offices, hospitals, and local health departments. In many communities, the health departments, which have long been active in the respiratory disease field because of prior experience with tuberculosis, also provide emphysema clinics, which offer comprehensive care for those sufferers whose financial situation precludes care by the private sector or where physicians knowledgeable in the care of emphysema and chronic bronchitis may be in short supply. Medical schools and larger private hospitals may become involved in care for the emphysema or chronic bronchitis patient by providing the initial specialized inpatient care needed by the more seriously ill, usually in "respiratory intensive care units," and also by developing a full spectrum of services such as social service consultation, respiratory therapy and chest physiotherapy instruction, and patient education classes, as the patients progress from the hospital to the home stage of care. State and local health departments may also be key providers of certain home therapy needs, specifically, home oxygen and IPPB machines, the high cost of which may be beyond the means of sufferers without some form of third-party medical support.

Rehabilitation

Vocational rehabilitation goals must be highly individualized, recognizing that many patients with chronic obstructive pulmonary disease do not become enrolled in rehabilitation programs until the disease is advanced, the sufferer is past the "vocational prime" age, and reversibility of the physical handicap is minimal.

Ideally, if the disease is detected early and if the patient ceases cigarette smoking, controls weight, and takes medication to reduce bronchospasm and treat infection promptly, the degree of cough, wheeze, sputum production, and exertional breathlessness may be markedly reduced, permitting the return to former level of physical work and former job.

The next most acceptable vocational goal is relocation of the patient-employee to another work area within the same general occupational field or within the same employer organization. Thus, "dusty trade" construction workers, welders, miners, or similar employees with chronic obstructive pulmonary disease (or a related occupational condition, such as black lung disease) might, by means of enlightened personnel policies, be reassigned to certain dust- and fume-free jobs not requiring strenuous physical activity. Such a policy would enable them to remain gainfully employed in the same industry or for the same employer, but at a job more suited to their physical capabilities.

A further vocational goal would be to encourage the redevelopment of previous avocational skills or hobbies that might provide at least partial financial support for the severely incapacitated emphysema or chronic bronchitis patient. There are a number of skilled and semiskilled activities that may be performed in the office or home which, if in demand by the community, can provide a source of income for patients even with advanced disease.

Formal job retraining and reemployment in another, related field may prove most helpful when the prior work conditions include exposure to dusty or fume-ridden environments which markedly worsen the patient's symptoms. Sometimes the undesirable work conditions may be obvious, such as in the case of an allergic asthmatic who works in a sportswear factory and cannot avoid exposure to goose down feathers, which cause asthmatic attacks. However, many patients with chronic obstructive pulmonary disease find that "nonspecific" dusty or fume-ridden environments likewise cause worsening cough, sputum production, and exertional breathlessness; hence, workers in certain "dirty" occupations such as welding may markedly benefit by retraining or relocation in a "clean air" occupation. A difficulty for many individuals may be a lack of previous educational skills and vocational experience, further compounded by the fact that they often become aware of disabling obstructive pulmonary disease rather late in life, usually in their fifties and early sixties, at a time when comprehensive job retraining may prove unrealistic. If the sufferer has no prior potential educational or vocational talents or experience to fall back upon and if no sheltered workshop program with clean air exists, then the vocational rehabilitation goal may become a maximal level of self-care at home, utilizing existing community resources such as visiting nurse associations, outreach programs from local health departments or medical institutions, and enrollment in an appropriate disability program for financial support.

Long-Range Goals

With the increasing interest in the environment, various organizations sponsor such activities as clean air coalitions and nonsmokers' rights organizations which are mainly concerned with effective lobbying to enforce or implement new laws regarding atmospheric pollution, regulation of cigarette smoking in public places, etc.

Appliances, Devices, and Aids

These consist mainly of IPPB machines, hand-held or compressor-type aerosol nebulizers, and home oxygen therapy. Local information as to availability of these devices can be obtained directly from medical equipment rental agencies; through voluntary agencies such as the American Lung Association and its local affiliates; from state and local health departments, particularly chronic disease and vocational rehabilitation sections; or from local "chest clinics" operated by health departments in conjunction with tuberculosis control programs.

Research and Recent Projects

A variety of research programs are constantly investigating various genetic and environmental factors related to chronic obstructive pulmonary disease, its early detection, and the effects of various treatment modalities. However, overall progress has been slow, and at the moment the most effective derived information is the strong relationship between cigarette smoking and the development of chronic obstructive pulmonary disease; thus, antismoking goals appear to be the most effective method of prevention at this time.

Organizations and Government Assistance

The main voluntary organization concerned with chronic respiratory disease is the American Lung Association (1740 Broadway, New York, NY 10019), which sponsors a wide variety of national, state, and local programs related to patient education, antismoking, upgrading of physician and community standards for the care of patients with chronic lung problems, and the support of respiratory disease research and training of chest-oriented physicians. The American Lung Association was founded in 1973 as the successor to the National Tuberculosis Association, which dates back to the turn of the century and is still well known as the "Christmas Seal organization."

Emphysema Anonymous is a service, educational, and mutual assistance organization with headquarters at Fort Myers, FL 33902.

Government assistance in research directed toward respiratory disease programs is centered in the National Heart, Lung and Blood Institute, a branch of the U.S. Public Health Service located in Bethesda, Maryland. Additional governmental training grants for support of medical school respiratory disease teaching programs are also available through the National Institutes of Health, also a major branch of the Public Health Service.

SELECTED REFERENCES

FOR PHYSICIANS AND RELATED HEALTH PROFESSIONALS

Asthma: A Practical Guide for Physicians, American Lung Association, 1740 Broadway, New York, NY 10019.

Chronic Obstructive Pulmonary Disease: A Manual for Physicians, National Tuberculosis and Respiratory Disease Association (since 1973, American Lung Association), 1740 Broadway, New York, NY 10019.

"Chronic Respiratory Diseases," *Medical Clinicians of North America* (Benjamin Burrows, ed.), vol. 57, no. 3, May 1973.

"Definitions and Classification of Chronic Bronchitis, Asthma, and Pulmonary Emphysema: A Statement by the American Thoracic Society," *American Review of Respiratory Diseases*, vol. 85, no. 5, May 1962.

The Health Consequences of Smoking, U.S. Department of Health, Education and Welfare, Public Health Service Publication no. 1696, Superintendent of Documents, Government Printing Office, Washington, DC 20402, 1968.

"Modern Management of Respiratory Disease," *Medical Clinicians of North America* (William M. M. Kirby, ed.), vol. 51, no. 2, March 1967.

"Rehabilitation of the Pulmonary Cripple," *Chest* (Thomas L. Petty, ed.), vol. 60, no. 2, supplement, August 1971.

FOR PATIENTS AND FAMILIES

Emphysema: The Battle to Breathe, Public Health Service Publication no. 1715, Superintendent of Documents, Government Printing Office, Washington, DC 20402.

The Facts about Your Lungs, and pamphlets on asthma, chronic bronchitis, emphysema, and cigarette smoking, available without charge through state and local affiliates of the American Lung Association (headquarters, 1740 Broadway, New York, NY 10019).

Haas, Albert, *Essentials of Living with Pulmonary Emphysema: A Guide for Patients and Their Families*, Patient Publication no. 4, Institute of Physical Medicine and Rehabilitation, New York University Medical Center, 400 E. 34th St., New York, New York.

If You Have Emphysema or Chronic Bronchitis, Public Health Service Publication no. 1726, Superintendent of Documents, Government Printing Office, Washington, DC 20402.

Petty, Thomas L., and Louise M. Nett, *For Those Who Live and Breathe with Emphysema and Chronic Bronchitis*, Charles C. Thomas, Springfield, Illinois, 1967.

49

Speech and Language Disorders

LOIS KRIEGMAN, M.A., Cofounder, Kriegman Clinic,
Richmond, Virginia

The significance of speech and language disorders can hardly be overestimated. Through vocal communication and its integration with gesture, facial expression, and general body movement, we express our feelings and ideas, make known our wants, and maintain our interpersonal relationships. The ability to communicate also contributes to the development of personality and to participation as a functioning member of society. In contrast, defective speech or language ability interposes a barrier between the self and others, generates feelings of self-consciousness and inadequacy, frustrates self-expression, and makes it difficult to achieve vocational goals. Therefore, when communication defects persist without correction or compensation, they can be appropriately classed as disabilities or handicaps, for they greatly limit the individual's ability to meet basic demands of life.

Speech and Language Development: Normal and Abnormal

The development of normal speech is dependent on a complex and exquisite synchronization of many mechanisms. A large number of structural components, such as the lungs, palate, vocal cords, and speech muscles, must be present and in good working order; but it is not always recognized that the "primitive" processes of breathing, sucking, chewing, swallowing, and crying also prepare the way for speech production. Prior to making intelligible sounds the child must, in addition, be able to oppose the tongue to the hard and soft palate and to the upper and lower lips. If any of these functional steps are lacking, due to structural defect or inadequate cerebral control, the capacity to develop normal speech will be seriously compromised.

In addition, if speech is to develop normally, the organs of hearing, neural auditory pathways, and auditory areas of the brain must also be intact. Just as important is the intellectual and perceptual apparatus. A mentally retarded child will have a limited capacity to develop the understanding, memory, and other cognitive processes required for learning the names of objects and the meanings of words used in speech. Likewise the child with a perceptual or other learning disability due to brain damage or dysfunction will have great difficulty learning to communicate, since the data received from the world will be distorted and many of the concepts required for verbal expression will be faulty or nonexistent.

Finally, a healthy social and emotional life is a prerequisite to normal speech and language development. The child who is in stimulating contact with both adults and peers will not only learn words from them, but will be motivated to communicate wishes and ideas. And if experiences at home and outside are basically enjoyable and satisfying, the child will have the emotional security to express feelings and needs in words. On the other hand, the child who is deprived of social contact or who is brought up in a cold or tense environment will almost inevitably withdraw from others and be unable to establish the human relationships required for normal speech development.

General Etiology of Speech and Language Disorders

The causes of communication disorders fall into two general categories: organic and functional. Deafness, aphasia, cerebral palsy, cleft lip, and cleft palate are among the most common organic factors involved in multiple speech and language disorders. In their milder forms, speech may be normal or only slightly affected, but the more extreme forms produce severe and complex disturbances. It is also important to recognize that age of onset, specific type of disorder, the individual's mental ability and flexibility, and the quality of family life and early influences all contribute to the severity of the communication problem and the readiness to respond to treatment.

A wide variety of factors also contribute to the development and persistence of functional speech disorders. Among the most important are emotional tension, parental pressure, anxiety, and unconscious conflict. Less widely recognized is selective inattention—that is, the tendency not to listen to the speech of other people and to one's own vocalizations. Learning to speak requires collaboration with others and concentration on what they are saying. Nonfluency (as in stuttering), abnormal voice patterns, misarticulation, and in fact any speech and language disturbance may therefore be due in large part to a degree of noncollaboration or nonlistening, and these conditions will go uncorrected unless direct steps are taken to alert the individual to the essential role of listening in speech, voice and language development, and correction. The non-collaborative speech-disabled individual may need to become aware of the fear of being found at fault, feelings of discouragement and, at times, of resistance that perpetuate the problem. In some cases the lack of collaboration brings secondary gains in the form of negative attention from parents and others. This reinforces the speech disorder, and the individual may choose to continue faulty speaking despite all efforts at correction.

Incidence

All speech and language disorders fall into four major categories: articulation, time (or rhythm), voice, and symbolization (language). A single individual may show symptoms of one or more of these problems. In general, the incidence of speech disorders in the school population has been estimated at about 10 percent. From kindergarten through the fourth grade roughly 12 to 15 percent of the children have seriously defective speech, while above the age of fourteen the incidence is estimated at 4 to 5 percent. There has been no report on the extent of additional language disorders such as those involving symbolization, although it is recognized that many learning disabilities in children are associated with disorders of communication. These disorders may become manifest in a child's inability to read, listen, or write, as well as in vocal communication, and may be responsible for grade failure and occupational difficulties as well as social and emotional adjustment problems of the child. The incidence of speech disorders in adults has been estimated at 4 to 5 percent. (See CHAPTER 37: LEARNING DISABILITIES.)

TYPES OF DISORDER

There may be disorders of (1) articulation, (2) time and rhythm, (3) voice, or (4) language usage.

Disorders of Articulation

These are characterized by the substitution, omission, addition, or distortion of speech sounds. They range from mild misarticulation through various degrees of severity to complete unintelligibility. Articulatory disorders are regarded as primarily functional when no apparent organic or physiological cause can be discovered. This diagnosis is made when there is no evidence of abnormality of the nervous system, mental functioning, or physical development of the speech organs, or when a former abnormal condition has been corrected which might have been associated with the disorder. L. E. Travis found in 1957 that 75 to 80 percent of all speech defectives in the school population can be regarded as primarily suffering from functional articulation disorders. In regard to functional causes for misarticulation, the amount and kind of speech stimulation given a child and general management of the child's speech learning seem to be significant.

Articulatory disorders may also be primarily organic. In these cases it should be possible to demonstrate that the speech problem is associated with organic etiology, such as cleft palate, cerebral palsy, or other forms of brain damage. According to a report of the National Institute of Neurological and Communication Disorders and Stroke, articulatory defects caused by physiological conditions occur at a rate of 40 to 60 per 1,000 school children.

In the first grade 15 to 20 percent of children are likely to be described as having defective articulation. Estimates are unstable after the third grade, but all surveys indicate a predominance of males about two to one over females. In general there is a marked improvement in articulatory skills up to and through the fourth grade. It appears, however, that in the absence of speech therapy there is likely to be little improvement in articulation after the fourth grade.

It should be noted that all children produce some sounds defectively when first learning to talk. This is developmentally quite normal. Defective articulation up to the age of two is rarely considered a serious problem. By the age of three the child seldom has difficulty being understood outside the family, although there are still traces of infantile pronunciation in varying degrees. Substitution of sounds despite evidence of the ability to make them is common in three-year-olds. However, these children usually talk normally by the age of five or six. According to J. E. Bryant, a child is considered to have a speech problem if he or she is unable to say the following sounds at the ages listed:

Age	Sounds
3½	m, b, p, h, w
4½	k, g, i, d, n, ng, y
5½	f, v
6½	sh, zh, e, th voiced
7½	s, z, v, th voiceless, ch, j

The child of eight years of age is usually able to articulate without omissions, substitutions, additions, or distortion of sounds. The most common types of articulatory disorders after this age are described below.

A. *Misarticulation of specific speech sounds or groups of sounds.* This involves omissions, substitutions, distortions, or additions of speech sounds.

1. *Omissions.* The individual leaves out a speech sound at a place where it should occur, such as "tar" for "star," "cay" for "clay," and "baw" for "ball." Omissions are common in preschool and primary school children.

2. *Substitutions.* The individual substitutes one speech sound for another. The substituted sound is usually one that has been learned earlier. "Y" or "w" can be substituted for "l" or "r," such as

"yady" for "lady" or "Woy" for "Roy." Substitutions are also common in preschool and primary school children.

3. *Distortions.* A distortion is an inaccurate approximation which does not sound like the correct sound. It is impossible to record the characteristics of this type of misarticulation since there are no sound equivalents for the distortions used. These are relatively less frequent at early age levels, but tend to be the dominant type of misarticulation at later ages.

4. *Additions.* Sounds or entire syllables may be added to words, such as in the combination of substitutions and additions in "mowah" for "more" or "dowah" for "door." The addition of linking sounds as in "buhlue-guhreen" for "blue-green" or "spuhruce" for "spruce" frequently occurs.

B. *Oral inaccuracy.* There are some cases of articulatory disorder which show general rather than specific misarticulation. Some of these may be due to imprecise speech movements or slow, weak, and underenergized movements. At times this speech can be described as indistinct, but oral inaccuracy can be so severe that it is unintelligible.

As with all speech and language disorders in children, misarticulation and oral inaccuracy in the simple forms may be regarded at times as "cute" or relatively unimportant, while the most handicapping and unintelligible forms become complicated by misunderstandings and frustrations. Negative attention-getting in the form of misbehavior can ensue when a child cannot be understood due to unclear speech. Moreover, as with many undesirable and infantile behavior patterns, faulty articulation or baby talk can enable the child to dominate or exercise the power necessary to stand up to parents who insist on ego separation before the child is ready.

1. *Lisping.* Six sounds in English are classified as sibilant consonants and have in common some form of the *s* sound. They are *s, z, sh,* soft *j, ch,* and hard *j.* The misarticulation of one or more of these can occur as a result of faulty tongue adjustment or faulty auditory production, and in combination with various dental conditions. These misarticulations may begin when the teeth are irregular and usually seem to persist despite the visual and acoustic unpleasantness they create for the listener. Occasionally, organic deviations can be responsible for these misarticulations of specific sounds or groups of sounds.

2. *Lalling.* Characterized by sluggish and insufficiently energized tongue movements, lalling is a distortion of the sounds *l* and *r* primarily, although *t* and *d* can also be involved. In this disorder there can be functional as well as past or present organic causes. It is usually the case, however, that even after surgical modifications of the tongue, the child will need speech training to correct the speech disorder. Cerebral palsy, with its potential for interfering with innervation of tongue muscles, may also result in lalling.

C. *Delayed speech.* Closely related to infantile perseveration (baby talk) but a more complex and profound disorder, this condition usually goes along with little or no effort at speech until past two years of age, meager vocabulary, single-word communication instead of sentences or phrases, and heavy reliance on gestures and nonspeech vocalizations.

The causes of infantile perseveration and delayed speech range from deviations in intelligence to hearing disorders, perceptual interferences, and minimal brain dysfunction. Both are found in children with brain damage but may also occur when the purposes and style of the child are satisfied by such speech behavior. Faulty auditory concentration, resistance to the learning process, overwhelming separation anxiety, sensitivity, and instability may contribute as nonorganic causes. The stages of speech learning occur during a period of life when the child is being required to respond to inner and outer stimulation, and when mastery of motor skills, establishment of the self, and general ability to relinquish early sensations of power act as antagonists to the reception and internalization of the necessarily corrective and instructive process of learning to speak as others do. Sometimes these speech disorders are the result of imitation of others in the environment who are themselves affected by faulty speech production.

D. *Misarticulation of other sounds*. A careful study of the many sounds of English reveals that many of them can be grouped as to the formal process that normally occurs when they are produced. Occasionally, some dental, facial, bony, muscular, or soft tissue deformity of the oral cavity interferes with the movement of the organs of articulation and contributes to speech disorder. Notable among these are the conditions known as cleft palate and cleft lip. It has been estimated that 5,000 school children in the United States have defective speech caused by these conditions. Such deformities occur as a result of failures or disturbances of growth during prenatal development. Articulation errors and voice disorders (see below) are the two most significant problems associated with these deformities.

Cerebral palsy also produces misarticulation. It has been estimated that 65,000 school children in the United States have defective speech caused by this disorder, which is probably the largest group of paralytic articulatory cases. The problem stems from the profound effect of the brain injury on the speech musculature, so that many sounds may be misarticulated at times or consistently. This condition, as with clefts of the lip and palate, may produce multiple speech disorders.

Disorders of Time and Rhythm

In these disorders the timing of sounds and syllables and the prosodic patterns are so off the standard that speech is conspicuous, unpleasant, or unintelligible.

The most common disorder of rhythm is stuttering, the repetition and prolongation of syllables or sounds. It occurs at the rate of 6 to 10 per 1,000 school children, and in most cases has its onset in the preschool years, ages two to four. Ninety percent of stuttering occurs under the age of ten, but acute onset can occur at any age.

Most cases of stuttering are considered nonorganic (functional), but disorders of time and rhythm similar to the functional type occasionally accompany some physiological conditions. Usually the functional disorder can be distinguished by the selective manner in which it occurs — that is, there are almost always periods of fluency — whereas consistent speech disturbance plus other motor difficulty are usually demonstrable when the cause is organic.

As pointed out above, in the early stages of speech learning, almost all children produce some sounds defectively. Most instances of early childhood stuttering reflect a lack of concentration on the part of the child. Such lapses in concentration should become less frequent under normal conditions and by the time some mastery of speech and language has occurred. It is only when nonfluency persists beyond the learning stage, or when children begin to adopt avoidances and mechanisms to help themselves get started, that the tendency to stutter requires therapeutic intervention.

When stuttering goes untreated, it frequently develops from repetition or prolongation of sounds such as "a-a-a-I want cake" or "k-k-k-can I ride with you" to severe forms of blocking, facial tics, and body movements, as well as stuttering on every word, holding the breath, tremors, and other unpleasant behavior. The reaction of the listener may become an embarrassment to the stutterer, and withdrawal from and avoidance of social situations can strongly influence the nature of interpersonal experiences. Furthermore, the puzzling aspects of the occurrences and absences of stuttering may lead to mistaken hypotheses and unsuccessful efforts at self-correction, and well-meaning advice on the part of concerned friends, teachers, and family. "Stop and think before you speak" and "take a deep breath" are such directives. Efforts at control and general overconcern, as well as constant admonition to get more rest, refrain from excitement, or not to speak may undermine the child's self-confidence and naturalness in relating and communicating. The stutterer's self-image frequently incorporates these "special directives." Many individuals who stutter become enslaved by the disorder and may even become dominated by feelings of shame and guilt.

Frequently stuttering is intermittent, occurring only at times or under special conditions. Often individuals who stutter report that they have no trouble speaking when no one else is present. Choral speaking is also usually free of the speech disorder. Some individuals have been able to engage in theatricals and, when acting a role that has been memorized, they do not stutter. Some speakers read fluently but cannot speak without difficulty, and vice versa. There are no two people who stutter in exactly the same way. Rarely does the person who stutters decide to stop speaking. Frequently stutterers have a lot to say, and some have been early in certain aspects of their language development.

In adults, stuttering becomes even more complicated as a result of misconceptions, attempts to disguise, and secondary emotional reactions to the disorder. Adult stutterers complain about being restricted in their activities or excuse themselves from various activities. Sometimes these secondary reactions are mistaken for causes of the difficulty, and the true cause is overlooked. In many cases the adult stutterer is merely continuing a speech pattern which camouflaged earlier problems of identification, separation, and general communication. Occasionally one encounters an acute onset of stuttering which is purely functional, but traumatic emotional events cannot always be demonstrated to have preceded the outbreak.

Disorders of Voice

Defects of tone with regard to pitch, loudness, or quality can be organically or functionally caused. In the case of organic voice disorders, the symptom can lead to early identification of a physical disorder and the prevention of a more serious condition (see CHAPTER 36: LARYNGEAL CANCER).

Voice disorders seem to occur in approximately 1 percent of the total population. These individuals constitute between 5 and 15 percent of cases of defective speech.

A. *Disorders of pitch.* Pitch level refers to the general highness or lowness of the voice on the musical scale, and is directly related to the frequency of movement of the vocal cords located in the larynx. Heavier cords vibrate slowly and produce a low-pitched voice while the more elastic cords vibrate faster and produce a high pitch. Pitch level should be appropriate for age and sex. The disorders of pitch are of three types: too high; too low; and other deviations such as monotone, tremulousness, and idiosyncratic, irregular melody patterns.

While a high- or low-pitched voice does not interfere directly with communication, inappropriateness of pitch can suggest a lack of masculinity in males and a lack of femininity in females. The effects on self-image and sexual adjustment are often severe. Pitch abnormalities can be due to variations in the size of the larynx resulting from general structural retardation, characteristic familial body size, or endocrine disorder. Another cause of high-pitched voice is laryngeal web, which may be small enough not to interfere with breathing, yet large enough to interfere with normal voice production. This condition may be accompanied by hoarseness and vocal strain when the individual attempts to adjust to a lower pitch. Still another organic cause may be an abnormal approximation (bringing together) of the vocal cords. Growths anywhere on the vocal cords can also produce both pitch and quality voice disorders. Likewise, damage to the nerve supply of the larynx may cause paralysis and consequently low pitch. Tremulousness is sometimes associated with deterioration or injury to the central nervous system.

Anxiety and concomitant tension frequently give rise to vocal abuse, and when persistent may produce organic lesions in the vocal cords, which are ordinarily remarkably resistant to trauma. In an indirect way other functional factors can adversely affect pitch production. Among these are the conscious or unconscious control of voice pitch to enhance an individual's idealized self-image. For example, a boy or girl who unconsciously wishes to hold on to the dependent role of a child and delay the responsibilities of growing up may retain a childlike voice.

B. *Disorders of loudness.* The loudness of the voice depends primarily on air pressure. Adequate loudness is in part a matter of adequate breathing, particularly control over the outgoing air. As with pitch, the disorders of loudness are of three types: too loud; too soft; and other deviations and irregularities.

Voice disorders involving loudness are more often functional than organic in origin. Among the organic causes, hearing loss is especially common, but a weak voice may also be due to paralysis in the larynx or the muscles of respiration. As for functional causes, it is generally accepted that a high degree of emotionality or excitement goes hand in hand with loudness of voice, and sadness, restraint, apathy, and timidity are often associated with soft-spokenness. Some cultural groups are noted for louder voice production than others, and people who grow up in a noisy environment usually speak loudly. As with pitch disorders, severe vocal strain due to emotional stress or unconscious conflict may be a factor, producing tense and whisperlike labored speech. Psychologically based causes can be emotional need displacements or anxiety reactions and may in some cases be related to the individual's self-image or life-style. Frequently the anxious individual who is in conflict over self-identity may adopt a loud voice in an effort to cover up or appear self-confident and secure.

C. *Disorders of quality.* Quality of voice is determined both by vocal cord vibration and resonance. Voice quality may be clear, breathy, harsh, hoarse, or nasal. There can also be complete or near-complete absence of voice. Loss of voice, breathiness, hoarseness, and resonance problems can have multiple causes, organic and functional. Misuse and subsequent damage to the vocal cords, structural abnormalities, neuromuscular lesions, physical disease, and effects of drug therapy can cause disorders of voice quality. The most common and complex of these disorders are the following.

1. *Loss or absence of voice.* In this condition the vocal cords fail to vibrate properly, and the voice is reduced to a whisper and, in some cases, may be halting and arhythmic. The voiced portions of speech are usually of defective quality, either breathy or hoarse. This condition, when functionally caused, is more common in women than in men and occurs most often between the ages of eighteen and thirty-four.

The absence of vocal sound may occur when the cords cannot be approximated sufficiently to be set in motion by the air stream, or when they are not capable of vibrating even when approximated. Such a condition may be caused by paralysis, stiffening of the joint (or joints) of the larynx, or abnormal mass that prevents approximation of the cords. Far more frequently the cause is functional and may require extensive psychological exploration. As one example among many, the individual may be creating a defense against the invasion of conscious awareness by ego-threatening feelings. The isolation and withdrawal provided by the speech loss are regarded as a means of screening out experiences associated with guilt, fear, anxiety, or hostility.

2. *Breathy voice.* This disorder is characterized by an excessive output of airflow along with voice production. It is apt to suggest a lack of physical vitality. In this condition the vocal cords vibrate but are unable to hold back the air stream long enough for much increase in pressure. The resultant voice is therefore weak. The organic causes are similar to those producing voice loss, but one cord may be involved rather than two, and small growths may result in more restricted areas of pathology.

Sometimes generalized emotional tension is severe enough to hamper the operation of the vocal cords. In other cases breathiness serves in a defensive capacity against unacceptable feelings, or may be adopted for attention-getting purposes. Here the individual may unconsciously maintain faulty voice production to prevent unacceptable and destructive impulses from becoming known. Mood disturbances, feelings of weakness during convalescence, loneliness, worry, fears, and guilt may result in or promote persistent or recurring breathiness.

3. *Hoarseness.* Hoarseness is a combination of harsh (vocal strain) and breathy voice quality, due in some cases to improper pitch levels. Children who yell at the top of their voices on the playground commonly suffer chronic hoarseness. Baynes (1969) found that 7.1 percent of children exhibit this disorder, with the highest incidence among boys and in the first grade of school.

Hoarseness requires careful diagnosis to determine the presence or absence of organic causes. Some cases may be traced to disturbances on the surfaces and edges of the vocal cords due to excessive sticky mucus, relative flabbiness of one or both cords, or additions to the mass of the cord. Vocal strain caused by chronic laryngitis, general weakness or tiredness, as well as asthma, laryngeal web, or endocrine disorders, may also be responsible. Babies who are noticeably hoarse after excessive bouts of crying may develop chronic hoarseness throughout childhood. Occasionally the disorder appears as the first sign of tumor or other abnormal growth. More often it is caused by smoky, dusty, overdry or nonhumidified atmosphere or by excessive smoking.

Hoarseness can have functional causes as well. While the symbolic connection between the personality and the voice may be obscure, it is an accepted fact that anxiety can lead the voice to quality disorders. The conversion of emotional disturbance to a vocal symptom usually accomplishes some purpose which is rarely clear to the individual or others.

4. *Resonance voice problems.* Nasality and denasality are the

most common resonance disorders. These defects are related to the appropriate openness or closedness of the nasal passage. In the case of nasality there is failure of the proper closure, whereas in denasality there is an obstruction in the nasal passage. The latter is exhibited by normal speakers who are suffering from a severe head cold.

The air-filled cavities, varying somewhat in size, shape, and material composition, act as resonators for the human voice. The larynx, pharynx, and oral and nasal chambers, as well as the chest, affect the quality of resonance of the voice. Any interference with these resonators can cause a problem.

Openness or closedness of the nasal passage depends on velopharyngeal function, neuromuscular action, and the presence or absence of obstruction such as enlarged tonsils, polyps, deflected septum, or inflammation. Another organic cause is cleft lip or palate, a congenital deformity which can result in velopharyngeal inadequacy even when repaired in infancy. In this condition the two halves of the lip or of the hard and soft palates fail to fuse completely during the first three months of prenatal life.

Following the removal of the adenoids, the presence of a congenitally short palate may give rise to a nasal resonance disorder. Likewise in cases of cerebral palsy, of an isolated paralysis, or following bulbar poliomyelitis, the palate will be inactive and cause nasal speech. A temporary paralysis of the palate may occur after diphtheria; this may cause anxiety, which in turn may prolong the voice disorder. Organic causes of nasality cannot be completely described without reference to the nasality that may accompany congenital severe global hearing loss.

Finally, nasal speech can also be due to emotional disturbance, without any structural or neurological abnormality. In these cases it usually serves some obscure need gratification.

Disorders of Language Usage

These disorders are characterized by difficulty in comprehending speech or in expressing ideas through the medium of speech. While most of the recognized disorders of language have been identified with organic conditions, such as deafness, brain damage (as in traumatic aphasia or cerebral palsy), or mental retardation, there are a vast number of individuals who present functional disabilities of comprehension and expression. Mild or severe disorders may appear in any category. According to the National Institute of Neurological and Communication Disorders and Stroke, an estimated 600,000 adult Americans are affected with aphasia. Among deaf children, there is a 100 percent incidence of delayed speech development, in which language problems play a major part. Large numbers of children in the retarded category also demonstrate delay in speech development, including language. Childhood aphasia has been estimated at a maximum of 0.6 percent of the school population.

A. *Aphasia.* Aphasia is defined as the loss of symbolic formulation and expression due to brain lesion. Either the ability to speak or the ability to comprehend, or both, may be affected as a result of injury, disease, or maldevelopment of the brain. When the disorder occurs in adults, there are complex problems stemming from the way the individual copes with the effects of brain damage as well as the direct effects of the damage itself. Frequently there are secondary symptoms of mood disturbance, emotional instability, and efforts to compensate and cover up the disorder. The disturbed functions often have to do with intellectual and abstract meaning, while automatic memorizations and social gestural forms such as songs, numerical and letter sequences, and phrases such as "hello" and "how are you?" remain relatively intact. Likewise words spoken under the influence of strong emotion appear to escape the effects of the disorder. However, individuals with aphasia may have trouble understanding what they hear or read, or both (receptive impairment). On the expressive side, aphasia is often characterized by word-finding difficulty and errors and omissions in speaking or writing. The voice may also be affected; the aphasic person often talks without the "tonal color" normally provided by vocal inflections.

The brain lesions which cause aphasia may be due to head injury, tumors, cerebral vascular disorders, infectious diseases, or degenerative disorders. There may or may not be pervasive emotional side effects, but when they do occur they present a difficult challenge to the patient, family, and speech pathologist. Among these are a sense of abandonment and a loss of mutuality with others due to impairment of the ability to make oneself known and understood by others (D. W. Abse, 1972).

In children, aphasia appears to be caused by brain damage occurring either prenatally or at birth. When the damage occurs prior to birth, receptive aphasia frequently follows, while postnatal traumatic aphasia is more apt to interfere with linguistic expression and may not affect understanding and integration of language. Oxygen deprivation, Rh incompatibility, rubella, cerebral hemorrhage due to birth injury, and encephalopathic diseases such as meningitis and encephalitis are the most common causative factors.

In adults the most frequent causes of aphasia are strokes due to hardening of the arteries, blood clots which block off nourishment of the nerve cells in the brain, and cerebral hemorrhages. Other causes are brain inflammation, severe head injuries such as those occurring in automobile accidents, and brain surgery required because of tumors or gunshot wounds.

B. *Language disorders associated with deafness.* Since the basic language system in any human being is essentially auditory and oral in nature, it can readily be understood that deafness, particularly as it occurs prior to or during the stage of language learning, has a profound effect on symbolic activity and communication. The resourcefulness of deaf individuals is particularly on trial, since they must attempt to develop a personal style of comprehension, expression, and of self-communication. It is useful to recognize that individuals may have mild or severe hearing loss from birth, that a sudden or gradual onset of loss may occur during childhood, adulthood, or old age, and that there are different types of hearing disabilities. (See CHAPTER 33: HEARING DISORDERS.)

Deafness can be caused by some of the same conditions that produce general language disorder, such as a disease process, trauma, or congenital abnormality. Furthermore, the deafness can involve peripheral (conduction deafness) or central (neural deafness) disturbances. Congenital malformations, acquired lesions, otosclerosis (hardening of the ear mechanism), bone diseases, infections, birth trauma, physical trauma, and drug damage may affect areas critical for adequate hearing. Particularly as these disorders occur prenatally or in the early years of life, they cause sensory deprivation that may be irreversible. The educative process requires very special broadening for such individuals. Early diagnosis has an influence on the extent to which an individual with hearing loss stands to compensate for the inability to learn speech and language concepts through ordinary channels. In the process of concept formation, the absence of audible signs leaves gaps in the imagery and associative processes. Generalization of ideas, personal individuation and separation, and emotional life-style may become grossly affected. The full joy of sound and music will not be experienced, and self-identification may suffer. Furthermore, children who wear hearing aids sometimes react with inadequacy feelings and an exaggerated sense of helplessness. They may also feel ashamed and guilty and fear ridicule. And in the presence of prejudicial adults who tend to disbelieve the disability, they may develop unhealthy emotional attitudes and disturbances in interpersonal relationships due to faulty basic trust.

C. *Cerebral palsy.* This congenital disorder, due to damage to the motor region of the brain, involves speech and language defects of varying severity and complexity in over half of the cases. The language problem is not unlike that of other individuals, such as aphasia victims, who have undergone an insult to the brain. Not only speech but powers of abstraction and concept formation may be impaired. Cerebral palsy patients, therefore, require a multiple approach in terms of language, speech production, and a combination of phonation, articulation, resonance, and rhythm.

While physiological problems usually take priority in the approach to this disorder, the individual's self-image, sense of security, interpersonal relationships, and general attitude toward life are bound to be affected when communication difficulties are experienced. Moreover, a secondary thought and language disturbance can evolve out of the emotional distresses associated with this disability. In spite of these problems, many of the cerebral palsied are able to lead productive and happy lives when intensive efforts are made to help them overcome their speech and language problems, and when proper measures are taken by their families and friends to satisfy their basic needs and encourage optimum functioning in all other areas of life.

D. *Language disorders associated with mental retardation.* These disorders develop when speech development is slow or incomplete, and when unintelligibility of speech can be correlated with a history of retardation in overall development. The differentiation of language disorder due to mental retardation from disorder due to other causes requires evaluation by specialists. The specific nature and degree of communication defect must also be determined by careful testing procedures. Mildly retarded individuals can usually express themselves with some degree of clarity, though on a simple, pragmatic level. The more severely retarded may use monosyllabic words such as "man," "eat," and "cat," but be unable to form sentences. Most of the profoundly retarded cannot use words at all.

The incidence of speech disorders among the mentally retarded is considerably higher than in the rest of the population. However, there is no evidence to suggest that the speech defects of the mentally retarded differ in kind from those of a nonretarded speech-defective population. With regard to symbol formation, however, low intelligence appears to place an immutable limitation on the individual's ability to deal with abstract concepts and to express emotions. The capacity to perceive, recall, generalize, and integrate sensations relating to the external world or themselves may be more or less affected depending on the degree of retardation. In mental deficiency there has been a failure in the development or an irreversible impairment of areas of the brain required for normal learning.

Individuals who are mentally retarded or mentally deficient, therefore, may develop intelligible speech but may not be able to grasp abstractions of a tangible or intangible nature. They may also be unable to conceptualize those emotional reactions to which, on a stimulus-response level, they can learn to react negatively or positively. Again, it should be noted that there is more or less severity in these conditions, and only in the case of the severest subnormality is there a complete absence of symbolic activity and language conception. On the other hand, there is growing evidence that many severely and even profoundly retarded individuals can be taught to use and respond to gestures — and gesture is a form of language. (See CHAPTER 39: MENTAL RETARDATION.)

E. *Language disorders associated with mental illness.* Mental illness can affect any system, and symbolic language is frequently influenced. By stress in the production of speech, by slips of the tongue, by misunderstandings and personalized concepts as well as the entire style of language and communication, the mentally ill person demonstrates the expressive and receptive problems associated with the illness. As the skills of therapists grow, much of the resolution of mental disorders may occur as the language phenomenon is more completely understood and utilized. A study of symbolic usage by the trained observer can reveal experiences in early childhood that presently influence the disorder, and through a study of the patient's style of language it is sometimes possible to

plan and institute appropriate treatment with ultimate improvement and recovery.

Greater degrees of disordered language occur with patients who
are suffering more extensive forms of emotional distress. This
phenomenon is described by Abse (1971) as he points out that verbal expression may be personalized communication that resembles
the "double-talk" often satirized by comedians. The language is
disconnected and incoherent but can sometimes be deciphered
when a thorough knowledge of the patient is obtained by a therapist.

Distorted language is particularly common in schizophrenia—in
such symptoms as echolalia (automatic repetition of the words of an
interlocutor); verbigeration (repeated utterance of apparently
meaningless phrases or sentences); word salad (garbled words);
acataphasia (use of inappropriate words); neologisms (invented
words); aboiement (involuntary animallike sounds); and clang associations (words strung together by sound rather than meaning). In
retarded depressions speech is extremely slow and labored, while
in manic states it is likely to be rapid and "pressured," shifting unpredictably from topic to topic (flight of ideas). Patients with senile
brain diseases frequently dwell interminably on trivial details
(circumstantiality or labyrinthine speech), and may fabricate events
to fill gaps in memory (confabulation).

TREATMENT OF SPEECH AND LANGUAGE DISORDERS

In recent years there has been a gradual but consistent broadening of the scientific treatment of these disorders to include and integrate speech with interpersonal relationships. Efforts have been
made to structure treatment programs and yet maintain respect and
consideration for the unique needs of the individual apart from the
disorder. The therapeutic atmosphere, tools for evaluation and
treatment, and opportunities for practice and reinforcement of
healthy speech behavior have all been expanded and improved.
Furthermore, in speech therapy there needs to be full recognition
of the interdisciplinary approach as well as the essential role that
the disabled individual plays in effecting self-improvement.

Attention will be paid in this section strictly to speech therapies,
since the basic disorders that result in speech problems are discussed elsewhere. Psychotherapy, physical therapy, and other
techniques can be understood as adjunctive and at times prime
treatment, but the specialist in speech disorders furnishes a unique
aspect of treatment that may not be available in any other discipline.

Treating Articulation Disorders

Three principal methods are employed in articulatory correction.
In the phonetic-placement method, the individual is given training
in specific placement of the articulators (tongue, jaws, lips, and soft
palate) for the production of each sound. Faulty placement is point-

ed out by the therapist, and the patient is instructed to make those changes required to produce sounds correctly. This method presupposes that there is a standard way to produce each sound.

In the motor-kinesthetic method, the therapist manipulates the articulators so that the individual produces the correct sound. At the same time the therapist also produces the correct sound.

The auditory-training method is dependent on the primary sensory basis, hearing and listening, for correction of articulatory disorders. The object of this method is to increase the individual's awareness of speech sounds and to apply that awareness to speech production. As a basis for treatment, the therapist, therefore, attempts to develop the individual's auditory discrimination ability, which can then be applied to listening to his or her own speech.

All three of these methods may be combined, but most therapists rely heavily on the auditory approach. The most effective therapy comprises three phases: training in auditory discrimination, training in articulatory production, and carry-over outside the treatment situation.

Treating Disorders of Time or Rhythm

Speech therapy for stuttering has customarily been symptomatic in nature. It is frequently based on uninhibited stuttering, which the individual may have been consciously avoiding, and which can be discouraging. But once the patient has been permitted to stutter freely, some therapists proceed to a technique called cancellation. In this treatment the patient is required to come to a complete halt after the stuttered word has been finally uttered, pause a moment, and then attempt to say the word again with less struggle and avoidance (C. Van Riper, 1957). The next stage of this therapy occurs when instead of cancellation the patient is instructed to make a deliberate attempt to "pull out" of the stuttering during the nonfluency. The next stage consists of deliberate nonfluency, and finally the technique aims at tolerance for stuttering fluently.

Some type of voluntary stuttering has become the major symptomatic therapy but brief mention should be made of operant conditioning—that is, rewarding or reinforcing fluent speech when it occurs. As with all situations where this therapeutic procedure can be applied, it works most effectively when it is a part of an overall treatment plan.

General psychotherapy has had questionable success in the treatment of stuttering, but when a person is treated with a combination of speech therapy and psychotherapy it has sometimes been possible for a nonfluent speaker to develop fluency.

The young child who stutters is usually experiencing primary or simple nonfluency and is not attempting to avoid stuttering. Much can be done for such a child if the parents are interested in helping. Counseling of such families, and instructing the parents to recognize the moments of stuttering at times of inadequate concentration, together with efforts to clarify the role that the parents play in the disorder, can result in some success in prevention of secondary symptoms and nonfluency. When feelings of helplessness are conveyed to a stuttering child, and when the parents are reluctant to respond to the child's need for help, they may set up a pattern of mistrust and inadequacy which may persist into adulthood. It is therefore essential that families get help in dealing with stuttering, and that they do not become discouraged or alienated from the child by their own sense of helplessness.

Treating Voice Disorders

In cases of organic voice disorder, the physical condition must be improved as much as possible before active voice therapy begins. There are two approaches to organic voice problems: restoration and compensation. Whenever possible, a normal structure should be provided (usually through surgery) before vocal therapy is applied, in order to reestablish normal voice sound production. In cases of irreversible structural limitations, voice therapy proceeds along compensatory lines to establish the greatest possible efficiency, to develop physiological compensations, and to help the patient accept a "different" voice.

When the cause of the voice disorder, whether it be a defect in pitch, loudness, or quality, has been vocal abuse, a period of education is required for the patient to become acquainted with the effects of the misuse and the necessity for correct use of the voice. Moreover, the individual is usually instructed to remain silent when the contributing factors cannot be controlled. The therapist also emphasizes the slowness of the rehabilitation process and provides continuous encouragement. Silence sometimes creates great difficulty for an individual, but the process of using paper and pencil and maintaining muteness is a major phase of the therapy. Usually from two weeks to several months of this phase are required. The next step is training and reeducation in relaxed phonation. Included in this phase of therapy are general physical relaxation and learning to distinguish adequate and inadequate voice production.

Learning to hear one's own voice requires a good teacher and a good recording machine. Critical listening must be related to the subjective sensation and ultimately to the control necessary for direct vocal training. Control is usually achieved through exercises designed to produce a breathing process that prevents vocal abuse.

In compensatory therapy the patient is trained to acquire as effective a voice as possible. This approach does not usually require a period of silence, and the therapy may begin immediately. The initial phase consists of helping the patient become acquainted with methods of compensating for whatever deficiency exists in the vocal apparatus.

All voice disorders require the utmost participation by the patient with the therapist. The person with a voice disability needs to be motivated to correction, and with the help of the therapist must learn to be aware of the voice defect before any remedial procedure can be effective. Analysis and training are required, and in many cases supportive therapy as well, since with increased awareness the patient may begin to feel that the voice is deteriorating.

Following these general procedures of educating for detection, the next step involves discovery of a new voice. Apparently without realizing it, one's own voice, however it is heard by the owner, is subjectively incorporated in the idealized self-image and may be rigidly held on to. Thus the discovery of a new voice involves risk-taking, experimentation, and varying the possible ways of producing phonation.

Of all the disorders in language, those caused by brain damage in cases of aphasia and cerebral palsy lend themselves most fully and urgently to speech therapy. The key principle in therapy is to begin with the least impaired functions, since the disorder often renders a patient anxious and lacking in confidence. Hope and optimism are the primary attitudes to be fostered. The actual program is educative in nature, and involves eight basic activities, according to Van Riper. (1) *Stimulation* is achieved through such simple tasks as copying letters, tracing, echoing, and filling in missing words. These tasks are repeated until there is less confusion and the functions that are lost or missing can be formed or developed. (2) *Inhibition* may be difficult, since a form of involuntary repetition may occur in aphasia. The patient may cry, laugh, or talk as if a needle were stuck in the groove of a damaged record. The therapist can help the individual interrupt these perseverative patterns and develop control or inhibit the useless behavior. (3) The *translation* objective is more than an effort to help the patient generalize from one experience to others. It is a studied effort to assist in conceptualization, which frequently is a major area of disturbance when brain damage has occurred. (4) *Memorization* of sequential material, be it tasks, directions, words, or phrases, provides the patient with the opportunity to restore concentration and collaboration. (5) Through a process of simple comparisons of likenesses and differences, the mental skill of *scanning and concentration* may need to be emphasized. (6) *Formulation* of categories by finding similar objects is a method of achieving this function. Self-talk is relied on heavily to assist the patient to organize and formulate. (7) *Body image integration* is a process of reacquainting the patient with the self through pictures, self-exploration, and conscious movements of the parts of the body. (8) *Psychotherapy* is implicit in all procedures. Without the effective awareness and clarification provided by the process of talking with someone and gaining insight, it would be impossible to achieve modification in this difficult form of retraining.

Whether brain damage is due to birth injury or later trauma, therapy is aimed at the restoration or development of all aspects of the mental-perceptual apparatus. This usually requires close cooperation with a physical therapist and medical advisor. The speech therapist can assist in the process, but complete restoration is also dependent on group processes outside the speech clinic. For this reason the rehabilitation approach is a total one, focused on the appropriate satisfaction of all the patient's basic needs.

Speech therapy with the mentally retarded has always been much in demand. Therapists, however, have been reticent to invest much time and effort with this group of individuals in view of their limited perceptual and conceptual functions. Parents of mentally retarded children are inclined to regard the child's communication and speech problem as of major importance and will therefore seek speech therapy and feel disappointed when they are turned down. When this occurs, it would be helpful if some explanation were given of the limited gains made by speech therapy, and a generalized mental health program should be outlined instead. In recent years there has been a healthy emphasis on prevocational and recreational programs which hold greater promise for the future. These retarded children must receive emotional support, and when basic trust is established as a result of need fulfillment, many of them can achieve considerable success and even a measure of insight. Speech and language processes may then reach a degree of satisfaction if the overall adjustment of the retarded individual is improved.

SELECTED REFERENCES

Abse, D. Wilfred, *Speech and Reason: Language Disorder in Mental Disease*, University Press of Virginia, Charlottesville, 1971.

ASHA, journal of the American Speech and Hearing Association.

Greene, Margaret C. L., *The Voice and Its Disorders*, 3d ed., Pitman Press, Belmont, California, 1972.

Ostwald, Peter F., *The Semiotics of Human Sound*, Mouton, Atlantic Highlands, New Jersey, 1973.

Penfield, Wilder, and Lamar Roberts, *Speech and Brain-Mechanisms*, Princeton University Press, 1959.

Travis, Lee Edward, ed., *Handbook of Speech Pathology*, Appleton-Century-Crofts, New York, 1957.

Van Riper, Charles, *Speech Correction: Principles and Methods*, Prentice-Hall, Englewood Cliffs, New Jersey, 1963.

50

Spina Bifida

LINDA HOWELL, M.A., Group Health Cooperative of
Puget Sound, Seattle

Reviewed by the Spina Bifida Association of America

Spina bifida (also known as open or split spine) is a birth defect
that results from failure of the vertebral canal to close normally
around the spinal cord. The failure is due to a defect in the development of the vertebrae during the gestation period. In *spina bifida
occulta* the problem is minimal since the spinal cord itself is essentially normal despite the fact that some of the vertebrae are defective. In *spina bifida with myelomeningocele* (spina bifida manifesta
or spina bifida cystica), one part of the spinal cord is like a flat plate
instead of a tube, and protrudes from the body's surface covered
only by the membranes (meninges) which surround the spinal cord.
Also, the nerves extending from the spinal cord at this point to other
parts of the body have fewer nerve fibers than normal.

There is wide variation between the extremes of this condition.
The greater the protrusion and exposure, and generally the higher
the spinal defect, the more serious the condition. In addition, spina
bifida is frequently associated with other anomalies of the skeletal
system and the viscera, and only within the last two decades have
the more seriously involved babies survived beyond infancy.

Incidence and Prevalence

It is estimated that spina bifida occurs in from 2 to 4 out of 1,000
live-born babies, for a total of more than 11,000 new cases each year
in the United States. It is one of the most common of all birth defects, and occurs in males and females with equal frequency.

Causal Factors

Spina bifida develops during the first three months of pregnancy, the period in which the spinal column forms and closes. It has not been related to any untoward events of pregnancy, nor to characteristics of the mother or father. However, there is a slight tendency for the condition to recur in families — that is, the probability that spina bifida will occur again in a family which already has one child with the problem is higher than the probability for the general population. For this reason genetic counseling is recommended for families planning more children after the birth of a child with myelomeningocele. Amniocentesis can be used to diagnose myelomeningocele with great accuracy in the third fetal month. (See CHAPTER 19: BIRTH DEFECTS; GENETIC COUNSELING.)

Symptoms

Spina bifida is a highly complex disorder. Lack of proper innervation of the lower part of the body causes weakness, even flaccid paralysis, of the muscles of the legs and feet. This condition can in turn lead to deformities, among the most common being club feet and dislocated hips. In addition, sensation may be abnormal or absent in the lower back and extremities.

There will also be problems of urination and bowel control, since the child with myelomeningocele usually cannot sense when bladder and bowel are full and need emptying. Muscle control and strength necessary to empty the bowel and bladder properly may also be lacking.

A serious complication of spina bifida, occurring in 80 percent of children with myelomeningocele, is hydrocephalus. Normally the cerebrospinal fluid travels inside and around the brain and spinal cord and is eventually absorbed into the bloodstream. In spina bifida there is usually some interference with the circulation and absorption of this fluid, and it therefore increases in volume and exerts pressure on the brain and skull. As a result, the head is enlarged (hydrocephalus) and the brain is compressed and damaged, leading to many other developmental difficulties, including mental retardation in some cases. Another serious problem is that the cerebrospinal fluid may leak through the sac protruding from the spinal cord, and an unclosed sac is susceptible to infection (meningitis). (For hydrocephalus, see CHAPTER 39: MENTAL RETARDATION.)

Diagnosis and Treatment

The serious forms of spina bifida are easy to detect, but the occult type, which may result in milder symptoms or none at all, is frequently overlooked. A proper diagnosis requires x-rays of the spine.

Today surgical techniques have been developed to hide or bury the protruding spinal cord below the skin surface. This is usually done soon after birth. The child can then lie on the back, and the susceptibility to meningeal infection is reduced. To counter the build-up of cerebrospinal fluid and possible hydrocephalus, a shunting procedure is frequently performed. This is a surgical process in which a tube is inserted into one of the large, hollow cavities (ventricles) of the brain where the fluid originates. The tube, which is thin and unobservable, drains the fluid into the bloodstream through the jugular vein, peritoneal cavity, or gall bladder, and in this way pressure build-up is avoided. This procedure is well accepted and generally has good results. (For other conditions involving hydrocephalus, see CHAPTER 22: BRAIN DAMAGE.)

Problems of stool and urinary incontinence become especially apparent at the time when most children are toilet-trained, but treatment should begin well before this point. Normally a young child reflexively empties the bladder, but in the child with spina bifida the reflex may not be operative, and as a result urine builds up and overflows the bladder, gradually leaking out. Continual pressure on the bladder also causes dilation of the ureters which connect the kidneys to the bladder, and eventually irreversible destruction of the kidneys will take place, and it will not be possible to filter waste products from the bloodstream. To prevent such damage, repeated tests must be performed to determine the condition of the urinary tract. These tests include an intravenous pyelogram, or x-ray of the kidney and ureters; cystoscopy, an internal examination of the bladder; and a cystogram, or x-ray of the bladder to determine its size and shape.

Treatment is aimed at relieving pressure on the bladder and avoiding infection. To relieve pressure, a catheter or tube may be inserted into the bladder through the urethra to drain off urine. Careful urological follow-up is extremely important, since the urinary tract is highly susceptible to infection and may prove to be the most difficult management problem in spina bifida. Many systems and devices are available for dealing with this problem. (See CHAPTER 51: SPINAL CORD INJURY.)

Where sensation is diminished, care of the skin in the lower areas of the body is particularly important, since these areas become highly susceptible to injury and pressure sores.

The problems of muscle weakness of the lower extremities must be anticipated from the very beginning to avoid the development of joint deformities. This can be accomplished by proper positioning and by giving the child range-of-motion exercises for the affected limbs. The extent of muscle weakness and the ability to be mobile depend upon the initial amount of damage and the regularity and thoroughness of treatment. Some children may be able to walk without assistance. Others may require braces and assistive devices such as canes or crutches. Ambulation and weight-bearing are important to prevent disuse osteoporosis, which may lead to easy fracturing. (See CHAPTER 45: ORTHOPEDIC DISORDERS.) A few patients, essentially paralyzed in the lower extremities (paraplegic), may need to use a wheelchair. As for other complications, orthopedic attention has recently been focused on spinal curvatures secondary to myelomeningocele and aggressive treatment has shown good results.

In any case of spina bifida a qualified pediatric specialist should be consulted, and in the more severe cases it is necessary to arrange for multidisciplinary care at a regional center or at a research or teaching hospital. The importance of maintaining a close working relationship between the individual or family and the physicians cannot be overestimated.

Educational and Vocational Aspects

If the effects of spina bifida are severe and irreversible, the child will probably require a special educational program. In cases where mobility is a problem, a facility which can accommodate limited mobility may be required. Ramps and proper toilet facilities are needed for some of these children. A regular program of physical therapy to maintain and develop muscle strength is also desirable. Such facilities are available in progressive public school systems, and today many children with spina bifida are integrated into regular schools.

A child who has some degree of mental retardation as a result of an early hydrocephalic condition should be placed in an appropriate public school class. Later on, vocational guidance and training are available through State Offices of Vocational Rehabilitation. (For details of educational programs, see CHAPTER 39: MENTAL RETARDATION.)

With such complex problems, the child or adult and the family need much supportive help and understanding so as to reach the highest potential level of functioning. Fortunately, today's total approach to rehabilitation enables many people with spina bifida to maintain their basic health and to marry, hold jobs, and have children.

Research

The most pertinent basic research is focused on the development of the nervous system beginning at conception, and relates this development to environmental and especially to maternal factors on a time schedule. Other areas of research include factors relating to the intelligence of children with myelomeningocele; teratogenic (deformity-producing) factors in embryology; immunological factors in families with a history of myelomeningocele; methods of management for neurogenic bladders; light-weight and cosmetically acceptable orthosis materials; methods of determining the prognosis of the child very early in infancy; improved ventricular shunt designs; and early intervention to develop visual-motor coordination.

Organizations

The Spina Bifida Association of America, with headquarters at 343 South Dearborn Avenue, Chicago, IL 60604, is a voluntary organization consisting of 120 chapters throughout the United States dedicated to providing information, making resources available to families and professionals, and increasing opportunities for all individuals with this disorder. More specifically, the Association seeks (1) to promote the well-being of children and adults with spina bifida through a program focused on care, treatment, education, socialization, recreation, and vocational adjustment; (2) to stimulate research into the causes, management, and prevention of spina bifida; (3) to promote the training of competent treatment and rehabilitation personnel; and (4) to increase public awareness of this condition.

The National Foundation (P.O. Box 2000, White Plains, NY 10602) is concentrating its efforts on birth defects, including spina bifida. It supports research, medical and other diagnostic services, and supportive and rehabilitative services, and provides educational materials to both professionals and the public. The National Easter Seal Society for Crippled Children and Adults is also deeply involved in the problem of spina bifida. Another major resource is the Children's Bureau of the U.S. Department of Health, Education and Welfare, which provides funds to divisions of children's services of the various state departments of health for services to children with spina bifida.

(See CHAPTER 55: ILLUSTRATIVE CASES, A. A Sack on His Back.)

SELECTED REFERENCES

Bunch, Wilton H., et al., *Modern Management of Myelomeningocele,* Warren Green, II, St. Louis, 1972.

Freeman, John M., ed., *Practical Management of Meningomyelocele,* University Park Press, Baltimore, 1974.

Henderson, Marcia, and Diane Synhorst, *Care of the Infant with Myelomeningocele (Spina Bifida) and Hydrocephalus,* Campus Stores, University of Iowa, Iowa City.

Pieper, Betty, *Straight Talk, Parent to Parent,* Illinois Spina Bifida Association, P.O. Box 1974, Elmhurst, IL 60126.

Sugar, Miklos, and Mary D. Ames, "The Child with Spina Bifida Cystica: His Medical Problem and Habilitation," *Rehabilitation Literature,* December 1965.

Swinyard, Chester A., *The Child with Spina Bifida,* Institute of Rehabilitation Medicine, New York, NY 10016.

51

Spinal Cord Injury

LINDA HOWELL, M.A., Group Health Cooperative of Puget Sound, Seattle

Reviewed by AARON ROSENTHAL, M.D., Physical Medicine and Rehabilitation, Fox River Hospital, Chicago

The spinal cord is the large nerve fiber tract which extends from the base of the brain down through the bones of the spinal column (vertebrae) to the lumbar vertebrae level. It consists of many parallel nerve tracts which serve to conduct messages from the body to the brain and from the brain to the body. Severe injury to the spinal cord through accident or disease causes loss of sensation and loss of voluntary motion (enervation of muscles) below the level of the injury. If the injury is to the upper part of the spine in the region of the cervical vertebrae, the condition is called quadriplegia, as there is involvement of all four extremities. If the injury is lower, in the thoracic or lumbar area of the spine, the result is paraplegia, involving only the lower extremities.

This is only a gross differentiation. The specific symptoms depend on the level of the lesion—thus there are significant differences among quadriplegics and among paraplegics corresponding to differences in lesion level. There are also differences in the degree of paralysis (total or partial) and in the amount of sensation lost, both related to the amount of destruction of the spinal cord and nerve roots at the point of injury.

Until World War II, survival from spinal cord injury (SCI) was rare, primarily due to uncontrollable infections of the urinary tract which developed very easily, and also due to respiratory failure, especially in quadriplegics. The mortality rate for quadriplegics in the acute phase is still very high, but today spinal-cord-injured individuals who have competent medical care and a good understanding of their condition, and who participate in their own care, will usually be able to live full and productive lives.

Causes

Injury to the spinal cord can result from either disease or trauma. Among the diseases are cancer and other tumors of the spinal cord, infections and abscesses of the spine, arthritis, some congenital defects (such as spina bifida), multiple sclerosis, and poliomyelitis. In the United States traumatic spinal cord injury is primarily a result of automobile accidents, and secondarily of sports injuries, industrial accidents, falls, and gunshot wounds.

Incidence and Prevalence

There are no reliable statistical studies of spinal cord injuries in the United States at this writing. It is estimated that there are 5,000 to 10,000 new cases per year, with a total of approximately 150,000 paraplegics and quadriplegics in the population, according to the National Center for Health Statistics. Nearly three-fourths of the injured are male. The age period in which injury is most likely to occur is from fifteen to thirty. Victims of industrial accidents tend to be older on the average than victims of automobile or sports accidents and gunshot wounds.

Symptoms and Complications

A spinal cord injury affects many systems of the body. The complex results require extremely good care in order to prevent complications and greater disability than necessary. The basic impairments are in the areas of sensation and voluntary movement. The inability to move half or most of one's body makes ambulation impossible without human or mechanical assistance. Paralyzed individuals may be unable to change position without assistance. Quadriplegics and even paraplegics with high-thoracic-level lesions often have difficulties with independent sitting. Eating and self-care may be difficult. In the paraplegic, however, the ability to use one's arms makes it possible to compensate in large part for lower-extremity paralysis.

When sensation is impaired, the patient may be unaware of the paralyzed portion of the body—that is, insensitive to heat, cold, wetness, sharp objects, or pressure—and therefore may incur additional injury unless problems are constantly anticipated and compensated for. Due to the inability to move voluntarily and to sense changes occurring in the body, the individual is highly susceptible to the development of pressure sores (decubitus ulcers), especially on parts of the body which are bony and relatively unprotected by other tissue. If left untreated, these sores can become very large, deep, and difficult to heal.

Eliminative processes are often affected, since the person with an injured spinal cord may lose the ability to sense when it is time to empty bowel or bladder, and may not be able to control elimination of wastes. This problem creates a susceptibility to urinary tract infections and to gradual deterioration of bladder and kidney function. Sexual functioning is also affected by paraplegic and quadriplegic conditions, but there is wide variation from case to case depending upon the level and extent of the lesion, as well as the attitudes and inventiveness of the individual and the sexual partner.

Relative immobilization of parts of the body has a tendency to produce deformities unless proper preventive measures are taken. That is, when joints are inactive, their supporting muscles, capsules, and ligaments tighten up and produce contractures. The joints can become relatively frozen into position and are very hard to loosen again. Contractures are most likely to occur in the ankle (foot drop), hips, and knees, and in quadriplegics, in the fingers and elbows as well.

After the acute stage of this illness, the spinal cord injured may be subject to frequent involuntary muscle jerks or spasms below the level of lesion. These reactions are caused by essentially random stimulation of the motor nerves leading to the muscles, rather than stimulation that originates in the brain. Spasms may also affect internal organs, the bladder in particular. They may be just minor twitching or may be very strong. It is not uncommon for the spinal-cord-injured patient to be thrown from a bed or wheelchair by leg spasms.

The irony in this condition of impaired sensation is that most paraplegics and quadriplegics live with some degree of pain, particularly in relation to spasms or concentrated about the area of the lesion. The quadriplegic who has had an injury to the neck is likely to experience much neck strain. In incomplete lesions of the cord, pain and spasms may be a major problem.

Patients may also experience respiratory and gastrointestinal problems, especially in the early phases of the injury. Lack of activity of the whole body tends to produce some demineralization, which weakens the skeletal structure and may produce stones in the urinary system.

The psychological stress on the person with a spinal cord injury is immense, as is the adjustment which must be made to the disability in order to survive, let alone to become productive again.

Treatment

Immediate Medical Care (First Aid). In the event of traumatic damage to the spine, significant additional damage may be done by those who attempt to help the injured person. Immediate first-aid care must be performed very carefully. Accident victims who report loss of sensation or movement, or complain of back or neck pain, or lose consciousness should be handled as if the spinal cord has been injured—that is, they should be moved flat to avoid any change in alignment of the vertebrae. If the arms are involved, suggesting neck injury, the head and neck must be held steady while the patient is moved to a stretcher or transported to a hospital. If any bending must be done to transport the injured person, this should be only to the hips or knees, never to the back or neck.

Acute Medical Care. When the patient arrives at the hospital (ideally at a spinal cord injury center), a physician will perform a clinical examination and x-rays, and possibly a myelogram will be taken to determine the extent and level of injury. Additional injuries will be noted and treated. Treatment for shock may be necessary, and in any case the patient must be immobilized. A decision may be made to operate in order to stabilize the spine or free the nerve roots or remove bony fragments. Conservative methods of treatment, such as traction, are, however, more commonly employed (and research shows these methods produce better end results on the average than the more drastic techniques). New techniques have been developed to minimize swelling, hemorrhaging, and lack of oxygen (anoxia) associated with the injury, since these conditions may produce further tissue destruction.

Much of the early work with the patient is designed to prevent complications and unnecessary damage. A catheter is inserted into the bladder to control urine flow. Urine output is carefully checked, and the patient is strongly encouraged to drink extra fluids. The patient is positioned, turned, and padded in such a way as to prevent pressure sores and deformities. A patient with a neck injury may undergo skeletal traction and be positioned on a rotating bed called a Stryker frame. Once the spine is stabilized (this may take six to twelve weeks in some cases), placement on a water bed or some kind of alternating pressure pad is desirable. In the acute injury stage, respiratory and gastrointestinal distress may occur suddenly and must be anticipated by the hospital staff.

Active Rehabilitation—Goals and Assistive Devices

It is estimated that the initial cost of hospitalization (excluding later follow-up care) of spinal-cord-injured patients ranges from $15,000 to $35,000. These patients need specialized emergency and acute care, as well as rehabilitation, which is extensive both in terms of variety of services and duration of care. Almost invariably, some unexpected complications develop to delay recovery and increase costs. The medical-rehabilitation program described here is not truly representative, as few institutions have the sophistication and equipment to deal effectively with the spinal cord injured. To remedy this problem, the Rehabilitation Act of 1973, as a special project, authorized funds to establish Model Spinal Cord Injury Systems across the United States to demonstrate a system of delivery of compehensive care from the point of injury, including emergency medical services; intensive care; rehabilitation management; vocational, educational, and psychological services; and long-term community follow-up. In early 1977 there were eleven such model systems based in the following institutions: Boston University Medical Center, New York University Medical Center, the University of Virginia and Woodrow Wilson Rehabilitation Center in Fishersville, Virginia, the University of Alabama Medical Center, Northwestern University Medical Center in Chicago, the University of Minnesota School of Medicine, Craig Rehabilitation

Hospital in Denver, Texas Institute for Rehabilitation and Research in Houston, Santa Clara Valley Medical Center in San Jose, the University of Washington Department of Rehabilitation Medicine, and the Good Samaritan Hospital in Phoenix (this last is also the site of the National Spinal Cord Injury Center set up to evaluate the program). (See CHAPTER 55: ILLUSTRATIVE CASES, B. Lawyer and Quadriplegic; CHAPTER 56: REHABILITATION FACILITIES AND SERVICES, C. Vocational Rehabilitation Center.)

The primary objective of any rehabilitation program for paraplegics and quadriplegics is to help the individual reach a maximal level of independent functioning. Range of motion must be actively maintained (by the therapist/nurse). Existing muscle power must be strengthened and weakened muscles retrained. Specifically, the patient needs to become independent in self-care. This may mean feeding oneself (a complex task for a high-level quadriplegic), which is usually accomplished with the use of a hand splint which promotes grasping. It may mean developing control or regulation of bladder and bowel activity—to be catheter free, ideally; to use an external catheter; or to care for one's own internal catheter. In some cases it may be necessary to undergo a surgical procedure known as an ileal conduit (see CHAPTER 46: OSTOMIES for a description of ureterostomy). It means taking care of one's skin, which requires special pads, cushions, and mattress, and above all *foresight*.

Independence also means developing the capacity for mobility or ambulation. Learning transfer techniques is a major goal of any program. Some individuals may be able to use crutches, walker, or cane, and short- or long-leg braces for some activities, others may be independent of the wheelchair, and some may not even require assistive devices. Most, however, require the use of a wheelchair full time or at least part time. Wheelchairs are expensive, as they must be specially fitted for the individual to ensure comfort and proper positioning, as well as to permit ease of movement. For those unable to operate a manual wheelchair independently, a battery-powered chair can be used. Regardless of the patient's ability to ambulate, regular weight-bearing is important to prevent the demineralization which takes place with inactivity. (See CHAPTER 5: INDEPENDENT LIVING: WAYS AND MEANS.)

Spasms may develop over time. If these are very strong and troublesome, they can be controlled in part by medication. Sometimes surgery must be resorted to if spasms become too painful and start to cause contractions.

Since a spinal cord injury can be devastating to the spirit of the individual, at some point in the long rebuilding process a good deal of supportive help must be given by the staff involved with the patient, and by family and friends as well. Counseling should be provided to assist the patient in adjustment and to help maintain or build self-motivation to deal with this complex and drastic condition. Much education and concentration on prevention of further problems are required if the patient is to cope effectively. The development of an optimistic and productive attitude may require considerable experience and time. The importance of the understanding, willingness to learn, patience, and encouragement of persons who are especially close or significant to the paraplegic or quadriplegic cannot be underestimated as a factor in successful rehabilitation.

Educational and Vocational Rehabilitation

Since victims of traumatic spinal cord injury are generally young, helping them to be socially and financially, as well as physically, independent is of crucial importance. Educational and vocational training should be available. Some preliminary aspects of this process may be started within a rehabilitation facility, but the major steps are usually taken after discharge, often under the State Department of Vocational Rehabilitation. In the young patient, the emphasis may be on academic work if the individual shows a potential for educational achievement. In the case of an older individual, the emphasis is on retraining, unless the paraplegic or quadriplegic is fortunate enough to possess skills and experience which do not require now-impossible physical activity. A licensed driver with limited use of the lower extremities can have hand controls put into a car, and after appropriate training will usually be able to drive to work or school.

A paraplegic with ability and adequate training can handle most types of "sit-down" jobs — accountant, assembly line worker, receptionist, social worker, or draftsman, to name only a few. A quadriplegic with little use of upper extremities must capitalize on mental abilities. These persons are usually young and have much to offer society. A number are self-employed and in the business of designing and manufacturing equipment for the handicapped.

Yet the statistics show the situation far from optimal. The problem of accessibility to work and educational facilities is a real one, which is only very gradually diminishing. It is one thing for an employer to want to hire a paraplegic in a wheelchair, and quite another for the facility to provide ramps, wide doorways, accessible toilets, and close-in parking that will make it possible for such an employee to travel to and function at work independently. (See CHAPTER 10: REMOVING ENVIRONMENTAL BARRIERS.)

The United States rehabilitation rate for the spinal cord injured is less than that of several other developed countries, because the care here is seldom comprehensive enough. Persons in rural areas, for example, do not have excellent care available to them unless they travel great distances. Also, the Veterans Administration financial benefit system for those injured while in the armed services unfortunately has the effect of decreasing the disabled person's need for vocational achievement, thereby lowering traditional ratings of rehabilitation success.

Prevention

Prevention of spinal cord injury is possible to some degree. Since automobile accidents are the major cause, diminution of speed and greater use of seat belts can make a significant difference in the statistics. It has been shown that in nearly all injuries of this type, the victims were *not* wearing safety belts. Better protective equipment for sports participants can prevent serious injury, as can safer industrial working conditions. If handguns were less accessible, there would be fewer spinal cord injuries. Worldwide peace would certainly lower the incidence of traumatic injury. Spinal injuries caused by disease may be prevented in some cases by regular medical checkups with early diagnosis and treatment of the problem, and also by inoculation, as in the case of polio. The prevention of more extensive injury, once the initial injury has occurred, is another very important area of current research work. (See CHAPTER 50: SPINA BIFIDA.)

Research

The long-range goal of research in spinal cord injury is the regeneration of the spinal cord. Regeneration in the central nervous system was once thought to be impossible. Although researchers are a long way from reaching this goal, their determination and conviction that it can be accomplished in time are strong. This research is at a very basic physiological and biochemical level, and will have implications for the whole range of nervous system function and dysfunction. The hope is, of course, that not only the newly injured but those with injuries of years' duration may someday be candidates for cord regeneration.

A major focus of research is on the acute period and prevention of additional damage which may occur at this critical stage. Physiological and chemical changes which take place immediately after injury to the cord are being observed and measured, and steps are being taken to alter or minimize these changes. This work and basic regeneration research are performed primarily on other animal species or on tissue cultures.

Applied research in this field involves refinement of techniques of surgery, improved treatment of spastic bladder, study of the sexual functioning of spinal cord injured, and the development of more effective devices and therapies for rehabilitation (such as biofeedback treatment) and for independent living. Much of the research is being carried out under the sponsorship of the National Institutes of Health, specifically the National Institute of Neurological and Communication Disorders and Stroke, which has been instrumental in planning and coordinating the efforts of acute spinal cord injury clinical research centers.

Organizations

The National Paraplegic Foundation (333 North Michigan Avenue, Chicago, IL 60601) was founded in 1948. It is a voluntary health agency whose members are paraplegics, quadriplegics, and other interested persons. The goals of the organization are (1) to bring about the best possible medical care; (2) to stimulate research toward a cure for paraplegia; and (3) to help individual paraplegics achieve personal goals. The Foundation advocates the development of a network of care centers. It sponsors scientific conferences and rewards researchers interested in the problems of spinal cord injury; publishes and distributes a considerable amount of helpful literature; and supports legislation to eliminate architectural barriers. It also arranges personal contacts among paraplegics and quadriplegics and sponsors recreational activities. Information about local chapters may be obtained from the national office.

Paralyzed Veterans of America, Inc. (3636 Sixteenth Street N.W., Washington, DC 20010) was founded in 1947 as a national organization of veterans who had incurred an injury or disease affecting the spinal cord. It is essentially a self-help group whose members have furthered the development of wheelchair sports, adequate housing, and appropriate training programs. They have sponsored legislation which has brought benefits (primarily financial) for its members. This organization also provides pertinent literature, which is useful to the spinal cord injured and to those who participate in rehabilitation.

SELECTED REFERENCES

Edward, William H., and Harry A. Schweikert, *An Introduction to Paraplegia*, Paralyzed Veterans of America, 1965.

Innovations in the Total Care of the Spinal-Cord Injured (conference), National Paraplegia Foundation, 1973.

Johnson, H. E., and W. H. Garton, *A Practical Method of Muscle Re-education in Hemiplegia: Electromyographic Facilitation and Conditioning*, Casa Colina Hospital for Rehabilitative Medicine, Pomona, CA 91767.

Saltman, Jules, *Paraplegia: A Head, A Heart and Two Big Wheels*, Public Affairs Pamphlet.

Self-care for the Hemiplegic, Sister Kenny Institute, 1800 Chicago Avenue, Minneapolis, MN 55404.

Spinal-Cord Injury: Hope through Research, National Institute of Neurological and Communication Disorders and Stroke, National Institutes of Health, 1971.

University of Illinois, *Quadriplegic Functional Skills* (dressing, elimination, etc.), films available from Media Resources Branch, National Medical Audiovisual Center, Atlanta, GA 30324.

Valens, E. G., *A Long Way Up: The Story of Jill Kinmont*, Harper & Row, New York, 1966.

52

Stroke

LINDA HOWELL, M.A., Group Health Cooperative of Puget Sound, Seattle

Reviewed by AARON ROSENTHAL, M.D., Physical Medicine and Rehabilitation, Fox River Hospital, Chicago

A stroke is due to a disruption of the blood supply to the brain. When the blood does not supply oxygen and other nutrients to cells, the nerve cells in the affected area of the brain cannot function properly. These nerve cells control consciousness, thought, and motor activity, including speech, coordination, sensation, and perception. Therefore, if blood supply is changed, some of these processes may be temporarily or permanently impaired. A common sign of such disruption of blood flow to and through the brain (the so-called cerebrovascular accident or episode) is weakness or paralysis on one side of the body, which may be accompanied by loss or change of sensation. There may be limitations of vision and some degree of speech impairment. There may also be loss of consciousness for a period of time. Some confusion in time and place and some problem with memory may occur, especially immediately after onset. The relative suddenness of onset of these symptoms accounts for the common name of the disability — stroke.

Incidence

The average age of onset of stroke is sixty years old, but it may happen at any age, in both sexes, and across all races and socioeconomic levels (this is not to say it occurs with equal frequency in all such groups). Stroke afflicts 600,000 individuals per year in the United States, killing approximately one-third of them. In recent years, with improved medical diagnosis and treatment, the mortality rate has been decreasing at a significant rate.

Causes

Nearly all strokes originate in one of two ways. Either there is a closing off (occlusion) of one of the brain (cerebral) arteries or of one of the arteries in the neck which leads to the brain; or there is bleeding (hemorrhage) of a diseased cerebral artery. An artery may be blocked, or occluded, by a blood clot called a thrombus. This tends to occur when the artery itself has become damaged through the gradual depositing of material on the inner walls of the arteries (atherosclerosis), which causes narrowing of the space for the blood to flow through and stimulates the blood to form clots. This is referred to as cerebral thrombosis and is the commonest known cause of strokes. Also, a blood clot may travel from some other part of the body through the bloodstream to the brain, closing off an artery and causing a stroke. This kind of clot, called an embolus, usually detaches from (or is thrown off by) a heart damaged by disease.

In hemorrhage, a diseased or weak artery may rupture, flooding the local brain tissue with blood. Nerve cells which receive blood from the artery are cut off from the supply, and the blood itself may accumulate and cause pressure on the tissue in the area, thereby doing additional damage. Hemorrhagic strokes occur much less frequently than occlusive strokes, and have a much higher death rate.

The seriousness of the resulting stroke condition tends to depend upon many factors—the importance of the blood vessel involved, the location of the affected area in the brain, how efficiently the body can repair itself, etc.

The cerebrovascular disease process tends to occur along with some other disease processes which may or may not be causal factors. For example, three-fourths of stroke victims have been diagnosed as having high blood pressure (hypertension). Arteriosclerosis (hardening of the arteries) and especially atherosclerosis (narrowing of the arteries due to fat deposits) are usually found in the stroke victim. Cardiac disease, high cholesterol levels, overweight, heavy smoking, and diabetes are known to be contributing factors.

Diagnosis

Sometimes there are warning signs of stroke—temporary, mild versions of the major stroke symptoms. Many people have no such warning, however. A diagnosis is made by taking a careful history where possible, and by performing certain laboratory procedures such as examination of the urine and cerebrospinal fluid; examination of the eyes; checking respiration, temperature, pulse, and blood pressure; and neurological testing for motor and sensory function, and for mental and language functioning. Sudden onset is usually suggestive of stroke, but toxicity, tumor, or infection should be ruled out. (See CHAPTER 22: BRAIN DAMAGE.) Such tests as the electroencephalograph (EEG) and brain scan are often used in diagnosis. Arteriography of the internal carotid vessels and the vertebral arteries may also be helpful in diagnosis. Physicians are often able to determine the particular blood vessels involved from the pattern of symptoms, as these tend to follow certain known patterns based on localization of function in the brain.

Significant (Common) Symptoms

The effects of a stroke may be severe, moderate, or very slight; and temporary or permanent. Improvement occurs in nearly all cases, but recovery is usually a slow process.

The most distinguishing and usually the most incapacitating symptom of stroke is its effect on the motor power of one side of the body. (The side involved is the one opposite to the side of the brain affected, because most nerve fibers cross from one side to the other within the pathways to and from the brain.) When there is a total loss of muscle power (paralysis), the condition is called hemiplegia. Partial loss of muscle power is termed hemiparesis. In some cases a single arm or leg may be affected—a monoparesis. Frequently the face is partially paralyzed or weakened as well. Involvement of one side of the body may make independent ambulation difficult or impossible at first. Loss of active function of one arm limits the patient in a highly frustrating way. Facial paralysis or paresis may make swallowing and the formation of words difficult, so that the person mumbles or slurs words; this condition is called dysarthria. If in addition there is sensation loss, the patient's ability to compensate for motor loss is greatly limited, that is, there will be almost total unawareness of the position of limbs so that vision must be used to compensate for loss of touch and sense of position. With impaired control over the lower extremities, muscles may have no tension or strength, become tense and even rigid, or move involuntarily. The stroke may, in addition, affect the centers of the brain which regulate balance.

Another type of sensation impairment involves vision. Eye muscle paralysis and double vision occur in some instances. More commonly, the stroke patient's field of vision may be narrowed somewhat, usually on the side of the hemiplegia or motor impairment (each eye's vision to that side is constricted somewhat). Or there may not be an actual loss of vision, but instead there may be a tendency to ignore that side, just as the rest of that side of the body does not interact with the environment in a normal way. This last tendency is a psychological or perceptual manifestation of the underlying brain damage.

One type of stroke tends to produce a great deal of pain—that is, when there is damage to pain centers within the brain. Typically, stroke patients experience relatively little pain.

A significant problem may develop in the patient's ability to communicate verbally with other people. The ability to communicate or understand language (written or oral) may be impaired. This condition is called aphasia, and is found most typically in a right-hemiplegic patient (one with damage to the left side of the brain). (See CHAPTER 49: SPEECH AND LANGUAGE DISORDERS; CHAPTER

55: ILLUSTRATIVE CASES, H. Aphasia: A Personal Account.)

The person who suffers a stroke may experience visual perceptual disturbances. Essentially, this means that there is a reduced capacity to make visual discriminations. In addition, depth and spatial judgment may be affected. Thus interaction with the environment is likely to be uneven, and may seem to reflect poor judgment when actually it indicates changed perception. This may be manifested in writing, which may be impaired as a result of problems with spatial planning and form perception. Perceptual problems are especially common in patients with hemiplegia of the left side of the body.

Other "mental" problems may manifest themselves and are most evident soon after the stroke occurs. These and other symptoms of stroke tend to abate to some degree in time with the natural and spontaneous process of healing. In some individuals there may be rapid variations in mood, with some of the emotionality expressed but not felt, or not felt deeply (therefore sometimes becoming embarrassing to the stroke patient). Depression is usually experienced by the patient who has had this life-threatening experience and is left with residual impairment. This reaction may be especially acute in individuals with multiple problems and responsibilities, or in those who find themselves abruptly cut off from a particularly active, independent life-style. In a few cases, mental control and general orientation may be quite disturbed, depending upon the severity of the brain insult and the premorbid condition of the patient. Concentration is likely to be poor for some time, and there may be problems with recent and short-term memory. Some patients tend to deny obvious impairment, and therefore are particularly slow in learning how to compensate for their problems. The degree of denial seems related to the severity of the cerebral insult and to the characteristic personality of the individual prior to the stroke.

Prevention

The best means of prevention of strokes is through competent, regular medical care in which blood pressure is checked and the other possible contributing conditions are checked and treated where necessary. Hypertension can be controlled through regular medication; cholesterol level can be lowered through diet. Blood-clotting tendencies can be countered with anticlotting medication (anticoagulants). Diabetes can be regulated by diet or medication in many cases. Smoking can be eliminated. Surgery is sometimes performed on the arteries which lead to the brain if they have become clogged. Weight reduction may be helpful. Tension and stress should be reduced as much as possible.

Treatment

Some stroke victims recover so quickly that they need very little treatment. Others may require an intense course of rehabilitation, and there are many gradations between the two extremes. As a general rule, therapy should be initiated soon after the stroke occurs. In a general hospital this starts with "passive" treatment, in which a nurse or therapist exercises the affected and unaffected limbs of the stroke patient to prevent loss of flexibility of joints and possible deformity of the affected limbs. The patient is carefully positioned in bed to aid in preventing problems. Active exercises are prescribed as soon as the patient can carry them out. At this point the patient may be transferred to a hospital or hospital unit which specializes in treatment of stroke patients and others who require relatively intense retraining.

Rehabilitation Program

The emphasis in a rehabilitation setting is on independence rather than convalescence. The stroke patient is helped to compensate for losses, regain function where possible, and become independent again by learning new techniques and utilizing various compensatory devices. Muscle strength and range of motion of the shoulder, wrist, hip, ankle, etc. are measured, a therapy program is devised accordingly, and improvement is charted. Balance is noted, and problems in this area require special efforts at compensation. Exercises are done regularly, and ambulation training is begun when the patient is ready. In addition, the "activities of daily living"—hygiene, dressing, eating, getting in and out of bed and chair, using the toilet and bath, etc.—are all worked on in systematic ways. Many patients must initially use a wheelchair, and training in its use is needed. Crutches, canes, walkers, and other devices are introduced as the patient develops more strength and coordination. Bowel and bladder retraining may be necessary in some cases.

Many stroke patients require some speech or communication retraining. The degree of visual impairment—perceptual and sensory—is noted, and special forms of therapy may be instituted to compensate for these problems if natural compensation is insufficient. Supportive therapy to help the patient sort out emotional reactions may also be helpful. Families are usually encouraged to become familiar with the patient's condition, therapy regimen, and its rationale, so that they may provide emotional support during and after hospitalization. Sensitive, caring family members can be instrumental in making possible recovery to the patient's fullest potential.

Some patients may not require intensive rehabilitation training, or it may not be available to them. Some degree of physician-guided care may be provided at home by family members, friends, and visiting nurses who can apply basic principles of rehabilitation therapy.

Vocational Assistance

If the stroke victim has been actively employed, or now wishes to enter the labor market, evaluation of work skills and vocational counseling may be very helpful. Involvement in a sheltered workshop may be beneficial (see CHAPTER 8: THE SHELTERED WORK-

SHOP). As the peak incidence of stroke is near the period of retirement, vocational rehabilitation is a less significant aspect of recovery than it is in many other conditions. But the Department of Vocational Rehabilitation statistics for 1969, which show that less than 1 percent of their rehabilitated clients had stroke-caused disability, do suggest a disinterest in stroke victims far out of proportion to their numbers in the work-force age range.

Aids and Devices

Among the aids which make it possible for patients to get from one place to another, the first device to be used in most cases of completed stroke is a wheelchair. Usually an individual will progress to walking with a walker or a four- or three-legged cane, or a straight cane, or to no device at all. Long and short leg bracing may be helpful to support a weak hip, knee, or ankle. Bracing may be needed only temporarily until strength is regained. Various types of slings may be used to support a paralyzed arm, protect it from injury, and help in the control of swelling (edema). Splints may be applied to prevent contractures, especially of the hand, fingers, or feet. Other devices may be used in performing the activities of daily living. Many are designed to compensate for the inability to use one side of the body effectively. For example, to help in eating, a special knife allows the patient to cut with one hand. Dressing devices help extend reach in putting on and taking off clothing. Special fasteners aid in buttoning or closing articles of clothing. In the bathroom, a person may need a raised toilet seat to minimize bending. Bars or railings can be installed to provide support. A stool for sitting in the shower or a chair in the tub will help to minimize the difficult maneuver of getting in and out of the bath.

There are aids to reading and writing, such as stands on which to do work or special holders which attach to a hand which is too weak to grip a pen properly. Housework and especially cooking are areas in which a good deal of ingenuity has been applied. Many kitchen organizers are available even in ordinary hardware stores. Furniture around the house may need to be raised or lowered to minimize bending. (See CHAPTER 5: INDEPENDENT LIVING: WAYS AND MEANS.)

Research

Basic science research into stroke is a part of the larger study of the cardiovascular system as a whole, and includes the system's susceptibility to disease, hereditary factors which predispose a person to certain problems, and the aging process. Attempts are being made to determine whether controlling significant variables — blood pressure levels, diet, blood sugar levels, and emotional stress — will prevent strokes from occurring. More attention is being paid to warning signs, and especially to what appear to be "ministrokes," which if detected may allow for preventive treatment such as surgery.

To understand what causes strokes, it is most helpful to know as much as possible about stroke victims. Statistics about the incidence and types of strokes (such as clot or hemorrhage) occurring in various areas, among various races, within different age groups, in certain types of environments, etc. are hard to obtain and to analyze. Better forms of data collection and analysis should greatly improve our understanding of this disorder.

Research into the development of labor-saving and self-help devices, as well as evaluation and retraining methods, goes on continuously in rehabilitation centers and in industry.

Organizations

Nationally there are two organizations which take a significant interest in stroke. The American Heart Association (7320 Greenville Avenue, Dallas, TX 75231) has many local branches which provide information to stroke patients and families about services available to them. Local associations may sponsor classes for families and lecture series on stroke for physicians. The Association publishes several informative booklets about the condition, home care, aids and devices, and therapy activities. The emphasis in this literature is on getting good medical advice for all phases of recovery.

The National Easter Seal Society for Crippled Children and Adults (2023 West Ogden Avenue, Chicago, IL 60612) concerns itself with stroke as well as many other conditions, and provides rehabilitation care for stroke patients at Easter Seal Centers. There are many local chapters which offer a broad range of services, including home services, equipment loan pools, speech therapy, workshops for vocational experiences, job placement, recreational programs, referral services for patients and families, lobbying, and public pressure to improve environmental conditions for the handicapped.

The National Heart Institute and the National Institute of Neurological and Communication Disorders and Stroke are federal research institutes which deal with the problems of stroke.

Stroke Clubs have been started in many communities by stroke victims. The Easter Seal Society has resolved to encourage and support this effort. The Visiting Nurse Association can be contacted if home nursing care or home health teaching is needed after hospitalization. Home Health Services under the Medicare Act are available to all stroke victims over the age of sixty-five. These include physical, occupational, and speech therapy services, which can be provided in the patient's home.

SELECTED REFERENCES

American Heart Association: *Aphasia and the Family; Do It Yourself Again: Self-help Devices for the Stroke Patient; Strike Back at Stroke; Strokes: A Guide for the Family.*

Buck, McKenzie, "Life with a Stroke," *Crippled Child,* December 1957.

Hodgkins, Eric, *Episode: A Report on the Accident Inside My Skull,* Atheneum, New York, 1968.

National Easter Seal Society: *Developing an Out-Patient Treatment Program for*

Stroke Clients; First Aid for Aphasics, by Joseph S. Keenan; *Handy, Helpful Hints for the Handicapped,* by Julius D. Lombardi; *Home Care of the Stroke Patient* (annotated references); *Publications of Families of Adult Aphasics: A Review of the Literature,* by Mary Pannbacker (reprinted from *Rehabilitation Literature,* March 1972); *Speech Problems of Hemiplegic Patients,* by Martha L. Taylor, 1972; *Stroke Clubs: How To Organize a Group Program for Stroke Patients and Their Families; Stroke Rehabilitation,* by Rehabilitation Study Group, Joint Committee for Stroke Facilities, 1972.

U.S. Department of Health, Education and Welfare, *Cerebral Vascular Disease and Strokes,* Superintendent of Documents, Government Printing Office, Washington, DC 20402.

Wilbert, E. Fordyce, and Roy S. Fowler, *Stroke: Why Do They Behave That Way?,* State Heart Association, Seattle, 1974.

53

Venereal Disease

The American Social Health Association, Palo Alto,
California

Venereal disease is an experiential classification for a number of
etiologically and pathologically different infections that share one
common aspect—they are sexually transmissible. [Sexually transmissible disease (STD) and venereal disease (VD) are today considered interchangeable terms.]

The increasing incidence of the various forms of venereal disease
makes these disorders extremely serious problems of our time. Although in their early stages they present medical and social rather
than rehabilitative challenges, in their later stages they can result
in major disability.

With regard to incidence, among the most common forms of venereal disease are gonococcal urethritis (GU or gonorrhea), nongonococcal urethritis (NGU), trichomoniasis, genital herpes
(herpesvirus hominis type 2, or HVH-2), and syphilis. In addition to
these five, which are incontrovertibly sexually transmissible, a
sixth, cytomegalovirus (CMV), bears consideration as recent evidence suggests it too is sexually transmissible. It must also be noted
that there are at least fourteen other sexually transmissible diseases
and conditions.

Historically there is known to have been a serious outbreak of
syphilis in Europe after Columbus returned from his discovery of
the New World, and this led some historians to hypothesize that the
disease originated in the West Indies. However, it is more likely
that it existed in Europe prior to that historical event, but was rela-

tively rare. Gonorrhea, without question, has been with humans throughout recorded history.

Of the six venereal diseases to be discussed, reported incidence data are available on only two, gonorrhea and syphilis [though according to the U.S. Public Health Service (USPHS), these reported data understate the extent of their actual incidence due to underreporting and underdiagnosis].

The incidence of gonorrhea in the United States has quadrupled since 1962. At that time there were roughly 260,000 reported cases; now reported cases stand at over 1 million. And according to USPHS estimates, actual gonorrhea incidence is closer to 3 million cases annually. Reported early syphilis (primary, secondary, and early latent cases) has also registered an increase over that same time period, though not as steadily or as dramatically as gonorrhea. Presently there are nearly 52,000 cases of early syphilis reported annually, as compared with 40,000 in 1962.

Annual incidence estimates have been made relative to nongonococcal urethritis, trichomoniasis, and genital herpes. Extrapolations from samples conducted in both the public and private sectors as well as data derived from Great Britain and some of the Scandinavian countries suggest estimated annual occurrence in the United States at the following levels: nongonococcal urethritis — 2.5 million cases; trichomoniasis — 3 million cases; genital herpes — 300,000 cases. No reasonable estimate of annual CMV incidence level is available.

As stated previously, these several diseases are etiologically and pathologically different, although it is possible to be infected with them all at the same time. One of the greatest dangers associated with five of the six diseases is that women seldom exhibit any noticeable symptoms during the early stages of infection. As a result, they often do not know they are infected until told by their male contacts or diagnosed medically. (Trichomoniasis is the one infection with which women can be expected to be noticeably symptomatic.)

Gonorrhea

Only 20 percent of women with gonorrhea experience any symptoms of infection. Such symptoms generally consist of a burning sensation in the genital area or some vaginal discharge. Men, however, generally experience noticeable symptoms of infection, usually within two to seven days after contact. Such symptoms consist of pain during urination or pus discharge from the penis. (Recent data suggest that a small but significant proportion of urethrally infected males may experience no noticeable symptoms at all.) If left untreated, serious complications can arise, often resulting in loss of fertility in male or female.

Complications of gonorrhea in women include various inflammatory diseases of the reproductive tract and general pelvic area, including inflammation of the fallopian tubes (salpingitis), inflammation of the lining of the uterus (endometritis), and gonococcal pelvic inflammatory disease (PID). Extragenital (disseminated) gonococcal complications are rare, but have been observed and include inflammation of the lining of the heart (endocarditis), other problems of the heart and aortic valves, and gonococcal arthritis. In men, complications tend to occur less frequently since the early symptoms of the disease are more noticeable and more painful, and therefore generally lead to earlier treatment. When they occur, disseminated gonococcal complications follow the same pattern as in women. With respect to genitourinary tract complications, the foci in males are usually the testicles, prostate gland, and seminal vesicles.

Syphilis

The first symptom of syphilis is a painless sore or hard chancre developing at the site of inoculation and appearing about three weeks after exposure to the infected person (though incubation periods of as little as ten days and as long as three months are possible). A sore of this type is also present in infected women, but is usually located internally. Since no pain is associated with the chancre, women are not likely to realize they have become infected. The chancre will generally disappear without treatment, usually within one to five weeks, but that does not mean the disease is cured. A second stage begins several weeks later and is characterized by such symptoms as multiple sores, skin rashes, hair loss, sore throat, fever, and headache. The disease is particularly insidious because these symptoms also disappear in time, even without treatment. Secondary symptoms may recur for up to two years, after which no outward signs will be experienced (with the exception of gummatous lesions — symptomatic of late infection).

The period of latency is characterized by the lack of any outward signs or symptoms. It is during this stage that the attack on internal organs such as the lymph glands, spleen, blood vessels, heart, spinal cord, and brain begins. It may be a long time (ten to twenty years) before the damage begun in the third stage manifests itself, if it does at all. Data indicate that as many as two-thirds of potential victims escape serious consequences owing to spontaneous cure or life-long latency (in which, although the infection persists, no complications arise). It may be that in this age of widespread antibiotic use, inadvertent therapy (even at subtherapeutic levels) may further reduce one's likelihood of experiencing complications — although it must be stressed that they do still occur.

One of these complications is meningovascular syphilis, a form of cerebral syphilis in which the blood vessels and brain coverings (meninges) are attacked by the causative spirochete. This condition takes two forms: syphilitic meningitis and vascular neurosyphilis. Syphilitic meningitis is divided into three types: (1) basilar meningitis, an inflammation of the base of the brain leading to such symptoms as headache, memory impairment for recent events, dulled mentality, drowsiness and, in some cases, confusion, double vision, and deafness; (2) vertical meningitis, which involves more extensive areas of the brain, and produces such manifestations as dizziness, severe headaches, retarded thought and speech, irritability, and sometimes confusion and delirium, but without serious disturbance of personality or behavior; and (3) acute syphilitic hydrocephalus, a rare condition involving impairment in the absorption of the cerebrospinal fluid, and characterized by headache, nausea, vomiting, and stiff neck.

The other form of meningovascular syphilis, vascular neurosyphilis, usually accompanies the early stages of syphilitic meningitis, and is characterized by intermittent headaches, insomnia, dizziness, emotional instability, increasing apathy, and memory impairment, which may in later stages be followed by vascular accidents resulting in temporary neurological disturbances such as aphasia and hemiplegia, with some loss of intellectual capacity.

An even more severe complication of untreated syphilis is general paresis (also called general paralysis or meningoencephalitis), an inflammatory disease in which the neural tissue of the brain is damaged. During its early stages the symptoms are relatively mild and easily overlooked: forgetfulness, headaches, disturbed sleep, fatigue, exaggeration of previous personality traits, and deterioration of manners, morals, and judgment accompanied by total unconcern and lack of insight. As the disease advances, personality deterioration sets in, and the patient tends to fall into one of three categories: (1) the demented or simple type, characterized by mental deterioration, loss of interest and alertness, vacant expression, and withdrawal; (2) the depressed type, characterized by increasing despondency over failing abilities, loss of insight, and hypochondriacal or nihilistic delusions in which the patient comes to believe the internal organs have ceased functioning or have disappeared, leaving only a hollow shell; and (3) the expansive type, characterized by euphoria developing into grandiose ideas of untold wealth and power. These mental symptoms are accompanied by a variety of physical symptoms: sluggish pupils (Argyll-Robertson pupil), sagging facial muscles and an "ironed-out" facies, slurred speech, poor handwriting, tremors, unsteady gait, and in some cases sudden fevers, paralysis, and convulsions. In the terminal period the patient gradually sinks to a vegetative level of existence, until infection produces a final breakdown of all body functions, ultimately resulting in death.

There are several other types of neurosyphilis. In Lissauer's type, cerebral destruction is localized on one side of the cortex, resulting in a moth-eaten appearance called status spongiosis. The major symptoms are aphasic speech disorders, deafness, epileptic attacks, and paralysis on one side of the body. In taboparesis patients are afflicted not only with brain tissue damage but with a degeneration of the posterior nerves of the spinal cord (tabes dorsalis). They exhibit the usual mental symptoms of general paresis, but in addition experience shooting pains in the legs, an unsteady gait (locomotor ataxia), abdominal pain, incontinence, impotence, and in some cases optic atrophy that may lead to blindness. In juvenile paresis the child has contracted the infection from the mother during pregnancy, but due to the long developmental period of the disease, may not begin to show symptoms (in less than 1 percent of cases) until between the ages of five and twenty. In about one-third of these cases physical development is retarded, and in over 40 percent there is some degree of congenital mental retardation, usually followed by progressive dementia. Some of these children become increasingly restless and confused, and many of them experience convulsions. Treatment is less effective than in adult paresis, and remissions are uncommon. The child gradually becomes mute, untidy, and emaciated, and usually dies within four to five years after acute onset. Fortunately this disorder is now rare due to administration of tests to pregnant women and the efficacy of penicillin treatment.

Syphilis may also affect the cardiovascular system, causing serious heart problems, including inflammation and aneurysms of the aorta and involvement of the coronary arteries. In some cases infection of the vascular system may lead to nerve destruction, and a sudden strokelike hemiplegia may occur on one side of the body due to inadequate oxygen supply to the brain. Also there may be paraplegia, or paralysis of the lower extremities due to lack of blood supply to the spinal cord.

Nongonococcal Urethritis

There are many agents of infection of the lower urogenital tract other than the gonococcus (the bacterium that causes gonorrhea). *Chlamydia trachomatis* and *Ureaplasma urealyticum* (also known as T-mycoplasma) are currently regarded as the major etiological agents in nongonococcal urethritis.

While the true incubation period has yet to be conclusively determined, it is generally considered to be eight to fourteen days. In the male, the usual presentation is with low-grade urethritis, with scanty or moderate mucopurulent urethral discharge and variable dysuria. Symptoms often subside spontaneously over a period of two to three months without treatment, though such cessation of symptoms is not necessarily indicative of spontaneous cure. Rather, clinical complications of urethral stricture, epididymitis, and prostatitis indicate that spontaneous cure should not be assumed.

In women, the disease is often asymptomatic (similar to gonorrhea), although hypertrophic erosion and endocervical mucopus may be noticeable upon internal examination. Complications of prolonged infection may include bartholinitis and pelvic inflammatory disease.

Herpesvirus Hominis Type 2

Herpesvirus hominis type 2, or HVH-2 (not to be confused with HVH type 1, commonly referred to as cold sores), is a sexually acquirable condition characterized by painful and recurrent genital lesions.

Approximately two to twenty days after exposure, the first symptoms of HVH-2 infection can be expected to occur in the form of minor rashes or itching in the genital area. The symptoms then commonly develop into one or more painful blisterlike, fluid-filled lesions or cluster of lesions lasting for about twenty days. Dysuria, inguinal lymphadenopathy, vaginal discharge, and occasionally systemic manifestations accompany HVH-2 lesion development. Dysuria is more common in women than in men, and is correlated with recovery of HVH-2 from the urethra. The lesions eventually disappear as do the accompanying symptoms.

However, symptoms remisson is not indicative of cure. Most patients who have primary genital herpes develop recurrent genital lesions, with each recurrence presenting in roughly the same manner as did the primary episode, though somewhat less severely. There is no apparent pattern of recurrent infection; the duration and frequency vary with the individual and may be triggered by a variety of physical or even emotional factors.

HVH-2 infection has been shown to be associated with cervical cancer by seroepidemiologic and cytohistopathic studies, and by demonstration of HVH-2 DNA fragments and HVH-2 antigens in cervical carcinoma tissue. The oncogenic potential of HVH-2 is further suggested by evidence of transformation of tissue cells in culture by HVH-2, and by the known oncogenicity of other herpesviruses in other animals.

HVH-2 early in pregnancy has been associated with fetal wastage. Studies have indicated that one-third of pregnancies associated with cytologic evidence of maternal herpetic infections early in pregnancy resulted in spontaneous abortion. Maternal genital herpetic infection during the third trimester also presents a problem. Upwards of two-thirds of infants born to women who have clinically apparent HVH-2 infections at term develop neonatal herpetic infection. In most cases the organisms apparently are transmitted to the fetus during passage through the birth canal or by ascending infection following rupture of the membranes. The great majority of infected infants die or develop serious neurological complications. Some physicians attempt to protect the infant from infection by performing an elective caesarean section before or as soon as possible after the membrane has ruptured and by isolating the infant from the mother following delivery.

Trichomoniasis

Trichomoniasis has been well established as a sexually transmissible disease. In women, inoculation with *Trichomonas vaginalis,* the causative protozoan, generally results in prominent symptoms after an incubation interval of four to twenty-eight days. Such symptoms include severe itching, vulvar edema and irritation, and a copious discharge. Inguinal adenopathy may be present. In men, infection with *T. vaginalis* is frequently a symptomless state. Occasionally, slight itching and discomfort inside the penis may occur. Also slight moistness at the tip of the penis may be present. Generally these symptoms disappear spontaneously, although the organism remains in the urethral tract.

In women, complications associated with trichomoniasis tend to be correlated with repeated rather than prolonged infection, as the severity of symptoms generally promotes rapid diagnosis and treatment. Repeated trichomonal infection frequently precipitates cervical erosions and may predispose cervical tissue to malignant transformation. In men, prostatic involvement, epididymitis, and urethral stricture can result from infection with *T. vaginalis.*

Since men are generally symptomless, therapy extended to symptomatic females must coincide with treatment for all male sexual partners, as repeated infection in women is most frequently the result of reinfection rather than therapeutic failure.

Cytomegalovirus

Cytomegalovirus (CMV) is the most common viral cause of mental retardation, surpassing even rubella virus. It is estimated that 1 out of every 1,000 infants — that is, more than 3,000 per year in the United States alone — is seriously retarded as a result of congenital CMV infection.

Evidence now exists supporting the hypothesis that CMV is sexually transmissible. The organism has been demonstrated in seminal fluid.

Cytomegalovirus appears widely distributed in human populations throughout the world. In the United States, up to 80 percent of some study populations acquired antibodies that are indicative of infection with the virus by the age of thirty-five or forty years. Effects are minimal for most healthy individuals who acquire the infection after birth; they may have no symptoms at all, but may continue to shed the virus in their body secretions for months.

The severe consequences of cytomegalovirus are associated with congenital infection of neonates. Transplacental spread of the virus from an infected mother to the developing fetus appears to pose a greater threat than infection of the neonate with the virus at birth. In addition to serious mental retardation, neonatal complications may include blindness, deafness, cerebral palsy, enlargement of the spleen, and blood abnormalities. Occasionally, neonatal mortality is a direct or indirect result of disseminated CMV infection.

Diagnosis and Treatment

Diagnosis of the aforementioned (and other) sexually transmissible diseases can be established clinically and in concert with a variety of laboratory supports. Diagnostic techniques and laboratory tests are generally specific to the particular disease.

All sexually transmissible diseases of a bacteriologic nature are fully treatable with antibiotics. Specific antibiotics and dosages vary with the disease. Those sexually transmissible diseases of viral origin are not subject to curative therapy, although symptoms may be relieved in some instances.

Research

Research on the sexually transmissible diseases is currently being conducted by the National Institutes of Health, the Center for Disease Control, the Venereal Diseases Research Fund of the American Social Health Association, the National Foundation, and the American Cancer Society. Research efforts are currently focused on basic biology of the agents, better diagnostic tests, better therapeutic agents, and vaccines.

Organizations

The Venereal Disease Control Division of the Center for Disease Control of the Department of Health, Education and Welfare is the federal agency responsible for venereal disease control in the United States. City, county, and state public health officers and venereal disease clinics are also involved.

The American Social Health Association (ASHA), founded in 1912, is a national nonprofit organization that has as its major objective the control and elimination of venereal disease. ASHA works in cooperation with interested local agencies, sponsors research, and acts as a clearinghouse for information on venereal disease control. Among the many periodical publications available to members of ASHA are *VD News* and *VD Alert*. In addition, all special reports and monographs produced by the Association are available to members. Membership information is available from ASHA National Headquarters, 260 Sheridan Avenue, Palo Alto, CA 94306.

Many of those involved in venereal disease control in the United States and abroad are members of the American Venereal Disease Association, whose main purpose is dissemination of information on the subject.

SELECTED REFERENCES

Holmes, K. K., "Sexually Transmitted Diseases," *University of Washington Medicine*, vol. 21, no. 1, Winter 1976.

King, A., and C. Nicol, *Venereal Diseases*, F. A. Davis, Philadelphia, 1969.

Nalimias, A., "The TORCH Complex," *Hospital Practice*, May 1974.

VD Fact Sheet 1975, U.S. Department of Health, Education and Welfare, Public Health Service, edition 32.

VD News, American Social Health Association, vol. 1, no. 2, June 1976.

"Venereal Disease in Obstetrics and Gynecology," *Clinical Obstetrics and Gynecology*, vol. 18, no. 1, March 1975.

"Venereal Diseases," *Medical Clinics of North America*, vol. 56, no. 5, September 1972.

Today's Venereal Disease Control Problem, 1975, American Social Health Association, March 1975.

54

Other Disorders

Sections A, C-E, and G-K by ROBERT M. GOLDENSON, Ph.D.

A. Arthrogryposis Multiplex Congenita

Reviewed by JUDITH G. HALL, M.D., Associate Professor, Pediatrics and Medicine, University of Washington School of Medicine, Seattle

Arthrogryposis (literally "crooked joint disorder") multiplex congenita is a birth defect characterized by congenital rigid contracture or limitation in movement of joints. In the past the term has been used as a single specific diagnosis, but recent research suggests that it is a symptom seen in a number of different conditions. An estimated 500 new cases occur each year in the United States. Bilateral clubfoot, the most common congenital skeletal deformity, is regarded as a minimal form of the syndrome, which usually involves several joints in different body areas—hence the term "multiplex." The articular elements (bones and cartilage) are all present and normal, but they are fixed, often in distorted positions, by surrounding soft-tissue structures, including tendons, ligaments, and skin. Although the foot is most often affected (in about 90 percent of cases), the hips are involved at least half the time (often with dislocation), and the wrists, elbows, and knees somewhat less often. The severely involved infant is sometimes likened to a wooden doll, and may have flexed or extended joints.

The most seriously affected patients die in infancy, due to feeding and respiratory problems. Among those who live, the condition is generally nonprogressive, but in many cases there is marked muscular weakness and atrophy in addition to joint contractures. Congenital limitation of joint movement is known to occur in a number of specific disorders such as meningomyelocele, spinal tumor, trisomy 18, diastrophic dwarfism (in this chapter, see SECTION C, Dwarfism), and congenital myotonic dystrophy. Thus confusion has arisen because the term AMC has also been used to describe these conditions. (See CHAPTER 41: MUSCULAR DYSTROPHY; CHAPTER 50: SPINA BIFIDA.)

Autopsy studies of cases of AMC in which no other syndrome is recognized have revealed significant abnormalities at some level of the neuromuscular system, frequently changes in the motor neurons (anterior horn cells), which probably led to skeletal muscle paralysis at an early stage of prenatal development. The disorder may be related to other conditions involving loss of motor neurons, especially the congenital form of Werdnig-Hoffmann disease, in which joint contractures occur in about one-third of cases; and the Möbius syndrome, characterized by congenital paralysis of facial and eye muscles and often by clubfoot and AMC as well. In still other cases abnormalities of the muscle or connective tissue early in intrauterine development seem to be primarily responsible for fixation of joints.

Observations and experiments performed by Daniel B. Drachman, of Johns Hopkins University, suggest that the joint malformations may result from relatively brief immobilization of the developing embryo. This is indicated by the fact that "in almost all cases of AMC, there is a clear history of weak or absent fetal movements." To test this hypothesis, Drachman administered paralyzing drugs intravenously to chick embryos for twenty-four to seventy-two hours at various developmental stages, and found that all of them exhibited joint deformities when born, and "a comparison of the anatomical findings in these joints with the reported findings in human cases of congenital clubfoot and AMC reveals that the conditions are pathologically identical." Moreover, the particular deformity was "attributable to moulding by the walls of the confined space available to the developing embryo," and appeared to reflect the position of the embryo at the time the immobilization occurred.

Drachman concludes that "there is strong evidence that impairment of embryonic movements causes AMC in man," and that studies have shown that the impairment, or paralysis, can be due to a "defect in the neuromuscular system." There is apparently not a single cause for this defect; it can be due to intrauterine neuropathy, myopathies, abnormalities of connective tissue, or limitation of space. In some cases it may be traced to a spinal cord lesion which can only be detected microscopically; in others, the lesion may be far more evident, as in meningomyelocele (see CHAPTER 50: SPINA BIFIDA). Cases of decreased fetal motility may also be associated with congenital muscular dystrophy, prenatal brain damage, or extraembryonic conditions that might interfere mechanically with embryonic movement, such as oligohydramnios (deficiency in amniotic fluid) or polyhydramnios (excess of amniotic fluid).

Familial cases of AMC have been reported but most cases are sporadic, and as yet it is not possible to distinguish which types are definitely familial. When there is a family history, the inheritance pattern is usually obvious (autosomal dominant, recessive, or X-linked); but when there is no family history, it is generally felt that there is about 5 percent chance of recurrence. In some cases there is a history of abnormality during gestation, such as maternal exposure to rubella, high fevers, viral illness, or premature delivery, and in these cases there would be little risk of recurrence. Werdnig-Hoffmann disease may also be one of the causes of AMC. However, at this point the majority of cases, especially those involving neural damage, cannot be related to any known hereditary or prenatal factors. All that can be said with certainty is that the disorder has diverse etiology.

Just as there is no single cause, so there is no single approach to treatment and rehabilitation, since there are many types of AMC which may be associated with many other disabling conditions. A study of the various types, etiologies, and treatment approaches is being conducted by Judith G. Hall and associates at the Children's Orthopedic Hospital and Medical Center in Seattle. Preliminary findings indicate that three groups of patients may be distinguished. The first group consists of those with involvement only of limbs, with normal head and trunks, but with muscle absence probably due to defective development of the limbs. These patients do not respond well to physical therapy. Radical surgery is usually required to give them stabilization, but they develop very little useful movement in the involved arms and legs. Intelligence is usually normal.

The second group shows more generalized involvement, including the head, face, or trunk; the arms and legs are often fixed in a bent position (flexion contractures) from birth. Surgery may not be required, since these patients are often quite responsive to physical therapy and often achieve good use of arms and legs in time. However, they may be afflicted with other congenital anomalies, such as ptosis, cleft palate, or scoliosis. Some show mild mental retardation. They probably represent diverse etiologies, and about a third have a family history of other affected individuals.

The third category, termed CNS (central nervous system), includes patients with severe brain damage, often with microcephaly, who have a very poor prognosis. These patients are not responsive to either surgery or physical therapy and may have progressive contractures.

An organization of AMC individuals and their families has recently been formed: Arthrogryposis Association, Inc. (106 Herkimer Street, North Bellmore, NY 11710).

B. Ataxia

LAWRENCE J. SCHUT, M.D., Medical Director, National
Ataxia Foundation, and PHYLLIS ROSS PANTELL

Many forms of ataxia are known. Friedreich's ataxia strikes the younger person, often below ten years of age or in the teens. Marie's ataxia (which includes many variations) generally attacks the adult. There is also a late onset form of ataxia which does not lead to premature death but often is disabling. Ataxia is generally an inherited disorder but may occur spontaneously.

Ataxia is basically a disorder of coordination due to spinocerebellar degenerative disease. "Spino" refers to the spinal cord, which transmits messages between the brain and the body. "Cerebellar" refers to the cerebellum (little brain), in the lower back portion of the skull, which controls muscular coordination. As the cells of the spinal cord and cerebellum degenerate, messages sent from the cerebellum are transmitted less and less clearly, until coordination fails and the brain can no longer effectively control the muscles. Thus persons with hereditary ataxia gradually become helpless.

From the onset of ataxic symptoms, there is progressive disability. It affects balance and coordination first, impairs speech, and interferes with swallowing and, finally, breathing and clearing of secretions. From the onset, the victim has possibly a ten-to-thirty-year life expectancy. People with ataxia do not die of ataxia, but (most often and prematurely) from its complications.

Hereditary ataxia is commonly misdiagnosed as multiple sclerosis because of the many similarities between the symptoms and signs of the two. Hereditary ataxia should not be confused with locomotor ataxia, which is associated with syphilitic infection of the nervous system. Hereditary ataxia is not contagious, nor is it a mental disorder. The cause is generally a defective gene, and there is no known cure.

Incidence

Ataxia respects no one. Hereditary ataxia victims are both male and female; the disease strikes all races and ethnic groups, and is found in every country of the world. At least 50,000 Americans are afflicted with the disease. Some regions have a greater number of victims, due to the fact that families with ataxia tend to remain close together.

Etiology

Hereditary ataxia is passed from one generation to the next and is due to a defective gene. The diagram shows how a dominant hereditary disease, which can affect a male or female, is passed on through three generations. The key fact is that in each pregnancy, whether the husband or wife is affected by the disease, there is a 50 percent chance that offspring will be born with the abnormal gene.

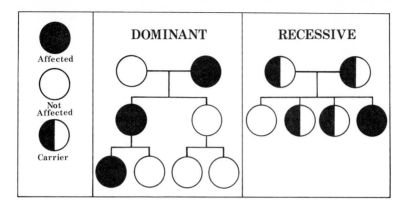

Any child receiving this abnormal gene will develop the disease at some point in life.

The diagram also shows the inheritance pattern for a recessive disease. In this case an affected person receives a defective gene from both parents, who are carriers but are often unaware of that fact. Each child has a 25 percent chance of acquiring both defective genes and inheriting the disorder. This person will, in turn, be capable of passing one defective gene to each child in the next generation. Two carriers can also produce a child with no defective genes (again a 25 percent chance) or a child who is merely a carrier (a 50 percent chance) and not show any significant signs of the disorder.

Marie's ataxia is passed on as a dominant hereditary disease, which means that each child of a parent with Marie's ataxia has a 50 percent chance of getting the disease. A child who does not receive the defective gene cannot become ataxic, nor can he or she pass this form of ataxia on; generations thereafter are thus free of the disease.

In Friedreich's ataxia the parents do not have ataxic symptoms, but each carries the recessive gene which can produce ataxia in approximately one out of four of their children. (The exception, although very remote, could occur if an afflicted parent married a carrier of the recessive gene. Each of their children would have a 50 percent chance of being afflicted; all offspring would be carriers.) It is impossible to predict whether Friedreich's ataxia will strike a youngster. The recessive gene may be dormant for generations and then suddenly reveal itself when two unsuspecting carriers marry and have children.

Symptoms

Ataxia cannot be diagnosed before the symptoms appear. There is no prenatal test to determine whether the disease is present in the fetus, nor is there a neurological or other diagnostic study that will give early warning of the disease.

Most forms of ataxia begin with a gait disturbance. In Friedreich's ataxia this disturbance is often associated with pes cavus (a foot with an abnormally high longitudinal arch) and scoliosis (lateral curvature of the spine). It may first be noted by poor performance in sports or awkwardness in negotiating stairs. As the disease progresses, there is great difficulty in walking. The gait is wide-based, with a drunken stagger and a tendency to fall frequently. This may be accompanied by severe instability of the trunk and a nodding of the head. Occasionally, the muscles in the lower extremities become spastic or tight. Muscular wasting occurs in some ataxia victims and may be accompanied by general weakness. Locomotion eventually can be accomplished only with the use of a cane, then a walker, and finally a wheelchair.

The ataxias vary with respect to other symptoms. Incoordination of the upper extremities or severe tremor may eventually disable the patient completely. Speech gradually becomes slurred, slow, and halting, with gradual deterioration culminating in total unintelligibility. Swallowing becomes difficult; the cough is weak and breathy; and choking is a major hazard. Sensory loss (light touch, pain, temperature) may be found in more advanced cases. Some persons with ataxia may experience reduced vision, which may progress to blindness. Mental deterioration may also occur to some degree, but is not a striking feature. Bladder control is usually not lost until the disease is far advanced.

Those ataxias, such as Marie's, which begin in young adulthood or middle age tend to progress more rapidly, while those which begin in later life generally have a more benign course. Those who succumb to the disease usually die of overwhelming pneumonia, which may occur within ten to thirty years after the onset.

In Friedreich's ataxia there is a high association rate with diabetes, perhaps up to 20 percent. The heart is often affected, with minor changes in the electrocardiogram seen in the majority of patients. Some persons develop an irregular rhythm, congestive heart failure, or even heart attacks.

Treatment

There is no reliable amelioration of this condition. Symptoms, such as spastic or tight muscles and twitching, may be controlled by medication to a certain degree. Propranolol has proved to be effective for some of the particularly distressing symptoms of tremor. Dantrium sodium may be of limited help for those patients with muscle tightness of the lower extremities.

Prevention of pneumonia is a constant challenge in the care of ataxic patients. Instruction in proper swallowing techniques, postural drainage, chest percussion, and discreet use of antibiotics is helpful. Foods which tend to precipitate choking spells should be avoided. Milk and related products tend to be poorly handled.

Prevention

There are many facts to know and many important decisions to be made by persons afflicted with hereditary ataxia and the significant people (spouse, children, immediate family members) in their world. Correct diagnosis of the disease and a knowledge of the type of inheritance (dominant or recessive) involved is basic to making these decisions. Genetic counseling, based on medical facts, offers the best way to make decisions about family planning. Most forms of ataxia are inherited and defective genes are passed from generation to generation. The frequency of ataxia could be lessened if those who are known to have the defective gene would not reproduce. In order to prevent passing the disorder to future generations, these persons can decide to have no children by using birth control methods or by undergoing sterilization; or in the case of the dominant form of ataxia, can delay having children until the person is certain of not developing the disease. This may be a quite unreliable method, as the age of onset varies significantly.

Research efforts are directed toward early detection of the disease, discovery of the biochemical defect, and further understanding of its genetic basis. Studies include muscle, nerve, and cerebellar biopsies. The funds available for this type of research are limited.

Rehabilitation

A rehabilitation program has limited value for patients because ataxia is a progressive deteriorating disease. An effort to maintain a state of good nutrition and muscle tone, and to use help with ambulation, as long as possible, are of some benefit.

Adjustment to the disease is extremely difficult. The patient with hereditary ataxia may have lived in fear of developing the disease, even before the earliest manifestations, because a parent or sibling had the disorder. This person requires a great deal of family support, medical supervision, and family physician concern, as well as community awareness. The patient is often dependent on governmental means of family support, such as welfare, aid to dependent children, Social Security Disability, and Medicaid. This can be a devastating threat to the ego. Encouragement of the patient, maintenance of morale, and freedom from mental and emotional stress and fatigue are important.

Usually, the spouse or others close to the victim need counseling in learning to cope with changes occurring in the patient. They too need encouragement and support in handling the additional responsibilities. They must be educated about the disease in order to understand and cope with its various stages, to participate in decisions, and to carry out treatment. Genetic counseling is extremely important for the victim and close relatives. There are, in most localities, professionals (neurologists, geneticists, nurses, etc.) who can offer encouragement and helpful advice to the ataxic person and family.

Organizations

The National Ataxia Foundation (4225 Golden Valley Road, Minneapolis, MN 55422) is engaged in all phases of the field: service, prevention, education, and research. Through chapters located in many parts of the country, it encourages all victims and possible victims to have a complete neurological examination and makes arrangements for genetic counseling. Two free clinics are sponsored every year at its headquarters, and clinics are held from time to time in other sections of the country. Data obtained at these clinics are used to further the understanding of ataxia and to assist in developing early detection techniques. The clinic staff recognizes the needs of the victim and family, and tries to offer ways of dealing with the stress and strain (social, physical, spiritual, emotional, and financial).

The National Ataxia Foundation shares a common medical and scientific board with the Friedreich's Ataxia Group in America (P.O. Box 1116, Oakland, CA 94611), which is also dedicated to education, research, and patient care for the different types of ataxia. The Muscular Dystrophy Association (710 Seventh Avenue, New York, NY 10019) is also deeply involved with the problem, and conducts both a research and a service program. Patient services, including referrals and information about aids and appliances, as well as genetic counseling, are provided by many of its local chapters. Grants-in-aid are awarded to specialists and centers engaged in investigating the basic pathological processes that give rise to peripheral nerve disorders such as Friedreich's ataxia, including studies of the close electrochemical relationship between muscle and nerve, the transmission of motor impulses from the spinal cord to the muscle cells, and the biochemical substances involved.

C. Dwarfism

Reviewed by JUDITH G. HALL, M.D., Associate Professor, Pediatrics and Medicine, University of Washington School of Medicine, Seattle

A dwarf is an individual with disproportional, short stature. The disproportion may be primarily in the trunk or in the limbs. Some types of dwarfism are characterized by both short trunks and short limbs. Overall height is generally under 4 feet 10 inches (147 centimeters). In contrast, the midget is characterized by extremely short stature, but the body proportions are normal.

There are an estimated half million American adults of short stature, many of whom are dwarfs. Over fifty specific types of dwarfism are now distinguishable. Some are present at birth, others do not become evident until the child is two or three years old. Most recognized types of dwarfism are hereditary disorders. Some are due to a recessive gene, others to dominant inheritance, and still others are X-linked. Most dwarfs are fertile and can have children. However, dwarfed women frequently require caesarean section. The particular type of inheritance depends on the specific diagnosis, and so genetic study and counseling are strongly advised for any dwarfed individual thinking of having children.

Dwarfism is not in itself considered a disabling condition, since most dwarfs are able to live a normal life—holding jobs, marrying, and raising families. However, some types of dwarfism are known to develop serious complications involving the musculoskeletal system, the spinal cord or nerve roots, eyes, heart and respiratory system, and these complications may drastically interfere with health and adjustment to life. Some of these conditions can be corrected surgically; others respond to physical therapy, bracing, or other forms of treatment; still others are so severe that they cause lifetime incapacitation. As Steven Kopits ("Orthopaedic Complications of Dwarfism," *Clinical Orthopaedics*, vol. 114, 1975) points out:

> At this point in our experience, and faced with our present inability to change the basic etiology of these conditions, we accept the syndromes of dwarfism and their primary characteristics as variations of normal development, but differentiate as abnormal or pathological those features which are *complications* of their basic condition and which cause disability.

The description below of six well-defined types of dwarfism is based on a study of 248 cases conducted by Kopits and others at the Moore Clinic, Johns Hopkins University, between 1969 and 1974. The emphasis in this study was on musculoskeletal pathology occurring in patients referred for orthopedic consultation—that is, individuals in whom the condition was most disabling. Twelve types of orthopedic pathology were found in varying frequency and degree in the six types: (1) atlantoaxial problem (instability of the head due to defective joint at upper end of spine); (2) scoliosis (spinal curvature, including kyphosis, or humpback, and lordosis, or a combination of the two); (3) hyperlordosis (extreme hollow back); (4) spinal stenosis (narrowing of spinal canal); (5) hip dislocation; (6) hip flexion contracture (hip fixed in distorted position); (7) coxa vara (hip deformity, with neck of femur at right angle); (8) malaligned lower limbs (out of alignment with trunk); (9) foot deformity (especially clubfoot); (10) hand deformity; (11) joint laxity (loose or double joints due to weak ligaments); and (12) joint stiffness. In the outline below, these symptoms will be referred to without further explanation. It should also be noted that the six types of dwarfism are by no means exhaustive—first, because each has many variants and subtypes; and second, because there are many other, but rarer, types of dwarfism.

Achondroplasia

This is the most frequent type, evident at birth and transmitted by autosomal dominant inheritance (see CHAPTER 19: BIRTH DEFECTS; GENETIC COUNSELING). About 80 percent of cases, however, are new mutations, that is, the parents are of normal size but because of a change in genetic information (mutation) they produce a dwarfed child. These new mutations are often associated with advanced paternal age. The milestones of development (holding head up, sitting, standing, etc.) may be somewhat delayed due to joint laxity, weak muscles (hypotonia), and the size and weight of the head. However, this does not reflect delayed mental development. Severe thoracolumbar kyphosis is frequent in infancy, but usually improves when the child begins to weight-bear and walk. Other common characteristics are lax knee joints with knock or bowed knees, which also improve over the years; bowlegs in varying degree due to relative overgrowth of the fibula; and, in 85 percent of cases, spinal stenosis. In about 40 percent of adults the spinal compression may require surgery (laminectomy, foraminotomy) to free the nerve roots, since this condition often leads to sensations of tiredness about the hips; paresthesias, pain, and weakness in the lower limbs which interfere with ambulation; and in rare cases, paraplegia. The upper limbs are quite short, particularly in the upper part of the arm, and in most cases there is limitation in extension of the elbows, making it difficult or impossible to comb the hair and perform personal sanitary needs. Upper-limb surgery is rarely required and usually makes the elbow joint worse.

In addition to these orthopedic problems, achondroplasts have a number of common characteristics: a prominent forehead, nose with a flat or depressed bridge, protruding jaw, crowded and poorly aligned teeth, tendency toward excess weight, frequent middle ear infections due to short eustachian tubes, and in rare cases hydrocephalus which rarely requires surgical treatment. Affected adult males average 51.8 inches (132 centimeters) in height, and females 48.6 inches (123 centimeters). Height cannot be increased by administration of hormones or any other treatment.

Pseudoachondroplasia

This type of short-limb dwarfism, also known as pseudoachondroplastic spondyloepiphyseal dysplasia or PAD, is distinguished from achondroplasia by the normal shape and size of the head, relatively normal length of the trunk with short arms and legs, greater degree of joint laxity, and greater severity and progressive nature of lower-limb deformity. There are several types of pseudochondroplasia, some with dominant and others with recessive inheritance. Affected individuals are normal at birth but begin to develop disproportion between two and four years of age. In addition they begin to develop a "windswept" deformity or bowing of the lower limbs by three or four years. In time, the knees may turn outward on one side and inward on the other (valgus, varus), the hips and pelvis become malaligned, scoliosis develops, and the patient may find it hard to stand without falling over. Repeated surgical correction (osteotomy) of the lower limbs is required to improve alignment because the deformities recur. The scoliosis can usually be managed through the use of a Milwaukee brace. Other symptoms are minor atlantoaxial instability; instability of the wrists; and flatfoot deformity. These conditions do not impair functioning enough to require surgical correction.

Diastrophic Dwarfism

This is a short-limb syndrome recognizable at birth and of recessive inheritance. It is characterized by a variety of musculoskeletal problems that require extensive orthopedic care: severe clubfoot deformity; "hitchhiker" hands; flexion deformities of thirty to forty degrees in the hips, knees, and elbows; and spinal deformity progressing to great severity. The clubfeet require casts, but the condition will recur unless the hip and knee deformities are corrected also. Severe osteoarthritis of the hip joint may develop, and total hip replacement may be the only solution. The feet are short and broad, and special shoes may be required. Spinal deformity (scoliosis, kypholordosis) is more severe than in any other form of dwarfism, and early spinal fusion may have to be performed. In addition, atlantoaxial instability is known to occur and requires fusion. Surgical correction of the hands is not indicated, since the patient usually adjusts well to the deformity.

Metaphyseal Chondrodysplasia

In this disease, abbreviated MCD, the major characteristic is a slowly progressive bowing of the long bones, particularly in the legs, resulting in malalignment in about half the cases. Corrective surgery is often performed, resulting in greater ease in walking and increased work tolerance. There are many different types of metaphyseal chondrodysplasia.

Morquio Syndrome

This type of dwarfism is also known as mucopolysaccharidosis IV, and is transmitted by autosomal recessive inheritance. The shortness of stature becomes evident in the second year of life and is marked particularly by a short trunk. At three years pectus carinatum ("pigeon breast") as well as knockknee (genu valgum) deformities begin to develop, and become progressively severe. Joint laxity is also severe, and the child becomes weaker and may have increasing difficulty in walking on uneven or slippery terrain. Absence of odontoid (a toothlike process of the axis on which the atlas rotates) is the rule, and complications may be seen even in infancy. At about seven or eight years of age there may be signs of cervical spinal cord compression and atlantoaxial instability. If untreated, many individuals lose their ability to walk in their teens, develop progressive weakness of the upper limbs and trunk, and may die in their twenties due to paralysis of the respiratory muscles. The breastbone (sternum) may continue to protrude, and spinal deformities (scoliosis and kyphosis) may develop to a moderate degree. Damage to the upper cervical cord is the most severe complication of this syndrome, resulting in contractures (clonus) and spasticity, predominantly on one side of the body and most severe in the lower limbs. Cervical fusion may be required to stabilize the head. The hips are frequently dislocated but do not usually require treatment. Knockknee deformity is most severe in this syndrome and often reaches disabling proportions; surgery is often indicated. Laxity of the wrists is also severe and often disabling, and splints may be required. With aging, patients develop corneal clouding and deafness. Late in life cardiac complications occur.

Spondyloepiphyseal Dysplasia Congenita

This condition, transmitted by autosomal dominant inheritance, is characterized by a short trunk, round face with undeveloped midface, a protuberant abdomen and broad chest due to a disproportionately small pelvis, exaggerated lumbar lordosis, and bowing of legs or knockknees. Attempts to correct the lordosis by bracing are sometimes made. Coxa vara is frequently observed, producing a waddling gait which is usually progressive and may require surgery. The bowleg deformity is usually of mild to moderate degree and does not necessitate correction. Many individuals have severe myopia and retinal detachments. Cleft palate and hearing problems are frequent.

Other Types of Short Stature

There are many other types of short stature besides dwarfism. A missing or malformed chromosome may be responsible in some cases. The best-known example is probably Turner's syndrome, which affects only girls, who show short stature (less than 4 feet 10 inches or 147 centimeters) and underdeveloped ovaries. Contrary to earlier reports, mental retardation is not a frequent feature, although their verbal IQ exceeds their performance IQ and involves perceptual difficulties. These girls develop feminine interests and have well-proportioned bodies, but usually fail to develop breasts, pubic hair, and menstrual bleeding unless treated with hormones. They are generally unable to have children but frequently adopt instead. Anabolic steroids given in childhood may add several inches to their height.

In addition to chromosomal disorders, there are no fewer than 100 bone diseases, such as hypophosphatasia and osteogenesis imperfecta (fragile bones; see SECTION H, Osteogenesis Imperfecta), which may stunt growth and lead to deformity. Some serious diseases, such as kidney failure, may also inhibit growth. Other causes are malnutrition, particularly protein deficiency, which is especially prevalent in underdeveloped countries; and hypopituitarism, which may be reversed by replacement of missing hormones such as human growth hormone.

Problems Encountered

Dwarfs and other individuals of excessively short stature encounter many practical, social, and emotional problems. Elevator buttons, mail boxes, drinking fountains, and door handles become environmental barriers which, it is hoped, will be reduced in number when accessibility standards are more widely adopted. Sports activities must be adapted to their limitations of height and movement. The psychological problems are often harder to handle, and professional assistance may be required in some cases. However, understanding parents and friends often help dwarfed individuals cope with teasing and jokes when they are children, and participation in Little People groups helps them face their problems as teen-agers and adults.

Organizations

There are two national organizations, each with a full program of helpful activities. The Human Growth Foundation, with headquarters in the Maryland Academy of Science Building, 601 Light Street, Baltimore, MD 21230, provides opportunities to share experiences and resolve mutual problems, both medical and psychological; supports research, training, and treatment programs; furnishes information on growth problems to physicians and the community; and assists the National Pituitary Agency in the collection of human pituitary glands for use in research and treatment. Little People of America (LPA; Box 126, Owatonna, MI 55060) is organized to provide fellowship, solutions to problems unique to the membership, moral support, and information. Activities include an annual national convention; district and local chapter meetings; special programs for the children (Little Littles) and teen-agers; publication of *LPA News*, distribution of a handbook containing practical suggestions on clothes, jobs, and devices for convenient living; and the LPA Foundation, established to gather and disburse funds for vocational training, research, and assistance to placement agencies which arrange for the adoption of children.

D. Familial Dysautonomia

Reviewed by the Dysautonomia Foundation

Familial dysautonomia is a rare hereditary disorder of the central and autonomic nervous systems and appears to be found exclusively in Jewish children of East European ancestry. It is also known as the Riley-Day syndrome, after C. M. Riley and R. L. Day, who first described it in 1949. Symptoms consist of wide-spread sensory-motor defects combined with autonomic nervous system dysfunction. Although symptoms are present in varying degrees of severity and varying combinations, the first sign is frequently the inability to shed tears; other common characteristics are the absence of taste buds (fungiform papillae), relative insensitivity to pain, absent or hypoactive tendon reflexes, poor motor coordination, vasomotor instability, and emotional lability. As a result of the autonomic dysfunction, patients are frequently subject to corneal ulceration due to diminished lacrimation and corneal anesthesia, defective swallowing and bronchial pneumonia caused by aspiration of fluids, excessive perspiration (hyperhidrosis), sudden body temperature changes, and vomiting attacks. About 60 percent of patients are afflicted with spinal curvature (scoliosis, kyphosis), which may result in respiratory difficulties and cardiac strain.

The disorder follows an autosomal recessive pattern of inheritance, but its exact etiology is unknown. There are, however, several theories, such as a defect in the neurotransmitter acetylcholine, or improper nerve development in the embryo. The diagnosis cannot be made prenatally or through the carrier, but can sometimes be made within the first week of life by means of tests (histamine injection, methacholine infusion of the eye) and examination of the tongue for absence of papillae. Any of the complications of this disorder, such as pulmonary disease or severe vomiting attacks, may prove fatal, and the mortality rate is high.

There is no specific treatment, but life may be prolonged by controlling as many of the symptoms as possible through medical and nursing care. Some of the more frequent measures are the following: special nipples for young children who have trouble sucking or swallowing; baby foods for children who cannot chew well; avoidance of hot foods and objects if the child is unable to detect temperature differences; addition of table salt to food if there is profuse perspiration; early treatment of infections that may produce high fever; use of a respirator to prevent pulmonary disorder; administration of chlorpromazine to control vomiting; application of eye drops or other lubricants to prevent corneal ulcers; use of the Milwaukee brace and in some instances spinal fusion for scoliosis.

Dysautonomic children are subject to frequent, unpredictable illnesses that pose serious educational, vocational, and adjustment problems. Although not classified as mentally retarded, they are usually somewhat delayed in verbal development and are frequently handicapped in motor and perceptual functions. School performance may therefore be below intellectual capacity, and special training or a special school may be necessary. In addition, sexual maturation is also delayed, emotional immaturity and body image disturbance are common, and participation in strenuous sports is impossible. After graduation from high school or college these young people are often beset with so many illnesses that they do not have the stamina for a full day's work; nevertheless many can function well in sedentary jobs or sheltered workshops.

Parents of dysautonomic children need special training in handling the many physical, emotional, and psychosocial problems. They must also be made aware of all the manifestations and life-threatening complications of this multifarious disorder. Almost inevitably they need help in learning to take necessary precautions without becoming overprotective, and in view of the hereditary character of dysautonomia, they usually require genetic counseling as an aid in family planning. For further information, and a booklet, "Caring for the Child with Dysautonomia," contact the Dysautonomia Foundation, 370 Lexington Avenue, New York, NY 10017.

E. Geriatric Rehabilitation

Reviewed by LEONARD D. POLICOFF, M.D., Chairman, Department of
Rehabilitation Medicine, Rutgers Medical School

Although old age cannot be described as a sickness or disorder in
itself, it is nevertheless true that the number of elderly people with
severe limitations due to chronic conditions is relatively great and
has been on the increase for some time. The basic reason is that the
lengthening of the life-span has markedly increased the number of
older Americans and, as a consequence, the prevalence of disorders
that have a high incidence in the later years. Statistics published by
the National Center for Health Statistics indicate that in 1920 the
life expectancy was 53.6 years for males and 54.6 for females; in
1940 these figures were 60.8 and 65.2, respectively; and by 1972
they had risen to 67.4 and 75.2. Today, due not only to these increases in life expectancy but also to general population growth,
more than 20 million Americans—over 10 percent of the population—are 65 years of age or older, and it has been predicted that this
percentage will double by the end of the century.

Prevalent Disorders

In the *Bulletin of the New York Academy of Medicine* for December 1973, Howard A. Rusk states that "the largest percentage of disability occurs in elderly persons." Whether we accept the arbitrary
figure of 65 as the onset of old age or, as he suggests, think in terms
of "physiology, not chronology," we still have to recognize that
impairments do, in general, increase in later life. A national sampling of patients in 2,100 nursing homes for 1973–1974 revealed
that the following chronic conditions were most prevalent (many
individuals were afflicted with more than one disorder): arthritis
and rheumatism (367,907 cases); heart trouble (360,223); mental
illness (200,277); paralysis other than arthritis (188,092); amputation or deformity of limbs (149,871); senility (146,519); diabetes
(142,613); glaucoma or cataract (110,818); chronic back or spine
trouble (105,974); neoplasms (25,624); and respiratory diseases
(22,179). The incidence of these conditions was shown to increase
regularly between the ages of 65 and 85. It should be borne in
mind, however, that even though these figures represent typical
disorders that afflict the aged, they are not exclusively "geriatric
disorders," and that the statistics do not reflect the large number of
basically healthy elderly individuals.

Details on these disorders are given in this volume, but a few
comments are in order here. The most crippling, and often the most
painful, disorder affecting elderly people is arthritis, which ranks
second only to heart conditions as a cause of activity limitation. Its
most common forms, rheumatoid arthritis and osteoarthritis, are particularly prevalent among old people. Certain orthopedic disorders,

such as osteoporosis (thin, brittle bones) and osteomalacia (soft bones) are due, at least in part, to diet deficiencies often found in old people who live alone. Many fractures (and hip replacements) could be prevented by early treatment. Cerebral arteriosclerosis, which can be retarded in many cases, reduces blood flow to the brain and may lead not only to strokes and paralysis but also to such mental symptoms as memory defect, inability to concentrate, clouding of consciousness, and incoherence. Senile brain disease (senile dementia) is a state of mental, emotional, and social deterioration resulting from degeneration of the brain; common symptoms are loss of interest and alertness, egocentricity, forgetfulness for recent events, and preoccupation with bodily functions, progressing in some cases to extreme memory impairment, confusion, untidiness, and disorientation. In neglected cases the patient may develop a senile psychosis. These psychoses fall into more or less well-defined types, such as paranoid, depressed and agitated, delirious and confused, and presbyophrenic (characterized by excessive joviality, rambling talk, confabulation, and aimless repetitive behavior).

As Myrtle L. Reiner points out in the *Journal of Rehabilitation* for September-October 1974:

> Gerontologists claim that elderly patients are reporting illness too late, and that many of the diseases of old patients are to some extent preventable if they are detected early and treated immediately. The complex organization of hospitals creates a staff that is not sufficiently understanding of the older citizen's needs. Medical and rehabilitation facilities are needed specifically for the purpose of serving the elderly.

A growing number of physicians are advocating geriatric health centers comparable to maternity and child health centers. Such centers, staffed by geriatric specialists, would go far toward preventing or alleviating the disorders of the aged, especially if they attended to the social and emotional as well as the medical needs of these individuals.

Present Facilities

The first term that comes to mind when the question of care of the aged is raised is frequently "nursing home." However, there are many provisions for medical care of geriatric patients other than in nursing homes. In an article "Types of Geriatric Institutions" in *The Gerontologist* (Autumn 1973), George G. Reader summarizes the various types and their functions. He quotes estimates that from 8 to 15 percent of individuals over 65 in the United States and other countries are either bedfast or housebound but living in their own homes, and an additional 6 to 16 percent go outdoors only with difficulty. In the United States certified home health agencies have been on the increase under the impetus of Medicare, and over 2,000 now provide skilled nursing care at home, plus at least one other service such as physical therapy. A major advantage of this type of care is that it enables the patients to live at home. The same is true of geriatric day hospitals, which are relatively rare in this country but are more common in Great Britain.

Most homes for the aged have beds available for infirmary care, but they are usually minimally staffed. Some extended-care facilities, including nursing homes, provide adequate medical and nursing care, but others are inadequate, and in 1972 the White House ordered an upgrading of all these facilities under the threat of withdrawing federal reimbursement. Many elderly people are treated in chronic disease hospitals, but it is important to recognize that high-quality ambulatory care will often reduce the number and length of hospitalizations. In addition, approximately 16 percent of first admissions to mental hospitals in 1965 were over 65, but the present trend is to keep as many elderly patients as possible in the community, treating them in community mental health centers or other local facilities. Also, many elderly people with neuromuscular disorders, particularly stroke, or with chronic heart or pulmonary disease are now being treated in rehabilitation centers affiliated with hospitals. As Reader's account indicates, geriatric health care is fragmented and there is great need for an integrated system that emphasizes ambulatory and domiciliary care "to keep people in their own homes and functioning as long as possible."

The concept of keeping the elderly in the community and out of institutions is the basis of a forward-looking program developed by Neil Solomon, Secretary of Health and Mental Hygiene for the State of Maryland. In an interview published in *Geriatrics* (September 1973), he describes the state's ombudsman program in which elderly persons and their families are invited to discuss their medical, Social Security, and other problems with specialists. They are also encouraged to investigate nursing homes and other facilities to see if these offer the kind of social activities, medical care, and rehabilitation programs they need, and to take advantage of noninstitutional care whenever possible. Such noninstitutional care includes home visits by physicians, nurses, and social workers; regular visits to day care centers; a meals-on-wheels program; group homes for those who cannot live alone; and geriatric screening and evaluation centers equipped to provide physical examinations and psychological and financial counseling. A case-by-case review of all people over 65 in mental hospitals has been conducted throughout the state, with the result that 50 percent of elderly patients were moved out of the hospitals and back into the community. In addition, an Administration of Aged and Chronically Ill has been established, on a par with the state's Health and Mental Hygiene and Juvenile Services, and Solomon strongly advocates "establishing a Department of Gerontology in every medical school in the United States as a means of training medical students in this form of care so they will be oriented to the field when they leave."

Rehabilitation

Those who view the aging process in terms of inevitable decline, and the chronic disorders of the elderly as completely irreversible, are apt to ask: How can the concept of rehabilitation apply to the aged at all? But the fact is that the basic principles can be applied to all but the most incapacitated, and even then some measure of restoration is often possible. Every technique of rehabilitation has a place in geriatric rehabilitation, although not all procedures can be applied equally to all patients and all types of disabilities. The total, team approach is as applicable to rehabilitation of the old as it is to rehabilitation of the young, and the emphasis should be the same: on ability rather than disability, on what is left, not on what is lost.

Reduced functions can usually be at least partially restored by mild forms of physical therapy such as massage, hydrotherapy, and exercise. Occupational therapy is often effective as a means of retraining the patient in the activities of daily living. Recreational therapy in the form of a planned program of entertainment, visits to museums or libraries, and parties and celebrations helps to maintain morale, provide needed stimulation, and open new avenues of interest and activity. Although the emphasis is frequently on hobbies and other avocational pursuits, it is often possible to apply vocational retraining to elderly people with functional impairment. In a paper, "Dynamic Rehabilition in Geriatrics" (*Bulletin of the New York Academy of Medicine*, December 1973), Howard Rusk reported on a study of 3,000 patients with stroke whose average age was 66 and whose average period of hospitalization was seven weeks. Through the rehabilitation program conducted at Bellevue Hospital and the Institute of Rehabilitation Medicine, 35 percent of these patients were able to return to some kind of gainful work, including a federal judge who went back to the bench for another seventeen years of distinguished service.

Other studies conducted at the Institute showed that retraining procedures were, on the whole, equally effective with victims of chronic obstructive lung disease, orthopedic disabilities, and cardiac disorders. And even where geriatric patients are not capable of full-time employment, they can often serve as social service volunteers or as consultants to business, industry, or social agencies. Through these activities, which enable society to call upon their years of accumulated experience, they can regain a feeling of usefulness and dignity. Unfortunately, however, as Dr. Rusk points out,

> Our present policies toward the aged are wasting the most precious human resource we have: wisdom . . . If I had one universal medication or therapeutic tool to give to people over 65, it would do more than all the medicine in the world; it would be to give the aged the feeling of being wanted and needed, so that when they awake in the morning they would have something to look forward to.

In "Rehabilitation of the Aged Disabled" (*Journal of the Medical Society of New Jersey*, August 1973), Leonard D. Policoff, Chairman of the Department of Rehabilitation Medicine at Rutgers Medical School, outlines a number of basic guidelines for a geriatric program. He points out that "we sometimes conceptualize aging as an inexorable process of erosion, an expenditure of fixed reserves with closure of the account when the reserves have been totally depleted, [but] this does not fit the facts at all." Instead of deterioration in all body systems at once, "the human animal includes complexly interdependent biologic systems whose capabilities vary independently on an irregular and unpredictable chronological basis." This means that the functional efficiency of some systems may be relatively intact even though others may be greatly or even catastrophically impaired — and much of the rehabilitation program can be focused on the more intact functions.

At the same time, as Dr. Policoff points out, physical rehabilitation in general is usually limited by certain common factors, including a slowing of replacement and repair; a tendency toward disuse, weakness, and atrophy; loss of muscle force, endurance, and skill; slowed reflex response; narrowed sensorial perception capability; and some decline in the intellectual energy required to cope with environmental demands, especially when major illness or disability occurs. The loss of capability may cause the individual to "retreat into a posture of limited competence [and to] appear to have lapsed into intellectual senility." He states that "with poor management, the problem may become fixed, [but] with proper management, such individuals are restorable."

But how is restoration to be achieved? Here Dr. Policoff enumerates several medical principles on which physical rehabilitation depends: prevention of secondary disorders such as decubitus ulcers and pressure sores; avoidance of unnecessary bed rest which may result in pulmonary congestion, pneumonia, cardiac insufficiency, muscular atrophy and weakness, or accelerated osteoporosis; and avoidance of frequent catheterization wherever possible because of its adverse effect on bladder capacity. In addition, treatment sessions should be short because of lowered fatigue tolerance, and practice sessions for the relearning of lost skills (for example, walking after leg amputation) should also be short, slow-paced, and repetitious. Goals should be realistic: when a prosthesis is used, a stable and safe gait pattern is more important than walking without a trace of a limp. But whatever the goals, they should be "set as small achievable increments which will produce enough success to encourage an approach to the next incremental goal." At the same time, "the wise physician will also have handy some alternate goals so that if the current objective appears on experience to be unattainable, one can deftly substitute a less arduous one."

The setting of realistic but flexible goals is an important factor in maintaining morale and in the prevention of discouragement, withdrawal, and depression. In other words, though physical restoration is of fundamental importance, it cannot be achieved in a psychological and social vacuum. As Dr. Policoff says:

> Whatever the physical goals, they can never be separated from socialization, family participation and community relationships. Outreach programs which encourage the patient to consider the rehabilitation center or the extended care facility as transient stops on the way to the broader life style of the outside world are an integral part of restorative services and may involve institutional psycho-social and recreational therapeutic personnel working in close harmony with family, friends and community resources. It does little good to restore the function of an extremity if one cannot restore the total organism to its environmental relationships and communications. . . . It is important not to be deterred from our rehabilitation goals by the apparent frailty of the aged. They have been tough enough and survived long enough to reach this problem age. They often have greater resources both physically and emotionally than superficial observation would suggest and we must never deny them a trial at the restorative process, despite appearances which may be surprisingly deceptive!

It is also important to remember the oft-quoted statement that "a society which fosters research to save human life cannot escape responsibility for the life thus extended."

(For organizations concerned with aging and the aged, see PART 4, SECTION 2: VOLUNTARY ORGANIZATIONS—Geriatric Rehabilitation. For a case history, see CHAPTER 55: ILLUSTRATIVE CASES, G. Mrs. Y.: A Case of Geriatric Rehabilitation. For rehabilitative procedures applied to specific disabilities, see the following chapters: 17, AMPUTATIONS; 18, ARTHRITIS; 24, CANCER; 25, CARDIAC DISORDERS; 29, DIABETES MELLITUS; 38, MENTAL ILLNESS; 45, ORTHOPEDIC DISORDERS; 47, PARKINSON'S DISEASE; 48, PULMONARY DISEASE; and 52, STROKE.)

F. Hansen's Disease (Leprosy)

OLIVER W. HASSELBLAD, M.D., Medical Consultant, American Leprosy Missions, Inc.

Like many other infectious diseases, Hansen's disease (leprosy) is caused by bacteria, in this case *Mycobacterium leprae*. Indeed, leprosy was the first disease found to have an identified causative bacterium, discovered more than 100 years ago in Norway by Gerhard Armauer Hansen. The bacteria have a special affinity for skin, mucous membranes, and peripheral nerves. So far as is known, *M. leprae* causes infection only in humans. It may be transmitted from person to person by close, prolonged contact or may possibly be inhaled from nasal discharge. There is no known intermediary animal host.

Signs and Symptoms

Usually the first sign is a spot (macule), or a variety of them, appearing on any part of the body and of varying sizes. There are two characteristics of such spots. First, the pigment of the skin is altered: in dark-skinned people the spot becomes lighter, and in light-skinned people the macule tends to be darker than the surrounding skin. Second, careful examination shows a loss or change in sensation at the center of the spot. There is insensitivity to light touch, to heat or cold, and eventually to pain. A third sign is often present: the thickening of certain peripheral nerves in selected locations, with pain and tenderness. Invariably the sites are at those points where nerves are just under the skin, for example the ulnar nerve at the elbow. All these signs and symptoms are due to the bacilli entering the skin and attacking first the tiny nerve endings and then the larger nerve trunks. This eventually becomes the root cause for the complications and disabilities that may arise.

Major Types

There are three main types of leprosy, determined by the degree of defensive immunity the human host can produce against the invading bacteria. Patients who develop the *tuberculoid* type of the disease have the strongest immunity or resistance, but have a tendency for greater damage to peripheral nerves and hence the development of crippling disabilities. *Lepromatous* leprosy occurs in patients with little or no immunological resistance. It is by far the more infectious of these two polar types. In between is a zone where a third type may occur, called *dimorphous* leprosy, usually showing some characteristics of the two polar types. This type may remain fixed or it may move toward either pole, with or without treatment. In any case, the first lesion is the macule described above. This macule is very often not diagnosed, and is termed *indeterminate* leprosy. This original lesion may spontaneously heal itself, particularly in children. It may also gradually progress to any one of the three major types.

Prevalence

Leprosy is widely and seemingly indiscriminately distributed throughout the world. The greatest numbers of victims are found along the Equator. However, climate is not a decisive factor in the spread of leprosy; it is also found in cold climates albeit in fewer numbers. Poor housing, hygiene, sanitation, and nutrition, as well as poverty, may well be contributing factors but to no greater extent than in a host of other diseases. It is generally believed that unknown genetic factors determine the degree of immunity and hence the spread of leprosy. Estimates of the total number in the world with leprosy vary from 10 to 20 million. Statistics in many of the less-developed countries are notoriously unreliable. It is safe to say that wherever a sound country-wide control program is initiated, the estimated number of patients usually has to be revised upward as much as 75 percent or higher. In the United States it is estimated that there are 3,000 patients, but many authorities believe there are many more unknown cases, for it may take as long as four years to have the disease correctly diagnosed after the onset of symptoms.

Complications

As with many diseases, possible complications are the source of greatest danger. In all major types, involvement of the peripheral nerves is frequent and usually critical. As the nerves of the hands, feet, face, and eyes become involved, the motor muscles supplied by these nerves become paralyzed, causing many types of deformity such as drop foot, claw hand, lagophthalmos, and facial paralysis. The secondary results of nerve damage are equally critical because anesthesia of body surface develops. Anesthesia results in the inability to feel pain and in a loss of the sense of touch. Thus burns, blisters, or cuts may occur on hands and feet, but because there is no pain they are neglected. In turn they may become secondarily infected with other bacteria, destroying the soft tissues and even entering the bone to cause osteomyelitis. Leprosy does not "eat" away tissues; fingers and toes do not "drop off"; they are worn away, hastened by secondary infections and repeated trauma. Ulceration of the mucous membrane of the nose may result in secondary infection of the supporting cartilage, allowing the nose to collapse; it is not destroyed. The bacilli may enter the deeper structures of the eye, carried by the blood and lymph circulation. Without prompt treatment with corticosteroid internally or locally and with atropine drops, serious damage to vision and even loss of eyesight will occur. Since the facial nerve is often involved, lagophthalmos sometimes occurs, resulting in an inability to close the eyes. Subject to the effects of dryness of the cornea and foreign bodies entering the eye, corneal ulceration frequently develops. The involvement of the facial nerve may also lead to paralysis of the cheeks similar to Bell's palsy.

Another critical danger is acute lepra reaction, erythema nodosum leprosum, a sudden exacerbation in which numerous inflamed nodules develop under the skin. Without prompt and radical measures, irreversible deformities may develop in a few hours.

Treatment

Today there are effective drugs that can cure leprosy. As with all diseases, much depends on early diagnosis and prompt regular treatment. The most commonly used and least expensive drug is Dapsone, a sulfone medication given either orally or by injection. Newer drugs (Clofazimine, Rifampicin) act much more quickly and, in combination with the sulfones, more effectively. However, they are too expensive for general use in countries where the total health budget may be $1 or less per person per year. They should be used in the presence of complications that may cause permanent disabilities.

The disabilities of leprosy are not just physical. Because of the almost universal stigma of "spoiled identity," the patient is very often socially isolated, and thus disabled psychologically, socially, and vocationally. These problems are often more difficult to cope with than the disease itself. This has been particularly true when patients were forcibly segregated, often for life, in leprosariums. Long institutionalization exaggerated many existing psychosocial problems and created new ones. Today the vast majority of patients are treated while continuing their normal life through the use of health centers managing major health problems in the community. Stationary and mobile dispensaries and clinics are also being used. Persons who develop complications are increasingly being admitted to general hospitals. Nevertheless, the fight against leprosy will never be won until it is accepted in the mainstream of medicine and until leprosy becomes a part of comprehensive community health planning.

Prevention of Disabilities

Most disabilities in leprosy are *preventable*. If early danger signs of impending complications are taken seriously with immediate treatment, they will never require costly programs of rehabilitation. If leprosy patients come for help because of a first or early deformity, much can be done. The skills of physicians, surgeons, nurses, physical therapists, occupational therapists, prosthetists, social workers, and vocational counselors are required.

After the patient is carefully prepared by the therapists, a surgeon can restore function to a clawed hand by substituting undamaged tendons for damaged ones. Even the smallest ulcer on the plantar surface of an anesthetic foot must be taken seriously. Simple sandals with an insole of microcellular rubber will permit the ulcer to heal. Larger or multiple ulcers will need complete rest of the foot to bring healing, usually accomplished by immobilizing and enforcing rest with a plaster cast. Properly made footwear measured before the cast is made must be used as soon as the foot is out of the cast to prevent recurrence. If infection has entered the bones, more radical surgical procedures may be required, and molded footwear constructed. The surgeon can correct lagophthalmos, improve facial palsy, correct deformity of the nose, restore eyebrows, and reshape deformed ear lobes. These may seem to be minor disabilities, but are often sufficient to prevent loss of the patient's job.

Education, Training, and Rehabilitation

Health education in which patients and their families participate in their own care and prevention of disability is extremely important. Education about the disease to dispel myths, superstitions, and ignorance will restore courage and confidence; patients can become community health educators themselves. Health education can also be a primary instrument of preventive rehabilitation, and of rehabilitation itself, for the patient, but it must be internalized to the extent that it becomes a way of life. The following international training centers offer courses and practical experience in the prevention of disabilities and rehabilitation:

All Africa Leprosy & Rehabilitation Training Center, Addis Ababa, Ethiopia.

American Leprosy Missions Leprosy Atelier, University of Hawaii, Honolulu.

International Center for Training and Research in Leprosy and Related Diseases, Caracas, Venezuela.

Institute of Leprology, University of Dakar, Senegal.

Sanatorio de Fontilles, Alicante, Spain.

William J. Schieffelin Leprosy Research Sanatorium, Karigiri, South India.

United States Public Health Service Hospital, Carville, Louisiana.

Many other institutions and general hospitals also offer training and experience at the local level. Every effort is being made to persuade existing rehabilitation centers dealing with disabilities arising from many causes to also accept patients with disabilities arising from leprosy on a fully integrated basis. Equally important is the integration of vocational training centers. Where facilities for leprosy patients exist, they too must take responsibility for those in the community with disabilities arising from other causes.

Research Areas

An encouraging development is the greatly expanded research work in many countries to improve techniques of rehabilitation and to solve the remaining unknowns about leprosy. Many medical universities, at an increasing rate, are becoming involved in leprosy research.

There are two remaining problems that await a breakthrough: a vaccine or other means that will make a preclinical diagnosis of leprosy possible; and a vaccine by which the disease can be prevented. Only in recent years has successful multiplication of the bacilli in specially bred laboratory mice been possible. This has been of tremendous importance in the testing of new drugs. More recently, it has been found that when injected with *M. leprae*, a certain percentage of armadillos will develop leprosy very similar to lepromatous leprosy, and will die from the disease. This permits even greater experimentation and also provides, under controlled laboratory conditions, an unlimited supply of the bacilli and the antigens that develop in the animal.

G. Narcolepsy

This lifetime, often progressive, neurological disorder is more prevalent than is generally recognized, since it affects between 50,000 and 250,000 Americans. There are two primary symptoms, sleep attacks and cataplexy, both of which usually have their onset during puberty, and which slowly develop to a maximum degree.

Sleep attacks are generally the first symptom to appear, starting with a gradual increase in daytime drowsiness and a tendency to fall asleep in situations where many normal people fall asleep, such as after meals, during a dull lecture, or while reclining in a comfortable chair. In time they occur in less appropriate situations, such as while driving a car or watching a play; and finally they progress to dramatically inappropriate situations, for example, in the middle of a conversation or even in the middle of a sentence. After a few seconds or minutes of sleep, the conversation or sentence may be continued where the patient left off. In some cases there is little or no forewarning of an attack; in others an approaching attack can be detected and resisted for minutes or even hours, although the individual may feel drowsy or tired while fighting off sleep. But when the sleep attack does occur—which may be occasional or many times a day— it is usually accompanied by vivid, realistic dreams which may be confused with actual events; and by automatic behavior, such as completing a meal, driving a car to an unintended destination, putting used plates into a clothes dryer, or writing meaningless sentences—all of which are performed without awareness or recall.

The second major symptom, cataplexy, consists of a rapid or abrupt loss of voluntary muscle control leading to partial muscle weakness or complete body collapse. The attack is frequently precipitated by outbursts of laughter or anger, but may be induced by stress, fatigue, or a feeling of elation while reading a book or watching a movie, or even by visualizing emotionally charged situations. While it is in progress, the individual may experience blurred vision, convulsive jerking movements, and difficulty in speaking. In some instances the person may fall heavily, but usually without injury. Some individuals experience cataplectic attacks only one or two times a year, while others may have hundreds of attacks a day. The attacks generally last from a very few seconds to as long as thirty minutes, and in contrast to sleep attacks, normal awareness is maintained throughout.

Both cataplexy and sleep attacks are essential to a diagnosis of narcolepsy. In addition, many individuals experience three other symptoms: (1) sleep paralysis, during which the muscles cannot be moved or controlled—a frightening condition that usually occurs while falling asleep or waking up; (2) fear-inspiring hypnagogic hallucinations, which usually occur at the beginning of nighttime or daytime sleep, and consist of perceiving a threatening figure or event, or the feeling of leaving one's body; and (3) disrupted nocturnal sleep, often accompanied by terrifying dreams and, in about 20 percent of male patients, by a temporary suspension of breathing (sleep apnea). These three symptoms are usually not disabling, but the primary symptoms of sleep attacks and cataplexy can be severe enough to interfere with the individual's ability to hold a job and lead a normal educational, social, and emotional life.

Several studies have indicated that narcolepsy tends to run in families, although children of a patient are not certain to develop the disorder. The specific cause is not fully known, but is believed to involve an impairment in the brain mechanism which regulates the sleep-waking cycle. Where diagnosis is in doubt, a laboratory test is conducted in which the presence of narcolepsy is confirmed by an electrical recording of rapid eye movements during the onset of sleep (sleep onset REM). This is a unique characteristic of narcolepsy, since these movements do not occur in normal individuals during the first sixty minutes of sleep. There are also differences between the brain waves of narcoleptics and normal persons. But unfortunately studies have shown that an average of fifteen years elapses between the first symptoms and a correct medical diagnosis—partly because of the subtle nature of the early symptoms, and partly because many physicians have not had experience with this disorder. This situation is gradually improving, since the number of sleep specialists and sleep clinics in the United States has been increasing.

Treatment of narcolepsy has to be tailored to the individual, since some have more sleep attacks and others more cataplexy attacks. Analeptics (invigorators, stimulants) such as methylphenidate (Ritalin) are administered for sleep attacks and sleepiness, and imipraminic compounds (such as chlorimipramine and Tofranil) are effective in controlling cataplexy. They are usually prescribed only in severe cases because of possible side effects and withdrawal problems. Some individuals, however, are able to reduce the severity of their symptoms by learning to control their emotions, while others experience only mild symptoms which are little more than an inconvenience.

The above summary is based upon material provided by the American Narcolepsy Association (Box 5846, Stanford, CA 94305). This organization encourages private and governmental research, and distributes information to both the general public and the medical profession to enable physicians, families, and patients to recognize the symptoms of narcolepsy and to assure appropriate treatment. It also publishes a list of sleep disorder clinics and conducts a referral service.

H. **Osteogenesis Imperfecta**

The most characteristic manifestation of this genetic defect is fragility of bone, commonly referred to as "brittle bones." Fractures of the long bones frequently occur after trivial injury. Other signs are blue sclera (white of the eye), loose and easily dislocated joints, flat feet, bowing of bones, sweating, constipation, misshapen teeth, and progressive deafness. The exact number of cases is unknown, with estimates varying between 10,000 and 30,000 in the United States.

The disorder has two major variations. Osteogenesis imperfecta congenita, the more severe form, is usually diagnosed at birth by the presence of multiple fractures which have occurred in utero or during delivery. Many severely affected children do not survive, and those who live are subject to numerous fractures, multiple deformities, and growth retardation which may be confused with achondroplasia (see SECTION C, Dwarfism). In most instances they have to spend their lives in bed or in a wheelchair. However, fractures and deformities can sometimes be prevented by the "rodding" or "shish kebab" operation. The hollow, central portion of the long bones is removed and cut into short segments, which are next threaded onto steel rods with space between. The bones are then returned to the body and the limb is placed in a cast until the segments grow together. The operation can be performed as early as one year of age, but must be repeated every three years or so while the child is growing.

The second variation, osteogenesis imperfecta tarda, is milder and often unrecognized until a fracture occurs days, months, or years after birth. Affected individuals are often close to normal in height and weight and experience a minimum of fractures. There is no clear-cut division between the two forms, since all degrees of severity exist. The only signs of the defect may be the blue sclera, poor teeth, or increasing deafness later in life. In some cases the disorder remains undetected until fractures begin to occur at an advanced age, or appear in an offspring.

Osteogenesis imperfecta sometimes occurs in families with no known history of the defect. Nevertheless, it is classed as an hereditary defect, usually autosomal dominant but possibly recessive in some cases.

A recently established organization, Osteogenesis Imperfecta, Inc. (1231 May Court, Burlington, NC 27215) focuses on service, dissemination of information, and stimulation of research on this disorder.

I. Poliomyelitis

Reviewed by the National Foundation

Poliomyelitis, or infantile paralysis, is an acute viral infectious disease of the nervous system which is spread from person to person. The virus causes inflammation of the throat, intestine, and occasionally the central nervous system. The primary area of attack is the spinal cord, nerve bundles attached to the cord, and areas of the brain surrounding the cord's upper end. The attack causes degenerative changes which result in muscular paralysis or weakness. Children are more susceptible to the infection than adults, but are less likely to develop severe paralysis. Historically, summer and fall have been the seasons of highest incidence.

Three types of virus have been isolated from human subjects: Brunhilde (I), Lansing (II), and Leon (III). They are all believed to enter the body through the oral cavity and multiply in the intestinal tract.

Incidence and Prevalence

Polio is an ancient disease with a world-wide distribution. The first evidence of its existence has been found in a drawing on an Egyptian tablet dating back 3,500 years. An incidence of up to 38,000 cases per year was reported in the United States until 1955, when the vaccine developed by Jonas Salk was proved effective and began to eliminate epidemic polio. This vaccine consists of killed cultures of strains of the three polio viruses and is administered by injection. In 1962 the oral polio vaccine of Albert Sabin, containing live but attenuated, nonvirulent strains of the viruses, was licensed by the U.S. Public Health Service. It is now universally administered in the United States, although the Salk vaccine is still used in Scandinavia.

The number of new cases of polio in the United States has declined to less than fifty per year. However, the disease has left many disabled victims, practically all of whom are still in need of special rehabilitative services and equipment.

Symptoms and Diagnosis

Mild, nonparalytic cases of polio may avoid detection, and differential diagnosis may be difficult. This is particularly true during the early phases, since polio may be confused with other infectious diseases of rapid onset, such as meningitis, influenza, and diphtheria. Other disorders that simulate polio are cerebral and spinal neoplasm, pulmonary infections, encephalitis, and Guillain-Barré syndrome.

The typical early stage of the infection is characterized by such symptoms as sore throat, elevated temperature, headache, drowsiness, vomiting, some rigidity of neck and spine, pain in the back and legs, and muscle tenderness. Confirmation of polio is based on evidence of flaccid muscle paralysis, absence of tendon reflexes in affected areas, abnormal spinal fluid, and isolation of the virus. There may be no residual symptoms of this acute stage. On the other hand, shortly after this stage there may be sudden signs of central nervous system involvement, especially muscle paralysis beginning in the legs and spreading to the trunk. In some cases the paralysis involves the muscles of respiration and the vital centers of the brainstem. It is seldom symmetrical in nature, as is likely in other kinds of spinal cord damage.

Within about the first six months after onset, there may be considerable recovery of function, but the muscles of the legs may sustain permanent changes. The individual is left essentially paraplegic or paraparetic, but without the sensory involvement that occurs in most cases of spinal cord injury. Cases in which muscle weakness lasts longer than two or three weeks are termed paralytic.

More specifically, paralytic polio is classified into three types: spinal (70 percent), bulbar (10 percent), and bulbospinal (20 percent). The spinal form is characterized by weakness of the trunk, pelvic or shoulder girdle, neck, or extremities. Some patients may experience urinary retention for a few days, and if there is extensive paralysis the diaphragm and chest muscles may be so severely affected that artificial respiratory aid may be required. The bulbar form most commonly involves impairment of facial movements, phonation, and swallowing, as well as disturbances of respiration, circulation, and cardiac functions. The bulbospinal form is characterized by diffuse involvement. These patients are the most seriously affected and the most difficult to manage, due to loss of respiratory independence associated with loss of protective cough and swallowing reflexes.

Treatment and Rehabilitation

There is no specific treatment which destroys the virus or controls the spread of the disease once it has developed. If patients enter the paralysis stage, hospitalization is necessary. They must be positioned carefully, usually with pillows, and turned at intervals to relieve painful spasms and avoid the development of swellings and deformities. Moist heat is applied to relax the muscles, and patients are usually placed in a warm-water Hubbard tank as soon as physical therapy can be applied. If there are significant signs of a respiratory problem, mechanical aid is called for, such as a tank respirator (iron lung), rocking bed, or chest respirator. In cases of respiratory paralysis, respiration is maintained by positive pressure, and a tracheostomy may be performed. Appropriate medications are administered to relieve pain and help reduce motor activity and spasms. Some paralysis of the bladder, with urine retention, may occur, but this condition is usually temporary and can be cleared up since it is often due to urinary tract infection. Hypertension and other cardiovascular problems may develop, requiring special treatment.

After the condition has stabilized, careful testing must be performed to determine the extent of involvement. At this point a program of muscle reeducation and rehabilitation is usually instituted, including carefully graded range-of-motion and progressive-resistive exercises. Orthopedic surgery may be deferred until after adolescence, and may include tendon transplants or other means of joint stabilization. Leg braces, hand and wrist splints, overhead slings for the shoulders, and corsets or spinal braces may be required. Crutches, canes, or a wheelchair may be needed for ambulation. These devices are used during the convalescent period, but supportive equipment may in some cases be needed on a permanent basis. Various self-help devices may be required, and a home care program is usually planned. The occupational therapist develops this program and provides training in the activities of daily living. Vocational retraining may also be necessary. Psychiatric or psychological assistance is indicated if the patient develops anxiety or confusion during the acute stage, or such reactions as passivity, dependence, regression, or hostility during the convalescent stage. The development of all these rehabilitative procedures was greatly advanced during the years when polio was rampant. (See CHAPTER 51: SPINAL CORD INJURY.)

National Foundation

The National Foundation for Infantile Paralysis was chiefly responsible for the conquest of poliomyelitis. Through its March of Dimes campaigns, this organization raised funds which supported all major research projects, including those of Jonas Salk, Albert Sabin, Thomas Weller, John Enders, and Frederick S. Robbins. It supported the development of the polio vaccines, including the field trials. The organization was renamed the National Foundation in 1958 and now focuses on birth defects.

J. Prader-Willi Syndrome

The Prader-Willi (Prader-Labhart-Willi) syndrome, first described in 1956, will be used as an example of a rare birth defect (only about 500 current cases in the United States) with clear-cut manifestations. Significant symptoms include marked obesity, particularly in the face, lower trunk, and buttocks; short stature; hypotonia (lack of muscle tone); a weak cry and poor sucking reflex in infancy; and hypogonadism (small genitals in the male, scanty menstruation and small breasts in the female). Developmental milestones are delayed, with sitting at about twelve months, walking at thirty months, and talking at forty-two months. Mental retardation, usually mild or moderate, is the general rule, although some patients show specific learning disabilities instead. Other characteristics are small, often puffy hands and feet, crossed eyes (strabismus), and sometimes diabetes, heart disorders, and scoliosis. Prader-Willi children are generally affectionate and happy in their early years, but usually become irritable and stubborn as they grow older.

There is no cure or specific treatment for this syndrome. The obesity is particularly hard to control, and a rigid dietary regimen must be prescribed in order to avoid diabetes and maintain mobility. Children with the disorder often require special schooling and social-psychological guidance. The risk that a parent with an afflicted child will have another child with the same disorder is not great; nevertheless genetic counseling is recommended.

An organization, Prader-Willi Syndrome Parents and Friends (P.O. Box 252, Long Lake, MN 55356), has recently been formed to maintain communication among parents and professionals who are attempting to understand and cope with this condition.

K. Tuberous Sclerosis

Reviewed by the National Tuberous Sclerosis Association

Tuberous sclerosis (TS) is an uncommon neurocutaneous disorder. Also known as epiloia, it is characterized by four sets of symptoms: (1) convulsive seizures, (2) skin lesions, (3) mental retardation, and (4) tumors, or "tubers," of calcified (hardened, sclerotic) tissue within the brain and other organs such as the kidneys and lungs. The specific symptoms vary with the individual, and the condition is often difficult to diagnose since there are many incomplete forms (formes frustes). However, recent studies indicate that a noninvasive radiologic technique, computer-assisted cranial tomography (using the CAT scanner), can be effective in identifying the disorder in infants and young children who do not exhibit the classic symptomatic triad of epilepsy, skin lesions, and mental retardation.

More specifically, epileptic seizures have been found to occur in over 70 percent of cases, and may take a variety of forms: grand mal, petit mal, akinetic, or psychomotor. The skin lesions also take many forms. Most characteristic is adenoma sebaceum, a persistent butterfly rash over the bridge of the nose, which usually appears during the first decade of life. Other skin lesions are depigmented "ash leaf" spots on the trunk, detectible under ultraviolet light; pebbly "sha-green" spots on the back; small wartlike tumors (ungual fibromas) along the nail beds; and in some cases light brown "café au lait" areas. Most but not all TS children are mildly to severely retarded, especially in cases where seizures are difficult to control early in life. The tumors may become malignant and reduce life expectancy. On autopsy, the brain shows not only calcification but the presence of overgrown "monster" cells in nerve fibers and supportive tissue.

The incidence of tuberous sclerosis is still conjectural, but appears to be on the order of 1 in 10,000. Exact figures are hard to obtain because the spectrum of symptoms is so wide and their severity so varied that many cases are probably overlooked.

The precise etiology of TS is also obscure, although it is known to affect both sexes equally and is believed to be trasmitted genetically as an autosomal dominant. This means that if either parent carries the gene by heredity — or, in cases where there is no family history, by mutation — there is a 50 percent chance of having a TS child with each pregnancy. No laboratory tests have as yet been developed to detect these carriers or to detect the disorder in offspring before birth. However, some individuals who appear to be completely normal may, on careful examination, be found to exhibit signs of the disorder, especially in the form of faintly depigmented spots (ash leaf) or increased pigmentation (café au lait). If these signs are found, they indicate that these persons may be carriers. Genetic counseling is strongly recommended, whether or not they have already had a TS child.

Neurological treatment of TS is primarily directed toward the control of seizures through medication. It is often necessary to try many types of anticonvulsant drugs, and different dosages as well, since the seizures are so varied. In some patients the seizures may be completely controlled; in others, only partially. Dermatological treatment is administered where adenoma sebaceum is severe. The mentally retarded TS child will usually profit from attending a school for exceptional children, and if the brain damage results in motor impairment, physical therapy will often be of value.

A recently formed organization, the National Tuberous Sclerosis Association (P.O. Box 159, Laguna Beach, CA 92652), has been conducting an active campaign directed toward maintaining a national registry of patients and families, promoting exchange of information through a newsletter, and furthering research into this enigmatic, disabling disorder. The organization and its medical advisory board have been successful in obtaining a grant from the California Department of Health to be used in setting up a model research, education, prevention, and service project.

On the opposite page: A child with spina bifida is assisted by a physical therapist in practicing stair climbing. (National Foundation/March of Dimes)

3

Cases, Facilities, and Professions

55

Illustrative Cases

Compiled by ROBERT M. GOLDENSON, Ph.D.

I f the excitement of attending the International Rehabilitation Conference in 1972 in the burgeoning cosmopolitan city of Sydney, Australia, caused you to be somewhat flustered, then you, too, might have arrived late at the opening session and missed the introduction of the keynote speaker, Dr. Harold Wilke. After we settled in the back of the crowded hotel hall for general assemblies and focused attention on Dr. Wilke, it didn't take long to recognize his charisma and become absorbed in his well-prepared speech articulating an enlightened and stimulating approach to the field of rehabilitation. Standing at a podium, he turned a page of his manuscript, but somehow it didn't seem that he moved the arms of his dark blue suit. The text of his talk was engrossing, and the odd notion about the way he turned the page faded out of consciousness until he came to the end of the next page and one saw that he swiftly and gracefully turned the page with his foot—his *left* foot. Then you noticed that he wore his watch on his ankle—the left one. "I am left-footed," he later explained.

Dr. Wilke was born with no arms and is one of those individuals who has made a remarkable accommodation and adjustment to his physical difference. He can, for example, write on a blackboard while standing, or shave himself while standing in a moving railroad car with "nary a nick." At the banquet he dines gracefully, toasting with wine glass so that companions are soon unaware that he is armless. It seems as though he is managing his utensils with a black-gloved "hand." When, however, he goes to the buffet because his companions lament having missed some delicious pine-apple and returns to the table with enough napkin-covered slices for all, one is once again inspired by the height of accommodation to disability of which a human being is capable.

In just a brief glimpse of Dr. Wilke, the depth of his maturity and character is only to be surmised, but nevertheless seems evident. The satisfying, close relationship with his intelligent and accomplished wife and their mutual pride in each other; and the involvement with their five children are apparent even during casual dinner conversation. Dr. Wilke's accomplishments as pastor of his church in White Plains, New York; the national recognition evidenced by his post as one of three Chief Armed Services Chaplains; his leadership in rehabilitation as board member of Goodwill Industries and the National Easter Seal Society; and the international acclaim as evidenced by his task as keynoter to the Sydney Congress give some indication of his productivity. But perhaps as impressive as these glimpses of the man is the steady stream of people from every corner of the world who come by his table to warm themselves a moment, interacting with the personality and zestful humanity of this remarkable man.

Because everyone is not gigantic of spirit, superior in intellectual endowment, or blessed with the effects of support and enablement, there is always a danger in writing about the brilliant, exceptional people. Dr. Thomas Cutsforth rocked work for the blind when he wrote iconoclastically in *The Blind in School and Society* (1951) about the revered Helen Keller. His purpose and, indeed, his effect were to bring attention to the more ordinary people who are blind—to focus on genuine personal experience and perceptions of the world with whatever equipment one has, rather than parroting what others have taught about experience as one's own. Dr. Cutsforth was a courageous, early example of a self-aware, disabled individual who could face and work through the difficulties of a disability, and not gloss over the situation for the comfort of others.

The struggle for identity, for a concept of self-worth and integrity, is common to all human beings. As society is more or less honest, more or less romantic and denying about the real world, we seem to give individuals more or less room to grow. It is not surprising that in Victorian times or at the turn of the century when chivalrous roles and Horatio Alger success stories prevailed, people who were different, less than perfect, were hidden or shipped away from view. It has seemed that since the 1940s there has been an accelerated trend toward genuine social equality. Minorities, women, the physically different, indeed, everybody's children are increasingly insisting on their equal rights to getting their needs met in the scheme of things.

In this climate there are signs of moving away from false expectations of perfection, but it remains difficult to do. Deep-rooted fears make it necessary to work in order to accept individual differences comfortably. As a part of the larger society, any of us who becomes disabled, has a disabled child or spouse or parent, or works with a disabled colleague, or is trying to help an individual or family cope with disability, needs to examine his or her own feelings and attitudes.

The personal accounts which follow have been selected with several purposes in mind: to provide a human touch that will help to counterbalance the necessary emphasis on objective, factual information in this book; to illustrate different ways in which people learn to rise above their limitations; to show the rehabilitation process in action; and, above all, to increase awareness of the disabled as individuals — as persons, not as problems.

[CHARLIS S. DUNHAM]

A. A Sack on His Back

Excerpted from *A World to Care For: The Autobiography of Howard A. Rusk, M.D.,* Random House, New York, 1972; with permission

His name was Johnny. He was three years old, and he had been born with what we call "a sack on his back." In other words, he was a spina bifida case. He had a congenital defect in the vertebrae from which an undeveloped spinal cord protruded in a sack filled with spinal fluid. Sometimes in such cases, pressure develops in the brain from the excess amount of cerebral spinal fluid, and the patient's head becomes enlarged — he becomes what we call hydrocephalic. Little Johnny had a tiny, emaciated body with a sack the size of a grapefruit attached to it, and he had a head too big for the rest of him. He looked definitely hydrocephalic. He was in the last bed of the children's ward. It was pointless to put him where he would get more intensive care. He was not acutely ill, and there was nothing they could do for him there. He had a beautiful face but he was very pale. He didn't talk. He only whimpered softly as he stared out at the world around him from a bed that was constantly wet. Spina bifida cases usually have no control over their bowels or bladders or their lower extremities.

I was there the day one of our therapists rolled Johnny into our clinic for evaluation. His skin was as white as paper. He was wearing diapers. He didn't say a word. He just gazed into space. He was such a forlorn creature his own parents had become despondent looking at him and rarely came to the hospital to see him. We brought him down for evaluation, and as the therapist lifted him off the stretcher onto the examining table, he put his arms around her neck and gave her a pathetic little squeeze. It was the most fortunate thing little Johnny had ever done. From that moment on he owned the therapist. She insisted we keep him, even though his situation looked hopeless, and she lavished her love and care upon him. She gave him the first real understanding love he ever had.

Within a month, he could say about thirty words. In two months, his bladder came under control. He had been emaciated when he came to us because he was eating poorly, but now he was eating like a little pig and we began to realize he was not hydrocephalic. His head had looked big only because his body was so small. He grew now almost as fast as he ate. He stopped whimpering and began to smile. He even laughed a little. When we put him on the floor he began to crawl toward us and pull himself up. We wanted to strengthen his arms but we didn't have any parallel bars for children, so we built some, two feet high. We also had braces made for him, the first time, to my knowledge, that had ever been tried on this type of spina bifida patient. Dr. Deaver got him special braces with a band around the pelvis, and both knee and hip locks, so he could sit down.

We started training him on the bars, then taught him to use crutches, and within three months or so, he began walking on his crutches away from the bars. By this time, his family eagerly followed his progress and when he finished his training, they took him home.

Although Johnny came back periodically for checkups, I didn't see him again for six or seven years, and then accidentally. One day I went to a meeting at a public school in Brooklyn. It was recess time and the kids were running up and down the halls screaming at each other. Among them was this fine-looking boy who came stumping along at a great rate on his crutches, yelling at the top of his voice. Since I have more than a passing interest in people on crutches, I took a good look at him and suddenly I realized it was Johnny. He didn't remember me, of course, but I remembered him. So I went to see his teacher.

"There is a little boy named Johnny out in the hall," I said, "a paraplegic. I understand he's one of your pupils. Could you tell me how he is doing?"

"Johnny?", the teacher smiled. "He's at the top of the class."

Johnny was our first spina bifida case. We now have between four and five hundred such cases under our care, and they all should be thankful to Johnny because he proved to us that even such a disability can be managed. It is worth noting that about thirty years ago a distinguished neurosurgeon used to advocate calculated neglect for such cases to encourage their death. Today, almost 90 percent of our spina bifida cases are living at home with their families, and about 80 percent are in school.

(See CHAPTER 50: SPINA BIFIDA.)

B. Lawyer and Quadriplegic

Excerpted from Winthrop Rockwell, "Curtis Brewer Can Do Nothing for Himself . . . But He's Accomplishing Quite a Bit for Others," *Today's Health,* December 1975; with permission

"Because I've been paralyzed for twenty years, I'm an expert in the problems that handicapped people face. As a lawyer, with my training in public administration, I can serve as a catalytic agent to help disabled people bring their problems to the experts who can solve them," says Curtis Brewer, founder of Untapped Resources, in New York City, and ombudsman for the disabled.

The first signs of Curt Brewer's paralysis came on suddenly in the winter of 1955. At the time, he was working for the U.S. Postal Service in New York City.

"It was absolutely frightening. I didn't know what was happening," recalls Brewer, who was 29 at the time. "My left forearm began stiffening, then the fingers. Then came pressure on my chest and tingling in my toes. I lost sensation in my hand so that it became difficult to get the subway tokens out of my pocket."

For six weeks the paralysis steadily advanced until he was forced to enter a hospital where he remained for five months.

Brewer's paralytic condition is known as transverse myelitis, which is an inflammation across the spinal cord. At first, his physicians believed that there might be hope for recovery if he could get physical therapy.

Before long, however, Brewer began to lose ground physically, until he was confined to a wheelchair. For the next twelve years he pursued a succession of odd jobs, from selling magazines over the phone, to selling insurance (for which he studied and passed the licensing exam). Then he decided to continue on to graduate school in public administration at New York University.

But by 1968 he had lost virtually all movement below his neck. And shortly thereafter his doctors became aware of a severe respiratory problem. Because none of his voluntary muscles function, the rise and fall of his diaphragm (which helps to draw air into the lungs and then expel it) is entirely dependent on involuntary muscles.

What this means is that Brewer has only about 23 percent of the breathing capacity of a normal person. Whenever he overexerts and increases his body's conversion of oxygen to carbon dioxide (CO_2), his lungs do not have the capacity to remove all the CO_2 and it builds up in his body and acts like a sedative, making him weary and slowing the functioning of his brain.

In order to offset the CO_2 buildup, at least partially, Brewer wears a respirator most of the time. The respirator resembles an air-filled doughnut around his lower chest; it rhythmically puffs up with air, then collapses, providing a mechanical assist to the breathing action of his diaphragm. This respirator operates from electrical current or the batteries mounted on Brewer's wheelchair.

Curtis Brewer's life is immaculately organized. At his present home in New York's East Village, four attendants work full or part-time in the apartment. In the morning one of them must literally pull back the covers on his special hospital bed and then bathe him, shave him, dress him, shave his head (twice a week), adjust a special urinary device that he wears almost constantly, move him into the wheelchair, and get him ready to meet the day. This process alone takes two to three hours.

Then he must be fed, one spoonful at a time. When he drinks, the glass must be lifted to his mouth.

Other than his respirator, there is no special treatment for Brewer's condition of paralysis. He takes no medication. He does not even take aspirin because it has a negative effect on his ability to breathe.

Bettie Brewer has been Curt's tireless supporter ever since they were married in 1955 – the same year his paralysis began. For years she had to do everything for Curt, carrying all of the responsibilities that are now borne by attendants. In spite of the strains, Mrs. Brewer is a warm and outgoing person, seemingly unhurried in the face of the never-ending needs of her husband.

In 1968 Dr. Sidney Weinstein hired Brewer to be the administrator of his neuropsychological research laboratory on upper Fifth Avenue in New York. In the $12,000-a-year position, he was supervising 50 employees, purchasing, hiring, and doing some fund raising. But before long, the lab became involved in designing equipment that would assist quadriplegics like Brewer.

Under Weinstein's direction and with a $20,000 grant from an interested corporation, a pioneering system was developed to enable Brewer to operate his wheelchair and certain electrical appliances from a switch mounted in front of his chin and operated by pressure from his tongue. The system, which was the first of its kind, worked moderately well but there were problems.

Then Richard Doherty, chief engineer at a Manhattan electronic design and manufacturing company, appeared on the scene to redesign and improve the entire system.

Doherty combined a radio receiver of an automatic garage door opener with a small computer that then was wired to electric terminals. The terminals could be connected to any device run by electricity such as a light, a radio, a tape recorder, or even the latch on the front door of Brewer's apartment.

Perhaps the most invaluable equipment to Brewer's law practice is a van that is set up as a mobile law office. Brewer can be hoisted into the van on a special lift without leaving his wheelchair. The interior of the van is furnished with a couch and chair for visitors, a small round conference table, a special air conditioning unit to hold the temperature within Brewer's comfort range, a special taping system so that he can dictate notes, a flip-down bulletin board for displaying materials, and a portable respirator unit that operates off the van's battery. Donated by a Michigan furniture research company, the van is driven by one of Brewer's attendants. In it, Brewer can comfortably travel almost anywhere he needs to go to represent his clients.

Brewer got the idea of going to law school in the late 1960s when he was working as what is called a "private ombudsman" — a problem solver for handicapped and nonhandicapped clients. He had two main concerns when he was looking for a law school: doorways and steps. As it turned out, Brooklyn Law School had no architectural barriers, so it was there that he attended classes and received a full tuition scholarship.

For most people, law school is demanding. For Brewer it demanded every ounce of energy he had. In class he had a special prop on which his books and papers were spread out so that he could follow the lecture. A classmate, Nancy Erickson (who has since become an assistant professor of law at New York Law School), sat next to him each day and turned the pages in his books during the class period. She was paid $50 a week by the New York State Department of Education, Office of Vocational Rehabilitation, to tape every lecture, take extensive notes in class, and summarize every case studied. Each night she would go home and correct her notes, copy them, and give them to Brewer so that he could study them the following evening.

But most of his books contained more than 1000 pages, and legal study often requires flipping back and forth from one page to another. Before long, the physical strain of flipping the pages began to take its toll on Brewer's fragile constitution. Unless he could find a different way of reading his books, it looked as if Brewer might have to give up law school.

Then, by word of mouth, two men, John Robertson and John Milward, heard about Brewer's problem. Both were members of the National Microfilm Association and committed themselves to finding a solution. The result was the loan of a sophisticated $10,000 Eastman Kodak microfilm reader and the microfilming of some 35,000 pages of textbooks and legal materials.

Another man, Milton Mandel, then head of the National Microfilm Corporation of America, paid for much of the processing out of his own personal funds because of his admiration for Brewer.

In addition to everything else, Brewer had to petition to the highest New York state court for special permission to take four years instead of the normal three to complete his legal education. He also had to arrange to take his exams at home so that he could take part of the exam, rest, take another part, rest, and so on until he finished.

With his law degree, with the long involvement in his pet project, Untapped Resources [UR], with his efforts to reduce architectural barriers, and with his network of contacts built up carefully over the years, Curtis Brewer is a man on the move.

[Editor's Note: In an article on Curtis Brewer (*Rehabilitation Gazette*, 1975), Donna McGwinn gives the following illustration of his activities: "An example of a case that UR handled concerns that of a middle-aged client disabled by heart disease. He had been a superintendent of an ironworks firm and performed other tasks in the industry. The rehabilitation agency in his state, where funds were exceedingly limited, had rejected him as a client. UR's job was two-fold: To combat the client's fear that his eighth-grade education was a bar to his performing suitably in a clerical or administrative capacity, and, secondly, to establish in the minds of rehabilitation authorities that he had sufficient medical tolerance, experience and training to function in a sedentary job. To do this UR developed a resumé of the client's experience and education which emphasized that despite his eighth-grade education the client had risen from a worker to a superintendent. The client was also urged to obtain a medical evaluation of his probable work tolerance. Having succeeded in these two objectives, UR persuaded the Federal-State Employment Service to search for jobs in terms of the client's experience in administration. An administrative position in the ironworks industry was found for him."]

C. Sensory Feedback Therapy

Excerpted from Joseph Brudny, Julius Korein, Lucie Levidow, Bruce B. Grynbaum, Abraham Lieberman, and Lawrence W. Friedmann, "Sensory Feedback Therapy as a Modality of Treatment in Central Nervous System Disorders of Voluntary Movement," *Neurology,* vol. 24, no. 10, October 1974; with permission

The current study was initiated in 1971 as a practical clinical attempt to use audiovisual sensory feedback from muscle to treat disorders of voluntary movement that were not significantly benefited by other forms of therapy. The group studied included patients with torticollis, dystonia, and hemiparesis or quadriparesis with spacticity and/or weakness related to a variety of etiologies . . . All patients had their illness for at least nine months, with no further improvement using conventional forms of therapy, except for four who were treated early in the study. All patients had some component of volitional motor activity present, which could not be utilized in any meaningful manner.

The patients' ability and motivation to cooperate and understand instructions were essential for the therapy. The presence of aphasia, organic mental syndrome, or mental deficiency that impaired patients' ability to follow instructions were reasons for exclusion from the study. The age of the patients ranged from 13 to 68 years. The duration of their illness was 9 months to 25 years, with the exception of four patients with hemiparesis. Each of these patients was independently evaluated by a physiatrist and a neurologist before acceptance into the study.

Several modifications of the electromyograph (EMG), designed to detect, amplify, rectify, integrate, and display the myoelectric potential were used in this study. The transducers were skin electrodes. The integration technique provided quantification of changing EMG signal levels continuously. This change was reflected in both visual and auditory displays. The visual display provided information by means of a dial pointer on a calibrated scale, or oscilloscopic display of two-dimensional changes of the electric potentials (amplitude and rate), or digital readout of integrated muscle potential measured in microvolt-seconds. The auditory display provided rising and falling intensity of sound or a changing click rate. All these displays are proportional to the integrated EMG activity, over a selected time period.

We found that little time was needed for the patients to understand the relationship between muscle contraction or relaxation and the corresponding changes in the audiovisual display. A brief demonstration of technique often was carried out on a normal muscle in order for the patients to understand the concept. Therapy was directed toward two major goals: volitional decrease of spasm in spastic or spasmodic muscles and volitional increase of contraction and strength of the atrophied and/or paretic muscles. The therapeutic goals were achieved in a step-by-step fashion with a set of controls allowing for gradual change in the gain loop of the sensory feedback, thus demanding progressively better performance from the patient. The reward for performance was the achievement of voluntary control, confirmed directly and often by mirror viewing.

The therapeutic sessions usually were scheduled three times a week and lasted a half-hour, on the average. When a patient could volitionally change abnormal activity, usually after one to three sessions, and could maintain such control over several sessions, including functional improvement of the preexisting deficit, gradual withdrawal of feedback was instituted by decreasing the number and duration of reinforcement sessions.

Initially, photographs and occasionally motion pictures were taken before and after treatments. Currently all patients are videotaped prior to their entry into the study to demonstrate the degree of their functional impairment or movement disorders. In addition, a base line of physiologic parameters including electroencephalogram, EMG, and integrated EMG activity of the involved and contralateral muscles are recorded and taped with quantification of the integrated EMG expressed in microvolt-seconds. The measures are obtained with muscles relaxed (at rest) and during maximal activity (voluntary or involuntary).

After treatment, repeat videotapings as well as physiologic parameters are recorded for comparison . . . A functional scale of activity of daily living also was developed for comparing the effects of therapy.

The results were evaluated in terms of the patients' ability to modify their longstanding motor disorders, first with feedback, then when feedback was withdrawn. For example, in patients with hemiparesis, gains were measured in terms of upper extremity function: (1) relief of spasms with no functional component, (2) assistive function of the extremity, and (3) actual prehension. In patients with spasmodic disorders like torticollis, results were considered in terms of duration of the patients' ability to maintain a neutral neck position, first with feedback and then when feedback was withdrawn. Changes of the EMG and integrated EMG activity of the involved muscles before and after therapy also were noted.

In the two patients with injuries of the spinal cord at the C-5, C-6 level, there was total paralysis of lower extremities, and the upper extremities had some minimal degree of nonfunctional movement for up to three years. Improvement occurred in both patients and is exemplified by the following case report.

Case 1. This patient is a 28-year-old electrician with a fracture dislocation of C-5, C-6 vertebrae, resulting in paraplegia and marked weakness of both upper extremities. The patient had a laminectomy with limited improvement. For three years he received conventional physical therapy and was treated for multiple decubiti. He was a total care patient.

Sensory feedback therapy was initiated with two specific goals: relaxation of the right spastic biceps and pronation of the forearm for use of a wrist-driven splint. Within two weeks the patient achieved both goals, step by step. The same progress took place concurrently in the left arm without sensory feedback therapy. Two years later, the patient has retained these functions and can feed and groom himself, type, and drive an electric wheelchair . . .

Case 2. The patient is an 18-year-old high school girl who has a left spastic hemiparesis observed from the age of one. Previous treatment included right cryothalamectomy with some improvement. She also had several release and reconstruction procedures on both upper and lower extremities. Sensory feedback therapy was tried for relief of painful, constant, "dystonic" contractions of the left peroneal muscle group that failed to respond to use of cast and brace.

Within two weeks she achieved voluntary control of her lower extremity, was free of pain, and discarded the brace. Subsequently, treatment to relieve her spastic clenched hand was started. This hand never had been used in any functional manner. Within six weeks of sensory feedback therapy she learned to control opening her left hand and later used her hands to cut meat, tie her shoelaces, and cook.

Case 3. This is a 57-year-old sculptor who had a cerebrovascular episode two years ago that resulted in aphasia and right hemiplegia. The patient gradually recovered except for marked somatosensory and kinesthetic disturbance of his right hand. He had no functional use of his right hand, which was continuously showing "athetoid-like" involuntary movement. With sensory feedback therapy, he learned to control the involuntary movements. He began to use the right hand for meaningful functions, such as drawing and painting, within four weeks . . .

The next group of patients consists of those with primary torticollis. Of the 13 patients with torticollis, most had gone through a large variety of treatments. Medications used included diazepam, haloperidol, levodopa, and amantadine hydrochloride, while surgical procedures performed were cryothalamectomy and direct section of muscles. Psychotherapy had been attempted in eight of the patients.

Prior to sensory feedback therapy none of the patients could maintain voluntary neutral neck position for longer than a few minutes while seated. After 8 to 12 weeks of sensory feedback therapy, all the patients, with feedback, could maintain head position in neutral state for the duration of the session with minor fluctuations; without feedback, nine could maintain the neutral head positions for significant periods . . .

Case 4. This patient is a 55-year-old assembly worker who had had spasmodic torticollis for three years. He could not work during this period. His chin and face were virtually fixed to the right, with hypertrophy of the left sternocleidomastoid and right trapezius muscles. He occasionally was able to turn his head to neutral position by touching his left chin with his finger.

After eight weeks of sensory feedback therapy, he learned voluntary control of his neck muscles, regaining and maintaining neutral neck position. Treatment included learning both relaxation of the hypertrophied muscle and strengthening of the opposite, relatively atrophied muscle. The resulting improvement has lasted for approximately two years without feedback. Occasional sessions for reinforcement were useful. The patient has been back to work during this period . . .

Although the results of early stages of our study appear promising and at times dramatic, the mechanism of sensory feedback therapy is not clear and future studies will require further serious, cautious, and statistically significant evaluations . . . In our patients, despite a varied etiology and different levels of anatomic interruption (in the central nervous system) of the normally closed loop sensory motor interaction, the response to indirect sensory feedback was relatively uniform. In the early stages of therapy most patients were able volitionally to change the displays of EMG activity rather promptly. In the subsequent stages of therapy, when spatial displacement resulted from an increasingly larger degree of volitional change of the functional activity of the muscle, direct feedback by observation of the moving limb or mirror viewing of the altered position seemed to enhance the effects of ongoing indirect auditory feedback. If the final stages of therapy were reached, the control of movement was maintained when all external feedback was eliminated . . .

Further investigations under controlled circumstances are required to determine whether the results obtained are specific to sensory feedback therapy, and if so, to determine more precisely the characteristics of motor performance, learning and retention curves, the most appropriate time for reinforcement in different types of disorders, and an appropriate rationale for initiating therapy . . .

D. Amyotrophic Lateral Sclerosis

By Robert G. Dicus, *Rehabilitation Gazette*, vol. 16, pp. 11–13, 1973; with permission

Henry Louis Gehrig of the New York Yankees played in 2,130 consecutive baseball games. For this accomplishment, plus the accumulation of many records which still prevail in baseball today, Lou Gehrig was called an "iron man."

Lou Gehrig succumbed to the ravages of amyotrophic lateral sclerosis (ALS) in 1938. Then, as is still the case today, baseball fans could hardly pronounce the tongue-twisting ALS name. Almost as a final tribute to this great athlete's memory, the public coined their own name to describe it. That name survives today, both in the public sector and in medical circles, as "Gehrig's disease."

ALS is one of the more common diseases of the central nervous system (CNS). ALS has an incidence equal to multiple sclerosis and is four times more prevalent than muscular dystrophy. However, ALS is virtually unknown to the general public.

"There is no known cause, or cure for ALS," most neurologists pronounce to the victims. "There is nothing anyone can do," the doctor continues. "Most ALS patients can expect to die in the first 12 to 18 months. Some survive five years and a very few make it beyond 10 years."

The patient is given some medication to relieve the severe muscle cramping and instructed to return for reevaluation in six months. It is suggested that the patient might wish to "put his personal affairs in order." No definitive course of long-term planning or therapy is offered.

During my 10 years of direct combat with ALS, as a patient, I have come to know that there is HOPE of survival from ALS and that there is a great deal which the patient and his family must do to survive.

Considerations of medical descriptions of ALS disease types are well documented. While these scholarly writings provide the roadmap for the medical community, they offer nothing to the patient or his family to help guide them and prepare them for what lies ahead.

Conditioned by this "no hope" prognosis, many ALS patients return to their homes to await the final decision. Periodically, the American press will document actual newspaper stories of the helpless, first-person accounts of how these ALS patients exhibit great courage in the face of this disease. In my view, the press is making a big mistake by glorifying only the personal interest point-of-view. It is in this context that I now present some additional considerations about Gehrig's disease.

Gehrig's disease presents a rather consistent victim profile. The person to be attacked is a man near fifty, the head of a household, a father of school-age children; usually very active and vigorous in his chosen field of endeavor, having achieved above average athletic and business success. Males are afflicted more often than females in the proportions of two-to-one.

But what about ALS itself? The medical community has as many pseudonyms for ALS as gangsters have aliases. They include: progressive bulbar palsy, primary lateral sclerosis, progressive muscular atrophy, "motor neuron disease," and anterior horn cell disease (similar to polio).

With the exception of unique geographical concentration of ALS in Guam and another focus in southern Japan, ALS occurs in a rather even distribution throughout the world. While the world-wide incidence of ALS is well documented, insight into the cause is still speculative.

Three major types have been identified: (1) the sporadic form, which accounts for over 90 percent of the cases occurring in North America and Western Europe; (2) the familial or hereditary form, which has a dominant transmission pattern; (3) the Guam type which is the major cause of death among Chamorro people.

Before you accept your doctor's ALS diagnosis, have it confirmed by at least two other medical specialists who are recognized experts in the neuromuscular disease. Your state or county medical association can assist you.

When the ALS diagnosis has been clearly proven, you should accept that diagnosis and begin some practical long-range planning. By the term "acceptance" I do not mean surrendering and giving up. Instead, I mean learning everything you can about the different effects this disease can impose upon your personal health, your family, and your future. Learn what different courses of action you can take to *prevent* or *minimize* these impositions on your person and then prepare to repulse the invader. You must plan for not only survival from crisis, but also for long-term survival as a possible severely physically disabled person. You must prepare for dramatic changes upon the life style of both yourself and your family.

Stop running around the world seeking a miracle cure for Gehrig's disease. These miracle cures do not exist in reality; they exist only in the plans of those who would separate you from your money under false pretenses. Save your money and your energy because you are going to need every bit of it if you expect to give a good accounting of yourself in the ALS contest. Unless you are a wealthy person going in, what material possessions you presently have will not be enough.

Prevent the temptation to give in to the implied "no hope" prognosis. Fear can kill a person too! Get your emotions under your control as fast as possible and use your head to think with, not your heart. Prevent fear.

Prevent the secondary debilitating effects of anything and everything which would tend to weaken your personal health defense mechanisms. There is a very real possibility that the cause of ALS might be a heretofore undetected toxin which gains entry into the body by the liquid or food intake route. Why not give your body with its excellent natural defense system the optimum chance to win?

Practice good nutrition. Prevent the secondary atrophy of muscles. Atrophy results from normal disuse of your muscles. Maintain your muscle strength and endurance through a properly balanced activity and exercise program. Avoid fatigue, especially in the acute phase of ALS. Once the disease burns itself out, this consideration of avoiding fatigue will become less important.

Prevent colds and upper respiratory infections. Prevent secondary urinary and bowel complications.

All of these preventative considerations can be effectively dealt with by consultation with a team of medical experts, not just your physician. This medical team should include, in addition to the supervising physician, the registered nurse, the registered physical therapist and occupational therapist, the social worker, the medical equipment engineer, and the immediate members of the patient's family. Vitally important is the necessity for keeping the family unit intact and teaching each other how to cope with the problem. The medical team will be primarily important in the early stages of ALS onset to deal directly with medical emergencies; and then to teach the patient and his family how to assume the continuing care and prevention of further crisis events. The family and the patient must adjust quickly together to these traumatic occurrences. They must learn to assume the responsibility for implementing preventative measures, especially when the patient returns to the home environment.

As the patient is able to survive the initial insults of respiratory failure and total paralyzing quadriplegia, treatment emphasis shifts from just saving the patient's life to now determining how to live together in a world society which knows very little about the needs of severely disabled persons. Most people are ill equipped to deal with the problems of chronic illness or disability. They naturally have an inclination to change any unpleasant situation by taking some action to do something about it. Just what to do and how to do it is another problem. No one can tolerate living in a purgatory of chronicity.

Prevention and long-term planning become a continuing way of life for every paraplegic and quadriplegic, regardless of how their disability was caused. This is especially true for the ALS patient and family survivors.

Spinal cord injury (SCI) and spinal cord disease (SCD) cause paraplegia and quadriplegia. Put them both together and you have the acronym (SCID), coined and pronounced by me as SKID.

ALS survivors will probably be respiratory quadriplegics and SCIDS. From the date of onset, the patient will experience a progressively accelerating downhill course. Initial symptoms may include: (1) extreme fatigue, (2) severe muscle cramping like a large "Charley horse," (3) persistent worm-like twitchings of muscles known as muscle fasciculations, and (4) loss of skeletal reflexes with increasing muscle weakness progressing to full paralysis. Thus does the ALS patient become a SCID.

Those SCIDS having the loss of voluntary breathing control will have to adjust to the further trauma of a possible tracheostomy and a life-long dependence upon some form of respirator life-support. While no one welcomes this further insult, the ALS patient might view the tracheostomy as one of the key reasons for his being able to survive Gehrig's disease. Without an unobstructed airway or trachea, and the ability to suction out accumulating chest mucus or fluids, the ALS patient will either drown in his own juices or ultimately perish from upper respiratory infections, such as pneumonia. The tracheostomy and the portable positive-pressure respirators developed during the polio years are one of the best hopes for ALS survival. Preventative postural drainage techniques and breathing exercises taught by physical therapists further increase the survival capability. Antibiotics for control of respiratory infections should be prescribed by the team physician.

SCIDS are faced with a multitude of living problems which vary in relationship to the cause of their condition. These common problem areas include: economics, employment, transportation, housing, architectural and social barriers, and recreation needs. ALS survivors and families should look to other ALS patients for guidance and assistance in dealing with their long-term planning needs.

Central Nervous System Regeneration Research. Research efforts to find a cure for SCIDS should be a source of hope and a program worthy of ALS families' tangible support.

The NPF (National Paraplegia Foundation, 333 N. Michigan Ave., Chicago, Illinois 60601) took the lead in a crusade to find a cure for SCIDS. The NPF sponsored a symposium in 1970 on the enigma of CNS regeneration which was attended by world authorities in the fields of genetics, neurology, anatomy, immunology, physiology, and molecular biology.

These areas for future research are reported and discussed in terms of their present levels of knowledge with particular reference to collateral sprouting, growth of the neuron, neurotrophic interactions, and nerve specificities.

Since its initial breakthrough, NPF has continued to support the quest for a cure by offering an annual $10,000 reward for outstanding research efforts in this area . . .

Families with ALS members have incorporated the ALS Foundation, Inc., 10212 Noble Ave., Mission Hills, California 91340, as a non-profit California corporation. This group will provide direct support of research, education and patient services.

I have successfully survived ALS for 10 years. In those 10 years, I have produced about 50 medical-educational motion pictures and written many medical abstracts and articles. My wife, Shirley, and I have been able to keep our family unit intact. Our son just graduated from San Diego University and our daughter is finishing her freshman year there. I am just completing my formal training as a computer programmer in COBOL language. Because of all these things we have been able to achieve in spite of ALS, I remind you that there is hope for ALS survivors and families.

ALS takes away everything if you permit the "no hope-no cure" philosophy to lead you into a life of self-pity, fear, and dependence. On the other hand, if you believe that a cure of ALS is possible, then you should join us.

In the final analysis, it will only be through overt acts by people-oriented groups that the resolution of problems like Gehrig's disease will be achieved. We should help others to help us to help ourselves. Who is more worthy of our help?

(See **CHAPTER** 43: **NEUROLOGICAL DISORDERS**.)

E. Shali: Educational Therapy

MARIANNE FROSTIG, Ph.D., The Marianne Frostig
Center of Educational Therapy, Los Angeles

Shali is an 8½-year-old girl whose intelligence scores are in the low normal range. She is small for her age, narrow-boned and slender. Her tiny face is flanked by two bushy, blonde ponytails. She has a compliant demeanor, and seems to want to appear obedient and polite. So long as no demands are made of her, she gives no indication of her mastery of techniques of refusal and escape from any situation that confronts her with a task she dislikes.

School History. Shali's parents state that they noticed no problems until she entered kindergarten. Her developmental milestones were all in the average range, and her behavior as a preschooler was described as that of a "cute little girl, sometimes a bit mischievous." In her kindergarten year, however, Shali often came home from school upset, especially when her regular teacher was ill and there was a substitute. On these occasions she said that she did not want to go to school. In the first grade the teacher felt that Shali was slow in learning. She therefore recommended that she repeat the first grade, but her mother refused. During the next year she was reported to be well below grade level and unwilling to participate in reading, math, and other academic subjects.

All the reports of Shali's teachers were similar: Shali resisted schoolwork. When she felt a task to be too hard and thought that she might not succeed, she indulged in the pretense that she did not care how her work was executed, and substituted scribbling, looking at pictures in a book, or any other activity connected with the task except doing the task itself. But her favorite escape was to let her gaze rove around the room instead of looking at her work. "Pretend performances" and frank evasion were evident whenever Shali felt afraid of failure.

Home Environment. For a long time Shali's mother had been thought to be unable to have children, and the parents therefore adopted two children. These children, a girl now 17½ and a boy 16½, seem to be well-adjusted teen-agers.

When Shali was born, her parents were overjoyed and lavished affection on her. But this happy state lasted only until about the time she entered school, when the mother's physical and mental health, which had been borderline, began to break down. Both parents continued to love and to fondle her, but at times when the mother was ill Shali was totally ignored. She would then withdraw and become fidgety and restless, to which the parents would respond by admonishing her. This state of affairs accounted for her dependence upon the presence of her regular teacher in kindergarten. It was unfortunate that this teacher, like her own mother, was often ill and absent. Whenever this was the case, Shali cried, pouted, and resisted all discipline. She felt isolated at home, insecure at school, and often abandoned in both places.

When Shali was in first grade, she developed temper tantrums, which were controlled at home by putting her to bed and in school by not requiring any work. In the second grade her mother's health became worse, and so did Shali's depression and fits of anger. Whenever the mother felt pressured, she fainted, and she finally made a suicide attempt. During the height of the mother's illness, the parents became very hostile to each other.

About a year ago the parents began psychological treatment, and according to the therapist's report, they are now better able to discuss differences of opinion and to treat Shali more consistently. Nevertheless the mother is still rather anxious and tense, there are still differences of opinion between her and her husband, and Shali remains an essentially lonely little girl.

Evaluation. Because of her inability to function in school, Shali has been tested numerous times from kindergarten on. Each time the psychologist has reported that her I.Q. test score was about 90, but that it might well be higher because she was unwilling to try. She also showed definite lags in certain abilities as indicated by her test results. Her very poor performance in tasks requiring fine motor coordination, her deficits in verbal areas and in auditory and visual perception, and the reports received from various clinicians all indicated a probably neurological dysfunction. But these deficits in psychological functions might not have impaired the child's school performance so severely had they not been accompanied by her emotional reactions to the school environment as well as to her own deficits. Her motivation had been particularly affected, and in her anxiety she tried to escape learning.

Educational Planning. The public school authorities had decided that transfer to a special school was necessary because Shali's achievement was far below the required minimum and her behavior was unsatisfatory. She was therefore transferred to the Marianne Frostig Center of Educational Therapy, while the parents remained in treatment with the therapist they had engaged.

As Shali's emotional disturbance was strongly tied in with her learning difficulties, it was decided to undertake her whole treatment within the classroom, at least for a few months.

Sensorimotor Functions. The evaluation of sensorimotor functions with the Frostig Movement Skills Test Battery showed that Shali was far below the expected proficiency in tasks requiring fine motor coordination — bead stringing and transferring blocks from the left to the right side of her body. Low scores in these skills are found very frequently in children with learning difficulties. At the Frostig Center we try to ameliorate the disturbance by emphasizing exercises which require crossing the midline, and bimanual exercises.

The difficulty in crossing the midline was also observed in the classroom. For example, when Shali wanted to pick up with her left hand a crayon that lay to the right on the desk, she would turn her body so as to avoid reaching across the midline. Also, her hand dominance was not yet established, though she usually preferred her left hand. Her perception of position in space, which is frequently disturbed in children who have no established dominance, was poor, and she could not differentiate between such letters as *b* and *d* or *p* and *q*.

Observation also showed that Shali's difficulty in fine motor coordination seemed to stem from a lack of right-left coordination, rather than from lack of finger dexterity. She therefore needed practice in manipulating small objects with both hands. It was suggested that in arithmetic she work with blocks which can be clipped together and taken apart only by using both hands.

Shali's ability to skip and jump was also observed. She needed practice with movements requiring leg strength, but she had no difficulty with asymmetrical movements, such as those involved in galloping.

Visual Perception. Visual perception was evaluated with the Frostig Developmental Test of Visual Perception and with the Bender-Gestalt Test. Her scores on these tests were poor. On the Bender-Gestalt she showed numerous distortions, rotations, and general spatial confusion. Her score on the eye-motor subtest of the Frostig was low, confirming the evidence from the Frostig Movement Skills Test Battery: Shali had poor fine motor coordination. Figure ground perception, perception of position in space, and perception of spatial relationships were also impaired. It was therefore decided to introduce visual perceptual training, using the worksheets and "Teacher's Guide" of the Frostig Developmental Program for Visual Perception.

Evaluation of Language and Higher Cognitive Functions. Higher cognitive functions were evaluated with the Wechsler Intelligence Scale for Children (WISC). With the exception of similarities, digit span (memory for auditory stimuli), block design (analysis and synthesis of patterns), and picture completion (memory for details), Shali's scores were slightly or markedly below average, with lowest scores in information and vocabulary. The discrepancy between verbal and performance scores was thirteen points, and indicated that Shali's major difficulties were in the verbal area, although she also had significant sensorimotor and visual perception difficulties.

Systematic teaching in science and social studies, using multimodal presentation (listening to explanations while looking at filmstrips, slides, pictures, maps, and so on, making graphs, drawings, and pictographs, and writing down or discussing what she learned) was suggested as a means of developing Shali's vocabulary and information.

Arithmetic was Shali's lowest score. Mathematics is difficult for children with poor visual perceptual skills. It was hoped that visual perceptual training would help to improve her scores. On the other hand, auditory sequential memory and digit span were high.

Illinois Test of Psycholinguistic Abilities (ITPA). Shali's ITPA scores showed many deficits, especially in visual sequential memory, associational skills (auditory association and visual association), and expressive abilities (verbal expression, grammatic closure, and manual expression). These scores gave additional indications regarding this child's training needs. Since visual sequential memory was low, while auditory sequential memory was high (as indicated by the ITPA subtest and the digit span subtest of the WISC), it was suggested that memory tasks during academic learning be presented to Shali auditorially. Number triads ("number facts") and measurement tables and spelling are examples. It was also suggested that Shali's deficits in verbal expression and grammatic closure (grammatically correct speech) could be ameliorated through much practice in speech and writing. Specific exercises in phonetic spelling (often with the use of nonsense words) which introduce consonants, vowels, and blends systematically were planned. It was suggested to her teacher that she should always speak slowly, distinctly, and simply when giving instructions to Shali.

Evaluation during the Initial Tutoring Hour. The deficits in information, comprehension, vocabulary, verbal expression, and grammatic closure indicated that language activity should accompany all training in visual perceptual and sensorimotor areas, and that ample opportunity for language activities, including oral language, should be provided. Such integrative ability training was begun during the observation-tutoring hour. Shali was given Worksheet No. 56 (Advanced Pictures and Patterns, Frostig, 1972), which was chosen because it focuses on figure-ground perception, in which she scored low, and because the picture related to a poem which Shali was asked to read. First she was asked to name the animals she saw, to count them, and to say what sounds they made. A transparent plastic (acetate) sheet was then placed over the pic-

The subject is presented with this worksheet from the Frostig Visual Perception Program and is asked, "What animals do you see?" (Marianne Frostig Center of Educational Therapy, Los Angeles)

ture, and Shali was asked to trace the outline of each animal, in turn. Using a sheet on which erasures could easily be made protected her from failure and also gave the opportunity for extra practice in eye-motor coordination. She at first omitted the duck's foot, but when asked to which animal the foot could belong, she was able to use her ability to visualize to connect it correctly. Training in eye-hand coordination and figure-ground perception, and language and conceptual thinking were thus integrated.

The teacher and Shali then discussed briefly how each of the animals moved in its natural environment. Shali was asked to move like a duck on land and then like a duck in water; these exercises in motor expression she enjoyed greatly. She was then asked if she had any of the animals as a pet, and was encouraged to talk about her cat. Training in coordination, flexibility, in motor planning and expressive movement, and in visualization and verbal expression were integrated in this task.

Since Shali's lowest scores on the WISC were information and vocabulary, and the ITPA scores also indicated her very poor use of language, the greatest emphasis had to be put on language training, and reading material had to be used which supplied terms and concepts adequate for Shali's ability. During one of the first hours, a poem of a few lines was read by the child and teacher together. The poem gave her the vocabulary to denote the noises animals make, an exercise she had done before when working with the visual perception sheet as described above. She learned that a chicken clucks, a dog barks, a lion roars, etc. Then a game was played in which the words for the animals and for their vocal productions had to be paired. The teacher then wrote the name of the animal, and Shali wrote a word indicating the "noise"; then the roles were reversed. This was done because of Shali's apparent difficulties in forming associations, which were evidenced by her responses to the WISC vocabulary subtest and the association subtest of the ITPA.

Although auditory memory was Shali's greatest asset, a method of learning to spell and to read was employed which made use of both auditory and visual memory simultaneously. According to this method, each new word is color-coded, each successive sound being written in a different color (for instance *r ea ch*: black *r*, red *ea*, brown *ch*). Digraphs, diphthongs, and silent letters are pointed out. Silent letters are written in a stippled fashion. After the words were written in color, they were written in black ink, so that synthesis followed the analytic process. The whole word was read after it had been divided into sounds. Shali learned to look at the words, to memorize the nonphonetic elements by remembering their graphic representation, and to reproduce them from memory.

Teaching Reading. At the beginning of instruction, high first-grade material was chosen for Shali. She made only one mistake while reading two stories, but her reading was so labored that it was decided not to use more difficult material for the next three or four weeks, until she had achieved some fluency and a better ability to pay attention. Shali read one story a day by reading in alternation with another child who was a good reader; that is, Shali read a short paragraph, then the other child read the next one, and so on. This method was indicated because Shali seemed to tire very easily while reading alone, and when reading with a group her attention wandered.

Teaching Math. Observation showed that Shali could not add or subtract because she did not understand partial counting. She drew a new numberline for each new addition problem (for instance, for $7 + 4$ she drew seven dots in a line, and then four dots in a line) and counted all the dots. This cumbersome procedure had made it impossible for her to keep up with the other children. Partial counting forward and backward was taught successfully during the first two lessons, using step-by-step procedures. She first solved problems involving adding and subtracting 1, and learned that the correct solution of these problems was the same as counting forward and backward. Then she learned to "skip" one or two numbers and thus to add or subtract 2 or 3. She was required to write the problems; and finally they were practiced again in a card game.

Writing. Shali could not form all letters but could copy them. As she had difficulties with differentiating between *b* and *d*, the teacher made the following drawing: b-e-d. "These letters make a picture of a bed," she said. "Do you see how there is a board at each end, and the rest of the picture makes a mattress: You could not write the *b* or the *d* any other way or the mattress would fall down. So when you hear *b* or *d* in a word, always ask yourself if the letter sounds like the first or last letter in the word *bed*. Then you will be able to write it correctly."

Since Shali had fair visualization skills and could hear single beginning or final consonants in short words, she was able to write without mistake the phonic words beginning or ending with *b* or *d* that the teacher dictated: "bed, mad, Dan, ball, dab, bud, did, dot." No reversals were noted during the remainder of the hour.

Summary. Shali's deficits were multiple. In addition to her disabilities, there were attitudinal factors which made progress in public school impossible. But in a clinical school the prognosis for Shali was good, provided she could be induced to apply her energy to the learning task instead of evading it. She had to accept help before she could gain the skills in which she was lagging. This was possible in a small class, especially one with a "family" structure, where she could obtain attentive help from the teacher and from the older, more advanced children. She also had to learn to put forth consistently a real, not a "pretend," effort. After the first tutoring-observation session she said spontaneously, "I learned a lot. I kept my eyes on the work. I like that." This attitude was maintained throughout the seminar.

(See CHAPTER 37: LEARNING DISABILITIES.)

F. Employing the Handicapped

Excerpted from "Honors to Tektronix in Employing the Handicapped," *Modern Manufacturing*, vol. 3, pp. 14–15, May 1970; with permission

Tektronix, Inc., the Beaverton, Oregon manufacturer of oscilloscopes, has been cited for its significant achievement in employing the handicapped. Through a comprehensive, positive, and continuing effort, the firm can boast of disabled employees who are full-fledged productive workers holding their own with nonhandicapped personnel doing the same type of work.

Howard Vollum, Tektronix president, said the firm's basic employment philosophy is to "select and place individuals on the basis of their abilities." All applicants are considered equally; the same employment policy applies to both handicapped and non-handicapped.

The only time concern is shown for a disability is when it might impair the employee's performance in standard jobs, when it would affect the individual's safety, or affect the safety of his co-workers.

Ever since the firm's inception in 1946, management has always made an effort to use qualified handicapped people. Then, in 1961, it decided to emphasize this type of hiring by adding a person to the employment staff to oversee these special placements. While it never was and still is not a company policy to give preference to the handicapped, this addition to the employment staff was a move to ensure that appropriate and equal consideration was given to qualified handicapped applicants.

One of the first projects Norman H. Silver, in charge of special placements, undertook was to identify all jobs within Tektronix. The purpose of the survey was to determine those jobs at which people with certain types of handicaps and with the proper job qualifications might be employed. He wanted to find out the jobs in which a disability would not inhibit the employees' performance. The entire list was then circulated to interviewers, plant managers, supervisors, and others concerned with selecting people to fill openings.

The program's success is evident in the types of handicapped people who have been hired. Among the disabled are deaf, blind, amputees, paraplegics, and the mentally retarded. There are also those afflicted with muscular dystrophy, epilepsy, and orthopedic disabilities. At Tektronix, the handicapped number just over 200 in a workforce that is approaching 9000.

Throughout the history of Tektronix, the policy that all positions and advancements are open to all is a viable, active one. Here are some examples:

An individual confined to a wheelchair started as an assembler. He then advanced to a technician's post and was responsible for testing, calibrating, and troubleshooting. Today, he is training candidates for field engineering positions.

Two deaf employees were upgraded to the most complex assembly job in the company from their previous assembly positions. Within a short time both rose to the top 10% in terms of productivity and work quality. Now, they have progressed still further into inspecting and semi-technical functions.

With polio, a severe back injury, and being a cardiac, this former assembler now is a production manager, supervising a 30-woman assembly line.

A blind employee was asked which job he preferred. To everyone's surprise, he selected a cabling position (assembling harnesses). He set up a board with braille indicators on pattern. He also set up a braille dog-house (holder of individual wires). Before long he was producing at a rapid rate — without using the braille indicators. He also suggested a more efficient way of making the cables that sighted people now follow.

Once the handicapped individual is placed in a job at Tektronix, all efforts are geared to assimilate him into the workforce. He receives the prevailing rate of pay for the specific job assigned and participates in the firm's profit sharing program from his first day on the job.

Tektronix has a comprehensive education program in which disabled employees are encouraged to participate. Courses range from those of general development (art, music, human relations) to specifics, such as electricity and electronics, materials and processes, data processing, and computer technology. Generally, no special efforts are made on behalf of specific handicapped groups. However, special courses are instituted whenever it is obvious that members of a specific group need to have their horizons broadened or their abilities and talents upgraded. For example, Tektronix has a series of in-house programs geared to the deaf and hard-of-hearing. The purpose is to upgrade the education of these people so they can participate in regular courses offered by the company and other sources.

Phase one of the educational program provides remedial and communications skills courses. Typical subjects include language building, mathematics, etc. In phase two, the deaf and those who are severely hard-of-hearing will be integrated into regular classes with assistance, when necessary, from sign language interpreters.

One course—telephone communications for the deaf—has already been an overwhelming success. The deaf person attaches a meter to the side of a phone. Once the other party picks up the receiver, the deaf person controls and directs the conversation. He explains that he is deaf and tells the person to respond with a "no," "yes, yes," or "please repeat." The needle on the meter moves with each syllable spoken. Thus, the deaf person gets an answer.

In addition to the curriculum for the deaf, Tektronix also offers an in-house course in sign language for hearing co-workers and supervisors. This course, in particular, has always been well attended.

In addition to educational opportunities, special counseling is provided. Occasionally, communications and other problems occur between the handicapped worker and his supervisor; or the individual has a personal problem. Both could and usually do affect the employee's performance. Therefore, Tektronix offers special counseling to the employee and, if needed, the manager. The handicapped person can also consult with a psychologist who is available.

In addition to educational and psychological assistance, company facilities have been geared to aid the handicapped. One such modification was lowering work-benches in assembly areas to accommodate workers confined to wheelchairs. Also, disabled employees are able to ride in freight elevators to second-story work areas. In addition, ramps are available for entry into the buildings. Parking spaces, too, are specially reserved for wheelchair employees and others with impaired mobility.

The facility also has six conveniently located first aid stations each staffed by a registered nurse. Each station has a list and the medical records of disabled personnel working nearby. The nurses are equipped to handle any emergency in their area and provide continuous care to those handicapped employees who require it, e.g. massages, medication and bandage changes.

(See CHAPTER 37: VOCATIONAL REHABILITATION; EMPLOYMENT; SELF-EMPLOYMENT.)

G. Mrs. Y.: A Case of Geriatric Rehabilitation

CHARLIS S. DUNHAM, M.A.

Mrs. Y., a seventy-year-old widow, was referred to an agency for the blind by a neighbor because of depression precipitated by vision loss due to retinal hemorrhage. The condition was not treatable by laser beam, and at the time of intake Mrs. Y.'s vision was progressively deteriorating. She had been told, however, that the loss would stabilize at some time in the future but had no idea when this would be.

A social worker visited Mrs. Y. at home and found her deeply despondent and considering suicide. Although a formerly active woman (enjoying golf, bowling, civic work, and card playing), she sat nearly immobile during the intake interview. Occasionally she punctuated her withdrawn silences with bitter outbursts directed toward the physician, who she felt had "dismissed" her, or toward her daughter, who "abandoned" her by failing to offer permanent residence in the daughter's home. Mrs. Y. was not interested in rehabilitation and even rejected an offer of talking books during the initial interview. She insisted that her situation was "hopeless," and was planning to move immediately into a nursing home, where she believed she would quickly die. Only after persistent persuasion did she agree to allow the social worker to return.

After seeing Mrs. Y., the case worker arranged a meeting with Mrs. M., Mrs. Y.'s only child, who resided in another state. Mrs. M. was generally concerned about her mother, but was overwhelmed by her mother's enormous dependency needs and stated that her mother's moving into her home would precipitate a divorce. The worker helped the daughter define her mother's dependency needs realistically and in so doing reduced the daughter's panic. Together they set limits to protect Mrs. M.'s own emotional resources, and defined concrete services which she felt able and willing to provide for her mother. The worker also made clear to Mrs. M. that she was not responsible for her mother's emotional well-being.

When the worker returned to see Mrs. Y., the two agreed on a four-month delay before making any change in her living situation. During this period the social worker visited Mrs. Y. twice weekly, presenting herself as the appropriate object for Mrs. Y.'s intense dependency wishes, and in so doing assumed a role formerly filled by her daughter. Intensive work was done around Mrs. Y.'s anger, depression, dependency wishes, and need for all-or-nothing perfectionism. A sister of Mrs. Y.'s and a granddaughter, both living locally, helped with meal preparation, shopping, and transportation. A friend was hired at Mrs. M.'s expense to help with housework. Six weeks after intake Mrs. Y. allowed the worker to request a "talking book."

Toward the end of the four-month period Mrs. Y. began to interest herself in her former active life-style. She initiated (with help) a search for a Braille teacher so that she could continue with her favorite pastime, bridge. She spontaneously began to brush up her typing and purchased a cassette tape recorder so that she could communicate privately with her daughter. She began to keep a cassette phone directory, and started, at her sister's urging, to transcribe recipes onto tape. With support, she was able to begin cooking, was offered activities-of-daily-living (ADL) training, and was helped to obtain appropriate aids and appliances. She also began to initiate contact with other people (primarily around bridge), and to reassume more normal interpersonal relationships.

By the end of the four months, Mrs. Y. felt that her wish to move into a nursing home had perhaps been premature. Interviews were reduced to once weekly. Between the fourth and eighth month of casework, Mrs. Y. consolidated previous gains, learned to crochet, and explored more fully her feelings about blindness. Of specific concern was her unconscious association of blindness with mental retardation. During the eighth month she began limited mobility training (to the grocery store, drug store, bank, park), using a swagger stick instead of the more traditional (but still unacceptable to her) white cane.

After one year Mrs. Y.'s sister announced plans to leave the city. At about the same time her daughter gave birth to her second child, and several friends moved to other parts of the country. Mrs. Y. coped well with these "abandonments" and felt able to carry on independently. She began to take over cleaning duties that before had been managed by her friends.

During the second year Mrs. Y. saw the worker once or twice monthly. Mobility training was continued toward concrete and progressively more difficult goals. Functioning during this year was excellent, but complete termination was felt to be inappropriate only because of Mrs. Y.'s deep-seated characterologic dependency problems.

(See CHAPTER 54: OTHER DISORDERS, E. Geriatric Rehabilitation.)

H. Aphasia: A Personal Account

Excerpted from Mary Pannbacker, "Aphasia According to an Expert," *Rehabilitation Literature,* October 1971; with permission

The purpose of this article is to present a written self-account, the return to life, of a 30-year-old engineer who became aphasic. No attempt has been made to edit Mr. K.'s statements; they are presented just as he wrote them . . .

Medical History. On July 13, 1969, Mr. K. was admitted to the hospital with complaints of severe girdle headache, left retrobulbar pain, and associated nausea with projectile vomiting. The illness started about 10 days prior to admission as a spontaneous intermittent prostrating headache with associated visual changes involving the left optical pathway. The admission diagnosis was choriolymphocytic meningitis.

Headaches were progressive and additional studies were made, including brain scan and carotid arteriography. A diagnosis of left subdural hematoma was made because of arterial changes and brain shift. On July 28 a bur hole procedure was performed with drainage of a subdural hematoma through the temporal, parietal, and frontal areas. Postoperatively, the patient had bizarre motor signs with localization on the right and speech characterized as inappropriate, prepositional, and violent with associated exasperation. During a left craniotomy procedure on August 3 an organized subdural hematoma with secreting membrane was removed.

The patient was referred for physical medicine and rehabilitation consultation on August 12 with regard to a possible rehabilitation program. Mr. K. was admitted to the Rehabilitation Center because of *a*) "residuals, head injury, with subdural hematoma"; *b*) "residuals, craniotomy, left, secondary to bur holes for drainage, subdural hematoma," and *c*) "aphasia, mixed, with hyperkinesis." Language was further described as motor boat in fashion, gestures suggested exasperation in connection with speech difficulty, and reception was approximately normal. The patient's chief complaint was: "Can't talk, can't talk, can't talk."

Mr. K.'s Description of the Return to Life. On 7-27-69, I had an operation on the left side of my head to remove a Blood-Clot. This was my second operation, the first one being done on 7-21-69. This operation lasted 6 hours 15 minutes.

As a result of this operation, I lost my speech, reading, writing, and ability to understand (comprehend) fully what people were saying to me. I found out the day they took me out of the Intensive Care Unit that I had lost these four things. What a shock this was! What a bitter and frustrated feeling I had. I just sank into utter despair for a day or two.

The third day after my operation, my close friend came to see me. He talked to me, got me a coke, and the best thing of all — my first cigarette since before the operation. While he was talking to me, I couldn't understand everything he said, which was a bit frustrating. At one point, he printed on an envelope if there was anything I wanted him to bring me. So, I tried to write pillow on this envelope and couldn't [see illustration]. This was so frustrating, that I just broke down and cried.

After he left, I decided that I better try and do something about this situation. I realized that it all was up to me. Especially if I wanted to go back to my job, and lead a normal life, and also retain my social life and activities.

So I started to try and pronounce words, but I couldn't get any-

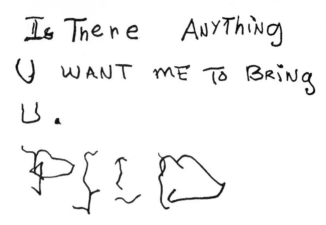

thing out except a laugh, yes and no. I then realized if I worked at it, that it could all come back.

One of the Student Nurses, I forgot when, but she wrote out the alphabet for me. After she left, I started to copy the alphabet. It took me 15 minutes to write "A," which came out crooked, but you could tell it was an "A." This really made me feel good, but I had written it with a ball-point pen, and decided a pencil would be better to work with. So I went to the Nurses Station and got a pencil. On the way back to my room, I dropped that pencil about 3 or 4 times. This was due to my right arm still slightly paralyzed, which eventually disappeared. Anyhow, I started on the rest of the alphabet, and it took me about 3 hours to complete. In the next 2-3 days, I conquered the alphabet.

Then I started to work on pronouncing the letters of the alphabet. It took me 3-4 days, but I still couldn't pronounce — F, I, L, N, R, U, W, X, Y — when Dr. Jones came in the 4th day and found out I was having trouble with these letters, he spent a ½ hour with me working on them. *Bang!* They came around, I could curl my tongue around all the letters now. What a great feeling, progress is being made, I thought to myself. Then I went through the alphabet, constantly repeating the letters.

However, as I taught myself to write and pronounce the letters of the alphabet, my ability to understand wasn't coming along at the same pace. I still couldn't look at a sentence and have it make sense to me. So, no reading. Thus, still many frustrations.

The weeks of 8/6-12 and /13-19/69 was when I really made progress. The week of 8/6-12 was when I finally was able to pronounce completely all the letters of the alphabet. Also, 2 Student Nurses helped me to say — Hi Dr. Smith and Hi Mrs. Brown. Mrs. Brown was the head nurse on my ward at the hospital. After the student nurses helped me pronounce her name the best I could, which was a little slurred, they brought her back to my room. I said to her, "Hi Mrs. Brown," and she cried. I was elated over the fact that I could say more than just the letters of the alphabet. The next morning when Dr. Smith came in to remove the rest of my stitches, I said to him, "Hi Dr. Smith," and he shook my hand and said to keep up the good work.

However, during all this time, until the 18th of August, I still couldn't keep track of the dates and days. No matter, if I looked at the date and day on a newspaper. This was slightly frustrating, but not really important since I realized that when I got my speech and reading back, that I could be able to retain the days and dates as one normally does.

On the 16th of August, I was transferred from the hospital to the Rehabilitation Center. The first thing they did was to take my B.P., Temp., and Pulse Rate. Then they did the most important thing (as far as I was concerned). They asked me questions, and where I had scars and what size, and the cause of the scars. So, I had to talk in order to answer their questions, and I did to the best of my ability, but, they were able to understand me.

This was the end of frustration for me. I could make people understand me. Great feelings again. Everything was coming along fine.

On 8/17 and 18/69, my Mother, Sister and small brother came up to see me. This really helped, because we talked and talked both days.

Also on the 18th, I had a session with the psychiatrist. This was also good for me, since I had to answer his questions, copy diagrams, and assemble a set of blocks in various patterns.

The evening of 8/18, I finished writing a letter which I had started on 7/20/69. I only wrote two sentences, and had to use a dictionary for almost every word. I almost let this frustrate me, but I thought—why become frustrated again since I was progressing so quickly. Later on that evening, I decided I would read the last 3 chapters of the "Dirty Dozen." As I started to read, I found that I had some difficulty at first finding my way through a sentence. I would then re-read the sentence, or just re-read the paragraph.

After I read and re-read these 3 chapters, my reading improved and to increase my reading and writing abilities, I looked up words in the dictionary. I also just leafed through and would read a page wherever I stopped.

When I started Speech Therapy on 8/21/69, the speech therapist gave me a series of tests. I guess they were the standard ones. The speech therapist also worked with me twice a day. One of the projects she had me do, was to write "the story of my life." While doing this project, I noticed that it was helping to improve my writing. She then had me start on this summary report of my Dysphasia. While writing this report, it has really helped me to recall what's happened to me since my second operation. However, the speech therapist has really helped me with my speech problem.

To sum it all up, *"It's great to be alive again."*

(See CHAPTER 49: SPEECH AND LANGUAGE DISORDERS.)

I. Independence?

Excerpted from "Independence?", *Exceptional Parent*,
September-October 1974; with permission

Mr. and Mrs. Conners first consulted me ten years ago when their
daughter Alice was sixteen. From the time she was hit by a car and
suffered brain damage when she was four years old, they had spent
a great deal of time and money on evaluations, private schools, tutors — and yet it seemed, at that time, that no one had made the effort to help them to understand their daughter's special problems in
the context of her overall development.

Their own observations turned out to be sensitive and accurate. I
remembered Mrs. Conners saying, "Even though Alice looks sixteen — and that's a problem in its own right — her conversations
aren't really those of a sixteen year old. At least not after the first five
minutes. She can say a few words about rock 'n' roll stars and
clothes, but I don't think she understands what she's talking about.
Certainly not when I compare her with my neighbor's daughter —
and she's only thirteen.

"And Alice has always had a hard time in school. She learned to
read, and she does read the comics in the newspaper. But she
doesn't really catch on. And she doesn't seem to remember the details well enough to follow the ones that continue from day to day.

"Her teachers say she fools around too much, even in the special
class. But in their opinion she isn't as retarded as the rest of the
kids. And she looks fine. Some of the other kids, you know, they
really look different."

The results of periodic psychological and neurological examinations that had been done over the years were consistent. As a result
of her accident, Alice was considered mildly mentally retarded.
However, directly or indirectly, the brain damage also contributed
to some other, more specific problems. First, Alice had a memory
deficit that was directly attributable to her brain injury. That is, her
memory was much poorer than that of others her age who were also
mildly mentally retarded. She had trouble with short-term tasks
such as remembering a shopping list or set of simple directions, as
well as more complex long-term recollection, like remembering a
story or past events. This type of memory deficit usually affects the
mastery of complex skills such as reading which depends on remembering many specific details. Thus, as the school reports
showed, although Alice gradually learned to read, she progressed at
a rate much slower than might be expected of a mildly retarded
child. Eventually, and with great effort, she was able to read at
about a fourth grade level.

Alice enjoyed helping her mother with household chores. However, when given the task of dusting a particular room, Alice might
skip something and not be aware of her omission. Alice's judgment

in social situations was also affected by her disability. This problem stemmed from a combination of at least three factors: her impaired memory, her limited intellectual capacity, and the fact that she had been placed in special classes and special schools throughout her life, which limited the range of her social experiences. The comments of the teachers suggested that Alice was very accepting of the opinions of others, that she was gullible and eager to please and, thus, often taken advantage of. Furthermore, they thought she "overreacted" to criticism.

Nonetheless, Alice was secure and rather competent whenever the task was simple or the situation uncomplicated—when she knew specifically what was being asked of her and when she was not required to remember a series of details. However, when she felt uncertain about what was expected of her or when the challenge was beyond her ability, she would become rather silly.

After discussing these findings, Mr. and Mrs. Conners confronted the sad fact that Alice was disabled by these several specific limitations inside of her, and these were not going to change. This did not mean that she could not lead a useful and happy life but rather that she would require help along the way, throughout her life, from concerned and knowledgeable people.

Then Mr. and Mrs. Conners, Alice and I met together to discuss how Alice might take fullest advantage of the vocational training programs available in her community, while she was still in school. My objective was to help plan ways in which Alice could develop vocational skills and have additional social experiences under careful supervision. We were hopeful that in the years to come group counseling would become a part of such programs because Alice needed help in understanding social situations. Specifically, we hoped she would come to understand that people might criticize her and even be angry with her and at the same time be concerned about her well-being and truly like her. We knew that this would be a difficult lesson for her to learn and she would need repeated opportunities to do so. In thinking aloud together about the future, we agreed that a sheltered protected setting would enable Alice to live as full a life as possible for her, and that it was unlikely she could ever "make it" in the outside world without supervision.

We did not meet further because the resources in the Conners' community seemed likely to provide the programs and counseling Alice needed, and because of the great distance involved between their home town and my office. Thus, a referral was made to the local agency which seemed well equipped to work with Alice and her parents.

"That was ten years ago," Mrs. Conners was saying. "Three years ago Alice was living with us and going to a sheltered workshop. She had been going there for a few years. The other people were retarded or physically handicapped; and some were mentally ill. She was learning to make beds, to do some simple cooking and other kinds of domestic work. Her counselor told us that one of the motels nearby was willing to give the girls from the workshop a chance for jobs as maids. Alice was one of the three girls from the workshop who started working at the motel. Mrs. White, the workshop supervisor, went with them every day.

"It was wonderful for a while. Alice was thrilled. She had to get to the workshop by 8 AM. Then they would go with Mrs. White to the motel and work straight through until 1 PM. They were getting paid the minimum wage and they had lunch in the motel kitchen.

"Then Mrs. White decided that Alice and two other girls were doing so well that they should take responsibility for getting to the motel by themselves and getting started at the motel. Mrs. White would come later.

"On the first day of this new arrangement Alice came home in tears. She had had a dispute with one of the regular maids about something she had apparently forgotten to do. Well, we never really found out all the details, but Alice refused to go back to the motel.

"Mrs. White came over once and told Alice — in front of us — that it was time to grow up and take responsibility for herself. Alice just cried. We tried to suggest that she go back to the workshop but Mrs. White thought that would be babying her. She said we should insist that Alice go back to the motel — that the manager had not fired her and would be understanding. But this didn't help. She just cried some more.

"It took six months before she was ready to consider going back to the workshop. She just stayed around the house and watched television and helped me a little bit with my housework. We didn't have Mrs. White to turn to anymore, because we didn't see things her way. But a few months later she got a new job elsewhere and a new young man took over her job at the workshop. Mr. Park was so enthusiastic and persuasive — full of new ideas. He invited Alice back to the workshop and she agreed to go. I really think she had a crush on him and that's why she went.

"About a month later, Alice seemed to be in much better spirits. Then we went to a parents' meeting at the workshop, and Mr. Park told us about plans for beginning a group home near the workshop.

"Two months later Mr. Park asked us to come in and meet with him. He suggested that Alice move into the group home near the workshop. I believe he, like Mrs. White, thought we were over-protecting Alice.

"Mr. Park asked us to visit the home to look it over. It really was nice. And clean too. A dozen young adults from the workshop were going to live there — both men and women. A young couple, both students at the seminary, were going to be the 'house parents.'

"In a few weeks Alice was accepted and she moved in. At first it was fine. Alice shared a nice room with another girl. She came home for dinner once a week and spent some weekends with us. And, of course, she was continuing at the workshop where she seemed to be doing fairly well.

"But gradually we began to notice that the house was getting sloppy. Nobody was reminding the girls to tidy up. I always had to do that at home, or Alice's room would never have been clean. I asked Mr. Park about the house and he said they were teaching the girls to be independent and it was best not to interfere.

"Alice continued living there for two years. She made some friends and participated daily in the workshop. Things were going well. There were problems—but nothing serious. We would give her spending money and sometimes she would lose it; or she would forget to do things like pick up her clothes at the laundry. But all in all, she was happy and we were very relieved.

"Three months ago Mr. Park called us. He was all excited. The workshop had received a grant from the state to help young adults like Alice to live independently in the community. Alice was going to move into an apartment with two other girls. The idea was that the girls would do their own shopping and cooking and attend the workshop during the day. They would go to the group home for meetings and social functions. Alice was very excited.

"We helped Alice move into the apartment. Mr. Park was there and he was very helpful and optimistic. He said what Alice needed most was a chance to prove herself on her own.

"She called us that night. She sounded a little strange but we thought it was us. A week later, the supervisor at the workshop called me and asked if there was something wrong at home. She said Alice went around mumbling under her breath and seemed to be very tired and nervous.

"We visited her on Saturday and she wasn't her usual self at all. She was snappy to us and even swore at us—she had never done that before. She said one of her roommates was mean and was bugging her. We thought she'd better see someone. Mr. Park said he would arrange an appointment with one of their psychiatric consultants.

"On Friday they called us again and said we'd better come and get her. She hadn't shown up at the workshop, so they sent someone over to the apartment. She was uncontrollable. We saw the psychiatrist that afternoon, and he recommended that we put her in the psychiatric ward of the county hospital because she might hurt herself.

"Thank God she's okay now. She really snapped out of it at the hospital. Of course the medication and the therapy helped a lot. But it was just as you had said. She needs a protective setting. When she moved to the apartment she just fell apart—just like at the motel.

"Mr. Conners was angry. 'Now what do we do? Should we go back to the workshop and have some bright-eyed enthusiastic staff member push her right back out into the goddamn real world? What for? What's so great about the real world anyway? Who the hell is all that independent?' "

Mr. and Mrs. Conners were right. A careful review of Alice's history over the past years confirmed that whenever she was faced with new responsibilities without skilled and sensitive supervision, she would take a step backward. Although Mr. and Mrs. Conners understood this and worked accordingly to help plan for Alice's future, they held on to the human wish of any parent that their children will grow up and establish themselves on their own. As a result, when Mrs. White and then Mr. Park came along with their enthusiasm to help Alice establish her independence, Mr. and Mrs. Conners went along with the plans. But unfortunately, their commitments to certain goals of the new programs ignored Alice's unique needs which her parents had come to understand over an extended period of time.

Now Alice is living at home and helping with the housework. Mrs. Conners has taken a part-time job. Mr. and Mrs. Conners are trying to save some extra money for a trust fund for Alice's future which will supplement the Social Security benefits she now receives.

Psychologically, Alice is much better. The Conners, very carefully, are looking into some new community residential programs, including some privately supported ones. Hopefully, they will find a place where Alice can live her own life and be dependent too.

(See **CHAPTER 22: BRAIN DAMAGE.**)

J. Three Vocational Rehabilitation Cases

CHARLIS S. DUNHAM, M.A.

I.

H.Z., a triple amputee, was referred to the Department of Rehabilitation by the Veterans Administration. Before enlisting in the armed services he had attended college for one year, after which he had worked briefly as a grocery clerk, farm worker, and truck driver.

H.Z. served in Vietnam for ten months before being wounded so grievously that an arm and both legs had to be amputated. He was given field emergency treatment and flown to a veterans' hospital in the United States. During his first week at the hospital he was unable to sit in a wheelchair or carry on the activities of daily living, but at the end of seven months he had progressed to such an extent that he was fitted with a prosthetic device for his left arm, which had been removed near the shoulder, and also with prosthetic equipment for both legs. However, because the leg stumps were extremely short he had difficulty walking, but could do so for very short distances using a single cane. He was able to dress himself, to move about freely with both electric and regular wheelchairs, and could write and type. His dominant arm was not injured, and at the present writing he drives a car with hand controls.

During therapy and rehabilitation in the veterans' hospital, H.Z.'s interests suggested that he had a strong orientation toward people and that he might do well in social work or a related field. He planned to return to college when he was released from the hospital and work toward a B.A. degree, after which he would consider working toward a master's degree in social work. His vocational goals were judged to be realistic in terms of his handicap, since he would be able to handle a social work job physically. Tests indicated that his interests were high in art, religious activities, social service, and office practices. At the time of testing he was somewhat immature, but was cooperative and pleasant and seemed to have made a reasonable adjustment to his disabilities. He was good company and was well liked by both the staff and fellow patients. An intelligence test placed him in the bright-normal range and possibly a bit higher, for at the time of testing he was in a "low" period and also hampered by the limited use of his arms.

Because H.Z. felt that he was not particularly "academically inclined" during the one year he had attended college, he thought it would be best to enroll in a junior college for a year and raise his grade point average before applying to a university. After leaving the hospital he followed this plan, and achieved his B.A. degree in psychology in 1974.

When H.Z. approached the Department of Vocational Rehabilitation (DVR) in 1975, he was in training with a Social Security office and had started in its information trainee program. It was felt, however, that he would need further training in various situations in order to qualify for a position with permanency. After consultation with the Social Security office, and with their enthusiastic approval, DVR provided funds so that he could attend an on-the-job training program held at the Regional Training Center for two months. He completed this course with no difficulty and is now employed as an information officer on a full-time basis.

II.

DVR initiated an in-depth study of B.M. when he came to the program because of his history of alcoholic addiction. At forty-seven, he had been a heavy drinker most of his adult life, but his excessive drinking had accelerated as he came under increasing job and personal pressures. In his own words, "The more problems I have, the more I drink—and the more I drink, the worse my problems become."

When asked about his background and early history, B.M. said his mother was of middle European origin and his father was a Scandinavian who drank heavily. He expressed warm feelings toward his father, who raised him rather sternly, drilling into the youngster that "Scandinavians don't cry." He seems to have enjoyed joining his father at work, and as he grew older actually worked under his father for a time.

During the depression B.M. held a number of jobs and showed complete willingness to work. When World War II was in progress, he was accepted into the armed services, but just as he was about to get into his preferred area of military training the war ended and this possibility did not materialize. He was deeply disappointed, and an even greater loss occurred at the same time—his mother died. Although he was not as articulate about his mother, and did not appear to have been influenced by her as much as by his father, nevertheless he was fondly attached.

After the war B.M. fulfilled a life-long ambition and obtained his college degree. He then proceeded to go into advertising. However, his job involved considerable drinking and traveling, and shortly after marrying he and his wife agreed that he should give up advertising and start a new career. He did this most successfully and held a mid-level management job for fifteen years with a large manufacturing plant.

During these years he continued to drink heavily, and in 1967 his problems were aggravated by a new set of stresses—all most traumatic. He was shot in the abdomen by a friend during a drinking spree; he lost his job (due to large-scale job layoffs and somewhat due to his drinking); he was divorced and his six children were temporarily lost to him; and he experienced several grand mal seizures. B.M. seriously contemplated suicide at the time, but after hours of reflection realized how desperately he needed help, and contacted a mental health clinic. With the assistance of the doctors there as well as the county alcoholic center, he managed to get his drinking under control and began to understand some of his problems.

Because of his contact with the alcoholic center, B.M. had had intermittent contact with DVR over the years, and when he lost one job after another, he sought help from this agency. DVR provided a complete psychiatric examination, a complete physical, and a job evaluation, and saw to it that his teeth, which were in a shocking condition, received attention. Moreover, inasmuch as he was a well-qualified white-collar worker and had to present himself at his best to prospective employers in the upper-management field, the agency saw to it that he had some decent clothes.

B.M. has an unforgiving attitude toward himself—possibly based on the theme of "Scandinavians don't cry"—but his self-esteem and sense of purpose were strongly tied to work. Because DVR recognized that he was strongly motivated, had a good record of tenure on the job for many years (despite the drinking), and had developed insight into his problems, his counselor concluded that he was likely to benefit from help with job placement. This DVR proceeded to do. B.M. was an intelligent man and was approached as such by advisory agencies and personnel.

He has successfully terminated his drinking and has obtained a salesman's job. He has also regained contact with his ex-wife (who is a nurse), and they seem to have achieved a friendly relationship, although both have doubts about remarrying. But what was especially vital to this man has been the opportunity to resume his relationship with his children as well.

III.

V.L. had his first psychiatric hospitalization when he was in college. He could not complete the practicum teaching requirement for his degree in education, although he accomplished all course work well. He was very shy, with halting, stammering speech; and extremely close to his mother, but with almost no peer relationships. He was diagnosed schizoid personality.

V.L. did not exhibit bizarre ideation or acute illness, but limped along on the fringe of life. In his late thirties, at his mother's urging, he applied for help from the Department of Vocational Rehabilitation and was placed in a sheltered shop doing machinist work. For seven years he had a record of poor attendance and poor interpersonal adjustment. Though he attained the top of the shop's job family, he did not appear to be a candidate for placement in competitive employment.

V.L. became discouraged because he was "getting nowhere," and sought help from a community mental health rehabilitation program where he was evaluated anew. Psychological testing pointed to exploration of the clerical field, since he proved to be good at details, of average intelligence, rigid and systematic, and had middle-class, white-collar values. He was placed on job samples in the community where there were not only opportunities to gain experience in clerical work, but where he would be welcome to lunch with coworkers and attend staff parties. He engaged in supportive group therapy as well and received goal-directed counseling regarding his dress, job performance, behavior on the job, etc.

After almost three years of steady effort, V.L. was hired as a mail clerk by the federal government under the special hire-the-handicapped program. He proved himself to be a conscientious, responsible worker, and within a few years received a "most valuable employee" award. At present V.L. volunteers one night a week, filing at the mental health center where he received help. He has accumulated some $12,000 in savings, goes to concerts and blue grass hootenannies with his tape recorder, and has helped to organize a social club for sheltered-shop workers in which a small but faithful group meet monthly for fun together.

K. Huntington's Disease

Excerpted from "She Mobilizes a Battle on a Brain Disease," *The National Observer,* June 3, 1972, copyright Dow Jones and Company; with permission

Huntington's disease killed Marjorie Guthrie's husband, folk-balladeer Woody Guthrie, when he was 55. Now she lives with the certainty that each of their children — singer-actor Arlo, Joady, and Nora — stands a 50-50 chance of dying from the same hereditary disease.

Spurred by this personal tragedy, Marjorie Guthrie has spent her life since Woody's death in 1967 helping families facing the same crisis and prodding scientists into greater research efforts against the brain-destroying disease. Her singular efforts have produced amazing results.

"Until Marjorie, Huntington's disease was like cancer 50 years ago; nobody talked about it," says Dr. Thomas N. Chase, a neurologist at the National Institute of Mental Health in Bethesda, Md. "Through the force of her personality and her rapidly expanding expertise, she has been very effective in mobilizing increasing research in this area and in getting families to deal with their problems in a realistic way . . ."

Shortly after her husband died, Mrs. Guthrie began asking doctors what she could do in the fight against Huntington's disease (HD). "Each told me different things, but they all agreed that the one thing I could do was to show it wasn't as rare as the statistics said," she says. Toward this goal, Mrs. Guthrie established the Committee to Combat Huntington's Disease, a volunteer group that now has 18 chapters nationwide [47 in 1976], with tiny, cluttered headquarters at 250 West 57th St. Her initial list of 6 HD families has grown to over 1775 [7,000 by 1976].

"She demonstrated there were more than we thought," says Dr. Harold Klawans of Rush Medical College in Chicago. No one is yet sure how many HD sufferers there are in the United States. Some authorities figure 25,000, four times the 6,000 estimate given when Mrs. Guthrie began her work. Mrs. Guthrie thinks the actual number is around 100,000.

The problems of a family afflicted by HD are terrifying. There is no cure and no means of determining who will fall victim. And in many communities a tremendous stigma is placed on HD families. They have difficulties with jobs and insurance, leading normal social lives, and even in getting hospital beds for family members suffering from the disease.

The ailment, sometimes called Huntington's chorea, is named for Dr. George Huntington, a New York physician who first described it in 1872. Researchers now know its cause: a defective dominant gene, which means that every person who had a parent with HD stands a 50-50 chance of getting it too.

Woody Guthrie inherited the disease from his mother. His widow emphasizes that HD never skips a generation, an important fact: Though Guthrie's mother died of HD, if he had not been afflicted, none of his children would be in danger.

HD, for some unknown reason, kills the nerve cells in the brain areas that control body movements and intellectual processes. All of us have dying brain cells; it is part of aging. But in HD, the cells die much faster.

It generally strikes adults between 30 and 45, an age when many already have passed on their defective genes to offspring. Death comes slowly. Guthrie lived 15 years after his diagnosis with the disease, which became increasingly worse. Early symptoms are frequently confused with those of other ailments, such as nervousness. Often the first signs are jerky, twitchy, involuntary muscle movements and a slurring of speech. "People thought Woody was drunk when he hadn't been drinking," recalls Mrs. Guthrie.

The muscle spasms grow progressively worse and patients become bedridden. A total loss of speech usually follows. In his final years, Guthrie communicated with his wife by flopping his hand atop widely spaced cards she set on his bed. And at the end, he could only blink his eyes. HD patients often lose their mental agility. They grow indifferent, irritable, and careless about personal habits and responsibilities; they display memory loss and poor judgment. "At one point, when we knew he had something wrong but didn't know what, Woody threatened suicide," Mrs. Guthrie says.

Many researchers seek a test to diagnose the disease in advance of its onset. Three researchers — Dr. Klawans in Chicago, Dr. Andre Barbeau of the University of Montreal, and Dr. George Paulson of Ohio State University — think they have developed a drug test that will predict HD in about half its victims. Other researchers are trying to find HD indicators in the blood and chromosomes of HD patients. "It looks like these things are working out, but it will be a long time before people are sure," says Chase.

An accurate early detection test would have two advantages: It would ease the anguish of those from HD families who are not destined to get HD, and it would allow those who will contract the hereditary disease to decide whether to have children. Researchers ultimately hope to develop a prenatal test so parents can, if they wish, have an HD fetus aborted.

Most scientists don't talk about curing the disease, but they are trying to find better ways to treat it. There are now some drugs that are, as one neurologist puts it, "moderately to reasonably effective" in controlling the involuntary muscle movements and behavior problems of HD.

"I'm confident that in the next few years we will have a better control drug," says Mrs. Guthrie. "If we can push the onset back from 35 or 40 to 50 or 55, that's a help."

Woody Guthrie left a rich legacy of songs in praise of America and the dreams of its people. His death, and its influence on Marjorie Guthrie, may provide an even greater legacy to families stricken by Huntington's disease.

L. A Multihandicapped Child

By Martin C. Stone, in Barbara B. Hauck and Maurice
F. Freehill, eds., *The Mentally Retarded: Case Studies,*
William C. Brown, Dubuque, 1972; with permission

At the time of referral, Bobby is a ten year old nonambulatory youngster with cerebral palsy who has difficulty maintaining good sitting balance because of inability to keep his knees flexed. In addition, when Bobby is agitated or very happy, he expresses his emotions by wiggling and kicking, which causes him to slip from his seat. Thus he has to be strapped in his wheelchair. He is physically able to use his hands and can perform such gross motor tasks as throwing a ball and propelling his own wheelchair. However, he has difficulty performing fine motor tasks which require visual-motor integration. For example, Bobby is able to identify and recognize shapes, letters, and numbers, but he cannot reproduce them; he is aware of the proper placement of simple puzzle shapes, but has difficulty fitting them into their respective areas. Thus Bobby understands and sees what he wants to do, but he cannot adequately carry out the motor task, although physically able to do so.

The same dysfunction is indicated in his inability to speak. It is clear that he has developed inner language and can comprehend concrete and simple directions, instructions, and conversations relating to his daily routines and activities. Yet he cannot organize and produce a verbal response. He has learned to indicate "yes" and "no" by nodding his head. Again, this is an organic disability but is not due to damage to the vocal apparatus.

In the area of activities of daily living, Bobby is not toilet trained. The family has attempted toilet training many times, but Bobby's reaction to being taken to the bathroom leads to screaming; so he has been kept in diapers. He can feed and undress himself, but cannot dress himself or take care of other hygienic needs.

An educational evaluation administered five months after Bobby started to school, and the Peabody Picture Vocabulary Test, given in 1968 when Bobby was eight years old (results of which suggested an M.A. of 3.1 and an I.Q. of 38), corroborated these learning dysfunctions. The evaluation suggests that Bobby was functioning five to six years below his age level and that skills which rely on hearing have higher scores than those which rely on vision. This appears to indicate that Bobby has obtained most of his knowledge through auditory cues.

This evaluation and past history suggests that Bobby has a variety of disabilities which include visual motor dysfunctions, lack of communication, lack of environmental experience, inability to generalize and to accept change from a learned routine. Thus, if any change at all is made in his daily schedule, Bobby becomes confused. This may explain in part his difficulty in separating from his family and adjusting to new situations and routines. His disabilities, along with infantilism and inability to be away from his mother, plus the use of inappropriate behaviors to gain attention and to get his way, all interfere with optimal learning and development.

However, before academic learning geared to Bobby's interest, developmental age level, and specific learning problems could be attempted, procedures had to be devised which would teach Bobby to tolerate separation from his mother. He also had to learn that crying, kicking, pulling his hair, and other such inappropriate behavior would not bring him the attention he desired.

It is Bobby's first day at school. He is wheeled into the classroom by his mother. His thin face appears quite anxious and he looks fearfully about as he repeatedly nods his head. His right hand is clutching his mother's arm so that Bobby is almost standing in his chair. He is beginning to cry as his mother, with some desperation in her voice, attempts to calm him.

The teacher dismisses Bobby's mother and asks her to wait in a room at the end of the hall. Bobby is taken to a small room off the classroom. (The classroom is being supervised by the assistant teacher.) Planned half-hour sessions have been established in order to attempt to substitute the teacher as someone new with whom Bobby could become familiar. Also, an attempt would be made to alleviate his anxiety by providing him with structured experience. The teacher sits next to Bobby, holding his hand and talking to him quietly, in a very friendly manner, mentioning how glad he is to see him, how much he likes him, and that he hopes they will be good friends. At times, he also shows Bobby several pull toys. However, Bobby screams, cries, kicks, wiggles about, and waves his hands continuously for the first half hour. At the end of the session he is returned to his mother and again told how glad the teacher was to see him and that he would see him again in the room tomorrow.

This procedure continued for about fifteen more sessions, with Bobby screaming constantly. It should be noted that although he screamed during the sessions, he did not cry or protest when his mother got him ready for school and put him in the car. The crying began when he entered the classroom and subsided once he returned to his mother. During the sixteenth session, there were various momentary lapses in Bobby's crying. During the lapses he began to touch and pick up some of the toys and once nodded in response to the teacher's questions. By the eighteenth session, there were more frequent moments of silence.

Bobby now seemed quiet enough to listen to new instructions. A decision was made to incorporate behavior modification techniques as the next step in the program. Behavior modification refers to that process in which the individual is rewarded for correct responses and not rewarded for inappropriate responses.

Colored pieces of tape were placed on the floor. The teacher's chair was positioned just ahead of Bobby's chair. A timer was presented and set to ring within five minutes. Bobby's task was to sit without crying until the bell rang and then he could move his chair next to the teacher, who would talk to him and give him a toy.

However, if he cried he stayed where he was and was ignored. This procedure was repeated after each ring of the bell. For the first three trials Bobby cried. At trials four and five he succeeded in moving up two spaces, but then cried for the rest of the half hour. However, within two weeks Bobby was able to sit through a session without crying.

The next procedure was to employ the same method, but to extend sessions to forty-five minutes and extend the tape marks from the small room into the classroom. Bobby did not cry until the door was opened and he saw the other children in the room. However, after four more sessions he succeeded in sitting forty-five minutes without crying, fifteen of these in the classroom at his desk.

Within three months, Bobby was able to remain in the classroom for two hours, at which time his mother came for him. He adjusted well to the class routine, displayed no anxiety, and began to show an interest in the academic materials which were presented. Reinforcement was then terminated, with no regression to former behavior.

Each week, arrangements were made to have Bobby picked up fifteen minutes later. In this manner, he learned to remain in school for lunch and by the end of the first school year he was able to participate in a full class day without anxiety.

All educational materials which were presented to Bobby were designed so that he could achieve immediate success. In the visual motor area, his first attempts were scribbles. Gradually he began to structure his work and was able to connect dots. Later he could draw a line and circle on his own. Recently, he was able to print the word Mommy. However, Bobby is not able to reproduce a square or a triangle, and any attempts at reproducing these and more complicated letters cause extreme frustration. Thus, in order to expedite Bobby's writing skills and to end his anxiety (which could terminate his desire to learn), he was provided with an electric typewriter with large type. The typewriter proved to be a great learning aid. It not only gave Bobby the ability to copy words easily, but increased his inner vocabulary, enhanced his spelling and reading ability, and proved to be another tool to improve his eye-hand coordination.

Bobby took a great interest in words. He quickly learned to identify his printed name and those of his classmates. Because of this interest, two one-half hour weekly speech therapy sessions were recommended and established. Bobby was enrolled at a speech therapy clinic where he adjusted to the teacher and the new situations on the first day and showed no signs of distress. The program was designed to establish a communication board with many everyday words and experiences written on it. As Bobby learned the words new ones were introduced. He soon had a working vocabulary of over forty words, and was beginning to form sentences with them. Thus, if one asked, "How are you Bobby?" he would take his board and point to "Bobby feels good." When wishing to indicate his needs or desire for some objects, he would now use his board to express himself.

Bobby's conceptual knowledge of the use of numbers was increased through the use of the Stern Arithmetic Program. Also included in his program were social skills (learning about his home, neighborhood, classmates, and community), and physical education which provided group game participation and needed physical activities. A special program also was designed to teach Bobby to transfer to and from his wheelchair and to learn to crawl up and down stairs. As Bobby grew older, taller and heavier, this program became increasingly important because he had to be carried up and down a flight of stairs to the family's second-story apartment.

Bobby has been in school for two and a half years. Since that time there has been significant growth in his social and educational development. All inappropriate behavior disappeared once he adjusted to the school routine. It reappears only if situations become too frustrating, or if a sudden change in routine is not carefully explained to him.

Bobby participates in all group games and experiences. He will now accompany his classmates on field trips with no anxiety. Formerly, the sight of a bus brought on screaming. He has become more sociable and concerned with others. If one of his classmates needs to have a chair held in order to sit down, Bobby will volunteer to hold it. He has developed a sense of humor and will appropriately laugh at humorous situations. He has learned to recognize the complete upper and lower case letters of the alphabet. His reading and spelling vocabularies are increasing weekly, and he has gained more conceptual knowledge about his environment. He has learned to count and recognize the numbers one to ten and can place them in proper sequence. Recently he has begun to comprehend the rudiments of addition and can add one plus one, one plus two, and one plus three.

At the end of Bobby's second year, the Ammons Full Range Picture Vocabulary Test (FRPV) and the Pictorial Test of Intelligence (PTI) were administered. The results indicated that his mental age had advanced two and one-half years since his last psychological examination.

Toilet training, which had not been attempted since Bobby was five, was tried again. Through the use of a modified behavior shaping technique, toilet training was accomplished both at school and at home.

Although Bobby is a willing participant in the physical education program, he has not made significant progress toward the goal of wheelchair transfer and going up and down stairs.

Bobby's mother continues to bring him to and from school, because she does not want him riding on the school bus. The school psychiatric social worker has initiated conferences with the parents to discuss their objections to bussing and other problems related to child rearing. These sessions have been regularly attended and have provided the family with more insight as to how to handle and to understand the boy and his disabilities.

Bobby is allowed to do more on his own at home, such as dressing himself. He has almost accomplished this skill. Bobby is responding by being less demanding, spending more time on his own, playing with a variety of educational toys, showing less inappropriate behavior, and even has begun to play games with his sisters. Family outings have been planned in which Bobby now can be an eager participant.

(See CHAPTER 26: CEREBRAL PALSY.)

M. Charcot-Marie-Tooth Syndrome

By Bruce H. Scott, *Rehabilitation Gazette,* vol. 11, p. 53, 1974; with permission

"You have Charcot-Marie-Tooth peroneal muscular atrophy. Drs. Charcot, Marie, and Tooth isolated the symptoms of this malady many years ago, hence we refer to it by their names. Peroneal muscular atrophy means that the nerve cells that connect to the muscles become dormant or die, we're not sure which, causing the muscles to do nothing because they aren't told to do anything. Therefore, they atrophy."

That conversation took place over twenty years ago with the head neurosurgeon at the University of Kansas Medical Center in Kansas City, Kansas. Then I had only numbness in my toes, now I am in a wheelchair and unable to use my arms or legs.

I wasn't completely ignorant of the C-M-T syndrome. My mother had been diagnosed at the same medical facility in 1941 and had been in a wheelchair since 1949. My brother began showing symptoms shortly after I did, although he is seven years younger. Another brother has not shown any symptoms.

It is a rare condition. Only a few hundred in the U.S. are known to have the malady.

For some unexplained reason the peripheral nerves cease to function. One at a time, beginning at the tip of the toes and fingers, they stop conducting impulses to and from the skin and skeletal muscles, progressing up the legs and arms and finally to the back, chest, and neck muscles. Progress is very slow. There is no illness, no trauma, no pain.

My condition began when I was 19 with an itchy, burning numbness in my toes and soles of my feet. Two years later I needed short leg braces to correct toe drop, hammer foot, and ankle weakness. I first noticed the numbness in my fingers in late 1956. I added long leg braces in 1964, lost the use of my hands in 1967, elbows in 1969, and hips in 1970. I've been in a wheelchair since then.

I worked my way through college by working at a supermarket, first as a sack boy and then as an assistant buyer.

In June of 1955, after my junior year, I went to the National Institutes of Health in Bethesda, Maryland, for 26 days of tests and examinations. They confirmed the K.U. diagnosis, but could offer no cure or treatment.

I graduated in 1956 with a B.S. in Business Administration (Retailing) and worked for four years for a wholesale grocery warehouse in Kansas City, Missouri. I was married; we had twins. My wife worked and I worked for a food brokerage firm until it went out of business two years later, then for a self-insurance group.

After a few years I became restless and decided to return to college to obtain a teaching certificate. It took 4½ years of night school to get the required credits to teach Social Studies on the junior high level.

I quit my job, took my student teaching and did substitute teaching for two years before I realized that a handicapped teacher would have to fight like hell and be twice as smart to obtain a contract in a period when school population was declining.

My body was getting weaker. Walking became more difficult and driving almost impossible. After a bout with the flu at Christmas time 1968, the paralysis in my legs and arms progressed at a faster pace and due to my general weakened condition I decided to "retire" and draw Social Security Disability compensation.

For the past few years I have been an active member of the local chapter of National Paraplegia Foundation, now serving as president of the Greater Kansas City chapter. As chairman of the Architectural Barriers Committee, I influenced changes in design of new public buildings and was the editor of *Access*, a booklet of graphic illustrations showing how to make public buildings accessible.

I have a working wife, 15-year-old twin daughters, a house in suburbia, and an electric wheelchair. I could be complacent but I'm not. I'm going to keep on doing what I can to make this city, this county, this state a better place to live for all handicapped people. I'm 39. That's a long way from my first symptoms at 19. I hope I'm around long enough to get everything done. Dammit C-M-T, slow down!

(See CHAPTER 43: NEUROLOGICAL DISORDERS.)

N. David and Donny Share a Room, and Much More

The Arthritis Foundation

It is suppertime at Seattle's Children's Orthopedic Hospital and Dr. Jane Schaller, a tall curly-haired woman, whose youth belies the fact that she is one of the United States' top specialists on childhood arthritis, drops in to see how "her boys" are doing.

"I am glad that you are eating now," she says to David, who alternately spears bites of meatloaf and coconut cream cake on his fork. "How is your stomach today?"

David, who is 5½, indicates by making faces, that he is not all that happy because the IV needle that sticks in his hand hurts.

David is from Oregon. He started having symptoms of juvenile rheumatoid arthritis (JRA) a year ago. The condition was diagnosed correctly by his pediatrician, and the child was treated with the appropriate doses of aspirin. Unfortunately he failed to respond. David, like a certain number of children with JRA, also started to develop a serious eye condition called iridocyclitis, which when neglected can cause blindness. The eye disease is treated with steroid eye drops, but these did not help David, so his doctor prescribed corticosteroids by mouth.

Both corticosteroids and aspirin are hard on anybody's stomach, and one morning, when David's mother came to wake him up, she found that his pillow was covered with blood. David obviously had developed stomach ulcers.

Gold, a good drug for many patients with rheumatoid arthritis and JRA, was tried next, but special laboratory tests showed that for David gold would probably result in kidney disease.

At this point all medication was discontinued and David was simply kept in bed.

This regimen did not agree with the little boy. He stopped talking, and according to Dr. Schaller "got contorted like a pretzel." "When we first saw him," she added, "he also seemed to have no muscles left anywhere in his body and was a severe behavior problem."

Both David's mother—who has other small children to look after—and his doctor became overwhelmed with the child's problems and took him to the Children's Orthopedic Hospital of the University of Washington, in Seattle.

"He was quite a mess," Dr. Schaller recalled. "Our first job was to get to know him and get him to trust us."

"I have found," she said, "that if you feel confident in your method of treatment, your child patient will usually do well. At present doctors in Oregon are really not equipped to deal with a patient like David, who reacts adversely to most medications."

In Seattle, David unbent both physically and mentally. His legs straightened. His eye disease was controlled. He received physical therapy, and just as important, he went to the kindergarten at the hospital. He did so well that when he returned home he rose to the top of his class.

But David remains a problem from a medical point of view. Not that his arthritis is all that bad — Dr. Schaller is confident that he will "outgrow" the disease — but he does not seem to be able to take any of the medications indicated for his condition.

Dr. Schaller put him on antimalarials and then, cautiously, on some type of aspirin — but he again started to complain of pain in his stomach. And then there always is an eye problem.

The doctors in Oregon, who are very conscientious, feel ill equipped and nervous to handle such a complicated case, and David is back in the hospital in Seattle whenever his eyes, his joints, or his stomach seem to act up.

Donny, David's roommate, also would not need to spend so much time in the hospital if medical care near his home were better.

Originally he came to the hospital with a foot problem, but the admitting nurse was knowledgeable enough to suspect that he had JRA. She called Dr. Schaller, who confirmed the diagnosis. As she recalled: "Donny had one of the worst knees I ever saw, it was totally out of joint. I suspect that somebody must have mishandled it."

With good care Donny got better. He is a cheerful little kid who seems at ease in the hospital. He was readmitted recently because his hip hurt badly and Dr. Schaller suspects that he has ankylosing spondylitis, a disease which unlike JRA is usually not outgrown.

"The problem with Donny is that *all* the drugs that are useful for the treatment of ankylosing spondylitis, like Butazolidin or indomethacin, are not cleared for use in children."

Dr. Schaller hopes that the situation will change soon. In the meantime Donny's brother Tommy seems to also have developed a problem with his hip. This unfortunately supports the suspicion that both children have ankylosing spondylitis — a disease that definitely runs in families.

Contrary to popular belief, arthritis in childhood is not a rare disease. It accounts for more cases annually than paralytic polio did in any ten of the prevaccine years, and children with arthritis outnumber those suffering from leukemia. Fortunately about 75 percent of these young victims outgrow their disease without permanent damage, but as the cases of David and Donny demonstrate, the going can be rough and much damage can be wrought by improper care.

(See CHAPTER 18: ARTHRITIS.)

O. A Bridge between Hospital and Home

Excerpted from Norma H. Davies and Elaine Hansen,
"Family Focus: A Transitional Cottage in an Acute-Care
Hospital," *Family Process*, vol. 13, no. 4, December 1974;
with permission

The following case illustrates the operation of Family Focus, an innovative transitional program designed to bridge the gap between hospital treatment and home care. Sponsored jointly by the Mental Research Institute and the Stanford University Medical School Division of Physical Therapy, this program has to date served patients ranging in age from four months to 92 years, with such diagnoses as cardiovascular accident, total hip replacement, heart transplant, and carcinoma. These patients, together with their families, move into a comfortable, barrier-free cottage on the Stanford Hospital grounds for a three-day period just before discharge to the home, and physical therapists, as well as other staff members as needed (occupational therapist, social worker, dietitian, nurse, psychologist, etc.) teach them the rehabilitative and preventive skills required for care of their particular disorder.

This program reduces the anxiety of both the patient and the family, and shortens the period of post-hospital adjustment. As stated in the article from which the case is drawn, "The Family Focus philosophy enlarges the scope of hospital services in two important ways. First, family members, as well as patients, are recognized as affected by the patient's disability. Their lives, too, may require considerable readjustment. The manner in which they cope is not unrelated to the patient's ability to accept, or overcome, his disability. Second, difficulties do not terminate with hospital discharge. Rather, they often escalate when the family must assume functions previously performed by hospital personnel. We believe that hospital care should look beyond the discharge date and prepare the patient and family with the skills and support necessary for optimum out-of-hospital living." Here is the case:

The B.'s, a middle class Philippine couple, had lived in the United States for six years when Mrs. B., age 26, gave birth to their first child. The delivery and the baby were normal. Several hours later, however, Mrs. B. had a subarachnoid hemorrhage that left her with a right hemiplegia and severe expressive aphasia.

During the course of her month in the hospital, she learned to walk and to care for herself independently despite remaining weakness and sensory deficits. She continued to have difficulty writing, performing simple calculations, and occasionally remembering appropriate words. Her greatest problem, however, centered around her relationship to her newborn child. Shortly after the delivery, her mother, Mrs. S., arrived from the Philippines and cared for the infant daughter at the B.'s home. Although Mrs. S. brought her granddaughter to the hospital daily, Mrs. B. played little part in her care. In her hospital bed she sometimes held the child and gave her a bottle at feeding time, but on only one brief occasion was she left alone with her. Mr. B. visited after work and then took his mother-in-law and daughter home.

"I don't feel like her mother," Mrs. B. said despondently. To be a mother, Mrs. B. believed that she should be able to do everything for her daughter. Her sense of detachment began with her inability to recall the delivery and was accentuated by her lack of experience in caring for and comforting her child. The fear of being an inadequate mother was coupled with her more general concerns about whether she would ever be normal again: able to drive a car, to climb steps in their newly purchased home, to prepare a meal, and eventually to return to work. In capsule, her anxieties centered around her competence as an independent person and her role as a mother.

Mrs. B.'s expressed apprehensions and the hospital staff's concerns about potential problems of role-definition for the B.'s and Mrs. S. were the basis for referral to Family Focus.

The B.'s, the baby, and Mrs. S. lived in the Family Focus cottage for the last three days of Mrs. B.'s hospitalization. Mr. B. was employed during the day and returned each evening. The B. family slept in the bedroom, while Mrs. S. used a convertible sofa in the family room.

From the first moment Mrs. B. was eager to experiment with all the activities she had been unable to perform on the hospital ward; caring for her daughter, cooking, keeping house. In the course of accomplishing a task that required organized planning, she viewed herself as extremely slow and forgetful. She was afraid to use pins to diaper her baby or to prepare food on a hot stove, believing that her sharp-dull and hot-cold sensations were impaired. Each minor stumbling block simply reinforced her notion that she would be inadequate to the demands of the situation and those she was making upon herself.

During the early part of her residence, steps were taken by the Family Focus physical therapists to clarify and delineate her weaknesses. As it turned out, she could feel a pin prick and a hot stove but could not identify the position of her arm unless she observed it. Isolating and learning to cope with this specific problem relieved some of the vague, ill-defined apprehension she was experiencing. In other instances it was difficult to determine whether problems encountered were the result of stroke-related disabilities or confusion normally faced by a new mother unaccustomed to caring for an infant and a household. In her case this confusion was accentuated by the prolonged hospitalization. While the staff were careful to be realistic in their appraisal of Mrs. B.'s special difficulties and accepting of her fears, they attempted to refocus her self-concept from "disabled patient" to "new mother adjusting to a novel and complex role."

If Mrs. B. were to become "mother," it was necessary that Mrs.

S., who until this time was in complete charge of the infant's care, accept a different role. Mrs. S.'s importance as helper was reinforced throughout this period so as to strengthen and reward this view of herself and to prevent her from maintaining the role of the baby's primary caretaker. At one point Mrs. S. suggested that another relative from the Philippines replace her when she departed. Mrs. B. asserted that she would hire someone for the job. This idea was encouraged, since establishing Mrs. B. as independent mother and household manager had been a major goal and it was deemed a simpler task to dismiss a paid employee than to dislodge a relative.

By the second day Mrs. B.'s attempts to experiment with every conceivable household and child-care responsibility had taken its toll. She looked exhausted, her frustration becoming increasingly apparent. She spoke again of her feelings of inadequacy as a mother and was generally depressed and tearful. She was overwhelmed by her high expectations of functioning immediately as expert mother and housewife. Among other things, we were concerned that her mother might be interfering with child care when no observers were present. It was suggested that if Mrs. S. were extremely busy with household duties she would be too tired to care for the baby. This idea that Mrs. B. had the power to control her environment and the relationships within it was reinforced throughout the physical therapy sessions. On this particular occasion she calmed down and expressed gratitude for having the opportunity to discuss her discouragements and anxieties. Her new outlook was reflected in her conclusion, "This is the way I am, so I'll have to figure things out." Now she was eager to begin learning the program of rehabilitation activities that she would continue to follow at home.

By the third day, Mrs. B. reported that the previous night had gone exceedingly well. Mrs. B. had responded to her infant's cry in contrast to the night before when her husband had tended to the baby's needs because his wife was too exhausted. Her optimism was still guarded, but her tone and appearance were brighter and more hopeful. During the evening of her departure she expressed some apprehension about adjusting to her own home, but she was eager and ready to leave when her husband arrived from work.

At this juncture Mrs. B's attending physician arrived for a final hospital visit. He first spoke to the Family Focus therapist in the adjoining office. He mentioned his discomfort of the previous evening when he had appeared in formal white laboratory coat to find a warm, comfortable, home atmosphere. Now he was attired in street clothes and during the family visit answered questions while sitting comfortably and smoking his pipe.

On the physical therapist's first follow-up visit two weeks later, Mrs. B. answered the door holding her daughter comfortably in her arms. The observed interaction between Mrs. B. and her mother gave the impression that Mrs. B. was in complete control, although she might occasionally request assistance. As far as her progress was concerned, she was physically stronger but still dissatisfied with her slowness and disorganization. Although acknowledging her improvements, Mrs. B. wanted more immediate results.

The second home visit, approximately five weeks later, took place at the B.'s new home. Mrs. B. was doing all the housework, cooking and child care. Her mother had been ill for two weeks. This circumstance coupled with continued physical improvement prompted the final steps towards complete independence.

56

Rehabilitation Facilities and Services

Compiled by ROBERT M. GOLDENSON, Ph.D.

A. Rehabilitation Medicine Institute

Prepared in cooperation with the Institute of
Rehabilitation Medicine, 400 East 34th Street,
New York, NY 10016

T he Institute of Rehabilitation Medicine (IRM) has been chosen
as a prime example of a multidimensional rehabilitation center because of its unique position as a pioneer and continuing leader in
the field. Founded in 1948, it has from its inception operated under
the direction of Howard A. Rusk, M.D., who is widely recognized
as the originator of the discipline of physical medicine and rehabilitation.

The Institute's manifold services group themselves into three
principal areas of activity. As a treatment center, it offers a full
range of diagnostic and restoration services conducted by interdisciplinary teams. IRM also serves as a training institution for medical and supportive personnel in the rehabilitation field. And as a
research center, it conducts ongoing studies and projects directed
to the development of innovative techniques and devices. The Institute is a unit of the New York University Medical Center.

The IRM treats patients on both an inpatient and outpatient basis. The inpatient division consists of 152 beds for patients with
such conditions as stroke, spinal cord injury, amputation, or neuromuscular disorder. The Institute has been designated a Model Regional Center for Spinal Cord Injury by the federal government.
Trauma to the spinal cord is a leading cause of catastrophic and
permanent injury. Therefore comprehensive rehabilitation treatment is of vast importance. All patients receive a wide variety of
therapies, geared to individual needs, to help them reach their potential. The average stay at the Institute is sixty-two days.

Members of the Institute staff work closely with the staff of University Hospital, also part of the New York University Medical Center complex. When the patient is taken there during the acute phase of illness or for surgery, members of the Institute staff provide appropriate therapy as soon as possible, sometimes at the bedside. As Dr. Rusk has stated, "When the fever is down and the stitches are out, the rehabilitation process begins." Patients are also brought to the Institute from other acute care centers.

When the patient has progressed to the point where transfer is possible, one enters the inpatient program in which all aspects of rehabilitation are involved as well as the supportive services which enable the patient to return as a productive member of the community.

At the IRM the rehabilitation process is adapted to the individual needs of each patient, and is based upon the coordinated efforts of many specialists and departments. The physiatrist is a physician specializing in rehabilitation medicine and has the responsibility of deciding which of the many types of therapy will enable the patient to function to maximum potential. The therapeutic modalities which the physiatrist supervises are based on a total care concept which involves the collaboration not only of specialists (neurologists, orthopedists, plastic surgeons, etc.) but supportive personnel whose activities are described below.

The physical therapist starts treatment at the acute stage of illness. First, efforts are directed at assisting bed positioning to aid circulation and thus prevent many of the problems that occur from circulatory disorders. Patients are given breathing exercises when needed. As soon as possible, range-of-motion exercises are initiated to maintain joint mobility, and manual testing is started to evaluate the patient's muscle strength.

When the individual is transferred to the Institute, physical therapy retests for range of motion and muscle strength to establish a baseline for the patient's rehabilitation program. Treatment consists of exercise techniques for strengthening muscles, coordinating body movements, and maintaining and increasing joint mobility.

For those patients who need surgery, therapists work with presurgical and postsurgical patients, who are taught proper breathing mechanisms and movement to prevent complications.

Training in activities of daily living is part of the physical therapy program. When the patient is able, therapy is geared to providing a certain amount of independence despite the disability. Practice is given in getting into and out of bed from the wheelchair, dressing and undressing, and taking care of normal daily grooming and personal needs.

The Occupational Therapy Service is an important unit of the rehabilitation team. The occupational therapist's primary concern is to improve the patient's functional skill. Specific techniques are used to meet goals and will vary from patient to patient depending on the diagnosis and disability. Improving functional skills by increasing strength and improving coordination may be one technique. Improving or developing skill in functional activities such as eating, grooming, writing, and typing may require selection of special devices or equipment. These special devices may provide one method by which the patient can be independent. The occupational therapist has the expertise to appropriately select or design such devices.

In addition to retraining of specific functional activities, the Occupational Therapy Service provides training in homemaking techniques and evaluation of vocational potential. Home planning is a unique service which provides the patient and family an opportunity to discuss and work on problems related to the home environment. Visits are made to assess the home situation and later plans are drawn for necessary modifications and for solving other specific problems.

The Psychology Department is responsible for making an evaluation of the patient's emotional condition, intellectual status, and any psychological obstacles that might impede the rehabilitation process. If indicated, psychotherapy is administered as a supportive measure. The psychologist may also suggest approaches which other members of the staff might use for the patient's benefit. Special programs for patients with pain have been developed.

The Behavioral Sciences Program has developed psychological methods to compensate for impaired function due to brain damage from illness or trauma. Such brain damage can leave the patients with perceptual and cognitive disturbances.

In both the Psychology and Behavioral Sciences programs there are interdisciplinary seminars on personal functioning for the disabled and on approaches to the management of psychosocial problems of individuals with illness such as cancer or heart disease.

The Nursing Department focuses upon the restoration of functional potential and self-fulfillment within those individuals whose health status has been altered significantly. The basic nursing philosophy fosters a one-to-one relationship with each patient and emphasizes nursing therapy. The latter consists of the application of techniques and encompasses physical, psychological, and emotional care based on assessed priorities. Since the nature of nursing entails daily contact with the patient, the nurse is in a unique position to recognize emotional difficulties, and deal with feelings of frustration, anger, bewilderment, and helplessness. The nurse therefore plays an essential role in teaching and caring for the patient and maintaining morale.

The Speech Pathology Service is a combined clinical, research, and teaching program. That is, it provides diagnostic and treatment services to patients, conducts research concerning communication disorders, and provides training for graduate students and professional workers.

The majority of patients referred to the service for diagnosis or treatments are adults who have aphasia, a disorder affecting the ability to produce and understand language in both spoken and written form, or dysarthria, a disorder of the motor speech system which affects the ability to produce the sounds of speech. These disorders are generally caused by strokes or brain damage incurred in accidents. Approximately 500 different patients from the in- and outpatient services are seen each year.

Children who are referred to the Speech Pathology Service frequently present communication problems which resemble those of the adults, although the causes are often different and include cerebral palsy and other congenital and development disorders.

Diagnostic evaluations generally consist of special tests of language, speech, and hearing. When treatment is provided, it generally consists of speech therapy on an individual or group basis. Its purposes are to assist patients in acquiring the greatest possible improvement in speech and in adjusting to and compensating for permanent deficits.

The Social Service Department helps both the patient and the family deal with the emotional stresses which result from disability. Community referrals are made in handling such practical problems as medical bills, obtaining attendant-housekeeper services, visiting nurse service, mental health counseling, education, and accessible housing or funds for modification of existing housing. These are done in direct work with the patient and family through the individual and group processes, or through consultation with other team members. A community social worker helps to raise consciousness of the community and consumers in dealing with problems of architectural barriers and equal rights in housing, education, employment, transportation, and recreation. Playing an advocacy role, this worker maintains contact with legislators on all levels of government, consumers, and various social welfare agencies.

The Vocational Services Department provides a program of counseling, development of educational and training plans, and job placement and follow-up, all designed to enable patients to realize their fullest potential for work. In carrying out this program, the counselor helps the patient explore skills, talents, and interests. Placement services try to put the patient into a productive job.

The Institute has also developed a summer employment program for severely disabled students. These students not only get experience and receive a salary for it, but they demonstrate their capacities and capabilities to school personnel and potential employers.

The Therapeutic Recreation Program is designed to provide patients with the ability to interact with the community and to use the situations to deal with the many facets of becoming an active member of that community. Among the recreational activities are participation in the arts, music, sports, the theatre, and various other cultural centers, as well as the development of new hobbies suited to the individual preferences and abilities of each patient. The program is carried out on two levels, one designed for adults and the other designed for children.

Volunteers serve the varied areas of the Institute at all times. Among their activities are: helping patients get settled and oriented, giving reassurance to patients and their families, reading to patients and writing their letters, helping them select books from the Institute library, taking them to classes, religious, and recreational activities, and arranging for child patients to attend summer camp.

Research at the Institute is extremely varied and reflects the emphasis of rehabilitation medicine on *total* care. Research studies, therefore, range from basic investigations into mechanisms of disease to applied investigations directly relevant to patient care.

Core areas of research are in the following fields: (1) neuromuscular diseases, (2) behavioral science, (3) orthotic-prosthetics, (4) bioengineering, and (5) cardiopulmonary. Examples of research in each area are neuromuscular: electrophysiological studies in neuromuscular diseases; behavioral science: rehabilitation of cognitive and perceptual deficits in people with traumatic brain damage; orthotic-prosthetic: orthotic and prosthetic design improvements; bioengineering: development of electronic systems to provide increased vocational independence and recreational facilities for high-level quadriplegics; cardiopulmonary: a controlled study of inhalational therapy in the rehabilitation of patients with chronic obstructive lung disease.

The IRM Biomechanics Program focuses on body function and its relationship to working situations. The Center for Safety Biomechanics Laboratory at the IRM conducts research, professional services, and academic instruction in occupational biomechanics. Application of biomechanics to working situations can be termed industrial preventive medicine, since this field deals with disability prevention, maintenance of occupational safety and health, work tolerance, and effectiveness of human performance.

Finally, the Institute of Rehabilitation Medicine has become a dynamic force in rehabilitation not only in this country but on an international scale as well. Physicians from all parts of the world have trained at the Institute. Almost all have returned to their own land to conduct rehabilitation programs. It is therefore appropriate to end this profile of the IRM with a statement made by its founder, Dr. Howard A. Rusk, in his recent autobiography, *A World to Care For:*

> The sooner the people of the world demand rehabilitation services the sooner they will get such services. If I sometimes become impatient at the slowness of the total acceptance of rehabilitation needs, it is because millions of valuable lives are wasting away unnecessarily. At this moment throughout the world millions of handicapped people lying in their beds could be up and about doing constructive things. It has now been proved beyond question that 90 percent of even the severely disabled have the capacity, if they get training, to take care of their own daily needs, and in many cases, to return to gainful employment in a competitive society.

B. Cerebral Palsy Centers

The 290 affiliates of United Cerebral Palsy Associations comprise one of the largest and most highly developed networks of rehabilitation centers for the physically disabled. The reason for the scope of this agency is twofold: first, now that poliomyelitis has been all but conquered, cerebral palsy represents the largest single group of neuromuscular disorders; and second, in areas where facilities are lacking or inadequate, its centers frequently offer rehabilitation services to other groups, such as those afflicted with muscular dystrophy, multiple sclerosis, or mental retardation, as well as the multiply handicapped.

The programs provided by these centers differ in detail due to such factors as availability of funds; administrative policies; relationship to hospitals, government agencies, and community facilities; and the fact that the central headquarters in New York City provides general guidelines and information rather than specific directives. But in spite of individual variations, practically all cerebral palsy centers have several things in common. They are organized by a board of directors composed of leading citizens who contribute their services. They are supported by funds from government agencies, as well as funds raised by community campaigns, a small part (2 to 5 percent) of which goes to the support of the state association and 25 percent to the national organization for research and public education. They have an active corps of volunteers who participate in fund-raising, clerical, and auxiliary activities. They maintain a working relationship with the Office of Vocational Rehabilitation and other state or local agencies, and in many cases with the local public school system, camps for the handicapped, nearby hospitals, and colleges or universities, whose students satisfy practicum requirements in special education and allied health by working as aides.

But most important, each of these centers is staffed by a multidisciplinary group of professional workers who collaborate fully in meeting the needs of each individual client, and who subscribe to the principle that rehabilitation is a total process involving every aspect of life—physical, social, emotional, recreational, educational, and vocational.

The programs and services offered by cerebral palsy centers are based directly on the special character of this multifaceted disability. Since the disorder is basically congenital, and the typical symptoms are not outgrown and cannot be fully reversed, service must be provided from the beginning of life through adulthood. In concrete terms, this means that a fully developed cerebral palsy center must include a developmental school, a variety of training and educational programs for middle childhood and adolescence, a prevocational program for teen-agers, and a vocational program for adults, which usually includes a sheltered workshop. Recreation, residential living programs, and health services are often found in well-rounded center programs. Moreover, since multiple handicaps are the rule rather than the exception in cerebral palsy, the rehabilitation process must be geared to a wide variety of limitations and dysfunctions, and not to a single clearly defined symptomatology. This means that the center must offer physical therapy, occupational therapy, educational therapy, sociotherapy, psychotherapy, speech therapy, and vocational counseling. It must also make provisions for comprehensive medical evaluation and treatment by pediatricians, physiatrists, orthopedic surgeons, ophthalmologists, otologists, podiatrists, neurologists, dentists, psychiatrists, and other specialists. In addition, since cerebral palsy is bound to have an impact on the total life of the individual, the center must maintain contact with the family, and with community resources such as mental health and residential facilities as well as government agencies. Many of the centers also initiate or participate in research projects, and take an active part, often with client advocacy groups, in promoting legislative programs for the disabled.

Perhaps the best way to convey the comprehensive character of a cerebral palsy operation is to focus on a single facility. The Brooklyn Rehabilitation Campus of United Cerebral Palsy of New York City, Inc., has been chosen for this purpose since it incorporates many features which, it is hoped, will serve as a model for other centers throughout the country. Although some of these features cannot be easily duplicated, they may nevertheless suggest modifications suited to a more limited budget.

The campus occupies a 3-acre (1.2-hectare) site in the heart of Brooklyn, and therefore provides ready access not only to the manifold facilities of that borough, but to all New York City. Because of its central-urban location, clients do not feel isolated from the community. They have many opportunities to enrich their lives through visits to libraries, museums, and recreational activities of all kinds. The scope of the operation is further widened by its proximity to colleges, clinics, and hospitals; medical consultants and student aides are therefore readily available.

The core of the Brooklyn center is a modern two-story Education Center of 68,000 square feet (6,300 square meters), fully equipped to serve more than 250 multihandicapped individuals from infancy through adulthood. The 95 full-time staff members consist of specialists in early childhood education, special education, and physical education; physical, occupational, speech, and learning disability therapy; psychology; and social work, with a full corps of teacher assistants, aides, and administrative, clerical, and maintenance personnel. An adjacent transportation building houses a service garage, a driver's ready room, and a dispatching area for a fleet of forty minibuses. Between the two buildings are grassy spaces for outdoor play, and roof areas are used as terraces. Both buildings have been constructed with the cooperation of many governmental agencies, particularly the New York State Department of Mental Hygiene, which provided one-third of the financing. An apartment residence for singles and couples, connected to the Education Center and other buildings by an indoor passageway, is now in the planning stage. The residents will have easy access to the cafeteria and training and recreational facilities, and will be provided with special services, such as homemakers, so that even the most severely disabled will be able to live reasonably independently.

Every effort has been made to avoid an institutional feeling. The central reception area resembles an attractive hotel lobby, with plantings in the center, a skylight above, and paintings on the walls. All classrooms, therapy rooms, kitchens and cafeteria, and physical education and recreational areas are spacious and contain the most modern furnishings and equipment. Bright colors predominate throughout, and all furniture is designed to combine beauty with comfort and utility. Throughout the building there are many features which point the way to the rehabilitation center of the future. Among them are the following:

1. Wide corridors with rounded corners and double-level handrails.

2. Ground-level entrances with tread-operated exterior doors and elimination of steps and other architectural barriers.

3. Oversize elevators which can carry as many as ten or twelve wheelchairs at one time.

4. Automatic toilets (Clos-O-Mats) designed for complete independence, even for the most severely handicapped; grab bars and wide wheelchair "turn-around areas" in all bathrooms.

5. A specially engineered indoor "self-motivating" activity room for children, containing varied play materials and large, soft mats which can be inflated by pushing a button.

6. One-way mirror and audio observation rooms in the preschool section.

7. A complete video system with remote-controlled cameras in classrooms, for teaching and recording of client progress.

8. A fully equipped studio for videotaping of client productions and activities, as well as research projects and demonstration of therapeutic techniques for use in other cerebral palsy centers.

9. A multipurpose room with projection booth and stage designed to be accessible to performing wheelchair clients.

10. A completely furnished three-room apartment for training in activities of daily living and homemaking skills.

11. A specially designed home economics kitchen with individual cooking stalls built to accommodate wheelchair as well as ambulatory clients.

12. A creative arts and crafts center with a fully equipped darkroom.

13. A large heated swimming pool with a movable bottom at one end which can be automatically raised or lowered to accommodate very young children or severely handicapped clients who would benefit from rehabilitation activities in varying depths of water.

14. An attractive lounge area overlooking the pool for use by handicapped adults engaging in recreation programs.

The Center's program is carried out on three levels. Clients in the Children's Division range from six months to twelve years. The program is geared to individual abilities, and every effort is made to prepare each child for public school—but where this is not possible, the objective is to develop the child to fullest potential through physical rehabilitation and educational techniques. The goal of the Teen-age Division is to help young people between the ages of thirteen and twenty-one to acquire knowledge and independence which will enable them to meet life situations and accept an adult role in society. The program includes prevocational experiences and activities to develop social competencies. The Adult Division offers opportunities for remedial education, socialization, and training in independent living skills and vocational activities.

In addition to these three divisions and their special programs, the Center is organized into several major departments. The Physical Education Department provides a varied program of adapted games, sports, exercises, and aquatics in which every individual can participate regardless of the degree or type of handicap. The Social Service Department provides support and counseling to parents to help them cope with the many social and emotional problems associated with the disability, and to enlist their aid in carrying out the rehabilitation plan for their son or daughter. The Health Services Department conducts a coordinated program of evaluation, treatment, and medical management directed toward both physical and mental problems encountered by the clients. The personnel of this department include physical therapists, occupational therapists, speech therapists, and psychologists, and in addition each division has the services of part-time medical consultants in the fields of physical medicine, psychiatry, neurology, psychology, and dentistry.

Although both children and adults receive periodic attention from the health services therapists, the thrust of the program is to incorporate therapeutic goals and recommendations into their daily activities, thereby creating a constant therapeutic environment. The physical therapists work to improve functional movement and balance skills throughout all stages of motor development, and special training is given in crawling, sitting, standing, and ambulation. They also make evaluations and recommendations for orthotic appliances and other equipment, and help to train the client in their use. This department works closely with the Bio-Engineering Department, which is responsible for adapting equipment and devising mechanical apparatus for special needs.

The occupational therapists provide training in perceptual motor skills and the functional activities of everyday life such as eating, dressing, and writing. The speech therapists are primarily concerned with the development of effective communication through prespeech training in chewing, sucking, and swallowing, as well as analysis and correction of defective speech, audiological testing, and training in the use of language boards, gesturing, and sign language where intelligible speech is lacking. The psychologists evaluate intellectual development, emotional status, and educational readiness, and recommend procedures and activities that will promote learning, social adjustment, and overall development. Short-term individual and group counseling are also provided when needed. The recreation specialists also contribute to the well-being of the clients by organizing play and sports activities as well as a wide range of activities for teen-agers and adults on weekday and Saturday nights, including bowling, chess, dramatics, films, dinners, and parties.

Well-designed physical facilities and a multidiscipline staff, such as at the Brooklyn Rehabilitation Campus, must unite in bringing the best of rehabilitation services to the handicapped. This is the challenge of good supervision and team coordination in this field. It is often the intangible quality that makes a vital difference in the effective operation of rehabilitation facilities.

(See CHAPTER 26: CEREBRAL PALSY.)

C. Vocational Rehabilitation Center

From *Rehabilitation Gazette,* 1972; with permission

"We were the first comprehensive rehabilitation center in the world," said the attending surgeon, Dr. J. Treacy O'Hanlan, as he conducted us through the Woodrow Wilson Rehabilitation Center in Fishersville, Virginia. "We operate in the black because we need few doctors on our staff," he went on. "Primarily we are a rehabilitation center. We never lose sight of the reason for our students being here: to be prepared to go home and to work and to live as independently as possible.

"One of the reasons for our success with the rehabilitation of students with spinal cord injuries is our separation from care in the initial, acute stage. We think it is a positive step forward to move here into an entirely different setting as soon as the acute phase is over. We feel there is therapeutic value in living with other students of varied disabilities [cerebral palsy, polio, spina bifida, blindness, deafness, brain damage, etc.]. Here one can always find someone else who is worse off physically and who is also working hard at rehabilitation."

WWRC is a former Army hospital, seven miles from Staunton and Waynesboro, which the State of Virginia purchased from the War Assets Administration in 1947. The meandering old buildings are gradually being replaced by modern facilities. The most exciting was the activities building which contains a dining room, a basketball court, auditorium, bowling alleys, shooting and archery gallery, craft rooms, lounge, library, and a heated swimming pool. Scuba diving and canoeing are taught in a nearby lake.

The average daily enrollment is more than 500. Most of the students [patients] are from Virginia, but students from 39 other states and ten foreign countries have attended. The staff numbers about 375, including professional and service personnel. Currently there are 73 spinal cord injured in training. Over the years, 6,000 of them have been through WWRC.

While we were waiting to see Dr. O'Hanlan, we had an informative visit with the director of physical therapy, Mrs. Patty Altland. She explained the procedure at WWRC: "First, a student is sent to the Evaluation Department. He is given a series of tests and interviews which narrow his fields of interest to about three areas. Through the use of work samples, he may try various jobs such as drafting, operating business machines, dressmaking, tailoring, auto repairing, etc. While the student is narrowing his choice of work areas, WWRC contacts his state vocational rehabilitation counselor to ascertain whether the student can be placed if he is trained in his chosen area. When a job field has been chosen and his local job market has been assessed by his field counselor, he is ready to begin training.

"On the other hand, if the Evaluation Department concludes, after extensive testing, that an individual cannot be trained, then he is sent home," Mrs. Altland said.

"We all try to build independence into our student quads. We're tough! We try to make our center as tough as the world will be. We have found that it is not the abilities a quad has that determine his accomplishments, but what is expected of him (and we expect a great deal). As soon as possible we send students home on weekends so they will start to find the problems of adaptation and learn to meet them. We expose them to all kinds of recreational activities, including music and art appreciation, languages and all types of wheelchair sports, including camping out.

"Soon after they are up in a wheelchair, we start taking them to town," she continued. "Quads must learn to tell people how to handle them! On the first trip we take them to a department store, where we leave them for a while. They have to learn to ask people to open doors, to wait on them and the like. The very next Saturday they can go to town with a group of students to eat in the pizza shop and wander around town.

"Quads are taught to change their own catheters and to empty their urinal bags. We teach them to deal with their own bowels and teach them to instruct any type of person to help with any bathrooming and dressing problems they cannot manage by themselves."

Everyone we talked to was enthusiastic about the housing arrangements which encourage independence. Initially, a cord-injured student is assigned to the infirmary. Here are those who need a lot of nursing care. The rooms can accommodate two, four or six students.

As he develops independence, a student moves forward to the intermediate wing. Here, they are divided into units of six, housed

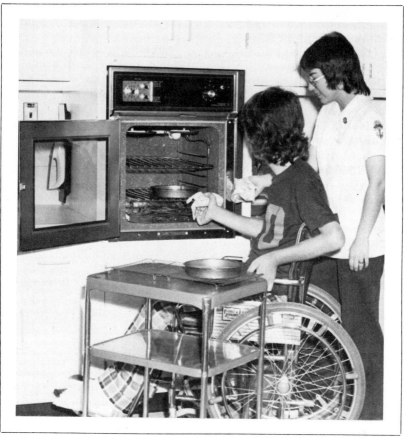

Cooking is among the skills taught at this comprehensive rehabilitation facility. (Woodrow Wilson Rehabilitation Center, Fishersville, Va)

in attractive two-bed rooms. Each room has an intercom to the nursing station, which handles about 32 individuals. Students are expected to direct their own care and to make appointments with a nurse for specific help.

The cost per day, including tuition, is $50 — in both the infirmary and the intermediate wing. This cost includes therapy and medical care.

Finally, when a student has reached a functional level he moves to the dormitory suites. This is the goal from the time a student enters the center. Here he takes the final step to living again in the world with maximum independence. The costs here are $13 a day. Therapy is an extra charge. The staff is minimal; the student is in complete charge of his own care. Vocational training courses are conducted 12 months a year. They range from auto body repair to woodworking, and special courses can be arranged. We saw a number of quads in the business education and drafting courses whose hand splints are activated by CO_2. Academic courses in reading, writing, and arithmetic are available as needed.

"One of the biggest obstacles to employment is the problem of getting to and from work," Dr. O'Hanlan said. "Therefore we put great emphasis on teaching our paras and quads to transfer and to drive. One of our most valuable departments is our driver-training program. Our 12 driving simulators are in constant use."

Physical and occupational therapy as well as speech therapy and a program for the deaf are available. Braces, splints, adaptive devices, artificial limbs as well as the services of an orthotist and a prosthetist are also available. Consultants include a general surgeon, a urologist, and a dentist.

WWRC is a vital part of the communities it serves. Volunteers from service organizations and clubs are coordinated in a Council of Organizations which stimulates and channels community interest. The Council provides funds for equipment (such as a hydraulic-lift bus), entertainment, and services in recreational, training, and living areas.

Student government provides opportunity for experience in democratic processes, and for development of a concern for civic matters. The student association meets once weekly. It elects new officers quarterly. Every student has the right to vote, and the opportunity to serve.

The In-Services Director described the center's discharge planning: "Independence is the aim of our whole program. Independence is achieved by carrying out procedures oneself, or by learning them so well that one can instruct another person in their performance. A well-trained quad will never need a highly skilled attendant; he can work with any pair of willing hands. When we are ready to discharge a student, we send a referral to his local public health nurse, and to his field counselor of rehabilitation. We work very closely with both. Four times a year we have a public health nursing workshop here.

"If needed, a team of two physical therapists and two occupational therapists will visit the student's home. Usually these visits are not needed because the local public health nurse has taken over."

Applications for admission are submitted through a state vocational rehabilitation counselor. To be considered for admission, a disabled individual must have a reasonably good prognosis for benefiting from WWRC services and have some means for defraying costs, such as department of vocational rehabilitation payments.

(See CHAPTER 51: SPINAL CORD INJURY.)

D. Educational Therapy Center

JEFFREY S. BISAGA, Ph.D., Staff Psychologist, The Marianne
Frostig Center of Educational Therapy, Los Angeles

The Marianne Frostig Center of Educational Therapy, in Los Angeles, California, has been established to help children overcome learning disabilities through the application of two approaches: (1) educational techniques designed to facilitate the acquisition of knowledge, skills, and attitudes valued in our culture; and (2) therapeutic procedures directed to specific deficits in sensory-motor, language, perceptual, and higher cognitive functions, and to social adjustment and emotional development. Such deficits usually become apparent when the child enters school, and therefore most of the children treated at the Center are referred by public schools, though referrals are also received from clinics, social agencies, parents, and private physicians.

The Center offers a multifaceted program of highly individualized remediation. Its diagnostic program, which must be carried out before the child is admitted, employs a team approach utilizing psychiatrists, psychologists, social workers, and educational specialists. It is designed to gain a picture of the child's emotional and academic functioning as well as to identify specific learning disabilities. The Director of Psychological Services is responsible for the psychological evaluation, and the Medical Director, for the final diagnosis and treatment plan.

The Center's educational services, under the supervision of the Director of Educational Services, are conducted on different levels. Since early treatment is a great advantage because of the plasticity and responsiveness of the young child and because school failure should be prevented if at all possible, preschool children are accepted for individual or group instruction. The Center's elementary day school is designed for the child who cannot progress in public school, but who can be expected to reenter regular classes after appropriate training. In the day school program, children are taught in small groups, following the standard school curriculum whenever possible. Educational methods are chosen which take each child's pattern of specific strengths and weaknesses into account, as well as special interests. The classroom atmosphere is designed to foster a positive self-concept and sensitivity to the needs of others.

At the junior or senior high level some of the students attend public school classes in which they can keep pace with their peers, but come to the Center for supplementary assistance in skills or subjects that present learning problems. Individual training and tutoring, an after-school activities program, and an intensive summer session, as well as remedial movement education and a recreational therapy camp program after school, are offered.

In addition to these services, the Center provides psychotherapy for emotional disturbances that contribute to the child's learning difficulties; individual or group counseling sessions for one or both parents; professional training of educators, therapists, and other personnel in the field, including a two-year master's degree program with Mount St. Mary's College; a publications, teaching materials, and film production resource; a research program; and lectures, demonstrations, and instructional sessions for both professionals and lay community.

Since the formulation of the individual educational program for each child is completely dependent on the diagnostic evaluation, a brief outline of this step in the process will be given here. After referral and preliminary consideration, an intake interview is set up with the parent or parents covering the presenting problem, an extensive social history including previous evaluations, and arrangements for diagnostic sessions. The child then comes for testing (usually for four sessions, and usually with at least two different examiners) in order to assess sensory-motor, perceptual, language, higher cognitive, and academic functioning. The test battery includes the Frostig Movement Skills Test Battery, the Frostig Developmental Test of Visual Perception, the Bender-Gestalt Visual-Motor Test, the Wepman Auditory Discrimination Test, the Illinois Test of Psycholinguistic Abilities, a Wechsler Intelligence Test (WPPSI or WISC-R), and appropriate achievement tests. An audiological screening and a visual screening are also given, as well as projective personality tests whenever indicated.

A complete profile of test results is then constructed, and a staff conference is held, in which all test data, relevant social or medical history, and prior evaluations are drawn together. Recommendations for initiating multidimensional training and therapeutic measures are made, and a summary report is written. This report is discussed with the parents during a conference with the intake worker. When a final decision has been made, the recommendations are implemented.

(See CHAPTER 37: LEARNING DISABILITIES; CHAPTER 55: ILLUSTRATIVE CASES, E. Shali: Educational Therapy.)

E. Recreation Center

The Recreation Center for the Handicapped, founded by Mrs. Janet Pomeroy in 1952, is a private, nonprofit corporation dedicated to the principle that handicapped people are entitled to the same opportunities for personal growth and fulfillment that are available to persons who are not handicapped. It is probably the only center in the United States that offers a full range of indoor and outdoor recreation and camping programs, year-round, for multihandicapped, mentally retarded, physically handicapped, and emotionally disturbed children, teens, and adults, with no restrictions as to age, race, creed, or severity of handicap. Activities include arts and crafts, drama, dance, music, socials, parties, physical fitness, games and sports, camp, trips, excursions into the community, swimming, fishing, boating, and horseback riding. No one is deprived of the opportunity to participate. The Center absorbs the cost of those who are not sponsored by a funding agency and who are unable to pay.

The program is conducted in a specially designed facility located at 207 Skyline Boulevard in San Francisco, California. The building is 18,000 square feet (1,675 square meters) in area and includes a day care room, an arts and crafts room, drama and music rooms, a multipurpose room with stage and audio-visual services, and an adjacent kitchen, staff offices, and related facilities. A large, heated, therapeutic swimming pool complex, 16,000 square feet (1,490 square meters) in area, includes a large swimming pool, ramp for wheelchairs, and steps into a wading pool for small children. The balance of the site permits day camping during warm weather and provides outdoor recreation areas with a variety of surfaces for wheelchairs, play vehicles, and day care play yards. (See CHAPTER 14: RECREATION FOR THE DISABLED.)

The Center also conducts an Outreach Program to serve the needs of infants, children, teens, and adults who cannot participate in programs at the Center. Activities are offered to these individuals in their own homes, in board and care homes for the mentally handicapped, in boarding homes for the aged, and in senior citizen complexes.

Virtually every disability is represented among those who participate at the Center or through the Outreach Program. The majority are mentally retarded. Some are also partially sighted, deaf, hard of hearing, neurologically handicapped, or emotionally disturbed, or have a combination of these handicaps. Others are handicapped as a result of accidents, arthritis, cerebral palsy, epilepsy, congenital malformations, multiple sclerosis, muscular dystrophy, and other conditions. Some are in wheelchairs, on crutches, and even bedfast. Many are unable to feed themselves and require assistance with bathroom needs. Speech impairments are a common handicap.

The Center owns and operates a fleet of sixteen buses and station wagons which are in operation every day from early morning to late evening. All buses are equipped with straps and harnesses for holding severely handicapped persons. Drivers work under a transportation coordinator and are carefully selected for their safe driving practices and special abilities for working with severely retarded and handicapped persons. A transportation aide supervises children at all times on their trips to and from the Center.

The Center is governed by a board of directors of lay and professional persons, broadly representative of both public and private organizations and agencies in recreation, education, health, medicine, welfare, and business. Parents of the handicapped also serve on the board. Janet Pomeroy, who has volunteered full-time services since the inception of the Center, has responsibility for its overall direction. A program director is responsible for operation of the program, and a business manager oversees all business aspects. Programming is offered through four divisions: Children's, Adult/Teen, Outreach, and Swimming.

The San Francisco Recreation and Park Department, the Community Mental Health Services, the Department of Social Services, and the State Department of Education subsidize a portion of the Center's budget on a contractual basis. A large proportion of the operating budget is raised by the board of directors through personal and organizational solicitation and fund-raising events, such as horse shows, luncheons, and bazaars. Parents assist the board in all fund-raising events, organize telephone and clerical work, and conduct an annual fiesta and a Christmas bazaar. They also build special equipment and furnish some foods and program supplies to the Center. The Parents' Auxiliary meets monthly for discussion and for talks by community speakers.

The San Francisco Community College District provides adult education instructors with a variety of expertise to supplement the services of the Center staff. Community Mental Health Services provides a psychologist, and the County Social Service Department provides a social worker who consults with staff about special problems and needs of the participants and their families. Special education personnel from the Unified School District provide evaluation services for children in the Day Care Program. Other consultants from various disciplines are made available on request, by Children's Hospital, the Easter Seal Society, and other agencies. Recreation specialists from Bay Area colleges and universities provide consultation and demonstrations.

The Center has served as a laboratory for graduate and undergraduate students from universities and colleges throughout the United States. Locally, students from Departments of Special Education and Recreation of California State University, San Francisco, and the University of California spend a full semester gaining practical experience at the Center, and many other students volunteer twenty-five hours or more each semester to fulfill class requirements for agency experience. Throughout the year, seminars, workshops, and discussion groups are conducted to encourage professionals in the field of recreation to initiate programs in their immediate community. The Center distributes written materials, films, and slides to various groups and individuals interested in recreation for the handicapped, and a book, *Recreation for the Physically Handicapped* (Macmillan, New York), written by the director, is being used as a college text throughout the country.

F. Mental Hospitals

Adapted from "Mental Hospital," in Robert M.
Goldenson, Ph.D., *Encyclopedia of Human Behavior,*
Doubleday, New York, 1970; Dell, New York, 1975

In 1972 there were 592 hospitals exclusively devoted to mental patients in the United States. Of these, 434 were government hospitals and 158 were private. In addition, approximately 653 community general hospitals had separate psychiatric units, about 500 other general hospitals admitted psychiatric patients to their regular medical facilities, and another 2,000 admitted mental patients on an emergency basis. Many mental patients were also housed in old-age homes and institutions for the chronically diseased and disabled. In all, about 76 percent of beds devoted to psychiatric patients were in public hospitals (in contrast to 98 percent in 1965) and 3 percent in private institutions. Taking turnover into consideration, approximately 1,750,000 mental patients received hospital care and treatment in the course of a year.

In recent years practically every aspect of the mental hospital has undergone modification, with the prime purpose of transforming it from a largely custodial institution to a center for intensive care. Massive, prisonlike buildings are being gradually replaced by facilities with less than a thousand beds. Large wards are being broken up, and an increasing number of patients are living in smaller units with a more intimate and homelike atmosphere. Greater attention is being paid to décor, and hard hospital benches are being replaced by comfortable chairs. More rooms are being set aside for special activities such as music, art, and dance sessions, and more emphasis is placed on occupational, recreational, and industrial therapy.

Administration is less centralized, and many staff roles have been redefined—for example, the attendant has been upgraded to "psychiatric aide," and recreation specialists and rehabilitation counselors participate in staff conferences as members of the therapeutic team. The patients themselves are now conceived as participants in the therapeutic process, advancing their own recovery by engaging in group discussions, psychodrama, and committees which make recommendations affecting their lives in the hospital. All these changes help to make the entire institution a therapeutic milieu.

The barriers between hospital and community are being broken down by wider use of volunteers, frequent visits of patients in the community, and attendance by local citizens at hospital social events.

Barred windows, locked wards, and forceful methods of restraint are rapidly disappearing, along with excessive use of such sedation techniques as tub baths, wet sheet packs, and heavy doses of hypnotic drugs. Seclusion is still occasionally required for violent episodes, but on a short-term basis. "Maximum security units" have been largely eliminated, except for some hospitals for the criminally insane. Three factors are primarily responsible for these changes: tranquilizing drugs, the idea of the therapeutic community, and the concept of the patient as a sick person rather than a madman.

Admission procedures are now designed to allay the patient's anxiety and to assure that one's rights and privileges will be respected. After admission, steps are taken to orient the patient to the hospital organization and help one adjust to ward life. Discharge procedures have been eased in many places, largely because many patients can be maintained on drugs. Readmission has also been simplified.

The most important newer facilities are the day hospital, in which the patient is treated in the hospital during the day but lives in the community at night; the night hospital, which offers evening or overnight treatment for patients who work during the day; the halfway house; the sheltered workshop; the therapeutic farm; the five-day hospital; and the foster family during convalescence.

An increasing number of state and general hospitals and community centers are also offering special emergency care. One study has shown that 40 to 50 percent of patients who receive emergency treatment are able to stay out of the hospital.

Finally, modern treatments and the use of community facilities have had a significant effect on the mental hospital picture in America. In 1971 only 17.9 percent of all psychiatric patients were treated in state institutions, as contrasted with 75 percent two decades before. This change was due primarily to an increase in the use of general hospitals, outpatient clinics, community mental health centers, and private office care. The number of resident patients has been dropping every year since the introduction of psychotropic drugs. Yet in spite of this decrease, the actual number of patients treated each year has risen 15 percent, since the average length of stay for new patients has been materially shortened. This is particularly true of the more advanced hospitals where intensive techniques are employed. In these institutions 80 percent of newly admitted patients are discharged within six months to a year. In some states, notably Iowa, California, Connecticut, and Kansas, the average hospital stay of all first admissions is now about two months. For schizophrenic patients, who occupy half the beds in mental hospitals, the chances for release within a year have risen from 20 to 80 percent. Moreover, readmission rates are now as low as 10 percent for patients receiving continuing aftercare and rehabilitation.

G. Day and Night Hospitals

As a facility for the treatment and rehabilitation of mental patients, the day hospital (also called the day care program) provides an alternative to the isolation of a residential institution and enables the patient to maintain contact with family and friends. It has the further advantages of relieving the patient's family of providing care during the day, reducing the cost of hospital treatment, and offering a transition from the community to the hospital or from the hospital back to the community. In the last case it has the psychological effect of assuring patients that they are getting well, and gives them an opportunity to gain self-confidence at their own pace. It may also be used to replace residential treatment and encourage patients to think of the hospital merely as a center for temporary treatment rather than permanent care. This has a positive effect on their morale and probably on their recovery as well.

In some instances the day care program is part of an outpatient clinic; in others it is a separate center; in still others day patients receive care and treatment along with residential patients. All types of ambulatory treatment and rehabilitation procedures are applied: medications, in some cases electroshock, individual and group psychotherapy, and engagement in the hospital's activity program according to the patient's needs and interests. When the family transports the patient to and from the hospital daily, the staff has a special opportunity to acquaint them with the individual's needs and enlist their collaboration in the rehabilitation process.

The day hospital concept is also being applied in treatment and rehabilitation centers for the physically disabled. This type of facility differs from outpatient clinic programs in offering more intensive medical, nursing, and rehabilitation services than most outpatient clinic programs, and in involving the patient for a longer period, usually from four to eight hours one or more times per week. A program of this kind has a number of special advantages, some of which are shared by day care facilities for mental patients: a chance for the patient to get out of the house and mingle with other people; a less expensive alternative to inpatient care; a special opportunity to train the family in the care of the patient; and participation of the patient in programs of occupational therapy, speech therapy, physical therapy, and other activities designed to encourage independence and meet emotional needs. Many severely disabled patients would deteriorate at home both physically and psychologically if they did not have such opportunities, especially if an adequate home care program is not available.

Selection of patients for a day hospital of this type is based on a diagnosis of disability or chronic illness which necessitates continuing medical evaluation, treatment, and nursing care, as well as a host of other needs: personal assistance in such daily living activities as feeding, bathing, toileting, transfers, and ambulation; supervision because of communication difficulties, behavior, or psychological problems; rehabilitation services to improve or maintain the level of independent function; socialization and psychological treatment due to depression, withdrawal, and other emotional symptoms; treatment to prevent deterioration that would lead to admission to an institution; treatment to prevent or correct disuse atrophy, deformities, decubitus ulcers, urinary tract infection, and deterioration of behavior; training in taking drugs, special diets, catheter management, and bowel and bladder control; surveillance because of problems of hearing or vision; repeated x-ray examinations, electrocardiograph, and laboratory tests as needed; planned exercise and self-care and home management training. In addition, the family usually receives special training in the management of the special needs of the patient.

A comprehensive program of this kind requires the coordinated services of practically all the rehabilitation professions described in Chapter 57.

In night psychiatric hospitals (or night care programs), mental patients either reside at the hospital or live in the community and come to the hospital in the evenings for psychotherapy and supportive activities, such as recreational or occupational therapy. A program of this kind has many advantages. Designed primarily for patients on the road to recovery, it enables them to make a gradual transition from hospital to community; provides help without interrupting their jobs or other daytime responsibilities; and in many cases makes it possible for them to be discharged sooner. It also encourages disturbed individuals to apply for the help they need on an outpatient basis, since they do not have to reveal to their employers that they are receiving treatment. Finally, the night operation makes fuller and therefore more economic use of hospital facilities, and also provides overnight psychiatric emergency service.

H. Community Mental Health Centers

The community mental health center is one of the most significant recent developments in the psychiatric picture, dating from President John F. Kennedy's demand for a "bold new approach" and the Community Mental Health Centers Act of 1963. The object of these centers, now numbering over 300, is to offer comprehensive, community-based treatment as a practical alternative to "the strange and lonely mental hospital which for years has been a world apart." This alternative has been made possible not only by the use of psychotropic drugs, but by concrete evidence that many types of patients who were once sent to a residential hospital as a matter of course can be more effectively treated on an outpatient or part-time inpatient basis in their own community.

Most community mental health centers get their start through an expansion and integration of the services of existing agencies, such as clinics, local hospitals, or county health department treatment units; but some have been newly built, with federal funds financing up to two-thirds of the cost of construction. In either case they are designed to offer a broad spectrum of coordinated services (though not necessarily under one roof) with the aim of tailoring treatment to individual patients and enabling them to obtain this help without leaving family, job, or school. The overall goal is to provide readily accessible treatment to a wide variety of patients, including those with acute disturbances and personality disorders, and a growing number with chronic disorders.

In general, the services of a community mental health center include the following: (a) outpatient programs providing individual and group therapy to children, adults, and entire families; (b) inpatient treatment for emergency cases or those requiring twenty-four-hour care for a limited period; (c) partial hospitalization on a day, night, or weekend basis; (d) vocational, educational, and social rehabilitation of both current and former mental patients; (e) precare and aftercare in hostels and foster homes, as well as home visits; (f) specialized and outreach programs for such groups as alcoholics, drug addicts, abused children and their parents, and individuals living in deprived neighborhoods; (g) consultation to physicians, clergymen, health departments, welfare agencies, and schools; (h) training of professional and paraprofessional mental health personnel; and (i) ecological research and evaluation of programs. In its full development, a comprehensive program of this kind requires the services of a wide range of mental health workers (psychiatrists, clinical psychologists, rehabilitation counselors, psychiatric social workers, etc.) as well as specialists in community psychiatry, social psychology, and demography. (See CHAPTER 57: REHABILITATION PROFESSIONS.)

Various studies reported by the National Institute of Mental Health indicate that these centers are having a constructive effect on the total mental health problem. Collaboration between all types of community mental health resources has been stimulated. Full and long-term hospitalizations have been obviated in a large number of cases. The per-patient cost of treatment has been materially reduced. The morale of patients has been lifted, and recovery has been speeded. Many groups, such as those living in "ghetto" areas, are receiving more adequate care. The concepts of early detection and early treatment have been put into wider effect, and this is cutting down the incidence of severe and chronic mental illness. In addition, a number of promising innovations have been introduced by these centers, such as the mobile crisis intervention and suicide prevention unit of the Lincoln Community Mental Health Center in the Bronx, New York.

I. Mental Health Clinics

Today there are approximately 2,000 outpatient mental health clinics in the United States, serving a total of almost 1 million patients per year. Most of them are operated by community mental health centers, state and Veterans Administration hospitals, and voluntary agencies, although nearly 400 are under private auspices. They are usually located within the community, often in neighborhoods where the need is greatest, for their purpose is to provide help as close to home as possible. Their significance in the mental health picture has been increasing with the recognition that (a) early treatment will often forestall chronic illness that requires long-term hospitalization, and (b) patients who have already been hospitalized can frequently be discharged to the community sooner if outpatient treatment is available to them.

A representative clinic has a psychiatrist in attendance at regularly scheduled hours and also employs psychologists and psychiatric social workers—all of whom function as a team. The primary emphasis is on relatively short-term psychotherapy, group and individual, as well as the prescription of the milder types of psychotropic drugs. A few clinics serve children or adults exclusively, but by far the greatest number serve both. Patients with narcotics addiction, mental retardation, and chronic alcoholism may be referred to appropriate agencies and centers. Referrals are also frequently made to various rehabilitation resources, such as the Office of Vocational Rehabilitation, foster family agencies, sheltered workshops, or nursing homes.

Mental health clinics accept clients with a wide variety of emotional difficulties, including depression, anxiety, behavior problems, marital conflict, and psychiatric emergencies. During the present drive to reduce the population of large public institutions, more and more patients are being referred to clinics for aftercare, although patients diagnosed as actively psychotic still require hospitalization. A statistical study has indicated that the most common diagnoses for children seen at these centers are transient situational disorders without underlying personality disturbance, personality disorders or behavioral defects with little evidence of anxiety or stress, and mental deficiency. Boys outnumber girls by a ratio of 2 to 1, but the number of adult males only slightly exceeds the number of females. The most common diagnoses for adult patients are personality disorders, psychoneurotic disorders, and psychotic disorders, particularly schizophrenic reactions. The psychoneurotic patients, in general, receive the greatest amount of treatment and make the greatest progress, with 70 to 80 percent improved.

In 1962 the Joint Commission on Mental Illness and Health stated that mental health clinics occupy a "pivotal position" for early treatment on an outpatient basis and for aftercare of discharged mental patients. That position has been maintained, even though many clinics are now functioning as an integral part of a total community program instead of independently. (See SECTION H, Community Mental Health Centers.)

J. Halfway Houses

Halfway houses are temporary residences which provide mental patients and ex-patients with a bridge between the hospital and community life. These facilities have been established for a variety of reasons. Long-term patients have often adjusted so completely to the routines and restrictions of institutional life that they need to relearn the living skills demanded by society at large. Many of them do not have families they can count on, and are not yet prepared for a totally independent existence. They may also need the additional psychiatric care and social work services that halfway houses provide. Moreover, many proponents of this concept feel that these residences allow more freedom and encourage more independence than other transition arrangements, such as foster family care.

Halfway houses and other forms of group residences have been rapidly increasing during the past few years. One of the developments which makes them possible is the widespread use of psychoactive drugs that enable many patients to function on maintenance doses outside the hospital. A second reason for their growth is that experience in a protected transitional setting significantly reduces the relapse rate and therefore increases the patients' chances of remaining out of the hospital. Another is the current revolt against huge, impersonal "warehouses" and the consequent drive to disperse as many patients and ex-patients as possible into smaller, familylike facilities.

There are three general types of halfway houses. One is the *treatment-oriented facility,* in which the residents are still patients who have not been discharged from the mental institution, but who are far enough along in the recovery process to live in a group residence outside the hospital. As patients, they are under supervision by the hospital staff and visit the hospital regularly for psychiatric treatment and occupational, industrial, and other forms of auxiliary therapy. They are not expected to assume much responsibility in the halfway house, or to participate actively in community life, but usually engage in group sessions designed to prepare them for full discharge.

The second type is the small residence for ex-patients, sometimes called a *cooperative urban house,* though it may be established in small communities as well as large or medium-sized cities. These halfway houses are usually limited to ten to thirty residents of the same sex who need minimum supervision and who are potentially employable or nearly ready to enroll in academic programs or assume homemaking responsibilities. An example is Futura House, in White Plains, New York, which has a section for men and one for women, all of whom have been referred by mental hospitals, social agencies, or psychiatrists in private practice. This facility offers the residents an opportunity to try their wings and broaden their social life in a secure atmosphere before embarking on a fully independent life. But at the same time they must assume certain responsibilities, such as getting up at a reasonable hour and assisting in household chores. In addition, the residents hold meetings in which day-to-day activities are discussed, consult with the staff social workers about personal and vocational problems, and receive outside psychiatric assistance as needed.

A third type of halfway house is the somewhat larger *rural work-oriented house,* sometimes called a ranch, farm, or homestead. Ex-patients of both sexes are accepted, as well as individuals who have emotional disorders that do not require hospitalization. An example is Gould Farm, in Monterey, Massachusetts, which accommodates approximately forty troubled individuals who need help but do not require special care or close supervision. The staff consists of a director, counselors, and a resident nurse, with medical and psychiatric facilities within easy reach. Group and individual counseling are both available, but "most basic to our therapeutic program is provision of a warm and friendly caring atmosphere in which a healing process takes place, and experience has shown us that working with one's hands and with the earth and nature's processes and creatures is helpful in encouraging guests to look beyond themselves and to gain a new perspective on their lives" (Kent Smith, Director). The work, however, is counterbalanced with such activities as square dances, films, discussions, concerts, hikes, and weaving and other crafts.

K. Group Homes

In some sections of the United States there is a trend toward the establishment of small group residences for the emotionally disturbed and mentally retarded, as well as for other individuals outside the scope of this book, such as homeless persons or victims of child abuse. Their overall objective is to keep these people out of institutions and enable them to live in familylike settings where they are encouraged to establish healthy relationships, cooperative behavior, and increased self-acceptance. In one New York county, Westchester, the Community Services Council has reported that the number of group homes, some of which are called hostels, has grown from thirty-six in 1970 to ninety-two in 1975, with another forty-seven in the making. A special branch of the Council has been organized to provide information about these homes, as well as to help agencies find suitable sites, and to draw up a model zoning ordinance, since in some instances group homes meet local opposition from real estate interests and municipalities (even though there is little evidence that they lower property values). Most of the residences for children are located in smaller communities where the young people can attend local schools, use parks and playgrounds, and join organizations such as the Scouts. Cities are favored for adults due to availability of transportation, employment, and recreational facilities. In both cases efforts are made to integrate the residents with the rest of the community rather than provide a social island within it.

L. Foster Families

The foster family is a well-recognized living arrangement for both children and adults who are without homes, or whose homes are broken beyond repair or unalterably detrimental to their health and well-being. When selected and supervised by social agencies, the foster family is a constructive alternative to institutionalization, for it offers the benefits of a warm and accepting home to the neglected, the abused, the friendless, and the lost. But it is also of particular value to two other groups of special relevance to this volume: mental patients (or ex-patients) and retarded children.

Foster family care is provided by many mental institutions, both private and public, as an aftercare service for patients who no longer require the specialized program of the hospital but still need additional treatment and supervision. It is available to many kinds of individuals on either a temporary or permanent basis, such as recovered or partially recovered patients who need help in making the transition to independent life but who cannot get this help from their own family; victims of convulsive disorders who must receive medication on a maintenance basis or who have difficulty gaining acceptance from society; and homeless men and women of advanced age with chronic, irreversible disorders. All these types of patients, and others as well, receive special care from the hospital or clinic while they reside with the foster family—for example, supervision of medication, periodic evaluation, group or individual psychotherapy, or assistance in finding recreational activities or part-time work.

In developing a foster family program, the hospital social work department searches for suitable homes by contacting appropriate agencies or by arranging a publicity campaign. Prospective families, or "caretakers" as they are sometimes called, are interviewed and, if accepted, receive group instruction in patient care and hospital requirements. The patients themselves must be given careful preparation and orientation, as well as an opportunity to voice their preferences before being assigned to a home. In some cases arrangements are made for selected hospital services, such as occupational therapy, to be carried out in the home, and in many instances arrangements are made with appropriate social agencies for vocational rehabilitation for the patient or homemaking services for the family.

As stated in Robert M. Goldenson's *Encyclopedia of Human Behavior* (Doubleday, New York, 1970):

> A well-run family care program offers many benefits. It helps to release hospital beds for the acutely ill. It enables the community to assume responsibility for patients, and it spreads the idea that people who have recovered from mental illness can take part in everyday activities. It gives the families an opportunity to be of valuable service and to receive some financial return. But most important of all, it gives the patients themselves a chance to live as normal a life as possible.

Most of these benefits apply to foster family care for the retarded as well. When children are placed in a carefully selected home, there is every chance that they will develop further than they would in an institution, and in so doing they will demonstrate that mental deficiency is not necessarily a fixed, hopeless condition. As Gerard W. O'Regan states in an article in *Children Today* (January-February 1974), "Foster family care can provide a child with parent surrogates who, within the setting of their own homes, may supply the individualized care, attention and love that institutions can rarely offer." Moreover, most foster parents say they enjoy retarded foster children and do not find them an excessive burden. Nevertheless it cannot be denied that they must have an extra degree of patience, understanding, and an ability to face the questioning attitudes of others. Too often these attitudes are shared by professionals who take it for granted that retarded children are "hard to place"; and it is not unusual to hear them complain, "We can't even find foster homes for *normal* children."

Mr. O'Regan, executive director of Retarded Infants Services, in New York City, has proposed a new and promising approach to placement. He points out that many parents have chosen to keep their retarded child at home — and these parents would often make ideal parents for foster children as well. The reasons? They have already learned to cope with the problems of the mentally retarded, and this "on-the-job training" can be applied to other atypical children. What is more, a second retarded child would provide companionship for their own retarded son or daughter on an equivalent level, and in so doing ease the burden on normal brothers and sisters as well as on the parents. Also, the parents could spread their attention more evenly, instead of concentrating an excessive proportion on the retarded child to the detriment of the rest of the family, as well as to the child.

Studies conducted by Retarded Infants Services have shown that these children are usually compatible and happy to spend most of their time together, and the added companionship frequently results in unexpected progress. The agency, however, regards parents of the retarded only as one additional resource for a full foster parent program to explore. Through its efforts a large number of foster care agencies in the New York area are now recognizing their responsibility to retarded children, and it is to be hoped that the same will be true in other sections of the country as well.

M. Nursing Homes

In 1973 approximately 1,200,000 Americans resided in nursing homes. By far the greatest number were age sixty-five or older, and were confined to nursing homes for the disabled and chronically ill. Their disorders ran the gamut of conditions affecting the elderly, including stroke, heart disease, Parkinson's disease, rheumatoid arthritis, osteoporosis, atherosclerosis, Alzheimer's disease, laryngectomy, amputation, and colostomy. Some of these disorders may strike at an earlier age, and for this reason approximately 12 percent of residents are younger than sixty-five. Currently a few of these homes are also accommodating physically disabled young adults and, in some cases, ex-mental patients on the road to recovery. These groups generally occupy a separate wing or department.

Nursing homes are long-term care facilities designed to provide medical and social supports to their residents. Despite abuses which have recently come to light in some of these institutions, the concept itself is widely accepted and the need for these homes is increasing, due to the extension of life and the relatively high incidence of disorder among the aged. Many of these individuals do not require hospitalization, yet do not have the necessary financial and social resources to live independently. They need professional help and a place to live and socialize, and a superior nursing home may be the answer on both counts. A well-organized facility provides medical supervision, day-to-day nursing service, a rehabilitation program, activities programs, nutritious meals served in pleasant surroundings, homelike rooms, and specially equipped bathrooms and lounges. Special efforts are made to assist residents in remaining active and integrated in the community. A nursing home, in the best sense of the term, is a facility designed for enriched living and comprehensive care and rehabilitation.

Nursing homes are licensed under social welfare or other government agencies, and their physical plants and health services are subject to periodic inspections. Facility resources are often a function of size. Smaller homes often operate on a minimal basis in all respects and differ little from other senior citizen residences, except for employment of a practical nurse and regular visits by a physician. On the other hand, some are so large that the term "home" is a euphemism, since the atmosphere tends to be impersonal and institutional. Between these two extremes are the medium-sized facilities which provide a spectrum of services and activities carried out by a number of departments under the guidance of an administrative office and board of directors.

The various departments in a well-run nursing home are organized to deliver effective and efficient patient care. The Social Work Department, sometimes aided by a part-time psychologist, conducts intake and family interviews, compiles the patient's case history, evaluates the patient's suitability for the home, and provides counseling on personal problems. The Nursing Department consists of a nursing supervisor, registered nurses, licensed practical nurses, and nursing aides. There is a nursing station on each floor or in each wing, with a staff equipped to administer everyday care and handle emergencies. Medications are prescribed by physicians, and a link to a local hospital is maintained for emergency care. Some homes have their own pharmacies.

The Dietary Department is responsible for planning and preparing meals under the direction of a professional dietitian. Attention is paid to the general nutritional needs of older men and women as well as prescribed diets. The Occupational Therapy Department trains residents in the use of rehabilitation aids and assistive devices as well as in daily living activities, with the common purpose of preserving or restoring independent functioning. This department also provides guidance and instruction in arts, crafts, and other hobby activities. The Recreational Therapy Department arranges outdoor and indoor games, folk dances, films, talks, concerts, parties, and visits to theaters, museums, libraries, and other community resources. The Physical Therapy Department administers prescribed rehabilitation procedures, using such equipment as exercise bicycles, whirlpool baths, parallel bars, and adjustable weights. Training may also be given in the use of a cane, crutches, walkers, or wheelchairs. The Housekeeping Department is responsible for laundry, bedmaking, and cleaning; and the Maintenance Department keeps the entire residence in working order.

The physical plant plays an integral part in the quality of life which the nursing home establishes. Comfortable chairs in groupings that encourage social interaction, a well-decorated dining room resembling a good restaurant, varied colors in halls and bedrooms, interesting prints on the walls—all these can have a constructive effect on the residents. In addition, the newer homes are usually designed with the elimination of architectural barriers in mind. Ground floor public rooms open directly onto patios or courtyards, with no steps between. Pedestal-type tables are often preferred to the four-legged variety that pose an obstacle to legs and wheelchairs. Floor coverings are chosen with wheelchair mobility in mind, and ramps are constructed wherever possible in place of steps. The needs of wheelchair patients also determine the height of chairs, beds, and toilets. For the same reason light switches are placed 36 inches (90 centimeters) above the floor, and closet shelves, storage cabinets, desks, washbasins, and public telephones are designed to be used from a sitting position. Handrails are frequently installed along both sides of corridors and around recreation rooms, and grab bars are placed near showers, tubs, and toilets. In a few homes, doorknobs have been replaced by levers, since stroke and arthritis victims find knobs hard to manage. In addition, many of the devices helpful in independent living (listed in Chapter 5) are now found in nursing homes — for example, built-up handles on eating and writing utensils, long-handled shoehorns, gadget bags for wheelchairs, and bathtub lifts.

There is no doubt that assistive devices, well-chosen furnishings, and the ecological arrangement of the nursing home can have a positive influence on the patients. Together with physical, occupational and recreational therapy programs, they can help the disabled and chronically ill remain active and relatively independent, and in so doing retard the degenerative processes often associated with aging (see CHAPTER 54: OTHER DISORDERS, E. Geriatric Rehabilitation).

While the above description applies to a great many nursing homes, it is important to recognize that different long-term care facilities (LTCF) provide different levels of nursing care. Skilled nursing facilities (SNF) provide continuous medical nursing service on a twenty-four-hour basis for convalescent patients, plus restorative therapy, physical therapy, and occupational therapy. Residential or intermediate care facilities (ICF) provide regular medical, nursing, and social services in addition to room and board for persons incapable of fully independent living, but the level of nursing care is less than that provided by skilled nursing facilities. The SNF and ICF are both recognized for participation in Medicaid and Medicare programs. In addition, the role of long-term care has expanded in recent years to include child care of chronically ill children, including rehabilitation, education, and other services such as nursing, nutrition, and recreation; adult day care, for persons who are able to maintain personal residence but who require assistance in the activities of daily living, as well as nursing, nutritional, recreational, and social services; and mental health care through local mental health services, for persons with mental health problems or developmental disabilities.

The principal objective of all these long-term care facilities, as expressed by the professional association in the field, the American Health Care Association, is "to preserve the dignity and worth of every individual and to meet the total emotional, physical, social, and spiritual needs of the residents." According to AHCA and government statistics, there were 6,539 facilities with a total of 172,000 beds in 1954, and by 1974 these figures had risen to 16,139 certified facilities with 1,187,973 beds. This growth is primarily due to increasing population and longevity; increasing incidence of chronic disease typical of an aging population; reduction in family size, with fewer members available to care for the elderly and incapacitated; availability of funds for investment, construction, and skilled personnel; and federal funding of long-term care programs through Medicare and Medicaid.

N. University-Affiliated Retardation Facilities

During the past decade thirty-eight university-affiliated centers have been created to provide services to the retarded as well as to train professionals and paraprofessionals. This program has been implemented by the Mental Retardation Facilities Construction Act of 1963 and the Developmental Disabilities Act of 1970 and its 1974 continuation, and now operates in cooperation with the Association of University Affiliated Facilities. It is the first major, coordinated approach to meeting the pressing needs of all developmentally disabled persons.

This section will be based primarily on a pioneer participant in the program, the Mental Retardation Institute, operated by New York Medical College in New York City and Valhalla, New York. Its basic components in the two campuses consist of two outpatient clinics, an inpatient clinic, a preschool facility, a school unit, the Hale Matthews Research Laboratories, and an administrative section. In addition, the Institute conducts a Community Outreach Program which provides services on a team basis to retarded individuals and their families who cannot readily utilize existing health resources, and sends interdisciplinary teams to many day care centers, head start centers, clinics, and public schools.

The activities and interdisciplinary character of the Institute can best be described by outlining the work of its many departments. The Medical Services Department is responsible for the case history of each patient, a full physical examination, a developmental evaluation, laboratory studies, and special tests. Members of this department include many specialists in diagnosis and treatment: neurologists, otolaryngologists, geneticists, physiatrists, radiologists, and ophthalmologists. Surgeons and other specialists are available on a consultant basis, and pediatric fellows rotate throughout the various components of the Institute.

The services of the Psychology Department include comprehensive assessment of both children and adults, a treatment program involving a variety of techniques (play therapy, behavior modification, etc.), consultation to schools and other agencies, and an educational program for teachers, parents, and volunteers, as well as a medical college training program for doctoral candidates specializing in mental retardation. The Department of Psychiatry provides services relative to the diagnosis, study, and treatment of emotional problems of the child and his family. The psychiatrists also consult with other staff members, such as counselors and speech therapists, and participate in the training programs of other disciplines, including child psychiatrists concerned with the retarded.

The Social Work Department is responsible for evaluation of the family unit and provision of such services as intake interviews, counseling, environmental manipulation, and case coordination in cooperation with other disciplines. It also offers a training program for graduate and undergraduate students, and coordinates the community outreach programs, in which trainees participate. The Department of Clinical Communicology evaluates practically all patients in language, speech, and hearing, and takes remedial action as needed. It also instructs parents in techniques to be employed in the home, functions in the outreach programs, conducts a training program for doctoral candidates and masters level students as well as paraprofessionals, and carries out numerous research projects.

The Occupational Therapy Department provides an evaluation and treatment program involving motor skills, arts and crafts, and activities of daily living for inpatients, outpatients, and school participants, as well as clinical training for students and the professional staff. The Physical Therapy Department provides evaluation and treatment directed to improved motor development and behavior, and also participates in in-service training for other staff members. Recently this department has been providing intensive infant developmental stimulation for Down's syndrome babies from the age of two weeks onward, seeking to extend and enrich their physical and motor development from the earliest possible age.

The Dance Therapy Department uses body expression as a means of inducing physical and emotional changes, and gives courses to selected students. The Music Therapy Department conducts group and individual sessions in all the components of the Institute, and trains interns in the techniques of paraverbal therapy developed for children with communication disorders. The Nursing Department also provides both patient services and student training. The Media Department produces educational video tapes for trainees and staff, develops techniques and materials to be used as therapeutic aids, and operates a closed-circuit TV network throughout the Valhalla campus.

The director of the Institute, Margaret J. Giannini, M.D., who is also its founder, guides its total program (administration, funding, relationships with the parent New York Medical College and cooperating agencies) and maintains a close relationship with the staff, patients, trainees, and members of the advisory board.

O. Communities for the Retarded

A number of facilities for the mentally retarded have been organized on a community basis. An excellent example of this concept is the recently developed New England Village in Pembroke, Massachusetts, which is designed to "provide a setting in which the retarded adult can live in dignity, with appropriate independence, work in a job suited to his interests and capabilities, and spend his leisure time with his peers in a manner that provides him with enjoyment and a sense of belonging." The Village consists of a number of houses which function as independent units, each establishing its own routines consistent with personal needs and work schedules. Assisted by staff members, the residents plan meals, purchase food, share in its preparation, participate in routine housekeeping chores, and can make and receive calls on the house telephone. Retarded individuals in the area may participate with them in both the occupational and social-recreational programs.

The occupational program at New England Village is divided into three phases: (1) evaluation, to enable each individual to pursue employment in keeping with his abilities and interests; (2) training, to help develop the required skills, work attitudes, and interpersonal relationships; and (3) paid work on several different ability levels. The first level is geared to individuals who cannot meet the pressures of production, and consists of packaging and hand assembly jobs subcontracted from industry, or working in the Village greenhouse or outdoor horticulture program. The second level consists of services to the community, such as animal care, cleaning and maintenance, and lawn and yard care. The third consists of competitive jobs in the community, but performed under close supervision. Those who function well can graduate to the fourth level of independent employment obtained with the assistance of the Village staff. Individuals who earn the minimum wage or more and who are receiving fee assistance from the Village are expected to contribute a reasonable amount for room and board.

The social-recreational program makes maximum use of community as well as Village resources and is designed to encourage participation in all activities normally available to adults, such as visits to athletic events, beaches, and restaurants; hobby clubs and groups (photography, sewing, painting, etc.); religious services; political discussions and voting; driver education classes; partaking of alcoholic beverages outside the Village and in the houses on special occasions; trips, outings, and parties arranged by the Village; cards and other table games played in the recreation lounges.

Another example is Innisfree, Virginia—well described by *Washington Post* staff writer George F. Will, and reprinted here with permission.

> Nestled on what was, 200 years ago, an American frontier, this village is an outpost on a new frontier. The frontier is social and moral, not geographical: Innisfree is pioneering a new way of caring for a minority that has been all too easy to neglect.
>
> Innisfree is a self-contained working community with mentally handicapped adults, built on 400 acres of rolling farmland adjacent to the Shenandoah National Forest in the foothills of the Blue Ridge Mountains. Today it has residential and work facilities for about thirty handicapped adults and about half as many nonhandicapped coworkers and their children. It is a haven from the complexity and competitiveness of an urban society. But it offers enriching, dignified labor and life.

Villagers provide a substantial portion of their food from their dairy and beef herds, poultry, gardens, and orchards. In their workshop they produce safe, sturdy toys. In their weavery they produce purses, shawls, and scarves. And in their bakery they produce something that is almost as much of an American rarity as is Innisfree: good bread. These activities are commercially promising and will be more so when the village can afford to expand its facilities. For example, the bakery capacity will expand from 350 loaves per week to 1,500.

Innisfree is an example of how small private resources in the service of a private vision can produce a model for public policy.

Approximately 3 percent of American citizens are mentally retarded. When their families are considered, the problem of retardation can be said to directly affect upward of 20 million Americans. An undetermined but large number of mentally retarded or otherwise handicapped adults are living with elderly parents in an environment that may be oversheltered today, and may at any time be shattered by parents' deaths. Such parents are haunted by the lack of alternatives to the impoverished living environments of public institutions.

Hundreds of thousands of retarded citizens are in public institutions which offer only what is decorously called custodial care, which often means the warehousing of human beings. Often the warehousing is facilitated by the heavy, regular use of tranquilizing drugs—chemical straightjackets. Many of the retarded or otherwise handicapped could function in community environments like Innisfree, minimizing their handicaps and their cost to society.

The sublime physical setting of Innisfree—a small bear recently wandering in from the forest—is a temptation to romanticism. But such sentimentality would not be respectful of the strength of hand and soul required of the serene but unsentimental nonhandicapped people here. Their sinewy idealism causes them to shun distinctions—even salaries—that would put social distance between themselves and the villagers whose personhood they are here to affirm.

The usefulness of Innisfree as a model for public policy is limited only by this: Government money can purchase professional competence, and can increase society's supply of such competence. But the mysterious dedication that makes Innisfree a community is, like all love, mysterious: it is not a price-elastic commodity, expanding with the size of government appropriations.

Indeed, as the world becomes richer but more secular, handicapped people become more vulnerable. Money can build the large impersonal institutions that are limbos of cool neglect in affluent societies. But the humble cottages of an Innisfree are, like Chartres, manifestations of something like a religious vocation.

A society's ascent from barbarism can be measured, in part, by the care it shows for the defenseless, like mentally handicapped people. It also is true that societies are propelled upward, slowly, by the astonishing energies of moral pioneers operating in little platoons.

Innisfree is one of those little platoons, conquering the nation's inner frontier of caring, unsung except, in a sense, by William Butler Yeats, from whose poem the village took its name:

I will arise and go now, and go to Innisfree,
And build a small cabin there . . .
And I shall have some peace there,
    for peace comes dropping slow . . .
I will arise and go now, for always night and day . . .
While I stand on the roadway, or in the pavement's grey
I hear it in the deep heart's core.

P. A Training School for the Retarded

Even at a time when deinstitutionalization is a trend, it must be recognized that there is no viable alternative to residential facilities for many markedly retarded persons. Most families cannot cope with the manifold problems of care and training posed by the child with an I.Q. below 50, and in some cases above that level. Even if they have a high degree of patience and understanding, they would have to devote vast amounts of time and effort to such a child at great sacrifice to themselves and at the expense of their other children. But most important, they would rarely, if ever, possess the many specialized skills required to help this child develop maximum potential and live a satisfying and useful life.

The concept of the training school has been developed as a basic answer to the problem of the intellectually handicapped individual and the family. In its most advanced form it provides the retarded boy or girl with an opportunity to live in pleasant, homelike surroundings; to obtain medical and psychological care; to be fully evaluated in every area of personality, with emphasis on strengths rather than weaknesses; to enjoy a full social and recreational life; and to develop vocational or homemaking skills to the best of the individual's ability. As with other forms of rehabilitation, the training school approach is based on the coordinated efforts of an interdisciplinary team of professionals and aides trained especially for this manifold task.

In recognition of the need for special facilities, the Office of Mental Retardation of Connecticut has established ten regional centers and two training schools, which serve every area of the state. This article presents a profile of the Southbury Training School, which now has a residential population of 1,650, consisting of 5.8 percent borderline I.Q. or above, 12.4 percent mildly retarded, 20.6 percent moderately retarded, 23.3 percent severely retarded, and 37.9 percent profoundly retarded individuals. The objectives of the school, as stated by its superintendent, Frank R. Giliberty, are:

. . . to provide sheltering protection for retarded individuals; to provide an opportunity for them to grow physically, mentally, emotionally and socially to the full limits of growth; to restore and rehabilitate them both within their own limitations and the limitations of the knowledge and culture of their times; to train and educate them insofar as their capacities allow; and to permit them to live their lives whether in the institution or returned to the community with as much dignity, happiness and usefulness as is inherent in them.

The Southbury school is organized into five departments in addition to administrative, business, plant, and maintenance services required by an institution consisting of 138 buildings and 1,200 full-time employees. The Cottage Life Department is responsible for providing a warm, understanding home atmosphere in each of the thirty-nine cottages dotting the landscape of the school's 200 acres (80 hectares) of rolling, rural land. In the Boys' and Girls' Villages fourteen to fifty-two individuals live in each unit, and the units for the severely and profoundly retarded accommodate from twenty-two to sixty-six. All residents, boys, girls or adults, are grouped by age, developmental level, and personality. The cottages are decorated in Colonial style, and each has a kitchen, dining room, living room, playroom, and sleeping areas. As with all other facets of this facility, the accent is on education and training. The younger boys and girls are taught all phases of self-care, and all the residents learn to live in a group, accept direction, establish routine habits, and assume responsibility. The Cottage Life Department also works closely with the parents, who actively participate in the lives of their children through visits and cottage organizations. The child is not simply "put away" at Southbury.

The Medical Department is responsible for all phases of medical care, including maintenance of public health standards; preventive immunizations; reparative and rehabilitative procedures; medical, surgical, and dental therapy; and diagnostic procedures to determine the nature of the aberration responsible for the mental retardation. A well-equipped hospital is located on the grounds, and physicians make daily rounds in the cottages for the severely and profoundly retarded, after which they conduct a clinic. The department also conducts research and laboratory studies, and works closely with Yale Medical School, Yale – New Haven Hospital, and Waterbury Hospital, actively participating in intern and resident programs which train future physicians in the problems of the retarded.

The Education and Training Department designs, implements, and supervises individualized, meaningful programs for all residents. Formal classes are held in the Roselle School, centrally located on the grounds. Remedial instruction is available in all basic subjects. The recreation programs, comprising arts, crafts, and music, help all residents develop new interests, skills, and sources of enjoyment. The Activity and Sheltered Workshop buildings are focused on post – school age residents. The physical education program is geared not only to the health of all the children, but to the special needs of the physically handicapped. Programs have been developed for the neurologically impaired and the adult retarded, and deaf/blind classes and gestural language groups are conducted for individuals with these special needs. Emphasis is placed on the development of useful work attitudes and skills in the industrial arts classes, institutional service programs (maintenance, laundry, etc.), and the work training programs. These programs not only train residents for productive work, but help to bring the institution and the community together. A recent study showed that over $17,000 was earned in one year by residents in the Resident's Earning Program and off-campus work.

The Psychological Services Department serves not only the residents directly, but other departments concerned with child care and training. In particular cases it also serves parents of residents and parents of agencies seeking outpatient diagnostic evaluation. The specific functions of the department include psychological studies of the residents, a personal adjustment program, use of behavior modification techniques, a speech and hearing clinic, an outpatient clinic, research projects, and graduate and postgraduate training for students in the field. The department is also involved in the Neurologically Impaired Program, in which a psychologist is assigned to evaluate impairments and serve as consultant.

The Department of Education and Training has initiated a number of innovations. One is a successful Gestural Language Program, in which manual signs are used in conjunction with speech (simultaneous method). Members of this program are profoundly retarded or physically handicapped individuals who have serious communication problems. A second project is the development of the Functional Education Evaluation, which lists seventeen areas of functional skills organized according to developmental progression. An individualized curriculum is based on the student's performance on the evaluation. A third project is the Developmental Task List, used to assess severely and profoundly retarded residents, and to record slight but significant changes in feeding, dressing, language, etc., as they occur.

The Social Service Department maintains a liaison between the school and the home, and between the school and the community. Its specific functions include casework with residents and their families, placement counseling and supervision, discharge planning, and locating and supervising of boarding homes. A recent census indicated that 500 boys, girls, men, and women were on placement in the community, a large number of whom were self-supporting and working toward final discharge. An additional 64 were on placement in boarding homes of two types, private homes and extended-care facilities, under the supervision of the department. In working with the residents, the emphasis is on individual counseling, monitoring their progress, and working with other departments to help the individuals reach the full limits of their ability. In working with the family, one major objective is to help them recognize that residence at Southbury is dynamic, not static, and that movement through the total program of treatment, training, and social development may be necessary in order to achieve the best results. Another phase of the department's work is the training of future social workers. A Graduate Training Unit from the University of Connecticut School of Social Work has been in operation at Southbury since 1961.

Another major function of the school is to maintain a close working relationship with the parents of the residents and with the community at large. Its Home and School Association, consisting of parents and friends of residents, is affiliated with the Connecticut Association for Retarded Children. The fact that parents and friends live in nearby communities provides many opportunities for involvement in school activities. It also makes it possible to involve a large corps of volunteers who work on a one-to-one basis with cottage residents, helping them to feed, write letters, read, etc., and organizing parties and other recreational activities, knitting and cooking projects, sports events, a boutique which offers handmade items for sale, and an Adoption-by-Mail Program.

Q. Deinstitutionalization of Retarded Adults

By Saul S. Leshner and Sally A. Wells, in
Programs for the Handicapped, Office for Handicapped
Individuals, Washington, D.C., August 11, 1975

One day in 1968, a middle-aged woman left her efficiency apartment in Philadelphia, boarded a city bus, and rode to the electronics assembly plant where she worked. Few who witnessed this scene would have suspected that for 38 years, this woman had lived in an institution for the mentally retarded.

Until the 1960's, few believed the retarded had any possibilities for development. The traditional solution for those who were orphaned, abandoned, or unwanted was institutionalization and custodial care. Over 275,000 mentally retarded adults and children were in institutions across the country in 1960. Society was more than willing to pay a high price — $1¼ billion annually — not to be reminded of the retarded among them.

In 1964, the Elwyn Institute of Elwyn, Pennsylvania, challenged that tradition. Among its 1,100 inmates, who ranged in age from 7 to 90, some had been there almost 50 years. Many were capable of learning, as were over 60,000 of all the retarded housed in institutions.

Elwyn staff believed in growth for everyone. They devised a program through which clients of all abilities progressed according to performance. The easy tasks came first. Occupational therapy preceded assignment to the sheltered workshop; vocational training came before an outside job. Adult and community education courses taught the social skills which are not developed in the environment of institutional life.

The Elwyn method stressed concrete, practical, manual, and vocational skills. Since abstract and verbal ability had little relationship to success or adjustment, a learn-by-doing method replaced textbook instruction. Vocational training and work experience available within the institution were sufficient to prepare the retarded for success in community employment.

Elwyn Institute was transformed. The laundry, the kitchen, the grounds, and the maintenance department became job training sites. Clients in the Community Work Program, who held outside jobs, returned to Elwyn in the evening until they were used to the transition. If they had adjustment problems they would withdraw from work temporarily without jeopardizing apartment leases.

By 1968, 128 former "inmates" were living on their own in the community. They ranged in age from 20 to 55, had IQs from 50 to 80, and had been at Elwyn an average of 15 years, some as little as two years, and some as long as 49 years. All of the 65 who were contacted for a follow-up study after 6 months to 3 years in the community were well-adjusted. Ninety-five percent were employed and most had worked steadily. They were handling their jobs well, avoiding legal difficulties, and making friends. They rented apartments, paid their bills, and married. All were optimistic that they had the skills to remain independent.

But there were problems, too. Most were working at semi-skilled or unskilled jobs, earning around $3,000 a year. Budgeting was a problem. Tests measuring satisfaction with various aspects of community life indicated that the retarded were sensitive to their low socioeconomic position. Since lowered intellectual ability does not mean blind acceptance of low economic and prestige positions, it is extremely important that prestige rehabilitation workers instill realistic aspirations in the retarded client before he attempts the outside world.

A cohesive, therapeutic atmosphere helped transform Elwyn from a custodial institution to a rehabilitation facility, as did strong leadership and management support. Elwyn's federal funding ended in 1968, but the project's sound philosophy is basic to the Institute's continuing programs and research. All Elwyn clients now receive services toward independent living and the concepts of permanent care and a ceiling on development belong to the past. As proof of its commitment, Elwyn has invested in a new Vocational Rehabilitation Center. Here clients receive an array of services — from medical evaluation through speech therapy to vocational counseling, training, sheltered workshop experience, and job placement. A permanent half-way house has been established for Elwyn clients in Philadelphia.

The local community now sends over 400 retarded public school students to attend educational and vocational classes at Elwyn daily. Local colleges send special education majors for practicum experiences and graduate schools use Elwyn as a site for internship training.

The national network of institutions for the retarded has also been affected. Major institutions such as Horizon House in Philadelphia, and large service organizations such as the Veterans Administration have adopted the Elwyn method. A substantial number of agencies use Elwyn tests and evaluation instruments in their programs for deinstitutionalization of the retarded.

Professional training goes on almost daily at Elwyn. Professionals and students come from all over the United States and many foreign countries to attend Elwyn training programs and seminars.

Elwyn has produced several "tools of the trade" which are now in widespread use. Their three volume *Guide to the Community* is a simple learning test covering the ins and outs of the independent life, from renting an apartment and setting up a checking account to taking a bus or a cab.

The Elwyn method also works for the non-institutional client. Children and adolescents in need of special education and training in social skills can benefit from exposure to methods and staff who believe in rehabilitation and the ability of the retarded.

A program of Elwyn's scope and magnitude costs $50,000 to rehabilitate 30 clients. Compare this one-time cost to an annual cost of $216,000 for non-rehabilitative institutionalization of the same 30 clients. Or step outside the realm of cost-efficiency, and compare life in an institution to life outside. Which would you choose?

R. Foster Grandparent Program

By Jerry L. Smith (Administrative Officer of the State Home and Training School of Grand Junction, Colorado), in *Programs for the Handicapped,* Office for Handicapped Individuals, Washington, D.C., November 28, 1975

At 9:17 Monday through Friday, a shiny new 19 passenger bus pulls up in front of the house of Mary Werner of Grand Junction. Mary is one of a select group of 43 community members who participate in ACTION's Foster Grandparent Program.

Forty-three minutes later Mary's face breaks into a broad smile as she sees Mark, her foster grandson. Seeing the love in both faces, it is almost impossible to believe that this relationship has existed for only two years. Mark, confined to a wheelchair because of cerebral palsy, is a developmentally disabled child who lives at the State Home and Training School at Grand Junction, Colorado.

Mary and her 42 fellow foster grandparents became a part of the ACTION program for varied reasons. Most were senior citizens who felt they needed to add meaningful activity to their lives.

Many were of limited income and were first attracted by the small cash stipend provided low income participants. Four were former employees of the school who felt a need to return to the students with whom they had worked.

The Foster Grandparent Program was established in the mid 60's as a federal program with a dual nature. First, the program provides assistance to persons over the age of 60. This assistance goes far beyond the small stipend of $1.60 per hour paid low income participants. It draws the senior citizen out of his home and thrusts him back into the rumble tumble world of raising and caring for children. Not to be overlooked are the social ramifications of meeting and sharing concerns with new friends. The sharing of experiences while riding the bus to work, or while dining family style in the school cafeteria, do much to blast Grandma and Grandpa into a rejuvenated living style unmatched by their contemporaries. As the ACTION recruitment brochure claims, "This is retirement *to,* instead of a retirement *from* . . ."

Of equal importance to the program is providing children with special needs the love and affection more fortunate children enjoy with their natural families. When circumstances force families to be separated, younger children cannot receive the special affection and attention to which children are normally exposed. To these children a caring foster grandparent is a miracle almost beyond imagination.

Nonambulatory boys and girls suddenly have legs — their grandma pushing the wheelchair. Infants have laps on which to sit and be held. Lonely girls find they have a special friend with whom to hold hands. Older boys have an audience for their Crayola drawings. Time to stop and pay special attention to one of these children is the greatest resource the Foster Grandparent Program has at its disposal.

Foster Grandparents came to the State Home and Training School in the Fall of 1973. Community Social Services of Colorado West, a local nonprofit social services agency, holds the grant for the program. Currently all active participants are assigned to the State Home and Training School, a residential facility for developmentally disabled children and adults. Beginning with a "pilot" training class of five grandpas and grandmas the program has grown to its present scope.

Each new group of foster grandparents underwent an intensive forty hour training class to provide them with the skills and attitudes necessary for success. The major focus of the training program was to reorient the attitudes prospective grandparents had towards disabled children. Throughout the training period grandparents voiced their concerns over whether they "could make it." By the end of the two-week training class most of the apprehension and misinformation had been eliminated and the grandparent was ready to begin his relationship with his or her children.

Daily activities of foster grandparents vary. The abilities of the children vary greatly, and the grandparent must accommodate his planning to the skills his child possesses. [A grandmother and child] may visit the Foster Grandparent Center, a converted staff housing duplex, and complete a jig-saw puzzle. Other grandmas may take their nonambulatory or limited ambulatory students to the campus park for outdoor play. Always the maximum effort is to get the children out of the dormitories where they spend so much of their lives and into the world of varied experiences. Sitting or rolling on the grass becomes possible. Climbing a slippery slide with grandpa's help or using a swing become everyday accomplishments. Increased mobility and access to new experiences is perhaps the single greatest accomplishment the program can document. Not statistically provable, but nonetheless important, are the social and emotional changes a child may go through because he is developing a consistent long term affectional relationship with an adult who has a primary interest in his personal welfare and has daily contacts with him.

Once a week all foster grandparents return to the training center for "in-service" sessions. These classes vary in content from familiarization with the latest Social Security benefits to classes in sign language. Learning to "talk" after sixty can be a unique experience. It is also very rewarding to say "Hello, how are you?" to one of the deaf clients of the training school.

Although grandparents are assigned to individual students, they soon became the appropriated property of all campus residents regardless of chronological age. "Hello, Grandma" and "Hi, Grandpa" can be heard all over the campus as the bus arrives and the respective grandparents seek out their assigned children.

Grandparents spend 4½ hours a day on the campus, including a 30 minute lunch period, and are assigned to two children who can benefit from the program. They work with all levels of the school population from the lower functioning resident to the more capable. At the beginning of the program state staff members were concerned about the willingness and the ability of senior citizens to work effectively with severely physically and mentally handicapped children. Happily, foster grandparents have outperformed all expectations with children at all levels of functioning.

When asked to comment on the effect of the program, state staff reflected the view that grandparents were performing a vital role in providing the emotional and social support necessary for optimum growth and development of the residents. The fact that Grandma and Grandpa are appropriately "spoiling" their children is viewed as a positive factor rather than a negative one.

As the Foster Grandparent Program celebrates its tenth anniversary nationally and its second on the State Home campus, it is appropriate to remember the words of one State Home and Training School student who told his grandma, "You are the best thing that ever happened to me."

57

Rehabilitation Professions

Compiled by ROBERT M. GOLDENSON, Ph.D.

Currently an estimated 3.8 million men and women work in the health field, including approximately 350,000 physicians. Many of these individuals are directly involved with disabling disorders and the rehabilitation process, playing either key or auxiliary roles in a multidisciplinary approach. Although practically every medical and paramedical field may be called upon, the following professions and paraprofessions appear to be especially relevant. The qualifications for each field, as well as their contributions to the process of diagnosis, treatment, and rehabilitation, are outlined below, but their collaboration with other workers is indicated in the chapters on each disabling disorder in Part 2, in the illustrative cases presented in Chapter 55, and in the descriptions of rehabilitation facilities and services in Chapter 56.

A. Medical Specialists

Family physicians play a key role in the rehabilitation picture, since they usually serve as the first point of contact for the disabled patient, evaluate the total health needs, and refer the individual to appropriate specialists. Today twenty-two specialties are recognized by the American Medical Association, each requiring a hospital residency, after the internship, of two to four years' duration, followed by an examination for certification as a diplomate. They include anesthesiology, colon and rectal surgery, dermatology, family practice, general practice, general surgery, internal medicine, neurological surgery, neurology, obstetrics and gynecology, ophthalmology, orthopedic surgery, otolaryngology, pathology, pediatrics, physical medicine and rehabilitation, plastic surgery, preventive medicine and public health, psychiatry and neurology, radiology, thoracic surgery, and urology. Many subspecialties are also recognized, such as cardiology, occupational medicine, and geriatrics. Although every type of medical specialist may become involved in the treatment and rehabilitation of disabled individuals, the seven described below play especially important roles.

PHYSIATRIST*

The physiatrist is a specialist in physical medicine and rehabilitation with a basic understanding and training in various specialties: medicine, physiology, pathology, biochemistry, pharmacology, the behavioral and social sciences. This knowledge, combined with therapeutic aids such as drugs, exercise, and mechanical or motorized devices, is applied to bring patients to the best possible medical, physical, mental, social, and vocational condition. In the care of the patient, the physiatrist designs a comprehensive plan of treatment which is based on the special characteristics of the patient, and continually guards against secondary complications.

In the practice of medicine, some overlapping of content between specialties is inevitable. The rehabilitation specialist shares with other physicians the general skills and knowledge required of all medical practitioners. This doctor also has certain skills in common with several medical specialists, and like most medical specialists, patients are frequently referred by other physicians. The physiatrist may assume complete medical responsibility for general as well as special care, or may play a consultative role.

The physiatrist works very closely with various allied health professions such as physical and occupational therapy, rehabilitation nursing (visiting nurse), social service, psychology, speech pathology, vocational rehabilitation, and job placement. The functions of these individuals are performed on a delegated basis, for the ultimate responsibility of the patient care rests upon the shoulders of the physiatrist. Though not directly administering therapy, the physiatrist prescribes appropriate modalities of physical therapy, occupational therapy, activities of daily living, prevocational training, drivers' education, and psychosocial therapy, and truly directs the comprehensive rehabilitation of an individual. Within this context it is apparent that the primary aspect of human disability is a medical problem which demands that a well-trained physician plan and control the overall supervision and care of the patients.

*By Kamla Iyer, M.D., Institute of Rehabilitation Medicine, New York.

The most common disabling conditions referred by the nonsurgical specialties of internal medicine, neurology, pediatrics, rheumatology, and dermatology include patients with strokes, cerebral palsy, spina bifida, arthritis, multiple sclerosis, neuromuscular disorders, amyotrophic lateral sclerosis, peripheral vascular disease, pulmonary disease, cardiovascular disease, myelopathies, and radiculopathies. These referrals are usually made when the acute stage is well past, hence the diagnosis of the pathologic process has been established. The referral requires a diagnosis of the consequences of the medical condition, assessment of residual capacities, and the designing and implementing of a plan of restoration of function.

The surgical specialties such as general surgery, orthopedics, plastic surgery, and neurosurgery refer patients with such conditions as amputations, fractures, dislocations, burns, tumors, mutilating and deforming injuries, spinal cord traumas, postreconstructive surgery (tendons, nerves), and other diseases and insults to the central nervous system. The physiatrist outlines the goals and therapeutic regimen, including medical and psychosocial aspects of rehabilitation, as well as the use of prosthetics and orthotics and other assistive devices.

The physiatrist in turn frequently refers patients to other specialists—for example, the surgical specialist for restorative surgical procedures—whenever they are indicated to improve the function or capabilities of individual patients. For example, a posttraumatic quadriplegic patient (paralysis of all four extremities) who has regained some muscle power in the shoulder and arm muscles but is unable to use the hands because of lack of muscle power would be referred to a reconstructive surgeon for tendon transfers to restore function in the upper extremities. Subsequently this patient would require therapy or reeducation of the transferred muscles to achieve adequate and appropriate function and return to the supervision of a physiatrist.

In summary, a physiatrist serves in the role of a "medical manager" or "director" in which one evaluates, advises, and directs the total care of disabled persons and learns to exploit the ever-increasing knowledge and technology, as well as to utilize fully the services of a full array of experts.

After completing a year of rotating internship, the physician enters a residency training program in an approved rehabilitation center or department of physical medicine and rehabilitation of a hospital. Upon completion of three years of this postgraduate program, the candidate is eligible for the written examination (part 1) of the American Board of Physical Medicine and Rehabilitation. Following a subsequent interval of clinical experience, the physician may sit for the oral examination (part II) of the Board. The doctor may either work in the Department of Rehabilitation Medicine as a junior attending physician or engage in fellowship or instructorship in an academic rehabilitation program for the two-year period between parts I and II of the examination.

Certification as a diplomate in the specialty practice of physical medicine and rehabilitation follows successful completion of both parts of the board examination.

PSYCHIATRIST

Psychiatrists are physicians who specialize in the diagnosis, treatment, and prevention of mental and emotional disorders. Psychiatrists may engage primarily in private practice, but may at the same time act as consultant to a clinic, court, school for disturbed children, industrial concern, health department, or specialized rehabilitation center. On the other hand, they may be full-time members of the staff of a private or public mental hospital, psychiatric department of a general hospital, or community mental health center. In these facilities they function as the head of an interdisciplinary treatment and rehabilitation team, which includes clinical psychologists, psychiatric social workers, rehabilitation counselors, occupational therapists, and others. They supervise and integrate their activities through case conferences, and serve as an internal consultant when they encounter special problems with individual patients.

The psychiatrist is uniquely equipped to treat the entire range of mental and emotional illnesses, including psychoneuroses, character disorders, functional and organic psychoses, and both acute and chronic conditions. In a rehabilitation center the psychiatrist may make a special study of the effects of physical disability on the personality of the client, and may be involved in the community and public health aspects of mental disorder.

The psychiatrist is also uniquely equipped to conduct a full psychiatric examination; to formulate a comprehensive treatment plan for the severely disturbed; and to prescribe psychotropic drugs and apply other somatic treatments such as electroconvulsive therapy. In a growing number of settings his major role is becoming that of consultant with legal responsibility for treatment programs, which are carried out by psychologists and case managers; as one psychiatrist has phrased it, "In this community mental health center the psychiatrists are on tap, not on top."

NEUROLOGIST

The neurologist, or nerve specialist, diagnoses and treats organic diseases and disorders of the nervous system, such as epilepsy, multiple sclerosis, amyotrophic lateral sclerosis, Charcot-Marie-Tooth disease, the Guillain-Barré syndrome, polio, spinal cord injury, stroke, and Parkinson's disease. This doctor administers a general neurological examination, interprets cerebrospinal fluid tests as well as the electroencephalogram (EEG) and new CAT (computerized axial tomography), prescribes medications, and if also a neurosurgeon, performs surgery. (See CHAPTER 43: NEUROLOGICAL DISORDERS.)

719

ORTHOPEDIST

The orthopedist, or orthopedic surgeon, treats diseases and deformities of the spine, bones, joints, muscles, or other parts of the skeletal system through the use of medical, surgical, and physical therapy procedures. The disorders may be congenital or acquired from illness or injury, and include such disabling conditions as spinal curvature, clubfoot, hip dysplasia, foot drop, amputation, muscular dystrophy, osteoporosis, and arthritis. (See CHAPTER 45: ORTHOPEDIC DISORDERS.)

OPHTHALMOLOGIST

The ophthalmologist, or eye physician, diagnoses and treats diseases and injuries of the eyes, many of which may lead to chronic reduction or loss of sight requiring special rehabilitative measures. Among these disorders are cataract, glaucoma, detached retina, ophthalmia neonatorum, and retinitis pigmentosa. The eye specialist determines the nature and extent of the disorder, prescribes and administers appropriate medication, performs surgery such as corneal transplantation, executes a variety of tests to determine loss of vision, directs medical and rehabilitative procedures designed to improve sight or fully utilize remaining sight, writes prescriptions for corrective glasses or contact lenses, and may also instruct patients in eye exercises. (See CHAPTER 20: BLINDNESS AND VISUAL IMPAIRMENT.)

PATHOLOGIST

Pathologists investigate the nature, cause, and development of diseases, as well as structural and functional changes produced by all types of physical disorders. They are also specialists in diagnoses, basing their findings on laboratory procedures performed on body tissues, fluids, secretions, and other specimens which enable them to determine not only the presence but also the stage of disease. They frequently act as a consultant for other medical practitioners. In addition, they perform autopsies to determine the nature and extent of disease, the cause of death, and the effects of treatments which were administered.

RADIOLOGIST

Radiologists specialize in the use of x-rays and radioactive substances in diagnosis and therapy. They take x-ray pictures, or radiographs (or supervise technicians who take them), which they then use to reveal and evaluate such conditions as skull fracture, bone injury, malignant or nonmalignant tumors, or cardiac enlargement. In addition to reading x-rays, radiologists also use the radioactive isotopes as tracer agents which enable them to follow the action of medications and other substances on bodily organs, as well as the effects of different levels of radiation on the organism. Radioactive isotopes are also used in the treatment of carcinoma—for example, radioactive phosphate may help to control abnormal red cell proliferation (polycythemia) or white cell growth (leukemia); and radioactive iodine is used not only in the diagnosis of thyroid function but in the treatment of hyperthyroidism.

B. Nonmedical Specialists

REHABILITATION PSYCHOLOGIST*

Psychologists who devote time to rehabilitation typically consider themselves as primarily clinical, counseling, school, or academic psychologists. Rehabilitation is very often seen as a secondary identity with widely varying levels of interest and commitment. The field of rehabilitation psychology was oriented to physical restoration of lost functions for many years. In the mid-1940s, legislation for the first time included the mentally and emotionally handicapped among the potential clientele, but the full impact of change was not felt for some years. By the mid-1960s, millions of "disadvantaged" and "behaviorally disordered" had become high-priority clients so that the primary focus was no longer on restoration of lost functions, but on making up for massive behavioral deficits.

Since 1960, psychological and social factors have been increasingly emphasized. Mary Switzer, the first Commissioner of Vocational Rehabilitation, has pointed out that individuals' drive to avail themselves of agency services and to help accomplish their own rehabilitation must be awakened. Counseling must therefore focus on motivation and attitude. Along these lines, H. J. Mandl indicates in "Psychological Aspects of Disability and Rehabilitation" (1962) that frequently the task in aiding individuals' growth is to help them look at the here and now instead of what might have been or what they might have become. Effective rehabilitation depends on restricting the intrusion of ghosts of the past, getting disabled persons to deal with the actual limitations and freedoms associated with their impairment. Indeed, a classic text in this field (B. A. Wright, "Physical Disability: A Psychological Approach") discusses such aspects as inferior status position, salutary status position, frustration and uncertainty, value changes in acceptance of disability, development of the self-concept, grievances and gratifications in everyday relationships, attitudes toward persons with atypical psyche, and training in social skills.

---

*By Raymond A. Ehrle, Ed.D., Secretary, Division 22 (Rehabilitation Psychology), American Psychological Association.

Direct service in rehabilitation includes counseling in individual and group sessions, and consultation to obtain needed services and assessment. The rehabilitation psychologist is the preferred person to administer and interpret projective personality tests, but psychometrists trained at the Master's level should probably administer paper and pencil tests.

The psychologist's role in the rehabilitation center differs widely from agency to agency. Among possible functions are consultation to staff on a broader level, supervision of personnel, administration, training, and research. Some rehabilitation psychologists are also involved in behavior modification and biofeedback programs.

There are strong demands for both consumer involvement and involvement on the part of self-help groups. Client groups such as the blind and the parents of the mentally retarded have gained considerable sophistication in developing social action effort. Their success has led to the formation of other self-help groups. This has caused some role strain on the part of rehabilitation psychologists since they have been more evaluators than brokers. Problems of community participation have traditionally been perceived as the responsibility of the social worker or rehabilitation counselor.

In a 1970 article in *Rehabilitation Record*, S. C. DiMichael predicted that the emotionally disabled would increasingly outnumber the physically disabled as clients. This prediction seems to be coming true, particularly in consideration of state Office of Vocational Rehabilitation caseloads which indicate an increasing number of clients with emotional or behavioral deficits. He also felt that greater attention would be given to the seriously disabled; the 1974 federal legislation seems to support this prediction.

Most rehabilitation psychologists are employed by publicly funded agencies such as Veterans Administration hospitals, rehabilitation centers such as the Pennsylvania Rehabilitation Center, Regional Rehabilitation Research Institutes such as the one at the University of Florida, Rehabilitation Research and Training Centers, and university graduate training programs. Many others, however, are employed by teaching hospitals and private rehabilitation centers such as the Institute of Rehabilitation Medicine.

Most research and publication is either directly or indirectly supported through government funding and is carried out in cooperation with the employment sites outlined above. Studies are reported either in monograph form or in such journals as *Rehabilitation Psychology, Journal of Rehabilitation,* and *American Rehabilitation,* and occasionally in specialized journals on physical medicine, mental deficiency, or guidance.

In "Rehabilitation Psychology" (1971; edited by W. S. Neff), B. Kutner notes that areas of research which appear to be understudied include the attitude of the disabled toward the disabled and toward others, interpersonal relations of the disabled in the course of therapy, intrafamilial relationships, the origins of attitudes toward disability, and experimental attitude change especially in natural settings.

The National Rehabilitation Counseling Association, a division of the National Rehabilitation Association, was founded in 1958. This association is particularly likely to be chosen by persons employed by state Divisions of Vocational Rehabilitation. The American Rehabilitation Counseling Association was also established in 1958, and is a division of the American Personnel and Guidance Association. Its emphasis is on counseling, and its membership is predominantly from private rehabilitation agencies and academic settings.

Although the American Psychological Association was founded in 1892, the National Council on Psychological Aspects of Disability (now APA Division 22 — the Division of Rehabilitation Psychology) was not established until 1949. In 1970, membership in this division was nearly 1,000; however, as of this writing there are no more than 800 members. No one knows how many psychologists in rehabilitation are not members of Division 22; however, the division certainly constitutes the largest single interest group. About half of the division members are active in direct service programs in rehabilitation, 30 percent are primarily involved in academic activities, and about 10 percent are in research.

The current Division 22 platform defines Division 22 as:

> . . . an organization of psychologists having a common concern with problems of disability and deprivation, with the prevention of these problems, and with the rehabilitation process as a method for helping to deal with these problems. Division 22 members recognize that rehabilitation is a multi-disciplinary process which must be concerned with the interplay of physical, social, psychological, environmental and vocational factors. Division 22 has two general objectives with respect to its area of concern: to expand knowledge and understanding of the problems relating to disability and deprivation and to the rehabilitation process, and to seek solutions to these problems toward enriched lives for persons having such problems. To achieve these objectives, attention must be focused both on individuals and their environments.

Efforts are also being made to ensure the accreditation of training institutions and certification of individual working counselors. The Council of Rehabilitation Education (CORE) has spearheaded this effort. Division 22 is a constituent member, as well as appointees from ARCA, NRCA, the Council of State Administrators of Vocational Rehabilitation, the Council of Rehabilitation Counselor Educators, the Association of Rehabilitation Facilities, and a representative from a national consumer organization.

The Division of Rehabilitation Psychology has independently become involved in attempting to provide legislative input to the most recent rehabilitation legislation and has also attempted to work with such advocate groups as the Council for the Advancement of Psychological Professions and Services and the Association for the Advancement of Psychology.

SOCIAL WORKER

Two areas of social work are particularly relevant to the rehabilitation process: medical social work and psychiatric social work. Since these two fields have a common basis in personal and educational qualifications, these will be outlined before their special roles and functions are presented. But whether the social worker is primarily involved with patients affected by physical or psychiatric disorder, he or she is an integral and essential member of the rehabilitation team.

By profession and training, the social worker is a highly skilled specialist in helping individuals and families deal with personal problems that arise when they are faced with illness or disability — problems having to do with such areas as work, finances, living arrangements, social life, marriage, child care, and emotional reactions. Most of these problems are complex, and special personal qualifications, knowledge, and expertise are required to meet them.

The most important personal qualifications are warmth and empathy, interest and faith in people of all backgrounds and all types of personality, a capacity to consider all sides of human problems, sound judgment, and the ability to work as a member of a team. The knowledge and expertise can be acquired only through rigorous education and training. For both the medical and psychiatric social worker, a bachelor's degree must be granted by one of two hundred accredited colleges and universities in the United States and two in Canada which offer programs in social welfare. A master's degree can be obtained upon completion of a two-year program at one of seventy-three accredited colleges and universities in the United States and four in Canada, with one-third to one-half of the semester hours devoted to field instruction. A doctor's degree is available in twenty-three accredited colleges and universities in the United States and two in Canada, and is required for university teaching, policy formulation, and administration. In general, courses in the field cover five major areas: human behavior and the social environment, social welfare policy and services, techniques of social work, research, and field practice in service situations. The medical social worker usually takes specialized courses in the medical aspects of casework, and the psychiatric social worker takes specialized courses in mental illness and usually engages in field practice in a psychiatric center or hospital.

Medical social workers apply their knowledge and experience to helping the patient and family handle personal problems arising from severe or lengthy illness or disability. They recognize that a congenital or acquired disability may affect an individual's self-acceptance and self-image as well as relationships with other people; and a chronic illness may produce emotional, financial, and family problems that can retard recovery. In cases of disability, the social worker offers practical and psychological assistance in such areas as finding a job that will not be overtaxing, locating a suitable place to live, encouraging constructive helpful attitudes on the part of parents and other family members, making appointments for medical examinations or treatments, arranging for transportation to and from a doctor's office or service facility, checking to see whether the patient or client is taking medications or adhering to diet. Another extremely important area is contacting a homemaker, home health aide, or nursing service for the client. Social workers must also be fully acquainted with available facilities and service agencies which offer help in solving the manifold problems of the disabled: rehabilitation centers, health associations, hospitals, halfway houses, sheltered workshops, recreational facilities such as camps and bowling clubs, specialized educational institutions for such disorders as learning disability and mental retardation, and government organizations such as social service and the Office of Vocational Rehabilitation. They may also serve on committees which advocate new facilities or changes in existing services.

Medical social workers are generally employed in hospitals, clinics, rehabilitation centers, public health departments, military and veterans' hospitals, and voluntary health agencies for the blind, deaf, cerebral palsied, etc. They work closely with physiatrists, physicians, psychologists, rehabilitation counselors, and physical therapists. Psychiatric social workers, on the other hand, are employed primarily by mental hospitals, mental health centers and clinics, child guidance agencies, general hospitals with mental health departments, and rehabilitation organizations or hospitals for the retarded, epileptic, or persons afflicted with organic brain disorders. They are members of a team headed by a psychiatrist and consisting also of psychologists, psychiatric nurses, and occupational and recreational therapists. One of their major responsibilities is to interview the patient and family, and provide the psychiatrist with information about the patient's background and relationships, education, work experience, and social contacts, as well as immediate symptoms and attitudes, and events which might have precipitated the breakdown. Such information is of key importance to the psychiatrist in trying to understand the patient's illness and plan an effective treatment program.

Since the psychiatric patient may require months of treatment, it is also essential for the social worker to keep in touch with the family in order to help them understand the nature of the illness, and to enlist their cooperation in giving the patient the support needed during the process of treatment. The social worker also helps both the patient and family with special job or financial problems, as well as fears and worries which may impede recovery. As the patient improves and is about to be discharged, the psychiatric social worker paves the way for a smooth return to the family and community. This usually means providing practical assistance with problems involved in readjusting to the activities and demands of daily life outside the hospital, as well as difficulties encountered in returning to a job or finding a new one. The worker is also prepared to help the patient make new living arrangements, if necessary, and to advise on Medicaid and other public assistance.

REHABILITATION NURSE*

Rehabilitative nursing is goal-directed, personalized care that encompasses preventive, maintenance, and restorative aspects of nursing as a form of therapy. The rehabilitation-oriented nurse utilizes knowledge of the mechanisms of adaptation to impairment and skills as a nursing diagnostician in the evaluation of complex symptomatology before formulating a plan of nursing care based on a nursing assessment. This evaluation will need to be congruent with the multidiscipline team's assessment and plan of care. The nurse assesses the disabling effects of the disease process, the residual functions, and the potential for improved function of each patient. One needs to do this with perceptive insight into and involvement with the whole person within the environment in which the individual will be functioning.

The plan of care will need to include alternative means of helping a patient and family strengthen their physical, social, psychological, and vocational resources so they may effectively utilize residual capacities with which the patient must continue to live. For those patient losses which are irreversible, the nursing process and the patient's plan of care must concern itself with helping the patient to achieve optimal function at the highest possible level of adaptation. This implies the importance of planning for continuity of care that is rehabilitative in nature through all the phases of a patient's illness.

Rehabilitation nursing is nursing with an awareness of the patient's tomorrows, and the relationship between what does and does not happen today and the tomorrows that follow. It is a moving, ever-changing process led forward by the patient's development, interest, and ability to achieve newer and higher goals. The patient's active participation in the personal care program is a key theme in rehabilitation.

The nurse who is rehabilitation-oriented is primarily a therapist who understands and uses a great variety of therapeutic tools or measures in the care of patients. The basic skills and the know-how for carrying out the rehabilitative aspects of nursing should be the armamentarium of every nurse. However, it cannot be expected that every nurse is a rehabilitation nurse. The rehabilitation nurse is a specialist who through intensive theory and practice courses, as well as experiences, has gained expertise in rehabilitation. The elements of rehabilitative nursing need to be viewed as part of basic nursing. They are those factors that should be considered during the acute and intermediate phase of any patient's illness so as to

---

*By Lena M. Plaisted, R.N., P.T., M.S., Professor Emeritus, Boston University, and former chairperson of the Graduate Program in Rehabilitation Nursing. Condensed from an article requested by the American Nurses' Association and available for publication.

maintain health and prevent complications, such as pressure sores, or the development of dysfunction which may later require intensive rehabilitation services.

The concepts of rehabilitative nursing should be applied to patients regardless of their pathology or residence; for example, the acute patient in intensive or coronary care units, the diabetic patient, the patient on kidney dialysis, the patient with respiratory or cardiovascular disease, as well as the patient with a stroke placed in various intermediate care units in general hospitals or in a long-term care facility, a nursing home, or rehabilitation setting, or receiving services at home or at an ambulatory care unit. Of equal concern is the rehabilitative nursing care of surgical patients, such as those having an amputation, a mastectomy, an ileostomy or colostomy, to mention only a few. Patients with orthopedic, neurological, or neurosurgical conditions are of special concern to the rehabilitative-oriented nurse because of the complexity of these patients' residual problems which necessitates their learning to do as much as possible for themselves but with an altered life-style.

More specifically, rehabilitation nurses help the patient maintain proper positioning of body parts and apply their knowledge of anatomy, physiology, and functioning as they plan for individualized protection of joints either to prevent joint stiffness and contracture or to encourage a desirable functioning position. They help bed patients maintain mobility and teach them to utilize unimpaired extremities or mechanical supports to assist in moving. They encourage active exercise of uninvolved extremities and the trunk so that musculature remains strong during bedrest or immobilization, in order that patients who will need aids in transfer or ambulation can perform. For those patients unable to assist in position change, they know how to move patients manually or by mechanical lifts in a manner that will prevent trauma. They are also alert to the importance of assisting patients to maintain continency of bladder and bowel. For patients with aphasia or communication problems they will need to grossly assess if the patient has a problem of expression (speaking and writing) or reception (understanding of speech or writing). If the patient experiences pain and discomfort, they must be aware that relief can be gained from psychological support as well as physical measures, and that medication is not always necessary. And since the basis of the functional ability of all organs is use, they must be aware not only of the disuse phenomena possible for each body system, but more importantly, the effect of a dysfunction in one system on all other systems.

One may ask how a nurse can carry out these activities that have been emphasized along with other life-saving responsibilities for acutely ill patients. It is not an easy task, and priorities within the nursing care needs of patients must be established. How well each nursing team member's abilities are assessed and matched with the patient's nursing needs will make a difference in the patient's progress in rehabilitation. The nurse who is knowledgeable in rehabilitation is able to make use of the know-how that should be available from other disciplines on the health team. The importance in this instance is that the know-how be translated into *nursing action*.

Nursing must therefore play an active part in the total rehabilitation program. Someone on the nursing team must be responsible for assessing each patient's nursing needs and developing a nursing plan of care. Someone in nursing must be designated as a resource to the patient—a patient's advocate. This would be the person with whom other nursing team members, as well as other health workers, including the physicians, would communicate about a patient's progress. This would be the one who in concert with others would plan therapeutic nursing and modify the strategies based on the patient's behavior and feedback from other team members. This nurse would implement the plan of care if it called for special skills which other nursing team members did not have; otherwise the nurse would direct their activities.

A myriad of levels of nursing practice have emerged over the last twenty years. Nursing assistants, nurse aides, and home health aides are usually taught in on-the-job training programs in the institutions and agencies that employ them. Licensed practical or vocational nurses are trained in hospital or in public school vocational programs, which vary in length, content, and quality; most last about one year and include didactic and clinical instruction. There are currently three types of educational programs preparing registered nurses, and they vary in scope, depth, and length of curricula. These are diploma programs in hospital schools of nursing, associate degree programs in junior colleges, and baccalaureate generic programs in colleges and universities. A new nursing role, clinical specialist in rehabilitation, has come into being. This title is usually applied to a nurse who has had graduate education at the master's level in rehabilitation nursing. Increasing numbers of nurses are also receiving doctoral preparation. The primary focus of this program is on research, which should have impact on the improvement of nursing practice.

Although there are many levels of nursing care, and many levels of preparation, they all share in one urgent need today—the need for greater knowledge and skill in the field of rehabilitation.

REHABILITATION COUNSELOR

The rehabilitation counselor is a professional worker who is specially trained and equipped to evaluate and guide physically, mentally, and emotionally handicapped individuals in all major phases of the rehabilitation process. These phases include not only vocational rehabilitation, which has historically received the greatest amount of attention, but also such areas as special training and education, social and personal adjustment, government benefits, community facilities, opportunities for recreation, and activities and devices which contribute to independent living.

The rehabilitation counselor does not carry out these manifold functions in isolation; rather, the counselor is usually a key member of a rehabilitation team which may include physicians, psychiatrists, psychologists, social workers, nurses, physical and occupational therapists, recreation specialists, specialized teachers, and volunteers. The counselor's major task is to identify the special needs of a particular disabled individual, to help the person understand why specific types of assistance are needed, and to coordinate the various services into a well-planned program aimed at helping one overcome the disability, make the most of capacities and opportunities, and in general lead a more satisfying life.

The rehabilitation counseling field has been rapidly expanding ever since Congress passed the first Vocational Rehabilitation Act in 1920. In 1943 this act was broadened to include not only the physically disabled but the mentally ill and mentally retarded. In 1968 Congress authorized substantial increases in aid to states for vocational rehabilitation, and as a consequence many of the states were able to double or even quadruple their staffs. An estimated 20 percent of the counselors are women, some of whom are young college graduates and others housewives with grown children. An important feature of this field is that it offers a job opportunity to many disabled people themselves, who have the advantage of personal insight into the needs of the handicapped.

A survey conducted in 1965 indicated that approximately 2,700 out of a total of 3,600 rehabilitation counselors were employed by state and local vocational rehabilitation agencies, and an additional 350 worked in offices of the Veterans Administration. The rest were employed in rehabilitation centers, hospitals, clinics, insurance companies, labor unions, training schools, courts, prisons, and sheltered workshops run by private agencies. Although they must be equipped to counsel all types of disabled people, including the multihandicapped, many counselors specialize in one group, such as the blind, deaf, epileptic, mentally retarded, mentally ill, or cerebral palsied. In 1965 Congress amended the Vocational Rehabilitation Act to make socially handicapped persons eligible for rehabilitation. As a result, a growing number of counselors hold positions in agencies which deal with drug addicts, alcoholics, school dropouts, prison inmates, and the poverty stricken.

The National Rehabilitation Counseling Association lists the following major "specifications": a basic understanding of human behavior and ways of reaching people; an awareness of the medical and psychological aspects of disabilities; a fund of knowledge about occupational and vocational opportunities; broad information on community resources for the handicapped; thorough awareness of the rehabilitation philosophy and program; a belief in the client's capacity for self-improvement and self-development; ability to communicate with individuals who may be socially inhibited or who may lack verbal skills; ability to relate to all kinds of people; sensitivity to persons with many types of handicaps, and ability to perceive their needs; a high capacity for empathy; ability to keep personal problems from interfering with the client's rehabilitation; objectivity in appraising the client's strengths, weaknesses, and problems; patience and perseverance. Other important qualities, some of which are implicit in the above, are a deep interest in helping other people; acceptance of the client no matter what the limitations or personal characteristics; an ability to maintain and impart enthusiasm; a capacity for imagination and resourcefulness in helping the client overcome obstacles.

The essential preparation for rehabilitation counseling is carried out on a graduate level, although a few colleges offer courses which may lead to introductory positions such as employment interviewer or counselor trainee. The graduate program usually requires an undergraduate major in any of the social science fields, but in some cases appropriate experience gained in industry or in work related to rehabilitation counseling may be accepted in lieu of academic preparation.

Over fifty colleges and universities now provide appropriate graduate preparation, usually with partial financial assistance from the Social and Rehabilitation Services Administration. Most of these institutions offer two-year programs leading to a master's degree, or a certificate in rehabilitation counseling if the student already holds a master's degree in a related field. The graduate program is generally offered in either the education or psychology department, and derives its content from a variety of disciplines, including sociology, psychology, medicine, education, human growth and development, and guidance and counseling.

SPECIAL EDUCATOR

A special educator (also known as a teacher of the handicapped, or a teacher of special or exceptional children) is trained to serve as a teacher of children with either unusually high intellectual potential or children who are handicapped by emotional illness, specific learning disabilities, or pervasive mental retardation. The latter three categories are particularly relevant to the process of rehabilitation, in which the special educator frequently plays an essential role. The reason is that the disabled child's self-image, acceptance by peers, emotional stability, ability to communicate with others, and potential for employment all depend heavily on academic progress.

Most special educators organize and conduct programs for the handicapped in regular schools or in developmental centers for children with special disabilities, such as blindness, deafness, or cerebral palsy. Others function in hospital settings, and some teach children at home or in private practice. Most of their work is carried out on an elementary or secondary grade level, and includes teaching academic subjects, selecting or devising special instructional materials and aids, and planning extracurricular programs designed to broaden the children's interests and experience.

Preparation for this profession includes all standard courses offered by college departments of education, plus special courses in such subjects as the psychology of the exceptional child, behavior problems, tests and evaluations, mental retardation, learning disorders, and techniques and materials involved in teaching handicapped children. Many candidates specialize in particular disorders such as blindness, deafness, impaired speech, or minimal brain dysfunction. Most of these courses are taken on a graduate level, and most positions require a master's degree as well as a practicum in special classes, or a developmental school or other center for the handicapped. A Ph.D. degree is often required for a position as director or administrator of a center with a comprehensive program. Fortunately, considerable financial assistance is available for scholarships, fellowships, and traineeships. Grants totaling $30 million were provided by the U.S. Office of Education for the 1970 – 1971 academic year, and substantial aid was available from private sources as well. (For information, write to the Bureau of Education of the Handicapped, Box 1492, Washington, DC 20013).

More than 7 million school- and preschool-age children have been identified as needing special education, not to mention those whose needs remain undetected. The need for special educators is correspondingly great, both in terms of the personal adjustment of these children and the interests of society. Many of them can be saved from institutional life with its often unfortunate effects for both the child and family. Also, the cost of institutional care for a retarded child is more than seven times as much as the cost of a public school education, and a nonpublic school program for a deaf child is just as expensive. Beyond these dollar savings is the even more important fact that children who have been helped to overcome a handicap, even if incompletely, can become contributing citizens and an asset to society as well as themselves.

SPEECH PATHOLOGIST AND AUDIOLOGIST

Speech pathology and audiology will be considered together because the American Speech and Hearing Association, the basic organization in the field, views them as different aspects of a single area. The Association, however, recognizes that "some workers concern themselves primarily with speech disorders or with hearing disorders; nevertheless, speech and hearing are so interrelated that professional competence requires familiarity with both." The reason for this integral relationship is that both fields are concerned with problems and disorders of human communication in both children and adults. The child with a communication disorder, such as deafness or dysarthria, may encounter overwhelming obstacles to learning and may find it difficult to establish satisfying relationships with other children. The adult who acquires a speech or hearing disorder may find it hard to earn a living, and may also develop a negative self-image and withdraw from his friends and community life. These effects are so important, and so complex, that a single integrated profession is required to deal with them.

Despite the overriding importance of communication in human

life, professional identity did not emerge until the 1920s, when speech and hearing services were first offered in public school systems and universities began to offer clinical and research programs in the field. During World War II the profession was further advanced by military rehabilitation programs designed to retrain servicemen who suffered speech and language impairments or hearing problems resulting from head wounds or exposure to blasts. Since that time, specialists in electronics have created new instruments and techniques for research and treatment. As a result of these advances and wider recognition of the field of rehabilitation as a whole, there are today at least ten times as many speech pathologists and audiologists as at the end of World War II. Yet in spite of this steep increase, over four times the number of available clinicians would be required to meet the needs of the 8 million individuals with speech and hearing problems in the United States alone.

In the field of rehabilitation the speech pathologist–audiologist functions in a variety of settings. These include (a) medical rehabilitation facilities, which assist patients in overcoming physical handicaps resulting from birth defect, illness, or injury; (b) vocational rehabilitation centers, which prepare the disabled for productive employment; (c) specialized community speech and hearing centers, devoted exclusively to children and adults with problems of speech, learning, or hearing; (d) hospitals, where this specialist is a member of departments of otolaryngology (ear, nose and throat), pediatrics, neurology, physical medicine and rehabilitation, or where this specialist is a member of a separate speech and hearing clinic; (e) public school systems (with visits once or twice a week to each school), and special schools for handicapped children; (f) health departments, with special emphasis on hearing conservation programs in schools, though preschool children and senior citizens may also be served. In addition, hearing conservation programs are conducted by audiologists in many industries, and a number of colleges and universities conduct speech and hearing clinics and research centers in the field. A growing number are also engaging in private practice on a full- or part-time basis, while others are active in special research centers dealing with the physiology of the ear and speech organs, electronics, psychology, communication, and space medicine.

In general, most speech pathologists and audiologists concentrate on at least two of the following activities: clinical work, research, teaching, administration. A hospital worker may, for example, administer a variety of tests to determine hearing level, the site of damage to the auditory system, the amount of social disability resulting from hearing loss, and the need for a hearing aid or special training. Another specialist, working in five schools, identifies children with speech and hearing problems, works with teachers, and counsels parents on methods of overcoming these difficulties, and may also work with individual children or groups of children on the more severe problems resulting from such conditions as cleft palate or extreme hearing loss. Still another may serve in a rehabilitation division of a county hospital, helping to retrain patients with losses in language usage or speech production following stroke, head injury, or cancer surgery, or speech and hearing disorders associated with cerebral palsy or other congenital defects.

Personal qualifications for this growing field include such characteristics as emotional stability, sensitivity, and warmth, intellectual curiosity, a scientific attitude, and the ability to interact constructively with disabled individuals. High academic ability is also essential, since the profession requires a master's degree, and many members go on to the Ph.D. On the high school level, courses in biology, physiology, physics, and mathematics are particularly relevant, and on a college level, advanced courses in these subjects should be taken, plus anatomy, child and adolescent psychology, sociology, and possibly anthropology. Undergraduate courses in speech pathology and audiology specifically may also be available, as well as special work in such areas as linguistics, semantics, and phonetics. Graduate degrees may be offered by schools of arts and sciences, speech, education, or medicine, with courses covering such areas as anatomy, physiology, acoustics, psychological aspects of communication, speech and hearing disorders, measurement and evaluation of speech production, language ability and auditory processes, clinical treatment of children and adults, and research methodology. The American Speech and Hearing Association awards a certificate attesting to professional qualifications, and special credentials are also issued by state departments of education to individuals working in public school programs. Many scholarships, fellowships, and assistantships are available.

OPTOMETRIST*

Optometry as a profession is concerned with the problems of human vision. Optometrists examine the eyes and related structures to determine the presence of vision problems, eye diseases, or other abnormalities. They prescribe and adapt lenses or other optical aids and may use visual training (orthoptics), when indicated, to preserve or restore maximum efficiency of vision.

In recent years electrodiagnostic techniques have been developed in the laboratory which have become an invaluable adjunct to the delivery of vision health care services to the public. These procedures do not replace traditional methods but provide additional support in gaining a much clearer concept of the patient's visual abilities and disabilities. They include: (a) electroretinography, or ERG: recording of light-evoked electrical activity originating in the retina; (b) electro-oculography, or EOG: the recording of changes in the resting potential of the eye which are initiated by predetermined movements of the eye(s): (c) visual evoked response, or VER: recording of electrical cortical activity from the visual cortex

*By Leo A. Roman, O.D., formerly Clinical Program Coordinator, American Optometric Association.

initiated by various visual stimuli and computer-averaged over time; (d) dark adaptometry, which allows the optometrist to evaluate the night vision performance of the patient; and (e) visual fields: a perimeter which allows static and dynamic visual fields is used to examine the patient's visual field with precision.

A license for the practice of optometry is required in all fifty states. Requirements include graduation from an accredited school or college of optometry and passing an examination on theoretical and clinical subjects. These procedures are administered in each state by a legally constituted board of optometry. There is also a National Board of Examiners in Optometry, passage of whose examinations is accepted by thirty-four states in lieu of the written theoretical part of the state examination.

Early university programs in optometry were in departments of physics, but the curricula of the schools of optometry have moved steadily away from physics, though not abandoning it, for the past forty years and toward psychology, physiology, biology, and medicine. The length of preparation has increased from one or two years to a minimum of six years of collegiate training: two years of preprofessional prerequisites and a four-year professional curriculum. Internship is included in the degree program, and graduates, all of whom receive the doctor of optometry (O.D.) degree, are prepared to take the state board and National Board examinations and practice their profession.

There are currently twelve schools or colleges of optometry in the United States: seven are in universities, while five are independent nonprofit institutions. All are accredited by the Council on Optometric Education, an affiliate of the National Commission on Accrediting.

Optometrists are primarily concerned with human visual performance, its maintenance and enhancement. As primary providers, they are trained to recognize general health problems through detection of ocular disease (such as cataract or glaucoma) and ocular manifestations of systemic disease (such as hypertension, arteriosclerosis, diabetes, or renal disease) and refer such patients to appropriate professionals. This decision is made on the basis of examination of the physical, physiological, and functional aspects of the eyes and the visual system (ophthalmoscopy, biomicroscopy, tonometry, visual fields, visual acuity, binocular coordination and neurological evaluation, etc.) as well as a comprehensive visual health history.

The treatment methods employed by optometrists are primarily related to enhancing visual performance. Optometrists employ spectacle lenses, contact lenses, low vision aids, vision therapy, and perceptual training procedures as appropriate. Some optometrists have specialized in the visual perceptual problems of children, others in the visual efficiency and eye safety requirements in industry and motor vehicle operation, still others in the visual care and functional restoration of the partially sighted, and some in the visual problems of the geriatric patient. The nature of optometric education is such that all graduates are prepared to render basic services in all these specialty areas.

Epidemiological studies indicate that vision problems have the lowest frequency and severity rates at about five years of age and increase regularly with age, with an increasing percentage of the aging population requiring attention. Fortunately the treatment procedures of optometrists, while not eliminating or "curing" chronic conditions, can largely compensate for the deleterious effects and restore function.

Finally, optometrists perform a preventive function: prevention of blindness through the early detection of potentially blinding conditions and prevention of behavioral decrements through restoration or maintenance of visual function.

RECREATION SPECIALIST (THERAPEUTIC)

Therapeutic recreation is a specialized field within the recreation profession. The specialist (also called hospital recreation director, recreation instructor, or adjunctive therapist) plans and directs recreational activities for patients recovering from physical and mental illness or coping with a temporary or permanent disability. He or she works as a member of a treatment or rehabilitation team in a hospital, health agency, mental institution, nursing home, or facility for the retarded.

Recreational therapy is based on the concept that the enjoyable use of leisure time can contribute to both the mental and physical well-being of the disabled by keeping them occupied constructively, by restoring their self-confidence, by encouraging group participation and interaction, and by enabling them to develop avocational interests which will permanently enrich their lives. The therapist must therefore have strong leadership qualities, versatility, understanding, patience, and the ability to maintain congenial relationships with patients of different ages and backgrounds.

Preparation for this allied health profession must not only stimulate insight into the personality needs of the sick and disabled, but provide a thoroughgoing acquaintance with a wide variety of activities such as games, sports, camping, nature study, arts, crafts, and other hobbies. High school and college courses in physical education, arts, dramatics, public speaking, as well as involvement in music, sports, clubs and other group activities, are especially important. A bachelor's degree from an accredited college offering an approved program in recreation therapy is considered the minimum level of preparation for professional service in the health and hospital field. A master's degree with a major or special emphasis on therapeutic recreation is considered the optimal level of preparation for executive positions involving administration, teaching, research, and the conduct of training programs. An associate degree or certificate in therapeutic recreation from an accredited junior or community college may meet requirements for therapeutic recreation aide or assistant. A position of this type involves limited responsibility for programming and may focus on specific activities, such as athletics, drama, music, or arts and crafts. A list of colleges offering courses in therapeutic recreation can be obtained from the National Therapeutic Recreation Society. (For the address of this organization and others in the field, see PART 4, SECTION 2: VOLUNTARY ORGANIZATIONS. See also CHAPTER 14: RECREATION FOR THE DISABLED; CHAPTER 56: REHABILITATION FACILITIES AND SERVICES, E. Recreation Center.)

CORRECTIVE THERAPIST

Corrective therapy (also called adapted physical education) is the application of medically prescribed therapeutic exercises and physical education activities in the treatment of the mentally or physically ill patient. Administered under a physician's guidance, the conditioning exercises are used to develop such capacities as strength, coordination, and agility according to the individual patient's needs. Similarly, the physical education activities are geared to treat the specific disabilities. Both types of procedures are used not only to improve the patient's physical condition, but to maintain morale, restore self-confidence, and stimulate resocialization.

Corrective therapy became a separate discipline during World War II when physical reconditioning units were established in army hospitals to combat the harmful effects of prolonged bedrest and shorten the hospital stay. Pioneers in the movement were Surgeon General Norman T. Kirk and Dr. Howard Rusk. During the past thirty years a broad spectrum of procedures has been developed, including postural exercises, mat exercises, therapeutic swimming, gravity exercises, orthopedic exercises, stump strengthening, gait training, and elevation techniques. Other forms of treatment include functional ambulation, self-care training, and specific exercises for the paraplegic, blind, arthritic, amputee, cardiac patient, stroke victim, and the aged. Treatment may take place in a bed, at bedside, in a chair or wheelchair, on a ramp or stairway, in a swimming pool, or on an exercise table. In addition, corrective therapists may also give driving lessons in specially equipped automobiles; guide the blind in the initial stages of training for independent moving and travel; and train patients in the use of braces, artificial limbs, and other devices.

Today corrective therapists are active members of the treatment team in public and private rehabilitation centers, Veterans Administration hospitals, nursing homes, mental institutions, and centers for cerebral palsy, arthritis, and other disabling disorders. Those who specialize in adapted physical exercise concentrate on sports and games, and are more likely to work in schools, camps, and colleges than in hospitals. However, the two fields are closely allied and use the same tools, techniques, and methods. Candidates for examination for certification by the American Board of Certified Corrective Therapists must have completed an approved four-year curriculum leading to a bachelor's degree in physical education. A fifth year, including 400 hours of clinical experience, under the supervision of a certified corrective therapist, is required for specialization in corrective therapy. Advanced degrees are available from some higher institutions. For information on colleges offering courses in the field and on available scholarships, contact the American Corrective Therapy Association, Veterans Administration Hospital, 1030 Jefferson Avenue, Memphis, TN 38104.

PHYSICAL THERAPIST

The physical therapist plays an essential role in the rehabilitation of the physically disabled, and is responsible for evaluation of physical capacities and limitations, and for administering treatments designed to alleviate pain, correct or minimize deformity, increase strength and mobility, and improve general health. The treatment program is planned on the basis of test findings, and is implemented in collaboration with a physician with whom continuous contact is maintained. In addition, the physical therapist helps to motivate and instruct the patient, family, and others who may be of assistance in carrying out the treatment and rehabilitation program.

The following is a sampling of specific activities for which the physical therapist has primary responsibility: planning and supervision of individualized treatment programs; application of testing and evaluation procedures; recording and reporting results of these procedures; evaluating orthotic and prosthetic devices; making a gait analysis; supervising or carrying out a predetermined exercise program; development of ambulation and elevation skills; training in the use of braces, crutches, prostheses, and other assistive and supportive devices; application of specialized treatment procedures, such as hot and cold packs, paraffin, moist air, infrared, diathermy, ultrasound, ultraviolet, massage, traction, vascular apparatus, and electrodiagnosis and treatment; application of specified hydrotherapy treatment, such as whirlpool, Hubbard tank, contrast baths, and therapeutic pool.

At present over 30,000 men and women function as physical therapists, and the demand is expected to exceed the supply for years to come. They hold positions in a wide variety of settings, including departments of physical therapy in general and specialized hospitals, schools for crippled children, clinics, rehabilitation centers, physicians' or physical therapists' offices, hospitals and nursing homes for the chronically ill or disabled, the Armed Forces, the U.S. Public Health Service, research centers, universities offering educational programs for professional physical therapy, junior colleges offering physical therapist assistant programs, and a growing number of industrial firms.

Since the physical therapist works with disabled persons who may become anxious or discouraged, he or she must therefore have a basic interest in helping others and be able to maintain a cheerful, pleasant, and accepting attitude. In addition, the profession requires physical stamina, manual dexterity, and the patience required to work toward long-range goals even when progress is slow.

The practice of physical therapy is regulated by fifty states, the District of Columbia, Puerto Rico, and the Virgin Islands, all of which require a license or registration on the basis of state examinations and other legal requirements, the details of which may be obtained from the Board of Medical Examiners of the state in question. Seventy-six colleges and universities offer fully accredited educational programs for this profession. They generally require at least four years of study, including the equivalent of two or three years of study in the humanities and social studies, biological sciences, and physical sciences; specialization courses in the knowledge and skills required to treat patients; and supervised clinical practice in a hospital or other treatment center. A certificate program, which usually takes twelve to sixteen months, may be available for students who already hold a bachelor's degree in a major other than physical therapy, and is considered equivalent to the bachelor's degree in physical therapy. The master's degree program leading to qualification in physical therapy requires a bachelor's degree for admission and usually takes two years to complete. Master's degree programs for qualified physical therapists are usually one year in length. A list of approved schools may be obtained from the American Physical Therapy Association.

The physical therapist assistant works with the physical therapist in treatment programs and related activities performed by a physical therapy service. Thus far only seventeen states require a license or registration, but others will be added in the near future. A growing number of junior and community colleges offer two-year programs toward an associate degree in physical therapy. The course of study includes biology, physical and social sciences, the humanities, and a physical therapy technical course as well as clinical experience.

The physical therapy aide is a nonlicensed worker at least eighteen years of age who has completed an on-the-job training program and has received special instruction offered by a local hospital, approved home health agency, public vocational school, or approved rehabilitation center. Working under the supervision of a professionally qualified physical therapist, the aide performs designated routine tasks and patient-related activities. These tasks vary from institution to institution, but usually include maintenance of equipment and supplies; transporting patients, records, equipment, and supplies; supervised clerical work; assistance in preparing patients for treatment; assembling and disassembling equipment; assisting patients in activities related to the development of strength and endurance; and performing selected treatment procedures under supervision.

Scholarships and loans are available from many colleges and universities offering a physical therapy program. During the final year, outstanding students may be eligible for a McMillan Scholarship, which is administered by the American Physical Therapy Association through the directors of physical therapy at educational institutions. Many traineeships for juniors, seniors, and certificate students are available from the Rehabilitation Services Administration, U.S. Department of Health, Education and Welfare. In addition, the Association has compiled a list of private sources of financial assistance limited to special groups, and a list of local sources which are usually limited to state residents.

The American Physical Therapy Association, the professional organization, located at 1156 15th Street N.W., Washington, DC 20005, has enrolled approximately 25,000 members in fifty-three chapters. Its many-sided program includes publication of the monthly journal *Physical Therapy;* assistance in accreditation of physical therapy educational programs; administration of the McMillan scholarship program; a placement service for recent graduates through the Association's chapters; assistance to foreign physical therapists in the United States; and distribution of monographs, reprints, career-related publications, video tapes, and films on the field.

OCCUPATIONAL THERAPIST*

Occupational therapy is a health profession whose primary purpose is assisting individuals to achieve or maintain their capacities to function in daily living activities at a level which allows as much independence as possible.

Occupation here refers to those activities and tasks which each individual must perform as determined by age and role in the family and community, including self-care activities (eating, dressing, personal hygiene, grooming, and handling objects), work activities (related to school, home management, and employment), and play/leisure (games, sports, hobbies , and social activities).

Because all activities in daily life require, to some degree or other, the ability to use one's body (motor and sensory-integrative functioning), to think, understand, and learn (cognitive functioning), and to relate to others in an appropriate way (psychological and social functioning), the occupational therapist must have knowledge and understanding of these components of functioning and how they are involved in the performance of daily life tasks. Thus the therapist must be able to analyze daily living performance tasks and determine what is required to successfully carry out these tasks.

The inability of the individual to perform is of concern to occupational therapy. There are many reasons why a person may have performance problems: one may have suffered from an accident or

*By Madelaine Gray, O.T.R., American Occupational Therapy Association, 6000 Executive Boulevard, Rockville, MD 20852.

injury, disease, or emotional illness, or may be delayed in development because of deprivation or congenital deficits or defects.

In those instances in which the problem appears to be due to lack of experience or failure to develop in a particular component of functioning, such as motor skills, the occupational therapist will use activities in assisting the individual to develop skill functions. Sometimes this requires the use of special equipment or devices as an aid to limited functioning. Through practice, one can become more independent and capable of self-care and carrying on one's work and leisure-time activities.

Other individuals have problems because of an injury or illness which has impaired their functional abilities. For example, arthritis is a disease which causes swelling in joints, pain upon movement, and deformities which can severely hamper independent functioning. With these individuals, the therapist uses activities to restore and maintain as much function as possible, teaches the individuals ways to do things which will protect their joints, and often will design special splints, particularly for the hands, to reduce or prevent deformity and yet allow for use of the hands in carrying out activities.

Still other people have difficulty in pursuing their daily lives in a satisfying way for psychological or social reasons. The stresses of modern-day living, the impact of poverty, unemployment, and restricted social environment are all factors which a good many people find overwhelming or which they do not have the means to resolve. For such individuals, occupational therapy provides an opportunity to examine their daily life schedules and environment and to determine some alternative ways of living and coping which will be more satisfying and less stressful. For some this may require the learning of new work skills, for others the opportunity to experience positive relationships with people, and for still others a readjustment of their daily living schedule to provide time for leisure and play which are necessary for a healthy balanced life.

The child with problems in school and the aging citizen are a part of this client population. The disadvantaged and the developmentally disabled child are often not ready for the intellectual and social demands of schooling. The occupational therapist has the knowledge and skills to stimulate or develop those underlying functions necessary to establish readiness for academic learning and performance either in special education programs or in the regular classroom. The therapist works closely with the classroom teacher to provide readiness activities or adaptations to the regular school environment to make learning and performance possible.

The older citizen is confronted with decreasing physical abilities and an increasing sense of uselessness, which require special attention. Through the provision of purposeful and stimulating activities, the older citizen can be assisted in maintaining physical and intellectual functioning, and be involved in meaningful social interactions and productivity which enhance one's sense of worthwhileness and encourage a positive perspective toward living.

Occupational therapy services may be provided in the home, hospital, rehabilitation center, outpatient clinic, special school setting, nursing home, or work environment.

There are two entry levels of occupational therapy personnel: the occupational therapy assistant, certified (C.O.T.A.), and the occupational therapist, registered (O.T.R.).

The C.O.T.A. is a highly- skilled technician who is qualified to carry out programs for individuals and groups for which the primary goals are prevention of performance problems or maintenance of functioning (as in the aging population). In addition, under the supervision of the O.T.R., the assistant provides activities for those individuals requiring restoration of functioning and rehabilitation.

The assistant is trained in an academic and field experience program approved by the American Occupational Therapy Association and upon satisfactory completion of the program is recommended for certification. There are presently thirty-nine assistant programs; some are located in vocational technical schools and others in colleges and universities offering the associate degree or its equivalent.

The occupational therapist is educated in professional programs accredited by the American Occupational Therapy Association and the American Medical Association.

Upon satisfactory completion of the academic field experience curriculum, the graduate is recommended to sit for the national certification examination conducted by the American Occupational Therapy Association. Successful completion of the examination qualifies the therapist to use the designation O.T.R. and to be admitted to the Registry maintained by the American Occupational Therapy Association. There are presently fifty programs for occupational therapists located in four-year colleges and universities. The majority of these are baccalaureate degree programs; some are postbaccalaureate-level programs for individuals who have undergraduate degrees in other fields, and grant either a certificate in occupational therapy or the master's degree.

The O.T.R. serves the individual client or patient by evaluating performance capacities and deficits, selecting tasks or activity experiences appropriate to defined needs and goals, facilitating and influencing client participation and investment, evaluating client response, assessing and measuring change and development, validating assessments, sharing findings, and making appropriate recommendations. The experienced therapist, in addition, provides consultative services and administrative and supervisory leadership, and participates in community health planning and research.

In addition to the two entry-level educational programs, there are a number of graduate programs in occupational therapy which provide therapists with additional knowledge and skills required to work with particular client populations, in specialty areas or in administration, professional and technical education, and research.

ART THERAPIST*

Art therapy includes a range of activities. At one end of the spectrum, art as a means of nonverbal communication in a psychotherapeutic process is stressed. In conjunction with verbal associations and interpretations, art products are used to assist the understanding and working through of emotional problems. At the other end of the spectrum, therapy derives from experience of the artistic process itself. Here, artwork is encouraged for its special psychological value. Its usefulness depends on the age-old power of the arts to reconcile conflicting forces within the individual and between the individual and society.

Art therapy may be used to help deal with a wide variety of mental, emotional, and social problems, and in the alleviation of psychological stress accompanying physically handicapping conditions. Art therapists work in psychiatric and other hospitals and clinics; community mental health centers; schools and residential centers for emotionally disturbed, mentally retarded, and brain-damaged children; special educational facilities in ordinary schools; prisons; residential facilities and day programs for old people; growth centers for normal adults; and rehabilitation facilities for alcoholics and drug addicts.

Art therapists often make special contributions to the diagnosis as well as the treatment of psychological disorders. Some of them conduct private practice, often in conjunction with treatment offered by a referring psychiatrist or psychologist. Art therapy may be part of a psychiatric team endeavor, it may serve as an independent mode of psychotherapeutic treatment, or its use may lie outside the medical field — in the areas of special education and the prevention of mental or emotional disturbance.

The national professional association in the field is the American Art Therapy Association, with headquarters at 3607 South Braeswood Boulevard, Houston, TX 77025. The Association approves the master's degree in art therapy as the professional entrance level requirement. Prerequisite to graduate studies are proficiency in the fine arts — drawing, painting, and clay sculpture — and preparation in the behavioral and social sciences. Elective studies may be in the fields of art education; esthetics; clinical psychology; and psychoanalysis and other systems of psychotherapy. For the registration of individuals by AATA, professional experience in the field is required in addition to credit allowed for relevant graduate study. Appropriate experience may be substituted for special educational preparation.

The professional journal representing the field is the *American Journal of Art Therapy*, which became an affiliate of the AATA in 1974. Subtitled "Art in Education, Rehabilitation, and Psychothera-

* By Elinor Ulman, editor, *American Journal of Art Therapy*, 6010 Broad Branch Road N.W., Washington, DC 20015.

py," it provides a forum for art therapists, psychologists, teachers, psychiatrists, and others interested in the relationship of art to human understanding and mental health.

MUSIC THERAPIST*

Healing through music is not new; there is evidence that it was practiced in the biblical and classical periods. But it was not until quite recently that music therapy became an important contributor to the rehabilitation process, used to facilitate physical, emotional, intellectual, and psychological growth in disabled or impaired people of all ages.

Prior to 1944 few hospitals had music programs and there was no formal college training for music therapists. About that time a surge of interest began in hospitals caring for war victims, and by 1950 a few universities offered degree programs in music therapy, and the use of music in hospitals had grown to the extent that the National Association for Music Therapy was formed in Lawrence, Kansas. In the past ten years the number of institutions offering music therapy programs, and the number of graduates from each, has rapidly increased. As an indication of the size of the field, it may be pointed out that total membership in the Association is roughly 1,650, and approximately 2,200 people are now employed as music therapists in the United States.

Students of music therapy are required to take courses in biological sciences, psychology, sociology, and anthropology as well as theory, history, education, and major instrument courses in music. Added to these are specialized music therapy courses such as psychology of music, influence of music on behavior, music in recreation, and music in therapy. A three-month clinical experience and a six-month internship at a recognized institution under the supervision of a registered music therapist are also required before students are eligible for registration through the National Association for Music Therapy. Once registered, a student may go on for master's and doctoral degrees in music therapy at some universities. Emphasis in music therapy coursework is not on musical competition and performance, but on the student's ability to present music in such a way as to establish communication, elicit changes in behavior, motivate learning, and improve health.

In the beginning, music therapists were employed mainly in psychiatric hospitals. Today they are employed in regular hospitals, day care and special service facilities, community mental health centers, clinics, special education programs, homes for the retarded and emotionally disturbed, convalescent centers, and private practice. They work with cerebral palsied, deaf, blind, crippled, emotionally disturbed, retarded, and multiply handicapped people.

*By Penny E. Bigelow Wight, condensed.

Music therapists usually work with physical, occupational, speech, and recreation therapists in a rehabilitation therapy team. Dance, art, and drama might also be included in recreation therapy. Each therapist uses his or her own particular talents and tools for helping the medical staff achieve specific goals. These may range from providing pleasurable and socially acceptable use of leisure time to promoting socially acceptable behavior, overcoming illness, or even preventing disabilities from occurring.

One of music therapy's best attributes is that goals can be set which even the most severely impaired people can achieve. Another is that it can be a positive experience and thus help to create a positive self-image. But perhaps the first gift of music therapy to rehabilitation is its ability to draw people into a therapeutic setting. Before people can benefit from rehabilitation medicine, they must feel comfortable with and accept help from rehabilitation professionals. Music, as an all-encompassing, nonverbal, nonthreatening form of communication, helps exceptional people feel comfortable and can even make work toward wholeness fun.

Music's place in rehabilitation does not stop here, however. Its inherent structure and very wide spectrum of activities allows everyone to participate in it. Learning music involves motivation, listening, attention span, correlation, memory, and mental and physical participation just as other learning disciplines do. Since music involves concepts of up-down, fast-slow, loud-soft, long-short, and smooth-rough, these can be learned from it. Also, words to music can teach colors, body parts, numbers, self- and non-self-oriented concepts, and many other things which can serve to motivate exceptional people to learn self-help skills and thus help them to lead more independent and fulfilling lives.

The physical process of participating in music can be used to improve gross to fine motor coordination, strengthen muscles, and increase physical endurance. For example, special piano lessons for the cerebral palsied can better their arm, hand, and finger coordination. Movement to music can be geared to exercise certain muscles. Singing can improve breath control and lung capacity, and stutterers often do not stutter when singing. Because music is a sensual medium, it can be used to develop senses which are left to people who lack sight, hearing, or balance. The blind can hear and feel musical instruments in order to play them. Special methods for giving music lessons to the blind have been developed by using Braille. The deaf can see and feel the vibrations and move to the rhythm of music. And since music improves motor coordination and deals with the senses, it can be helpful to those who have perceptual-motor disabilities.

Music accomplishes both psychological and social goals. It helps people to relate to others on a one-to-one basis and in group settings in which they must learn socially acceptable behavior: sharing, taking turns, making friends, dealing with things or people who are "different," accepting others, helping others, listening, expressing opinions confidently, sometimes leading, sometimes following, always being a part of the group rather than apart from the group.

Finally, music helps people to deal with themselves as well as with others. It helps create self-acceptance and understanding of personal goals and develops the feeling of self-worth, a very important aspect of wholeness which in turn is a very important aspect of rehabilitation medicine.

DANCE THERAPIST*

Dance therapy is the psychotherapeutic use of movement to further the emotional and physical integration of the individual. It is used in the treatment of those who require special services because of emotional, behavioral, perceptual, or physical disorders. Dance therapists work with people of all ages, in groups or with individuals. They are employed primarily as clinicians, working in psychiatric hospitals, clinics, geriatric settings, special schools and other treatment centers, correctional facilities, and private practice. They engage in research and are involved in professional education, teaching in universities and colleges, and serving as consultants for schools and agencies.

In 1966 dance therapists throughout the United States formed the American Dance Therapy Association. The organization has facilitated communication and the exchange of ideas that is so critical to the development of a new profession. The ADTA has also been influential in establishing and maintaining specific professional standards through Registry procedures, encouraging the growth of graduate academic programs in dance therapy, developing a body of literature through its publications, and securing recognition from such bodies as the Joint Commission on Accreditation of Hospitals.

A dance therapist works with patients or clients using a form of nonverbal psychotherapy within the framework of a therapeutic contract. As in any therapeutic relationship between people, a therapist must have attained some degree of skill and self-awareness to be of service. Therefore a dance therapist must go through an indepth process to achieve this learning and maturation. There are many ways to become a dance therapist, but common to all is an intensive and extensive background in dance. Movement is the primary therapeutic tool in dance therapy, and in order to use it as a means of communication, freely and spontaneously, a wide range of movement experience is necessary.

In addition to developing a creative awareness of the body, a student must acquire physiological knowledge and understanding. An undergraduate degree in dance will usually provide this. However, undergraduate degrees may be in other related disciplines, such as special education or psychology, as long as the student has also

*By Joan Smallwood, D.T.R., and Sharon Chaiklin, D.T.R., American Dance Therapy Association, 1000 Century Plaza, Columbia, MD 21044.

experienced the necessary years of dance and movement studies, anatomy and physiology, and a liberal arts background with an emphasis on the social and behavioral sciences. Practical experiences such as teaching, the theater, personal psychotherapy, peer counseling, working with children, etc., provide opportunities for the development of qualities needed to work in therapy. One must expand one's sensitivity to the needs of others and be aware of one's own personality in such interactions.

Professional preparation is usually on the graduate level. It is here that intensive learning experiences can be focused, building on previous knowledge and experiences. The content should include dance therapy theory and practice, with specific clinical applications of dance therapy in treatment settings. Systems of movement observation, awareness of one's own movement style, mastery of the principles of psychosocial processes, and an understanding of the nature of therapy are all incorporated. A clinical internship at the completion of course studies should be minimally the equivalent of six months of full-time work.

Dance therapy differs from dance education, recreational dance, and adaptive dance. Dance education and recreational dance occur in the usual school and social situations. Adaptive dance (at times called therapeutic dance) usually occurs in special settings for those with mental or physical handicaps. Although all have therapeutic components, only dance therapy is a form of psychotherapy. In educational, recreational, or adaptive dance, there is a mutual understanding that the participants are learning dance techniques and forms which give them tools to use for improved body coordination, personal expression, or social interaction. Dance therapy includes such purposes secondarily, but its main assumption is that the participant is using movement and the body experience to focus on difficulties in behavioral and communicative functioning. Through the interventions of the therapist, the patient works toward integrating movement experiences and new awareness about self toward a defined therapeutic goal. Material from the individual's unconscious and intrapsychic processes will begin to surface and must be used to further those goals.

The body in movement often calls forth strong emotional feeling. The immediacy of that moment allows the patient to explore those feelings and the unique meanings attached to them for that individual. Anger, guilt, love, and grief are often inadequately experienced and frequently overlaid with other fears. Through movement, it is possible to work through these emotional experiences toward some resolution to allow more satisfaction in life.

Basic goals in dance therapy, adapted to each specific population and treatment facility, include development of body image and self-concepts, a wider range of movement to draw upon for adequate coping, increased awareness of inner physiological sensations and their psychological counterparts, awareness of body tensions, alternatives for verbal and nonverbal behavior, means to express a total body-mind integration, social interaction with clarity in one's own

verbal and nonverbal statements, and ability to participate successfully in group interactions.

The goals described are primary for the emotionally disturbed,
but specific needs of individuals lay emphasis on particular aspects
of dance therapy. Work with the mentally retarded stresses physical
coordination and control and further behavioral and expressive
uses of movement. When working with the physically disabled, the
thrust is toward healthier self-concepts and new means of expressive communication. Children and adults with any kind of disability usually have some emotional overlay to their problem due to the
stresses encountered. The dance therapist works toward an awareness of the strengths and potentialities of the individual and builds
upon these for healthier functioning.

MANUAL ARTS THERAPIST

Manual arts therapy utilizes a broad range of work activities to
further the recovery and readjustment of both mental and physical
patients. Wherever feasible, the work is performed under actual
working conditions; but if this cannot be done, the therapist sets up
a work situation that is as realistic as possible. Examples of these
activities are printing, metal and woodworking, radio and TV repair, agriculture, and animal care. The work program is based on
the interests, experiences, and needs of the individual patient, and
on suggestions and recommendations made by physicians, psychologists, vocational counselors, and other members of the rehabilitation team.

The primary objectives of manual arts therapy are restoration of
confidence, a sense of achievement, and motivation for recovery. At
the same time it serves the practical purpose of retraining patients
in their own skill or trade, or training them in a new field in keeping
with the disability. The work may be prescribed at any stage of
hospitalization, depending upon the patient's condition and vocational goals, and it may be performed in the wards, on the hospital
grounds, in maintenance shops, or in a manual arts workshop.

Qualifications for manual arts therapist consist of a college degree with a major in industrial arts, agriculture, or a related field,
plus two to seven months of clinical training in a hospital or rehabilitation center. The majority of therapists work in Veterans Administration facilities, but an increasing number are engaged by
psychiatric hospitals, prisons, and drug addiction rehabilitation facilities. For further information, contact the American Association
for Rehabilitation Therapy, P.O. Box 93, Little Rock, AR 72116.

INDUSTRIAL THERAPIST

Industrial therapy consists of medically prescribed work performed by mentally ill patients in a hospital setting. Its primary
objectives are to lift morale, build self-esteem, and provide a bridge
to outside employment. The work is carefully chosen for the indi-

vidual patient, by keeping in mind the particular disorder and personality needs, interests, and level of skill and ability; but in contrast to occupational therapy, the activities are utilitarian in nature and performed in a work environment. Examples are painting, repairing, building and grounds maintenance, gardening, and work in the laundry or kitchen. To motivate patients and bring them closer to the real world, they are always paid for their work.

The industrial therapist handles the payroll, evaluates the patient's progress, and participates in staff conferences in order to coordinate efforts with those of other members of the rehabilitation team. The minimum educational requirement for this field is a college degree in occupational therapy, manual arts, or a related field. For further information, contact the American Association for Rehabilitation Therapy, P.O. Box 93, Little Rock, AR 72116.

HOME ECONOMIST

Home economists are playing an important role in rehabilitation, since a great many disabled individuals, both male and female, need help in adapting themselves to the everyday activities and responsibilities of living. A woman who is deficient in manual control can retain a measure of self-dependence if her kitchen is rearranged and she is taught simplified techniques of cooking and cleaning. A man who is too disabled for outside employment may learn to occupy himself constructively with housekeeping responsibilities, perhaps releasing other family members for work outside the home. People of both sexes who have become debilitated by geriatric disorders may continue to live independently if they learn less strenuous ways of meeting their needs at home. Handicapped children and teen-agers can often be taught to do homemaking chores and thereby reduce the burden on the rest of the family.

Every phase of home economics has a place in the rehabilitation process: family finance, nutrition, clothing, child care, laundry, family relations, home furnishings, interior design. Problems arising in each of these areas can be solved through the concentrated efforts of a specialist, and life can be made easier and more gratifying for the blind, the arthritic, the paraplegic, the mentally retarded, and others.

Home economists counsel and train disabled individuals directly or serve as resource persons for a rehabilitation team. Most of their work in this field is performed in public agencies such as the Cooperative Extension Service and the state departments of health, social service, or vocational rehabilitation, or in private rehabilitation centers, hospitals, and heart associations. Basic preparation for the field consists of a four-year college education with a major or special courses in home economics, occupational therapy, or social work, plus graduate or in-service training in the education of the disabled. Practical experience in homemaking and child care is also extremely important. Information on rehabilitation traineeships leading to a master's or doctor's degree can be obtained from the

American Home Economics Association, 2010 Massachusetts Avenue N.W., Washington, DC 20036.

ORIENTATION AND MOBILITY INSTRUCTOR

The orientation and mobility instructor, also known as a peripatologist, trains the blind or near-blind in orienting themselves to their surroundings and moving about safely, independently, and confidently. Instruction generally begins with teaching the visually handicapped individual to use a sighted person as a guide, and to use one's own arms and hands for protection and location of objects and obstacles in familiar indoor settings. Later the blind person learns to use a long prescription cane to get around in both familiar and unfamiliar surroundings. One is also taught orientation skills which help in becoming acquainted with the environment, including the use of the senses of hearing, touch, and smell to the fullest extent possible. The instruction must be adapted to the special needs of each client; for example, a businessman may need to reach his office by subway, while an elderly woman may only need to move about in a nursing home. The field requires at least one year of graduate-level instruction at one of the eight colleges and universities offering special programs approved by the American Foundation for the Blind, and qualified instructors may also be certified by the American Association of Workers for the Blind. Orientation and mobility instruction may be given in the home, rehabilitation centers, hospitals, and nursing and convalescent homes, as well as in school systems.

EDUCATIONAL THERAPIST

Educational therapy is a special application of teaching techniques to individuals with emotional or physical disabilities. Its object is to overcome tendencies toward depression, withdrawal, and defeatism by arousing new interests and developing academic and practical skills which will help them build self-confidence, improve their self-image, and keep them in touch with the world of people and ideas. The courses are usually on a high school level and include such subjects as English, biology, chemistry, mathematics, typing, shorthand, and bookkeeping. They are chosen with full consideration of the patient's interests and goals, and the teaching methods are adapted to the particular disability.

Most educational therapists are employed in Veterans Administration hospitals, but an increasing number of private and state institutions are adding this modality to their rehabilitation programs. The field requires a high degree of sensitivity to changing moods and emotions, strong motivation to help the disabled, and an ability to reach and communicate with troubled people. Preparation for this career includes at least four years of college with emphasis on courses in education and specific subjects the student intends to teach, as well as an in-service or clinical practice program of two to seven months' duration. Several institutions offer postgraduate training in educational therapy. Information on educational and training centers for this field can be obtained from the American Association for Rehabilitation Therapy, P.O. Box 93, North Little Rock, AR 72116.

HOMEMAKER–HOME HEALTH AIDE*

Homemaker–home health aides are a relatively new addition to the ranks of health and rehabilitation personnel. They are paraprofessionals who are recruited, trained, and professionally supervised by an employing community agency, such as a visiting nurse association, a hospital with a home care unit, a public health or social service department, a voluntary family service or child care agency, or a "free-standing" agency, that is, an agency established specifically to provide homemaker–home health aide services. There are approximately 1,700 homemaker–home health aide programs in the United States and Canada, employing about 45,000 aides. It is estimated that there should be 300,000 aides for the need to be met adequately in the United States.

Homemaker–home health aide service is a development of a movement begun in the early 1900s to provide help in their homes to families with young children during a mother's illness or convalescence. Over the years the service grew to encompass the needs of the physically and mentally ill, the elderly, and disabled persons of all ages who require homemaking assistance, personal care, and help in carrying out rehabilitation regimens to avoid unnecessary institutionalization. Accordingly, aides are trained to carry out these functions under professional supervision.

An agency providing homemaker–home health aide service must meet fourteen basic standards set by the National Council for Homemaker–Health Aide Services, including the provision of at least forty hours of formal training and continuing in-service training for the aides. The training program must include the principles and techniques of personal care and rehabilitation. There are no educational requirements to qualify for this training beyond the ability to read, write, and communicate adequately. Personal qualities sought include a genuine concern for people, tolerance for people's differences, emotional maturity, willingness to give of oneself, flexibility, ability to accept supervision constructively, a neat personal appearance, and good physical health.

Personal care and rehabilitation tasks which homemaker–home health aides may perform within the plan of care established and under appropriate supervision may include assistance with mobility, help with bathing, and with prescribed exercises and the use of prosthetic equipment, braces, walkers, and the like. However, their role in the rehabilitative process is much more personal and far-

---

* By the National Council for Homemaker–Health Aide Services, 67 Irving Place, New York, NY 10003.

reaching than the tasks involved, for their teaching and motivating skills are often the key factor in encouraging the handicapped person — adult or child — to realize the full potential of one's abilities and to become as self-sufficient as possible.

Aides who are trained in methods of work simplification, body mechanics, kitchen planning, and use of special equipment can help disabled adults to function safely in their own homes and to achieve better self-care. Those trained in behavior modification techniques, cast care, gait training, and other disability management techniques can help retarded or disabled children to achieve maximum independent functioning and provide relief for their overburdened families. In addition to their core training program, aides may receive specialized training to equip them to work in special situations, such as with developmentally disabled children, the emotionally disturbed, confused elderly persons, the blind, or the paralyzed.

The goal of the National Council is availability of quality homemaker–home health aide services in all sections of the nation to help individuals and families in all economic brackets with services in their own homes when there are disruptions caused by illness, disability, social disadvantage, or other problems, or when there is need of help to achieve or maintain independent functioning and self-sufficiency.

VOLUNTEER WORKER

The volunteer worker deserves special consideration in a volume on disabilities and rehabilitation since she or he performs far more than the routine functions which predominate in short-term situations. As the American Hospital Association states:

> In long-term care situations, volunteers can become important members of the therapeutic team. While the professional staff concentrates on the patient's medical and health needs, the volunteer can help to fill his social and emotional needs . . . Also, the volunteer can give more attention to individual patients than the average staff member, who must cover an entire ward or service; and by performing needed non-technical duties, the volunteer can free the professional for tasks requiring special skills . . . The volunteer can serve as a major link between the patient and the community . . . and help him maintain his identity as an individual in the world where he fears he has become only a disease or impairment.

Among the activities performed by volunteers in centers for the mentally or physically disabled are the following: assisting nurses in seating and feeding patients; conducting informal classes or groups in arts and crafts, current events, or occupational skills; helping patients learn daily living skills; escorting patients on outings; assisting the physical therapist in nontechnical activities such as practice in operating a wheelchair or walking on crutches; planning and supervising recreational activities such as films, parties,

751

or concerts; working with patients on personal problems that do not require professional help; helping the patient's family become oriented to the situation; performing clerical duties for the hospital or agency, such as sending out mailings; assisting in fund-raising activities. Most of these functions are performed in institutions such as hospitals, rehabilitation centers, mental institutions, and facilities for the retarded. However, an increasing number of agencies are conducting coordinated home care programs for individuals with chronic illnesses and disabilities such as cardiac disorders, diabetes, pulmonary disease, cancer, and neurological conditions. Here the volunteer may serve as a friendly visitor to alleviate loneliness, and as an aide in solving personal problems and meeting practical needs.

Volunteer work in the rehabilitation field requires not only an "understanding heart," but such qualities as the ability to accept a patient's physical or mental incapacities and emotional reactions; to recognize the patient's capacity for growth even within limited areas; ingenuity in devising and providing constructive activities; patience when progress is slow; an encouraging and supportive attitude; an ability to work with the professional staff.

In larger hospitals and agencies there may be a director of volunteer services who organizes a many-sided program, recruits volunteers from local organizations and educational institutions, interviews candidates, orients them to the institution and staff, assigns tasks, gives them on-the-job training, and supervises their relationship to patients. In smaller facilities the social worker or other staff member may take responsibility for volunteer services. Many volunteers become so involved with the work that they take special training courses in their particular field of interest, and some become professional workers.

In recent years public funding of subsistence level of maintenance has enabled many persons to volunteer on a full-time basis. Religious organizations have also sponsored one- and two-year volunteer assignments in order that youth of their congregations may give public service and benefit from deeper understanding of the needs of fellow humans. These volunteers, along with the students from many helping professional groups who volunteer their services as a part of their training programs, constitute a large work force vital to the delivery of human services. Individuals with professional credentials also give of their services on a voluntary basis. Sometimes they do so in order to maintain a clinical orientation to their primary function; often they volunteer in order to offer public service as any citizen does.

Utilization of volunteer service gives many unique benefits to an agency and its clients. Foremost is the eloquent expression to clients that a fellow human being cares about them. The flow of volunteers through an agency does more than any educational campaign in public media to inform and enlighten persons in the community about the needs and actual capacities of the client population.

C. Allied Medical and Paramedical Professions

GENETIC COUNSELOR*

In a 1973 Princeton University study, 90 percent of 491 genetic counselors who returned questionnaires reported that they were M.D.'s. Some of the respondents also held a Ph.D., 11 percent held only the Ph.D., and 9 percent had neither. Of the M.D.'s, 63 percent were pediatricians, 17 percent were internists, and 5 percent obstetricians-gynecologists. Three-quarters (77 percent) were board-certified in at least one specialty.

Although most genetic counselors are physicians, master's-degree courses in human genetics and genetic counseling are offered at the following:

Human Genetics Program, Sarah Lawrence College, Bronxville, NY 10708.

Genetic Advising Program, Building T-7, University of California, Berkeley, CA 94720.

Department of Biological Sciences, Douglass Campus, Rutgers University, 32 Bishop Street, New Brunswick, NJ 08903.

Division of Development Disabilities and Clinical Genetics, University of California, Irvine, California College of Medicine, Irvine, CA 92664.

The courses are generally designed to train associates, a new level of professional, to serve in the rapidly growing fields of human genetics, birth defects, and inherited diseases. Graduates of these courses function as professional members of the medical genetics team.

The prerequisites for admission differ somewhat, but information from Sarah Lawrence College and Rutgers indicates that applicants must have completed college-level courses in some combination of the following: mathematics, physics, organic chemistry, genetics, and human or vertebrate physiology, general biology or zoology, developmental biology (human embryology), basic chemistry, and probability and statistics. The University of California at Irvine gives preference to students who have a baccalaureate degree in biology or chemistry. At Berkeley, applicants must have a B.A. or B.S. degree, at least one college-level course in each of certain areas (biology, chemistry, a social science), and experience in working with adults on a one-to-one basis.

Although the field has expanded, clear-cut job descriptions and professional guidelines governing who is qualified to do what remain in a fledgling state of development. Graduates are employed as associates to medical geneticists in counseling and in clinical

---

*By the National Foundation, P.O. Box 2000, White Plains, NY 10602.

and laboratory research; as administrators, developers, and counselors for community screening programs; as teachers; and as writers for public information departments and for scientific research.

Individuals can continue toward a Ph.D. degree in human genetics or some related field. They can also enter medical school or function in groups engaged in research or other activities directed toward health-care delivery in medical genetics. Genetic counseling associates may participate in various ways in hospitals, community health centers, private practice groups of physicians, institutions for the mentally retarded, and other medical or paramedical centers, always in conjunction with medical geneticists.

With the provision of counseling services to larger segments of the population, the need for appropriately trained nurses, social workers, or genetic associates within counseling units will greatly increase. These individuals can effectively act as the interface between medical geneticists and the patient population, making it possible for the geneticists' time and skills to be most efficiently utilized, and at the same time can enhance the processes of communication and assist patients and families in dealing with their problems. The field is growing rapidly. In 1959 genetic counseling was available in only ten institutions nationwide. By 1974 the number had increased to 272, according to the International Directory of Genetic Services, published by the National Foundation.

BIOMEDICAL ENGINEER

The biomedical engineer specializes in the application of scientific theory and technology to the development of devices and techniques for medical treatment, rehabilitation, and research. This rapidly developing field draws on many areas of physical science — for example, electronics, fluid dynamics, mechanics, optics, radiation, and thermodynamics — as well as on techniques, instrumentation, and materials developed in such fields as space exploration, the plastics industry, and computer technology.

At present, biomedical engineers are working in four main areas; a few illustrations will be given of what is being done in each of them:

1. *Development of new medical instruments* for measuring changes in organ size or activity from outside the body, that is, noninvasively. Among them are sonar devices that locate a brain tumor, measure an enlarged liver, or determine whether the head of an unborn baby is too large for normal birth. Other instruments are miniature transistorized radio transmitters which, when swallowed or worn, record fluctuations in body temperature, various kinds of chemical changes in the internal organs, digestive activities, or indications of internal bleeding; an intravenous microphone that enables the surgeon to diagnose specific heart murmurs; a laser beam device used in eye surgery; and the recently developed biofeedback instruments used to enable patients to alter bodily func-

tions involved in migraine, hypertension, spasticity, and other disorders.

2. *Replacement, repair, and rehabilitation devices,* such as a battery-powered artificial forearm and hand activated by nerves and residual muscles; a wheelchair operated by the eyes; an electrical obstacle detector for the blind; an artificial kidney machine with which fifteen patients may be treated at the same time; a miniature implanted cerebellar pacemaker used to control equilibrium; an electronic defibrillator for use in cardiac arrest; and plastic tubing for splicing damaged arteries.

3. *Computers and data processors* used for such purposes as compiling health statistics, keeping medical records, storing information for use in epidemiology, recording second-by-second changes in biofeedback applications, diagnosing obscure diseases with complex symptomatology, and providing immediate information retrieval for medical researchers and librarians.

4. *Research activities,* such as evaluation of the effects of medications on internal organs, mapping the brain, and investigating the operations of other parts of the nervous system, studying cell structure, analyzing genetic factors, simulation of complex biological systems, and identification of the effects of environmental conditions on body processes.

Biomedical engineers carry on their work in hospitals, rehabilitation centers, research foundations, colleges and universities, and industrial and governmental laboratories. Their educational background must give them a thoroughgoing foundation not only in all engineering fields (mechanical, electrical, chemical, etc.) but in biology, physiology, biochemistry, physics, and mathematics. An engineering degree is basic, but must be supplemented by on-the-job training in a laboratory or rehabilitation unit. A few universities now offer specialized courses in the field. In addition, there is a growing need for *biomedical engineering technicians* to assemble, adapt, and maintain the new instruments and devices. Some of them are working in the field of orthotics and prosthetics; others have had experience in such fields as glass blowing, electronics, watchmaking, or plastics. Further information on this field may be obtained from the Alliance for Engineering in Medicine and Biology, the American Association for the Advancement of Medical Instrumentation, and the Bioinstrumentation Advisory Council of the American Institute of Biological Sciences.

OSTEOPATHIC PHYSICIAN

This medical field is based on a system of therapy which stresses the importance of body mechanics and applies manipulation procedures to the detection and correction of faulty structure. Illness, injury, and musculoskeletal disabilities are also treated with drugs, surgery, physical therapy, and medical devices and aids. Most members of the profession conduct a private practice, but have access to the 310 osteopathic hospitals or other hospitals. Educational requirements include three years of professional courses in an accredited college or university, graduation from one of the seven colleges of osteopathic medicine accredited by the American Osteopathic Association which grant the degree of D.O., and in most cases a rotating internship of twelve months. A state license based on educational qualifications and an examination is also required.

DENTIST

The dentist plays an important role in the rehabilitation process, since many disabilities involve tooth, gum, and mouth disorders. Although most of these conditions are treated by general dentists, there are some who specialize in the problems of the physically handicapped, and at least one special organization exists for this purpose: the Dental Guidance Council for Cerebral Palsy. Individuals with cerebral palsy or other physical disabilities may require realignment of warped gums or correction of malocclusion. They may also be so severely incapacitated that they cannot take normal preventive measures, and therefore become cavity-prone and subject to mouth and gum diseases, and may eventually require artificial teeth or dentures. Educational qualifications for dentistry include a minimum of two years at an approved liberal arts college with emphasis on scientific subjects, after which a standard admissions test must be taken before enrolling in a four-year course at a dental school, which may lead either to the degree of D.D.S. (Doctor of Dental Surgery) or D.M.D. (Doctor of Dental Medicine). Before the graduate can practice, one must pass a written examination given by the state or by the National Board of Medical Examiners of the American Dental Association. At least two years of postgraduate training are required for such specialties as oral surgeon, orthodontist, prosthodontist (artificial teeth and dentures), and public health dentist, all of which have special relevance to rehabilitation.

PODIATRIST

The podiatrist, or foot specialist, diagnoses and treats diseases and deformities of the foot. Though podiatrists often deal with relatively minor ailments such as corns and ingrown toenails, they also treat major disabling conditions, including congenital or acquired deformities. They frequently use mechanical and electrical procedures (whirlpool baths, shortwave, etc.) in treating such conditions as flat or weak feet, or foot imbalance, and plastic casts may be used in correcting clubfoot and other deformities. In addition, they may fit prosthetic appliances and braces and prescribe corrective footwear. Preparation for this profession includes at least two years of undergraduate work, a four-year course at one of the five colleges accredited by the American Podiatry Association, leading to the degree of Doctor of Podiatric Medicine (D.P.M.). Before practicing, the graduate must pass a state board examination and obtain a license.

RADIOLOGIC TECHNOLOGIST

The field includes three types of technicians: (a) The *diagnostic x-ray technologist* operates equipment that produces radiographs of bones and interior organs of the body. X-ray films are read by the physician to determine the location and extent of illness or injury in cases of possible cancer, osteoporosis, tumors, etc. (b) The *nuclear medical technologist* operates radioscopic equipment such as scintillation detectors and scanners which produce scanograms and measure concentrations of radioisotopes administered by the physician for diagnostic or treatment purposes. (c) The *radiation therapy technologist* operates x-ray therapy machines and may prepare, administer, and measure radioactive isotopes as specified by the radiologist. Although each of these three disciplines has its own curriculum and its own certification examination administered by the American Registry of Radiologic Technologists, they all require a high school education with courses in the physical sciences, and technical training at an approved school conducted by a hospital or medical college. The duration of most courses in the field is two years, though some extend over four years and entitle the graduate to a degree of bachelor of science in x-ray technology. Tuition is usually free, and jobs can readily be found in public and private hospitals, private medical laboratories and clinics, public health laboratories, and physicians' and dentists' offices.

RESPIRATORY THERAPIST

Respiratory therapy, also known as inhalation therapy, is a rapidly growing allied health occupation based on the administration of oxygen and other gases and mists for medical purposes. The therapist sets up the equipment involved in this process, including respirators, and intermittent-positive-pressure breathing (IPPB) machine, masks, tents, catheters, cannulas, and incubators, and administers prescribed doses of therapeutic gases and aerosolized drugs to patients with such diseases as emphysema, tuberculosis, cardiac conditions, and asthma.

The responsibilities of the respiratory therapist include not only the actual administration of inhalants in the most suitable manner, but also explaining the treatment to the patient, instructing in breathing procedures, regulating the flow of gases at the required level, observing the patient's color and rate of respiration, and reporting adverse reactions to the nurse or doctor. In addition, the therapist may be required to conduct various pulmonary function tests such as lung volumes, gas flows, and blood gas analysis; must also keep the equipment clean, sterile, and in good working condition; order repairs and new equipment and supplies as needed; and in some cases conduct classroom and on-the-job instruction.

Qualifications for this occupation range from a high school education with courses in biology and chemistry, plus more than a year's on-the-job training, up to a B.S. degree. Hospital and college training programs should be approved by the Joint Review Committee for Inhalation Therapy Training sponsored by the American Medical Association and the American Association for Respiratory Therapy. Applicants who meet training, experience, and examination requirements may become registered therapists. Similar requirements are in effect for certification as a *respiratory therapy technician*.

ORTHOTIST AND PROSTHETIST

These rehabilitation occupations are grouped together because they require the same training and skills, and in many cases the responsibilities overlap. The prosthetist makes and fits artificial limbs for amputees, while the orthotist makes and fits orthopedic braces to support or correct body parts weakened or distorted by disease, injury, or congenital defect. Both work from the physician's prescription and under the physician's supervision. Before a brace or limb can be designed and built, the individual needs of the patient must be determined and accurate measurements must be made. Preliminary fittings generally lead to changes and adaptations, and a full evaluation of the appliance in use must be made by the prosthetist or orthotist, the patient, and the physician. A physical or occupational therapist then helps the patient learn to use the device.

These careers require manual and mechanical skill, inventiveness, patience, accuracy, concern for the welfare of the disabled, and ability to communicate effectively with patients and other members of the rehabilitation team. Special courses of two to five weeks' duration are available at several leading universities for individuals with practical experience. They include anatomy, biomechanics, engineering as related to orthotic and prosthetic devices, and practical shop experience. One university offers a four-year course, and others offer Associate of Arts degrees. Traineeships are available from the U.S. Social and Rehabilitation Service. A candidate for practitioner certification by the American Board for Certification in Orthotics and Prosthetics must now have an Associate of Arts degree in one or the other field, plus two years of clinical experience. An *orthotic-prosthetic assistant and technician* must have two years of nonformal apprenticeship and pass a certification examination. Further information may be obtained from the American Orthotic and Prosthetic Association, 1440 N Street N.W., Washington, DC 20005.

LABORATORY TECHNICIANS

The *medical technologist* matches blood samples for transfusions, performs blood tests, analyzes urine, grows bacteria cultures, tests for antibodies, and operates apparatus such as autoclaves, centrifuges, and electronic counters. Preparation for the field consists of three years of college followed by one year of clinical education in an approved school, usually located in a hospital. Many of the less complicated tests, however, are performed by the *medical laboratory technician*, who must have an associate degree from a community college plus clinical experience in an approved laboratory; and the routine laboratory procedures are usually performed by a *certified laboratory assistant*, who must qualify for the work by graduating from high school and completing a one-year training program in a certified school.

Other paramedical technicians who play auxiliary roles in the rehabilitation field are the following. The *cytotechnologist* detects signs of disease by staining cell samplings and examining them under the microscope; two years of college, at least six months of study in an approved school, and six months of supervised laboratory experience are required for this occupation. The *histologic technician* cuts and stains tissue specimens which are then examined microscopically by the pathologist; educational preparation for this field includes a high school diploma and a year of supervised training. The *blood bank technologist* collects, classifies, processes, and stores whole blood or plasma; one must be a certified medical technologist with an additional year of training in a school approved by the American Association of Blood Banks. The *electrocardiograph technician* records heart activity on the electrocardiograph (ECG, or EKG) instrument for interpretation by the physician; a high school education is required, plus three to six months of on-the-job training in a hospital. The *electroencephalograph technologist* records brain wave activity through which the neurologist diagnoses such conditions as epilepsy, brain tumors, and strokes; most of the training in this field is of the on-the-job variety, but a year of study and supervised practice is increasingly required. Three levels of personnel are concerned with the use of radioactive isotopes and scanners in diagnosing cancer and other diseases. First, a physician who specializes in nuclear medicine is responsible for the diagnosis itself. Second, the *nuclear medical technologist* performs the required laboratory tests and analyses; preparation for this field includes four years of college and sometimes graduate work, plus on-the-job training. Third, the *nuclear medical technician* performs the more routine tasks involved in the process; preparation for this field includes at least two years of formal technical training beyond high school.

Further information on these nine occupations can be obtained from the American Society of Medical Technologists. Also important are the American Medical Technologists, American Society of Clinical Pathologists, American Association of Blood Banks, American Association of EEG Technologists, American Society of Radiologic Technologists, Society of Nuclear Medical Technologists, American Hospital Association, and the American Medical Associa-

tion. (For addresses, see PART 4, SECTION 2: VOLUNTARY ORGA-
NIZATIONS.)

MEDICAL AND DENTAL AIDES AND ASSISTANTS

The *medical assistant* contributes indirectly to the rehabilitation
process by serving as the physician's receptionist, secretary, administrative aide, and clinical aide. Acting as a link between the physician and patients, the assistant can help to make disabled individuals comfortable, reassure them when they must undergo tests and
examinations, and take over the burden of filling out forms. The assistant also obtains medical histories, arranges for hospital admission, and assists in emergency situations. Many community colleges now offer one- or two-year courses in the field, including a
period of practical experience in a doctor's office. The two-year
program enables the student not only to obtain an associate degree
but to apply for certification by the American Association of Medical Assistants, 1 East Wacker Drive, Chicago, IL 60601.

The *psychiatric aide,* or ward attendant, assists mentally ill patients in a hospital setting. In close and continuous contact with the
patients, the aide is in a unique position to give them moral support
and to provide the psychiatrist and other staff members with information on their behavior, attitudes, and needs. Among the duties
are assisting them in bathing, dressing, and grooming; taking them
to and from wards for examination and treatment; administering
prescribed medications; encouraging them to participate in social
and recreational activities; persuading them to eat, and noting reasons for rejection of food; preventing injuries to themselves or
others; and escorting them off the grounds for outings or for medical
or dental treatment. Training is usually of the on-the-job or in-service type, but some community colleges are offering courses in the
field.

The *nurse's aide* assists in the care of hospital patients under the
direction of the nursing and medical staff. Duties include answering signal lights and bells to determine the patients' needs; bathing
and dressing them; serving food and helping them eat; taking them
to treatment units; draping them for examinations or treatment; and
holding instruments and lights for the physician. The aide also
keeps the patient's room clean, changes bed linens, directs visitors,
answers the telephone in the patient's room, and provides the physician with such assistance as taking and reporting temperature and
pulse and respiration rate, applying compresses, and cleaning, sterilizing, and storing packs, treatment trays, and other supplies. Like
the psychiatric aide, she can help materially in maintaining the patient's morale, and must be warm and interested in the total welfare
of individuals who are ill or disabled.

Three allied health fields play an auxiliary role in dentistry. The
dental hygienist, who specializes in cleaning and polishing teeth
and dental health education, usually takes a two-year program at a
community college, but must also pass a state licensing examina-

tion. The *dental assistant,* who performs such tasks as making the patient comfortable and sterilizing instruments, takes a one- to two-year course at a dental college, community college, or technical institute. The *dental laboratory technician,* who makes and prepares dentures, bridges, and crowns, either acquires skills through on-the-job training as an apprentice, or preferably enrolls in an approved program for a year of formal education followed by a year of supervised training in a commercial laboratory.

4

Data Bank

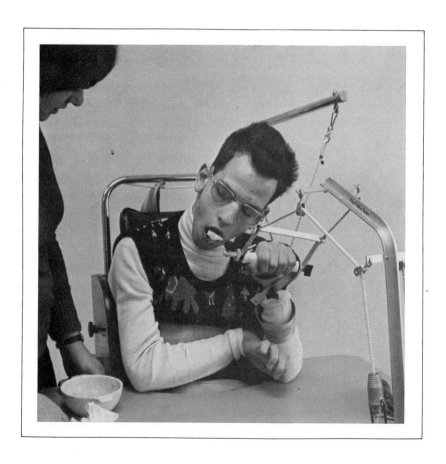

Section 1. Statistics

Sections 1–8 compiled by ROBERT M. GOLDENSON, Ph.D.

The major sources for the following statistics are publications of the National Center for Health Statistics and "Key Facts on the Handicapped" (April 1, 1975), compiled by the Education and Public Welfare Division of the Congressional Research Service from data submitted to Congress by a number of government agencies. The total population of the United States, according to the latest census figures, is approximately 215,000,000. All the following statistics are estimates.

Persons with activity limitation caused by chronic conditions, physical and mental (1972)		25,868,000
Percent with activity limitation		12.7
Persons sixty-five years and over with activity limitation		8,613,000
Noninstitutionalized disabled not in school (ages 16–64)		11,710,000
Percent of this universe, which totals 104,556,000		11.20
Number needing vocational rehabilitation (ages 16–64), 1975		6,500,000
Total served in 1975		1,326,000
Total rehabilitated in 1975		391,500
Mentally ill		131,900
Mentally retarded		45,400
Blind, visually impaired		30,200
Deaf, hard of hearing, speech-impaired		20,100
Heart, cancer, stroke		13,900
Other		150,000
Total handicapped youth (ages 0–21), 1970		9,550,000
Visually impaired		193,000
Partially sighted	180,000	

Legally blind	13,000	
Hearing-impaired		490,000
Deaf	50,000	
Hard of hearing	440,000	
Speech-impaired		2,200,000
Crippling or other health impairment		1,676,000
Mentally retarded		2,800,000
Emotionally disturbed		1,500,000
Learning-disabled		740,000
Multihandicapped		50,000
Handicapped children receiving special education, 1972–1973		3,046,000
Mentally retarded		900,000
Trainable	148,000	
Educable	752,000	
Hard of hearing		55,000
Deaf		28,000
Speech-impaired		1,383,000
Visually impaired		28,000
Emotionally disturbed		199,000
Crippled		128,000
Learning-disabled		230,000
Other health impairments		95,000
Physical disabilities and chronic disorders, all ages (selected)		
Severely visually impaired (including blindness)		1,306,000
Legally blind, 1973		479,000
Hearing-impaired, one or both ears		14,491,000
Significant bilateral impairment		6,548,842
Deaf, total, both ears		330,000
Chronic obstructive pulmonary disease		14,000,000
Rheumatoid arthritis		5,000,000
Paralysis, complete or partial		1,392,000
Chronic heart conditions, 1972		10,291,000
Orthopedic impairments, other than paralysis or absence of limbs, 1971		8,018,000
Speech defects, 1971		1,934,000
Parkinsonism (between 500,000 and 1,500,000)		1,000,000
Cerebral palsy		750,000
Multiple sclerosis		500,000
Muscular dystrophy		200,000
Mental illness		
Mentally ill and emotionally disturbed, needing treatment (10% of population)		21,500,000
Admission episodes to all mental facilities, 1971 (2/3 to public facilities)		2,700,000
Admissions to inpatient services (47%)		1,269,029
Admissions to outpatient services (50%)		1,378,822
Admissions to day treatment services (3%)		75,545
Patient care episodes (that is, number at beginning of year plus admissions during year)		4,190,913
Inpatient (41.9% of total, 1971)		1,755,816
State and county mental hospitals		745,259
Private mental hospitals		97,963
Veterans Administration psychiatric services		176,800

General hospital psychiatric services   542,642
Residential centers for disturbed children   28,637
Community mental health centers   130,088
Other multiservice facilities   34,427
Outpatient (55.3% of total)   2,316,754
Community mental health centers   622,906
Other outpatient services   1,693,848
Day care   118,343
Community mental health centers   43,653
Other day care services   74,690
Mental retardation
All categories (nearly 3% of population), estimated   6,000,000
Number in public institutions, 1971   181,009
Facilities
Rehabilitation facilities, defined as offering a
     variety of integrated services, all types, in-
     cluding 50% workshops, 1973   3,000
Mental health treatment facilities, all types, 1972   3,220
Free-standing outpatient clinics   1,123
    General hospitals with separate psychiatric
     services   771
    Psychiatric hospitals   601
     State and county   324
     Private   158
     Veterans Administration   119
    Residential centers for disturbed children   344
    Community mental health centers
     (543 in 1976), 1972   295
    Day hospitals   34
    Other multiservice facilities   33
Mental retardation facilities   372
    Public   190
    Private   182
Nursing homes, 1974   16,139
Number of beds   1,187,973
Annual social cost of selected disabilities, estimated
     (treatment, care, rehabilitation, loss of earnings)
Alcoholism $15 billion
Drug abuse   10 billion
Heart disease   20 billion
Rheumatoid arthritis   3.645 billion
Mental illness   21 billion
Annual cost of care for major chronic neurological and sensory disorders[*]
Amyotrophic lateral sclerosis (9,000 cases) $37 million
Cerebral palsy (750,000 cases)   1.6 billion
Epilepsy (2,000,000 cases)   2 billion
Friedreich's ataxia (4,000 cases)   8 million
Head injuries (3,053,000 cases)   1.6 billion
Huntington's disease (14,000 cases)   25 million
Mental retardation (6,000,000 cases)   3.5 billion
Multiple sclerosis and related diseases (500,000 cases)   1 billion

[*]From the National Institute of Neurological Diseases, Communication Disorders, and Stroke, National Institutes of Health, 1973.

767

Muscular dystrophy (200,000 cases)	400 million
Myasthenia gravis (30,000 cases)	94 million
Parkinson's disease (200,000 cases)	400 million
Reading disabilities (elementary, high school; 8,000,000 cases)	800 million
Spina bifida (27,500 cases)	55 million
Spinal cord injury (125,000 cases)	2.4 billion
Stroke (2,000,000 cases)	4 billion
Tumors of the brain and other parts of the nervous system (140,000 cases)	430 million
Hearing and speech impairments (23,500,000 cases)	800 million
Federal appropriations for programs serving the handicapped, 1975 (1976 estimates about the same)	
Civilian programs specifically for the handicapped°	10,649,902,000
Veteran programs for the disabled	8,654,851,000

°Total reached by adding appropriations for handicapped only, as listed in "Federal Assistance Programs for the Handicapped," 1975. This figure does not include appropriations for programs which serve both the handicapped and the nonhandicapped, such as maternal and child health services, certain educational and vocational services, public assistance, Medicare, Urban Mass Transit, Small Business Administration loans, and National Institutes of Health research and training programs (which alone came to $843,237,000 for 1975).

Section 2. Voluntary Organizations

REHABILITATION (GENERAL)

American Academy of Compensation Medicine, Box 336, Murray Hill Station, New York, NY 10016.

American Academy of Physical Medicine and Rehabilitation, 30 North Michigan Avenue, Chicago, IL 60602.

American Association for Rehabilitation Therapy, P.O. Box 93, Little Rock, AR 72116.

American Board of Physical Medicine and Rehabilitation, Suite J1A, Kahler E., Rochester, MN 55901.

American Coalition of Citizens with Disabilities, 1346 Connecticut Avenue N.W., Washington, DC 20036.

American Congress of Rehabilitation Medicine, 30 North Michigan Avenue, Chicago, IL 60602.

American Dental Association, 211 East Chicago Avenue, Chicago, IL 60611.

American Hospital Association, Rehabilitation and Chronic Disease Hospital Section, 840 North Lake Shore Drive, Chicago, IL 60611.

American Medical Association, Department of Environmental Public and Occupational Health, 535 North Dearborn Street, Chicago, IL 60610.

American National Red Cross, 17th and D Streets N.W., Washington, DC 20006.

American Public Health Association, 1015 18th Street N.W., Washington, DC 20036.

American Rehabilitation Committee, 28 East 21st Street, New York, NY 10010.

American Rehabilitation Foundation (Sister Kenny Institute), 1800 Chicago Avenue, Minneapolis, MN 55404.

Association of Medical Rehabilitation Directors and Coordinators, 3830 Linklea Drive, Houston, TX 77025.

Association of Rehabilitation Facilities, 5530 Wisconsin Avenue, Washington, DC 20015.

Association of University Affiliated Facilities, 1100 17th Street N.W., Washington, DC 20036.

Commission on Accreditation of Rehabilitation Facilities, 6510 North Lincoln Avenue, Chicago, IL 60645.

Council of State Administrators of Vocational Rehabilitation, 1522 K Street N.W., Suite 1110, Washington, DC 20005.

Federation of the Handicapped, 211 West 14th Street, New York, NY 10011.

ICD Rehabilitation and Research Center, 340 East 24th Street, New York, NY 10010.

Institute of Rehabilitation Medicine, 400 East 34th Street, New York, NY 10016.

International Association of Psycho-Social Rehabilitation Services, 501 South 12th Street, Philadelphia, PA 19147.

International Society for Rehabilitation of the Disabled, 122 East 23d Street, New York, NY 10010.

National Association of the Physically Handicapped, 76 Elm Street, London, OH 43140.

National Congress of Organizations of the Physically Handicapped, 7611 Oakland Avenue, Minneapolis, MN 55423.

National Easter Seal Society for Crippled Children and Adults, 2023 Ogden Avenue, Chicago, IL 60612.

National Foundation for the Handicapped and Disabled, 1643 West Ogden Avenue, Chicago, IL 60612.

National Health Council, 1740 Broadway, New York, NY 10019.

National Rehabilitation Association, 1522 K Street N.W., Washington, DC 20005.

Partners of the Americas Rehabilitation–Special Education Program, 2001 S Street N.W., Washington, DC 20009.

Rehabilitation International, 122 East 23d Street, New York, NY 10010.

Rehabilitation International USA, 17 East 45th Street, New York, NY 10017.

World Rehabilitation Fund, 400 East 34th Street, New York, NY 10016.

ADVOCACY

This list does not include organizations with advocacy departments or committees, such as the American Association on Mental Deficiency, Council for Exceptional Children, Epilepsy Foundation of America, Joseph P. Kennedy Jr. Foundation, National Association of Retarded Citizens, National Society for Autistic Children, and United Cerebral Palsy Associations.

Action League for Physically Handicapped Adults, P.O. Box 5223, Louisville, KY 40205.

American Bar Association, Commission on the Mentally Disabled, 1800 M Street N.W., Washington, DC 20036.

ACLU Juvenile Rights Project, 22 East 40th Street, New York, NY 10016.

Center on Human Policy, Syracuse University, Syracuse, NY 13210.

Children's Defense Fund, 1520 New Hampshire Avenue N.W., Washington, DC 20036.

Civil Rights Division, United States Department of Justice, 1121 Vermont Avenue N.W., Washington, DC 20005.

Institute for the Study of Mental Retardation and Related Disabilities, 130 South First, University of Michigan, Ann Arbor, MI 48108.

Mental Health Law Project, 1220 19th Street N.W., Washington, DC 20036.

National Center for Law and the Handicapped, 1238 North Eddy Street, South Bend, IN 46617.

National Coalition for Children's Justice, 613 National Press Building, Washington, DC 20045.

National Legal Aid and Defender Association, 1155 East 60th Street, Chicago, IL 60637.

President's Committe on Mental Retardation, Regional Office Building #3, Seventh and D Streets S.W., Washington, DC 20201.

Youth Law Center, 693 Mission Street, San Francisco, CA 94105.

CONSUMER

In addition to the national association, American Coalition of Citizens with Disabilities (1346 Connecticut Avenue N.W., Washington, DC 20036), there is a growing number of organizations of the disabled throughout the United States, such as the following.

Action League for Handicapped Adults, 3901 Atkinson Drive, Louisville, KY 40218.

Adult Handicapped Association of Pennsylvania, 1346 Connecticut Avenue N.W., Washington, DC 20036.

Alabama Physically Handicapped Association, Route 3, Box 317, Haleyville, AL 35565.

Boston Center for Independent Living, 51 Spring Street, Watertown, MA.

California Association of the Physically Handicapped, P.O. Box 22552, Sacramento, CA 95822.

Center for Independent Living, 2539 Telegraph Avenue, Berkeley, CA 94704.

Coalition for the Removal of Architectural Barriers, 182 Alpine Terrace, San Francisco, CA 94117.

Disabled in Action, P.O. Box 243, Paramus, NJ 07652; 175 Willoughby Street, Apt. 11H, Brooklyn, NY 11201; 1319 McKinley Street, Philadelphia, PA 19111; 243 Roosevelt Avenue, Syracuse, NY 13210.

Idaho Association for Physically Handicapped Adults, 3115 Sycamore Drive, Boise, ID 83703.

Independence for Impaired Individuals, 826 Payne Avenue, St. Paul, MN 55101.

League for Human Dignity, 1118 Sharp Boulevard, Lincoln, NE 68508.

Massachusetts Association of Paraplegics, P.O. Box 48, Bedford, MA 01730.

Massachusetts Council of Organizations of the Handicapped, P.O. Box 153, Boston, MA 02130.

Minnesota Council for the Handicapped, Metro Square, Suite 492, Seventh and Roberts Streets, St. Paul, MN 55101.

Ohio Coalition of Citizens with Disabilities, 10236 Marie Avenue, Pickerington, OH 43147.

Our Way, 4304 Bradley Lane, Chevy Chase, MD 20015.

People First, P.O. Box 5208, Salem, OR 97304.

United Handicapped Federation, 1951 University Avenue, St. Paul, MN 55104.

DISABILITIES

Alcoholism

Al-Anon Family Group Headquarters, 115 East 23d Street, New York, NY 10010.

Alcohol and Drug Problems Association of North America, 1101 15th Street N.W., Washington, DC 20005.

American Council on Alcohol Problems, 119 Constitution Avenue N.E., Washington, DC 20002.

American Medical Society on Alcoholism, 733 Third Avenue, New York, NY 10017.

American Temperance Society, 6840 Eastern Avenue N.W., Washington, DC 20012.

General Service Board of Alcoholics Anonymous, 468 Park Avenue South, New York, NY 10016.

National Committee for the Prevention of Alcoholism and Drug Dependency, 6830 Laurel Street N.W., Washington, DC 20012.

National Council on Alcoholism, 2 Park Avenue, New York, NY 10016.

Amputation

American Orthotic and Prosthetic Association, 1440 N Street N.W., Washington, DC 20005.

National Amputation Foundation, 12-45 150th Street, Whitestone, NY 11357.

Arthritis and Rheumatism

Arthritis Foundation, 3400 Peachtree Road N.E., Atlanta, GA 30326

Lupus Foundation of America, Inc., 150 North Merrimac, St. Louis, MO 63141.

National Lupus Erythematosus Foundation, 5430 Van Nuys Boulevard, Van Nuys, CA 91401.

Arthrogryposis

Arthrogryposis (Multiplex Congenita) Association, 106 Herkimer Street, North Bellmore, NY 11710.

Ataxia

Friedreich's Ataxia Group in America, Box 11116, Oakland, CA 94611.

Muscular Dystrophy Association, 810 Seventh Avenue, New York, NY 10019.

National Ataxia Foundation, 4225 Golden Valley Road, Minneapolis, MN 55422.

Birth Defects, Genetic Counseling

American Genetic Association, 1028 Connecticut Avenue N.W., Washington, DC 20036.

American Society of Human Genetics, Department of Medical Genetics, John Hopkins University, 601 North Broadway, Baltimore, MD 21205.

Genetics Society of America, Department of Zoology, University of Texas, Austin, TX 78712.

National Foundation — March of Dimes, Box 2000, White Plains, NY 10602.

National Genetics Foundation, 250 West 57th Street, New York, NY 10019.

Prader-Willi Syndrome Parents and Friends, P.O. Box 252, Long Lake, MN 55356.

Rubella Birth Defect Evaluation Project, c/o Roosevelt Hospital, 428 West 59th Street, New York, NY 10019.

Blindness, Visual Impairment

American Academy of Ophthalmology and Otolaryngology, 15 Second Street S.W., Rochester, MN 55901.

American Association of Ophthalmology, 1100 17th Street N.W., Washington, DC 20036.

American Association of Workers for the Blind, 1511 K Street N.W., Suite 637, Washington, DC 20005.

American Council of the Blind, 818 18th Street N.W., Suite 700, Washington, DC 20006.

American Federation of Catholic Workers for the Blind and Visually Handicapped, 154 East 23d Street, New York, NY 10010.

American Foundation for the Blind, 15 West 16th Street, New York, NY 10011.

American Optometric Association, 7000 Chippewa Street, St. Louis, MO 63119.

American Optometric Foundation, 1730 M Street N.W., Washington, DC 20036.

American Orthoptic Council, 555 University Avenue, Toronto, Ontario M5G 1X8, Canada.

American Printing House for the Blind, 1839 Frankfort Avenue, Louisville, KY 40206.

Associated Blind, 135 West 23d Street, New York, NY 10011.

Association for the Education of the Visually Handicapped, 919 Walnut Street, Philadelphia, PA 19107.

Association for Research in Vision and Ophthalmology, Albany Medical College, Albany, NY 12208.

Better Vision Institute, 230 Park Avenue, New York, NY 10017.

Blind Service Association, 127 North Dearborn Street, Room 1628, Chicago, IL 60602.

Braille Institute of America, 741 North Vermont Avenue, Los Angeles, CA 90029.

Christian Record Braille Foundation, 4444 South 52d Street, Lincoln, NE 68506.

Eastern Conference of Rehabilitation Teachers of the Visually Handicapped, 3003 Parkwood Avenue, Richmond, VA 23221.

Eye-Bank for Sight Restoration, 210 East 64th Street, New York, NY 10021.

Eye Research, 131 Fulton Avenue, Hempstead, NY 11550.

Fight for Sight, 41 West 57th Street, New York, NY 10019.

Hadley School for the Blind, 700 Elm Street, Winnetka, IL 60093.

Jewish Guild for the Blind, 15 West 65th Street, New York, NY 10023.

National Accreditation Council for Agencies Serving the Blind and Visually Handicapped, 79 Madison Avenue, Suite 1406, New York, NY 10016.

National Association for Visually Handicapped, 305 East 24th Street, New York, NY 10010.

National Braille Association, 85 Godwin Avenue, Midland Park, NJ 07432.

National Committee for Research in Ophthalmology and Blindness, University of Louisville, School of Medicine, Louisville, KY 40201.

National Council of State Agencies for the Blind, c/o South Carolina Commission for the Blind, 1400 Main Street, Columbia, SC 29207.

National Eye Research Foundation, 18 South Michigan Avenue, Chicago, IL 60603.

National Federation of the Blind, 218 Randolph Hotel Building, Des Moines, IA 50309.

National Foundation for Eye Research, 1100 Keith Building, Cleveland, OH 44115.

National Retinitis Pigmentosa Foundation, Rolling Park Building, 8331 Mindale Circle, Baltimore, MD 21207.

National Society for the Prevention of Blindness, 79 Madison Avenue, New York, NY 10016.

Protestant Guild for the Blind, 456 Belmont Street, Watertown, MA 02172.

Recording for the Blind, 215 East 58th Street, New York, NY 10022.

Research to Prevent Blindness, 598 Madison Avenue, New York, NY 10022.

Tapes for the Blind, 12007 South Paramount Boulevard, Suite 2, Downey, CA 90242.

Xavier Society for the Blind, 153 East 23d Street, New York, NY 10010.

Blood Disorders

American Association of Blood Banks, 1828 L Street N.W., Washington, DC 20036.

American Society of Hematology, c/o Dr. Thomas B. Bradley, Veterans Administration Hospital, 4150 Clement Street, San Francisco, CA 94121.

Children's Blood Foundation, 342 Madison Avenue, New York, NY 10017.

Cooley's Anemia Blood and Research Foundation for Children, 647 Franklin Avenue, Garden City, NY 11530.

Leukemia Society of America, 211 East 43d Street, New York, NY 10017.

Living Bank, P.O. Box 6725, Houston, TX 77005.

National Hemophilia Foundation, 25 West 39th Street, New York, NY 10018.

National Rare Blood Club, c/o Associated Health Foundation, 164 Fifth Avenue, New York, NY 10010.

National Sickle Cell Disease Research Foundation, Association for Sickle Cell Anemia, 521 Fifth Avenue, New York, NY 10036.

Society for the Study of Blood, New York Medical College, 1249 Fifth Avenue, New York, NY 10029.

Brain Damage

Brain Research Foundation, University of Chicago, 343 South Dearborn Street, Chicago, IL 60604.

Institutes for the Achievement of Human Potential, 8801 Stenton Avenue, Philadelphia, PA 19118.

National Easter Seal Society for Crippled Children and Adults, 2023 West Ogden Avenue, Chicago, IL 60612.

Burn Injuries

Action for Prevention of Burn Injuries to Children, P.O. Box 347, Burlington, MA 01803.

American Burn Association, c/o Charles E. Hartford, Department of Surgery, University of Iowa Hospitals, Iowa City, IA 52242.

National Burn Victim Foundation, 439 Main Street, Orange, NJ 07050.

National Fire Prevention and Control Administration, Department of Commerce, Washington, DC 20230.

National Fire Protection Association, 470 Atlantic Avenue, Boston, MA 02210.

National Institute for Burn Medicine, 909 East Ann Street, Ann Arbor, MI 48104.

Cancer

American Association for Cancer Research, Institute for Cancer Research, 7701 Burholme Avenue, Philadelphia, PA 19111.

American Association for Cancer Education, c/o Dr. Richard F. Bakemeier, Strong Memorial Hospital, 601 Elmwood Avenue, Rochester, NY 14642.

American Cancer Society, 777 Third Avenue, New York, NY 10017.

Breast Diseases Association of America, 3310 Rochambeau Avenue, Bronx, NY 10467.

Candlelighters, 123 C Street S.E., Washington, DC 20003.

Children's Cancer Fund of America, 15 East 67th Street, New York, NY 10021.

City of Hope, 208 West Eighth Street, Los Angeles, CA 90014.

Damon Runyon–Walter Winchell Cancer Fund, 33 West 56th Street, New York, NY 10019.

International Association of Cancer Victims and Friends, Box 7318, Beverly Hills, CA 90212.

National Cancer Foundation, 1 Park Avenue, New York, NY 10016.

United Cancer Council, 1803 North Meridian Street, Indianapolis, IN 46202.

Cardiac Disorders

American College of Cardiology, 9650 Rockville Pike, Bethesda, MD 20014.

American Heart Association, 7320 Greenville Avenue, Dallas, TX 75231.

Heart Disease Research Foundation, 963 Essex Street, Brooklyn, NY 11208.

Mended Hearts, 721 Huntington Avenue, Roxbury, MA 02115.

Cerebral Palsy

American Academy for Cerebral Palsy and Developmental Medicine, c/o James E. Bryan, 1255 New Hampshire Avenue N.W., Washington, DC 20036.

Dental Guidance Council for Cerebral Palsy, 122 East 23d Street, New York, NY 10010.

United Cerebral Palsy Associations, 66 East 34th Street, New York, NY 10016.

Cystic Fibrosis

Cystic Fibrosis Foundation, 3379 Peachtree Road N.E., Atlanta, GA 30326.

Diabetes

American Diabetes Association, 1 West 48th Street, New York, NY 10020.

Joslin Diabetes Foundation, Inc., 15 Joslin Road, Boston, MA 02215.

Juvenile Diabetes Foundation, 23 East 26th Street, New York, NY 10010.

Disfigurement

American Academy of Facial Plastic and Reconstructive Surgery, 2800 North Lakeshore Drive, Chicago, IL 60657.

American Society of Plastic and Reconstructive Surgeons, 29 East Madison, Suite 807, Chicago, IL 60602.

Debbie Fox Foundation for Treatment of Craniofacial Deformities, P.O. Box 11082, Chattanooga, TN 37401.

Institute of Reconstructive Plastic Surgery, New York University Medical Center, 550 First Avenue, New York, NY 10016.

Plastic Surgery Research Council, 11411 Brookshire Avenue, Suite 504, Downey, CA 90241.

Society for the Rehabilitation of the Facially Disfigured, 550 First Avenue, New York, NY 10016.

Dwarfism

Human Growth Foundation, Maryland Academy of Science Building, 601 Light Street, Baltimore, MD 21230.

Little People of America, Box 126, Owatonna, MN 55060.

Dysautonomia

Dysautonomia Foundation, 370 Lexington Avenue, New York, NY 10017.

Epilepsy

American Epilepsy Society, Division of Neurosurgery, University of Texas Medical Branch, Galveston, TX 77550.

Epilepsy Foundation of America, 1828 L Street N.W., Washington, DC 20036.

Geriatric Disorders

Aging Research Institute, 342 Madison Avenue, New York, NY 10017.

American Aging Association, c/o Dr. Denham Harman, University of Nebraska Medical Center, Omaha, NE 68105.

American Association of Homes for the Aging, 1050 17th Street N.W., Washington, DC 20036.

American Geriatrics Society, 10 Columbus Circle, New York, NY 10019.

American Health Care Association, 1200 15th Street N.W.,Washington, DC 20005.

Association for the Advancement of Aging Research, 309 Hancock Building, University of Southern California, Los Angeles, CA 90007.

Citizens for Better Care in Nursing Homes, Homes for the Aged and Other After-Care Facilities, 960 East Jefferson Avenue, Detroit, MI 48207.

Gerontological Society, 1 Dupont Circle, Suite 520, Washington, DC 20036.

National Council of Senior Citizens, 1511 K Street N.W., Washington, DC 20005.

National Council on the Aging, 1828 L Street N.W., Washington, DC 20036.

National Geriatrics Society, 212 West Wisconsin Avenue, Milwaukee, WI 53203.

Hansen's Disease (see Leprosy)

Hearing Disorders

Academy of Rehabilitative Audiology, c/o Dr. E. J. Hardick, Wayne State University, Department of Audiology, 261 Mack Boulevard, Detroit, MI 48201.

Alexander Graham Bell Association for the Deaf, 3417 Volta Place N.W., Washington, DC 20007.

American Organization for the Education of the Hearing Impaired, 1537 35th Street N.W., Washington, DC 20007.

American Otological Society, 221 Marshall Taylor Doctors Building, Jacksonville, FL 32207.

American Speech and Hearing Association, 9030 Old Georgetown Road, Washington, DC 20014.

Deafness Research Foundation, 366 Madison Avenue, New York, NY 10017.

International Parents Organization, c/o Alexander Graham Bell Association for the Deaf, 1537 35th Street N.W., Washington, DC 20007.

Junior National Association for the Deaf, Gallaudet College, Washington, DC 20002.

National Association for Hearing and Speech Action, 814 Thayer Avenue, Silver Spring, MD 20910.

National Association of the Deaf, 814 Thayer Avenue, Silver Spring, MD 20910.

Kidney Disease

American Society for Artificial Internal Organs, Box 777, Boca Raton, FL 33432.

Committee on Donor Enlistment, 2022 Lee Road, Cleveland Heights, OH 44118.

Medic-Alert Organ Donor Program, 1000 North Palm Street, Turlock, CA 95380.

National Association of Patients on Hemodialysis and Transplantation, 505 Northern Boulevard, Great Neck, NY 11021.

National Kidney Foundation, 116 East 27th Street, New York, NY 10016.

Laryngeal Cancer

International Association of Laryngectomees, c/o American Cancer Society, 777 Third Avenue, New York, NY 10017.

Learning Disabilities

Association for Childhood Education International, 3615 Wisconsin Avenue N.W., Washington, DC 20016.

Association for Children with Learning Disabilities, 5225 Grace Street, Pittsburgh, PA 15236.

National Association of Private Schools for Exceptional Children, 7700 Miller Road, Miami, FL 33155.

National Association of State Directors of Special Education, 1510 H Street N.W., Washington, DC 20005.

Orton Society, 8415 Bellona Lane, Towson, MD 21204.

Research and Demonstration Center for the Education of Handicapped Children and Youth, Teachers College, Columbia University, New York, NY 10027.

Leprosy (Hansen's Disease)

American Leprosy Missions, 1260 Broad Street, Bloomfield, NJ 07003.

Damien Dutton Society for Leprosy Aid, 616 Bedford Avenue, Bellmore, NY 11710.

Leonard Wood Memorial for the Eradication of Leprosy, 2430 Pennsylvania Avenue N.W., Washington, DC 20037.

Mental Illness

American Academy of Child Psychiatry, 1800 R Street N.W., Suite 904, Washington, DC 20009.

American Academy of Psychoanalysis, 40 Gramercy Park North, New York, NY 10010.

American Association of Psychiatric Services for Children, 1701 18th Street N.W., Washington, DC 20009.

American Group Psychotherapy Association, 1865 Broadway, 12th Floor, New York, NY 10023.

American Mental Health Foundation, 2 East 86th Street, New York, NY 10028.

American Orthopsychiatric Association, 1775 Broadway, New York, NY 10019.

American Psychiatric Association, 1700 18th Street N.W., Washington, DC 20009.

American Psychoanalytic Association, 1 East 57th Street, New York, NY 10022.

American Psychosomatic Society, 265 Nassau Road, Roosevelt, NY 11575.

American Schizophrenia Association, Huxley Institute, 1114 First Avenue, New York, NY 10021.

American Society of Group Psychotherapy and Psychodrama, 259 Wolcott Avenue, Beacon, NY 12508.

Association for Advancement of Behavior Therapy, 475 Park Avenue South, New York, NY 10016.

Group for the Advancement of Psychiatry, Western Psychiatric Institute, 3811 O'Hara Street, Pittsburgh, PA 15261.

International Association for Child Psychiatry and Allied Professions, Child Study Center, Yale University, 333 Cedar Street, New Haven, CO 06510.

International Association for Suicide Prevention, 1041 Menlo Avenue, Los Angeles, CA 90006.

Menninger Foundation, 3617 West Sixth Street, Topeka, KS 66601.

National Association for Mental Health, 1800 North Kent Street, Rosslyn, VA 22209.

National Association of Private Psychiatric Hospitals, 1 Farragut Square South, Suite 201, Washington, DC 20006.

National Association of State Mental Health Program Directors, 1001 Third Street S.W., Washington, DC 20024.

National Committee Against Mental Illness, 1101 17th Street N.W., Washington, DC 20036.

National Consortium for Child Mental Health Services, 1800 R Street N.W., Suite 904, Washington, DC 20009.

National Save-A-Life League, 815 Second Avenue, Suite 409, New York, NY 10017.

National Society for Autistic Children, 169 Tampa Avenue, Albany, NY 12208.

Neurotics Anonymous International Liaison, 1341 G Street N.W., Washington, DC 20005.

Recovery, 116 South Michigan Avenue, Chicago, IL 60603.

Social Psychiatry Research Institute, 150 East 69th Street, New York, NY 10021.

Society for Clinical and Experimental Hypnosis, 205 West End Avenue, New York, NY 10023.

Society of Biological Psychiatry, 2010 Wilshire Boulevard, Los Angeles, CA 90057.

Mental Retardation

American Academy on Mental Retardation, 1640 Roosevelt Road, Chicago, IL 60608.

American Association on Mental Deficiency, 5201 Connecticut Avenue N.W., Washington, DC 20015.

Association for Children with Retarded Mental Development, 902 Broadway, New York, NY 10010.

Council for Exceptional Children, 1920 Association Drive, Reston, VA 22091.

International Association for the Scientific Study of Mental Deficiency, c/o Dr. David Primrose, Royal Scottish National Hospital, Lambert, Sterlingshire, Scotland.

Joseph P. Kennedy Jr. Foundation, 1701 K Street N.W., Suite 205, Washington, DC 20006.

Mothers of Children with Down's Syndrome, 105 East Anandale Road, Falls Church, VA 22046.

National Association for Down's Syndrome, 628 Ashland, River Forest, IL 60305.

National Association for Retarded Citizens, 2709 Avenue E East, Arlington, TX 76011.

National Association of Coordinators of State Programs for the Mentally Retarded, 2001 Jefferson Davis Highway, Suite 802, Arlington, VA 22202.

President's Committee on Mental Retardation, 20th and D Streets N.W., Washington, DC 20201.

Multiple Sclerosis

National Multiple Sclerosis Society, 205 East 42d Street, New York, NY 10017.

Muscular Dystrophy

Muscular Dystrophy Association, 810 Seventh Avenue, New York, NY 10019.

Myasthenia Gravis

Muscular Dystrophy Association, 810 Seventh Avenue, New York, NY 10019.

Myasthenia Gravis Foundation, 230 Park Avenue, New York, NY 10017.

Neurological Disorders

American Narcolepsy Association, Box 5846, Stanford, CA 94305.

American Neurological Association, c/o Peritz Scheinberg, P.O. Box 520875, Biscayne Annex, Miami, FL 33152.

Amyotrophic Lateral Sclerosis Foundation, 2840 Adams Avenue, San Diego, CA 92116.

Amyotrophic Lateral Sclerosis Society of America, 11520 San Vincente Boulevard, Suite 206, Los Angeles, CA 90049.

Committee to Combat Huntington's Disease, 250 West 57th Street, Suite 2016, New York, NY 10019.

National ALS Foundation, 185 Madison Avenue, New York, NY 10016.

National Committee for Research in Neurological and Communicative Disorders, 927 National Press Building, Washington, DC 20045.

National Tay-Sachs and Allied Diseases Association, 122 East 42d Street, New York, NY 10017.

National Tuberous Sclerosis Association, P.O. Box 159, Laguna Beach, CA 92652.

Obesity

American Society of Bariatric Physicians, 333 West Hampden Avenue, Suite 500, Englewood, CO 80110.

National Council of Obesity, P.O. Box 35306, Los Angeles, CA 90035.

Overeaters Anonymous World Service Organization, 3730 Motor Avenue, Los Angeles, CA 90034.

TOPS Club, 4575 South Fifth Street, Milwaukee, WI 53207.

Orthopedic Disorders

American Association of Foot Specialists, 1801 Vauxhall Road, Union, NJ 07083.

American Fracture Association, 600 Livingston Building, Bloomington, IL 61701.

American Orthopaedic Association, 430 North Michigan Avenue, Chicago, IL 60611.

American Osteopathic Association, 212 East Ohio Street, Chicago, IL 60611.

American Osteopathic College of Rehabilitation Medicine, 1720 East McPherson Street, Kirksville, MO 63501.

American Podiatry Association, 20 Chevy Chase Circle N.W., Washington, DC 20015.

Association of Bone and Joint Surgeons, 2116 North 122d Street, Seattle, WA 98133.

Association of State Maternal and Child Health and Crippled Children's Directors, Division of Maternal and Child Health, 10003 O Street, Lincoln, NE 68508.

Osteogenesis Imperfecta, Inc., 1231 May Court, Burlington, NC 27215.

Ostomies

American Digestive Disease Society, 420 Lexington Avenue, New York, NY 10017.

National Foundation for Ileitis and Colitis, 295 Madison Avenue, New York, NY 10017.

United Ostomy Association, 1111 Wilshire Boulevard, Los Angeles, CA 90017.

Parkinson's Disease

American Parkinson Disease Association, 147 East 50th Street, New York, NY 10022.

National Parkinson Foundation, 1501 Northwest Ninth Avenue, Miami, FL 33136.

Parkinson's Disease Foundation, William Black Medical Research Building, Columbia Presbyterian Medical Center, 640 West 168th Street, New York, NY 10032.

United Parkinson Foundation, 220 South State Street, Chicago, IL 60604.

Pulmonary Disorders

Allergy Foundation of America, 801 Second Avenue, New York, NY 10017.

American College of Chest Physicians, 911 Busse Highway, Park Ridge, IL 60068.

American Lung Association, 1740 Broadway, New York, NY 10019.

Children's Asthma Research Institute and Hospital at Denver, 1999 Julian Street, Denver, CO 80204.

Emphysema Anonymous, P.O. Box 66, Fort Myers, FL 33902.

National Foundation for Asthmatic Children at Tucson, P.O. Box 50304, Tucson, AZ 85703.

Research and Education Foundation for Chest Disease, 911 Busse Highway, Park Ridge, IL 60068.

Speech Disorders

Academy of Aphasia, 1 Waterhouse Street, Massachusetts General Hospital, Pediatric Urology Unit, Boston, MA 02114.

American Cleft Palate Association, 331 Salk Hall, University of Pittsburgh, Pittsburgh, PA 15261.

American Speech and Hearing Association, 9030 Old Georgetown Road, Washington, DC 20014.

Council of Adult Stutterers, c/o Speech and Hearing Clinic, Catholic University of America, Washington, DC 20064.

Spina Bifida

Spina Bifida Association of America, 343 South Dearborn Avenue, Chicago, IL 60604.

Spinal Cord Injury

National Paraplegia Foundation, 333 North Michigan Avenue, Chicago, IL 60601.
Paralyzed Veterans of America, 7315 Wisconsin Avenue, Suite 300W, Washington, DC 20014.

Stroke

Stroke Club of America, 805 12th Street, Galveston, TX 77550.

Venereal Disease

American Social Health Association, 260 Sheridan Avenue, Palo Alto, CA 94306.
American Venereal Disease Association, 4716 Benton Smith Road, Nashville, TN 37215.
Operation Venus, 1213 Clover Street, Philadelphia, PA 19107.

EMPLOYMENT

AFL-CIO Department of Community Services, 815 16th Street N.W., Washington, DC 20006.
American Organization for Rehabilitation through Training Federation (ORT), 817 Broadway, New York, NY 10003.
Association of Handicapped Artists, 1134 Rand Building, Buffalo, NY 14203.
Council of State Administrators of Vocational Rehabilitation, 1522 K Street N.W., Suite 836, Washington, DC 20005.
EPI-HAB, L.A., 5533 Western Avenue, Los Angeles, CA 90062.
Federation Employment and Guidance Service, 215 Park Avenue South, New York, NY 10003.
Goodwill Industries of America, 9200 Wisconsin Avenue, Washington, DC 20014.
Handicapped Artists of America, 8 Sandy Lane, Salisbury, MA 01950.
Human Resources Center, Abilities, Inc., Willets Road, Albertson, NY 11507.
Industrial Home for the Blind, 57 Willoughby Street, Brooklyn, NY 11201.
International Association of Machinists and Aerospace Workers, 1300 Connecticut Avenue N.W., Washington, DC 20036.
Interstate Conference of Employment Security Agencies, 1329 E Street N.W., Washington, DC 20004.
Just One Break, 373 Park Avenue South, New York, NY 10016.
National Industries for the Blind, 1455 Broad Street, Bloomfield, NJ 07003.
National Industries for the Severely Handicapped, 4350 East-West Highway, Suite 1120, Washington, DC 20014.
Paraplegics Manufacturing Company, 304 North York Road, Bensenville, IL 60106.
President's Committee on Employment of the Handicapped, Washington, DC 20210.

RECREATION

American Alliance for Health, Physical Education and Recreation, 1201 16th Street N.W., Washington, DC 20036.

American Athletic Association for the Deaf, 3916 Lantern Drive, Silver Spring, MD 20902.

American Blind Bowling Association, 150 North Bellaire Avenue, Louisville, KY 40206.

Boy Scouts of America, North Brunswick, NJ 08902.

Camp Fire Girls, 1740 Broadway, New York, NY 10019.

The 52 Association, 147 East 50th Street, New York, NY 10022.

Girl Scouts of the U.S.A. 830 Third Avenue, New York, NY 10022.

Indoor Sports Club, 1145 Highland Street, Napoleon, OH 43545.

International Committee of the Silent Sports, Gallaudet College, Washington, DC 20002.

International Friendship League, 40 Mount Vernon Street, Boston, MA 02108.

International Handicapped Net (amateur radio), P.O. Box B, San Gabriel, CA 91778.

International Mailbag Club, 3641 Marydell Place, Cincinnati, OH 45211.

International Sports Organization for the Disabled, Stokes Mandeville Sports Stadium, Harvey Road, Aylesbury, Buckshire, England.

Letters Abroad, 209 East 56th Street, New York, NY 10022.

National Inconvenienced Sportsmen's Association, 3738 Walnut Avenue, Carmichael, CA 95608.

National Recreation and Park Association, 1601 North Kent Street, Arlington, VA 22209.

National Therapeutic Recreation Society, 1601 North Kent Street, Arlington, VA 22209.

National Wheelchair Athletic Association, 20-64 62d Street, Woodside, NY 11377.

National Wheelchair Basketball Association, 110 Seaton Building, University of Kentucky, Lexington, KY 40506.

Special Olympics (for retarded), 1701 K Street N.W., Suite 203, Washington, DC 20006.

United States Deaf Skiers Association, 2 Sunset Hill Road, Simsbury, CT 06070.

Voicespondence Club, P.O. Box 207, Shillington, PA 19607.

World Pen Pals, 1690 Como Avenue, St. Paul, MN 55108.

REHABILITATION PERSONNEL

Academy of Dentistry for the Handicapped, 1240 East Main Street, Springfield, OH 45503.

American Academy of Orthotists and Prosthetists, 1444 N Street N.W., Washington, DC 20005.

American Art Therapy Association, 3007 South Braeswood Boulevard, Houston, TX 77025.

American Association for Rehabilitation Therapy, P.O. Box 93, North Little Rock, AR 72116.

American Association for Respiratory Therapy, 7411 Hines Place, Dallas, TX 75235.

American Association of Certified Orthoptists, c/o Evelyn Tomlinson,

Department of Ophthalmology, Medical University of South Carolina, 80 Barre Street, Charleston, SC 29401.

American Association of Industrial Nurses, 79 Madison Avenue, New York, NY 10016.

American Association of Special Educators, 107-20 125th Street, Richmond Hill, NY 11413.

American Boards of Examiners in Speech Pathology and Audiology, 9030 Old Georgetown Road, Washington, DC 20014.

American College of Nursing Home Administrators, 4650 East-West Highway, Washington, DC 20014.

American Corrective Therapy Association, c/o Kirk Hodges, 6622 Spring Hollow, San Antonio, TX 78249.

American Dance Therapy Association, 1000 Century Plaza, Suite 216-E, Columbia, MD 21044.

American Dietetic Association, 430 North Michigan Avenue, Chicago, IL 60611.

American Home Economics Association, 2010 Massachusetts Avenue N.W., Washington, DC 20036.

American Medical Technologists, 710 Higgins Road, Park Ridge, IL 60068.

American Nurses' Association, 2420 Pershing Road, Kansas City, MO 64108.

American Occupational Therapy Association, 6000 Executive Boulevard, Suite 200, Rockville, MD 20852.

American Optometric Association, 7000 Chippewa Street, St. Louis, MO 63119.

American Orthoptic Council, 555 University Avenue, Toronto, Ontario M5G 1X8, Canada.

American Personnel and Guidance Association, 1607 New Hampshire Avenue N.W., Washington, DC 20009.

American Physical Therapy Association, 1156 15th Street N.W., Washington, DC 20005.

American Psychological Association, Division of Rehabilitation Psychology, 2658 South Elm Street, Tempe, AZ 85282.

American Rehabilitation Counseling Association 1607 New Hampshire Avenue N.W., Washington, DC 20009.

American Society for Medical Technology, 5555 West Loop South, Suite 200, Bellaire, TX 77401.

American Society of Allied Health Professions, National Center for Higher Education, 1 DuPont Circle N.W., Suite 300, Washington, DC 20036.

American Women's Voluntary Services, 135 East 65th Street, New York, NY 10021.

Association of Medical Rehabilitation Directors and Coordinators, 3830 Linklea Drive, Houston, TX 77025.

Association of Volunteer Bureaus of America, Box 7253, Kansas City, MO 64113.

Biomedical Engineering Society, P.O. Box 2399, Culver City CA 90230.

Convention of American Instructors of the Deaf, 5034 Wisconsin Avenue N.W., Washington, DC 20016.

Family Service Association of America, 44 East 23rd Street, New York, NY 10010.

Joint Commission on Allied Health Personnel in Ophthalmology, 1575 University Avenue, St. Paul, MN 55104.

National Association for Music Therapy, P.O. Box 610, Lawrence, KS 66044.

National Association for Practical Nurse Education and Service, 122 East 42d Street, New York, NY 10017.

National Association of Allied Health Schools, 1629 K Street N.W., Suite 520, Washington, DC 20006.

National Association of Disability Examiners, 1522 K Street N.W., Washington, DC 20005.

National Association of Human Services Technologies, 1127 11th Street, Main Floor, Sacramento, CA 95814.

National Association of Physical Therapists, P.O. Box 367, West Covina, CA 91793.

National Association of Social Workers, 1425 H Street N.W., Suite 600, Washington, DC 20005.

National Center for Voluntary Action, 1785 Massachusetts Avenue N.W. Washington, DC 20036.

National Council for Homemaker–Home Health Aide Services, 67 Irving Place, New York, NY 10003.

National Federation of Licensed Practical Nurses, 250 West 57th Street, New York, NY 10019.

National League for Nursing, 10 Columbus Circle, New York, NY 10019.

National New Professional Health Workers, 184 Fifth Avenue, New York, NY 10010.

Professional Rehabilitation Workers with the Adult Deaf, 814 Thayer Avenue, Silver Spring, MD 20910.

Society of Nuclear Medicine, 475 Park Avenue South, New York, NY 10016.

Volunteers (civic organizations, lodges): Demolay, Elks, Civitan, Jaycees, Junior Leagues, Kiwanis, Knights of Columbus, Knights of Pythias, Lions, Masons, Moose, Optimist International, Rotary, Volunteers of America.

VETERANS ORGANIZATIONS

American Legion National Rehabilitation Commission, 1608 K Street N.W., Washington, DC 20006.

American Veterans Committee, 1333 Connecticut Avenue N.W., Washington, DC 20036.

AMVETS, 1710 Rhode Island Avenue N.W., Washington, DC 20036.

Blinded Veterans Association, 1735 DeSales Street N.W., Washington, DC 20036.

Catholic War Veterans of the U.S., 2 Massachusetts Avenue N.W., Washington, DC 20001.

Disabled American Veterans, 3725 Alexandria Pike, Cold Spring, KY 41076.

Jewish War Veterans of the U.S.A., 1712 New Hampshire Avenue N.W., Washington, DC 20009.

Military Order of the Purple Heart, 1022 Wilson Boulevard, Arlington, VA 22209.

National Association of State Directors of Veterans Affairs, 211 West Campbell Avenue, Roanoke, VA 24011.

Paralyzed Veterans of America, 7315 Wisconsin Avenue, Washington, DC 20014.

Veterans of Foreign Wars of the United States, 34th and Broadway, Kansas City, MO 64111.

Section 3. Federal Organizations

Major Information Offices

National Center for Health Statistics (DHEW, Health Resources Administration), 5600 Fishers Lane, Rockville, MD 20852.

National Information Center for the Handicapped (DHEW), *Closer Look*, 1201 16th Street N.W., Washington, DC 20036.

National Institutes of Health (DHEW), Office of Information, 9000 Rockville Pike, Bethesda, MD 20014.

Office for Handicapped Individuals (DHEW), *Programs for the Handicapped*, 330 C Street S.W., Washington, DC 20201.

Veterans Administration Central Office, Washington, DC 20420.

ACTION (Foster Grandparents Program), 806 Connecticut Avenue N.W., Washington, DC 20525.

Committee for Purchase from the Blind and Other Severely Handicapped, 2009 14th Street North, Suite 610, Arlington, VA 22201.

Department of Agriculture, Extension Service, Washington, DC 20250.

National Industries for the Blind, 1511 K Street N.W., Washington, DC 20005.

National Industries for the Severely Handicapped, 4350 East-West Highway, Washington, DC 20014.

Civil Service Commission

Interagency Committee on Handicapped Employees, 1900 E Street N.W., Room 6514, Washington, DC 20415.

Office of Selective Placement, Washington, DC 20415.

Personnel Research and Development Center, 1900 E Street N.W., Washington, DC 20415.

DHEW, Office of Education

Bureau of Education for the Handicapped, 400 Maryland Avenue S.W., Washington, DC 20202.

Bureau of Occupational and Adult Education, Washington, DC 20202.

Bureau of School Systems, Division of Supplementary Centers and Services, 400 Maryland Avenue S.W., Washington, DC 20202.

DHEW, Office of Human Development

Architectural and Transportation Barriers Compliance Board, Room 1004, Switzer Building, Washington, DC 20201.

Children's Bureau, P.O. Box 1182, Washington, DC 20013.

Developmental Disabilities Office, Washington, DC 20201.

Office of Child Development/Head Start, P.O. Box 1182, Washington, DC 20013.

President's Committee on Mental Retardation, Washington, DC 20201.

Rehabilitation Services Administration, Washington, DC 20201.

DHEW, Office of the Secretary

Office of Surplus Property Utilization, Washington, DC 20201.

DHEW, Public Health Service

Bureau of Community Health Services (Crippled Children's Services, Family Planning Services, Office for Maternal and Child Health), 5600 Fishers Lane, Rockville, MD 20852.

National Institute of Mental Health, 5600 Fishers Lane, Rockville, MD 20852.

National Institute on Alcohol, Drug Abuse, and Mental Health Administration, 11400 Rockville Pike, Rockville, MD 20852.

National Institutes of Health, 9000 Rockville Pike, Bethesda, MD 20014.

DHEW, Social and Rehabilitation Service

Community Services Administration (Social Services), 330 C Street S.W., Washington, DC 20201.

Medical Services Administration (Medicaid), 330 C Street S.W., Washington, DC 20201.

DHEW, Social Security Administration

Bureau of Disability Insurance, Room 760, East Highrise, Baltimore, MD 21235.

Bureau of Health Insurance (Medicare), Room 700, East Highrise, Baltimore, MD 21235.

Bureau of Supplemental Security Income 108 West Highrise, Baltimore, MD 21235.

Department of Housing and Urban Development

Assistant Secretary for Housing Production and Mortgage Credit, 451 Seventh Street S.W., Washington, DC 20410.

Department of Labor

Employment Standards Administration, Washington, DC 20210.

United States Employment Service, Manpower Administration, Washington, DC 20213.

Department of the Interior

Division of Social Services, Bureau of Indian Affairs, 1951 Constitution Avenue N.W., Washington, DC 20245.

Department of Transportation

Federal Aviation Administration, Washington, DC 20590.

General Services Administration

General Services Administration (Removal of Architectural Barriers), Washington, DC 20205.
Office of Real Property, Public Buildings Service, Washington, DC 20405.
Utilization and Donation Division, Federal Supply Service, Washington, DC 20406.

Library of Congress

Division for the Blind and Physically Handicapped, 1291 Taylor Street N.W., Washington, DC 20542.

National Aeronautics and Space Administration

Technology Utilization Office, Code KT, NASA Headquarters, Washington, DC 20546.

Urban Mass Transportation Administration

Office of Capital Assistance, 400 Seventh Street S.W., Washington, DC 20590.

Other Agencies

President's Committee on Employment of the Handicapped, Washington, DC 20210.
Small Business Administration, 1441 L Street N.W., Washington, DC 20416.
Veterans Administration (all services and departments), Washington, DC 20420.

Section 4. Periodicals

The following list is divided into three sections: (1) periodicals on general rehabilitation; (2) periodicals on individual disabilities; and (3) abstracts and digests in the field. Except in a few instances, it does not include newsletters, bulletins, annual reports, or convention proceedings, all of which can usually be obtained free of charge from the organizations listed in Section 1.

REHABILITATION (GENERAL)

Academic Therapy (quarterly, $6.00), 1539 Fourth Street, San Rafael, CA 94901.

Accent on Living (quarterly, $3.50), P.O. Box 700, Bloomington, IL 61701.

Achievement (monthly, $2.00), The Achievement-Disabled Action Group, 9251 Northeast 122d Street, North Miami, FL 33161.

Active Handicapped (bimonthly, $3.00), Active Handicapped, Inc., 528 Aurora Avenue, Metairie, LA 70005.

American Archives of Rehabilitation Therapy (quarterly, $7.00), American Association of Rehabilitation Therapy, Box 93, North Little Rock, AR 72115.

American Corrective Therapy Journal, (bimonthly, $12.00), 4910 Bayou Vista, Houston, TX 77088.

American Journal of Art Therapy (quarterly, $10.00), Box 4918, Washington, DC 20008.

American Journal of Physical Medicine (bimonthly, $12.00), Williams and Wilkins Company, 428 East Preston Street, Baltimore, MD 21202.

American Rehabilitation (formerly *Rehabilitation Record;* monthly, $11.75), Rehabilitation Services Administration, P.O. Box 1533, Washington, DC 20402.

Amicus (bimonthly), National Center for Law and the Handicapped, 1235 North Eddy Street, South Bend, IN 46617.

Archives of Physical Medicine and Rehabilitation (monthly, $20.00), American Congress of Physical Medicine and Rehabilitation, 30 North Michigan Avenue, Chicago, IL 60602.

Canadian Journal of Occupational Therapy (quarterly, $10.00), 4 New Street, Toronto, Ontario M5R 1P6, Canada.

COPH Bulletin (quarterly, $2.00), National Congress of Organizations of the Physically Handicapped, 7611 Oakland Avenue, Minneapolis, MN 55423.

Closer Look, National Information Center for the Handicapped (DHEW), Box 1492, Washington, DC 20013.

The Independent (quarterly, $2.00), Center for Independent Living, 2539 Telegraph Avenue, Berkeley, CA 94704.

Informer, Office of Human Development, Rehabilitation Services Administration, Washington, DC 20201.

International Rehabilitation Review (quarterly, $5.00), Rehabilitation International, 122 East 23d Street, New York, NY 10010.

Journal of Applied Rehabilitation Counseling (quarterly, $8.00), National Rehabilitation Counseling Association, 1522 K Street N.W., Washington, DC 20005.

Journal of Health and Social Behavior (quarterly, $8.00), American Sociological Association, 1001 Connecticut Avenue N.W., Washington, DC 20036.

Journal of Health, Physical Education and Recreation (monthly, $25.00), American Alliance for Health, Physical Education and Recreation, 1201 16th Street N.W., Washington, DC 20036.

Journal of Music Therapy (quarterly, $7.00), National Association of Music Therapy, P.O. Box 610, Lawrence, KS 66044.

Journal of Physical Therapy (monthly, $18.00), American Physical Therapy Association, 1156 15th Street N.W., Washington, DC 20005.

National Hookup (monthly, $2.50), Indoor Sports Club, 31 Margaret Drive, RD 6, Ballston Spa, NY 12020.

National Star Newsletter ($1.50 per year), 6932 North Olcott Avenue, Chicago, IL 60631.

New Horizons (semiannual), 2150 Corbin Avenue, New Britain, CT 06050.

New World (monthly, $5.00), California Association for the Physically Handicapped, Box 229, Northridge, CA 91324.

Occupational Therapy (monthly, $8.00), American Occupational Therapy Association, 6000 Executive Boulevard, Rockville, MD 20852.

Performance, President's Committee on Employment of the Handicapped, Washington, DC 20210.

Perspectives in Long Term Care (quarterly), American Medical Association Council on Medical Service, 535 North Dearborn Street, Chicago, IL 60610.

Polling Magazine (quarterly), 122 East 23d Street, New York, NY 10010.

Programs for the Handicapped, Office for Handicapped Individuals, Washington, DC 20201.

Rehabilitation (quarterly, $6.00), British Council for Rehabilitation of the Disabled, Tavistock Square, London WC1, England.

Rehabilitation Counseling Bulletin (quarterly, $7.00), American Rehabilitation Counseling Association, 1607 New Hampshire Avenue N.W., Washington, DC 20009.

Rehabilitation Digest (quarterly, $3.00), Canadian Rehabilitation Council for the Disabled, 242 St. George Street, Toronto, Ontario M 5R 2NF, Canada.

Rehabilitation Gazette (1 per year, $3.00 to disabled, $5.00 to nondisabled), 4502 Maryland Avenue, St. Louis, MO 63108.

Rehabilitation in Canada (3 per year), Department of Manpower and Immigration, 305 Rideau Street, Ottawa, Ontario K1A OJ9, Canada.

Rehabilitation Literature (monthly, $12.50), National Easter Seal Society for Crippled Children and Adults, 2023 West Ogden Avenue, Chicago, IL 60612.

Rehabilitation Psychology (quarterly, $15.00) American Psychological Association, Box 26034, Tempe, AZ 85282.

Rehabilitation/World (quarterly, $7.50), Rehabilitation International U.S.A., 20 West 40th Street, New York, NY 10018.

Sports n' Spokes (quarterly, $4.00), 6043 North Ninth Avenue, Phoenix, AZ 85013.

Summary of Activities (quarterly), Mental Health Law Project, 1220 19th Street N.W., Washington, DC 20036.

Therapeutic Recreational Journal (quarterly, $8.00), National Therapeutic Recreation Society, 1601 North Kent Street, Arlington, VA 22209.

Worklife (monthly, $15.30), U.S. Department of Labor Employment and Training Administration, Washington, DC 20213.

DISABILITIES

Alcoholism

ICPA Quarterly Bulletin (membership), International Commission for the Prevention of Alcoholism, 6830 Laurel Street N.W., Washington, DC 20012.

Journal of Alcohol and Drug Education (3 per year, $4.00), Alcohol and Drug Problems Association of North America, 3500 North Logan Avenue, Lansing, MI 48914.

Journal of Studies on Alcohol (quarterly, $25.00), Center of Alcohol Studies, Rutgers University, New Brunswick, NJ 08903.

Amputation

The Amp (monthly, $3.00), National Amputation Foundation, 12-45 150th Street, Whitestone, NY 11357.

Bulletin of Prosthetics Research, U.S. Veterans Administration, Prosthetics and Sensory Aids Service, Washington, DC 20420.

Orthotics and Prosthetics (quarterly, $10.00), American Orthotic and Prosthetic Association, 1440 N Street N.W., Washington, DC 20005.

Arthritis

Arthritis and Rheumatism (bimonthly, $23.00), The Arthritis Foundation, 3400 Peachtree Road N.E., Atlanta, GA 30326.

Blindness and Visual Impairment

American Journal of Óphthalmology (monthly, $15.00), Ophthalmic Publishing Company, 233 East Ontario Street, Chicago, IL 60611.

American Optometric Association News (monthly, $15.00); American Optometric Association Journal (monthly, $7.50), American Optometric Association, 7000 Chippewa Street, St. Louis, MO 63119.

Braille Book Review (bimonthly), Division for the Blind and Physically Handicapped, Library of Congress, Washington, DC 20542.

Canadian Journal of Ophthalmology (quarterly, $15.00), Canadian Ophthalmological Society, Box 8650, Ottawa, Ontario, Canada.

Canadian Journal of Optometry, Canadian Association of Optometrists, 210 Gladstone, Ottawa, Ontario, Canada.

Education of the Visually Handicapped (quarterly, $6.00), Association for the Education of the Visually Handicapped, 919 Walnut Street, Philadelphia, PA 19107.

Home Teacher (in Braille, monthly, $2.00), National Braille Press, 88 Stephen Street, Boston, MA 02115.

Light (semiannual), Braille Institute of America, 741 North Vermont Avenue, Los Angeles, CA 90029.

New Outlook for the Blind (10 per year, $11.00), American Foundation for the Blind, 15 West 16th Street, New York, NY 10011.

Sight-Saving Review (quarterly, $10.00), National Society for the Prevention of Blindness, 79 Madison Avenue, New York, NY 10016.

Talking Book Topics (bimonthly), Division for the Blind and Physically Handicapped, Library of Congress, Washington DC 20542.

Cancer

Cancer (monthly, $25.00), **CA: A Cancer Journal for the Clinician, Cancer News** (semiannual), American Cancer Society, 777 Third Avenue, New York, NY 10017.

National Cancer Institute Journal (monthly, $58.45), Government Printing Office, Washington, DC 20402.

Cardiac Disorders

Cardiac Rehabilitation (quarterly, $4.00), American Heart Association, 7320 Greenville Avenue, Dallas, TX 75231.

Cardiovascular Diseases (quarterly), Texas Heart Institute, P.O. Box 20269, Houston, TX 77025.

Cerebral Palsy

Crusader (bimonthly); **Word from Washington** (monthly), United Cerebral Palsy Associations, 66 East 34th Street, New York, NY 10016.

Developmental Medicine and Child Neurology (bimonthly, $17.00), American Academy for Cerebral Palsy, 1255 New Hampshire Avenue N.W., Washington, DC 20036.

Cystic Fibrosis

National CF News Bulletin, Cystic Fibrosis Research Foundation, 3379 Peachtree Street N.E., Atlanta, GA 30326.

Diabetes

Diabetes Forecast (bimonthly, $5.00), American Diabetes Association, 1 West 48th Street, New York, NY 10020.

Facial Disfigurement

Society for the Rehabilitation of the Facially Disfigured News, New York Medical College, 550 First Avenue, New York, NY 10016.

Dysautonomia

Journal of the Dysautonomia Association (annual), Dysautonomia Association, 370 Lexington Avenue, New York, NY 10017.

Epilepsy

Epilepsia (quarterly, $34.00), American Epilepsy Society, Division of Neurosurgery, University of Texas Medical Branch, Galveston, TX 77550.

National Spokesman (monthly, $3.00), Epilepsy Foundation of America, 1828 L Street N.W., Washington, DC 20036.

Geriatrics

Aging (10 per year, $5.50), Administration on Aging, DHEW, Washington, DC 20201.

Geriatrics (monthly, $15.00), 4015 West 65th Street, Minneapolis, MN 55435.

Journal of the American Geriatrics Society (monthly, $21.00), 10 Columbus Circle, New York, NY 10019.

Journal of Geriatric Psychiatry (semiannual, $12.00), International Universities Press, 239 Park Avenue South, New York, NY 10003.

Journal of Gerontology (bimonthly, $30.00), Gerontological Society, 1 Dupont Circle, Washington, DC 20036.

The Gerontologist (quarterly, $20.00), Gerontological Society, 1 Dupont Circle, Washington, DC 20036.

Hearing and Speech Disorders

American Annals of the Deaf (bimonthly, $12.50), Conference of Executives of American Schools for the Deaf, 5034 Wisconsin Avenue, N.W., Washington, DC 20016.

ASHA (monthly, $28.00), American Speech and Hearing Association, 9030 Old Georgetown Road, Washington, DC 20014.

Cleft Palate Journal (quarterly, $20.00), 331 Salk Hall, University of Pittsburgh, Pittsburgh, PA 15261.

Hearing and Speech Action (bimonthly, $5.00), National Association for Hearing and Speech Action, 814 Thayer Avenue, Silver Spring, MD 20910.

IAL News (bimonthly), International Association of Laryngectomees, 777 Third Avenue, New York, NY 10017.

Journal of Auditory Research (quarterly, $8.00), C. W. Shilling Auditory Research Center, Box N, Groton, CT 06340.

Journal of Rehabilitation of the Deaf (quarterly, $8.00) Professional Rehabilitation Workers with the Adult Deaf, 814 Thayer Avenue, Silver Spring, MD 20910.

Journal of Speech and Hearing Disorders (quarterly, $28.00), American Speech and Hearing Association, 9030 Old Georgetown Road, Washington, DC 20014.

The Deaf American (monthly, $5.00), National Association of the Deaf, 814 Thayer Avenue, Silver Spring, MD 20910.

The Volta Review (9 per year, $15.00), Alexander Graham Bell Association for the Deaf, 3417 Volta Place N.W., Washington, DC 20007.

Hemophilia

Hemophilia Today (bimonthly), Canadian Hemophilia Society, 242 St. George Street, Toronto, Ontario, Canada.

Kidney Disease

The Kidney (bimonthly, $3.00), National Kidney Foundation, 116 East 27th Street, New York, NY 10016.

Transplantation (monthly, $40.00), Williams and Wilkins Company, 428 East Preston Street, Baltimore, MD 21202.

Learning Disabilities

Journal of Learning Disabilities (10 per year, $12.00), Executive Office, 101 East Ontario Street, Chicago, IL 60611.

Leprosy

International Journal of Leprosy (quarterly, $25.00), International Leprosy Association, 16 Bridgefield Road, Sutton, Surrey, England.

Leprosy Review (quarterly, $19.25), Academic Press, 111 Fifth Avenue, New York, NY 10003.

Mental Illness

American Journal of Orthopsychiatry (5 per year, $16.00), American Orthopsychiatric Association, 1775 Broadway, New York, NY 10019.

American Journal of Psychoanalysis (semiannual, $6.00), APS Publications, 150 Fifth Avenue, New York, NY 10011.

American Journal of Psychiatry (monthly, $18.00), American Psychiatric Association, 1700 18th Street N.W., Washington, DC 20009.

American Journal of Psychotherapy (quarterly, $16.00), 14 East 78th Street, New York, NY 10021.

Behavior Therapy (5 per year, $46.50), Academic Press, 111 Fifth Avenue, New York, NY 10003.

Canada's Mental Health (5 per year, $3.00), Department of National Health and Welfare, Mental Health Division, Ottawa, Ontario, Canada.

Community Mental Health Journal (quarterly, $35.00), Behavioral Publications, 2852 Broadway, New York, NY 10025.

Diseases of the Nervous System (monthly, $15.00), Physicians Postgraduate Press, Box 38293, Memphis, TN 38138.

Journal of Abnormal Psychology (bimonthly, $24.00), American Psychological Association, 1200 17th Street N.W., Washington, DC 20036.

Journal of the American Academy of Psychoanalysis (quarterly, $20.00), John Wiley and Sons, 605 Fifth Avenue, New York, NY 10016.

Journal of the American Psychoanalytic Association (quarterly, $20.00), International Universities Press, 239 Park Avenue South, New York, NY 10003.

Journal of Clinical Psychology (quarterly, $20.00), Clinical Psychology Publishing Company, 4 Conant Square, Brandon, VT 05733.

Journal of Consulting and Clinical Psychology (bimonthly, $20.00), American Psychological Association, 1200 17th Street N.W., Washington, DC 20036.

Journal of Counseling Psychology (monthly, $18.00), American Psychological Association, 1200 17th Street N.W., Washington, DC 20036.

MH/(Mental Hygiene) (quarterly, $10.00), National Association for Mental Health, 49 Sheridan Avenue, Albany, NY 12210.

Psychiatric Quarterly (quarterly, $8.00), New York State Department of Mental Hygiene, Hudson River Psychiatric Center, Poughkeepsie, NY 12601.

Psychoanalytic Review (quarterly, $6.00), National Psychological Association for Psychoanalysis, 150 West 13th Street, New York, NY 10011.

Psychosomatic Medicine (bimonthly, $17.50), American Elsevier Publishing Company, 52 Vanderbilt Avenue, New York, NY 10017.

Psychosomatics (quarterly, $20.00), Academy of Psychosomatic Medicine, 992 Springfield Avenue, Irvington, NJ 07111.

Mental Retardation

American Journal of Mental Deficiency (bimonthly, $20.00); **Mental Retardation** (bimonthly, $22.00), American Association on Mental Deficiency; order from AAMD Publications Office, 49 Sheridan Avenue, Albany, NY 12210.

Challenge: Recreation and Fitness for the Mentally Retarded (5 per year,

$4.00), Alliance for Health, Physical Education and Recreation, 1201 16th Street N.W., Washington, DC 20036.

Exceptional Children (8 per year, $20.00), Council for Exceptional Children, 1920 Association Drive, Reston, VA 22091.

The Exceptional Parent (bimonthly, $10.00), P.O. Box 964, Manchester, NH 03105.

Focus on Exceptional Children (9 per year, $9.50), Love Publishing Company, 6635 East Villanova Place, Denver, CO 80222.

Handy-Cap Horizons (quarterly, $3.00), 3250 East Oretta Drive, Indianapolis, IN 46227.

Journal for Special Educators of the Mentally Retarded (3 per year, $9.00), 107-20 125th Street, Richmond Hill, NY 11419.

Journal of Mental Deficiency Research (quarterly, $30.00), National Society for Mentally Handicapped Children, Pembridge Hall, Pembridge Square, London W2 4EH, England.

Journal of Special Education (quarterly, $15.00), 3515 Woodhaven Road, Philadelphia, PA 19154.

Special Children, with supplement, **The Retarded Adult** (quarterly, $15.00), American Association of Special Educators, 107-20 125th Street, Richmond Hill, NY 11419.

Teaching Exceptional Children (quarterly, $12.50), Council for Exceptional Children, 1920 Association Drive, Reston, VA 22202.

Multiple Sclerosis

MS Messenger (quarterly); **MS Briefs** (10 per year), National Multiple Sclerosis Society, 257 Park Avenue South, New York, NY 10010.

Muscular Dystrophy

Muscular Dystrophy News (6 per year), Muscular Dystrophy Association, 810 Seventh Avenue, New York, NY 10019.

Myasthenia Gravis

National Newsletter (quarterly), Myasthenia Gravis Foundation, 230 Park Avenue, New York, NY 10017.

Obesity

Obesity and Bariatric Medicine (bimonthly, $12.00), American Society of Bariatric Physicians, 333 West Hampden Avenue, Englewood, CO 80110.

Orthopedic Disorders

Journal of Bone and Joint Surgery (8 per year, $18.00), American Orthopaedic Association, 10 Shattuck Street, Boston, MA 02115.
See also Amputations, Arthritis, Cerebral Palsy, etc.

Ostomies

Ostomy Quarterly (quarterly, $7.00), United Ostomy Association, 1111 Wilshire Boulevard, Los Angeles, CA 90017.

Pulmonary Disorders

American Lung Association Bulletin (10 per year), 1740 Broadway, New York, NY 10019.

Batting the Breeze (bimonthly), Emphysema Anonymous, Box 66, Fort Myers, FL 33902.

Chest (monthly, $21.00), American College of Chest Physicians, 911 Busse Highway, Park Ridge, IL 60068.

Respiratory Therapy (bimonthly, $20.00), Brentwood Publishing Corporation, 825 South Barrington Avenue, Los Angeles, CA 90040.

Spina Bifida

The Spina Bifida Association of America Pipeline (bimonthly), 343 South Dearborn Avenue, Chicago, IL 60604.

Spinal Cord Injury

Caliper (quarterly, $2.00), Canadian Paraplegic Association, Toronto, Ontario, M 5 R-3A2, Canada.

Paraplegia Life (bimonthly, $4.00), National Paraplegia Foundation, 333 North Michigan Avenue, Chicago, IL 60601.

Paraplegia News (monthly, $4.00), Paralyzed Veterans of America and National Paraplegia Foundation, 935 Coastline Drive, Seal Beach, CA 90740.

Venereal Disease

VD News (monthly), American Social Health Association, 260 Sheridan Avenue, Palo Alto, CA 94306.

ABSTRACTS AND DIGESTS

Rehabilitation Literature, which is published monthly by the National Easter Seal Society, systematically indexes and reviews current literature.

Abstracts for Social Workers (quarterly, $10.00 to members, $30.00 to nonmembers), National Association of Social Workers, 49 Sheridan Avenue, Albany, NY 12210.

Alcoholism Digest (monthly, $75.00), P.O. Box 6318, 5632 Connecticut Avenue N.W., Washington, DC 20015.

Birth Defects (monthly, $7.00), National Foundation, P.O. Box 2000, White Plains, NY 10602.

Child Development Abstracts and Bibliography (quarterly, $10.00), Society for Research in Child Development, University of Chicago Press, 5750 Ellis Avenue, Chicago, IL 60637.

DSH Abstracts (quarterly, $15.00), Deafness Speech and Hearing Publications, American Speech and Hearing Association and Gallaudet College, 9030 Old Georgetown Road, Washington, DC 20014.

Exceptional Child Education Abstracts (quarterly, $50.00), Council for Exceptional Children, 1920 Association Drive, Reston, VA 22091.

Excerpta Medica (abstracts on arthritis and rheumatism, cancer, cardiovascular diseases, chest diseases, epilepsy, gerontology and geriatrics, muscular dystrophy, psychiatry, rehabilitation and physical medicine, etc.), 228 Alexander Street, Princeton, NJ 08540.

Geriatrics Digest (monthly, $15.00), Geriatrics Digest, Inc., 445 Central Avenue, Northfield, IL 60093.

Hospital Literature Index (quarterly, $10.00), American Hospital Association, 840 North Lake Shore Drive, Chicago, IL 60611.

Index Medicus (monthly, $173.05); **Cumulated Index Medicus** (annual), U.S. Superintendent of Documents, Washington, DC 20402.

Mental Health Digest (monthly, $6.50), National Clearinghouse for Mental Health Information, National Institute of Mental Health, U.S. Superintendent of Documents, Washington, DC 20402.

Mental Retardation Abstracts (quarterly, $8.00), Division of Developmental Disabilities, Rehabilitation Services Administration, Superintendent of Documents, Washington, DC 20402.

Psychological Abstracts (monthly, $190.00), American Psychological Association, 1200 17th Street N.W., Washington, DC 20036.

Section 5. Directories

General

Alliance of Information and Referral Services, *Directory of Information and Referral Services in the United States and Canada,* Phoenix, AZ.

American Board of Medical Specialties, *Directory of Medical Specialists,* Marquis Who's Who, Chicago, IL 60611.

American Medical Association, *Directory of National Voluntary Health Organizations,* and *Survey of State Medical Association Committees Concerned with Rehabilitation,* 535 North Dearborn Street, Chicago, IL 60610.

American Personnel and Guidance Association, *Directory of Approved Counseling Agencies,* 1607 New Hampshire Avenue N.W., Washington, DC 20009.

American Public Health Association, *Membership Directory,* and *Affiliated Societies,* etc., 1015 18th Street N.W., Washington, DC 20036.

American Public Welfare Association, *Public Welfare Directory,* 1155 16th Street N.W., Suite 201, Washington, DC 20036.

Council for Exceptional Children, *Directory of Federal Programs for the Handicapped,* 1920 Association Drive, Reston, VA 22091.

Health Insurance Institute, *Inventory of State and Areawide Health Planning Agencies and Related Organizations,* 277 Park Avenue, New York, NY 10017.

Health Organizations of the United States, Canada, and Internationally, McGrath Publishing Company, 821 15th Street N.W., Washington, DC 20005.

National Assembly for Social Policy and Development Service, *Directory of National Organizations, Voluntary and Governmental,* 345 East 46th Street, New York, NY 10017.

National Congress of Organizations of the Physically Handicapped, 7611 Oakland Avenue, Minneapolis, MN 55423.

National Exchange, *National Directory of Hotlines and Youth Crisis Centers,* Minneapolis, MN.

National Free Clinic Council, *Free Clinic List,* San Francisco, CA.

People-to-People Program, Committee for the Handicapped, *Directory of Organizations Interested in the Handicapped,* La Salle Building, Suite 610, Connecticut Avenue and L Street, Washington, DC 20036.

Rehabilitation International, *Compendium on the Activities of World Organizations Interested in the Handicapped,* 122 East 23d Street, New York, NY 10010.

United Way of America, *Directory of I and R Centers, United Way of America Directory,* 801 North Fairfax Street, Alexandria, VA 22314.

U.S. Public Health Service, *Consumer Health Education: A Directory,* and *Directory of State and Territorial Health Authorities,* Superintendent of Documents, U.S. Government Printing Office, Washington, DC 20402.

U.S. Rehabilitation Services Administration, *Directory of State Division of Vocational Rehabilitation,* Washington, DC 20201.

U.S. Social Security Administration, Office of Research and Statistics, *Social Security Programs in the U.S.* Superintendent of Documents, U.S. Government Printing Office, Washington, DC 20402.

Membership Directories and Registries (partial: see also Section 2)

American Academy for Cerebral Palsy and Developmental Medicine, 122 New Hampshire Avenue N.W., Room 1030, Washington, DC 20036.

American Occupational Therapy Association, 6000 Executive Boulevard, Rockville, MD 20852.

American Physical Therapy Association, 1156 15th Street N.W., Washington, DC 20005.

American Psychological Association, 1200 17th Street N.W., Washington, DC 20036.

American Registry of Physical Therapists, *Directory,* 30 North Michigan Avenue, Chicago, IL 60602.

Association of Medical Rehabilitation Directors and Coordinators, *Annual Directory,* 3830 Linklea Drive, Houston, TX 77025.

National Association of Social Workers, *Directory of Agencies,* and *Directory of Members,* 1425 H Street N.W., Washington, DC 20005.

President's Committee on Employment of the Handicapped, *Membership Directory,* Washington, DC 20210.

Facilities and Services

American Board for Certification in Orthotics and Prosthetics, *Registry of Certified Facilities and Individuals,* 1440 N Street N.W., Washington, DC 20005.

American Hospital Association, *Guide to the Health Care Field,* 840 Lake Shore Drive, Chicago, IL 60611.

Association of Rehabilitation Facilities, *Membership Directory,* 5530 Wisconsin Avenue, Suite 955, Washington, DC 20015.

Health Delivery Systems, Inc., *Allied Health Education Directory,* St. Louis, MO.

National Council for Homemaker Services, *Directory of Homemaker—Health Aide Services,* 1740 Broadway, New York, NY 10019.

National Easter Seal Society for Crippled Children and Adults, *Directory of Affiliated State Societies; Directory of Affiliated Sheltered Workshops,* 2023 Ogden Avenue, Chicago, IL 60612.

Disabilities

National Research Council–National Academy of Sciences, *Amputee Clinics in the United States and Canada,* Committee on Prosthetic-Orthotic Education, 2101 Constitution Avenue, Washington, DC 20418.

American Foundation for the Blind, *Directory of Agencies Serving the Visually Handicapped in the U.S.,* and *Professional Preparation Centers for Teachers of the Visually Handicapped,* 15 West 16th Street, New York, NY 10011.

Education

American Medical Association, *Allied Medical Education Directory,* 535 North Dearborn Avenue, Chicago, IL 60610.

American Trade Schools Directory, Croner Publications, 211-05 Jamaica Avenue, Queens Village, NY 11428.

National Home Study Council, *Directory of Accredited Private Home Study Schools,* 1601 18th Street N.W., Washington, DC 20009.

U.S. Office of Education, Bureau of Education for the Handicapped, *Selected Career Education Programs for the Handicapped,* Washington, DC 20202.

Genetics

National Foundation, *International Directory of Genetic Services,* P.O. Box 2000, White Plains, NY 10602.

Geriatric Disorders

American Association of Homes for the Aging, *Directory of Non-Profit Homes and Facilities,* 374 National Press Building, Washington, DC 20004.

National Council on the Aging, *A National Directory of Housing for Older People,* and *National Directory of Voluntary Agencies,* 1828 L Street N.W., Washington, DC 20036.

U.S. Administration on Aging, *National Directory of Senior Centers,* Superintendent of Documents, U.S. Government Printing Office, Washington, DC 20402.

Learning Disabilities

American Association of Special Educators, *Directory for Special Children,* 107-20 125th Street, Richmond Hill, NY 11413.

Association for Children with Learning Disabilities, *Directory of Educational Facilities for the Learning Disabled,* Academic Therapy Publications, 1539 Fourth Street, San Rafael, CA 94901.

Directory of Facilities for the Learning Disabled and Handicapped, Harper and Row, 10 East 53d Street, New York, NY 10022.

Directory for Special Children, and **The Underachiever,** Porter Sargent, 11 Beacon Street, Boston, MA 02108.

Mental Disorders

National Association for Mental Health, *Mental Health Programs for Pre-School Children,* 1800 North Kent Street, Rosslyn, VA 22209.

National Institute of Mental Health, *Directory of Halfway Houses for the Mentally Ill and Alcoholic, Mental Health Directory,* and *U.S. Facilities*

and Programs for Children with Severe Mental Illness: A Directory,
5600 Fishers Lane, Rockville, MD 20852.

Mental Retardation

American Association on Mental Deficiency, *Directory of Residential Facilities for the Mentally Retarded,* and *Directory of Members,* 5201 Connecticut Avenue N.W., Washington, DC 20015.

President's Committee on Mental Retardation, *In Service to the Mentally Retarded,* and *International Directory of Mental Retardation Resources,* Washington, DC 20201.

U.S. Department of Health, Education and Welfare, Secretary's Committee on Mental Retardation, *Directory of State and Local Resources for the Mentally Retarded,* Washington, DC 20201.

Speech and Hearing Disorders

American Speech and Hearing Association, *A Guide to Clinical Services in Speech Pathology and Audiology,* and *Directory* (annual), 9030 Old Georgetown Road, Washington, DC 20014.

Conference of Executives of American Schools for the Deaf, *Directory Issue of American Annals of the Deaf,* and *Directory of Programs and Services for the Deaf in the U.S.,* 5034 Wisconsin Avenue N.W., Washington, DC 20016.

Council of Organizations Serving the Deaf, *Council Membership Directory,* 4201 Connecticut Avenue N.W., Washington, DC 20008.

International Association of Laryngectomees, *Directory* (annual), 777 Third Avenue, New York, NY 10017.

Registry of Interpreters for the Deaf, P.O. Box 1339, Washington, DC 20013.

Summer Camps

American Camping Association, *Directory of Camping for the Handicapped,* Bradford Woods, Martinsville, IN 46151.

Association for Children with Learning Disabilities, *Directory of Summer Camps for Children with Learning Disabilities,* 5225 Grace Street, Pittsburgh, PA 15236.

Guide to Summer Camps and Summer Schools, Porter Sargent, 11 Beacon Street, Boston, MA 02108.

National Easter Seal Society for Crippled Children and Adults, *Easter Seal Directory of Resident Camps for Persons with Special Health Needs,* and *Easter Seal Guide to Special Camping Programs,* 2023 West Ogden Avenue, Chicago, IL 60612.

Section 6. Federal Programs: An Index to Government Assistance

The extent of federal support of programs and services for the disabled can be determined by consulting *Federal Assistance for Programs Serving the Handicapped*, a directory first compiled in 1975 by the Clearing House of the Office for Handicapped Individuals, Department of Health, Education and Welfare, and planned as an annual publication. Entries in the directory are excerpted from the *Catalog of Federal Domestic Assistance*, each entry consisting of the following subheads: Program Description, Uses and Use Restrictions, Types of Assistance, Formula and Matching Grants, Eligibility Requirements, Application Procedure, Appropriations, Program Accomplishments, Enabling Legislation, and Information Contact. Grants are usually made to state or federal agencies, not to individuals directly. A full digest of this publication will not be attempted here, but a list of programs, departments administering them, and 1975 appropriations may prove useful as an index to federal involvement. Many of these programs are designed specifically for handicapped individuals; others are more general but include the handicapped. The term "total" precedes the amount of appropriation where the latter is the case. Most addresses can be found in Section 3.

ACTION (Foster Grandparents Program): volunteer opportunities for low-income persons, and supportive person-to-person services to children in residential settings with special needs ($28,260,000).

Civil Service Commission:

Federal Employment for the Handicapped: assistance to handicapped persons in obtaining federal employment ($249,000).

Office of the Secretariat, Interagency Committee on Handicapped Employees: to review and report on federal employment of handicapped (none).

Personnel Research and Development Center: to enable blind, deaf, and other handicapped persons to compete for federal employment on written examinations ($32,090).

Committee for Purchase from the Blind and Other Severely Handicapped: for procurement by the government of commodities and services from qualified workshops, to increase employment opportunities ($252,000).

Department of Agriculture:

Extension Service: for rural home economics education, 4-H programs, agricultural production, and marketing training (total: $182,846,560).

Department of Defense:

U.S. Soldiers' and Airmen's Home: for certain elderly, invalid, or disabled servicemen ($15,391,000).

DHEW, Office of Education:

Educationally Deprived Children — Handicapped: to extend and improve programs in state-operated or -supported schools ($88,176,675).

Handicapped — Research and Demonstration: to improve the education of handicapped children through research and demonstration projects ($9,341,000).

Handicapped Early Childhood Assistance: to support experimental preschool and early childhood programs ($14,000,000).

Handicapped Innovative Programs — Deaf-Blind Children: regional centers for diagnosis, evaluation, education, and consultative services ($12,000,000).

Handicapped Media Services and Captioned Films: free loan service for the deaf, and for training of teachers, parents, and others in use of media ($13,000,000).

Handicapped Physical Education and Recreation Training: to improve the quality and increase the supply of trained personnel ($700,000).

Handicapped Preschool and School Programs: grants to states for initiation, improvement, and expansion of these services ($100,000,000).

Handicapped Regional Resource Centers: to establish centers which provide advice and technical assistance to educators of handicapped ($9,243,000).

Handicapped Teacher Education: training programs designed to improve the quality and increase the supply of personnel ($37,700,000).

DHEW, Public Health Service:

Crippled Children's Services: extension of medical and related services and special projects, especially in rural and distressed areas ($64,900,000).

Family Planning Projects: educational, medical, and social services involved in family planning and maternal and child health (total: $95,046,000).

Maternal and Child Health Research: projects relating to maternal and child health and crippled children's services (total: $6,571,000).

Maternal and Child Health Services: extension and improvement of these services, including services to the mentally and physically handicapped, especially in rural and low-income areas (total: $211,905,791).

Maternal and Child Health Training: to train personnel for maternal and child health care services, particularly for retarded and multihandicapped children (total: $18,575,818).

Alcohol, Drug Abuse, and Mental Health Administration:

Mental Hospital Improvement Grants: improved care, treatment and rehabilitation, and transition to open institutions and community ($5,575,200).

Mental Hospital Staff Development Grants: to increase staff effectiveness and promote back-up support for community programs ($1,674,300).

Community Mental Health Centers: to finance building of centers and improvement of organization, care, and treatment ($24,219,700 for construction; $172,053,000 for staffing).

Mental Health Fellowships: to provide training for research and to increase the competence and number of researchers ($9,560).

Mental Health Research Grants: for research into causes, treatment, control, and prevention, and to develop and test delivery systems ($61,527,973).

Mental Health Research Development Awards: to support research and raise the level of competence and number of researchers ($4,400,000).

Mental Health National Research Service Awards: individual awards and institutional grants for research training ($6,206,324).

National Institutes of Health: for research and training programs related to disabling diseases and disorders: National Heart, Lung, and Blood Institute; National Institute of Dental Research; National Institute of Arthritis, Metabolism, and Digestive Diseases; National Institute of Neurological and Communicative Disorders and Stroke; National Institute of Allergy and Infectious Diseases; National Institute of General Medical Sciences; National Institute of Child Health and Human Development; National Institute on Aging; National Eye Institute; National Institute of Environmental Health Sciences (total: $843,237,000).

DHEW, Social and Rehabilitation Services:

Medical Assistance Program: financial assistance to states for Medicaid program for the aged, blind, disabled, etc. (total: $6,788,017,000).

Public Assistance — Social Services: services oriented toward employment, self-care, and family stability (total: $1,891,905,000).

Public Assistance — Maintenance Assistance: to set state standards and provide the federal financial share to states (total: $4,861,927,000).

Handicapped Teacher Recruitment and Information: to encourage people to enter the special education career, and to disseminate information to parents on programs and services for their children ($500,000).

Vocational Education — Basic Grants to States: for improvement and extension of vocational programs of all types, including those for the educationally handicapped (total: $428,139,455).

Supplementary Educational Centers and Services — Special Programs and Projects: for demonstration projects on critical educational problems, including 15 percent for programs for the handicapped (total: $16,348,332).

Supplementary Educational Centers and Services — Guidance, Counseling and Testing: for innovative projects and services (total: $103,426,668).

Special Programs for Children with Specific Learning Disabilities: for model centers, research, and training ($3,250,000).

Regional Education Programs for Deaf and Other Handicapped Persons: for vocational, technical, postsecondary, and adult programs ($575,000).

Handicapped Innovative Programs — Programs for Severely Handi-

capped Children: for educational/training services and public acceptance ($2,826,000).

DHEW, Office of Human Development:

Child Development—Head Start: for comprehensive services to preschool disadvantaged children and their families (total: $414,300,000).

Child Development—Technical Assistance: to coordinate, develop, and advocate programs for children, youth, and families (total: $3,450,000).

Child Development—Child Welfare Research and Demonstration Grants: for projects in child and family development and welfare (total: $15,700,000).

Mental Retardation Evaluation: to advise and assist the President, evaluate nationwide efforts, help to coordinate federal activities, inform the public, and mobilize public support ($695,000).

Rehabilitation Services and Facilities—Basic Support: for vocational rehabilitation services, including small business opportunities for the blind ($680,000,000).

Vocational Rehabilitation Services for Social Security Disability Beneficiaries: to increase services for these disabled people ($83,000,000).

Rehabilitation Services and Facilities—Special Projects: for services over and above those provided by the Basic Support Program ($13,900,000).

Rehabilitation Research and Demonstrations: to discover, test, demonstrate, and promote new concepts and devices ($20,000,000).

Rehabilitation Training: projects to increase the number of trained personnel providing vocational rehabilitation services ($22,200,000).

Developmental Disabilities—Basic Support: for planning, services, and construction of facilities ($30,875,000).

Developmental Disabilities—Special Projects: to improve services, demonstrate new techniques, coordinate resources, and train personnel ($18,500,000).

University-Affiliated Facilities—Demonstration and Training Grants: for operating and developing personnel for developmental disabilities facilities ($4,250,000).

Sheltered Workshop Study: on the role of the workshop, number employed, funding, wage payments, etc. ($675,842).

Architectural and Transportation Barriers Compliance Board: to assure compliance with accessibility standards ($300,000).

Randolph-Sheppard Vending Facilities Program: economic opportunities for the blind on federal property (administered by Vocational Rehabilitation Funds).

DHEW, Office of the Secretary:

Surplus Property Utilization: to donate federal surplus property to health and educational institutions (total: $400,000,000).

DHEW, Social Security Administration:

Medicare—Hospital Insurance: for persons sixty-five and over and certain disabled persons (total: $10,325,000,000).

Medicare—Supplementary Medical Insurance: for persons sixty-five and over and certain disabled persons who elect this coverage (total: $3,750,000,000).

Social Security—Disability Insurance: to replace part of working income lost due to disability ($7,630,000,000).

Special Benefits for Disabled Coal Miners: for those totally disabled by black lung disease (pneumoconiosis) or their survivors ($939,000,000).

Supplementary Security Income: for the aged, blind, and disabled whose income falls below federal prescribed minimums or who are eligible for state income payments (total: $4,080,000,000).

Department of Housing and Urban Development:

Housing for the Handicapped and Elderly: for long-term financing to nonprofit sponsors for construction or rehabilitation of rental housing projects which provide health, educational, welfare, recreational, and homemaking services (total loans: $375,000,000).

Special User Research: to support research and demonstration projects for housing and other community services for the elderly, handicapped, and minorities (total: $593,215).

Department of Labor:

Manpower Administration, Employment Service: for handicapped individuals and potential employers, to assure equal opportunity and wages ($477,172,000).

Employment Standards Administration, Longshoremen's and Harbor Workers' Compensation: for disability or death due to injury or occupational disease ($5,040,000).

Employment Standards Administration, Minimum Wage and Hours Standards: to prevent curtailment of opportunity for handicapped individuals who normally could not command the minimum wage ($33,428,000).

Coal Mine Workers' Compensation: to provide benefits to miners totally disabled by black lung disease, or to their survivors ($3,986,000 for salaries and expenses; $7,172,000 for benefits).

Employment Standards Administration, Federal Employees Compensation Branch of Rehabilitation: payments to injured covered federal workers, along with vocational rehabilitation services ($3,100,000 for income maintenance; $720,000 for services).

Employment Standards Administration, Special Wage Standards for Sheltered Workshops—Research: to provide employment and demographic information to Congress ($300,000).

Employment Standards Administration, Employment Standards for Handicapped Workers: to advance nondiscriminatory hiring and advancement ($817,000).

Department of the Interior:

Bureau of Indian Affairs, Indian Social Service—Child Welfare Assistance: foster home and institutional care (total: $6,480,000).

Department of Transportation:

Urban Mass Transportation Administration, Capital Improvement Grants: for acquisition, construction, reconstruction, and improvement of facilities and equipment (total: $1,196,600,000).

Urban Mass Transportation Administration: projects oriented to the special needs of the handicapped (grants cut across the preceding entry).

Federal Aviation Administration, Air Carriage of the Handicapped: to provide greater mobility to the handicapped, with safety ($72,000).

General Services Administration:

Disposal of Federal Surplus Real Property: for park, recreation, public health, or educational purposes (total: $3,197,000).

Donation of Federal Surplus Personal Property: for education, public health, civil defense, and airport purposes (total: $4,793,000).

Removal of Architectural Barriers: to ensure that federal buildings are accessible to the handicapped (none; technical assistance only).

Library of Congress:

Books for the Blind and Physically Handicapped: books and musical scores in large type, recorded or in Braille ($11,339,824).

National Aeronautics and Space Administration:

Technological Utilization: to ensure that apparatus resulting from research and development is made available to amputees, spinal cord patients, and others (total: $5,500,000).

President's Committee on Employment of the Handicapped:

Handicapped Employment Promotion: to increase employment opportunities of the disabled ($1,297,000).

Small Business Administration:

Handicapped Assistance Loans: for nonprofit sheltered workshops and small businesses operated by handicapped individuals ($5,311,700 for direct loans; $1,335,400 for guaranteed loans).

Veterans Administration:

Community Nursing Home Care ($46,279,000).

Grants to States for Construction of State Nursing Home Care Facilities ($4,557,721).

Prosthetics Branch: to develop prosthetic devices, sensory aids, and related appliances for veterans, and also for use by the civilian disabled ($3,900,000).

Blind Veterans Rehabilitation Centers in Veterans Administration hospitals ($2,016,000).

Veterans Domiciliary Care: for independent living in the community or in a protective environment ($48,904,000).

Veterans Hospitalization: to provide all inpatient services ($2,238,190,-000).

Veterans Nursing Home Care: to accommodate those who need nonhospital care ($105,247,000).

Veterans Outpatient Care: for medical and dental care, medicines, and supplies ($603,335,000).

Veterans Prosthetic Appliances: for prosthetic appliances and related services ($33,048,000).

Veterans State Domiciliary Care: assistance to states for Veterans Homes ($11,009,000).

Veterans Nursing Home Care: for financial assistance to states ($9,371,000).

Veterans State Hospital Care: for financial assistance to states ($4,015,000).

Grants to States for Remodeling of State Home Hospital Domiciliary Facilities ($2,323,000).

Veterans Rehabilitation—Alcohol and Drug Dependency ($58,859,000).

Hospital-Based Home Care: medical, nursing, and rehabilitation services ($2,134,000).

Automobiles and Adaptive Equipment for Certain Disabled Veterans and Members of the Armed Forces ($15,900,000).

Pension for Nonservice-Connected Disability for Veterans with permanent and total disability ($1,572,883,990).

Specially Adapted Housing for Disabled Veterans: to assist them in acquiring housing with special fixtures and facilities ($13,813,000).

Veterans Compensation for Service-Connected Disability: direct payments according to impairment of earning capacity ($3,797,329,965).

Vocational Rehabilitation for Disabled Veterans ($72,730,648 for direct payments; $992,000 for loans).

Veterans Housing—Direct Loans to Disabled Veterans: to help them acquire housing with special features ($1,100,000).

Department of Medicine and Surgery, Mental Health Services to Veterans with Mental, Physical or Emotional Impairment: for treatment centers, crisis intervention clinics, halfway houses, etc. (no estimates available).

Department of Medicine and Surgery, Audiology and Speech Pathology: to restore communicative efficiency, conduct research on treatment modalities, and train specialists ($6,606,297 for basic services; $340,000 for research and technology; $1,064,265 for personnel training.)

Other Programs Not Specifically Directed toward the Handicapped but Providing Basic Services and Assistance Which They May Need:

Food Programs: Food Stamps, Distribution, Nonschool Program Public Assistance—Research: project grants, research contracts.

Public Assistance—Training: personnel for agencies.

Retirement Income: Social Security payments to workers and dependents.

Survivors Insurance: Social Security payments.

Housing: Rent Supplements for Low-Income Families, and Mobile Home Loans for Veterans and Certain Widows of Veterans.

Child Care for WIN Registrants: work incentive, child care, employment-related support.

Aging Programs: special programs for setting up Area Agencies.

Prevention of Neglect and Abuse of Children: DHEW Division of Child and Family Services, and DHEW National Center on Child Abuse and Neglect.

Veterans' Widows Pensions.

Life Insurance for Veterans.

Veterans Information and Assistance with claims and benefits.

Dependents Educational Assistance, for families of disabled or deceased veterans.

Income for Certain Persons Aged Seventy-two and Over: Social Security benefits for those who have had little or no opportunity to earn Social Security protection.

Section 7. Federal Programs: Projections

The thrust of federal programs for the disabled during the late 1970s and beyond can be gauged from the following summary of a study entitled *Long Range Projection for the Provision of Comprehensive Services to Handicapped Individuals,* prepared by the Department of Health, Education and Welfare Office for Handicapped Individuals in 1975. This study is based on projections made by eight federal agencies.

DHEW Office of Education, Bureau of Education for the Handicapped

The bureau has committed itself to six objectives aimed at providing equity and equality of education:

1. *Provision of appropriately designed education to every handicapped child,* since at present less than half of the 8 million children of school age with physical or mental handicaps are receiving the special education they need. Efforts to achieve this objective will be carried out in five main areas: (a) specific learning disabilities, through identification, model programs, and in-service teacher training; (b) support of research and demonstration projects for the speech- and hearing-handicapped, vision- and hearing-impaired, crippled, emotionally disturbed, and mentally retarded; (c) media services and captioned films and TV programs for the deaf, provided by the National Center for Educational Media and Materials and Area Learning Resource Centers in the states; (d) Regional Resource Centers for programming, training, and technical assistance to states; and (e) recruitment for careers in special education, and an information and referral service for parents, through *Closer Look* and radio and TV commercials.

2. *Assistance to states in providing a full range of services to handicapped children,* through (a) a State Grant Program which will increase the number of children served from 250,000 in 1976 to 406,000 in 1977 and

more in succeeding years; (b) Deaf-Blind Regional Centers; and (c) special projects for the severely disabled, as outlined below.

3. *Career vocational orientation and training for handicapped children* in the elementary grades, and sequential development of skills at secondary and postsecondary levels.

4. *Expansion of the number of training teachers and other resource personnel,* through a Personnel Preparation Program which provides financial assistance for preservice and inservice training, to meet the growing demand for special education.

5. *Enrollment of preschool-age children in day care programs,* since handicapped children can make exceptional gains if educational services are provided during the preschool years. The early childhood program will be greatly expanded through demonstration and outreach projects, and dissemination of materials developed by the Handicapped Children's Early Education Program and the Technical Assistance Development System.

6. *Comprehensive statewide programs for severely handicapped children,* who thus far have been largely overlooked by public school systems. Projects will be funded to provide plans for comprehensive services, model demonstration programs, and dissemination of information to professional and nonprofessional personnel. The operational plan for 1976–1980 focuses on: (a) mental, emotional, physical, social, and language development; (b) parent participation; (c) community awareness of their capacities and potentialities; (d) deinstitutionalization to home-based, community-centered intervention programs on an individual basis; and (e) early intervention to prevent temporary handicaps from becoming permanent, and to prevent the development of secondary handicapping conditions.

DHEW Office of Education, Bureau of Occupational and Adult Education

The bureau has established the following goals relative to the handicapped: (a) improvement and extension of existing programs, and development of new approaches in adult, vocational, and work force education; (b) integration of handicapped students into regular training programs; (c) extension of counseling, guidance, job placement, and follow-up services; (d) a research program to develop individualized and performance-oriented curricula, to identify emerging occupations and work force needs for different areas, and to identify basic skills needed for more occupational cluster areas; (e) gathering of information needed to improve vocational education and provide access to employment; and (f) extension of work experience programs.

DHEW Office of Human Development, Rehabilitation Services Administration

The target population for vocational rehabilitation is estimated at 6.5 million mentally or physically disabled persons in the working age group (sixteen years and over). A prime objective for the near future is to provide priority services to the severely disabled, increasing the proportion of rehabilitations for this group from 40 percent of the total for fiscal 1976 to 60 percent in 1980 through a concerted state-federal program involving fuller tracking and reporting, technical assistance, research and demonstration, training, evaluation, data collection, and job development. Some of the major specific goals for this group are: (a) application of rehabilitation engineering technology; and (b) improvement of vocational rehabilitation services (including homebound services) to individuals with spinal cord injury, chronic obstructive pulmonary disease, cardiovascular disease, neuro-muscular disease, and end-stage renal disease. During the period the reha-bilitation goal for the severely disabled will be increased from 144,000 persons in 1976 to 216,000 persons in 1980, and the goal for the less severe-ly disabled will be reduced from 225,000 to 150,000.

DHEW Office of Human Development, Division of Developmental Disabilities

The target population is estimated to increase from 5,295,000 persons in 1976 to 5,532,000 in 1980, and includes individuals disabled by cerebral palsy, epilepsy, mental retardation, and other neurological disorders be-fore age eighteen. The major objective during this period is to establish planning and evaluation capabilities within DHEW and the states for collection and analysis of baseline data on the characteristics and need for services of this population, on the utilization of existing services for meet-ing these needs, and on the resources required for supporting current im-provements and future needs for service. Specific problems include better utilization of present facilities, improved quality of care in community and institutional facilities, and development of appropriate alternatives to insti-tutionalization; identification of specific services needed by the above groups; and demonstration projects which will show how these needs may be met.

DHEW Office of Human Development, Office of Child Development, Head Start

The target population is preschool children (three to five years of age) of low-income families. Priorities for the period include recruitment and en-rollment of handicapped children (at least 10 percent of the total), including those with substantial and severe handicaps, into Head Start programs, and provision of health (medical, dental, nutritional, mental health), education-al, social, and parental services to meet their special needs. Specific train-ing materials will be developed to assist teachers working with handi-capped children, and experimental projects directed to mainstreaming these children will continue.

DHEW Alcohol, Drug Abuse and Mental Health Administration, National Institute of Mental Health

The institute will focus on three major areas. (a) The Center for Studies of Schizophrenia will concentrate on former institutionalized, still handi-capped patients in the community; high readmission rates; cases of unknown etiology; and minimization of disability, through increased de-ployment of funds for rehabilitation of former patients, creation of new services, and strengthening of existing broad-spectrum services in the community, development of pilot projects to test the effectiveness of var-ious alternatives to hospitalization, development of new modalities and training programs to meet rehabilitation needs of schizophrenics in a com-munity setting, and continuation of existing "high-risk studies" which attack the problems of etiology and prevention in children. (b) The Mental Health Services Development Branch, Division of Mental Health Service Programs will concentrate on patients' rights and consumer advocacy, com-munity alternatives to institutionalization, services to minorities, quality assurance experiments, mental health services to nursing home popula-tions, new approaches to consultation and education, and systematic analy-sis of needs for service improvement. (c) The Community Mental Health Centers Program, which comprised 543 centers providing coordinated, comprehensive services to an estimated 1,770,000 persons in 1976, will be extended to catchment areas not now served.

DHEW Bureau of Community Health Services, Maternal and Child Health Programs

These programs will continue to be focused on reduction of infant mortality, improvement of maternal health, reduction of incidence of mental retardation and other handicapping conditions associated with childbearing, and promotion of child health, especially in rural and distressed areas. Over 500,000 children were served by the Child Health Services– Crippled Children Services Program in 1975.

DHEW Social Security Administration, Bureau of Supplementary Security Income

The program will provide federal income benefits to an estimated 2,-470,000 disabled persons by the end of fiscal 1980, and all those under sixty-five who receive benefits will be referred to the appropriate state vocational rehabilitation agency for review of their need for and utilization of vocational rehabilitation services.

Section 8. Sources of Information and Supply

AIDS AND EQUIPMENT

Specific types of aids and equipment are described and listed in CHAPTER 5: INDEPENDENT LIVING: WAYS AND MEANS. A comprehensive guide to suppliers and manufacturers, comprising approximately 600 firms, can be found in Edward W. Lowman and Judith L. Klinger, *Aids to Independent Living*, pp. 749–787, McGraw-Hill, New York, 1969. New items are regularly reported in *Accent on Living, Rehabilitation Gazette,* and *Paraplegia News.* The following are a few representative firms in general and specialized categories.

General

Comprehensive catalogs are available to organizations.

American Hospital Supply Company, Rehabilitation Products, 2020 Ridge Avenue, Evanston, IL 60201.
Cleo Living Aids, 3957 Mayfield Road, Cleveland, OH 44121.
G. E. Miller, Inc., 484 South Broadway, Yonkers, NY 10705.
J. A. Preston Corporation, 71 Fifth Avenue, New York, NY 10003.
Medical Equipment Distributors, Inc., 1215 South Harlem Avenue, Forest Park, IL 60130.
Rehabilitation Equipment, Inc., 1556 Third Avenue, New York, NY 10028.

Aids for the Blind and Visually Handicapped

American Foundation for the Blind (catalog: *Ideas for Better Living*), 15 West 16th Street, New York, NY 10011.
American Printing House for the Blind, 1839 Frankfort Avenue, Louisville, KY 40206.

Sciences for the Blind Products, 221 Rock Hill Road, Bala-Cyn-Wyd, PA 19004.

Howe Press of Perkins School for the Blind, 175 North Beacon Street, Watertown, MA 02172.

Automobile Hand Controls

List of manufacturers will be supplied.

American Automobile Association, 1712 G Street N.W., Washington, DC 20015.

Clothing

Amputee Shoe and Glove Exchange, Dr. and Mrs. Richard E. Wainerdi, 1115 Langford Drive, College Station, TX 77840.

Clothing Research and Development Foundation, 1 Rockefeller Plaza, Suite 1912, New York, NY 10020.

Fashion Able, Rocky Hill, NJ 08553.

Handee for You, 7674 Park Avenue, Louisville, KY 13367.

Leinenweber, Inc., 69 West Washington Street, Chicago, IL 60602.

National Odd Shoe Exchange, 1415 Ocean Front, Santa Monica, CA 90401.

Home Elevators and Stair Lifts

American Stairglide Corporation, 1000 West 25th Street, Kansas City, MO 64108.

Dover Corporation, Elevator Division, P.O. Box 2177, Memphis, TN 38101.

Inclinator Company of America, 2200 Paxton Street, Harrisburg, PA 17111.

Homemaking Equipment

Ekco Products Company, 9234 West Belmont Avenue, Franklin Park, IL 60131.

Sears, Roebuck and Company (catalog).

Montgomery Ward (catalog).

See *A Manual for Training the Disabled Homemaker,* Institute of Rehabilitation Medicine; and *Mealtime Manual for the Aged and Handicapped,* Institute of Rehabilitation Medicine, Simon & Schuster, New York, 1970.

Hospital and Orthopedic Equipment

E. F. Brewer Company, 13282 West Carmen Avenue, Butler, WI 53007.

Guardian Products Company, 8277 Lankersheim Boulevard, North Hollywood, CA 91605.

Lumex Inc., 100 Spence Street, Bay Shore, NY 11706.

Orthopedic Equipment Company, Bourbon, IN 46504.

Posey Company, 39 South Santa Anita Avenue, Pasadena, CA 91107.

Play and Game Equipment

Creative Playthings, Princeton, NJ 08540.

General Sportcraft Company, 140 Woodbine Street, Bergenfield, NJ 07621.

Playskool Manufacturing Company, 200 Fifth Avenue, New York, NY.

Self-help Aids

B/K Sales Company, Fred Sammons, Inc., Box 32, Brookfield, IL 60513.

Invalex Company, 741 West 17th Street, Long Beach, CA 90813; 102 Lee Street, Lodi, OH 44254.

Telephone Equipment

American Telephone and Telegraph Company, 195 Broadway, New York, NY 10007.

Bell Labs, Inc., 20 Church Street, Montclair, NJ 07042.

Bell Telephone Company, 463 West Street, New York, NY 10014 (and local business office).

Wheelchairs

American Wheelchair Company, 5500 Muddy Creek Road, Cincinnati, OH 45238.

Everest and Jennings, 1803 Pontius Avenue, Los Angeles, CA 90025.

AUDIO-VISUAL MATERIALS

Many voluntary organizations offer films on a free-loan, rental, or purchase basis. Among them are the American Group Psychotherapy Association; American Alliance of Health, Physical Education and Recreation; American Heart Association; American Cancer Society; American Physical Therapy Association; Arthritis Foundation; Goodwill Industries; Muscular Dystrophy Association; United Cerebral Palsy Associations; and U.S. Wheelchair Sports Fund. An estimated 4,000 films (also other A-V materials) are listed in directories compiled by the following organizations:

American Foundation for the Blind, *Films about Blindness,* 15 West 16th Street, New York, NY 10010.

American Medical Association, 535 North Dearborn Street, Chicago, IL 60610.

American Speech and Hearing Association, *ASHA Film Theater Catalog,* 9030 Old Georgetown Road, Washington, DC 20014.

Association Films, 866 Third Avenue, New York, NY.

Association for Educational Communications and Technology, 1201 16th Street N.W., Washington, DC 20036.

A/V Publications Office, Sister Kenny Institute, 1800 Chicago Avenue, Minneapolis, MN 55404.

Bell and Howell, 7100 McCormick Road, Chicago, IL 60645.

R. R. Bowker Company, *Index to 16 mm Educational Films,* 1180 Avenue of the Americas, New York, NY 10020.

Bureau of Education for the Handicapped, Educational Media Distribution Center, *Catalog of Captioned Films for the Deaf,* 5034 Wisconsin Avenue N.W., Washington, DC 20016.

Educators Progress Service, *Educators Guide to Free Films,* Randolph, WI 53956.

Library of Congress, *Film Reference Guide for Medicine and Allied Services* (annual), Washington, DC 20542; *Catalog of Motion Pictures and Film Strips,* U.S. Government Printing Office, Washington, DC 20402.

Media Services and Captioned Film Program, Bureau of Education for the Handicapped, U.S. Office of Education, Washington, DC 20202.

Mental Health Film Board, 8 East 93d Street, New York, NY.

Mental Health Materials Center, *Selective Guide to Materials for Mental Health and Family Life Education,* 419 Park Avenue South, New York, NY 10016.

Modern Talking Picture Service, 45 Rockefeller Plaza, New York, NY 10020.

National Audio-Visual Association, *Audio-Visual Equipment Directory*, 3150 Spring Street, Fairfax, VA 22030.

National Easter Seal Society, *AV Research References for Hospital and Institution Libraries*, 2023 West Ogden Avenue, Chicago, IL 60612.

National Film Board of Canada, 1251 Avenue of the Americas, New York, NY 10020.

National Medical Audiovisual Center, *Motion Picture and Videotape Catalog*, National Library of Medicine, DHEW, Atlanta, GA 30333.

Psychological Cinema Register, Pennsylvania State University, University Park, PA 16802.

Region Two Regional Continuing Education Program Media Library, 489 Christopher Baldy Hall, SUNY at Buffalo, Amherst, NY 14206.

Rehabilitation International USA, *Rehabilitation Film Library Catalogue*, and *International Rehabilitation Film Review Catalogue*, 20 West 49th Street, New York, NY 10018.

Rehabilitation Research and Training Center No. 9, *Rehabilitation Training Materials Study* (lists A-V catalogs, etc.), George Washington University, 2300 Eye Street N.W., Washington, DC 20037.

Veterans Administration, Central Office Film Library, 810 Vermont Street N.W., Washington, DC 20420.

EDUCATIONAL MATERIALS

Aims Instructional Media Services, P.O. Box 1010, Hollywood, CA 90028.

American Guidance Service, Publisher's Building, Circle Pines, MN 55014.

American Printing House for the Blind, 1839 Frankfort Avenue, Louisville, KY 40206.

Appleton-Century-Crofts, 440 Park Avenue South, New York, NY 10016.

Argus Communications, 7440 Natchez Avenue, Niles, IL 60648.

Association for Childhood Education International, *Selecting Educational Equipment and Materials for School and Home*, 3615 Wisconsin Avenue N.W., Washington, DC 20016.

Brodhead-Garrett, X-L (Experience Learning) Programs, 4560 East 71st Street, Cleveland, OH 44105.

Childcraft Education Corporation, 20 Kilmer Road, Edison, NJ 08817.

Constructive Playthings, 1040 East 85th Street, Kansas City, MO 64131.

Coronet Learning Programs, Learning, Inc., Tempe, AZ.

Creative Playthings, Princeton, NJ 08540.

Developmental Learning Materials, 7440 Natchez Avenue, Niles, IL 60648.

Diagnostic Test and Teaching Aids, Consulting Psychologists Press, 577 College Avenue, Palo Alto, CA 94306.

Educational Developmental Laboratories, McGraw-Hill Book Company, Hightstown, NJ.

Educational Performance Associates, 563 Westview Avenue, Ridgefield, NJ 07657.

Educational Teaching Aids, 159 West Kinzie Street, Chicago, IL 60610.

Marianne Frostig Center of Educational Therapy, 5981 Venice Boulevard, Los Angeles, CA 90034.

General Learning Corporation, The Judy Company, 250 James Street, Morristown, NJ 07960.

Ideal School Supply Company, 11000 South Laverne Avenue, Oak Lawn, IL 60453.

Macmillan Arts and Crafts, 9520 Baltimore Avenue, College Park, MD 20740.

Modern Education Corporation, P.O. Box 721, Tulsa, OK 74101.

Modern Teaching Associates, 1506 West Pierce Street, Milwaukee, WI 53246.

National Center on Educational Media and Materials for the Handicapped, Ohio State University, Columbus, OH 43210.

J. A. Preston Corporation, Special Materials for Children, 71 Fifth Avenue, New York, NY 10003.

Scott, Foresman and Co., 99 Bauer Drive, Oakland, NJ 07436.

Special Education Materials, Inc., G. E. Miller, Inc., 484 South Broadway, Yonkers, NY 10705.

R. H. Stone Products, 18279 Livernois, Detroit, MI 48221.

Teaching Resources Corporation, The New York Times, 100 Boylston Street, Boston, MA 02116.

Word Making Productions, P.O. Box 1858, Salt Lake City, UT 84101.

Instructional Materials Network for Handicapped Children and Youth: American Printing House for the Blind; Colorado State College; George Washington University; Illinois State Department of Public Instruction, 410 South Michigan Avenue, Chicago, IL; Michigan State University; New York State Department of Education, Albany, NY; State University College at Buffalo; Hunter College; Boston University; University of Kansas; University of Kentucky; University of Oregon; University of South Florida; University of Southern California; University of Texas; University of Wisconsin.

READING MATERIALS AND AIDS

Association of Hospital and Institution Libraries (American Library Association pamphlet: *Reading Aids for the Handicapped* — sources for aids, large-type books and newspapers, talking books, etc.), 50 East Huron Street, Chicago, IL 60611.

American Foundation for the Blind (catalog of publications; also pamphlets on Braille publishers, publishers of large-type books, etc.), 15 West 16th Street, New York, NY 10011.

American Printing House for the Blind, Instructional Materials Reference Center (hand-transcribed textbooks), 1839 Frankfort Avenue, Louisville, KY 40206.

Hadley School for the Blind (correspondence courses), 700 Elm Street, Winnetka, IL 60093.

Library of Congress, Division for the Blind and Visually Handicapped (talking books, etc.), Washington, DC 20542.

M. C. Migel Memorial Library (American Foundation for the Blind), 15 West 16th Street, New York, NY 10011.

INFORMATION SOURCES

Governmental

See Section 3 for addresses.

Clearing House on the Handicapped, Office for Handicapped Individuals.

National Information Center for the Handicapped.

National Institutes of Health, Office of Information.

Veterans Administration, Central Office.

Health Resources Administration, Department of Health, Education and Welfare.

Nongovernmental

Accent on Information, P.O. Box 700, Bloomington, IL 61701.

Information and Research Utilization Center in Physical Education and Recreation for the Handicapped, 1201 16th Street N.W., Washington, DC 20036.

Information Center on Recreation for the Handicapped, Southern Illinois University, Carbondale, IL 62901.

Mental Health Materials Center, 419 Park Avenue South, New York, NY 10016.

National Easter Seal Society for Crippled Children and Adults, 2023 West Ogden Avenue, Chicago, IL 60612.

National Clearing House of Rehabilitation Materials, Oklahoma State University, 202 North Murray, Stillwater, OK 74074.

Rehabilitation Research and Training Center, George Washington University, Washington, DC 20037.

Rehabilitation Research and Training Center in Mental Retardation, Clinical Services Building, University of Oregon, Eugene, OR 97403.

RESEARCH REPORTS

Council for Exceptional Children, *Exceptional Child Education Abstracts* (quarterly), 1920 Association Drive, Reston, VA 22091.

Educational Resources Information Center (ERIC), *Resources in Education* (monthly; reports on research projects funded by Office of Education, and reports collected by the ERIC network of clearinghouses), Superintendent of Documents, U.S. Government Printing Office, Washington, DC 20402.

International Research Referral Service, Rehabilitation International, 219 East 44th Street, New York, NY 10017.

The Johns Hopkins Medical Institutions, *Information Sources in Hearing, Speech, and Disorders of Human Communication,* 310 Harriet Lane Home, Baltimore, MD 21205.

National Institutes of Health, Division of Research Grants, *Research Grants Index,* Bethesda, MD 20402.

National Technical Information Service (federally sponsored research clearinghouse), *Catalog of Health Services Research: Abstracts of Public and Private Projects, Health Services and Mental Health Administration, and U.S. Government Research and Development Reports,* 5285 Port Royal Road, Springfield, VA 22151.

Rehabilitation Unit for the Disabled, Bureau of Social Affairs, *Summary of Information on Projects and Activities in the Field of Rehabilitation of the Disabled* (annual), United Nations, New York, NY 10017.

Smithsonian Science Information Exchange, Inc. (current projects; computer searches), 1730 M Street N.W., Room 300, Washington, DC 20036.

U.S. Children's Bureau Clearinghouse on Early Childhood Education, *Research Relating to Children,* University of Illinois, 805 West Pennsylvania Avenue, Urbana, IL 61801.

U.S. Social and Rehabilitation Service, Division of Research and Demonstration Grants, *Research and Demonstration Projects: An Annotated Listing,* Washington, DC 20201.

U.S. Social and Rehabilitation Service, *SRS Research Information System:*

Cumulative Index of Projects, Superintendent of Documents, U.S. Government Printing Office, Washington, DC 20402.

Veterans Administration, Department of Medicine and Surgery, *Bulletin of Prosthetics Research,* 810 Vermont Avenue N.W., Washington, DC 20420; compilation of research projects available from Smithsonian Science Information Exchange.

STATISTICAL DATA

Gallaudet College Office of Demographic Studies, *Data from the Annual Survey of Hearing Impaired Children,* Gallaudet College Bookstore, Kendall Green, Washington, DC 20002.

Library of Congress, Congressional Research Service, *Key Facts on the Handicapped,* 10 First Street, Washington, DC 20540.

National Center for Health Statistics (vital and health statistics from the National Health Survey), Public Health Service, Rockville, MD 20852.

National Institute of Mental Health, DHEW, *National Institute of Mental Health Statistics Notes,* 5600 Fishers Lane, Rockville, MD 20852.

Office of Research and Statistics, U.S. Social Security Administration, 6401 Security Boulevard, Baltimore, MD 21235.

Ohio State University, Department of Physical Medicine, Division of Disability Research, *Disability in the United States: A Compendium of Data on Prevalence and Programs* (edited by L. E. Riley and S. Z. Nagi, 1970), 472 West Eighth Street, Columbus, OH 43210.

Statistical Abstract of the United States, Superintendent of Documents, U.S. Government Printing Office, Washington, DC 20402.

REHABILITATION ENGINEERING; BIOFEEDBACK

Biofeedback and Self-control, *Aldine Annual,* Aldine Publishing Company, 529 South Wabash Avenue, Chicago, IL 60605.

Biofeedback Research Society, University of Colorado Medical Center, 4200 East Ninth Avenue, Denver, CO 80220.

Engineering Design Center, Cybernetics Systems Laboratory, Case Western Reserve University, Cleveland, OH.

Krusen Center for Research and Engineering, Moss Rehabilitation Hospital, Philadelphia, PA 19141.

Ontario Crippled Children's Centre, *Rehabilitation Engineering Research,* 350 Rumsey Road, Toronto, Ontario M4G 1R8, Canada.

Rancho Los Amigos Hospital, University of Southern California, Rehabilitation Engineering Center, *Annual Report of Progress,* 7601 East Imperial Highway, Downey, CA 90242.

Sensory Aids Evaluation and Development Center, Massachusetts Institute of Technology, Boston, MA.

United Cerebral Palsy Associations, *Technology and the Neurologically Handicapped: Report of the UCP Research Foundation and NASA,* 66 East 34th Street, New York, NY 10016.

University of California, Biomedical Engineering Department, Santa Barbara, CA.

BIBLIOGRAPHIES

American Alliance for Health, Physical Education and Recreation, *Helpful Sources for Developing Physical Education and Recreation Pro-*

grams for the Handicapped; Adult Mentally Retarded and Contributions of Physical Education and/or Recreation to Social Development; Dance, Music, Arts and Crafts for the Handicapped; and *Physical Education and Recreation Programs for the Emotionally Handicapped, Mentally Ill, Seriously Maladjusted, and Severely Disturbed,* 1201 16th Street N.W., Washington, DC 20036.

Association of Children with Learning Disabilities, *Annotated Bibliography for Parents of Learning Disabled Children,* 2200 Brownsville Road, Pittsburgh, PA 15210.

M. C. Migel Library (American Foundation for the Blind; selected references on low vision, psychological testing of the blind, intelligence testing of blind children and adults; *Index of Publications Issued by International Research Information Service),* 15 West 16th Street, New York, NY 10011.

National Easter Seal Society for Crippled Children and Adults (References compiled by the library on architectural planning for the physically handicapped; brain injury and learning disorders in children; cerebral palsy; rehabilitation of the physically handicapped; recreation for the handicapped; self-help devices for the handicapped; home care of the stroke patient; vocational counseling, placement, and employment of handicapped workers), 2023 West Ogden Avenue, Chicago, IL 60612.

National Institute of Mental Health, *Annotated Bibliography of Mental Health in Schools* (ADM 74-107), *Art Therapy Bibliography* (ADM 74-51), and *Bibliography on Suicide and Suicide Prevention* (HSM 72-9080), 5600 Fishers Lane, Rockville, MD 20852.

Selected Publications Concerning the Handicapped, U.S. Government Printing Office, Washington, DC 20402.

PAMPHLETS

Many pamphlets are listed in individual chapters, under Selected References.

Public Affairs Committee, 381 Park Avenue South, New York, NY 10016 (pamphlets on aging, alcoholism, asthma, cancer, cardiac disorders, cerebral palsy, drug abuse, employment, hearing disorders, hypertension, independent living, mental illness and health, mental retardation, multiple sclerosis, obesity, occupational therapy, rehabilitation counseling, sex and the disabled, venereal disease, visual handicaps).

Section 9. Selected Books on Disability

DONNA McGWINN

The following list of books includes most of my favorites from the more than ten years I have been reviewing books for one of the finest magazines for the disabled, *Rehabilitation Gazette*. They were chosen because they taught, stimulated, or delighted me; they were the kind of books one wants to share with everybody.

My experience with disability resulted from polio in 1953 when I was seventeen, leaving me with totally paralyzed arms and hands and totally dependent on respiratory aid. This, strengthened by the information from the many books on disability I have read, taught me much about how my disability affects myself and others, and broadened my understanding of humans and their meaning, purposes, and values. The rise in numbers of the disabled and their increased participation in the mainstream of life indicate that there will be more books than ever about disability. Hopefully they will be widely read.

Cape to Cape by Wheelchair, by Ernest M. Gutman (Erncar Publications, Fort Lauderdale, 1959). A travel-by-wheelchair account of the 50,000-mile (80,000-kilometer) journey by the author and his wife through South Africa to Norway. Included are wheelchair travel hints.

Employment for the Handicapped: A Guide for the Disabled, Their Families and Their Counselors, by Julietta K. Arthur (Abingdon Press, Nashville, 1967). Anything you want to know about getting a job: suggestions and necessary data on aptitude, means of financing, and particulars of application, covering every disability and area of occupation. There are many examples of disabled people and their vocational experiences.

Experiments in Survival, compiled and edited by Edith Henrich, commentary by Leonard Kriegel (Association for the Aid of Crippled Children, New York, 1961). Thirty-three personal accounts of coping with disability, intended to help others who are disabled learn more about themselves and their interaction with society.

Games, Sports and Exercises for the Physically Handicapped, by Ronald C. Adams, Alfred Daniel, and Lee Rullman (Lea & Febiger, Philadelphia, 1972). Written by therapeutic recreation directors, this book describes all kinds of activities and for what disabilities they are most feasible. There are explicit details on how to construct game equipment and assistive devices, and information about such things as putt-putt golf courses for wheelchairs and table croquet with mouth mallets.

Helping the Handicapped Teenager Mature, by Evelyn West Ayrault (Association Press, New York, 1971). A therapeutic handbook based on the author's personal experience with cerebral palsy and her professional experiences as a psychologist specializing in the treatment of handicapped children and teen-agers.

Hilary, by Dorothy Clarke Wilson (Hodder & Stoughton, London, 1971). The impressive, inspiring story of a woman with myasthenia gravis who could not talk, swallow, breathe, open her eyes, or move any muscles other than those in her big toes. She nonetheless managed to communicate, write poetry, letters, and articles, sell Christmas cards, and control electrical appliances.

Joni, by Joni Eareckson with Joe Musser (Zondervan Publishing House, Grand Rapids, 1976). An athletic girl of seventeen breaks her neck in a diving accident and goes through the horrors and sorrows of nearly total paralysis until she finds purpose and meaning as a Christian. Honest treatment of relationships and feelings gives the book deep meaning.

Life Together: The Situation of the Handicapped, compiled by Inger Nordquist (Svenska Centralkommitten for Rehabilitating, Fack/Broma 3, Sweden, 1969). The purpose of this widely read classic is to outline the practical problems, prejudices, and complexes that complicate the personal relationships of the orthopedically handicapped and, where possible, to suggest solutions. Sexual relationships are emphasized because of their importance and the strong prejudices and difficulties concerning them.

A Long Way Up: The Story of Jill Kinmont, by E. G. Valens (Harper & Row, Hagerstown, Md., 1966). *The Other Side of the Mountain* (Warner Paperback Library, New York, 1975). The story of a glamorous skier with Olympic promise who severs her spinal cord in a ski jump. Her life and loves were the basis for the movie for which the paperback was named.

The Man Who Had Everything, by Donald Murray (New American Library, New York, 1974). A novel of the marital consequences and psychological machinations that result when a man who literally has everything becomes paralyzed from the neck down.

New Light of Hope, by Bill Kiser (Keats Publishing Company, New Canaan, Conn., 1974). In a life characterized by relentless struggle to overcome the problems resulting from severe cerebral palsy, Kiser describes frankly and personally the experiences and people he has encountered. Winner of the President's Trophy as 1976 Handicapped American of the Year, he is a regularly syndicated columnist in five newspapers and on twenty radio stations.

Pat and Roald, by Barry Farrell (Random House, New York, 1969). The story of Hollywood actress Patricia Neal and her author husband, Roald Dahl, and their experiences after her series of near-fatal strokes. Here is a beautiful demonstration of love in the daily struggles of rehabilitation.

Personal Relationships: The Handicapped and the Community; Some European Thoughts and Solutions, edited by Derek Lancaster-Gaye (Routledge & Kegan Paul, Ltd., London, in association with the International Cerebral Palsy Society, Boston). Essays by fourteen rehabilitation professionals from Denmark, Sweden, England, and Holland on relationships of the disabled. The first part concerns the total setting within which personal and more formal relationships between the disabled themselves and the disabled and the able-bodied are developed, and the second part deals with sexual relating.

Physical Disability: A Psychological Approach, by Beatrice A. Wright (Harper & Row, Hagerstown, Md., 1960). This study of the interaction and interdependence of appearance and personality serves to debunk certain myths regarding physical imperfection and to increase understanding of the psychological effects of disability on oneself and others.

The Raging Moon, by Peter Marshall (Hutchinson & Co., London, 1964). A popular story of wheelchair lovers that was made into a movie, *Long Ago Tomorrow.* Two strong-minded individualists meet in a Cheshire-like home and passionately ignore the taboos against the disabled and romance.

Recovery with Aphasia: The Aftermath of My Stroke, by C. Scott Moss (University of Illinois Press, Urbana, 1972). The analytical expertise of a practicing psychologist in his forties who suffers a stroke and aphasia focuses on how the effects change him physically, emotionally, and mentally, as well as his family, his work, and his future. Lists other literature by aphasics.

Silent Victory, by Carmen McBride (Nelson-Hall, Chicago, 1969). The wife of a stroke victim shares the ways in which she and her husband readjusted to daily living without his ability to speak. A tender, moving love story of a couple who, in a marriage of fifty years, reached their deepest level of communication after the stroke.

Stigma: The Experience of Disability, by Paul Hunt (Geoffrey Chapman Ltd., London; Herder & Herder, New York, 1966). An exciting collection of essays by the disabled on their social status. These are eloquent writers with handicaps ranging from heart disease to muscular dystrophy who carefully examine all aspects of human relationships between the disabled and able-bodied.

Take One Step, by Evelyn West Ayrault (Doubleday, New York, 1963). A psychologist who has lived with the problems of cerebral palsy all her life tells of her experiences with family relationships, romances, jobs, and the challenges of society.

To Race the Wind, by Harold Krents (hardback: G. P. Putnam's Sons, New York, 1972; paperback: Bantam Books, New York, 1973). An autobiography full of the tender and hilarious experiences of the childhood and adulthood of the blind person who was the subject of the Broadway play *Butterflies Are Free.*

Understanding Paraplegia, by J. Walsh (Tavistock Publications, London, 1964). A general handbook by the Deputy Director of the National Spinal Injuries Center of Stoke-Mandeville Hospital that covers most of the problems faced by paraplegics and quadriplegics, including sex, how to buy wheelchairs, and the prevention and treatment of decubiti.

Winning, by Robin F. Brancato (Knopf, New York, 1977). A fast-reading, believable novel about the feelings, relationships, and rehabilitation of a high school football player who tackles hard enough to permanently injure his spinal cord and become a quad.

You Still Have Your Head, by Franz Schoenberner (MacMillan, New York, 1957). His neck and spinal cord broken by assault when he was fifty-nine, Schoenberner writes of the new energy that physical immobility gives to the mind, freeing it to the endless fields of reflection, imagination, and memory.

Postscript

Progress — and Problems

ROBERT M. GOLDENSON, Ph.D.

Today rehabilitation is one of the most fluid of all fields. After centuries of neglect and indifference on the part of society as a whole, disabled members of the population are beginning to be accorded the attention they deserve — and this attention is not merely in the form of sympathy and solicitude, important as these are, but of concrete projects and practical efforts designed to bring them out of the shadows and into the mainstream of society. The day when the mentally and physically handicapped are "put away" in cold, impersonal institutions, or simply "filed and forgotten," is rapidly passing, and enormous social and scientific energy is being directed toward improving their well-being, increasing their independence, and releasing their potential as contributors to society.

The objective of this volume has been not only to provide basic information on the major disabilities and the many phases of the rehabilitation process, but to bring the reader up to date on the nationwide effort to see that the disabled secure their place in the sun. The questions to be addressed in this final chapter are therefore: what are the areas in which the most significant progress is being made, and where does the field of rehabilitation stand at this time? In attempting to answer, this postscript will cite representative examples of promising developments and indicate pressing problems that remain to be solved.

The Research Effort

The National Institutes of Health (NIH) are spending over $2 billion a year on research projects and facilities, and major voluntary agencies an estimated $100 million more. Where do we stand in this essential area? If we insist on measuring progress in terms of breakthroughs such as polio vaccines, rubella immunization, kidney transplants, and heart surgery, we must admit that dramatic advances are few and far between, and we may even begin to wonder what these huge investments of time, talent, and resources are producing. But when we recognize, as we must, that the human organism is infinitely more complex than we ever imagined, we will begin to measure progress in terms of a slow accumulation of knowledge accruing from lengthy, tedious investigations in hundreds of laboratories and research centers. One indication of the scope of this massive effort is the fact that, in addition to its intramural programs, the National Institutes of Health supported projects conducted by 175,000 nonfederal scientists in more than 10,-000 different institutions during fiscal 1974 alone. And anyone who questions the $2 billion plus spent each year on medical research should be reminded that "American society allots about 4 percent of the amount it spends for all health purposes to medical research and development" (*Research Advances,* National Institutes of Health, 1975).

There are specific reasons for the immensity of this effort. At this point in the history of medicine, the human organism is still in process of exploration, and most research is therefore basic rather than applied in nature. There are innumerable unanswered questions about the composition of blood, the biochemistry of enzymes, the substances that control neural transmission, the action of muscle, the processes of digestion and metabolism, the makeup and interaction of hormones, the mechanisms of genetic transmission, and the cerebral circuitry involved in cognition, memory, and perception.

Much of research, then, is focused on basic problems of physiology and biology. But when we enter the field of pathology and disability, the basic subject matter of this book, the number of unanswered questions multiplies geometrically. Though the symptoms and types of epilepsy are fairly well known, most cases must still be described as idiopathic: "of unknown origin." The major types of leukemia have also been identified, and many cases can be arrested at least temporarily by the newer treatments; but we do not know why this disease suddenly develops in one individual and not in another. Sickle cell anemia is characteristically ethnic, but the nature of the inborn error that produces it is still a mystery — and the same is true of Tay-Sachs and familial dysautonomia. We are equally in the dark about the precise mechanisms responsible for muscular dystrophy, multiple sclerosis, cystic fibrosis, myasthenia gravis, Parkinson's disease, Huntington's disease, the myriad forms of cancer, and the two disorders that make up the bulk of serious mental disease, schizophrenia and manic-depressive reaction.

A more concrete idea of the range of research problems can be gained by citing some of the projects reported in the NIH publication mentioned above. Among them are development of immunity against meningitis, the leading cause of acquired mental retardation in the United States, by feeding newborns with a single dose of live, harmless intestinal bacteria; healing of refractory, disabling fractures through electrical stimulation carried by electrodes implanted within the bone; use of continuous positive airway pressure (CPAP) with premature infants suffering respiratory distress (hyaline membrane disease) which might otherwise lead to brain damage or death; experiments with the transplantation of insulin-producing beta cells from immature pancreases of newly born animals to older animals (and in time, it is hoped, to human beings) as a means of controlling diabetes; development of two-dimensional echocardiography, a safe, painless, noninvasive technique in which reflected ultrasound waves are used to detect structural defects in the heart; a new method of tracing visual pathways in the brain by labeling neuron cell bodies with injected radioactive material; development of faster and less expensive procedures for identifying cancer-causing chemicals in the environment (at present each chemical requires two to three years of investigation involving more than 500 animals); development of an extremely sensitive test for detecting a cancer-related protein (alpha-fetoprotein, or AFP), to be used both in diagnosis and in assessment of the progress of treatment; synthesis of the active component of human parathyroid hormone for use in experimental studies of its role in metabolic bone disease and potentially in therapy; development of enzyme replacement therapy for application to such genetic diseases as Tay-Sachs and Gaucher's; a series of double-blind tests of carbamazepine (Tegretol), the first new epilepsy drug to be approved by the Food and Drug Administration in 14 years; preliminary research on an "auditory prosthesis" for the profoundly deaf, consisting of an electrode implanted in the cochlea and capable of transmitting signals to the brain via the acoustic nerve; studies of immuno-senescence, the decline in the immune system which increases susceptibility of the aged to infectious diseases and cancer, through interchange of lymphoid cells between old and young mice; and application of behavior modification techniques to juvenile delinquents by taking them out of reformatories and institutions for the retarded and placing them in normal homes where they are rewarded with special privileges for responsible behavior.

Prevention of Disorders

Significant strides are being made in the all-important area of prevention. The vaccination program in the United States has all but eliminated polio and has substantially reduced the incidence of cerebral palsy. Vaccines are also helping to control many potentially disabling diseases such as diphtheria, mumps, whooping cough, and tetanus. On the other hand, recent surveys (1977) indicate that due to the apathy of parents and sometimes of physicians about one-third of all children under fourteen have not been adequately immunized. Here is a case where we have the tools but are not doing a complete job.

Recent advances in the study of genetic disease have also opened up new avenues to prevention. Over 1,500 of these diseases have been identified, and new applications of genetic counseling are constantly coming to the fore. Amniocentesis makes it possible to determine congenital defect in the thirteenth or fourteenth week of pregnancy, when therapeutic abortion is still possible; but so far this technique can be applied only to a minority of birth defects. Biochemical tests to determine carriers of a number of disorders (such as Duchenne's dystrophy, hemophilia, sickle cell anemia, Tay-Sachs) are now available; but tests have not yet been developed for scores of other genetic disorders, though many research projects are in progress.

Prevention of disorder can also be achieved by immune globulin (in Rh incompatibility cases); control of nutrition (such as a low phenylalanine diet for babies afflicted with phenylketonuria); infant and child surgery (such as for spina bifida and hydrocephalus); and through a psychosocial approach to mental health. Many current research projects have a bearing on prevention. Examples are the recently reported use of synthetic retinoids (vitamin A–like substances) in treating precancerous growths in the lining of the bladder, lungs, colon, breasts, and pancreas; investigation of a possible link between change in the balance of the sex hormones (testosterone and estradiol) and heart attacks in men; and the much publicized "genetic engineering" experiments on recombinant DNA and the synthesis of working genes—which at this point are being pursued on the level of basic research, but which may later be applied to the correction or prevention of genetic defect.

Progress is also being made in secondary prevention—that is, prevention or reduction of disability resulting from existing disorders. New lightweight plastic braces, molded to the limb, are replacing heavy metal-and-leather devices that are disabling in themselves. Operations for drop foot and drop wrist are now highly developed, and surgery is being applied with some success to correction of scoliosis and to cases of osteogenesis imperfecta before deformity develops. The physical therapy procedures described in several chapters of this volume also serve as preventive measures, since they help to strengthen weak muscles that might lead to further disability or even deformity.

Artificial Body Parts and Assistive Devices

Replacement of body parts represents another rapidly developing means of dealing with disability. While two or three decades ago the only commonly replaced components were teeth, today the list of transplants, implants, and prostheses is long and constantly growing. Over 15,000 kidney transplants were performed between 1953 and 1977 (but 8,000 people are waiting for them). Cataract surgery, followed by implantation of a plastic lens (or more frequently, special eyeglasses or a contact lens), restores effective vision in 95 percent of cases, including the aged. Although transplants from animals and human beings are often unavailable or create problems of rejection, a wide variety of artificial implants have been devised. These replacements are available in unlimited quantities and appropriate sizes, and are made of long-wearing materials not readily rejected by the organism, such as Silastic, Vitallium, Teflon, and Dacron.

The most widely used "spare parts" are joint replacements (arthroplasty) designed to overcome the effects of rheumatoid arthritis, cancer, and traumatic injury. Artificial substitutes are available today for practically every joint in the body: finger, toe, hand, ankle, elbow, knee, shoulder, hip, and wrist. Other functional substitutes are the artificial kidney, the cardiac pacemaker, heart valves, Eustachian tube, artificial larynx, mandibular (jaw) implant, mid-ear stapes (for otosclerosis), skull plate (cranioplasty), and urinary sphincter. Since 1964 the National Heart, Lung and Blood Institute has allocated more than $50 million in grants and contracts for development of an artificial heart—and an externally powered polyurethane heart has already kept a calf alive for ninety-four days.

Some artificial parts, such as the myoelectric arm, are both functional and cosmetic; others, such as remarkably lifelike chins, noses (rhinoplasty), cheeks, fingers, and ears, are designed primarily to overcome congenital or acquired disfigurement.

Another area in which notable advances are being made is bioengineering and biomechanics. Many of the products of recent applied research in these fields are already in use—for example, a "floating mattress" filled with a mudlike compound, which prevents bed sores in patients with severe burns or neurological dysfunctions; an electric stimulator that activates paralyzed muscles of the lower leg to enable the patient to walk without dragging his foot; a voice-controlled computer terminal which can be operated over telephone lines without the use of the hands, to convert spoken words into machine-readable code; a device which uses carbon dioxide to power the fingers so that quadriplegics can write; a "talking typewriter" which helps blind people learn to type by instantly echoing the sound of every letter they press; a surgically implanted bladder pacemaker operated by a small, hand-held transmitter, to overcome incontinence; miniaturized computers called microprocessors, each with thousands of transistors and circuits in one wafer-thin chip, which make it possible to trigger natural-appearing, coordinated movements of a prosthesis through a sequence of signals; and the first small vehicles that can be entered and driven by an individual confined to a wheelchair.

Innumerable other devices are still in the developmental or prototype stage. Three examples are a computerized reading machine for the blind, capable of scanning a line of print and translating it into speech; a wearable artificial kidney which will greatly enhance the mobility and rehabilitation of patients with kidney failure; and a "low-floor bus" with a single step, a ramp that can be extended to the curb, and a door wide enough to accommodate a wheelchair.

Rights of the Disabled

There is a continuous flow of new developments in every phase of rehabilitation discussed in this book. Advocacy groups are multiplying, and more than twenty national organizations or departments of organizations have been established expressly for the purpose of defending and extending the rights of the disabled. A body of legal precedent is being continuously accumulated on such basic questions as the right to education, provision of adequate treatment, confidentiality of health records, guardianship, and readmission to jobs after psychiatric treatment—and new rights are constantly being sought and won on such questions as the refusal of schools to hire blind teachers, inaccessibility of polling places, and the establishment of small group homes for the retarded in single-family residential zones. Though many victories have been achieved, the process is a gradual one, since rights gained in one part of the country do not always apply to other areas, and there is often a gap between court decisions and the implementation of these decisions, just as there are many instances where legislation is enacted but not fully carried out.

Accessible Transportation

An example of an area in which progress is particularly slow is accessible transportation facilities. Though some airlines and airports make provision for disabled people, others do not; and as of this writing, the Civil Aeronautics Board has not issued its long-promised regulations. Only a handful of cities have ordered barrier-free buses, and only a few railroad stations provide ramps and raised platforms. Specially equipped vans are available in a limited number of communities, but in general the cost is high and Medicaid will not always pay for this service—and where it does, payment is usually provided only for visits to physicians and clinics, and not for transportation to colleges, shopping centers, and recreational facilities.

Employment and Housing

In the area of employment, sheltered workshops have been increasing in number, but in many instances insufficient effort is made to place trained clients in business and industry. There is also an increase in the number of private firms which hire only the disabled and operate on a completely competitive basis. Such concerns are proving that disabled individuals make competent, reliable, highly motivated employees. The nationwide affirmative action program is also providing conclusive evidence of this fact, and it is important to note that some of the stumbling blocks in this program are being eliminated—for example, the requirement that the disabled applicant "has reasonably benefitted from vocational rehabilitation services." These are all indications of progress; but it must also be recognized that thousands of qualified workers are still being denied job opportunities due to fear, prejudice, and misconceptions.

The situation in housing can only be described as critical. Practically everywhere in the United States, disabled individuals are forced to live with their families because there is no alternative. They are therefore being denied the fundamental right to independence, and are haunted by the fear of what is going to happen to them when their parents are no longer able to take care of them. However, a few barrier-free apartments and homes are becoming available, and a number of communities, rehabilitation centers, and action groups are exploring alternative solutions. In addition, several federal agencies, such as Housing and Urban Development and the Veterans Administration, are prepared to offer help with the crucial problem of financing.

Voluntary Organizations

One of the most promising developments in the entire field is the establishment of new voluntary organizations to deal with disorders which have hitherto received little attention from the public and in some instances scant attention from the medical profession as well. The initiative in forming these groups is usually taken by victims' families who have sought in vain to find the help they need. Among the conditions that have given rise to new organizations are osteogenesis imperfecta, amyotrophic lateral sclerosis, arthrogryposis, tuberous sclerosis, Prader-Willi syndrome, and Huntington's disease—all of which are represented in this volume. In some cases, too, existing organizations have broadened the scope of their concern to include disorders more or less related to their primary focus—for example, the Muscular Dystrophy Association now covers thirty-five muscle diseases. The informational services and fund-raising campaigns of these organizations have begun to awaken the general public to the existence of these little-known but highly disabling disorders, and have helped to focus the attention of physicians and research scientists upon them. Moreover, it is a significant fact that when they do receive greater attention, the incidence of these conditions is almost invariably found to be larger than previously recognized.

Action Organizations

Still another important forward step is being taken by the disabled themselves. They are not only starting to address their own problems through advocacy and consumer committees in established agencies, but are forming action-oriented organizations of their own. These groups are rapidly multiplying across the country (see PART 4, SECTION 2: VOLUNTARY ORGANIZATIONS), and their membership lists often number in the hundreds. They study methods of influencing legislators, business groups, and government agencies, acting as their own ombudsmen or enlisting the services of professional advocates. Some of their major areas of activity include elimination of architectural barriers in public buildings as well as private structures such as colleges; accessibility of buses and other means of transportation; ramped sidewalks; barrier-free housing; job placement and implementation of affirmative action laws; improved care and social services; and establishment of camps and other recreational facilities. A few of these organizations also offer services of their own, such as peer counseling, attendant referrals, wheelchair repair, advice on insurance and social security problems, and specialized vocational training. This new and promising movement should be measured not only in terms of solutions to practical problems, but in terms of a new image, and self-image, of disabled persons as effective individuals who are ready, willing, and able to contribute to society's progress as well as their own. A striking example is the 1977 White House Conference on Handicapped Individuals, in which 83% of the persons who assembled to deal with a total of 3,500 questions were themselves disabled.

Self-help and Social Contribution

These, then, are some of the growth points in the vast field of disabilities and rehabilitation. It is all too apparent that though advances are being made, we have a long, long way to go in every one of them. But while the slow, cumulative process of research and application is going on, there is one never-failing area of progress, and that is the successful efforts of the disabled themselves to surmount their limitations and contribute to society. This volume could have no more appropriate ending than to cite concrete evidence of this fact: the man with advanced multiple sclerosis who earns a living as a caricaturist, holding the pencil in his mouth, and spends his spare time reading textbooks to blind children; the respiratory polio victim who runs a gift shop stocked entirely with items made by the disabled; the electronics engineer who has spent years perfecting a control system for himself and his fellow quadriplegics which makes it possible to operate a TV set, typewriter, lights, telephone, page turner, and the front door with a single microswitch activated by breath or voice; the blind mechanic who specializes in repairing and overhauling automatic transmissions; and the many spinal-injured individuals who have successfully changed their occupations, including the truck driver who shifted over to dispatcher, the internist who took special courses to become an outstanding allergist, and the eye surgeon who went back to medical school to study psychiatry.

In thousands of such examples, the rehabilitation program would never have succeeded had it not been reinforced by a second process: self-rehabilitation.

Index